CIVIL JURISDICTION AND JUDGMENTS

SIXTH EDITION

BY

ADRIAN BRIGGS

Professor of Private International Law, Oxford University
Sir Richard Gozney Fellow and Tutor in Law, St Edmund Hall, Oxford
Barrister, Blackstone Chambers, Temple

LLOYD'S COMMERCIAL LAW LIBRARY

Civil Jurisdiction and Judgments
Sixth edition
by Adrian Briggs
(2015)

EU Competition Law and the Financial Services Sector
by Andrea Lista
(2013)

Rules of Evidence in International Arbitration: An Annotated Guide
by Nathan D. O'Malley
(2012)

Civil Jurisdiction and Judgments
Fifth edition
by Adrian Briggs and Peter Rees
(2009)

Deceit: The Lie of the Law
by Peter MacDonald Eggers
(2009)

Financial Crisis Management and Bank Resolution
Edited by John Raymond LaBrosse,
Rodrigo Olivares-Caminal and Dalvinder Singh
(2009)

Arbitration Act 1996
Fourth edition
by Robert Merkin and Louis Flannery
(2008)

Practice and Procedure of the Commercial Court
Sixth edition
by Anthony Colman, Victor Lyon and Philippa Hopkins
(2008)

Freezing and Search Orders
Fourth edition
by Mark S. W Hoyle
(2006)

Commercial Agents and the Law
by Severine Saintier and Jeremy Scholes
(2005)

CIVIL JURISDICTION
AND
JUDGMENTS

BY

ADRIAN BRIGGS

SIXTH EDITION

informa law
from Routledge

Sixth Edition published 2015
by Informa Law from Routledge
2 Park Square, Milton Park, Abingdon, Oxon OX14 4RN

And by Informa Law from Routledge
711 Third Avenue, New York, NY 10017

Informa Law from Routledge is an imprint of the Taylor & Francis Group, an Informa business

First Edition published 1993 by LLP
Fifth Edition published 2009 by Informa

British Library Cataloguing in Publication Data
A catalogue record for this book is available from the British Library

Library of Congress Cataloging in Publication Data
Briggs, Adrian, author.
   Civil jurisdiction and judgments / by Adrian Briggs, Professor of Private International Law, Oxford University, Sir Richard Gozney Fellow and Tutor in Law, St Edmund Hall, OxforD, Barrister, Blackstone Chambers, Temple. -- Sixth edition.
      pages cm. -- (Lloyd's commercial law library)
   "First Edition published 1993 by LLP."
   Includes index.
   ISBN 978-1-138-82560-4 (hardback) -- ISBN 978-1-315-73630-3 (ebook) 1. Conflict of laws--Jurisdiction--England. 2. Conflict of laws--Jurisdiction--Europe. I. Title.
   KD681.J87B75 2015
   347.42'012--dc23

                                                                                      2014045464

ISBN 978-1-138-82560-4
eISBN 978-1-31573-630-3

Typeset in Bembo Std
by Servis Filmsetting Ltd, Stockport, Cheshire

Printed and bound in Great Britain by
TJ International Ltd, Padstow, Cornwall

TABLE OF CONTENTS

xvi

PREFACE TO THE SIXTH EDITION

The recast version of the Brussels I Regulation, Regulation 1215/2012, was published in the Official Journal just before Christmas 2012, giving those with an interest in such things two years plus 20 days to ready themselves for new European rules of jurisdiction. But the recast version of the Statutory Instrument made to tie up the loose ends was something else entirely: two years went by before the United Kingdom managed to produce it. Had it been otherwise, this edition could have come out as the Regulation came in. But one might as well have been wishing for the moon on a plate.

As things turned out, the recast Regulation was not quite the radical instrument which had been forecast or feared. For judgments obtained in proceedings instituted on or after 10 January 2015 it removed the requirement that a judgment creditor apply for a judicial order giving the green light to enforcement of a judgment from another Member State. But the cost of having to apply for a judicial order, which served as a costly *terminus a quo* for challenges to recognition which were hardly ever made, was out of all proportion to the benefit achieved thereby; and once that was acknowledged its days were numbered. Maybe getting rid of it was so mighty an accomplishment that other matters, which might also have been attended to, could be put off, though some of the proposed changes which were not eventually made were opportunities timidly lost. Of the changes which were made, most, though not all, were for the better, though when one considers what was done to clarify the relationship between the Regulation and arbitration, it is hard to say whether it was all much ado about nothing, or nothing done about much, or both at the same time. Yet though we did not get everything we might have wanted, and were given a couple of things we would have been better off without, the law took two steps forward, one step back. When the recast Regulation is looked at again, as is promised for its tenth birthday, a further edition of this book will, *deo volente*, be there to deal with it.

The European Court has been busy with the original version of the Regulation: as national courts at all levels may now make references for a preliminary ruling on it, this was only to be expected. In spite of the fact that it seems increasingly prepared to get by without the assistance of an Opinion from an Advocate General, judgments now tend to be more predictable just as, ironically, these Opinions appear to be going increasingly wild. Predictable also was the Court's decision to give up the struggle to publish its Reports in hard copy. No doubt the cost of producing upwards of a dozen slab-like volumes a year, in 20-odd official languages, was unsustainable, but whatever tipped the balance, official publication is now in digital form only. The Court's adoption of a neutral citation for its judgments is a helpful, if inelegant, addition: it has been used in this edition for decisions published by the Court from 1 January 2012, from which date no new European Court Report will see the light of day.

It should not be thought that the common law, or the common non-Brussels law, has lost its vigour. In one particularly heady period of 12 months, give or take a week, the Supreme Court had a good look at *forum conveniens*, service out of the jurisdiction, the law applicable to liability in tort and its impact on jurisdiction, anti-suit injunctions, estoppel by *res judicata*, foreign judgments generally; and, in the context of insolvency in particular, the things one cannot do to the corporate veil, and what it is that makes jurisdiction exorbitant. It quelled any remaining doubts about the soundness of a claim for damages for breach of a jurisdiction or arbitration agreement with *dicta* of such studied calm that one wonders how there could ever have been any doubt about it; and it still found time to deal with the complexity of parallel and tactical litigation in the framework of the Brussels I Regulation. And the Court of Appeal did all this, and far more besides. There is life in the old law yet, which is just as well, for the to-do list still has plenty on it. One cannot help but be struck by the number of cases in which artificial corporate and corporate-like structures make it so much harder than it should be to attach and enforce legal liability where it ought to belong. Whether these are devised to conceal the ownership of assets, or to obfuscate the performance of civil obligations, or to provide insulation from the need to comply with orders made by the court, or to avoid tax, or all of the above, it is all part of a virulent modern plague. The Supreme Court recently confiscated the shears with which lower courts might have set about these corporate veils. But the law on privity or sufficiency of interest, and on what should be the duty of friends and relations to assist the court, rather than treating its judgments and orders with disdain or indifference, now needs some serious attention. When this happens, and when individuals and entities play the conflicts card to get out of jail free, it will be necessary to think through some deep and serious issues of private international law; given the tools, we are ready to get on with the job.

In 2009, when we signed off on our fifth edition, Peter Rees and I expected to be back for a sixth edition, but also recognised that the time had come for the book to lose some weight. Things did not work out quite that way. The change which took place was not one that had been foreseen, but Peter's various and new professional commitments led him to relinquish his role in the book. If truth be told, though, the flood of legislative and judicial material, and the explosive jostle of reactions to it, is always on the point of overwhelming the other compartments of normal life. As only one of us had the exhausting privilege of sabbatical leave, the grant whereof by St Edmund Hall and the University of Oxford is hereby acknowledged, the labour on this edition was all mine, as may be any praise and will, inevitably, be all the blame.

The change which had been intended, alas, does not appear to have taken place: the book has not lost weight (or its bulk, which may not be quite the same thing). That is a consequence of the huge spread of tempting new law laid before us over the last five years. As with cake, so with judgments: it takes unimaginable self-discipline to plead *quantum sufficit*, enough is enough. Despite the terrible warning of *Mylward v. Weldon* 21 ER 136 (1596), few writers are completely impervious to the occasional, slightly tart, observation that a point has been made for which no authority is cited. As to that, of course, a rolled-up plea of justification and fair comment will just have to suffice; and as to the rest, it is in the nature of diets to begin tomorrow.

This volume endeavours to describe the law as it appeared to me as the recast Regulation, 1215/2015, went live.

Adrian Briggs

Oxford, 10 January 2015

TABLE OF CASES

TABLE OF STATUTES

TABLE OF STATUTORY INSTRUMENTS

TABLE OF CIVIL PROCEDURE RULES

TABLE OF EUROPEAN LEGISLATION

CHAPTER 1

Introduction

NATURE OF THE SUBJECT AND SCHEME OF THE BOOK

1.01 General introduction

Few things complicate the law as much as a project to simplify it. Not so long ago, a statement of the rules that defined and regulated the jurisdiction of an English court could be made, and explained, in a modest number of pages. If the defendant was in England and was served with the writ, the fact of service founded the jurisdiction of the court; and if the court had jurisdiction, it would exercise it. If the defendant was not in England, making service upon him would depend on first obtaining leave,[1] the process for doing (or for subsequently defending) which was a little more involved; but by and large a single set of rules applied to all defendants alike, and to all actions *in personam*.

It now seems hard to believe that it really was that simple. Today, the law on civil jurisdiction and the enforcement of foreign judgments has many, and much more complicated, jurisdictional rules. The simplicity and uniformity of the old design is a thing of the past, and new terminology has had to be invented to explain the modern law. The engine of change has been irresistible pressure from the institutions of Europe. In the field of civil and commercial matters, great leaps or lurches have taken us towards common rules to determine the jurisdiction of courts and the effect of judgments from Member States of the European Union.[2] Two footnotes to this should be mentioned. First, a derivative set of rules was made to cover the States still party only to the European Free Trade Association (EFTA) to bring them into line with the law of the Member States; and second, the internal jurisdictional law of the United Kingdom was altered to resemble, as between England, Scotland and Northern Ireland, the rules of international jurisdiction by which the United Kingdom is bound as a Member State. But the common law has not been eradicated, just pushed aside from some areas in which it used to be untrammelled.

The result is a complex web of statutory schemes which has substantially, but not wholly, displaced the common law rules of jurisdiction developed by the courts and adjusted, from

---

1 Unless specific legislation makes provision for it to be done, it is contrary to common law to serve a 'claim form', or 'process' (formerly, a 'writ') out of the jurisdiction without the leave (now, 'permission') of the court.

2 The original basis for the Conventions was Art. 220 of the Treaty of Rome. This was concerned only to pave the way for the free movement of judgments, but the goal was achieved by creating clear and common jurisdictional rules as a result of which the unimpeded movement of judgments would follow. The current basis for the Council Regulations is Art. 81 of the Treaty on the Functioning of the European Union (TFEU). This is also the basis for the development of harmonised rules for identification of the applicable law, but other than for incidental reference, this field of activity lies beyond the scope of the present work.

time to time, by Parliament. Because the new rules are legislatively European rather than legislatively English, courts outside England deal with and contribute to their interpretation, and the principles by which they do so are not principles of English domestic law. It all makes for an elaborate system, though one which is justifiable, and which is justified, by the increased degree of harmonisation of the law of civil jurisdiction and the enforcement of judgments across the European Union.

Sometimes these European instruments do not set out the precise jurisdictional powers of national courts, but authorise and direct instead the application of domestic legal rules. The result is that the traditional jurisdictional rules of the common law[3] now have two distinct roles to play. In cases which fall right outside the domain of the Regulations they are the sole and untrammelled source of the law on jurisdiction. But in cases within the domain of those instruments into which they are co-opted, or incorporated by reference, they operate as rules of residual Regulation jurisdiction, and where this happens, their content and their operation is modified.

In fact, before all this European development got going, the common law had embarked on a radical reassessment of its basic assumptions about the law and exercise of jurisdiction. Until 1974 it was assumed, almost without question, that a claimant was entitled to decide whether a defendant would be summoned to court in England, and that a defendant had practically no say in the matter. In 1974 it was finally admitted that this was just too one-sided to be proper. Not only did it pay too little attention to the fact that a defendant should have a right to be heard on the issue of where he should defend himself,[4] but it also paid less attention than it should to the role of the court, acting in the public interest to regulate the conduct of litigation with a cross-border element. A series of cases refining the idea of the 'appropriateness' of an English forum, in the sense of place for trial, emerged from the House of Lords, in a superb illustration of how a court with inherent jurisdiction may refurbish its jurisdictional rules without the need for a legislature to get involved. The result was, and is, that as a matter of common law, it is necessary, but is no longer sufficient, to catch up with one's defendant and serve process upon him. Though this gives the court jurisdiction in a technical sense, if the defendant disputes it – that is, he disputes the jurisdiction itself, or the appropriateness of its exercise – the court must rule on the jurisdictional arguments, and may do so in such a way that the claimant is left to bring his case before the courts of another country. The details of this broad reorientation of the common law have been much litigated and refined. Some, including the occasional judge, argue that the rules have become over-engineered; but whatever the truth of that, mapping of the relationship between the European and the common law schemes of jurisdictional rule has required considerable work, not all of it easy.

This book will attempt to state the jurisdictional rules of the English courts[5] to show how the various systems of jurisdiction organise themselves and fit together, and to show which rules have priority over which others. Chapters 2 and 3 examine the jurisdictional rules which operate in England through the adoption of various European treaties, Conventions,

---

3 The detail of which is examined in Chapter 4.

4 If the issue is seen as where *the claimant's claim* should be litigated, it seems to follow that the claimant should be entitled to decide where to prosecute it. But if instead it is seen as *the dispute between the parties*, it is unclear why the claimant alone should decide where to have it adjudicated.

5 And, to the extent that the Regulation applies identical rules to the civil jurisdiction of the courts of Member States, to describe the rules as they equally apply there.

and other instruments. Chapter 4 explains what happens in those cases in which the traditional jurisdictional rules of the common law continue to apply, whether residually within the scope of the Regulation or outside the scope of the Regulation altogether: in a perfect world, they would be dealt with separately and twice, but this would test the patience of writer and reader alike. Chapter 5 deals with the procedure for serving process and for objecting to jurisdiction, and with other strategies for practising and preventing 'forum shopping'. Chapter 6 deals with interim and interlocutory measures which may be obtained or enforced.

It is often as important to know the consequences of taking (or defending, for that matter) proceedings in a foreign court. In deciding where to sue, close attention will presumably be given to whether the judgment is capable of being enforced elsewhere. Chapter 7 explains the rules which govern the recognition and enforcement of foreign judgments in England. To the extent that these rules are also common to the laws of other European States, this account will also give an indication[6] of whether an English judgment would be enforceable there as well.

No account of this subject can be regarded as complete if it ignores the fact that many commercial agreements provide for, and many commercial disputes are settled by, arbitration. Though that subject requires a large book in its own right, the Arbitration Act 1996 calls for a concise account of how and when an English court will give effect to, and will support, an agreement that a dispute should be settled by arbitration. This is discussed in Chapter 8.

ENGLISH COMMON LAW AND COMMON EUROPEAN LAW

1.02 General

An understanding of the institutional relationship between the pan-European rules, which may be looked on as a common European law, and the English common law, is the key requirement. It has become increasingly clear that the European rules on private international law – on jurisdiction as well as on applicable law – cannot be understood as bringing about the amendment of the rules of the common law. That view, which would risk 'domesticating' European law into the common law system, would denature rules which were devised and made, and which take effect, as rules of European law, whomping down on national legal systems and pushing aside everything which gets in their way. It would tend to construe the legislative changes made as working within an existing system, rather than as rules which make a fresh start by creating something entirely new. In civil and commercial cases, the new basic law of jurisdiction is established by the various European instruments, which are drafted in Europe and elucidated by the Court of Justice of the European Union[7] in Luxembourg. The most important of these is the Brussels I Regulation, 'recast' in

---

6 And really only that. In each country there will also be a national (private international) system of rules for the recognition of judgments, operating alongside and in addition to the European rules.

7 This will be referred to, in most contexts, as 'the European Court', or as 'the Court', with an upper case initial, to underline the fact that it, and it alone, has the power to give rulings on the interpretation of Regulations which are authoritative and binding in all Member States.

its most recent form as Regulation 1215/2012.[8] For the most part, these instruments contain 'direct' or 'primary' rules of jurisdiction, that is, rules which directly determine whether the courts of a particular Member State, or of a particular place within that State, have jurisdiction in a particular case.

As said above, there are circumstances in which these instruments provide their answer to the immediate question in a different way. Rather than providing a direct or primary rule of jurisdiction for the claim against the particular defendant, they may direct a national court to apply its own traditional, pre-European, jurisdictional rules instead. This is done, by and large, in cases where the defendant does not have a domicile in a Member State, and none of the extraordinary facts for which a particular jurisdictional rule is provided is present. The result is a patchwork of jurisdictional rules for claims against those not established in the Member States, which makes the position of those not domiciled in Member States far more difficult than it should be. Although an attempt was made, in the process leading up to the adoption of what became Regulation 1215/2012, to establish more uniform rules for claims against defendants who lacked a domicile in or relevant connection with any Member State, the proposal failed to secure acceptance: this looks like a very serious misjudgment. Still, in providing that these various rules of jurisdiction found in and taken from the national laws of the Member States apply in circumstances which it specifies, the Regulation gives them the status of 'residual' rules of jurisdiction, having the force of law by virtue of these European instruments which in turn have authority in England by virtue of an Act of Parliament,[9] and not as part of the inherent jurisdiction of court at common law.

Outside the field of civil or commercial matters, as well as in those civil and commercial matters from which it expressly excludes itself, the Regulation has no immediate application. Even so, general rules of European law still do apply to an English court exercising jurisdiction, and it is for this reason that a court exercising jurisdiction in a matter of arbitration, to which the Regulation does not apply, may still be prevented, by a rule of European law, from making an order of a kind which its law of arbitration might otherwise have allowed or required it to make.[10] But the focus of this book lies with jurisdiction and the enforcement of judgments in civil and commercial matters in general, which substantially means that the main focus of this book is on the Brussels I Regulation.

1.03 Relationship between jurisdictional systems

This puts the common law rules in their place. There is a clear sense in which the common law rules are precarious: they continue to apply in civil and commercial matters only insofar as these European instruments have not laid down jurisdictional rules which contradict them. If proceedings in a civil or commercial matter are commenced in England against someone who has no relevant connection with any of the Member States, the English court will have jurisdiction in accordance with the common law and civil procedure rules, via Article 6 of the Regulation. In such circumstances it cannot be said

---

8 Published in the Official Journal of the European Communities: [2012] OJ L351/1. This is described as a 'recast' of the original Brussels I Regulation, Regulation 44/2001, [2001] OJ L12/1.

9 European Communities Act 1972.

10 C-185/07 *Allianz SpA v. West Tankers Inc* [2009] ECR I-663.

that the Regulation 'has no application' to such a case.[11] In such a case the Regulation prevents the courts of another Member State taking jurisdiction over the same case,[12] even if the traditional jurisdictional laws of that State would have permitted it. It permits the claimant to seek provisional or protective relief from the courts of other Member States;[13] and it will provide, in due course, for the recognition and probable enforcement of the English judgment in all other Member States. Given this, it is neither helpful nor correct to contend that the Regulation 'has no application'. It does have application, and that is that.[14]

In any case which may come before the courts of a Member State one must start by asking whether (and if so, on what basis) the Regulation confers jurisdiction on the court. It may in principle do three things: it may give the English[15] court jurisdiction over the dispute; it may potentially give jurisdiction to the courts of England and to those in another Member State; or it may give jurisdiction to the courts of another Member State, and deny it to the English courts. In the first case the court may, and generally must, hear the case if called upon by the claimant to do so. In the second case, the court may hear the case if it is seised first in time, but may not do so if the courts of the other Member State were seised first and still remain seised. In the third case, the court may not hear the case at all.

The jurisdiction conferred by the Regulation is statutory, legislated, jurisdiction. It is, in a very fundamental way, very different from the jurisdiction – the inherent jurisdiction – which the English courts have as a matter of common law. It is, as English lawyers now understand, unsurprising that rules of judicial procedure which apply when a court is dealing with a case over which it has inherent jurisdiction do not find a place when a court is dealing with a case in which it has been given legislative, statutory jurisdiction. It may have taken a while to appreciate this, but there seems to be little remaining doubt about it.

PRIMARY SOURCES OF THE LAW

1.04 The Conventions

Though the Brussels I Regulation is the starting point for the determination of the jurisdiction of the English courts, it is necessary to list the instruments which formed the stepping stones to these rules. There were five editions of the Brussels Convention: (a) the original Brussels Convention, made between the six original members of the EEC; (b) the

---

11 See Jenard [1979] OJ C59/1, 20–21. (As to Jenard, see para. 1.15 below.)

12 Suppose the defendant to the English proceedings wished to bring a counter-action in France.

13 Suppose the defendant has a bank account in France, and it is wished to freeze it to prevent his spiriting the money away and frustrating a later attempt to enforce the judgment.

14 Jurisdiction taken by virtue of certain other specialist Conventions (see Art. 71 of the Regulation) is similarly justified.

15 As will be seen, the Regulation generally allocates jurisdiction to the courts of the United Kingdom, which is the Member State, not to the courts of England, for England is not currently a State, never mind a Member State. Where this happens, the identification of a court within the United Kingdom is generally a matter of domestic United Kingdom law. But to maintain the purity of this structure would be cumbersome and tedious; from time to time reference will be made to the English courts which should more correctly be understood as a reference to the United Kingdom (and within these, the English) courts.

amended Brussels Convention, to which Denmark, Ireland and the United Kingdom became Contracting States; (c) the re-amended Brussels Convention, to which Greece also became a party; (d) the re-re-amended Brussels Convention, to which Portugal and Spain also became party; and (e) the re-re-re-amended Brussels Convention to which also Austria, Finland and Sweden became party. The designation of 'the Brussels Convention' may be taken to refer to any or all of these versions of the Brussels Convention, as the context may require. Alongside these, the original Lugano Convention was made between the States of the expanded EEC and the members of the European Free Trade Association. It was amended once, to allow the accession of Poland.

A significant change was made by the Brussels I Regulation, Regulation 44/2001, which came into force on 1 March 2002. The Regulation had and has direct effect in the Member States according to the law of the European Union, and has effect in English law by virtue of the European Communities Act 1972. It was, and still is, occasionally and misleadingly referred to[16] in England as 'the Judgments Regulation', but the nomenclature of 'the Brussels I Regulation' is now universal. On the accession of 10 new Member States on 1 May 2004, it became directly applicable in and to those States as well; on the accession of Bulgaria and Romania on 1 January 2007 it became directly applicable in and to those States; and it took effect in relation to Croatia on 1 July 2013. All these States are, from the date on which the Regulation became directly effective in relation to them, 'Member States'. The Brussels I Regulation supplanted and overrode the Brussels Convention except where it left a gap for the continued operation of the Convention.

In principle this means that the Brussels Convention applied to proceedings instituted before 1 March 2002, or until 1 July 2007 in any case in which Denmark was concerned, for Denmark originally exercised its right to opt out of the Regulation,[17] agreeing to accept it only as from 1 July 2007.[18] It continues to apply to proceedings which relate to a small scattering of non-European territories of the Member States to which the Regulation does not extend but to which the Conventions did and continue to apply. The Regulation had no direct impact on the Lugano Convention, though the revised Lugano Convention, 'Lugano II', is in effect a copy of Regulation 44/2001.

A further change was made when the Brussels I Regulation was 'recast'. Though it was both claimed and conceded that the Regulation had worked well, there was some evidence that it had not succeeded in making the enforcement of judgments as smooth and automatic as it was possible for it to be; and it was further arguable that certain aspects of its jurisdictional rules were in need of attention. An updated text, made to take effect as Regulation 1215/2012, was adopted in 2012, two years prior to its taking effect on 10 January 2015. This version of the Regulation supplies the text which is used in this book to organise the law on civil jurisdiction.

The judicial decisions which will be used to assist the interpretation of Regulation 1215/2012 will all have been decided on the basis of corresponding provisions of one or

---

16 The nomenclature derives from SI 2001/3929, which makes various alterations to English law in the light of the Regulation. SI 2001/3929 was itself amended by SI 2014/2947, to take account of the recast Regulation 1215/2013, and the amended text is from time to time referred to in this book as the 'recast' Statutory Instrument.

17 Denmark was therefore a Contracting State to the Brussels (and Lugano) Conventions, but was not originally a Member State in which the Regulation was in effect.

18 For this to be brought about, a parallel agreement was required: [2006] OJ L120/22; for implementation in the United Kingdom, see SI 2007/1655. Aside from any issue about the material dates (the parallel agreement with Denmark does not have retrospective effect) Denmark may now be regarded as a Member State.

other of the editions of the Conventions or of Regulation 44/2001. As this book is intended as a guide to the future rather than a record of the past, and for convenience of future use, references in the following text have tried to use the terminology and the numbering system of Regulation 1215/2012, even when discussing cases decided on the basis of an earlier text. On those few occasions on which it felt as though this would just be wrong, an older numbering may have been used; but signposts have been planted where they appeared to be most needed. Awareness of the context will almost always dispel confusion, but for those cases where this claim proves to be too optimistic (to say nothing of those in which the process of updating and renumbering has failed to meet the target it set for itself), it is hoped that the reader will be forgiving.

With that explanation, the particulars of the various jurisdictional instruments can be given.

1.05 The Brussels Convention

The original Brussels Convention was signed on 27 September 1968. The parties to it were France, Germany, Italy, Belgium, the Netherlands and Luxembourg. It was published in the Official Journal.[19]

1.06 Accession of Denmark, Ireland and the United Kingdom

When the United Kingdom, Ireland and Denmark joined the European Community they acceded to the system of civil jurisdiction and judgments created by the Brussels Convention. The opportunity was taken to make some changes to the Convention, and an Accession Convention was entered into on 9 October 1978. It was published in the Official Journal,[20] but the most accessible place to find the amended text of the Brussels Convention is in Schedule 1 to the Civil Jurisdiction and Judgments Act 1982.[21] It came into force in the United Kingdom on 1 January 1987, upon which date the United Kingdom became a Contracting State.

1.07 Accession of the Hellenic Republic

When Greece joined the European Community it acceded to the scheme of civil jurisdiction and judgments. This was done by an Accession Convention, which incorporated Greece and its courts, but which made no other changes to the Convention. It was signed on 25 October 1982, and was published in the Official Journal.[22] The Brussels Convention, as re-amended to take account of the accession, appears in the Civil Jurisdiction and Judgments Act 1982 (Amendment) Order 1989.[23] It came into force in the United Kingdom on 1 October 1989.

---

19 [1978] OJ L304/36.

20 [1978] OJ L304/77.

21 Referred to throughout this book as 'the 1982 Act'. It should be noted that the English language text is only one of several language versions which are equally authentic: see Art. 68 of the Convention. The English text appears in Sch. 1 to the 1982 Act 'for convenience of reference': see s. 2(2) of the 1982 Act.

22 [1982] OJ L388/1.

23 SI 1989/1346.

1.08 Accession of Portugal and Spain

When Spain and Portugal joined the European Community they acceded to the scheme of civil jurisdiction and judgments. This was done by an Accession Convention, signed on 26 May 1989, which incorporated Spain and Portugal into the scheme, but which also made some substantive changes to the text of the existing Brussels Convention. The text was published in the Official Journal,[24] and the Brussels Convention as re-re-amended to take account of these changes appears in the Civil Jurisdiction and Judgments Act 1982 (Amendment) Order 1990.[25] It came into force in the United Kingdom on 1 December 1991.

1.09 Accession of Austria, Finland and Sweden

When Austria, Finland and Sweden joined the European Union, as it had by then become, they acceded to the scheme of civil jurisdiction and judgments. This was done by an Accession Convention signed on 29 November 1996, which incorporated Austria, Finland and Sweden into the scheme, but which made no other substantive changes to the text of the existing Brussels Convention. The re-re-re-amended text was published in the Official Journal,[26] and also appears in the Civil Jurisdiction and Judgments Act 1982 (Amendment) Order 2000.[27] It came into force in the United Kingdom on 1 January 2001. This represented the final chapter in the development of the law by means of adjustment to the original Brussels Convention.

1.10 The Lugano Convention

As the European Community expanded, a parallel Convention was entered into, in Lugano, between the then States of the European Community and those States party to the European Free Trade Association ('the EFTA': Norway, Sweden, Finland, Iceland, Austria and Switzerland) which at that date were not also members of the European Community. The substance of the Convention was very substantially the same as the Brussels Convention as re-re-amended on the accession of Portugal and Spain, but as it was not part of the family of Brussels Conventions, the European Court had no jurisdiction to interpret it. Austria, Finland and Sweden then joined the European Union, and from 1 March 2002 they were Member States bound by the Brussels I Regulation. However, in relation to Iceland, Norway and Switzerland, the Lugano Convention remained the relevant jurisdictional text.[28] On the accession of Poland,[29] it applied in relation to that State also, though from 1 January 2004, Poland was a Member State of the European Union. It was published in the Official Journal,[30] and appeared as Schedule 1 to the Civil

---

24 [1989] OJ L285/1.

25 SI 1990/2591.

26 [1997] OJ C15/1.

27 SI 2000/1824.

28 Liechtenstein became a full member of the EFTA in 1991, but it did not accede to, and has shown no sign of wishing to accede to, the Lugano Convention. The reasons are not hard to guess.

29 Pursuant to Art. 62; and see Civil Jurisdiction and Judgments Act 1982 (Amendment) Order 2000: SI 2000/1824, in force in the United Kingdom from 1 August 2000. But since 1 May 2004, Poland was a Member State of the European Union, bound by the Brussels I Regulation.

30 [1988] OJ L319/9.

Jurisdiction and Judgments Act 1991.[31] It came into force in the United Kingdom on 1 May 1992.[32]

1.11 The Brussels I Regulation: Regulation (EC) 44/2001

Proceeding from the view that it had power to legislate directly in the field of civil jurisdiction and judgments, that power then being conferred by Article 65 of the Treaty establishing the European Community, the Council of the European Union adopted a Regulation which took direct effect in the Member States of the European Union. The term 'Member States', when used in this context originally excluded Denmark, which did not agree to be bound by the Regulation until 1 July 2007.[33] It was published in the Official Journal,[34] and took effect in all Member States on 1 March 2002. Its practical effect was to supersede the Brussels Convention as between the Member States in relation to proceedings instituted on or after that date.

There were a number of occasions of minor and technical amendment to the Brussels I Regulation. First, some minor corrections were made to the Regulation by a Corrigendum,[35] and minor alterations by Regulation.[36] Second, on 1 May 2004, ten States acceded to membership of the European Union: Cyprus, the Czech Republic, Estonia, Hungary, Latvia, Lithuania, Malta, Poland, Slovakia and Slovenia. The necessary adjustments to the Regulation, which were mechanical and procedural, were made by the Act of Accession which was published in the Official Journal.[37] Third, on 1 January 2007, Bulgaria and Romania acceded to membership of the European Union. The necessary technical adjustments to the Brussels I Regulation were made by Regulation;[38] so also, fourth, when Croatia acceded to membership on 1 July 2013.[39]

1.12 The Lugano II Convention

Meanwhile, the text of the Lugano Convention was amended to bring it substantially into line with the Brussels I Regulation 44/2001.[40] Formally speaking, the parties to the new Convention, 'Lugano II', were the European Union, which had by then acquired the external competence for the negotiation of such Conventions which the Member States

---

31 The 1991 Act amended the 1982 Act by the addition of a new s. 3A and Sch. 3C, and made other consequential changes. The effect is that the 1982 Act, as amended, is the statutory basis for the operation of the Lugano Convention in the United Kingdom.

32 SI 1992/745.

33 Article 1(3) of the Regulation (for the original opting out); [2006] OJ L120/22 for the subsequent opting in; and SI 2007/1655 for the incorporation of this Decision into English law.

34 [2001] OJ L12/1.

35 Published in [2001] OJ L307/28.

36 To take account of some reorganisation of courts in Germany and the Netherlands. It was made as Council Regulation (EC) 1496/2002, published in [2002] OJ L225/13.

37 [2004] OJ L236/33.

38 Council Regulation (EC) 1791/2006, [2006] OJ L363/1. The consolidated, post-2002, amendments to the Annexes were published as Council Regulation (EC) 280/2009, [2009] OJ L93/13. From time to time a further (unofficial) consolidated version is published.

39 [2013] OJ L158/1.

40 For the text, [2007] OJ L339/1. For a comparison with the 1988 Convention, see Pocar (2008) 10 *Yearbook of Private International Law* 1.

no longer have,[41] and the Contracting States of Iceland, Norway and Switzerland.[42] It is practically identical to the Brussels I Regulation, and the most helpful report on the Lugano II Convention by Professor Pocar is the closest thing we have to an explanatory report on the Brussels I Regulation 44/2001. The Convention took effect in relation to Norway on 1 January 2010, Switzerland on 1 January 2011, and Iceland on 1 May 2011.

1.13 The Brussels I Regulation 'recast': Regulation 1215/2012

A project to refurbish the Brussels I Regulation was commenced after five years of operation of Regulation 44/2001. The principal basis for the work was a Report coordinated at the University of Heidelberg.[43] The broad aims of the recast Regulation 1215/2012 were less wide-ranging than the Heidelberg Reporters may have hoped for, but they included four points above all: (i) to make the enforcement of judgments quicker and more straightforward; (ii) to give greater power to the court designated by an agreement on jurisdiction; (iii) to reduce the complications caused by the untidy relationship between arbitration and the Regulation; and (iv) to take a step towards the harmonisation of rules for taking jurisdiction over defendants not domiciled in Member States. Of these, the first was successful and rational; the second successful if less obviously rational; the third only partly successful; and the fourth a failure which appeared to be rather ahead of its time. The Regulation was published in 2012, which meant that there was plenty of time to prepare for its coming into force on 10 January 2015.[44]

The jurisdictional provisions of the recast Regulation 1215/2012 apply to proceedings instituted on or after 10 January 2015: for this reason this book is organised on the basis that this is the legislative text which states the law. The provisions for the enforcement of judgments, however, apply only to judgments given in proceedings commenced after that date, and for this reason it will be several years before Regulation 1215/2012 will serve as the basic text for the enforcement of judgments. For this reason, Chapter 7 of this book will not precisely reflect the structure of Chapter 2, but will assume that any recognition and enforcement of judgments from other Member States will, for some years, be governed in practice by Regulation 44/2001.

SECONDARY SOURCES OF THE LAW

1.14 General

The text of the Regulation and of the Conventions is the primary source of the rules on jurisdiction and the effect of foreign judgments. But these instruments are written in all official languages of the European Union, and all of them are equally authentic.[45] On occasions,

---

41 See 1/03 *Lugano Opinion* [2006] ECR I-1145.

42 Liechtenstein appeared to play no part in the process.

43 Published as Hess, Pfeiffer & Schlosser, *The Brussels I Regulation 44/2001* (Beck, Munich, 2008).

44 Denmark agreed to be bound by Regulation 1215/2012 by agreement with the European Union: [2013] OJ L79/4. An amendment to the original text of Regulation 1215/2012, to provide for the Unified Patent Court, was made by Regulation 542/2014, [2014] OJ L163/1.

45 See, for illustration of the technique, C-347/08 *Vorarlberger Gebietskrankenkasse v. WGV-Schwäbische Allgemeine Versicherungs AG* [2009] ECR I-8661, [25]–[28].

there are minor differences between them, and where these have significance they are pointed out. In general and from day to day, the English language versions are sufficient.

1.15 Official Reports on the Brussels and Lugano Conventions

The Brussels and Lugano Conventions were each supplemented by a Report giving background and explanation to the text.[46] These Reports had significant influence in the interpretation of the Conventions and therefore bear on the construction of corresponding provisions of the Brussels I Regulation.[47] The Brussels Convention was accompanied by the Report signed by Mr Jenard;[48] the Accession Convention for the United Kingdom by the Report signed by Professor Peter Schlosser;[49] the Accession Convention for the Hellenic Republic by the Report of Professors Evrigenis and Kerameus;[50] the Accession Convention for Portugal and Spain by the Report of Messrs Almeida Cruz, Desantes Real and Jenard;[51] the Lugano Convention by the Report of Messrs Jenard and Möller;[52] and the Lugano II Convention by the Report signed by Professor Pocar.[53] So far as English law is concerned, the legislation which implemented the relevant Conventions expressly provided[54] that the English courts were entitled to consider the Reports and to give them such weight as was appropriate in the circumstances. As a matter of fact, the English courts have tended to follow the advice given in the Reports. So too has the European Court: there are rather few cases where the Court has chosen to depart from the expressed views of the Reporter.[55]

There is no equivalent, nor other *travaux préparatoires* worthy of the name, to assist with the interpretation and construction of the Brussels I Regulation, original or recast. The preambles contain a number of recitals of rather general and unspecific content.

1.16 References to the European Court for a preliminary ruling

In order to establish uniformity in the interpretation and application of the Conventions, the Court of Justice was given jurisdiction to take references for a preliminary ruling on the interpretation of the provisions of the Brussels Conventions from national courts. The national courts which had this power were once restricted to those exercising appellate jurisdiction; but Article 267 of the Treaty on the Functioning of the European Union, which makes provision for references for a preliminary ruling on the interpretation of the Brussels I Regulation, now states:

---

46 In England, it is usual to refer to these as 'the Jenard Report', 'the Schlosser Report', etc: see s. 3(3) of the 1982 Act, as amended. But the named individual was no more than the *Rapporteur* for the meeting of experts, and it is unfair to ascribe to the named individuals personal responsibility for the common or agreed text of the Report: a point arguably overlooked by the Advocate General in C-190/89 *Marc Rich & Co AG v. Società Italiana Impianti SpA* [1991] ECR I-3855.

47 *Cf* C-533/07 *Falco Privatstiftung v. Weller-Lindhorst* [2009] ECR I-3327.

48 [1979] OJ C59/1.

49 [1979] OJ C59/71.

50 [1986] OJ C298/1.

51 [1990] OJ C189/35.

52 [1990] OJ C189/57.

53 [2009] OJ C319/1.

54 See, for example, s. 3 of the 1982 Act.

55 One example of such departure was 241/83 *Rösler v. Rottwinkel* [1985] ECR 99.

'**[TFEU, Art 267]** The Court of Justice of the European Union shall have jurisdiction to give preliminary rulings concerning: (a) the interpretation of the Treaties; (b) the validity and interpretation of acts of the institutions, bodies, offices or agencies of the Union. Where such a question is raised before any court or tribunal of a Member State, that court or tribunal may, if it considers that a decision on the question is necessary to enable it to give judgment, request the Court to give a ruling thereon. Where any such question is raised in a case pending before a court or tribunal of a Member State against whose decisions there is no judicial remedy under national law,[56] that court or tribunal shall bring the matter before the Court...'

The power to make a reference to the European Court is not now restricted to courts exercising an appellate jurisdiction: any national court may make a reference requesting a preliminary ruling on the interpretation of the Brussels I Regulation. This will have added considerably to the workload of the Court; it may explain why it is increasingly (and not always obviously wisely) prepared to dispense with an Opinion from an Advocate General, the numbers of whom have not kept up with the increasing workload of the Court.

The practical question for the national court called on to make a reference for a preliminary ruling is whether it is necessary to invoke the reference procedure to obtain a ruling in the context of the dispute pending before the national court. The question is, after all, not an abstract or theoretical one: the fact that it may take somewhere between one and two years for a referring court to receive its answer forms part of the data which inform the decision whether to make a reference.

That said, the duty of the national court is to apply European law, and to apply it properly. It follows that if there is a rule of national law by which a court is bound by the decision of a superior court which cannot be properly distinguished, but which it considers to be wrong, it cannot be allowed to call into question the obligation arising from Article 267 TFEU. Though the point has not always been appreciated in England,[57] the constant jurisprudence of the European Court has made it clear that a national law principle of precedent or of *stare decisis* does not override the duty of a national court to make a reference if it considers that Article 267 otherwise requires it to do so. Of course, if a national court considers that a ruling from the European Court will not be necessary to enable it to give judgment, on the basis that its judgment will be the same whatever answer to the question referred might be given,[58] or because it is clear[59] in its own mind what the correct answer is, it has no duty, and, if Article 267 is taken literally, no power, to make a reference. By contrast, if a judge apprehends that the national rules of judicial precedent might result in the misapplication of Union law, a reference should be made for a ruling from the European Court. For as the European Court put it, 'a rule of national law whereby a court is bound on points of law by

---

56   In England, that means the Supreme Court, not the Court of Appeal: *Chiron Corp v. Murex Diagnostics Ltd* [1995] All ER (EC) 88; *cf* C-99/00 *Lyckeskog* [2002] ECR I-4839.

57   *Dar Al Arkan Real Estate Development Co v. Majid Al-Sayed Bader Hashim Al-Rifai* [2013] EWHC 4112 (QB), and *The Conde Nast Publications Ltd v. HMRC* [2006] EWCA Civ 976, must be considered to be wrong so far as European Union law is concerned: the point was not raised on appeal in the former case: *Dar Al Arkan Real Estate Development Co v. Majid Al-Sayed Bader Hashim Al-Rifai* [2014] EWCA Civ 715, [2015] a WLR 135. The position in relation to the European Convention on Human Rights, on which see *Kay v. Lambeth LBC* [2006] UKHL 10, [2006] 2 AC 465, [40]–[45], is different.

58   On the footing, for example, that it is bound to apply a decision of the Court of Appeal or Supreme Court which it is unable to distinguish.

59   Bearing in mind that what may be clear from the English language version of the Regulation may not be so clear when equally authentic versions in other languages are looked at: 283/81 *CILFIT v. Ministry of Health* [1982] ECR 3415.

the rulings of a superior court cannot deprive the inferior courts of their power to refer to the Court questions of interpretation of Community law involving such rulings... if inferior courts were bound without being able to refer matters to the Court, the jurisdiction of the latter to give preliminary rulings and the application of Community law at all levels of the judicial system of the Member States would be compromised.'[60]

The reference procedure is the principal[61] mechanism by which uniform definitions of legislative terms are produced. When it is dealing with a matter in which it has to apply a term of art of European private international law, but on which the European Court has not established the basis for the uniform interpretation, a national court will guide itself by asking how the European Court would be expected to answer if the question were to be put to it; and must be prepared to make a preliminary reference for a ruling if it is less than sure of the answer.[62]

1.17 The authority of decided cases

The most authoritative of judicial decisions are those of the European Court: its rulings which bind the courts of all Member States.[63] In relation to the Brussels I Regulation, this is provided for by European Communities Act 1972. The European Court does sometimes deliver rather narrow rulings, tailored for the particular case in which the reference has been made, but from which it is not always easy to generalise; there is, therefore, scope for the interpretation of decisions of the Court, which tend to be referred to cumulatively as the 'jurisprudence' of the Court.

Decisions of the Court were officially reported in the European Court Reports. Every decision of the Court was so reported, but the speed of production became slower and slower and eventually ground to a halt when in 2014 it was decided to discontinue the publication of the European Court Reports with effect from the end of 2011. In place of these reports, the official version of the judgment is published in electronic form on the EUR-lex website. A system of 'neutral citation' was introduced at the same time, with the intention that this also be applied with retrospective effect. According to this system as publicised by the Court, a decision which had been reported, identified, and previously referred to as C-281/02 *Owusu v. Jackson* [2005] ECR I-1383 will instead be identified as 'Judgment in *Owusu*, C-281/02, EU:C:2005:120', and on subsequent occasions as 'Judgment in *Owusu*, EU:C:2005:120'. In

---

60   166/73 *Rheinmühlen-Düsseldorf v. Einfuhr- und Vorratsstelle für Getreide und Futtermittel* [1974] ECR 33; C-396/09 *Interedil Srl v. Fallimento Interedil Srl* [2011] ECR I-9915. For a similar ruling, that national procedural law as to *res judicata* must not impair (and on the facts, did impair) the European principle of effectiveness, see C-32/12 *Duarte Herros v. Autociba SA* EU:C:2013:637, [2014] 1 All ER (Comm) 267. For a ruling that a rule of national procedural law restricting rights of appeal on a question of jurisdiction must not impair (and on the facts, did not impair) the principle of effectiveness in EU law, see C-413/12 *Asociación de Consumadores Independientes de Castilla y León v. Anuntis Segundamano España SL* EU:C:2013:800; also C-112/13 *A v. B* EU:C:2014:2195. It must follow that a rule of English procedural law to the effect that a national court is bound by a rule of *stare decisis* to apply a decision of a superior court in circumstances in which it considers the precedent may be wrong as a matter of European law is itself contrary to European law: if that was not clear before, C-112/13 *A v. B* EU:C:2014:2195 means that it is clear now.

61   The decisions of national courts, and the writings of commentators, play a gap-filling role.

62   For a detailed analysis by the Supreme Court of the problems which arise when the European Court appears to have ignored the proper interpretation of European legislation, and the difficulty which this poses for a national court, see *R (on the application of HS2 Action Alliance Ltd) v. Secretary of State for Transport* [2014] UKSC 3, [2014] 1 WLR 324, [161] *et seq.*

63   European Communities Act 1972, s. 3.

this formula, 'EU' indicates that the judgment was given by a European court;[64] 'C' indicates that it was given by the Court;[65] '2005' indicates the year in which the item – judgment, opinion – was handed down;[66] and '120' indicates that it was the 120th published item to have a serial number attached to it in that year. It seems unnecessary to add these neutral citations to decisions published in the European Court Reports,[67] but proper to use them for decisions handed down from 1 January 2012. Although some references may have slipped through the net, this is the approach sought to be applied in this book.

Decisions of English courts have the effect that they normally do: subject to what was said above, the ordinary principles of *stare decisis* apply to them. Decisions of courts of other Member States may have some influence. There have been cases[68] in which English judges have made reference in their reasoning to a decision given by a court in another Member State, but as there is no real way to be sure that those decisions from other courts cited by counsel are representative of the whole range of judicial decisions in Member States, and as they will often lack the status of *stare decisis* in the State of origin, caution is needed when using them in an English court.

1.18 Academic sources

There has been an observable tendency for courts to refer to academic sources as making some contribution to the proper interpretation of the Conventions.[69] Upon the interpretation of the common law rules, where these still govern, academic sources have rather less influence.

HUMAN RIGHTS AND DISCRIMINATION

1.19 European Union law and the Human Rights Act

It is now apparent that the law which prohibits discrimination on grounds of nationality, and the Human Rights Act 1998, have the potential to modify or annul certain rules of

---

64 It is intended that the system be capable of use by national courts as well.

65 As distinct from the Court of First Instance ('Tribunal', or 'T').

66 For example, the Opinion of the Advocate General in *Owusu* will be cited as 'Opinion in *Owusu*, C-281/02, EU:C:2004:798'.

67 Though they can be found in the Table in Appendix III to this book.

68 For example, *Kurz v. Stella Musical Veranstaltungs GmbH* [1992] Ch 196.

69 A number of English works are standard on this topic, but Dicey, Morris and Collins, *The Conflict of Laws*, 15th edn, 2012, plus cumulative supplements, holds the rank of *princeps liborum*. Reference may also be made to Layton and Mercer, *European Civil Practice*, 2nd edn (Sweet & Maxwell, London, 2004) (the first edition appearing *sub nom* O'Malley and Layton); Cheshire, North and Fawcett, *Private International Law*, 14th edn (Oxford University Press, 2008); and Hill and Chong, *International Commercial Disputes*, 4th edn (Hart, Oxford, 2010), though all predate Regulation 1215/2012. On jurisdiction and arbitration agreements, see Joseph, *Jurisdiction and Arbitration Agreements and their Enforcement*, 2nd edn (Sweet & Maxwell, London, 2010).

A leading French commentator, Gaudemet-Tallon, is the author of *Compétence et exécution des Jugements en Europe*, 4th edn (LGDJ, Paris, 2010), which offers probably the most useful civilian perspective on the scheme of the Conventions and Regulation 44/2001. A commentary in English, edited by Magnus and Mankowski, *Brussels Ibis Regulation*, 2nd edn (Sellier, Munich, 2011) calls to mind the curate's egg, but it does offer indirect access to some non-English material. Finally, a comparative analysis by Van Lith, *International Jurisdiction and Commercial Litigation* (Asser, The Hague, 2009) contains a lot of interesting material, though more in the form of a scholarly study than as a guide to the busy practitioner.

law in the field of civil jurisdiction and judgments. The precise extent of this is still being worked out, but at this stage it is necessary to indicate the general lines of argument.

The principal source of law prohibiting discrimination on grounds of nationality is Article 18[70] TFEU, which provides that 'Within the scope of application of this Treaty, and without prejudice to any special provisions contained therein, any discrimination on grounds of nationality shall be prohibited'. As the law on jurisdiction and enforcement of judgments in civil and commercial matters falls under Article 81 TFEU, the provisions of Article 18 TFEU may be applied to rules of civil jurisdiction and judgments. Article 18 TFEU does not prevent differentiation on grounds of nationality in circumstances where there is an objective justification for the distinction; the issue therefore resolves into two limbs: does the rule of law lead to discrimination on grounds of nationality; and if it does, whether there are objective reasons to justify it.

An illustration of the working of this principle can be seen in the rules which allow a court to order a claimant, or appellant, to provide security for costs in the event that he is unsuccessful and is held liable to his opponent in costs.[71] Once upon a time[72] such an order would be easily obtained against a claimant who was ordinarily resident out of the jurisdiction, on the footing that the costs of enforcing a costs order against someone who may have no assets within the jurisdiction would be greater than where the claimant was local. But it came to be understood[73] that this was unjustifiable where the claimant was resident in a Contracting State to the Brussels or Lugano Conventions, or a Member State in which the Brussels I Regulation was in force, where the enforcement of an English costs order would in principle be little more problematic than at home. The rule was held (in this respect) to be unlawful; and the Civil Procedure Rules were subsequently amended to bring them into line with the requirements of what is now Article 18 TFEU.

But other examples exist. Some national systems, such as the French, allow for a form of service of process on a defendant[74] not domiciled in France to be made by *remise au parquet*, or delivery of the document to the court office, from which it is supposed to be transmitted to the defendant. But if the document never reaches the defendant, it appears that the fact of *remise* is still sufficient to establish due service. A German court once ruled[75] that this could not constitute due service for the purpose of the Brussels Convention, or Regulation, as it discriminated on grounds of nationality against non-French defendants, contrary to what is now Article 18 TFEU. The reasoning was that the pretended service by *remise* will be made much more frequently against foreign defendants than against those who are French

---

70 Formerly Art. 12 TEU.

71 CPR rr 25.12–15.

72 When the procedure was contained in RSC Order 23.

73 *Porzelack KV v. Porzelack (UK) Ltd* [1997] 1 WLR 420; *De Bry v. Fitzgerald* [1990] 1 WLR 552; *Berkeley Administration Inc v. McLelland* [1990] 2 QB 407; *Fitzgerald v. Williams* [1996] QB 657; and see C-398/92 *Mund & Fester v. Hatrex International Transport* [1994] ECR I-467; C-43/95 *Data Delecta Akt v. MSL Dynamics Ltd* [1996] ECR I-4661.

74 Maybe the point is better understood as service *to* the defendant.

75 *Re the Enforcement of a French Interlocutory Order* (9W 67/97) [2001] ILPr 208. Another German court, whose decision is not available in English, made a reference concerning the same points, to the Court of Justice. By its decision in C-522/03 *Scania Finance France SA v. Rockinger Spezialfabrik für Anhängerkupplungen GmbH & Co* [2005] ECR I-8639, the Court ruled that the document instituting the proceedings was required to be served in accordance with Art. IV of the Protocol Annexed to the Brussels Convention, and that as a result it was not necessary to go on to consider whether the French rule permitting 'pretend service' was unlawful as discriminating against non-French nationals.

nationals; and this discrimination cannot be justified by objective factors when, in reality, all it does is show a bias that favours French defendants, who will generally receive service personally, faster, and more reliably. It seems clear that the German view was well founded; and it has since been held[76] that such service is incompatible with the Service Regulation.[77] The extent to which Article 18 TFEU may be used to attack other rules of jurisdiction and civil procedure which show conscious or unconscious bias against nationals of other Member States remains to be explored. Likewise, it remains to be seen whether the Charter of Fundamental Rights of the European Union, Article 47 of which deals with the right to a fair trial, will have any impact, other than rhetorical, on the interpretation of the Brussels I Regulation.[78]

1.20 The European Convention on Human Rights

Separate and distinct from the provisions of the European Treaty, the European Convention for the Protection of Human Rights and Fundamental Freedoms ('ECHR') was given the force of law in the United Kingdom by the Human Rights Act 1998. It came into force in the United Kingdom in October 2000. It has made and will make a further contribution to the issues to be examined in this book. The details of the Act, and of the jurisprudence of the European Court of Human Rights and European Commission of Human Rights, represent a major study in their own right, and there exist a number of detailed and thorough treatises to which reference may be made. For present purposes it is proposed to give a very brief outline of the scope and effect of the 1998 Act; and then to identify a number of points which may have a noticeable impact on the particular legal issues which arise in the context of civil jurisdiction and judgments.

The Act extends its various forms of protection to 'persons': an expression which encompasses natural and legal persons, so an association of individuals, and a corporate body, are entitled to the rights secured by the ECHR and the 1998 Act in the same way as a natural person. There is no limitation on grounds of nationality, or to particular nationalities, or on grounds of place of establishment: the fundamental rule is that if the person is within the power or jurisdiction of the English court then the protections of the Act will be applicable to him, her, it, or them.

The precise formulation of this aspect of the scope of the Convention, and what it means in an individual case which has points of contact with non-Contracting States,

---

76 C-325/11 *Alder v. Orłowska* EU:C:2012:824, though on the basis that the procedure of Polish law in that case failed to protect the rights of the defence, as distinct from the challenge being directly based on discrimination on grounds of nationality.

77 Regulation 1393/2007.

78 It was mentioned in the recitals to Regulation 805/2004 on the creation of a European Enforcement Order [2004] OJ L143/15, which is examined in Chapter 7, below, but has made no impact beyond this. It is probably fair to say that the European Union is scrambling to make up ground on, or steal the ground from, the European Convention on Human Rights, which has had a much more significant impact on civil procedure, and which is not formally part of the constitutional structure of the European Union. And although Art. 6 of the Treaty on the Functioning of the European Union paved the way for the European Union to accede to the European Convention on Human Rights, in its Opinion 2/13, EU:C:2014:2475, the Court ruled that the proposed accession of the EU to the ECHR was incompatible with European law, for reasons which boil down to the assertion that the possibility that European law would be subordinated to the decisions, control, and law of a body which is not established by the European Union was itself incompatible with European law. In the light of Art. 6 TFEU, this will come as a surprise only to those who consider that treaties mean what the States which made them intended them to mean.

is not free from difficulty. In *Soering v. United Kingdom*[79] it was stated in clear terms by the European Court of Human Rights that the duty of Member States was to secure the freedoms guaranteed by the Convention to those within their jurisdiction, but also, and rather unsurprisingly, that the Convention was not applicable to States not party to it and that it was not designed as a means of imposing Convention standards on such a State. *Soering* was a case in which it was argued that the deportation of a person from England to the United States of America may involve a breach of his human rights, by reason of the treatment to which he would then be exposed: it dealt with the argument that, if an English court took a particular step, a consequence of it might be something which would violate Article 6. But for Article 6 to be applied, prospectively and predictively, as it were, by a national court, it is only reasonable to expect or require that the evidence before the court, tending to show that there may be a violation of the standards of the ECHR by the foreign court, must be very convincing, or that the nature of the anticipated violation will be flagrant.

The issues are different, and the judicial approach may also be different, when no anticipation is involved, but a court has instead to consider whether, when called upon to enforce a judgment from a State which is not party to the ECHR, the enforcement of that foreign judgment would violate Article 6 ECHR. One would suppose that it would be permissible to show that the procedure before that foreign court was of a quality which fell short of the guarantees of the ECHR in support of a contention that recognition of the judgment would give effect in England to a violation of the guarantees of the ECHR. However, in *Government of the United States of America v. Montgomery*[80] the House of Lords declined to accept an argument formulated along such lines. It considered that, for Article 6 ECHR to be used to prevent the recognition and enforcement of a judgment from a court in the United States, the degree of the failure by the American court to conduct itself in accordance with the right to a fair trial was also required to be a 'flagrant' one. This is puzzling, and it is far from clear that it should represent the last word on the point. For a national court to hold that the proceedings in a foreign court *did* fall short of the standards of Article 6, but then to go on to recognise and enforce the judgment resulting from such defective procedure, on the basis that the violation was not a particularly flagrant one, does not involve (as, by contrast, the deportation cases necessarily did) a prediction of how a foreign court will behave. It simply requires a judgment to be made about what the foreign court actually did. In this context, a requirement of 'flagrancy' does not seem to be apt. For an English court to recognise as *res judicata* a judgment falling demonstrably short of what Article 6 requires, bristles with difficulty.[81] The question is examined further below,[82] as is the related question whether the ECHR may be used to justify the non-recognition of an appellate judgment from a non-Contracting State which had set aside,

---

79 (1989) 11 EHRR 439, esp. at [86].

80 [2004] UKHL 37, [2004] 1 WLR 2241; noted (2005) 121 LQR 185.

81 See *Pellegrini v. Italy* (2002) 35 EHRR 2, where an Italian court was held to be bound to ask whether the recognition of a judicial order from the Vatican City would place the Italian court in breach of its obligations under the ECHR. Note also that the rights of an individual under the ECHR may be sufficiently respected by a judicial decision to refuse to recognise a judgment. There is no need for an English court to go further and order an anti-suit injunction to restrain the foreign court from conducting proceedings, even if there is a strong chance that they will fall short of what Art. 6 expects and requires: *Al-Bassam v. Al-Bassam* [2004] EWCA Civ 857, [2004] WTLR 757.

82 See para. 7.73, below.

on objectionable grounds, the decision of a lower court to which objection could not otherwise be taken.[83]

1.21 Article 6 of the ECHR and the right to a fair hearing

The most significant Convention right for present purposes[84] is in Article 6(1) of the ECHR, which provides in material part that:

> '[6.1] In the determination of his civil rights and obligations or of any criminal charge against him, everyone is entitled to a fair and public hearing within a reasonable time by an independent and impartial tribunal established by law.'

The right of access to justice may be endangered or lost when a jurisdiction agreement or agreement to arbitrate is enforced and English proceedings are stayed without limit of time; and if it will be significantly problematic for proceedings to be brought in the nominated court, the right conferred by Article 6(1) may be infringed by a stay.[85] If so, the court, in the exercise of its discretion, may be expected to decline to stay the proceedings. In general, if the court is sufficiently certain that the parties did freely and voluntarily agree in the terms of the clause, there should be no objection to its enforcement. Rights conferred by the Convention may in general (though not where this would conflict with an important public interest) be waived;[86] and in particular, arbitration agreements have been held to be valid and enforceable.[87] But if the alleged agreement is not founded on an actual and voluntary consensus, this analysis may not be applicable.[88] Within the context of Article 25 of the Brussels I Regulation there may be no room for such a challenge: as will be seen,[89] the requirements for a jurisdiction agreement to be valid and binding under Article 25 will appear to satisfy whatever condition is required to constitute an effective waiver of Article 6(1) ECHR. On the other hand, the proposition that a person who was not party to a bill of lading or other contract may be bound by a jurisdiction agreement contained within it[90] is less obviously correct. It may be commercially convenient for the law to require that the person who in due course acquires a bill of lading is bound by its terms, but the effect of such a rule is that a person who was not privy to, or maybe even aware of, an exclusive jurisdiction agreement finds that he is bound by it and, in consequence, may be debarred from suing in England: at this point, a step towards an argument based on Article 6(1) ECHR has been taken. It may also be argued that the effect of such a provision is not to deprive a claimant of a court, but just of the right to sue in the court he would prefer. But the proposition that he can be denied by an agreement *inter alios* is not a very attractive one.

In the context of jurisdiction agreements falling outside the scope of Article 25, such as those for the courts of non-Member States, there is more room for doubt. The decision

---

83 See *Merchant International Co Ltd v. NAK Naftogaz* [2012] EWCA Civ 196, [2012] 1 WLR 3036.

84 See Fawcett (2007) 56 ICLQ 1; Juratowich (2007) 3 JPIL 173.

85 Though if *Government of the United States of America v. Montgomery* [2004] UKHL 37, [2004] 1 WLR 2241 is applied, the nature of the prospective violation will need to be flagrant.

86 *Pfeiffer and Plankl v. Austria* (1992) 14 EHRR 692. As the English courts consider there to be an important public interest in enforcing agreements on jurisdiction and dispute resolution, this is not an issue here.

87 *Deweer v. Belgium* (1979–80) 2 EHRR 439; *R v. Switzerland* (1987) 51 *Decisions and Reports* 83.

88 *Malstrom v. Sweden* (1983) 38 Decisions and Reports 18.

89 Paragraph 2.130, below.

90 See the discussion at para. 2.135, below.

of the Privy Council in *The Pioneer Container*[91] had the effect that a jurisdiction agreement between a bailee and sub-bailee of goods was valid and enforceable against the owner of the goods when he brought proceedings against the sub-bailee. The fact that the owner had consented to sub-bailment 'on any terms' was held to establish his consent, *vis-à-vis* the sub-bailee, to a jurisdiction clause about which he did not otherwise know. Although this can hardly be seen as a case of 'involuntary agreement' to a jurisdiction clause, it is at least arguable that this application of the principles of bailment, an arrangement which has been held not to amount to an agreement for the purposes of what is now Article 25 of the recast Regulation,[92] may not be sufficient to constitute an express and unequivocal waiver of the right of access to a court, at least an English one.

When it comes to the staying of actions on the ground of *forum non conveniens*, it was the opinion of Lord Bingham of Cornhill in *Lubbe v. Cape plc*[93] that the principles of English law set out in *Spiliada Maritime Corp v. Cansulex Ltd*[94] accorded with Article 6 ECHR. As the House of Lords refused to stay proceedings in favour of a court in which the claimant would manifestly have been unable to sue – the complexity of the case and the absence of financial provision to support the bringing of the claim ensured this – there was no basis in justice for a stay of English proceedings. Had the court been otherwise inclined to order a stay, there would have been an arguable violation of Article 6(1).[95] The general principles by which Article 6(1) is illuminated appear to be that the right of access to a court is not unlimited and may be restricted, but the restriction must be proportionate to the purpose secured by the restriction, and must not be of such an extent that the very essence of the right is impaired.[96]

But it is important to remember that Article 6 ECHR does not confer an unlimited right of access to any and every court of the claimant's choosing. It is not, therefore, a violation of Article 6 ECHR for an English court to issue an injunction to require a respondent to desist from bringing proceedings in a foreign court,[97] for it is implicit in doing so that England is available as a forum for the hearing and that it is either the most appropriate forum, or the one on which the parties contractually agreed in advance.[98] It seems to follow that, even if the claimant will lose if he is confined to England for the bringing of his claim, this does not infringe his right of access to a court: his guarantee is of the right to a hearing, not of the right to be victorious.[99]

If an intending litigant is denied legal standing or legal personality, this may involve a violation of Article 6(1) ECHR;[100] exclusion from a scheme for multi-party litigation may also violate Article 6(1) unless the person excluded has the right to claim outside the

---

91 [1994] 2 AC 324.

92 *Dresser UK Ltd v. Falcongate Freight Management Ltd* [1992] QB 502.

93 [2000] 1 WLR 1545.

94 [1987] AC 460.

95 A possibility foreshadowed by Sir Thomas Bingham MR in *Connelly v. RTZ Corp plc* [1997] ILPr 643, upheld on other grounds [1998] AC 854.

96 *Lithgow v. United Kingdom* (1986) 8 EHRR 329; *Golder v. United Kingdom* (1979) 1 EHRR 524; *Prince Hans-Adam II of Liechtenstein v. Germany*, 12 July 2001.

97 Known for convenience as an 'anti-suit injunction'.

98 *OT Africa Line Ltd v. Hijazy* [2001] 1 Lloyd's Rep 76 (a very strong, and commercially sensible, judgment, though on the particular point for decision, now effectively overruled by C-159/02 *Turner v. Grovit* [2004] ECR I-3565).

99 Even so, it may just be objected that a choice of law rule may offend the guarantees of the ECHR: see, for example, *X v. Belgium and the Netherlands*, Commission Decision, 10 July 1975, (1975) 6 *Decisions and Reports* 75.

100 *Canea Catholic Church v. Greece* (1999) 27 EHRR 521.

scheme.[101] Limitation periods do not in themselves violate Article 6(1),[102] but, if a limitation provision appears to be applied inflexibly, it may be that there is room for the argument that there is a breach.[103] Orders for security for costs are not a violation of Article 6(1) if they are made in a manner which is proportionate to the interest which is to be protected.[104] Access to legal aid may raise an Article 6(1) argument, but only where the assistance of a lawyer, who could not otherwise be retained, is 'indispensable for effective access to court', either because legal representation is compulsory, or because of the complexity of the procedure or the case.[105] And it is accepted that legal aid funding is limited, and as long as the rules that are put in place to determine which cases and parties will obtain it, the decision not to award it will not constitute a violation of Article 6(1).[106] A stay of proceedings in favour of trial in a court in which the procedure will be substantially delayed may infringe Article 6(1).[107]

A claimant, when seeking permission to serve a claim form out of the jurisdiction, may argue that if permission is not given he will not in practice be able to sue, and that this triggers the application of Article 6(1). Whether this argument should succeed is far from clear. The law can hardly be that there is an absolute obligation to grant permission, but, if there is clear evidence to support the contention that if a trial does not take place in England it will not be heard at all, the reasoning in *Lubbe v. Cape plc* may suggest that permission will now be more likely to be granted.[108]

In the context of orders made without notice, the right to be present and heard[109] is probably no threat to the granting of interim remedies. In general there is such a right,[110] but, as in England, the court may set aside any order which it made in the hearing without notice, and as the evidence relied on must be disclosed[111] to the respondent, there should be no basis for challenge. Even so, Article 6 ECHR will provide further support for the argument that, when the respondent applies for the setting aside of the order made without notice, he should not face any disadvantage which arises as a result of the hearing at which he was not entitled to be present.[112] In the broader context of the recognition and enforce-

---

101 *Taylor v. United Kingdom* (1997) 23 EHRR 132.

102 And, hence, it may be supposed, staying an action for a forum in which it will be barred by limitation.

103 *Stubbings v. United Kingdom* (1997) 23 EHRR 168.

104 *Tolstoy Miloslavsky v. United Kingdom* (1995) 20 EHRR 442. The case was one of an order for security for the costs of an appeal; it would undoubtedly have been more difficult to justify an order for security before the trial at first instance.

105 *X and Y v. The Netherlands* (1975) 1 *Decisions and Reports* 66; *Airey v. Ireland* (1979) 2 EHRR 305; *Winer v. United Kingdom* (1986) 48 *Decision and Reports* 154; *Munro v. United Kingdom* (1987) 52 *Decisions and Reports* 158; *Andronicou and Constantinou v. Cyprus* (1998) 25 EHRR 491; *X v. United Kingdom* (1980) 21 *Decisions and Reports* 95.

106 *X v. United Kingdom* (1980) 21 *Decisions and Reports* 95.

107 See generally, on the effect of delay, *Stogmuller v. Austria* (1979) 2 EHRR 155; *H v. France* (1990) 12 EHRR 74; *Robins v. United Kingdom* (1998) 26 EHRR 527; *Union Alimentaria SA v. Spain* (1990) 12 EHRR 24; *Buchholz v. Germany* (1981) 3 EHRR 597.

108 See, for example, *Cherney v. Deripaska* [2009] EWCA Civ 849, [2010] 2 All ER (Comm) 456 (a decision not directly based on Art. 6 of the ECHR, but consistent with the proposition in the text). Even so, this may tend to suggest that a Contracting State to the ECHR is under some sort of obligation to allow itself to become courthouse to the world, which cannot be correct: *cf EM (Lebanon) v. Home Secretary* [2008] UKHL 64, [2009] 1 AC 1198, relying on *Z and T v. United Kingdom* (Application No 27034/05; unrep.).

109 *Brandstetter v. Austria* (1993) 15 EHRR 378; *Ruiz Mateos v. Spain* (1993) 16 EHRR 505.

110 *Dombo Beheer BV v. The Netherlands* (1994) 18 EHRR 213.

111 See, for example, CPR 25 Practice Direction – Interim Injunctions, para. 5.1(2); *Feldbrugge v. The Netherlands* (1986) 8 EHRR 425; *McGinley and Egan v. United Kingdom* (1998) 27 EHRR 1.

112 See further, para. 6.22, below.

ment of foreign judgments, the application of Article 6 of the ECHR is examined in detail in Chapter 7.

To return to our first concrete example, we revert to orders for security for costs. Within the context of Article 65 of the EC Treaty, the provisions of Article 18 TFEU were shown to have prevented the making of such orders against nationals of other Member States, it being no more difficult in principle to enforce a costs order in the state of the defendant's residence than it would be in England. But where the enforcement of the order will not fall within the provisions of the Brussels I Regulation, because it will have to be enforced in a non-Member State, and an order for security may be made, Article 6 ECHR still limits the amount of security that may be ordered: it may not exceed the extra sum which will have to be found by reason of the fact that the enforcement must be overseas: an estimate of the extra costs incurred serves as the proper limit. To order more than that, just because the respondent is resident out of the jurisdiction, will be likely to discriminate against him on grounds of nationality, to a degree which cannot be objectively justified, and in a way which will deprive him of his right to a fair trial under Article 6 ECHR.[113] But if it can be objectively justified – if, for example, the respondent has been evasive about identifying his place of residence or secretive about his assets, and there is a well-founded fear of difficulty in the enforcing of a costs order, no difficulty should be presented by Article 6 ECHR or Article 18 TFEU.[114]

Finally, it is necessary to mention a more difficult case, where it is hard to deny that there is discrimination on grounds of nationality but which, because it may not have the effect of depriving a person of his right to a fair trial, is not prohibited. As will be seen below, under the Brussels I Regulation a defendant who is not domiciled in a Member State is liable to be sued in any Member State on the basis of the traditional and exorbitant jurisdictional rules which are not made available in relation to claims raised against those domiciled in a Member State. Not only are such non-domiciled defendants denied the protection of the restricted jurisdictional rules which apply to defendants domiciled in a Member State, they are disadvantaged when it comes to the enforcement under Chapter III of the Regulation of a judgment obtained in such proceedings: they may not raise a retrospective challenge to the exercise of jurisdiction by the adjudicating court,[115] and so cannot object, at the original hearing or afterwards, to the way in which the court exercised jurisdiction over them.

One might have thought that this inequality of treatment was a form of discrimination on grounds of nationality, which was forbidden by law. But this view of first impression may be wrong. If the defendant is not a national of a Member State, Article 18 TFEU will not help him; and if he is such a national, the rules of the particular State in which he is sued still cannot be said to discriminate against all defendants of that nationality, nor to discriminate against them in relation to the freedoms secured by the European Treaty. Nor is it clear that his rights under Article 6 of the ECHR have been infringed, either. True, he will have been deprived of a jurisdictional defence which is offered to defendants from Member States, but if the effect of this cannot in his case be said to deprive him of a right to a fair trial, he appears to have no recourse to the ECHR to vouch for a complaint. If this is correct, a species of unequal treatment will have been permitted to survive, untouched by this new legislation. It

---

113 *Nasser v. United Bank of Kuwait* [2002] 1 All ER 401.
114 *Goodacre v. Bates* [2000] ILPr 527.
115 Regulation 1215/2012, Art. 45(3); Regulation 44/2001, Art. 35(3).

remains only to say that it remains there because the Member States wish it to remain: in the proposals to reform the Brussels I Regulation, the Commission had proposed measures which would have moved towards harmonisation of the jurisdictional rules for claims against defendants domiciled in non-Member States. This would have gone a considerable way to remedy a flaw in the Regulation; it was apparently ahead of its time.

CHAPTER 2

Jurisdiction under the Brussels I Regulation

INTRODUCTORY MATTERS

2.01 General

When a case is brought or to be brought in the courts of the United Kingdom, and a question of jurisdiction arises, the point of departure will be the impact of the Brussels I Regulation. For proceedings commenced before 10 January 2015 this will mean Regulation 44/2001,[1] the basic jurisdictional provision for all proceedings instituted on or after 1 March 2002.[2] For proceedings commenced on or after 10 January 2015, this will mean the recast Regulation 1215/2012,[3] the jurisdictional rule for all proceedings in civil and commercial matters instituted on or after that date.[4]

The Brussels I Regulation was the successor in title to the Brussels Convention,[5] and save where there are obvious and apparently deliberate alterations to the text found in the Convention, it is intended to reproduce, and will be interpreted as though it reproduced, the law established by the Convention.[6] The same will be true where the recast Regulation 1215/2012 reproduces the text of Regulation 44/2001.[7]

In any case in which jurisdiction is an issue there are, in broad terms, four possibilities. The first is that the Regulation does not apply at all, because the claim falls outside its domain: this may be because the claim is outside the material, or the subject matter, or the temporal, scope of the Regulation. In such a case, the traditional jurisdiction rules as set out in this book in Chapter 4[8] will govern. The second is that the claim is within the domain

---

1 [2001] OJ L12/1.

2 Articles 66 and 76.

3 [2012] OJ L351/1.

4 Article 81.

5 Civil Jurisdiction and Judgments Act 1982, Sch. 1 (as amended).

6 It became a boilerplate paragraph in judgments in 2009: C-533/07 *Falco Privatstiftung v. Weller-Lindhorst* [2009] ECR I-3327; C-167/08 *Draka NK Cables Ltd v. Omnipol Ltd* [2009] ECR I-3477; C-180/06 *Ilsinger v. Schlank & Schick GmbH (in liq)* [2009] ECR I-3571; C-111/08 *SCT Industri AB (in liq) v. Alpenblume AB* [2009] ECR I-5565; C-198/08 *Zuid-Chemie BV v. Phillippo's Mineralenfabriek NV/SA* [2009] ECR I-6917; C-298/08 *German Graphics Graphische Maschinen GmbH v. Holland Binding BV (in liq)* [2009] ECR I-8421. It continues to be: C-533/08 *TNT Express Nederland BV v. AXA Versicherung AG* [2010] ECR I-4107; C-478/12 *Maletic v. lastminute.com GmbH* EU:C:2013:735, [2014] QB 424; C-548/12 *Brogsitter v. Fabrication de Montres Normandes EURL* EU:C:2014:148, [2014] QB 753; C-302/13 *flyLAL-Lithuanian Airlines AS v. Starptautiskā lidosta Rīga VAS* EU:C:2014:2319, [2015] I-L pr 28.

7 Recital (34) to Regulation 1215/2012, second sentence.

8 But if there is some other legislative scheme, it will apply instead. In relation to insolvency and matrimonial causes, for example, Regulations 1346/2000, and 2201/2003 (replacing Regulation 1347/2000) will apply their special rules, and these will also displace the rules of the common law.

of the Regulation but the Regulation provides that the traditional jurisdictional rules, as set out in this book in Chapter 4, are to be applied, by incorporating them by reference within the broader framework of the Regulation where they operate as residual jurisdictional rules. The third is that the claim falls within the domain of the Regulation, and the Regulation identifies, by the rules set out in its Chapter II, the specific court (as distinct from merely identifying the Member State), which is to have jurisdiction; and if this is so, there is no need to look any further. The fourth is that the claim falls within the domain of the Regulation, but the Regulation specifies, by means of the jurisdictional rules set out in its Chapter II, that the courts of a Member State are to have jurisdiction. If that Member State is the United Kingdom, a further set of rules, internal to the United Kingdom, will be needed to identify the particular part (England and Wales, Scotland, Northern Ireland) of the United Kingdom whose courts have jurisdiction. It is the third and fourth of these cases, and the rules which apply to them, which are examined in this chapter.

The third category of case is more complex than it seems for, though the Regulation is the most important, it is not the only instrument which governs the jurisdiction of the courts in civil and commercial matters. In other words, the Regulation has a territorial scope as well. It yields to the Brussels and Lugano Conventions, which continue to apply principally where there are jurisdictional connections with States and territories which were covered by these Conventions but which are not, for various reasons, bound by the Regulation. Until 2007 these non-Regulation States and territories included Denmark, which had opted out of the Regulation and in relation to which the Brussels Convention rather than the Brussels I Regulation continued to govern.[9] On 1 July 2007, Denmark became bound by Regulation 44/2001;[10] it agreed to be bound by Regulation 1215/2012 by a declaration to this effect.[11] Non-Regulation territories still include the non-European possessions of France,[12] the Netherlands,[13] and the United Kingdom,[14] to which the Brussels Convention may apply but the Regulation does not.[15] Iceland, Norway, and Switzerland remain outside the European Union, and in relation to them, the Lugano Convention[16] applies. So today, when there is a possible jurisdictional connection with Iceland, Norway, or Switzerland, or to the non-European territories of the Member States, there may be need to refer to the rules of these Conventions. For the sake of completeness, it should be noted that Gibraltar counts as part of the United Kingdom for the purposes of the Regulation,[17]

---

9 Recital (22) to the Regulation.

10 The 'parallel agreement' is at [2006] OJ L120/22; it was given effect in the United Kingdom by SI 2007/1655. So far as the Brussels Convention was concerned, it was never extended to Greenland or the Færoe Islands.

11 [2013] OJ L79/4.

12 Neither Convention nor Regulation applies to Monaco or to Andorra. The *Regulation* applies in Guadeloupe, French Guiana, Martinique and Réunion, which are overseas departments of France. The *Brussels Convention* applies in the French Overseas Collectivities (formerly Territories) of New Caledonia, French Polynesia (which includes Tahiti), Mayotte, the Wallis & Futuna Islands, and in St Pierre & Miquelon.

13 The *Regulation* applies in the Netherlands; the *Brussels Convention* in Aruba; neither instrument applies in the Netherlands Antilles.

14 The *Regulation* applies to Gibraltar; neither the Regulation nor the Convention applies to the Isle of Man, the Channel Islands, the Sovereign Bases on Cyprus, or any non-European territory of the United Kingdom.

15 Recital (23) of Regulation 44/2001.

16 Regulation 1215/2012, Art. 73.

17 Article 60 of the Brussels Convention permitted the United Kingdom to extend it to Gibraltar, but the Spanish courts, in an exhibition of anarchy, refused to recognise Gibraltar judgments as judgments from the courts of the United Kingdom: see the note of the decision in [2003] ILPr 9.

albeit that it was not within the Brussels Convention. But the Isle of Man and the Channel Islands are outside the territorial scope of the Regulation, just as they were, and are, outside the territorial scope of the Conventions; the same is true for Monaco, Andorra, San Marino, the Vatican City and Liechtenstein: for jurisdiction and judgment purposes they are just about as foreign as China or Peru.

For the purposes of exposition, it makes most sense to deal with the jurisdictional regime established by Regulation 1215/2012, and to reserve to Chapter 3 the examination of those particular details in which the rules of the Brussels and Lugano Conventions (and Regulation 44/2001), diverge from the corresponding provisons of the Regulation. If this leaves the impression that the result is more complex than it should be, the impression is entirely accurate: but the world has become a complex place, and the law reflects this. Even though in most cases the enquiry can begin and end with the Brussels I Regulation, the continuing, if diminished, survival of these earlier instruments may make the determination of jurisdiction trickier than the ideal would have been.

The most problematic jurisdictional interface is the one between the Regulation and the jurisdictional rules of the common law which, as explained above, may be applicable for two quite distinct reasons but which also, for reasons also explained above,[18] understand jurisdiction and its exercise in very different ways. However, if the case falls within the scope of the Regulation, the Regulation, and it alone, governs the taking of jurisdiction. This will mean, among other things, that the traditional means of asserting jurisdiction, by serving the defendant with proceedings while he is within the jurisdiction, or by obtaining permission[19] to serve the defendant outside it, will no longer be applicable. Article 5 of Regulation 1215/2012 emphasises that these traditional rules for asserting jurisdiction may be resorted to only insofar as the Regulation permits it. The Regulation is therefore the point of jurisdictional departure in every civil or commercial case in which the jurisdiction of the courts of the United Kingdom is in question. It has mandatory effect. It obviously does not need to be pleaded; it is the law of England, even if it is not English law.

As a matter of English civil procedure, however, it is always *necessary* to serve the defendant with proceedings for the English court to have jurisdiction: it is not inaccurate to respresent the common law as proceedings on the basis that where there is service there will be jurisdiction.[20] But the Regulation is organised the other way around: where there is jurisdiction, there may be service. In cases where the defendant is within the jurisdiction, and the Regulation provides that there is jurisdiction, he may be served, and there is no more to be said. In cases where he is outside the territorial jurisdiction of the court, and the Regulation provides that the English courts have jurisdiction, he may be served: it is not necessary to seek the permission of the court to serve the defendant *ex juris*: rules 6.32[21] and 6.33[22] of the Civil Procedure Rules provide, in effect, that the defendant may be served as of right in a case where the Regulation provides the statutory basis for the jurisdiction of the court.[23]

---

18 At the beginning of this paragraph.

19 Under Part 6 of the Civil Procedure Rules 1998 (abbreviated hereafter as 'CPR'), as amended.

20 How and when service is lawful, and how a defendant may challenge service of process upon him, is examined in Chapter 5, below.

21 Service in Scotland and Northern Ireland.

22 Service outside the United Kingdom.

23 As long as he has a domicile in a Member State, or Arts 18(1), 21(2), 24 or 25 give the court jurisdiction over a defendant who is not so domiciled. The claimant must also file and serve a notice containing a statement of the grounds on which he is entitled to serve out of the jurisdiction: CPR r. 6.34(1). Practice Form N510 will

It is therefore no longer true that if the defendant is within the jurisdiction, he may be proceeded against as of right, or that, if he is outside the jurisdiction, the assertion of jurisdiction by the English courts is a matter controlled by judicial discretion. The Regulation defines the cases when a claimant has a right to sue the defendant, and the cases where he has no such right: and if he has the right to sue he has the right to serve. By and large, discretion has no part to play in the operation of the rules.

2.02 General principles of interpretation of the Regulation

The jurisdiction of English courts has been governed by European legislative texts, of one form or another, since 1 January 1987. Since then, a number of overriding general principles of interpretation applicable to those texts have emerged. It is convenient to identify four or five such general principles, though there are certainly others of narrower or of less precise operation.

The fundamental rule is clear enough: if the case falls within the provisions of the Regulation, the Regulation alone allocates jurisdiction over the defendant. It may do so by giving jurisdiction to the courts of the United Kingdom, or by giving jurisdiction to the courts of another Member State or States. If the Regulation, as properly interpreted, gives jurisdiction to the courts of the United Kingdom, those courts must exercise that jurisdiction when called upon to do so by the claimant, unless the rules of the Brussels I Regulation which deal with a situation of *lis alibi pendens*[24] are applicable, or unless the jurisdiction is founded on what is now Article 6 of the Regulation. If the Regulation allocates jurisdiction to the courts of another Member State, and also to the courts of the United Kingdom, either court, though generally not both courts at the same time,[25] may exercise jurisdiction. But if the Regulation allocates jurisdiction to the courts of another Member State and not to those of the United Kingdom, the courts of the United Kingdom do not have jurisdiction.[26] The Regulation must therefore be considered before the traditional rules of civil jurisdiction in English (and Scottish and Northern Irish) law.

2.03 The terms of the Regulation are given an equal and uniform interpretation

The substance of the preceding paragraph could (one imagines) equally be found in a book on private international law in other Member States. There is an obvious practical benefit in the provisions of the Regulation bearing, to the greatest extent possible, a meaning which is common and uniform across the Member States. It would rather diminish the

---

be used: see CPR PD 6B, para. 2.1. For the question of how certain or well-established must be the facts which confer jurisdiction under the Regulation, see para. 4.86, below. If the claimant is in doubt whether he can meet this standard, it makes practical sense to make a concurrent application for permission to serve out, just to be on the safe side: see further below, para. 5.20; see also *Mercury Communications Ltd v. Communication Telesystems International* [1999] 2 All ER (Comm) 33. It may be appropriate to explain in the witness statement in support of the application for permission to serve out the basis for the difficulty and the circumstances in which the application is made.

24 Articles 29 to 34 of Regulation 1215/2012, discussed in paras 2.260 *et seq.*, below.

25 Because the court seised second will in general be required to apply the rules of the Regulation on *lis alibi pendens*.

26 Article 5(1) of Regulation 1215/2012 states that persons domiciled in a Member State shall be sued in the courts of another Member State only in accordance with the provisions of the Regulation.

practical effect of the scheme for there to be a single text, but one which meant something different in every Member State of the European Union. This need for a uniform interpretation is met in two ways: first, by the power and the duty of certain national courts to make references to the European Court for a preliminary ruling on the proper interpretation of the Regulation, as described in the preceding chapter.[27] Second, it has been met by the development of autonomous, or independent, meanings for the basic definitional terms of the Regulation: this is, beyond doubt, the most characteristic feature of the jurisprudence of the Court.

The point may be illustrated by a simple example.[28] Suppose a German manufacturer sells goods to a French buyer, who sells them on to a French sub-buyer. Suppose the goods are not fit for the purpose for which they were originally sold, and that the sub-buyer wishes to sue the manufacturer. In German, as in English, law any action would lie in tort, whereas in French law the claim may be regarded as contractual.[29] If in the particular case jurisdiction is to be based on Article 7 of Regulation 1215/2012,[30] it is necessary to ask whether the action is one relating to a contract or to tort. Whatever the answer is, it is *not* 'contract if the claim is brought in France, but tort if it is brought in Germany'. Instead, the jurisdictional question has to be answered by use of an independent, or uniform, or autonomous, or anational, or delocalised, definition of the terms: not by recourse to national law.

To take another example, suppose a house buyer sues the surveyor who was negligent in reporting its condition to the mortgage lender, but who was well aware that the report could be shown to the intending buyer who had in any event paid for the survey. As a matter of English domestic law, such an action would be seen as lying in tort. But in other systems it may be seen as contractual in nature, on the footing that the contract between mortgage lender and surveyor was also made for the benefit of (and the service paid for by) the house buyer. It may, therefore, be wrong to assume too quickly that for special jurisdictional[31] purposes the action is not to be regarded as a 'matter relating to a contract' and as falling within Article 7(1).

To take a third example, if commercial partners fall out, one accusing the other of disloyalty and unfair competition, national law may permit a claim to be framed as one in tort or delict, from which it may be argued that special jurisdiction may be available under Article 7(2) of the Regulation. But if the complaint could have been pleaded as a claim for breach of contract, or if it is necessary to plead the contract in order to establish the

---

27 Paragraph 1.16, above.

28 See C-26/91 *Jakob Handte & Co GmbH v. Soc Traitements Mécano-Chimiques des Surfaces* [1992] ECR I-3967.

29 Warranties of quality being considered to pass with title to the goods: not such a crazy idea, when you reflect on it. It is said that the French courts now accept that the claim of the sub-buyer is not contractual: *Soc Donovan Data Systems Europe v. Soc Dragon Rouge Holding* (Cass 6 July1999), [2000] Rev crit DIP 67. But the general point is still valid.

30 In other words, the defendant is sued in a Member State other than that in which he has a domicile.

31 Until very recently, there was no reason to suppose that if the claim were seen as relating to a tort for jurisdictional purposes it had to be resolved on the merits by the law of tort of the court seised. The reverse was true: a court with jurisdiction over a claim would then apply whatever substantive law its rules of the conflict of laws told it to: see C-26/91 *Jakob Handte & Co GmbH v. Soc Traitements Mécano-Chimiques des Surfaces* [1992] ECR I-3967, at [24] of the Opinion of the Advocate General (a view which was entirely sound, even in the absence of the explicit confirmation of the Court). But as the applicable law for contractual and for non-contractual obligations is now specified by Regulation (Rome I and Rome II, respectively), the relationship between the Regulations governing jurisdiction and the applicable law may be much closer than it was, and divergence acknowledged by the Advocate General will be less likely to result. For further consideration, see below, para. 2.163.

unlawfulness of the acts complained of, the matter will be one relating to a contract for the purposes of special jurisdiction over a defendant domiciled in another Member State, and hence within Article 7(1), despite the view taken by domestic law.[32]

2.04 The nature of autonomous interpretation

Autonomous meanings have been (or will be, as soon as the opportunity arises) given to practically all the definitional terms used in the Regulation. In earlier editions of this book a lengthy and lengthening list was given, but it now makes no sense, for the point is general and perfectly clear, and it is made and illustrated on practically every page of this chapter. Indeed, the Court has recently expressed the view that the need to proceed on the basis of uniform interpretations is, if anything, more entrenched than ever. As it said in *Re Roda Golf & Beach Resort SL:*[33]

> 'The objective pursued by the Treaty of Amsterdam of creating an area of freedom, security and justice, thereby giving the Community a new dimension, and the transfer, from the EU Treaty to the EC Treaty, of the body of rules enabling measures in the field of cooperation in civil matters having cross-border implications to be adopted testify to the will of the Member States to anchor such measures firmly in the Community legal order and thus to lay down the principle that they are to be interpreted autonomously.'

The road to a completed dictionary of definitional terms and uniform meanings for terms of art in the Regulation will be long. The road is paved with rulings from the European Court, but there is much paving still to be done. But the direction of legal development is clear, and to put forward an argument in a case which relies upon a term in the Regulation being given a meaning which is derived from the idiosyncrasy of national law is to advance an argument which exposes itself to attack.

2.05 A purposive interpretation of the Regulation

The Regulation is the latest incarnation of a legislative text designed and drafted by civil lawyers trained in the continental legal tradition, and subject to authoritative interpretation by judges who are almost all civilian lawyers. It was made, and has to be understood, to be interpreted according to the European canons of construction, at least if it is to be understood in a way which will conform to the views of the European Court.

The English approach of interpreting, more or less literally, the precise relevant words, following the prior decisions of earlier courts, is not exactly the European way.[34] Instead, the Regulation must be interpreted purposively, or 'teleologically'; that is to say, with a view which gives predominant weight to achieving the overall purposes of the instrument as a whole, as distinct from seeking to ascertain the natural meaning of a single provision taken in isolation from the rest of the text. This is important: in the paragraphs which follow attention is given to principles which apply to the interpretation of the individual

---

32 C-548/12 *Brogsitter v. Fabrication de Montres Normandes EURL* EU:C:2014:148, [2014] QB 753.

33 C-14/08, [2009] ECR I-5439. The case concerned the interpretation of the Service Regulation, Regulation 1348/2000; the passage from which the quotation is taken is [48]. This observation appeared first in C-433/03 *Götz Leffler v. Berlin Chemie AG* [2005] ECR I-9611, [45].

34 Indeed, it is not the approach taken to the construction of international treaties by the English courts.

Article; but the framework within which all of this is done is the purpose or purposes of the instrument as a whole. The point may be made by reference to a recent judgment, in which the Court put it this way:[35]

> 'By its questions, which should be examined together, the referring court asks, in essence, how, in the case where a manufacturer faces a claim of liability for a defective product, Article 5(3) of Regulation No 44/2001 is to be interpreted for the purpose of identifying the place of the event giving rise to the damage. In order to answer that question, it should be borne in mind, first, that, according to settled case-law, the provisions of Regulation No 44/2001 must be interpreted independently, by reference to its scheme and purpose.'

The fourth-from-last word in the passage shows that the interpretation, which will yield a uniform interpretation of the particular provision in respect of which the national court has sought a ruling, is to be found by reference to the scheme and purpose of the Regulation as a whole. The Court did not say that it was concerned to find the scheme and purpose of the particular Article or sub-Article which had been of concern to the referring court and in relation to which it had made its reference. The Court was instead required to make a broader and more comprehensive assessment of the scheme and purpose of the entire Regulation.[36] It is this approach which will guide the Court to its answer, and which will be manifested in more particular ways in the principles of interpretation discussed below.

It should not be thought that the European Court does not regard itself as bound by its own decisions, though no doubt this is correct. It does routinely refer to previous judgments, but what it draws from these tends to be a recitation of general principles of interpretation, rather than the ratios of individual judgments which it then proceeds to apply to the matter before it. The general principles of interpretation represent the continuing force of the judgments of the Court; the answers given to questions referred for a preliminary ruling are presented as the logical consequence of those principles.

For this reason, attention to the general principles underpinning the Regulation, as the European Court has declared them and as set out above, is the proper first step in the interpretation of any individual provision: they must be taken as read in all cases in which a question of construction arises for decision. Where they point in different directions, an argument which is well founded by reference to the purpose of the Regulation as a whole has the greatest prospect of being found to be correct.

2.06 Where the Regulation has general rules and exceptions, the latter are construed narrowly

In previous editions of this book, the 'construction of exceptions' principle stated that exceptions to the principle of domiciliary jurisdiction were to be construed restrictively. This version of the principle remains good law: almost from the beginning, the Court has said that provisions of the Regulation which allow a defendant to be sued, against his will, in a Member State other than that of his domicile are to be construed narrowly, or, at any

---

35 C-45/13 *Kainz v. Pantherwerke AG* EU:C:2014:7, [2015] QB 34, [18]–[19]. The same point is made in any number of judgments, including those cited in that case; also in C-548/12 *Brogsitter v. Fabrication de Montres Normandes EURL* EU:C:2014:148, [2014] QB 753.

36 See further, C-533/08 *TNT Express Nederland BV v. AXA Versicherung AG* [2010] ECR I-4107, [44].

rate, no more broadly than is required to give effect to the purpose of the provision.[37] In other words, the principle that a defendant may expect[38] to defend himself at home is the fundamental principle of civil or commercial jurisdiction. Other jurisdictional rules are to be seen as exceptions, to be given no wider an interpretation than is necessary to achieve the purposes of the Regulation in general and the individual Article in particular.

A claimant who, for example, wishes to rely on Article 7 of Regulation 1215/2012 to sue the defendant in a Member State other than that of the latter's domicile, may find it less easy than may be suggested by the first reading of the text.[39] While many of the individual provisions of the Regulation prevail over the domiciliary principle, the protection of the primacy or centrality of the domiciliary rule, by the narrowing of these other provisions, is a clear trend. On occasion, the narrow construction of exceptions to the domiciliary principle appears to have been applied without proper reflection, especially where the consequence of adopting a narrow interpretation of a particular provision increases the risk of inconsistent adjudications and irreconcilable judgments.[40]

The principle that exceptions to the rule of domiciliary jurisdiction are construed narrowly makes sense within the Regulation. Indeed, the Court has even interpreted the relationship between what is now Article 7(1)(a) and 7(1)(b) as being one of general principle and particular exception: part of the justification for the conclusion that a licensing agreement was not within Article 7(1)(b) was that this provision was to be seen as an exception to Article 7(1)(a).[41] There is, so far as can be ascertained, no suggestion that the legislator intended this to be the nature of the relationship between the two provisions, though it may be assumed that those drafting the Regulation were aware of this canon of construction.

It has been suggested, and is probably correct, that the exceptions to the material scope of the Regulation which are stated in Article 1(2) are to be construed restrictively, on the footing that they constitute subject-specific exceptions for certain civil and commercial matters which derogate from the more general scheme for jurisdiction and judgments in civil and commercial matters established by the Brussels I Regulation.[42] Such an approach is defensible when the material question is whether a matter is a 'general civil or commercial' one, or one of the 'special civil or commercial' matters listed in Article 1(2).

---

37 Under Art. 24, see C-115/88 *Reichert v. Dresdner Bank* [1990] ECR 27; C-261/90 *Reichert v. Dresdner Bank (No 2)* [1992] ECR I-2149. Under Article 7, see 189/87 *Kalfelis v. Bankhaus Schröder Münchmeyer Hengst & Co* [1988] ECR 5565; C-220/88 *Dumez France SA v. Hessische Landesbank* [1990] ECR I-49; C-68/95 *Shevill v. Presse Alliance SA* [1995] ECR I-415; C-364/93 *Marinari v. Lloyds Bank plc* [1995] ECR I-2719. As to Art. 8, where it is less obvious that a restrictive interpretation should be adopted, see paras 2.223 *et seq.*, below.

38 It would be possible to represent the same point in terms of the defendant having a *right* to defend himself at home. But for reasons explained below, at para. 2.21, it is misleading to use the terminology, and to draw conclusions which depend on the terminology, of rights.

39 On the other hand, it has been acknowledged that Arts 7(1) and 7(2) are, as they have been interpreted, not especially narrow in material scope: see C-27/02 *Engler v. Janus Versand GmbH* [2005] ECR I-481. The restrictiveness has been supplied within, rather than to, the operation of these Articles: see below, para. 2.188. A claimant seeking to interpret a provision of the Regulation so as to allow him to sue in his home court should expect to find the law particularly unaccommodating: C-88/91 *Shearson Lehmann Hutton Inc v. TVB* [1993] ECR I-139, [17]; C-364/93 *Marinari v. Lloyds Bank plc* [1995] ECR I-2719; C-220/88 *Dumez France SA v. Hessische Landesbank*; C-168/02 *Kronhofer v. Maier* [2004] ECR I-6009.

40 Especially in relation to Art. 8: see further below, para. 2.223.

41 C-533/07 *Falco Privatstiftung v. Weller-Lindhorst* [2009] ECR I-3327.

42 C-292/08 *German Graphics Graphische Maschinen GmbH v. Holland Binding BV (in liq)* [2009] ECR I-8421; C-157/13 *Nickel & Goeldner Spedition GmbH v. Kintra UAB* EU:C:2014:2145, [2015] QB 96; C-295/13 *H v. HK* EU:C:2014:2410.

This principle would, however, not justify giving a broad interpretation to the expression 'civil and commercial', on the pretended basis that matters which are not civil or commercial are exceptions to the Regulation which must, for that reason, be given a narrow scope: any such reasoning would be fundamentally flawed. Matters which are not civil or commercial in the first place were never within the scope of the Regulation. They are not excluded from the Brussels Regulation by being relocated to a separate Regulation, at least not in the sense in which this explains the function of Article 1(2), because they were not even potentially within it in the first place. Not until the end of 2014 did the Court say anything to cast doubt on this; but its decision in *flyLAL-Lithuanian Airlines AS v. Starptautiskā lidosta Rīga VAS*[43] that 'civil and commercial' must be interpreted broadly so as to ensure that the scope of 'not civil and commercial' is made narrow, as befits an exception, does not appear to be based on careful reflection on the development of the law. If it ever matters, it should not be taken as correct.

2.07 Interpretation must help keep the risk of irreconcilable decisions to a minimum

The Brussels I Regulation seeks to facilitate the easy, almost automatic, enforcement of judgments across the Member States. It is therefore necessary to prevent, as far as possible and from the outset, the existence of concurrent proceedings in the courts of two or more Member States. This has led the European Court to deliver forceful judgments[44] insisting upon a broad and purpose-driven application of the provisions for dealing with *lis alibi pendens*. It has also meant that the Court will not favour an interpretation of a rule which would lead to the conclusion that there was an unavoidable multiplicity of courts with jurisdiction over a claim, or over parts of a claim.

2.08 Interpretation should promote legal certainty, predictability and proximity

The principle of 'legal certainty' means that the interpretation adopted should be one which contributes, or is not damaging, to the idea of legal certainty. There are several aspects to the principle of legal certainty, of which five in particular call for mention.

First, legal certainty is the basis for objection to the common law's approach to questions of jurisdiction in general, and to its understanding that judicial discretion is a necessary or desirable element of jurisdictional law in particular.[45] For this reason, arguments which seek to show that a jurisdictional rule, otherwise applicable, should not be applicable because its underlying purpose does not apply to the instant case will be unprofitable.[46] More generally, a definition of a term such as 'consumer' which was liable to require the court to decide whether a person deserved that privileged status, by reference to a variety of socio-economic factors, is unlikely to be favoured.[47]

Second, and rather more justifiably, the principle will tell against a proposed construction of the Articles which would have the effect of leaving an intelligent claimant uncertain

---

43 C-302/13, EU:C:2014:2319, [2015] ILPr 28.

44 144/86 *Gubisch Maschinenfabrik KG v. Palumbo* [1987] ECR 4861; C-351/89 *Overseas Union Insurance Ltd v. New Hampshire Insurance Co* [1991] ECR I-3317; C-406/92 *The Tatry* [1994] ECR I-5439.

45 For the most obvious example, see C-281/02 *Owusu v. Jackson* [2005] ECR I-1383, [38]-[46].

46 C-288/92 *Custom Made Commercial v. Stawa Metallbau GmbH* [1994] ECR I-2913.

47 See further, para. 2.101, below.

about where he will be able to sue, or a well-informed defendant unable to predict where he may be liable to be called to account. The existence of autonomous definitions of the terms used in the Regulation contributes to this certainty, but approaches to interpretation, put forward especially in relation to special jurisdiction, may find that they are measured against the requirement that they also make an individual contribution to legal certainty. Accordingly, the Court has declared itself in favour of interpretations of the special jurisdiction provisions, in particular, which would tend to prevent the multiplication or fragmentation of jurisdiction where claims arise within a single legal relationship; it has also rejected approaches which would require a national court to conduct an investigation of issues of applicable law in order to decide whether it had jurisdiction.[48] It has also used this as a justification for excluding the national law of the court seised from adding to or otherwise contradicting the jurisdictional rules set out in the Regulation.[49]

Third, the Court may invoke objectives of 'proximity and predictability',[50] which are perhaps best seen as particular manifestations of the general principle of legal certainty. The 'proximity' component of this, especially in relation to the rules of special jurisdiction in Article 7, may be used to support an interpretation of a particular provision which will tend to mean that, generally,[51] the court with special jurisdiction is one which will have a close and foreseeable connection, a close link, to the facts which give rise to the dispute. This will, at least in principle, tend to improve the quality of the adjudication. Even so, it is important to appreciate the abstract nature of the reasoning at this point. A court will not have special jurisdiction simply because it has a close link to the dispute; and a court will not lack special jurisdiction if, on the facts of the instant case, the application of Article 7 gives jurisdiction to a court which, atypically perhaps, does not have a close connection to the facts.[52]

Fourth, the interpretation and application of the rule of European law must conform to the principle of effectiveness. Or, to put it another way, rules of national procedural law may not encroach on a rule of European law in such a way as will undermine the application and intended effect of the rule of European law: where European law has laid down a rule, the rule must be effective. The principle of effectiveness is probably separate and distinct from the principle of legal certainty, but they are undoubtedly linked, and together they militate against clever or creative (or self-serving) readings of European law which are designed to give advantage to one side or the other in litigation at the expense of the clarity and effectiveness of rules and principles of European law.

And fifth, the Court has made it clear that there is to be continuity of interpretation as between the Brussels Convention and the Regulation: unless it is plain that a change in the wording of the two instruments was meant to produce a different outcome, the answers and

---

48 C-269/95 *Benincasa v. Dentalkit Srl* [1997] ECR I-3767; C-381/08 *Car Trim GmbH v. KeySafety Systems Srl* [2010] ECR I-1255.

49 150/80 *Elefanten Schuh GmbH v. Jacqmain* [1981] ECR 1671.

50 For the recent examples, see C-204/08 *Rehder v. Air Baltic Corp* [2009] ECR I-6073; C-157/13 *Nickel & Goeldner Spedition GmbH v. Kintra UAB* EU:C:2014:2145, [2015] QB 96.

51 Without prejudice to the specific case: C-288/92 *Custom Made Commercial v. Stawa Metallbau GmbH* [1994] ECR I-2913.

52 C-288/92 *Custom Made Commercial v. Stawa Metallbau GmbH* [1994] ECR I-2913 (a case decided on an earlier version of Art. 5(1)).

interpretations given in relation to the Convention continue to be reliable for the purposes of the Regulation.[53]

2.09 All national courts are of equal authority, and none has institutional superiority

The court of one Member State may not speak ill of a court in another Member State: *de iudice nil nisi bonum*, as one might say. The Court has become increasingly emphatic that it is impermissible for a court in one Member State to find fault with the proceedings or process before the courts of another Member State, and to draw the conclusions which might be thought to follow from such a finding of fault.

Insofar as there is a textual basis for this principle, it is elusive:[54] it would not be helpful, in this context, to repeat the mantra of obviousness and authority being in inverse relation to each other. A court called upon to recognise the judgment of a court in another Member State is absolutely forbidden to review the substance of the judgment.[55] So far as the exercise of jurisdiction by the other court is concerned, the court called upon to recognise a judgment may not review the jurisdiction of the court which gave the judgment; and where jurisdiction has been based on Article 6, it may not find this rule of jurisdiction, or its exercise, to be contrary to its public policy.[56]

From this statutory basis, an intermediate principle was deduced by the Court: that a court in one Member State is forbidden to review the jurisdiction of a court in another Member State outside the context of the recognition of judgments; and that it follows that a court may not take any step or make any order which is predicated on its having reviewed the jurisdiction of the courts of another Member State: it may not adjudicate as a consequence of its conclusion that the courts of the other Member State do not have or should not exercise jurisdiction, because that conclusion is one which involves a judgment which the court is almost always forbidden to make.[57] The justification is that the Regulation is part of the law of all 28 Member States, and as there is no reason to suppose that any national court is blessed with superior skills in the art of interpretation, a court may decide whether it has jurisdiction, but may not decide whether another court had or has it.

This led to the final and definitive statement of the principle: to the proposition that the courts of the Member States were required to repose and demonstrate trust in each other's legal systems and judicial institutions.[58] Not only did that explain the intermediate principle mentioned above, but 'mutual trust' was the principal reason why the grant of an anti-suit injunction, ordered to restrain a person from bringing proceedings before the courts of another Member State whose only purpose was to undermine the jurisdiction of the English

---

53 For a recent example, see C-548/12 *Brogsitter v. Fabrication de Montres Normandes EURL* EU:C:2014:148, [2014] QB 753, [19]. But the point is now made as a matter of routine.

54 An attempt to isolate the source of the principle in the broader scheme of European law was made by Blobel and Späth (2005) 30 Eur LR 528, but the truth really is that there is no better source than that identified here.

55 Article 52 of Regulation 1215/2012.

56 Article 45 of Regulation 1215/2012. It has also been suggested that the duty imposed by Art. 4(3) TFEU, of 'sincere cooperation', may contribute to the principle, but this is not really persuasive.

57 C-351/89 *Overseas Union Insurance Ltd v. New Hampshire Insurance Co* [1991] ECR I-3317; C-163/95 *Von Horn v. Cinnamond* [1997] ECR I-5451; Opinion C-1/03 *Lugano Convention* [2006] ECR I-1145, [163].

58 C-116/02 *Erich Gasser GmbH v. MISAT Srl* [2003] ECR I-14693.

courts and to oppress the impecunious claimant in those English proceedings, was impermissible.[59] It was also a part of the justification explaining why an English court, seised of an arbitration matter which fell outside the material scope of the Regulation, was forbidden to grant an injunction to require the party, breaching the arbitration agreement by bringing proceedings before the courts of another Member State, to cease his offending activity and comply with his contractual agreement.[60]

It may be surprising that trust and confidence in the courts of all Member State courts is an obligation imposed from above, rather than a ground-level principle. And it will not have escaped notice that there are some courts, in parts of the European Union, whose reputation for impartial excellence and adjudicatory expertise is not quite so easily vouched for. But the membership of the European Union requires one to take the rough with the smooth, the bitter with the sweet, and not always in balanced or measured quantities.

2.10 The hierarchy of jurisdictional rules

The key to understanding the Brussels I Regulation is to recognise that its various jurisdictional rules reflect a hidden hierarchy of application. If a particular Article gives jurisdiction to the courts of a particular Member State, it is often[61] unimportant that another provision, lower in the hierarchy, would have allowed the courts of a different Member State to take jurisdiction. The prudent course is to approach the Regulation in the order in which the provisions are set out in this chapter. The danger in adopting a less thorough approach (leaping to the conclusion, for example, that because the defendant is domiciled in the United Kingdom he may be sued in England) is that another provision, appearing later in the text of Regulation but occupying a higher position in its internal hierarchy, may override this conclusion. For this reason, the following set of 15 questions, considered in detail below, should guide the reader to answer the question whether the English[62] courts, or, for

---

59 C-159/02 *Turner v. Grovit* [2004] ECR I-3565.

60 C-185/07 *Allianz SpA v. West Tankers Inc* [2009] ECR I-663. It is not clear from the judgment whether the obligation not to interfere with the right of a court to take its own decision on a matter of jurisdiction is a principle which is independent of the duty to extend mutual trust and confidence, or is instead a particular manifestation of it. However, the English courts have held that an award of damages for breach of a contractual undertaking not to invoke the jurisdiction of a court in another Member State does not infringe the principle, for it respects the jurisdictional decision of the foreign court but merely uses this as the basis for further reasoning: *Starlight Shipping Co v. Allianz Marine & Aviation Versicherungs AG* [2014] EWCA Civ 1010, [2014] 2 Lloyd's Rep 554. Proceeding from this, it has been held that a decree of specific performance, framed as one to enforce an obligation to abide by the terms of a contractual agreement which carried with it the obligation not to bring further judicial proceedings in any court, anywhere, may be awarded without there being any allegation of interference with a foreign court, which will be assisted by the clarification offered by the English judgment: *Starlight Shipping Co v. Allianz Marine & Aviation Versicherung AG* [2014] EWHC 3068 (Comm), [2014] 2 Lloyd's Rep 579. This seems very challenging indeed, for the consequences of disobedience are practically identical to those which result from disobedience to an injunction.

61 But not always. In cases where, according to the Regulation, the courts of two or more Member States would have jurisdiction, the court first seised, not necessarily the court which derives its jurisdiction from a rule higher in the hierarchy, may exercise it.

62 The Regulation deals with the jurisdiction of the courts of the *United Kingdom*, generally (but not always) drawing no distinction between the courts of the various national jurisdictions within the Kingdom. By Sch. 4 to the 1982 Act, as substituted by Civil Jurisdiction and Judgments Order, SI 2001/3929, Sch. 2, para. 4 (itself amended in only minor details by Civil Jurisdiction and Judgments (Amendment) Regulations 2014, SI 2014/2947), a set of rules closely following, but not exactly reproducing, those of the Regulation allocates jurisdiction, as a matter of the internal law of the United Kingdom, between the three national jurisdictions. For ease

that matter, the courts of another Member State, have jurisdiction over a particular defend-ant which they may or must exercise when called on to do so. The sixteenth question arises only when the applicable question from the list of 15 gives jurisdiction to the courts of the United Kingdom. The consequential question, whether that means England and Wales, or Scotland, or Northern Ireland, or some combination of these, is not the concern of the Regulation, but has to be answered; it is dealt with at the end of the Chapter, as though it were the sixteenth question. That is convenient; though, as this question is, technically at least, nothing to do with the Regulation, it is not quite right.

Q1: Are the proceedings within the domain of the Regulation?

That means to ask whether the proceedings are within the scope of the Regulation so far as the subject matter of the claim is concerned (scope *ratione materiae* and in other respects as defined by Article 1) and so far as the scope of the Regulation is defined by the date of institution of proceedings (scope *ratione temporis*, as defined by Article 66).

Unless these questions are answered in the affirmative, the Regulation makes no claim to apply, and no further reference is made to the Regulation. The traditional jurisdictional rules (those of English law are set out in Chapter 4) will apply. But if these questions are both answered in the affirmative, the Regulation will determine, in accordance with Q2 to Q11 below, which court or courts have jurisdiction. Once this has been determined, and account has been taken of Q14 and Q15, it will be known whether the court has jurisdiction.

If the dispute falls within the domain of the Regulation, the next question is:

Q2: Does a particular Convention which governs jurisdiction in relation to particular matters, or some other international instrument, give jurisdiction to the English court?

If the answer is yes, Articles 67–71 of the Regulation provide, in effect, that jurisdiction may be exercised in accordance with the particular Convention or instrument. But if there is no such particular Convention which applies, the next question is:

Q3: Do the courts of the United Kingdom, or do the courts of another Member State, have exclusive jurisdiction regardless of domicile?

If the answer is yes, Article 24 provides that the courts of that Member State, and only the courts of that Member State, have jurisdiction over the defendant in relation to the claim.[63] But if Article 24 does not apply, the next question is:

---

of explanation, unless the contrary is stated, the expression 'English court' may be used here to signify the courts of the United Kingdom, on the footing (i) that as a matter of pure statistics, the vast majority of cases allocated by the Regulation to the courts of the United Kingdom will in turn be allocated by s. 16 of and Sch. 4 to the 1982 Act, as amended by SI 2001/3929, to the English courts, and (ii) that this is primarily intended as a textbook on English law.

63 If, exceptionally, this Article identifies two courts with *exclusive* jurisdiction, Art. 31(1) resolves the clash of exclusive jurisdictions on the basis of temporal priority.

Q4: Has the defendant entered an appearance before the court in which the claimant wishes to sue?

If the answer is yes, Article 26 provides that the court has jurisdiction over the defendant.[64] But if Article 26 does not apply, the next question is:

Q5: Does the claim arise out of a contract of insurance?

If the answer is yes, Articles 10 to 16 provide that the court or courts identified by those provisions, and no other courts, have jurisdiction.[65] But if Articles 10 to 16 do not apply, the next question is:

Q6: Does the claim arise out of a contract made by a consumer?

If the answer is yes, Articles 17 to 19 provide that the court or courts identified by those provisions, and no other courts, have jurisdiction.[66] But if Articles 17 to 19 do not apply, the next question is:

Q7: Does the claim arise out of an individual contract of employment?

If the answer is yes, Articles 20 to 23 provide that the the court or courts identified by those provisions, and no other courts, have jurisdiction.[67] But if Articles 20 to 23 do not apply, the next question is:

Q8: Has there been an agreement, in a prescribed form, that a court or the courts of a Member State are to have jurisdiction?

If the answer is that there has been, Article 25 provides that that court has, or those courts have, exclusive[68] jurisdiction[69] unless the parties' agreement was otherwise. But if Article 25 does not apply, the next question is:

---

64 Other courts may also, from provisions lower in the hierarchy: Art. 26 jurisdiction does not exclude the jurisdiction of other Member States.

65 In other words, the provisions of Arts 10 to 16 exclude jurisdictions which might have been, but now may not be, derived from provisions lower in the hierarchy. The special rules about insurance contracts do not apply within the intra-UK scheme of jurisdiction.

66 In other words, the provisions of Arts 17 to 19 exclude jurisdictions which might have been, but now may not be, derived from provisions lower in the hierarchy.

67 In other words, the provisions of Arts 20 to 23 exclude jurisdictions which might have been, but now may not be, derived from provisions lower in the hierarchy.

68 This is what the Regulation says. But it is misleading, for the meaning of exclusive jurisdiction in Art. 25 (which falls within Section 7 of Chapter II of the Regulation, sub-titled 'prorogation of jurisdiction') is different from the meaning of exclusive jurisdiction regardless of domicile as derived from Art. 24 (which comprises Section 6 of Chapter II of the Regulation, sub-titled 'exclusive jurisdiction'). It is not 'exclusive' in the most absolute sense of the term. Whenever the term 'exclusive jurisdiction' is encountered, care must be taken to see which Article, and which sense of exclusivity, is being referred to.

69 In other words, a court which might have derived jurisdiction from provisions lower in the hierarchy may not do so: Art. 25 jurisdiction excludes the jurisdiction of the courts of other Member States unless the agreement of the parties was for non-exclusive jurisdiction.

Q9: Does the defendant have a domicile in the United Kingdom?

If the answer is he does, Article 4 provides that the courts of the United Kingdom[70] have general jurisdiction.[71] But if Article 4 does not apply, the next question is:

Q10: Does the defendant have a domicile in another Member State?

If the answer is that he does, Articles 7 to 9 may provide that the English[72] court has special jurisdiction[73] over him in respect of the claim, though jurisdiction on this basis is confined to so much of the claim as falls within Articles 7 to 9, as the case may be. If the defendant is domiciled in another Member State, but Articles 7 to 9 do not give the English court special jurisdiction, the court has no jurisdiction and the enquiry is at an end. But if the defendant is not domiciled in another Member State:

Q11: If the defendant is someone who does not have a domicile in a Member State, does the court have residual jurisdiction?

If the defendant does not have a domicile in a Member State, Article 6 provides that the court may exercise jurisdiction in accordance with its traditional jurisdictional rules: those of English law are set out in Chapter 4. Article 6 incorporates these by reference into the body of the Regulation, where they operate, in effect, as residual rules of jurisdiction.[74]

Q12: Is the application for provisional or protective relief?

If the court does not have jurisdiction over the defendant in respect of the substance of the claim, Article 35 provides that the court may have jurisdiction to grant provisional, including protective, measures. In this book this is examined in detail in Chapter 6.

Where these rules lead to the conclusion that the English court appears to have jurisdiction, a number of further questions arise:

---

70 The Regulation is concerned only with the domicile in the United Kingdom, for the United Kingdom, not England is the Member State. If Art. 2 gives jurisdiction to the courts of the United Kingdom, the defendant cannot be sued in the courts of the United Kingdom as such, but only in the courts for a part of the United Kingdom. The rules which determine the part of the United Kingdom in which he may be sued, but as a matter of internal United Kingdom law, are at the end of this Chapter.

71 Jurisdiction based upon Art. 4 is not in any sense exclusive, and a jurisdiction based upon provisions lower in the hierarchy may still be asserted by the courts of another Member State, so long as it is asserted first in time.

72 Note that Arts 7 and 8 mainly give jurisdiction to the courts for a *place* having the relevant connection. As the High Court has jurisdiction over the whole of England, the present formulation is precise enough. But in the context of the corresponding jurisdiction of foreign courts, it is the courts for the place, rather than the courts of the State in general, which have special jurisdiction by virtue of the Regulation.

73 But not exclusively: at least one other Member State, namely that of the defendant's domicile, must also have jurisdiction. This jurisdiction must therefore be asserted first in time.

74 In other words, the jurisdictional rules directly legislated by the Regulation do not apply to govern jurisdiction, but the indirectly-provided rules do. But these apply by virtue of Art. 6 of the Regulation, and their operation is not identical with that of the same rules of the common law as applying to a case which (under Q1) falls wholly outside the scope of the Regulation.

Q13: Is the court required to check for itself that it has jurisdiction according to the Regulation?

The court which appears to have jurisdiction has a limited obligation, according to Article 27 and, if the defendant (who is domiciled in another Member State) has not entered an appearance, Article 28, to confirm that its jurisdiction is consistent with the Regulation. If this check does not lead the court to the conclusion that it does not have jurisdiction, the next question is:

Q14: Are there concurrent proceedings before the courts of another Member State?

If there are, Articles 29 to 31 may affect any affirmative answer given to Q2 to Q11 in three possible ways.[75] First, if the court would have jurisdiction according to Q2, or according to Q4 to Q11, Article 29 will remove that jurisdiction if proceedings on the same cause of action, between the same parties, had been commenced earlier in time before the courts of another Member State: a rule memorably[76] described as 'first come, first served'. Second, if the court would have jurisdiction according to Q2, or according to Q4 to Q11, but a related action had been commenced earlier in time before the courts of another Member State, Article 30 allows the court to stay its proceedings or to decline jurisdiction to allow the claim to be consolidated with the related action (or to do neither of these). Third, if the court would have exclusive jurisdiction according to Q3,[77] Article 31 may alone remove this jurisdiction, and it will do so if, but only if, an action was commenced earlier in time in another Member State which also had exclusive jurisdiction in accordance with Q3.

Q15: Are there concurrent proceedings before (or other facts and matters pointing to a material connection with) the courts of a non-Member State?

If there are, Articles 33 and 34 may affect any affirmative answer given by, but only by, Q10 or Q11. If the proceedings before the courts of a non-Member State were in respect of the same cause of action and between the same parties, and were already pending when the English proceedings were instituted, Article 33 allows the court to stay its proceedings. If the proceedings before the courts of a non-Member State are related to the English proceedings, and were already pending when the English proceedings were instituted, Article 34 allows the court to stay its proceedings. The Regulation makes no other apparent provision for proceedings before, or for material connections to, a non-Member State. The question whether any account may be taken of such points of contact awaits an authoritative answer.

---

75 If the English courts have jurisdiction because Q1 means the case falls outside the domain of the Regulation, no other rule of the Regulation may take it away again, and a *lis pendens* in another Member State can be disregarded.

76 Though not altogether accurately: it would be better to observe that there is no prize for coming second.

77 C-438/12 *Weber v. Weber* EU:C:2014:212, [2015] 2 WLR 213.

Q16: When the Regulation gives international jurisdiction to the courts of the United Kingdom, which national part or parts of the United Kingdom have jurisdiction?

Where the rules in Chapter II of the Regulation lead to the conclusion that the courts of the United Kingdom, rather than the courts of a place within the United Kingdom, have international jurisdiction, the Regulation does not care whether the proceedings are brought in England and Wales, or Scotland, or Northern Ireland. Insofar as it is necessary to decide whether the courts of the individual parts of the United Kingdom have jurisdiction in the particular matter, the answer is to be found in rules of national law made to fill in the detail which the Regulation left blank. These rules are examined at the very end of this Chapter, as they relate to, but are not part of, the jurisdictional rules laid down by the Regulation.

2.11 Disputing the jurisdiction of the English court

A defendant who considers that the English court does not have jurisdiction over him in relation to the claim set out in the claim form may, when he has been served, take steps to dispute the assertion of jurisdiction over him.

If the defendant takes a step in the proceedings other than to dispute the jurisdiction, he may well be taken to have submitted to, and to have conferred jurisdiction upon, the court in accordance with Article 26. If he wishes to dispute the jurisdiction, English procedural law requires that he first acknowledge service of process, and then within 14[78] days apply under Part 11 of the Civil Procedure Rules for orders declaring that the court does not have jurisdiction and granting the appropriate consequential relief. This procedure is outlined in Chapter 5 below. If he does nothing, judgment may be given by default, and this will[79] in principle be entitled to recognition throughout the European Union, with little or no regard to whether the jurisdiction of the court might have been successfully challenged: the recognition of judgments under Chapter III of the Regulation does not depend upon the absence of error in the original court's decision to exercise jurisdiction. The philosophy of the Regulation is that if the defendant believes the court does not have jurisdiction over him, he should declare it, or else thereafter hold his peace.

2.12 The need to be first to commence proceedings

These questions will let a prospective litigant know whether he is able to sue, or liable to be sued, in a Member State. However, they will not completely answer the question. There may be cases in which two or more courts may have jurisdiction to try a particular dispute: the simplest example is when the litigants have domiciles in different Member States. Clashes or potential clashes of jurisdiction are resolved by the rather blunt instrument of Article 29 and its rule of temporal priority: *qui prior est tempore, potior est jure*, or 'first come, first seised', according to taste. This means that, for a prospective litigant who has a preference for litigation to take place in a particular forum, it is essential to be first out of the starting blocks, and by being the first to start proceedings, to be *dominus litis*.

---

78 In the Commercial Court, 28 days.
79 Subject to certain restricted exceptions, see Chapter 7, below.

2.13 Prospective claimant

Suppose a dispute has arisen in connection with a contract for the sale of goods between parties domiciled in different Member States. If one party wishes proceedings against his opponent to be heard in a particular court, he would be well advised to move silently and without delay to commence[80] them as claimant. If he does otherwise, he gives his opponent chance to institute such proceedings as the latter may wish to bring, as claimant, with the possible result that the entire[81] dispute may be heard in a court other than that of the former's choice or entitlement. And worse, from the would-be claimant's point of view, is the fact that once the opponent, whom he envisaged as defendant, has become claimant and *dominus litis*, any challenge to the jurisdiction has to be brought in the court first seised,[82] and not in the court preferred by the would-be, or would-have-been, claimant who is now defendant.

It follows that, in cases where there may be claims and counterclaims, a prospective claimant may be unwise to delay the institution of proceedings before the courts of the Member State of his preference: he who hesitates is lost. It may be unwise to send the customary, and otherwise professionally proper, letter before action, for this may give the game away:[83] careless talk costs *lis*, as one might be tempted to say. It cannot be denied that this puts a prospective claimant in a difficult position. Where negotiations towards a settlement have a prospect of success, there is a danger that, if the prospective claimant delays, an opponent may seize the initiative and commence proceedings of his own, thereby depriving the prospective claimant of the choice of court. On the other hand, the unannounced institution of proceedings, to preserve the claimant's position upon the question of which court should hear the case, is an inherently untrusting act, which may have a jarring effect on the chances of settlement. If the dispute is a contractual one, and if the contract contained a jurisdiction agreement which complied with Article 25, it is now less dangerous than it was to defer the institution of proceedings,[84] but there are still many questions which may

---

80 For the purposes of the Brussels Convention, an English court was held to be seised only when process had been served on the defendant, and not before: *Dresser UK Ltd v. Falcongate Freight Management Ltd* [1992] QB 502; *The Sargasso* [1994] 3 All ER 180; *Phillips v. Symes (No 3)* [2008] UKHL 1, [2008] 1 WLR 180. For the purposes of the Brussels Convention, therefore, the jurisdictional race was not won merely by issuing the claim form: it had to be served before the other court was seised. Under the Brussels I Regulation, an English court is seised at an earlier point: on issue of process, as long as the claimant does not fail to take the steps necessary to serve the defendant: Regulation 1215/2012, Art. 32(1). But this only means that a goalpost has moved; it does not mean that there is any less of a race to get the ball into the net. The right advice must be to issue proceedings, to save the position under the Regulation, *and* to serve, to avoid the indolence trap at the end of Art. 31(1)(a).

81 The claims will be reduced to the status of a counterclaim.

82 C-351/89 *Overseas Union Insurance Ltd v. New Hampshire Insurance Co* [1991] ECR I-3317 (except where the court has exclusive jurisdiction under Art. 24: C-438/12 *Weber v. Weber* EU:C:2014:212, [2015] 2 WLR 213. And it may take an age for the procedure to complete the appellate processes of the court seised, especially if a reference to the European Court is made along the way. Add to that the fact that a party which eventually succeeds in its jurisdictional challenge may not recover its costs (in some systems at least), and the disadvantage of being defendant should be evident, especially if one would have been entitled to litigate in a different court if one had not been so slow off the mark.

83 Indeed, it is believed that a number of reported cases involved the sudden and pre-emptive commencement of proceedings by an opponent to whom had been sent a letter before action. It also follows that, if reliance is to be placed on Art. 29 to prevent another court considering that it has jurisdiction, claims for relief need to be drafted sufficiently widely for there to be no room for the opponent to frame a claim of his own which is not directly covered by the claim brought. A claim for a declaration in appropriately broad terms may suffice; see para. 2.265, below.

84 See below, para. 2.277.

be deployed to undermine the effect of a jurisdiction agreement.[85] The soundest general advice has to be that the would-be claimant who foresees the possibility of proceedings being commenced elsewhere by his opponent should institute proceedings first, becoming *dominus litis* himself.[86]

A distinct problem arises if a claimant is uncertain where he may sue the defendant.[87] He may be unsure which of the Member States will have, or will accept it has, jurisdiction in respect of the claim he wishes to bring. He may not know where the defendant is domiciled for the purposes of Article 4; or be uncertain whether a jurisdiction agreement will be considered as effective to confer jurisdiction on, or to exclude the jurisdiction of, a particular court under Article 25; or he may self-question whether a court has, or will accept that it has, special jurisdiction under Article 7, and so forth. His dilemma is that, if he guesses wrongly, or mis-predicts, and commences proceedings in a court which later rules that it has no jurisdiction, he may find himself out of time in the court in which it now appears he should have brought the action;[88] but if he institutes proceedings in respect of the same claim in more Member States than one, those brought before the court seised second would appear to lack jurisdictional foundation.

The answer should be that Article 29[89] is not designed to deprive the claimant of access to a court, and that the court seised second should merely stay its proceedings until the jurisdiction of the court seised first has become established. If the jurisdiction of the first court is established, the second court will then dismiss its proceedings; and there may be a costs penalty for the claimant. Alternatively, if the jurisdiction of the first court is not established, the second court may proceed to confirm that it has jurisdiction.[90] As a result the claimant, if he has the luxury of time to do what he wishes to do without pressure from his opponent threatening to bring counter-proceedings in a Member State of his choosing, may be well advised to seise the courts in more than one of the Member States in which he may have a case for being able to sue.

2.14 Prospective defendant

The advice to be given to the party who apprehends that he is about to be made a defendant to a claim reflects those which apply to the claimant. If he fears that proceedings may be

---

85 See para. 2.124 *et seq.*, below.

86 That this advice was sensible, if not altogether welcome, was confirmed by Lord Woolf MR in *Messier-Dowty Ltd v. Sabena SA* [2000] 1 WLR 2040, 2048.

87 The question of how convincingly the claimant needs to show that he satisfies the jurisdictional provision on which he relies is dealt with in Chapter 5, as part of the procedural framework which supports and surrounds the rules of jurisdiction. The short answer is that he will have to have the better of the argument on the point on which he relies.

88 This is because the court which finds that it does not have jurisdiction does not 'transfer' the case and the process which originated it on a particular date to another court. It simply dismisses the proceedings and leaves it to the claimant to figure out where to start again.

89 Which regulates the problem of *lis alibi pendens*, and which is examined at paras 2.260 *et seq.*, below.

90 *Cf Internationale Nederlanden Aviation Lease BV v. Civil Aviation Authority* [1997] 1 Lloyd's Rep 80, discussed at para. 2.272, below. Until the jurisdiction of the first-seised court is established, the second court has (stayed) jurisdiction and is therefore free to grant provisional measures: *J P Morgan Europe Ltd v. Primacom AG* [2005] EWHC 508 (Comm), [2005] 2 Lloyd's Rep 665 without the need for the claimant to rely on what is now Art. 35. But there is no need for a formal decision from the foreign court to state that its jurisdiction is to be regarded as established: if it has not been challenged by the time of the first defence, it is established: C-1/13 *Cartier parfums-lunettes SAS v. Ziegler France SA* EU:C:2014:109, [2014] ILPr 359.

commenced against him in a court not of his preference, he has a number of options open to him. If he himself has a claim for substantive relief against his opponent, he may start his own proceedings, and wrest control of the issue of jurisdiction by becoming claimant. If he has no claim for substantive relief of his own, but has grounds to dispute the liability threatened against him, he may be able to institute proceedings for a declaration that he has no liability to the claimant.

Despite some early doubts in relation to the Brussels Convention, which were quickly dispelled,[91] the Regulation does not find fault with proceedings brought to seek a declaration of non-liability.[92] In certain areas of the law it is commercially necessary that such actions are available, and the Regulation should not call them into question. An insurer or reinsurer will often need to know if he is exposed to liability to an insured or reinsured; such declaratory actions allow the uncertainty to be dispelled.[93] A supplier of goods may be faced with a demand that he supply goods when he believes that he has no obligation to a particular buyer or distributor, but where he needs urgently to know where he stands and what he may lawfully do. Moreover, even an action in a modest civil case claiming that a contract has been rescinded is, in essence, an action for a declaration of non-liability. It must surely be possible to bring these in a court with personal jurisdiction over the opposite party. Not only that: it would impair the principle of legal certainty if a court could be called upon to examine which of two litigating parties was the 'real' claimant.

The guidance offered by the European Court has made it clear that, as long as the proceedings are permitted by the national law of the court seised, and as long as the defendant to the claim for negative declaratory relief is subject to the personal jurisdiction of the court in which the party who brought the proceedings started them, there is no objection, so far as the Regulation is concerned, to the declaratory form of the proceedings. In *The Tatry*,[94] proceedings had been commenced in the Netherlands for a declaration of non-liability; subsequently, proceedings were brought in England between the same parties[95] for damages for damage allegedly done to the cargo. The Court of Appeal referred a question[96] which was designed to ascertain whether the Dutch proceedings were to be seen as having been commenced first for the purposes of what is now Article 29 of Regulation 1215/2012; the Court answered that they were. The judgment of the Dutch court in the proceedings before it would furnish a conclusive answer to the issues raised in the claim later brought in the English courts; and for that reason the two sets of proceedings had the same cause of action. It is plain that the Court saw nothing objectionable in the nature of the proceedings brought in the Netherlands. It therefore follows that the Convention did, and the Regulation will, simply respect, as being first seised for the purposes of Article 29, a court hearing a claim in proceedings which seek no more relief than a declaration of non-liability.

The English courts duly accepted that, as long as the claim for a declaration is not an abusive or improper use of the process of the court (as would be the case if it were seen to stir up a

---

91 C-406/92 *The Tatry* [1994] ECR I-5439.

92 C-133/11 *Folien Fischer AG v. Ritrama SpA* EU:C:2012:664, [2013] QB 523.

93 For instance, the insurer may need to know whether to take over the defence of the claim brought by the claimant against the insured.

94 C-406/92, [1994] ECR I-5439. For further authority, see C-133/11 *Folien Fischer AG v. Ritrama SpA* EU:C:2012:664, [2013] QB 523 (negative special jurisdiction under what is now Art. 7(2); see further, para. 2.200).

95 But insofar as the proceedings were not between the same parties, they were not covered by what is now Art. 29; see para. 2.267, below.

96 It was the fifth question referred by the Court of Appeal.

controversy when there was no need to), any criticism which suggests that it is motivated by a desire to forum shop is inadmissible: proceedings brought in a court having jurisdiction under the Regulation is brought before a court whose jurisdiction is by definition appropriate.[97]

That said, an English court is not bound to grant declaratory relief, just because it has jurisdiction to entertain the claim. It is one thing to conclude that the Regulation poses no jurisdictional obstacle to the bringing of such proceedings; it is quite another to debate, by reference to English procedural law, whether such proceedings should be permitted to continue. There may be cases where the applicant for a declaration has commenced proceedings in circumstances where his opponent has never threatened to commence any of his own, and in circumstances where it would really be an abuse of the process of the court to require the opponent to defend himself in relation to a claim for declaratory relief in relation to a claim which he had never threatened to bring. A court may apply its own rules to determine whether to allow such a claim to proceed.[98] In doing so, it may draw a distinction between claims which are timely and useful and should be allowed to proceed to judgment, and those which are premature, pointless and should not be allowed to proceed any further.[99] But if the court purports to do so on grounds that the claim should be brought in another Member State, its decision will be legally unsound, for it will have been based on discretionary *forum non conveniens* grounds, which have no part to play within the jurisdictional scheme of the Regulation.[100]

2.15 The absence of other means of preventing a court from exercising jurisdiction

It is worth asking whether there are other ways to prevent a court taking jurisdiction under the rules of the Regulation. If we take as an example the case of proceedings, which themselves fall within the domain of the Regulation, being brought in another Member State, in circumstances where the defendant to those proceedings wishes the dispute to be resolved by the English courts, he could try to persuade the court seised first that it does not have, or should not exercise, jurisdiction. If he wishes instead to achieve his goal by recourse to the English courts, the prospects are limited unless the English court has exclusive jurisdiction regardless of domicile or there is an exclusive jurisdiction agreement for the English court which satisfies the requirements of Article 25 of Regulation 1215/2012.

2.16 Bringing substantive proceedings notwithstanding those in another court

It is not generally an option to respond to proceedings commenced in another Member State to start proceedings in England and to seek to persuade the English court, sesied second, to exercise jurisdiction on the basis that the other court was wrong to have taken jurisdiction. The decision of the European Court in *Overseas Union Insurance Ltd v. New Hampshire Insurance Co*[101] makes it plain that a court (in that case, the English court) which

---

97 *Messier-Dowty Ltd v Sabena SA* [2000] 1 WLR 2040.
98 CPR r. 40.20 provides that the making of a declaration is a matter for the discretion of the court.
99 *Messier-Dowty Ltd*, at 2050–2051. And see further, para. 5.64, below.
100 *Boss Group Ltd v. Boss France SA* [1997] 1 WLR 351. For a more detailed examination of the issues which arise when the claimant seeks to commence proceedings for a negative declaration, see Chapter 5, below.
101 C-351/89, [1991] ECR I-3317.

was seised second in time is forbidden to act on the basis of its opinion, even if such opinion is undeniably correct, that the court seised first erred in taking jurisdiction. Subject to what is said below, Article 29 obliges a court seised second to stay proceedings in respect of the same cause of action and between the same parties until the court seised first has determined its own jurisdiction. If the first court determines that it has jurisdiction, the court seised second must dismiss its proceedings; such is the disadvantage of being the claimant in a court seised second. There is no prize for being second.

There are two exceptions to note. The first applies to Regulation 44/2001 and therefore also to Regulation 1215/2012. It arises when the court seised second has exclusive jurisdiction regardless of domicile. In such a case, any judgment from the court seised first is liable to be refused recognition, and in those circumstances there would be no sense in waiting for it to do anything. The court seised second may proceed to exercise jurisdiction,[102] even if the court seised first has refused to accept that it has no jurisdiction. It does not appear that the answer depends on the court seised second concluding that the court seised first was in error. If the court seised first has taken jurisdiction in violation of what is now Article 24, the court seised second may and must proceed; if the court seised first has not taken jurisdiction in violation of Article 24, it must be seised of a different cause of action from that over which Article 24 gives the second court exclusive jurisdiction regardless of domicile. The second court should therefore proceed to adjudicate.

The second exception applies where the court seised second has or should have jurisdiction by reason of an agreement to prorogate its jurisdiction, but the exception applies only where the the jurisdiction of the court seised second is derived from Regulation 1215/2012, but to understand it, a little history is required.

Where the jurisdiction of a court was derived from Regulation 44/2001, as with the Conventions which preceded it, it followed from a clear decision of the European Court that there was no material exception to the rule that the court seised second had to wait for and abide by the decision of the court seised first.[103] This reflected the apparent distinction, drawn by the Regulation, between 'exclusive jurisdiction regardless of domcile', which comprises Section 6 of its Chapter II, and Section 7 of that Chapter which groups jurisdiction by agreement and jurisdiction by appearance as 'prorogation of jurisdiction'. The Court bolstered its conclusion, that the court seised second had to wait for and accept the decision of the court seised first, with the observation that every court, prorogated or not prorogated, was as able as any other to apply the Regulation, as the provisions of the Regulation on prorogation of jurisdiction were part of the law of every Member State alike.[104]

That conclusion contradicted earlier decisions of the English courts, most notably *Continental Bank NA v. Aeakos Compania Naviera SA*,[105] which had taken the robust view that if the English court found that it had jurisdiction by reason of an agreement, it might

---

102 C-438/12 *Weber v. Weber* EU:C:2014:212, [2015] 2 WLR 213, confirming the existence of an exception to the general rule established in C-351/89 *Overseas Union Insurance Ltd v. New Hampshire Insurance Co* [1991] ECR I-3317 and which had been left open in that case.

103 C-116/02 *Erich Gasser GmbH v. MISAT Srl* [2003] ECR I-14693.

104 The choice of court clause may be contained in a contract governed by the domestic law of the court seised second, from which it might be argued that the court seised second is, in fact, better placed to determine the jurisdictional issue. However, the application of Art. 23 of Regulation 44/2001 (so also Art. 25 of Regulation 1215/2012) does not depend on the law governing the contract between the parties, and this argument has little or no substance.

105 [1994] 1 WLR 588.

and should proceed to hear the case without regard to proceedings having been commenced in another Member State. That approach was uneniably pragmatic and compelling, for if two commercial parties have agreed to the exclusive jurisdiction of the courts of a Member State, it should not be open to one of them to vex or harass the other by commencing proceedings in a different Member State: that other party will have to contest the jurisdiction in the court in which proceedings have been wrongly instituted;[106] appeals[107] may allow the day to be put off when the merits of the dispute are litigated. But these points were put to, and specifically rejected by, the European Court in *Erich Gasser GmbH v. MISAT Srl*.[108] It was no more relevant that the proceedings in the court seised first (*in casu*, Italy) were likely to last for ever and a day before there being any dismissal on jurisdictional grounds.[109]

There was a widely-held view that the decision in *Erich Gasser*, whether considered to be right or wrong as a matter of legal interpretation, was undesirable, as it allowed proceedings brought in bad faith to undermine the agreement of the parties. As a result, Article 31(2) of Regulation 1215/2012 reverses the effect of *Erich Gasser* in cases to which it applies.[110] It provides that a court seised first is required to stay its proceedings where it has been agreed, in accordance with Article 25 of Regulation 1215/2012, that the courts of another Member State have exclusive jurisdiction. The details of this are examined below,[111] and they are not all easy to deal with. It does, however, mean that the party who commences proceedings second in time may be able to proceed in the second court if he is able to use Article 31(2) to persuade the court seised first to stay its proceedings and to give priority to the court designated, or allegedly designated, by agreement. This, therefore, widens a little the category of cases in which proceedings may be brought second, and still proceeded with.

2.17 Application for an injunction to restrain the bringing of proceedings in other Member States

If the defendant has failed to seize the jurisdictional initiative, he may consider applying to the English courts for an injunction to restrain his opponent, who is bringing the foreign proceedings, from continuing with his action.[112] In *Continental Bank NA v. Aeakos Compania*

---

106 Because if he does not, that court being seised first will exclude the jurisdiction of all other Member State courts, whether chosen or not.

107 Which themselves may be delayed by a reference to the European Court.

108 C-116/02, [2003] ECR I-14693.

109 This aspect of the judgment of the Court was disappointing. There was a perfectly sound argument that the dilatory nature of proceedings in Italy would prevent the claimant from obtaining 'a fair and public hearing within a reasonable time', so violating the guarantee given by Art. 6 of the European Convention on Human Rights. As the ECHR is a part of the law of the Member States, and is also apparently a part of European law, an argument based on Art. 6 ECHR could not properly have been dismissed by reference to the Regulation, unless one takes the view that the jurisdiction of the European Court was strictly limited to an interpretation of the Brussels Convention, and did not extend beyond this to consider the impact on it of other European instruments. It presumably followed that although the Brussels Convention did not permit the Austrian court to proceed to hear the case, the international obligations of the Austrian Republic under Art. 6 ECHR may have been seen by the Austrian court as overriding the answer given by the European Court (in which case there was no need for the reference to have been made in the first place).

110 This must mean that the proceedings in the court seised first were instituted on or after 10 January 2015, for unless this is so, Art. 31(2) of Regulation 1215/2012 will not touch the court seised first.

111 Paragraph 2.127, below.

112 Of course, if the opponent has not yet commenced such proceedings, the obstacles standing in the way of the applicant will be one fewer (but still sufficient).

Naviera SA[113] the Court of Appeal swept all objections aside, and granted such an injunction to restrain a party from continuing proceedings in Greece in (as it saw the matter) breach of contract.

It was never easy to see how this view was compatible with the Conventions or the Brussels I Regulation. So far as jurisdiction over the respondent was concerned, he was immune to the jurisdiction of the English court unless the Regulation gave the court personal jurisdiction over him. As on this hypothesis the proceedings in the foreign court will already have begun, it was strongly arguable that its status as court seised second would annul any jurisdiction the English court might otherwise have had.[114] For even though the English proceedings would not involve an examination of the merits of the dispute, and would not result in a judgment strictly irreconcilable with the decision of the foreign court, there was a clear potential for conflict between the conclusions of the two courts. And quite apart from that, it was not easy to defend the substance of the reasoning[115] deployed in the case, not least because the Greek court might have applied its law, faithfully and correctly, to come to the conclusion that the proceedings before it were not within the material scope of an agreement for the jurisdiction of the English courts.

All that came to an end when the European Court held in *Turner v. Grovit*[116] that the granting of an anti-suit injunction against a respondent, which had the indirect effect of preventing an action being brought in a civil or commercial matter before the courts of another Member State, was incompatible with the relationship of mutual trust and confidence to and by which the Member States have bound themselves. The reasoning underpinning this decision will be examined later, but the decision of the Court left no room for injunctive relief to restrain the bringing of proceedings (whether actually pending or otherwise) before the courts of another Member State. *Continental Bank* has in effect been overruled; and what one may call the 'anti-European-suit injunction' has had its day.[117]

On the other hand, though it does not prevent the exercise of jurisdiction, a claimant who can show that the institution of legal proceedings before the courts of the other Member State was a breach of contract may bring proceedings for damages for breach. This involves no interference with the foreign court and its exercise of jurisdiction, merely drawing the legal conclusions which follow from that exercise of jurisdiction.[118]

---

113 [1994] 1 WLR 588. The decision was followed and approved in *The Angelic Grace* [1995] 1 Lloyd's Rep 87.

114 Though in the light of Art. 31(2) of Regulation 1215/2012, this conclusion may now be avoided and jurisdiction established.

115 Examined in detail in Chapter 5, below.

116 C-159/02, [2004] ECR I-3565. The reference for a preliminary ruling was made by the House of Lords: [2002] 1 WLR 107.

117 In *Through Transport Mutual Insurance Association (Eurasia) Ltd v. New India Assurance Co Ltd* [2004] EWCA Civ 1598, [2005] 1 Lloyd's Rep 67, the Court of Appeal had considered that an anti-suit injunction could still be ordered where the breach was of an arbitration agreement. That conclusion is not reconcilable with the decision in C-185/07 *Allianz SpA v. West Tankers Inc* [2009] ECR I-663, in which the Court ruled that an injunction to restrain a party acting in breach of an arbitration agreement fell within the principle laid down in *Turner v. Grovit*, and that was that. See further below, paras 2.30 and 2.274.

118 *Starlight Shipping Co v. Allianz Marine & Aviation Versicherungs AG* [2014] EWCA Civ 1010, [2014] 2 Lloyd's Rep 554. Likewise, perhaps, if the claim is for a decree of specific performance: *Starlight Shipping Co v. Allianz Marine & Aviation Versicherungs AG* [2014] EWHC 3068 (Comm), [2014] 2 Lloyd's Rep 579.

2.18 Bringing proceedings in a non-Member State

The foregoing discussion has concentrated upon the competition between the courts of two Member States: the conclusion must be that it is highly desirable to be the first to institute proceedings before the courts of a Member State, and that save for narrow exceptions, it is difficult to circumvent or defeat the jurisdiction of the court first seised unless that court is persuaded that it has no jurisdiction. What is less clear is whether a similar step, namely commencing one's proceedings first, in the courts of a non-Member State has a corresponding effect.

Suppose that A commences proceedings against B in the courts of New York, and that at a later date B commences proceedings in England, against A, who is domiciled in England, pursuant to what is now Article 4 of Regulation 1215/2012. The material question is whether the existence of the prior New York proceedings has any effect on the exercise of jurisdiction by the courts of a Member State, so as, for example, to furnish grounds to have the proceedings in a Member State stayed.

Where jurisdiction is taken under Regulation 1215/2012, and the basis for taking it is general jurisdiction under Article 4 or special jurisdiction under Articles 7 to 9, the court is permitted by Articles 33 and 34 of the Regulation to accede to an application to stay proceedings in view of prior proceedings already commenced before the courts of a non-Member State. This is a limited improvement on Regulation 44/2001,[119] which made no equivalent provision of any kind. It is true that Articles 33 and 34 apply on a discretionary basis, but that seems sensible. By contrast, Regulation 44/2001 made no provision for such cases, which might suggest that proceedings in New York, not being brought before the courts of a Member State, have no relevance to, or effect upon, proceedings in a Member State. On the other hand, the legal protection of persons established within the European Union[120] is hardly strengthened if no regard is given to legal proceedings actually taking place in courts outside the European Union, especially when these judgments may be enforceable within one or more of the Member States. The broader question is whether a court which has or appears to have jurisdiction under the Regulation may ever decline to exercise it, which is one aspect of a complex question which is examined in detail at the end of this chapter.[121] For present purposes, it is sufficient to say that the institution of proceedings before the courts of a non-Member State may prevent a court in a Member State from allowing subsequent proceedings to proceed to final judgment.

2.19 What a defendant should do if served with process in a case to which the Regulation applies

The rules contained in this chapter describe whether the court has jurisdiction under the Brussels I Regulation. In other words, if the claimant seises the court, these are the rules which will be applied if the defendant disputes the propriety of the exercise of jurisdiction over him. If the defendant believes that a challenge, based upon the rules in this chapter, will succeed, he may take the steps prescribed by national procedural law to make the challenge.

---

119 Not so much half a loaf as half a croissant.

120 See the preamble to the Brussels Convention. This is not reproduced in terms in the Recitals to the Regulation.

121 At para. 2.299 *et seq.*, below.

Those of English law are set out in Chapter 5; they apply equally to cases where jurisdiction is asserted under the Regulation, under the Conventions and under the common law.[122] A defendant who follows that procedure will be safe from the allegation that he has inadvertently conferred jurisdiction, under what is now Article 26 of Regulation 1215/2012, by his entering an appearance. If he wishes the court to rule that it has no jurisdiction, he must apply to it for the relief he seeks, at the outset of proceedings.

If he disregards the service he may make his position irretrievably worse. In principle, if the defendant does not appear, the court may of its own motion declare that it has no jurisdiction,[123] but if it fails to do so and judgment is entered, a later objection made to a court called on to recognise the judgment, complaining that the court which gave judgment did not have jurisdiction, is usually inadmissible. It follows that, if proceedings in a civil or commercial matter are instituted before the court of a Member State, almost all jurisdictional challenges available to a defendant must be made immediately or not at all.

2.20 What a claimant may do if the defendant does not enter an appearance

If the defendant does not appear, the claimant may proceed to enter judgment. In principle, the court will be obliged to satisfy itself that, if the non-appearing defendant is domiciled in another Member State,[124] it nevertheless did have jurisdiction over him.[125] The degree or quality of evidence required from the claimant is a matter for national law, but something more than a bare assertion in a witness statement should be called for.[126] The court will also be required to satisfy itself that the defendant received the document instituting the proceedings in sufficient time for him to be able to arrange for his defence.[127]

A question, slightly unexpected in England at least, has also arisen as to whether an order made in such circumstances is to be seen as a judgment for the purposes of its enforcement under Chapter III of the Regulation. The problem, if it is a problem, is that the order made by the court is simply to permit the claimant to enter judgment in terms of the claim. There is no significant judicial scrutiny of the claim or of the basis for it; there is no judicial determination of the issues raised by the claim, and therefore no statement of the grounds on which the court found the claim to be justified. In the absence of such judicial scrutiny and statement of reasons, the administrative order which results might be thought to lack the essential quality of a 'judgment', that is, that be the product of adjudication. To put the point another way, it may be a decision without being a judgment. This objection was

---

122 Though it may be argued in the light of *Kurz v. Stella Musical Veranstaltungs GmbH* [1992] Ch 196 that when the challenge is made in a case to which the Regulation applies, the rules are applied in a slightly less rigid manner.

123 Articles 27 and 28 of Regulation 1215/2012.

124 No such requirement exists if the defendant was not so domiciled.

125 Article 28.

126 Jenard [1979] OJ C59/1, 39; 38/81 *Effer SpA v. Kantner* [1982] ECR 825.

127 Article 28. Alternatively, it suffices that all necessary steps were taken to this end, or if there had been service pursuant to Council Regulation (EC) 1393/2007 (which replaces Regulation (EC) 1348/2000), or in accordance with the Hague Convention of 15 November 1965 on Service Abroad of Judicial and Extrajudicial Documents in Civil and Commercial Matters. In order to forestall difficulties which may later arise when it is sought to enforce the judgment in another Member State, it may well be a prudent step to warn the defendant by letter, prior to the entering of judgment, that judgment is about to be entered. Although the court called upon to recognise a judgment is entitled to decide for itself whether the defendant was duly and timeously served (as to which, see para. 7.17, below), the giving of such a warning should ensure that the recognising court concludes that the defendant had sufficient time to arrange for his defence.

raised before the European Court in *Gambazzi v. Daimler Chrysler Canada Inc*,[128] where the defence had been struck out as a response to contempt of court. The objection was rejected, on grounds which appear to owe more to pragmatism than to principle,[129] for the contention that the order is not a 'judgment' is a serious one:[130] how, one may ask, can a defendant decide whether to appeal if there is no judicial determination of the basis on which the claim was sustained?[131] To guard against this, a claimant may be well advised to apply for summary judgment, rather than judgment in default, if the defendant elects not to appear.

2.21 The nature of the jurisdictional rules of the Regulation

The Regulation lays down the rules which determine the jurisdiction, and the absence of jurisdiction, of courts of the Member States. From this perspective, it states rules in the nature of rules of public law; legislative instructions to the judge which tell him whether he has jurisdiction or not. If the judge has jurisdiction, he may be required to exercise it, because that is what he has been told to do. Of course, the attitude of the parties will provide important data for a court in deciding whether it has jurisdiction. The fact that the defendant is prepared to submit by appearance has the consequence, as the European legislator has told the judge it shall, that the court has jurisdiction in all but a narrow class of cases in which such submission does not have that decisive effect. If the parties have made an agreement for the jurisdiction of a court, the judge in the court so designated will discover that he has been told to accept jurisdiction if the claimant invokes it; and a judge in another, undesignated, court will find that he has been told to find that he has no jurisdiction if the defendant to the claim disputes the jurisdiction by reference to that agreement. If the court has jurisdiction according to these legislative rules, it must be exercised when the claimant invokes it unless the courts of another country were seised first, in which case the judge will find that he has no jurisdiction after all. That, as far as one may tell, is roughly the way it works and was designed to work. It is a statutory scheme, which confers or imposes jurisdiction on the court, which has that jurisdiction by legislative instruction.

The nature of common law jurisdiction is very different. The jurisdiction of the courts is inherent, wide, and open. If the defendant is present within the jurisdiction, he may be served as of right; if he is not, the claimant needs the permission of the court to serve out. That is pretty much that.

The common law accepts that the parties may make agreements as to the exercise of the inherent jurisdiction of the court. Such agreements do not create or establish jurisdiction, for jurisdiction is inherent and depends on service. Instead, they give rise to private, and enforceable, rights and obligations in relation to the issue of proceedings, which the court may enforce in the same way as any other enforceable agreement as to the behaviour of

---

128 C-394/07, [2009] ECR I-2563.

129 If the defendant may default and, by so doing, deprive the claimant of the right to obtain an enforceable order, some may be tempted to think that the world has gone slightly mad.

130 And it seems to have been accepted by the Privy Council in *Keymer v. Visvasantam Reddi* (1916) LR 44 Ind App 6. The decision was based on s. 13 of the Indian Code of Civil Procedure, but on this point it declared the common law as it was then and is now.

131 *Cf* C-619/10 *Trade Agency Inc v. Seramico Investments Ltd* EU:C:2012:531. The weakness of this point, however, is that recourse against a judgment in default is not by appeal (on the merits) but by application to set aside.

parties. A contract may therefore give rise to a right to sue or to not be sued. The common law accepts instinctively that parties may create enforceable contracts concerning the inherent jurisdiction of a court at common law. This encourages the common law to understand that the exercise of jurisdiction, the asking of a court to accept jurisdiction over a case, is not simply a question of public law, of whether that court is bound or entitled to adjudicate, important though that question is. It may also be about the exercise and enforcement of rights to sue (the defendant having promised the claimant to defend in the court in question), or rights not to be sued (the claimant having made a promise to the defendant not to invoke the jurisdiction of that court). This in turn explains why injunctions may restrain the unlawful invocation of jurisdiction (because if that jurisdiction is invoked in breach of contract, the breach of contract should be restrained), and why damages may also be ordered in the aftermath of an invocation of jurisdiction in breach of contract (because the personal obligations which the parties assume *inter se* sound in damages if they are broken). The apparatus of private obligations operates alongside, but is conceptually distinct from, the larger, public law, framework of rules on jurisdiction. These rights and agreements about jurisdiction do not establish that a court does or does not have jurisdiction; but they do amount to promises, intended to be legally binding, about what parties will and will not do in courts which do and do not have jurisdiction.

It is not clear how easily this understanding translates to the context of jurisdiction which is created and imposed by legislation or Regulation. But this way of thinking about the law and jurisdiction has sometimes led common lawyers to think about the Regulation as a source of jurisdictional rights. It has been said, for example, that what is now Article 4 of Regulation 1215/2012 gives a defendant a right to defend in the courts of his domicile; that Article 25 gives the parties to the agreement a right to insist that only the designated court has jurisdiction. This appears to be a mistake.[132] The European Court does not use this language; and it probably does not think about jurisdiction in the idiom of rights. Defendants shall, according to Article 4, be sued in their home courts, but they do not have a *right* to defend there. The parties may make an agreement about the jurisdiction of courts, but that does not give them rights: the jurisdiction of a court is prorogated, that of another court is derogated; but whatever is happening, it is not the creation of rights, still less rights enforceable as a matter of private law.

Some of the issues which have emerged as the most troublesome are precisely those in which the common law's instinct, that there are judicially enforceable private rights, is fundamentally at odds with the view of others, that jurisdiction is a matter of public law and whether judges may be asked to adjudicate, in relation to which the preferences of the parties may be data, but do not make the law. Accordingly, this chapter tries to avoid using terminology which suggests that parties have rights or duties in relation to the jurisdiction of courts. This chapter deals with jurisdictional rules in a public law sense: it is, after all, concerned with the Regulation, which owes nothing to the common law. The extent to which the parties

---

132 An early recognition that it was not helpful, or not English, to speak of a defendant having a 'right' that the Brussels Convention be applied properly to him was made by Potter J, as he then was, in *Soc Commerciale de Réassurance v. Eras International Ltd (No 2)* [1995] 1 Lloyd's Rep 64. The contrary view, that the Regulation directly confers rights, enforceable even in relation to proceedings before the courts of non-Member States, and even when the parties have made an agreement for the courts of a non-Member State, which is to be ignored, led to the decision of the Court of Appeal in *Samengo-Turner v. J & H Marsh & McLennan (Services) Ltd* [2007] EWCA Civ 723, [2008] ICR 18, on which see [2007] LMCLQ 433: the decision, on that point, cannot be taken as correct.

have rights in relation to jurisdiction, and may make and call upon a court to enforce private agreements about matters relating to jurisdiction, will be examined in Chapter 5.[133]

2.22 The hierarchy of jurisdictional rules established by the Regulation

With that introduction, the remainder of this chapter examines the structure and detail of the Regulation, by organising the provisions of the Regulation into the order in which logic requires them to be assessed. The point of departure is, therefore, to determine whether the matter before the court falls within the domain of the Regulation.

(1) THE DOMAIN OR SCOPE OF THE BRUSSELS I REGULATION

2.23 General

For the Brussels I Regulation to regulate jurisdiction in a particular matter, the claim which is made must fall within its domain. If it does *not* fall within its domain, the Regulation[134] applies neither directly to regulate, nor indirectly[135] to affect, the jurisdiction of the court: in such cases, courts will apply their national law rules on jurisdiction, including those rules of exorbitant jurisdiction referred to by Article 5 of Regulation 1215/2012. But if the claim made *does* fall within the domain of the Regulation, the Regulation regulates the taking, and the non-taking, of jurisdiction. Everything, therefore, turns upon an accurate mapping of the boundaries which mark out the domain of the Regulation. This may be examined by reference to three aspects of its scope: (i) its temporal, geographical, personal and international scope; (ii) its material scope; and (iii) its relationship with other instruments.

2.24 Temporal, geographical, personal and international scope of the Regulation: Article 66(1)

Article 66(1) of Regulation 1215/2012 provides that

> *This Regulation shall apply only to legal proceedings instituted, to authentic instruments formally drawn up or registered, and to court settlements approved or concluded on or after 10 January 2015.*

Article 66 of Regulation 44/2001 had been to the same effect, with a commencement date of 1 March 2002.

2.25 Temporal scope

The recast Brussels I Regulation, Regulation 1215/2012, takes effect in relation to proceedings instituted on or after 10 January 2015, even though the cause of action arose prior to that

---

133 It is also examined in greater depth in Briggs, *Agreements on Jurisdiction and Choice of Law* (Oxford, 2008).

134 The Brussels and Lugano Convention will not apply either, and the material in Chapter 3 will not be relevant.

135 145/86 *Hoffmann v. Krieg* [1988] ECR 645, (1988) 8 YEL 265. For another example in support of this proposition, see the manner in which the Regulation does not apply to judgments ordering payment of an arbitration award (see paras 2.42 and 7.09, below), or judgments declaring enforceable a judgment from a non-Member State (see paras 2.37 and 7.07, below).

date. The position in relation to Regulation 44/2001 was a little more tricky, for though it had an effective commencement date of 1 March 2002, a number of Member States acceded to the European Union after that date.[136] The amendments to Regulation 44/2001 which incorporated Cyprus, the Czech Republic, Estonia, Hungary, Latvia, Lithuania, Malta, Poland, Slovakia and Slovenia came into effect on 1 May 2004, and for the purpose of legal proceedings instituted on or after that date, those States were also Member States bound by Regulation 44/2001. The same, *mutatis mutandis*, was true for proceedings which relate to Bulgaria and Romania, which became Member States on 1 January 2007, and for Croatia, which became a Member State on 1 July 2013.

For the purposes of this rule, it seems certain that the date on which an action is instituted in England is the date of issue of the claim form, which is to say the date stamped on it by the Registry out of which it is issued.[137] Prior to the coming into force of Regulation 44/2001, when the law was contained in the corresponding provision of the Brussels Convention,[138] it was debatable whether the relevant date was that of issue or of service.[139] But as an English court is now deemed to be seised on the issue of the claim form,[140] it seems plain beyond argument that the date of issue of the claim form will determine which version of the Regulation, original or recast, will apply to the proceedings in question.

2.26 Geographical scope

In principle, the geographical scope of the Brussels I Regulation is the territory of the Member States of the European Union. For the purpose of Regulation 1215/2012, there are 28 Member States. In order of seniority they are France,[141] Germany, Italy, Belgium, the Netherlands[142] and Luxembourg; the United Kingdom[143] and Ireland; Greece; Portugal[144] and Spain;[145] Austria, Finland[146] and Sweden; Cyprus,[147] the Czech Republic, Estonia,

---

136 And Denmark, which exercised its right to opt out, signed up to Regulation 44/2001 only in 2007.

137 CPR r. 7.2(2).

138 Article 54 of the Brussels Convention.

139 A court was not seised until service had been effected: *Dresser UK Ltd v. Falcongate Freight Management Ltd* [1992] QB 502, though the date for determining whether a jurisdictional fact was satisfied was the date of issue rather than service: *Canada Trust Co v. Stolzenberg (No 2)* [2002] 1 AC 1; and a decision at first instance had held that the operation of the 'date of service' rule was confined to what is now Art. 29 of Regulation 1215/2012, and did not apply more generally: *Arab Monetary Fund v. Hashim (No 4)* [1992] 1 WLR 1176 (see also *Trade Indemnity plc v. Försäkrings AB Njord* [1995] 1 All ER 796, 821, where the issue was discussed but not resolved).

140 Article 32(1) of Regulation 1215/2012.

141 Which includes Guadeloupe, French Guiana, Martinique, Réunion, St Barthélemy and St Martin, but which excludes New Caledonia, French Polynesia, Mayotte, Wallis & Futuna Islands, St Pierre & Miquelon; and see also Art. 355(1) TFEU.

142 It does not apply to Aruba or to the Netherlands Antilles.

143 Which for this purpose includes Gibraltar, as a European territory of the United Kingdom for which the United Kingdom has responsibility for external relations: Art. 355(3) TFEU. It does not include the Channel Islands or Isle of Man, or the sovereign base areas of Akrotiri and Dhekelia: Art. 355(5) TFEU. It is not completely clear whether Gibraltar or the United Kingdom is the Member State for the purposes of Art. 4 of the Regulation. The better view is that the United Kingdom is the Member State and that Gibraltar is a part of it, the allocation of jurisdiction to which is a matter of the internal law of the United Kingdom.

144 Which includes Madeira and the Azores: Art. 355(1) TFEU.

145 Which includes the Canary Islands: Art. 355(1) TFEU.

146 Including the Åland Islands: Art. 355(4) TFEU.

147 The Regulation applies in principle to the whole territory of the Republic of Cyprus, but while the northern part of the island remains under the illegal occupation of the armed forces of the Turkish Republic and under the administration of a rebel junta, the application of European law in that part of the Republic of Cyprus is

Hungary, Latvia, Lithuania, Malta, Poland, Slovakia and Slovenia; Bulgaria and Romania; and Croatia.[148]

Denmark[149] became bound by Regulation 44/2001 from 1 July 2007,[150] and has agreed to be bound by Regulation 1215/2012, presumably from 10 January 2015.[151] Iceland, Norway and Switzerland are not Member States, though they remain Contracting States party to the Lugano II Convention.[152] But Andorra, Liechtenstein, Monaco and San Marino are not Member States, nor are they otherwise within the geographical scope of the Regulation. Nor, needless to say, is the Vatican City.

2.27 Personal scope

The personal scope of the Brussels I Regulation is not specifically limited. It applies to all persons who are defendants in proceedings falling within its domain, and it may be relied on by all persons who are claimants in proceedings falling within its domain. It is certainly not limited to claims against defendants who have a domicile in a Member State, though these will be the most frequent of defendants, and is certainly not restricted to proceedings instituted by claimants having a domicile in a Member State.[153] Though the recitals to the Regulation indicate that the defendant will in principle be domiciled in a Member State, and that a defendant not domiciled in a Member State will in general not be subject to the detailed jurisdictional rules of the Regulation,[154] there are exceptions for which specific provision is made, and this point in the Recitals should not be taken too seriously. Moreover, as there is no reason to suppose that the jurisdictional protections put in place by the Regulation are available to defendants only when they are sued by claimants who are themselves domiciled in Member States, it must follow that the Regulation applies without regard to the domicile of the claimant. The European Court held that this was so under the Brussels Convention,[155] and the same is surely true for the Brussels I Regulation.

2.28 International scope

At this point it is necessary to consider another aspect of the material scope of the Brussels I Regulation: its 'international scope'. The issue requires a little history to explain the rather odd conclusions which appear to be required to be drawn; but the conclusion will be that unless the issues are wholly internal to the United Kingdom, the Regulation applies.

The Brussels Convention, according to its preamble, stated that the parties thereto were 'anxious to strengthen in the Community the legal protection of persons therein established',

---

curtailed, and the Government of the Republic of Cyprus is not in dereliction for failing to secure its application in the occupied territory. See C-420/07 *Apostolides v. Orams* [2009] ECR I-3571.

148 Albania, Iceland, Macedonia (Former Yugoslav Republic of), Montenegro, Serbia and Turkey are, according to the European Union, 'on the road to EU membership'. They are not all at the same point along that road.

149 Not including the Færoe Islands or Greenland.

150 Recital 21; and Art. 1(3). For the change of status, see [2006] OJ L120/22; SI 2007/1655.

151 [2013] OJ L79/4.

152 On which, see Chapter 3, below.

153 C-412/98 *Universal General Insurance Co v. Groupe Josi Reinsurance Co SA* [2000] ECR I-5925.

154 Regulation 44/2001, Recitals (8) and (9); Regulation 1215/2012, Recitals (13) and (14).

155 C-412/98 *Universal General Insurance Co v. Groupe Josi Reinsurance Co SA* [2000] ECR I-5925; on this point the decision is consistent with C-351/89 *Overseas Union Insurance Ltd v. New Hampshire Insurance Co* [1991] ECR I-3317.

and considered it 'necessary for this purpose to determine the international jurisdiction of their courts…'. It followed that the Convention attended to jurisdictional issues which were international in the sense of implicating the courts of more Contracting States than one. It was arguable that it did not govern jurisdiction in two other classes of case: first, where the issue was one of national jurisdiction, namely of whether the courts of one city or another, or one part of the United Kingdom or another, had jurisdiction; and second, where the only question was whether the courts of a single Contracting State or a non-Contracting State had jurisdiction. What these cases have in common is that in neither was there any issue as to which of two or more Contracting States had jurisdiction in the matter.

The proposition that questions of jurisdiction which were purely internal to a single Contracting State were not touched or affected by the Convention was supported by Jenard, who stated[156] that the Convention was not to affect[157] the jurisdiction of courts where the facts lacked any international[158] element: in such a case the domestic law of that State alone governed the jurisdiction of the courts. To answer any question of internal or national jurisdiction arising in such cases, for example, to allocate jurisdiction as between the parts of the United Kingdom, a court would look only to rules of national law. In the United Kingdom, these were made by Civil Jurisdiction and Judgments Act 1982, section 16, and Schedule 4. These rules of United Kingdom law were to apply where the Brussels Convention allocated international jurisdiction to the courts of the United Kingdom as a Member State and the question was which part of the United Kingdom had national jurisdiction. They were, for convenience, also to apply where the issue of jurisdiction was wholly internal to the United Kingdom, providing the rules which determined jurisdiction within the United Kingdom. When Regulation 44/2001 came into force, the provisions of Schedule 4 to the 1982 Act were amended and remade; they remain operative in relation to the recast Regulation 1215/2012.

According to the case law established under the Convention, the jurisdictional rules of the Convention were not restricted so as to apply only to claims against defendants having a domicile in a Contracting State. Where a court had exclusive jurisdiction regardless of domicile, for example, the Convention governed jurisdiction without regard to domicile; where there was a jurisdiction agreement for the courts of a Contracting State, the Convention applied if one of the parties – it did not matter which party – to it was domiciled in a Contracting State. And even though the claimant had no connection with any Contracting State, the jurisdictional rules of the Convention still applied to claims which he might bring, so as to allow jurisdiction to be asserted against a defendant domiciled in a Contracting State, and also to protect that same defendant from jurisdictional rules wider than those contained in the Convention when he was sued by a claimant who was not domiciled in a Contracting State.[159]

Despite that, there was in England a tendency, or temptation, to argue that the Convention did not apply, and was an irrelevance, where the only jurisdictional connections were between the United Kingdom and a non-Contracting State, on the footing that in such a case the issue for decision was not concerned with international jurisdiction in the sense of

---

156 [1979] OJ C59/1, 8.

157 In civilian systems, the courts for the defendant's domicile will always be competent, and for the Regulation to provide that they have jurisdiction will not alter the law in force.

158 Of course, everything turns on the meaning of 'international'.

159 C-412/98 *Universal Groupe Insurance Co v. Groupe Josi Reinsurance Co SA* [2000] ECR I-5925 (Convention applies where Canadian claimant sues a French defendant in a French court).

inter-Contracting State jurisdiction. This perception led the English courts to hold that the Convention 'did not apply' to an application for a stay of proceedings, brought against an English-domiciled company, in favour of the courts of Argentina;[160] and it was also considered that nothing in the Convention prevented a stay of proceedings, in favour of the courts of Greece, which had been brought against a defendant who did not have a domicile in any of the Contracting States.[161]

The European Court disposed of this restrictive English approach to the international scope of the Brussels Convention by its judgment in *Owusu v. Jackson*.[162] In that case a claim was made against six defendants, one domiciled in the United Kingdom and five in Jamaica, in a personal injury claim arising out of a holiday accident in Jamaica. It was contended that as the facts meant that the only Contracting State with jurisdiction was the United Kingdom, and no other Contracting State had jurisdiction, any 'internationality' was only as between the United Kingdom and a non-Contracting State, with the result that the matter fell outside the material scope of the Convention. The European Court disagreed, ruling that the requisite international element could be found in connection to a non-Contracting State. It rejected the argument that, as the original justification for the Convention was to secure the free movement of judgments within the community of Contracting States, the jurisdictional rules established to that end were inapplicable where there was no issue of internationality as between the Contracting States. Rather, the Court said[163] that the uniform rules of jurisdiction contained in the Brussels Convention:

> 'are not intended to apply only in situations in which there is a real and sufficient link with the working of the internal market, by definition involving a number of Member States. Suffice it to observe in that regard that the consolidation as such of the rules on conflict of jurisdiction and on the recognition and enforcement of judgments, effected by the Brussels Convention in respect of cases with an international element, is without doubt intended to eliminate obstacles to the functioning of the internal market which may derive from disparities between national legislations on the subject... It follows from the foregoing that Article 2 of the Brussels Convention applies to circumstances such as those in the main proceedings, involving relationships between the courts of a single Contracting State and those of a non-Contracting State rather than relationships between the courts of a number of Contracting States.'

And that was that: there was a requirement of internationality, and this was satisfied by an actual connection to Jamaica or its courts.

The Brussels I Regulation does not explicitly state that its purpose is to determine the international jurisdiction of the courts of Member States, and it may therefore be asked whether this makes any appreciable difference to the operation of its rules of jurisdiction. The answer appears to be that there is a requirement of internationality, but that the manner in which this may be satisfied may be arbitrary. It is certain that *Owusu* would be decided the same way under the Regulation as it was under the Convention, for continuity of

---

160 *Re Harrods (Buenos Aires) Ltd* [1992] Ch 72; see also Collins (1990) 106 LQR 535. In the later decision in *Lubbe v. Cape plc* [2000] 1 WLR 1545, the House of Lords acknowledged that the law was unclear and that, in an appropriate case, a reference to the European Court would have been appropriate.

161 *Haji-Ioannou v. Frangos* [1999] 2 Lloyd's Rep 337, where the point was *obiter*, as the defendant was eventually held to be domiciled in Greece. But even so, if what is now Art. 6 jurisdiction is derived from the Regulation, it is hard to see how the Regulation could be said not to apply to it. What solution the Regulation prescribes if it does apply is considered at the end of this chapter, under Question (15).

162 C-281/02, [2005] ECR I-1383.

163 At [34]–[35].

interpretation is understood to be required by the principle of legal certainty.[164] Although the European Court has indicated that a requirement of internationality still applies to define or to limit the material scope or operation of the Regulation, it may be satisfied by an inessential point of contact with a foreign country, such as where a claim is advanced against a local defendant at the same time as a claim is made against a co-defendant who is not local.[165] This appears to mean that the answer would have been the opposite, and the Regulation would not have applied, if the non-local co-defendant had not been sued, or had been sued but in separate proceedings, which as an outcome seems more arbitrary than it should be.[166] It is satisfied if the defendant is a foreign national and it is not possible to determine where he has a domiciled.[167]

The result is that if a matter is demonstrably wholly internal to the United Kingdom, so that the only jurisdictional question which may arise is as to the part of or place within the United Kingdom which has jurisdiction, it is not one in which the Regulation is designed to have any role. The point may be illustrated this way. Suppose a defamatory statement is made by a person domiciled in the United Kingdom about another such person, and is published in newspapers in England and Scotland. If the question is whether the claimant may or must sue in England or Scotland, or whether the courts of England or Scotland may stay proceedings on grounds of *forum non conveniens* in favour of the other jurisdiction, the Regulation has no role in answering the question, for the matter before the court is wholly internal to a single Member State. But as soon as the claim is broadened to include complaint of publication by a person outside the United Kingdom, whether the defendant or another, it appears that the Regulation would then apply to all aspects of the jurisdiction of the court.[168]

2.29 Material scope of the Regulation: Article 1

Article 1 of Regulation 1215/2012[169] provides that:

> *(1) This Regulation shall apply in civil and commercial matters whatever the nature of the court or tribunal. It shall not extend, in particular, to revenue, customs or administrative matters or to the liability of the State for acts and omissions in the exercise of State authority (acta iure imperii). (2) This Regulation shall not apply to: (a) the status or legal capacity of natural persons, rights in property arising out of a matrimonial relationship or out of a relationship deemed by the law applicable to such relationship to have comparable effects to marriage; (b) bankruptcy, proceedings relating to the winding-up of insolvent companies or other legal persons, judicial arrangements, compositions and analogous proceedings; (c) social security; (d) arbitration; (e) maintenance obligations arising from a family relationship, parentage, marriage or affinity; (f) wills and succession, including maintenance obligations arising by reason of death.*

---

164 C-533/07 *Falco Privatstiftung v. Weller-Lindhorst* [2009] ECR I-3327, [49]–[51]; C-167/08 *Draka NK Cables Ltd v. Omnipol Ltd* [2009] ECR I-3477, [20].

165 C-478/12 *Maletic v. Lastminute.com GmbH* EU:C:2013:735, [2014] QB 424.

166 See also C-328/12 *Schmid v. Hertel* EU:C:2014:6, [2014] 1 WLR 633, holding that the Insolvency Regulation, Regulation 1346/2000, is applicable to proceedings (in that case, to set aside a transaction on the basis of insolvency legislation) in which the only non-local element is that the defendant does not have a domicile in a Member State. It seems to confirm that the Insolvency Regulation also requires an international element.

167 C-327/10 *Hypoteční Banka AS v. Lindner* [2011] ECR I-11543. See also C-292/10 *G v. De Visser* EU:C:2012:142, [2013] QB 168 (special jurisdiction where EU citizen with unknown domicile).

168 *Cf* C-478/12 *Maletic v. lastminute.com GmbH* EU:C:2013:735, [2014] QB 424.

169 The material scope of Brussels and Lugano II Conventions, and of the intra-UK rules which allocate Regulation jurisdiction conferred on the courts of the United Kingdom to England or to Scotland or to Northern Ireland, is practically identical.

Article 1 of Regulation 44/2001 had been to the same effect, with a small number of immaterial differences.[170]

2.30 Matters excluded from the Regulation: broad, neutral or narrow interpretation

According to its title, the Brussels I Regulation applies to regulate jurisdiction in, according to Article 1, 'civil and commercial matters whatever the nature of the court or tribunal'. The meaning of 'jurisdiction' may appear to be uncontroversial, but the European Court in *Kongress Agentur Hagen GmbH v. Zeehaghe BV*[171] stated that it did not extend to cover matters of procedure properly so called, which continue to be governed, in principle at least, by the national law of the court seised. The significance of this will appear in various places below. Article 1 then proceeds to specify certain matters which are specifically excluded from the material or subject matter scope of the Regulation.

As will be seen below, the idea that the Regulation applies to certain matters but not to others is not free of complexity. The questions which arise when a claim is based on matters which fall within the scope of the Regulation but the defence raises an issue which falls outside it, or vice versa, are probably to be answered by focusing on the claim and not on the defence. The questions which arise when a claim is based on matters which fall within the scope of the Regulation but a subordinate or subsidiary part of that claim would fall outside it, or vice versa, are probably answered by focusing on the main issue, or the principal issue, and not on the incidental or subordinate part of the proceedings. Though not always completely easy to operate, this approach is practical and sensible.

The European Court has given little[172] support to the contention that the expression 'civil and commercial matters' should be given an expansive meaning on the supposed ground that matters which are not civil or commercial are exceptions to the general rule, which should therefore be interpreted narrowly. Such a contention would be wrong in principle, because the jurisdictional rules which apply to civil and commercial matters do *not* constitute a general rule to which the rules applicable to matters which are not civil or commercial are exception. The line defined by 'civil and commercial matters' in Article 1 is a line of demarcation between two spheres: inside and outside the domain of the Regulation. This was confirmed by the Court, which has stated that:[173]

---

170 Regulation 44/2001: Art. 1(1): 'This Regulation shall apply in civil and commercial matters whatever the nature of the court or tribunal. It shall not extend, in particular, to revenue, customs or administrative matters. (2) The Regulation shall not apply to (a) the status or legal capacity of natural persons, rights in property arising out of a matrimonial relationship, wills and succession, (b) bankruptcy, proceedings relating to the winding-up of insolvent companies or other legal persons, judicial arrangements, compositions and analogous proceedings, (c) social security, (d) arbitration.'

171 C-365/88, [1990] ECR I-1845; *cf* also, C-68/93, *Shevill v. Presse Alliance SA* [1995] ECR I-415.

172 The only statement which appears to be at odds with the view in the text is C-302/13 *flyLAL-Lithuanian Airlines AS v. Starptautiskā lidosta Rīga VAS* EU:C:2014:2319, [2015] ILPr 28. It is too early to tell whether this will mark a change in interpretive policy by the Court.

173 C-190/89 *Marc Rich & Co AG v. Soc Italiana Impianti* [1991] ECR I-3855, [16]. The case is concerned with the Brussels Convention, which owes its genesis to what was Art. 220 of the Treaty of Rome; but the principle is common. Its statement to contrary effect, in C-302/13 *flyLAL-Lithuanian Airlines AS v. Starptautiskā lidosta Rīga VAS* at [27], appears to have been made without reference to its earlier, and more principled, position. The newer decision cannot be regarded as soundly based.

'it does not follow that the Convention, whose purpose is in particular the reciprocal recognition and enforcement of judicial decisions, must necessarily have attributed to it a wide field of application. Insofar as the Member States are called upon, by virtue of Article 220, to enter into negotiations "so far as necessary", it is incumbent on them to determine the scope of any agreement concluded between them.'

However, the approach to interpretation is different when a court considers the interpretation of Article 1(2). For although the matters referred to in that provision are in some sense also part of the broad definition of the scope of the Regulation, they are all civil or commercial matters, and the material question for the court is the allocation of a civil or commercial matter to one jurisdictional category or another. Where the matter before the court is civil or commercial, but the question is whether it falls within one Regulation or another, it is more obviously legitimate to regard – for example – the Insolvency Regulation as an exception to the Brussels I Regulation. Both Regulations deal with civil and commercial matters: one for general matters and the other for particular matters; and the legislative intention appears to be that all the numbered exclusions, with the possible exception of social security, should be governed by particular, specialist, Regulations. Settling the line between these exclusions and the general Brussels I Regulation is closer in nature to the internal ordering of provisons, not an external question of scope.[174]

If a court concludes that the Regulation does not apply to a matter before it, this does not, however, mean that the court may proceed as though somehow freed from all the constraints of European law: it does not have licence to run amok. According to the European Court in *Allianz SpA v. West Tankers Inc*,[175] a court in a Member State may not apply its own law on a matter excluded from the Regulation if by doing so it would 'have consequences which undermine [the Regulation's] effectiveness, namely preventing the attainment of the objectives of unification of the rules of conflict of jurisdiction in civil and commercial matters and the free movement of decisions in those matters'.[176] It is important not to read too much into this, lest it be deduced that the decision in *Marc Rich & Co AG v. Soc Italiana Impianti*[177] was wrong because it allowed an Italian party to be hauled before the English courts and deprived of a form of judicial protection to which it was entitled;[178] or that *Hoffmann v. Krieg*[179] was wrongly decided, and that a Dutch court should not have applied its law on status to prevent the judgment creditor of a German maintenance judgment enforcing that order. The Court in *Allianz SpA v. West Tankers Inc*[180] did not refer to these decisions, which is not terribly helpful, but there is no reason to suppose that they have become wrong.[181]

---

174 In C-292/08 *German Graphics Graphische Maschinen GmbH v. Holland Binding BV (in liq)* [2009] ECR I-8421, the Court, at [23]–[25] indicated that the subject-matter scope of the Brussels I Regulation *was* intended to be expansive, at least when the question is whether the civil or commercial matter before the court falls within the (general) Brussels I Regulation or the (specialist, and in this sense exceptional) Insolvency Regulation. For a general discussion, albeit without specific conclusions, see *Sabbagh v. Khoury* [2014] EWHC 3233 (Comm).

175 C-185/07, [2009] ECR I-663.

176 C-185/07 *Allianz SpA v. West Tankers Inc* [2009] ECR I-663.

177 C-190/89, [1991] ECR I-3855.

178 C-185/07 *Allianz SpA v. West Tankers Inc* [2009] ECR I-663, [31].

179 145/86, [1988] ECR 645.

180 C-185/07, [2009] ECR I-663.

181 For the sake of completeness, one should note that in his Opinion, the Advocate General in C-536/13 *Re Gazprom OAO*, EU:C:2014:2414 invited the Court to conclude that its decision in *Allianz v. West Tankers Inc* was inapplicable to cases falling within the scope of Regulation 1215/2012, and that the decision should be taken

The better explanation for the decision in *Allianz SpA* is that there is a rule of European law, common to and applicable in all Member States, that every court in a Member State, exercising jurisdiction in civil and commercial matters, is entitled to respect and non-interference, from the judicial authorities of all other Member States, and not just from the courts of Member States when they happen to be exercising jurisdiction in civil and commercial matters.

2.31 Civil and commercial matters: proceedings brought by public authorities against private parties

The phrase 'civil and commercial matters' has an autonomous meaning, rather than one drawn from national law. As English law has not generally adopted this expression as a term of art, this conclusion is a mainly welcome one, though the content of the autonomous meaning is, in some respects, elusive. The best way to appreciate the nature of the reasoning of the Court is to gather it from the cases.

The point of departure is the importance of the distinction between private law rights and public law rights. To take an early example, in *Netherlands State v. Rüffer*,[182] a local council had removed a sunken barge which had been obstructing the Bight of Watum. It did so in the exercise of powers given to it, under Dutch[183] law. It proceeded to bring proceedings against the German defendant, in the Dutch courts, evidently under the Dutch private law of tort,[184] to recover the cost incurred in the operation. The defendant objected that the claim was a civil or commercial one, and that as it was domiciled in Germany, general jurisdiction lay with the German, not the Dutch, courts.[185] The European Court ruled that the Brussels Convention did not apply *ratione materiae*, and therefore did not affect jurisdiction in the case, as the claim did not arise in a civil or commercial matter. The view taken by Dutch law was not decisive, for when one surveyed the laws of the various Contracting States, their general view would be that such a claim was a matter of public, not private, law. The decision accorded with the earlier decision in *LTU GmbH v. Eurocontrol*.[186] The organisation

---

to have been wrongly decided even in relation to Regulation 44/2001. If this rather surprising invitation were to be accepted, neither a court seised of a matter properly seen as arbitration, nor an arbitral tribunal, would be prevented by the Regulation from ordering an injunction by way of enforcement of an agreement to arbitrate and not to litigate. It is far from clear that the Court will be persuaded by this analysis, not least because the question which the Lithuanian referring court actually needed to answer was concerned with the recognition of arbitral awards under the New York Convention: it was, therefore, not one in which the Brussels I Regulation had any part to play. Rather than distend the present text with excited comment about a bracingly challenging Opinion, it is noted here but will not be further discussed.

182 814/79, [1980] ECR 3807. The analysis below will suggest that the Court has departed from its approach in *Rüffer*, but in C-292/05 *Lechouritou v. Germany* [2007] ECR I-1519 the Court expressed no dissatisfaction with the decision in *Rüffer*.

183 In accordance with the Ems-Dollard Treaty of 8 April 1960, a treaty between the Netherlands and Germany, which imposed this duty upon the Netherlands.

184 This may look strange to English eyes. But if the action were thought of as a restitutionary one, based on a non-contractual obligation (see Regulation 864/2007, Rome II), it would be much easier to appreciate the basis on which Dutch law dealt with the claim.

185 He also contended that if he was wrong, and the action was in a civil or commercial matter, the Dutch court did not have special jurisdiction under what is now Art. 7(2) of Regulation 1215/2012, either.

186 29/76, [1976] ECR 1541. By contrast, for a case in which proceedings, brought against the state-owned operator of an airport in respect of unfair or unlawful charges levied by it for the use of the airport, were considered to be civil or commercial in nature, see C-302/13 *flyLAL-Lithuanian Airlines AS v. Starptautiskā lidosta Rīga VAS* EU:C:2014:2319, [2015] ILPr 28.

which regulates European civil aviation brought proceedings against Lufthansa, a German airline, before the Belgian courts to recover sums due in respect of unpaid invoices. The defendant argued that general jurisdiction lay with the German courts; the European Court ruled that the claim did not arise in a civil or commercial matter, with the result that it fell outside the material scope of the Convention.[187]

By contrast with these decisions, if the town council engages a private contractor to refurbish the mayor's office, a claim by or against the contractor for breach of contract would undoubtedly be a civil or commercial matter:[188] the making, performance, and enforcing of a contract by a public authority involves no more than the exercise of private law powers. This conclusion is, at first sight, reinforced by the decision in *Sonntag v. Waidmann*.[189] A German schoolteacher had failed to guard a child in a party which was supposed to be under his supervision from wandering off and falling to its death. In a claim for compensation brought against the schoolteacher,[190] it was contended that, as a German State employee, the duties which he owed to the pupils in his care were part of public law,[191] but not private law. As a matter of domestic German law this may have been correct, but the European Court ruled that the claim was made in a civil or commercial matter. The substance and content of the duty of care imposed by law on German teachers is no different from that owed by all other persons, State employees or not, to those individuals in their care. It followed that the claim against the teacher was to be regarded as arising as a civil or commercial matter. Had the powers under which the teacher had been acting been exorbitant when contrasted with those vested in private individuals, the result would have been otherwise: this proposition is examined below.[192]

If this were the point at which the case law had stopped, it would have indicated that a national court should ask whether a claim of the kind brought in the individual case would, under the laws of the various Member States, tend to be seen as based on public law rights (in the claimant) and public law duties (upon the defendant). The answer given by the national law of the particular court seised would have no decisive effect: after all, the claim in *Rüffer* was not in a civil or commercial matter though Dutch law would have taken the opposite view; the claim in *Sonntag* was in a civil or commercial matter though German law would have taken the opposite view.

But such a question would be difficult to answer conscientiously, especially as the number of Member States increased; and more recent cases have moved quietly away from the approach in *Rüffer* and *Sonntag*. Its place has been taken by an approach which requires a court to isolate and focus upon the legal right on which the claimant relies and seeks to enforce, and to characterise it as civil or commercial, or not, within the context of the law of the national court seised.

---

187 It followed that the Belgian court was entitled to apply its national law (including the provisions of any treaty which related to the case in question) to the taking of jurisdiction. Another way of saying the same thing may be to ask whether the body concerned is a public law body acting in pursuance of its public law powers.

188 The reverse of this, namely a claim by a private entity against a public authority, is considered below, para. 2.33.

189 C-172/91, [1993] ECR I-1963.

190 In fact, the claim was advanced in the Italian criminal proceedings for manslaughter, and fell within the special jurisdiction of the Italian courts by reason of what is now Art. 7(3) of the Regulation.

191 Under a limb of German administrative law.

192 Paragraph 2.36, below.

For example, in *Gemeente Steenbergen v. Baten*[193] a husband and wife had been divorced by a Belgian court. The husband, however, failed to perform an agreement according to which he would make maintenance payments in respect of a child of the marriage. The former wife, now settled in the Netherlands, applied for and obtained financial support from her municipality; the municipality then brought a claim for recovery of the sums, paid by it by way of social assistance, from the former husband. It was held that the claim against the husband, which was based on a right of recourse which Dutch law characterised as being in a civil matter, and which was analogous to the claimant State being subrogated to the wife's right to maintenance[194] was, on that account, brought as proceedings in a civil or commercial matter. It fell within Article 1, even though the particular claim could have been brought by the municipality alone. The nature and extent of the defendant's liability to pay was governed by the ordinary law of maintenance; his legal liability to make payment to the entity which had discharged the maintenance debt for which he was primarily responsible was, as a matter of Dutch law, an ordinary private law liability. If, by contrast, the State had power, when bringing the proceedings, to disregard a binding agreement between the parties under which they had agreed on the level of maintenance, it would be exercising powers peculiar to it as a State, and if that were so, the claim advanced by reference to such ability would not arise in a civil or commercial matter.

The same principle explains *Freistaat Bayern v. Blijdenstein*.[195] In that case, a father had failed to meet his liability, under German law, to make financial support for his children. Such support had therefore been provided to the child by the Bavarian State which then brought proceedings against the delinquent father, based on the Federal Law on Educational Support, which subrogated the State to the right of the child against the father. It was held that the claim of the State was to be regarded as arising in a civil or commercial matter, as the right to subrogation, to which the Federal Law made reference, was one which arose under and was governed by ordinary German civil law. As the original liability to pay was based on rules of ordinary civil law, the matter was to be regarded as a civil or commercial one, even though the claimant was a public body bringing a claim which, in fact, only a public body could bring.

The principle deduced from these decisions was followed and applied in *Frahuil SA v. Assitalia SpA*.[196] F made an agreement with V by which V would pay customs duty on F's behalf. But rather than do this itself, V contracted with A for the payments to be made by the latter. A made the payments, but was not reimbursed. It therefore brought proceedings against F for reimbursement, claiming to be subrogated to V's claim against F. It was held by the Court that the material issue was the legal relationship between A and F, and the claim which gave effect to it. This was based on the right to subrogation in respect of a debt claim, and as such was governed by ordinary civil law: it arose out of a relationship governed by private law, not from some special or public law. As a result it fell within Article 1.

According to this approach, therefore, if the claim is based upon the defendant's liability to perform obligations and duties cast upon him by private law, then even if the claimant

---

193 C-271/00, [2002] ECR I-10489.

194 Maintenance was a civil or commercial matter not excluded from the Brussels Convention. Maintenance is now a civil or commercial excluded from the Brussels I Regulation (Regulation 1215/2012, Art. 1(2)(e)), but that fact does not affect the point made here.

195 C-433/01, [2004] ECR I-981.

196 C-265/02, [2004] ECR I-1543.

is a public authority, relying upon a right of action which happens to be vested in it, as a public authority, alone, it will still be enforcing duties and rights which bind the defendant according to the private law of the State in question, and the proceedings are to be regarded as arising in a civil or commercial matter. The fact that the claimant is prosecuting the claim in its capacity as a public authority is irrelevant to the jurisdictional issue. Striking confirmation of this approach may be seen in *Verein für Konsumenteninformation v. Henkel*.[197] Austria implemented the European Directive on unfair terms in consumer contracts[198] by giving to VfK, a consumers' rights organisation, the right to take legal proceedings against a trader alleged to be using unfair terms in consumer contracts.[199] Proceedings were accordingly brought in Austria by VfK against a German trader. It was contended that, among other things, the proceedings were not brought in respect of a civil or commercial matter. The Court disagreed, reasoning that the obligations of a trader to his consumer-clients were a matter of contract law, and that as the trader was being held to account by reference to his legal obligations under consumer contract law, the proceedings were in respect of a civil or commercial matter, even though only VfK had standing under Austrian law to bring such proceedings. The action was brought against a defendant to compel him to deal fairly with his consumer clients, which was enough to make the matter a civil or commercial one.[200]

In *Préservatrice foncière TIARD SA v. Netherlands*,[201] an insurance company made an agreement with the Dutch State to discharge customs duties for which certain importers were liable. An action by the Dutch State to enforce the payment obligations of that contract was held to be made in a civil or commercial matter. The fact that the claimant was a public authority did not contradict the fact that the defendant company had chosen to enter into a voluntary, contractual relationship as part of its commercial business, and the obligations of that contract were enforced as civil or commercial obligations.

In *Land Berlin v. Sapir*,[202] the public body charged with making compensation payments to those who, or whose ancestors, had their property confiscated by the Nazi State made an overpayment, and brought proceedings before the civil courts, relying on the general law of unjust enrichment, for its recovery. The claim was therefore made in a civil or commercial matter; and even if it was necessary to place the claim for restitution within the broader framework, the original claim for compensation by a dispossessed property owner was an ordinary civil claim which any property owner might bring. The proceedings were therefore in a civil or commercial matter.

---

197 C-167/00, [2002] ECR I-8111.

198 Council Directive (EC) 93/13.

199 In England, the right is given to the Director-General of Fair Trading: SI 1999/2083.

200 *Cf* the State Immunity Act 1978, which draws an analogous distinction between commercial and governmental transactions. It was held in *R v. Harrow Crown Court ex parte Unic Centre Sàrl* [2000] 1 WLR 2112, that proceedings brought by a local authority, having a duty to prosecute by virtue of Trade Marks Act 1994, for the seizure of property alleged to infringe a trademark was brought in a civil or commercial matter. Though the trademark dispute, if later fought, might well have been, it seems doubtful that the local authority was acting otherwise than under a public law duty, albeit that the benefit of its doing so was for the private individuals who held the property right. But the obligations on the defendant were owed by it as a matter of intellectual property law, not public law; and in the light of the decision in *VfK*, in particular, the decision seems to be correct. More generally, for claims brought in the public interest under modern consumer law, see *Robb Evans v. European Bank Ltd* (2004) 61 NSWLR 75 (on which, see [2004] LMCLQ 313), which held that such judgments could be enforced at common law on the footing that they were not attempts to enforce the public law of a foreign State.

201 C-266/01, [2003] ECR I-4867.

202 C-645/11, EU:C:2013:228, [2013] ILPr 481. For the relationship between this decision and the claim for compensation from Germany for acts of wartime barbarity, see below, para. 2.33.

The case which takes this approach to its furthest point is *HMRC v. Sunico ApS*.[203] The tax-collecting arm of the Government of the United Kingdom brought proceedings alleging a conspiracy to defraud against a defendant accused of participating in a tax-evasion scheme; the sum claimed as damages was the tax evaded. The Court held that the proceedings were brought in a civil or commercial matter, as conspiracy is an ordinary tort liable, in principle, to be committed by anyone against anyone else. The fact that the victim and claimant was a State was incidental to the question whether the right (not to suffer loss by tortious conspiracy) and the correlative obligation (not to cause loss by commission of a tortious conspiracy) was a civil matter. The State relied on the ordinary law of tort, which meant that its claim was made in a civil matter. To similar effect, if in mirror image, is the decision in *flyLAL-Lithuanian Airlines AS v. Starptautiskā lidosta Rīga VAS*,[204] that a claim for damages for economic conspiracy is a civil or commercial matter, even where it relates to the unlawful conduct of a State-owned company which determines the charges at a national airport: the civil right relied on is that created by the economic competition law of the European Union.

Almost all decisions now seem to fit into this new methodology of looking at the actual legal relationship relied on in the proceedings.[205] The decision of the Court in *Re C (a child)*[206] is perhaps the only awkward decision, but it depends on its own special facts. In the context of litigation following the decision of the Finnish police to remove a child from its family on the ground that this was necessary to protect the child, it was held that this arose in a 'civil matter' for the purposes of the Brussels II Regulation.[207] As that Regulation expressly applies to parental responsibility, the Court felt able to reason that as the issue was one of parental responsibility, this sufficed to ensure that it was to be seen as a civil matter.[208] It rejected the contention that the exercising by the State of public law powers – it is hard to see that they could be conceived of in any other way – meant that the case fell outside the Brussels II Regulation. The case is, it is submitted, best seen as confined to the special issues which arise under the Brussels II Regulation in general and in the context of urgent measures for child protection in particular, and as having no broader application to the Brussels I Regulation.

2.32 Civil and commercial matters: proceedings brought by private parties against private parties

A claim by one private party against another may be founded on rules of public law, and if it is, it will fall outside the material scope of the Regulation. Where, for example, a claimant contends that its right to freedom of establishment under European law has been wrongfully interfered with by another, proceedings for relief in relation to the alleged wrong may fall outside the material scope of the Regulation on the ground that the *jus actionis*, the legal right relied on, is in essence a matter of public law, not of private law.[209] This is not to

---

203 C-49/12, EU:C:2013:545, [2014] QB 391.
204 C-302/13, EU:C:2014:2319, [2015] ILPr 28.
205 It seems inevitable that *Netherlands State v. Rüffer* would today be decided the other way.
206 C-435/06, [2007] ECR I-10141. Applied in C-523/07 *Re A (a child)* [2009] ECR I-2805.
207 Regulation 2201/2003.
208 Which, according to Art. 1 of the Regulation, is what the Regulation applies to.
209 *British Airways plc v. Sindicato Español de Pilotos de Lineas Aereas* [2013] EWHC 1657 (Comm). See also *Viking Line ABP v. International Transport Workers' Federation* [2005] EWHC 1222 (Comm), [2005] 3 CMLR 29: on appeal to the Court of Appeal, a reference was made to the European Court, but it did not relate to the application

say that the provisions of the Treaty on the Functioning of the European Union may not give rise to rights and obligations which operate in private law, but the right of freedom of establishment and of the right to provide services is, in cases in which it is alleged that this has been infringed and this is the direct source of the right to relief, liable to be seen as a matter of public law.

The analysis is otherwise if the claimant relies on a cause of action which is obviously one of private law. If the claim is advanced as a common or garden claim in tort, it will fall within the material scope of the Regulation. Allegations that trades unions are committing tortious wrongs by exercising their alleged freedom to withdraw their labour and to interfere with the freedom of everybody else to go about their business, will be brought within the material scope of the Regulation where the cause of action relied on by the victim of the trades union is part of the ordinary law of tort.[210] As it so often does, the application of the Regulation depends on the cause of action relied on, much more than it does on the broader 'flavour' of the disagreement or dispute. A claim brought to enforce rights under European competition law, generally regarded as being actionable in England in the form of a private law, tort, claim, is plainly brought in a civil or commercial matter.[211]

2.33 Civil and commercial matters: proceedings brought against public bodies

Where proceedings are brought against public authorities, the reasoning described above cannot be applied without modification. The point of departure may be the same: that the focus of attention is on the legal liability of the defendant to the claimant, and on the nature of that liability. So if the liability sought to be enforced is the same as that owed by ordinary individuals in their private capacity, the claim against the authority should be seen as one arising in a civil or commercial matter. If, therefore, the contractor engaged to refurbish the mayoral office has not had his bill paid, his claim against the council for payment will arise in a civil or commercial matter. If, by contrast, the authority is sued on the basis of a claim which is one peculiarly concerned with the liability of a public body for acts done by it in the exercise of public authority, the proceedings will not be seen to arise in a civil or commercial matter. The principle is clear; its application is less straightforward.

The difficulty is illustrated by *Lechouritou v. Germany*.[212] Proceedings were brought before the Greek courts by claimants who alleged that they had sustained loss and damage at the hands of the armed forces of the German State in the Second World War,[213] it being argued that the German State was subject to the special jurisdiction of the Greek courts as Greece was the place of the harmful event in question.[214] The Court, however, ruled that the claim against Germany was not brought in respect of a civil or commercial matter, as it arose out of the exercise of public powers by a State. The fact that the claim could be formulated and pleaded in private law terms – that a person who wrongfully damages the property of

---

of the Regulation. The proposition that a matter of public law may be relied on against a private individual or entity is not remarkable (C-438/05 *International Transport Workers' Federation v. Viking Line ABP* [2007] ECR I-10779), but that does not somehow convert it into a matter of private law.

210 C-18/02 *DFDS Torline A/S v. SEKO* [2004] ECR I-1417.

211 C-302/13 *flyLAL-Lithuanian Airlines AS v. Starptautiskā lidosta Rīga VAS* EU:C:2014:2319, [2015] ILPr 28.

212 C-292/05, [2007] ECR I-1519.

213 The problems posed by state immunity and the limitation of claims as these applied to the instant case are not pursued here.

214 Now Regulation 1215/2012, Art. 7(2).

another commits a civil wrong in the nature of a tort, and where this is done by an individual for whom another is vicariously liable, civil liability may be enforced against that other – did not support the contention that the proceedings arose in a civil or commercial matter, for the fact that the claim arose out of acts done in the exercise of public authority displaced the view from that perspective.

The outcome makes some sense, for liability for acts of war must be a matter of public law, and the legal consequences a matter of international or treaty law, not private law. It is, in effect, now reinforced by the express exclusion of 'the liability of the State for acts and omissions in the exercise of State authority (*acta iure imperii*)', now inserted into Regulation 1215/2012.[215] It must also be likely that in any case in which a sovereign State, or an organ of the State, is sued and is entitled to plead immunity from the jurisdiction of the court, the claim is likely to be one which would have fallen outside the material scope of the Regulation in any event, though in cases in which the immunity is invoked, the soundness of this proposition will not be put to the test.[216] It must follow, therefore, that even if the claim may be advanced by the claimant on the basis of private law obligations which are owed by every man – not to damage property without lawful excuse, not to injure persons without lawful excuse – alike, if the obligation arises from what is, in fact, the exercise of public authority, proceedings brought in relation to it will not fall within the material scope of the Regulation. The exercise of public authority may be more significant than the principle which focuses attention on the legal right relied on as the basis of the claim.

States, and State authorities, discharge functions more humdrum than waging war. It is not clear whether the general approach in *Lechouritou*, which overrides the approach of concentrating on the content and nature of the legal relationship relied on, applies in more modest contexts. Take for example a claim brought against a local authority or other public body charged with the statutory duty to inspect the quality of building work,[217] or to ensure the compliance of a care home with standards of safety and quality.[218] It may[219] be complained that the local authority was negligent in the discharge of its duties, and this negligence may have resulted in financial and other loss, and that liability for negligence is a matter of ordinary civil law. But where the local authority acts in the performance or misperformance of the obligations imposed on it as a public authority, it is more difficult to see a claim against it as one arising in a civil or commercial matter, even if it also true that the standard of care or liability sought to be enforced is one entirely familiar to the civil law of negligence.[220] The law cannot yet be regarded as completely clear.

---

215 One supposes that the real point of the litigation in *Lechouritou* was not the jurisdiction of the Greek court (for if the matter were not within Art. 1 of the Regulation, this would then be a matter of Greek national law, which might well give the Greek court jurisdiction), but the fear that if the matter were a civil or commercial one, a judgment in favour of the Greek claimants would have been open to enforcement in all other Member States under Chapter III of the Regulation, which would have been a much larger problem, the apprehension of which must have meant that the Court was bound to arrive at the conclusion it did, no matter the means by which it got there.

216 See *Grovit v. De Nederlandsche Bank NV* [2007] EWCA Civ 953, [2008] 1 WLR 51 (action against Dutch Central Bank).

217 *Murphy v. Brentwood DC* [1991] 1 AC 398.

218 *Trent Strategic Health Authority v. Jain* [2009] UKHL 4, [2009] 1 a.c. 853.

219 For the purpose of defining the scope of Art. 1 of the Regulation, it is irrelevant whether domestic law gives a cause of action in negligence or breach of statutory duty to the claimant, so the fact that no tort was committed by the Trent Strategic Health Authority when it behaved with appalling carelessness is nothing to the point.

220 If one were to concentrate on this aspect of the matter, the approach in C-172/91 *Sonntag v. Waidmann* [1993] ECR I-1963 would tend to the conclusion that the claim was in a civil or commercial matter.

2.34 Civil and commercial matters: proceedings brought against private persons exercising public functions

The identification of acts as done in the exercise of public authority or State authority will not always be straightforward. For example, in *Land Oberösterreich v. ČEZ AS*,[221] proceedings were brought by an Austrian local authority against a Czech energy supply company in the majority ownership of the Czech State. The claimant sought an order that the company close down a nuclear power plant on the supposed ground that it was irradiating part of Austria. The referring court did not ask whether the proceedings were brought in respect of a civil or commercial matter. The Court considered it unnecessary to say anything on the question, as what is now Article 24(1) of Regulation 1215/2012 did not give the Austrian court jurisdiction in any event.[222] In principle, the obligation not to commit a nuisance applies to any owner or occupier of neighbouring land. If the proceedings were seen as having been brought against a private party, the legal basis of the proceedings would lie in private law, even if the claimant were a body exercising authority under public law.[223] But if the defendant were to be seen as acting in the exercise of public powers, the principle in *Lechouritou* would override this provisional conclusion, and carry the proceedings outside the material scope of the Regulation after all.[224]

The problem is that the provision of utility services by, or under licence granted by, the State is not easy to categorise. In principle, a company limited by shares should be presumed to be acting as a private entity,[225] even where the shares are in the hands of the State;[226] but where the entity is acting under authority granted by the State, it is more tempting to see it (though not inevitable that it will be seen) as acting in the exercise of a delegated public authority: if a public authority can act by the exercise of private powers, it may be that a private body may sometimes act in the exercise of public powers, whether these are undertaken within a scheme of public regulation, or take the form of public powers delegated to a private provider.

For example, a claim against a private company charged with transporting accused persons to court, or with the running of prisons, or against the company (in which the State has a 49 per cent share) which runs the national air traffic control system, may plead and rely on ordinary civil law duties of care.[227] The approximate question is whether the liability of the defendant is the kind of liability which any defendant might owe, or which is peculiar to this defendant because it is 'doing the State's job'; and as the line between governmental and private functions becomes increasingly blurred, the answer is extremely difficult to sense.[228]

---

221 C-343/04, [2006] ECR I-4557.

222 However, for further proceedings, concerning whether the Austrian courts might issue an injunction on a *quia timet* basis, and by so doing infringe the rules of EU law on freedom of establishment (i.e. freedom to establish near the borders of the Austrian Republic), and also risk the non-recognition of any such judgment on the ground of public policy, see C-115/08 *Land Oberösterreich v. ČEZ AS (No 2)* [2009] ECR I-10265. It is not apparent on what basis the Landesgericht Linz considered itself to have jurisdiction, but what is now Art. 24(1) cannot have been it.

223 As in C-167/00 *Verein für Konsumenteninformation v. Henkel* [2002] ECR I-8111.

224 Once again, it is more likely that the fear of an Austrian judgment being enforceable under Chapter III of the Regulation was more compelling than the actual question of jurisdiction.

225 The principle of separate corporate personality appears to require this conclusion.

226 C-302/13 *flyLAL-Lithuanian Airlines AS v. Starptautiskā lidosta Rīga VAS* EU:C:2014:2319, [2015] ILPr 28.

227 By contrast, a claim for beach of statutory duty would be less obviously civil or commercial, even though it sounds in tort.

228 For illustration, C-302/13 *flyLAL-Lithuanian Airlines AS v. Starptautiskā lidosta Rīga VAS* EU:C:2014:2319, [2015] ILPr 28.

2.35 Civil and commercial matters: the activity from which the claim arises

From what has been said above, it will be seen that there are a number of strands which help, but no clear single principle which determines, whether proceedings are brought in respect of a civil or commercial matter. By way of summary and recapitulation, the following three points may capture the essence of the law as it has been explained.

First, if the claim is one based on ordinary civil law duties, which is to say, it originates in a private law relationship (contract, tort, maintenance), it will be a civil or commercial one, even when enforced by a public law entity. It retains this character even if the only claimant which could bring the present proceedings is a public law entity, for it is the character of the right or obligation relied on, rather than the nature of the claimant doing the relying, which determines the impact of Article 1.

Second, if the claim is brought against a defendant which performs the functions out of which the claim is brought as a matter of public law, it is unlikely, though not impossible, that the proceedings will be in a civil or commercial matter. This will be so even if the allegation made against the defendant is that it was negligent, or acted without legal excuse for what it did, in a way which is, in terms of its content, practically identical with duties owed by other persons in other contexts.[229]

Third, if the claim is brought against an individual who is placed in the position in which he finds himself as a matter of public law,[230] *and* the duty which he owes is enforced against him by an entity exercising the rights which only it has, the claim will not be a civil or commercial one. In other words, a dual test may show the non-civil or non-commercial law character of the claim.[231] For example, proceedings brought against an airline which is required by legislation to make payments for air traffic control services, or an individual who is required by law to pay the BBC a licence fee to own a television (whether or not the BBC's programmes are actually watched), on pain of imprisonment if this fee is not paid, should not be regarded as arising in a civil or commercial matter.

It bears repeating that claims brought by, or against, a utility company provide a good example of the potential difficulties. In England, water and electricity services are provided, and the railways and the postal service[232] are run, or at any rate owned, by private, or semi-private, companies performing the functions which were until fairly recently, and which in a decent world would still be, and which may in other Member States still be, performed by public bodies or statutory boards. It appears from the *Land Oberösterreich* decision that electricity supply in the Czech Republic is, as it is in many Member States, undertaken by entities which do not fit easily into the categories of public or private entity. A claim against one of these providers alleging that it has, in some respect, failed to supply clean water, or power at a steady voltage, or rails which are properly maintained, is hard to place on one or the other side of the line. The supply to customers may be technically contractual,[233]

---

229 It has to be admitted that *Sonntag* is not easy to reconcile with this, if it is correct to say that, as a matter of German law, the defendant schoolteacher was acting in the exercise of public authority.

230 It is arguable that this could have been said of the defendant in *Netherlands v. Rüffer*. It will depend on whether one focuses on the defendant's liability for obstructing an international waterway, or on his liability to reverse the unjust enrichment which resulted from his liability to remove the obstruction having been discharged by a public body.

231 As will be seen below, it is the claim, rather than the claim-and-defence, which is determinative.

232 And practically anything else which the Government fancied it owned and dared to sell.

233 In the sense that a customer may decline the service and avoid the obligation to pay.

and in England the supplier, though subject to statutory regulation, supplies in accordance with some sort of contract, but that does not inevitably mean that it is civil or commercial. There may be no alternative to asking the rather blunt question whether the cause of action appears to be a private law claim, asserting rights and duties which arise in private law, even though a party to the legal relationship may be a public law entity.

It cannot be correct, for example, to regard utility supply as a matter of public law just because at some point in the past the supply was a matter of state monopoly, and still less because it may be a state monopoly in other Member States. It may be preferable to ask whether there is any real difference between this case and any other purchase from a powerful, or quasi-monopoly, supplier which can dictate the terms on which it deals. If there is none, consequent disputes should be seen as being in civil or commercial matters, at least unless and until the rights and powers relied on by the supplier are not those in the contract, but are created by legislation to be exorbitant and unique to the utility company.

2.36 Civil and commercial matters: excluded matters which arise only incidentally

A question which has arisen on a couple of occasions, the answer to which is now tolerably clear, is whether the identification of a claim as one in a civil or commercial matter is affected by the fact that a point may arise in the course of the adjudication which would, if taken in isolation, be seen to fall outside the scope of the Regulation. Ths issue here is different from that which arises when the whole of the claim or defence tests the definition of civil and commercial matters. Here the concern is with a case which is civil or commercial but which may, along the way, raise a matter which would, if taken in isolation, be excluded from the material scope of the Regulation. It appears that where such a matter arises incidentally as part of the defence,[234] it will not affect the application of the Regulation.

The point is illustrated by *Préservatrice Foncière TIARD Compagnie d'Assurances v. Netherlands*.[235] In that case, the State sought to enforce a contractual promise to pay another entity's customs liabilities, suing on a contract of guarantee which the guarantor insurance company had made. As was explained above, it was held that the claim was not excluded from Article 1, for the rights enforced were those of a private and voluntary legal guarantee. It was then contended, as against this, that a distinct question of customs law would arise if the guarantor were to dispute the validity of the underlying customs levies, and that this should take the entire matter outside the scope of Article 1. The Court disagreed, saying it would make no difference, for pleas raised by way of defence did not bear on the proper application of Article 1, which has its focus solely on the claim advanced by the claimant. The subject matter of the claim was civil or commercial, and it would be unsatisfactory for that to be contradicted by an issue, raised as part of the defence.[236] The Court proposed this answer to avoid the awkwardness of a claim being found to fall inside the material scope of the Regulation, only for the defence to take it back outside, and so on as the pleadings developed. It makes some sense, though the contrast with *Lechouritou*, where it certainly appears that it was the defence raised

---

234 Though the same principle must apply where the excluded issue forms an incidental part of the claim, as in C-49/12 *HMRC v. Sunico ApS* EU:C:2013:545, [2014] QB 391, where the computation of tax lost was a step in the quantification of damages.

235 Case C-266/01, [2003] ECR I-4867.

236 See in particular at [40]–[43].

by the German State which took the matter outside the scope of the Regulation, is clear. The reconciliation may be that the defence in *Lechouritou* actually overwhelmed the claim, rather than being an incidental issue, or that in *Lechouritou*, the claim itself had to be seen as a matter of public law, that is, that it sought to enforce legal duties owed by a warmonger.

Similarly, in *Realchemie Nederland BV v. Bayer CropScience AG*,[237] proceedings were brought on the basis of an infringement of intellectual property rights. Along the way, the court ordered the defendant to pay a fine for failure to comply with an order which it had made. When the claimant came to enforce the judgment, it was held that the whole of the judgment was within the material scope of the Regulation and enforceable under it. The relationship between the parties was a private law one, entirely based on the civil law of intellectual property. The incidental[238] imposition of a fine could not call that conclusion into question.

Collateral support may also be derived from the decision in *Gantner Electronic GmbH v. Basch Exploitatie Maatschappij BV*.[239] In that case, which concerned the application of what is now Article 29 of Regulation 1215/2012 on *lis alibi pendens*, the Court held that the proper application of that provision was made by reference to the claims raised in the two proceedings, and was unaffected by the defences raised in answer to them: if the claim was not already the subject of proceedings before another court, the fact that issues raised by way of defence were so subject was irrelevant to the application of what is now Article 29. As matters now stand, the dominant concern appears to be to establish whether the Regulation gives the court jurisdiction at the earliest possible stage of proceedings, and to not have the answer alter as the case develops. That being so, *TIARD* makes sense, and *Gantner* is consistent with it.

2.37 Civil and commercial matters: the principle that the greater includes the less, or the 'umbrella' principle

Cases may arise in which the claimant brings proceedings which at first sight appear to take the form of a civil or commercial matter, but which, when seen in a broader context than the narrowly pleaded case, also appear to be embedded in subject matter which does fall outside the scope of the Regulation. If that happens, the matter falls wholly outside the Regulation. That slightly clumsy formulation may be made clearer by illustration.

In *Owens Bank Ltd v. Bracco*[240] it was held that proceedings brought before the courts of a Member State to obtain an order for the enforcement of a judgment from the courts of St Vincent and the Grenadines, a non-Member State, fell outside the scope of what is now the Brussels I Regulation. It followed that the decision of an Italian court in such proceedings which determined whether the judgment from St Vincent had been obtained by fraud and forgery, would also fall outside the Regulation. It further followed that when the same general issue of fraud or forgery sufficient to prevent recognition of the judgment in England arose before the English courts, what is now Article 29 of Regulation 1215/2012 had no application to it. In other words, the subject matter of the case was the enforcement of judgments from a non-Member State. Any proceedings or procedure which arose within and formed part of that question also fell outside the scope of the Regulation even though, if taken out of context and viewed in isolation, the incidental procedure might be presented

---

237 C-406/09, [2011] ECR I-9773.
238 The term is not used in the judgment, but it appears to reflect the approach of the Court.
239 C-111/01, [2003] ECR I-4207.
240 C-129/92, [1994] ECR I-117.

as having arisen in a civil or commercial matter. This principle may also explain why in proceedings which were principally concerned with status, a Dutch court had no obligation to recognise a German maintenance decree, even though this, taken in isolation, was a matter which fell within the material scope of the Regulation.[241]

By contrast, but to the same effect, a fine imposed in proceedings which were concerned with intellectual property rights is a civil or commercial matter, because the broad context of the litigation was rights of intellectual property.[242] The incidental issue, the fine, assumes the character of the broader relationship between the parties, of the broad issue which has arisen. To use another idiom, the lesser issue accedes to the greater.

That general understanding of the way Article 1 works would also justify the result in *Lechouritou v. Germany*.[243] For if proceedings against the German State for damages or reparation for its wartime depredations would not be a civil or commercial matter, a claim which was in truth a small part of that larger excluded subject matter could not properly be torn from its context in order to be given the opposite characterisation. Likewise, and prefiguring a question which will be examined below, if a court is seised with proceedings which have arbitration as their subject matter, in and to which the Regulation has no application, it might be contended that there should be no obligation to recognise a judgment from another Member State, even in a civil or commercial matter, and even though that question, if arising in another context, would have required recognition. The broad subject matter is arbitration, and the fact that a sub-issue within it might have arisen in and as a civil or commercial matter is irrelevant. Accordingly, it might be argued, a court dealing with the question whether parties have made a legally binding agreement to arbitrate is not obliged to recognise a judgment on a civil or commercial matter between the same parties as part of the process of its adjudication, even where this would materially affect the decision to be reached by the English court. As will be seen, however, this application of the broad principle is not widely accepted as correct.

The decision of the Court in *Apostolides v. Orams*[244] might have taken, but did not obviously adopt, a similar approach. A claim by a dispossessed landowner, ethnically cleansed from the north of the Republic of Cyprus invaded and occupied by the armed forces of Turkey, brought proceedings for trespass against defendants who had purported to purchase his land from a vendor who had only a stolen title to it. Having obtained judgment in the courts of the Republic of Cyprus, the claimant sought to enforce it in England. The European Court confirmed that there were no grounds within Chapter III of the Regulation upon which recognition of the judgment could be refused. It declined to take the view that proceedings brought to obtain damages or other relief for trespass to land were brought in anything other than a civil or commercial matter. In doing so it appears to have spurned the argument, but which may not have been directly put, that the subject matter of the case was the legal rights and illegal wrongs flowing from the Turkish invasion of Cyprus and the installation of a junta to administer the occupation and to sell off looted assets, and that the claim was merely a sub-issue, part of a much broader issue which fell entirely outside the scope of the Regulation. The Court may have been right to decide as it did, but one cannot help but observe that if litigation about effect of the belligerent invasion of Greece on the

---

241 145/86 *Hoffmann v. Krieg* [1988] ECR 645.
242 C-406/09 *Realchemie Nederland BV v. Bayer CropScience AG* [2011] ECR I-9773.
243 See above, para. 2.33.
244 C-420/07, [2009] ECR I-3571.

property rights of individual landowners falls outside the Regulation, litigation about the effect of the belligerent invasion of Cyprus on the property rights of individual landowners might have done as well.

The actual proceedings in *Lechouritou* were conceived as narrow, and were framed as an attempt to vindicate private, patrimonial, rights and to claim damages for their infringement; but they had to be seen as part of a broader picture which was excluded from the material scope of the Regulation. Had that been the method of approach in *Apostolides*, the result might have been different from that actually reached by the Court. There are obvious differences between the two cases. In *Lechouritou*, the claim was brought against the German State which had invaded Greece, whereas in *Apostolides*, it was brought against a private individual, albeit one who claimed to have acquired title from the illegal regime installed by the invaders, with the result that no State was party to the proceedings in *Apostolides*. But it is not obvious that this is or ought to be enough to justify the difference in approach or outcome. It would be unsettling if there were to be a distinction according to whether the aggressor State which was the ultimate cause of the claimant's loss was a previous incarnation of a Member State or the present incarnation of a non-Member State.

2.38 Matters specifically excluded from the domain of the Regulation by Article 1

Article 1 specifically excludes 'revenue, customs or administrative matters' as well as 'the liability of the State for acts and omissions in the exercise of State authority (*acta iure imperii*)' from the Regulation. These terms will bear autonomous or uniform meanings, but no particular difficulty is likely to arise in connection with them. It may well be that their express mention adds little to what has already been deduced from the definition of 'civil and commercial' matters.[245] If *HMRC v. Sunico ApS*[246] is any guide, a State which is able to formulate its claim under ordinary civil law may be able to bring within the Regulation proceedings which have the economic object of remedying of a shortfall in taxes. That may open the door to some creative pleading, but so what? If a defendant has conspired to injure another in its economic activity, or has acted in such a way as causes another to incur expense which it then seeks to recover by private law action (such as where the State has to provide medical treatment to those injured by the wrongdoing of others), there is no reason of principle why the Regulation should not apply to judicial proceedings brought in respect of it.[247]

Article 1 goes on to exclude from its scope six specific areas of law, each of which must be briefly examined.

2.39 Matters of personal capacity and status, family property and succession

It is convenient to take three of the six specific exclusions from the material scope of Regulation 1215/2012 together, because they were, in effect, grouped together as a single exclusion from the material scope of Regulation 44/2001. In Regulation 1215/2012 the exclusions are: the status or legal capacity of natural persons, rights in property arising out

---

245 *QRS 1 ApS v. Frandsen* [1999] 1 WLR 2169, citing Schlosser [1979] OJ C59/71, 82–83.
246 C-49/12, EU:C:2013:545, [2014] QB 391.
247 C-302/13 *flyLAL-Lithuanian Airlines AS v. Starptautiskā lidosta Rīga VAS* EU:C:2014:2319, [2015] ILPr 28.

of a matrimonial relationship or out of a relationship deemed by the law applicable to such relationship to have comparable effects to marriage (Article 1(2)(a)); and maintenance obligations arising from a family relationship, parentage, marriage or affinity (Article 1(2)(e)); and wills and succession, including maintenance obligations arising by reason of death (Article 1(2)(f)). It is clear that these are civil matters which, were it not for the express exclusion, would have fallen within the material scope of the Regulation.

Divorce, nullity, and matters of parental responsibility are in principle governed by the Brussels II Regulation;[248] it is therefore rational that they be excluded in their entirety from the Brussels I Regulation. Maintenance is in principle governed by the Maintenance Regulation.[249] It was originally a civil matter within the domain of the Brussels I Regulation,[250] but it is rational that it is is now excluded. Wills and succession will be, in Member States other than the United Kingdom,[251] principally governed by the Succession Regulation;[252] it is rational that it is now excluded.

It is important to note that the exclusion of these matters from the Brussels I Regulation is not conditional. The reason for the exclusion will have been that it was intended that they be dealt with – as some already have – by a specialist Regulation which would comprehend jurisdiction, applicable law, and the effect of orders from other Member States; but the exclusion from the material scope of Brussels I is not dependent on the existence of such other special Regulation, or upon its having been adopted by a Member State which had the right to not do so. The exclusions are to be understood according to their terms, though, as suggested above, it is arguable that as these are all civil matters, the exclusion of these special matters from the Brussels I Regulation which deals with civil matters generally may be approached on the basis that a special Regulation which makes an exception to a general rule is to be given an interpretation which is no wider than is necessary to secure the aims of the special Regulation.

If the issue before the court is directly linked with a matter excluded by Article 1(2), it appears that the issue is excluded in its entirety. If proceedings are brought by or in the name of a person under legal incapacity for judicial authorisation to sell property, the proceedings are so closely linked to the question of personal capacity that they musy be considered to fall within the exclusion in Article 1(2)(a). This is not quite the same as saying that the exclusion will apply if the matter of personal capacity is the principal issue before the court. Rather, if the whole basis for the application, and in this sense the central legal issue with which the proceedings are concerned, is one of personal capacity, the matter is excluded by Article 1(2)(a) from the scope of the Regulation.[253]

Article 1(2)(a) excludes rights in property arising out of a matrimonial or quasi-matrimonial relationship.[254] The extent of the exclusion, though generally clear enough, is not free

---

248 Regulation 2201/2003, which is not further discussed in this book.

249 Regulation 4/2009, in effect from 18 June 2011, and by which the United Kingdom has chosen to be bound, is not further discussed in this book.

250 See Art. 5(2) of Regulation 44/2001, which provided a rule of special jurisdiction for claims by a maintenance creditor.

251 Which has exercised its privilege not to be bound by the Regulation.

252 Regulation 650/2012, applicable to those who die on or after 17 August 2015.

253 C-386/12 Re Schneider EU:C:2013:663, [2014] Fam 80.

254 Civil partnership, and marriage between persons of the same sex are included (though the second of these is marriage, plain and simple); cohabitation will not be unless the law of the Member State in question deems cohabitation to be comparable to marriage, as in England it does not.

from all doubt. Would it extend, for example, to a dispute as to whether a spouse or civil partner who contributed to the purchase price, or to the discharge of the mortgage debt, had thereby acquired a share in the ownership of the matrimonial home? In principle, the resolution of a dispute of this sort may be found in the application of the general law of property, applying to all persons alike, or in special laws applicable only to those in a matrimonial relationship.[255] Principle would suggest that the answer should be found by asking whether the rules of law resorted to and relied on by the claimant are those of the general law of property, or those peculiar to matrimonial or quasi-matrimonial law. The result may be that a dispute arising between spouses may fall outside the domain of the Brussels I Regulation, whilst one on identical facts, differing only in that the parties are not in a matrimonial or equivalent relationship, will fall within it.[256]

2.40 Bankruptcy and insolvency

Article 1(2)(b) excludes bankruptcy, proceedings relating to the winding-up of insolvent companies or other legal persons, judicial arrangements, compositions and analogous proceedings. The exclusion reflects the fact that special provision was intended to be made, and was made, for insolvency and bankruptcy proceedings. If the debtor's centre of main interests is in a Member State, jurisdiction and the recognition of judgments given in insolvency or bankruptcy proceedings are governed by the Insolvency Regulation, Regulation 1346/2000, which provides its own jurisdictional framework. In cases in which the Insolvency Regulation does not apply, which will tend to mean that the debtor's centre of main interests is not in a Member State, the application, or not, of the Brussels I Regulation is determined, in principle, by asking whether the right asserted is peculiar to the law of insolvency; whether the obligation to be enforced, is founded on the law of bankruptcy or winding-up. The material question is not whether the proceedings are brought by or defended by the company acting through its administrator or liquidator: there is no other way for an insolvent company to act. Rather, the question is whether the right relied on as the foundation of the claim is a right which exists because, but only because, of the insolvency.[257] Save in those cases in which the body in administration is not formed under private law, the general scheme is that the nature of the proceedings will fall either under the Brussels I Regulation or under the Insolvency Regulation, which are meant to fit neatly and cleanly together.

The approach of the European Court has been clear and consistent. It held in *Gourdain v. Nadler*[258] that the terms used in Article 1(2)(b) had uniform or autonomous meanings. In accordance with the principle set out above, it followed that the proceedings in that case, which invoked French insolvency law to obtain an order that the director of an insolvent company ordered to contribute to the assets of the insolvent estate, were excluded from Article 1(1) because they fell squarely within the wording of Article 1(2)(b). The right

---

255 In England it is found partly in the general law relating to trusts of land, and partly in the Matrimonial Proceedings and Property Act 1970. The categorisation of the claim by reference to English domestic law would therefore be problematic. See Schlosser [1979] OJ C59/71, [43]–[50].

256 See C-220/95 *Van den Boogaard v. Laumen* [1997] ECR I-1147.

257 C-292/08 *German Graphics Graphische Maschinen GmbH v. Holland Binding BV (in liq)* [2009] ECR I-8421 (action by owner to recover property from liquidator on the basis of *Romalpa* clause not intrinsic to insolvency); applied *Byers v. Yacht Bull Corp* [2010] EWHC 133 (Ch), [2010] BCC 368.

258 133/78, [1979] ECR 733.

asserted was unique to the administrator; the liability of the director existed (and the cause of action to enforce it arose) because, and only because, of the insolvency. Likewise in *Seagon v. Deko Marty Belgium NV*,[259] in which proceedings were brought against a recipient or payee to compel the restoration of property to the estate of the bankrupt on the ground that the transfer had been made in fraud of creditors: the right to bring the claim arose on and only because of the insolvency; the liability to make the payment claimed was part and parcel of the administration of the insolvent estate.[260] The proceedings were therefore excluded from the Brussels I Regulation.

Similarly, a judgment from the courts of another Member State, ordering the cancellation of a transfer of shares which had been obtained by the liquidator of an insolvent company on the ground that a foreign liquidator had no authority to act as such, falls within Article 1(2)(b), and therefore falls outside the Brussels I Regulation, as litigation concerning the powers of a liquidator concerns matters which are the 'direct and indissociable consequence of the exercise by the liquidator' of powers which he has only by reason of his status as liquidator.[261] Likewise, a claim for compensation from a bankruptcy trustee who is alleged to have committed various faults in the discharge of his duties will be sufficiently connected to the insolvency to fall within the exception and so outside the Brussels I Regulation.[262]

By contrast, a claim by a liquidator of an insolvent company seeking to recover commercial debts due and owing to the company,[263] is not excluded from the scope of the Brussels I Regulation,[264] for the substance of the legal claim, or of the defendant's obligation, has nothing to do with the insolvency of the company.[265] Likewise, proceedings by a seller of goods who has reserved title to them by a *Romalpa* clause, or the like, to recover them from the liquidator, are not within Article 1(2)(b), and are not excluded from the Brussels I Regulation, because the fact that the defendant is insolvent has nothing to do with a claim to retrieve goods from a buyer who has not paid for them and who, according to the contractual agreement under which possession was transferred, has no title to them.[266]

---

259 C-339/07, [2009] ECR I-767.

260 Such proceedings may (therefore) be brought before the court which is seised of the bankruptcy proceedings in accordance with the Insolvency Regulation. This is obviously sensible, as it concentrates all the proceedings arising in the administration of the bankruptcy before the one court.

261 C-111/08 *SCT Industri AB (in liq) v. Alpenblume AB* [2009] ECR I-5565. Insolvency proceedings opened in Sweden preceded the coming into force of the Insolvency Regulation, with the result that the effect of the Austrian judgment in the Swedish insolvency proceedings was governed by the Brussels I Regulation alone. The passage quoted is at [28] of the judgment.

262 *Polymer Vision R&D Ltd v. Van Dooren* [2011] EWHC 2951 (Comm), [2012] ILPr 249.

263 Or property belonging to the insolvent: *Re Hayward* [1997] Ch 45; *Re Ultra Motorhomes International Ltd* [2005] EWHC 872 (Ch).

264 C-214/89 *Powell Duffryn plc v. Petereit* [1992] ECR I-1745; *UBS AG v. Omni Holding AG* [2000] 1 WLR 916 (claim on pre-liquidation agreement not a matter relating to insolvency, even if there is a dispute as to its admissibility in the insolvency itself).

265 Even if, it is to be supposed, the non-payment of this outstanding debt is what tipped the company into insolvency in the first place.

266 C-292/08 *German Graphics Graphische Maschinen GmbH v. Holland Binding BV (in liq)* [2009] ECR I-8421; applied in C-157/13 *Nickel & Goeldner Spedition GmbH v. Kintra UAB* EU:C:2014:2145, [2015] QB 96. In C-295/13 *H v HK* EU:C:2014:2410 proceedings were brought in Germany by the liquidator against the managing director of an insolvent German company. As a matter of German law, it was possible for such a claim to be made when the company was insolvent but had not been made subject to liquidation proceedings; but this (perhaps rather theoretical) possibility did not displace the conclusion that the actual claim was so closely tied up with the insolvency proceedings that it should be considered part of them and therefore as falling within the material scope of Art. 1(2)(b) of the Regulation (or, as it was in that case, as the defendant was Swiss, the Lugano II Convention).

It is inherent in the nature of the proceedings which fall within Article 1(2)(b), and therefore outside the scope of the Brussels I Regulation, that they are brought (or defended, if the action is against the insolvent company) by the liquidator in the interest of the general body of creditors. It follows that if the liquidator has assigned the right to bring proceedings for the return of property to another, proceedings brought by the assignee against the defendant will not fall within Article 1(2)(b), for the claimant will be acting in his private interest, vindicating the right which he has purchased from the company for his own benefit.[267] Likewise, proceedings brought by a creditor of a company against a director of a company which has gone into insolvency, seeking compensation for loss to him resulting from the negligence of the office-holder, are not within Article 1(2)(b), as they are brought in the interest of the individual claimant, and not for the general body of creditors.[268]

In *Ashurst v. Pollard*,[269] it was held that an action by a trustee in bankruptcy to perfect his title to foreign land, of which the bankrupt was registered proprietor, was not within Article 1(2)(b), and was therefore within the scope of what is now Regulation 1215/2012. To the extent that the action was an assertion of the rights of civil ownership, albeit at the behest of a trustee in bankruptcy in whom the property in question had vested, it was not excluded from Article 1(1), even though the trustee derived his *locus standi* to bring the proceedings from the law of bankruptcy, because the claim was also in the nature of a patrimonial claim. Even so, the decision appears to be close to the line. It would not have been altogether surprising if the court had decided, instead, that the provisions under which the trustee acted 'derogate from the general rules of private law, and in particular, from property law. In particular, such provisions provide that, in the case of insolvency, debtors lose the right freely to dispose of their assets and the liquidator has to administer the assets in insolvency on behalf of the creditors, which includes effecting any necessary transfers'[270] and that the claim was 'the direct and indissociable consequence of the exercise by the liquidator' of powers which he has only by reason of his status as liquidator,[271] and that, as a result, the claim by the trustee fell within the exception and outside the Regulation. But the point was, in the end, not decisive of the outcome in the case, and it may be open to re-examination.

It is to be noted that proceedings for the judicial winding-up of solvent companies are *not* excluded from the Regulation, for it is the actual solvency or insolvency of the company, rather than the precise ground upon which it is sought to wind it up, that determines whether the case falls within the material scope of the Regulation. Lastly, as voluntary winding-up is not within the scope of the term 'proceedings',[272] incidental applications which may arise in the course of a voluntary winding-up do not fall within Article 1(2)(b), and are therefore within the material scope of the Brussels I Regulation.

As indicated above, jurisdiction over collective insolvency proceedings, which entail the partial or total divestment of a debtor and the appointment of a liquidator, where the

---

267 C-213/10 *F-Tex SIA v. Lietuvos-Anglijos UAB 'Jadecloud-Vilma'* EU:C:2012:215. It is not quite as odd as it may at first sight appear: the assignee of the right to proceed against the defendant was the sole creditor of the company, and who had the most obvious interest in pursuing the defendant.

268 C-147/12 *ÖFAB v. Koot* EU:C:2013:490, [2015] QB 20; C-519/12 *OTP Bank Nyilvánosan Működő Részvénytársaság v. Hochtief Solution AG* EU:C:2013:674.

269 [2001] Ch 595. Whether the claim was, therefore, within what is now Art. 24 of the Regulation will be examined below.

270 C-111/08 *SCT Industri AB (in liq) v. Alpenblume AB* [2009] ECR I-5565, [27].

271 *Ibid.*, [28].

272 'Proceedings' is to be read as meaning 'legal proceedings'.

centre of main interests of the debtor is in a Member State, is governed by the Insolvency Regulation 1346/2000. The detailed jurisdictional rules of the Insolvency Regulation are beyond the scope of this book, but a useful illustration was provided in *Mazur Media Ltd v. Mazur Media GmbH*.[273] Insolvency proceedings in respect of a German company were opened in Germany, but an alleged English creditor had previously brought a claim against it for breach of contract or conversion.[274] On the footing that the English court had jurisdiction under the Brussels I Regulation in the conversion claim, the decision whether to allow the English proceedings to proceed to judgment was a matter for English law to determine. This followed from Articles 4(2)(e) and 15 of the Insolvency Regulation, but it would in principle also have followed from the exclusion in Article 1(2)(b).[275] On the other hand, the Insolvency Regulation[276] would have applied German law to the question whether the insolvency had any effect (and if so, what effect) on proceedings commenced in accordance with the Brussels I Regulation after the opening of the insolvency proceedings.

2.41 Social security

The combined effect of its having so close a connection with revenue and administrative matters, and the intensely national character of the social policies involved, is enough to explain the exclusion of social security from the Brussels I Regulation by Article 1(2)(c); there may be further reasons, but the effect is clear. Apart from the presumed need to give the term an autonomous meaning, it must be clear that a claim for a payment by way of social security is not within the scope of the Regulation.

A difficulty may arise where a claim is brought against the recipient of a social security payment for the repayment of sums that were paid to him as a result of the mistake of the paying body. The claim for repayment will be a civil or commercial matter; the question is therefore whether Article 1(2)(c) excludes it from the scope of the Regulation. In accordance with the methodology examined above, if the legal basis for the claim for repayment is the general civil law, such as that which provides for restitution from those to whom money was paid under a mistake, or the recovery of money from someone to whom it was paid on a supposed basis which was non-existent, the claim will be based on ordinary law rather than on the particular law of social security, and the proceedings will not be excluded from the Regulation by Article 1(2)(c). It will be otherwise if the claim arises under special provisions of social security legislation which imposes a liability to repay which is peculiar to the law of social security.[277]

---

273 [2004] EWHC 1566 Ch, [2004] 1 WLR 2966.

274 In fact, the two claims were two ways of advancing precisely the same claim, and special jurisdiction over it was governed by what is now Art. 7(1) and not Art. 7(2) of Regulation 1215/2012.

275 Whether the proceedings should be stayed was a matter for English law (not as set out in Insolvency Act 1986, s. 130, as the insolvency was foreign, but under the inherent discretion of the court or Senior Courts Act 1981, s. 49(3)); but this stay was not to be imposed to prejudice the operation of the Brussels I Regulation.

276 Insolvency Regulation, Art. 4.

277 Under English law there is a statutory right to recover, but the question whether there is a parallel claim for restitution at common law does not have an easy answer. For consideration of the broader issue of parallel claims for recovery of sums which should (not) have been paid, though not in relation to social security, see *Deutsche Morgan Grenfell plc v. IRC* [2006] UKHL 49, [2007] 1 AC 558 (recovery of corporation tax wrongly levied); *Total Network SL v. HMRC* [2008] UKHL 19, [2008] 1 AC 1174 (recovery of avoided VAT by means of conspiracy claim).

In *Gemeente Steenbergen v. Baten*[278] an action was brought under Dutch law for the recovery from a defendant of sums equivalent to payments of social assistance made by the State to a former spouse: the claim was therefore analogous to those described above, but in the context of a case in which the original payment was made to support a person for whose support the defendant was legally responsible. The Court drew a distinction between claims by a claimant for social assistance, which may well fall within Article 1(2)(c), on the one hand, and claims for reimbursement in respect of sums paid, which are governed by the general law and which were therefore not to be seen as excluded from the material scope of the Regulation. The particular claim for reimbursement fell within the latter category, and therefore within the material scope of what is now the Regulation.

2.42 Arbitration: the broad principle

Particular importance attaches to the exclusion of arbitration from the Brussels I Regulation by Article 1(2)(d). Although the dispute which is to be resolved by arbitration is almost always civil or commercial, Article 1(2)(d) demonstrates and means that the Brussels I Regulation makes no claim to apply to the arbitration of civil and commercial matters, or to arbitrators discharging their function.

So far as jurisdiction is concerned, this is of small importance, as the jurisdiction of the arbitral tribunal will be founded on the agreement of the parties to it, and insofar as there is dispute about it, the law of the seat of the arbitration will determine whether the tribunal may rule on its jurisdiction, and whether and at what point such a ruling may be challenged in judicial proceedings. The significance and relevance, if any, of there being legal proceedings before the courts of another Member State will be a matter for the tribunal and law under which it operates, and not for the Brussels I Regulation. It also follows that Chapter III of the Regulation, which obliges courts in Member States to recognise judgments from other Member States, has no direct effect upon, or application to, an arbitration tribunal.[279] Of course, if the law under which the arbitral tribunal is operating obliges it to apply rules of English private international law, any obligation to recognise a judgment from another Member State is imposed, if at all, by the law which applies to the arbitration, rather than by the Regulation itself.

The effect of the Regulation in relation to legal proceedings which are connected to arbitration is more complex; and there are significant differences between Regulation 44/2001 and Regulation 1215/2012. But the point of departure is easy enough. Legal proceedings may arise prior to, during, or after an arbitration; all such procedures which may be seen as integral to the arbitration, and as arising only because of the arbitration (by reason of their supervisory, supportive, or enforcement character) are excluded from the domain of the Regulation. To put the matter another way, such proceedings have arbitration as their object, or their subject matter. So judicial proceedings to set up a tribunal, or to remove an arbitrator, are within Article 1(2)(d), and are therefore excluded from the material scope of the Regulation. Neither does the Regulation apply to or in

---

278 C-271/00, [2002] ECR I-10527; see also C-433/01 *Freistaat Bayern v. Blijdenstein* [2004] ECR I-981.

279 It follows that an arbitral tribunal may award damages for breach of an agreement to arbitrate, where the breach consists of bringing proceedings before the courts of a Member State: *West Tankers Inc v. Allianz SpA* [2012] EWHC 854 (Comm), [2012] 2 Lloyd's Rep 103. The tribunal was required to apply English law, but not a rule of English law which, *ex hypothesi*, did not apply to arbitration.

judicial proceedings to secure the setting aside, or the enforcement, of arbitral awards, not even if these awards are to be incorporated into and given the force of law by a court judgment.[280] As international arbitration is itself covered by the New York Convention, it would be most unfortunate if the extent of the exclusion of arbitration from the Brussels I Regulation were to be drawn so narrowly as to prejudice the operation of the New York Convention. This principle is, it seems, now clearly accepted by Regulation 1215/2012, which provides that the Regulation 'shall not affect the application of the 1958 New York Convention'.[281]

2.43 Arbitration and Regulation 44/2001: problems of interpretation and application

Other court procedures are not so closely connected to the process of arbitration, and the application of Article 1(2)(d) to them depended on the width ascribed to the exclusion of 'arbitration'. It is generally accepted that the exclusion, as understood in relation to Regulation 44/2001, was narrower than applies to Regulation 1215/2012, and in order to understand the effect of Regulation 1215/2012, it is necessary to say something about the earlier jurisprudence.

Support for the view that the exclusion of arbitration was to be construed amply was provided by the European Court in *Marc Rich & Co AG v. Soc Italiana Impianti PA*,[282] which held that judicial proceedings to appoint an arbitrator were excluded from the Brussels Convention, and could be brought in England against an Italian domiciliary: measures adopted by States as part of the process of setting an arbitration in motion were excluded from the scope of the Convention, and that was that. The respondent could not circumvent the exclusion of arbitration by denying *ab initio* the existence of the arbitration agreement;[283] the subject matter of the dispute before the Court was arbitration, and that excluded the proceedings from the material scope of what became the Regulation. It followed that the exclusion covers litigation to determine whether the parties have bound themselves to settle disputes by arbitration.

As long as there existed a genuine dispute as to whether there was an obligation to proceed to arbitration, judicial proceedings aimed at a resolution of that dispute were excluded from the scope of the Regulation, for their subject matter is arbitration, pure and simple.[284] The logic of this analysis had been considered in England to lead to a further conclusion: that proceedings in which the applicant claimed, or also claimed, an injunction to restrain the respondent, found to be bound by an agreement to arbitrate, from bringing judicial proceedings before the courts of another Member State in breach of an agreement to arbitrate, also had arbitration as their principal subject matter and should be unhindered by

---

280 Jenard [1979] OJ C59/1, 13; Schlosser [1979] OJ C59/71, [65]; see further, para. 7.09.
281 Regulation 1215/2012, Art. 73(2).
282 C-190/89, [1991] ECR I-3855. In fact, while this was going on, the party seeking appointment of an arbitrator submitted to the Italian courts, who had been seised first and had determined that there was no binding arbitration clause; they gave judgment, and this was – because the defendant had submitted to the Italian courts – entitled to be recognised in England: *Marc Rich & Co AG v. Soc Italiana Impianti PA (No 2)* [1992] 1 Lloyd's Rep 624.
283 For a similar point in another context, see 38/81 *Effer v. Kantner* [1982] ECR 825.
284 C-185/07 *Allianz SpA v. West Tankers Inc* [2009] ECR I-663.

the Regulation.[285] By its decision in *Allianz SpA v. West Tankers Inc*[286] the Court confirmed the premise but denied the conclusion. It accepted that an application for an injunction to enforce an agreement to arbitrate had arbitration as its subject matter. But it relied on its earlier decision in *Turner v. Grovit*,[287] in which it had held that an English court, seised of a civil or commercial matter, may not grant injunctive relief in order to interfere with proceedings brought in a civil or commercial matter before the courts of another Member State, to deny that the English court was free to grant the injunction applied for. Its reason was that an injunction, which sought to prevent a damages claim being brought for damage done to the claimant's property, before a Sicilian court, was impermissible for the very same reason: it sought to intrude in a civil or commercial matter before the courts of another Member State. It was true that the English court was seised of proceedings in a civil or commercial matter which fell outside the scope of the Regulation, but that did not mean that it could treat the Sicilian court as though the Regulation did not exist. The decision did not go down well in England, but its logic was impeccable.

It was still surprising that the Court in *Allianz SpA* made no reference to its judgment in *Hoffmann v. Krieg*,[288] and the principle there established: that when dealing with a civil or commercial matter which fell outside the Regulation (in that case, one of personal status), a national court was not prevented from applying its own law to the full, even where this led to a result which, according to the Regulation, would otherwise have been prohibited (in that case, the refusal to recognise a judgment to which the Regulation applied). Even so, from the perspective of the Sicilian judge, he was seised of proceedings in a civil or commercial matter, and the application of *Turner v. Grovit*, to allow him to deal with the civil proceedings before him without interference from London, will have struck him as normal and proper. Attention may therefore turn to alternative means of enforcing personal obligations assumed by the parties who agree to arbitrate, with the result that the decision in *Allianz SpA* is a rather minor detail of the effect of Regulation 44/2001.[289] The immediate controversy is now at an end.[289A]

A further logical deduction from the judgment of the European Court in *Hoffmann v. Krieg*[290] and which is examined shortly, might be that if a court in another Member State has assumed jurisdiction contrary (in English eyes) to an arbitration agreement, an English court should be free, notwithstanding anything in the Regulation, to apply English arbitration law as set out in section 32 of the 1982 Act. This would allow it to refuse to recognise the foreign judgment,[291] and to refuse to recognise the view of that foreign court upon the

---

285 *Through Transport Mutual Insurance Association (Eurasia) Ltd v. New India Assurance Co Ltd* [2004] EWCA Civ 1598, [2005] 1 Lloyd's Rep 67, approving in particular *The Ivan Zagubanski* [2002] 1 Lloyd's Rep 106; *cf Toepfer International GmbH v. Société Cargill France* [1997] 2 Lloyd's Rep 98.

286 C-185/07, [2009] ECR I-663.

287 Case C-159/02, [2004] ECR I-3565. The case was not concerned with arbitration, but with judicial proceedings before the courts of England and Spain.

288 145/86, [1988] ECR 654.

289 After all, the Sicilian proceedings had no effect on (and did not torpedo) the arbitration; and the idea that one requires an injunction to prevent proceedings in Sicily making any discernible progress is not grounded in reality.

289A Though see n181, above, for the possible effect of C-536/13 Re *Gazprom OAO* (not yet decided).

290 145/86, [1988] ECR 645.

291 But if the defendant submits to the jurisdiction of the foreign court, he waives the argument upon the arbitration clause, and s. 32(1)(c) does not require non-recognition: *Marc Rich & Co AG v. Soc Italiana Impianti PA (No 2)* [1992] 1 Lloyd's Rep 624.

validity of the arbitration clause itself. The question whether there has been a breach of an arbitration agreement, and the further question of which remedies may lie for that breach, still has arbitration as its subject matter, and therefore should fall outside the scope of the Regulation.[292] The question whether this is affected by *Allianz SpA* would be answered negatively if the point is taken to have been decided by *Hoffmann*; but the issue is more appropriately examined in Chapter 7.

2.44 Arbitration and Regulation 1215/2012

It was understood that the approach taken in relation to arbitration under Regulation 44/2001 was resented by those who took the view – entirely rationally – that the very purpose of agreeing to arbitration was to provide for a forum and mechanism for the settling of disputes which was consensual, private, and tailor-made for the issues as the parties saw them, and that to relegate an arbitration agreement to the status of a mere defence which might be raised in legal proceedings in a civil or commercial matter was fundamentally wrong. Though Regulation 1215/2012 made no alteration to the text of the Regulation – it is ironic that perfectly sensible-looking proposals to do so were also objected to on the ground that they gave the courts a role in relation to arbitration – Recital (12) made a statement of principle which was intended to strengthen the policy of allowing arbitration to proceed, and where necessary, to be supported, without interference from the Regulation. In material part (and with sentences numbered for convenience of reference), it reads:

> '[1] This Regulation should not apply to arbitration. [2] Nothing in this Regulation should prevent the courts of a Member State, when seised of an action in a matter in respect of which the parties have entered into an arbitration agreement, from referring the parties to arbitration, from staying or dismissing the proceedings, or from examining whether the arbitration agreement is null and void, inoperative or incapable of being performed, in accordance with their national law. [3] A ruling given by a court of a Member State as to whether or not an arbitration agreement is null and void, inoperative or incapable of being performed should not be subject to the rules of recognition and enforcement laid down in this Regulation, regardless of whether the court decided on this as a principal issue or as an incidental question. [4] On the other hand, where a court of a Member State, exercising jurisdiction under this Regulation or under national law, has determined that an arbitration agreement is null and void, inoperative or incapable of being performed, this should not preclude that court's judgment on the substance of the matter from being recognised or, as the case may be, enforced in accordance with this Regulation. [5] This should be without prejudice to the competence of the courts of the Member States to decide on the recognition and enforcement of arbitral awards in accordance with the Convention on the Recognition and Enforcement of Foreign Arbitral Awards, done at New York on 10 June 1958 ("the 1958 New York Convention"), which takes precedence over this Regulation. [6] This Regulation should not apply to any action or ancillary proceedings relating to, in particular, the establishment of an arbitral tribunal, the powers of arbitrators, the conduct of an arbitration procedure or any other aspects of such a procedure, nor to any action or judgment concerning the annulment, review, appeal, recognition or enforcement of an arbitral award.'

The first sentence simply repeats what Article 1(2)(d) provides, though it must be taken to re-enforce the conclusion that arbitrators are not required by the Regulation – what the law

---

292 The question was left open when the United Kingdom acceded to the Brussels Convention: Schlosser [1979] OJ C59/71, [62]. But it has now been held that the Regulation is no impediment to an award of damages *by an arbitral tribunal* for breach of the agreement to arbitrate: *West Tankers Inc v. Allianz SpA* [2012] EWHC 854 (Comm), [2012] 2 Lloyd's Rep 103. Whether a court would have a similar power is debatable.

of the seat may tell them to do is a separate issue – to take any account of the Regulation. The second sentence provides, in effect, that when dealing with a matter of arbitration, a court shall ignore proceedings before the courts of another Member State, whether or not it was seised first, but should get on with the matter before it without distraction. It is not clear whether this changes the law, but it is a welcome clarification of the position. The third sentence builds on that, to allow the court to be about its business unhampered by any obligation from the Regulation to take account of any decision by the courts of a Member State on the validity, scope, or effect of the arbitration agreement. Of course, there is nothing to say that the national law of the court seised – that is to say, its ordinary law on the effect of foreign judgments – may not take account, but in England, section 32 of the 1982 Act is left to operate without contradiction.

The fourth sentence is problematic, but it is best examined in the context of foreign judgments, with which it is most directly concerned. One should be open about it, though: if a dispute arises in a civil or commercial matter, judicial proceedings in relation to it are within the material scope of the Regulation unless they are excluded by other provisions; and if there is a judicial disagreement as to whether the parties bound themselves to arbitrate, there is no particular reason for supposing one court rather than the other to be correct. Once the Member States were persuaded to abandon a proposal that the decision on the validity and scope of the arbitration agreement be taken by the courts of the seat (a proposal which is little use when the seat is not in a Member State), the possibility of judicial disagreement is inevitable. The fourth sentence of the Recital might be thought to illustrate the proposition that one should be careful what one wishes for.

The fifth sentence is uncontroversial; and the sixth reinstates the ample reading of the exception for which the decision in *Marc Rich* stood, though the idea that it might have opened the door to the possibility of an anti-suit injunction (and the reversal of the effect of *Allianz SpA*) ordered in aid of the arbitration is most implausible.

Of course, proceedings for damages for breach of a contractual agreement to resolve differences by arbitration will fall outside the scope of the Regulation. If a claim for damages for breach of a jurisdiction agreement, when the breach is the bringing of proceedings before the courts of another Member State, is not precluded by the Regulation,[293] damages in the case of the breach of an arbitration agreement must be an *a fortiori* case.

2.45 Conclusion

If the proceedings before the court fall outside the domain of the Regulation,[294] the court will apply its traditional rules on jurisdiction[295] without more ado: not because the Regulation directs it to, but because the Regulation says nothing at all. Nothing in the Brussels I Regulation, not even the rules on *lis alibi pendens*,[296] will be applicable.[297] The eventual judgment will not be entitled to recognition or enforcement under Chapter III

---

293 *Starlight Shipping Co v. Allianz Marine & Aviation Versicherungs AG* [2014] EWCA Civ 1010, [2014] 2 Lloyd's Rep 554; for further proceedings see *Starlight Shipping Co v. Allianz Marine & Aviation Versicherungs AG* [2014] EWHC 3068 (Comm), [2014] 2 Lloyd's Rep 579.

294 This will mean that it falls outside the scope of the Brussels and Lugano Conventions as well.

295 But including any special statutory rules, such as apply to insolvency, matrimonial proceedings, etc.

296 C-129/92 *Owens Bank Ltd v. Bracco* [1994] ECR I-117; *Moore v. Moore* [2007] EWCA Civ 361, [2007] ILPr 481.

297 The rules will be found in Chapter 4.

of the Regulation.[298] But if the case falls within the domain of the Regulation, jurisdiction will be determined by the Regulation, and the next question must therefore be addressed.

(2) JURISDICTION UNDER ANOTHER CONVENTION OR INSTRUMENT

2.46 General

The Brussels I Regulation is an instrument made under the authority of a Treaty. The Regulation cannot, any more than its predecessors could, properly abrogate any prior treaty or other international instrument dealing with jurisdiction and the recognition of judgments, except to the extent that it is one to which only Member States are party. The Regulation makes express provision to preserve the continued operation of: (a) the Brussels Convention and Lugano Convention, to the extent that they are not superseded by the Brussels I Regulation; (b) other international Conventions which govern jurisdiction and the recognition of judgments; and (c) other Union legislation (or national laws implementing Union legislation) dealing with specific matters and which provide for jurisdiction and the recognition of judgments.

For present purposes it is not proposed to deal with the Brussels Convention and Lugano Convention. These Conventions continued to operate after the coming into force of the Regulation, but the precise manner and extent of their doing so, and the countries in relation to which they have effect, are more conveniently and very shortly examined in Chapter 3. At this point in the analysis of the Brussels I Regulation it is convenient to examine only Conventions on particular matters, and community instruments.

2.47 Conventions on particular matters

Article 71 of the Brussels I Regulation, original and recast alike, provides that:

> *(1) This Regulation shall not affect any conventions to which the Member States are parties and which in relation to particular matters, govern jurisdiction or the recognition of judgments. (2) With a view to its uniform interpretation, paragraph 1 shall be applied in the following manner: (a) this Regulation shall not prevent a court of a Member State, which is a party to a convention on a particular matter, from assuming jurisdiction in accordance with that convention, even where the defendant is domiciled in another Member State which is not a party to that convention. The court hearing the action shall, in any event, apply Article 28[299] of this Regulation ... .[300]*

The Article goes on to provide that where jurisdiction is assumed on this basis, a judgment resulting from it shall be recognised and enforced in the other Member States, pursuant to the Brussels I Regulation.[301] It is for this reason that if proceedings are taken in a civil or commercial matter, falling within Article 1 of the Brussels I Regulation, they are regarded as

---

298 As to whether the court addressed may examine this question for itself, see para. 7.08, below.

299 In Regulation 44/2001, the reference is to Art. 26. The substance is identical.

300 The remainder of the Article deals with the recognition of judgments, providing that judgments in cases where the jurisdiction of the court was derived from Art. 71 may be enforced under and in accordance with the procedures set out in Chapter III of the Regulation.

301 But such a Convention may also deprive a court of jurisdiction conferred by the Regulation. For the operation of the Brussels and Lugano Conventions in this regard, see Chapter 3, below.

being and treated as having been within the scope of the Regulation, even though the actual jurisdictional rule relied on is peculiar to cases which fall under the particular Convention. And it is for this reason that Article 71 is not to be read as opening a doorway which leads out of the domain of the Regulation.

Article 71 means that the jurisdictional rules of the Brussels I Regulation cannot be used to override or deny the jurisdiction authorised for exercise by the particular Convention. For this reason, jurisdiction pursuant to Article 71 prevails over the other jurisdiction-creating rules of the Regulation discussed below.

To begin with there had been some uncertainty whether the effect of taking jurisdiction under a particular Convention might carry the case outside the scope of the Regulation altogether. The practical significance of the question was whether jurisdiction asserted on the basis of a particular Convention was subject to, or removed from, the *lis alibi pendens* rules of what are now Articles 29 to 34 of Regulation 1215/2012. But when it is seen that the recognition of such judgments falls within Chapter III of the Regulation, and that what are now Articles 29 to 34 are designed to facilitate the free movement of judgments, the conclusion that jurisdiction taken under Article 71 was taken within the scope of the Regulation was inevitable. To put the matter another way, jurisdictional rules found in a particular Convention are incorporated by reference into the Regulation by means of Article 71, and are in this sense derived from the Regulation.[302] The technique is not dissimilar from that which is used by Article 6 of Regulation 1215/2012 to refer to and incorporate jurisdiction taken from rules of national law.

Article 71 refers to Conventions which 'govern jurisdiction'. That expression obviously includes rules in Conventions which provide in terms for the taking of jurisdiction, but a Convention may 'govern' jurisdiction is less direct ways. An example might be seen in *The Hollandia*.[303] In that case, the parties had made a jurisdiction agreement for the courts of the Netherlands which, if given effect, would have resulted in the application of rules on the limitation of liability which were inconsistent with the Hague-Visby Rules. These Rules provided that a term which had the effect of limiting liability to below the level fixed by the Rules was null and void. The House of Lords interpreted that aspect of the Hague-Visby Rules, given effect by Carriage of Goods by Sea Act 1971, as requiring it to override the jurisdiction agreement so as to forestall an outcome which the Rules proscribed. On the footing that the Rules are a particular Convention,[304] and that the House of Lords was correct to understand the Rules as requiring a court to exercise jurisdiction in order to prevent the circumvention of the Rules,[305] it is arguable that it could be decided in the same way today, even though Article 25 of Regulation 1215/2012, which would otherwise require the court to give effect to the Dutch jurisdiction agreement, does not make express provision for such reasoning to be applied, and does not allow rules of national law to override the validity of an agreement on jurisdiction.

---

302 C-148/03 *Nürnberger Allgemeine Versicherungs AG v. Portbridge Transport International BV* [2004] ECR I-10327.

303 [1983] 1 AC 565. At that date the Brussels Convention had not taken effect in the United Kingdom.

304 Which they certainly are: International Convention for the Unification of Certain Rules of Law Relating to Bills of Lading, as amended by the Visby Protocol (1968).

305 Which is more arguable, as the Rules do not deal specifically with jurisdiction, rather with contract terms more generally but in a way which could relate to jurisdiction.

2.48 Incorporation by reference of jurisdiction authorised by a particular Convention

The question whether the rules of a particular Convention actually give the court jurisdiction is not examined here. The question is a technical one, governed in its entirety by the particular Convention, and most appropriately examined in specialist works in which the relationship between the jurisdictional provisions and the substantive provisions of the particular Convention can be explored. But a problem arises when proceedings are commenced in a court on the basis of a particular Convention, and there are proceedings before the courts of another Member State which considers itself to have jurisdiction – under the particular Convention or otherwise – to hear them. The answer to the question depends on the proper relationship between the Regulation and the particular Convention.

The starting point is the decision of the European Court in *The Tatry*.[306] In that case, proceedings had been commenced in the Netherlands[307] by a shipowner against owners of cargo for a declaration that it owed no liability to those interested in the cargo for any loss or damage which had been sustained. Proceedings were then commenced in England, by the arrest of a sister ship, followed by service of process upon it, for compensation for damage to the cargo. When the jurisdiction of the English court was challenged, the cargo owners argued that the claim in England should proceed, notwithstanding prior Dutch proceedings, as the jurisdiction of the English court was derived from the provisions of a particular Convention, and in the circumstances, there was nothing in the particular Convention to cause or allow the English court to decline to exercise jurisdiction.[308] Had this argument been accepted, it would have meant, in effect, that a claim brought on the jurisdictional basis of a particular Convention was immune from what are now Articles 29 and 30 of Regulation 1215/2012, or even that it fell outside the scope of the Regulation altogether. The European Court disagreed, holding that what is now Article 29 of Regulation 1215/2012 prevented the English court hearing the case.[309]

The argument that if a case falls within the scope of a particular Convention it falls outside the domain of what is now the Brussels I Regulation has therefore been rejected. So far as concerns the particular issue of *lis alibi pendens*, the position adopted was that if the particular Convention contained its own provisions for dealing with situations of *lis alibi pendens*, they may apply, effectively in place of the Brussels I Regulation; but if the particular Convention made no provision to deal with the issue – or the problem, as it might be seen – then the provisions of the Regulation would apply, *faute de mieux*, 'to fill the gap'. The latter was the case in *The Tatry*.

On the face of it, there are problems with the interpretation of Article 71 adopted in *The Tatry*, and especially with the proposition that an international Convention left a 'gap', almost as though this were a careless oversight. If what is now Article 29 of the Regulation can apply to require an English court to decline jurisdiction, it creates friction with Article

---

306 C-406/92, [1994] ECR I-5439. The proposition that Art. 71 jurisdiction is, in this sense, derived from the Regulation and subject to its control, is confirmed by C-148/03 *Nürnberger Allgemeine Versicherungs AG v. Portbridge Transport International BV* [2004] ECR I-10327, [17].

307 On the basis of the Dutch domicile of some defendants, and what is now Art. 8(1) of Regulation 1215/2012 in relation to the others.

308 International Convention relating to the arrest of sea-going ships (1952).

309 And, to the extent that the conditions of what is now Art. 29 were not satisfied, Art. 30 (as it now is) would permit the court seised second to grant jurisdictional relief.

71(2)(a), as it seems to 'prevent a court of a Member State which is party to a convention on a particular matter from assuming jurisdiction in accordance with that convention'. It might be argued that the European Court did not deny that the English court was entitled to assume jurisdiction, merely holding that it was not entitled to proceed to exercise the jurisdiction which it had been entitled to assume. It is true that the prospect of irreconcilable judgments from the courts of the Netherlands and the United Kingdom was unattractive, but the fact remains that a provision of what is now the Regulation prevented the English court from hearing a case over which the Arrest Convention gave it jurisdiction, and which, as a matter of public international law, it had been obliged to permit the claimant to bring.

The proposition that the provisions of the Regulation would apply if the particular Convention had no mechanism for dealing with *lis alibi pendens*, but would be sidelined if the particular Convention did, proved to be unsatisfactory; and the position now adopted by the European Court is that the provisions of the Brussels I Regulation will be applied unless those of the particular Convention are even more stringent in their operation. In *TNT Express Nederland BV v. AXA Versicherung AG*[310] the jurisdiction of the national court was to be taken in the basis of the CMR Convention,[311] and the question was whether what is now Article 29 of Regulation 1215/2012 would apply in circumstances in which Article 31(2) of the CMR Convention may not have prevented the second set of proceedings. The reasoning of the European Court was striking.[312] It held that the CMR Convention 'cannot compromise the principles which underlie judicial cooperation in civil and commercial matters in the European Union' in general, and those which secure the free movement of judgments in particular. Article 71, as a part of the Regulation, had to be interpreted in the broad context of the Regulation as a whole, and could not be allowed to conflict with it, as a result of which 'rules governing jurisdiction, including the *lis pendens* rules, set out in specialised conventions... can be applied in the European Union only to the extent that... they are highly predictable, facilitate the sound administration of justice and enable the risk of concurrent proceedings to be minimised.'[313] As a result, the *lis pendens* provision of the CMR Convention 'can be applied in the European Union only if it enables the objectives of the free movement of judgments in civil and commercial matters and of mutual trust in the administration of justice in the European Union to be achieved under conditions at least as favourable as those resulting from the application of the Regulation'. In particular, if the CMR Convention were to permit proceedings in two Member States to proceed, because it did not consider them to have the same cause of action in circumstances in which the Regulation would have considered the cause of action to be the same, the untrammelled application of the CMR Convention would undermine the Regulation, and would on that account not be given effect.[314]

It goes further. It is arguable, at least, that other provisions of the Regulation are designed to serve the broad aims of the Regulation, such as the power to join co-defendants under

---

310 C-533/08, [2010] ECR I-4107. Applied in C-452/12 *Nipponkoa Insurance Co (Europe) Ltd V. Inter-Zuid Transport BV* EU:C:2013:858, [2014] 1 All ER (Comm) 288.

311 Convention on the Contract for the International Carriage of Goods by Road (1956), as amended by the Protocol signed at Geneva on 5 July 1978.

312 'Delphic', in the opinion of the Court of Appeal in *British American Tobacco Switzerland SA v. Exel Europe Ltd* [2013] EWCA Civ 1319, [2014] 1 WLR 4526, [81].

313 At [45]–[56].

314 C-452/12 *Nipponkoa Insurance Co (Europe) Ltd v. Inter-Zuid Transport BV* EU:C:2013:858, [2014] 1 All ER (Comm) 288.

Article 8(1) into proceedings in which they could not otherwise be sued. If an international convention were to be interpreted as preventing a co-defendant from being joined to proceedings, it is at least arguable that Article 8(1) of the Regulation would override this as well.[315] However, it does not follow that the jurisdictional rules of (for example) the CMR Convention may be relied on only when they are identical with those of the Regulation, for if that were so Article 71 would be without sensible effect. Rather, the particular convention's jurisdictional rule must be sufficiently analogous to that of the Regulation that it can be said that it is consistent with the scheme, if not the detail, of the Regulation.[316]

It follows that jurisdiction taken from a particular convention enjoys much the same status as other rules of jurisdiction, made outside the Regulation but incorporated into it by reference. This may not be what Article 71(2) says, but it is what it means.

2.49 Particular Conventions and jurisdictional privilege

A distinct shortcoming arises from the curiously limited wording of Article 71, in that it appears to be engaged only if the particular Convention permits or requires a court to exercise jurisdiction. It appears to say nothing where a particular Convention would require a court to refrain from exercising jurisdiction. Yet, if the particular Convention is drafted to this effect, the international obligation to act in accordance with its provisions would appear to be just as strong, and Article 71 ought to permit the court to do as required and to refuse to hear the case, without contrary instruction from the Brussels I Regulation. Or so one might think.[317]

In the particular context of arbitration, where there may[318] well be an obligation under the New York Convention to refuse to hear a claim which the parties have agreed to arbitrate, it should have been provided by Article 71 of the Regulation, and its predecessors, that this obligation to refuse to exercise judicial jurisdiction prevails over any contradictory answer which may be derived from the Brussels I Regulation or its predecessors. Likewise where, for example, Article 28 of the Warsaw Convention[319] provides that a claim against a carrier may be brought 'either before the court of the domicile of the carrier, his principal place of business, or of the place where he has an establishment... ', one would have thought that it meant that the proceedings may not be brought elsewhere. And where the CMR Convention[320] gives the claimant the right to choose between certain jurisdictions, it also presumably means that the defendant may not be summoned before the courts of any

---

315 The point was raised in *British American Tobacco Switzerland SA v. Exel Europe Ltd* [2013] EWCA Civ 1319, [2014] 1 WLR 4526, but was not eventually decided. The international Convention in that case (CMR) was interpreted as permitting the joinder of the co-defendants in any event. It is fair to say that this interpretation was driven by awareness of the fact that if it were not arrived at, a submission that what is now Art. 8(1) of the Regulation would supervene to provide jurisdiction in any event would be hard to reject.

316 C-157/13 *Nickel & Goeldner Spedition GmbH v. Kintra UAB* EU:C:2014:2145, [2015] QB 96.

317 *British American Tobacco Switzerland SA v. Exel Europe Ltd* [2013] EWCA Civ 1319, [2014] 1 WLR 4526 might suggest that this is not so.

318 The 1958 New York Convention does oblige (Art. II.3) a court to give effect to an arbitration agreement and to cease hearing the claim, though it does not, in express terms, oblige it to refuse to enforce an award which violated it. For discussion not leading to a clear conclusion, see (2001) 18 *Journal of International Arbitration* 13, 27.

319 Convention for the Unification of Certain Rules relating to International Carriage by Air (1929).

320 Convention on the Contract for the International Carriage of Goods by Road (1956), given the force of law in the United Kingdom by Carriage of Goods by Road Act 1965.

other place. It would have been natural to read this as meaning that in such a case, Article 71 would exclude the possibility that the rules of the Brussels I Regulation might be employed to bring the carrier before the courts of another Member State. But Article 71, as presently drafted and interpreted,[321] is inadequate to give firm support to this analysis. It is rather surprising, but it appears to be the law.

2.50 Maritime and other Conventions

Some of the most important particular Conventions to which Article 71 will apply will be in the sphere of maritime law: the 1952 Arrest Convention and the 1952 Collision Convention.[322] Under the Arrest Convention, jurisdiction in relation to certain claims may be founded by the arrest of a ship; if this arrest takes place,[323] Article 71 of the Regulation will authorise the taking of jurisdiction. But it will still be necessary for jurisdiction *actually* to be taken as a matter of English law: jurisdiction in an admiralty action *in rem* in English law requires the claim form to be served. Arrest does not itself found jurisdiction in English law (nor is it a precondition for it), but it appears that it is the fact of arrest, in accordance with the Arrest Convention, which permits the court to exercise jurisdiction upon the basis of service of process, and to be permitted by Article 71 to do so.

Under the Collision Convention, jurisdiction in relation to certain claims may be asserted if the ship could have been arrested, but security is instead given for the claim. If this takes place, the Collision Convention permits the court to take jurisdiction,[324] and to do so under the authority of Article 71 of the Brussels Convention. But once again, the claim form must be served before jurisdiction can be said to have been asserted.[325]

The 1999 Montreal Convention for the Unification of Certain Rules for International Carriage by Air provides for certain jurisdictions to be made available to a passenger with a claim against an air carrier; and these are not abridged by the Brussels I Regulation. But where the passenger brings a statutory claim under the Compensation Regulation 261/2004,[326]

---

321 And as the Court of Appeal seemed to consider that it had to be understood, in *British American Tobacco Switzerland SA v. Exel Europe Ltd* [2013] EWCA Civ 1319, [2014] 1 WLR 4526, that the Regulation takes little account of an argument that a defendant is not liable to be brought before the court if the Regulation would provide a basis for the assertion of jurisdiction.

322 Also the Warsaw Convention governing carriage by air, in relation to which, see *Milor Srl v. British Airways plc* [1996] QB 702, where it was held that the Warsaw Convention itself precludes the imposition of a stay of proceedings. See also *Deaville v. Aeroflot Russian International Airlines* [1997] 2 Lloyd's Rep 67, where it appears to have been held that the Warsaw Convention allowed the action to proceed in England, and proceedings in France did not affect the English action. By contrast, the European Patents Convention does not deal with issues of jurisdiction and is, therefore, not an Art. 71 Convention: *Fort Dodge Animal Health v. Akzo Nobel NV* [1998] FSR 222.

323 If the claimant does not arrest the ship, but instead commences proceedings by service of process without an arrest, there has been no arrest and the Arrest Convention does not apply: *The Deichland* [1990] 1 QB 361. But *cf The Prinsengracht* [1993] 1 Lloyd's Rep 41, *The Anna H* [1995] 1 Lloyd's Rep 11.

324 *The Po* [1991] 2 Lloyd's Rep 206. Technically the Collision Convention, though signed by the United Kingdom, is not part of the domestic law of the United Kingdom; instead the Senior Courts Act 1981 contains rules corresponding to those of the Collision Convention. It was held that the English had taken jurisdiction 'in accordance with' that Convention, even though not directly under it.

325 On this see generally, Hartley (1989) 105 LQR 640, and *The Po* [1991] 2 Lloyd's Rep 206. That case decides that jurisdiction derived from the Collision Convention, though confirmed by the Brussels Convention, may be the subject of a stay of proceedings for a non–Contracting State. This aspect of the decision may require reconsideration in the light of C-281/02 *Owusu v. Jackson* [2005] ECR I-1383.

326 Regulation (EC) 261/2004 of 11 February 2004: [2004] OJ L46/1.

claiming a payment in respect of delay inflicted by the airline, this operates outside the framework of the Montreal Convention, and is subject to the ordinary rules of the Brussels I Regulation.[327]

2.51 The European Convention on Human Rights as an Article 71 Convention

The European Convention for the safeguard of Human Rights and Political Freedoms[328] ('the ECHR') is not, on the face of it, a Convention which governs jurisdiction or the recognition of judgments, and so it is not obvious that Article 71 of the Regulation might apply to it. Neither, more specifically, does it provide clear or precise rules for the taking of jurisdiction, with the consequence that Article 71(2)(a) looks equally inapplicable to it.

On the other hand, the ECHR is a Convention to which all Member States are party, and its Article 6[329] guarantees those persons within its scope access to a court: it provides that 'everyone is entitled to a fair and public hearing within a reasonable time by an independent and impartial tribunal established by law…'. The wording of Article 6, read as it is written, is a guarantee of access to a court, enshrined in an international Convention. While it may be going far too far to contend that this rather general statement of the right of access to a court has the potential to overthrow the restrictions imposed by national rules of civil jurisdiction,[330] it is less clear that the ECHR is silent when a court with jurisdiction is said to be prevented from exercising it, in a manner which appears to violate the ECHR.

The case which brought this proposition into rather sharp focus is *Erich Gasser GmbH v. MISAT Srl.*[331] An Austrian claimant who wished to bring proceedings in Austria against an Italian defendant was prevented from doing so by what is now Article 29 of the Regulation, because the defendant had already seised the Italian courts. The particular objection to the behaviour of the defendant lay in the fact that, not only did it involve a breach of his apparent contractual agreement to litigate only in Austria, but also in the evidence that procedure before the Italian court was liable to be so slow that it was capable of amounting to, so the claimant contended, a violation of his rights under the ECHR. The Austrian court appeared to see merit in this last point, that for the claimant to be shut out of the Austrian courts and stranded in interminable Italian indecision was a violation of Article 6 ECHR. It referred a question on the point of how the ECHR might affect the jurisdictional rules of the Brussels Convention, as it then was, to the European Court.

It received a dismissive answer:[332] the Brussels Convention made no reference to Article 6 ECHR, and that there was therefore no basis in the Brussels Convention for a court seised second, as the Austrian court was, to exercise jurisdiction as a response to a conclusion that the ECHR required it to. It followed that the ECHR had no bearing on the Austrian court's obligation under the Brussels Convention to stay its proceedings while waiting for the procedure in Italy to grind its way to an end.

---

327 C-204/08 *Rehder v. Air Baltic Corp* [2009] ECR I-6073.
328 Given effect in England by Human Rights Act 1998.
329 See above, para. 1.20.
330 For example, it surely cannot require a court to exercise a jurisdiction which the rules for service out of the jurisdiction would otherwise deny.
331 C-116/02, [2003] ECR I-14693. But if Regulation 1215/2012 had been in force, Art. 31(2) would have solved the problem.
332 At [71]–[72].

This cannot be the last word on the issue. It may be that the Court, with jurisdiction to rule only on the interpretation of the Brussels Convention, and without formal power to rule on the ECHR, considered that its hands and tongue were tied by the lack of reference to the ECHR in the Brussels Convention. But an Austrian court may have taken the view that the international obligations of the Austrian Republic, created by its ratification of the ECHR and the incorporation of its guarantees into Austrian law, required it to accept jurisdiction over the proceedings brought by Erich Gasser GmbH. It is beyond the scope of this book to assess whether the Austrian court would have been right or wrong about such a matter of Austrian law, though it may well be argued that a State which had ratified the ECHR before it became a Contracting State to the Brussels Convention, or Member State for the purposes of the Regulation, is bound to give primacy to the obligations created by the ECHR. Article 71 of the Regulation would not have needed to be stretched very far, if stretched at all, to allow the Austrian court to discharge its international obligations by assuming jurisdiction over the claim. If the ECHR were understood to require the Austrian court to allow the claimant to proceed with his claim, what is now Article 71(2)(a) of the Regulation could be read to cover the case more or less precisely. Article 351 TFEU tends to point to the same conclusion. Of course, the point made in *The Tatry*, that what is now Article 29 of the Regulation will still apply if the particular Convention makes no provision for the regulating of parallel proceedings,[333] could still be raised. But the response to be made in a case like *Gasser* is that the ECHR would indeed make provision, but by refusing to regard the existence of moribund parallel proceedings as something which could override and in practice oust the guarantees of a right to a hearing given by Article 6 ECHR.

If this is not accepted, then the problem for the Austrian courts is how to proceed if their international obligations under the ECHR point in one direction, and their international obligations under the Brussels Regulation in another. On this, the judgment of the European Court in *Gasser* is not the answer, for all it does is to confirm that what is now the Brussels I Regulation does not yield to contradiction by the ECHR. It is possible, at least in theory, that the European Court of Human Rights could be expected to take the opposite point of view.[334] Faced with such data, the decision for the Austrian court is one of a higher legal order. It therefore remains to be decided whether the ECHR may yet be regarded as a Convention on a particular matter which may modify or override the rules of the Brussels I Regulation; or what a national court may yet do if it perceives there to be a simple clash between the two instruments. *Erich Gasser GmbH v. MISAT Srl* offered an opportunity for a thorough analysis of the issues; and it is disappointing that the European Court failed to rise to the challenge.

2.52 Other Union *leges speciales*

Article 67 of the Brussels I Regulation[335] provides that:

---

333 See above, para. 2.48.

334 However, for the argument that compliance with obligations created by European law will be presumed not to conflict with the ECHR, see *Bosphorus Hava Yollari Turizm ve Ticaret AS v. Ireland* (ECtHR, 30 June 2005). For the Austrian court to give effect to what is now Art. 29 of the Regulation may therefore not infringe the ECHR.

335 The text of Regulation 44/2001 is practically identical, differing only in referring to Community instruments rather than instruments of the Union.

> *This Regulation shall not prejudice the application of provisions governing jurisdiction and the recognition and enforcement of judgments in specific matters which are contained in instruments of the Union or in national legislation harmonised pursuant to such instruments.*

A growing number of legal instruments, made by the competent bodies of the European Union, contain their own special provisions for jurisdiction and the recognition of judgments.[336] The jurisdictional provisions of these instruments, these *leges speciales*, may displace any conflicting provisions of the Brussels I Regulation.

For example, provisions of national law adopted to implement Council Directive 96/71/EC on the posting abroad of workers within the framework of the provision of services, Article 6 of which contains a special jurisdictional rule, will displace any conflicting answer which might have been derived from the Regulation.[337] Moreover, it appears that the provisions of Directive 93/13 on Unfair Terms in Consumer Contracts,[338] which may deprive an arbitration[339] or jurisdiction[340] clause of effect, will operate even where its provisions would contradict the otherwise plain words of Article 25.[341]

Other instruments which will have this effect have been enacted in the context of the unification of the law on intellectual property, where the separate and territorial nature of rights and of jurisdiction can give rise to practical problems. Regulation 207/2009,[342] which is a codification of the various amendments to Regulation 40/94[343] on the Community Trade Mark, seeks to ensure that the validity and infringement of Community Trade Marks was effective, and that decisions are uniform, across the Member States. It requires the Member States to designate courts as 'Community trade mark courts', and provides in Title X detailed rules of jurisdiction which, in certain respects, displace the Brussels I Regulation from application.[344] But where the *lex specialis* of the Regulation on the Community Trade Mark is not made to apply, the provisions of the Brussels Regulation will continue to apply.[345]

---

336 For present purposes, this does not include the Insolvency Regulation (EC) 1346/2000 or the Brussels II Regulation, Regulation 2201/2003, as these deal with subject matter which lies outside the domain of the Brussels I Regulation.

337 This Directive has not been specifically enacted in the United Kingdom, the view apparently being that other legislative changes have discharged the obligation which the Directive placed on the United Kingdom: HC Deb. 1998–1999, vol. 336, col. 1. The legislation will have to be interpreted to meet this aim: *Lawson v. Serco Ltd* [2006] UKHL 3, [2006] ICR 250.

338 Given effect in England by SI 1999/2083.

339 C-240/98 *Océano Grupo Editorial SA v. Quintero* [2000] ECR I-4941 (arbitration clause, not otherwise within the domain of the Regulation).

340 *Standard Bank London Ltd v. Apostolakis* [2001] Lloyd's Rep Bank 240 (jurisdiction clause, but held to be invalid without the need to have recourse to the Directive). For subsequent proceedings in Greece, which held that claimants had not made the contracts in question as consumers, that the jurisdiction clause for the English courts was therefore effective, and that the English courts were wrong, see the note at [2003] ILPr 342. It is understood that an appellate tribunal reversed the decision at first instance but the judgment does not appear to be published in any English form.

341 However, the proposition in *Snookes v. Jani-King (GB) Ltd* [2006] EWHC 289 (QB), [2006] ILPr 433, that the Unfair Contract Terms Act 1977, a rule of domestic English law, can deprive a jurisdiction agreement, otherwise (according to the judge) valid by reference to what is now Art. 25, of legal effect is challenging.

342 [2009] OJ L78/1.

343 [1994] OJ L11/1.

344 For the details, see Title X to Regulation 207/2009; and otherwise see specialist works on trade mark law.

345 For illustration, see C-360/12 *Coty Germany GmbH v. First Note Perfumes NV* EU:C:2014:1318 (proceedings on infringement of Community Trade Mark fall within jurisdictional provisions of Regulation 40/94, the jurisdictional rules of which apply in place of those of the Brussels I Regulation; proceedings for infringement of law against unfair competition not within jurisdiction of Community Trade Mark Court as established by Regulation 40/94, and therefore within jurisdictional provisions of Brussels I Regulation).

Title IX of Council Regulation 6/2002 on Community Designs[346] sets out detailed rules which modify the application of the Brussels Convention[347] and in particular require a national court to be designated as a 'Community Design Court'. The details of these substantial but specialist provisions are beyond the scope of a general work. At the time of writing, it is expected that provision of an analogous kind may be made for European patents.

And the Hague Convention on Choice of Court Agreements will take effect under Article 67 when it has completed its legislative progress through the mechanisms of the European Union and the instrument of approval is deposited.[348]

In addition to these specialist instruments, the European Union has enacted a number of instruments which are designed to make it easier for small claims to be prosecuted, and for judgments in certain types of proceedings to be enforced in other Member States.[349] In particular, the Regulation establishing a European Order for Payment ('EOP'),[350] and the Regulation establishing the European Small Claims Procedure ('ESCP')[351] make provision for jurisdiction in the cases to which they apply; but their impact is, in this respect, small. The EOP Regulation applies in civil and commercial matters in cross-border cases. Where proceedings fall within it, jurisdiction is, in fact, determined by the Brussels I Regulation, except where the claim relates to a contract concluded by a consumer for a purpose which lies outside his trade or profession, and the defendant is the consumer, the only court with jurisdiction is that of the Member State of the consumer's domicile.[352]

The ESCP Regulation applies to proceedings in civil and commercial matters in cross-border cases. Where the value of a claim does not exceed €2000, the procedure, which is innovative in that it is almost entirely carried out in writing, may be invoked. But the question of which court has jurisdiction is answered by the provisions of the Brussels I Regulation.[353] These instruments, therefore, make little difference to the jurisdictional rules otherwise set out in the Brussels I Regulation.

2.53 Conclusion

If the court has jurisdiction pursuant to a particular Convention within the scope of Article 71, or European instrument within the scope of Article 67, it may exercise that jurisdiction, subject to the provisions of that particular Convention, or of the Brussels I Regulation, as to *lis alibi pendens*. If no such Convention or instrument applies, the next question in the hierarchy must be asked.

---

346 [2002] OJ L3/1.

347 See Art. 79; this will now also apply to the Brussels I Regulation.

348 This will be within a month of 5 June 2015: Council Decision 2014/887/EU, [2014] OJ L353/5.

349 So far as these instruments deal with the recognition and enforcement of judgments, they are dealt with in Chapter 7.

350 Regulation (EC) 1896/2006, [2006] OJ L399/1, in force from 12 December 2008. See also CPR Part 78.

351 Regulation (EC) 861/2007, [2007] OJ L199/1, in force from 1 January 2009. See also CPR Part 78.

352 Article 6. For a case which shows how strictly the opportunities for the defendant to object are to be interpreted, in order to secure the advantages which are intended for the claimant, see C-324/12 *Novontech-Zala kft v. Logicdata Electronic & Software Entwicklungs GmbH* EU:C:2013:205.

353 Article 4(1) and Annex I, s. 4.

(3) EXCLUSIVE JURISDICTION, REGARDLESS OF DOMICILE

2.54 General

Article 24 of Regulation 1215/2012, which is functionally identical to Article 22 of Regulation 44/2001, forms Section 6 of Chapter II of the Regulation. Article 24 of the Regulation opens by stating that:

The following courts shall have exclusive jurisdiction, regardless of domicile:

Certain proceedings which fall within the scope of the Brussels I Regulation are assigned by what is now Article 24 to the exclusive jurisdiction of the courts of a particular Member State. A number of points emerge immediately from the wording of the Article itself. If the claim[354] before the court falls within this Article, the courts of the Member State so identified have exclusive jurisdiction over it. The domicile of the parties is an irrelevance: even if none is domiciled in a Member State, Article 24 is still applicable. An agreement on jurisdiction which purports to contradict Article 24 does not confer jurisdiction on the agreed-to court.[355] The purported submission of either or both of the parties to the jurisdiction of the courts of another Member State does not confer jurisdiction on the submitted-to court.[356] Not only that: if the exercise of jurisdiction by a court in a Member State conflicts with Section 6 of Chapter II, a court in another Member State called upon to recognise that judgment must refuse to do so:[357] this is one of the few cases where the jurisdiction of the court which gave judgment must be reviewed by a court called upon to recognise the judgment. The provisions of Section 6 of Chapter II, which provide for this exclusive jurisdiction, override all others within the domain of the Regulation; and there are five of them. It should be noted that if the relevant connection is with a Lugano Convention State, the Lugano Convention may operate to override the Regulation.[358]

It is also worth making a number of preliminary observations which have emerged from the jurisprudence of the European Court, for the case law can be more puzzling than the wording of the Article might suggest it should be.

First, Article 24 should be interpreted restrictively, or, at least, be given no wider an interpretation than is required to promote the purpose for which the rule was enacted. Considering the overall structure of the Regulation, although it is an important rule, it should not encroach excessively upon the general jurisdiction of the courts of the defendant's domicile, or override more than strictly necessary an agreement made by the parties on the jurisdiction of a court.[359] Second, it cannot be correct that a defendant, say to an ordinary commercial contractual claim, may simply plead a defence which

---

354 But this is not to say that the claim, as distinct from the defence to it, is the determinant.

355 Regulation 1215/2012, Art. 25(4).

356 Regulation 1215/2012, Art. 26.

357 Regulation 44/2001, Art. 35(1), on which see para. 7.10, below. If the proceedings were ones to which Regulation 1215/2012 applied, the same result would follow on an application for refusal of recognition: Art. 45(1)(e)(ii), on which, see para. 7.40, below.

358 See Chapter 3, below. In the case of connections to a territory to which the Brussels Convention applies but the Regulations do not, it will be the Convention which applies: Regulation 1215/2012, Art. 68.

359 See in particular C-294/92 *Webb v. Webb* [1994] ECR I-1717; C-372/07 *Hassett v. South Eastern Health Board* [2008] ECR I-7403; C-144/10 *Berliner Verkehrsbetriebe v. JP Morgan Chase Bank NA* [2011] ECR I-3961.

raises a point which would, if taken in isolation, have fallen within the material scope of Article 24, and thereby undermine the jurisdiction of the court in which proceedings in respect of the claim had been commenced. But third, and on the other hand, if the purpose of Article 24 is that certain issues must be determined by a particular court, and the point is simply one about adjudication, it is not obvious why it would matter whether the material issue, to which Article 24 applies, would arise by way of claim or defence. Fourth, the sub-rules which make up Article 24 may not apply in a strictly uniform manner: in particular the provision that the validity of patents is within the exclusive jurisdiction of the courts of the Member State of grant may raise concerns which are specific to that context. Fifth, the correct general approach to Article 24 may be, at least in cases in which several issues arise for decision, to ask with what the case, as distinct from the claim, is 'principally' concerned.[360] Sixth, if the matter before the court for decision will require the specific application of land law or housing law, or corporations law, or patent law, and so on, for its determination, it is more likely that it will fall within Article 24 than if the case is liable to be disposed of by the application of general law. Not all of these principles emerged at the same time; and in any individual case, it may not be possible for them all to be given equal prominence. But they run, if unevenly, through the case law.

2.55 Title to, and tenancies of, immovable property in a Member State: Article 24(1)

Article 24 of the Regulation goes on to provide:

> *The following courts shall have exclusive jurisdiction, regardless of domicile:*
> *(1) in proceedings which have as their object rights in rem in immovable property or tenancies of immovable property, the courts of the Member State in which the property is situated. However, in proceedings which have as their object tenancies of immovable property concluded for temporary private use for a maximum period of six consecutive months, the courts of the Member State in which the defendant is domiciled shall also have jurisdiction, provided that the tenant is a natural person and that the landlord and tenant are domiciled in the same Member State.*

In the original version of this provision in the Brussels Convention, this rule was limited to what now appears as the first sentence of the Article; the second sentence was added in 1990.[361] In some intuitive, fundamental, sense, disputes concerning title to land, or tenancy law, belong in, and only in, the courts of the State in which the land is situated. However, as the European Union has legislative power to impose exclusive jurisdiction only on the courts of Member States, Article 24(1), as with the rest of Article 24, is confined to immovable property in Member States. The European Court has held that some at least of the concepts used in this Article bear an autonomous interpretation or have a uniform meaning, but it has generally held that this uniform meaning is narrow,[362] so as not to call into question the primacy of the rule in Article 4, that a defendant shall be sued in the courts of the Member State in which he has a domicile.

---

360 C-144/10 *Berliner Verkehrsbetriebe v. JP Morgan Chase Bank NA* [2011] ECR I-3961.
361 Its effect is dealt with at para. 2.61, below.
362 C-115/88 *Reichert v. Dresdner Bank (No 1)* [1990] ECR I-27.

2.56 Proceedings having as their object rights *in rem* in immovable property

Proceedings have as their object rights *in rem* in immovable property if they are brought to determine that the claimant has a title to immovable property which is good against the whole world.[363] By contrast, proceedings do not have as their object rights *in rem* where the claimant asserts that he is entitled to have such a right transferred to and vested in him. Proceedings do not have as their object rights *in rem* where the claimant claims to have a right *in personam* against the defendant, even though this existing and vested right would also be enforceable against third parties, and even though its enforcement would result in his becoming the proprietor of a right *in rem*: this conclusion follows from the decision of the Court in *Webb v. Webb*,[364] and although it may need to be reconsidered,[365] it is still reliable. It may also be that the claimant must show that his entitlement derives from rules of land law properly so called: this may follow from *Webb* as well as from the decision in *Reichert v. Dresdner Bank*.[366]

Both aspects of the rule – the meaning of 'having as their object' and 'right *in rem*' – were dealt with in *Webb v. Webb*. An English father had conveyed land in the south of France to his English son. Though the father had paid for the land and for its subsequent maintenance out of his own pocket, title had been conveyed into the name of the son. In due course the father demanded the re-conveyance of legal title to the land. He commenced proceedings in England for a declaration that the son held the land for him on resulting trust, and for an order that the son, as bare trustee, re-convey the land. The son disputed the jurisdiction of the English court, contending that the claim brought by the father had as its object rights *in rem* in French land, and that, in consequence, it fell within the exclusive jurisdiction of the courts of France. The European Court rejected the son's analysis of the matter, with the result that the proceedings were properly brought in England, where the son had a domicile.[367]

Two arguments advanced by the son were separately rejected by the Court. In the first place, the son argued that as the father was seeking to obtain legal title to the land, the proceedings which he had brought had legal title to the land as their object. But the Court considered the litigation to show that the father did *not* have legal title to the land, and therefore that the proceedings did not have a right *in rem*, as their object. Proceedings may be regarded as having such rights as their object only where the claimant asserts that he has such rights already[368] and seeks relief on the basis of that vested right.

In the second place, and focusing on equitable title to the land, the son argued that the father was relying on and seeking to enforce his existing right as sole beneficiary of a bare trust of the land: he was claiming to be equitable owner of the land and was claiming relief on the basis of that equitable right. No doubt it was correct to say that the proceedings had this equitable right as their object. But the Court observed that equitable rights were not rights *in rem*, for equity operates *in personam*, and rights *in personam* are not rights *in rem*.

---

363 A claim to recover land which one claims one *does* already own will therefore be within the Article: *Re Hayward* [1997] Ch 45.

364 C-294/92, [1994] ECR I-1717. For further comment, see (1994) 110 LQR 526, (1994) 14 YEL 563. For the earlier English proceedings, see [1991] 1 WLR 1410, [1992] ILPr 374.

365 C-438/12 *Weber v. Weber* EU:C:2014:212, [2015] 2 WLR 213 (though there is no sign that the Court intended to cast any doubt on the decision in *Webb*).

366 C-115/88, [1990] ECR I-27.

367 It is difficult to see what the son sought to achieve by his challenge to the jurisdiction, except to irritate his father, which may be all the explanation one needs.

368 *Cf Re Hayward* [1997] Ch 45.

Even a bundle of rights *in personam* is, on this view, no more than a number of individual rights *in personam*.

The reasoning is not especially convincing, even if the result is not indefensible. The general point in its support is that the interpretation favoured by the Court will mean that the scope of Article 24(1) is narrow: it will not be enough just to make a passing reference to 'title to land' in order to invoke this exclusive jurisdictional rule. One then turns to the two aspects of *Webb*. So far as the first explanation is concerned, one may accept that proceedings do not have as their object rights *in rem* if existing and vested rights *in rem* are not relied on as such as the legal foundation for the claim made, but are sought to be acquired as the goal of, and after, the proceedings,[369] or (to put it another way) are the *objet* of the proceedings, the end the proceedings have in view, but are not the *cause* of the proceedings, the facts and matters relied on as the basis of the proceedings.[370] Even so, it is surprising that the *objet* of the proceedings is not that which the proceedings have as their object.

But the second explanation is more difficult. The proposition that the claim made by the father, relying on his existing equitable title to the land, had as its object only a right *in personam* is debatable. To be sure, there is an historical sense[371] in which equity operates only *in personam*. As a matter of legal history, such sophistry allowed the medieval Chancellor to outflank the rules of the common law and to make orders more in keeping with the demands of conscience. And as another matter of legal history, if the recalcitrant defendant failed to comply with the Chancellor's order, he could be committed to prison, and his body harshly treated, until he submitted to the will of the court: measures of constraint operated *in personam* in a particularly direct, occasionally gruesome, sense. But it would be surprising if this shone a light on the interpretation of the Brussels I Regulation. The equitable owner of land has a claim to the land which can be enforced against everybody,[372] against all third parties, save for the *bona fide* purchaser of a legal estate in the land for value without notice or his modernised equivalent; the idea that he has a single right *in personam*, or has a bundle of individual rights *in personam*, but nothing more, is not persuasive. If it were to be argued that the potential defeasibility of equitable title prevents the right being seen as one *in rem*, this also is unsustainable: a legal owner may also be defeated by (for example) the claims of an adverse possessor. All that being said, though, it must be admitted that weakness in the reasoning in *Webb* may not be the fault of the Court. English lawyers tend to use the expression '*in personam*' with only an imprecise idea of what they actually mean by it; doubtless they have no idea at all what a foreign lawyer might take them to be meaning to mean. But the result of *Webb* is that only a claimant who asserts that he is already holder of legal title to the land (or of a legal interest in it) brings proceedings which have as their object rights *in rem* in immovable property.

In *Land Oberösterreich v. ČEZ AS*,[373] the Court explained that proceedings which have as their object rights *in rem* in immovable property were those which 'seek to determine

---

369 For acceptance of this argument in the analogous case of what is now Art. 24(2), see *Newtherapeutics Ltd v. Katz* [1991] Ch 226; *Grupo Torras SA v. Sheikh Fahad Mohammed Al-Sabah* [1996] 1 Lloyd's Rep 7.

370 See C-406/92 *The Tatry* [1994] ECR I-5439 for this distinction which is implicit in Art. 29 of the Regulation; see further below, para. 2.265.

371 For the analysis, see Yale, *Lord Nottingham's Two Treatises* (CUP, 1965) at 7–45.

372 *Cf* a case where the claim really is only available against a single individual (claim for an occupation rent brought by legal owner against occupant of land): C-292/93 *Lieber v. Gobel* [1994] ECR I-2535.

373 C-343/04, [2006] ECR I-4557.

the extent, content, ownership or possession of immovable property, or the existence of other rights *in rem* therein, and to provide the holders of those rights with protection for the powers which attach to their interest'.[374] This may have encouraged the claimant, bringing proceedings to restrain a neighbouring landowner from committing a nuisance and so interfering with the claimant's occupation of its land, to suppose that its claim was one which sought protection for the powers which attached to its ownership of land in Austria; but the Court disagreed. According to it, the proceedings were not brought on a dispute about title to land;[375] the claimant's right of ownership of land was of marginal significance; the fact that the claimant was a landowner would have no influence on the issues which would need to be investigated and determined at trial;[376] and, in fact, there were two parcels of land – those of claimant and defendant, as there will usually be in a nuisance case – which might be thought to point to the court with jurisdiction, which would be inconvenient.[377] The reasoning does not do justice to the result. It may be that the Court was not willing to allow an Austrian court to summon the operators of a Czech nuclear power plant and to order the plant to be closed down; and that the rule of jurisdiction relied on was approached in that light. A less challenging view would be that unless the action is one to be determined by the application of principles of land law of the Member State in which the property is, it will fall outside Article 24(1). The claim against ČEZ would not depend on rules of Austrian land law, as distinct from rules of Austrian law about delict more generally, or Czech law; it did not fall within what is now Article 24(1). The point is developed below.

2.57 Claims based on personal obligations relating to land

It follows naturally from the decision in *Webb* that proceedings to enforce or to dissolve, or otherwise deal with, a contract for the sale of land do not fall within Article 24(1).[378] According to Schlosser,[379] the personal character of the action, the fact that it is an action against a vendor to enforce or to annul the obligations of a contract, is decisive. It overshadows the fact that in English law, and in some other systems as well, the purchaser under a contract for the sale of land may be regarded, prior to completion and in some sense at least, as the equitable owner of the land.[380] *Webb v. Webb* means that as the obligation relied on by the claimant is one owed to him *in personam*, proceedings based on it do not have a right *in rem* as their object. Accordingly, in *Gaillard v. Chekili*,[381] proceedings brought to dissolve a contract for the sale of land were held to fall outside what is now Article 24(1).

---

374 At [29], citing its earlier decision in C-115/88 *Reichert v. Dresdner Bank (No 1)* [1990] ECR I-27.

375 As if that proved anything: this was the very characterisation of proceedings falling within Art. 22(1) which had been proposed by the son in *Webb v. Webb* and rejected by the Court.

376 At [30]–[34].

377 It seems to have been supposed at [36]–[38] that this disqualified the case from coming within Art. 22(1); it was not suggested that this would have meant instead that there were two courts with exclusive jurisdiction.

378 This is without prejudice to the possibility of combining it with an action falling within Art. 24(1) pursuant to Art. 8(4) of Regulation 1215/2012.

379 [1979] OJ C59/71, [171].

380 The vendor holds the legal estate as trustee for the purchaser-beneficiary. Although the beneficiary is therefore equitable owner, this is indissociable from his status as contractual purchaser, entitled to obtain a decree of specific performance. His status as owner is therefore coloured by his personal rights against the vendor.

381 C-518/98, [2001] ECR I-2771. The action was for rescission for non-performance and damages for consequential loss.

It also follows that a claim for a declaration that (for example) the family home is held on constructive trust for the non-registered spouse or partner is not within Article 24(1). The claim in such proceedings seeks to establish only an equitable claim to a share in property arising from an agreement, and in any event does not depend on rules of law peculiar to land.[382] A claim that a person under disability should be given permission to dispose of land in his name does not depend on rules of land law, but is wholly based on the law of personal capacity.[383] And it may also be thought to follow that claims brought in respect of a tort or other non-contractual obligation which relates to land, which are based on the personal obligation of the tortfeasor not to commit a wrong and the right of the claimant not to be wronged, are for the same reason outside Article 24(1). This would be consistent with *Land Oberösterreich v. ČEZ*, and might be thought to offer a smoother path to the conclusion actually reached by the court.

If proceedings brought to rescind a contract for the sale of land are not within Article 24(1), it might be supposed that proceedings which seek to determine whether a pre-emptive right to purchase land was enforceable against a proprietor, or which seek a determination that it is not enforceable,[384] would also fall outside the Article. But in *Weber v. Weber*[385] the Court proceeded on the basis – it is not clear how hard the contrary was seriously pressed – that such proceedings had a right *in rem* in German land as their object. The explanation offered was that the exercise of the right of pre-emption in that case would have had effect on all the parties involved in the proceedings, but that was precisely true in *Webb v. Webb*, where it counted for nothing. It is correct that the litigation in *Weber* was designed to settle which of two persons was entitled to the land and to be registered as proprietor of it, but that also had been true, and irrelevant, in *Webb*. The Court in *Weber* appears to have accepted that the registration of a right of pre-emption meant that it could be enforced against the world, but English land law produces the same result, not always by means of registration.[386] In the end, the Court may have been swayed by the sensible perception that a dispute over the right to be owner of land in Germany should not be determined by the courts of Italy. That is all very well, but it does not fit the pattern of the law which had been laid down beforehand, and that is a problem.

The decision in *Webb* was used[387] to explain why a trustee in bankruptcy, bringing proceedings in England against the bankrupt and his wife as registered proprietors of an estate in Portugal, was able to obtain an order that they take the steps which were required to enable the trustee to sell the land with vacant possession. The trustee's claim against the proprietors, the *jus actionis*, was a personal right that they co-operate with him; it was not based on a right which sought or was designed to be enforceable against third parties. Even so, if the trustee was to be seen as bringing the proceedings to perfect a title which he had, as a matter of English law, already acquired on becoming trustee in bankruptcy, it is less easy to see why the action was not one brought by the

---

382 *Cf Prazic v. Prazic* [2006] EWCA Civ 497, [2006] 2 FLR 1125.

383 C-386/12 *Re Schneider* EU:C:2013:663, [2014] Fam 80, though the issue of personal capacity removes the case from the material scope of the Regulation in any event.

384 It cannot make any difference, in principle at least (as explained below), whether the principal object of the proceedings is presented to the court in positive or negative form.

385 C-438/12, EU:C:2014:212, [2015] 2 WLR 213.

386 The Land Registration Act 2002 provides for the registration of legal titles and some interests; protection of the priority of interests which are not registrable is by other means specified in the act.

387 *Ashurst v. Pollard* [2001] Ch 595.

owner of land, to give effect to and vindicate his rights of ownership.[388] On the other hand, the reasoning used to justify the trustee's claim would presumably have been just the same if the property had been registered shares in a Portuguese company, or a yacht in a marina on the Algarve; and in this respect the case did not raise any issues of land law, properly so called.

2.58 A dispute which requires the application of principles of land law

The cases discussed above appear to demonstrate that proceedings are unlikely to fall within Article 24(1) unless they depend for their resolution on principles of land law. The principle may not be rigid and absolute, but it does reflect a noticeable theme in the judgments of the Court. From this rather different perspective, *Webb* and *Land Oberösterreich* make perfect sense. In *Webb*, the rules which would have been relied on were not rules peculiar to land law: had the property in question been shares in a French bank, or a yacht lying at Cap d'Antibes, the substantive arguments advanced by the claimant against his son would have been exactly the same: it may have been a case about land, but it was not a case about land law. Likewise in *Land Oberösterreich*, where the issues were about cross-border nuisance and the effect of licences to carry out industrial operations, the case was about land, but it was not about land law. By contrast, the litigation in *Weber v. Weber* might well have been seen as a dispute about the nature and effect (and therefore the consequences) of an interest in land: it was a land law case, not just a case about land.

This approach to Article 24(1) is consistent with *Reichert v. Dresdner Bank (No 1)*.[389] A bank, creditor of a father, brought an action in the French courts for a declaration that the gift and transfer of land in France by father to son was ineffective against the creditor bank. Although the bank did not seek to establish that title to the land was vested in it, it applied for an order which would reduce the title of the registered proprietor, the son, from absolute to partially defeasible. To achieve this, the bank relied on its personal right against the father.[390] The substantive right on which the bank relied was not specifically part of French land law, but was instead part of the law of credit and security: a form of action available to all potential creditors, in respect of disposals of all forms of property in potential fraud of creditors. Its judicial examination did not require the special land law expertise of the courts of the *situs*. The Court considered that the claim did not fall within the Article.[391] This supports the view that Article 24(1) aims to apply to land law disputes, properly so called, and if the dispute does not raise issues of land law it is less likely to be within the Article.[392]

It may seem odd to use the source and nature of the rules of substantive national law which will be applied by the court at the place of the land to determine jurisdiction

---

388 The property of the bankrupt vests in the trustee by operation of law: Insolvency Act 1986, s. 306.

389 C-115/88, [1990] ECR I-27. Subsequent proceedings, in C-261/90 *Reichert v. Dresdner Bank (No 2)* [1992] ECR I-2149, are dealt with elsewhere.

390 To similar effect, see *Jarrett v. Barclays Bank plc* [1999] QB 1. A claim against a creditor who provided credit for the purchase of a time-share interest in land, and who was liable under the Consumer Credit Act 1974, ss 75 and 56(2), for misrepresentations made by the seller, did not have as its object a right *in rem*; it had as its object the personal liability for misrepresentation of the creditor.

391 Similar reasoning led to its exclusion from what is now Art. 7(2): para. 2.187, below.

392 *Ashurst v. Pollard* [2001] Ch 595. See also C-73/04 *Klein v. Rhodos Management Ltd* [2005] ECR I-8667, [17].

according to a rule whose elements have a uniform definition. But it can be defended. The rational policy which justifies the Article is that local courts alone should determine land law disputes properly so called, and tenancy disputes, considered below, because land law and tenancy law do not travel well. In many cases, a registrar has to be called up to amend the public register of titles. The true basis of Article 24(1) should be, it is therefore submitted, that it covers disputes where the court is called upon to resolve disputes as to title to land in a Member State, or to adjudicate upon the relative enforce-ability of claims of title to land, by the application of rules of local land law. Upon that basis, *Reichert (No 1)* probably failed both criteria[393] and therefore fell outside what is now Article 24(1).

2.59 Proceedings having as their object tenancies of immovable property

The expression 'having as their object... tenancies of immovable property' will bear an autonomous meaning. However, there is no decision of the European Court which gives a comprehensive definition of 'tenancies'. The jurisprudence has instead dealt with the question whether the proceedings have such a relationship as their object, or their prin-cipal object.[394] In *Jarrett v. Barclays Bank plc*,[395] the Court of Appeal suggested that if the relationship fell within the English definition of a tenancy, which requires the grant of exclusive possession for a definite and not indeterminate period of time,[396] it would satisfy the autonomous definition, whatever that was. As a temporary rule of thumb this is work-able; however, the Court of Appeal did not go on to suggest that unless the relationship fell within the English definition of a tenancy it could not fall within what is now Article 24(1). No case has addressed how this expression might relate to claims involving licences to occupy land; but on the footing that the lease/licence distinction, and the degree of protection given to licences, is in substance a matter of land law, proceedings which have as their object licences to occupy land should, for the purposes of the Regulation, and despite the restrictive interpretation of Article 24(1), probably be treated as though they were tenancies.[397]

In *Klein v. Rhodos Management Ltd*,[398] German claimants had quickly repented of their rash decision to join a 'time-share' scheme, operated in respect of a Greek holiday devel-opment by an entity from the Isle of Man. The contract of club membership gave them the right to occupy one of many flats in the complex for the thirteenth week of every calendar year. When they brought proceedings in Germany, the defendant contended that what is now Article 24(1) required the proceedings, which sought the avoidance[399] of the membership contract and the return of the money paid, to be brought in Greece. The

---

393 The right being relied upon was a personal one against the father alone.

394 C-144/10 *Berliner Verkehrsbetriebe v. JP Morgan Chase Bank NA* [2011] ECR I-3961 (a decision on what is now Art. 24(2), but of general application within Art. 24).

395 [1999] QB 1.

396 See *Street v. Mountford* [1985] AC 809.

397 Time-share interests were held to be capable of being tenancies for this purpose in *Jarrett v. Barclays Bank plc* [1999] QB 1. The decision in C-73/04 *Klein v. Rhodos Management Ltd* [2005] ECR I-8667 does not directly contradict this, as the package of rights in that case was complex and, insofar as they allowed the right to occupy land, they did not relate to a particular parcel of land.

398 C-73/04, [2005] ECR I-8667.

399 The fact that the claim was brought to secure the annulment of the contract did not prevent the application of the Article; the fact that the contract was not, or not principally, about a tenancy did prevent its application.

Court dismissed the defendant's jurisdictional objection. Not only were the occupation rights contained in the contractual package for club membership a minor part of the whole, economically speaking, but also, the contract of membership did not entitle or confine the claimants to a single or specific flat.[400] That all pointed to the conclusion that the proceedings did not have a tenancy as their object. Beyond that, the definition of the term awaits further clarification.

When it comes to whether the proceedings have the alleged tenancy as their object, the jurisprudence offers more guidance. In *Sanders v. Van der Putte*,[401] a dispute concerning an alleged agreement to take over the goodwill and running of a florist's business in a rented shop was held to fall outside what is now Article 24(1) of Regulation 1215/2012, on the basis that, although tenancy disputes should be assigned to the courts of the *situs* of the tenanted land, those arising, or equally capable of arising, out of other commercial contracts did not need to be. There was a tenancy of immovable property, but the proceedings were not based on the tenancy, as distinct from the commercial business conducted from the demised premises, and as a result they did not have the tenancy as their object. In *Rösler v. Rottwinkel*,[402] a dispute arose from the letting of a holiday cottage. The Court held that whereas landlord and tenant disputes, extending to actions for possession, repair, rent and utility charges, fell under what is now Article 24(1) of the Regulation, more remote or ancillary matters, such as loss of travel expenses, or of enjoyment, did not. In other words, litigation founded on issues essentially or naturally connected with the relationship of landlord and tenant is comprehended by Article 24(1); those not so founded will not be. This same reasoning led to the conclusion that proceedings brought by a landlord against a tenant who had lived like an animal and made a ruin of the premises demised, and which were brought by the landlord to recover the cost of cleaning and refurbishment, fell within the Article.[403]

The requirement that the usual obligations of the tenancy form the central core, or perhaps the principal economic element, of the proceedings also explains why Article 24(1) will not be engaged in certain kinds of holiday letting. In *Hacker v. Euro-Relais GmbH*[404] a travel agent had sold a holiday package which included the use of a holiday cottage[405] in Denmark. The disappointed client wished to sue the travel agent in Germany, where both were domiciled, for relief resulting from the fact that the house was smaller than had been advertised and that the holiday had, therefore, been spoiled. The Court confirmed that the Article did in principle apply to short holiday lettings,[406] but that it did not apply in the context of a contract for a holiday package, where accommodation formed only a part of the package of services provided. Though the decision was motivated by a desire to restrict

---

400 At [24].

401 73/77, [1977] ECR 2383.

402 241/83, [1985] ECR 99. It had been argued, following, that short holiday lets were outside the scope of what was then Art. 16(1) of the Brussels Convention, but the Court refused to accept the argument. Note that the amended Art. 8(4) may allow an action based on ancillary matters to be combined with an action under what is now Art. 24(1); para. 2.244, below.

403 C-8/98 *Dansommer A/S v. Götz* [2000] ECR I-393. A suggestion in *Wellington Pub Co plc v. Hancock* [2009] 3 EGLR 45, that an action by a landlord against the tenant's financial guarantor fell within Art. 24(1), seems plainly wrong.

404 C-280/90, [1992] ECR I-1111.

405 Which it did not own. But the contract was made between Hacker and Euro-Relais GmbH; it was not doubted that this fact was irrelevant to the potential application of the Article: *sed quaere*.

406 Thereby confirming *Rösler v. Rottwinkel*. But now see the second sentence of Art. 24(1).

the material scope of the Article, the actual reasoning was not as convincing as it might have been, for the actual complaint was confined to the inadequacy of the accommodation aspect of the contract. But the claim was for damages for misrepresentation and for disappointment. That would not require the application of principles of tenancy law. It was therefore uncontroversial that it fell outside the scope of what is now Article 24(1), for the reasons given in *Rösler*, and deduced from *Reichert (No 1)*.

The result of *Klein v. Rhodos Management Ltd*,[407] which was discussed above, is certainly consistent with this. Of the total fee paid by the claimants for club membership, the Court calculated that only one-sixth of it was paid for the use of an apartment.[408] The right of accommodation, whatever its legal nature, was a minor part of the benefit supplied to the claimants, and as a result, the claim could not fall within the Article, any more than it did in *Hacker*. Moreover, the benefits supplied went further[409] and less far[410] than a tenancy would have done; the result was that the proceedings did not have the tenancy as their object. It is also possible, though it is not clear, that the Court took the view that as the claim for repayment was predicated on the contention that the contract was void, the basic assumption on which Article 24(1) is founded, that there was a dispute as to a matter of local land law, was not sustained by the facts.[411]

2.60 Proceedings in which Article 24(1) is prompted by the defence, not the claim

Some cases have been excluded from what is now Article 24(1) because the portion of the claim which has as its object rights *in rem* in, or tenancies of, immovable property in a Member State, is not the principal part of the claim. If, therefore, a matter within the scope of Article 24(1) arises only incidentally, Article 24(1) has no application. Although it has been noted that this test will not always be clear and easy to apply, it makes sense in principle, for otherwise a claim in which a question of title to land arises only incidentally would fall under the exclusive jurisdiction of Article 24(1)[412] in circumstances which may go far beyond the rationale of that provision. But the point needs to be treated with care.

A question arises if the claim is not brought by someone who claims to have a right *in rem* in, or a tenancy of, land in a Member State, but in answer to it the defendant pleads that, because he was proprietor of the land, he was entitled to act as he did, say by ejecting the claimant as a trespasser. The proceedings brought by the claimant, for example for damages for assault, do not have as their object rights *in rem* in, or a tenancy of, immovable property, but the defence may well do so. The question is whether Article 24(1) applies in such a case to give exclusive jurisdiction to the courts of the *situs*. If the answer is that it may do, one will also need to ask whether the case is one in which the defendant's title is subject to serious contention. And it is necessary to observe that the proper application

---

407 C-73/04, [2005] ECR I-8667.

408 At [18]–[20]. The actual basis for this conclusion is not clear from the judgment, but it does tend to show what a rotten proposition these arrangements often are.

409 Other services were made available at the complex.

410 The right of occupation in the thirteenth week of each year was not related to a specific apartment.

411 See the judgment at [17].

412 And the obligation to deny recognition to a judgment which violated it.

of the Regulation cannot be called into question by the fact that a defence to proceedings seeking a declaration of non-liability may have as their object rights *in rem* in land. Not all defences are alike. A preference for a restrictive construction of Article 24(1) might suggest that such a case would not fall within Article 24(1): the claim advanced does not have as its object a right *in rem* in immovable property. But if the purpose of Article 24(1) is to ensure that genuine questions of land law, properly so called, are resolved in the courts for the *situs* of the land, then the cases in which Article 24(1) should apply will not be limited to cases in which the issue of land law is raised by the claim rather than the defence, not least because of the declaratory proceedings referred to above.

It is tentatively suggested that the court should look at the defence and ask this question: suppose the substance of this defence had been formulated as the basis for a claim for declaratory relief, would Article 24(1) have applied to it? If the answer to that notional question is affirmative, the court should conclude that the proceedings fall principally within Article 24(1), and will be within the exclusive jurisdiction of the Member State indicated by Article 24(1). Though this has the plain disadvantage that a court which appeared to have jurisdiction over the proceedings when the claim was issued discovers that it does not once the defence is set out, this must be set against the prospect that the courts of other Member States would refuse to recognise a judgment given in proceedings in which, as it seems to them, the adjudicating court acted in conflict with Section 6 of Chapter II. After all, Article 24 speaks of 'proceedings which have as their object', not 'claims which have as their object'.

Article 24(1) is not rendered inapplicable simply because the defendant denies the existence of the tenancy, or the right *in rem*, claimed as the object of the proceedings.[413] As in any other case in which the jurisdictional fact which would give the court jurisdiction is challenged by the defendant, the court must satisfy itself, to its own standard of civil proof on such questions, that it has jurisdiction to hear the case.[414] No more is required of it.

2.61 Short private lettings: concurrent exclusive jurisdiction

The obvious inconvenience of requiring, for example, parties domiciled in the United Kingdom to litigate against each other in Bulgaria or Greece if there is a dispute concerning, for example, non-payment of rent for a fortnight's letting of a holiday flat, led to the legislative reversal of the decision in *Rösler v. Rottwinkel*.[415] Though the precise terms in which the amendment was formulated varied as between the Brussels and Lugano Conventions, the Regulation now confers additional exclusive jurisdiction on the courts of the Member State in which the defendant is domiciled if the claimant is also domiciled there and the tenant is a natural person. A short letting for these purposes is a tenancy of immovable property concluded for temporary private use for a maximum period of six consecutive months, which will cover the average summer holiday. Its potential

---

413 158/87 *Scherrens v. Maenhout* [1988] ECR 3791. This decision is also authoritative on questions relating to a tenancy of land straddling the border of Member States, which is hardly a major social problem in the United Kingdom (even though it has a theoretical possibility of occurring across the border between Northern Ireland and the Irish Republic).

414 38/81 *Effer v. Kantner* [1982] ECR 825; C-68/93 *Shevill v. Presse Alliance SA* [1995] ECR I-415. That means, in England, to the standard of a good arguable case: *Canada Trust Co v. Stolzenberg (No 2)* [2002] 1 AC 1.

415 See above, para. 2.59.

application to time-shares[416] may be problematic, as each period of occupation is usually less than six months, but the contractual arrangement is designed to last for many years. However, a contractual arrangement which entitled the occupant to two weeks' accommodation every year for 20 years would not appear to fall within the wording of the second sentence of this provision.

The jurisdiction conferred by this provision is also exclusive, with the consequence that there will be concurrent or alternative exclusive jurisdictions.[417] In the event of there being a situation of *lis alibi pendens* as between them, Article 31 of Regulation 1215/2012 will give exclusive jurisdiction to the court first seised.

2.62 Immovable property in the United Kingdom

Article 24(1) gives international jurisdiction to the courts of a Member State, but not to the courts for a particular place within that Member State. Accordingly, where the land in question is within the United Kingdom, the Regulation gives exclusive jurisdiction only to the courts of the United Kingdom. It is therefore necessary, as a matter of internal United Kingdom law, to allocate national jurisdiction to the separate law districts which comprise the United Kingdom.

In relation to Regulation 44/2001, section 16(1) of, and Schedule 4 to, the 1982 Act, as amended,[418] allocate jurisdiction to the part of the United Kingdom in which the land is situated. The original textual version was amended to harmonise it with the provision for short private lettings.[419] As will be explained in greater detail below, the subject-matter scope of Article 11(a) of Schedule 4 will be interpreted as being the same as Article 24(1) of the Regulation.[420]

2.63 Immovable property in a non–Member State

The discussion of how the Regulation might still make a contribution to the issues which arise when proceedings have as their object rights *in rem* in or tenancies of immovable property in a non-Member State will be found below.[421] The apparent silence of the Regulation on this issue seems likely to proceed from the fact that the Regulation cannot dictate the jurisdiction of a non-Member State. But if an English court has no jurisdiction to adjudicate in proceedings which have as their object the tenancy of French land, it would be most surprising to be told that the result was otherwise, and they did have jurisdiction and could be required to adjudicate in proceedings which sought to establish and enforce legal title to land in China or Peru.

---

416 If these create tenancies, which is debatable.

417 Jenard and Möller [1990] OJ C189/75, [52].

418 As amended by Civil Jurisdiction and Judgments Order 2001, SI 2001/3929. The new rule appears as r. 11(a) of Sch. 4 to the 1982 Act (as inserted by SI 2001/3929, Sch. 2, para. 4).

419 SI 2001/3929, Sch. 2, para. 4, discussed in greater detail in this chapter under Q16.

420 This follows from the wording of s. 16 of the 1982 Act and the decision in *Kleinwort Benson Ltd v. Glasgow City Council* [1999] 1 AC 153, and *Agnew v. Länsförsäkringsbolagens AB* [2001] 1 AC 223. As a result, there will be no real scope for an argument that the reasoning in C-294/92 *Webb v. Webb* [1994] ECR I-1717 should be denied application within the intra-United Kingdom scheme for allocation of jurisdiction.

421 In fact what is said in this paragraph applies equally to the other rules of Art. 24(2), but at this point it is said once, not five times.

2.64 Companies with their seat in a Member State: Article 24(2)

Article 24 of the Regulation goes on to provide that:

The following courts shall have exclusive jurisdiction, regardless of domicile:
(2) in proceedings which have as their object the validity of the constitution, the nullity or the dissolution of companies or other legal persons, or associations of natural or legal persons, or the validity of the decisions of their organs, the courts of the Member State in which the company, legal person or association has its seat. In order to determine that seat, the court shall apply its rules of private international law.

2.65 General

Article 24(2) applies to certain proceedings brought in respect of companies and partnerships;[422] it may also extend to other unincorporated associations such as clubs. But the question of which proceedings fall within its scope is not as plain as may appear at first sight. Though the original Article 16(2) of the Brussels Convention had not been worded quite as clearly as the Regulation now is, the English courts had held[423] that it required the *validity* of the decisions, rather than just the decisions themselves, of the company's organs to form the object of the action brought, which in turn may have required the principal subject matter of the proceedings to be identified.[424]

However that may have been, the position under the Regulation has been clarified by the addition of the words 'the validity of' before the reference to 'the decisions of their organs'. It follows that if the proceedings are founded on a dispute about the constitutionality or regularity of internal company procedures, such as the validity or invalidity of the appointment of directors, the composition of the board and so forth, Article 24(2) should be engaged. Issues of internal corporate management and governance are most sensibly determined by the courts of the seat applying their own company law. No other court is likely to be able to make a good job of what may be a complicated legal task; no other court is likely to be able to impose the remedy which will meet the needs of the case. By contrast, the Article does not apply where the legal proceedings which are brought against the corporation concede that the corporation had the legal power to make the decision of which complaint is made, with the consequence that the validity of its decision is not in question, but complaint is made that the company, or a corporate officer,[425] should not have exercised its powers in the way in which it did.[426] It has been held[427] that proceedings which seek to challenge or establish the legality of the composition of the board of directors fall within the Article, for this is an inevitable precondition to the validity of the decision of this particular corporate organ; and even if this were to involve a slight loosening of the

---

422 Schlosser [1979] OJ C59/71, [162]; see also *Phillips v. Symes* [2002] 1 WLR 853, whether the partnership was created formally or informally, and as including the winding up of its affairs.

423 *Newtherapeutics Ltd v. Katz* [1992] Ch 226; see Kaye (1991) 10 CJQ 220. But in *Grupo Torras SA v. Sheikh Fahad Mohammed Al-Sabah* [1996] 1 Lloyd's Rep 7, the Court of Appeal doubted the significance of the distinction drawn by Knox J in *Newtherapeutics Ltd v. Katz*. Stuart Smith LJ had expressed the view that, even if it was the *validity* of the decisions which was in issue, this expression should be interpreted so as to include within it 'consideration of the meaning and effect of decisions of the relevant organs'. See also *FKI Engineering Ltd v. Dewind Holdings Ltd* [2007] EWHC 72 (Comm), [2007] ILPr 17, affirmed on other grounds, [2008] EWCA Civ 316, [2009] 1 All ER (Comm) 118.

424 *Cf* para. 2.60 (in the context of Art. 24(1)), above.

425 *Chaudhary v. Bhatter* [2009] EWCA Civ 1176, [2010] 2 All ER 1031.

426 C-372/07 *Hassett v. South Eastern Health Board* [2008] ECR I-7403.

427 *Speed Investments Ltd v. Formula One Holdings Ltd (No 2)* [2004] EWCA Civ 1512, [2005] 1 WLR 1936.

interpretation given to Article 24(2), it is rational that such issues of company law should be resolved by the courts and in accordance with the law of the seat of the company. The law, at this point, probably reflects the sense that, in the legal systems of most Member States, matters of corporate indoor management and general corporate constitutionality belong in, and only in, the courts of the seat.

2.66 The issue of corporate validity as the principal element in the proceedings

It is now reasonably well established that Article 24(2) will not apply if the issue of the validity of an act of the corporation is not the issue with which the proceedings are principally concerned. This appears from a combination of *JP Morgan Chase Bank NA v. Berliner Verkehrsbetriebe*[428] and *Berliner Verkehrsbetriebe v. JP Morgan Chase Bank NA.*[429] In the English proceedings, a German corporation was sued on account of its failure to pay sums due under a contract which it had made. It disputed the jurisdiction of the English court on the ground that, as it alleged, the making of the contract was *ultra vires* the corporation; and that as a result, though the contract was void, the English court lacked jurisdiction over the proceedings. The Court of Appeal rejected the challenge to the jurisdiction on the ground that it was required to identify the principal issue raised in the proceedings, and this was the enforceability of the contract rather than the acts of the corporation.[430] While the English proceedings were pending at first instance the corporation brought proceedings against the Bank before the German courts, seeking a declaration that the contract was *ultra vires* the corporation, together with various additional or consequential relief. It argued that what is now Article 24(2) gave the German court jurisdiction,[431] but the European Court rejected the contention. According to the European Court, the validity of the decision of the corporation to make the contract was neither the sole nor the principal subject of the analysis, but was rather merely ancillary to the contract claim. Quite apart from everything else – the fact that Article 24 should have a scope no wider than necessary to meet the purpose of the rule; the fact that an interpretation which would negate the effect of an agreement on jurisdiction will be viewed with particular wariness; the fact that the courts of the seat are best placed to deal with proceedings which are predominantly concerned with issues on which they have the most obvious expertise – this was enough to explain why what is now Article 24(2) had no application to such a case.

2.67 The jurisdictional effect of imperfections in corporate decision-taking

A distinct problem arises when proceedings are brought in which a claim is founded on acts done by those who hold office in the corporation, but who have acted otherwise than

---

428 [2010] EWCA Civ 390, [2012] QB 176. Applied in *Depfa Bank plc v. Provincia di Pisa* [2010] EWHC 1148 (Comm), [2010] ILPr 930; *UBS AG v. Kommunale Wasserwerke Leipzig GmbH* [2010] EWHC 2566 (Comm), [2010] 2 CLC 499.

429 C-144/10, [2011] ECR I-3961.

430 It also confirmed, entirely correctly, that the fact that proceedings had been started in the German court furnished no basis for a contention that the English court should stay its proceedings while the German court made a reference to the European Court. See also *Depfa Bank plc v. Provincia di Pisa* [2012] EWHC 687 (Comm); [2012] ILPr 458.

431 And that as a result the prior English proceedings could be disregarded.

strictly in accordance with what the *lex incorporationis* permits and requires. In the light of the *Berliner Verkehrsbetriebe* decisions, the issue of the validity of the acts of the corporate organ must form the principal subject matter of the proceedings, and the reasoning which was deployed in those cases will apply in this context as well.

Where complaint is made about or against the acts of officers of a corporation, and it is said that those officers have not acted in full and unchallengeable conformity with their powers and the general law, the proceedings will, in some sense, impugn the validity of these acts. The acts themselves may or may not be lawful, and they may or may not bind the corporation; but the question whether this can be said to raise a question of their validity is more difficult. It is, perhaps, to be doubted if the question is not whether the act was valid or invalid, but whether it binds the company: there may be a distinction to be drawn between the *validity* of acts and the *legality* of acts.

A claim that an act purportedly done by the directors was a nullity because it required (and did not have) the prior sanction of a board meeting, could fall within Article 24(2), because it does plainly raise a matter of corporate constitutional law. However, for reasons set out above, it will not do so unless this point arises as the principal element in the proceedings, no matter how they are constituted. As it was earlier explained in *Grupo Torras SA v. Sheikh Fahad Mohammed Al-Sabah*,[432] what is now Article 24(2) confers exclusive jurisdiction to determine questions concerning 'the capacity of the company, the composition and powers of various organs of the company, the formalities and procedures laid down for them, the extent of an individual member's liability for the debts and liabilities of the company, and other matters of that kind'.[433] It does not encompass all disputes between shareholder and company, or officer and company, even if these are inward-looking and do not involve third parties.[434] An allegation that a corporate officer has acted fraudulently and dishonestly, and has thereby defrauded – rather than bound – the company may not bring the subject matter of the proceedings within Article 24(2), for if the validity of acts is not in dispute, Article 24(2) makes no claim to apply. The position is no different if it is *all* the corporate officers, rather than merely some of them, against whom the accusation lies.

Challenges to legal validity of corporate acts will therefore fall under Article 24(2) in some instances but not in others: it depends on both the nature of the imperfection in corporate acting and on the nature of the proceedings themselves. According to the European Court in *Hassett v. South Eastern Health Board*,[435] the application of Article 24(2) is intended to be restrictive and is not meant to swallow up other jurisdictional rules. This is perhaps no surprise, for though it may be correct that one cannot infringe an invalid patent, one can hold a company to an *ultra vires* act. In other words, the invalidity of a patent is more obviously 'what the infringement claim is all about' than it is the case that the invalidity of a corporate act may be said to be 'what the damages claim is all about'.

It is less clear whether the Article applies where proceedings are brought under Part 30 of Companies Act 2006,[436] alleging unfair prejudice to a shareholder in the running of the company and seeking relief in consequence of it. One available form of relief is

---

432 [1996] 1 Lloyd's Rep 7.
433 At 15.
434 *Blue Tropic Ltd v. Chkhartishvili* [2014] EWHC 2243 (Ch), [2014] ILPr 501.
435 C-372/07, [2008] ECR I-7403, [2009] ILPr 479.
436 Replacing Companies Act 1985, s. 459.

a compulsory buy-out of the shares,[437] but alternative forms of relief may include orders altering the company's constitution; it is also common for the petitioner to apply for the company to be wound up on the ground that it is just and equitable for this to be done:[438] for a well-known example of a case in which both forms of relief were sought, one might see *Re Harrods (Buenos Aires) Ltd*.[439] It may be that the nature of the relief sought brings proceedings of this sort within the Article.[440] On the other hand, where altering the constitution of the company, or winding it up on the just and equitable ground, is merely one of the possible remedies, as opposed to a process which is taking place and in the context of which a dispute has arisen, analogy drawn from *Webb v. Webb*[441] would suggest that the proceedings do not have the alteration of the constitution, or a winding up, as their object. The true position may, therefore, be that the court may entertain a petition under Part 30 of the 2006 Act, but that if the company does not have its seat in the United Kingdom, the court may not make an order for its winding up.

It has been held that the power of the court to approve a scheme of arrangement in respect of a (still solvent) company is unaffected by the jurisdictional rules in Chapter II of the Regulation.[442] The court has power, as a matter of substantive law, to approve such a scheme if the company is liable to be wound up. The Brussels I Regulation was designed to apply to claims against defendants, but in the case of a scheme of arrangement, no one was really suing anyone else, and on that basis neither Article 24(2) nor any other provision of the Regulation stood in the way of the exercise of jurisdiction by the court.[443]

2.68 The identification of the seat of the company

To determine where a company has its seat for the purpose of this provision, Article 24(2) instructs a court to apply its rules of private international law. Though the Brussels I Regulation[444] contains an autonomous definition by which to determine where a company, other legal person, or association of natural or legal persons, has its *domicile*, the provisions of Article 24(2) specify that exclusive jurisdiction is conferred upon the courts of the State of the *seat*, not the domicile; and the two must not be confused.[445]

---

437 Companies Act 2006, s. 996(2).

438 Insolvency Act 1986, s. 122(1)(g).

439 [1992] Ch 72.

440 The House of Lords, on the appeal from the decision in the Court of Appeal in *Re Harrods (Buenos Aires) Ltd*, referred questions upon this point to the Court; C-314/92 *Ladenimor SA v. Intercomfinanz SA*. But the case settled and the reference was withdrawn.

441 C-294/92, [1994] ECR I-1717, discussed above in the context of Art. 24(1).

442 See also *JSC BTA Bank v. Ablyazov* [2012] EWHC 2698 (Comm) (application for appointment of a receiver to allow the company to instruct a representative to defend the claim not within Art. 24(2), as it is merely an application made in proceedings in which the company is already being sued in England).

443 *Re Rodenstock GmbH* [2011] EWHC 1104 (Ch), [2011] Bus LR 1245; *Re Primacom Holding GmbH* [2011] EWHC 3746 (Ch), [2013] BCC 201. The practical benefit of this conclusion is plain. On the other hand, the making of a judicial order which has the effect of reducing the legal rights of a person with a claim does look rather like suing that person. It may be for this reason that in *Re Vietnam Shipbuilding Industry Groups* [2013] EWHC 2476 (Ch), the court confirmed that if the matter was one which fell within the material scope of the Brussels I Regulation, the court had (by prorogation) jurisdiction over all the parties concerned. The law cannot be regarded as finally settled, though it seems fair to say that this kind of corporate procedure is not the kind of thing for which the Regulation was obviously devised.

444 Regulation 1215/2012, Art. 63.

445 Note that the definition of domicile in Art. 63 makes references to a 'statutory seat', which is a different concept.

The definition of 'seat', for the purpose of this exclusive jurisdictional rule in Article 24(2) is contained in Civil Jurisdiction and Judgments Order 2001, Schedule 1, paragraph 10.[446] According to it, a company or association has its seat in the United Kingdom if, and only if, it was incorporated or formed under the law of part of the United Kingdom, or its central management and control[447] is exercised in the United Kingdom.[448] A corporation or association has its seat in another Member State only if it was incorporated or formed under the law of that State, or its central management and control is exercised from that State;[449] but it will not have its seat in that Member State if it was incorporated or formed under the law of the United Kingdom, or the courts of the Member State in question would not regard it as having its seat there for the purposes of Article 22(2).[450]

2.69 Company with seat in the United Kingdom

As Article 24(2) of the Regulation allocates international jurisdiction to the courts of the United Kingdom, it is thereafter a matter for the internal law of the United Kingdom to identify the particular law district having such internal or national jurisdiction. According to section 16(1) of, and Schedule 4 to, the 1982 Act, exclusive jurisdiction is given to the part of the United Kingdom in which the company, legal person or association has its seat.[451] It has its seat in a particular part of the United Kingdom if and only if it has its seat in the United Kingdom and was incorporated or formed under the law of that part, or being incorporated or formed under the law of a State other than the United Kingdom, its central management and control is exercised in that part.[452] But if it was incorporated or formed under an enactment forming part of the law of more than one part of the United Kingdom, or under an instrument having effect in the domestic law of more than one part of the United Kingdom, it shall, if it has a registered office, be taken to have its seat in the part of the United Kingdom in which that office is situated, and not in any other part.[453]

2.70 Validity of entries in public registers in Member States: Article 24(3)

Article 24 of the Regulation continues:

> *The following courts shall have exclusive jurisdiction, regardless of domicile:*
> *(3) in proceedings which have as their object the validity of entries in public registers, the courts of the Member State in which the register is kept.*

---

446 As amended by SI 2014/2947, Sch. 2, para. 3(12). This is closely modelled on s. 43 of the 1982 Act, which continues to apply to cases where international jurisdiction is determined by the Brussels or Lugano Conventions, and also where a seat has to be located within one of the parts of the United Kingdom.

447 On central management and control, see *The Deichland* [1990] 1 QB 361; *The Rewia* [1991] 2 Lloyd's Rep 325; *Latchin v. General Mediterranean Holidays SA* [2002] CLC 330; *Royal & Sun Alliance Insurance plc v. MK Digital FZE (Cyprus) Ltd* [2006] EWCA Civ 629, [2006] 2 Lloyd's Rep 110; *Vava v. Anglo America South Africa Ltd* [2013] EWHC 2131 (QB).

448 Paragraph 10(2) of SI 2001/3929, Sch. 1.

449 Paragraph 10(3).

450 Paragraph 10(4).

451 1982 Act, Sch. 4, r. 11(b).

452 1982 Act, s. 43(3). On central management and control, see *The Deichland* [1990] 1 QB 361; *The Rewia* [1991] 2 Lloyd's Rep 325.

453 1982 Act, s. 43(5).

Article 24(3) of the Brussels I Regulation calls for little elaboration. In the context of the original Brussels Convention, Jenard said[454] that what is now Article 24(3) will apply mainly to land registers and commercial registers. In *Re Hayward*[455] it was held that proceedings which sought an order against the registered proprietor of land in Spain, that he take steps to secure the rectification of the entry in the land register, fell within this provision. At first sight, this makes sense: it resembles the view of English law that the place to obtain an order for the rectification of a public register is the courts in the place where that register is kept.[456] However, at second sight, *Re Hayward* poses more of a difficulty. The order applied for was not that the register be rectified, for the land registrar was not party to the proceedings. The application was rather for an order that the defendant be ordered to procure its registration. It might therefore have been argued that, on the basis of an analogy with *Webb v. Webb*, the proceedings did not have as their object the validity of the register as such. Rather, they had as their object the personal obligation of the registered proprietor to apply to the registrar for rectification, which meant that they would fall outside Article 24(3). If it is argued that the reality of the matter was that this was a claim to obtain inscription on the register, the response is that this is exactly the same as the point which was rejected in *Webb v. Webb*.

The true position is made no clearer by the decision in *Ashurst v. Pollard*.[457] In that case, the defendant proprietor was ordered to cooperate with the claimant trustee in bankruptcy in procuring a sale by the latter of the defendant's land in Portugal. It may have seemed plain that a necessary preliminary was that the register of title be amended so that the trustee, already regarded as owner according to the English law of insolvency, could sell the land; but the court barely glanced at what is now Article 24(3) in rejecting the submission that the claim was within the exclusive jurisdiction of the Portuguese courts. As the entire basis for the claim made in the proceedings was that the trustee was already legal owner of the land, and that the register should presumably be rectified to reflect this, the case for saying that what is now Article 24(3), or even Article 24(1), of the Regulation applied to the case was not trivial. However, an analysis which shows that a claim is really one to enforce a personal obligation will always have the capacity to divert attention from this way of looking at the facts.

It has been held that a register maintained by a public limited company which is open to public inspection is a public register for the purposes of this provision.[458]

2.71 Registers in the United Kingdom

As Article 24(3) of the Regulation gives international jurisdiction to the courts of the United Kingdom, it will be a matter of internal United Kingdom law to allocate national jurisdiction to the courts of a part of the United Kingdom. By section 16 of, and Schedule 4 to, the 1982 Act,[459] jurisdiction is conferred on the courts for the part of the United Kingdom in which the register is kept.

---

454 [1979] OJ C59/1, 35.
455 [1997] Ch 45.
456 *International Credit and Investment Co (Overseas) Ltd v. Adham* [1994] 1 BCLC 66 (register of shares).
457 [2001] Ch 595.
458 *Re Fagin's Bookshop plc* [1992] BCLC 118 (register of shareholders).
459 1982 Act, Sch. 4, r. 11(c) (as inserted by the Civil Jurisdiction and Judgments Order 2001, SI 2001/3929, Sch. 2, para. 4).

2.72 Intellectual property rights registered in Member States: Article 24(4)

Article 24 of the Regulation goes on to provide:

> *The following courts shall have exclusive jurisdiction, regardless of domicile:*
> *(4) in proceedings concerned with the registration or validity of patents, trade marks, designs, or other similar rights required to be deposited or registered, the courts of the Member State in which the deposit or registration has been applied for, has taken place or is under the terms of a community instrument or an international convention deemed to have taken place. Without prejudice to the jurisdiction of the European Patent Office under the Convention on the Grant of European Patents, signed at Munich on 5 October 1973, the courts of each Member State shall have exclusive jurisdiction, regardless of domicile, in proceedings concerned with the registration or validity of any European patent granted for that State.*[460]

2.73 General

An easy and straightforward aspect to the exclusive jurisdiction conferred by Article 24(4) is illustrated by *Duijnstee v. Goderbauer*,[461] which shows that the Article is engaged only where the validity of the right in question, or of its registration, is raised as a substantial issue in the proceedings; but the Article is not applicable where the validity or registration is incidental to the proceedings. With this is mind, a claim by an employee that he was entitled to a right or lien over an employer's patent, the validity of which was not in question, did not fall under Article 24(4). The same will be true more generally of disputes over ownership of such rights in which the validity of the right is not contested or disputed.[462] And in a simple action founded on an allegation of infringement, which does not call into question the validity of the right, Article 24(4) will likewise have no part to play.[463] Moreover, the provision applies only to those intellectual property rights which depend on deposit or registration, and will therefore not extend to copyright, which does not.

If it were to be judged by reference to the English language text alone, it might be argued that Article 24(4) is wider than the first three heads of Article 24 jurisdiction, for it uses the language of the proceedings being 'concerned with' the validity of the patent or other right, rather than having this as the object of the proceedings. But no such distinction appears in the French[464] or German[465] language versions of Article 24, and it would be sensible to follow where they point.[466] Accordingly, Article 24(4) will apply when the proceedings have as their principal object the validity of the right. Proceedings brought by way of petition seeking the revocation of a patent will clearly fall under Article 24(4).[467]

---

460 The second sentence of the sub-Article is new, and did not appear in the original Art. 16(4) of the Brussels Convention.

461 288/82, [1983] ECR 3663.

462 *Napp Laboratories v. Pfizer Inc* [1993] FSR 150.

463 *Mölnlycke AB v. Procter & Gamble Ltd* [1992] 1 WLR 1112.

464 All use the formula *'en matière de...'.*

465 All use the formula *'für Verfahren, welche... zum Gegenstand haben...'.*

466 See *JP Morgan Chase Bank NA v. Berliner Verkehrsbetriebe* [2009] EWHC 1627 (Comm), [2010] QB 276 (on appeal, [2010] EWCA Civ 390, [2012] QB 176) (a case on what is now Art. 24(2)).

467 *Ibid.*

2.74 Invalidity raised as a defence to an infringement claim

The issue arises in a more acute form in the context of proceedings for patent infringement, in defence of which claim the defendant may plead the invalidity of the patent, for it is something of a mantra in patent litigation that one cannot infringe an invalid patent. Assuming that the defence of invalidity of the right cannot be struck out summarily as having no realistic prospect of success, one may suppose that there are three possible responses. The first would be to say that the raising of a defence does not alter the character of the claim advanced in the proceedings, and if the claim did not bring the proceedings within Article 24(4), it is not dragged back within its range by the particular defence, or by one of them. The second would be to say that the infringement proceedings should be stayed, and the parties left to go to the court with exclusive jurisdiction under Article 24(4) for a determination of the validity of the right, the stay being lifted and the infringement action resumed in the light of that ruling. The third would be to hold that, once the issue of validity is squarely raised, or is raised as the principal concern of the action, Article 27 of Regulation 1215/2012 divests the court of jurisdiction over the infringement action, which is then and thereafter vested in the court identified by Article 24(4). For reasons explained below, the third of these is correct.

As a matter of principle, the first possibility would not be easy to accept, for if the policy which underpins Article 24(4) is taken as seriously as the structure of the Regulation suggests it should be,[468] it cannot be made to depend upon the accident of who sues whom first, and therefore upon the particular procedural context in which the issue of validity comes to be raised. If the claimant's claim can succeed only if the property right is valid, and will be defeated if the defence of invalidity succeeds, the proceedings do have as their object, are founded on, the existing validity or invalidity of the right, and are certainly concerned with the right. The second possibility would not be obviously wrong, but it would be procedurally inconvenient. Bifurcated procedure will generally delay the final resolution of the claim, and in the context of intellectual property disputes, very large sums of money can be put at risk if one or the other of the parties can stall proceedings and fend off the day of judgment, all the while shovelling up money from the alleged infringement. The third represented the practice of the English courts.[469] It had the merit of practical wisdom about it, combining respect for what is now Article 24(4) with the need to obtain a prompt, efficient and coherent resolution of the entire dispute.

When the issue eventually came before the Court in *GAT v. LuK*,[470] it was not dealt with in a wholly satisfactory way. The claimant, a German company, was warned by the defendant that an industrial process which it was proposing to develop infringed two French patents of which the defendant was the proprietor. The claimant brought proceedings before the German courts for declarations that no infringement would be committed and that the patents were invalid. The European Court confirmed that the validity of patents could, whenever[471] that was in dispute, be determined only under the law of, and in, the

---

468 In particular, the obligation to refuse recognition to the judgment of a court which has exercised jurisdiction in violation of Art. 24: see further below, para. 7.10.

469 *Coin Controls Ltd v. Suzo International (UK) Ltd* [1999] Ch 33; *Fort Dodge Animal Health Ltd v. Akzo Nobel Ltd* [1998] FSR 222.

470 C-4/03 *Gesellschaft für Antriebstechnik mbH & Co KG v. Lamellen und Kupplungsbau Beteiligungs KG* [2006] ECR I-6509.

471 Though 'wherever' may be preferable.

Member State in which the right was granted;[472] and it followed that the Member State under whose law the right was granted had exclusive jurisdiction to determine validity, no matter the procedural context in which the issue had arisen for decision;[473] it said no more. This meant the rejection of the first of the three possible solutions discussed above, but offered no guidance on whether the second or third was correct, or on whether the national court was free to choose between them. As the two possibilities were canvassed in the Opinion of the Advocate General,[474] it was disappointing that the Court did not give any guidance.

The answer should be that once the issue of validity is genuinely[475] raised, Article 31(1) of the Regulation is engaged, and the court seised of the infringement claim should consider that the proceedings are to be understood as principally concerned with, or as having as their object, the issue of validity, no matter that the validity of the right is not the basis of the claim, and grant jurisdictional relief accordingly. Because one cannot infringe an invalid patent, it may very well be that issues of validity are more central or fundamental to an infringement case than they are to a damages claim in which the lack of corporate capacity is raised as a defence,[476] and that as a result, the raising of a defence which Article 24(4) allows to override the jurisdictional basis on which the claim was brought will be easier and more frequent than is the case under Article 24(2).[477]

2.75 Claims involving multiple national patents

Though it is not directly based on the interpretation of Article 24(4), it is convenient at this point to mention some related issues of difficulty with patent litigation, which derive from the historical proposition that patents, and intellectual property rights in general, are strictly territorial in their grant and in their operation. This means that it is not a breach of an English patent to perform acts in Italy. It is neither a breach of English law nor an infringement of an English patent to infringe an Italian patent which is in precisely identical[478] terms to the English one. Given the development of European patents,[479] the national patents derived from which will in substance frequently be identical, or practically identical, in each national territory, there is a risk of cumbersome and inefficient litigation for the holder of such a patent who finds that a defendant, or group of defendants, intends to infringe the protected rights by acting in several Member States.[480] If the several national infringements are carried out by different defendants, there are problems in seeking to justify their joinder into proceedings before a single court under Article 8(1) of Regulation 1215/2012,[481] for although the defendants may be acting in concert, and claims against them may be

---

472 At [22].

473 At [25].

474 At [46] in the Opinion of Geelhoed A-G, where he seemed to consider that the court hearing the infringement claim could follow either the second or the third of the possibilities mentioned earlier in this paragraph.

475 A value judgment will be called for in order to decide whether the issue of validity is 'genuinely' raised.

476 C-144/10 *Berliner Verkehrsbetriebe v. JP Morgan Chase Bank NA* [2011] ECR I-3961.

477 See *JP Morgan Chase Bank NA v. Berliner Verkehrsbetriebe* [2009] EWHC 1627 (Comm), [2010] QB 276, [52] (on appeal, [2010] EWCA Civ 390, [2012] QB 176).

478 Save as to the territory.

479 Though for the special regime of jurisdictional rules applicable to Community Trade Marks and Community Designs, see above, para. 2.52.

480 This likelihood appears to be reinforced by the second paragraph of the Article.

481 See further, para. 2.225, below.

connected, it is difficult to say that the actions need to be tried together to avoid the risk of legally irreconcilable judgments resulting from separate trials. Each patent is a separate property right, so that there is, technically, no risk of irreconcilability resulting from separate trials, highly inconvenient though this may be.[482]

In response to this, Dutch law evolved a principle that, if the principal infringer is Dutch, it may be regarded as the 'spider in the web', and the other infringers joined under what is now Article 8(1) as co-defendants to the Dutch proceedings, which would then deal with all the national patents, Dutch and non-Dutch. The result, which is convenient from the perspective of achieving a speedy and efficient resolution of disputes, was not easy to reconcile with the rather restrictive jurisprudence on Article 8(1).[483] In *Roche Nederland BV v. Primus*[484] the proprietor of a European patent brought proceedings in the Netherlands against companies from eight countries who were, as he alleged, infringing his national patents in their separate jurisdictions. The defendants were all members of the Roche group, based in the Netherlands.[485] The claimant was therefore bringing proceedings against eight defendants who had each infringed a different patent: at least, different in terms of legal identity, albeit practically identical in substance. The European Court therefore held that the Dutch court had jurisdiction over only the Dutch defendant, who was sued in relation to the Dutch patent: the other defendants were not (co-)defendants to the allegation that the Dutch patent had been infringed, and as they were each defendants to a claim arising from distinct facts and patents, it was not expedient that they be tried in a single judicial proceeding to avoid the risk of irreconcilable judgments which might result from separate trials. The acts of the defendants did not overlap; in any event, issues of validity of non-Dutch patents could not be decided by the Dutch courts;[486] and legal certainty would be at risk if acts in relation to a patent granted and allegedly infringed in one Member State could be brought before the courts of another Member State simply because another defendant was infringing another patent there.

There was nothing obviously wrong with the logic which the Court used to interpret the provisions of what is now the Regulation; there was everything wrong with the parallel litigation which it gave rise to. This seems to have been appreciated in several places. It led the Court of Appeal to observe how poorly the Regulation deals with intellectual property issues, as well it might:[487] the reasoning in *Roche* means that Article 29 cannot treat separate national proceedings in respect of parallel patents as involving the same cause of action, for each patent, even if substantively identical to the others, will give rise to a separate *jus actionis*, a separate cause of action. The result is that they will not be, as *Roche* confirms, within the jurisdiction of a single court for the purpose of ordering a dismissal under Article 30(2).

The next development was a rather puzzling judgment in *Solvay SA v. Honeywell Fluorine Products Europe BV*.[488] Proceedings were brought in the Netherlands against a Dutch and

---

482 Nor will the foreign infringers be regarded as joint tortfeasors in the infringement of the English patent: *Coin Controls Ltd v. Suzo International (UK) Ltd* [1999] Ch 33. See also, to this effect, *Prudential Assurance Co Ltd v. Prudential Insurance Co of America* [2003] EWCA Civ 327, [2003] 1 WLR 2295.

483 It is also difficult to reconcile with the principle that Art. 8(1) does not depend on one defendant being identified as the principal target of the claim. But see, for an insight into the Dutch position, *Expandable Grafts Partnership v. Boston Scientific BV* [1999] FSR 352.

484 C-539/03, [2006] ECR I-6535.

485 Which made Roche Nederland BV the 'spider in the web'.

486 C-4/03 *Gesellschaft für Antriebstechnik mbH & Co KG v. Lamellen und Kupplungsbau Beteiligungs KG* [2006] ECR I-6509.

487 *Research in Motion UK Ltd v. Visto Corp* [2008] EWCA Civ 153, [2008] 2 All ER (Comm) 560.

488 C-610/10, EU:C:2012:445.

two non-Dutch defendants, in relation to their infringement of the national part of a European patent. The European Court seemed to consider that as all three, including a Dutch company, had infringed the national part of a European patent, the joinder of the non-Dutch defendants under what is now Article 8(1) was permissible. The judgment also allowed an application for interim injunctive relief to be brought in the Netherlands without reference to Article 24(4). It appears that the Court was aware of the shortcomings of this part of the Regulation, and went as far as it could to meet them. But that was no distance at all, for it reaffirmed its judgment in *Roche*.

The third is that a 'Unified Patent Court' will be created and given jurisdiction. At the date of writing, the Unified Patent Court Regulations have been adopted by almost all of the Member States, under the procedure for enhanced cooperation;[489] and a proposal for the creation of a Unified Patent Court has been published.[490] The Brussels I Regulation 1215/2012 has been amended to make provision for the new court.[491]

The result is that until such time as there is a relaxation of the strictness of the rules on joinder of actions, or a specific amendment of the Regulation to provide for the more expeditious trial of patent proceedings, the course of litigation may very well be troublesome and duplicative. In this respect the problems associated with Article 22(4) are the tip of an iceberg.[492]

2.76 Deposit or registration in the United Kingdom

The Regulation gives international jurisdiction in such proceedings to the courts of the United Kingdom. If this happens, it is a matter of internal United Kingdom law to allocate the case to the internal, national, jurisdiction of the courts of a part of the United Kingdom. The answer is found in the Patents Act 1977,[493] Trade Marks Act 1994,[494] Registered Designs Act 1949[495] and Copyright, Designs and Patents Act 1988.[496]

2.77 Enforcement of judgments from the courts of Member States: Article 24(5)

Article 24 of the Regulation goes on to provide:

> *The following courts shall have exclusive jurisdiction, regardless of domicile:*
> *(5) in proceedings concerned with the enforcement of judgments, the courts of the Member State in which the judgment has been or is to be enforced.*

And in relation to this, Article 2 provides that:

---

489 Regulation 1257/2012.
490 COM(2013) 554 Final, 26 July 2013.
491 Regulation 542/2014, [2014] OJ L163/1.
492 For the view that the existence of what is now Art. 24(4) prevents the recognition in England of a French judgment on a French trademark, for fear that recognition would amount to constructive breach of Art. 24(4), see *Prudential Assurance Co Ltd v. Prudential Insurance Co of America* [2003] EWCA Civ 327, [2003] 1 WLR 2295. But it is not clear that this is correct, for even if it will only rarely arise, Art. 24(4) does not preclude the recognition of judgments which are otherwise entitled to recognition under Chapter III of the Regulation.
493 Section 72.
494 Sections 32 and 66(1).
495 Sections 20 and 45.
496 Sections 115, 149 and 287–289.

For the purposes of this Regulation: (a) 'judgment' means any judgment given by a court or tribunal of a Member State, whatever the judgment may be called, including a decree, order, decision or writ of execution, as well as a decision on the determination of costs or expenses by an officer of the court.

2.78 General

The manner and form of, and disputes which arise incidentally in the context of, the enforcement of judgments from other Member States are so closely connected to the State in which enforcement is being sought that they fall within the exclusive jurisdiction provisions.[497] Regulation 1215/2012 defines 'judgment', in Article 2, as a judgment from a court or tribunal of a Member State; Regulation 44/2001 had given the same definition in its Article 32. According to Jenard,[498] the corresponding rule in the Brussels Convention was intended to cover disputes as to methods of execution in the course of enforcement: practical enforcement, as opposed to theoretical right to enforce. The Court followed this expression of opinion in *Reichert v. Dresdner Bank (No 2)*,[499] in ruling that the Article had no application to proceedings brought to obtain certain measures prior to the obtaining of judgment, even though the purpose of making the application was to pave the way to a more effective later enforcement of a judgment. The Article is therefore of relatively narrow scope.

The provision applies to the enforcement of judgments regardless of the domicile of the person against whom they are to be enforced. Although the Court of Appeal has questioned whether this can really be correct,[500] there is no reason to doubt that the language of the Article means what it says. It does not matter where the judgment debtor is domiciled; Article 24(5) applies to the enforcement in England of judgments from Member States, including English judgments. It follows that service out of the jurisdiction, if any is needed, is available as of right.

The most problematic part of the rule is that it supposes that judgments are easily seen as being enforced in one or another State. It is not clear that matters are quite so straightforward. It is not unusual for orders to be made in relation to or aid of enforcement, whose effect is to be felt overseas, but whose purpose is to assist the enforcement of a judgment which might or might not take place in England. The short point is that judgments are enforced, or are enforced by processes; it is not always possible to say that they are enforced in a particular place. The point is developed in relation to the orders which can be made to assist the enforcement of judgments; the position is more subtle, and more complex, than Article 24(5) might suggest.

2.79 Orders made in relation to judgments from other Member States

An English court has power to order a person who is within its jurisdiction, and who owes money to the judgment debtor, to pay the sums instead to the judgment creditor: the

---

497 See 220/84 *A-S Autoteile Service GmbH v. Malhé* [1985] ECR 2267; C-129/92 *Owens Bank Ltd v. Bracco* [1994] ECR I-117.

498 [1979] OJ C59/1, 36.

499 C-261/90, [1992] ECR I-2149.

500 *Choudhary v. Bhatter* [2009] EWCA Civ 1176, [2010] 2 All ER 1031. Criticism (academic, and by the judge below) of the decision in that case was regarded in *Dar Al Arkan Real Estate Development Co v. Al Refai* [2014] EWCA Civ 715, [2015] 1 WLR 135, as 'compelling'.

process traditionally known as garnishment is now a 'third party debt order', governed by CPR Part 72. It had once been thought that an order against the third party might be made even though the assets representing the debt were not in England; and that even if that other jurisdiction were another Member State, there was no violation of what is now Article 24(5) if the order was made, for the procedure was still to be regarded as the enforcement of a judgment in England. If the third party, or garnishee, within the jurisdiction were to plead that the Regulation protected him from the jurisdiction of the English court, Article 24(5) would serve to answer it.

In 2003 the House of Lords held that this understanding was erroneous. On the footing that a third-party debt order was to be understood as the judicial seizure of intangible property by way of enforcement of the judgment, it was beyond the proper powers of the English court to make it in relation to property (including bank debts) considered to be located outside England. Accordingly, a French judgment could not be enforced in England under what is now Chapter III of the Regulation by making a third-party debt order in respect of a bank account credit (or debt) situated in Hong Kong;[501] and an English judgment may not be enforced by making a third-party debt order in relation to a bank debt situated in Switzerland, for the ordering of judicial measures of enforcement by way of confiscation of assets treated as being located in Switzerland is something which falls within the exclusive jurisdiction of the Swiss courts.[502] A suggestion that the enforcement is in England because the order operates *in personam* against a person who is in England will not be persuasive.

2.80 Enforcement orders made in aid of English judgments

At this point, it is convenient to say something about the orders which an English court may make after it has given judgment. Article 24(5) is not expressed to be confined to the enforcement of foreign judgments; it appears to apply to the enforcement of English judgments just as much as it applies to the enforcement of judgments from other Member States. In this context, the explanation of Jenard[503] as to what is comprehended by the Article is particularly important, for the English court has several powers which are useful as part of the broad process of enforcement, but which, unlike the third-party debt order, do not purport to seize or strike at property and which, therefore, appear to fall foul of Article 24(5).

An English court may in certain circumstances make orders against persons who were not party to proceedings before it. These orders are designed to make the judgment, which has already been given, more effective. Most striking, perhaps, is the power to grant a freezing injunction against a non-party if there is found to be a 'sufficient connection' between him and the defendant.[504] Also significant is the power to order a non-party to pay all or some of the costs ordered to be paid by the unsuccessful claimant to a successful

---

501 That is to say, the bank account in question was held in Hong Kong: *Soc Eram Shipping Co Ltd v. Hong Kong and Shanghai Bank Corp* [2003] UKHL 30, [2004] 1 AC 260. See further Cuniberti [2008] JDI/Clunet 963.

502 *Kuwait Oil Tanker Co SAK v. Qabazard* [2003] UKHL 31, [2004] 1 AC 300. For comment on both cases, and the question whether the court was right to focus on the situs of the assets (the debt) as opposed to the law governing the contractual obligation under which the (third party) debt was created, and which was said to be liable to be discharged by the English court's order, see Dickinson (2004) 120 LQR 16; Briggs [2003] LMCLQ 418, (2003) 74 BYBIL 511; Cuniberti [2008] JDI/Clunet 963.

503 [1979] OJ C59/1, 36.

504 *C Inc plc v. L* [2001] 2 Lloyd's Rep 459. See further below, para. 6.03.

defendant.[505] Where English law confers such powers on the court, it does not seem difficult to argue that such applications, though not made against those who were defendants to the proceedings which led to the original judgment, are part of the process of enforcement of that judgment. As Article 24(5) does not state that it is restricted to the enforcement of judgments from a Member State other than the one in which the enforcement is to take place,[506] it can be used as the jurisdictional basis for asserting personal jurisdiction over non-parties not otherwise subject to the jurisdiction of the English court, where proceedings against them are, and are only, part of the process of enforcement of the original judgment.[507]

Even if it were correct to say that the (non-) party against whom such orders are made is 'sued' for the purpose of Chapter II of the Regulation, which is questionable,[508] and even if Article 24(5) does not provide the jurisdictional justification for the order,[509] it can still, or may alternatively, be justified on the basis that the court with jurisdiction to entertain the claim may make any order it sees fit against a defendant. The fact that an English court may make orders which significantly assist the enforcement but which do not amount to execution, appears to mean that such orders may be made even though the assets on which execution will ultimately fasten are in another Member State. None of which addresses the distinct question whether an English court has the power in the individual case to make the order applied for.[510]

The principle is therefore clear enough: an English court may make orders which secure or assist in the securing the enforcement of an English judgment; and the only limitation imposed on this by Article 24(5) is that the court may not decree measures of enforcement in the territory of another Member State. But if 'measures of enforcement' is interpreted to mean 'measures which confiscate or otherwise seize property', as *Kuwait Oil Tanker Co SAK v. Qabazard*,[511] and Jenard,[512] suggest in their separate ways that it does, it will not preclude the making of orders against persons subject to the personal jurisdiction of the court which may in due course have a consequence for assets outside the territorial jurisdiction of the English court.

The point was made with particular clarity in the aftermath of the judgment in *Masri v. Consolidated Contractors International (UK) Ltd.*[513] The court had ordered the defendant to

---

505 Usually on the ground that the non-party was responsible for the action or the way it was conducted by the claimant: the power is in the Senior Courts Act 1981, s. 51, applied in *The Ikarian Reefer (No 2)* [2000] 1 WLR 603.

506 The proceedings in *Kuwait Oil Tanker* were in respect of an English judgment.

507 In *The Ikarian Reefer (No 2)*, the court considered that what is now Art. 8(1) of Regulation 1215/2012 furnished a basis for asserting personal jurisdiction over the non-party, or (alternatively) that he was not being sued at all, with the result that there was no jurisdictional impediment. The submission advanced in the text does not appear to have been advanced to the court, but see further (2000) 71 BYBIL 435, 450.

508 The proposition that the respondent to such an application was 'sued' was rejected by the Court of Appeal in *Masri v. Consolidated Contractors International Co SA (No 4)* [2008] EWCA Civ 876, [2009] 2 WLR 699. The House of Lords did not address this question of European law, instead deciding that the power under CPR Part 71 did not extend to making orders against persons who held office in a judgment debtor who were outside the territorial jurisdiction of the court: *Masri v. Consolidated Contractors International Co SAL (No 4)* [2009] UKHL 43, [2010] 1 AC 90.

509 As the order made is not one by way of execution. The proposition that Art. 24(5) does not prevent the making of the order, because the order does not purport to seize assets by way of execution, also means that it does not provide the jurisdictional basis for it either.

510 *Masri v. Consolidated Contractors International Co SAL (No 4)* [2009] UKHL 43, [2010] 1 AC 90.

511 [2003] UKHL 31, [2004] 1 AC 300.

512 [1979] OJ C59/1, 36.

513 [2007] EWHC 3010 (Comm).

pay the claimant a colossal sum by way of damages. When the defendant indicated that it had not the slightest intention of paying, the Court of Appeal upheld orders made by the judge: (i) appointing a receiver by way of equitable execution, who would then take steps to recover for the benefit of the claimant sums due in the course of business from third parties to the judgment debtor;[514] (ii) restraining the defendant from bringing proceedings before the courts of Yemen or elsewhere to contest the liability which had been adjudicated against it;[515] and (iii) summoning individuals who had held office in the judgment debtor to give evidence as to the whereabouts of assets.[516] Although *Turner v. Grovit*[517] meant that the injunction in (ii) had to be restricted to the restraint of proceedings brought outside the Member States, this limitation was of little practical effect as a court in another Member State would be required to recognise the English judgment under Chapter III of the Regulation in any event.

The appointment in England of a receiver by way of equitable execution was the appointment of a person who was then commissioned to seek to recover assets outside England. As the order asserted no right or proprietary claim in relation to the assets, but merely appointed a person to seek to collect trade debts owed to the judgment debtor, it did not involve the enforcement of the English judgment in other Member States. No execution was decreed by the English court; no specific assets were decreed or identified by order of the English court as being liable to be paid over to the judgment creditor; indeed, the order was really made to assist the enforcement in England. Similarly, the summoning of a corporate officer-holder to give evidence which might help trace assets was not a measure of enforcement, in the sense of execution against assets. Because it was only an order which paved the way for a future enforcement of the judgment, Article 24(5) did not apply to it, and Article 24(5) therefore did not stand in the way of the court exercising jurisdiction to make it if that jurisdiction could otherwise be established. The House of Lords did not comment on this element of the judgment of the Court of Appeal, as it interpreted the material provision of the Civil Procedure Rules as extending only to office-holders who are within the territorial jurisdiction of the court, and that as the application for relief was unfounded as a matter of English domestic law,[518] the question of jurisdiction did not arise.[519]

---

514 *Masri v. Consolidated Contractors International (UK) Ltd (No 2)* [2008] EWCA Civ 303, [2009] QB 450.

515 *Masri v. Consolidated Contractors International (UK) Ltd (No 3)* [2008] EWCA Civ 625, [2009] QB 503.

516 *Masri v. Consolidated Contractors International (UK) Ltd (No 4)* [2008] EWCA Civ 876, [2009] 2 WLR 699. But the House of Lords held that the English courts had no power to make an order against an office-holder who was not within the jurisdiction (and who, *ex hypothesi*, could not be served with the summons) as CPR Part 71 did not apply to such persons, and set aside the order made by the Court of Appeal: *Masri v. Consolidated Contractors International Co SAL (No 4)* [2009] UKHL 43, [2010] 1 AC 90. However, if such an order is applied for against a person who is within the jurisdiction but who has a domicile only in another Member State, the question will arise again. However, as to service of notices on a non-party, see now CPR r. 6.39. For an application of the principle in *Masri*, see *Serious Organised Crime Agency v. Perry* [2012] UKSC 35, [2013] 1 AC 182. For another view of the issue in *Masri*, not agreeing with its acceptance of territorial limitation on the power to issue a summons, see *Burgundy Global Exploration Corp v. Transocean Offshore International Ventures Ltd* [2014] SGCA 24.

517 C-159/02, [2004] ECR I-3565.

518 *Masri v. Consolidated Contractors International Co SAL (No 4)* [2009] UKHL 43, [2010] 1 AC 90.

519 For further consideration of this, see *Dar Al Arkan Real Estate Development Co v. Al Refai* [2014] EWCA Civ 715, [2015] 1 WLR 135. It seems that the issue of 'where' enforcement is taking place is liable to be tricky, if orders are made which relate to and have their immediate impact overseas, but are made to assist enforcement in England.

2.81 Judgments from non–Member States

As the Regulation defines 'judgment' as 'any judgment given by a court or tribunal of a Member State', Article 24(5) has no application – because the Regulation as a whole has no application[520] – to proceedings to enforce a judgment from the courts of a non–Member State. This applies equally to, and also excludes, proceedings in a Member State seeking a declaration that a judgment from a court in a non–Member State is entitled to be recognised in its territory. The recognition of a non–Member State judgment in a Member State, under its national rules of private international law, does not give the judgment a passport to Chapter III of the Regulation. As the original substantive adjudication was not one made by a judge in a Member State, the order made upon the issue of liability is simply different in quality from a judgment within the sense of the Regulation. The same reasoning probably explains why judgments which decree the enforcement of an arbitral award do not constitute judgments for the purpose of the Regulation.

2.82 Enforcement of judgments from courts of other Member States in the United Kingdom

The Brussels I Regulation gives international jurisdiction in such proceedings to the courts of the United Kingdom. If it does, it is a matter of internal United Kingdom law to allocate the case to the national jurisdiction of the courts of a part of the United Kingdom. By section 16 of, and Schedule 4 to, the 1982 Act, jurisdiction is conferred on the courts for the part of the United Kingdom in which the judgment has been or is to be enforced.[521]

2.83 Article 24 and connections which would point to a non–Member State

It is clear that autonomous, and relatively narrow, interpretations are given to the concepts in Article 24, reflecting their exceptional nature within the broad scheme of the Brussels I Regulation. The connections are with Member States: the Article cannot and does not apply if the land is in a non–Member State, or if the company has its seat in a non–Member State, or if the patent is granted under the law of a non–Member State, and so on. Of course, if there is such a connection with Iceland, Norway, or Switzerland, the corresponding provision of the Lugano Convention will give exclusive jurisdiction to the courts of that Contracting State.[522] But otherwise the Regulation, having no power to direct a court in a non–Member State to exercise jurisdiction, says nothing direct. At least, Regulation 44/2001 said nothing. In fact, as will be seen below, Articles 33 and 34 of Regulation 1215/2012 may be read as making even less than no allowance for the existence of an 'Article 24 connection' with a non–Member State, for insofar as they deal – as Regulation 44/2001 did not – with *lis pendens* before the courts of a non–Member State, it may be implicit that they intend no account to be taken of a connection, which would have justified exclusive jurisdiction, in or to a non–Member State. It follows that at this point a court

---

520 C-129/92 *Owens Bank Ltd v. Bracco* [1994] ECR I-117.
521 1982 Act, Sch. 4, r. 11(d), as inserted by Civil Jurisdiction and Judgments Order 2001, SI 2001/3929, Sch. 2, para. 4.
522 See para. 2.288, below, and Chapter 3. The same will be true for those non-European territories for which the Brussels Convention still applies.

which would otherwise have jurisdiction must ask itself whether it is entitled or bound to decline to exercise it. That issue goes beyond the analogy with Article 24, and is therefore dealt with below.[523]

2.84 Conclusion

If Article 24 gives exclusive jurisdiction to the courts of a Member State, then those courts alone[524] have jurisdiction. If the English court has jurisdiction on this basis, service out (if required) may be made as of right.[525] But if Article 24 does not apply, the next question must be asked.

(4) JURISDICTION BY ENTERING AN APPEARANCE

2.85 General

Article 26 of the Regulation provides that:

(1) Apart from jurisdiction derived from other provisions of this Regulation, a court of a Member State before which a defendant enters an appearance shall have jurisdiction. This rule shall not apply where appearance was entered to contest the jurisdiction, or where another court has exclusive jurisdiction by virtue of Article 24. (2) In matters referred to in Sections 3, 4 or 5 where the policyholder, the insured, a beneficiary of the insurance contract, the injured party, the consumer or the employee is the defendant, the court shall, before assuming jurisdiction under paragraph 1, ensure that the defendant is informed of his right to contest the jurisdiction of the court and of the consequences of entering or not entering an appearance.

The corresponding provision of Regulation 44/2001 did not have the second paragraph, which was added to deal with a particular issue which is explained below. Together with Article 25, which deals with jurisdiction agreements, Article 26 forms part of Section 7 of Chapter II, entitled 'Prorogation of jurisdiction'.

Apart from those cases excluded from the possibility by Article 24, the court of a Member State before which the defendant enters an appearance – unless this appearance is made to contest the jurisdiction – has jurisdiction. This is so even though there may be a valid and binding choice of court agreement for another court, for a voluntary appearance by the defendant in response to the summons will amount to a consensual variation of the agreement, as the Court held in *Elefanten Schuh GmbH v. Jacqmain*.[526] It is so even though the case might otherwise have fallen under the insurance, or consumer, or employment contract provisions, which would not have given the court jurisdiction[527] though awareness of this fact prompted the addition of the second paragraph of what is now Article 26. It is so even though the defendant might have disputed the jurisdiction but elected not to do so. And it is so even though the jurisdiction actually invoked by the claimant, in response to which

---

523 Paragraph 2.298.

524 And if more than one court has exclusive jurisdiction under this Article, Art. 31 applies a 'first come, first served' rule: para. 2.271, below.

525 CPR r. 6.33.

526 150/80, [1981] ECR 1671.

527 C-111/09 *Česká podnikatelská pojišt'ovna as, Vienna Insurance Group v. Bilas* [2010] ECR I-4545.

the defendant appears, is one of those otherwise proscribed[528] jurisdictional rules referred to by Article 5 of the Regulation;[529] no injustice is done to defendants who choose to appear: *volenti non fit injuria*. It is obviously otherwise in the context of a procedure of national law under which an absent defendant may have a person appointed on his behalf, the participation of that person being deemed to be that of the defendant, for this cannot be seen as the voluntary appearance of the defendant who, *ex hypothesi*, will not have tacitly accepted the jurisdiction for himself.[530]

It has not been decided, and it is not altogether clear, whether the 'defendant' to whom Article 26 refers is confined to those who have a domicile in a Member State. There is no compelling reason why such a limitation should be read in: as Article 25 now applies without reference to the domicile of any party, coherence in the law of jurisdiction by prorogation, under Section 7 of Chapter II, would support the view that Article 26 also applies regardless of domicile. Moreover, if both parties are willing to resolve their dispute before the court of a Member State, it is hard to see why they should not now be entitled to do so. On the other hand, Article 6 of Regulation 1215/2012 is stated to be inapplicable where Articles 18(1), 21(1), 24 and 25 apply to the claim against the defendant, but no equivalent mention is made of Article 26; and it may be argued that the European Union has not shown its proper interest in laying down the jurisdictional law on whether a civil or commercial dispute between parties, none of whom has any relevant connection with the Member States, should be brought before the courts of a Member State. From this it might be taken to follow that Article 26 has no application to defendants who are not domiciled in a Member State, whose amenability to jurisdiction is otherwise left to the national law of the court seised. The cases in which it will matter are few; but if jurisdiction over such a defendant is based on Article 6 rather than Article 26, a national court will be permitted to apply other elements of its law on jurisdiction and procedure in order to decline to exercise jurisdiction,[531] whereas if jurisdiction is held to be based on Article 26 this will not be allowed.

2.86 Entering an appearance, rather than submission

The concepts of entering an appearance, and submission, are not always quite the same. According to English domestic law, it is possible to submit to the jurisdiction of a court by a contractual choice of court, or by a contractual agreement to accept service of process. Neither of these would, by itself, bring a defendant within Article 26. Whether a defendant has in fact entered an appearance must in principle be governed by the procedural law of the court concerned: an autonomous meaning may be given to entering an appearance,[532]

---

528 In relation to defendants domiciled in a Member State.

529 Jenard [1979] OJ C59/1, 38.

530 C-112/13 *A v. B* EU:C:2014:2195.

531 In England, in particular, the traditional rules by which certain matters are not justiciable in an English court (para. 4.05 *et seq.*), and the new rule about the absence of jurisdiction in certain instances of cross-border defamation (para. 4.12, below).

532 It does not include the formal opposition of a claim for payment under the European Order Procedure, even if the opposition to that demand set out the substantive grounds on which the liability was contested. The two procedures are sufficiently distinct that participation in the one has no relevance to the application of the other: C-144/12 *Goldbet Sportwetten GmbH v. Sperindeo* EU:C:2013:393, [2013] Bus LR 1115.

but precisely how and when this takes place is a matter of procedural law[533] which the Regulation does not govern.[534]

It has been held that a defendant who enters an appearance and so submits to the jurisdiction in respect of the claim set out in the writ does not necessarily submit to the jurisdiction in respect of other claims which, in the exercise of its procedural discretion, the court allows to be introduced by later amendment of the claim.[535] One can see why this ought to be the answer: it would not appear obviously right that if a defendant enters an appearance in relation to a narrowly-drafted claim, he has no opportunity to re-consider his position if the claimant later seeks to add new claims, or if other parties seek to be added to the claim: to put it in homely terms, it does not seem right that a claimant should be allowed to use a sprat to catch a mackerel. On the other hand, a defendant does not have a right to pick and choose which claims in a writ he is prepared to submit to if he has no basis for, and does not make, a jurisdictional challenge:[536] if he chooses to appear when summoned to an English court, he opens himself up to the full range of procedural possibilities for which English law makes provision. It may be that the best answer is that the court should exercise its rules of procedural law to prevent allow new claims to be added in such a way as to prevent the jurisdiction, originally established by the entering of an appearance, being abused.

By contrast, where a defendant has a 'representative' appointed on his behalf by a court, that 'representative' then purporting to appear on his behalf, he is not to be held to have entered an appearance for the purpose of the rule. It could hardly be otherwise when the fundamental basis of Article 26 is that of voluntary appearance by the defendant.[537] Although the power of a court to make such an appointment in respect of a defendant who cannot be located and whose domicile is unknown is not necessarily contrary to European law,[538] a deduction that the defendant may thereby be treated as having entered an appearance is wrong.

2.87 Contesting the jurisdiction of the court: principles

Article 26 provides that a defendant who makes an appearance to contest the jurisdiction of the court does not enter an appearance in the sense of Article 26, no matter what the

---

533 In England this is by acknowledging service of the claim form in accordance with CPR Part 10, or if this is not done, by filing a defence: CPR r. 10.2. But if within 14 days of filing an acknowledgement of service the defendant makes an application to contest the jurisdiction, pursuant to CPR Part 11, the acknowledgement of service ceases to have effect; the defendant will be entitled to file a further acknowledgement after the application has been dealt with: CPR r. 11(7). See para. 5.23 *et seq.*, below. However, there are specialist bodies with adjudicatory jurisdiction, such as the Intellectual Property Office (see *Future New Developments Ltd v. B&S Patente und Marken GmbH* [2014] EWHC 1874 (IPEC)), and the Competition Appeal Tribunal (see *Deutsche Bahn AG v. Morgan Advanced Materials plc* [2013] CAT 18), in which the procedure for appearing, and for objecting to the jurisdiction, is much less clearly separated from the procedure for defending the claim on the merits. In relation to these bodies, a test of outward appearance may be the best guide.

534 At least, so long as this does not jeopardise the jurisdictional rules of the Convention or Regulation: C-365/88 *Kongress Agentur Hagen GmbH v. Zeehaghe BV* [1990] ECR I-1845; C-68/93 *Shevill v. Presse Alliance SA* [1995] ECR I-415; *cf* C-159/02 *Turner v. Grovit* [2004] ECR I-3565.

535 *Maple Leaf Macro Volatility Fund v. Rouvroy* [2009] EWHC 257 (Comm), [2009] 1 Lloyd's Rep 475. For the corresponding position in national law, see para. 4.58 *et seq.*, below.

536 Unless, of course, he can challenge the jurisdiction of the court in respect of certain causes of action in the claim form. This point was examined in *Deutsche Bahn AG v. Morgan Advanced Materials plc* [2013] CAT 18 in a slightly different context.

537 C-112/13 *A v. B* EU:C:2014:2195.

538 C-327/10 *Hypoteční Banka AS v. Lindner* [2011] ECR I-11453.

procedural law of the court might have said. This aspect of Article 26 will certainly apply where the defendant appears to object to the international jurisdiction of the court: that is, by objecting that the courts of the United Kingdom, rather than France, for example, do not have jurisdiction. It is less obvious that it applies when the objection is to the national or internal jurisdiction of the court: that is, by pleading that the courts of Bordeaux rather than Paris do not have jurisdiction in a case in which the Regulation simply gives jurisdiction to the French courts, and the jurisdiction actually objected to is a national jurisdiction as defined by French internal law. The Brussels Convention was made to determine the international jurisdiction of the courts of the then-Contracting States, and it is generally accepted that the Regulation works on the same basis: a challenge to the jurisdiction, in the sense of Article 26, would be a challenge to the jurisdiction by reference to the jurisdictional rules of the Regulation.[539] Of course, where the Regulation is more prescriptive, and gives jurisdiction to the courts for a place within, rather than just to, a Member State, as it does for Article 7, for example, there is no reason to doubt that a challenge to the jurisdiction of a court which, as the claimant asserts, is derived from the Regulation, is covered by the second sentence of Article 26.[540]

If the purpose of the appearance is to contest[541] the jurisdiction of the court, the defendant's appearance does not confer jurisdiction upon it. In some systems, however, it is inadvisable to object to the jurisdiction of the court without also putting forward the substantive defences upon which the defendant will rely if the jurisdictional point is lost. If the defendant, heeding this advice, files a defence by way of objection to the jurisdiction as well as answering the merits of the claim against him, it could be said that the purpose of the defendant's appearance was not *solely* to contest the jurisdiction. When the provision which is now Article 26 first appeared, as Article 18 of the Brussels Convention, the English-language version of the rule did indeed require that the appearance of the defendant be *solely* for the purpose of contesting the jurisdiction:[542] a fact which created a problem for a defendant whose initial pleading both contested the jurisdiction and set out his defence on the merits. To have held that he had forfeited the protection of the Article would have been unacceptable, for it would have put in jeopardy the right of a defendant to ensure that the Convention was being interpreted and applied correctly in relation to him.

In the Regulation, the word *solely* does not appear. It is clear that its omission is deliberate. The law will remain as stated by the European Court in *Elefanten Schuh GmbH v. Jacqmain*[543] and *Rohr SA v. Ossberger*.[544] Both cases establish that the defendant, who wishes

---

539 Including those incorporated by reference in Arts 71 and 6. It has been held that if a defendant does not object to a determination by the Intellectual Property Office, but when the hearing officer transfers the matter to the court for hearing then objects to the jurisdiction, this will have already counted as a submission to English jurisdiction: *Future New Developments Ltd v. B&S Patente und Marken GmbH* [2014] EWHC 1874 (IPEC). This tends to suggest that the objection has to be made to the jurisdiction of the Member State, and that objection to a particular court is not enough.

540 For example, if in a tort claim it is objected that the courts of England do not have jurisdiction under Art. 7(2) but the courts of Scotland do.

541 This expression must include making misguided or unfounded challenges, such as where it is argued that the English court, which would otherwise have jurisdiction under the Regulation, is a *forum non conveniens*.

542 In this respect (unconsciously, no doubt) reflecting the view of English procedural law that a defendant who takes any step in the proceedings other than one to dispute the jurisdiction of the court submits to the jurisdiction of the court.

543 150/80, [1981] ECR 1671. A qualification added by C-144/12 *Goldbet Sportwetten GmbH v. Sperindeo* EU:C:2013:393, [2013] Bus LR 1115, does not call into question what was said in that case.

544 27/81, [1981] ECR 2431.

to contest the jurisdiction but to be guarded from having entered an appearance under what is now Article 26, may put forward his defence to the merits of the claim at the same time. What is required of him is that he make his contest to the jurisdiction at the first opportunity which is given to him under the procedural law of the court seised,[545] and not, as happened in *Elefanten Schuh*, as decidedly late afterthought. It is difficult to believe that this provision should now give rise to any practical difficulty. If the plea to object to the jurisdiction is made at the first practical opportunity and no later than the time for filing the first defence, and in accordance with the procedural rules of the court or tribunal concerned, neither concurrently entering a defence upon the merits, nor taking procedural steps, such as applying for an extension of time to make the jurisdictional challenge, or seeking discovery of documents in order to demonstrate the facts which show the court not to have jurisdiction,[546] in the course of the adjudication upon the jurisdictional plea, will prejudice the position of the defendant. By contrast, taking further voluntary steps, not themselves consistent with the original and continuing intention to challenge the jurisdiction, but which deal instead with the merits of the claim, will be liable to forfeit the protection of Article 26, and will amount to the entering of an appearance.[547]

There may also be in-between cases as where, for example, a defendant states that it 'reserves its right' to contest the jurisdiction but does not actually invoke the mechanism to do so at the first opportunity. In these cases, the best guide may be to ask whether it outwardly appears that the jurisdiction of the court is being contested. And as to that, a jurisdiction can be uncontested even though a person asserts that he is still wondering whether to contest it. It may be significant that to 'contest' appears to require something to be done, as distinct from something being merely threatened, and that an airy assertion of the reservation of rights does not operate, as it has been tellingly put, as a 'get out of jail free' card.[548] It follows that if the defendant initially indicates an intention to contest the jurisdiction but then fails to make his challenge within the period and by the procedure specified by the rules for him to do so, the indication was a false alarm and the defendant is taken simply to have entered an appearance.[549]

545 Though in England, failing to tick the relevant box on the acknowledgment of service form is not fatal, as long as the challenge to jurisdiction under CPR Part 11 is made within the timetable provided by the rules: *IBS Technologies (Pvt) Ltd v. APM Technologies SA (No 1)*, 7 April 2003: and quite right, too, for the law should not punish for the smallest procedural imperfection. Continuing to appear and participate in the proceedings while still contesting jurisdiction, where this is permitted by the rules of the court or tribunal in question, does not amount to submission by appearance, for it will not appear as a plain and unequivocal submission: *Harada v. Turner (No 2)* [2003] EWCA Civ 1695 (applied in *Deutsche Bahn AG v. Morgan Advanced Materials plc* [2013] CAT 18 Civ 1484), which was evidently approved in *AES Ust-Kamenogorsk Hydropower Plant LLP v. Ust-Kamenogorsk Hydropower Plant JSC* [2011] EWCA Civ 647, [2012] 1 WLR 920 (not referred to on this point in the Supreme Court). It seems sensible to allow a degree of flexibility, for the procedure in every country is different, and it may also differ as between courts and tribunals in the one country (on which in particular, see *Deutsche Bahn AG v. Morgan Advanced Materials plc* dealing with the procedural rules of the Competition Appeal Tribunal; *Future New Developments Ltd v. B&S Patente und Marken GmbH* [2014] EWHC 1874 (IPEC), dealing with the procedural rules for matters which start before the Intellectual Property Office).

546 Illustrated by *Kurz v. Stella Musical Veranstaltungs GmbH* [1992] Ch 196.

547 *Alfred C Toepfer International GmbH v. Molino Boschi Srl* [1996] 1 Lloyd's Rep 510, 514.

548 *Future New Developments Ltd v. B&S Patente und Marken GmbH* [2014] EWHC 1874 (IPEC); see also *Global International Multimedia Ltd v. ARA Media Services* [2006] EWHC 3612 (Ch), [2007] 1 All ER (Comm) 1160.

549 *Maple Leaf Macro Volatility Fund v. Rouvroy* [2009] EWHC 257 (Comm), [2009] 1 Lloyd's Rep 475; *cf* in the context of recognition of foreign judgments: *Starlight International Inc v. Bruce* [2002] EWHC 374 (Ch), [2002] ILPr 617, discussed below, para. 7.32.

2.88 Contesting the jurisdiction of the court: procedure

The above account states the law. It does not precisely describe how a party, served with process issued by an English court, should conduct himself in order to make the challenge while avoiding being held to have entered an appearance. Chapter 5 outlines the procedure which governs the application, though it is important to bear in mind that the procedure may vary, even in England, as between courts of general jurisdiction and specialist tribunals.

2.89 Appearance by insured, consumer or employee

The conclusion in *Česká podnikatelská pojišťovna AS v. Bilas*,[550] that an appearance by a consumer who may not have realised that he had a plausible basis for contesting the jurisdiction was still effective to confer jurisdiction, and was not inconsistent with Section 4 of Chapter II,[551] was plainly correct, but it had the potential to be harsh on the under-resourced defendant. The second paragraph of Article 26, which is fine in abstract principle, was added to respond to this point. But how a court is supposed to discharge the duty laid upon it if the defendant makes no effort to challenge the jurisdiction and does not actually appear in person before the court until the hearing of the substance of the claim, is not clear.

2.90 Conclusion

Apart from cases covered by Article 24, if the defendant enters an appearance before the courts of a Member State, those courts have jurisdiction, and may exercise it subject to the rules of the Regulation on *lis alibi pendens*. Unless the defendant has entered an appearance and does not challenge the jurisdiction, the next question has to be addressed.

(5) JURISDICTIONAL PRIVILEGE IN MATTERS RELATING TO INSURANCE

2.91 General

Article 10 of the Regulation provides that:

> In matters relating to insurance, jurisdiction shall be determined by this Section, without prejudice to Article 6 and point 5 of Article 7.

The Section referred to in Article 10 is Section 3 of Chapter II of the Regulation, which for the purposes of Regulation 1215/2012 means Articles 10 to 16, entitled 'jurisdiction in matters relating to insurance'. The term 'insurance' is not defined, but according to *Universal General Insurance Co v. Groupe Josi Reinsurance SA*,[552] it does not include reinsurance. The saving provision for Articles 6 and 7(5) needed to be spelled out, for those jurisdictional rules

---

550 C-111/09, [2010] ECR I-4545.

551 With the consequence that there was no basis for a refusal to recognise the judgment.

552 C-412/98, [2000] ECR I-5925, clarifying a point which had hitherto been unresolved by the Court, but agreeing with the House of Lords: *Agnew v. Länsförsäkringsbolagens AB* [2001] 1 AC 223.

come lower in the hierarchy than those forming Section 3 of Chapter II. It goes without saying, though, that these rules do not prejudice the application of Articles 24 and 26, which are of a higher order. For matters which fall within Article 10, Articles 11 to 16 spell out in detail the particular jurisdictional rules which apply to claims falling within the Section. They are essentially unchanged from the corresponding provisions in Regulation 44/2001, and they[553] provide:

> 11. *(1) An insurer domiciled in a Member State may be sued: (a) in the courts of the Member State in which he is domiciled; (b) in another Member State, in the case of actions brought by the policyholder, the insured or a beneficiary, in the courts for the place where the claimant is domiciled; or (c) if he is a co-insurer, in the courts of a Member State in which proceedings are brought against the leading insurer. (2) An insurer who is not domiciled in a Member State but has a branch, agency or other establishment in one of the Member States shall, in disputes arising out of the operations of the branch, agency or establishment, be deemed to be domiciled in that Member State.*
>
> 12. *In respect of liability insurance or insurance of immovable property, the insurer may in addition be sued in the courts for the place where the harmful event occurred. The same applies if movable and immovable property are covered by the same insurance policy and both are adversely affected by the same contingency.*
>
> 13. *(1) In respect of liability insurance, the insurer may also, if the law of the court permits it, be joined in proceedings which the injured party has brought against the insured. (2) Articles 10, 11 and 12 shall apply to actions brought by the injured party directly against the insurer, where such direct actions are permitted. (3) If the law governing such direct actions provides that the policyholder or the insured may be joined as a party to the action, the same court shall have jurisdiction over them.*
>
> 14. *(1) Without prejudice to Article 13(3), an insurer may bring proceedings only in the courts of the Member State in which the defendant is domiciled, irrespective of whether he is the policyholder, the insured or a beneficiary. (2) The provisions of this Section shall not affect the right to bring a counter-claim in the court in which, in accordance with this Section, the original claim is pending.*

Proceeding from the view that the context of insurance is one in which inequality of bargaining power is to be suspected or presumed, the Regulation contains special and detailed rules for jurisdiction in cases concerned with insurance contracts. The existence of inequality may or may not be present in individual cases, but it is generally unnecessary to show (and equally irrelevant to deny), that inequality existed in the particular case in order to bring the proceedings within Section 3 of Chapter II.[554]

2.92 Structure and importance of Section 3 of Chapter II

Section 3 of Chapter II forms a self-contained code of jurisdiction in insurance cases, though as what is now Article 6 of Regulation 1215/2012 remains applicable to claims under insurance contracts, the jurisdictional privilege established by the rules is generally confined to claims against defendants who have a domicile,[555] or who are treated as though they had a domicile,[556] in a Member State.[557] Defendants who do not have a domicile in a Member State are subject to the traditional jurisdictional rules of the national law of the court seised, by reason of Article 6. It is only the exclusive jurisdiction provisions of Article 24, and the

---

553 Article 15 appears below, para. 2.95; but Art. 16, on account of its length, only in the Appendix.

554 *New Hampshire Insurance Co v. Strabag Bau AG* [1992] 1 Lloyd's Rep 361.

555 See Arts 10, 11(1) and 14(1).

556 Article 11(2). For the deemed domicile provisions of English law, see SI 2001/3929, Sch. 1, para. 11 (as immaterially (*sic*) amended by SI 2014/2947, Sch. 2, para. 13.

557 The widening of the rules for consumer and employment cases as they stood in Regulation 44/2001, by Arts 18(1) and 21(2) of Regulation 1215/2012, has no counterpart in Section 4 of Chapter II.

power of a defendant to waive the jurisdiction of the court which would otherwise have had competence over the claim against him, by entering an appearance under Article 26, which may override the particular rules of Section 3.

The importance of the rules in Section 3 of Chapter II is further entrenched by the rules on the enforcement of judgments from another Member State in insurance matters. By way of exception to the general rule, the court in which enforcement is sought must refuse[558] to recognise the judgment if the jurisdiction of the original court conflicted with the provisions of Section 3 of Chapter II. Though this last point might suggest that the judgment of a court, which had taken jurisdiction on the basis of the defendant's entering an appearance before a court not otherwise having jurisdiction under Section 3, may not be recognised, this is not so.[559]

The term 'insurance' is not defined in the Regulation. No doubt it will be held to have an autonomous meaning, but so far no case has needed to grapple with it, save for the decision that it does not extend to reinsurance.[560] The Section refers to the parties to the insurance relationship, other than the insurer, as the insured, the policy-holder and the beneficiary. The policy-holder[561] refers to the contracting party who originally took out the insurance. All others with an interest in the insurance will presumably fall within one or other of the other two terms.

So far as concerns the kinds of claim which will count as matters falling within the scope of the Section, the phrase 'matters relating to' denotes a material scope which is wider than claims which are founded on, or seek the enforcement of, the contract of insurance itself. For example, direct claims brought by an injured party against the insurer of a tortfeasor may not always be understood as the enforcement of the contract, as distinct from a direct statutory entitlement, but such claims are included within Section 3. It therefore seems probable that a matter may relate to insurance even though the claim between the parties does not have the contract of insurance as its object, or basis: again, a claim by an injured person against the insured motorist who injured him may be said to have the alleged negligent driving as its foundation and as the matter which needs to be established, even though legislation allows the claim, in certain circumstances, to be laid at the door of an insurer.[562] In the absence of guidance from the European Court, it may not be helpful to seek to paraphrase the Regulation, and to leave the question of when a matter relates to insurance to the common sense of the judge hearing the jurisdictional application.

The general principle, that rules which would remove a defendant from his or its home court will be given a construction which is no wider than is needed to secure the aims of the provision in question, has played little part in the insurance cases. Indeed, in the one case in which it might have had an effect, *FBTO Schadeverzekeringen NV v. Odenbreit*,[563] the

---

558 Regulation 44/2001, Art. 35(1); Regulation 1215/2012, Art. 45(1)(e)(i).

559 C-111/09 *Česká podnikatelská pojišťovna AS, Vienna Insurance Group v. Bilas* [2010] ECR I-4545.

560 C-412/98 *Universal General Insurance Co v. Groupe Josi Reinsurance SA* [2000] ECR I-5925.

561 A more accurate, if inelegant, translation may have been 'taker-out of insurance'.

562 But if the victim makes a direct claim against the insurer, the insured may be joined into those proceedings by reference to Art. 13(3): *Hoteles Piñero Canarias SL v. Keefe* [2013] EWHC 4279 (QB). The question whether the claim against the insured is a matter relating to insurance does not really need to be addressed, given the clear wording of Art. 13(3).

563 C-463/06, [2007] ECR I-11321.

decision of the Court led to what is now Article 13(2) being given a rather wider interpretation than might have been expected in advance of the decision.

2.93 Professional and non-professional insurance relationships

The rules in Section 3 of Chapter II work well, and make sense, where the relationship actually is one of inequality between insurer and insured, for this is what they were designed for. There is more difficulty when the insurance relationship is one between professional parties who, one might think, can look after themselves: this perception provided a justification for the European Court to rule that Section 3 does not extend to reinsurance.[564] But there is nothing on the face of Section 3 to suggest that it does not apply to insurance relationships in which all parties are professionals. Quite the contrary: the provisions on jurisdiction agreements referred to in Article 15(5) and dealt with in detail in Article 16, will in many cases deal with risks which will only ever arise as between professional operators. Section 3 therefore applies to insurance disputes as between professional entities; and if this were not correct, the line of division could be a difficult one to draw. However, it appears that there are some jurisdictional privileges within Section 3 which will be limited in their operation so that they do not apply to a professional claimant, and this elasticity in interpretation needs to be taken as given.

The starting point is the decision in *FBTO Schadeverzekeringen NV v. Odenbreit*.[565] In that case, proceedings were brought by an injured victim directly against the insurer of the tortfeasor. The insurer contended that the combined effect of what is now Article 13(2) and Article 11(1)(b) was that the injured party could only bring his direct claim against the insurer in the court in which the *insured* could have sued. The European Court rejected the proposed interpretation, taking the view that as the purpose of Section 3 was to give protection to weaker parties (and not just to insureds) in litigation against insurers, it had to be read as allowing the injured party to sue the insurer where he was domiciled, rather than allowing him to sue where the insured had been domiciled.[566] Such reliance on the technique of discerning the broad purpose of the Regulation at the expense of the literal wording of individual Articles is a familiar procedure, but it can give rise to trouble.

In *Vorarlberger Gebietskrankenkasse v. WGV-Schwäbische Allgemeine Versicherungs AG*,[567] the injured party's direct claim against the insurer of the tortfeasor had passed to a State provider of social security which contended, rather opportunistically, that it too had the privilege of suing in the place of its domicile, as though it were in every respect the claimant in a direct claim for the purpose of what is now Article 13(2). This time the European Court rejected the argument, saying that in the same way that the jurisdictional privileges of Section 3 had no application in the context of reinsurance, which was a relationship created between businesses, they did not apply where the claim of a private party against an insurer had passed, in accordance

---

564 C-412/98 *Universal General Insurance Co v. Group Josi Reinsurance SA* [2000] ECR I-5925.

565 C-463/06, [2007] ECR I-11321; *Cf* C-89/91 *Shearson Lehmann Hutton Inc v. TVB* [1993] ECR I-981 (a case on the assignment of claims by a consumer to a professional or an organisation, on which, see para. 2.100, below).

566 And Art. 13(3) will therefore allow the insured to be joined into the proceedings in that court, even though the claim against the insured is, from one point of view, not an insurance matter: *Hoteles Piñero Canarias SL v. Keefe* [2013] EWHC 4279 (QB).

567 C-347/08, [2009] ECR I-8661.

with the principle of subrogation, to a professional organisation: it could not be said that the claimant–insurer was an 'injured party' for the purposes of what is now Article 13(2). It would be different, however, if the claim had passed to an ordinary assignee or to the heirs of the victim.[568] This may produce a defensible outcome, for there was no reason of legal policy to extend a helping hand to a professional body standing in the rather frailer shoes of an insured. The Court suggested that the 'protective role fulfilled' by Section 3 'implies that the application of the rules of special jurisdiction laid down to that end by [the Regulation] should not be extended to persons for whom that protection is not justified'.[569] The key to the judgment must lie in the proposition that it would have 'extended' the scope of Section 3 if it had allowed a professional assignee of a claim to take advantage of jurisdictional rules which were made for the benefit of the assignor and which were, in this respect, not assignable.

Something similar may explain *GIE Réunion Européenne v. Zurich España*,[570] in which it was held that an insurer, in proceedings brought by a professional insured, could not rely on what is now Article 13(1) to join another insurer as third party for the purpose of claiming an indemnity from it. The Court observed that in the circumstances of the case, 'no special protection is justified since the parties concerned are professionals in the insurance sector, none of whom may be presumed to be in a weaker position than the others'. But this cannot be taken to mean that Section 3 was inapplicable, only that it did not accommodate the particular joinder which the insurer sought to make, and for which a justification had to be found elsewhere in the Regulation.[571] It is undeniable that the width and generality of some of the observations of the Court made in relation to Section 3 of Chapter II is problematic. It appears to be necessary to approach Section 3 on the basis that it does apply to disputes between professionals, but to accept that it is inherent in the nature of some of the individual jurisdictional provisions that they are confined in their operation to cases in which they are relied on by non-professionals.

2.94 General jurisdictional rules: Articles 11 to 14

The jurisdictional rules are sufficiently involved for it to be difficult for them to be explained by reference to principle. But, as is the case with the Regulation itself, the complex rules for jurisdiction in insurance cases also fit into a structure and order: a special sub-hierarchy of their own. The text of the Article, and the broad purpose of the Regulation, obviously comes first, but, the following synopsis describes the sense and general structure of the law. It is to be noted that some rules are unaffected by whether the defendant to the claim is the insured or the insurer, but that others are specific to claims against one or the other side to the insurance contract.

The jurisdictional rules fall into four categories of proceedings, within which various sub-rules are established.

First, there are jurisdictional rules which apply generally, that is, mostly without regard to which party to the insurance is the defendant in the proceedings; they are defined by

---

568 At [43], [44].
569 At [41].
570 C-77/04, [2005] ECR I-4509.
571 It was, however, entitled to rely on what is now Art. 8(2). That being so, it is not easy to see what the fuss was about.

reference to the defendant. If the defendant enters an appearance, Section 3 does not apply at all: it does not matter whether the defendant is insurer or insured, for jurisdiction derived from the appearance of the defendant is of a higher order than the provisions set out in Section 3. Article 26 of Regulation 1215/2012, which does not exclude itself from insurance matters, provides that the court before which the defendant enters an appearance will have jurisdiction.[572] Article 26(2) qualifies this with a (new) requirement that the court make sure that a policy-holder, insured, or beneficiary of the insurance, sued in a court to the jurisdiction of which Section 3 would allow him to object, is made aware of this fact; but otherwise, appearance confirms jurisdiction.

If the defendant does not have a domicile in any of the Member States, Articles 6 and 10 together provide that the residual or traditional jurisdictional rules of the national law of the court will apply to the proceedings, and there is no need to be concerned with the remaining rules of Section 3.[573] This rule applies whether the defendant is the insurer, or the insured, the policy-holder, or the beneficiary. However, if the defendant is an insurer which does not have a domicile in a Member State, Article 11(2) provides that it may be treated as domiciled in a Member State if the dispute arises out of the operations of a branch, agency, or other establishment in that Member State.[574] This 'deeming' of a domicile in a Member State will operate only within the context of the provisions on insurance. It will not, therefore, extend to reinsurers who are sued as reinsurers, or to parties to litigation who happen to be insurers but who are not being sued in that capacity. It is the nature of the contract or relationship from which the claim arises, rather than the general business of the defendant, which determines the application of the Article.

If the defendant, whether the insurer, or the policy-holder, insured or beneficiary, is domiciled in a Member State, Articles 10 and 7(5) provide that he or it may also be sued in another Member State if he or it has a branch, agency or establishment in that other Member State, and the dispute arises out of the operations of that branch.[575]

Second, there are jurisdictional provisions which deal generally with claims made against an insurer domiciled or deemed to be domiciled in a Member State. They deal with claims in general, and with claims in proceedings which are particular to certain kinds of insurance.

The general provision is that claims which are made against an insurer domiciled, or deemed to be domiciled, in a Member State may be brought: (a) in the Member State in which the insurer is domiciled;[576] or (b) in the Member State in which the claimant policy-holder, claimant insured or claimant beneficiary, is domiciled.[577] This provision applies equally to direct claims against an insurer by a person injured by the insured.[578]

The particular provision is that claims against an insurer domiciled, or deemed to be domiciled, in a Member State may also be brought: (a) if the defendant is a co-insurer,[579] in the Member State in which proceedings are brought against the leading insurer; or (b) if the

---

572 See above, para. 2.85.

573 Cf C-318/93 Brenner & Nöller v. Dean Witter Reynolds Inc [1994] ECR I-4275. But the rules of lis alibi pendens, which are found in Section 9 of Chapter II, will still apply.

574 For the definition, for these purposes, of a domicile in the United Kingdom, see SI 2001/3929, Sch. 1, para. 11, as immaterially (sic) amended by SI 2014/2947, Sch. 2, para. 13.

575 See further below, paras 2.213 et seq.

576 Article 11(1)(a).

577 Article 11(1)(b).

578 Article 13.

579 Article 11(1)(c).

insurance is liability insurance or insurance of immoveable property,[580] in the courts for the place where the harmful event occurred; or (c) if the insurance is liability insurance, in the proceedings in the Member State in which the injured party is suing the insured if the court which is seised of the action will permit the joinder of the insurer;[581] or (d) if the insurance is liability insurance, and if the claim is brought directly by an injured party against the insurer, and if the law[582] permits such direct actions to be brought, in the Member State in which the policy-holder could himself have sued the insurer,[583] or in the Member State in which the injured party is domiciled.[584]

Third, the jurisdictional provision which makes provision for claims made by an insurer against an insured, policy-holder or beneficiary domiciled in a Member State: the claim must be brought in the Member State in which the defendant is domiciled.[585]

Fourth, a final set of jurisdictional provisions makes provision for two discrete issues. A counterclaim may be brought in a court which is, in accordance with these rules, seised of the main action. However, a 'counterclaim' is, for this purpose, a counterclaim against an original party. A counterclaim against a new party may not deprive the latter of any jurisdictional protection which he would have enjoyed had he been sued in separate proceedings.[586] And an agreement on jurisdiction is effective, and will displace the jurisdictions identified by the provisions stated above, but only when the agreement complies with the conditions now set out in Regulation 1215/2012, Articles 15 and 16, and which are examined next.

2.95 Agreements on choice of court: Articles 15 and 16

The provisions dealing with agreements on choice of court, in matters falling within Section 3 of Chapter II, are complex. They state:

> 15. The provisions of this Section may be departed from only by an agreement: (1) which is entered into after the dispute has arisen; (2) which allows the policyholder, the insured or a beneficiary to bring proceedings in courts other than those indicated in this Section; (3) which is concluded between a policyholder and an insurer, both of whom are at the time of conclusion of the contract domiciled or habitually resident in the same Member State, and which has the effect of conferring jurisdiction on the courts of that Member State even if the harmful event were to occur abroad, provided that such an agreement is not contrary to the law of that Member State; (4) which is concluded with a policyholder who is not domiciled in a Member State, except in so far as the insurance is compulsory or relates to immovable property in a Member State; or (5) which relates to a contract of insurance in so far as it covers one or more of the risks set out in Article 16.
>
> 16. ... [omitted; refer to Appendix 1]

---

580 Article 12.

581 Article 13(1). But an insurer, sued as such, may not use this provision to join a co-insurer as third party for a contribution or indemnity: C-77/04 *GIE Réunion Européenne v. Zurich España* [2005] ECR I-4509. The co-insurer may instead be joined in accordance with Art. 8(2) if the conditions of that Article are met.

582 *Thwaites v. Aviva Assurances* [2010] Lloyd's Rep IR 667 interprets this to mean the law which governs the policy of insurance, but Rome II Regulation, Art. 18, would suggest that either the law governing the insurance or the law applicable to the tort may be relied on for this purpose.

583 Article 13(2). For joinder of the insured to such proceedings, by reference to Art. 13(3), see *Maher v. Groupama Est* [2009] EWCA Civ 1191, [2010] 1 WLR 1564; *Hoteles Piñero Canarias SL v. Keefe* [2013] EWHC 4279 (QB).

584 C-436/06 *FBTO Schadeverzekeringen NV v. Odenbreit* [2007] ECR I-11321.

585 Article 14(1). See *New Hampshire Insurance Co v. Strabag Bau AG* [1992] 1 Lloyd's Rep 361.

586 Article 14(2). See *Jordan Grand Prix Ltd v. Baltic Insurance Group* [1999] 2 AC 127.

By contrast with the treatment of an arbitration agreement, which falls outside the domain of the Brussels I Regulation and which is not otherwise regulated or restricted by it, an agreement on choice of court, or jurisdiction agreement, may be given effect in relation to a claim which otherwise falls within Section 3 of Chapter II only if it satisfies Article 15. It may be surprising that Article 15 may prevent parties, who may be fully aware of what they are doing and who have taken independent legal advice, from including in their contract of insurance an agreement as to the court which will adjudicate disputes which may arise. But the fear was, no doubt, that it would be difficult, at the jurisdictional stage, to separate cases of genuine agreement, or cases in which each side can be expected to look after itself, from those relationships in which the freedom to make an agreement was liable to be impaired. With that said, there is little room for a court to manoeuvre within the straitjacket of Article 15 when dealing with an agreement on choice of court, made before the dispute arises, by which it is contended that the parties are bound. For the purpose of Article 15(2), as the Article states that the agreement must allow the consumer to bring proceedings in courts other than those permitted by the other rules, an agreement which is validated by it must be in non-exclusive form: an exclusive jurisdiction agreement does not allow, but requires, proceedings to be brought in a named court.[587]

Although it is nowhere expressly so stated, there is little reason to doubt that Article 15 governs only the substance of such agreements, or the cases in which it is open to the parties to make an agreement, and is without prejudice to the distinct need for a valid agreement to comply with the formal requirements now set out in Article 25 of Regulation 1215/2012, which are considered below.[588] It has also been held that, even though a jurisdiction clause may be valid as between the insurer and the policy-holder, it cannot be extended so as to impose it as a burden on the beneficiary of the insurance, a conclusion which may appear to take hostility to jurisdiction agreements in insurance contracts further than it needed to go.[589] However, if Article 15 is taken to place an undue restriction on the power of the parties to determine jurisdiction in advance, a provision for arbitration will be effective in removing the resolution of the dispute from the scope and restrictive rules of the Regulation altogether.[590]

The obvious effect of Article 15 is in relation to agreements for the jurisdiction of a court in a Member State. It is implicit in the Article that it determines when a court other than one identified by Articles 10 to 14 may exercise jurisdiction, which therefore means that it must be confined to agreements for the courts of a Member State. Where it is contended that a court with jurisdiction under Section 3 should give effect to an agreement for the courts of a non-Member State, there appears to be no reason why it should not, always assuming that the agreement otherwise conforms to Article 15. For Article 15 does not say that it is limited to choices for the courts of Member States; and if it is correct that a

---

587 *Sherdley v. Nordea Life & Pension SA* [2012] EWCA Civ 88, [2012] Lloyd's Rep IR 437.

588 *Cf* Schlosser [1979] OJ C59/71, [161]; see also *Tradigrain SA v. SIAT SpA* [2002] 2 Lloyd's Rep 553; *Sherdley v. Nordea Life & Pension SA* [2012] EWCA Civ 88, [2012] Lloyd's Rep IR 437.

589 C-112/03 *Soc Financière & Industrielle de Peloux v. Soc AXA Belgium* [2005] ECR I-3707, where it was held that the burden of the agreement on jurisdiction could not be extended unless there had been a distinct acceptance of the agreement on jurisdiction by the beneficiary of the insurance. The broader principle of which this is one aspect, namely whether a person who takes substantive advantages under a contract which is, by some mechanism, transferred to him is *ipso facto* bound by an agreement on jurisdiction which bound the transferor, is discussed below, para. 2.135.

590 C-190/89 *Marc Rich & Co AG v. Soc Italiana Impianti PA* [1991] ECR I-3855.

choice of court for a non-Member State, which otherwise fits the template of the Article, is effective in the case of an employment contract, it is hard to see why it would not be so in an insurance contract.[591]

Article 15 provides for five cases in which an agreement[592] on jurisdiction may be given effect. The first is where the agreement is entered into after the dispute has arisen. The point at which a dispute arises for these purposes must be somewhere between the occurrence of the facts which will give rise to the claim and the service of process. But it is not possible, at this stage, to be any more precise about it.[593] The second is where the agreement allows[594] proceedings against the insurer to be brought by the policy-holder, insured or beneficiary in a court in addition to those open to the claimant pursuant to Section 3. Where this is the provision on which reliance is placed, the agreed-to jurisdiction can hardly be an exclusive one; and an agreement which purports to *require* the claimant to sue in the nominated court will, therefore, fall outside the ambit of this rule

The third case is where, on the date on which the insurance was taken out, the policy-holder and insurer were domiciled or habitually resident in the same Member State, and jurisdiction was lawfully conferred upon the courts of that Member State even if the harmful event were to occur abroad.[595] The fourth case is where the policy-holder is not domiciled in a Member State, except insofar as the insurance is compulsory or relates to immovable property situated in a Member State.[596]

The fifth case is where the policy of insurance relates to a marine, aviation, or other 'large risk' as specified by Article 16,[597] the terms of which it is sufficient to set out in Appendix 1.

2.96 International jurisdiction in the courts of the United Kingdom

Some of the provisions of Articles 10 to 16 will give international jurisdiction to a particular court;[598] others will give international jurisdiction only to the courts of a Member State. Where that Member State is the United Kingdom, it is a matter of internal United Kingdom law to identify the part of the United Kingdom in which proceedings may be brought. In the case of an insurer which is not domiciled in any Member State and which, because it operates through a branch or agency or other establishment in the United Kingdom, is deemed by Article 11(2) to be domiciled in the United Kingdom, it is deemed to be

---

591 See further, in the context of employment contracts, below, para. 2.121, discussing C-154/11 *Mahamdia v. People's Democratic Republic of Algeria* EU:C:2012:491, [2013] ICR 1.

592 On the meaning of 'agreement', see para. 2.146, below.

593 In the context of the original Brussels Convention, which this Article reproduces without material alteration, Jenard [1979] OJ C59/1, [33], stated that it meant that the legal proceedings are imminent or contemplated. This may be thought to be too vague, or if not, too late in the day.

594 Rather than 'requires'.

595 On whether it may be asserted against the beneficiary of the insurance who did not personally agree to it, see C-112/03 *Soc Financière & Industrielle de Peloux v. Soc AXA Belgium* [2005] ECR I-3707.

596 *Tradigrain SA v. SIAT SpA* [2002] 2 Lloyd's Rep 553.

597 See *Charman v. WOC Offshore BV* [1993] 2 Lloyd's Rep 551, on risks 'connected to' those in Article 16. See also *Denby v. Hellenic Mediterranean Lines Co Ltd* [1994] 1 Lloyd's Rep 320; *Minister for Food, Agriculture & Forestry v. Alte Leipziger Versicherung AG* [2001] IR 82.

598 Especially under Arts 13 and 14. But also under Art. 11(1)(b), where the policy-holder, insured or beneficiary may sue in the courts for the *place* where he is domiciled; Art. 12, where proceedings may be brought in the courts for the *place* where the harmful event occurred.

domiciled in the part of the United Kingdom in which the branch, agency or other establishment in question is situated.[599]

Otherwise, the allocation of jurisdiction over a defendant domiciled in, and sued in, the United Kingdom is dealt with by the 'general' provisions of Schedule 4 to the 1982 Act.[600] There is no counterpart of Articles 8 to 14 of the Regulation to be found in Schedule 4 to the 1982 Act; accordingly there is no distinct set of jurisdictional rules, applicable to insurance contracts, which allocates national jurisdiction within the United Kingdom in the case of insurance contracts. Presumably this is because the United Kingdom does not really see contracts of insurance as an area of civil or commercial life characterised by inequality of bargaining power.

2.97 Conclusion

If the provisions on insurance contracts give the English court jurisdiction, service out (if needed) is available as of right.[601] If they operate to exclude the jurisdiction of the English courts, that will mark the end of the enquiry. But if they do not apply, the next question must be addressed.

(6) JURISDICTIONAL PRIVILEGE IN MATTERS RELATING TO CERTAIN CONSUMER CONTRACTS

2.98 General

Section 4 of Chapter II of Regulation 1215/2012 is entitled 'Jurisdiction over consumer contracts'.[602] Articles 17 and 18 identify the contracts[603] to which the Section applies, and the courts which have jurisdiction over proceedings relating to them, as follows:

> 17. *(1) In matters relating to a contract concluded by a person, the consumer, for a purpose which can be regarded as being outside his trade or profession, jurisdiction shall be determined by this Section, without prejudice to Article 6 and point 5 of Article 7, if: (a) it is a contract for the sale of goods on instalment credit terms; (b) it is a contract for a loan repayable by instalments, or for any other form of credit, made to finance the sale of goods; or (c) in all other cases, the contract has been concluded with a person who pursues commercial or professional activities in the Member State of the consumer's domicile or, by any means, directs such activities to that Member State or to several States including that Member State, and the contract falls within the scope of such activities. (2) Where a consumer enters into a contract with a party who is not domiciled in a Member State but has a*

---

599 Civil Jurisdiction and Judgments Order 2001, SI 2001/3929, Sch. 1, para. 11, which corresponds to 1982 Act, s. 44.

600 That is, the rules found in Sections 1, 2, 6 and 7 of Chapter I of the Regulation (as modified and appearing in the corresponding sections of Sch. 4 to the 1982 Act as amended by SI 2001/3929, Sch. 2, para. 4). Insurance contracts are not treated as consumer contracts (as to which see para. 2.92, below) for the purposes of Sch. 4: see 1982 Act, Sch. 4, r. 7(2) as inserted by SI 2001/3929, Sch. 2, para. 4.

601 CPR r. 6.33.

602 For an excellent and detailed analysis of the issues raised by consumer contracts, in terms of jurisdiction, choice of law, and the various needs for reform, see Hill, *Cross-Border Consumer Contracts* (OUP, Oxford, 2008); and (with a focus more on what is now Art. 17) Cachia (2009) 34 ELR 476. See also, on certain aspects, Gillies, *Electronic Commerce and Private International Law* (Ashgate, Aldershot, 2008), ch. 5.

603 Though some of the detail has been supplied by case law to supplement the definitions provided by the Section.

branch, agency or other establishment in one of the Member States, that party shall, in disputes arising out of the operations of the branch, agency or establishment, be deemed to be domiciled in that Member State. (3) This Section shall not apply to a contract of transport other than a contract which, for an inclusive price, provides for a combination of travel and accommodation.

18. *(1) A consumer may bring proceedings against the other party to a contract either in the courts of the Member State in which that party is domiciled or, regardless of the domicile of the other party, in the courts for the place where the consumer is domiciled. (2) Proceedings may be brought against a consumer by the other party to the contract only in the courts of the Member State in which the consumer is domiciled. (3) This Article shall not affect the right to bring a counter-claim in the court in which, in accordance with this Section, the original claim is pending.*

Article 19, which is set out separately below, deals with agreements on jurisdiction and their application to contracts which fall within Article 17. The provisions of the corresponding rules of Regulation 44/2001 were substantially the same, save that Article 18 of Regulation 1215/2012 differs from Article 16 of Regulation 44/2001 in one particular detail, which is mentioned below.

2.99 General scope and purpose of Section 4 of Chapter II

Contracts made by consumers with professionals form the second category of subject matter given its own largely self-contained code of jurisdictional rules. This is justified by the perception that there is liable to be such inequality of arms that the jurisdictional playing field should be tilted so that the professional has to play uphill. The similarity to the structure of rules for matters relating to insurance is noticeable: the jurisdictional rules exclude the application of much of the remainder of the Regulation; there is considerable restriction on the right of parties to agree and to hold each other to an agreement on choice of court; and a court has a duty to deny recognition to a judgment from a court in another Member State in which the taking of jurisdiction conflicted with these jurisdictional rules.

In one respect the wording of Article 17(1) is apt to mislead. The reference to its being 'without prejudice to Article 6' would suggest that where the defendant is not domiciled in a Member State, jurisdiction over him is governed by the residual or traditional rules of jurisdiction. But this is not so: a professional without a domicile in any Member State may, or may also, be sued at the place in a Member State where the consumer is domiciled. This makes provison for jurisdiction in the courts of the consumer's home State, which was not provided by Regulation 44/2001, and it means that a professional may be sued in a Member State even though Article 6, and the rules it incorporates by reference, would not have given the court jurisdiction.[604]

Whereas Section 3 of Chapter II applies to all insurance and insurance contracts, there is a more restrictive definition, or identification, of consumer contracts to which Section 4 applies. This is partly statutory and partly judicial. In this context the Court has been more open about proceeding on the basis that Section 4 of Chapter II makes an exception to the general rule that a defendant should be sued in the courts of his domicile and that the Section should be construed accordingly, restrictively rather than generously.[605]

---

604 This will have the effect of reversing C-318/93 *Brenner & Noller v. Dean Witter Reynolds Inc* [1994] ECR I-4275, [16] in cases to which Regulation 1215/2012 applies.

605 C-464/01 *Gruber v. Bay Wa AG* [2005] ECR I-439, [32], reiterating a point made in C-269/95 *Benincasa v. Dentalkit Srl* [1997] ECR I-3767, and C-99/96 *Mietz v. Intership Yachting Sneek BV* [1999] ECR I-2277, [26].

The material which is available to explain which cases will fall within the framework of Section 4 of Chapter II may be organised by reference to three issues. The first is the general definition of 'contract... concluded by a... consumer'. The second concerns the three categories of contract into which the 'contract... concluded by a... consumer' must fall. The third concerns the range of claims, not all of which may seek the judicial enforcement of contract admitted on all sides to be valid and binding, which fall within the material scope of Section 4 of Chapter II.

2.100 The parties to the contract and to the litigation: Article 17

The special jurisdictional regime applies to certain contracts made by consumers: the contracts are referred to here, for convenience only, as 'consumer contracts'. The principal identifier of a consumer contract, according to Article 17, is the purpose of the contract as being one which is outside the trade or profession of the putative consumer.[606] After that, the Regulation sets out the three categories of contract into one of which the actual contract must also fall.[607] The Regulation also excludes a contract of transport except where this is part of a holiday package.[608] But judicial interpretation has provided further detailed specification of what brings a contract within, or keeps it outside, the material scope of Section 4 of Chapter II.

The question of what it means to be acting outside a person's trade or profession is not at all free from trouble. The issue has arisen with particular pointedness in cases in which an individual investor makes investment contracts, by which he aims to become richer. No doubt it is true that the pensioner with a couple of small savings accounts can make a convincing claim to have dealt as consumer, but what of the more comfortably off retired person who reads the financial pages of the daily papers and who fancies that he may make money from investment? It is unclear whether investment contracts made in such circumstances are capable of falling within Section 4 of Chapter II. The dominant view in England, at least, is that the definition of a consumer is not limited in a way which would serve to exclude middle-class investors, or similar individuals, from the definition of a consumer:[609] individuals who make investment agreements do not *ipso facto* exclude themselves from the category of persons who make their contracts as consumer. It may be a fair reading of references made by the German courts that they tend to the same view.[610] But

---

See also C-27/02 *Engler v. Janus Versand GmbH* [2005] ECR I-481; C-180/06 *Ilsinger v. Schlank & Schick GmbH (in liq)* [2009] ECR I-3571.

606 For an example of a case in which the contract, even if made for private gain, was not outside (subject matter of) the trade or profession of the individual, see *Maple Leaf Macro Volatility Master Fund v. Rouvroy* [2009] EWHC 257 (Comm), [2009] 1 Lloyd's Rep 475.

607 See para. 2.103, below.

608 Regulation 1215/2012, Art. 17(3). See also C-585/08 *Pammer v. Reederei Karl Schlüter GmbH* [2010] ECR I-12527 (voyage by freighter not excluded by what is now Art. 17(3), as it provided a combination of travel and accommodation for an inclusive price). The Court at [38]–[46] held that what is now Art. 17(3) should be interpreted in harmony with Regulation 593/2008 and Directive 90/314.

609 *Standard Bank London Ltd v. Apostolakis* [2001] Lloyd's Rep Bank 240.

610 C-89/91 *Shearson Lehmann Hutton Inc v. TVB* [1993] ECR I-139; C-318/93 *Brenner & Nöller v. Dean Witter Reynolds Inc* [1994] ECR I-4275. And in C-375/13 *Kolassa v Barclays Bank plc* EU:C:2015:37 the reason the claim was not covered by Section 4 was not because the purchase of financial bonds fell outside the Section, but because the claimant did not have a contractual relationship with the issuing bank.

it is equally evident that a different mentality prevails in Greece,[611] and that (for example) a doctor who pursues a profitable sideline in financial speculation has two professions.

However, even if were to be accepted that such a contract was made by the speculator outside any trade or profession of his, the contract must still fall within the purposive definition of a consumer contract, which is discussed further below: not every contract made by a person who could be a consumer is a contract made by a consumer for the purposes of the Regulation. It will be necessary to enquire further into the characteristics of a contract made by a consumer; and in this respect the correct analysis of those who make small-scale investment contracts may need to be revisited.

By contrast, a person who gives a guarantee of the financial liabilities of a company with which he is associated cannot be regarded as a consumer, even if the giving of guarantees is not his trade or profession.[612] The giving of the guarantee is, in effect, allied to the business liability of the company, albeit that it is given by an individual.

Though Article 17 provides a partial definition of the person who may be a consumer, the Section simply refers to the counterparty as 'the other' party to the contract.[613] It might appear to follow that, if a student in Oxford buys a second-hand bicycle from another who is about to return home to Germany, the contract is within the initial words of Article 17(1). This would be wrong. First, contracts made between private individuals are outside the mischief of Section 4. Second, in *Ilsinger v. Schlank & Schick GmbH (in liq)*,[614] the Court referred to the counterparty as a 'professional', in this respect following the usage of the Rome I Regulation,[615] which states the applicable law for consumer contracts by defining the other as someone 'acting in the exercise of his trade or profession'. Third, it has now been held that in Regulation 805/2004, which establishes the European Enforcement Order,[616] the reference to a consumer implies that the other party must be a professional.[617] It was surprising that the text of Article 17 was not amended to make this explicit, but it is clear that the 'other party' must be acting in the course of a[618] trade, profession, or business.

It is not yet clear whether a person may be held to be making the contract in question as a consumer if the counterparty does not realise, or had no reason to suppose, that the person he was dealing with was in this sense a consumer. The answer may depend on the extent to which Section 4 of Chapter II is understood to be an exception to the general jurisdictional rules of the Regulation; but on the face of it, there is no requirement of knowledge on the part of the professional.

In order to claim the jurisdictional privilege which Section 4 of Chapter II extends to a consumer, the consumer must also be party to the proceedings brought on the contract

---

611 In the *Standard Bank London* litigation, the Greek courts found the individual investors not to be making contracts as consumers: [2001] ILPr 766; see further below. See also *Maple Leaf Macro Volatility Master Fund v. Rouvroy* [2009] EWHC 257 (Comm), [2009] 1 Lloyd's Rep 475, [208]–[209]; *AMT Futures Ltd v. Marzillier et al GmbH* [2014] EWHC 1085 (Comm), [2015] 2 WLR 187.

612 C-419/11 *Česká spořitelna as v. Feichter* EU:C:2013:165, [2013] ILPr 375.

613 For the case in which the 'other party' appears to be one party who arranges for the contracted-for performance to be provided by a partner company, in which case both may be regarded as the 'other party', see C-478/12 *Maletic v. lastminute.com GmbH* EU:C:2013:735, [2014] QB 424.

614 C-180/06, [2009] ECR I-3571, [50]. The terminology of 'professional' to describe the other party now appears to have become standard: C-419/11 *Česká spořitelna AS v. Feichter* EU:C:2013:165, [2013] ILPr 375.

615 Regulation (EC) 593/2008, [2008] OJ L177/6, Art. 6.

616 On which, see below, para. 7.31.

617 C-508/12 *Vapenik v. Thurner* EU:C:2013:790, [2014] 1 WLR 2486.

618 There is no reason to suppose that a person cannot have more than one of these.

which he made. In *Shearson Lehmann Hutton Inc v. TVB*,[619] a private investor, considered to be a consumer, had entered into a speculative investment contract which had turned out to be disastrous. However, by the time a claim was brought against the investment adviser, whose professional performance was alleged to be inadequate, the rights of the contracting party had been assigned to an entity which was in the business of enforcing such claims. The European Court held that the proceedings did not fall within Section 4 of Chapter II, as the claimant was no longer the weak and disadvantaged party for whose benefit the jurisdictional rules had been framed.[620]

It follows that proceedings against rogue traders brought in the general interest of consumers, by bodies such as a Consumers Association, Offices of Fair Trading, or various financial services regulators,[621] etc., will not be within Section 4. Thus, in *VfK v. Henkel*,[622] an Austrian entity charged with taking action to prevent the use of unfair terms in consumer contracts took proceedings[623] against a professional who was using such terms in his dealings with consumers. It was held that the proceedings brought by VfK fell outside Section 4 of Chapter II, as the claim for relief was not being advanced by a consumer. There was no material sense in which the claim brought by VfK related to a contract made by a consumer, even though VfK was applying for orders in respect of contracts which the professional trader proposed to make with consumers.[624] Neither did the particular institutional claimant need the special jurisdictional advantages from which a consumer claimant would have benefited.

2.101 The purpose for which the contract was made

Though the types of contract which attract the special protective jurisdictional rules are specified in Article 17 (there are three of them, and they are examined below), there is an additional, preliminary, and general limitation which has been laid down by the European Court by reference to the purpose for which the contract was made. It will not fall within the material scope of Section 4 of Chapter II unless it secures the needs of an individual, final, consumer, in terms of private consumption.

It was held in *Benincasa v. Dentalkit Srl*[625] that a contract, by the terms of which Mr Benincasa became a franchisee of various dental products manufactured by Dentalkit, was not a contract made by a consumer, even though Benincasa was not a franchisee at the instant of signature. It was indicated[626] that the contract did not supply the needs of a private final consumer in terms of private consumption; it was instead made to allow him to go into

---

619 C-89/91, [1993] ECR I-139.

620 *Cf* C-347/08 *Vorarlberger Gebietskrankenkasse v. WGV-Schwäbische Allgemeine Versicherungs AG* [2010] ECR I-8661; C-433/01 *Freistaat Bayern v. Blijdenstein* [2004] ECR I-981; *Hatzl v. XL Insurance Co Ltd* [2009] EWCA Civ 223, [2010] 1 WLR 470. Likewise, if the claimant consumer does not have a direct contractual relationship with the defendant, but has a contractual relationship with an intermediary who, in turn, has a contract with the professional, Section 4 is inapplicable: C-375/13 *Kolassa v Barclays Bank plc* EU:C:2015:37.

621 The use of language is deliberate, as the identity of the body or bodies charged with bringing such proceedings is liable to change as the various regulatory regimes are reviewed and improved.

622 C-167/00, [2002] ECR I-8111.

623 Pursuant to Austrian legislation implementing Directive 93/13 on Unfair Terms in Consumer Contracts.

624 It followed that as the claim was not a contractual one, it fell within what is now Art. 7(2) of Regulation 1215/2012, on which see further below, para. 2.186.

625 C-269/95, [1997] ECR I-3767.

626 It would be for the referring court to make the final decision by applying the interpretation given by the Court to the facts of the case.

business. The notion of an individual final consumer is not, in the final analysis, a challenging one. But the concepts of 'needs' and of 'private consumption' are more open to debate. If this aspect of the decision in *Benincasa* is definitional rather than merely rhetorical, we must ask what it means. Does it apply to the contract made by an individual with an architect by which a house will be extended, or a loft converted, in order to allow the client to take in a lodger or two? Elderly and retired people who eke out their savings and pensions in this way may do so with a view to raising the cash to pay their heating and medical bills, and in this sense with a view to financing their needs, but they achieve this goal by making a contract which will permit them to run what is, in effect, a very small business; and if the contract has two purposes, as will be seen below, the trade or professional element has to be negligible if the contract is to fall within the Section. The answer to the question whether the contract with the architect is made to secure the needs of the individual in terms of private consumption is, it is submitted, too unclear for a firm view to be taken. That is certainly not to say that the test is incoherent. Rather, the line sought to be drawn is, almost certainly, one that cannot be defined with simplicity. It may, therefore, be preferable to regard the statement in *Benincasa* as a signpost but not necessarily as a boundary mark.

As hinted above, the English courts have not drawn the limits of 'needs' and 'private consumption' with puritan or socialist zeal.[627] It has been held that the private investor, or retired person with a private income and time on his hands, makes a contract with his broker which falls within Section 4 of Chapter II, even though he may not exactly be boiling stones to make soup. Even if the proposition, that those who engage in such activities are not so much needy as wanty,[628] is superficially attractive, any definition of a consumer which sought to exclude the wealthy or greedy from its scope would have been quite challenging, for even a millionaire must buy milk.[629] At least, this is what one supposes.

But the Greek courts have expressed a more severe opinion. In *Standard Bank London Ltd v. Apostolakis*,[630] two Greek investors had placed significant sums of money with investment advisers in London. They had signed jurisdiction agreements for the High Court from which they wished to resile; the English courts declared that they lacked jurisdiction on the basis that the investors had made their contracts which fell within Section 4 of Chapter II, as a result of which the jurisdiction agreements were invalid. The bank therefore sued them in Greece, only for the Greek court to disagree: it considered serial investment activity to be entrepreneurial, far removed from contracts by which the investors satisfied their needs in terms of private consumption. The question is problematic,[631] for each side has something to be said for it. The view tentatively preferred here is that the approach of the Greek court

---

627 It has been assumed by the European Court to extend to contracts for Alpine holidays (C-144/09 *Hotel Alpenhof GmbH v. Heller* [2010] ECR I-12527) which, on any sensible use of language or understanding of the human condition, cannot be seen as a need.

628 Attrib. Randolph Heard, *The Tick* (2001), Episode 8.

629 C-318/93 *Brenner & Nöller v. Dean Witter Reynolds Inc* [1994] ECR I-4275; *Standard Bank London Ltd v. Apostolakis (No 2)* [2001] Lloyd's Rep Bank 240.

630 [2001] Lloyd's Rep Bank 240.

631 Especially for the bank, which was told it could not sue in England (which considered the Greek courts only to have jurisdiction) or in Greece (which considered the English court only to have jurisdiction). It is not a satisfactory outcome by any manner of means. As to whether the practical answer was that the Greek court should have recognised the English judgment as to the ineffectiveness of the jurisdiction agreement, whether it liked it or not, one should now see C-456/11 *Gothaer Allgemeine Versicherung AG v. Samskip GmbH* EU:C:2012:719, [2013] QB 548. But in the light of Regulation 44/2001, Art. 35(1) and Regulation 1215/2012, Art. 45(1)(e), this might not provide the whole answer.

accorded more closely with the purpose of the Regulation, and that if a contract is made by which an investor[632] seeks to make financial gain which may or may not be used to make other contracts for the satisfaction of private needs, it is mercantile in nature, and is not itself a consumer contract.[633] It is, in this sense, similar to the case of Mr Benincasa: the contract is entered into as a small or medium-sized business venture.

It is, however, undeniable that if this view is taken, there will be marginal cases which are difficult to predict and which may not be few in number; and this definition may exclude from Section 4 litigation resulting from a contract made by an individual who has been lured, by fraud,[634] into an objectively unsuitable financial transaction. But if any income is liable to income tax as income arising from a trade or profession, there is an argument for saying that the contract which generated it was not made by the taxpayer for the purposes of consumption. If the income is liable to tax as the rental income from property, there is a case for saying that the contract which generated it was not made by the taxpayer as consumer. Of course the fiscal legislation of the United Kingdom cannot influence, still less dictate, the proper interpretation of the Regulation. But any temptation to see small-scale profit-generation as resulting from contracts made by a consumer is, in the present submission, one which should be resisted, for if one asks whether these are the people whom Section 4 of Chapter II was designed to privilege, the answer is that they are not.

2.102 Contracts made for mixed purposes

The question of how one is to deal with contracts entered into for mixed or marginal purposes is no easier to deal with in this context than it is elsewhere in the law. The individual who buys a computer on which to work from home, but which is also used by him and his family for their own private entertainment, or who buys clothes and shoes, or a car, which are used for work and leisure, is far from being a rare case. Whether a contract of sale entered into for such mixed purposes would fall within Section 4 of Chapter II is not easy to ascertain from the wording of the Regulation; and case law does not fully resolve the doubts.

The issue arose most directly in *Bay Wa AG v. Gruber*.[635] A farmer entered a contract to have roof tiles laid on his farmhouse and his farm buildings. It was clear that this indivisible roofing contract was one entered into for mixed purposes. The Court, following the advice of its Advocate General, ruled that where the contract was entire or indivisible and was entered into for both private and trade purposes, it was necessary to ask of the trade or professional element whether it was 'marginal to the point of having a negligible role' in the overall context. Unless it could be said that it was, the contract did not fall within, and

---

632 Or anyone else, for that matter. An employee's contract of employment is, after all, usually entered into to secure the needs of the employee in terms of his consumption, but it would be surprising to see it treated as a contract made by a consumer. It is rather a contract made and performed to allow a person to make other contracts which he may make as consumer.

633 For tentative support for this view, see *Maple Leaf Macro Volatility Master Fund v. Rouvroy* [2009] EWHC 257 (Comm), [2009] 1 Lloyd's Rep 475, [209]; *AMT Futures Ltd v. Marzillier et al GmbH* [2014] EWHC 1085 (Comm), [2015] 2 WLR 187.

634 Though the perpetration of such fraud is called 'mis-selling' when conducted by banks and other institutions of a similar kind. It is a deceitful name for a deceitful practice. And see now C-375/13 *Kolassa v Barclays Bank plc* EU:C:2015:37.

635 C-464/01, [2005] ECR I-439. And see also *Général de Banque v. Dumont* (Cass, 18 July 2000) [2001] Rev crit DIP 135 (*note* Gaudemet-Tallon).

therefore fell outside, the scope of Section 4 of Chapter II. An alternative 'predominant purpose' test was rejected; but the result is that one has to make an assessment of whether the non-consumer element of the contract was more than marginal.

Despite what the Court may have supposed, this solution will not promote legal certainty. It also has the potential to lead to troublesome arguments. At first sight, one might suppose that a person who goes to a shop to buy shoes or a bicycle makes a contract as a consumer, even though he wears the shoes and uses the bicycle to cycle to and from college. Yet if travelling to work is regarded as trade or professional activity, the contracts of sale would fall outside Section 4, whether or not they satisfied the other components of the definition. It is hard to believe that this is correct, though it is not easy to formulate the convincing argument which will refute it. This fact suggests, in turn, that the idea of use which is 'marginal to the point of having a negligible role' ought to be operated and applied with some flexibility. One notes in passing that the justification offered by the Court for its unexpectedly restrictive answer to the question referred by the national court was the derogatory[636] nature of the jurisdictional scheme for consumer contracts.[637]

2.103 The three classes of contract to which the Section applies

If analysis of the contract, and of the situations of the parties to it, survives the various tests just described, so as to qualify as a contract concluded by a consumer, it is next necessary to show that it falls within one of the three categories of contracts set out in what is now Article 17(1). The first two categories are types of contract; the third is defined in terms of the manner of its making rather than its content.

2.104 Contracts of sale on instalment credit terms

The first of the three categories of contract identified in the Article, a contract for the sale of goods on instalment credit terms, will not be difficult to identify. The concept of the sale of goods should not be difficult to apply. Its uniform meaning is liable to include contracts of hire purchase, even though these are not strictly sales of goods at common law.[638] The European Court held in *Soc Bertrand v. Paul Ott KG*,[639] that 'instalment credit terms' has an autonomous meaning which excluded payment by two bills of exchange. Its reasoning, based on an early and long-superseded version of what is now Article 17(1)(a) of the Regulation, was to the effect that those sophisticated enough to pay by bills of exchange did not require, and so stood outside, the protection of the Article. That may well be so; but as a cheque is, in English law, a bill of exchange, this decision should, perhaps, be treated with caution.[640] However, if the price is paid in instalments but the buyer does not take possession until the last instalment has been paid, the sale is not regarded as being on instalment credit terms.[641]

---

636 In that it reduced the scope of Art. 4.

637 C-464/01, [2005] ECR I-439, [32].

638 Schlosser [1979] OJ C59/71, [157], regards hire purchase as tantamount to an instalment sale.

639 150/77, [1978] ECR 1431.

640 After all, although cheques are falling into disuse, the complexity of the financial arrangements actually made or brought about by a customer who pays with a cheque or credit card does not generally indicate sophistication on the part of the customer.

641 C-99/96 *Mietz v. Intership Yachting Sneek BV* [1999] ECR I-2277.

2.105 Contracts made to finance the sale of goods

The second category of contract, identified in Article 17(1)(b), is a contract for a loan payable by instalments, or for any other form of credit, made to finance the sale of goods. When dealing with a contract of loan, repayable by instalments, or for other credit, made to finance the sale of goods, it appears that the purpose for which the loan was made is the crucial factor. It is not clear whether this is confined to cases where the permitted use of the money advanced is stipulated as a term of the contract by the supplier of credit, or extends to any case where credit is obtained and is then used to purchase goods. The former is the preferable view; in the latter case the provider of credit would have no reason to suppose that the contract was a consumer one.

2.106 Contracts made with those who direct activity to, or pursue activity in, Member States

The third category of protected consumer contracts, as it is now stated in Article 17(1)(c), has undergone more substantial alteration when put alongside its predecessor in the Brussels Convention:[642] this is important when reading decisions which were concerned with a predecessor text. Its current component elements are that the supplier carries on commercial or professional activities in the Member State of the consumer's domicile, or directs his activities to that Member State, or to several Member States including that one; and the contract falls within the scope of those activities.

By contrast with its predecessor, Article 17(1)(c) of the Regulation does not require the contract in question to be one for goods or services. Instead, it opens with the words 'in all other cases the contract… ', which is not so limited, and which makes it wider in material scope.[643] Moreover, it is no longer necessary to ask where the consumer took the steps necessary to conclude the contract.[644] Instead, the rule is stated in terms of the professional's[645] carrying on of activities in, or directing its activities to, the Member State in which the consumer has a domicile, or is at home.[646] The provision is best approached in fairly general terms and then by an examination of the detail as this has been drawn out by the European Court.

Article 17(1)(c) appears to be targeted at those professional suppliers who project their activity, their availability as would-be contracting parties, into the consumer's home State or actual home. It will cover those who carry on their business in person as well as those who act through agents, but may also extend to those whose activities – such as advertising their goods and services – fall short of making contracts in the consumer's home State. Its application to contracts made over the internet by home computer users is tricky, for there is a balance to be struck between the interests of the individual consumer and the business of the professional. For though the internet made a modest contribution to consumer life a generation ago, its use by consumers to make contracts has increased at a tremendous rate.

---

642 It was more concerned with showing that a specific invitation, or advertising, had been directed into the State of the consumer's domicile. As to this, see *Rayner v. Davies* [2002] EWCA Civ 1880, [2003] 1 All ER (Comm) 394, making the point that 'advertising' required initial conduct by the seller, and that the test of invitation also asks who invited whom to do business, so excluding cases where the first approach was made by the buyer.

643 C-180/06 *Ilsinger v. Schlank & Schick GmbH (in liq)* [2009] ECR I-3571, [50].

644 On this, see the Opinion of the Advocate General in C-464/01 *Bay Wa AG v. Gruber* [2005] ECR I-439: the Court did not refer to the point.

645 Though the Article does not use the terminology of 'professional'.

646 For an illustration, *Oakleaf Conservatories Ltd v. Weir* [2013] EWHC 3197 (TCC).

The Brussels Convention version of what is now Article 17(1)(c) had as its paradigm the professional who visited the consumer at home. This tended to mean that the consumer who stayed at home was liable to be privileged in a dispute with a professional who should have realised, in making a metaphorical journey to the consumer's door, that he might be forfeiting jurisdictional advantage. The sense in which Article 17(1)(c) is intended to operate is less immediately apparent when all parties stay – notionally – in their own jurisdiction and make contracts by remote communication. Take, for example, the case of a seller who maintains a website to which consumers have access, such as an internet bookseller. On the footing that the website (wherever it may be thought of as being) can be accessed from the spare bedroom of a computer-literate English consumer, but also by a consumer from any other Member State, or by a consumer who is domiciled in a Member State but who is temporarily overseas, the strain which is to be taken by Article 17(1)(c) is considerable.

There is no sense in trying to locate internet servers, and the like, not least because Article 17(1)(c) is concerned with how, not where, the contract is made. The most useful guidance was given by the European Court in the joined cases of *Pammer v. Reederei Karl Schlütter & Co KG*[647] and *Hotel Alpenhof GmbH v. Heller*.[648] In each case an individual had booked a cruise and a holiday, respectively, with a professional, using the internet to do so. Pammer, who was Austrian, had booked his sea passage[649] with a German shipping company through a German intermediary company, making his communications by internet. The shipping company denied that it pursued any professional or commercial activity in Austria. Heller, who was German, contracted with an Austrian hotelier, all communications being by email, Heller's initial awareness of the hotel having come from its website. When Heller left the hotel without settling his bill the hotel commenced proceedings in Austria. In each case the principal issue was whether the circumstances in which the contract was made brought it within what is now Article 17(1)(c).

The first question was whether the professionals had directed their activity to the home States of the consumers, and whether this required a conscious or deliberate targeting of (customers in) one or more Member States. By way of answering the question which it had framed, the Court held that it was not enough that the website was accessible by customers in their home States; what was required was that the professional have manifested its intention to establish commercial relations with consumers in the Member State in question, or in several Member States but including this one. The question was therefore whether the German shipping company had manifested its intention to deal with Austrian consumers; whether the Austrian hotelier had shown that it intended to deal with German consumers. The answer to that question was liable to be intensely fact-specific, and it was for the national court to find. As to the evidence which would and would not help the national court to find the answer, it is expedient to quote directly from the ruling: 'The following matters, the list of which is not exhaustive, are capable of constituting evidence from which it may be concluded that the trader's activity is directed to the Member State of the consumer's domicile, namely the international nature of the activity, mention of itineraries from other Member States for going to the place where the trader is established, use of a language or a currency other than the language or currency generally used in the Member State in which the trader is established with the possibility of making and confirming the reservation

---

647 C-585/08, [2010] ECR I-12527.
648 C-144/09, [2010] ECR I-12527.
649 On a rather spartan-sounding freighter, notably short of the usual pleasurable diversions of cruising.

in that other language, mention of telephone numbers with an international code, outlay of expenditure on an internet referencing service in order to facilitate access to the trader's site or that of its intermediary by consumers domiciled in other Member States, use of a top-level domain name other than that of the Member State in which the trader is established, and mention of an international clientele composed of customers domiciled in various Member States. It is for the national courts to ascertain whether such evidence exists.'

It is hard to quantify the guidance this actually gives. The reference to currency is liable to be distorted by the fact that many Member States use the euro, but traders in those which do not will often express a price in, or offer a conversion into, euros. It would be odd if that amounted to evidence that an English company had directed its activities to Austria but was not evidence that a German company had done likewise. It would be odd if the application of Article 17(1)(c) turned on whether a telephone number was stated with the +44 prefix, or whether the trader used .co.uk rather than .com or .eu, for example, as the last part of its web address. Yet it is not obvious what else the European Court could have said by way of elaboration of what it means to direct activities and how this is to be shown.

Opinions will legitimately differ on the question whether this is the place to try to draw the limits of Article 17(1)(c). It is still tempting to say that a supplier directs its activities to every consumer who can, without leaving the house, easily download everything the supplier has made electronically available and conduct all his communications in his own language. The idea that the consumer went and looked for the information, as distinct from his finding that it had been directed to his home State,[650] is not convincing; the proposition that a professional does not direct his activities to a consumer in circumstances where he exposes himself to that jurisdiction, by making his availability to contract fully and immediately available to a consumer who does not get up from the kitchen table, is not convincing either.

The last point taken by the hotelier in *Hotel Alpenhof GmbH v. Heller* was that the Article could not apply as the contract had not been concluded until the consumer arrived at the reception desk, handed over his credit card, and took his key. The Court should have said that the place of making the contract was an irrelevance, not referred to in Article 17(1)(c). Unfortunately, it rejected the point with observation that the parties had become bound to each other by exchange of email. This encouraged some to interpret the judgment as limiting the contracts covered by Article 17(1)(c) to those concluded at a distance. This had to be corrected in *Mühlleitner v. Yusufi*,[651] which confirmed the irrelevance of the place of making the contract.

The final point to consider is whether it is implicit – it is not explicit – in Article 17(1)(c) that the contract be made by the consumer as a result of the directing of activity to, or the pursuit of activity in, the consumer's home State. The short answer, that the Article does not say so, and that such a requirement would be a horrible thing to read in, comes from *Emrek v. Sabranovic*.[652] Whatever the merits of the point might otherwise have been, the need to demonstrate causation at the jurisdictional stage of proceedings which, in most cases, will be in actions for very modest sums, would have put the weaker party at a severe disadvantage; the Court did well to reject it. So long as the professional is shown to have

---

650 Note that it is to the Member State (or States), and not to the consumer's actual home, that the activity needs to be directed.

651 C-190/11, EU:C:2012:542. The judgment contains what is, in effect, a warning about too easily reading from one Regulation to another.

652 C-218/12, EU:C:2013:666, [2014] Bus LR 104.

directed its activity at the Member State in which the consumer has a domicile, the contract is liable to fall within Article 17(1)(c).

2.107 Matters relating to a contract: 'congratulations, you have won a prize' cases

The Court has sanctioned the application of Section 4 in some rather surprising cases, to the satisfaction of some, but not all, of those who are pestered by unsolicited communications from complete strangers, telling them that they have just won some improbably large prize if only they will do one little thing. In *Gabriel v. Schlank & Schick GmbH*[653] the Austrian recipient of one such letter responded and then claimed his prize, complying with the apparently minimal conditions set by the offeror by entering a contract to buy goods of minimal value, only for the offeror to refuse to hand over the prize. Austrian law gives a statutory cause of action to a consumer who has been so wronged or disappointed, to obtain an order that the offeror perform what it appeared to have promised to do.[654] The claimant therefore sued for his prize in the Austrian courts. It was held that the claimant had entered into a contract for the sale of goods, which satisfied the criteria laid out in *Benincasa*, and the prize offered was indissociable from that contract. The way in which the offeror had targeted its business at consumers in Austria by advertising there was sufficient to satisfy the predecessor to what is now Article 17(1)(c). Proceedings brought to claim the undelivered prize therefore fell within the Section.

By contrast, in *Engler v. Janus Versand GmbH*,[655] the claimant, to whom the letter was sent was not required to enter into any form of qualifying contract for the supply of goods or services in order to meet the conditions specified for the claiming of the prize. Once again the consumer invoked the Austrian statutory cause of action; this time she failed to show that her claim fell within what is now Article 17. It was held that the statutory claim under Austrian law for the prize did not bring the proceedings within the Section, as there was no contract otherwise falling within Article 17 and from which the claim to the prize was indissociable. However, even though there was no contract of sale or supply to which the claim for the prize could be linked, there was still an invitation from the supplier which had been accepted by the customer.[656] It was held that the proceedings did not fall within the predecessor of Article 17(1)(c), for Article 13(3) of the Brussels Convention, as it then stood, was expressly restricted to contracts for the sale of goods or services preceded by advertising or invitation.[657] But as the limitation in Article 13(3) has not reappeared in Article 15(1)(c) of the Regulation, the claim advanced by the consumer in *Engler* might now be decided differently.

The view that *Engler* might be decided differently today is also supported by *Ilsinger v. Schlank & Schick GmbH (in liq)*.[658] In that case it was accepted that the claimant

---

653 C-96/00, [2002] ECR I-6367.

654 That is to say, to do what the large print promised and never mind the small print.

655 C-27/02, [2005] ECR I-481. The decision was effectively followed and applied by the German Federal Supreme Court in its decision of 1 December 2005 in Case III ZR 191/03, [2006] IPrax 602.

656 With the result that what is now Art. 7(1) of the Regulation might apply.

657 It did, however, fall within what is now Art. 7(1), because it still created a contractual relationship.

658 C-180/06, [2009] ECR I-3571. The report does not record whether the defendant's liquidation was caused or contributed to by the fact that it found itself the defendant in three separate cases which went right up through the Austrian judicial system, thence to Luxembourg, and then back to the Austrian courts: in addition to this, there had been C-96/00 *Gabriel v. Schlank & Schick GmbH* [2002] ECR I-6367, and C-234/04 *Kapferer v. Schlank & Schick GmbH* [2006] ECR I-2585. At the very least, this will have stopped it sending out those bothersome letters.

may[659] be found to have made a contract in respect of the prize offered by the other party even in a case in which all that was required of the consumer was that she return a slip of paper to claim the prize offered. Even so, two doubts remain. The first arises from a comment by the Advocate General in *Engler*'s case, who observed that the aim of the provisions now compromising Section 4 of Chapter II was 'to protect the consumer and not to facilitate his enrichment'.[660] This was said as part of a preference for a restrictive construction of Section 4. The Court duly agreed that a restrictive interpretation was called for, though did not expressly endorse its Advocate General's rather glib statement of legislative purpose.[661] The point did not appear to surface in *Ilsinger*, and its status is therefore uncertain.

The second problem is created by the passage in the judgment in *Ilsinger*, which seems to intend to limit the material scope of what is now Article 17(1)(c) in a way which will exclude some cases in which the consumer lays claim to a prize by simply responding to the invitation, or doing what is asked of her, without undertaking any distinct obligation of her own.[662] The judgment states that if there was a contract to hand over the 'prize',[663] this will bring the claim within the rule. But if, by contrast, the communication from the professional was not a contractual offer,[664] or for some other reason there was no contract[665] to provide the prize, then Article 17(1)(c) will not apply. The principle of the matter is sensible: not all offers of 'free gifts' and prizes are contractual in nature or foundation; the challenge is to work out how to distinguish between them. And it is also true as a matter of English law that the contractual analysis of such cases is not always completely straightforward;[666] and it is plausible that it may also vary from law to law and country to country. In this context, though, the proposition that there must be a contract does not, perhaps, benefit from excessive elaboration; and the national court's principles of contractual formation should be sufficient to deal with the detail of whether the claim advanced is for a benefit which the offeror contracted to provide or deliver.

2.108 Matters relating to a contract: rescission and repayment claims

Other claims which might be brought, and which raise some difficulty, are those which do not affirm and seek to enforce a contract, but seek to rescind the contract and recover money paid. These must surely fall within the Section, especially where the consumer brings or defends the proceedings on the basis of special legislation for the protection of consumers.

A further category of case might involve a claim against a supplier who has not acted in good faith or who has failed to conclude a contract with the consumer. As to this last, there is room for more doubt whether a claim by a consumer against a supplier who is alleged to have caused loss by failing to conclude a contract with the consumer would fall within the scope of Article

---

659 It is for the national court to make this determination for itself, but by reference to which precise (national, autonomous) criteria is not clear.

660 At [29] of the Opinion.

661 At [43].

662 At [54]–[59].

663 In English terms, at least, an offer of a prize, which was intended to become binding on the communication of acceptance by the consumer, which was coupled with an intention to be legally bound, and for which something of value in the eye of the law was asked for in return.

664 Presumably some promotional material, for the wrongful sending of which other laws may make provision.

665 Such as (when it is governed by English law) an absence of consideration.

666 See, for illustration from the domestic law of contract formation, *Chappell & Co Ltd v. Nestle Co Ltd* [1960] AC 87; *Esso Petroleum Co v. Customs & Excise Commissioners* [1976] 1 WLR 1.

17. As the European Court has held[667] that claims which are founded on such legal obligations, predicated on the absence of a contract, do not raise matters relating to a contract, but are instead matters relating to a tort, it would be at least arguable that the text of Article 17, which speaks of matters relating to a contract *concluded* by... a consumer, could not extend to them.[668] Whether the opening words of Article 15 may be allowed a wider scope than those of Article 7(1) must be open to some doubt,[669] but there can be little doubt that it would be desirable for such a purposive construction, favouring the weaker party, to be adopted.

The result should be that wherever the relationship between consumer and professional was that of parties to an actual contract, a disputed contract, an avoided contract, a supposed contract, a failed contract, etc., the claim should have the potential to fall within Article 17. It would be convenient if this extended to a situation in which the parties tried but failed to conclude a contract, and that this is the fact which founds the claim. It is not yet known whether this, or any of it, will commend itself to the European Court.

2.109 Jurisdictional rules: Article 18

With that unhappily lengthy introduction to the nature of contracts made by a consumer, Regulation 1215/2012 establishes the rules which determine jurisdiction over proceedings falling within Section 4 of Chapter II as follows.

First, where the defendant, whether the consumer or the professional, enters, or will enter, an appearance, Article 26 provides that the courts of that Member State have, or will have, jurisdiction.[670] Article 26 is a superior rule in the hierarchy of the Regulation; where the defendant is the consumer, the court has an unparticularised duty to inform the consumer of the right he may have to contest the jurisdiction of the court.[671]

Second, a consumer may sue a professional in the Member State in which the professional has a domicile;[672] a professional may sue a consumer in the Member State in which the consumer has a domicile.[673]

Third, where the consumer sues a professional who does not have a domicile in a Member State, the professional may be treated as though he had a domicile in a Member State, and sued there, if he has a branch, agency or other establishment in a Member State and the dispute arises out of the operations of that establishment.[674]

---

667 C-334/00 *Fonderie Officine Meccaniche Tacconi SpA v. Heinrich Wagner Sinto Maschinenfabrik GmbH* [2002] ECR I-7357. In C-234/04 *Kapferer v. Schlank & Schick GmbH* [2006] ECR I-2585, an Austrian court referred a question concerning pre-contractual liability in relation to consumer contracts and what is now Art. 17. But the question was not answered, as the Court answered the first question before it in a way which meant that the question on Art. 17 did not require an answer. The Advocate General had proposed the answer that the claim advanced by the claimant fell outside Art. 17(1)(c) as the point of departure was that no contract whatever had been entered into, and as a result, the words 'in all other cases a contract has been concluded ...' could not be satisfied.

668 This may be thought to follow from C-180/06 *Ilsinger v. Schlank & Schick GmbH (in liq)* [2009] ECR I-3571

669 Especially in the light of *Engler v. Janus Versand GmbH* and C-180/06 *Ilsinger v. Schlank & Schick GmbH (in iq)* [2009] ECR I-3571, the latter of which seems perfectly sure that what is now Art. 7(1) is *broader* in scope than Art.17.

670 C-111/09 *Česká podnikatelská pojišťovna AS, Vienna Insurance Group v. Bilas* [2010] ECR I-4545.

671 Regulation 1215/2012, Art. 26(2).

672 Regulation 1215/2012, Art. 18(1).

673 Regulation 1215/2012, Art. 18(2). In the rare case in which the consumer has renounced his domicile, and has vanished in circumstances which mean that his current domicile is unknown, the prior domicile will apply in proceedings brought by the professional: C-327/10 *Hypoteční Banka as v. Lindner* [2011] ECR I-11453.

674 Regulation 1215/2012, Arts 17(2) and 18(1).

Fourth, where, but only where, the consumer is domiciled in a Member State, and sues a professional who neither has nor is deemed to have a domicile in a Member State, the consumer may sue the professional in the courts of the Member State in which the consumer is domiciled.[675] This rule applies when, but only when, Regulation 1215/2012 applies to the proceedings. He may, also, rely on the residual or traditional jurisdictional rules which operate in the court proposed to be seised.[676]

Fifth, if neither the consumer nor the professional has a domicile in a Member State, jurisdiction over the defendant will be determined by Article 6, which provides that jurisdiction over a defendant may be based upon the national law of any State which will exercise it.[677]

Sixth, any court which is seised with a dispute according to these rules has jurisdiction to entertain a counterclaim.[678]

Seventh, jurisdiction agreements are effective only in accordance with the restrictive conditions of Article 19, and which is examined below.

2.110 Agreements on choice of court: Article 19

As is the case with insurance contracts, a jurisdiction agreement, or agreement on choice of court, is enforceable in relation to a matter falling within Section 4 of Chapter II of the Regulation only in limited circumstances. These are set out in Article 19 of Regulation 1215/2012, which states as follows:

> *The provisions of this Section may be departed from only by an agreement: (1) which is entered into after the dispute has arisen; (2) which allows the consumer to bring proceedings in courts other than those indicated in this Section; or (3) which is entered into by the consumer and the other party to the contract, both of whom are at the time of conclusion of the contract domiciled or habitually resident in the same Member State, and which confers jurisdiction on the courts of that Member State, provided that such an agreement is not contrary to the law of that Member State.*

It is irrelevant that the parties may have been content to make a different and binding agreement as to choice of court. For it to be valid at all, the jurisdiction agreement must comply with the formal requirements of Article 25.[679]

For the purpose of Article 19(1), it is again difficult to identify the precise moment at which a dispute arose.[680] The date of the fact which gave rise to the alleged breach of contract may help to identify it, though in English law it is the acceptance that the contract has been breached, rather than the wrongful conduct, which is decisive. For the purpose of Article 19(2), as the Article states that the agreement must allow the consumer to bring proceedings in courts other than those permitted by the other rules, an agreement which is validated by reference to this rule must be non-exclusive in form: an exclusive jurisdiction agreement does not allow, but requires, proceedings to be brought in a named court.[681] For the purpose of Article 19(3), the text speaks for itself.

---

675 Regulation 1215/2012, Art. 18(1).
676 Regulation 1215/2012, Art. 17(1).
677 Regulation 1215/2012, Art. 17(1).
678 Regulation 1215/2012, Art. 18(3).
679 Schlosser [1979] OJ C59/71, [161]. For the validity of non-exclusive (that is, additional) jurisdiction agreements for a non-Member State, see the discussion at para. 2.121, below.
680 See above, para. 2.95.
681 *Sherdley v. Nordea Life & Pension SA* [2012] EWCA Civ 88, [2012] Lloyd's Rep IR 437.

The effect of Article 19 is that a jurisdiction agreement will be of limited effect in a contract made by a consumer. But there are two respects in which these controls may not go far enough. The definition of a consumer contract is too restrictive to include all contracts which may be made by a consumer; and the conditions stated in Article 17 may not always serve to exclude agreements which are unfair and contrary to the interests of the consumer. In such cases in particular, therefore, the Unfair Terms in Consumer Contracts Regulations[682] may operate to deprive such a term[683] of effect, even if it were to survive the scrutiny of Article 19.

2.111 Further legislative provision for small claims

As said above,[684] the European Union has enacted a number of instruments which are designed to make it easier for small claims to be brought, and for judgments in certain types of proceedings to be enforced, in other Member States.[685] In particular, the Regulation establishing a European Order for Payment ('EOP'),[686] and the Regulation establishing the European Small Claims Procedure ('ESCP')[687] make provision for jurisdiction in the cases to which they apply. Their jurisdictional impact is generally small, as they adopt and use the jurisdictional rules of the Brussels I Regulation. The ESCP Regulation applies to proceedings in civil and commercial matters in cross-border cases. Where the value of a claim does not exceed €2000, the ESCP procedure, which is almost entirely carried out in writing, may be invoked. But the question of which court has jurisdiction is answered by the provisions of the Brussels I Regulation.[688]

The EOP Regulation applies in civil and commercial matters in cross-border cases. Where proceedings fall within it, jurisdiction is, in fact, determined by the provisions of the Brussels I Regulation.[689] However, where the claim relates to a contract concluded by a consumer for a purpose which lies outside his trade or profession, and the defendant is the consumer, the only court with jurisdiction is that of the Member State of the consumer's domicile.[690] The definition of the contracts to which this provision applies is therefore broader than Article 17 of the Brussels I Regulation, but otherwise proceedings taken under the aegis of these Regulations in respect of matters relating to contracts made by consumers are subject to the jurisdictional rules of the Brussels I Regulation.

---

682 SI 1999/2083, enacting Directive 93/13; and as the European Union makes increasing provision for unfair terms and practices in contracts and dealings with consumers, legislation of this kind will cast a larger shadow over jurisdiction agreements which would otherwise have been valid: cf C-240/98 *Océano Grupo Editorial SA v. Quintero* [2000] ECR I-4941; *Standard Bank London Ltd v. Apostolakis (No 2)* [2001] Lloyd's Rep Bank 240; and see Withers [2002] LMCLQ 56.

683 Though in practice, its impact on arbitration clauses will be greater, for these are outside the scope of, and therefore never restricted by, the Brussels I Regulation.

684 Paragraph 2.52, above.

685 So far as these instruments deal with the recognition and enforcement of judgments, they are dealt with in Chapter 7.

686 Regulation (EC) 1896/2006, [2006] OJ L399/1, in force from 12 December 2008. See also CPR Part 78.

687 Regulation (EC) 861/2007, [2007] OJ L199/1, in force from 1 January 2009. See also CPR Part 78.

688 Article 4(1) and Annex I, s. 4.

689 See for illustration of the approach of the Court to the exhaustiveness of the provisions of the Regulation C-215/11 *Szyrocka v. SiGer Technologie GmbH* EU:C:2012:794; but for the limits of that (holding in effect that the restrictive Regulation scheme for opposing the order is not exclusive where the defendant had not been served in the first place, for otherwise the rights of the defence would be imperilled), see C-119/13 *eco cosmetics GmbH v. Dupuy* and C-120/13 *Raiffeisenbank St Georgen reg. Gen. mbH v. Bonchyk* (joined cases) EU:C:2014:2144, [2015] 1 WLR 678.

690 Article 6. Cf C-508/12 *Vapenik v. Thurner* EU:C:2013:790, [2014] 1 WLR 2486 (a case on Regulation 805/2004).

2.112 International jurisdiction in the courts of the United Kingdom

Some of the provisions of Articles 17 to 19 give jurisdiction to a particular court,[691] whereas others will give international jurisdiction only to the courts of a Member State. Where that Member State is the United Kingdom, it is then a matter of internal United Kingdom law to go on to identify the particular part of the United Kingdom in which proceedings may be brought. In the case of a professional who is not domiciled in a Member State but who, because he operates through a branch, agency or other establishment in the United Kingdom, is deemed in accordance with Article 17(2) to be domiciled in the United Kingdom, he is deemed to be domiciled in the part of the United Kingdom in which the branch, agency or other establishment in question is situated.[692] If the consumer is domiciled in the United Kingdom and sues there on the basis of Article 16(1), he is deemed to be domiciled in the part of the United Kingdom in which he is domiciled.[693] Otherwise jurisdiction is determined by rules 7 to 9 of Schedule 4 to the 1982 Act as inserted by SI 2001/3929 Schedule 2, paragraph 4, which reproduce in large part the provisions of what are now Articles 17 to 19 of the recast Regulation, but with reference to a 'part of the United Kingdom' in place of a 'Member State'.

2.113 Conclusion

If these provisions give the English court jurisdiction, service out (if needed) will be available as of right.[694] If these provisions apply and give the answer that the English court does not have jurisdiction, the enquiry ends there. If these provisions do not apply, the next question must be asked.

(7) JURISDICTIONAL PRIVILEGE AND CONTRACTS OF EMPLOYMENT

2.114 General

Section 5 of Chapter II of Regulation 1215/2012 is entitled 'Jurisdiction over individual contracts of employment'. Articles 20 to 23 spell out the jurisdictional rules which apply to proceedings which fall within this Section, as follows:

20. *(1) In matters relating to individual contracts of employment, jurisdiction shall be determined by this Section, without prejudice to Article 6, point 5 of Article 7 and, in the case of proceedings brought against an employer, point 1 of Article 8. (2) Where an employee enters into an individual contract of employment with an employer who is not domiciled in a Member State but has a branch, agency or other establishment in one of the Member States, the employer shall, in disputes arising out of the operations of the branch, agency or establishment, be deemed to be domiciled in that Member State.*

21. *(1) An employer domiciled in a Member State may be sued: (a) in the courts of the Member State in which he is domiciled; or (b) in another Member State: (i) in the courts for the place where or from where the employee habitually carries out his work or in the courts for the last place where he*

---

691 Especially Art. 19.
692 SI 2001/3929, Sch. 1, para. 11, which corresponds to 1982 Act, s. 44.
693 SI 2001/3929.
694 CPR r. 6.33.

did so; or (ii) if the employee does not or did not habitually carry out his work in any one country, in the courts for the place where the business which engaged the employee is or was situated. (2) An employer not domiciled in a Member State may be sued in a court of a Member State in accordance with point (b) of paragraph 1.

22. *(1) An employer may bring proceedings only in the courts of the Member State in which the employee is domiciled. (2) The provisions of this Section shall not affect the right to bring a counter-claim in the court in which, in accordance with this Section, the original claim is pending.*

23. *The provisions of this Section may be departed from only by an agreement: (1) which is entered into after the dispute has arisen; or (2) which allows the employee to bring proceedings in courts other than those indicated in this Section.*

2.115 General scope and purpose of Section 5 of Chapter II

The provisions of Regulation 44/2001, Articles 18 to 21, are to substantially the same effect as those in Regulation 1215/2012, save for two important facts. The first is that the jurisdictional rule contained in Article 21(2) of Regulation 1215/2012 is new, and had no counterpart in Regulation 44/2001. The second is that, for reasons which reflect no credit on the European Union, Regulation 44/2001 allowed a judgment to be recognised even though it had been given by a court whose taking of jurisdiction conflicted with Section 5 of Chapter II. In this respect, Regulation 44/2001 did not reinforce the jurisdictional privileges of the employee in the way which it did for insured parties and for consumers. That lingering trace of anti-employee bias has now been removed for judgments in proceedings commenced on or after 10 January 2015, where recognition is governed by Regulation 1215/2012, but otherwise the shortcoming in Regulation 44/2001 remains in a sorry place.

That point aside, the structure of Section 5 of Chapter II is reasonably similar to that of Sections 3 and 4. The jurisdictional rules are tilted in favour of the employee, who may only be sued in the Member State in which he has a domicile but who, as well as being able to sue the employer where the employer is domiciled, has the option of suing in the place where he carries out his work;[695] and restrictions are placed on the effectiveness of jurisdiction agreements. As is the case with the consumer contract provisions, and as distinct from the insurance provisions, the jurisdictional provision which allows an employee to sue somewhere other than where the employer is or is deemed to be domiciled applies even where the defendant employer does not have a domcile in any Member State.[696] The significance of the fact that the matter before the court must be one 'relating to' an individual contract of employment is examined below, though it suffices at this point to observe that the form of words may describe a looser or broader relationship with a contract than that the proceedings be brought to enforce the contract of employment properly or narrowly so called.

The original version of the Brussels Convention made no special provision for claims arising and made in the context of the employment relationship, which always seemed strange: the exploitation of the weakness of employees by the bosses was more of a social ill than anything ever dreamed up by insurers or professionals who dealt with consumers. When the Contracting States failed to stir themselves, the European Court confected a protective jurisdictional rule by interpreting the original version of what is now Article 7(1),

---

695 He does not have the option of suing in the Member State in which he is domiciled. The suggestion in C-154/11 *Mahamdia v. People's Democratic Republic of Algeria* EU:C:2012:491, [2013] ICR 1, [45], which seems to say that the employee may sue in the Member State in which he is domiciled, must be wrong.

696 Regulation 1215/2012, Art. 21(2).

which provided for special jurisdiction over a defendant domiciled in another Member State, in a way which would make it easier for an employee to sue his employer, domiciled in another Member State, in the courts for the place where he carried out his work.[697] This was fine as far as it went, but this could have no effect on the validity of choice of court agreements, and it could not prevent actions by the employer being brought wherever the employer could found jurisdiction against the employee. More organised measures to improve the jurisdictional position of the employee came with legislative confirmation of the special jurisdiction of the courts for the Contracting State in which he worked, and with limitations on the effect of agreements on choice of court.[698] But it was not until Regulation 44/2001 that the individual contract of employment achieved its status of junior parity alongside insurance contracts and certain contracts made by consumers; and it was not until Regulation 1215/2012 that it was, in effect, put on a par with contracts made by consumers.

2.116 The working relationships to which Section 5 of Chapter II applies

Section 5 of Chapter II applies to matters relating to individual contracts of employment. It has application neither to collective agreements nor to contracts for the provision of services.[699] No doubt these expressions all enjoy autonomous or uniform meanings, though the possibility that they will depart significantly from the definition of employment in English domestic law is perhaps unlikely. It is necessary to take care to separate the 'employee', to which Section 5 applies, from the broader category of 'worker', which may include, for example, some members of Limited Liability Partnerships who are workers but not employees, and to which Section 5 should not be taken to apply unless and until the European Court clarifies the true position.[700]

The distinction between employment, and the provision of services which is not employment, was examined in *WPP Holdings v. Benatti*.[701] The decision was that the individual in that case was a self-employed management consultant, even though he worked under the constraints of a very detailed brief. It may be helpful to look at the contract to see whether the individual had freedom to decide when and where to work, when to take a holiday, whether remuneration was paid on a commission basis, and so on. But in the end the question whether the individual was employed or self-employed is no easier to answer in this context than it is elsewhere in the law.

The line which separates conracts of employment from contracts of service leads to another problem when it is asked how Section 5 of Chapter II applies in certain artificially contrived circumstances. In some areas of economic activity, a person who is admitted to be

---

697 133/81 *Ivenel v. Schwab* [1982] ECR 1891: a rule held to have been limited to contracts of employment: 266/85 *Shenavai v. Kreischer* [1987] ECR 239.

698 Adjustments made on the accession of Spain and Portugal, and largely reproduced in the Lugano I Convention (1988).

699 On whether commercial agents are to be seen as employees, see Mankowski (2008) 10 *Yearbook of Private International Law* 19, who concludes that the answer will be 'rarely'.

700 See Employment Rights Act 1996, s. 230(3); *Clyde & Co LLP v. Bates van Winklehof* [2014] UKSC 32.

701 [2007] EWCA Civ 263, [2007] 1 WLR 2316. It is to be noted that Sir Anthony Clarke MR was of opinion, at [100], that the European Court may be expected to take a broader view than the common law as to when a contract is one of employment. Subject to the observation that this would conduce to a narrow interpretation of Section 5 of Chapter II, the view of the Master of the Rolls may well prove to make an accurate prediction. Remember, though, that Art. 20 simply requires the matter before the court to be one 'relating to' an individual contract of employment.

an employee may be required to be party to more than one contractual relationship, these being interdependent but legally distinct. The fundamental question is whether to respect, or to be prepared to look past, the formal contractual structures put in place to secure the labour of the employee and entrench his loyal performance. For example, in *Samengo-Turner v. J&H Marsh & McLennan (Services) Ltd*[702] it was held that an 'incentive agreement', concluded between an employee and a company associated with the employer, was to be treated as though it was, or was all part of, an individual contract of employment. The court took this approach to deprive an agreement on jurisdiction contained in the 'incentive agreement' of effect by virtue of its failure to meet the conditions which are now set out in Article 23.[703] And in *Duarte v. Black & Decker Corp*[704] it was held, in effect, that if the relationship between company and worker was one of employment, a separate agreement which was entered into within the broad context of that employment was itself to be seen as a contract of employment. Proceedings brought in respect of a separate agreement not to disclose confidential information, concluded in such circumstances, may therefore 'relate to' a contract of employment for the purpose of the Regulation.[705] But if this is correct, and an 'individual contract of employment' will be understood to mean any[706] contract which forms part of the contractual relationship of individual employment, its scope may be surprisingly wide.

It has yet to be decided how far this reasoning, which is all taken from domestic sources and which is therefore subject to confirmation, can be made to go: whether, for example, it applies in cases in whch an individual is retained by a company which then provides his services to another. In such a case, the company to which the services are provided does not employ the worker, but the degree to which the worker is independent of the control of the company may be close to zero. And it has yet to be decided whether the European Court would accept any of it, or would instead confine the material scope of Section 5, which is an exception to the broad structure of the Regulation, to such individual contracts, and to only such individual contracts, as are drafted as contracts of employment, between employer and employee.

A further problem, which may also be a reflection of modern labour practices, is the application of Section 5 in cases in which the employee is not rooted to a single place of work, but is lent or seconded by one employer to the service of another, or is sent to which-ever place the employer needs him to work from time to time. Accordingly, the problems which arise from the mobile nature of some employments will be considered after the rules have themselves been examined.

---

702 [2007] EWCA Civ 723, [2008] ICR 18. See [2007] LMCLQ 433.

703 This is open to criticism at several levels. But to the extent that it closes a door to a possible evasion of Art. 25 by crafty employers, there is a pragmatic defence of it to be made. The question whether the court was right to read what is now Art. 23 as applying to a jurisdiction agreement for a non-Member State is considered below, para. 2.121.

704 [2007] EWHC 2720 (QB), [2008] 1 All ER (Comm) 401 (a case on choice of law under the Rome Convention).

705 Another way to make the same point would be to reason that if, on the facts, this obligation would have not bound the parties if there had been no contract of employment to which they were (also) bound, the obligation is one which relates to the employment; *cf* C-548/12 *Brogsitter v. Fabrication de Montres Normandes EURL* EU:C:2014:148, [2014] QB 753.

706 Even so, it is hard to believe that, say, a contract by which an employer leases a car to an employee, as a perk of the job, is a contract of individual employment, even if its purpose is to encourage the employee to stay.

2.117 Former employment

A question to which the Section does not immediately furnish the answer is how its rules apply when the proceedings are brought after the termination of the employment, for example, as a claim against a former employee. No case has held that the Section is inapplicable if there is no longer an employment relationship; and in some cases at least, the claim will be brought by reason of the allegedly-wrongful termination of the employment. It must surely be correct in principle that the ex-employee should continue to benefit from the jurisdictional rules of Section 5. An employer may be able to dismiss an employee, and the employee may have no real choice but to accept the *fait accompli*,[707] but this should not call into question the application of Section 5. If the former employee sues the employer, maybe decades after the termination of the employment, such as when it becomes clear, long after the event, that a condition like mesothelioma was contracted during the employment and that the employer was at fault, the Section must in principle apply, though its operation may be awkward in cases in which the original employer has been merged or taken over.

It is harder to see what is to happen if the employee changes his domicile after the termination of the employment: retiring to live in Spain, for example. It might seem surprising that he should now have Spain as the Member State of his domicile for the purposes of Section 5 of Chapter II, with the consequence that claims brought against him by his former employer would have to be brought in Spain,[708] especially if this was not a domicile he ever had as employee. Yet it appears to be the answer given by Article 22: it is difficult to interpret Article 22 as giving jurisdiction in claims against a former employee to the courts of the Member State in which he was domiciled on the cessation of the employment, even if this might be said to accord more closely with the broad scheme of the Section. Clarification will have to come from the Court or from legislative amendment to Article 22.

2.118 The relationship between the claim and the employment

Whether a matter relates to an individual contract of employment only if it is founded on the relevant contract is debatable. There is no reason why proceedings on a claim formulated by the employee as one in tort but which arises from and because of the contractual employment relationship – based on an allegation that the employer has breached a statutory duty to maintain a safe system of work, for example – would not fall within the Section, and every reason why it should fall within it. Likewise, claims which seek to enforce fiduciary duties, or to restrain the misuse of confidential information by an employee, should fall within the Section.[709] Where it is alleged that an employee has stolen property from the employer, or from another employee, and faces legal proceedings from

---

707 *Cf Societé Générale, London Branch v. Geys* [2012] UKSC 63, [2013] 1 AC 523.

708 Article 20. But the courts for the Member State of the employee's domicile do not, as such, have jurisdiction in proceedings brought by the employee under Art. 21.

709 If such proceedings, when brought against a joint venturer, are a matter relating to a contract (as they are: C-548/12 *Brogsitter v. Fabrication de Montres Normandes EURL* EU:C:2014:148, [2014] QB 753) for the purpose of special jurisdiction under Art. 7(1), they must also be matters relating to a contract of employment for the purpose of this Section. The legal or conceptual basis of substantive liability appears to have nothing to do with the matter of jurisdiction under Chapter II.

the employer as a result, the Section should apply, as the matter relates to the contract of employment, at least as a matter of language. But would it apply to a claim for personal injury by an employee who is knocked off his bicycle by the works bus on the road leading away from the factory? Would it make any difference whether the bus driver was an employee or an independent contractor? The factual variations are endless. The Court of Appeal, perhaps seeing this, criticised an attempt to gloss or paraphrase the expression 'relating to individual contracts of employment', saying that the statutory wording laid down a broad test which should be comparatively easy to apply.[710] Time will tell,[711] but in the absence of guidance from the European Court there are bound to be cases to which the plain, unvarnished language of Article 20 does not work in a wholly predictable way. For the present, however, if the allegation could be presented as a breach of contract by the employee or employer, that may bring it within Section 5 of Chapter II, no matter how the claim is actually formulated; where this is not so, it will be very much more difficult to come within the Section.

2.119 Jurisdictional rules: Articles 20 to 23

The jurisdictional rules put in place by Articles 20 to 23 of Regulation 1215/2012 may be stated in the following form.

First, where the defendant, whether employer or employee, enters or will enter an appearance, Article 26 of the Regulation, which is a superior jurisdictional rule, provides that the courts of that Member State have jurisdiction.[712] But in cases to which Regulation 1215/2012 applies, the court must inform the employee that he may be entitled to object to the jurisdiction of the court.[713]

Second, if the case is one to which Directive 96/71, on workers posted abroad, applies, the jurisdiction specified by that Directive will be applicable,[714] in accordance with Article 67.

Third, proceedings against an employee who has a domicile in a Member State may be brought only before the courts of that State.[715] Proceedings against an employee who does not have a domicile in a Member State may be brought on the basis of the residual or traditional rules of jurisdiction applicable in the court proposed to be seised, in accordance with Article 6.[716]

Fourth, if an employee wishes to bring proceedings against an employer who has a domicile in a Member State, he may bring them in that Member State.[717] But if the employee wishes to sue the employer in a different Member State, he may do so (i) if this Member State is the place where he habitually carries out his work or in the last place where he did so,[718] or (ii) if he does not or did not habitually carry out his work in any one

---

710 *Alfa Laval Tumba AB v. Separator Spares International Ltd* [2012] EWCA Civ 1569, [2013] 1 WLR 1110, [24], [25], disapproving (and on this point, overruling) *Swithenbank Foods Ltd v. Bowers* [2002] EWHC 2257 (QB), [2002] 2 All ER (Comm) 974 and *CEF Holdings Ltd v. Mundey* [2012] EWHC 1524 (QB).

711 No doubt in 1932 there were those who thought that the 'who is my neighbour?' question, asked by *Donoghue v. Stevenson* [1932] AC 652 would be just as straightforward to answer.

712 C-111/09 *Česká podnikatelská pojišťovna AS, Vienna Insurance Group v. Bilas* [2010] ECR I-4545.

713 Regulation 1215/2012, Art. 26(2).

714 Article 6 of that Directive; Art. 67 of the Brussels I Regulation is examined at para. 2.52, above.

715 Regulation 1215/2012, Art. 22(1).

716 Regulation 1215/2012, Art. 20(1).

717 Regulation 1215/2012, Art. 21(1)(a).

718 Regulation 1215/2012, Art. 21(1)(b)(i).

country, if this is the place in a Member State where the business which engaged him is or was situated.[719]

Fifth, if an employee wishes to bring proceedings against an employer who does not have a domicile in a Member State, but who has a branch, agency or other establishment[720] in a Member State out of the operations of which the dispute arises, he may sue in the courts of that Member State.[721]

Sixth, if the employee wishes to join the employer, who has or is deemed to have a domicile in a Member State, in proceedings brought against another defendant who is being sued in the Member State in which he has a domicile, he may do so if the conditions of Article 8(1) of the Regulation are satisfied.[722]

Seventh, if an employee wishes to sue an employer who does not have a domicile in a Member State, he may still sue in a Member State at the place in which he habitually carries out his work or in the last place where he did so, or (if he does not or did not habitually carry out his work in any one country) in a Member State at the place where the business which engaged him is or was situated.[723] He may instead sue the employer on the basis of the residual or traditional jurisdictional rules of the court proposed to be seised in accordance with Article 6.[724]

Eighth, any court which is seised with a dispute according to these rules has jurisdiction to entertain a counterclaim.[725]

Ninth, a jurisdiction agreement will be effective only if it is entered into after the dispute has arisen, or where it allows the employee to bring proceedings in courts other than those indicated by these rules.[726]

2.120 Employment in more than one Member State

The jurisdictional rule which allows an employee to seise the courts of a Member State other than that in which the employer is domiciled,[727] may sometimes be tricky to apply because it requires the court to identify the Member State in which, and sometimes the place at which,[728] the employee habitually carries on his work. Regulation 1215/2012 is at this point rather challenging, though it may simply reflect the untidy reality of some employments. Article 21(1)(b)(i) appears to make it necessary to identify a single place at which the

---

719 Regulation 1215/2012, Art. 21(1)(b)(ii).

720 An expression which may extend to the embassy of a non-Member State: C-154/11 *Mahamdia v. People's Democratic Republic of Algeria* EU:C:2012:491, [2013] ICR 1. There appears to be a misprint in [45]: if it means that the employee may sue in the Member State in which he is domiciled, it is wrong.

721 Regulation 1215/2012, Art. 20(2).

722 Regulation 1215/2012, Art. 20(1). This reverses, for matters to which Regulation 1215/2012 applies, the practical effect of the woeful decision in C-462/06 *GlaxoSmithKline v. Rouard* [2008] ECR I-3965, which held that jurisdiction by joinder was unavailable to an employee in matters which fell within Section 5, but which presumably remains reliable on the interpretation of Regulation 44/2001.

723 Regulation 1215/2012, Art. 21(2). This provision applies to Regulation 1215/2012, but is not available in proceedings to which Regulation 44/2001 applies.

724 Regulation 1215/2012, Art. 20(1).

725 Regulation 1215/2012, Art. 22(2).

726 Regulation 1215/2012, Art. 23, which is considered further below.

727 Or, indeed, when the employer does not have a domicile in a Member State at all: Art. 21(2).

728 Article 21(1)(b)(i), for example.

employee habitually carries out his work;[729] Article 21(1)(b)(ii) then provides for the case in which this cannot be done as the case in which he 'does not habitually carry out his work in any one country'.[730] As a preliminary observation, it is submitted that the first reference to 'place' will generally work better if interpreted as though it had said 'Member State', and that 'does not' would be better understood as 'cannot be considered to'.

It is not just the drafting which is untidy: the duties of the employment may also be. In the straightforward case, if the employee carries on all his work in a single Member State, the courts of that State will have jurisdiction if the employee elects to sue there. When the duties of the employment are not concentrated in a single Member State, one might think that it does not matter where the work is done,[731] for the connection with 'the' place of work is not significantly strong if there is no such place at all. It is for these cases that Article 21(1)(b)(ii) offers an alternative connection: to a Member State where this State is where the business which engaged him is or was situated.[732] The trouble with this alternative is, however, that it may point to a connection which arose years, or decades, ago; and in any event, it is hard to see how the application of the law of the place where the employer was then established serves to protect the present interests of the employee.[733]

Perhaps in the light of this, in cases in which the employee performs the duties of his employment across several Member States – as sales representative in the Low Countries, for example – the European Court has shown notable willingness to find that there is *a* place at which, or at least a Member State in which, the employee habitually carries out his work, notwithstanding the availability of Article 21(1)(b)(ii). No doubt this proceeds from a view that the duties of the employment, even where dispersed, make for a closer and more real connection to the dispute than the place where the employer which first took the employee on was established. In such cases, according to the Court, it may be possible to regard the employee's work as being habitually carried out in the one Member State which represents the base or effective centre of his working obligations, or which may be seen as the principal place of his activities as employee,[734] or the place where the greater part of his duties are discharged.[735]

In *Mulox IBC v. Geels*,[736] a marketing director had his base of operation in France, but travelled to several other countries in the discharge of his duties. In order to justify

---

729 Article 21(1)(b)(i). The reference to 'place' will include the continental shelf adjacent to a Member State: C-37/00 *Weber v. Universal Ogden Services Ltd* [2002] ECR I-2013.

730 Article 21(1)(b)(ii).

731 It is suggested in the Report of Almeida Cruz, Jenard and Desantes Real that, if the employee carries out all the duties of his employment in a single State which is a non-Member State, he will not fall within what is now Art. 21(1)(b)(ii), because if he does carry out his business in one country, the jurisdiction of the place of the business which engaged him will not be available. It is, however, hard to see the sense of a rule which applies if he works in non-Member States A and B, but not if he works only in non-Member State A: but see [1990] OJ C189/44–45.

732 This reflects the argument in 266/85 *Shenavai v. Kreischer* [1987] ECR 239, that the justification for a special jurisdictional rule is the way in which the employee is integrated into the structures of his employer.

733 C-29/10 *Koelzsch v. Luxembourg* [2011] ECR I-1595 (a case on the identification of the governing law, but which will be of general application); C-384/10 *Voogsgeerd v. Navimer SA* [2011] ECR I-13275 (also a case on governing law).

734 It has adopted a similar technique for the identification of the governing law for contracts of employment: see C-29/10 *Koelzsch v. Luxembourg* [2011] ECR I-1595, directing the court to look for the Member State in which the employee carries on the greater part of his duties to the employer.

735 C-29/10 *Koelzsch v. Luxembourg* [2011] ECR I-1595; C-384/10 *Voogsgeerd v. Navimer SA* [2011] ECR I-13275.

736 C-125/92, [1993] ECR I-4075. The case was decided under an older version of the jurisdictional rule in Art. 5(1) of the Brussels Convention. But the principle of interpretation is general and robust.

permitting him to sue his employer in France, it was held that special jurisdiction existed in courts of the place from which the employee principally discharged the duties of his employment. As the employee did this from a base and office in France, the court at that place had special[737] jurisdiction. The Court observed that jurisdiction was conferred on the courts of a place,[738] as distinct from a Member State; and that it was important to avoid the multiplication of jurisdictions as would result, it is to be supposed, from an analysis which allowed the employee to sue in every place in which a part of the duties of the employment were discharged. In *Rutten v. Cross Medical Ltd*,[739] the Court held that if the employee were to maintain an office in one of the countries in which his duties were performed, from which he goes out and to which he returns to write up his paperwork and keep his records, this may be regarded as the place at which he has established the centre of his working activities and therefore as the place where he habitually carries out his work.

So much for white-collar workers. But the centre of gravity approach also applies to blue-collar workers whose employment rarely gives them the privilege of establishing a centre of work for themselves. In the case of a lorry driver directed to drive all over the place, the Court said that the national court 'must, in particular, determine in which State is situated the place from which the employee carries out his transport tasks, receives instructions concerning his tasks and organises his work, and the place where his work tools are situated. It must also determine the places where the transport is principally carried out, where the goods are unloaded and the place to which the employee returns after completion of his tasks'.[740] It follows that the centre of gravity approach extends to those employees who are directed to go from place to place at the employer's whim. In *Weber v. Universal Ogden Services Ltd*,[741] in which case the employee had been sent from site to site, the place where the employee habitually carried out his work was said to be identified by looking to see where he performed the essential part of his duties, this being assessed by reference to the entire duration of the employment relationship, and which may in turn indicate the place where he has worked the longest, unless the subject matter of the dispute is more closely connected with another place.[742] The case law therefore appears to require a place to be identified by these centre of gravity, or centre of history, tests. It is implicit, where it is not explicit, that an employee should not be at liberty to pick any place in which he has habitually worked as the place to sue: the test is designed to force the facts to disclose a single such place.

---

737 Because the case was concerned with special jurisdiction under what was then Art. 5(1) of the Brussels Convention.

738 Article 5(1) of the Brussels Convention gave special jurisdiction to the courts of a place, rather than to the courts of a Member State; Regulation 1215/2012, Art. 7(1) does the same. The issue, and the general desirability of such interpretation, may still be open to debate.

739 C-383/95, [1997] ECR I-57.

740 C-29/10 *Koelzsch v. Luxembourg* [2011] ECR I-1595, [49] (a case on governing law); C-384/10 *Voogsgeerd v. Navimer SA* [2011] ECR I-13275 (also a case on governing law).

741 C-37/00, [2002] ECR I-2013.

742 In the rare case in which Employer 1 allows an employee to work for Employer 2, after which the employee falls into a dispute with Employer 1, the action against Employer 1 may be brought where the work for Employer 2 is habitually performed only if Employer 1 had from the outset an interest in the performance of the contract with Employer 2, which must be established 'on a comprehensive basis, taking into consideration all the circumstances of the case': C-437/00 *Pugliese v. Finmeccanica SpA* [2003] ECR I-3573. Though the case may apply more generally to cases of secondment, the problem will surely be a rare one.

It remains to be seen whether this conclusion is affected by the decision in *Color Drack GmbH v. Lexx International Vertriebs GmbH*.[743] That case was concerned to identify the courts of the place with special jurisdiction under what is now Article 7(1)(b) of Regulation 1215/2012, in proceedings brought in relation to a contract for the sale and delivery of goods in several places within the one Member State. The decision was that special jurisdiction lay in the court for the place of the principal delivery, but if there was not such a place, it could be asserted at a place of delivery of the claimant's choice. The Court said that its decision was confined to a case in which there were deliveries at several places within the one Member State, and did not extend to a case where there was delivery in several Member States.[744] If that were taken at face value, it would be of no relevance to the case of an employee who is required to work in several Member States, but the extension of the decision in *Color Drack* to situations which appear to be analogous is not unimaginable. But the centre of gravity approach, designed to yield one jurisdiction rather than a choice of jurisdictions, seems likely to prevail.

In the rare case in which an employee has two employers with domiciles in separate Member States, and has a claim against them both, one would expect that Section 5 of Chapter II would allow him to sue one of them in the court with jurisdiction under these rules, and to join the other as a co-defendant by reference to what is now Article 8(1). The issue arose in *GlaxoSmithKlein v. Rouard*,[745] in which case the Court refused to arrive at so sensible a conclusion. It held, to the wholly irrational disadvantage of the employee, that Section 5 of Chapter II made no allowance for a claim to be brought against a co-employer on the basis of what is now Article 8(1). In cases to which Regulation 1215/2012 applies, this witless decision has been superseded by the final clause of Article 20(1): good riddance to the horrible thing.

2.121 Agreements on jurisdiction

The provisions on jurisdiction agreements set out in Article 23 of Regulation 1215/2012 appear straightforward. An agreement on jurisdiction will be effective only if entered into after the dispute has arisen (there remains the difficulty, common to Sections 4 and 5, of identifying the precise point at which a dispute has arisen) or if it allows the employee to bring proceedings in a court other than one indicated by the rules of the Section: that is, it widens his jurisdictional options, by providing that a court will have non-exclusive jurisdiction, rather than restricting them.[746] Otherwise the privilege conferred on the employee would be too easily lost.

It had been held in *Samengo-Turner v. J&H Marsh & McLennan (Services) Ltd*[747] that what is now Article 23 required the court to disregard an exclusive jurisdiction agreement, entered into before the dispute arose, for the courts of New York. That was perhaps surprising, as the most obvious purpose of Article 23 is to prevent a court in a Member

---

743 C-386/05, [2007] ECR I-3699.
744 At [16].
745 C-462/06, [2008] ECR I-3965.
746 C-154/11 *Mahamdia v. People's Democratic Republic of Algeria* EU:C:2012:491, [2013] ICR 1. This conclusion had already been reached in relation to jurisdiction agreements in consumer contracts: *Sherdley v. Nordea Life & Pension SA* [2012] EWCA Civ 88, [2012] Lloyd's Rep IR 437.
747 [2007] EWCA Civ 723, [2008] ICR 18. See [2007] LMCLQ 433.

State taking jurisdiction by reference to a jurisdiction agreement which does not conform to its requirements, and to prevent a court otherwise having jurisdiction under Section 5 being required to refuse it by reference to an agreement for the courts of another Member State. Insofar as the court had to decide whether it had jurisdiction under Section 5 of Chapter II, the real issue in *Samengo-Turner* was whether a court with jurisdiction under the Regulation may decline to exercise it on the ground that there was a material connection to a non-Member State. There could certainly be no objection in principle to a court, in considering whether to grant relief on the basis of an agreement for the courts of a non-Member State, taking into account the general structure of Article 23 as part of the background which should inform the exercise of its discretion.

But Article 23 does not specifically limit its impact to jurisdiction agreements for Member States. And in *Mahamdia v. People's Democratic Republic of Algeria*[748] the Court accepted that a jurisdiction agreement, entered into before the dispute arose, for the courts of a non-Member State would be effective for the purposes of Article 23 if it reflected Article 23(2) by widening the employee's choice of court,[749] but would not be effective if, by purporting to narrow that choice, it did not comply with it. After all, Article 23 gives effect to a jurisdiction agreement, but does not expressly limit its effect to jurisdiction agreements for the courts of a Member State. Accordingly, where the employee was privileged by the jurisdictional rules of Section 5 of Chapter II, that privilege could be surrendered by agreement on jurisdiction, but only in accordance with Article 23. It follows that a non-exclusive jurisdiction agreement entered into before the dispute had arisen would be effective under Article 23, even if for the courts of a non-Member State; and it appears to follow that a jurisdiction agreement for the courts of a non-Member State, entered into after the dispute has arisen, will also be made effective by Article 23(1), even if exclusive. At least, there is nothing in *Mahamdia v. Algeria* to suggest the contrary.

2.122 International jurisdiction in the courts of the United Kingdom

Where Section 5 of Chapter II confers international jurisdiction on the courts for a place, there will be no need for a further identification of the part of the United Kingdom in which the action may be brought. But where they confer international jurisdiction only on the courts of a Member State, and that Member State is the United Kingdom, internal rules of United Kingdom law are required to further identify the particular part of the United Kingdom whose courts have national jurisdiction. These rules are contained in Schedule 4 to the 1982 Act,[750] and in relation to employment claims they are very closely based on Section 5 of Chapter II of the Regulation, with the references being instead to a part of the United Kingdom.

---

748 C-154/11, EU:C:2012:491, [2013] ICR 1, [65].

749 It did not say whether the same would be true if the agreement were proposed to be validated by Art. 23(1), but there is no reason to doubt it for the language of Art. 23 is not restricted to agreements for the courts of Member States, at least on the face of it.

750 For the deemed domicile in (and in a part of) the United Kingdom of a non-domiciliary employer, see SI 2001/3929, Sch. 1, para. 11, as amended by SI 2014/2947, Sch. 2, para. 13. For the rules of internal United Kingdom jurisdiction in an employment contract case, see r. 4 of Sch. 4 to the 1982 Act (as inserted by SI 2001/3929, Sch. 2, para. 4, discussed in greater detail under Q16 at the end of this Chapter.

2.123 Conclusion

If these provisions give the English court jurisdiction, service out (if needed) will be available as of right.[751] If they deny jurisdiction to the English courts, that is the end of the matter. But if they are inapplicable, the next question must be addressed.

(8) AGREEMENTS ON JURISDICTION FOR COURTS OF MEMBER STATES

2.124 General

Article 25 of Regulation 1215/2012, which forms the other[752] part of Section 7 of Chapter II, which is entitled 'Prorogation of Jurisdiction', provides as follows:

> *(1) If the parties, regardless of their domicile, have agreed that a court or the courts of a Member State are to have jurisdiction to settle any disputes which have arisen or which may arise in connection with a particular legal relationship, that court or those courts shall have jurisdiction, unless the agreement is null and void as to its substantive validity under the law of that Member State. Such jurisdiction shall be exclusive unless the parties have agreed otherwise. The agreement conferring jurisdiction shall be either: (a) in writing or evidenced in writing; (b) in a form which accords with practices which the parties have established between themselves; or (c) in international trade or commerce, in a form which accords with a usage of which the parties are or ought to have been aware and which in such trade or commerce is widely known to, and regularly observed by, parties to contracts of the type involved in the particular trade or commerce concerned. (2) Any communication by electronic means which provides a durable record of the agreement shall be equivalent to 'writing'. (3) The court or courts of a Member State on which a trust instrument has conferred jurisdiction shall have exclusive jurisdiction in any proceedings brought against a settlor, trustee or beneficiary, if relations between those persons or their rights or obligations under the trust are involved. (4) Agreements or provisions of a trust instrument conferring jurisdiction shall have no legal force if they are contrary to Articles 15, 19 or 23, or if the courts whose jurisdiction they purport to exclude have exclusive jurisdiction by virtue of Article 24. (5) An agreement conferring jurisdiction which forms part of a contract shall be treated as an agreement independent of the other terms of the contract. The validity of the agreement conferring jurisdiction cannot be contested solely on the ground that the contract is not valid.*

The wording of Article 25 differs from the counterpart provision in Article 23 of Regulation 44/2001, in three principal respects. First, Article 25 applies regardless of the domicile of the parties: Article 23 of Regulation 44/2001 was limited to cases in which one of the parties was domiciled in a Member State.[753] Second, the wording in Article 25(1), which provides that the designated court will have jurisdiction 'unless the agreement is null and void as to its substantive validity under the law of that Member State' is new, and may have a significant impact on the reasoning of a court which is called upon to apply Article 25 rather than the predecessor provision. Third, Article 25(5) is a new provision, though as it is in substance a statutory confirmation of the constant jurisprudence of the European Court, as well as of English law, its practical significance is probably small.

---

751 CPR r. 6.33.

752 Article 26, dealing with jurisdiction by entering an appearance, was dealt with above.

753 And therefore gave rise to questions as to when that domiciliary connection was required to be satisfied.

2.125 The general effect of an agreement on jurisdiction

If there is an agreement[754] to confer jurisdiction upon a court or the courts of a Member State,[755] which complies with the requirements of what is now Article 25 of Regulation 1215/2012, the court or courts so designated will have jurisdiction: the jurisdiction will be exclusive unless the agreement provides otherwise.[756] There are many points of detail on which the law has become rather complex, but the basic idea is simple enough: parties may exercise their autonomy to identify a court which is to have jurisdiction, and subject to clear and precise exceptions, that court should adjudicate and other courts should not.

The first thing to say is that Article 25 does not require the parties to have made a *contract* which contains among its terms a provision that the courts of a Member State are to have jurisdiction: the parties may agree in this manner if they wish, but there is no obligation on them to do so. Even if many of the reported cases before the English courts appear to have interpreted the question 'did the parties make an agreement?' as though it actually meant 'did the parties make a contract?' it is sufficient for the purposes of Article 25 that there is an *agreement*. There is no reason to interpret this as 'an agreement which takes the form of a contract which contains this as a term'; and in the light of Article 25(5), there is even less reason to read the word 'agreement' as though it meant 'contract'.

The second thing to say is that it may not be necessary that the *parties* have made the agreement, as distinct from its being required that the *party who is said to be bound* has communicated, to the other, *his* agreement to accept the jurisdiction of the named court in respect of the present proceedings. It may prove to be very significant indeed that what is required to prorogate and to derogate from the jurisdiction of a court in a Member State is an agreement, which may be understood to be unilateral, and which need not be formed by an exchange of promises. It may follow from this that if the parties have made a contract which also deals with the issue of the jurisdiction in which any proceedings will be brought, this creates and establishes a set of mutual performance undertakings which are, conceptually and functionally separate and distinct from, outside and clear of, the agreement which was effective to prorogate jurisdiction.[757]

The third thing to say, which follows from the first two, is that a person may depart from his agreement on jurisdiction; whether he is free to do so will be determined by reference to the Regulation, with such incidental reference to national law as may be required to secure the correct application of the Regulation. But if he has also *contracted* not to sue in a particular court, in which he then institutes proceedings, he breaches his contractual promise. It may not be – probably is not – helpful to describe this as the breach of a jurisdiction

---

754 The issue of what may be meant by 'agreement' in this context, and especially whether it is to be understood as bilateral and contractual in nature, or more in the nature of a unilateral waiver of jurisdictional privilege, is further examined at paras 2.128 and 2.129, below.

755 If there is an agreement for the courts of Iceland, Norway or Switzerland, Art. 73(1) of Regulation 1215/2012 means that its validity and effect are dealt with by the Lugano II Conventions, as to which see Chapter 3. The same principle applies if the agreement is for the courts of a territory in relation to which the Brussels Convention still applies: Regulation 1215/2012, Art. 68(1).

756 Note that if there is a choice of court agreement for the courts of Iceland, Norway or Switzerland, the Lugano Conventions, as the case may be, will govern jurisdiction in virtue of that agreement; and the effect will be broadly, though not exactly, the same; the same is true if the agreement is for the courts of a territory in relation to which the Brussels Convention still applies.

757 See further below, paras 2.128, 2.129; *JSC Aeroflot-Russian Airlines v. Berezovsky* [2013] EWCA Civ 784, [2013] 2 Lloyd's Rep 242. See also Briggs, *Agreements on Jurisdiction and Choice of Law* (Oxford, 2008), [7.35].

agreement, because it is bound to confuse two conceptually distinct legal propositions: a public law rule about whether the court has jurisdiction to adjudicate; and a private law rule about abiding by contractual promises or paying damages as the consequence of breach.

Fourth, one should note the relative position in the hierarchy of jurisdictional rules which is occupied by agreements on jurisdiction for the courts of a Member State. Such agreements may not override the exclusive jurisdiction conferred by Article 24.[758] Prorogation of jurisdiction by voluntary appearance before the courts of another Member State will override them;[759] and their effect in relation to insurance, consumer and employment contracts is restricted. The fact that a court in a Member State has taken jurisdiction in conflict with Article 25 does not lead to its judgment being refused recognition in Member State: the opposite is the case.[760] In this sense Article 25 is misleading when it describes the chosen court as having *exclusive*[761] jurisdiction. It confers a jurisdiction which may exclude the jurisdiction, based upon rules lower down in the hierarchy, of courts which might otherwise have had it, but not a great deal more. The adoption of Article 31(2)[762] is a modest step to ameliorate this, but it remains clear that prorogated jurisdiction is not exclusive jurisdiction properly so called.

Fifth, it is no longer necessary for one of the parties to be domiciled in a Member State. Article 23 of Regulation 44/2001 had limited the direct effect of jurisdiction agreements to cases in which such a condition was met; where it was not, the courts of other Member States might exercise jurisdiction, on whichever basis may be open to them under their various national laws, only if the court upon which there was 'such an' agreement had declined jurisdiction.

And sixth, the matter before the court must obviously fall within the four corners of the agreement, but there is no reason to suppose that the Article is unavailable to a claimant who relies on the jurisdiction agreement to seise a court with proceedings which seek a declaration that the substantive contract is in fact invalid.[763] Though the statutory limits are drawn very widely, so that Article 25 may apply to 'any disputes which may arise or have arisen in connection with a particular legal relationship', the question whether the particular dispute is one which the parties did indeed agree to subject to the jurisdiction of the court chosen is one of construction. It was confirmed in *Powell Duffryn plc v. Petereit*[764] that the task of construction was laid on the court seised or proposed to be seised. It may be implicit in this that it should apply the rules of contractual construction of its own law, including private international law. Though the Court did not say so, it is hard to see how else it could be done. It will also be a question of construction, resolved by the application of the law which governs the agreement, to identify those mentioned in it.[765] In England, this question of

---

758 Article 25(4).

759 As a consensual variation of the agreement: 150/80 *Elefanten Schuh GmbH v. Jacqmain* [1981] ECR 1671.

760 Neither Regulation 44/2001 nor Regulation 1215/2012 makes reference to judgments which conflict with Section 7 of Chapter II of the Regulation: see para. 7.13, below.

761 The word 'exclusive' will be seen to have different meanings in different contexts. In the context of Art. 25 it means 'relatively exclusive'. Those who move in the weird world of gentlemen's clubs or in the institutions which educate class enemies, will recognise such shades of meaning.

762 Below, para. 2.127.

763 *Ryanair Ltd v. Bravofly* [2009] IEHC 41, [2009] ILPr 701.

764 C-214/89, [1992] ECR I-1745.

765 *Breitenbücher v. Wittke* [2008] CSOH 145 (jurisdiction agreement in German contract in German language stated to be binding on the parties if they had the status of *Kaufmann* (translated as 'merchant'): German law was applied to determine whether this condition was satisfied and jurisdiction prorogated accordingly.

construction[766] is referred to the law governing the substance of the jurisdiction agreement. To the extent that an English court may take a more ample view of the material scope of a jurisdiction agreement than may be found in the law of a Member State which is more wary of such clauses, especially when they are used outside mercantile contracts, there will be scope for some difference of view, and some consequent unevenness in the manner in which Article 25 may apply.[767] But if this is a problem, it is not obvious what may be done to alleviate it, unless there are uniform or abstract rules of interpretation to which all courts may refer, which has not yet happened.

2.126 Managing jurisdictional disputes: agreement for English court

It is convenient to address at the outset the practical difficulty which faces a court which has to decide whether it has jurisdiction in a case in which there is disagreement between the parties as to whether there is a valid and effective agreement on jurisdiction. Suppose there is a disputed agreement for the English courts, which would not otherwise have jurisdiction over the defendant; suppose that if the agreement is not effective, the courts of another Member State will have jurisdiction. The point of departure is that as a matter of common law, jurisdictional facts, which means the facts and matters which justify the English courts in taking jurisdiction, are generally required to be shown to the standard of a good arguable case.[768] This is capable of meaning that though the court would accept that the argument for its having jurisdiction may not be as persuasive as the argument that it does not, there is still enough of a case for the taking of jurisdiction, for the facts may, at this stage, be incomplete and untested.

The 'good arguable case' test had been developed to deal with questions concerning the inherent jurisdiction of the English court, and to regulate those cases in which English legislation permitted service out of the jurisdiction with the leave of the court. There is no particular reason to suppose that it applies where jurisdiction is not inherent but is conferred (or imposed) by a European instrument;[769] and no particular reason to suppose that it is applicable to questions which concern the validity or otherwise of an agreement to which Article 25 attaches jurisdictional consequences.

It could not be correct for an English court to exercise jurisdiction, and by doing so to displace the jurisdiction of the court of another Member State, by finding only a good arguable case that it has jurisdiction by virtue of an agreement. It would amount to its saying that 'we consider that on balance we do not have jurisdiction and that another Member State does, but the case for saying that the agreement is inapplicable is not hopeless, so we will proceed to confirm our jurisdiction to hear the case'. If the question is

---

766 Notice that the present submission is concerned with questions of construction of wording used in a clause which is taken for valid, and not with questions of validity, which are principally governed by the wording of Art. 25 itself, and which are examined below.

767 For the application in this context of the general (broad) principles of construction favoured by English law, articulated in *Fiona Trust & Holding Corp v. Privalov* [2007] UKHL 40, [2007] Bus LR 1719, see *Deutsche Bank AG v. Asia Pacific Broadband Wireless Communications Inc* [2008] EWCA Civ 1091, [2008] 2 Lloyd's Rep 619; *Maple Leaf Macro Volatility Master Fund v. Rouvroy* [2009] EWHC 257 (Comm), [2009] 1 Lloyd's Rep 475.

768 Indeed, its very flexibility is the source of the problem with it.

769 The English courts cannot be faulted for applying English procedural law to the question whether jurisdiction under the Regulation has been established when this is contested by the defendant: C-68/93 *Shevill v. Presse Alliance SA* [1995] ECR I-415; cf C-375/13 *Kolassa v Barclays Bank plc* EU:C:2015:37 (4th Question). The question considered here is what those rules of English law should be taken to require.

whether an agreement has displaced the jurisdiction of the courts of another Member State, that would not be a satisfactory answer. In the context of Regulation jurisdiction, therefore, the English courts adopted a rule or practice which asks whether the party who – in this context, by reference to an agreement – seeks to show that the court has jurisdiction has 'the better of the argument' on the issue of jurisdiction. The question will be whether the arguments advanced to demonstrate the existence of jurisdiction (in the context of an Article 25 agreement for the jurisdiction of the English courts) are more persuasive than those advanced in order to establish its unavailability or invalidity. A test which asks who has the better of the jurisdictional argument is neutral as between the litigating parties. As there are likely to be two Member States whose courts may have jurisdiction, a position of neutrality as between the parties is the only principled stance. There is no good reason to interpret the Brussels I Regulation as giving an advantage to the claimant or the defendant; no reason to lean in favour of the party seeking to uphold or to deny the agreement on jurisdiction. And there is no reason to interpret a test of 'who has the better of the argument?' as though it required either party to establish their case on jurisdiction as meeting the more robust standard of a balance of probability. In many cases the court will be all too aware that it can do no more than decide whose contentions on jurisdiction are the more persuasive, or the least unpersuasive, while entertaining significant doubts about what the facts will prove to be if the matter proceeds. The question of who has the better of the argument, on the basis of whatever material was available at the time, is a rational, comprehensible, manageable, standard.

That much is clear. However, a further strand in the English jurisprudence proposes that the court may be required to ask whether one party has '*much* the better of the argument'.[770] This is most unwelcome. A test which requires one party to have *much* the better of the argument immediately prompts the question of which party carries the burden which 'much' suggests, and there is no sensible answer to it. The European Court has repeatedly stated that where the question arises, the requirements of what is now Article 25 must be 'clearly and precisely demonstrated'. That makes sense, and may be aligned with a requirement that the party seeking to show that there is an effective and applicable jurisdiction agreement have the better of the argument on the issue. Requiring one party – claimant or defendant? party who says that the English court has jurisdiction or party who says that another Member State has jurisdiction? – to bear a greater burden is not rational, and it should not be the law. It is time for the qualifier 'much', if it ever meant anything, to be erased.

The rule should be, and may already be, that the party who seeks to rely on an agreement on jurisdiction, to establish or to remove the jurisdiction of the English court must have the better of the argument, on such material as is before the court, on all those points which go to determine the existence of the agreement and which are not conceded by his opponent. The 'better of the argument' test is preferable to 'a good arguable case', for even if the latter is open to a flexible interpretation, the law will only benefit from use of a form of words

---

770 The origin of the expression, as useful in this context, appears to be the judgment of Waller LJ in *Canada Trust Co v. Stolzenberg (No 2)* [1998] 1 WLR 547, which was affirmed: [2002] 1 AC 1. But *Canada Trust* was not a case involving a jurisdiction agreement. The leading case on the 'much the better' test, in the context of agreements on jurisdiction, is *Bols Distilleries BV v. Superior Yacht Services Ltd* [2006] UKPC 45, [2007] 1 WLR 12 (a case on the law of Gibraltar). The statement of principle in *Bols Distilleries* has been approved several times since, though this has not always endorsed the qualifier 'much'.

which states its meaning with clarity and without ambiguity;[771] and it is clearly preferable to any enquiry into who may have 'much the better of the jurisdictional argument'.

A question which is closely connected to this is whether a party seeking to deny that he is bound by an agreement on jurisdiction may support his contention by pointing to the fact that the substantive contract in which, as is said, the agreement on jurisdiction was contained, was never agreed to, or was agreed to but has now been rescinded. The issue is examined below, but the answer is clearly negative.[772]

2.127 Managing jurisdictional disputes involving an agreement for the courts of a Member State

One of the shortcomings of the Brussels Convention, carried forward into Regulation 44/2001, was that if the parties had agreed on the jurisdiction of the courts of a Member State, there was little that could be done if one of them, apprehending the institution of legal proceedings to which he had little or no defence, brought proceedings before the courts of another Member State for relief which might be genuine but might also be entirely spurious. If the court in which these proceedings were brought was chosen with care, the wrecking or blocking proceedings could be kept in a persistent vegetative state for years, but their technical pendency would prevent the court designated by agreement from taking and exercising jurisdiction.

The rule of priority for the court seised first, even where it had been seised in a matter in which it was practically certain that it had no jurisdiction, opened the door to those of low ambition. In *Erich Gasser GmbH v. MISAT Srl*[773] the European Court ruled that a court in whose favour the parties had made an exclusive jurisdiction agreement, but which had been seised second, had no jurisdiction to hear the case while the same action was still pending between the same parties before another court, even if that other court were to have been seised in blatant breach of contract. This practice, of starting proceedings in a court before which the proceedings could be kept alive but immobile, came to be known as the 'Italian torpedo', which seems alarmingly inapt for something whose purpose is to move as slowly as possible; but the egregious behaviour which it permitted was widely thought to be intolerable.

Regulation 1215/2012 adopted, in Article 31, a corrective measure, which reads as follows:

> *(2) Without prejudice to Article 26, where a court of a Member State on which an agreement as referred to in Article 25 confers exclusive jurisdiction is seised, any court of another Member State shall stay the proceedings until such time as the court seised on the basis of the agreement declares that it has no jurisdiction under the agreement. (3) Where the court designated in the agreement has established jurisdiction in accordance with the agreement, any court of another Member State shall decline jurisdiction in favour of that court.*

The effect of this is straightforward enough, and a little odd, at the same time. If proceedings are before an English court, on the footing that the court has jurisdiction and there is

---

771 *JSC Aeroflot-Russian Airlines v. Berezovsky* [2013] EWCA Civ 784, [2013] 2 Lloyd's Rep 242. For this reason, the support given to the 'flexible' version of the 'good arguable case' test in *Kolden Holdings Ltd v. Rodette Commerce Ltd* [2008] EWCA Civ 10, [2008] Bus LR 1051, is not altogether welcome. If the court actually means 'the better of the argument', it is helpful if it simply says that.

772 Paragraph 2.146, below.

773 C-116/02, [2003] ECR I-14693, a reference from the Austrian courts.

no impediment in the form of a jurisdiction agreement for the courts of another Member State, the court will have jurisdiction on the basis of voluntary appearance unless Article 24 applies. If the defendant objects to the jurisdiction of the English court on the basis that there is an agreement for the courts of another Member State, it appears that he has a choice of tactic. If he considers that the English court is more likely to conclude that the jurisdiction agreement is valid and binding, he may challenge the jurisdiction of the English court in accordance with Part 11 of the Civil Procedure Rules. The English court will address the question whether it has jurisdiction by using the 'better of the argument' test described above. If the English court rules that it does not have jurisdiction because the agreement gives jurisdiction to the courts of another Member State, that ruling should be recognised under Chapter III of the Regulation.[774] If the English court rules that it does have jurisdiction because the alleged agreement on jurisdiction does not apply to remove its jurisdiction, it ought to follow that its decision is also entitled to recognition.[775]

Alternatively, the defendant may prefer to seek his ruling from the court which he says is designated by the agreement. If he takes that step, the English court must stay its proceedings and abide by the eventual decision of the allegedly-designated court.[776] It is not clear from the wording of the Article, but it seems likely that the defendant is required to seise the allegedly-designated court with substantive proceedings, even if these are for a declaration of non-liability. There is a time limit on this, of course: the proceedings in the court first seised may not be later disrupted if the defendant has already entered an appearance in accordance with Article 26. But otherwise, it appears that when the designated court is seised, the proceedings in the first-seised court must be stayed. It would be sensible if this were understood to mean that if the court first seised has not yet confirmed its jurisdiction, it is required to act in accordance with Article 31(2), but that if there has been an unsuccessful challenge to its jurisdiction, or an appearance and submission to its jurisdiction, Article 31(2) is no longer applicable.

Article 31(2) applies when a court 'on which an agreement as referred to in Article 25 confers exclusive jurisdiction' has been seised. A claimant may therefore respond to a defendant, who has seised a court in another Member State, which the defendant says was the designated court, by contending that the agreement on which he relies does not conform to Article 25, or that it does not confer exclusive jurisdiction, or even that there was no such agreement as alleged or at all, and that Article 31(2) is therefore inapplicable. Though there is an obvious textual justification for such an argument, it should not be lightly accepted. The purpose of Article 31(2) was to allow the allegedly-designated court to decide whether it had been materially designated. It would serve no proper purpose for a court to undermine this scheme by allowing a party of the sort encountered in *Erich Gasser* to contend, before the Italian court, that the agreement was not one which Article 25 would validate, and that the procedure described in Article 31(2) was therefore not applicable. It would undo such good as was sought to be done; it should be repudiated if ever it is tried on.

---

774 C-456/11 *Gothaer Allgemeine Versicherung AG v. Samskip GmbH* EU:C:2012:719, [2013] QB 548, below, para. 7.07.

775 It is not certain whether, though it should be concluded that, C-456/11 *Gothaer Allgemeine Versicherung AG v. Samskip GmbH* EU:C:2012:719, [2013] QB 548 applies in this case as well.

776 Though perhaps not if the English court considers that it has exclusive jurisdiction, regardless of domicile: C-438/12 *Weber v. Weber* EU:C:2014:212, [2015] 2 WLR 213.

2.128 The nature of agreement on the jurisdiction of courts: prior to 2015

English lawyers have tended to speak of choice of court agreements or of choice of court or jurisdiction clauses. This conveys and confuses a number of ideas. One is that contracting parties are entitled to make a choice of court: the court chosen may or may not accept that agreement as effective; the court whose jurisdiction is chosen against may or may not accept that its jurisdiction has been excluded; but the parties make an agreement, a choice. The agreement is seen as, and is to be treated as, contractual in nature. Each side may be held to it by the other. Either may be restrained from breaching it or ordered to pay damages for breaching it: all this is in the nature of contracts. Issues of validity of such clauses are approached in contractual terms. Those facts and matters which impugn the validity of a contract may be used to impugn the choice of court agreement; and a serious structural question has to be addressed when the statement on choice of court is a term of a contract which, on analysis, turns out not to be a legally enforceable contract after all. No particular stress is placed on formal validity – indeed, there are no formal requirements. Instead, the rules and legal principles which determine the validity of contractual agreements control the validity of choice of court agreements.

This can leave English lawyers puzzled by the manner in which the substantive validity of agreements on jurisdiction, whose effect was determined by the Brussels Convention or by Regulation 44/2001, did not appear to be regulated by ordinary contractual rules. Issues like duress and misrepresentation, which might be thought to prompt recourse to a *lex contractus*, did not do so. Instead, formal requirements served as the guarantee that the agreement was valid and binding; and because this was the means by which a court ascertained that the agreement was genuine, the formal requirements were interpreted strictly. The approach is quite different, culturally different, from that of the common law. From a common law perspective, it can be hard to understand how the European Court can ignore the need to explain which law should be applied to assess the substantive validity of the agreement; hard to understand how the problems of substance may be resolved by the application of formal requirements.

An explanation – for this there is no direct authority, but it seems to be plausible – is that the scheme of the Regulation is not to look at agreements on jurisdiction as contractual agreements, liable to be understood, controlled, and enforced as contracts. Jurisdiction agreements, for the purposes of what is now Article 25, do not need to be, or to be approached as, contracts. The Regulation may look on them as formal decisions made by a party (and communicated to another) to waive the provisions, privileges, and protections of the Regulation which would otherwise determine jurisdiction in proceedings brought against him. The proper nature of the enquiry is to ascertain that the party sued has agreed to waive the objection he could have taken to the jurisdiction of the court named; has agreed to waive the jurisdiction of the court in which he could have would otherwise have been sued. It is an agreement, but not in the sense of a contractual agreement. Rather, it is a willing, in-advance, submission to jurisdiction, which is why it appears in Section 7 of Chapter II.

If that is so, if for the purposes of prorogating or derogating from the jurisdiction of courts in a Member State the agreement need not be contractual, it does not need a governing law. It makes sense that it be done with some formality – being done in writing or with evidence in writing – but it is not necessary that it be incorporated as or into a contract. A waiver, an acceptance, of jurisdiction need be no more than that. If one were to understand the agreement on jurisdiction as the acceptance of one party, communicated formally or with equivalent seriousness of purpose to another, of the jurisdiction of a court which would not otherwise have it, there is no reason to enquire whether it meets contractual conditions of validity; and there is no reason to suppose that it is dependent on the validity or invalidity of the substantive legal relationship between the parties. From this perspective it would be an error to think about it in contractual terms, and an error to assess its jurisdictional validity in contractual terms. Rather, it is better to consider it as closer in philosophy to a written nomination of a lawyer authorised to accept service of process. It is a unilateral act, enforceable when, and because, that unilateral act appears to be deliberate and serious.

Article 25, as it now is, does use the language of 'agreement', and can certainly be read as though it were describing a contractual or quasi-contractual[777] relationship. But it may be preferable to interpret 'if the parties... have agreed' as meaning that if one or more parties have agreed on the jurisdiction of a court, that court shall have jurisdiction in accordance with that agreement. In other words, there may be more than one unilateral agreement to accept jurisdiction.

There are several advantages to this understanding of agreements on jurisdiction. One is that it explains why issues of *substantive* validity in relation to agreements on jurisdiction need not be approached as though they were issues of *contractual* validity; the proposition that these agreements on jurisdiction are unaffected by the validity or invalidity of the substantive agreement is plain and obvious; the idea that they are severable from the substantive contract misses the point entirely, because they are not contractual in the first place. Another is that it explains why the formality requirements, the importance of which the Court has always maintained, are to be seen as a proper test of the validity of the agreement of the party whose consent to jurisdiction is to be asserted and held against him. Third, it may also explain why the Court is hostile to the idea that the court whose jurisdiction has been agreed to may do anything where proceedings are brought before the courts of another Member State. If the agreement to the jurisdiction of a court is not contractual in nature, the proposition that the seising of another court is a breach of contract is also wrong: the true position is that the other court will have been seised in circumstances where there is a basis for objecting to it: the effect of that on the jurisdiction of the court which has been seised is a matter for it to assess.

Fourth, however, it allows us to understand that where the parties have made a contract about where proceedings will be brought, they may be seen to have done two quite separate things: by writing, or with written evidence each has, by *unilateral* act, waived jurisdictional objections to the designated court, so that that court may find that it has a jurisdiction which it would not otherwise have had; and they have made *bilateral* promises about where proceedings will be issued. The second of these, the distinct promise about where writs will and will not be issued, will not itself determine whether a court has jurisdiction, but it will determine whether a person has bound himself to act in a certain way, and will pave the way to further analysis. It will follow from this that if a court considers that it has jurisdiction, its conclusion must be accepted without question. But the decision of the court on the question whether it has jurisdiction does not say anything – because it is another question, entirely – about whether the parties made a mutually-binding agreement to invoke that

---

777 Not in the sense that this term was used in the age before the law of restitution and the doctrine of unjust enrichment were invented.

jurisdiction or not. This will be especially important when considering the scope, if there is a scope, for the action for damages for breach of an agreement about where to sue (and not, be it noted, for departure from a unilateral agreement to accept the jurisdiction of the courts of a Member State).[778]

These ideas may be debatable. They cannot be said to state the law in terms which are yet clearly established. But they show how to distil into separate legal elements the complexity not always noticed in the idea of an agreement upon the jurisdiction of a court.[779]

2.129 The nature of agreement on the jurisdiction of courts: after 2015

The true position is complicated, but perhaps not fatally, by the incorporation of the phrase 'unless the agreement is null and void as to its substantive validity under the law of that Member State' into Article 25(1) of Regulation 1215/2012. The explanation for this addition comes in two parts. The first is that the years of puzzling over why there was no clearly prescribed rule for addressing issues of substantial validity took their toll; and the second is that the Hague Convention on Agreements on Choice of Court, agreed to in 2005 but not likely to be of any real significance for some time, contained such a provision. As the participants in the discussions at The Hague included more common lawyers than are found in meetings of the European Council, it was to be expected that a distinct rule to respond to issues of substantive validity was incorporated into that Convention. As the European Union will incorporate the Convention into its own law,[780] to make further[781] provision for agreements on choice of court for non-Member States party to the Convention,[782] it appears that Article 25 was adjusted to align it in this respect with Article 5(1) of the Hague Convention.

If the designation of a court in a Contracting State is considered by the law of that State to be a nullity, it would be surprising if it had any effect on a court before which proceedings had been instituted. Insofar as this is the effect of Article 25(1), there is no reason to object: if the law of the State in which the designated court is located would regard the provision as being without effect, it should not be given effect by the court seised either. But if it means that the law of the Member State who courts have been chosen has a greater role in assessing the substantive validity of an agreement on jurisdiction – as it is accepted that it probably does – it poses more of a problem.

A taste of what may lie in store may be seen in the decision of the French Supreme Court in *Soc Banque privée Edmond de Rothschild Europe v. X*.[783] An agreement between a bank and its customer contained an agreement on jurisdiction by which the customer agreed to bring

---

778 *Starlight Shipping Co v. Allianz Marine & Aviation Versicherungs AG* [2014] EWCA Civ 1010, [2014] 2 Lloyd's Rep 554.

779 For a fuller consideration of this question, and of the legal consequences which may flow from it, see Briggs, *Agreements on Jurisdiction and Choice of Law* (Oxford, 2008), esp. ch. 7.

780 It will take effect under Art. 67 of the Regulation. It will enter into force after the deposit of the instrument of approval, within a month of 5 June 2015: Council Decision 2014/887/EU, [2014] OJ L353/5.

781 As to whether this means better, there is room for differences of opinion. See generally Hartley, *Choice-of-Court Agreements Under the European and International Instruments* (Oxford, 2013).

782 At the date of writing, this means Mexico. The United States has signed, but its signature has not been ratified. So has the European Union, and the laborious process of securing the agreement of the institutions to the adoption of the Convention into European law is underway. But it seems highly improbable that the Convention will apply to jurisdiction agreements for the courts of a Member State, on which the Regulation states the law.

783 Cass I civ, 26 September 2012; [2013] JDI/Clunet 175 (note Brière), [2013] ILPr 181; disapproved in *Mauritius Commercial Bank Ltd v. Hestia Holdings Ltd* [2013] EWHC 1328 (Comm), [2013] 2 Lloyd's Rep 121.

proceedings against the bank only in Luxembourg, while the bank was to be permitted to sue the customer in any court which had jurisdiction over her. The customer sued the bank in France; the French Supreme Court refused to dismiss the proceedings by reference to what was then Article 23 of Regulation 44/2001, applying a principle of French (and quite possibly of Luxembourg) law, to the effect that an agreement which was so lop-sided ('potestative') was not legally enforceable. This was a calamitous decision, which imposed the idiosyncrasy of national law into the assessment of validity of a jurisdiction agreement, in the very way which the European Court had denounced in case after case. A jurisdiction agreement which was exclusive if A sued B, but non-exclusive if B sued A, would appear to fit comfortably within what is now Article 25(1). The clause was agreed to in writing in a complex banking contract. It could be regarded as 'potestative' only if it were severed from the rest of the contract; but if that were to be a permissible question to ask, a provision that a bank may demand repayment of an overdraft at any time would also be potestative and void. It is all nonsense, but at least it was possible to point to the wording of Article 23 of Regulation 44/2001, and to the constant jurisprudence of the Court, to show how wrong it is. But when Article 25 is in effect, and recourse to the 'substantive' law of a particular Member State is permitted to an extent which before 2015 it was not, the door to such chicanery will have been opened a little wider.

2.130 Formal requirements for an agreement on jurisdiction: general

Article 25 of Regulation 1215/2012 stipulates certain requirements which an agreement on jurisdiction must satisfy before it can be valid and legally effective to confer jurisdiction on the nominated court, and (if on its true construction, it is exclusive) to exclude the jurisdiction of other courts.

Over the course of the successive amendments of the Brussels Convention, and now the Regulation, these formal requirements have been adjusted and improved. It means that older authorities need to be read with some care. The purpose of these requirements is plain. Unless some formality is insisted upon, a jurisdiction agreement may be alleged, or an inconspicuous clause may be slipped, all unnoticed, into the relationship created by the parties. If they are viewed in this way, the formality rules reflect what is achieved at common law by a requirement that proper notice of an onerous term be given to the party against whom it will be invoked. If it is going to be said against a defendant that he had agreed to the jurisdiction of the court in question, or had agreed to give up the jurisdiction of another court, it is reasonable that the law should require this to be done in a demonstrably plausible fashion.

A basic tension still remains between two opposed ideas: that there is a need for strict compliance with the formality rules so as to protect the party against whom the agreement is sought to be invoked; and that an insistence on strict compliance with written forms may sometimes allow an unmeritorious argument to prevail. It will be no surprise, therefore, that the jurisprudence of the Court has experienced trouble in holding to a clear line, probably because there is no clear line to be held.

If one searches for a case in which a party signed a contract which contained[784] an agreement on jurisdiction but was not bound by it, one may not be found. The European Court

---

784 Or contained an express reference to other written provisions which contained: 24/76 *Estasis Salotti di Colzani Aimo e Giannmario Colzani snc v. RÜWA* [1976] ECR 1831.

might not have said, as clearly as it had been said in *L'Estrange v. Graucob*,[785] that a party is for all practical purposes bound by the contents of a document to which he puts his signature, but signature has a public, declaratory effect, and in an appropriate case, this should be the answer to the question posed by the formality issue.

2.131 Agreement of the party to be bound, in writing, or evidenced in writing

It has been stated by the European Court[786] that the purpose of the formality rules now in Article 25(1), is to establish 'clearly and precisely' the existence of consensus between the parties as to the jurisdiction of the particular court. In early case law, this led the Court to insist upon a strict application of the requirements, but it may be that the rules may, in certain circumstances, be interpreted more as signposts towards the existence of a consensus, which must be established, rather than as being mandatory in every case. For this reason, the older case law upon this point needs to be relied on with a little care. There is also a risk, not always appreciated, that the formal requirements are a means to an end; and that it is the end, not the means, which is the important thing.

According to the earliest decisions of the Court, it was not enough that the reference to the jurisdiction of a court was written on paper. Rather, it was the agreement to it, or acceptance of it by the party to be bound, which was required to be in writing or evidenced in writing: to put the point simply, a jurisdiction clause may be in A's standard written terms, and B may have been furnished with a copy of these, but that does not establish B's (as distinct from A's) agreement to the designated court. The cases illustrate the development of the law. In *Estasis Salotti v. RÜWA*,[787] it was held that a statement as to the jurisdiction of a court, clearly printed upon the reverse side of a written contractual document, did not satisfy the requirement of what at that time was Article 17 of the Brussels Convention that it be agreed in writing, so as to be binding on the other party.[788] The gist of the reasoning was that, although the printed clause identified the court which was to have jurisdiction, the fact that it was so printed furnished no guarantee that it had come to the other party's attention, and offered no guarantee that he had agreed to it.

Accordingly, and in the language of what is now Article 25 of the Regulation, it could not be said that the agreement on jurisdiction was in writing or evidenced in writing. To the same effect was *Galeries Segoura v. Bonakdarian*,[789] where a 'confirmation in writing had been sent by one party to the other, stating that a sale was made upon general trading conditions,

---

785 [1934] 2 KB 394. See also, on the durability of the signature rule, *Toll v. Alphapharm Pty Ltd* (2004) 219 CLR 165. Of course, if the analysis properly is that it is agreements, rather than contracts, which prorogate jurisdiction, the application of the rule in *L'Estrange v. Graucob* [1934] 2 KB 394 is by analogy rather than strict authority. But that does not seem to be conceptually difficult. For plain, unvarnished adoptions of a 'signed-bound' rule, see *O'Connor v. Masterwood Ltd* [2009] IESC 49; *Coys of Kensington Automobiles Ltd v. Pugliese* [2011] EWHC 655 (QB), [2011] 2 All ER (Comm) 664; *Sherdley v. Nordea Life & Pension SA* [2012] EWCA Civ 88, [2012] Lloyd's Rep IR 437 (failure to alert consumer to the fact that the jurisdiction and law provision of the document they were about to sign was materially different from the clause in the document which they previously had).

786 In 24/76 *Estasis Salotti di Colzani Aimo e Gianmario Colzani snc v. RÜWA* [1976] ECR 1831 and in 25/76 *Galeries Segoura Sprl v. Bonakdarian* [1976] ECR 1851, both decided upon the version of the Brussels Convention in force prior to the accession of the United Kingdom, but which raised the same general issue. Their continuing validity was confirmed by the Court in C-106/95 *MSG v. Les Gravières Rhénanes Sarl* [1997] ECR I-911.

787 24/76 *Estasis Salotti di Colzani Aimo e Gianmario Colzani snc v. RÜWA* [1976] ECR 1831.

788 Article 17, as it then was, required that there be an 'agreement in writing or ... an oral agreement confirmed in writing'.

789 25/76, [1976] ECR 1851.

172

which themselves contained a provision on choice of court. It was held that this would not satisfy the requirement that the agreement of the parties to the choice of jurisdiction be evidenced in writing unless accepted in turn in writing by the other party. In other words, the acceptance by the other party of the proposed jurisdiction had to be in writing, or had to be evidenced in writing. As it was put in *The Tilly Russ*:[790] 'where a jurisdiction clause appears in the conditions printed on a bill of lading signed by the carrier, the requirement of an "agreement in writing" within the meaning of Article 17 of the Convention is satisfied only if the shipper has expressed in writing his consent to the conditions containing that clause, either in the document in question itself or in a separate document. It must be added that the mere printing of a jurisdiction clause on the reverse of the bill of lading does not satisfy the requirements of Article 17 of the Convention, since such a procedure gives no guarantee that the other party has actually consented to the clause derogating from the ordinary rules of the Convention.'

In other words, the acceptance of the other party's written jurisdiction provision had to be in writing or evidenced in writing. If, therefore, a party signs a document which refers plainly enough to trading conditions which themselves contain an agreement on jurisdiction, this should satisfy the requirements of the Article.[791] This is entirely consistent with the contention above, that it is the consent to or acceptance of it by the party to be bound to it, rather than the statement (by the other party) that a court is to have jurisdiction, which is required to be in writing. Though a party may propose written terms to another, these including among them an agreement on jurisdiction, the crucial question is whether the party against whom that jurisdiction is to be asserted signified his acceptance in a form which complies with what is now Article 25(1).

However, for every case in which formality is insisted on, there will be another in which it is inappropriate to do so. In *Berghöfer GmbH & Co KG v. ASA SA*[792] the Court accepted that an oral agreement, later confirmed in writing by one party and not apparently objected to by the other, could in principle be taken to satisfy what is now Article 25(1), even though there was no written consent from one of the parties. The basis for this result was thought to lie in the general principle of good faith:[793] that it would in those circumstances be bad faith or bad form for the party seeking to take a point about the lack of formality to do so. In *Iveco Fiat SpA v. Van Hool NV*[794] it was held that, where parties to a written contract

---

790 See, for example, 71/83 *The Tilly Russ* [1984] ECR 2417, [16].

791 24/76 *Estasis Salotti di Colzani Aimo e Gianmario Colzani snc v. RÜWA* [1976] ECR 1831, [9]–[10]; *Credit Suisse Financial Products v. Soc Gen d'Enterprises* [1997] CLC 168, 172; *7E Communications Ltd v. Vertex Antennentechnik GmbH* [2007] EWCA Civ 140, [2008] Bus LR 472 (taking a sensible and practical approach to whether the signed documents evidence consent to the agreement, which they plainly did); *Polskie Ratownictwo Okretowe v. Rallo Vito & C snc* [2009] EWHC 2249 (Comm), [2010] 1 Lloyd's Rep 384; *Chester Hall Precision Engineering Ltd v. Service Centres Aero France* [2014] EWHC 2529 (QB), [2014] ILPr 571.

792 221/84, [1985] ECR 2699; see also *Kolmar Group AG v. Visen Industries Ltd* [2009] EWHC 3765 (QB), [2010] ILPr 449.

793 The basis of the doctrine appears to be a kind of estoppel: after his apparent acquiescence, the defendant would be acting in bad faith were he to turn round and rely on the strict formal requirements of Art. 25 against his opponent, and to argue that the agreement on a choice of court was neither written nor evidenced in writing. This principle may also mean that one party is precluded from relying on the absence of the other side's written agreement to a term put forward by the former, so that the party whose standard form term it is will always be bound by it if it is invoked by his opponent. Jenard [1979] OJ C59/1, 37, appears to suggest that it is sufficient that *one* of the parties has confirmed in writing an oral agreement. This is questionable, but it may be that cases of writing which follows an oral agreement are different from cases in which the only form of agreement is the allegedly written one.

794 313/85, [1986] ECR 3337.

which had contained an agreement on jurisdiction and by which is was clear that each was bound, continued to deal with each other without the written renewal which the contract provided for, the agreement on jurisdiction in the original contract continued to bind. The Court observed, in as clear a statement of principle as one may hope to find, that the 'sole purpose of the formal requirement... is to ensure that the consensus between the parties is in fact established and it imposes on the national court the duty of examining whether the clause conferring jurisdiction upon it was in fact the subject of such a consensus, which must be clearly and precisely demonstrated'.[795] If the party responsible for drawing the contractual documents does not alert the customer to the fact that there has been a material change to the governing law and jurisdiction clause, with the consequence that the customer signs a contract in ignorance of this alteration from previous drafts, it may be bad faith to seek to hold the customer to his signature.[796]

In *Powell Duffryn plc v. Petereit*,[797] it was held that a jurisdiction provision contained in a company's articles of association bound shareholders in the company according to its terms, and that this proposition was unaffected by how or when the shares were acquired. The reasoning was that company's constitutional documents are in the public domain, and that the shareholders agree to be bound by their contents. If it were to be asserted that the shareholder did not actually know what these documents contained, the retort is that he had the means of knowledge, and that is enough.[798] If it follows from this that a party is bound by a written provision stipulating a court for the resolution of disputes, simply because it may be truthfully said that he had the means of knowledge of it,[799] the law would have moved a very long way from its original position. The Court observed that the issue in *Powell Duffryn plc* was quite different from that which arises in connection with a printed and standard-form clause contained in another's standard conditions of trade;[800] the proposition that a member of a company accepts and is bound by all the terms of his membership is quite distinct from the proposition that a person who makes a single contract on another's terms is, in the same way, bound by them. This seems correct.

The requirement that the party to be bound have sufficiently agreed, in writing or in a way which is evidenced in writing, is principled, even where the facts make its application less so. A question may arise as to what is meant by 'writing'. Some legal systems have rules which withhold effect from a jurisdiction agreement if the print in which it is written is too faint or is too small for it to be reasonably legible. At first sight, there is no room for such reasoning within the framework of Article 25 for, as we shall see, national legal rules prescribing the formalities required for the validity of an agreement may not be added to those set out in Article 25.[801] But if the writing is too small or otherwise illegible, or is written in an exotic language which means that it is completely camouflaged from the other party, even if there is writing by the party to be bound, it could be argued that it would be bad faith for the *proferens* to rely on it. If this is accepted, it may also offer a way forward to the

---

795 At [5].

796 *Sherdley v. Nordea Life & Pension SA* [2012] EWCA Civ 88, [2012] Lloyd's Rep IR 437.

797 C-214/89, [1992] ECR I-1745.

798 At [26]–[29].

799 At [28]. For the view that if a party signs a document which refers to printed conditions which do themselves contain a choice of court agreement, then he is bound by reason of the signature, see *Crédit Suisse Financial Products v. Société Générale d'Enterprises* [1997] ILPr 165.

800 At [25].

801 See below, para. 2.145.

problem which arises when the agreement on jurisdiction is printed in a language which, to the knowledge of the *proferens*, the other party cannot read or understand. The overriding need is to demonstrate that the agreement on jurisdiction was the subject of consensus; and the requirement of writing is, as was said above, a means to an end, rather than an end in itself. If the party proposing the term knows that the other cannot have known what he was being invited to consent to, it would arguably be wrong to hold the other to the jurisdiction which, as the proposer knows, the other did not agree to.

Article 25(2) extends the scope of 'writing' to include communication by electronic means which provide a durable record of the agreement. This doubtless includes fax and (if anyone still uses it) telex transmission. It must include email, on the footing that the message is stored, or is capable of being stored, and can also be printed to make a hard and durable copy of what has been agreed. It is less likely that it extends to a voicemail or text message, neither of which provides a durable, as opposed to an ephemeral, record, even if voice recognition software may produce a written version of the spoken word. It may also explain why a jurisdiction agreement, appearing or made accessible by clicking on a service provider's website, will bind a person who makes a contract on, or otherwise uses, that website.[802] If the general question is whether the customer appears to have agreed to the jurisdiction, and the answer is affirmative, that should be sufficient to meet the requirements of Article 25.

2.132 Agreement according with the parties' established practices

The wording which now appears as Article 25(1)(b) was introduced into the Brussels Convention in 1990 to relax the uniform requirement of writing or evidence in writing. It validates an agreement on jurisdiction in the absence of writing recording the assent of the party to be bound, so long as there is evidence of a practice having been established between the parties.[803] The reference to practices which the parties have established between themselves has in mind, no doubt, a situation in which the history of past dealings would suggest that it would be bad faith on the part of a party who sought to rely on the lack of writing to challenge the formal validity of the agreement, or to argue that there was no notice of the proposed agreement on jurisdiction.[804] This legislative version of formal validity was in fact ushered in by the decision of the European Court in *Iveco Fiat SpA v. Van Hool NV*,[805] where a written agreement, which had contained a choice of court clause, had lapsed without the parties noticing. It was held that the jurisdiction agreement could in principle continue to operate, though the precise reasoning in the case, that the clause did comply with the need for writing, would now be redundant. The proposition that the party to be bound had accepted the jurisdiction of the named court, and had done so in writing, remained true despite the fact that the parties' contractual relationship had become less formal. It may be that the wording of Article 25(1)(b) is more easily understood as a pointer

---

802 This was not quite the way it was put by the High Court of Ireland in *Ryanair Ltd v. Billigfluege.de GmbH* [2010] IEHC 47, [2010] ILPr 439, but the point is substantially the same. If by contrast the jurisdiction provision was well hidden and so practically invisible to the ordinary website user, it would not be binding.

803 For illustration, see *OT Africa Line Ltd v. Hijazy* [2001] 1 Lloyd's Rep 76 (liner services); *SSQ Europe SA v. Johann & Backes OHG* [2002] 1 Lloyd's Rep 465 (sales of slate). See also the approach of a German court in *Jurisdiction in the Case of a Sale Involving the Carriage of Goods* (5U 99/07) [2010] ILPr 529.

804 See *Calyon v. Wytwornia Sprzetu Komunikacynego PZL Swidnik SA* [2009] EWHC 1914 (Comm), [2009] 2 All ER (Comm) 603, esp. at [83].

805 313/85, [1986] ECR 3337.

to a principle of reasonable notice, rather than as requiring a strict analysis of the meaning of 'practices' and 'established'.[806]

2.133 Agreement according with the practices of international trade

The major relaxation of the original requirement of writing was made to accommodate those engaged in international trade, and who may be expected to assume that a jurisdiction agreement in common form will apply to them and to each of them. In its present version, Article 25(1)(c) provides that it is sufficient if, in international trade or commerce, the agreement is 'in a form which accords with a usage of which the parties are or ought to have been aware and which in international trade or commerce is widely known to, and regularly observed by, parties to contracts of the type involved in the particular trade or commerce concerned'. This formulation is relatively new, the two leading authorities on this issue having been decided on the basis of an earlier, less prescriptive, form of words. With that qualification, though, the guidance which they give is still reliable.

In *MSG v. Les Gravières Rhénanes Sarl*,[807] and in *Trasporti Castelletti Spedizioni Internazionali SpA v. Hugo Trumpy SpA*,[808] the Court stated that, where it was established that there are commercial practices in a particular branch of international trade or commerce, and that the parties were or ought to have been aware of them, their agreement to the jurisdiction of the court will be presumed to have been established. Indeed, the current version of the Article may even dispense with the presumption: the parties are bound if it can be said that the practice exists and is generally known in the trade, and that the parties should have been aware of it. International trade means just that, so in *MSG* itself, river transport on the Rhine between France and Germany qualified.[809]

As to how widely the practice must exist, whether it must be shown to exist in particular Member States, or whether there must be publicity, the Court explained that all that is required is a practice which is generally observed in the trade, eschewing any more prescriptive limitations. So if it is customary in the particular trade to use documents with a printed choice of court in them, which are otherwise unsigned and often unread, or if it is customary to send a letter of confirmation to which a response is not expected, assent (and in this sense, agreement) to the choice of court will be deemed to be present as long as the parties should have been aware of it. The parties in such a case are far from the predicament of the hapless private buyer who is not prompted to read the off-puttingly small print on the back of a delivery note.[810]

2.134 Agreement to jurisdiction incorporated from one document into another

Article 25(1)(c) may also point the way to a sensible analysis of the problems which arise when it is alleged that there has been an incorporation of an agreement on jurisdiction for

---

806 This may be the lesson to be drawn from *Calyon v. Wytwornia Sprzetu Komunikacynego PZL Swidnik SA* [2009] EWHC 1914 (Comm), [2009] 2 All ER (Comm) 603.

807 C-106/95, [1997] ECR I-911.

808 C-159/97, [1999] ECR I-1597.

809 It includes associated insurance: *Standard Steamship Owners' Protection & Indemnity Assurance (Bermuda) Ltd v. GIE Vision Bail* [2004] EWHC 2919 (Comm), [2005] 1 All ER 618.

810 Though this will sometimes be catered for under the rules for certain consumer contracts, the restricted range of contracts to which Art. 17 applies will limit the protection given.

the courts of a Member State from one contract into another, such that it may be said that there has been agreement of the jurisdiction of the court in question. In various areas of commercial activity a contract – for example, in the field of insurance and reinsurance – will provide that 'all terms' are to be 'as original'. If the 'original' contract contained an agreement on jurisdiction, it may be argued that these general words of incorporation fetch and carry that agreement on jurisdiction from the first into the second contract. As far as English[811] domestic law is concerned, it is sometimes held that words of such generality do not incorporate the agreement on jurisdiction into the new contract. There are several reasons. For one, it may be said that the jurisdiction agreement is ancillary to the subject matter of the contract, which is the 'risk', and not germane to it,[812] and that more specific reference to the jurisdiction[813] agreement will be needed to achieve its incorporation.[814] There may also be a problem if the clause in the first contract between A and B would, if copied *verbatim*, make little sense in the second contract between B and C. Such reasoning may be used to explain why a bill of lading, which purports in general terms to incorporate the terms of the charterparty into the bill, may not incorporate a jurisdiction or arbitration agreement from that charterparty: incorporation from one contractual document to another is easier where the parties to each are the same.[815]

While this may be well understood as a matter of the common law of contract, it is not so certain that the rules of the common law (or, if it is alleged that the bill or reinsurance is governed by a foreign law, the rules of the private international law) provide a satisfactory answer. For it may be that the question whether a jurisdiction provision has been incorporated into a contract, in such a way that a party to that contract may be said to have agreed to it, is actually an issue on which Article 25(1) frames the analysis. It may be shown that a contract term has been incorporated from one document to another, but that is not the precise point: the question is whether the party to be bound has agreed, in writing or in other effective form, to the jurisdiction of the court in question, and the law on incorporation of terms into contracts has little to do with it. Of course, if this form of incorporation is practised in the particular trade, and satisfies the further requirements of Article 25(1)(c), this may be effective to establish the validity of the agreement.

The more recent approach of the English courts, at least, has been to regard the question as one on which what is now Article 25 provides the answer, but to interpret the requirements of Article 25 in this context as requiring it to be shown that there was 'a clear and precise determination that the jurisdiction clause was the subject of consensus'. This may not be exactly how Article 25 puts it, but it may well be what it means; and a test framed

---

811 In principle it may be different if the second contract is governed by something other than English law.

812 *Crédit Suisse v. Association Générale d'Enterprises* [1997] CLC 168; *AIG Europe (UK) Ltd v. The Ethniki* [2000] 2 All ER 566; *AIG Europe SA v. QBE International Insurance Ltd* [2001] 2 Lloyd's Rep 268; *Assicurazioni Generali SpA v. Ege Sigorta A/S* [2002] Lloyd's Rep IR 480; *Evialis v. SIAT* [2003] EWHC 863 (Comm), [2003] 2 Lloyd's Rep 377; *Siboti K/S v. BP France SA* [2003] EWHC 1278 (Comm), [2003] 2 Lloyd's Rep 364; *Welex AG v. Rosa Maritime Ltd* [2003] EWCA Civ 938, [2003] 2 Lloyd's Rep 509; *7E Communications Ltd v. Vertex Antennentechnik GmbH* [2007] EWCA Civ 140, [2008] Bus LR 472; *Africa Express Line Ltd v. Socofi SA* [2009] EWHC 3223, [2010] 2 Lloyd's Rep 181; *Habaş Sınai ve Tıbbi Gazlar İstihsal Endüstrisi AS v. Sometal SAL* [2010] EWHC 29 (Comm), [2010] Bus LR 880.

813 Or arbitration.

814 For example, *Welex AG v. Rosa Maritime Ltd* [2003] EWCA Civ 938, [2003] 2 Lloyd's Rep 509.

815 *TW Thomas & Co Ltd v. Portsea Steamship Co Ltd* [1912] AC 1; *Habaş Sınai ve Tıbbi Gazlar İstihsal Endüstrisi AS v. Sometal SAL* [2010] EWHC 29 (Comm), [2010] Bus LR 880.

in these words has the potential to find the common ground beneath the common law approach and that set out in Article 25.

2.135 Article 25 and strangers to the original agreement

The operation of Article 25 where the matter before the court involves someone other than the original contracting parties can present some difficulty where the question is whether the non-party is or is not entitled to, or bound by, the agreement on jurisdiction which the original contracting parties made.[816] The beginning and the end of the enquiry will be to ask whether the non-party has agreed, or is to be treated as though he had agreed, to the jurisdiction of a court which he himself did not originally select.

It is established that a third party who succeeds to the rights or obligations of an original contracting party may rely upon the jurisdiction agreement which bound the original contracting parties and which was valid in point of form as between them. This will be so without the need for any further writing, or other demonstration of acceptance, by the non-party. In *Gerling v. The Italian State Treasury*,[817] a third-party beneficiary was held to be entitled to rely upon an agreement on jurisdiction contained in a contract which had been made for his benefit: but then, the law has never encountered insuperable difficulty with the proposition that the benefit of a contract may in certain circumstances be claimed by a third party.[818]

When it comes to the mirror image, the question whether a third party may be bound by or held to an agreement on jurisdiction which he did not make, the analysis and the answer will be different. The point of departure is *The Tilly Russ*.[819] In that case, it was held that a third-party holder of a bill of lading was liable to be held bound by an agreement on jurisdiction to which the shipper, the original contracting party, had subscribed 'in so far as the third party... has succeeded to the shipper's rights and obligations under the relevant national law'. It was the duty of the referring court in that case to determine for itself whether that condition had been satisfied in the matter before it. In other words, if the formal validity of the agreement on jurisdiction has been established as between the original contracting parties, its effect on third parties appears to be a matter for the national law, including its conflict of laws rules, of the court seised with the dispute, in particular its rules about succession and privity. As to this, it should not be supposed that the reference to 'succession' is limited or restrictive: a statutory mechanism of transfer and vesting by operation of law, by which a lawful holder of a bill of lading acquires all rights of suit,[820] will fall within the notion of 'succession' to which the Court referred.

---

816 See also *Bank of Scotland v. Banque Nationale de Paris* [1996] ILPr 668.

817 201/82, [1983] ECR 2503.

818 That is not to say that the doctrine of privity never made life difficult, but the right of a third party to claim a benefit is a good deal easier to justify than the proposition that a third party may be affected by the burden of a contract to which he was not party.

819 71/83, [1984] ECR 2417, applied in *Middle East Tankers & Freighters Bunker Services (Offshore) SA v. Abu Dhabi Container Lines PJSC* [2002] EWHC 957 (Comm), [2002] 2 Lloyd's Rep 643. *Cf* the position of bailor and sub-bailee, which is quite different: *Dresser (UK) Ltd v. Falcongate Freight Management Ltd* [1992] 1 QB 502. See also *Firswood Ltd v. Petra Bank* [1996] CLC 608.

820 Carriage of Goods by Sea Act 1992, s. 2(1). See also *AP Moller Mærsk A/S v. Sonaec Villas Cen Sad Fadoul* [2010] EWHC 355 (Comm), [2011] 1 Lloyd's Rep 1.

The point was reaffirmed in *Trasporti Castelletti Spedizioni Internazionali SpA v. Hugo Trumpy SpA*[821] and in *Coreck Maritime GmbH v. Handelsveem BV*,[822] and it is, therefore, established beyond doubt that where a non-party succeeds as a matter of fact and law to the contractual rights and liabilities of one who was also bound by an agreement which met the requirements of Article 25, he succeeds as well to the agreement on jurisdiction. He is not, separately and on his own behalf, required to agree in writing to it.[823] This accords with principle, for a true successor should not have greater rights or freedoms than the party to whose rights he has succeeded. The question whether there has been such a succession, in the sense in which *The Tilly Russ* used the expression, was said by the Court to be for 'the relevant national law', and this, presumably, indicates the law which governs the bill of lading or other contract succeeded to. In *Refcomp SpA v. AXA Corporate Solutions Assurance SA*[824] the Court used another idiom: the question was whether the non-party was in law substituted for the contracting party. But whatever the idiom, the legal principle is the same.

The apparent practical reason for this repeated emphasis by the Court was a series of decisions in which the French Supreme Court had denied that a person to whom a bill of lading had been indorsed or transferred, typically a French buyer, could simply be bound by receipt of an agreement on jurisdiction without independently 'accepting' the agreement on jurisdiction for himself.[825] The Court in *Coreck Maritime* therefore drew a distinction between the case in which the indorsee or other non-party was alleged to be bound by succession (or substitution), and the case in which he is said to be bound otherwise than by means of succession. In the latter, it is necessary to show that the third party has, for himself, agreed to the nominated jurisdiction in a manner which itself met the requirements of what is now Article 25(1). The distinction will turn on what is included within the concept of 'succession' in the sense in which it was used in *The Tilly Russ*, and this is a question of substance, not of form. By contrast with what happens when a bill of lading is transferred, a sub-buyer of goods, who lies outside the original contractual relationship, does not normally 'succeed to' or 'substitute' the person who sold to him in a relationship with the manufacturer or retailer: he makes a sub-contract. If that is so, the sub-buyer will be held to a jurisdiction provision in the contract of sale only if he has made his own acceptance in writing or otherwise in a form which satisfies Article 25(1).[826]

The principle, that only in the case of 'succession' will the third party be bound by an agreement on jurisdiction made *inter alios*, so there is no need for a separate act of individual acceptance, was also applied in *Soc Financière & Industrielle de Peloux v. Soc AXA Belgium*.[827] In that case, it was held that in order for the burden of a jurisdiction provision, contained in a contract of insurance, to be imposed on the beneficiary of the insurance, the beneficiary needed to accept the clause on his own behalf, and that he was not otherwise bound by it. Although this might appear to contradict the principle that *qui sentit commodum sentire debet*

---

821 C-159/97, [1999] ECR I-1597.

822 C-387/98, [2000] ECR I-9337.

823 *Knorr-Bremse Systems for Commercial Vehicles Ltd v. Haldex Brake Products GmbH* [2008] EWHC 156 (Pat), [2008] 2 All ER (Comm) 448.

824 C-543/10, EU:C:2013:62, [2013] 1 Lloyd's Rep 449. Perhaps 'standing in the shoes of' would make the point as well.

825 For example, *Insurance Co of North America v. Soc Intramar* [1999] ILPr 315.

826 C-543/10 *Refcomp SpA v. AXA Corporate Solutions Assurance SA* EU:C:2013:62, [2013] 1 Lloyd's Rep 449.

827 C-112/03, [2005] ECR I-3707.

et onus, the beneficiary did not succeed to the insurance, and did not therefore assume the obligations of the agreement on jurisdiction.[828]

It remains to be seen how this may apply in the context of the Contracts (Rights of Third Parties) Act 1999 which allows, where English is the governing law, a non-party to enforce in his own right a contract to which he was not privy but which was made for his benefit. The conclusion to be drawn from *Gerling v. The Italian State Treasury* is that, where the contract is made for the benefit of a non-party and is intended to be enforced by him, but that contract contains an agreement on jurisdiction which, as between the original contracting parties, satisfies Article 25(1), the non-party beneficiary will be entitled to rely on the agreement on choice of court; and[829] will be bound by it, without the need for an independent acceptance of it.[830] Though the agreement on jurisdiction may be seen as a burden, in that it may restrict the non-party to bringing an action in the nominated court, and therefore be said to fall outside the scope of the 1999 Act, it is submitted that this would be wrong, for if the burden is an integral part of the benefit which the contract confers, the principle that *qui sentit commodum sentire debet et onus* should apply.[831]

2.136 The possibility of 'lifting the veil of incorporation' and then applying Article 25

A particular issue, which has not yet been addressed by the European Court, arises where a jurisdiction agreement is made between a claimant and a company, and the claimant wishes to proceed against an individual who, he contends, is concealed by the veil of incorporation but who should be made liable alongside the company. The process is described, graphically if misleadingly, as lifting or piercing the corporate veil; and despite several attempts to bring the principles governing the practice under control, the material rules of English substantive law are not entirely settled.[832] In particular, English domestic law remains uncertain whether the effect of meeting the requirements of the doctrine may be that the person said to be found behind the veil is liable on the undertakings of the company, as though he were an original contractor, or is liable to have a judgment entered only against the company enforced against his separate assets. English private international law does not make it clear whether, when the

---

828 It is also clear that the Court was motivated by the general principle that agreements on jurisdiction in insurance cases are subject to severe limitation; and for the beneficiary of the insurance to become bound to an agreement which, as far as he was concerned, had never been adopted, was unacceptable. See also, in the context of a direct claim by a victim against the insurer of the tortfeasor, the tortfeasor's insurance containing a jurisdiction agreement and being governed by English law, *Through Transport Mutual Insurance Association (Eurasia) Ltd v. New India Assurance Co Ltd* [2004] EWCA Civ 1598, [2005] 1 Lloyd's Rep 67, where a Finnish court held that the claimant was not bound by the dispute resolution agreement, but the English court reached the contrary conclusion. The case was discussed but distinguished in *Shipowners' Mutual P&I Association (Luxembourg) v. Containership Denizcilik Nakliyat ve Ticaret as* [2015] EWHC 258 (Comm) which involved a jurisdiction agreement for a non-Member State.

829 Here the analysis goes beyond *Gerling*'s case.

830 And *cf Nisshin Shipping Co Ltd v. Cleaves & Co Ltd* [2004] 1 Lloyd's Rep 38, accepting and applying this broad argument in the context of an arbitration agreement in a charterparty which promised a payment to a non-party shipbroker.

831 He who claims the benefit must accept the benefit together with its burden: *Halsall v. Brizzell* [1957] Ch 169. But this would require C-112/03 *Soc Financière & Industrielle de Peloux v. Soc AXA Belgium* [2005] ECR I-3707 to be understood as turning on the fact that it concerned a contract of insurance. See also *Dresser (UK) Ltd v. Falcongate Freight Management Ltd* [1992] QB 502 (authorised sub-bailment).

832 See in particular *VTB Capital plc v. Nutritek International Corp* [2013] UKSC 5, [2013] 2 AC 337; *Prest v. Petrodel Resources Ltd* [2013] UKSC 34, [2013] 2 AC 415.

issues arise before an English court, the material rules are those of English domestic law, or may be referred to a foreign law whether *lex contractus* (because the usual context is that the company has made a contract which has given rise to the proceedings), or *lex incorporationis* (because the issue is one of company law in general, and of the rigidity or permeability of the principle of separate corporate personality), or the *lex fori* (as the matter is one of procedure, either generally or as one pertaining to the enforcement of judgments of the court).[833]

The idea that any of this should be relevant at the point of jurisdiction is, obviously, appalling. Where the jurisdiction of the English court has depended on the residual jurisdictional rules now taken up into Article 6 of the Regulation, and the question has arisen whether a person is liable to service out of the jurisdiction in a matter relating to a contract, where that contract was made by 'his' company but not, on the face of it, by him, the message from the Supreme Court appears to be that this is not an issue which can be gone into and resolved on a jurisdiction application.[834] Quite right, too: if the doctrine exists at all, it is dependent on a detailed analysis of fact and quasi-fact, bound to be highly contentious and quite unsuitable for any sort of investigation, never mind resolution, on a jurisdiction application.

If that is true in relation to Article 6 jurisdiction, which, as will be seen, can appear to be over-engineered, it is all the more true of jurisdiction on the basis of Article 25. To invite a court to consider the domestic and private international law of lifting the corporate veil, and then to investigate the facts which apply in relation to that law, would contradict the approach taken by the Court in *Benincasa v. Dentalkit Srl*.[835] It follows that if a claimant wishes to bring proceedings[836] against a person who is alleged to be, and to be liable as, the *alter ego* of a company which has made an agreement on jurisdiction, the simple question is whether he has, in writing or otherwise in accordance with Article 25(1), given his agreement to be sued in the court prorogated in the agreement his company made.[837] The view taken here is that the answer is that he has not: he may[838] have agreed that someone else should be sued in a particular named court, but as a matter of plain fact, he has not agreed, in writing or otherwise, that he should be sued there, and neither has the counterparty agreed to enter into legal relations with him at all, still less sue him before a particular court.

What may be said against this? One possibility is that it indulges bad faith for this stance to be permitted to be adopted. But arguments about bad faith are admissible to prevent a person who has agreed to the jurisdiction of a court taking an unmeritorious point about the absence of formality;[839] it will in other contexts be very hard to determine at the jurisdiction stage, and recourse to it is unlikely to be fruitful. Another might be to 'interpret' the agreement as meaning that there was one agreement to jurisdiction, and that the company

---

833 The issue was raised as one of potential significance, but did not need to be addressed, in *VTB Capital plc v. Nutritek International Corp* [2013] UKSC 5, [2013] 2 AC 337. In *Prest v. Petrodel Resources Ltd* [2013] UKSC 34, [2013] 2 AC 415, no question of applicable law appears to have been put before the court for its consideration; the court simply applied rules of English domestic law. See also *Antonio Gramsci Shipping Corp v. Lembergs* [2013] EWCA Civ 730, [2013] 2 Lloyd's Rep 295.

834 *VTB Capital plc v. Nutritek International Corp* [2013] UKSC 5, [2013] 2 AC 337.

835 C-369/95, [1997] ECR I-3767.

836 Other than for the enforcement of a judgment from the courts of a Member State, to which Art. 24(5) applies.

837 See *Antonio Gramsci Shipping Corp v. Lembergs* [2013] EWCA Civ 730, [2013] 2 Lloyd's Rep 295.

838 The decision-taking processes of the company will not be liable to be known or agreed at this point, so it cannot be said that *he* has agreed what the company will accept.

839 221/84 *Berghöfer GmbH & Co KG v. ASA SA* [1985] ECR 2699.

agreed on its behalf and on behalf of those who controlled it. But this cannot be correct: in the absence of special circumstances it would be absurd to argue that shareholders' consent to be sued by third parties in the court in which the company of which they are members has agreed that it should be sued.

Although it may leave the claimant with the sense that the individual has got away with it, at least in jurisdictional terms, there are two responses to make. The first is that this is a risk which everyone knows, or ought to realise, is run when dealing with companies without taking an enforceable promise or guarantee of performance from someone else with substance and jurisdictional accessibilty. The second is that if there were to be a legislative amendment to Article 8(1), to allow co-defendants domiciled in another Member State to be joined to proceedings brought against a defendant in the courts prorogated in accordance with Article 25, most jurisdictional difficulty would dissolve.

2.137 Subrogation by insurers and the effect of agreements made by their insured

A distinct, but related, issue arises when the claimant is subrogated to the contractual rights of another who was party to a contract which contained an agreement on jurisdiction. The question has arisen most frequently in cases of insurance,[840] when the insurer pays out to its insured and is then subrogated to the rights of the insured against the wrongdoer. If the insured and the wrongdoer were parties to a contract which contained an agreement on jurisdiction, the question is whether the subrogated claimant is bound, as the party to whose rights he is subrogated was bound, by the agreement on jurisdiction.

Where the dispute resolution provision in question is an arbitration agreement, the English courts have taken the approach that the question is answered by reference to the law which governed the arbitration agreement, which is likely to be the law of the contract in which the arbitration agreement was contained, as distinct from the law which governed the contract of insurance under or as a result of the performance of which the subrogation took place. If this law is English law, the conclusion is likely to be that if the rights of the insured against the tortfeasor were only enforceable in arbitration, the subrogated insurer is similarly bound:[841] the right to which the insured becomes subrogated will be defined in part by the obligation to proceed by arbitration in respect of it. This makes sense in the context of arbitration, for the question whether there is a valid and binding agreement to arbitrate is an unambiguously contractual issue, and only ever a contractual issue.

To similar effect, but in the case which combined subrogation to the rights of the insured and the bringing of a direct action against the insurer of the tortfeasor, is *Through Transport Mutual Insurance Association (Eurasia) Ltd v. New India Assurance Association Company Ltd*.[842] In that case, A had insured B who had been caused loss by C who had been insured by

---

840 The authorities have usually involved an arbitration agreement, rather than an agreement on jurisdiction, but the point is still worth consideration.

841 See, for example, *West Tankers Inc v. RAS Riunione Adriatica di Sicurta* [2005] EWHC 454 (Comm), [2005] 2 Lloyd's Rep 257 (not challenged on this point: [2007] 1 Lloyd's Rep 391), following and applying *Schiffahrtsgesellschaft Detlev von Appen v. Vöst Alpine Intertrading (The Jay Bola)* [1997] 2 Lloyd's Rep 279. See also *Hatzl v. XL Insurance Co Ltd* [2009] EWCA Civ 223, [2010] 1 WLR 470 (on the question whether the assignment or subrogation alters the identity of the court with jurisdiction).

842 [2004] EWCA Civ 1598, [2005] 1 Lloyd's Rep 67. cf *Shipowners' Mutual P&I Association (Luxembourg) v Containership Denizcilik Nakliyat ve Ticaret as [2015] EWHC 258 (Comm)*.

D. A settled with B and was subrogated to his claim against C; C had become insolvent and A proceeded directly against D in Finland.[843] The contract of insurance between C and D contained an arbitration clause for London, where the tribunal would have probably applied English law according to which A would lose: it therefore made sense for A to sue in Finland instead. The Court of Appeal held that A was in principle bound by the agreement to arbitrate, but ruled that it was inappropriate to reinforce it by anti-suit injunction.[844] No doubt the explanation was that, although legal reasoning led to the conclusion that A was bound to the arbitration agreement, it was simply not correct to say that A had agreed to it by his own individual act.

Had these various contracts contained agreements on jurisdiction,[845] rather than arbitration agreements, the reasoning could not have been the same. In *Through Transport*, for example, it is hard to see how a court could properly find that A and D had agreed, clearly and precisely, on the jurisdiction of a court for the purposes of what is now Article 25: to be more specific, it is hard to see how A could have been bound by C's jurisdiction agreement with D.[846] The correct approach appears to be that as between A and B, A may be taken to have assumed the rights of B in a manner which may be regarded as succession. If B had been bound by an agreement on jurisdiction made with C, A should be bound to it without further ado. But the question whether a jurisdiction agreement between C and D may be imposed on B, when B brings the direct action which A would otherwise have been entitled to bring, must be answered in the negative. The claimant in the direct action does not succeed to the position of the wrongdoer, C: whatever statutes creating direct actions may do, they do not mean that the person bringing the direct claim succeeds to the rights of the wrongdoer against the wrongdoer's insurer. As a result, a distinct act of acceptance of the agreement on jurisdiction would be required of the injured party, or his liability insurer after a subrogation, before a jurisdiction agreement in the tortfeasor's insurance could bind him in a direct action.

2.138 Content of the jurisdiction agreement: choosing the courts of two Member States

Article 25 of Regulation 1215/2012 appears to validate only agreements to choose the courts of a single Member State, and so a choice for the courts of two Member States would not appear to conform to the Article. So literal an interpretation was, however, rejected in *Meeth v. Glacetal Sàrl*.[847] In that case, an agreement on jurisdiction provided for all actions against M to be brought in Germany, where M was domiciled, and all actions against G to be brought in France, where G was domiciled. In upholding the validity of this agreement, the Court observed that the structure of the clause consecrated in express terms the

---

843 On the basis of a provision of Finnish law corresponding to the Third Parties (Rights Against Insurers) Act 1930.

844 However, in further proceedings reported at [2005] EWHC 455 (Comm), [2005] 2 Lloyd's Rep 378, the Commercial Court held that D could ask the English court to appoint an arbitrator, and that as a matter of English law, A was bound to arbitrate at D's behest even though it was not an assignee of the rights of C. The reasoning appears to be that the obligation to arbitrate was indissociable from the rights created by the original insurance which, as a matter of common sense, seems sound.

845 It is to be recalled, however, that the enforceability of jurisdiction agreements in cases falling within Section 3 of Chapter II of the Regulation is restricted.

846 *Cf* the position of bailor and sub-bailee, which is in many respects similar: *Dresser (UK) Ltd v. Falcongate Freight Management Ltd* [1992] 1 QB 502.

847 23/78, [1978] ECR 2133.

fundamental general principle that each party should be sued in the courts of its domicile, and that what is now Article 25 could not prejudice its validity. It is also clear that it gave rise to no uncertainty: if G wished to sue M it was clear which single court had jurisdiction, and vice versa. It was a wholly rational decision.

The principle said to be derived from *Meeth* may validate a clause which purports to give exclusive jurisdiction to the courts of two or more Member States concurrently. Had the clause in *Meeth* provided that actions could, without other restriction, be brought in the courts of France or Germany, its effectiveness would have been only marginally less certain. There are arguments which tend to oppose the validity of such a clause: it will not be clear in advance which court is to be competent; the clause no longer gives effect to the principle that defendants should be sued where they are domiciled; and to give exclusive jurisdiction to two courts is inelegant, even self-contradictory. On the other hand, a choice of concurrent exclusive jurisdictions may be taken as a case in which the parties have agreed that the jurisdiction should not be exclusive, as Article 25(1) accepts that they may. It will still be perfectly clear which courts have been derogated from and, in that sense, excluded from jurisdiction. And in any event, if the purpose of what is now Article 25 is to embody the principle that the parties have autonomy, and that the Article should respect the common intention of the parties so far as it is not clearly overridden by other rules of law, then if this is what the parties agreed to there is no good reason to withhold effect from it. This perspective, reinforced by Article 25(1), must be correct. Such an agreement will clearly exclude the jurisdiction of any non-chosen courts which would have had jurisdiction derived from provisions lower in the hierarchy of the Regulation, and the intention of the parties is not clearly contrary to the policy of the law.

However, the agreement of the parties for the jurisdiction of two courts cannot be allowed to call into question the application of the *lis alibi pendens* rule in what is now Article 29 of the Regulation. It is not uncommon to find a term in a contract to the effect that one party – typically a bank – is allowed to bring proceedings against the defendant in more than one court concurrently. There is no reason why the parties should not make that agreement if they wish, but they cannot expect a court in a Member State, seised second in time but in respect of the same cause of action as the court seised first, to give effect to it. What is now Article 29 of Regulation 1215/2012 makes no provision for the parties to agree that it shall be inapplicable to litigation between them, and in this respect, party autonomy has its limits.

2.139 Content of the jurisdiction agreement: non-exclusive jurisdiction

A little history is unavoidable. Prior to Regulation 44/2001, it was not clear that the Brussels and Lugano Conventions gave legal effect to an agreement which was expressed to indicate non-exclusive jurisdiction in the courts of the particular State. The problem was created by the wording of the then rule which provided for the chosen court to have exclusive jurisdiction, and which, therefore, provided a rather awkward basis for the conclusion that a designated court might have non-exclusive jurisdiction. Despite this, the English courts managed to persuade themselves that such an agreement should be given effect according to its terms.[848] Indeed, it was possible to simulate a non-exclusive jurisdiction

---

848 *Kurz v. Stella Musical Veranstaltungs GmbH* [1992] Ch 196; *Gamlestaden v. Casa de Suecia SA* [1994] 1 Lloyd's Rep 433.

clause by drafting an exclusive jurisdiction agreement but expressing it to be for the benefit of only one of the parties: the Brussels Convention, by a provision not reproduced in the Regulation, allowed the benefiting party to hold the other to the agreement, but to depart from it if he chose.[849]

It was clear that the idea of non-exclusive jurisdiction was more familiar in some Member States than others; and that its uncertain status was unsatisfactory. As far as the Member States were concerned, the difficulties were swept away by what is now the second sentence of Article 25(1) of the Regulation, which provides that the jurisdiction of the court nominated 'shall be exclusive unless the parties have agreed otherwise'. The alteration is beneficial, even though no indication is given to explain how 'agreement otherwise' is to be demonstrated. The answer must presumably be that the language in which the parties have expressed their agreement is construed in accordance with the law which governs the substance of the agreement.[850] This, being a matter for the national, including conflicts, rules of the court seised, and not one of European law, is best examined in Chapter 4. It does not appear helpful to read the Regulation as imposing a presumption of exclusivity on an exercise which depends on national law, save in the case in which the parties offer no evidence as to their actual intention. Where that evidence is put before the court, the determination of what the parties actually agreed is a matter of substantive law which a court will determine in the usual way; as to this it is clear that national laws are not uniform on the construction of jurisdiction agreements as exclusive or otherwise. It would, of course, be different if the construction of a jurisdiction agreement were held to be a matter for uniform rules, but that does not yet appear to be the case.

Of course, once a court has been seised in accordance with a non-exclusive jurisdiction clause, Article 29 of the Regulation will transform its jurisdiction so that it will become indistinguishable from exclusive jurisdiction.

2.140 Content of the jurisdiction agreement: lop-sided agreements

As has been noted above, it is not uncommon for a contract to provide that in litigation between A and B, A must bring proceedings against B in a designated court, whereas B may bring proceedings against A in that court or in any other court which has jurisdiction over A. An English court has rarely encountered any difficulty in giving effect to such a provision. Where the Brussels Convention applied, this would be an exclusive jurisdiction agreement for the single designated court which by its express words was for the benefit of B which therefore had the option of bringing proceedings elsewhere. Where the Regulation applied, the clause would be exclusive to the extent that A sued B, and non-exclusive where B sued A, as that was the extent to which the parties had agreed on something other than exclusive jurisdiction, plain and simple.

In *Soc Banque privée Edmond de Rothschild Europe v. X*,[851] the French Supreme Court disagreed. A contract between bank and customer contained an agreement on jurisdiction

---

849 On service of suit clauses taking effect as non-exclusive jurisdiction clauses, see *Ace Insurance SA-NV v. Zurich Insurance Co* [2001] EWCA Civ 173, [2001] 1 Lloyd's Rep 618; also *Excess Insurance Co Ltd v. Allendale Mutual Insurance Co* [2001] Lloyd's Rep IR 524.

850 *British Sugar plc v. Fratelli Babbani di Lionello Babbani* [2004] EWHC 2560 (TTC), [2005] 1 Lloyd's Rep 332.

851 Cass I civ, 26 September 2012, [2013] ILPr 181, [2013] JDI/Clunet 175 (note Brière). For further comment, see [2013] LMCLQ 137. The judgment appealed from had purported to find a basis for its decision

by which the customer agreed to bring proceedings against the bank only in Luxembourg, while the bank was to be permitted to sue in any court which had jurisdiction over the customer. The customer sued the bank in France; the French Supreme Court refused to dismiss the proceedings on the basis that the jurisdiction agreement was wholly void: a principle of French and probably of Luxembourg law,[852] meant that a provision which imposed obligations on one party but not on the other was not legally enforceable. It is doubtful that the decision is consistent with the Regulation, for the content of the agreement appeared to fit the template presented by the second paragraph of what is now Article 25(1). On the other hand, if it is correct that the meaning of the agreement has to be understood and construed by reference to its governing law, if that law decided that the agreement is empty of content, no agreement at all, then there is nothing to which Article 25 can apply.

The immediate solution is to ensure that any such lop-sided agreements on jurisdiction are contained in contracts governed by laws which do not share the doctrine which was applied by the French Supreme Court, in the hope that a court called upon to give effect to such an agreement will not look to the law governing the contract to find a basis for invalidating it. But in the light of the final part of the first sentence of Article 25(1), it may now be dangerous to designate a court which finds fault with such agreements, as it now appears that some Member States do. This does make it appear that the law has taken a big step backwards.

It may also be necessary to reconsider whether the construction of jurisdiction agreements by reference to national laws is, after all, such a good idea, for not all national laws are a good idea. If it were possible to regard the second sentence of Article 25(1) as a complete statement of the principles of construction necessary to deal with this individual point,[853] the opportunity for idiosyncratic or maverick principles of national law to undermine an agreement otherwise clear and precisely expressed would be reduced. The risks associated with that are, however, considerable.

2.141 Content of the jurisdiction agreement: non-geographical designation of court

It is not uncommon for a agreement on jurisdiction to identify the country, the courts of which are to have jurisdiction, not by name but by description. A common one is to nominate 'the courts of the country in which the carrier has[854] its principal place of business'. According to the Court in *Coreck Maritime GmbH v. Handelsveem BV*,[855] this may be effective as an agreement on choice of court; and it will be if the wording used identifies

---

to the same effect in the fact that the provision of the Brussels Convention which has been referred to was not reproduced in the Regulation. The point that it did not need to be because the Regulation had made better provision of its own does not appear to have been appreciated.

852 The court did not indicate which, if either, of the two national laws it was applying. It is possible, though not very likely, that it thought it was applying an autonomous interpretation of 'have agreed' in the first line of Art. 25(1).

853 Questions of material scope would also need to be dealt with; on this it is very hard to see how recourse to national law can be avoided or substituted.

854 No attention was given to the issue which might arise where the carrier's principal place of business is moved between the making of the agreement on jurisdiction and the institution of proceedings.

855 C–387/98, [2000] ECR I-9337.

objective factors which are sufficiently precise to allow the court to determine whether it has jurisdiction: *id certum est quod certum reddi potest*.[856] In *Coreck Maritime* itself, a case on carriage of goods by sea, it appears[857] that there was no dispute as to which party was the carrier, nor as to the place which counted as its principal place of business. There, words used to designate the court with jurisdiction were sufficiently precise to allow the national court to determine its jurisdiction.

But the facts may not always be so accommodating. It is clear that national laws may disagree as to who actually is the carrier,[858] and may disagree as to which of the places in which it has a presence represents the principal place of its business.[859] Had these matters been in dispute in *Coreck Maritime*, the national court might have concluded that it was unable to ascertain the effect of the agreement on jurisdiction. The issue of interpretation is, so far as is known, still one for reference to national law, including conflicts rules, of the court seised.[860] But in *Coreck Maritime*, the agreement in question provided that any disputes 'shall be decided in the country where the carrier has his principal place of business and the law of such country shall apply except as provided elsewhere herein'. In other words, the governing law was to be defined by reference to the principal place of business, but the principal place of business may have to be identified by reference to the governing law. Though there may be ways for a national court to cut the circle of argument, none is particularly convincing; and it may be that the answer is that the agreement on choice of court is not, in the circumstances, sufficiently intelligible to be accepted as clear, precise, or effective. Despite the evident attraction which these clauses appear to have for certain draftsmen, a jurisdiction provision which is set out in the form of a riddle has little to be said in its defence, because it risks failing to do the very thing which it is supposed that such clauses are intended to accomplish.

An agreement on jurisdiction may be found to have been made in very short form. A provision in a contract which stated 'Court: DK-6100 Haderslev, Denmark' was held to be an agreement on jurisdiction validated by what is now Article 25.[861] For the court to approach the construction, or interpretation, of the provision from the vantage point of the professional reasonable man was sensible enough; the fact that the terse wording did not make it clear whether the court designated was to have exclusive or non-exclusive jurisdiction, and that no evidence appears to have been placed before the court, may mean that the presumption of exclusivity resolves the issue.[862]

2.142 Content of the jurisdiction agreement: the courts of the United Kingdom

A jurisdiction agreement for the courts of the United Kingdom is not straightforward. Article 25 of the Regulation would appear to be satisfied, but the question of what effect it has is more involved.

---

856 It is certain if it is capable of being ascertained.
857 The issue was one for the national court to determine, and not for the European Court.
858 The party who undertakes with the shipper to carry, or the owner of the ship which does the physical carriage.
859 See *The Rewia* [1991] 1 Lloyd's Rep 69 (overruled on other grounds): [1991] 2 Lloyd's Rep 325.
860 See the answer to the fourth question submitted to the Court.
861 *Nursaw v. Dansk Jersey Eksport* [2009] ILPr 263. 'DK-6001' is a postcode.
862 See above, para. 2.139.

As there are no courts 'of the United Kingdom' as such,[863] there appear to be two broad possibilities. The first, suitable if the agreement is expressed as a term of a contract, would be that the law governing the contract must construe the language by which the parties have expressed their intention.[864] If the contract is governed by English law,[865] the parties may be taken as meaning the English courts are to have jurisdiction, on the footing that the courts of England, as distinct from the courts of Scotland or Northern Ireland, were in all probability what they had in mind.[866]

The second possibility would be to start from the proposition that Article 25 requires the wording of the agreement to be taken at face value and (in the absence of evidence to the contrary)[867] to mean that the defendant will not be in a position to complain, so far as the Regulation is concerned, if proceedings are instituted in the courts of any law district within the territory of the United Kingdom. It would then be up to the claimant to decide which court within the United Kingdom to elect to seise.[868] And if he then seises the English court, there is no problem.

It is submitted that, notwithstanding *The Komninos S*,[869] the latter is the better view.[870] It operates by treating the clause as binding and as taking effect according to, or as close as possible to, the letter of its drafting. It will also mean that other choices of court which may be founded on an erroneous assumption, such as a choice for the courts of Switzerland,[871] can be given effect. The difficulty with the former possibility would be that the law which governs the contract may have no reliable means of imposing a meaning upon such a clause. Certainly, English law does not have a reliable statutory rule to achieve this end, and the assumption that if parties elected the courts of the United Kingdom what they really meant was England is, however accurate it may be, an uncomfortable proposition to defend within the United Kingdom itself.[872]

---

863 On the footing that the House of Lords did not have, and the Supreme Court of the United Kingdom does not have, trial jurisdiction in civil and commercial matters.

864 Which would be the general approach to the interpretation of a choice of court clause.

865 But if the question of which law governs is affected by the question of how the clause is to be interpreted, this will not much help. *Cf The Komninos S* [1991] 1 Lloyd's Rep 370, where a reference to 'British courts' was assumed, in the context and without reference to any particular law, to mean 'English courts', and this was used as a pointer to the applicable law of the contract. There is a chicken-and-egg quality to this reasoning process. Even so, people still use these unhelpful expressions. For further support for reading 'UK law' as 'English law', see *Downing v. Al Tameer Establishment* [2002] EWCA Civ 721, [2002] 2 All ER (Comm) 545.

866 *Cf The Komninos S* [1991] 1 Lloyd's Rep 370, 374, where the reasoning is wholly sound, but the delicacy of putting it into print is undeniable.

867 If the law which governs the contract would allow the contract to be rectified, no doubt that would be permitted to resolve the issue.

868 If, as is submitted, the answer to the question of how this clause operates, is governed wholly by Art. 25 of the Regulation, there is no more to be said. If the clause gives jurisdiction to the courts of the United Kingdom, a defendant who is domiciled in another Member State, or in no Member State, is certainly liable to be sued in accordance with the clause. For completeness, however, there is a possible gloss upon this approach where the defendant is domiciled in the United Kingdom.

869 [1991] 1 Lloyd's Rep 370, where the identity of the chosen court was relevant only for the purpose of identifying the law applicable to the contract.

870 It is believed that the question is otherwise free of authority.

871 Although Switzerland is not bound by the Regulation, it is party to the Lugano II Convention, the corresponding provisions of which are, for practical purposes, identical. Original civil jurisdiction in Switzerland is believed still to be a cantonal matter. Accordingly 'the Swiss courts' is believed to pose the same problems as 'the British courts' or 'the courts of the United Kingdom'.

872 The more so if the identification of the chosen court is thought to indicate the applicable law. And this assumption would create special difficulty in the Supreme Court of the United Kingdom.

2.143 Content of the jurisdiction agreement: the courts of a non-Member State

Article 25 does not apply to an agreement for the courts of a non-Member State.[873] The Member States cannot legislate for the jurisdiction of courts in non-Member States, and have therefore left the issue untouched. The Schlosser Report[874] observed that agreements for the jurisdiction of a non-Member State will be enforced, or otherwise, according to the national procedural law of the court which has been seised with the dispute.[875] This makes perfect sense. If the claimant, party to such an agreement, were to invoke the jurisdiction of the courts of the defendant's domicile, Professor Schlosser supposed that the court would apply its own rules of private international law to decide whether to adjudicate or to dismiss the proceedings by reference to the clause. The European Court agreed. In *Coreck Maritime GmbH v. Handelsveem BV*[876] it observed that an agreement for the courts of a non-Member[877] State fell to be assessed by the conflicts rules of the court seised. It follows – for what otherwise would be the point of assessing its validity by any law? – that the court seised would give such effect to the agreement for the courts of a non-Member State as is allowed by its own rules of private international law. As a result, an English court will be entitled, but will not be bound, to give effect to a choice of court agreement for the courts of a non-Member State, by staying its proceedings, even if it might otherwise have jurisdiction from (say) Article 4 of the Regulation.

The principle of the matter is plain, and the observation of the Court is clear and uncomplicated. Yet others have managed to persuade themselves that it is actually more complicated than that, and that an agreement for the jurisdiction of the courts if a non-Member State is void of legal effect before a court which would otherwise have jurisdiction under the Regulation. It is nonsense, of course, but it will be necessary to say more about it as part of a broader analysis of the impact of connections with a non-Member State.[878]

2.144 Content of the jurisdiction agreement: the disputes falling within its scope

The examination of jurisdiction agreements has dealt with several issues, but has touched only incidentally on that of material scope. A very simple example may be taken. Suppose that an agreement on jurisdiction provides that 'this contract is governed by English law, and the English courts shall have exclusive jurisdiction over disputes arising from it', and that proceedings are brought which allege that a wrong was committed prior to the making

---

873 This passage was referred to with approval in *Winnetka Trading Corp v. Julius Baer International Ltd* [2008] EWHC 3146 (Ch), [24]. A choice for the courts of Iceland, Norway, or Switzerland will be validated and given effect by the Lugano Convention; a choice for a court in a territory to which the Brussels Convention still applies will be validated by that Convention.

874 [1979] OJ C59/71, [176].

875 Schlosser does not say whether such a clause would be required to comply with the formal requirements of Art. 25 before it could be given effect. The answer will depend on whether there is a remission of the question to national law, or the strict application, by reflexive effect, of Art. 25: see further below, para. 2.307. But to the extent that the effect of it is to prevent any Member State court from exercising jurisdiction, it may follow that the formal safeguards contained in Art. 25 would be held to apply here as well. See also *Ultisol Transport Contractors Ltd v. Bouygues Offshore SA* [1996] 2 Lloyd's Rep 140.

876 C-387/98, [2000] ECR I-9337.

877 It said 'non-contracting', for the case was governed by the Brussels Convention, not the Regulation.

878 See below, para. 2.307. For *lis pendens* in a non-Member State designated by agreement, see below, para 2.289 *et seq.*

of the contract, and that relief is sought in respect of it. This raises a question of scope – breadth or width – of the agreement; and requires an answer to the question of which rules determine that breadth or width.

Article 25 describes the issue, but the introduction of the Article with 'If the parties... have agreed that...' means that whether they have must be decided before the remainder of the Article can be applied to confirm or to remove the jurisdiction of the court in which the proceedings are to be brought. As said above, in *Powell Duffryn plc v. Petereit*[879] the Court simply said that the task of interpreting the agreement, to ascertain whether the proceedings in question fell within it, was a matter for the court seised. As the Court said no more than this, and did not explain whether this should be done by reference to the court's own rules of law, including private international law, the explanation for its silence is not clear. It may be that it saw no need to state the obvious; it may be that it considered no question of law to be involved, as a court would simply need to read Article 25, the words of the jurisdiction agreement, and see the answer. It is quite possible that the Court has never had to confront the issue directly; has never been made to appreciate that the interpretation of an agreement which parties have made does on occasion require recourse to rules of law.

Until the European Court gives clearer guidance, it appears that the English courts will and should construe the language of a jurisdiction agreement by reference to the substantive law which they consider to govern it. If the agreement is made as a term of a contract, it will be rare for the law governing the contract not also to be the law governing the interpretation of the jurisdiction agreement. If the agreement is not made as the term of a contract, but is freestanding, it will presumably be necessary for the court to ascertain the law by reference to which it was made, or if not, the law with which it has its closest and most real connection.[880]

2.145 Challenges to the formal sufficiency of the jurisdiction agreement and the (non-) role of national law

It is well established that a court, in dealing with a jurisdiction agreement, is not permitted to hold it unenforceable by reason of its failure to satisfy a requirement of a formal kind otherwise imposed by national law. The Court ruled in *Elefanten Schuh GmbH v. Jacqmain*[881] that a Belgian court was not entitled to hold an agreement invalid on the ground, well founded as a matter of Belgian law, that it was not written in the Dutch language.[882] The Court considered that what is now Article 25 of the Regulation established conditions relating to form which were necessary and sufficient to establish the validity of the agreement.

---

879 C-214/89, [1992] ECR I-1745.

880 In other words, by applying the choice of law rules applicable to contractual obligations, wills, etc., of the common law rules of private international law. The Rome I Regulation does not apply to jurisdiction agreements, so the answer to this particular question must be left to be answered by common law rules.

881 150/80, [1981] ECR 1671. See also *Denby v. Hellenic Mediterranean Lines Co Ltd* [1994] 1 Lloyd's Rep 320.

882 To this extent, the decision opposes the contention that an agreement on jurisdiction which is written in unintelligible writing should not be one to which a person may be held. The explanation may be that in *Elefanten Schuh* there was not the slightest doubt that the agreement on jurisdiction was perfectly well understood, and that the reliance on a rule of Belgian law was simply opportunistic.

The decision in *Sanicentral GmbH v. Collin*[883] is consistent with this. A provision of French employment law which would have invalidated an agreement on jurisdiction which purported to oust the jurisdiction of the French courts in employment cases was held to be inapplicable to a case where an agreement on jurisdiction, otherwise compliant with the requirements of what is now Article 25, selected the courts of Germany. The issue was seen by the Court as being one on which the formality rules of what was the Brussels Convention were exhaustive, and overrode those of national law,[884] even where the rule of national law in question was not a rule ostensibly concerned with the formal validity of agreements. There is no reason to suppose that the Brussels I Regulation will be treated any differently. Even so, though a court may not apply its own national law rules about the language, clarity of type, and so on, to the issue of validity of jurisdiction agreements, it may still be open to it to decide that the clause written in a language which it is plain one party could not read or understand is, one way or another, ineffective. But in the light of these authorities it may have to rest this conclusion on a refined interpretation of 'in writing', or on the principle that it may exhibit bad faith for the party responsible for the clause to take the point.[885] For all other purposes, satisfaction of the formal requirements set out in Article 25 is necessary and sufficient to establish the formal validity of the agreement.

2.146 Challenges to the substantive validity of the jurisdiction agreement: national law

Different considerations may arise where the clause is impugned upon grounds which are more obviously substantive, though it must be said at the outset that in *Sanicentral GmbH v. Collin*[886] the European Court drew no obvious distinction between formal and substantive objections to legal validity. It may therefore be argued that where these objections are derived from rules of national law they are excluded by Article 25 itself; but it may also be said that the law has moved on since the decision in that case.

Yet the distinction drawn between formal and substantial validity or invalidity is not so easily erased. For example, if one party alleges that the agreement on jurisdiction was procured by misrepresentation or duress, or that persons under the age of 18 have no capacity to bind themselves to an agreement on jurisdiction, it is far from obvious that the court should regard the contention as inadmissible, or look only at the presence of writing.

One may start by eliminating one argument which has no foundation. If it is alleged by one of the parties that the substantive contract in which the agreement was allegedly contained is itself invalid or void, this allegation, even if apparently well-founded, does not by itself invalidate the agreement on jurisdiction.[887] The point was made by the Court

---

883 25/79, [1979] ECR 3423.

884 It is thought that, although this wording of the explanation is at variance with later statements (such as in C-365/88 *Hagen v. Zeehaghe* [1990] ECR I-1845) to the effect that the Brussels Convention (now, Brussels I Regulation) does not affect procedure, the reasoning is still correct. It would also follow that such a clause could not be denied effect in England on the ground that it was rendered ineffective by virtue of Employment Rights Act 1996, s. 203; similarly, Consumer Credit Act 1974, s. 141, Carriage of Goods by Sea Act 1971, Sch. 1, art. III.8.

885 See above, para. 2.131.

886 25/79, [1979] ECR 3423.

887 See the substantial analysis of the Advocate General in C-288/92 *Custom Made Commercial Ltd v. Stawa Metallbau GmbH* [1994] ECR I-2913.

in *Benincasa v. Dentalkit Srl*,[888] accords with common sense (part of the reason to have an agreement on jurisdiction is to know in advance which court will have the task of deciding whether the contract was valid or invalid as a source of legal obligations), and it is now underpinned by Article 25(5). No more needs to be said about it.

But to say that arguments which challenge the validity of the substantive contract do not *ipso facto* challenge the agreement on jurisdiction is not to say that the jurisdiction agreement must always be taken to be valid if it appears in a form which complies with Article 25(1). It cannot be the law that a meritorious plea, that the agreement was procured by fraud or duress, or that the writing of consent to it is in fact a forgery, or that the person who assented to the jurisdiction had no authority to bind or commit another (company, principal, partner) to the jurisdiction, is inadmissible. Unless the issue is considered as one which can be dealt with without reference to rules of law,[889] which must be doubtful, it must be referred to a law or legal system for its assessment. As to that, there are two possibilities.[890]

The first would be to make reference to the law which the court seised considers as governing the agreement, as though it were a contract. This would mean the *lex contractus* if the agreement was made as part of a contract; its own, separate, governing law if it was not. After all, Article 25(1) says that if the parties 'have agreed'; and if one of them pleads that he did not agree, or that the law allows him to be treated as though he had not agreed, then the provisions of a law are needed to provide the apparatus for testing the contention that there was no agreement and nothing for Article 25(1) to apply to. The case for the *lex contractus* is, therefore, plausible. If that law were English law, it would be likely that an agreement obtained by fraud, or a voidable agreement, will be seen as an agreement for the purpose of Article 25(1), but an 'agreement' derived from a forgery, or a 'void agreement' will not.[891] The trouble with this is, though, that it may allow a party to lead the court into the maze of choice of law, so making a jurisdictional decision vastly more complex and costly than it needs to be.

The second possibility is that the issue, though not properly dealt with in Regulation 44/2001, has now been addressed in Regulation 1215/2012, and is referred to the law, including the rules of private international law, of the court whose jurisdiction has been agreed to.[892] It is undeniable that this offers a solution, in that it points to a system whose rules will be available for use to determine whether arguments of the kind considered at this point undermine the agreement which will otherwise be given effect. The strength of this solution is that it is not dependent on the view, and does not appear to assume, that an agreement on jurisdiction is a contractual creature, a contractual act. If it is accepted, as the scheme of the Regulation may appear to accept, that an agreement on jurisdiction is a formal unilateral acceptance of the jurisdiction of a court, or a formal unilateral waiver of the jurisdiction of a court, given in either case to the other party, it would be slightly jarring for it to be referred to a contractual governing law, or to a law identified as though it were

---

888 C-269/95, [1997] ECR I-3767.

889 By arguing, for example, that 'have agreed' has an autonomous or uniform meaning which is not assessed by reference to any rules of national law.

890 The third option, that it is not referred to any national law, is discussed in relation to Regulation 44/2001, below.

891 The argument is derived from *Fiona Trust & Holding Corp v. Privalov* [2007] UKHL 40, [2007] Bus LR 1719.

892 Article 25(1), as amplified by Recital (20) to the Regulation.

a contractual governing law. By contrast, a link to, and reference to the law of, the jurisdiction selected means that there will be reference to a law the identity of which is predictable, at least outside cases of alleged forgery.

It may be that this aspect of Article 25(1) provides a rule of reference which is open to criticism,[893] but it is justifiable on the basis that it gives a clear indication that so far as the Regulation is concerned, agreements to jurisdiction are *not* contracts. They are formal prorogations of the jurisdiction of a court; and the law with the greatest claim to determine whether that prorogation may be impugned on substantive grounds and shown to be a nullity, is the law of that jurisdiction. As to whether it should have been the law of the jurisdiction prorogated or the law of the jurisdiction derogated from, the answer is that the latter would be a much less sensible rule, as a jurisdiction agreement may derogate from the jurisdiction of several courts. True, an agreement which prorogates the jurisdiction of more than one Member State will be a little more problematic. But it will be relatively rare; and when it happens, the sensible reference will be to the court in which the proceedings are proposed to be brought. It is therefore considered that arguments which are based on the substance or substantive validity of the agreement, are to be referred to the law of the designated Member State, including its rules of private international law if it is shown that this is how the designated court would answer the question.

In the light of this, it is possible to deal rather briefly with the difficulties which face a court in having to assess arguments which challenge the legal basis for the agreement in cases which fall under Regulation 44/2001 rather than Regulation 1215/2012. Though there is a case to be made for alternatives, and despite the reservations expressed above, it is or was most likely that an autonomous or uniform conception of what comprises an effective 'agreement' will be held to apply in the context of Article 23(1) of Regulation 44/2001. Article 23 of that Regulation does *not* require that the parties have made a contract for the courts of a Member State to have jurisdiction, only that they *have agreed*. An agreement in contractual form is one form of agreement, but an agreement certainly does not need to be embedded in a contract. So, for example, where parties have exchanged drafts of a substantive contract, every version of which contained an unopposed provision that the English courts should have jurisdiction, there should be no particular difficulty in holding that the parties agreed on the jurisdiction of the English courts, even though there is dispute as to whether the terms of the substantive agreement were ever settled.[894]

The elements of a uniform definition of 'agreement' would, no doubt, include a requirement of consent, and will exclude duress and fraud; but the proper analysis of arguments as to the effect of the various kinds of mistake, or lack of personal capacity,[895] or misrepresentation (or non-disclosure) falling short of fraud, or illegality or the lack of consideration, for example, would be harder to forecast.[896] The laws of Member States may all agree that,

---

893 It does half-assume that the agreement on jurisdiction is effective, for it identifies the law to which the question will be referred from the agreement itself; it is liable to be complicated if a party invites or requires a court to apply the private international law rules of the Member State whose courts have been designated, in order to locate the rules of domestic law by which the validity of the designation will be tested.

894 For excellent illustration, see *Maple Leaf Macro Volatility Master Fund v. Rouvroy* [2009] EWHC 257 (Comm), [2009] 1 Lloyd's Rep 475, esp. [200].

895 It may be contended that Art. 1(2)(a) serves to exclude this question from the ambit of the Regulation, and that a national court may apply its own law to the issue of the contractual age of capacity.

896 On the other hand, the number of cases in which an English court has applied its doctrine of severability and yet held the agreement on jurisdiction or arbitration to be invalid is extremely small; and after *Fiona Trust &*

for example, the victim of duress should not be bound to an alleged agreement on jurisdiction, but not be as one on the precise edges of these concepts. As ever with autonomous definitions, devils lurk in the detail; and the prospect that the wording added into Article 25(1) may avoid this difficulty, by pointing to the law which should deal with objections on grounds of substance, makes the imperfection of that rule a cost worth bearing.

2.147 Agreements on jurisdiction in trust instruments

Article 25(3) of the Brussels I Regulation provides that, where a trust instrument confers jurisdiction upon the courts of a Member State, that court has exclusive jurisdiction in actions brought against a settlor, trustee or beneficiary within the (internal) scope of the trust relationship. No requirement as to form (though in a trust instrument this will not be a major concern) is imposed by this provision. Such agreements are not permitted,[897] however, to prevail over exclusive jurisdiction where this is conferred by Article 24, nor over Articles 15, 19 and 23.

Where the trust deed stipulates a choice of court for the courts of a non–Member State, there is authority[898] that this is irrelevant to a claim that the trust be varied in matrimonial proceedings: the financial matrimonial jurisdiction of the court is not ousted by an agreement on choice of court. In principle the same will be true when the trust instrument contains a provision giving jurisdiction to the courts of a Member State, as matrimonial matters fall outside the domain of the Brussels I Regulation and are not, therefore, prejudiced by its provisions.

2.148 Jurisdiction by agreement derived from other contractual terms

A contractual device, said to be more frequently used in civilian systems than it is seen in English cases, is to stipulate in the contract for a place of performance, and then to rely on what is now Article 7(1) of Regulation 1215/2012 to establish special jurisdiction in the courts of that place. It is clear that such a sensible provision should be respected, for it allows the parties to work out where they stand in terms of jurisdiction; and in *MSG v. Les Gravières Rhénanes Sarl*,[899] the Court duly held that such a term did not need to satisfy the particular formalities specified for agreements on the jurisdiction of a court.[900] But such a freedom from the constraints of formality may be used abusively if the contract stipulates for a place of performance which is manifestly unrealistic, or 'abstract',[901] and which is stated only for the purpose of creating jurisdiction in the courts of that place. If the term is open to criticism in those terms, it will be regarded, notwithstanding its form, as in

---

Holding Corp v. Privalov [2007] UKHL 40, [2007] Bus LR 1719 will be smaller still: see, for confirmation in (or extension to) the context of what is now Art. 25, *Deutsche Bank AG v. Asia Pacific Broadband Wireless Communications Inc* [2008] EWCA Civ 1091, [2008] 2 Lloyd's Rep 619. There is therefore a slight risk of appearing to make much ado about next to nothing, though the European Court has not yet approved the approach of the Court of Appeal in *Deutsche Bank AG v. Asia Pacific Broadband Wireless Communications Inc* and may, if this is seen as an exception to the general domiciliary rule of what is now Art. 4, pause before doing so.

897 Article 25(4).
898 *C v. C (Ancillary Relief: Nuptial Settlement)* [2004] EWCA Civ 1030, [2005] Fam 250.
899 C-106/95, [1997] ECR I-911.
900 56/79 *Zelger v. Salinitri* [1980] ECR 89.
901 Such as where a place for delivery is mentioned, but delivery there is impossible (for example, because it is not on the river and the contract provides for carriage by river only).

substance an agreement on jurisdiction, and required to comply with the formal and other requirements of Article 25.[902]

One might object that the decision in *MSG* involved a slight over-reaction, for the identification of the term as a sham, or as 'abstract' or 'fictitious', may not be straightforward; and in any case, as jurisdiction under what is now Article 7(1) is not in any sense exclusive, it seems unwarranted to force a clause of this type into the straitjacket of Article 25, and then to regard it as creating[903] an exclusive[904] jurisdiction because the parties have not agreed otherwise.

When the United Kingdom acceded to the Brussels Convention, provision was made that the courts of the United Kingdom might exercise jurisdiction over a contractual claim when that contract was made before 1 January 1987 and contained an express written term that English law was to govern.[905] This provision must have reached the end of its useful life; it does not appear in the Regulation.

2.149 Conclusion

If the rules on agreements on jurisdiction give the English courts jurisdiction, service out (if needed) is available as of right.[906] If they exclude the jurisdiction of the English courts, that is the end of the matter. But if there is no agreement upon jurisdiction to which Article 25 applies, the next question has to be addressed.

(9) GENERAL JURISDICTION OVER DEFENDANTS DOMICILED IN THE UNITED KINGDOM

2.150 General

Article 4 of Regulation 1215/2012 provides that:

> *(1) Subject to this Regulation, persons domiciled in a Member State shall, whatever their nationality, be sued in the courts of that Member State. (2) Persons who are not nationals of the Member State in which they are domiciled shall be governed by the rules of jurisdiction applicable to nationals of that Member State.*

Article 2 of Regulation 44/2001 was identical.

2.151 Scope and effect of general jurisdiction

It is often said that the fundamental jurisdictional rule of the Brussels I Regulation is that those with a domicile in a Member State may expect to be sued and to defend claims against them in their home courts. The jurisdiction of the courts of the defendant's domicile is sometimes referred to as 'general jurisdiction', that is, jurisdiction which is not specific to

---

902 C-106/95 *MSG v. Les Gravières Rhénanes Sarl* [1997] ECR I-911. See *7E Communications Ltd v. Vertex Antennentechnik GmbH* [2007] EWCA Civ 140, [2008] Bus LR 472, which would have applied the reasoning in *MSG* had it been necessary to decide the point.
903 Or if it fails to comply with the formal requirements, to fail to create.
904 Unless on a true construction it may be held to be non-exclusive, which seems plausible.
905 Article 35 of the Treaty of Accession; Sch. 3 to the 1982 Act.
906 CPR r. 6.33.

particular subject matter of relationships, or special to certain kinds of claim. The provisions of the Brussels I Regulation examined so far have been exceptional in that they operate regardless of domicile,[907] or constitute variations upon, but also prevail over, the ordinary domiciliary principle.[908] But if none of the prior rules is applicable, the courts of the United Kingdom will have general jurisdiction if the defendant has a domicile in the United Kingdom.[909]

As to the person being sued, it is not usually difficult to identify who is the defendant. But in a number of cases it is different. For example, in the case of an Admiralty action *in rem*, the traditional analysis is that the action is brought against the vessel upon which the claim form was served, event though the action may later continue as one *in rem* and *in personam* if a person with an interest in the action steps forward to enter an appearance and so become a defendant. However, for the purposes of what is now Article 4 of the Regulation, the English courts have held that the person being sued, whose domicile was decisive, was the person with an interest in the vessel, and not the vessel itself.[910] If this is what is required – that the 'reality' of the matter must be investigated and the 'real' defendant identified – there may sometimes be imperfect alignment between the claim and the jurisdictional rule which applies in relation to it. After all, in proceedings brought by a minority shareholder under Part 30 of the Companies Act 2006, the named defendant is the company,[911] though in some sense the target of the complaint is the majority shareholder. One imagines that the defendant is the company, not the majority shareholder; but the position is not entirely clear.

As to what it means to be sued, it may be that the expression excludes proceedings brought to seek some forms of relief, and in which contexts the defendant or respondent is not being sued. It has been suggested that in order to be sued, and therefore to have the advantage of the general jurisdictional rule in Article 4, it is necessary that the defendant is summoned to answer a claim by an opponent who advances a substantive cause of action; it is not sufficient that the defendant is summoned only to respond to an application for orders ancillary to substantive proceedings pending before a particular court.[912] If that were to be accepted, an application against a person who was not party to substantive proceedings, for an order that he pay all or some of the costs ordered to be paid to the winner by a losing party, would not involve his being sued. This would be so even though, as one must suppose, such an order gives rise to a judgment enforceable under Chapter III of the Regulation. It would also follow that on an application for post-judgment relief in the form of an application that a person be required to give evidence about the whereabouts of assets of a judgment debtor, the person summoned being an officer of that judgment debtor, is not being sued, and has no right to invoke the Brussels I Regulation by way of asserting a jurisdictional protection from the summons of the court.[913] There are liable to be problems with this analysis if taken

---

907 Articles 24 and 25 (and in some instances 18(1) and 21(2)); and possibly also Art. 26.

908 Sections 3, 4, 5 and 7 of Chapter II.

909 Of course, the Regulation refers only to the defendant being domiciled in the United Kingdom. It is a matter of internal national law to determine whether he is domiciled in England, or in another part.

910 *The Deichland* [1990] 1 QB 361; *The Indian Grace (No 2)* [1998] AC 878, 909–910.

911 See for illustration, *Re Harrods (Buenos Aires) Ltd* [1992] Ch 72: on the basis of the law as it then stood, the company was domiciled in England by virtue of being incorporated under English law; the majority shareholder was Swiss.

912 *The Ikarian Reefer (No 2)* [2000] 1 WLR 603, 615–616.

913 This was the analysis in *Masri v. Consolidated Contractors International Co Sal (No 4)* [2008] EWCA Civ 876, [2009] 2 WLR 699 (reversed without reference to this point: [2009] UKHL 3, [2010] 1 AC 90. Of course, the person against whom the order is sought may have no jurisdictional defence if either the application is seen as one

too far. A more realistic answer would accept that a person who is summoned to court as respondent to an application, and who stands at risk of being ordered by the court to pay money or perform an act unless he can persuade the court not to so order, is being sued.[914]

Article 4 contains the rule. The reference to nationality underlines the irrelevance of this fact or factor in the jurisdictional[915] scheme of the Brussels I Regulation. The statement that such persons *shall* be sued in these courts cannot, of course, be read as elevating Article 4 to the status of a mandatory provision. It means that they are liable to be sued in these courts if no provision of the Regulation says otherwise, but it also means that this is the central jurisdictional tenet of the Regulation.

If, therefore, the defendant is[916] domiciled in the United Kingdom according to the law of the United Kingdom, he may be sued in the United Kingdom. In order to determine where, more precisely, within the United Kingdom he may be sued, recourse must be had to the internal scheme of rules contained in section 16 of, and Schedule 4 to, the 1982 Act.[917] The basic principle of the domestic law of the United Kingdom in this area is that the defendant is entitled to be sued in the part of the United Kingdom in which he is domiciled. These rules are set out in detail in section 16 of, and Schedule 4 to, the 1982 Act. They will apply when the Brussels I Regulation confers international jurisdiction on the courts of the United Kingdom, but also when the case is wholly internal to the United Kingdom and the Regulation has no part to play in answering the jurisdictional questions which arise.

2.152 The determination of a defendant's domicile

Article 62 of Regulation 1215/2012 provides, in effect, that the question whether an individual (as distinct from a company, or other legal person, or association of legal persons) has a domicile in the United Kingdom is determined by the law of the United Kingdom. The question whether he has a domicile in France is determined by French law, and so on. Article 62 contains no provision to deal with whether a person is domiciled in a non-Member State, because that fact does not affect[918] the taking of jurisdiction under the Regulation: domicile within a Member State or Member States, and only that, is of jurisdictional significance.

---

for relief from a court which has substantive jurisdiction over the claim, or if it is seen as part of the enforcement of a judgment in England. However, the Civil Procedure Rules do not extend to allow an order to be applied for against a person who is physically out of the jurisdiction: *Masri v. Consolidated Contractors International Co Sal (No 4)* [2009] UKHL 43, [2010] 1 AC 90. The impact of European law was, in that case, irrelevant to the eventual decision of the House of Lords to set aside the order made by the Court of Appeal and considered wrongly by it to be capable of being served out of the jurisdiction.

914 In *The Ikarian Reefer (No 2)* it may have been preferable to see the case as one in which the respondent was being sued, but the English court had exclusive jurisdiction under what is now Art. 24(5).

915 And judgment recognition scheme, as is shown in Chapter 7.

916 The date for the determination of domicile is that of the institution of proceedings, which in England means by the issue of a claim form: *Canada Trust Co v. Stolzenberg (No 2)* [2002] 1 AC 1. For a slightly different approach, see the decision of the German Supreme Court in *Re Jurisdiction Based on Domicile of Defendant* (Case XI ZR 48/10), [2012] ILPr 12.

917 Schedule 4 to the 1982 Act was amended by Civil Jurisdiction and Judgments Order 2001, SI 2001/3929, Sch. 2, para. 4.

918 Except under Art. 72 of the Regulation, dealing with treaties for the non-recognition of certain judgments against persons domiciled in a specific non-Member State, where the jurisdiction asserted by the court was founded upon one of the rules of (arguably exorbitant) national jurisdiction to which Art. 5 of Regulation 1215/2012 refers: see para. 7.10, below.

It is a further consequence of Article 62 that a person may, contrary to the position which obtains under the common law rules of private international law, have a domicile in more Member States than one. Within the context of the Regulation, domicile is a factual connection of sufficient strength to justify the exercise of general jurisdiction by the courts of that Member State; and an individual may have such a connection with more than one Member State at the same time. The rules of the common law of domicile are wholly irrelevant to the determination of domicile for the purposes of the Regulation.[919]

For the purposes of the Brussels and Lugano Conventions, the 1982 Act set out the definition of domicile in the United Kingdom and under English law, with separate provision being made for individuals,[920] corporations and associations,[921] the deemed domicile in insurance and consumer cases,[922] trusts[923] and the Crown.[924]

But for cases to which the Brussels I Regulation (original and recast) apply, the corresponding definitions were provided by Civil Jurisdiction and Judgments Order 2001,[925] Schedule 1. Though these followed the provisions of sections 41 to 46 of the 1982 Act, they differ in some points of detail. In particular, section 42 of the 1982 Act, which provided for the determination of the domicile of a corporation, is largely superseded, as what is now Article 63 of Regulation 1215/2012 established a uniform definition of the domicile of corporations, legal persons and associations of persons. And the domicile of the Crown, dealt with by section 46 of the 1982 Act, has no counterpart in the Regulation, as this will also fall within the scope of Article 63 of the recast Regulation.

2.153 Domicile in the United Kingdom: individuals

Paragraph 9 of Schedule 1 to the 2001 Order[926] sets out the rules which determine whether an individual has a domicile in the United Kingdom. Paragraph 9(2) defines domicile in the United Kingdom; paragraph 9(3) defines domicile in a part of the United Kingdom in terms which are practically identical to it. For an individual to be regarded as being domiciled in the United Kingdom, two conditions must be satisfied: (a) he must reside there; and (b) the nature and circumstances of his residence must indicate he has a substantial connection with the United Kingdom.[927] For those individuals who satisfy condition (a), and who have been so resident for the last three months or more, condition (b) is deemed to be satisfied unless the contrary is proved.[928]

For an individual who is domiciled in the United Kingdom to be regarded as being domiciled in England (or in some other part of the United Kingdom), an identical test,

---

919 *Ministry of Defence and Support of the Armed Forces of Iran v. FAZ Aviation Ltd* [2007] EWHC 1042 (Comm), [2007] ILPr 538, [32].

920 Section 41 of the 1982 Act, which at s. 41(7) deals also with whether a person has a domicile in a non-Member State.

921 See below, for detail of where a corporation or association is domiciled.

922 Section 44.

923 Section 45.

924 Section 46.

925 SI 2000/3929. This instrument was amended by SI 2014/2947, but at this point the amendments are minor and technical only.

926 As immaterially (*sic*) amended by SI 2014/2947, Sch. 2, para. 11.

927 Paragraph 9(2). See *Bank of Dubai Ltd v. Fouad Haji Abbas* [1997] ILPr 308 (residence requires a settled place of abode); *Petrotrade Inc v. Smith* [1998] 2 All ER 346 (residence by force of bail conditions does not qualify).

928 Paragraph 9(6).

mutatis mutandis, is applied. In respect of those who are resident in a part of the United Kingdom, but whose residence, even with the benefit of the presumption applicable to residence of three months or more, fails to satisfy condition (b), their domicile is simply the part of the United Kingdom in which they reside.

At first sight, it may be thought that three months' residence in the United Kingdom is capable of establishing (and may well be sufficient to establish) the domicile of an individual in the United Kingdom, or, as the case may be, in England. This is indeed true. But in a number of cases involving very rich individuals,[929] mainly of Russian nationality or extraction, the courts have had to take a more detailed view of the legislation. Though the following are no more than indications, none of which is decisive, of whether the connection with the United Kingdom is sufficient to indicate that the defendant has a *substantial* connection with the United Kingdom, the court may be asked to look at, among other things: whether the individual has indefinite leave to remain or requires a visa and immigration clearance to enter the United Kingdom; whether HMRC[930] regards him as resident for tax purposes; the fraction of the year for which the individual is in the United Kingdom; whether he has places of residence elsewhere; the balance-sheet value of his United Kingdom assets in relation to the whole of his assets worldwide; whether it may actually be realistic to regard him as having such widely-scattered business interests that it may be said that he is not really resident anywhere. It is apparent that the court before which the question first arises will, in practice, have power to determine the issue with which an appellate court will be slow to find fault.

In the final analysis, the true meaning of 'substantial' is gathered from its consequences. A connection to the United Kingdom is 'substantial' if it suffices to make it appropriate that the courts of the United Kingdom exercise general jurisdiction, without the possibility of being able to stay proceedings in favour of a *forum conveniens* elsewhere, in any and all civil and commercial proceedings brought against the defendant.[931] Bearing in mind the formidable consequences of a finding that an individual has a domicile in the United Kingdom, the word 'substantial' is not to be interpreted as though it means 'not a lot more than minimal'.

2.154 Domicile of corporations and associations: scheme and purpose

By contrast with the rule laid down by what is now Article 62 in respect of individuals, the domicile of companies, other legal persons or association of legal persons is determined differently. Article 63 of Regulation 1215/2012 provides that a company, or other legal person, or association of natural or legal persons, is domiciled at the place[932] where it has its statutory seat, or its central administration or its principal place of business. Though Article

---

929 *High Tech International AG v. Deripaska* [2006] EWHC 3276 (Comm), [2007] EMLR 15; *Cherney v. Deripaska* [2007] EWHC 965 (Comm), [2007] 2 All ER (Comm) 785; *OJSC Oil Co Yugraneft v. Abramovich* [2008] EWHC 2613 (Comm).

930 Her Majesty's Revenue and Customs, formerly the Inland Revenue Commissioners.

931 *Ministry of Defence and Support of the Armed Forces of Iran v. FAZ Aviation Ltd* [2007] EWHC 1042 (Comm), [2007] ILPr 538; *OJSC Oil Co Yugraneft v. Abramovich* [2008] EWHC 2613 (Comm) (in this latter case, ownership of several large houses and the Chelsea Football Club did not amount to a sufficient connection to the jurisdiction to establish domicile. The conclusion is pleasingly dismissive of the national significance of the Chelsea Football Club, though whether it was influenced by the foreign ownership and largely foreign playing staff of the club was not made clear).

932 The reference is to a place, not to a Member State. The place, or one of the places, must be in a Member State, though, for the Regulation is not concerned to locate a domicile in a non-Member State.

63(1) talks of the place in singular terms, it follows from the definition given that a company may have a domicile in more than one Member State.[933]

This partial harmonisation of the definition of a company's domicile, first undertaken in Regulation 44/2001, departs from the corresponding provision of the Brussels Convention which had provided that the court seised of a dispute would apply its own rules of private international law, and not common and uniform rules, to determine the seat, and hence the domicile, of a company. The adoption of a common and uniform definition of corporate domicile is intended 'to make the common rules more transparent and avoid conflicts of jurisdiction'. But as will be seen below, this uniform definition of corporate domicile is inapplicable to Article 24(2) of Regulation 1215/2012, for the purpose of which a court is to apply its own private international law to ascertain the Member State in which the company or association has its 'seat'.

The expression 'corporation or association' requires a little elaboration. It extends to all juristic persons who are sought to be sued, other than individuals. One must interpret 'corporation' as covering all incorporated bodies, incorporated under English or foreign law, which, by virtue of the creative act of incorporation, enjoy legal personality separate from that of the individual members or corporators. An 'association' means an unincorporated body of persons.[934] In other words, Article 63 of the Regulation specifies the rules which determine where such bodies are domiciled for the purpose of actual or intended proceedings against them.

The 1982 Act, and the Brussels I Regulation, and the 2001 Order, determine jurisdiction: where defendants are liable, or are not liable, to be sued. The question of whether they can in law actually be sued, or be sued successfully, in the place where they are domiciled, and to whose courts they are amenable,[935] is a procedural and then substantive matter for the internal law of the country concerned. If, therefore, proceedings are instituted in England against an unincorporated association, which is domiciled in England according to this rule, as a body, the proceedings may not be validly constituted as a matter of English law,[936] and not permitted to proceed. This is not remarkable. The Regulation allocates jurisdiction to the various Member States without regard to the law or procedure which will be applied when the case is heard. If it allocates jurisdiction to a court in which the claimant is destined, by reason of the procedural or substantive law which that court will apply, to lose if he sues, nothing of jurisdictional significance turns upon that fact. To say that the Regulation confers jurisdiction upon the English court does not lead to the conclusion that there will be a cause of action available against that defendant in that court, any more than it leads to the conclusion that an action will succeed on the merits.

2.155 Domicile of companies or associations for general jurisdictional purposes

According to Article 63(1) of the Regulation, a company or other legal person or association of natural or legal persons is domiciled at the place or places where it has (a) its statutory

---

933 *Ministry of Defence and Support of the Armed Forces of Iran v. FAZ Aviation Ltd* [2007] EWHC 1042 (Comm), [2007] ILPr 538. This does not mean, of course, that there must be three separate countries in which the company may be considered to have a domicile.

934 Section 50 of the 1982 Act. It will include a partnership: Schlosser [1979] OJ C59/71, [162].

935 Unless an earlier provision of the Regulation has already allocated jurisdiction upon a basis superior to that of the domicile of the defendant.

936 See CPR Part 19 for the available procedure.

seat, or (b) its central administration, or (c) its principal place of business.[937] In the case of the United Kingdom and Ireland, for which the term 'statutory seat' is not a term of art, 'statutory seat' is to mean the registered office, or where there is no such office anywhere, the place of incorporation, or where there is no such place anywhere, the place under the law of which the formation took place. The first of these three possibilities will be easy enough to identify, almost always from the company's founding documents; and the third is, according to the Court of Appeal, identified by asking where the company does its principal business,[938] which – not, perhaps, completely helpfully – was said to be a question of fact more than anything else.[939]

On the particular problems raised by the second of these domiciliary possibilities, it is sensible to start with the proposition that each of these three provisions should be subject to uniform interpretation. As to whether 'central administration' is to be located by looking upward to the place of ultimate policymaking, or down to the place of day-to-day management, direction and control, the most recent judicial guidance would, in the particular light of German doctrinal writing, locate it at the place where the organs of the company in question take the decisions which are essential to the company's operations, or where entrepreneurial management takes place: these are to be seen as the same thing.[940] This approach to Article 63(1)(b) places its focus on the place at which the company takes its own decisions, even though it may be part of a corporate group as a result of which the taking of its own decisions is little more than implementation of instructions handed down from above. An earlier suggestion[941] that 'administration' had a rather lower-class, back-office, flavour to it, is not now reliable.[942]

2.156 Seat of company or association for purpose of Article 24(2)

It follows from Article 63 that a company or other legal person can be sued where it has a domicile, and it may be domiciled in more than one Member State. But this would be an unacceptable foundation for the operation of the jurisdictional rule in Article 24(2) of the Regulation which, in relation to certain company-constitutional matters, gives exclusive jurisdiction regardless of domicile to the courts of the Member State in which the company has its seat. Accordingly, Article 24(2) provides that, for this exclusive jurisdictional rule, a

---

937 If the company has ceased doing business, it is not permissible to rely on this aspect of Art. 63 by pointing to the place where it last did business: *Ministry of Defence and Support of the Armed Services for Iran v. FAZ Aviation Ltd* [2007] EWHC 1042 (Comm), [2008] 1 All ER (Comm) 372; jurisdiction may still be founded on the other limbs of Art. 60.

938 *Young v. Anglo American South Africa Ltd* [2014] EWCA Civ 1130, [2014] 2 Lloyd's Rep 606, [39].

939 This may underestimate the problems of choosing whether this is where the decisions about business are taken, or where the trading (in the case of a trading company) is actually performed, quite apart from the fact that a company may have several, and separated, aspects to its business. See also *The Rewia* [1991] 2 Lloyd's Rep 325.

940 *Young v. Anglo American South Africa Ltd* [2014] EWCA Civ 1130, [2014] 2 Lloyd's Rep 606, [40]. The approach of the second of the three options given by Art. 63 is consistent with 81/87 *R v. HM Treasury ex p Daily Mail and General Trust plc* [1988] ECR 5483, as well as being supported by German academic writing (which had been approved by German courts) to which the Court of Appeal was referred and which (evidently unfortunately) had not been placed before courts which had examined this question on earlier occasions.

941 *King v. Crown Energy Trading AG* [2003] EWHC 163 (Comm), [2003] ILPr 489.

942 The decision was doubted or disapproved in *Young v. Anglo American South Africa Ltd* [2014] EWCA Civ 1130, [2014] 2 Lloyd's Rep 606, as also was *889457 Alberta Inc v. Katanga Mining Ltd* [2008] EWHC 2679 (Comm), [2009] ILPr 14 (where the court had favoured a less sophisticated suggestion put forward in an earlier edition of this book but which is not now to be relied on).

Member State is to apply its own rules of private international law to the determination of the seat of the company or association in question. It follows, in principle at least, that there may be differences of view as to where a company has its seat for the purposes of this rule; and this is surprising. One might have been forgiven for thinking that Article 24(2) required there to be a single and uniform interpretation of the seat, and that over the issue of where a company could be sued, there was less need for a rigidly uniform view. But if clarity exists for the purposes of Article 24(2), it will have been reached despite, rather than because of, the Regulation.

It follows that for the Regulation to work properly, the law cannot properly conclude that there is Article 24(2) jurisdiction in more Member States than one. English law reflects this in Schedule 1, paragraph 10 to the 2001 Order[943] which deals with the seat of a corporation or association in the context of a case to which Article 24(2) applies. According to paragraph 10(2), a corporation has its *seat in the United Kingdom* if, and only if, either (a) it was incorporated or formed under the law of a part of the United Kingdom,[944] or (b) its central management and control is exercised in the United Kingdom. Whether a corporation, which has a seat in the United Kingdom, has its seat in one or other part of the United Kingdom is, however, determined by section 43 of the 1982 Act, as amended by Schedule 2, paragraph 16 to the 2001 Order: within the United Kingdom, a corporation has its *seat in a particular part of the United Kingdom* if, and only if, it has its seat in the United Kingdom, and either: (a) it was incorporated outside the United Kingdom, but its central control and management is exercised in that part of the Kingdom:[945] its seat is in that part; or (b) if formed under an Act which has effect across different parts of the United Kingdom,[946] it has its seat in the part of the United Kingdom in which it has its registered office, and not elsewhere; or otherwise (c) it was incorporated or formed under the law of a part of the United Kingdom: its seat is in that part.

According to paragraph 10(3), a corporation has its *seat in another Member State* if, and only if, either (a) it was incorporated or formed under the law of that State, or (b) its central management and control is exercised in that State; but not[947] if it was incorporated or formed under the law of part of the United Kingdom, nor if the courts of that other Member State would not, for the purposes of Article 24(2), regard it as having its seat there. In other words, a company incorporated in the United Kingdom has, for the purposes of Article 24(2), its seat in the United Kingdom, and not in any other State, whether a Member or a non-Member State.

2.157 Deemed domicile of non-Member State insurers, suppliers and employers

It will be recalled that for the purposes of the provisions of the Regulation which deal with jurisdiction in insurance[948] and consumer[949] and employment[950] contracts, an insurer or

---

943 SI 2001/3929. Only technical amendment is made by SI 2014/2947, Sch. 2, para. 12.

944 There being no additional requirement that it have a registered office or some other official address in the United Kingdom: *cf* s. 42(3).

945 Section 43(3).

946 Such as the Companies Acts, 1948–2006.

947 Paragraph 10(4).

948 Articles 10 to 16; paras 2.91 *et seq.*, above.

949 Articles 17 to 19; paras 2.98 *et seq.*, above.

950 Articles 20 to 23; paras 2.114 *et seq.*, above.

supplier or employer domiciled in a non-Member State may be deemed to be domiciled in a Member State[951] if the dispute arises out of the operations of a branch or agency which he has in that Member State. If a dispute arises in which an insurer,[952] not otherwise domiciled in a Member State, had established a branch or agency in the United Kingdom, out of the operations of which the dispute arose, paragraph 11 of Schedule 1 to the 2001 Order[953] provides that the insurer, supplier or employer will be deemed to be domiciled in the United Kingdom, and within the United Kingdom, in that part of the United Kingdom in which the branch, agency or other establishment, is.[954]

2.158 Domicile of trusts

A trust cannot, as a matter of English law, be sued. But what is now Article 7(6)[955] of Regulation 1215/2012 provides for certain actions to be brought in the courts of the Member State 'in which the trust is domiciled'; and Article 63(3) instructs the court seised to apply its own private international law to determine where that is.

According to Schedule 1, paragraph 12 to the 2001 Order, a trust is domiciled in the United Kingdom if, and only if, it is domiciled in a part of the United Kingdom. If the trust is, for these purposes, to be domiciled in the United Kingdom, it is necessary[956] to find that it has a domicile in one of the constituent parts of the United Kingdom. Paragraph 12 of Schedule 1 to the 2001 Order does this. According to these rules, if the system of law with which the trust has its closest and most real connection is the law of a part of the United Kingdom, the trust is domiciled in that part of the United Kingdom. Only if that condition is met is the trust domiciled in the United Kingdom.

An English court will therefore apply paragraph 12 to determine whether the trust is domiciled in England. If, when the trust was established, it was expressed to be governed by English law, then even if the property and the trustees are based or located in a country outside England, the trust will still be domiciled in England: indeed, if the settlor has chosen English law to govern the trust, it will be very difficult indeed[957] to show that the trust is more closely connected to another law.[958] An English court will never be called upon to decide whether the trust is domiciled elsewhere, because the trust gives rise to a separate head of jurisdiction only under Article 7(6) of the Regulation. Article 7(6) confers jurisdiction upon the courts of a particular Member State if the trust is domiciled in that State: it therefore operates to confer jurisdiction, but not to deprive a court of it; and it is therefore unnecessary for an English court to decide whether a trust is domiciled in another Member State.[959]

---

951 Article 11(2) in the case of insurers, Art. 17(2) in the case of professionals who deal with consumers and Art. 20(2) in the case of employers.

952 The same will apply, of course, to a supplier under a consumer contract within the provisions of Art. 15, and an employer under an individual contract of employment within the provisions of Art. 20.

953 As immaterially (*sic*) amended by SI 2014/2947, Sch. 2, para. 13.

954 It will be appreciated that the real significance of this section is to deal with the allocation of national jurisdiction between the separate parts of the United Kingdom.

955 See para. 2.218, below.

956 SI 2001/3929, Sch. 1, para. 7, as amended by SI 2014/2947, Sch. 2, para. 9.

957 The possibility that an evasive choice of law might be overcome was mooted in *Gomez v. Gomez Monche-Vives* [2008] EWCA Civ 1065, [2009] Ch 245, but the idea was not developed.

958 *Gómez v. Gómez Monche-Vives* [2008] EWCA Civ 1065, [2009] Ch 245.

959 It is a condition of jurisdiction under Art. 7 that the defendant be domiciled in another Member State, but the defendant in cases covered by Art. 7(6) will be the settlor, trustee or beneficiary, and not the trust itself.

2.159 Domicile of the Crown

Section 46(1) of the 1982 Act provided a definition of the domicile of the Crown: this stated that the Crown in right of Her Majesty's Government in the United Kingdom had its seat in every part of the United Kingdom.[960] But since the Crown is a legal person, it appears to follow that Article 63 of the Regulation[961] imposes its definition of domicile as the domicile of the Crown. It also follows that a court in another Member State may find that it has jurisdiction in an action against the Crown as it might in the case of any other defendant whose domicile is ascertained by Article 63.

Of course, if the matter is not a civil or commercial one, the Regulation will be wholly inapplicable, and the question of the domicile of the Crown will have no practical relevance to the taking of jurisdiction.

2.160 Conclusions

This part of the analysis of the Brussels I Regulation commenced by asking whether the defendant was domiciled in the United Kingdom. If the Regulation applies to the dispute in question, and none of the earlier provisions had settled the question of jurisdiction, Article 4 of Regulation 1215/2012 permits proceedings to be brought in the courts of the defendant's domicile. If according to these rules the English courts have jurisdiction, service out (if needed) is available as of right.[962] If the defendant does not have a domicile in the United Kingdom, according to English law, the next question must be asked in order to decide whether (and if so, upon what basis) the English[963] courts may still assert and exercise jurisdiction. The answer will turn upon whether the defendant has a domicile in another Member State, in which case Question 10 in this list will apply, or does not have a domicile in any Member State, in which case Question 11 will apply instead.

(10) SPECIAL JURISDICTION OVER A DEFENDANT DOMICILED IN ANOTHER MEMBER STATE

2.161 General

If, having reached this point, none of the previous rules has been shown to apply, the defendant will not be domiciled in the United Kingdom. Two alternatives remain: either he has a domicile in another Member State or Member States, or he does not have a domicile in any Member State.

In the former case, where the defendant is domiciled in another Member State but not in the United Kingdom, the courts of the United Kingdom may still have jurisdiction – called 'special jurisdiction' – by virtue of the rules set out in Section 2 of Chapter II of the Regulation, which are set out in Articles 7, 8 and 9 of Regulation 1215/2012. It is these

---

960 See *Tehrani v. Secretary of State for the Home Department* [2006] UKHL 47, [2007] 1 AC 521.

961 Discussed above, para. 2.155.

962 CRP r. 6.33.

963 In this context it is correct to say English, rather than the courts of the United Kingdom, because Arts 7 to 9 generally give jurisdiction to the courts of a place, not to the courts of a country. In other words, they specify both international and national jurisdiction.

rather complex rules which form the basis of this tenth broad question. If the English[964] court does have jurisdiction according to these rules, it may exercise it; but if under these rules the defendant is domiciled in another Member State, but it does not have jurisdiction, the enquiry has reached the end of the road, and the defendant is not liable to be sued in England. For the Regulation offers no further exception to the general jurisdiction of the courts of the domicile.

In the latter case, however, a defendant who is not domiciled in any Member State may be sued, but in accordance with the provisions of what is now Article 6 of Regulation 1215/2012: it is this hypothesis which will be examined after this tenth Question has been dealt with.[965]

2.162 Special jurisdiction under Article 7

The opening words to Article 7 of the Regulation state that

> *A person domiciled in a Member State may be sued in another Member State:*

and are followed by seven[966] matters in which this suing of a defendant away from the domicile of his home Member State may be be permitted.

It is therefore necessary to examine the grounds of special jurisdiction which may be asserted in proceedings brought against a defendant who has[967] a domicile in another Member State but not in the United Kingdom. The rules are reasonably intricate. This is because Article 7 represents an attempt to define the circumstances in which a particular court may be expected to have a close connection with the individual case, this reflecting, as the Court tends to put it, a principle of proximity.[968] Article 8 deals with jurisdiction in cases with multiple defendants, third parties and counterclaimants. Article 9 deals with the limitation of liability in shipping claims. It is unlikely that coverage of such large areas could ever be simple. Their practical importance in the scheme of the Regulation is obvious.

In Articles 7 and 8, the courts which are given special jurisdiction by the Regulation are usually those for a *place*, as distinct from the courts of a Member State in general. In other words, if the defendant is not domiciled in the United Kingdom but in France, he may be sued in the United Kingdom, under Article 7(1), in the court having jurisdiction at the *place* where the contractual obligation was required to be performed;[969] he may be sued,

---

964 In this context it is correct to say English, rather than the courts of the United Kingdom, because Arts 7 to 9 generally give jurisdiction to the courts of a place, not to the courts of a country. In other words, they specify both international and national jurisdiction.

965 Paragraphs 2.248 *et seq.*, below.

966 Regulation 44/2001, Art. 5(2) contained a rule for special jurisdiction in matters relating to maintenance. It ceased to have effect when the Maintenance Regulation, Regulation 4/2009, came into effect; and it has not been reproduced in Regulation 1215/2012. It it not disussed further in this edition.

967 Or who may be treated as though he had such a domicile, even if the true position is not known and not discoverable: C-292/10 *G v. De Visser* EU:C:2012:142, [2013] QB 168; C-327/10 *Hypoteční Banka AS v. Lindner* [2011] ECR I-11543; but *cf* C-112/13 *A v. B* EU:C:2014:2195 (defendant still entitled to say that the judgment was in default of (his) appearance, even if the court has appointed a lawyer to represent him.

968 See for example, C-19/09 *Wood Floor Solutions Andreas Domberger GmbH v. Silva Trade SA* [2010] ECR I-2121, [22], and cases there cited.

969 See Jenard [1979] OJ C59/1, 22. For illustration, see the opinion of the Advocate General in C-26/91 *Jakob Handte & Co GmbH v. Soc Traitements Mécano-Chimiques des Surfaces* [1992] ECR I-3967. As a result, it will rarely be necessary for internal United Kingdom law to identify the part of the United Kingdom in which proceedings may be brought. The concept of 'place' will extend to include the continental shelf adjacent to a Member State: C-37/00 *Weber v. Universal Ogden Services Ltd* [2002] ECR I-2013.

under what is now Article 7(2), at the place where the harmful event occurred. Where the Regulation itself gives jurisdiction to the courts for a specified place in, and not merely to the courts of, a Member State, there is neither room nor need for a rule of national law to supplement the provisions of the Regulation.[970] It also follows that in such a case there is no place for a rule of national law, such as the principle of *forum non conveniens*, to allow a court which has been given jurisdiction under Article 7 to stay proceedings in favour of the courts for another part of the United Kingdom and which, *ex hypothesi*, will have no international, and therefore no basis for national, jurisdiction at all.[971]

It is common to read in decisions of the Court that the special jurisdictional rules in what are now Articles 7, 8 and 9 are, as exceptions to the rule that defendants shall be sued where they are domiciled, to be given a narrow interpretation. It will be seen, however, that this is not consistently true: the material scope of Articles 7(1) and 7(2) taken together is wide. The Court has conceded that its interpretation of 'matters relating to a contract' is *not* a narrow one;[972] it may be more helpful to pay attention to the Court's concern that the special jurisdictional rules should not be permitted to extend beyond their proper limits in such a way as would call into question the role of general jurisdiction under what is now Article 4 of the Regulation, and to observe that it is met by other principles of interpretation which are applied within the context of each of these special jurisdictional rules.

2.163 Relationship to questions of applicable law

It is important to note that if a claim falls within Article 7, and special jurisdiction is given to, say, the English court, it means only that the court has special jurisdiction over the defendant in respect of the claim set out in the claim form. Once that has been decided, and attention turns to the task of determining the merits, and if it is not common ground that English domestic law should be applied, the court will have to identify the law which will be applicable to the substance of the claim. There is no necessary connection between the basis on which the court found that it had special jurisdiction, and the identifiation of the applicable law for resolution of the claim over which that special jurisdiction has been found to exist.

Until very recently the court's first step, in dealing with the substantive claim, would be to characterise the substantive issue or issues, so as to identify the law which is to be applied. In doing so, the court would not have been influenced by the rules of the Brussels I Regulation which had confirmed its jurisdiction. The court was free to adjudicate the merits of the dispute by applying its rules of contract, or rules of substantive law other than the law of contract if it found, according to its private international law of characterisation, that the dispute was not in substance a contractual one. It was as if the jurisdictional enquiry was completed and the page had been turned.[973]

---

970 C-386/05 *Color Drack GmbH v. Lexx International Vertriebs GmbH* [2007] ECR I-3699.

971 It may therefore be necessary to reconsider *Ivax Pharmceuticals UK Ltd v. AKZO Nobel BV* [2005] EWHC 2658 (Comm), [2006] FSR 888, and *Sunderland Marine Mutual Insurance Co Ltd v. Wiseman, The 'Seaward Quest'* [2007] EWHC 1460 (Comm), [2007] 2 Lloyd's Rep 308, in the light of the decision in *Color Drack*.

972 C-27/02 *Engler v. Janus Versand GmbH* [2005] ECR I-481, [48]. It expressed an opposite view in C-533/07 *Falco Privatstiftung v. Weller-Lindhorst* [2009] ECR I-3327, [37], but it did not seem to make anything of the point.

973 See the opinion of the Advocate General in C-26/91 *Jakob Handte & Co GmbH v. Soc Traitements Mécano-Chimiques des Surfaces* [1992] ECR I-3967, [23]–[24]. It may be that this will also have been the case in C-548/12 *Brogsitter v. Fabrication de Montres Normandes* EU:C:2014:148, [2014] QB 753, where the claim was a matter of special jurisdiction relating to a contract, but the substance of the claim was pleaded as a tort.

This made sense, and was probably inevitable, when a court with special jurisdiction would proceed to apply its private international law principles of characterisation and choice of law. But the picture is changing. In civil and commercial maters, the law applicable to contractual obligations arising from contracts made after 17 December 2009, and to non-contractual obligations arising from events which give rise to damage and which occur after 11 January 2009, will be common and uniform across the Member States. The Rome I[974] and Rome II[975] Regulations will apply uniform rules for applicable law across the Member States, with exclusions which are only minor.[976] It will mean the definition of matters relating to a contract in Article 7(1) will be very close indeed to that of 'contractual obligations' in the Rome I Regulation; and the definition of matters relating to tort, delict and quasi-delict in Article 7(2) will be close to that of 'non-contractual obligation' in the Rome II Regulation.[977]

We will examine this more closely in the context of each Article, below. At this point it is sufficient to say that although a court with special jurisdiction under Articles 7(1) or 7(2) may not be bound to apply the applicable law rules of the particular Rome Regulation which corresponds to the special jurisdiction, connection between special jurisdiction and applicable law will certainly be much tighter than it used to be.

2.164 Special jurisdiction in matters relating to a contract: Article 7(1)

Article 7(1) of Regulation 1215/2012 provides:

A person domiciled in a Member State may be sued in another Member State:
(1) (a) in matters relating to a contract, in the courts for the place of performance of the obligation in question;
(b) for the purpose of this provision and unless otherwise agreed, the place of performance of the obligation in question shall be:
— in the case of the sale of goods, the place in a Member State where, under the contract, the goods were delivered or should have been delivered,
— in the case of the provision of services, the place in a Member State where, under the contract, the services were provided or should have been provided;
(c) if point (b) does not apply then point (a) applies;

2.165 Development of special jurisdiction in matters relating to a contract

Article 7(1) of Regulation 1215/2012 is functionally identical to Article 5(1) of Regulation 44/2001.

In the form in which it appears as Article 7(1) of Regulation 1215/2012, the provision for special jurisdiction in matters relating to a contract has changed significantly from its predecessor in the Brussels and Lugano Conventions. These earlier texts made special provision for contracts of employment,[978] but otherwise contained only what now appears as sub-paragraph (a).[979] The detailed specification of the 'place of performance of the obligation

---

974 Regulation (EC) 593/2008, [2008] OJ L177/6.

975 Regulation (EC) 864/2007, [2007] OJ L199/40.

976 Article 1 of each Regulation.

977 For cross-reference between the Regulations generally, see Lein (2008) 10 *Yearbook of Private International Law* 177.

978 Because these instruments have not been amended to reflect the organisational change brought about by Section 6 of Chapter II of the Regulation.

979 C-533/07 *Falco Privatstiftung v. Weller-Lindhorst* [2009] ECR I-3327.

in question' in sub-paragraph (b) had no predecessor in the Convention. Sub-paragraph (c), which appears to do little more than state the obvious, is also new, but will call for little further examination.

The objections to the provision which now appears as Article 7(1)(a) were many, though not all were convincing. One major objection to a rule which simply gave special jurisdiction to the place of performance of the obligation in question, which found fault not with the rule but rather with its interpretation, derived from the interpretion that 'the obligation in question' was the obligation upon which the claimant based his claim. The court with special jurisdiction would therefore be that for the place where that obligation was, or was meant to be, performed. This was a satisfactory general rule in cases concerning delivery of defective or non-conforming goods: the aggrieved buyer would be able to sue a seller domiciled in another Member State in the courts for the place of delivery. But it was rather less satisfactory when it meant that an unpaid seller's claim for payment could be brought where payment was due to have been made. In allowing the unpaid seller to sue where he should have been paid, the Article gave special jurisdiction to a court which may have had little substantial connection with the facts which had given rise to the dispute and the issues which were required to be adjudicated: expressed in the idiom of the common law, the place of payment will rarely, and then only coincidentally, be the natural forum for such a claim.[980]

It also had a tendency to confer jurisdiction on the seller's own courts, either because a canny seller will have contracted for payment to be made at his place of residence or business, or because this was the default option provided by the *lex contractus*. In fact, the laws of four of the original six Contracting States generally provide for payment to be made at the debtor's, and hence at the defendant's, place of business.[981] The accession of the United Kingdom and Ireland, under the various laws of which payment is generally due where the creditor, not the debtor, is based,[982] showed this rule in a new light, because English sellers in particular were handed a surprise home advantage. The eventual result was not the abolition of the Article, as some had pressed for, but the adoption of Article 7(1)(b).

Article 7(1)(b) allowed Article 7(1) to become more predictable. But that goal would not be achieved simply by defining the place of performance of the obligation in question, for the question of *how* that place, under the contract, was to be pinpointed was not addressed. If it required a court to apply its substantive law of contract, including its rules of private international law, to discover the answer to that question, there would still be problems. Responding to this, the European Court created a principle of interpretation of contracts falling within Article 7(1)(b) which was designed to be less elaborate than that still applicable

---

980 For the proposition that this is in some sense the justification for the special jurisdictional *rule* in Art. 7(1), and for the decision that it is inadmissible to plead that Art. 7(1) should be inapplicable where it would confer jurisdiction on a court which in fact has little close connection, see C-288/92 *Custom Made Commercial Ltd v. Stawa Metallbau GmbH* [1994] ECR I-2913.

981 See Lando, in Tebbens, Kennedy and Kohler (eds), *Civil Jurisdiction and Judgments in Europe* (Butterworths, 1992), 29: France, Belgium, Luxembourg (Art. 1247 of the Civil Code); Germany (para. 270 of the BGB) specify the place of the debtor's residence; by contrast Italy (Art. 1182 of the Civil Code) and the Netherlands (Art. 1429 of the BW; Art. 6.116 of the NBW) specify the creditor's place of business.

982 *The Eider* [1893] P 119; *Bank of Scotland v. Seitz* 1990 SLT 584 (though *cf Deutsche Ruckversicherung AG v. La Fondaria Assicurazioni SpA* [2001] 2 Lloyd's Rep 621, making the point that the rule is general rather than absolute). But the same position obtains under the laws of Denmark, Finland, Iceland, Norway and Sweden (para. 3 of Law on Debt Instruments), Greece (Art. 321 of the Civil Code), and Switzerland (Art. 74 of the Law of Obligations). The position under the domestic laws of the States which acceded in or after 2004 is not known.

for Article 7(1)(a). Inch by inch the application of Article 7(1) is moving towards simplicity and away from obscurity.

There will be relatively few contracts for which Article 7(1)(b) will not specify the obligation in question and so identify the place whose courts have special jurisdiction. Apart from the sale of goods and the provision of services, and remembering that contracts of insurance, consumer sales and individual employment are separately dealt with, there is not very much left. Of course, not all contracts are sale, and not everything provided to a buyer will be goods or services. The precise demarcation will be examined at the point where it needs to be understood: that is, at the point at which it is necessary to identify the obligation in question.

2.166 Matters relating to a contract: development of an autonomous definition

The point of departure for the application of Article 7(1) is to understand the expression: 'matters relating to a contract'. This expression was not intended to indicate only those claims which are seen in English domestic law as being founded upon a contract, and it is not intended to exclude all those claims which are seen in English common law as not being based upon a contract. Its true meaning is neither derived from, nor very obviously inspired by, the common law of obligations.[983]

The expression has an autonomous, or uniform, meaning. This is to be expected: a European and autonomous rule for the exercise of special jurisdiction has a very different aim and purpose from those of the common law rules dealing with the characterisation of claims for the purpose of applying common law rules for choice of law. It is likely that the meaning of 'contractual obligation' in the Rome I Regulation, which deals with the law applicable to contractual obligations, will cover the same ground as Article 7(1) of Regulation 1215/2012. It is true that the Rome I Regulation determines the applicable law, while the Brussels I Regulation deals with special jurisdiction, but it is improbable that the meanings of core terms are intended to have divergent meanings. Accordingly, cross-reference from any decisions of the European Court on the Rome I Regulation and the Rome Convention which preceded it, to the Brussels I Regulation, and vice versa, would be sensible.[984] Even so, it is important to remember that the principles which ensure that the applicable law is the right one to apply, particularly where issues of contract and tort are intertwined, may diverge from those which are designed to ensure that the court with special jurisdiction is the right one to be given it. The exercises are connected, and similar; they are not the same.

The autonomous meaning of the expression 'matters relating to a contract' emerges, if not fully formed, from three decisions of the European Court in particular. In *Martin Peters Bauunternehmung GmbH v. Zuid Nederlandse AV*[985] a claim was brought in the Dutch courts by a trade association against one of its members, domiciled in Germany, for the payment of dues in accordance with the rules of the association. Dutch law regarded such a claim not as founded upon contract, but instead as being part of the law of associations. Upon the question whether the matter was one 'relating to a contract' for the purposes of what is now

---

983 Not least because it was first used in 1968, a generation before the United Kingdom acceded to the Convention and brought it into effect in its courts.

984 9/87 *Arcado v. Haviland SA* [1988] ECR 1539; C-96/00 *Gabriel v. Schlank & Schick GmbH* [2002] ECR I-6367.

985 34/82, [1983] ECR 987. See also C-214/89 *Powell Duffryn Ltd v. Petereit* [1992] ECR I-1745 (relationship between shareholder and company within the autonomous meaning).

Article 7(1), the European Court ruled that the expression had an autonomous meaning, and that the enforcement of the obligations of voluntary membership of an association by that association[986] against one of its members fell within it.

The Court returned to the question in *Arcado v. Haviland SA*,[987] on a reference from the Belgian courts. It reaffirmed its decision that the expression had an autonomous definition, without further particularisation, ruling that an action brought to recover compensation for loss resulting from the wrongful termination of a distributorship fell within this autonomous definition, even if Belgian law allowed a claim based on such an abusive exercise of legal rights to be framed as one which was tortious in nature.

Only in the third case did the outline of a definition begin to emerge. In *Jakob Handte & Co GmbH v. Soc. Traitements Mécano-Chimiques des Surfaces*,[988] a manufacturer had sold a piece of machinery to a buyer, who had sold it on to a sub-buyer. When the machine proved to be unfit for the purpose for which it had been first sold, the sub-buyer sued the manufacturer in the French courts, according to which the claim was said to be a contractual in nature.[989] The Court, however, ruled that the claim was not a 'matter relating to a contract' for the purposes of what is now Article 7(1). This was because a matter could not be seen as one relating to a contract 'in a situation in which there does not exist an undertaking freely entered into by one party in relation to another'.[990] In doing so, it appears to have approached the issue by reference to abstract principle, rather than by looking at the formulation of the cause of action advanced in the proceedings. If this is the way it is to be done, the contrast with the methodology for identifying a matter as civil or commercial, in which attention is focused on the analysis of the law of the court seised, is clear. It is not so clear that this is conscious and deliberate, but it appears to be the law.

In *Handte* the manufacturer had not, so far as he knew, entered into any form of undertaking to or with the sub-buyer, with the result that the sub-buyer's relationship with him was not contractual, and the claim against him was therefore not raised in a matter relating to a contract.[991] That was so even though the original contract of sale had triggered the

---

986 It is not so clear that what is now Art. 7(1) would have applied in the context of a claim to recover dues attributable to the obligatory membership of a professional association, such as the Law Society or the Bar Council. Though membership is voluntary in the sense that no one is obliged to carry on a particular profession, it is not voluntary in the sense that anyone who practises in the profession is obliged by law to pay the fees.

987 9/87, [1988] ECR 1539.

988 C-26/91, [1992] ECR I-3967.

989 It appears that the first buyer's rights against the manufacturer were assigned and pass, with title to the chattel, to the sub-buyer; the sub-buyer becomes subrogated to the rights of the first buyer under the original contract of sale: see the Opinion of the Advocate General, at [20]. It is as though the benefit of the covenant runs with the thing, which is sold on '*cum omni sua causa*', which makes perfect sense. But in the light of *Handte*, the French courts appear to have adopted the Court's definition of what makes a claim a contractual one: *Soc Donovan Data Systems Europe v. Soc Dragon Rouge Holding* (Cass, 6 July 1999), [2000] Rev crit DIP 67. And in C-543/10 *Refcomp SpA v. AXA Corporate Solutions Assurance SA* EU:C:2013:62, [2013] 1 Lloyd's Rep 449, the Court appears to have treated cases of purchase and on-sale as creating, at least in general cases, a chain of contracts, rather than the substitution of one person for another.

990 At [15]. It may be asked how this applies to the *Handte* decision itself. It presumably is true that if A assigns his contractual rights to B, B *can* enforce these in an action which falls within Art. 7(1).

991 It does not appear that the reasoning of the court would have been any different if the seller had been well aware that he was selling to a retailer who business was selling on: the subsequent purchaser is unascertainable. Even if that were not so – if the buyer had informed the seller that he was purchasing in order to sell on to an identified individual – it is unlikely, in the light of C-543/10 *Refcomp SpA v. AXA Corporate Solutions Assurance SA* EU:C:2013:62, [2013] 1 Lloyd's Rep 449, that this would have made a material difference.

dispute, and the claim in some sense[992] related to it, and even though the French courts would have understood the claim of the sub-buyer to have been contractual in nature. It follows that 'matters relating to a contract' will describe cases which can be said to be founded on an agreement between claimant and defendant. But it does not necessarily follow that in every case in which there is such an agreement, or which involves the voluntary assumption of a risk by one person in relation to another, proceedings between the parties are to be seen, for special jurisdictional purposes, as brought in a matter relating to a contract.

It follows, for example, that a person who holds office in a company, who is liable to be sued by a person dealing with the company who has sustained losses from the negligent or irregular supervision of the affairs of the company, is not sued in a matter relating to a contract. Even though he chooses to assume the responsibility of office, and must be taken to realise that those who deal with the company may, if things get out of hand, enforce the obligations which national law places on an office-holder, it could not be said that he has freely assumed a duty in relation to another (apart from the company, that is).[993]

2.167 The decision in *Handte*: claims involving strangers to the agreement

The cases which will be held to fall within the uniform definition proposed in *Handte* are not easy to identify with completeness. First, it should be noted that the definition propounded is essentially negative in its terms: that a matter will not relate to a contract in the absence of an obligation freely entered into by one party with another. It does not follow that whenever there is such an obligation, a claim founded on it must be seen as relating to a contract. But the point of departure in working out the details will certainly be to look for an obligation freely entered into with the other.

If a contractual claim or right has been assigned, or otherwise transmitted, to a third party, will the claim brought by the third party, which would have been contractual in the hands of the original beneficiary, remain contractual in the hands of this third party? A literal reading of the reasoning in *Handte* would suggest not. The defendant may be unaware that the assignment has taken place; he may not have foreseen that he would find himself contractually bound to the assignee.[994] If this were to have been the correct analysis, as a matter of French law, of the transmission of rights in *Handte*,[995] it could be argued that the assignee's claim is not one relating to a contract.

But it could not be correct. The proposition that a contractual claim ceases to be contractual would make no sense. On the footing that an assignee simply steps into the shoes of the assignor, and is entitled to the rights, but to no more than the rights, which the assignor had,[996] it is not obvious how the defendant is substantially prejudiced by the change

---

992 *Cf*, for a very different approach to a rule worded similarly, *Greene Wood & McLean LLP v. Templeton Insurance Ltd* [2009] EWCA Civ 65, [2009] 1 WLR 2013.

993 C-147/12 *ÖFAB v. Koot* EU:C:2013:490, [2015] QB 20; *cf* C-519/12 *OTP Bank Nyilvánosan Működő Részvénytársaság v. Hochtief Solution AG* EU:C:2013:674.

994 The law that governs the contract in question will determine whether the debtor needs to be notified to be bound.

995 Albeit that the assignment of rights took place by operation of law.

996 Or has the right to use the name of the assignor to bring the proceedings. See generally *Kolden Holdings Ltd v. Rodette Commerce Ltd* [2008] EWCA Civ 10, [2008] Bus LR 1051, which makes this assumption for the purposes of what is now Art. 29 of Regulation 1215/2012.

of creditor.[997] Such a suggestion would gain little support from other cases. In *Shearson Lehmann Hutton Inc v. TVB*,[998] a consumer had assigned his rights (contractual and non-contractual) against a dealer in financial futures, to an entity whose business appeared to be the enforcement of such claims. It was held by the Court that the claim was no longer to be seen as one falling within Section 4 of Chapter II of what is now the Brussels I Regulation, because the claimant was no longer a consumer. It did not suggest, still less did it decide, that the claim fell outside the consumer contract provisions because it was no longer contractual.

A transferee-holder of a bill of lading, if considered to succeed to the rights and liabilities of the transferor, is so closely regarded as bound to the original agreement that he is not required to make a separate act of acceptance of the jurisdiction provision set out in the bill:[999] the relationship between him and the issuer must relate to a contract. A transferee of shares presumably stands, for special jurisdictional purposes, in a contractual relationship with the company even though the company may, until he applies to be registered as a shareholder, have had no idea of his existence or identity.[1000] By contrast, it is not sufficient that both parties to a contract know that a non-party will perform some of the duties created by that agreement, and that the non-party will know for certain that he is performing within the context of a contract made between two others. To know that there will be another person involved in the factual matrix, who is involved because of the contract, is not sufficient to establish that an obligation was freely entered into in relation to that other. So a claim by the consignee of goods against the actual sea carrier, who had been appointed by the issuer of the bill of lading to undertake the contracted-for carriage, was not one relating to a contract.[1001] It should not be deduced that *Handte* generally excludes claims brought by assignees from the scope of Article 7(1).

If the dispute is in some sense concerned with a contract, but the claim is not between the parties to that contract, the claim will not be one relating to a contract. Proceedings brought by a consumer association to prevent the use of unfair contractual terms by a trader are not brought in a matter relating to a contract, for though the whole of the litigation will be concerned with a contract, the actual parties to the litigation are not parties to the contract with which the claim is concerned, and the particular *jus actionis* is not a contractual one.[1002]

If an agreement entered into by two parties as a contract provides for a third party to have directly enforceable rights under it, this will not prevent the claim being seen for jurisdictional purposes as falling within Article 7(1). The Contracts (Rights of Third Parties) Act 1999 provides that two contracting parties may confer a benefit on a stranger to the

---

997 All the more so if the law which governs the issue of assignment required the defendant to be notified of the assignment.

998 C-89/91, [1993] ECR I-139.

999 C-387/98 *Coreck Maritime GmbH v. Handelsveem BV* [2000] ECR I-9337.

1000 This will be so for bearer shares. But for registered shares, which are not so much transferred by the holder as surrendered to the company and issued afresh by the company, there is less room for the argument that the company might not know who its shareholder was. For the analogy between shareholding and contract, see C-241/89 *Powell Duffryn plc v. Petereit* [1992] ECR I-1745.

1001 C-51/97 *Réunion Européenne SA v. Spliethoff's Bevrachtingskantoor BV* [1998] ECR I-6511. And the issuer of a bond who issues it to an institution which has a contractual relationship with an 'investor', but who is not in a direct contractual relationship with the issuer, does not freely undertake obligations to that investor: C-375/13 *Kolassa v Barclays Bank plc* EU:C:2015:37.

1002 C-167/00 *Verein für Konsumenteninformation v. Henkel* [2002] ECR I-8111. It is therefore a matter relating to tort, delict or quasi-delict, even though the whole of the subject matter of the proceedings are the contractual terms used by the supplier in his contracts with consumers.

contract which that stranger may enforce in his own right, if their intention is demonstrable by reference to section 1 of the 1999 Act. A claim brought in such circumstances by the third party against the promisor is a matter relating to a contract for the purposes of Article 7(1) of the Regulation.[1003]

2.168 The decision in *Handte*: the nature of undertakings freely entered into

The proposition that there was no undertaking freely entered into with the other may or may not have been an accurate description of the situation, or of the *jus actionis*, in *Handte*.[1004] But the decision cannot be taken to mean that the individual right, or the specific *jus actionis*, on which the claim is based, must itself be one which was voluntarily, or freely, assumed.

For example, the obligations placed on a seller of goods in relation to title and quality may, according to the nature of the contract and the parties to it, be immune from exclusion by a term of the contract.[1005] They are in one sense not undertaken voluntarily; indeed, they are imposed on the parties by law, whether they like it or not, when parties make a contract of a certain type. But proceedings to enforce them cannot be said to fall outside Article 7(1). Likewise, an obligation to pay damages for breach of contract, or to pay or repay money when a contract is discharged by frustration, is not an obligation which is itself freely undertaken. But it arises within the framework, or as part and parcel, of an undertaking which was itself freely entered into[1006] and that will suffice for it to be seen as a matter relating to a contract.

Claims to enforce the obligations created by a unilateral contract must fall within the definition of matters relating to a contract, even though the offeror will not have the faintest idea who the other party or parties may be. If Mrs Carlill's claim against the Carbolic Smoke Ball Co is not to be seen as a matter relating to a contract, something will have gone terribly wrong.[1007] In *Engler v. Janus Versand GmbH*,[1008] a prize was offered to any customer who responded by claiming it, there being no condition that they conclude a separate contract to purchase goods from the offeror. Austrian law gave a statutory cause of action to the customer to demand the prize; and it was held that proceedings to enforce this statutory claim were within what is now Article 7(1)(a). The ultimate obligation on the seller was imposed by a statute, but the proximate cause of it was his volunteering by way of offer to give the prize, and the requested (and performed) response of the claimant asking for it to be supplied. The relationship between the parties was therefore a voluntary one, freely assumed by the one in relation to the other. This right to enforce the obligations of that relationship may have been reinforced by statute, but the matter was nonetheless one relating to a contract between the parties.[1009]

1003 It is put beyond doubt by *WPP Holdings Italy Srl v. Benatti* [2007] EWCA Civ 263, [2007] 1 WLR 2316 and which, at [54]–[55], approves the version of this statement which appeared in the 4th edition.

1004 For whether or not there was such an obligation, it had not been undertaken in respect of the actual claimant in the case.

1005 The obligations in ss 12–15 of the Sale of Goods Act 1979; for limitations on the right to exclude liability for breach, Unfair Contract Terms Act 1977, s. 6.

1006 As a secondary obligation thereunder.

1007 *Carlill v. Carbolic Smoke Ball Co Ltd* [1893] 1 QB 256.

1008 C-27/02, [2005] ECR I-439.

1009 C-180/06 *Ilsinger v. Schlank & Schick (in liq)* [2009] ECR I-3571, [54]–[57], may be read as suggesting that there is no contract unless each side assumes obligations to the other. But the Court was simply trying to distinguish between cases in which a gift is offered and accepted as a non-contractual gift, on the one hand, and

2.169 Matters relating to a contract: one party disputing the existence of a contract

A matter is not prevented from being one relating to a contract, and a court is not deprived of special jurisdiction, just because the defendant denies that there is a contract.

Two situations in which the existence of the contract is in issue need to be distinguished. If a claimant is suing a defendant, alleging that there is a contract between the parties, where performance was due in the court seised, the defendant may answer by pleading that there was no contract at all. Such a bare allegation does not deprive the court of special jurisdiction: there is no *a priori* reason to prefer the contention of the defendant to that of the claimant, or vice versa. In cases such as this, the sensible answer is (a) that the court must take a provisional view that there is in dispute between the parties a contract which contains an obligation such as would give it jurisdiction, and (b) that the required standard of certainty requires the claimant to show that he has to have the better of the argument that the facts are such as are needed to give the court jurisdiction under what is now Article 7(1).[1010]

The issue arose in *Effer SpA v. Kantner*,[1011] where a claim made was in respect of the non-payment of a contractual hiring fee, the defendant alleging that there was no contract between the parties at all. The Court said that, in deciding whether there was jurisdiction under what is now Article 7(1)(a) of the Regulation, the court seised was entitled to examine those facts which were preconditions to its having jurisdiction. It follows that, if the court were to decide *at the stage at which its exercise of jurisdiction is challenged* and to the standard of certainty imposed by its own procedural law that there was a contract, it will be entitled to proceed to hear the case; if it decides at this stage that there was no contract, it will not have jurisdiction to adjudicate the merits of the claim, and must decline jurisdiction. It plainly does not follow that if the court decides that it has jurisdiction, but at the trial of the substance of the dispute concludes that there was no contract after all, it will retrospectively declare that it had no jurisdiction. In England, at any rate, the jurisdictional issue is taken *in limine litis*, adjudicated upon then, once and for all, but without prejudice to any later decision upon the merits of the case. To hold otherwise would mean that, after a full hearing of the merits, a court would be obliged to say it had no power to reach a decision. As a matter of English procedural law, that could not be correct,[1012] though the implications for the standard of certainty which should, therefore, be insisted upon are explored below.

The approach indicated by *Effer* is further supported by the decision of the Court in *Marc Rich & Co AG v. Soc Italiana Impianti PA*.[1013] On the question whether a claim fell outside the Brussels Convention on the basis that it concerned arbitration, it was said that, if the subject matter of the dispute concerned arbitration, it fell outside the Convention, even though there was a dispute whether there was a binding obligation to arbitrate. The Court referred approvingly to *Effer*, from which it would follow that, if the dispute has a contract

---

in which a contractual agreement is made to supply a thing but for which practically nothing is asked in return save compliance with the terms of the offer, which is a perfectly sensible thing to do, but something which is not always easy to put into words.

1010 *Canada Trust Co v. Stolzenberg (No 2)* [2002] 1 AC 1.

1011 38/81, [1982] ECR 825.

1012 See also 158/87 *Scherrens v. Maenhout* [1988] ECR 3791, where a dispute about the existence of a lease of land was held to fall within the scope of what is now Art. 24(1), even though it was possible that the court would ultimately rule that there was no valid lease.

1013 C-190/89, [1991] ECR I-3855. See also, and to much the same effect, 73/77 *Sanders v. Van der Putte* [1977] ECR 2383; C-269/95 *Benincasa v. Dentalkit Srl* [1997] ECR I-3767.

as its subject matter, the jurisdictional rules of Article 7(1) of the Regulation may be resorted to even if the defendant contends that there was no binding contract. But in order to screen out frivolous or vexatious claims that a contract did exist, a court should apply its own procedural rules to determine whether the evidence in support of the allegation of a contract is serious enough to justify allowing proceedings to be brought against the defendant outside his domiciliary court. Its right and duty to apply its own procedural standards to determine whether the facts allow it to take jurisdiction was confirmed by the Court in *Shevill v. Presse Alliance SA*.[1014]

2.170 Matters relating to a contract: voidable contracts and 'void contracts'

One particular context in which the expression 'matters relating to a contract' has given rise to some difficulty of organisation is where the claimant asserts that he has rescinded a voidable contract, or that a supposed contract was void *ab initio*, and that judgment should be given accordingly with such relief as may follow from it. The starting point is to consider three cases in particular. A potential difficulty arises from the fact that the contract laws of the Member States diverge in their analysis of these faults, complaints, vices and impediments. It is not safe to assume that just because a particular complaint would, in English contract law, render the contract voidable, other systems will take the same view. It is probably best to examine the law before and after the impact of the Rome I and Rome II Regulations.

In *Kleinwort Benson Ltd v. Glasgow City Council*,[1015] it was common ground between the parties that a supposed contract, which they had purported to conclude, had been void *ab initio*, as being *ultra vires* the council.[1016] The bank sued to recover money which it had paid under this 'void contract'. A bare majority of the House of Lords held that the claim was not within what is now Article 7(1)(a) of Regulation 1215/2012. Such doubt as there is reflects the fact that the majority considered that whether or not the matter was one relating to a contract, the 'obligation in question' had to be a contractual one,[1017] and that because the obligation to repay or reimburse was not an obligation which was contractual in nature, the proceedings fell outside the Article.

The decision was controversial, for even if the parties had failed to create legally valid and binding contractual obligations, it had plainly been their intention to do so, and the potential application of Article 7(1) to a dispute between them would hardly have taken them by surprise.[1018] It would have been absurd for a court, called upon to enforce a contract in an action for damages but finding instead that it was void, to be prevented from making an order for such relief as followed from its substantive decision on contractual validity. In the context of consumer contracts it would have been worse still: to deprive the consumer of the jurisdictional privilege of Section 4 of Chapter II[1019] when claiming the return of his

---

1014 C-68/93, [1995] ECR I-415.

1015 [1999] 1 AC 153, a decision on the meaning of this term as it was used in Sch. 4 to the 1982 Act.

1016 It had been held, in an earlier test case, that such contracts were *ultra vires* the council, and therefore void.

1017 The issue is examined below.

1018 It would be different if the reason for impeaching the alleged contract were a mistake as to the identity of the other, where it would be much harder to say that the parties freely undertook obligations in relation to each other.

1019 Examined above, paras 2.102 *et seq.*

pre-payment or deposit would have been contrary to the purpose of the Regulation.[1020] Yet if the non-existence of a supposed contract, or the finding that the supposed contract was in fact void, were to take the proceedings outside the material scope of Article 7(1), there would have been a risk of such an unsatisfactory outcome. The minority saw this point and would have decided differently.

In *Agnew v. Länsförsäkringsbolagens AB*,[1021] a differently constituted House of Lords accepted unanimously that, in a case where the claimant brought proceedings for a declaration that it had been entitled to avoid a contract of reinsurance on the basis of material non-disclosure, the matter was one relating to a contract. The court also accepted that, in a case in which the claimant asserts that the alleged contract is void, or never was, but the defendant pleads its validity and existence,[1022] the matter was one relating to a contract:[1023] a dispute between the parties which had at its heart the question whether an alleged contract was valid and binding, naturally fell within Article 7(1). This seems right, not least because Article 7(1) speaks of a 'matter relating to a contract', rather than about a 'claim to enforce a contract'. It had the effect of confining *Kleinwort Benson* to those rare cases in which it is common ground from the outset of litigation that there never was a contract between the parties.

One such case is *Fonderie Officine Meccaniche Tacconi SpA v. Heinrich Wagner Sinto Maschinenfabrik GmbH*,[1024] in which parties had entered into negotiations aimed at concluding a contract of sale, but one had withdrawn before the anticipated contract had been concluded. Italian law evidently gave a cause of action to the wronged party for losses caused by the unjustified refusal to act in good faith by concluding the contract. On the question whether proceedings brought to claim damages for breach of that obligation fell within what is now Article 7(1), the Court ruled that it did not. This conclusion could, and probably should, have been rested on the simple proposition that where it is common ground that the parties did not conclude a contract, there is no contract in any sense which could have brought the case within Article 7(1). *Kleinwort Benson*, as explained above, would support this analysis.

It is not clear whether the Court shared this view. It said that though what is now Article 7(1) did not require a contract to have been concluded, it did require there to be an obligation, and on the facts there did not appear to be an obligation freely entered into by the defendant with the claimant. This seems wrong. There was an obligation between the parties, which each side had chosen to subject itself to in embarking on negotiation: there was an obligation to exercise good faith in doing so. It was freely entered into in the sense that neither was obliged to negotiate with the other, but once they had placed themselves in negotiation, the obligation arose and bound them. The conclusion

---

1020 And further, the French version ('*en matière contractuelle*') does not so obviously connote the idea of an actual contract as being the foundation of the action.

1021 [2001] 1 AC 223.

1022 Such as *Boss Group Ltd v. Boss France SA* [1997] 1 WLR 351.

1023 But it has been held that a claim for damages for misrepresentation leading to a contract is not a matter relating to a contract, but one relating to tort: *Alfred Dunhill Ltd v. Diffusion Internationale de Maroquinerie de Prestige Sarl* [2001] CLC 949. This is very problematic for damages awarded when tortious misrepresentation has led the victim to enter into a contract are assessed to put the victim in the position he would have been in if he had *not* entered into the contract. If the remedy is, in money terms, designed to avoid the contract, it is not so clear that the claim is a tortious one.

1024 C-334/00, [2002] ECR I-7357.

that the proceedings were not in a matter relating to a contract was right, but the better reason is that this conclusion was not in dispute, but was accepted by the parties as common ground.

However this may be, the issue will need to be reconsidered in the light of the Rome I and Rome II Regulations. In light of the fact that the scheme of those two instruments is to divide obligations in civil and commercial matters into contractual and non-contractual, and to specify the applicable law accordingly, it is likely to influence the drawing of the line between Articles 7(1) and 7(2) of the Brussels I Regulation. Non-contractual obligations arising from *culpa in contrahendo*, or pre-contractual faults, are within the Rome II Regulation,[1025] and although the applicable law will tend to be the law which governed or would have governed the contract, the clear message to be taken from the location of such matters within the Rome II Regulation so far as the applicable law is concerned is that proceedings based on non-contractual obligations which allege pre-contractual fault will fall within Article 7(2) of the Brussels I Regulation. In other words, proceedings which have the validity or invalidity of the contract as their focus will be within the scope of the Rome I Regulation, and if special jurisdiction is an issue, it will be dealt with by Article 7(1). But proceedings which seek compensation or other payment because of fault in negotiating or in failing to negotiate a contract, or as a response to a wrong which induced another to enter into a contract, will be within the domain of the Rome II Regulation, and is special jurisdiction is an issue, it will be provided by Article 7(2).

2.171 Matters relating to a contract: tortious misconduct by contracting parties

There are other areas of liability which, though not necessarily contractual as a matter of English domestic law, may nevertheless be seen as matters relating to a contract for the purposes of Article 7(1). The two most important examples are cases in which, as a matter of domestic law, the cause of action lies concurrently in contract and in tort, such as where a client sues the careless provider of professional services,[1026] and liability for negligent mis-statement under the rule in *Hedley Byrne & Co v. Heller and Partners*.[1027]

As to the first of these, suppose proceedings are brought by a client against his legal adviser, accountant, financial adviser or architect claiming that the professional services were performed without proper care. As a matter of English domestic law, the claims may be framed concurrently in contract and in tort, or in either, at the election of the claimant.[1028] But suppose the provider of services were domiciled in another Member State. If it is sought to sue him in England, is the claim to be seen as one relating to a contract? It seems that it is,[1029] for however the substantive claim is analysed as a matter of substantive law, there is only one obligation: to exercise reasonable care and skill. That obligation is one which arises out of (or is imposed upon the defendant by and because of) the agreement between

---

1025 Article 12.
1026 See, for example, *Henderson v. Merrett Syndicates Ltd* [1995] 2 AC 145.
1027 [1964] AC 465.
1028 *Henderson v. Merrett Syndicates Ltd* [1995] 2 AC 145. But there is an ongoing debate as to whether this is correct as a matter of the conflict of laws, or correct as a matter of the conflict of laws in cases in which the contract between the parties is governed by the Rome Convention. See in particular Briggs [2003] LMCLQ 12; *Base Metal Trading Ltd v. Shamurin* [2004] EWCA Civ 1316, [2005] 1 WLR 1157.
1029 As will be seen below (paras 2.192 *et seq.*), this will prevent its being seen, for jurisdictional purposes, as a matter relating to tort, delict or quasi-delict within Art. 7(2) of the Regulation.

the parties, and the agreement itself was freely entered into. That should locate it, for the purposes of special jurisdiction, within Article 7(1) of the Regulation.

This conclusion is supported by *Brogsitter v. Fabrication de Montres Normandes EURL*,[1030] in which a dispute between two commercial partners, making allegations of disloyalty and unfair competition, was framed as a tort claim. The Court, however, observed that if the contract had to be pleaded to establish the basis for a claim that the acts complained of were wrongful, and if the substance of the claim could have been put as a claim for breach of contract in any event, it fell within what is now Article 7(1). The decision reaffirms the point that the question is whether the claim could have been made on the basis of the contract; the answer to this question is quite independent of how the claimant chose or contrived to frame it.[1031]

As to the second, it may be necessary to distinguish cases where the parties are in a relationship equivalent to privity, where advice was given directly by defendant to claimant, as was the case in *Hedley Byrne*, from those where the claimant is not party to the advice-giving-and-receiving relationship, even though it is foreseen that he will rely on the advice given primarily to another.[1032] In the former case, it is only the absence of consideration which prevents the relationship being contractual as a matter of substantive English law: it is arguable, if not yet clear,[1033] that the relationship between the parties would satisfy the definition in *Handte*. In the latter case, it is much less clear, as the relationship between the parties is constituted less directly. But if one were to accept that the basis for the imposition of *Hedley Byrne* liability is that the defendant has voluntarily accepted the risk, or voluntarily assumed liability in relation to the third party, then the foundation exists for the argument that the matter is one which falls comfortably within the autonomous definition of matters relating to a contract offered in *Handte*.[1034]

Jurisdiction in an action to enforce fiduciary duties may be thought to raise further difficulties. It cannot be argued that claims to enforce fiduciary duties fall outside Article 7(1) by reasoning that fiduciary duties arise in equity rather than from the common law of contract. Neither can it be argued, it is submitted, that because fiduciary duties are imposed by equity on a defendant who has placed himself in a position where those duties are owed, then they are not to be seen as obligations freely undertaken. The preferable view[1035] is that if they result from a relationship which was freely entered into, such as between agent and principal, company and office-holder, or solicitor and client, their enforcement is, for jurisdictional purposes, within Article 7(1). If, by contrast, they are imposed on a defendant who has, without the agreement of the claimant, placed himself in a position where

---

1030 C-548/12, EU:C:2014:148, [2014] QB 753.

1031 See also *Source Ltd v. TUV Rheinland Holding AG* [1998] QB 54, which is to the same effect. It is otherwise, therefore, if the duty in tort is one which could only ever arise if it were found that there was no contractual duty to perform: *Domicrest Ltd v. Swiss Bank Corp* [1999] QB 548. See also *Raiffeisen Zentralbank Österreich v. National Bank of Greece* [1999] 1 Lloyd's Rep 408.

1032 *Cf Smith v. Eric S Bush* [1990] 1 AC 831.

1033 *Deutsche Bahn AG v. Petromena ASA* [2013] EWHC 3065 (Comm), which at [54] makes the fair point that there is no authority for the submission in the text. The matter is at this point one of analysis, rather than authority.

1034 *Source Ltd v. TUV Rheinland Holding AG* is not directly applicable here, as there is no actual contract as a matter of English law. But the obligation arises out of and only because of the obligations freely entered into, and that brings the case very close to that in *Source Ltd*. However, in *London Helicopters Ltd v. Heliportugal Lda-INAC* [2006] EWHC 108 (QB), [2006] 1 All ER (Comm) 597, it was accepted that a claim against an organisation which had negligently issued a certificate of airworthiness, which it knew would be relied on by all and sundry, fell under what is now Art. 7(2), not 7(1).

1035 But one which is believed to be free of authority.

equity requires him to act as a fiduciary, such as an accomplice to another's breach of trust, the matter will not fall within Article 7(1). And even if these two cases do represent the two sides of the argument, there will still be cases which appear to fall rather closer to the borderline, such as that of the company director who diverts a corporate opportunity to his own secret profit.

2.172 Matters relating to a contract: unjust enrichment and similar causes of action

It is convenient at this point to consider whether quasi-contractual or restitutionary or unjust enrichment claims, or some of them, or none of them, fall within Article 7(1) of the Regulation.[1036] As with the earlier discussion, it may be that the uncertainty of the law can be resolved by aligning the answer with the structure of the Rome I and Rome II Regulations.

It is too difficult to treat claims which are brought against a person accused of having unjustly enriched himself at the expense of another as though they formed a single, coherent and indivisible group, to be located within Article 7 as a single, coherent and indivisible group: they cover a diverse range of circumstances, and are linked, as much as by anything else, by an absence of something. On the other hand, they are also linked by a civil obligation to reverse the injustice of the enrichment, which obligation arises independently of the will of the defendant. If that is so, they do not fall within the definition in *Handte*, and therefore not within Article 7(1). They would therefore, in principle at least, fall within Article 7(2). This would align the law on special jurisdiction with the Rome II Regulation, which identifies the applicable law for non-contractual obligations,[1037] and makes particular provision for cases of unjust enrichment and *negotiorum gestio*, or intervention in another's affairs. That would also suggest that claims based on unjust enrichment should fall within Article 7(2).[1038]

A problem with this analysis, which will be noted below, is that the Rome II Regulation draws a distinction between tort and delict, on the one hand, and non-contractual obligations which do not arise from tort and delict, and it places unjust enrichment and *negotiorum gestio* in the latter category. But as will be explained, the view taken here is that proceedings which are based on non-contractual obligations will fall within Article 7(2), not least because they are not within the Rome I Regulation. The question of how the Rome II Regulation organises its rules for the identification of the applicable law is, in this respect, not a concern.

Insofar as the restitution of payments made is simply the logical consequence of proceedings in a matter relating to a contract, they will fall within the special jurisdictional provision for contractual obligations, as they are no more than the remedial consequence of proceedings which were in a matter of contractual obligation. But where they arise independently of proceedings which relate to a contract, they should fall under Article 7(2). Accordingly a claim for the recovery of money paid by a buyer who did not receive

---

1036 To the extent that they do not, it will be necessary to enquire whether they fall within Art. 7(2); as to which, see paras 2.197 *et seq.*, below.

1037 Regulation (EC) 864/2007.

1038 This is the analysis of the effects of 189/87 *Kalfelis v. Bankhaus Schröder Münchmeyer Hengst & Co* [1988] ECR 5565 which was put forward by the Advocate General in C-89/91 *Shearson Lehmann Hutton Inc v. TVB* [1993] ECR I-139, Opinion, [102]. The Advocate General in *Shearman Lehmann Hutton* had also advised the Court in *Kalfelis*, so it is rational that he understood what the Court had sought to achieve by its judgment when it rejected his advice in the earlier case.

the goods paid for would fall within Article 7(1), as it is a claim relating to an actual and admitted contract. A claim for the recovery of money repayable after the frustration of a contract for the sale of goods would fall within Article 7(1), as the claim relates to an actual contract and the effect of events in relation to it. The practical consequences of rejecting this analysis would be very inconvenient. It would mean that a buyer who sued for damages for failure of the seller to deliver or alternatively for the return of his money would be entitled to bring the first, but not the second, claim in the court with special jurisdiction under Article 7(1). This would not contribute to the rational development of the law: a single claim would be unnaturally and unnecessarily severed according to the theoretical basis for the various claims for relief made.

Other claims for restitution or in respect of unjust enrichment, such as may be brought by the benevolent intervener who has put out a blaze which threatened to consume his neighbour's house, would be unlikely to be found to relate to a contract.[1039] Claims for contribution between tortfeasors[1040] would also be unlikely to fall within Article 7(1), for there cannot really be said to be an implied contract between them to justify the claim. In the end the best advice must be that if the claim, though restitutionary or unjust enrichment-y in nature, arises out of, or in connection with, a real or supposed contract, it will fall within Article 7(1). Claims based on such obligations which do not so arise will be likely to fall under Article 7(2). And in making the judgment at this point, the particular analysis of the court which is seised, and of its national law, will not be decisive.[1041]

2.173 The obligation in question which points to special jurisdiction

If the matter is one relating to a contract, the court with special jurisdiction under Article 7(1) of the Regulation is that for the place of performance of the obligation in question. It is, therefore, necessary to elucidate the meaning of 'the obligation in question'. In the paragraphs which immediately follow, the main focus will be on 'the obligation in question' rather than on the question of its place of performance, which is discussed thereafter. But in analysing the manner in which the Court, in particular, has elaborated the meaning of 'the obligation in question', it will be impossible to avoid straying into the issue of where that obligation was to be performed.

Prior to the Brussels I Regulation, this expression was interpreted to mean the obligation upon which the claimant founded his claim.[1042] If he sued alleging non-delivery it would be the obligation to deliver; if he complained of non-payment it would be the duty to pay. If he alleged a failure to perform a professional duty, special jurisdiction lay at the place where that duty was to be performed.[1043] At one time, what is now Article 7(1)(a) was held to make separate treatment of contracts of employment, in matters relating to which the

---

1039 Obligations arising from *negotiorum gestio* are non-contractual obligations when it comes to the identification of the applicable law: Rome II Regulation, Art. 11.

1040 *Hewden Tower Cranes Ltd v. Wolffkran GmbH* [2007] EWHC 857 (TCC), [2007] 2 Lloyd's Rep 138 holds that they fall within what is now Art. 7(2).

1041 It is fair to point out that this technique is different from that currently used to decide whether a claim is within Art. 1, where the approach is to examine the particular *jus actionis* relied on. But nothing of significance turns on this difference in approach.

1042 14/76 *De Bloos Sprl v. Bouyer SA* [1976] ECR 1497; C-288/92 *Custom Made Commercial Ltd v. Stawa Metallbau GmbH* [1994] ECR I-2913.

1043 266/85 *Shenavai v. Kreischer* [1987] ECR 239.

obligation was that of the employee to work, no matter how the claim was framed or who was suing whom.[1044] But any need to tilt the playing field in favour of the employee is now met by Section 6 of Chapter II of the Regulation,[1045] and this modification of Article 7(1)(a) is no longer applied.

As indicated above, a rule which allowed an unpaid seller or supplier to sue in his own courts, simply because this was where the payment had been contractually due, ran contrary to the philosophy of what is now Article 7, which aims to give special jurisdiction to a court which is proximate to the facts and matters giving rise to the dispute and calling for adjudication.[1046] To overcome the problem it would have been necessary to adopt an autonomous interpretation of where obligations are to be performed, or an autonomous interpretation of which the defining obligation actually is. Acknowledging the impossibility of the former,[1047] Article 7(1) of the Regulation adopts the latter solution, by adopting a tripartite identification of the obligation in question and its place of performance. 'Unless otherwise agreed', in the case of a sale of goods the obligation in question is to deliver the goods; in the case of a provision of services it is the obligation to provide the services; and in each case the court with special jurisdiction is that of the place at which, under the contract, the delivery or the provision was done or should have been done. In all other cases the obligation in question will be, as it originally was, that on which the claimant founds his claim; and the court with special jurisdiction is that of the place where under the contract that obligation was to be performed.

It is not easy to see much in the words 'unless otherwise agreed'. It might suggest that the parties may agree on which is to be the obligation in question, or may agree what is the place of performance of it, but neither makes a lot of sense. If the parties stipulate a place for delivery or for provision of services, the courts of that place have special jurisdiction, because the place of delivery is specified by the parties: there is no conceptual opportunity for there to be a contractual place of delivery but with the parties agreeing that it is to be elsewhere.[1048] Neither are the parties likely to agree which is to be 'the obligation in question for the purposes of Article 7(1)': it would be a rather unusual term to find in a contract. It is possible that the words reflect the case in which the parties have made an agreement on jurisdiction to which Article 25 applied, but as Article 25 is a superior rule, it does not call for any reservation by Article 7(1). For the present, the words are best overlooked.

2.174 Identifying the contract as one for the sale of goods

Assuming that it has already been decided that the proceedings are brought in a matter relating to a contract, it is next necessary to decide whether the contract is one for the sale of goods or for the supply of services, in order to decide whether Article 7(1)(a) or 7(1)(b) will locate the place of performance of the obligation in question.

1044 133/81 *Ivenel v. Schwab* [1982] ECR 1891.

1045 Examined above, paras. 2.114 *et seq.*

1046 C-288/92 *Custom Made Commercial Ltd v. Stawa Metallbau GmbH* [1994] ECR I-2913; C-19/09 *Wood Floor Solutions Andreas Domberger GmbH v. Silva Trade SA* [2010] ECR I-2121, [22], and cases there cited.

1047 See also in this context, C-440/97 *Groupe Concorde v. Master of the Vessel 'Suhadiwarno Panjan'* [1999] ECR I-6307.

1048 And if they try to, it will be treated as abstract or fictitious, and treated as an agreement on jurisdiction requiring to be validated under Art. 25: C-106/95 *MSG v. Les Gravières Rhénanes Sarl* [1997] ECR I-911.

The meaning of 'for the sale of goods' will be an autonomous one, rather than one which follows the technicalities of the domestic law on sale of goods. In principle it will be found by ascertaining the obligation which is characteristic of the particular contract. In *Car Trim GmbH v. KeySafety Systems Srl*,[1049] an Italian customer required a German manufacturer to manufacture and deliver components for it to use in the manufacture of cars, to a very particular specification, in such a way that the German company might be seen as having obligations which went beyond the sale of goods. The Court observed that it was not unusual that a seller of goods did more than simply transfer title against payment, and the fact that the seller was required to manufacture the things to be sold did not prevent the contract being one of sale. It might have been different if the customer had provided the raw materials on which the other was to work, but where the party who is to be paid sources the materials, manufactures the goods, and delivers them, the contract is one for the sale of goods, even though there are contractual obligations additional to sale, strictly so called. The obligation of sale was characteristic of the contract, and that meant that the contract fell within Article 7(1)(b) as a contract for the sale of goods.

On the question of what counts as payment, it will be seen below in relation to contracts for the provision of services, the requirement that there be payment has been inferred from the Court, and then interpreted in a rather flexible manner. If this flexibility were to be applied within the definition of a contract of sale, it would not be necessary for there to be a consideration in money, as distinct from some other economic advantage being obtained by the seller in return for the transfer of title to the goods.

In other respects the uniform definition has not yet been made clear. But it is improbable that the complexity of the domestic law of sale is useful in this context. If the point of Article 7(1)(b) is to provide an improved version of the rule in Article 7(1), and not to fight against it, there is no need to confine it strictly or rigidly.[1050] If the Court meant what it said in *Car Trim GmbH*, that the contract in that case could be characterised as one of sale, the identification of a contract as one of sale will be by asking whether it is sufficiently like a contract of sale for this to be the appropriate rule of special jurisdiction for matters relating to it. That means, as it is submitted, that the contract should be one for the transfer of ownership in return for payment,[1051] or sufficiently analogous to it to attract the same rule of special jurisdiction. If the law is allowed to become any more complex than that, it is submitted, a wrong turn will have been taken.

2.175 Identifying the contract as one for the provision of services

In relation to the identification of a contract as one for the provision of services, some cases are simple and straightforward. No real difficulty arises with a contract for carriage of passengers by air,[1052] for example, or with the provision of professional services as a commercial agent,[1053] or with a contract for the delivery of another's goods,[1054] or with a

---

1049 C-381/08, [2010] ECR I-1255.

1050 Professor Schlosser considered hire purchase to be a form of sale: [1979] OJ C59/71, [157].

1051 Or for consideration having an economic function equivalent to payment.

1052 C-204/08 *Rehder v. Air Baltic Corp* [2009] ECR I-6073. The real issue in the case was as to the place of provision, as to which see below, para. 2.179.

1053 The search for a more elegant way of making that point was not crowned with success.

1054 C-386/05 *Color Drack GmbH v. Lexx International Vertriebs GmbH* [2007] ECR I-3699.

contract for the storage of another's goods.[1055] Assuming all these to be done for remuneration or reward, as to which see below, the person who performs provides services for the purpose of Article 7(1)(b).

For less obvioius cases, it is necessary to look to guidance which has been given by the European Court. In *Falco Privatstiftung v. Weller-Lindhorst*[1056] the Court explained why a licensing agreement relating to rights of intellectual property was not a contract for the provision of services: in being permitted to use the rights, the licensee did not undertake to do anything positive, only to refrain from defined misuse of the rights forming the subject of the contract. To be seen as a contract for the provision of services, the party said to be providing services must be carrying out a particular activity in return for remuneration.[1057]

These points of identification were applied to the question whether an exclusive distribution contract was a contract of sale (sales are part of the mechanism) or a contract for the provision of services (the distribution and the building of a market is part of the arrangement) or both (and in that case, whether both actually means neither). For such a contract is a hybrid. The approach of the Court in *Corman-Collins SA v. La Maison du Whisky SA*[1058] was to see the long-term nature of the distribution as more significant than the series of contracts of sale of materials to the distributor. It referred to the two elements of the definition given in *Falco Privatstiftung*, and suggested to the national court that they were satisfied. The positive activity part of the definition was plainly satisfied by the work done by the distributor. As to whether the distributor did this for payment, or in order to see whether there was remuneration for the service provided by the distributor, it is best to see how the Court put it: 'it must be stated that it is not to be understood strictly as the payment of a sum of money. Such a restriction is neither stipulated by the very general wording of the second indent of Article 7(1)(b) of the Regulation nor consistent with the objectives of proximity and standardisation'. Moreover, 'the distribution agreement is based on a selection of the distributor by the grantor. That selection, which is a characteristic element of that type of agreement, confers a competitive advantage on the distributor in that the latter has the sole right to sell the grantor's products in a particular territory or, at the very least, that a limited number of distributors enjoy that right. Moreover, the distribution agreement often provides assistance to the distributor regarding access to advertising, communicating knowhow by means of training or yet even payment facilities. All those advantages, whose existence it is for the court adjudicating on the substantive action to ascertain, represent an economic value for the distributor that may be regarded as constituting remuneration'. In other words, the economic advantages which were made available to the distributor were sufficient to meet the (non-statutory) requirement of remuneration.

As a result, the signpost to a contract for the provision of services will be the performance of a particular requested activity for remuneration, and on the latter point, the court may be creative. This is justifiable if the rule in Article 7(1)(b) is a modification by way of improvement on the more general rule in Article 7(1)(a). Though in *Falco Privatstiftung* the Court

---

1055 C-469/12 *Krejci Lager & Umschlagbetriebs GmbH v. Olbrich Transport und Logistik GmbH* EU:C:2013:788, [2014] ILPr 139.

1056 C-533/07, [2009] ECR I-3327.

1057 Likewise, making available capacity on an optical cable was held not to involve the provision of services in *Reliance Globalcom Ltd v. OTE International Solutions SA* [2011] EWHC 1848 (QB), because no discernible service was provided by the cable owner.

1058 C-9/12, EU:C:2013:860, [2014] QB 431.

suggested that Article 7(1)(b) should be given a narrow construction, on the footing that it was an exception to the more general rule in Article 7(1)(a), the Court plainly ignored its own advice in *Corman-Collins SA v. La Maison du Whisky SA*, and it is submitted that it was right to do so. There is no obvious need for judicial wariness in relation to Article 7(1)(b), for the jurisdictional rule does not call into question one which should be protected from being overshadowed.

2.176 Definition of the obligation in question in contracts of sale and provision of services

The identification of the obligation in question in those contracts which fall within Article 7(1)(b) will not usually be difficult, as the Article directs attention to the delivery of the goods or to the provision of the service, as the case may be. A general problem, which is certainly not confined to contracts which fall within Article 7(1)(b), arises when the obligation of delivery or provision, which is easy enough to identify, is required to be performed in more than one Member State: this is dealt with separately. It is unfortunate that this paragraph has to deal with an untidy collection of points which are not naturally coherent.

First, Article 7(1)(b) will apply easily to proceedings in which a person who says he is not bound, or not in breach, or otherwise not liable in relation to a contract, brings proceedings for a declaration of non-liability. It was sometimes difficult to see how the rule now in Article 7(1)(a) applied in cases in which the basis for the claim was that there was no breach of duty; no contractual term the breach of which was the foundation for the claim. The English courts approached the issue pragmatically, taking the approach that in the case of simple denial of contractual liability, the issue was to be approached by taking the contractual term on which the natural claimant would have relied if he had brought proceedings, and asking where that obligation required performance.[1059] In cases in which the claimant sought a declaration that he had been entitled to rescind or avoid a contract for non-disclosure, special jurisdiction was available at the place where disclosure should have been made.[1060] Both approaches were roughly consistent with the requirements of what is now Article 7(1)(a), but insofar as the contract is one which falls under Article 7(1)(b), these mental gymnastics will no longer be required. Special jurisdiction will lie at the place identified by reference to Article 7(1)(b) and the cases which interpret it, and will not be affected by the issue of who is suing who, or for what.

Next, there may be cases, particularly in the contract for the provision of services, in which it may not be clear which is 'the' service, the provision of which points the way to special jurisdiction. Cases decided under the Brussels Convention may be used to illustrate the issue. In relation to the jurisdictional rule which survives as Article 7(1)(a), it was held that the seller's obligation was to deliver fit or conforming goods at the place fixed for delivery, rather than to undertake to ensure their fitness on a continuing basis at the place of use,[1061] so if the claim was based on the failure to supply conforming goods, the obligation in question was to 'supply by delivery', to be performed at the place of delivery.[1062] It was

---

1059 *Boss Group Ltd v. Boss France SA* [1997] 1 WLR 351.
1060 *Agnew v. Länsförsäkringsbolagens AB* [2001] 1 AC 223.
1061 *Viskase Ltd v. Paul Kiefel GmbH* [1999] 3 All ER 362.
1062 *MBM Fabri-Clad Ltd v. Eisen-und Huttenwerke Thale AG* [2000] CLC 373.

held that the relevant obligation on a tax accountant to prepare papers in connection with a tax claim against the Inland Revenue was to liaise and deal with the Revenue in England, rather than to deal with the client and prepare the paperwork in Ireland.[1063] The obligation on an ex-employee not to contact former clients of the firm was to not make contact with the clients and, therefore, was to be performed or observed where the clients resided, rather than to refrain from instigating communication from the place where the employee lived.[1064] The obligation to use due diligence to ensure that a vessel is seaworthy is one to be performed at the start of the voyage, and performed at the place of loading or departure, but is not a continuing one to be performed wherever the vessel goes.[1065]

These cases are not directly reliable in relation to Article 7(1)(b), of course: they were addressing a different jurisdictional rule. But they do show, in particular with contracts for the provision of service, that the identification of the jurisdictionally-significant service may not always be straightforward. It may be that the Court would say that the service, provision of which points to the place with special jurisdiction, is the service which characterises the contract as one of service, and that in answering that question the court should remember that the search should be guided by the principle that Article 7(1) in general, and Article 7(1)(b) in particular, should lead to a court which reflects the principle of proximity.

Third, a distinct issue arises in relation to contracts for the sale of goods in which payment is made or arranged in the form of a documentary credit. The main contract, for which the payment arrangements are made, is still one for the sale of goods, but the standard-form letter of credit, by which the obligation to pay may be performed, is said to create five separate contractual relationships: buyer–seller; buyer–issuing bank; issuing bank–accepting bank; issuing bank–seller; accepting bank–seller. It is also a cardinal principle of the law and practice of letters of credit that the payment obligation which the credit creates is independent of and dissociated from the underlying contract of sale between buyer and seller. Should any problem arise in the transaction, which leads to non-performance of any of these contracts, it will have to be decided whether the fact that the principal contract was one for the sale of goods gives special jurisdiction only to the place of delivery of goods, no matter who is suing whom and for what relief, because these other contractual relationships are no more than a complicated mechanism of payment having no jurisdictional significance. The alternative would be that each separate and individual contractual relationship, put in place to result in payment, is to be dealt with individually and separately for the purposes of Article 7(1)(b).[1066] If that is correct, it may follow that the participants in the chain of payment obligations – that is to say, in the contracts other than the contract of sale – are providing services to their counterparty, and these have and dictate their own special jurisdiction for the purposes of Article 7(1)(b). It is suggested, very tentatively indeed, that this

---

1063 *Berry v. Bradshaw* [2000] CLC 455.

1064 *Kenburn Waste Management Ltd v. Bergman* [2002] EWCA Civ 98, [2002] ILPr 33.

1065 *The Sea Maas* [1999] 2 Lloyd's Rep 281.

1066 In a case decided under Art. 5(1) of the Brussels Convention, the Court of Appeal in *Chailease Finance Corp v. Crédit Agricole Indosuez* [2000] 1 Lloyd's Rep 348, held that where a bank was obliged to pay under a letter of credit against documents at the Swiss branch of the bank, payment to be as per the beneficiary's instructions, and the bank rejected the documents, the instruction for payment in London made that the place for performance of the obligation in question. There was no reference to the broader contractual network within which this contract had been made. And see, on choice of law, *PT Pan Indonesia Bank Ltd TBK v. Marconi Communications International Ltd* [2005] EWCA Civ 422, [2007] 2 Lloyd's Rep 72.

latter is to be preferred: just because these contractual obligations are put in place to facilitate the performance of a contract of sale, they remain independent and separately negotiated contracts, for the provision of financial services, unlike the payment obligation under the contract of sale itself, for consideration.

2.177 Definition of the obligation in question when the contract is not sale or provision of services: Article 7(1)(a)

Where the contract is within Article 7(1)(a) rather than Article 7(1)(b), the court with special jurisdiction will be identified by reference to the primary obligation on the basis of which the claimant brings the proceedings.[1067] In principle this will be the primary, or performance, obligation whose breach serves as the basis for the claim. It is convenient, therefore, to examine two aspects of the rule applying as Article 7(1)(a). The first is the 'primary or performance obligation' point; the second, the problems which arise when it is necessary to identify the obligation in question when several obligations have been broken and the claim relies on more than one of them. These are not confined to cases under Article 7(1)(a), but they exemplify some of the problems with that jurisdictional rule.

A contract falling under Article 7(1)(a), such as a licensing agreement,[1068] may provide for the performance of an obligation, and in default, for an obligation to pay a sum of money, perhaps by way of liquidated damages.[1069] If proceedings are brought after the failure to perform, claiming the sum agreed as damages, it may be necessary to decide whether the obligation which founds special jurisdiction under Article 7(1)(a) is the obligation to perform under the licensing agreement, or the obligation to pay damages. The question arose in *De Bloos Sprl v. Bouyer SA*.[1070] In that case, a distributorship agreement – but which would now be likely[1071] to fall under Article 7(1)(b) – had been terminated, and it had to be decided whether an action by the distributor for sums payable on termination could be brought in the distributor's own courts. It was possible to construe the obligation in respect of which the claim was brought as being either the duty of the supplier to permit the distributor to trade exclusively within the distributor's territory, or the duty of the supplier to pay a proper sum on the wrongful termination of the distributorship; it was also possible that these obligations were to be performed in different places. The Court appears[1072] to have held that the obligation referred to for the purpose of what is now Article 7(1)(a),[1073] was the obligation of the defendant supplier to perform the supply,[1074] rather than the later-arising obligation upon him to pay damages for failure to perform. In other words, the broken obligation was allowing the distributor to distribute in the designated territory rather than the obligation to pay damages for failure to do so: this latter was seen as a substituted, secondary, as distinct

---

1067 14/76 *De Bloos Sprl v. Bouyer SA* [1976] ECR 1497.

1068 C-533/07 *Falco Privatstiftung v. Weller-Lindhorst* [2009] ECR I-3327.

1069 Such as where a defined sum of money must be paid if a distributorship contract is terminated.

1070 14/76, [1976] ECR 1497.

1071 C-9/12 *Corman-Collins SA v. La Maison du Whisky SA* EU:C:2013:860, [2014] QB 431.

1072 It is not altogether clear what it did mean, but the interpretation offered here accords reasonably well with the judgment, and with logic.

1073 Article 7(1)(a) is to be interpreted in the same way as the earlier Art. 5(1) was: C-533/07 *Falco Privatstiftung v. Weller-Lindhorst* [2009] ECR I-3327.

1074 Corresponding to the concept of the 'primary' obligation of the English law of contract: *Photo Productions Ltd v. Securicor* [1980] AC 827: and not to 'secondary', or compensatory obligations.

from an alternative original, obligation. But if upon a proper construction the contract had provided that the supplier would furnish the distributor with a territory, and later, if he chose, pay a certain sum of money[1075] to terminate the distributorship, the obligation to pay money might be seen as an independent (primary, alternative) obligation, which is itself that in respect of which the action is brought. It must presumably be for the court seised with a claim to which Article 7(1)(a) may apply to use the law which governs the substance of the contract to decide whether an obligation to pay money is a secondary, or substituted, obligation or is instead an alternative primary obligation. One begins to see why this is a jurisdictional rule which stood to gain from legislative improvement.

In the case of actions for a declaration of non-liability, the obligation in question will be that which the defendant alleges should have been performed by the claimant, and which the claimant denies being bound by.[1076]

Where there is more than one such performance obligation on which the claimant founds his claim, the court may be able to see one of them as the principal obligation, which is jurisdictionally significant, to which the others are accessory and therefore jurisdictionally insignificant, and as a result, take jurisdiction over the whole of the contractual claim. But in cases in which the court is unable to do this, it will have special jurisdiction over only part of the claim. Two cases illustrate the point.

In *Shenavai v. Kreischer*,[1077] a German architect sued a Dutch client for his professional fees before the German courts. Of course, the contract would now fall within Article 7(1)(b), but the Court answered the question referred to it by stating that in the case of multiple broken obligations, it may be helpful, where it is possible, to regard ancillary obligations as following the principal obligation: *accessorium sequitur principale*. This would require the court seised to determine for itself which was the principal obligation to which the others could be regarded as ancillary. While that will tend to identify only one court as having special jurisdiction in respect of a party's claim, the identification of an obligation as the principal one may not always be straightforward.

When that happens, three possibilities suggest themselves. One would be to confine *Shenavai* to cases where there really is a principal and an ancillary obligation and, where this would distort the real structure of the contractual obligations, to accept that *Shenavai* cannot be applied. This was the approach of the Court in *Leathertex Divisione Sintetici SpA v. Bodetex BVBA*[1078] in which the national court described the two obligations in question as being of equal prominence. The European Court responded with the predictable, but calamitous, ruling that there was special jurisdiction only over that part of the claim which arose from the obligation which was to be performed within the territory of the referring court, and no jurisdiction over the remainder of the claim, which arose from the other. The second would have been to accept that in cases where there are multiple obligations, but none which may be seen as principal, there is no proper justification for giving special jurisdiction to a court under Article 7(1)(a) at all, for any answer arrived at will not satisfy the principle

---

1075 As liquidated damages.

1076 *Boss Group Ltd v. Boss France SA* [1997] 1 WLR 351; *Fisher v. Unione Italiana de Riassicurazione SpA* [1998] CLC 682; *Youell v. La Réunion Aerienne* [2009] EWCA Civ 175, [2009] 1 Lloyd's Rep 586.

1077 266/85, [1987] ECR 239; followed and applied in *Union Transport plc v. Continental Lines SA* [1992] 1 WLR 15; *Boss Group Ltd v. Boss France SA* [1997] 1 WLR 351; *Source Ltd v. TUV Rheinland Holding AG* [1999] QB 54; *Royal & Sun Alliance Insurance plc v. MK Digital FZE (Cyprus) Ltd* [2006] EWCA Civ 629, [2006] 2 Lloyd's Rep 110.

1078 C-420/97, [1999] ECR I-6747.

of proximity. The Court did say in *Shenavai* that the general justification for special jurisdiction under what is now Article 7 was the closeness of the relationship between the facts of the case and the court called upon to try it.[1079] Where there is no principal obligation, there may be no court whose connection to the facts of the case is so proximate that it should be seen as having special jurisdiction. The third would have been to argue that, by analogy with the decision of the Court in *Handelskwekerij GJ Bier BV v. Mines de Potasse d'Alsace SA*,[1080] the claimant may sue in any of those places in which a part of the obligations sued upon was due to be performed. But for the present, *Leathertex* rules out these two alternatives. The resulting incentive to force the obligations into a principal-accessory relationship must be very strong indeed.

2.178 Locating the place of performance of the obligation in question for contracts falling under Article 7(1)(a)

Having identified the obligation in question, it is next necessary to locate the place of performance within a Member State, so as to identify the court which has special jurisdiction. By contrast with the analysis of what counts as the obligation, in which Article 7(1)(b) was taken first, it is convenient to start with Article 7(1)(a) when dealing with the mechanism for locating the place of performance of the material obligation, the better to appreciate the way the law has developed.

The first port of call is to read the contract and see what it says about the place at which its obligations are to be performed. But if it is not helpful – if the contract states what must be done but not where it must be done – the place of performance must be found by other means. The rule is found in *Industrie Tessili Italiana Como v. Dunlop AG*.[1081] The Court said the national court before which the question had arisen should determine the place for the performance of the obligation which formed the basis for the claim by applying its own private international law to ascertain the law governing the legal relationship in question, and then using that law to identify the place for performance of the relevant obligation. In other words, a court was to apply its own law, including its conflicts rules if necessary, to identify the place of performance.[1082] Where *Tessili* applies, there was no such thing as an 'autonomous location'.

The decision in *Tessili* was much criticised, but the Court never doubted it. Its correctness was confirmed in *Custom Made Commercial Ltd v. Stawa Metallbau GmbH*,[1083] where the courts for the place of payment – as this was defined by the national law of the court seised – were held to have special jurisdiction under the rule which is now Article 7(1)(a). The Court approved *Tessili*, further rejecting the contention that, as the place of payment had, in fact, little to do with the contract or its performance, its courts should be denied special jurisdiction. It reaffirmed the correctness of *Tessili* in *Groupe Concorde v. Master of the Vessel 'Suhadiwarno Panjan'*.[1084] When it did so yet again in *Falco Privatstiftung v. Weller-Lindhorst*,[1085]

1079 See also C-106/95 *MSG v. Les Gravières Rhénanes* [1997] ECR I-911.

1080 21/76 *Handelskwekerij GJ Bier NV v. SA Mines de Potasse d'Alsace* [1976] ECR 1735; see below, para. 2.199.

1081 12/76, [1976] ECR 1473.

1082 See, for a general analysis of how the rule operates for executory contracts, negative contracts, provision of warranties: *Crucial Music Corp v. Klondyke Management AG* [2007] EWHC 1782 (Ch), [2008] Bus LR 327.

1083 C-288/92, [1994] ECR I-2913.

1084 C-440/97, [1999] ECR I-6307.

1085 C-533/07, [2009] ECR I-3327.

it confirmed that the approach to the location of the place of performance of the obligation which had been established in *Tessili* remained applicable to contracts falling within Article 7(1)(a).

The place for performance of a contractual obligation is a matter over which the contracting parties themselves have complete control, and nobody else has any control. If the contract specifies the place for performance, no difficulty will arise.[1086] If the parties have not done so, the law which governs the contract must be resorted to in order for its rules to fill in the gaps which the parties have chosen to leave. It is difficult to see a sensible alternative to this approach. An objection that *Tessili* leads to a lack of uniformity of a question of special jurisdiction is not especially convincing, for everything depends on the manner in which the parties have or have not used their power to select the place of contractual performance. And as the Member States have now harmonised their rules of private international law for contractual obligations,[1087] and hence their approach to identification of the law applicable to a contract made in civil or commercial matters, the prospect of disagreement about locating the place of performance under a contract in any given case diminishes.

Where the obligation in question is the payment of money,[1088] it is not uncommon to find that a contract makes no specific provision for the place of payment. In cases to which Article 7(1)(a) applies, the obligation to pay may be the obligation on which the claimant founds his claim, and in the absence of express specification, the place of payment has to be contractually determined. In English law, the general rule is that the debtor is obliged to seek out his creditor, and pay at the *creditor's* residence.[1089] A similar general rule prevails under the laws of Denmark, Finland, Greece, Italy, Ireland, Netherlands and Sweden. By contrast, the place of payment is generally the place of the *debtor's* residence under the laws of Austria, Belgium, France, Germany, Luxembourg and Spain.[1090] While it may be tiresome that the special jurisdiction of a court under Article 7(1)(a) may turn upon such haphazard rules, a rule is none the less clear for appearing arbitrary.

1086 If they do so, it is not necessary to comply with the formal requirements of Art. 25, even though the clause will indirectly attribute jurisdiction to the court in question: 56/79 *Zelger v. Salinitri* [1980] ECR 89; and see above, para. 2.148. For particular instances of the application of the principle in *Tessili*, see *Viskase Ltd v. Paul Kiefel GmbH* [1999] 1 WLR 1305; *Ferguson Shipbuilders Ltd v. Voith Hydro GmbH & Co* 2000 SLT 229; *Crucial Music Corp v. Klondyke Management AG* [2007] EWHC 1782 (Ch), [2007] Bus LR 327 (both cases on the place of performance of a warranty of quality: at the place of transfer of the thing to which it relates).

1087 The Rome I Regulation, and the earlier Rome Convention on the Law Applicable to Contractual Obligations, enacted in the United Kingdom by the Contracts (Applicable Law) Act 1990, mean that rules for determination of the applicable law in the Member States are pretty much uniform.

1088 The fact that a contract provides that 'general average shall be … adjusted in London' does not make London the place where payment of sums found due was obliged to be made: *The World Hitachi Zosen* (14 March 1996). According to *Mora Shipping Inc v. Axa Corporate Solutions Assurance SA* [2005] EWCA Civ 1069, [2005] 2 Lloyd's Rep 769, a contractual obligation to make a general average payment may be the obligation, but it will pinpoint special jurisdiction only if the obligation (rather than the option) is to pay in a single and identified Member State.

1089 Dicey, Morris and Collins, *The Conflict of Laws*, 15th edn (Sweet & Maxwell, London, 2012), 448; *The Eider* [1893] P 119; *Bank of Scotland v. Seitz* 1990 SLT 584. But *Royal Bank of Scotland v. Cassa di Risparmio* [1991] ILPr 411; aff'd *Financial Times*, 21 January 1992 makes the important point that it is a *general* rule, not an inflexible one; a point confirmed by *Deutsche Rückversicherung AG v. La Fondaria Assicurazioni SpA* [2001] 2 Lloyd's Rep 621. And as payment is now routinely made by electronic means, the idea that a debtor is required to set off in search of his creditor with a big bag of cash is rather unreal, and the rule is all the more easily set aside as a result: *Canyon Offshore Ltd v. GDF Suez E&P Nederland BV* [2014] EWHC 3810 (Comm). The current status of the rule is, therefore, in serious doubt.

1090 See Tebbens, Kennedy and Kohler (eds), *Civil Jurisdiction and Judgments in Europe*, 29.

2.179 Locating the place of performance of the obligation in question for contracts falling under Article 7(1)(b)

The logic of the rule in *Tessili* is obvious, and in a world where logic counted above all, there would be little else to say. The trouble is that if one understands that Article 7(1)(b) was designed to simplify and make more predictable the court with special jurisdiction in relation to contracts for the sale of goods and for the provision of services, and if one accepts that the obligation in question is not identified by reference to the manner in which the claimant elects to frame his claim, there needs to be a clear and predictable identification of the place where the material obligation was to be performed. *Tessili* does not always offer that: if a court finds that the contract with which it is concerned is governed by Ruritanian law, it may have to analyse Ruritanian law in order to decide whether it has jurisdiction to determine a question which will be governed by Ruritanian law. The sense of that will not leap to every mind. One cannot live, or litigate, by logic alone.

Article 7(1)(b) gives special jurisdiction to the courts for the place where, under the contract, the goods were delivered or should have been delivered, and to the place where, under the contract, the services were provided or should have been provided. The use of the words 'under the contract' makes it plain that the material question is where the contract required the goods to be delivered, and where the contract required the services to be provided. If these places are identifiable by plain sight, the court with special jurisdiction will have been identified.

But where that is not so, a uniform rule is applied, displacing *Tessili* from application in relation to what is now Article 7(1)(b). Among other things, this means that the decision of the House of Lords in *Scottish & Newcastle International Ltd v. Othon Ghalanos Ltd*,[1091] in which the court had applied *Tessili* to a contract for the sale of goods which were also to be carried by sea and delivered, is no longer reliable. Although the jurisprudence is not yet complete, it appears that the one thing which the identification of place of performance does *not* involve is recourse to the applicable law. The point emerges clearly from one case, and is implicit in the other.

According to the Court in *Car Trim GmbH v. KeySafety Systems Srl*,[1092] the place for performance will be the place of physical handing over of the goods. It is helpful to see why and how the Court did what it did. It said that the point of reforming the relevant rule on special jurisdiction was to remedy the shortcomings of applying the rules of private international law of the State whose courts are seised and to provide that 'pragmatic determination of the place of enforcement' was based on a purely factual criterion.[1093] It observed that 'the autonomy of the linking factors provided for in [Article 7(1)(b) of Regulation 1215/2012][1094] precludes application of the rules of private international law of the Member State with jurisdiction and the substantive law which would be applicable thereunder. In those

---

1091 [2008] UKHL 11, [2008] Bus LR 583. The contract will be seen as one for the sale of goods (albeit with delivery obligations); a contract simply for the carriage of another's good by sea will be a contract for the provision of services.

1092 C-381/08, [2010] ECR I-1255. The case was decided on the basis of Regulation 44/2001, but for clarity of exposition, the text of the judgment has been amended to make it read as though the judgment was dealing with Regulation 1215/2012. The two Regulations are, on this point, functionally identical. The case was followed and applied without significant alteration in C-87/10 *Electrosteel Europe SA v. Edil Centro SpA* [2011] ECR I-4987.

1093 At [52]. In other words, it was to provide an alternative to the *Tessili* approach.

1094 Article 5(1)(b) of Regulation 44/2001 in the original.

circumstances, it is for the referring court to determine first whether the place of delivery is apparent from the provisions of the contract. Where it is possible to identify the place of delivery in that way, without reference to the substantive law applicable to the contract, it is that place which is to be regarded as the place where, under the contract, the goods were delivered or should have been delivered'.[1095] But where the contract did not indicate the place of delivery, then: 'since the rule on jurisdiction provided for in Article 7(1)(b) is autonomous, it is necessary to determine that place in accordance with another criterion which is consistent with the origins, objectives and scheme of that regulation'.[1096] The conclusion of the Court was that

> 'the place where the goods were physically transferred or should have been physically transferred to the purchaser at their final destination is the most consistent with the origins, objectives and scheme of Regulation 1215/2012 as the "place of delivery" for the purposes of the first indent of Article 7(1)(b). That criterion is highly predictable. It also meets the objective of proximity, in so far as it ensures the existence of a close link between the contract and the court called upon to hear and determine the case. It should be pointed out, in particular, that the goods which are the subject-matter of the contract must, in principle, be in that place after performance of the contract. Furthermore, the principal aim of a contract for the sale of goods is the transfer of those goods from the seller to the purchaser, an operation which is not fully completed until the arrival of those goods at their final destination.'[1097]

If the place of performance, meaning the place of delivery in the sense of transferring physical possession to the buyer, is to be determined from the provisions of the contract, the court should examine all the contractual terms which bear on the issue; it may also pay attention to the general usages of the trade.[1098]

The robustness of the approach in *Car Trim GmbH* may be tested, but it should stand up. If the goods are collected by the buyer's agent, they may be taken to be delivered where the buyer's agent collects and takes possession of them, for even if the buyer does not have physical possession, the delivery of possession to his agent should be enough. It is the physical transfer, as distinct from the transfer of legal title, which is the decisive factor. If the goods are sold under a contract by which the seller retains title until payment has been made, or other obligation performed, the place of delivery will be where under the contract the goods were handed over, regardless of where legal title was at that point.

A uniform approach to the identification of the place where, under the contract, services were to be provided, will also apply to contracts for the provision of services. This is justified by the fact that the two kinds of contract are dealt with in Article 7(1)(b) without any indication that they diverge in any material – still less, major – way. But the leading case on the place of performance under a contract for the provision of services was not directly concerned with how to identify the place, for this was plain on the face of the contract.[1099] Instead, the question was how to proceed where it was evident from the face of the contract

---

1095 At [53]–[55].
1096 At [57].
1097 At [60]–[61].
1098 C-87/10 *Electrosteel Europe SA v. Edil Centro SpA* [2011] ECR I-4987.
1099 *Obiter dicta* in *Deutsche Bank AG v. Petromena ASA* [2013] EWHC 3065 (Comm) favour the place where the labour in performing the service was done over the place where the recipient of all that work received it: at [57]. This serves to highlight an issue which will need to be addressed on another occasion. The view taken here, however, is that it is not correct, and that the 'provision' of services is not the same as the 'performance' of service, and that Art. 7(1)(b) is focused on the former.

that there were to be several places of performance. It therefore makes sense to consider it in relation to the issue on which it is directly authoritative.

2.180 Concentrating the place of performance of the obligation under Article 7(1)(b) when the services are provided in several Member States

The jurisprudence of the Court suggests that a national court should try to find a single place as the place for provision of the service by looking at the contract and the manner in which the services have been provided. It should generally look for the centre of gravity of the obligation in question, but if that does not yield a solution, an alternative place – or even places – of provision may be found. It may be thought at this point that the ends are being allowed to justify the means, but that may be no bad thing if the end is rational and the means are comprehensible.

In *Wood Floor Solutions Andreas Domberger GmbH v. Silva Trade SA*,[1100] the contract called for the provision of services in several Member States; the question was how this affected or determined the place of performance of the obligation in question for the purpose of Article 7(1)(b). The Court indicated that the general need was to identify a single place which could exercise special jurisdiction over the entire contract for the provision of services. The general approach was that it was necessary to find the place of main provision of the services. The first thing to do was to read the contract; if that did not help, the court should look at where the services had been provided in the past; and if that did not help, another place of single reference would be found in the place where the service-provider was domiciled. It is sensible to set out its reasoning *in extenso*.[1101]

It said that:

'It is necessary to indicate the criteria according to which the place of the main provision of services must be determined, when those services are provided in different Member States. Having regard to the objective of predictability laid down by the legislature in recital [15] in the preamble to the regulation, and taking account of the wording of the second indent of Article 7(1)(b), according to which it is the place in a Member State where, under the contract, the services were provided or should have been provided which is decisive, the place of the main provision of services must be deduced, in so far as possible, from the provisions of the contract itself. Thus, in the context of a commercial agency contract, the place where the agent was to carry out his work on behalf of the principal, consisting in particular in preparing, negotiating and, where appropriate, concluding the transactions for which he has authority has to be identified, on the basis of that contract. The determination of the place of the main provision of services according to the contractual choice of the parties meets the objective of proximity, since that place has, by its very nature, a link with the substance of the dispute. If the provisions of a contract do not enable the place of the main provision of services to be determined, either because they provide for several places where services are provided, or because they do not expressly provide for any specific place where services are to be provided, but the agent has already provided such services, it is appropriate, in the alternative, to take account of the place where he has in fact for the most part carried out his activities in the performance of the contract, provided that the provision of services in that place is not contrary to the parties' intentions as it appears from the provisions of the contract. For that purpose, the factual aspects of the case may be taken into consideration, in particular, the time spent in those places and the importance of the activities

---

1100 C-19/09, [2010] ECR I-2121.
1101 The Court's references to Art. 5 of Regulation 44/2001 have been converted to Art. 7 of Regulation 1215/2012. Recital 11 to Regulation 44/2001 is essentially reproduced as Recital 15 to Regulation 1215/2012.

carried out there. It is for the national court seised to determine whether it has jurisdiction in the light of the evidence submitted to it. Fourth, if the place of the main provision of services cannot be determined on the basis of the provisions of the contract itself or its actual performance, the place must be identified by another means which respects the objectives of predictability and proximity pursued by the legislature. For that purpose, it will be necessary for the purposes of the application of the second indent of Article 7(1)(b) to consider, as the place of the main provision of the services provided by a commercial agent, the place where that agent is domiciled. That place can always be identified with certainty and is therefore predictable. Moreover, it has a link of proximity with the dispute since the agent will in all likelihood provide a substantial part of his services there.'

The case therefore stands for a number of propositions. First, the search for the place of performance of the obligation in a contract for the provision of service is designed to find, if this is possible, a single place of provision. Second, the default rule of the place of domicile of the service provider probably depends on this being a realistic interpretation of the facts. A commercial agent does, after all, have a home base which could be regarded as the centre of his professional operations; and though it is not only pedantry which would point out that he may not deliver his professional services there, the court at that place has a reasonable connection with the contract. Third, the decision at this point resembles that used in locating the place of performance of the duties of an employment in *Mulox IBC v. Geels*[1102] and *Rutten v. Cross Medical Ltd*:[1103] if all else has failed, a centre of gravity test is better than nothing.

The 'centre of gravity' approach will often work to organise the contract for the provision of services into a single place, but sometimes it cannot. In *Rehder v. Air Baltic Corp*,[1104] a claim against a passenger airline was subject to special jurisdiction under what is now Article 7(1)(b) at the place of departure or arrival, the passenger being free to select. The case was one in which the centre of gravity approach will not work. Neither the place of embarkation nor the place of disembarkation can be seen as *the* place where, under the contract, the services are provided: the service is provided in, and at all points in between, the two of them. There is no sensible centre of gravity, for if that were to be located at the place where the airline is established, it will fail the general test of proximity and predictability. An answer that there was no court with special jurisdiction would have defeated the purpose of Article 7(1); and in the end the solution adopted by the Court represented the triumph of pragmatism. But by parity of reasoning, it is to be supposed that a contract for the carriage of goods from A to B will be held to involve the provision of services at A and at B, and the principle in *Rehder* will allow special jurisdiction to be asserted in either Member State.

2.181 Concentrating the place of performance of the obligation under Article 7(1)(b) when the goods are to be delivered in several places

In *Color Drack GmbH v. Lexx International Vertriebs GmbH*[1105] a purchaser sued the seller under a contact for the sale of goods on terms of sale or return, complaining that the seller had refused to take back unsold goods and refund the price. It sued for the money due to it

---

1102 C–125/92, [1993] ECR I-4075.
1103 C–383/95, [1997] ECR I-57.
1104 C–204/08, [2009] ECR I-6073.
1105 C–386/05, [2007] ECR I-3699.

in the Member State in which the contract of sale provided for delivery, but it was objected by the seller that as the contracts had provided for delivery at several places within the one Member State, and as the Regulation allocated jurisdiction to the courts of the place, rather than the Member State, it was not open to the claimant to aggregate these and sue, in respect of all the deliveries, before the courts of a single place. The Court appears to have taken the view that the defendant's objection was technical and unmeritorious, for all the deliveries had been into a single Member State. The defendant was well aware that special jurisdiction under what is now Article 7(1)(b) would lie somewhere in Austria; for it to say that it was taken by surprise by being sued at St Johann-im-Pongau, as opposed to elsewhere in Austria, may have been true but was unedifying. The conclusion of the Court was that in such a case, the claim could be brought at the principal place of delivery;[1106] but where there was no such place the claimant could sue in respect of all of the delivery in any place of delivery, as it chose. Insofar as the Court applied the 'centre of gravity' approach to try and bring order to the jurisdictional issue, the primary part of its judgment was predictable and sensible. Less expected was the secondary conclusion for those cases in which the 'centre of gravity' approach did not work.

As to whether the principle in *Color Drack* applied where the places of delivery were in different Member States, the Court evidently did not wish its decision, allowing a claimant to select his court, to be taken as authority for such a case.[1107] But if this was a genuine limitation on the effect of the judgment, it did not last long. The reasoning in *Color Drack* was considered to be applicable in *Rehder v. Air Baltic*, which was a case of service provision in several Member States, and it was referred to without any reservation in *Car Trim GmbH* and in *Wood Floor Solutions Andreas Domberger GmbH*. The original limitation suggested by the Court seems to have been erased.

The result is that the court seised should try to marshal the places where under the contract the goods were to be delivered into a single place, and if it can do so, that will be the place at which special jurisdiction may lie. Where that is simply not possible on the facts, if the several places of delivery are in a single Member State, the claimant may sue in any of them; but where the several places of delivery are in several Member States, it is arguable, if not yet completely clear, that the claimant may sue in any one of those Member States in relation to the whole of the delivery.

2.182 Concentrating the place of performance of the obligation under Article 7(1)(a) when the obligation in question is to be performed in several places

It seems probable that the techniques used to locate or concentrate an obligation in a particular Member State will apply equally to cases in which the contract falls within Article 7(1)(a). Although the technique used to pinpoint the place for performance of the obligation in question will be different, and may involve use of the *lex contractus* to identify the place where the obligation was to be performed, once that place has been found, and has been shown to be two places, or even more than two, a centre of gravity approach will be applicable. This is because the authorities which developed a centre of gravity solution to the problem of multiple jurisdictions were decided on the basis of the

---

1106 This to be determined on the basis of economic criteria: at [40].
1107 C-386/05 *Color Drack GmbH v. Lexx International Vertriebs GmbH* [2007] ECR I-3699, [16].

Brussels Convention. This approach must, therefore, still be applicable to cases falling under Article 7(1)(a).

A distinct problem arises where there is a contractual obligation which is specified for performance, maybe over a period, in all Member States and in none, or to be performed once only, but in a Member State which may be selected from a list. As to the former, the Court in *Besix SA v. WABAG*[1108] ruled that where the obligation is one which calls for the defendant to perform an obligation under the contract in *all* Member (and non-Member) States, as may be seen in the case of a former office-holder's covenant against competing with the claimant, it cannot be accommodated by what is now Article 7(1)(a), which can therefore have no application to it. After all, it can hardly be that the claimant can make his own self-serving selection between the Member States for the purpose of bringing proceedings under Article 7(1)(a). This principle has been applied in a case[1109] in which the defendant had a contractual obligation to pay a sum of money to the claimant in either State A or State B.[1110] It was held that, as the contract did not, on a true construction, oblige the payment to be made in a single and identified Member State, what is now Article 7(1)(a) would not apply to it. The view apparently taken was that what is now Article 7(1)(a) applied only where there was a contractual obligation to perform in a single and identified Member State, as distinct from a contractual obligation to perform in a single Member State but which may be selected, after the date of contracting, from a list. While one must admit that the question was not an easy one to answer, this may be a construction of Article 7(1) which is more restrictive than is really necessary; and it has not been faithfully adhered to.[1111] After all, if a jurisdiction agreement may select two Member States, and be given effect according to its terms,[1112] a similar policy might be found to stretch to a case in which the place for performance is agreed to be in either of two Member States.

2.183 Locating the place of performance if one of the places indicated is in a non-Member State

In *Six Constructions Ltd v. Humbert*,[1113] the claimant in that case was employed on construction sites in various non-Member States, but was also required by his employer to

---

1108 C-265/00, [2002] ECR I-1699.

1109 *Mora Shipping Inc v. Axa Corporate Solutions Assurance SA* [2005] EWCA Civ 1069, [2005] 2 Lloyd's Rep 769 (payment of sums found due as general average; the court suggested that the solution was to employ a jurisdiction clause where the place of payment was not fixed). In fact, in *Mora Shipping Inc* the two States were the United Kingdom and Liberia (or possibly Norway), but the case was not regarded as one in which only the United Kingdom counted for the purposes of Art. 7(1) of what is now the Brussels I Regulation. The issue should not be regarded as settled.

1110 Contrast the case where the obligation in question is to (re)pay money on demand and therefore to pay it, as a matter of English law, at the place where the creditor resides on the date of the demand: the contract is one in which there is only one place of payment, even though it may not be known, prior to the making of the demand, which place that is: *Tavoulareas v. Tsavliris* [2005] EWHC 2140 (Comm), [2006] 1 All ER (Comm) 109, [48] *et seq*.

1111 *Canyon Offshore Ltd v. GDF Suez E&P Nederland BV* [2014] EWHC 3810 (Comm) concluded that where the obligation in question could be performed in either England or Scotland, the claimant was entitled to assert special jurisdiction in either place, according to his choice. This may be correct, but insofar as it increases the number of courts with special jurisdiction, it decreases legal certainty (and to say that the defendant can hardly claim to be taken by surprise is, it is submitted, rhetorical but insufficient as support). It may also be confined to cases of multiple special jurisdictions within the territory of a single Member State.

1112 See above, para. 2.138.

1113 32/88, [1989] ECR 341.

report periodically to the employer in Belgium. The Court interpreted the facts as amounting to a case in which the whole of the contractual duties which founded jurisdiction under Article 5(1) of the Brussels Convention, as it then was, namely the obligation of the employee to work, were performed, and were liable to be performed, outside the Member States. It therefore gave rise to no special jurisdiction in the courts of a Member State. On the facts of the case this was puzzling, for part of the relevant contractual obligation was to be performed in Belgium, and the rest in non-Member States. It may be that the principal obligation, to which the obligation to report was ancillary, was to be performed in non-Member States, but the Court did not say so, and the case is direct authority only for a case in which the whole of the relevant contractual obligation is to be performed in non-Member States.

In a case in which the obligation in question does involve some performance in non-Member States, a court will have to decide between two possible lines of analysis. One would require it to take the obligation in its entirety, and determine whether the centre of gravity is in a Member State. If it is, the court at that place will have special jurisdiction; if it is not, it will not have special jurisdiction. The other would be to ignore the performance in a non-Member State altogether, and to discern special jurisdiction from only that part of the performance as, under the contract, was to be performed in a Member State. In the absence of authority, it is submitted that the former is the correct approach, and the one which more precisely reflects the reason for special jurisdiction in the first place.

2.184 Joinder of contractual and non-contractual claims in the same proceedings

Suppose a claim which is based upon the special jurisdictional rules of Article 7(1) of the Regulation also contains another, *non*-contractual, claim,[1114] such as for the return of property.[1115] The question is whether the court has special jurisdiction over all aspects of the claim, or only over those parts of it which fall within the autonomous definition of 'matters relating to a contract' and over which it has jurisdiction under Article 7(1). The answer is the latter.

In general, the Brussels I Regulation does not permit special jurisdiction to be asserted over a claim over which the court would not otherwise have jurisdiction, on the sole basis that the claim is related to one over which it does have jurisdiction. It is true that the Court in *Martin Peters Bauunternehmung GmbH v. Zuid Nederlandse AV*[1116] emphasised the need to interpret what is now Article 7(1)(a) so as to prevent the court seised having to adjudicate upon some, but being unable to adjudicate upon other related, issues. From this it could be, and should perhaps have been, argued that, if the main body of the claim is one over which the court seised does have jurisdiction, it should also have jurisdiction over those ancillary

---

1114 That is, non-contractual for the purposes of Art. 7(1), whatever may be the substantive basis of the claim. It is assumed for present purposes that the court would not have had jurisdiction over this aspect of the claim if it had been brought alone. If it would have had jurisdiction over it upon the basis of a different provision of the Regulation, no problem will arise.

1115 On the footing that such a claim complaining of the wrongful detention of another's goods is not seen, even in this context, as a matter relating to a contract.

1116 34/82, [1983] ECR 987. See also C-214/89 *Powell Duffryn Ltd v. Petereit* [1992] ECR I-1745 (relationship between shareholder and company within the autonomous meaning).

or related aspects of it which are not in this sense contractual.[1117] Or, to put it another way, the matter not relating to a contract could be seen as accessory to the principal matter which did relate to a contract.

But there is a pervasive but unpersuasive argument against this, which derives from the need, sometimes expressed,[1118] to interpret what is now Article 7(1) restrictively, so that it does not call into question the general jurisdiction of the court of the defendant's domicile. In *Kalfelis v. Bankhaus Schröder Münchmeyer Hengst & Co*,[1119] the Court interpreted what is now Article 7(2) of Regulation 1215/2012, which governs special jurisdiction in cases of tort and delict, as permitting the court to assert[1120] jurisdiction only over such parts of the claim as related to tort or delict. The stated justification was to discourage claims from being brought outside the courts of the defendant's domicile. The Court built on this foundation in *Leathertex Divisione Sintetici SpA v. Bodetex BVBA*,[1121] in coming to the conclusion that where a commission agent brought an action against his principal for unpaid arrears of commission and for compensation for early termination of the agency, and relied on what is now Article 7(1)(a) of the Regulation to do so, the national court had special jurisdiction over only so much of the claim as was founded on an obligation which was to be performed within its territorial jurisdiction. As only one of the two obligations required performance to be within the jurisdiction of the court, the court had jurisdiction over only that fraction of the claim.

One may admit the logic of the decision but doubt the result. It does not seem to fit with the sensible and pragmatic advice in *Martin Peters* about not interpreting Article 7(1) so that a court had jurisdiction over only part of a claim. Rather, it seems to have been a casualty of the occasional urge to reduce the attraction of special jurisdiction. It may well have surprised the Court which decided *Martin Peters* to learn that, for jurisdictional purposes, *Leathertex* did not involve a single claim, but two separate ones. It also delivered the *coup de grâce* to the wisdom of the Advocate General, Mr Darmon,[1122] who had advised the Court of his opinion that, where there is a contractual claim over which the court has special jurisdiction, other related claims should be 'channelled' into the same jurisdiction, which will have been foreseen by the parties as competent in any event.

If the aim of Article 7(1) is to give jurisdiction to a court which is the proper forum for the claim, there is no excuse for reading it down. For all that, it follows from *Leathertex*, therefore, that if a court may not join a related contractual claim into proceedings which are founded on Article 7(1), the prohibition upon joining a non-contractual one is *a fortiori*. Of course, if the defendant does not make a fuss, and enters an appearance before the court, this fact will confirm the court's jurisdiction, by reason of Article 26, over the whole of the claim.

1117 Within the autonomous definition of the term. It is clear that they would be within a liberal interpretation of 'matters relating to a contract'.

1118 Though, notably, expressly contradicted by the Court in C-27/02 *Engler v. Janus Versand GmbH* [2005] ECR I-481, [48].

1119 189/87, [1988] ECR 5565; examined in detail in para. 2.188 *et seq.*, below.

1120 Unless, of course, the defendant enters an appearance, or does not otherwise object, in respect of those other parts of the claim.

1121 C 420/97, [1999] ECR I-6747.

1122 Advocate General in 189/87 *Kalfelis v. Bankhaus Schröder Münchmeyer Hengst & Co* [1988] ECR 5565; and C-89/91 *Shearson Lehmann Hutton Inc v. TVB* [1993] ECR I-139. And see references to 'canalisation' in *Knauf UK v. British Gypsum Ltd* [2001] EWCA Civ 1570, [2002] 1 Lloyd's Rep 199, [57].

2.185 International jurisdiction in the United Kingdom

As Article 7(1) of the Regulation gives jurisdiction to the courts for the place – not to the courts of the State – where the obligation was to be performed, international jurisdiction will be given directly to the courts of England, or Scotland or Northern Ireland. There is neither room nor need for rules of internal United Kingdom law to specify the part of the United Kingdom which has jurisdiction. Equally, if the Regulation gives jurisdiction to the courts of a place within, or part of, the United Kingdom, there can be no question of a rule of English law, such as *forum non conveniens*, being employed to obtain a stay of proceedings in favour of the courts of another part of the United Kingdom which, *ex hypothesi*, do not have jurisdiction according to the Regulation.[1123]

2.186 Special jurisdiction in matters relating to tort, delict and quasi-delict: Article 7(2)

Article 7(2) of Regulation 1215/2012 provides:

> *A person domiciled in a Member State may be sued in another Member State:*
> *(2) in matters relating to tort, delict or quasi-delict, in the courts for the place where the harmful event occurred or may occur.*

Article 7(2) of Regulation 1215/2012 is functionally identical to Article 5(3) of Regulation 44/2001. Article 7(2) is the counterpart to Article 7(1); the special jurisdiction which it confers is also the subject of some considerable complexity, and its relationship with Article 7(1) is not completely easy to determine.

The special jurisdiction established by what is now Article 7(2) is based on the proposition that, if jurisdiction is given to the courts at the place where the harmful event occurred, it will tend to give, in general and in principle, jurisdiction to a court which has a close connection with the facts giving rise to the dispute. This will give effect to the principle of proximity and will therefore make it likely that a defendant will know in advance where he is liable to be sued. It will also facilitate the sound administration of justice, the efficacious conduct of proceedings, and the taking of evidence. To some extent[1124] the detailed elucidation of Article 7(2) is undertaken with those general aims in mind.[1125]

2.187 Matters relating to tort, delict or quasi-delict: introduction

Mirroring the manner in which the expression 'matters relating to a contract' has been given an autonomous meaning, 'matters relating to a tort... ' likewise has an autonomous meaning. One effect of this is that the material scope of Article 7(2) does not correspond exactly to the English law of tort.

1123 C-386/05 *Color Drack GmbH v. Lexx International Vertriebs GmbH* [2007] ECR I-3699. Earlier decisions such as *Ivax Pharmaceuticals UK Ltd v. AKZO Nobel BV* [2005] EWHC 2658 (Comm), [2006] FSR 888 and *Sunderland Marine Mutual Insurance Co Ltd v. Wiseman, The 'Seaward Quest'* [2007] EWHC 1460 (Comm), [2007] 2 Lloyd's Rep 308 must be reassessed in the light of *Color Drack*.

1124 But where the proper application of Art. 7(2) gives special jurisdiction to a court which, on the particular facts, does not actually have so close a connection, this will not call into question the application of Art. 7(2). The Article may be inspired by, but does not enact, a rule of *forum conveniens* as such.

1125 See on this, C-189/08 *Zuid-Chemie BV v. Phillippo's Mineralenfabriek NV/SA* [2009] ECR I-6917, [24] and the cases there cited.

The starting point is the decision in *Kalfelis v. Bankhaus Schröder Münchmeyer Hengst & Co.*[1126] Claims were made in Germany against a bank domiciled in Luxembourg and against two German-domiciled intermediaries, alleging the commission of a tort,[1127] and unjust enrichment, by reference to the provisions of German domestic law. The question was whether it was, in principle, open to the German court to exercise special jurisdiction over all or any of these claims by reference to what is now Article 7(2). The Court held that the expression 'matters relating to a tort, delict or quasi-delict'[1128] had an autonomous meaning, and that this meaning comprehended 'all actions which seek to establish the liability[1129] of a defendant and which are not related to a contract within the meaning of Article 7(1)'.

It was inevitable that the expression should be held to have an autonomous meaning. But the content of that meaning may not be obvious at first sight: in particular, to the extent that the content of the autonomous meaning of 'matters relating to a contract' is uncertain, the meaning of 'matters relating to tort' will mirror it. In cases of difficulty, the point of departure is to ask whether the subject matter of the claim made relates to a contract in the sense of Article 7(1) of Regulation 1215/2012. That condition will be met if the claim could have been brought as a claim alleging breach of contract, or if the contract needs to be pleaded and proved to establish the cause of action even though the claim is not formulated as one for breach of contract.[1130] If it does, the claim cannot be brought as a matter of special jurisdiction within Article 7(2), even if national law would allow the substance of the claim to be pleaded as a tort, or as a claim in contract or tort or both. But if the matter does not relate to a contract in this sense, the proceedings may fall within Article 7(2).

It will be recalled that Article 7(1) is in principle applicable where the claimant seeks a declaration of non-liability to a party who alleges that a contractual obligation is owed to him and has been broken. The same principle applies to a claim for a declaration of non-liability brought by a person against another who alleges that the former owes liability in tort: Article 7(2) operates by reference to the components of the tort which are alleged against the person who appears as defendant but who contends that he is the victim of a tort.[1131] That may be surprising, but it is the law.

2.188 Matters relating to tort, delict or quasi-delict: the decision in *Kalfelis* and the meaning of liability

The definition put forward in *Kalfelis* is, at first sight, wide and uncomplicated in its scope. If all cases which seek to establish the liability of a defendant, but which do not relate to a contract within the meaning of Article 7(1), fall within Article 7(2), it might seem that

---

1126 189/87, [1988] ECR 5565. See also C-261/90 *Reichert v. Dresdner Bank (No 2)* [1992] ECR I-2149.

1127 Acting in bad faith.

1128 Abbreviated hereafter to 'matters relating to a tort.

1129 In French, *'responsabilité'*; in German *'Schadenshaftung'*. Each is said to convey more clearly than does the English paraphrase, the idea of liability for doing damage; as to which see further below. Note that the Court referred to Art. 5(1), not 7(1), as it was dealing with a Brussels Convention case; the quotation had been brought up to date for convenience of reference.

1130 C-548/12 *Brogsitter v. Fabrication de Montres Normandes EURL* EU:C:2014:148, [2014] QB 753.

1131 C-133/11 *Folien Fischer AG v. Ritrama SpA* EU:C:2012:664, [2013] QB 523. For an earlier English decision to the same effect, see *Equitas Ltd v. Wave City Shipping Co Ltd* [2005] EWHC 923 (Comm), [2005] 2 All ER (Comm) 301.

every claim raised against a defendant in a civil or commercial matter, so long as it is not one relating to a contract, will fall within Article 7(2). A definition drawn in these terms would have the advantage that it did not require any further lines to be drawn, but there is something counterintuitive about adopting such a solution, not least because the rest of Article 7, or even the rest of the Regulation, would be redundant or at least overlapped-with. It is therefore proposed to examine the reasoning in *Kalfelis*, then the proper interpretation of 'liability', and last, the extent to which (if at all) that definition can encompass actions against a defendant other than for the payment of damages for breach of a common law duty or its equivalent.

From time to time a decision would suggest that special jurisdiction under Article 7(2) is confined to claims which are in the nature of what an English court sees as a claim in the nature of a tort.[1132] Whenever this happened it provoked more doubt than anything else. The Court interpreted the expression 'matters relating to tort delict or quasi-delict' in what is now Regulation 1215/2012 as covering 'all actions which seek to establish the liability of a defendant and which are not related to a "contract" within the meaning of' what is now Article 7(1). This, rather than any other sense of what amounts to a tort, forms the basis for interpreting the words used in Article 7(2). A further question referred by the German court concerned the principles of accessory jurisdiction, to which the Court gave this answer: 'a court which has jurisdiction over an action in so far as it is based on tort or delict does not have jurisdiction over that action in so far as it is not so based'.[1133] Putting all this together, the ruling of the Court was that 'a court which has jurisdiction to establish the liability of a defendant in a case which is not related to a contract within the meaning of Article [7(1)] does not have jurisdiction over that action in so far as it does not seek to establish such liability'. There is no obvious room for a further restriction to claims which are in the nature of torts according to English (or some other) domestic law. Moreover, a number of language versions of the Brussels I Regulation simply define the subject matter of what is now Article 7(2) as 'non-contractual' matters;[1134] and there is the authority of the Advocate General in *Kalfelis* itself for the proposition that claims founded on unjust enrichment were located by reason that judgment within Article 7(2).[1135]

A more promising restriction of the material scope of Article 7(2) would focus on the concept of 'liability', and contend that this has a narrower meaning than simply being on the receiving end of a claim form.[1136] It may be said that the ideas of *'responsabilité'*, and of *'Schadenshaftung'*, which represent the original versions[1137] of the material words in the judgment in *Kalfelis*, connote more clearly than does the English term 'liability', the obligation to pay for wrongdoing. From this point of view, the obligation on a defendant bailee to return the bailed property would not be seen in this sense as liability. The obligation

---

1132 *Kleinwort Benson Ltd v. Glasgow City Council* [1999] 1 AC 153; *Agnew v. Länsförsäkringsbolagens AB* [2001] 1 AC 223, to the same effect.

1133 The referring court had asked the question in this form; it did not ask whether claims in respect of unjust enrichment fell within what is now Art. 7(2). Accordingly, the Court did not address the issue in direct words.

1134 In Portuguese, *'em matéria extracontratual'*; in Danish *'i sager om erstatning uden for contract'*. And note the reference in C-364/93 *Marinari v. Lloyds Bank plc* [1995] ECR I-2719, [18], to the scope of what is now Art. 7(2) as being 'non-contractual civil liability', and not something narrower than that.

1135 In C-89/91 *Shearson Lehmann Hutton Inc v. TVB* [1993] ECR I-139, at [102] of the Opinion.

1136 An alternative solution, which approaches that to be discussed below, is to confine Art. 7(2) to claims arising from the law of obligations.

1137 The Court drafts its judgments in French; the language of the case in *Kalfelis* was German.

upon someone who has unjustly enriched himself at the expense of another to disgorge the profit he has made, or the obligation imposed on a man whose blazing house was saved from conflagration by the intervention of another, to pay the person who has benevolently intervened in his affairs, does not exist to enforce a liability to compensate for wrongdoing, but to reverse the enrichment which it is unjust that he receive yet not pay for.

If that were accepted, claims to reverse unjust enrichment would not, or would not generally, fall within Article 7(2) of the Regulation, as they do not focus on 'liability' on the part of the defendant. Likewise, it may be argued, claims against a fiduciary who is held to be constructive trustee for another of the gains he has made, but whose status as such does not derive from an independent act of wrongdoing, would not involve the enforcement of liability by an order for compensation, rather the obtaining and delivery of what is already, in equity, the property of the beneficiary.

Such an interpretation would have limited attraction. If it is accepted that the philosophy of Article 7(2) is to give special jurisdiction to a court which is likely to have a close connection to the facts of the case, this is easy enough to see in a tort claim, but claims based on unjust enrichment are less likely to have a natural or proximate forum in the way a tort claim does. On the other hand, a claim by an owner for the return of chattels, brought in the form of an action for conversion or other tort, is framed in English law as an allegation of wrongdoing on the part of the defendant: in denying the title of the claimant he commits a wrongful act for which damages are payable. Next, a claim that a recipient of a sum, the retention of which unjustly enriches him, must hand it over, may require a prior demand with which the defendant has failed to comply. Would this refusal be seen as a wrongful act? Why is keeping something which you have no justification for keeping not itself a wrongful act? Third, a fiduciary who stands as constructive trustee for the claimant of the profit he has made or the bribe he has taken, is in this position because of his wrongful[1138] act; but the effect of his wrongful act is to constitute the beneficiary the equitable owner of the property. Is the action against such a defendant an attempt to enforce liability but with a remedial order calibrated by reference to the profit rather than the loss?

2.189 Matters relating to tort, delict or quasi-delict: subsequent jurisprudence of the Court

In the cases which came after *Kalfelis*, the Court said little to clarify what it meant, but also said little to cut down the apparent width of what it had said in *Kalfelis*. One plausible explanation for that is that the Court saw no need to elucidate something which was perfectly clear, and that it is no part of its job to take notice of over-excited academic quibbling.

In *Reichert v. Dresdner Bank (No 2)*[1139] an argument was made to the effect that a claim by a creditor for an order against a transferee of property from the debtor was not effective against the creditor[1140] and fell within what is now Article 7(2) of Regulation 1215/2012. The Court ruled that it did not; and it was plainly right to do so. The claim raised in the proceedings did not seek to establish the liability of anybody to anybody else, or seek the

---

1138 The inherently wrongful character of claims against a dishonest assister of another's breach of trust was established in *Royal Brunei Airlines Sdn Bhd v. Tan* [1995] 2 AC 378; for the proposition that the bribe accepted by a servant belongs immediately in equity to the master, see *Attorney-General for Hong Kong v. Reid* [1994] AC 324.

1139 C-261/90, [1992] ECR I-2149.

1140 Brought under Art. 1167 of the French Civil Code; also known as the *actio pauliana*.

handing over of property on any other basis. It made a note, lodged a caveat, against the property in the hands of the transferee, noting the fact that this property could, at a later date, be available to an unsatisfied creditor of the particular debtor. It was, if anything, part of the law of credit and security, but the proceedings did not seek to establish liability in any present or enforceable form. This means that it is of limited help in seeking to map the outer limits of the definition in *Kalfelis*.

In *Réunion Européenne SA v. Spliethoff's Bevrachtingskantoor BV*,[1141] a claim brought by the consignee of a cargo of fruit, damaged in the course of its carriage by sea, was held not to be a matter relating to contract, as there was no such relationship between the consignee and the actual sea carrier. The Court therefore applied the principle in *Kalfelis* to state that the claim fell within what is now Article 7(2): it simply said that as the matter did not relate to a contract, it fell within what is now Article 7(2). But as the allegation against the defendant was of wrongfully damaging another's property by fault, there was no need for it to say any more; and the decision does not really advance the argument.

In *Fonderie Officine Meccaniche Tacconi SpA v. Heinrich Wagner Sinto Maschinenfabrik GmbH*,[1142] a claim was made for damages on the basis that a defendant had acted in bad faith in failing to conclude a contract with his counterparty in negotiations. Having concluded that the claim was not to be seen as one relating to a contract, no doubt because it was common ground (and the very basis for complaint) that there was no contract between the parties, the Court referred to *Kalfelis* to establish, without further analysis, that the matter before the court fell within Article 7(2). But on any view the liability was based on fault; it therefore fell naturally within Article 7(2).

More data is provided by *VfK v. Henkel*.[1143] In that case, proceedings were taken by a body to prevent the use by a trader of unfair terms in his contracts with consumers. Having established that the matter before the court did not relate to a contract, as there was no contractual relationship between the authority and the trader, the Court said, almost immediately, that it was within the scope of what is now Article 7(2). But it did not do so by saying that it was 'therefore' within the scope of Article 7(2); it stated that 'by contrast' the matter satisfied the requirements of Article 7(2).[1144] It explained that the proceedings concerned the 'liability' of the trader. For though there was no loss which had been caused to anybody, still less a loss which called for compensation for the wrong, the proceedings against the trader were brought to establish liability, because, as the Court put it, 'the concept of "harmful event" within the meaning of Article [7(1) of Regulation 1215/2012] is broad in scope... so that, with regard to consumer protection, it covers not only situations where an individual has personally sustained damage but also, in particular, the undermining of legal stability by the use of unfair terms which it is the task of associations such as the VKI to prevent'. The judgment is a little opaque, but it does appear to proceed on the basis that the trader was committing a wrong, and that Article 7(2) applied as a result.

In *Engler v. Janus Verstand GmbH*[1145] the Advocate General doubted the rightness of what he called a 'simple binary' classification. He would have defined the material scope of Article 7(2) in positive terms, as requiring the breach of a legal rule, damage and

---

1141 C-51/97, [1998] ECR I-6511.
1142 C-334/00, [2002] ECR I-7357.
1143 C-167/00, [2002] ECR I-8111.
1144 At [41].
1145 C-27/02, [2005] ECR I-481.

compensation which may be reduced on account of fault or remoteness of harm, with the consequence that certain matters might be outside Articles 7(1) and 7(2). But the Court lent no support to the suggestion, simply repeating[1146] what it had said in *Kalfelis*.

The issue might have arisen but was not raised in *Freistaat Bayern v. Blijdenstein*.[1147] Proceedings were brought by the State of Bavaria to reclaim from a defendant sums which had been advanced by the State as financial support for the daughter whom the defendant had neglected. A question was referred to the Court on whether the proceedings fell within Article 5(2) of the Brussels Convention. The principal question was whether the State, subrogated to the rights of the daughter, who had a claim against the defendant for mainte-nance, was entitled to take advantage of the jurisdictional privilege which Article 5(2) would have extended to the daughter. The Court ruled that the State was not, on the footing that it had no need of the jurisdictional advantage which would have benefited the daughter, even though it was subrogated to her rights. One might have expected this to prompt the ques-tion whether, if Article 5(2) was not available, Article 5(3) might have been used instead, on the footing that the defendant had caused financial loss to the State. But the reference from the German court asked no question about Article 5(3), and the Court said nothing about it.

In *ÖFAB v. Koot*[1148] proceedings were brought against the managers of a company who, as it was alleged, had caused financial loss to the creditors of that company by their negligent conduct of its affairs. Having first concluded that there was no contract between the managers and the creditors, with the result that what is now Article 7(1) would not apply, the Court analysed the nature of the claim made in some detail before concluding that it fell within Article 7(2), on the basis that it sought compensation for harm caused by neglect of legal duty.

Pausing there, it is probably correct to say that the cases in which the Court has said, without further explanation, that Article 7(2) applies because Article 7(1) does not are cases in which it is common ground that the allegation against the defendant is of wrongdoing. The cases in which the Court has appeared to examine whether the criteria for the applica-tion of Article 7(2) are satisfied would tend to suggest that there are some claims which will fall outside Article 7(1) yet not fall within Article 7(2).[1148A]

In this respect, decisions of the English courts may be of secondary significance. Even so, it has been held that claims for infringement of patents are within what is now Article 7(2):[1149] the European Court would certainly agree. The same is true for claims which allege equitable liability for dishonest assistance of another's breach of trust, for on any view they are based on wrongdoing.[1150] Whether claims based on the receipt of trust property are within Article 7(2) may depend on whether the basis of liability is the wrongfulness of the receipt or the uncon-scionability of the failure to return or account for it.[1151] It does not seem difficult to say that the basis for liability is some form of wrongdoing which causes financial loss to the claimant,

---

1146 At [29] and [60].

1147 C-433/01 [2004] ECR I-981.

1148 C-147/12, EU:C:2013:490, [2015] QB 20.

1148A But in C-375/13 *Kolassa v Barclays Bank plc* EU:C:2015:37, at [44], the judgment suggests that evalu-ation is necessary to decide if Art. 7(2) applies, it having been held that Art. 7(1) did not. This seems to be a *faux pas* on the part of the Court.

1149 *Mölnlycke AB v. Procter & Gamble Ltd* [1992] 1 WLR 1112.

1150 *Casio Computers Co Ltd v. Sayo* [2001] EWCA Civ 661.

1151 *Bank of Credit and Commerce International (Overseas) Ltd v. Akindele* [2001] Ch 437, CA. The decision in *Dexter Ltd v. Harley*, *The Times*, 2 April 2001, to the effect that knowing receipt is based on a wrong and falls within Art. 7(2), cannot be taken to settle the matter; see on this Yeo (2001) 117 LQR 560.

with the consequence that such a claim may fall within Article 7(2) of the Regulation. So also will a claim which alleges conversion (whether by retention or by unauthorised use) of another's property. Though English courts have not quite decided the question,[1152] claims alleging breach of confidence, as between parties who have never made a contract with each other, should be seen as falling within Article 7(2).

On the other hand, a claim to assert title to a patent is not within Article 7(2), as it does seek to establish liability in the material sense.[1153] And a claim for the return of money paid under an admittedly void contract has been held not to fall within Article 7(2), on the footing that the claim was in substance restitutionary, and was not (or therefore not) based on tort or delict.[1154] Insofar as this conclusion was derived from the internal organisation of English domestic law it is not satisfactory. The fact that English domestic law does not characterise the claim as lying in tort, because money – unlike other property – is not converted by misuse, ought not to be relevant to the operation of Article 7(2). Had the House of Lords said that the claim fell outside Article 7(2) because it was not based on liability in the requisite sense, this would have been preferable, though not necessarily correct. After all, the proposition that, by reason of another's mistake, a person who receives money to which he was never entitled, and who proposes to keep every last penny of it even though the truth has now come to light, does not commit anything which could be considered as a wrong, would make most decent people rub their eyes in disbelief. The proposition that a claim for repayment could[1155] not fall within Article 7(2) is not convincing.[1156]

2.190 Matters relating to tort, delict or quasi-delict: the relationship between Article 7(2) and the Rome II Regulation

The decisions referred to in the previous paragraph were almost all handed down before the adoption of the Rome II Regulation. The vivid question which therefore arises is whether illumination is to be had from that instrument, and in particular the way it organises non-contractual obligations for the purpose of identifying the applicable law.

On one view, the material scope of Article 7(2) is aligned with Chapter II of the Rome II Regulation, which is entitled 'torts/delicts'. It would follow that Article 7(2) does not extend to 'unjust enrichment, *negotiorum gestio* and *culpa in contrahendo*', which form Chapter III of the Rome II Regulation, and which are therefore seen by the legislator as separate and distinct from obligations arising out of a tort or delict. But on another view, the material scope of Article 7(2) should be the same as that of the Rome II Regulation, that is, it covers the whole of non-contractual obligations in civil and commercial matters, whether these are torts/delicts within Chapter II of the Rome II Regulation or non-contractual obligations within Chapter III but which are not torts or delicts within Chapter II of the Rome II Regulation.

Although Recital (7) to the Rome II Regulation states that 'the substantive scope of this Regulation should be consistent with' the Brussels I Regulation, the Court rather read this

---

1152 *Kitechnology BV v. Unicor GmbH Plastmaschinen* [1995] FSR 765.

1153 *Future New Developments Ltd v. B&S Patente und Marken GmbH* [2014] EWHC 1874 (IPEC).

1154 *Kleinwort Benson Ltd v. Glasgow City Council* [1999] 1 AC 153 (a case on the same wording but in Sch. 4 to the 1982 Act, allotting jurisdiction as between England and Scotland. On this point there was no dissent.

1155 The issue is neither whether there is liability in the individual case, nor what the juristic basis for any claim might be, but the proper interpretation of a jurisdictional rule in a European instrument.

1156 See further, Briggs, 'Misappropriated and Misapplied Assets in the Conflict of Laws', in Degeling and Edelman (eds), *Unjust Enrichment in Commercial Law* (Thomson Reuters, Australia, 2008).

Recital down in *Kainz v. Pantherwerke AG*.[1157] The Court was called upon to identify the court with special jurisdiction under what is now Article 7(2) in circumstances in which a defective bicycle had been manufactured in one Member State, but sold and bought in another. In interpreting the relevant jurisdictional rule of the Brussels I Regulation, the Court refused to see the provision of the Rome II Regulation which identified the applicable law as having any relevance. This is, no doubt, correct; but it does not mean, and should not mean, that the Brussels I Regulation takes no account of the existence and structure of the Rome II Regulation. All that *Kainz* decides is that if the answer provided by the Brussels I Regulation is clear, the Rome II Regulation does not call it into question.

Having said that, there is some relationship between Article 7(2) and the Rome II Regulation, and the only question is what that relationship is. The Rome II Regulation has created, more formally than before, a legislative distinction between non-contractual obligations which are torts, and non-contractual obligations which are not torts. That distinction was not available to the Court in cases decided prior to *ÖFAB v. Koot*,[1158] with the result that it is not possible to say what the Court would have said in those cases if things had been different.

The answer proposed here, therefore, can be little more than an exercise in prediction. One must therefore tread lightly. But Rome II does articulate a distinction between torts and delicts, on the one hand, and non-contractual obligations which are not torts or delicts, on the other. It appears to draw a distinction between causes of action based on allegations of harmful conduct, and allegations of liability which is not imposed as a response to harmful conduct. If that is correct, one would expect Article 7(2) to apply to causes of action which fall within Chapter II of the Rome II Regulation, but would not necessarily expect it to apply to those causes of action which, for purposes of the applicable law, fall into the rather miscellaneous collection which makes up Chapter III of the Rome II Regulation.

However that may be, there is no clear decision from the European Court on whether a claim which alleges that the defendant has been unjustly enriched at the expense of the claimant, and should now be ordered to make payment to the claimant, falls within Article 7(2). Unless the claim is one which, as a matter of fact, relates to a contract (for example, it arises on the frustration, or rescission, or avoidance, or termination for total failure of consideration), it will fall within Article 7(2) only if it is based on wrongdoing giving rise to loss; and in this context, simple receipt and retention is not a wrong. It is extraordinary that the law on this point remains unsettled,[1159] but one cannot pretend that there is only one answer to which a court could properly come.

2.191 Matters relating to tort, delict or quasi-delict: pre-contractual liability, and proceedings which find fault with the making of a contract

Where the foundation of proceedings is a complaint of fault or wrongdoing in the negotiation of a contract, whether that is based on misstatement, or failure to make disclosure, or the application of improper pressure, English law allows for two broad, and non-exclusive, responses. One makes a direct challenge to the validity of the contract, and permits the

---

1157 C-45/13, EU:C:2014:7, [2015] QB 34.
1158 C-147/12, EU:C:2013:490, [2015] QB 20.
1159 It is also correct to observe that the cautious position taken here, which would mean that some claims based on unjust enrichment fall outside Art. 7 altogether, is not the view which was advanced in earlier editions.

injured party to rescind the contract and be restored to the position which he was in prior to the entry into the contract, with judicial assistance if necessary. The other takes the form of a money award, which is designed to put the claimant into the financial position which he would have been in today had he not entered into the contract.

While all this makes sense as a matter of domestic law, it gives rise to complication when an aggrieved contracting party in such a case seeks to rely on the special jurisdiction provisions of Articles 7(1) and 7(2). The reasons are many, but they include the following: (a) that the cause of action for a money judgment usually takes the form of a claim in tort – fraud, deceit, negligence, intimidation; (b) in such cases, the contract is not so much the foundation of the claim as it is the basis of the loss for which the claim seeks compensation, in the sense that without the contract there would be no loss; (c) the financial consequence of the claim in tort may be likened to the money equivalent of rescission;[1160] (d) rescission of a contract in English law is often a self-help remedy, the role of the court being simply to confirm that the party claiming to have rescinded was entitled to and did rescind; it is not correctly understood as a claim that a court should make an order annulling or dissolving the contract; (e) it is unlikely that the laws of other Member States deal with such issues in precisely the same way as the common law does; (f) the Rome II Regulation regards obligations arising from pre-contractual fault as non-contractual, but also as non-tortious; and (g) the Court has said, albeit very briefly, that liability for pre-contractual matters may be contractual and so within Article 7(1).[1161] The various ways in which complaints which allege misrepresentation, and other grounds of liability associated with a contract, are accommodated by the special jurisdictional rules of Articles 7(1) and 7(2) are, in some respects, problematic. But answers may be proposed.

To begin with, proceedings which seek a ruling on the validity or invalidity of a contract are matters relating to a contract. They will fall within Article 7(1), and not within Article 7(2). To put the same point another way, proceedings which have as their object the validity of invalidity of a contract must be seen as matters relating to a contract, even though they may seek to establish the invalidity of the contract as a source of legal obligation.[1162]

Proceedings which do not seek to have the contract adjudged to be invalid are less easy to deal with. If the validity of the contract is not directly in issue, but complaint is made of wrongdoing for which compensation is sought, it may be that the proceedings are not in a matter relating to a contract, but really are matters of tort, just as English domestic law says they are. But a number of points may be made against this. First, if the proceedings are really only the money equivalent of rescission, then although they may be framed in tort, and lead to recovery only on proof of wrong, they surely still *relate* to a contract. After all, the wording of Article 7(1) is that the matter be one relating to a contract. It is not required that the proceedings have the contract as their object. Second, it will not be possible to establish loss without pleading and proving the contract:[1163] the claim for damages will not succeed unless the contract said to have resulted from the misrepresentation is one which might have been rescinded.

1160 The possibility of damages taking notice of consequential losses is immaterial to this point.

1161 C-180/06 *Ilsinger v. Schlank & Schick GmbH (in liq)* [2009] ECR I-3571, [57].

1162 *Agnew v. Länsförsäkringsbolagens AB* [2001] 1 AC 223 (a case on the Lugano I Convention).

1163 *Cf* (albeit that the point is not identical) C-548/12 *Brogsitter v. Fabrication de Montres Normandes* EU:C:2014:148, [2014] QB 753. There, the claim framed in tort was a matter relating to a contract for the purpose of special jurisdiction, because the claim could not be made good without pleading and proving the contract. It is arguable that if the loss cannot be established without pleading and proving the contract, this has the same consequence for special jurisdiction.

It is also possible to imagine that lawyers from other legal traditions would be surprised to learn that English law deals with factors which would entitle a party to be released from a contract by alleging the commission of a tort and seeking monetary compensation. Particular difficulty may be presented by a claimant who seeks to rescind a contract but who, in the event that rescission was not available to him, claims in the alternative damages for misrepresentation or for intimidation. Bearing in mind the undesirability of a claim concerning a defective contract being partitioned between different courts, it would appear to be preferable that a misrepresentation claim, in which the effect of the wrongdoing was the conclusion of a contract, were held to fall within Article 7(1) and therefore not within Article 7(2).[1164]

No help is to be taken from the Rome II Regulation, which treats non-contractual obligations arising from pre-contractual fault as something other than torts,[1165] and identifies the *lex contractus* as the applicable law. It therefore delivers a muddled message, even if it were permissible to reinterpret the Brussels I Regulation in the light of the Rome II Regulation, which *Kainz* suggests that it may not be.

The view proposed here is that misrepresentation proceedings, in which the loss is the entering into a contract, are within Article 7(1), not Article 7(2). It will follow that certain kinds of complaint[1166] will be matters relating to a contract for the purposes of the Brussels I Regulation, but non-contractual obligations under the Rome II Regulation for the purpose of identifying the applicable law. The law can be untidy.

2.192 Matters relating to tort, delict or quasi-delict: concurrent causes of action and the relationship between Articles 7(1) and 7(2)

The decision in *Kalfelis* means that congruent claims may not – for special jurisdictional purposes – fall under Articles 7(1) and 7(2) at the same time. Neither, as *Brogsitter*[1167] makes plain, is it open to the claimant to exercise his own preference as to which of the two he would prefer to rely on. The result of the law on special jurisdiction being based on autonomous definitions of matters relating to contract and tort is that the court has to determine the jurisdictional category into which the claim falls for the purposes of the Brussels I Regulation. Some of the implications of this were discussed above;[1168] it may be helpful to revisit some of the more difficult cases. The following six numbered paragraphs do so; but in the end they do no more than apply the law as it has been sought to be understood.

2.193 Matters relating to tort, delict or quasi-delict: obligations based on a duty of care

Causes of action based upon simple *Donoghue v. Stevenson* negligence are firmly in the category of matters relating to a tort, and so covered by Article 7(2) of the Regulation. This was the basis of liability in *ÖFAB v. Koot*,[1169] after all.

1164 This submission is not consistent with *Alfred Dunhill Ltd v. Diffusion Internationale de Maroquinerie de Prestige Sarl* [2001] CLC 949, but which cannot be taken to settle the law.

1165 They are dealt with in Chapter III of the Rome II Regulation.

1166 That is, where a contract was concluded, but the proceedings claim damages for *culpa in contrahendo*.

1167 C-548/12 *Brogsitter v. Fabrication de Montres Normandes* EU:C:2014:148, [2014] QB 753.

1168 See esp. para. 2.168, above.

1169 C-147/12, EU:C:2013:490, [2015] QB 20.

Liability for negligent misstatement is more difficult to deal with. According to some, the substantive basis of liability for negligent misstatement in English law is that the parties were in a relationship 'equivalent to contract',[1170] but which was non-contractual because there was no consideration requested or given for the advice. But that may not be true in every case; and it has also been suggested that the basis of liability is that of the defendant's 'voluntary assumption of a risk' in relation to the claimant. That may come close to being based on an 'undertaking freely entered into with regard to another', and for the cause of action to be seen as relating to a contract for the purpose of Article 7(1).[1171] If so, where the claim is brought by the person who sought and obtained the advice, the claim will be contractual; where it is brought by a third party, who has relied on it, such a conclusion will be more difficult, though certainly not impossible, to reach.

One may also consider claims brought, for example, against a newspaper or magazine which has negligently published bad advice, on which a reader has relied to his detriment. Without entering into whether there actually is civil liability under any domestic law, the claim would, for special jurisdictional purposes, appear to fall under Article 7(2), on the footing that the publisher has no idea who will purchase the journal, still less take to heart what is printed. On the other hand, if the claimant is a subscriber, who receives the magazine by post, the relationship between the publisher and the reader is much closer to one which would fall within Article 7(1). It may be said that the publisher does not freely assume obligations to the other. But if the other is known to be a subscriber, the proposition that no obligations are assumed by the publisher appears to state a conclusion drawn from substantive national law, rather than offering an explanation of why the claim must still fall outside Article 7(1) and therefore into Article 7(2).

2.194 Matters relating to tort, delict or quasi-delict: claims against professional providers of services

In English law, actions against professional providers of services will lie in contract if there was a contract with them; in tort if they owed a duty of care in circumstances in which no contract created the relationship.[1172] If a contract imposed a duty of care, although domestic English law may permit the claim to be framed either in contract or in tort, or both, at the election of the claimant,[1173] it will be within Article 7(1) for the purposes of Regulation 1215/2012, on the basis that the claim could have been pleaded in contract, or on the basis that there would have been no liability if there had been no contract.[1174]

In the case where liability is imposed and affects a large number of third parties, such as where an auditor of a public company makes a statement of professional opinion about the state of the accounts, and this is relied on by a purchaser of shares in that company, any claim by the purchaser could not possibly fall within Article 7(1), as no undertaking to that unascertainable individual is freely undertaken by the defendant, whatever the foresight he may have as the possible impact of his advice; and the matter will fall under Article 7(2).

1170 *Hedley Byrne & Co v. Heller and Partners* [1964] AC 564.

1171 C-26/91 *Jakob Handte & Co GmbH v. Soc Traitements Mécano-Chimiques des Surfaces* [1992] ECR I-3967; and see para. 2.171, above.

1172 See, e.g., *Smith v. Eric S Bush* [1990] 1 AC 831.

1173 As a matter of domestic law, at least, *Henderson v. Merrett Syndicates Ltd* [1995] 2 AC 145.

1174 C-548/12 *Brogsitter v. Fabrication de Montres Normandes EURL* EU:C:2014:148, [2014] QB 753.

Liability may not have arisen if the auditor had not made a contract with the company, but the contract with the company is not one to which the purchaser is party. Any liability to him is not a matter relating to a contract, if, as *Handte* suggests, that means a contract with the claimant.

2.195 Matters relating to tort, delict or quasi-delict: claims in tort answered by contractual defences

In cases in which the parties to litigation have contractually agreed beforehand that in certain circumstances a claim otherwise available to the claimant will not be brought, the classification of the claim, for special jurisdictional purposes, is less difficult. In English law, the claim may be advanced in tort; the contractual promise operates, if at all, as a defence to that claim in tort. But for the purposes of the Brussels I Regulation it may be correct to start from the proposition that where there is a contract between the parties, the nature and extent of liability is defined by the contractual agreement between the parties. This leads to the conclusion that the entire matter is a matter relating to a contract for the purposes of Article 7(1). This will be all the more so if the claim could itself have been pleaded as a contractual claim.[1175]

2.196 Matters relating to tort, delict or quasi-delict: equitable obligations

The same principles of interpretation apply when one is dealing with proceedings in which the claimant seeks to rely on and enforce equitable obligations. It is for this purpose irrelevant that equitable obligations, derived ultimately from the unconscionable behaviour of the defendant, are understood in domestic law as being neither contracts nor torts. For the purpose of Articles 7(1) and 7(2), according to *Kalfelis*, if they are civil obligations, they are liable to be regarded as one or the other except in the rare case that they do not arise from a contract, and are not based on liability for wrongfully causing harm or loss.

The answer is, therefore, to be found by deciding whether the obligation which lies at the heart of the claim is rooted in an agreement between the parties, or on an allegation of wrongful behaviour which has caused loss to another. If the obligation arises from the unconscionable disregard of the duties of an agreement,[1176] such as those imposed upon a person who has with the agreement of the other party placed himself in a fiduciary relationship with that other, such as an agent to his principal, the matter should be seen as one relating to a contract, and the fiduciary aspect of the claim as going only to define or augment the remedies available to the claimant.

If by contrast the equitable obligation arises from the unilateral conduct of a defendant, such as the one who, by his dishonest assistance of another's breach of trust, or wrongful receipt of trust property, or wrongful acquisition and abuse of confidential information,[1177] owed a fiduciary duty to another, or participated in another's wrongdoing, the claim against

---

1175 C-548/12 *Brogsitter v. Fabrication de Montres Normandes EURL* EU:C:2014:148, [2014] QB 753.

1176 The making of a secret profit by a company director, who holds his office by reason of appointment by the company, and who by accepting the appointment agrees to discharge the duties of that office, should fall within this division of the law.

1177 Otherwise than where this arises from a contractual relationship, such as employment.

him is much more obviously a matter relating to a tort.[1178] In other words, the relationship between the parties, out of which the particular obligation arises, will have been either founded in agreement and the incidental obligations of that agreement, or based upon a wrongful act causing harm or loss, to which the law[1179] attaches its consequences. It will therefore be possible to accommodate equitable obligations into the jurisdictional framework of Articles 7(1) and 7(2).[1180]

2.197 Matters relating to tort, delict or quasi-delict: unjust enrichment

It has been shown above that claims which English law regards as being justified by the principle that unjust enrichment must be reversed will fall within Article 7(1) when they relate to a contractual relationship, and will in other cases fall within Article 7(2) where they are based on liability for causing harm or loss by a wrongful act; and in yet further cases, may appear to fall within neither special jurisdictional category.

2.198 Matters relating to tort, delict or quasi-delict: product liability

A claim against a manufacturer which is based on liability for a dangerous or defective product will be within Article 7(2) of the Brussels I Regulation unless the claimant is the party immediately contractually bound to the manufacturer.[1181] It will be seen that the places with special jurisdiction are those where the dangerous, damaging, or defective item is manufactured;[1182] and that where it is used by the party acquiring it and who, for instance, sustains damage to his person, or the spoliation of his property, as the case may be.[1183]

2.199 The harmful event: general interpretation

Once it has been decided that a case falls, for special jurisdictional purposes, within Article 7(2) of the Regulation, the task is to identify the place where the harmful event occurred.

In some cases this will be so obvious as to need no further analysis, such as where a pedestrian is knocked down by a car and treated in hospital in the same town, or where a fire carelessly started by the defendant destroys the claimant's house. But other cases may be rather more difficult. In some cases the damage and the events leading up to it will be geographically separated. In others the acts or omissions, or the damage, or all of these, may be hard to pin down to a physical location. As a result, the meaning to be given to the words 'the place where the harmful event occurred' requires elucidation.

1178 *Casio Computer Co Ltd v. Sayo* [2001] EWCA Civ 661, [2001] ILPr 694; *Dexter v. Harley, The Times,* 2 April 2001; *Cronos Containers NV v. Palatin* [2002] EWHC 2819 (Comm), [2003] ILPr 283.
1179 And if the obligations are equitable, severe.
1180 An analogous exercise is required to deal with issues of applicable law in cases in which the claim, in a wholly domestic context, would be seen as founded on equitable rights and liabilities: see, for example, *OJSC Oil Co Yugraneft v. Abramovich* [2008] EWHC 2613 (Comm).
1181 C-26/91 *Jakob Handte & Co GmbH v. Soc Traitements Mécano-Chimiques des Surfaces* [1992] ECR I-3967.
1182 C-45/13 *Kainz v. Pantherwerke AG* EU:C:2014:7, [2015] QB 34.
1183 C-189/08 *Zuid-Chemie BV v. Phillippo's Mineralenfabriek NV/SA* [2009] ECR I-6917.

The point of departure is that the words 'the place where the harmful event occurred' have a uniform meaning which permits the claimant[1184] to choose to sue in the courts for the place where the damage occurred, or in courts for the place of the event giving rise to that damage. This follows from the early decision of the Court in *Handelskwekerij GJ Bier NV v. SA Mines de Potasse d'Alsace*.[1185] In that case, a French industrial concern discharged toxic effluent into the River Rhine, with the eventual result that, when this water was used to irrigate a Dutch market garden, the crop perished. When the claimant sought to seise the Dutch courts with special jurisdiction over the French defendant, the question arose where the harmful event was to be seen as having occurred. Noting that national laws had already taken the view that the place of occurrence of the damage, and the place of the event giving rise to that damage, were equally likely to be competent, and that each was capable of constituting a significant connecting factor from the point of view of special jurisdiction, the Court accepted that what is now Article 7(2) 'must be understood as being intended to cover both the place where the damage occurred and the place of the event giving rise to it'. In accordance with general principle, this interpretation of the rule may be relied on even if, in a particular case, it gives special jurisdiction to a court whose actual connection with the facts of the case was not close. It also appears that, notwithstanding statements from the Court that Article 7 is to be given a restrictive interpretation, the jurisdictional generosity to the claimant inherent in the decision is, and remains, good law. The decision in *Bier v. Mines de Potasse d'Alsace* has not been called into question in any of the cases which came subsequently before the Court.[1186] It is, however, important to notice that the Court has insisted on a precise and literal application of the wording used in its ruling in *Bier*.[1187]

The decision in *Bier* is authoritative and applicable in cases in which the damage and the event giving rise to it (and in this sense, the harmful event) both occurred within the territory of the Member States. It is unclear whether or, if so, how it applies if the damage occurred outside the Member States, but the event giving rise to it occurred within a Member State. It would be premature, though not necessarily wrong, to conclude that, so long as either damage or event was located, or was principally located, in a Member State, the courts for the place within that Member State[1188] have special jurisdiction.[1189] The rule may instead be that unless the harmful event as a whole occurred, or perhaps principally occurred, within a Member State, Article 7(2), and therefore *Bier*, has no application. A justification for such an interpretation might be that a defendant should be deprived of the general jurisdiction of the courts of his domicile only if there is a strong connection with another Member State. To put it another way, the two limbs of *Bier* may only operate to confer special jurisdiction after, but not before, it has been decided that the harmful event occurred within the territory of the Member States. But the question appears to be free from authority.[1190]

1184 Whether victim (in the ordinary case) or alleged tortfeasor (in the case of proceedings brought for a declaration of non-liability): C-133/11 *Folien Fischer AG v. Ritrama SpA* EU:C:2012:664, [2013] QB 523.

1185 21/76, [1976] ECR 1735.

1186 See, for recent reaffirmation, C-228/11 *Melzer v. MF Global UK Ltd* EU:C:2013:305, [2013] QB 1112; C-360/12 *Coty Germany GmbH v. First Note Perfumes NV* EU:C:2014:1318. But there is hardly a judgment in which this statement is not made.

1187 As to which, see below.

1188 Note, however, that it is the courts for the place, and not for the State, which are given special (international) jurisdiction.

1189 Whether over all or the proportionate part of the claim would also need to be decided.

1190 For comparison with Art. 7(1), see 32/88 *Six Constructions Ltd v. Humbert* [1989] ECR 341, and para. 2.177, above.

It is therefore necessary to examine the two special jurisdictions authorised by the decision in *Bier*: the 'damage' limb, and the 'causal event' limb.

2.200 The harmful event and proceedings for declaratory relief

It is plausible to read *Bier v. Mines de Potasse d'Alsace* as offering a choice of forum to the victim of the alleged tort. Indeed, in the light of cases concerned with the infringement of personality by internet publication, which offer a still further option to the victim, one might well see in this a jurisdictional rule which was constructed for the purpose of giving a limited privilege to the victim of an alleged tort. But this quasi-privileged reading is contradicted by *Folien Fischer AG v. Ritrama SpA*,[1191] in which it was held that a person alleged to be a tortfeasor, but who had not been sued, was entitled to rely on what is now Article 7(2) to bring proceedings for a declaration of non-liability. The court seised could have jurisdiction on the basis of its being the place where the alleged damage had occurred, or on the basis of its being the place of the event giving rise to the damage. If either of those conditions was met, the court would have special jurisdiction; the fact that the proceedings were brought in a court which the actual defendant, but who was claiming to be the victim of a tort, would not have chosen to seise, was irrelevant.

On one view, this decision changes the nature of the jurisdictional rule which, as it was originally explained and developed, was intended to give the victim a choice of forum; but Article 7(2) is not worded in a way that suggests that it favours one party over the other: in *Kainz v. Pantherwerke AG*[1192] the Court repeated this point when declining to adopt an interpretation of Article 7(2) which might have tended to make it more likely that a victim of a tort would be entitled to sue at home.[1193] There may also be no sufficient reason for considering the person claiming to be the victim of a tort to be the one with right on his side;[1194] and if the courts identified by reference to the judgment in *Bier* are courts which have a connection sufficient to satisfy the principle of proximity, there is no reason to prevent one, but not the other, party from suing there. When one recalls that the rules for applicable law in non-contractual obligations are harmonised for causes of action which fall within the material scope of the Rome II Regulation, with the consequence that the selection of court with special jurisdiction should not affect the outcome of the case, the decision in *Folien Fischer* looks less wrong. But it still feels slightly unexpected.

2.201 The 'damage' limb of *Bier*: the damage which is relevant and that which is not

The first limb of the test in *Bier v. Mines de Potasse d'Alsace* gives special jurisdiction to courts for the place where the damage occurred. The problem is that the occurrence of damage is not always obligingly confined within a place which is easily and obviously identifiable.

1191 C-133/11, EU:C:2012:664, [2013] QB 523. See also (though special jurisdiction under this rule was not available) *McGraw Hill International (UK) Ltd v. Deutscher Apotheker- und Arztebank EG* [2014] EWHC 2436 (Comm), [2014] 2 Lloyd's Rep 523.

1192 C-45/13, EU:C:2014:7, [2015] QB 34, [31].

1193 Maybe so. But it is hard to avoid the suggestion that the Court which decided *Bier* would have agreed with this.

1194 The status of victim will only be determined by trial, which is what separates this case from that a contracts made by weaker parties to which Sections 3, 4 and 5 apply.

It can be challenging to locate the occurrence of the damage when a court is called upon to apply the rule in *Bier v. Mines de Potasse d'Alsace*; it can be no less problematic when it is applied as the applicable law rule for non-contractual obligations.[1195] The 'place where the damage occurred' is not always ascertainable by objective rules; and to the extent that legal certainty is a principle underpinning the interpretation of the Regulation, this aspect of special jurisdiction does not always contribute to it. The task of applying a general rule to untidy facts falls to the national court, which has to do the best it can.

The jurisprudence of the European Court establishes that the reference to 'damage' in *Bier v. Mines de Potasse d'Alsace* indicates the damage which is the immediate consequence of the harmful event. This excludes, as jurisdictionally insignificant for this purpose, damage which was done to indirect or secondary victims, or damage which may fairly be seen as the consequence of damage which occurred earlier. It also means that special jurisdiction is given to the courts at the place where the damage occurred, as distinct from where it was later suffered, felt, reflected or where it ramified or where its financial consequences were recorded. The words 'the damage occurred', which appear only in the judgment in *Bier* and not in the Regulation itself, have also been accorded an autonomous meaning.

The rule therefore works well enough where one is dealing with physical damage to person or property. It works less well where one is dealing with damage to the personality of the victim. It works least well where the consequence of the harmful event takes the form of pure financial loss rather than damage, that is to say, financial depletion which is neither preceded nor caused nor accompanied by any obvious impact on physical things or on personality. And in some cases, in which it is only realistic to admit that the damage occurs all over the place, an exceptional interpretation is required.[1196]

The identification of the relevant damage as that done to the immediate victim of the harmful act was established in *Dumez France SA v. Hessische Landesbank*.[1197] A German bank had withdrawn its financial support from a German subsidiary of a French parent company, with the result, among other things, that the parent sustained financial loss. The parent sought to sue the German bank in France, in a direct action, relying on the proposition that French law gave it a claim in quasi-delict for the financial loss which it had sustained. It argued that the damage of which it complained occurred in France, and that what is now Article 7(2) gave the French court special jurisdiction over the defendant. The Court disagreed, ruling that the damage which was jurisdictionally significant was that which was done to the immediate victim of the wrongful act, and not that which was done to indirect or more remote victims of it, even if the more remote victim asserted a cause of action which was based on its own independent loss. As a result, the jurisdictionally-significant damage, which applied equally to claims by immediate and more remote victims,[1198] occurred in Germany.

The decision in *Dumez France* applied to claims brought by indirect or secondary victims, but did not, in terms at least, cover other cases of indirectly-done, or consequential, or 'ricochet', damage resulting to the primary victim. But the Advocate General drew

---

1195 Rome II Regulation (Regulation (EC) 864/2007), Art. 4.

1196 See below, para. 2.204.

1197 C-220/88, [1990] ECR I-49. See also *Kitechnology BV v. Unicor Plastmaschinen GmbH* [1995] FSR 765. By parity of reasoning, where a claimant suffers a deterioration in his condition after a personal injury, and claims for an additional sum in damages, it is the original infliction of damage, not the later deterioration, which is jurisdictionally significant: *Henderson v. Jaouen* [2002] EWCA Civ 75, [2002] 1 WLR 2971.

1198 See *Deutsche Bahn AG v. Morgan Advanced Materials plc* [2013] EWCA Civ 1484.

attention to the distinction which exists in principle between the place where damage occurred, which court was identified by the Court in *Bier* as having jurisdiction, and the place where it was suffered, which was not.[1199] The significance of the distinction can be seen by considering *Marinari v. Lloyds Bank plc*.[1200] In that case, a claim was brought after the confiscation of promissory notes from the claimant[1201] had taken place in England. The claimant, who was domiciled in Italy, argued that the jurisdictionally-significant damage was located in Italy, on the footing that the Italian formulation of the delict, and of which he complained, was the diminution of his patrimony; and as he was domiciled in Pisa, his patrimonial estate was located there. The Court rejected the analysis proposed by the claimant, reasoning that when damage had been directly done in a particular place, the financial consequences of it were not the damage which was jurisdictionally relevant. The Court echoed the distinction drawn by the Advocate General in *Dumez France* when it said that Article 7(2) 'cannot be construed as including the place where… the victim claims to have suffered financial damage consequential upon initial damage arising and suffered by him in another Contracting State'.[1202]

It follows that the fact the claimant makes up his books and writes down his loss somewhere in a Member State is not enough to make that the place where the damage occurred.[1203] Likewise, in *Zuid-Chemie BV v. Phillippo's Mineralenfabriek NV/SA*,[1204] it was held that the damage occurred in the factory of the claimant, when and where it mixed its raw materials with corrupt ingredients which had been manufactured by another, so causing it to produce an unsaleable product.[1205] The damage was seen as being damage done to property, to the good raw material of the claimant, even though it might have been argued that the good material was not damaged as distinct from being mixed up with other material which would be very difficult to separate.[1206] It follows that the idea of 'damage' is to be treated as an autonomous concept, which does not invariably involve breaking or bleeding; it may sometimes be better understood as a 'spoiling'.[1207]

1199 At [51] of the Opinion: it was necessary to avoid any 'confusion between the place where the damage occurs (the very words used in the judgment) and the place where the damage was suffered': in the French original, *confusion entre le lieu où le dommage servient – termes mêmes de votre arrêt – et le lieu où le dommage est subi.* (The reference to 'the judgment' is to *Bier v. Mines de Potasse*.) French writers do not always stick to the precise terminology recommended by Darmon AG; but *survenir* and *subir* are two different ideas, corresponding to the occurring and the suffering of damage.

1200 C-364/93, [1995] ECR I-2719. The decision of the Court in C-168/02 *Kronhofer v. Maier* [2004] ECR I-6009 affirms the same principle, that the place of the damage cannot be understood in the sense of where the claimant keeps his assets and, in that sense, suffers depletion. But *Kronhofer* was a case of financial loss unconnected with any interference with physical person or physical property, and therefore raises different issues, which are discussed below, para. 2.203.

1201 By the police on information supplied by the bank.

1202 At [15], and the ruling. *Cf Batstone & Firminger Ltd v. Nasima Enterprises (Nigeria) Ltd* [1996] CLC 1902.

1203 See also *Future Investments SA v. FIFA* [2010] EWHC 1019 (Ch), [2010] ILPr 630.

1204 C-189/08, [2009] ECR I-6917.

1205 The claim in question was not against the immediate supplier and vendor, but against the manufacturer of the ingredient which the seller had acquired and then supplied.

1206 The Court refused to address a second question referred on the basis that the initial or immediate loss sustained might be seen as purely financial, on the basis that it was plainly not so and the question was therefore hypothetical.

1207 *Cf* the debate in Roman law as to the scope of the *lex Aquilia*. Although the *lex* allowed an action when property was broken (*ruperit*), the jurists understood it as meaning *corruperit*, generally translated as 'spoiling'. It was therefore considered to cover the case in which a man sowed thistles in another man's crop: the crop was spoiled even though the individual stalks of wheat were not themselves deformed; it covered the case in which sand was mixed with corn, something which was a nuisance to separate even though the individual grains of corn were

That said, the identification of damage as direct or indirect, or as occurring as distinct from being suffered, will not always be straightforward in cases in which there is physical damage which is combined with damage of a non-physical kind. Take, for example, a claim for damages for psychiatric injury, or for bereavement following the wrongful killing of a close relative. In the light of *Dumez France*, this aspect of damage may be seen as a consequence of damage done fatally and immediately to a direct victim. It might seem odd that in circumstances in which English law regards the wrong done to a person who has been bereaved or shocked as a free-standing tort, the damage done to such a person would be irrelevant to the application of the damage limb of *Bier*. Yet this must have been exactly what went through the mind of the French court in *Dumez France*: there was a cause of action available to the claimant parent company, but the damage done to it was not jurisdictionally significant for the purpose of this rule. By parity of reasoning, it may be said that the damage done to the bereaved claimant is not damage to the immediate victim.[1208] Similar reasoning may be applied to a claim by a dependent under the Fatal Accidents Act 1976. An English court may be receptive to a submission which would allow it to side-step the analysis set out here and to find that the damage done to a bereaved claimant was jurisdictionally significant; it is not clear it should.

More examples can be given. Suppose a defendant puts out a statement to the effect that the claimant's products are defective or that its financial position is perilous, with the result that the claimant also suffers a drop in business in other Member States, or suffers a sharp drop in its share price, or suffers financial strain as creditors panic and demand the repayment of loans. There is no doubt that financial losses result from the story. But which part of the loss is to be seen as the damage which identifies a court with special jurisdiction? Are any of these instances of indirect or consequential damage to the victim? It may be that the distinction between where the damage occurred and where it was suffered may offer a clearer guide than notions of the directness and immediacy of damage, but there will be cases in which it is difficult to say whether the damage to which a claimant points is jurisdictionally-significant damage, directly done to the immediate victim of the wrong.[1209]

2.202 The damage limb of *Bier*: locating the place where the damage occurred

Having defined the damage which is jurisdictionally significant, the next question is to pinpoint where it occurred. In many cases, especially where it takes the form of physical damage as distinct from financial loss, this question will already have been answered by the identification of the relevant damage. But where there is still a question where the relevant damage occurred, the answer appears to be that the location of the occurrence of the damage

---

not actually damaged: in short, there was Aquilian liability for spoiling the property of another: see Digest 9.2.27 (Ulpian).

1208 In C-220/88 *Dumez France v. Hessische Landesbank* [1990] ECR I-49, at [37] of the Opinion, the Advocate General appeared to regard damages for nervous shock, or severe psychological shock, as analogous to 'ricochet' damage, and therefore as having no jurisdictional role in the application of Art. 5(3): at [47] of the Opinion. It is not certain that this was material to the eventual conclusions of the Advocate General, and the point was not clarified by the judgment of the Court.

1209 A further example might be found in a case where a claimant takes a medicine in Member State A, but does not develop overt symptoms until he is in Member State B. It is unclear whether the damage occurs in, or was being directly done in, the State of original ingestion or that of manifestation of symptoms. See also *Kitechnology BV v. Unicor Plastmaschinen GmbH* [1995] FSR 765.

will be determined in a uniform manner. It is plain that the Court will generally view with scepticism any analysis which would tend to suggest that the courts for the place of the claimant's domicile have special jurisdiction, and will therefore scrutinise with care the proposition that that was where the damage occurred. Its general approach is clearly seen in *Dumez France*, and *Marinari*, where the Court observed that the principle of *forum actoris* was specifically discouraged by the scheme of the Regulation. But as will be seen, when damage has occurred all over the place, it may be better to deem it to be concentrated in a single place.[1210]

Réunion Européenne SA v. Spliethoff's Bevrachtingskantoor BV[1211] illustrates the way in which the place of the physical damage is to be identified in cases in which it is not immediately obvious. The damage done to a consignee's cargo of fruit, by a sea carrier who had failed to provide proper refrigeration, was held to occur at the place where the actual sea carrier was to hand over the goods, as distinct from the unknown place on the high seas where the rot first set in, and as further distinct from the place[1212] where the goods were when the consignee discovered that damage had occurred. Though there was financial loss, it was the consequence of physical damage, and the search was therefore for the place where that physical damage had occurred or was to be deemed to have occurred. The same technique will be applied in cases of product liability, even if the concept of damage requires a slight stretching.[1213] And the same technique applies in the case of damage to personality. For example, in the case of defamation, a modest adaptation of the rule as it applies to physical damage will allow the place[1214] of the damage to be located where the personality or reputation was trashed and lies in tatters.[1215] According to the Court in *Shevill v. Presse Alliance SA*,[1216] which was concerned with libel by defamatory statements appearing in a newspaper, the place where the damage occurred was where readers read the false information and so lowered their estimation of the victim. To the extent that there was a readership in England, the jurisdictional damage occurred in England.

2.203 The damage limb of *Bier*: locating the place where pure financial loss occurred

Cases in which 'damage' takes the form of pure financial loss, that is, financial loss which is not derived from or the result of personal injury, or damage to or loss of property, are harder to deal with. One may take as an example a case in which the claimant is supplied with advice[1217] which is negligent or fraudulent, on which he acts by instructing his agent to acquire an asset and instructing his bank to release the funds to pay for the property to

---

1210 See below, para. 2.204.

1211 C-51/97, [1998] ECR I-6511.

1212 They were then carried by road to the consignee's place of business, and this is where they were first found to be rotten.

1213 C-189/08 *Zuid-Chemie BV v. Phillippo's Mineralenfabriek NV/SA* [2009] ECR I-6917: the property of the claimant was not exactly damaged, but was rendered unusable, when tainted by admixture with corrupt material manufactured by the defendant.

1214 Where there are very many such places, a different rule may apply; see below, para. 2.204.

1215 The use of the vernacular is deliberate, for the tort of defamation is dealt with as though it were a case of personal injury or damage to property, and not as a tort of a distinct and different kind.

1216 C-68/93, [1995] ECR I-415.

1217 Assuming at this point that it is not supplied under a relationship which makes the claim contractual within the meaning of Art. 7(1).

be acquired. By the time the asset has been acquired, it is clear that several Member States may have been involved. The advice may be received in England; the decision to act on it is taken while the claimant is in Spain, from where he telephones his German agent to acquire securities in Belgium, he then giving instructions to his Swiss bank to transfer funds to a Luxembourg bank, after which the securities are delivered or transferred to his agent in Belgium. If at the end of all this the securities turn out to be worthless, with the undeniable result that loss has occurred,[1218] what was the place where it arose?

There is no generally right answer. The traditional response of the English lawyer[1219] might have been to look to the place where the advice was received and acted upon,[1220] but where that points in two directions the problem is not solved. Another view might be that if the real loss is parting with money,[1221] the place where the loss arises is the place where the money finally slipped out of the claimant's control, though this might allow the claimant to determine the place where the loss arises by careful selection of the bank account from which the payment will be made. On another view, if the loss is not seen as the payment out of money but as the acquisition of worthless paper or other property, the loss may arise where this is acquired, or where the proprietorship is electronically recorded.

The guidance available from the Court is limited. In *Kronhofer v. Maier*,[1222] an Austrian claimant had been induced by a German entity to make investments. The claimant transferred funds from Austria to an investment account in Germany, and this was then used by the defendant to purchase useless investments. The claimant sought to sue in Austria, on the ground that the ultimate or final damage, which was really loss, had occurred there. But according to the Court, this was not to be permitted, as the investments, and the loss of money from an account in Germany, had all been in Germany. The Court did not suggest that the loss might be seen as the earlier transfer of funds from the claimant's Austrian bank, observing without comment that that analysis had not commended itself to the referring court. The decision rejected the contention of the claimant that his loss occurred in Austria because that is where he was established. The judgment offers no firm guidance on the proposition that the loss occurred in Austria because it was from Austria that the wasted funds were pushed out onto a slippery slope. But it is to be inferred that this was not the place where the loss occurred: perhaps because, at that point, though loss had come a step closer it had not occurred for the claimant could still have recalled his money. Not until it was paid out of the German investment account was the money lost.

1218 No point is taken as to the point in time at which the loss occurs.

1219 To the extent that this was the technique for deciding where a cause of action for misrepresentation arose, it uses the techniques of the common law for choice of law to answer a question of autonomous European jurisdictional law, which is far from obviously right. An elaborate examination of the case law was undertaken in *AMT Futures Ltd v. Marzillier et al GmbH* [2014] EWHC 1085 (Comm), [2015] 2 WLR 187, but the answer derived by the court, that the damage, allegedly done by aiding and abetting breach of a jurisdiction for England by bringing legal proceedings in Germany, occurred in London, because that is where the 'contingent right to be sued' was located, is unconvincing. One only has to ask: 'what occurred in London?' to be given the answer that nothing occurred in London.

1220 Cf *London Helicopters Ltd v. Heliportugal Lda-INAC* [2006] EWHC 108 (QB), [2006] 1 All ER (Comm) 597 (receipt and reliance on certificate containing negligent advice).

1221 Or the equivalent of money, such as the debt owed to a customer by his bank.

1222 C-168/02, [2004] ECR I-6009. See also (on identification of the governing law) *Hillside (New Media) Ltd v. Baasland* [2010] EWHC 3336 (Comm), [2010] 2 CLC 986.

In *DFDS Torline A/S v. SEKO*,[1223] the proceedings arose from the campaign of economic sabotage organised by certain trade unions against companies carrying on business in international passenger shipping. In the case itself, an order that the claimants' sea ferry, the *Tor Caledonia*, be 'blacked' was issued by the trade union from Sweden.[1224] The result was that the claimant, a Danish company, had to hire another vessel to ply its North Sea route between Sweden and the United Kingdom. The loss of which it complained was the expenditure of money in making a contract of hire of a replacement vessel. As to the question where that damage, more properly loss, occurred, the Court observed that 'the damage allegedly caused to DFDS by SEKO consisted in financial loss arising from the withdrawal of the *Tor Caledonia* from its normal route and the hire of another ship to serve the same route. It is for the national court to inquire whether such financial loss may be regarded as having arisen at the place where [the claimant] is established'.[1225] That does not advance matters very far. Were it to be argued that the loss arose in Denmark, on the footing that the *Tor Caledonia* was flagged in Denmark, the Court suggested that this would not satisfy the rule unless the national court found that the loss arose on the *Tor Caledonia* itself.[1226] If the case is considered as one in which the economic loss is simply the consequence of the wrongful capture of the claimant's property, this is probably correct, if a little forced. In cases which do not conform to this template, it may have rather less to offer.

In *Kolassa v Barclays Bank plc*[1226a] an investor who asserted that false statements in a bond issuer's prospectus had caused him to invest, but who did not have a direct contractual relationship with the issuer, was entitled to say that a loss occurred where he held the bank account in which the loss occurred. But the Court, most unfortunately, did not explain whether the reference was to the account from which the purchase money had been paid out in the first place, or the investment account with a financial intermediary in which the customer's worthless entitlement in relation to the bond was recorded. Both accounts were in Austria, and the ambiguity in the judgment in a real problem.

In cases in which the damage takes the form of infringing an economic right to be protected from acts of unfair competition, it is open to the court to find that damage has occurred within the jurisdiction of the court. According to *Coty Germany GmbH v. First Note Perfumes NV*,[1227] the jurisdiction of the court is, in this case, defined by the damage occurring within the territory of the State.

Three other decisions contribute little more to our understanding of the law. First, in *VfK v. Henkel*[1228] the Court ruled that legal proceedings brought by a consumers' association against a trader, who was using unfair terms in his standard-form contracts, were brought in a matter relating to tort or delict, because they sought to enforce liability for wrongdoing

---

1223 C-18/02, [2004] ECR I-1417.

1224 This was, therefore, the place of the event which gave rise to the loss or damage.

1225 At [42]–[43].

1226 At [44].

1226a C-375/133, EU:C:2015:37. The effect was also to allow the investor to sue the Bank where the investor was domiciled, this being 'justified' on the basis that they should have been expected to be sued wherever an investor might invest: see at [54]–[56], which are extremely poorly reasoned. (*The Judgment in this case was handed down only as the proofs of this book were being corrected; it was not possible to integrate it fully into the text.*)

1227 C-360/12, EU:C:2014:911. But this identification of damage in terms of the protection of a right cannot be applied to a case like *AMT Futures Ltd v. Marzillier et al GmbH* [2014] EWHC 1085 (Comm), [2015] 2 WLR 187, for the damage when a jurisdiction clause for England is undermined by bringing legal proceedings in Germany is not the invasion of a right or a market in England.

1228 C-167/00, [2002] ECR I-8111.

where there was no contractual relationship between the claimant and the defendant. The Court was not asked specifically where the damage occurred (or loss arose), but observed that what is now Article 7(2) applied where 'the undermining of legal stability' resulted from the defendant's actions.[1229] It appears to follow that the undermining of legal stability was the damage, in the sense that it was the jurisdictionally-significant result of the event which gave rise to the damage, and that it occurred (if it was damage) or arose (if it was pure financial loss) in the place where the consumers would be expected to make[1230] their contracts only to have their stability undermined. The best interpretation appears to be that financial loss, independent of any personal or physical damage, arose in the place where the consumers were going to act, and that the courts at that place therefore had special jurisdiction as the courts for the place of occurrence of the damage or the loss.

In *Fonderie Officine Meccaniche Tacconi SpA v. HWS*[1231] the claim for damages for failure to negotiate a contract in good faith was held to fall within what is now Article 7(2), but as the referring court had not asked about the identification of the place where the harmful event occurred, or about where the loss arose, the Court said nothing about it. No help is to be had from *Dumez France SA v. Hessische Landesbank*[1232] either. The way in which the Court disposed of the case, ruling that the damage or loss which was significant had to be that which was done to the immediate victim, meant that the loss inflicted on the parent company had no jurisdictional significance, and any question of where it arose was immaterial.

Courts are therefore left to apply the general principle established by the European Court in the particular context of the claim which is brought with little robust guidance. They may take a pragmatic view in cases concerned with financial loss rather than material damage. In the case of passing off, it was held in *Mecklermedia Corp v. DC Congress Gesellschaft*[1233] that the place will be where the customers were deceived and the goodwill of the claimant was impaired: the decision really follows from the decision in *Shevill*, where financial loss may have resulted from the damage to reputation, but the damage to reputation was the jurisdictionally significant element.

In the case of loss by parting with money or other assets, the decision in *Domicrest Ltd v. Swiss Bank Corp*[1234] is useful. Advice was given by a banker to a seller of goods that it

---

1229 At [42].

1230 The Court, specifically and correctly, rejected a submission by the defendant that if there had been no loss caused to an actual consumer, there was no damage capable of satisfying what is now Art. 7(2). The avoidance of threatened loss was sufficient to trigger the application of the rule as giving special jurisdiction to the courts of the place where that damage was, unless restrained by judicial process, going to occur.

1231 C-334/00, [2002] ECR I-7357.

1232 220/88, [1990] ECR I-49.

1233 [1998] Ch 40; see also *Modus Vivendi Ltd v. British Products Sanmex Co Ltd* [1997] ILPr 654 (damage occurs where the passing off is effected, and not where the shortfall in sales takes place: the latter is where the damage is suffered, not where it occurs); *Raiffeisen Zentralbank Österreich AG v. Tranos* [2001] ILPr 85 (damage occurs where the disadvantageous transaction is entered into, not at the place from which is sent the instruction to enter into it); *London Helicopters Ltd v. Heliportugal Lda-INAC* [2006] EWHC 108 (QB), [2006] 1 All ER (Comm) 597 (loss or damage occurs at place of receipt of and reliance on certificate containing negligent advice); *Sandisk Corp v. Koninlijke Philips Electronics NV* [2007] EWHC 332 (Ch), [2007] Bus LR 705 (application of these principles to abuse of dominant position in relation to patent rights); *Crucial Music Corp v. Klondyke Management AG* [2007] EWHC 1782 (Ch), [2008] Bus LR 327 (place of damage when misrepresentation has induced buyer to take assignment of intellectual property rights is where and when the buyers entered into the obligation to take the rights, and not where they later did take them).

1234 [1999] QB 548. The approach in *Domicrest* was applied in *Maple Leaf Macro Volatility Master Fund Ltd v. Rouvray* [2009] EWHC 257 (Comm), [2009] 1 Lloyd's Rep 475 (place of damage was at the place where the claimant committed itself to the deal which sealed its financial fate, rather than some other place in which the financial

was financially safe for the seller-claimant to give an instruction to release goods, which it was holding, to the buyer without prior payment. This advice proved to be bad and was alleged to be negligent. The judge considered that, in many instances of negligent misstatement, the place where the damage occurs will be where the advice is received and acted on, but on the facts of the instant case,[1235] the loss occurred, or arose, at the place from which the goods were released, as distinct from the place where the advice was received and from where the instruction to release the goods was sent, and as further distinct from the place where the payment should have been, but was not, received. As an answer to the question where the loss occurred, it is certainly reasonable and probably right. It asks where the step was taken which was irrevocable and which in that sense caused financial loss to occur, then and there. Until the instruction was given there was neither loss nor the inevitability of loss. After it was acted upon, everything had changed. The decision is in this respect comparable with the view that in *Kronhofer*, the original transfer of money from Austria to Germany was not irrevocable, so there and then no loss had arisen, but the disbursement[1236] from the German account marked the point at which loss was inevitable for the claimant and unavoidable by him.[1237] This approach also allows the defendant to see where the immediate loss arose; it contributes to the principle of legal certainty, and does not ascribe jurisdiction to the place of such loss as was consequential. By parity of reasoning, in cases in which the loss takes the form of a non-receipt of funds or goods which should have been received, the loss occurs where the payment or delivery should have been received by the claimant.[1238]

---

consequences worked themselves out). The 'place of commitment' test will not depend upon the technicalities of the law of offer and acceptance, but it is possible to imagine cases in which it is not completely easy to identify that place as the place.

1235 The decision of the Court of Appeal in *Morin v. Bonhams & Brooks Ltd* [2003] EWCA Civ 1802, [2004] 1 Lloyd's Rep 702 is not directly relevant, concerned as it was with the question where, for purposes of choice of law, the most significant element of the tort of negligent misrepresentation was committed. The court took the view that it was where the bidder at auction committed himself irrevocably to a disastrous purchase. In the context of special jurisdiction under Art. 7(2), one might say that the place of the auction sale was the place where the damage occurred, even if the purchase money was paid from a bank account situated elsewhere, for when the auctioneer's hammer fell, the loss was inevitable and irreversible.

1236 Even so, the decision whether the place of the occurrence of loss is that from which money is paid out and irretrievably lost, or the place in which the (worthless) asset which is acquired by that payment is itself situated, has yet to be addressed by the Court. It could and should have done so in C375/13 *Kolassa v Barclays Bank plc* EU:C:2015:37, but it failed. In that case, as it happened, the two possible places were the same, but it is far from clear that the Court was even aware of this, or of the trouble liable to result from its failure to distinguish between them. And see also *Sunderland Marine Mutual Insurance Co Ltd v. Wiseman, The 'Seaward Quest'* [2007] EWHC 1460 (Comm), 2 Lloyd's Rep 308.

1237 Where, as in *Maple Leaf Macro Volatility Master Fund Ltd v. Rouvray* [2009] EWHC 257 (Comm), [2009] 1 Lloyd's Rep 475, the financial transactions to which the claimant committed were complex to the point of being impenetrable to the outside observer, this interpretation does allow special jurisdiction to be determined without the need to undertake a detailed analysis of the financial trading mechanisms into which the parties had plunged.

1238 *Dolphin Maritime Aviation Services Ltd v. Sveriges Angfartygs Assurans Forening* [2009] EWHC 716 (Comm), [2009] 2 Lloyd's Rep 123, [60] (non-receipt of money as result of tortuous interference with contract or conspiracy at the place where payment should have been received under the interfered-with contract); *cf* the analogy with economic loss which takes the form of non-delivery of goods, which occurs at the place of expected delivery of those goods; see also C-51/97 *Réunion Européenne SA v. Spliethoff's Bevrachtingskantoor BV* [1998] ECR I-6511. See also *Future Investments SA v. FIFA* [2010] EWHC 1019 (Ch), [2010] ILPr 630 (place where damage occurred is where the contract which would have been made was, by reason of the defendant's wrongful behaviour, not made; *X v. FIFA* (Cass I civ, 1 Feb 2012) [2012] JDI/Clunet 980 (place where business would have been carried on had it not been for the unlawful refusal of a licence).

2.204 The damage limb of *Bier*: damage occurring or loss arising in several Member States

There are torts in which the damage which occurs to the immediate victim is widely dispersed. A trader who is driven out of several markets by the unlawful acts of another, or a person whose good reputation is trashed by a newspaper with an international circulation, or a person whose privacy is broken by pictures published in several places at once, may all point to damage, the occurrence of which satisfies the requirements of the law laid down in *Dumez France SA*, in several Member States. The question which arises is where special jurisdiction may be found if the claimant wishes to rely on this, rather than on the event giving rise to the damage.

The point of departure is that a court will have special jurisdiction over only so much of the claim as concerns such damage as did occur within the territorial jurisdiction of the court. In general cases, there is no question of a single court having special jurisdiction in respect of all of the damage under the damage limb of *Bier* if that damage occurs in two or more Member States.[1239] There is therefore no requirement that all, or the majority of, the damage occur within the territorial jurisdiction of the court to be seised; but no possibility of asserting jurisdiction in respect of all the damage by showing that the greater part of it occurred within the territorial jurisdiction of the court.[1240] This follows from the decision in *Shevill v. Presse Alliance SA*.[1241] In that case, a French newspaper published a story which defamed the claimant. Copies of it were sold in several Member States; the claimant, who was domiciled in England, sought to sue in England, relying on the proposition that damage had occurred in England. It was held that she was entitled to do so insofar as she complained of sales of the newspaper in England, for the damage had, to that extent, certainly occurred in England.[1242]

Nevertheless, the proposition that the victim of defamatory publication, or of broadscale invasion of privacy, should be told that if he wishes to sue in the place where damage occurred, a separate claim must be brought in each Member State, has logic but no sense. The practical problem will not arise if the claim is brought instead where the defendant is domiciled, or in the Member State in which is the place of the event giving rise to damage. But if those places are in Member States in which the claim would be hard to bring and succeed in, or if the latter is in a non–Member State,[1243] a different solution may be available.

In *eDate Advertising GmbH v. X*,[1244] it was held that in the case of infringement of rights of personality by publication of material on an internet website, the place where the damage occurred may be considered to be the place where the centre of the claimant's interests

---

1239 But, of course, if the event giving rise to the damage was located in a single Member State, that court will have special jurisdiction under the second limb of *Bier*.

1240 Contrast with the position when it is sought to obtain permission to serve out of the jurisdiction under CPR 6B PD, para. 3.1(9): see para. 4.73, below.

1241 C-68/93, [1995] ECR I-415.

1242 In fact, at an early stage, the claimant amended her pleading to rely only upon the sales of the newspaper in England, presumably fearing that the gravitational pull of the sales in France might have deprived her altogether of the right to sue in England. It was accepted that she was entitled to proceed in this way (see at [1996] AC 959); but even if she had not, it would have been open to the court to conclude, if its special jurisdiction had been challenged by the defendant, that it had jurisdiction over some of the matters pleaded and not over others.

1243 Always assuming that, if this is so, Art. 7(2) still applies.

1244 C-509/09, [2011] ECR I-10269. The case was joined with C-161/10 *Martinez v. MGN Ltd*, and a joint judgment was delivered.

is based. The result was that there were two kinds of court with the potential for special jurisdiction: the court for each place in a Member State in which the damage to personality by publication occurred, or the court for the Member State in which the 'centre of interests' of the claimant was located, which would have jurisdiction in respect of damage occurring in all Member States. The Court admitted that the rules which worked for 'regional distribution' of print media, exemplified in *Shevill*, did not work so well for internet publication (even if it were possible to figure out where internet publication took place, which one could not always do). The centre of interests would often, though not always,[1245] correspond with the claimant's habitual residence. The Court was well aware that it was inventing a rule which had not been foreshadowed, but what else was it supposed to do? Its answer may owe something to a centre of gravity approach, and it seemed fair to assume that in most cases, the defendant who is caught by such a jurisdictional rule will only have himself to blame, as he is likely to have known (or to have had the means of knowledge) of the place where the victim had the centre of his interests.

The solution in *eDate Advertising* is therefore confined to torts in respect of rights of personality, which will mean defamation and privacy; it is unclear whether it will also apply to claims which allege breach of confidence, though in principle it should insofar as the breach causes damage to rights of personality. It is unclear also whether it is confined to claims by natural persons, or extends to damage done to the trade or institutional reputation of juristic persons. Insofar as this is an exceptional rule, it should be assumed that it has a narrow scope until the Court confirms that it is wider than the language of the judgment naturally suggests.

The other context in which the damage may be spread across a number of Member States is in the context of infringement of rights of intellectual property. The approach of the Court has been to seek to deal with such cases by the application, without significant modification, of the general rule in *Bier*, rather than by making an exception of the kind made in *eDate Advertising*, even where the infringement is committed on the internet.

In *Wintersteiger AG v. Products 4U Sondermaschinenbau GmbH*,[1246] the Court applied the traditional analysis to the infringement of a protected trade mark. It considered rights of personality to be different in kind from rights of intellectual property, not least because whereas rights of personality are naturally protected in all jurisdictions without the need for any protective act, rights of intellectual property which are protected by registration are closely linked to the territory of registration. The courts at that place should be considered to have jurisdiction over all of the damage said to have resulted from the infringement of the registered trademark which is, in the material sense, property which the acts of the defendant have damaged in the place in which it was resigtered and protected. The principle was applied, straightforwardly and uncontroversially, in *Coty Germany GmbH v. First Note Perfumes NV*,[1247] to damage which took the form of unfair competition within the jurisdiction of the court where the tort of unfair competition was committed by the infringement

---

1245 It would be particularly nauseating to discover that this allowed a 'celebrity' who claimed to be habitually resident in Jersey, Monaco, or the Isle of Man, or other strange little enclave, whenever the tax man came calling, to argue that the centre of his interests was in a Member State for the purposes of this aspect of Art. 7(2). It will not happen if the individual does not have a domicile in a Member State, but it is not hard to see how this condition might also be met.

1246 C-523/10, EU:C:2012:320, [2013] Bus LR 150.

1247 C-360/12, EU:C:2014:1318.

of a Community trademark. In essence, the Court encourages the national court to take a sensible approach to the 'localising' of the damage.

Copyright is rather more complicated, but the effect of *Pinckney v. KDG Mediatech GmbH*,[1248] and *Hi Hotel HCF Sarl v. Spoering*,[1249] is much the same. Special jurisdiction on the basis of its being the place where the damage occurred may be taken in the place or places in which the infringement is brought to fruition, but as copyright is territorial, it is confined to the damage which occurs within that jurisdiction. Insofar as the right is to control reproduction of that which is protected by copyright, the place where the damage occurs is the place where that right to regulate and control (and to charge a fee for) the right to copy has been trespassed on, even where the infringement has been committed by internet communication.

2.205 The 'causal event' limb of *Bier*: uniform interpretation of the event giving rise to the damage

The court with jurisdiction under the second limb of *Bier* is the court for the place of the event[1250] giving rise to the damage which is jurisdictionally significant under the first limb. The material question is which of the antecedent parts of the story *is* to be seen as the event giving rise to the damage; and this will be determined in a uniform manner which is not particularly tied to the elements of the cause of action pleaded before the court.

The point about its being approached in a uniform manner is important, because the legal systems of the Member States understand and construct their torts or delicts in differing ways. One may take product liability as an example. Suppose a defendant has designed, but has insufficiently tested, a pharmaceutical product in Member State A, and sold it, but without a warning of the harm it can do, in Member State B. And suppose it is acquired by a claimant-victim, and causes injury, in Member State C.[1251] As a matter of English private international law, at least as traditionally understood, there would be a tendency to see the event giving rise to the damage as being the sale without proper warning in State B.[1252] But it may well be the case that other legal systems would see the event as being the original design or manufacturing process, and would see special jurisdiction under the 'causal event' limb of Bier as properly founded in State A. Were jurisdiction under the 'causal event' limb of Bier to be viewed through the lens of national law, the application of the rule would be more likely to vary from Member State to Member State than it would if a different approach had been taken instead.[1253]

In order to reduce the possibility of inconsistent and unpredictable results in the operation of the Brussels I Regulation, the identification of the event giving rise to the damage will

---

1248 C-170/12, EU:C: 2013:635, [2014] ILPr 101.

1249 C-387/12, EU:C:2014:215, [2014] 1 WLR 1912. And see also C-441/13 *Hejduk v EnergieAgentur.NRW GmbH* EU:C:2015:28.

1250 This formulation is wide enough to encompass causes of action based on culpable inaction by a defendant, where it is presumably necessary to enquire where action was required so that it may be deduced that its failure to be delivered may be seen as the causative event.

1251 The issue might have arisen in C-198/08 *Zuid-Chemie BV v. Phillippo's Mineralenfabriek NV/SA* [2009] ECR I-6917, in which a toxic product was supplied to a victim who used it in an industrial process. But it was common ground that the place of the event which gave rise to the damage was not in the Member State whose courts were seised, so the only question referred and addressed was one concering the place where the damage occurred.

1252 See, for example, *Castree v. Squibb (ER) & Sons Ltd* [1980] 1 WLR 1248; and see para 4.71, below.

1253 With the unattractive possibility that State A thought State B had jurisdiction under this limb, and vice versa.

not be dependent on the peculiarities of the law of tort of the court proposed to be seised. This results from the decisions in *Shevill v. Presse Alliance SA*,[1254] and *Marinari v. Lloyd's Bank plc*.[1255] In *Shevill*, a case of defamation by newspaper, the Court stated that the event giving rise to the damage took place where the publisher of the newspaper was established and the production of a lying newspaper was organised, and not where the actual copies of it were shown to a third party. This is not how the English law of libel would have understood the matter: it would have been more inclined to see the dissemination of the newspaper as the event giving rise to damage, and the reception of the information gathered from it as the damage occurring: but a uniform approach was preferred.

A uniform approach was adopted in *Marinari*, in which the formulation of the *actio injuriarum* of Italian law was not taken as the framework for the identification of two limbs of *Bier*. The event giving rise to the damage was held to have taken place where the promissory notes were confiscated, and not where the depleted patrimony was eaten into or diminished. And in *DFDS Torline A/S v. SEKO*[1256] the harmful event was considered to be the giving of notice of industrial action to the employer: this was given and taken in Sweden, which was to be seen as the place where the harmful event had originated. In no case did the Court accept that the definition of the cause of action according to national law formed the basis and precondition for the application of what is now Article 7(2). On each occasion it decided for itself which was to be seen as the event giving rise to the damage.

This approach was inevitable. In many cases there is no need for a refined analysis of the cause of action: it is easy to identify the event which gave rise to the damage.[1257] In some it is less so: the case of product liability, given above, is a good example of a case in which only a ruling from the European Court can give a definitive answer to the question. No doubt something similar will be true of the so-called economic torts, in which national laws, no doubt, have very different ideas of what makes a good cause of action.

2.206 The 'causal event' limb of *Bier*: the significant event at the beginning of the story

The Court has tended to favour an interpretation of the event giving rise to the damage which enquires where the damage-causing event originated. If that can be understood to have had its centre of gravity in a single place, that will be the place of the event, but where it is not possible, the focus is on the event at the start, rather than at the end, of the story. The cases may not make the point with indisputable clarity, but a serviceable answer can still be obtained. In *Shevill v. Presse Alliance SA*,[1258] it was the production (editorial and printing) of the newspaper with its defamatory material, rather than the distribution or sale, which gave rise to the damage. In *DFDS Torline A/S v. SEKO*,[1259] it was the place where the notice of industrial action was given and received, since that was 'the place where the

---

1254 C-68/93, [1995] ECR I-415.

1255 C-364/93, [1995] ECR I-2719.

1256 C-18/02, [2004] ECR I-1417.

1257 In *Anton Durbeck GmbH v. Den Norske Bank ASA* [2003] EWCA Civ 147, [2003] QB 1160, the decision to arrest a ship was taken at the London branch of the mortgagee bank, and that identified the harmful event. An appeal to the House of Lords was withdrawn.

1258 C-68/93, [1995] ECR I-415.

1259 C-18/02, [2004] ECR I-1417.

harmful event originated'.[1260] If that is a fair reading of the guidance given by the Court, the judge in *Domicrest Ltd v. Swiss Bank Corp*[1261] was correct in looking for the act or omission which lay at the beginning of, not further along, the causal chain. He reasoned that the place of the event which gave rise to the damage was where the misstatement originated, not where it was received and acted on by the claimant.

And in *Kainz v. Pantherwerke AG*,[1262] a claim for damages for personal injury resulting from use of a bicycle which had been purchased and which was defective or dangerous, it was held that the place of manufacture, rather than of acquisition, was the place of the event giving rise to the damage. The Court considered that the place of manufacture was the best place to gather the evidence which would establish the defect in question, and was consistent with the requirement that rules governing jurisdiction should be predictable. If the gist of the case is that something went wrong in the manufacture, so that the thing was inherently dangerous, this is plainly correct.[1263] As to the argument that the place of purchase should be identified instead, the treatment by the Court was odd, for it seems to have elided the place of acquisition with the domicile of the claimant.[1264] A better point might have been that the case was not one in which the essence of the wrong lay in the absence of a warning – it was hardly as though there should have been a bright yellow sticker on the saddle saying 'do not ride this bicycle because the frame will shatter into pieces, the wheel will come off and you will be hurled into the oncoming traffic', or something like that. However, there will be other cases in which the proposition that the causative event really is the failure to give a proper warning, rather than the very manufacture, will make perfect sense. The pharmaceutical product which has nothing inherently wrong with it, but which should not be taken when pregnant,[1265] or with alcohol, or when operating heavy machinery, for example, gives rise to damage because of the lack of warning. It may therefore be that in other kinds of product liability, the case for arguing that the place of the failure to deliver a suitable warning is the place of the event which actually gives rise to the damage.

Whatever else it may have done, *Kainz* identifies an event at the beginning of the process, rather than a later one, as that which is the event which gives rise to the damage. Other cases involving more complex facts have generally kept to this line. In the case of the infringement of a trademark, the Court explained that 'in the case of an alleged infringement of a national trade mark registered in a Member State because of the display, on the search engine website, of an advertisement using a keyword identical to that trade mark, it is the activation by the advertiser of the technical process displaying, according to pre-defined parameters, the advertisement which it created for its own commercial communications which should be considered to be the event giving rise to an alleged infringement, and not the display of the advertisement itself'.[1266] That also lends further support to the view, pro-

---

1260 At [41].

1261 [1999] QB 548. See also *Waterford Wedgwood plc v. Nagli* [1999] 3 All ER 185; *McGraw Hill International (UK) Ltd v Deutscher Apotheker- und Arztebank EG* [2014] EWHC 2436 (Comm), [2014] 2 Lloyd's Rep 523.

1262 C-45/13, EU:C:2014:7, [2015] QB 34.

1263 See, for a further illustration, *Allen v. Depuy International Ltd* [2014] EWHC 753 (QB) [2015] 2 WLR 442 (a case on the event giving rise to the damage for the purpose of the Rome II Regulation, but identifying the place of manufacture of a defective hip, rather than the place of its sale, or sale without a warning).

1264 At [30]–[32].

1265 *Cf Distillers Co Ltd v. Thompson* [1971] AC 458.

1266 C-523/10 *Wintersteiger AG v. Products 4U Sondermaschinenbau GmbH* EU:C:2012:320, [2013] Bus LR 150. See also C-441/13 *Hejduk v EnergieAgentur.NRW GmbH* EU:C:2015:28.

posed above, that the substantial event at the beginning, not at the end, of the commission of that which gave rise to the damage is the pointer to special jurisdiction under this rule.

2.207 The 'causal event' limb of *Bier*: the person whose act or omission is material

The English courts always understood that the event which gave rise to the damage must be understood as being an event which had the defendant's own fingerprints on it.[1267] It was not enough to establish the special jurisdiction of a court over a defendant for it to be said that the event which gave rise to the damage took place within the jurisdiction of the court, and for the defendant to be said to be substantively liable. It was necessary to show that it was the defendant's act which was within the jurisdiction of the court, though always remembering that where one person acts through another, or where one of a number of joint tortfeasors did an act on behalf of all, that might be sufficient to implicate the actual defendant.

It now appears that the English courts were thinking along the right lines. In a couple of recent cases, in which the litigation strategy was quite mystifying, an attempt was made to assert special jurisdiction over a defendant in circumstances in which the defendant had done nothing within the jurisdiction of the court, while the person who did act within the jurisdiction of the court was not sued and was therefore not before the Court. In *Melzer v. MF Global UK Ltd*,[1268] a German firm had managed a client's trading account with a London futures broker in a way which lost the client a lot of money. The client complained that he had not been warned that he might sustain losses, or some such, and sued the broker in Germany, alleging that it had assisted the German firm to cause harm to him unlawfully. He did not sue the German firm, but contended that its acts were sufficiently attributable to the broker for the broker to be subject to the special jurisdiction of the German court under the 'causal event' limb of *Bier*. The Court disagreed. While it might be part of substantive law that the acts of one party justify the imposition of substantive liability upon another, the proposition that a court would be permitted or required to investigate substantive tort law in order to determine whether the act of a non-party was attributable to a defendant whose act it was not, was a recipe for confusion, and for divergence between the answers which would be given by different courts. It was therefore inadmissible. So also in *Coty Germany GmbH v. First Note Perfumes NV*,[1269] in which the only one among many participants in an act of unfair competition who was sued had not himself acted within the jurisdiction of the court, with the result that the 'causal event' limb of *Bier* was not available.

2.208 No 'accessory' special jurisdiction under Article 7(2)

It was established by *Kalfelis* that a court with jurisdiction over so much of a claim as falls within Article 7(2) does not have the right to assume jurisdiction over related parts of the claim, but over which it would not independently have had special jurisdiction. This prin-

---

1267 *Dexter Ltd v. Harley*, The Times, 2 April 2001.
1268 C-228/11, EU:C:2013:305, [2013] QB 1112. The principle was applied in C-387/12 *Hi Hotel HCF Sarl v. Spoering* EU:C:2014:215, [2014] 1 WLR 1912 without elaboration or comment, though the Court went on, in the latter case (as it had been asked to by the referring court) to consider the application of the 'damage limb' of *Bier*.
1269 C-360/12, EU:C:2014:911. But the damage limb was applicable.

ciple was applied in *Shevill* to explain why it was that the English court had jurisdiction over only so much of the claim as alleged damage occurring in England.

2.209 Special jurisdiction in respect of threatened or anticipated torts

The original rule in the Brussels Convention, where it appeared as Article 5(3), was drafted in the past tense, and therefore appeared at first sight to be inapplicable to claims based on torts which had not yet occurred. Even if it was unsafe to assume that such a construction was decisive – for the place in which a defendant is threatening to commit a tort is the most rational place for a court to have jurisdiction to decide whether he may be or should be impeded – it would have been difficult to overcome. It was obviously[1270] sensible for the courts for the place where the harmful event was threatened to occur, or was feared to occur, to have special jurisdiction, and Article 7(2) of Regulation 1215/2012 now makes express provision for it. Indeed, when the change was first made, in Regulation 44/2001, the Court actually saw that as justification for it to interpret Article 5(3) of the Brussels Convention in conformity with the incoming Regulation.[1271]

Article 7(2) of the Regulation, therefore, applies to threatened torts, as perhaps distinct from threats of damage within the jurisdiction resulting from a tort which has already been committed. As indicated above, it makes every sense for the courts of the place where it is feared that the damage will occur, as well as the place of the event threatened to give rise to it, to have jurisdiction over a claim in respect of the threatened tort, in just the same way as the court may have special jurisdiction after the tort is committed. The legislative amendment to confirm special jurisdiction in the courts of the place where it is feared that damage will occur is wholly welcome.

2.210 International jurisdiction in the English court

If Article 7(2) applies, it gives international jurisdiction to the courts of the place where the harmful event occurred. It does not simply give international jurisdiction to the courts of a Member State, but allocates special jurisdiction to the courts for the part of the United Kingdom in which the harmful event occurred. There is, therefore, neither room nor need for rules of internal United Kingdom law to specify the part of the United Kingdom which has jurisdiction. Equally, if the Regulation gives jurisdiction to the courts of a place within, or part of, the United Kingdom, there can be no question of a rule of English law, such as *forum non conveniens*, being employed to obtain a stay of proceedings in favour of the courts of another part of the United Kingdom which, *ex hypothesi*, do not have jurisdiction according to the Regulation.[1272]

1270 *Kitechnology BV v. Unicor Plastmaschinen BV* [1995] FSR 765. See also *Beecham Group plc v. Norton Healthcare Ltd* [1997] FSR 81 and *The Eras EIL Actions* [1992] 1 Lloyd's Rep 570.

1271 C–167/00 *VfK v. Henkel* [2002] ECR I-8111.

1272 This proposition was questioned in *Lennon v. Scottish Daily Record* [2004] EWHC 359 (QB), but assuming the case to be one to which the Regulation applies (that is, the case concerns the international jurisdiction of the court, as to which, see above, para. 2.28) the proposition in the text was well supported by the text of the Regulation, and is in effect confirmed by C–386/05 *Color Drack GmbH v. Lexx International Vertriebs GmbH* [2007] ECR I-3699 (where the case was clearly concerned with a matter of international jurisdiction).

2.211 Special jurisdiction over civil claims raised in criminal cases: Article 7(3)

Article 7(3) of Regulation 1215/2012 provides:

> *A person domiciled in a Member State may be sued in another Member State:*
> *(3) as regards a civil claim for damages or restitution which is based on an act giving rise to criminal proceedings, in the court seised of those proceedings, to the extent that that court has jurisdiction under its own law to entertain civil proceedings.*

Article 7(3) is identical to Article 5(4) of Regulation 44/2001.

A person domiciled in a Member State, who is the subject of criminal proceedings in the courts of another Member State, may be made subject to the special jurisdiction of that court to entertain civil claims in the course of those proceedings. Criminal proceedings as such fall outside the scope of the Regulation; but it was understood that to allow such a defendant to resist an order for compensation properly made in those proceedings on the basis of his having a domicile in another Member State would unduly interfere with the process.[1273] Even so, it may mean that an order for compensation may be made by a court which has asserted jurisdiction on the basis of a rule otherwise wholly incompatible with the scheme of the Regulation, such as the nationality of the victim of the crime.[1274]

Article 7(3) may raise a particular issue in relation to the date on which proceedings are to be regarded as begun if a civil claim is asserted during a criminal procedure which was instituted some time earlier. In principle, the date of seisin will be the date on which the civil claim is made, even if, for some purposes of the foreign system, the civil claim is backdated and treated as having been filed on the date on which the criminal proceedings were begun. It is clear that the issues will be very much dependent on the precise nature of the foreign process, but that a rule of strict chronology may cut through it.[1275]

2.212 Special jurisdiction over civil claims to recover a cultural object: Article 7(4)

Article 7(4) of Regulation 1215/2012 provides that:

> *A person domiciled in a Member State may be sued in another Member State:*
> *(4) as regards a civil claim for the recovery, based on ownership, of a cultural object as defined in point 1 of Article 1 of Directive 93/7/EEC initiated by the person claiming the right to recover such an object, in the courts for the place where the cultural object is situated at the time when the court is seised.*

The provision in Article 7(4) is new. Recital (17) to the Regulation does little more than recite the terms of the Article as a matter which should be provided for. It obviously makes sense that if proceedings are to be brought to recover property (presumably auction houses and galleries are the intended target) it should be possible to bring them where the property is located, even if the defendant is domiciled in another Member State, though whether there is a sufficient reason to confine the rule to items of cultural property is perhaps more

---

1273 See C-172/91 *Sonntag v. Waidmann* [1993] ECR I-1963.

1274 See, for example, C-7/98 *Krombach v. Bamberski* [2000] ECR I-1935. Article 64 of Regulation 1215/2012 contains provision as to legal representation and the right to be represented in such cases. See also Lowenfeld, 'Jurisdiction, Enforcement, Public Policy and Res Judicata: The Krombach Case,' in Einhorn and Siehr (eds), *Intercontinental Cooperation Through Private International Law* (TMC Asser, The Hague, 2004).

1275 See for illustration only, *Grupo Torras SA v. Sheikh Fahad Mohammed Al-Sabah* [1996] 1 Lloyd's Rep 7.

debatable and may in due course be debated. It appears from the wording of the rule that it does not permit proceedings to be brought for a declaration of non-liabilty, or for other proceedings to confirm title, to be brought by the person from whom any recovery might later be sought. Any such proceedings sought to be brought by a person whose title might be challenged will need to be based on other jurisdictional grounds.

2.213 Special jurisdiction over a defendant operating through a branch or agency: Article 7(5)

Article 7(5) of Regulation 1215/2012 provides that:

> A person domiciled in a Member State may be sued in another Member State:
> (5) as regards a dispute arising out of the operations of a branch, agency or other establishment, in the courts for the place where the branch, agency or other establishment is situated.

Article 7(5) is practically identical to Article 5(5) of Regulation 44/2001.

2.214 General

The explanation for Article 7(5), in general terms at least, is that if a defendant has set up a sufficient and permanent-looking establishment in another Member State, he has laid himself open to being sued there in just the same way as he would be if he were to have established a domicile there. The principal point which distinguishes special jurisdiction under Article 7(5) from the general jurisdiction conferred by Article 4 is, however, that Article 7(5) applies only to claims which arise out of the operations of the particular establishment, and does not extend to claims against the defendant generally. Moreover, whereas general jurisdiction under Article 4 may serve as the anchor for bringing claims against other defendants,[1276] Article 7(5), as a species of special jurisdiction, has no such power of gravitational attraction.

It is instructive to compare special jurisdiction under Article 7(5) of the Regulation with its approximate common law counterpart. English common law accepts that if a defendant is present within the jurisdiction of the English courts, or may otherwise be served within the jurisdiction, he may be sued in respect of all claims against him, whether or not these arise from activities which are local. As the presence of a corporation may be shown by pointing to a place at which its business is done, a defendant corporation may be sued in England, by reason of its having a place of business, in respect of claims which have nothing to do with that place of business or local establishment;[1277] and the common law will recognise a foreign judgment on the same basis.[1278] Under the laws of several of the United States, long-arm jurisdiction may be exercised over a defendant who has carried on business within the jurisdiction, or who has 'purposefully availed himself' of that jurisdiction;[1279] but whether

---

1276 Regulation 1215/2012, Art. 8(1); see further below, para. 2.225.

1277 Though the power to stay proceedings on the ground of *forum non conveniens* will limit the practical scope of this rule.

1278 *Adams v. Cape Industries plc* [1990] Ch 433 (with no limitation for considerations of *forum conveniens*: see further, para. 7.48).

1279 *International Shoe Co v. Washington* 326 US 310 (1945); *Asahi Metal Industry Co v. Superior Court of California* 480 US 102 (1987).

jurisdiction asserted on the basis of such a connection is general and unrestricted, or specific and limited to claims which arise out of the particular act of business, is less clear.[1280]

By contrast, the special jurisdiction under Article 7(5) is much more carefully defined and limited, and though it may provide an incentive for a defendant to conceal exactly which of its offices was or were involved in the facts which gave rise to a claim, the limited scope of the rule is welcome.

If the analogy with domicile were to be pressed to its logical conclusion, then although the claim would have needed to have arisen while the establishment was in operation, one would also expect that the establishment should be required still to be there on the date on which proceedings are commenced. After all, if a defendant has a domicile in England on the date on which a cause of action arose, but no longer has it by the time the proceedings are instituted, Article 4 does not allow him to be sued in England on the basis of his having earlier had a domicile there.[1281] On the other hand, most of the grounds of special jurisdiction in Article 7 are framed in terms of a connection to a cause of action; and if this is the basis for the analogy, it may suggest that as long as there was an establishment at the date on which the cause of action arose, out of the operations of which the dispute arose, the basis for special jurisdiction over the defendant will have been established, and will endure even if the establishment has ceased to function by the date of institution of proceedings.

No authority precisely deals with the point; the arguments would appear to be pretty evenly balanced. In *Lloyd's Register of Shipping v. Soc Campenon Bernard*,[1282] the Advocate General accepted that what is now Article 7(5) served two purposes: to allow a claimant, observing the appearance of permanency in the branch, agency or other establishment, to know that he need not deal with the head office of the defendant; and to approximate to the general jurisdiction given in what is now Article 4 of Regulation 1215/2012.[1283] The latter observation points to the conclusion that the establishment must still be present and functioning as such on the date on which the proceedings are instituted, and that if it has been closed down in the meantime, Article 7(5) will no longer be available.[1284] But it cannot be said that the point has been decided.

2.215 Branch, agency or other establishment

The Court has given guidance, but which falls short of being a dictionary definition, on the uniform definition of what constitutes a branch, agency or other establishment.[1285] The gist of it is that the entity must have a fixed place of business which has the appearance of permanence, that it is under and subject to the direction and control of the defendant, but that it also has the power to bind the defendant by its own acts. Too great a degree of independence will lead to the conclusion that the body is not a branch, etc., of the defendant, but an independent body whose acts are its own and not those of the defendant. From the

---

1280 *Helicopteros Nacionales de Columbia SA v. Hall* 466 US 408 (1984): as there is an overall constitutional requirement of due process, this issue tends to be dealt with on an individual, rather than a definitional, basis.

1281 *Canada Trust Co v. Stolzenberg (No 2)* [2002] 1 AC 1.

1282 C-439/93, [1995] ECR I-961.

1283 A conclusion echoed in *Anton Durbeck GmbH v. Den Norske Bank ASA* [2003] EWCA Civ 147, [2003] QB 1160, [43]: 'a quasi-defendant's domicile basis for jurisdiction'.

1284 But Arts 7(1) and 7(2) are not so restricted, and will in many cases simply provide an alternative basis for special jurisdiction in the place where the establishment was: *Lloyd's Register of Shipping*.

1285 It appears that although there appear to be three separate concepts here, they are in fact only one.

decisions of the Court, it appears that the branch or branch office is the paradigm for the application of Article 7(5). A distribution agency may therefore fall outside Article 7(5) by reason of its having too great a degree of independence in the manner in which it carries on its business.

Four principal decisions paint the overall picture of what constitutes a branch or agency. In *De Bloos Sprl v. Bouyer SA*,[1286] a French company appointed a Belgian company to be its exclusive distributor in Belgium: what is now Article 7(5) did not apply, with the result that the French company was not subject to the special jurisdiction of the Belgian courts. This was because the distributor was able to conduct its business without the direction and control from the French company. Indeed, if it had been in business as distributor for more than the one company's products, the case would have been all the stronger. In *Somafer SA v. Saar-Ferngas AG*,[1287] a French company had an employee who acted as its sales representative in Germany: what is now Article 7(5) did not apply, with the result that the French company was not subject to the special jurisdiction of the German courts. Although headed notepaper furnished some evidence of the French company's being present in Germany, there was no fixed place of business established or maintained in Germany. The Court observed that the Article, as an exception to the general jurisdictional rule now in Article 4 of Regulation 1215/2012, was to be construed restrictively.[1288] More significant, perhaps, was the fact that the representative in Germany had no power to bind the French company. The Article was therefore inapplicable.[1289] In *Blanckaert & Willems PVBA v. Trost*,[1290] an independent commercial agent had been appointed by the defendant, but was permitted also to represent other firms operating in the same sphere of business. She was entitled to fix her own conditions of work. It was held that an action brought against her principal did not fall within what is now Article 7(5) because the principal had insufficient control over the activities of a distinctly independent representative.

Lastly, in *SAR Schotte GmbH v. Parfums Rothschild Sàrl*,[1291] a German seller entered into contracts with a German company which appeared to be acting on behalf a French buyer. It was held that the French buyer could be sued in Germany under what is now Article 7(5), on the basis that the German company[1292] appeared to be acting on behalf of the French buyer and the French buyer was bound by the appearance it had created. In other words, if a company appears to have set up another to do its business, what is now Article 7(5) will allow the existence of the created entity to bring the defendant which created it within Article 7(5) of the Regulation. The principle is not, formally at any rate, one of estoppel,

---

1286 14/76, [1976] ECR 1497.

1287 33/78, [1978] ECR 2183.

1288 At [7].

1289 The English case law on the carrying on of business, for the purpose of jurisdiction and the recognition of foreign judgments (see *Adams v. Cape Industries* [1990] Ch 433), looks for similar factors in requiring the body present to have its own fixed place of business at which the business of the company is carried on, but does not require the transaction in question to have originated at that branch.

1290 139/80, [1981] ECR 819. See also *New Hampshire Insurance Co v. Strabag Bau AG* [1990] 2 Lloyd's Rep 61, affirmed on different grounds [1992] 1 Lloyd's Rep 361; *Latchin v. General Mediterranean Holdings SA* [2002] CLC 330.

1291 218/86, [1987] ECR 4905.

1292 Unusually, the German company was in fact the parent of the French company. But this did not prejudice the operation of Art. 7(5), as the relationship of control was sufficient to satisfy the requirements of the Article.

but the outcome of the cases is not very different from what a doctrine of estoppel by representation might have produced.[1293]

Once the test of permanence or apparency has been satisfied, the acid test may be to ask whether the body has been invested with the power to make contracts which bind the principal. This, certainly, was identified as the single most decisive factor by the Advocate General in *Shearson Lehmann Hutton Inc v. TVB*,[1294] and, though the Court did not need to deal with the particular point in disposing of that case, the acceptance of this as the touchstone for special jurisdiction would give an objective foundation to a test which is otherwise more impressionistic than perhaps it should be.

2.216 Dispute arising from the operations of the branch, agency or establishment

It is not sufficient that the branch or agency exists and satisfies the tests of apparency and permanence. The dispute must also arise out of the operations of that branch or agency. In *Somafer SA v. Saar-Ferngas AG*, the Court elaborated this element of the definition, saying that it encompassed actions concerning the running or management of the agency, and actions relating to business contracted in the name of the parent,[1295] and non-contractual cases arising from the activities of the agency. It plainly does not follow that a defendant which has carried on business in a particular Member State is necessarily exposed to the special jurisdiction of the courts of that Member State. The particular act or activity which gives rise to liability must[1296] fall within one of the three categories of activity – running, management, business done in the name of – given above.[1297]

It is not a requirement that the activity undertaken by the branch must be carried out in the Member State in which the branch is situated. A suggestion that there was such a further limiting condition was clearly present the judgment in *Somafer*,[1298] but it was rejected in *Lloyd's Register of Shipping v. Soc Campenon Bernard*.[1299] In that case, the French branch of the defendant, a classification society domiciled in the United Kingdom, contracted to provide services which would actually be performed for, and delivered to, the claimant by the defendant's sub-contractor in Spain. It was held that what is now Article 7(5) gave the French courts special jurisdiction over the defendant, even though the actual work was to be performed in Spain, because the claim arose out of the operations of the French branch. Had it not been so held there would, in contractual claims at least, have been such an overlap between Articles 7(1) and 7(5) that the latter would have been deprived of significant effect. This lends some support to the proposition that Article 7(5) reflects Article 4, in that it gives

---

1293 Subject to the point that as a matter of English law, estoppel generally does not establish jurisdiction where jurisdiction is defined by statute.

1294 C-89/91, [1993] ECR I-139, at [36] of the Opinion.

1295 This does appear to be unduly narrow. If the agency contracts in its own name, but it is known (but not expressly said) that it does so on behalf of its principal, should a claim against the principal not be seen to fall within the Article?

1296 At least, on the footing that *Somafer* correctly states the law. Though it is unlikely that the Court will widen the scope of what is now Art. 7(5), the definition given does seem rather narrow.

1297 See, for example, *McGraw Hill International (UK) Ltd v. Deutscher Apotheker- und Arztebank EG* [2014] EWHC 2436 (Comm), [2014] 2 Lloyd's Rep 523.

1298 At [13].

1299 C-439/93, [1995] ECR I-961; approved and applied in *Anton Durbeck GmbH v. Den Norske Bank ASA* [2003] EWCA Civ 147, [2003] QB 1160.

jurisdiction to the courts for a place of establishment, but less clearly reflects Articles 7(1) and 7(2), which give jurisdiction to the courts at the place in which the material acts or events took place. On the other hand, if special jurisdiction is limited to so much of the dispute as does arise out of the activities of the branch or agency, the distance between it and Article 4 is clear. The truth may simply be that Article 7(5) has to be taken at face value, and that deductions and analogies are not reliable.

2.217 International jurisdiction in the English court

As Article 7(5) gives international jurisdiction to the courts for the place where the branch, agency or other establishment is situated, it will give international jurisdiction to the English courts, rather than to those of the United Kingdom. Accordingly, there is neither room nor need for a further rule of internal United Kingdom law to allocate jurisdiction within the United Kingdom.

2.218 Special jurisdiction over a trustee, beneficiary or settlor sued as such: Article 7(6)

Article 7(6) of Regulation 1215/2012 provides that:

> A person domiciled in a Member State may be sued in another Member State:
> (6) as regards a dispute brought against a settlor, trustee or beneficiary of a trust created by the operation of a statute, or by a written instrument, or created orally and evidenced in writing, in the courts of the Member State in which the trust is domiciled.

Article 7(6) is identical to Article 5(6) of Regulation 44/2001.

2.219 General

When the United Kingdom first acceded to the Brussels Convention, a provision in terms of what is now Article 7(6) was added, for the six original Contracting States had not required a special jurisdictional rule for proceedings relating to trusts. The rule of special jurisdiction applies in relation to trusts created by operation of statute, or created by a written instrument, or created orally but evidenced in writing.[1300] In respect of all such trusts, special jurisdiction is available for actions against a trustee, beneficiary or settlor, who is sued as such and who is[1301] domiciled in a Member State, in the courts of the Member State in which the trust is domiciled. The rule applies, of course, only if the dispute falls within the material scope of the Regulation in the first place: in this respect it is of particular significance that wills, matrimonial property and bankruptcy fall outside it. Professor Schlosser was of opinion[1302] that a trust created by a contract for the sale of land does not fall within the provision, although as the contract must itself be made in writing in order to have any legal effect, it is not certain that this is correct.

1300 Thereby excluding remedial constructive trusts, if such things really exist. For the problems which have arisen, see *Williams v. Central Bank of Nigeria* [2014] UKSC 10, [2014] AC 1189.

1301 Probably at the institution of proceedings, not at the date of the setting up of the trust: *Chellaram v. Chellaram* [2002] EWHC 632 (Ch), [2002] 3 All ER 17.

1302 [1979] OJ C59/71, [117], [172].

According to Article 63(3) of Regulation 1215/2012, the domicile of a trust is ascertained by reference to rules of private international law of the Member State whose courts are seised of the case.[1303] In England, those rules are contained in paragraph 12 of Schedule 1 to the Civil Jurisdiction and Judgments Order 2001.[1304]

2.220 Trusts domiciled in the United Kingdom

Although Article 63(3) of the Regulation and paragraph 12(2) of Schedule 1 to the 2001 Order combine to mean that a trust is domiciled in the United Kingdom only if it is domiciled in a part of the United Kingdom, paragraph 12(3) provides that a trust is domiciled in a part of the United Kingdom if and only if the law of that part is the system of law with which the trust has its closest and most real connection.

As a consequence, if the law with which the trust has its closest and most real connection is English law, the trust will be domiciled in the United Kingdom for the purposes of the Regulation. When that is so, Article 7(6) will confer international jurisdiction upon the courts of the United Kingdom. It is therefore necessary for rules of internal United Kingdom law to specify the part of the United Kingdom which is to have special jurisdiction for the purpose of Article 7(6). Paragraph 7(2) of Schedule 1 to the 2001 Order[1305] provides that the proceedings shall be brought in the part of the United Kingdom in which the trust is domiciled. The course of this rather elaborate path leads to the broad conclusion that English law trusts are domiciled in England, and that no other trusts are.

The identification of the system of law with which a trust has its closest and most real connection will be straightforward if the settlor selected and expressed the law to govern the trust.[1306] Where this has been done, it is very hard to imagine that an express choice of law will not be the system of law with which the trust has its closest and most real connection. It was accepted in *Gómez v. Gómez-Monche Vives*[1307] that it was theoretically possible to imagine a case in which an express choice of law would not have this effect, but such cases, if they exist at all, will be very rare indeed. It also follows that factual connections with a country other than that of the chosen law will be unlikely to displace the chosen law as the system of law with which the trust is most closely connected, as the required connection is with a system of law, not a country.[1308]

2.221 The nature of the proceedings falling within Article 7(6)

More difficulty may arise if it is questioned whether the person being sued is being sued as settlor, trustee or beneficiary, as distinct from being sued in an individual capacity, as stranger to the trust. For not everyone who is trustee or beneficiary is sued as trustee or beneficiary. Where this question arises, it will be necessary to decide whether the proceedings

---

1303 Article 63(3).

1304 Which substantially replaces s. 45 of the 1982 Act: SI 2001/3929. See para. 2.158, above.

1305 As amended by SI 2014/2947, Sch. 2, para. 3(9).

1306 Recognition of Trusts Act 1987, enacting certain provisions of the Hague Convention on the Recognition of Trusts.

1307 [2008] EWCA Civ 1065, [2009] Ch 245.

1308 Although one may wonder why the words 'system of' were included in the 2001 Order. If all that was meant was 'the law with which the trust is most closely connected', then the words 'system of' are superfluous.

are brought against the defendant *as* settlor, trustee or beneficiary. In the *Gómez* case, proceedings were brought against the defendant, who was a discretionary beneficiary of the trust, to recover property which, it was said, was excessive and had been paid to her in breach of trust. The claim alleged that as she was not entitled to receive it, and knew that fact, she was liable to account as constructive trustee. The defendant argued that this meant that she was not being sued in her capacity as beneficiary but as an outsider who was liable to be treated as a constructive trustee, and that that took the proceedings outside what is now Article 7(6). The question whether she was sued as beneficiary appears not to have been answered on the basis of the wording of the claim as pleaded, but by discerning that, on a broad understanding of the claim as advanced, she was sued as an overpaid beneficiary, the gist of the complaint being that the distribution of property to her as beneficiary should not have been made, rather than as a stranger or appointee who had wrongly received trust property.

If the analysis of the claim was correct, the conclusion certainly follows. But it is hard to avoid the suspicion that, because the dispute would call for the application of English trusts law to determine its merits, it was convenient for the court to be able to reach the conclusion that the English court had special jurisdiction. For where there is a trusts dispute which arises from a trust which is governed by English law, it is so obviously sensible that it be heard in an English court that there is little else to be said. One imagines that the Spanish court of the defendant's domicile would appreciate the concern.[1309]

The claimant also alleged the defendant had acted unlawfully when, as donee of a power of appointment, she appointed herself as 'Appointor' of the trust. It was held that that allegation was not within what is now Article 7(6), but this is less easy to understand. It is true that the 'Appointor' is not a settlor, trustee or beneficiary, but the justification for Article 7(6) is that disputes which arise inside the circle of relationships created by the trust should be within the special jurisdiction of the court best placed to deal with them. Given that English trusts law will be pretty alien to a court in a Member State which does not have a law of trusts,[1310] the question whether the defendant had acted lawfully might well have been one impossible to determine before the Spanish court of her domicile. The court was unwilling to interpret the words of the Article in a broader sense than they are written, but even if this accords with a general principle that Article 7 is an exceptional jurisdiction, it conflicts rather sharply with the requirements of the sound administration of justice.

2.222 Jurisdiction over payment in respect of salvage claims: Article 7(7)

Article 7(7) of Regulation 1215/2012 provides that:

> *A person domiciled in a Member State may be sued in another Member State:*
> *(7) as regards a dispute concerning the payment of remuneration claimed in respect of the salvage of a cargo or freight, in the court under the authority of which the cargo or freight in question (a) has been arrested to secure such payment, or (b) could have been so arrested, but bail or other security has been given; Provided*

1309 Not only has Spain has not ratified the Hague Convention on the Recognition of Trusts, the Spanish Supreme Court recently refused to recognise a foreign trust (governed by the law of an American State) on grounds little more sophisticated than that the institution was not known to Spanish law: Tribunal Supremo (Section 1a) 30 April 2008, [2008] RJ 2685.

1310 See the previous footnote.

that this provision shall apply only if it is claimed that the defendant has an interest in the cargo or freight or had such an interest at the time of salvage.

Article 7(7) is identical to Article 5(7) of Regulation 44/2001. For the purposes of this book it is taken to be self-explanatory.

2.223 Special jurisdiction under Article 8

The opening words to Article 8 of Regulation 1215/2012 state that:

A person domiciled in a Member State may also be sued:

and are followed by four matters in which this possibility of suing of a defendant away from the domicile of his home Member State may be available.

2.224 General approach to Article 8

Article 8 provides for special jurisdiction over defendants domiciled in another Member State in certain – but certainly not in all – proceedings involving claims which are connected or interrelated. Its principal impact is in proceedings involving claims brought against two or more defendants, in relation to third-party proceedings, and in relation to counterclaims.[1311] To English eyes, at least, it has obvious and very significant shortcomings, for there are some contexts in which the efficient resolution of disputes would call for the joinder of claims into a single proceeding by which all will be bound, yet Article 8 does not allow for it. It was said in *Kalfelis v. Bankhaus Schröder Münchmeyer Hengst & Co*[1312] that what is now Article 8 must be given a narrow interpretation, so as not to call into question the general jurisdiction of the courts of the defendant's domicile. But in this respect the decision, and those subsequent decisions which have repeated this observation, is a bad one which ought to be reviewed and reversed. If the purpose of Article 8 is to secure the rational and efficient disposal of complex proceedings, and, in particular, to avoid the risk of irreconcilable judgments which would follow if co-defendants, or third-party claims, or counterclaims, were tried in separate proceedings, there is no reason to interpret it narrowly or to regard it as a threat to Article 4. One would have hoped to see the law develop in that light. But as will be seen, the signs are not promising.

2.225 Special jurisdiction over co-defendants: Article 8(1)

Article 8(1) of Regulation 1215/2012 provides that:

A person domiciled in a Member State may also be sued: (1) where he is one of a number of defendants, in the courts for the place where any one of them is domiciled, provided the claims are so closely connected that it is expedient to hear and determine them together to avoid the risk of irreconcilable judgments resulting from separate proceedings.

Article 8(1) is practically identical to Article 6(1) of Regulation 44/2001.

1311 It also applies to proceedings relating to a contract which are combined with matters relating to rights *in rem* in immovable property: see below, para 2.244.
1312 189/87, [1988] ECR 5565.

2.226 General

If there is a claim to be made against two or more defendants who have domiciles in different Member States,[1313] it is not possible for each defendant to defend at home without there being a waste of resources and a risk of two separate proceedings resulting in irreconcilable judgments. The Regulation therefore makes it possible, subject to conditions, for proceedings to be brought against all the defendants before the courts of the domicile of any one of them.

The special jurisdiction created by Article 8(1) is good as far as it goes. But it does not go far enough. It does not, for example, permit co-defendants to be joined into proceedings in a court in a Member State in which no defendant has a domicile but which is exercising jurisdiction in accordance with Article 25. The same is true, and Article 8(1) is unavailable, if proceedings are brought before a court which has jurisdiction over a defendant by reason of his voluntary appearance in accordance with Article 26, or if the court has special jurisdiction on the basis of Article 7. Only if the court into which it is proposed to join the co-defendants has jurisdiction over a defendant on the basis of domicile will the joinder be permitted. Article 8(1) provides for special jurisdiction over co-defendants only when one defendant is being sued in the courts of the Member State in which he is domiciled. It is arbitrary and makes no sense, but it is the law. The practical application, and the significance of this, is examined below.

One further point may be disposed of quickly. The meaning of 'tried together' was examined in *Masri v. Consolidated Contractors International (UK) Ltd.*[1314] It was held that what is now Article 8(1) allowed jurisdiction to be taken over a defendant domiciled in another Member State, if separate proceedings were instituted against a defendant in England, and an application were made to consolidate the proceedings. This looks rather odd if it means that proceedings over which the court did not have jurisdiction are retrospectively[1315] brought within its special jurisdiction by a procedural application for consolidation; but it looks eminently sensible if the alternative of applying to amend the proceedings against the English defendant, by adding a new claim against the co-defendant, would have brought the case within Article 8(1) in any event.[1316] However, if A has a claim against D1, and B has a claim against D2, then even if the claims against D1 and D2 are very closely connected indeed, Article 8(1) will not be available, as it is implicit in the Article that the two claims are brought by the same claimant.[1317]

Article 8(1) does not provide for special jurisdiction over another defendant unless the court has general jurisdiction over one defendant to the claim. That, however, is not enough,

---

1313 It is obvious that Art. 8(1) is not available to establish jurisdiction over a defendant who does not have a domicile in a Member State. The decision to this effect in C-645/11 *Land Berlin v. Sapir* EU:C:2013:228, [2013] ILPr 481, is an answer to a question which should never have been asked.

1314 [2005] EWCA Civ 1436, [2006] 1 WLR 830. A further appeal to the House of Lords was not proceeded with.

1315 This may be a significant point, because the Court has said, in other contexts, that jurisdiction is meant to be determined at the outset of proceedings, and not altered in the light of subsequent events, such as the filing of a defence: see para. 2.265, below.

1316 Moreover, the fact is that the Regulation does not harmonise procedure. Different national systems organise the structure and nature of their courts and adjudications differently, and nothing of importance ought to turn on the question whether there are bifurcated, conjoined, or otherwise-organised proceedings: see C-18/02 *DFDS Torline A/S v. SEKO* [2004] ECR I-1417.

1317 *Madoff Securities International Ltd v. Raven* [2011] EWHC 3102 (Comm), [2012] ILPr 275.

for additional requirements must also be satisfied, some of which are apparent from the text of the Article, but some others of which are not. It will be seen that Article 8(1) is the one part of the Regulation which works badly. This is not surprising. The common law, which allows jurisdiction to be taken over a defendant who is a necessary or proper party to a claim against another defendant depends for its successful operation on a number of textual requirements, and on a flexible judicial discretion which is capable of responding to all manner of issues and sub-issues which need to be considered before a proposed co-defendant is subjected to a jurisdiction from which he is otherwise safe. Article 8(1) works as it does with a very terse text and no opportunity for a judge to weigh and balance the case for and against jurisdiction. The comparison shows that the common law has nothing to learn from Article 8(1), but that Article 8(1) would have a lot to learn from the common law.[1318]

2.227 The claim against the 'anchor' defendant: jurisdictional basis

The claim against the anchor defendant must be brought before the court of a Member State in which that defendant has a domicile.

It has been held that the date for testing the domicile of the anchor defendant is that of the institution of proceedings against him, which will mean the date of issue of the claim form which names him as defendant.[1319] It follows from the wording of Article 8(1) that if the anchor defendant does not have a domicile in that Member State, Article 8(1) is unavailable to the claimant.[1320] However, it is not material to the existence of special jurisdiction under Article 8(1) that the anchor defendant might have had grounds to challenge the general jurisdiction of the court over him but elected not to do so.[1321] Of course, his submission by appearance in accordance with Article 26 is not enough, by itself, to make him the anchor defendant. But so long as the claimant has the better of the argument on the issue – if it is in contention – that the anchor defendant has a domicile in the Member State in which proceedings are to be brought, Article 8(1) may allow special jurisdiction to be taken over a co-defendant domiciled in another Member State.[1322] It follows that the passivity of the anchor defendant may in practice jeopardise the position of a co-defendant who may have difficulty in seeking to show that the anchor defendant did not have the domicile on which the claimant relies.

It may be surprising that, if the anchor defendant is sued in a Member State other than one in which he is domiciled, but on the basis of a jurisdictional rule which has a higher place in the system of jurisdictional rules, the proceedings will not suffice for Article 8(1) to be applied. Jurisdiction which is founded on progogation in accordance with Articles 25 or 26, for example, is at least as proper as general jurisdiction which is based on domicile. Special jurisdiction as authorised by Article 7 is provided for because of the close connection between

---

1318 For the common law – relevant here only for the purpose of comparison – see *AK Investment CJSC v. Kyrgyz Mobile Tel Ltd* [2011] UKPC 7, [2012] 1 WLR 1804.

1319 *Canada Trust Co v. Stolzenberg (No 2)* [2002] 1 AC 1.

1320 If authority is needed for this proposition, see C-51/97 *Réunion Européenne SA v. Spliethoff's Bevrachtingskantoor BV* [1998] ECR I-6511, where the anchor defendant was sued on the basis of what is now Art. 6, the claims were described by the referring court as 'indivisible', and it was held, inevitably, that what is now Art. 8(1) was not available.

1321 For example, on the basis of a jurisdiction agreement for the courts of another Member State.

1322 Of course, they may seek to establish that the anchor defendant was not domiciled in the Member State where the action is brought, but in the absence of that defendant's cooperation, the establishing of the material facts may be very problematic: *cf Canada Trust Co v. Stolzenberg (No 2)* [2002] 1 AC 1.

the facts and matters liable to be in dispute and the court called upon to deal with them. All these jurisdictional rules are rational and integral to the scheme of the Regulation, yet they do not provide a basis for the joinder of a co-defendant who is domiciled in another Member State. One has to wonder why this should be. From the perspective of the co-defendant proposed to be joined, he faces the prospect of being sued in a Member State other than one in which he has a domicile. The proposition that it makes any real difference to him whether the anchor defendant, to whose case it is proposed that he be joined, is being sued where he is domiciled or is being sued on another basis for which the Regulation makes provision, is fanciful. But there it is: jurisdiction over the anchor defendant must be based on Article 4.

The unintended consequences of that last point are illustrated by the astonishingly bad decision in *GlaxoSmithKline v. Rouard*.[1323] The case was one in which an employee had two employers, each part of the GSK group, one being domiciled in France and the other in the United Kingdom. He brought proceedings against the French employer in the French courts, as Section 5 of Chapter II allowed him to do, and sought to join the latter as a co-defendant, relying on what is now Article 8(1) to do so. No doubt he considered that as he was suing the French defendant in the courts of its domicile, he was entitled to assert special jurisdiction over the second employer. The Court held that he was not entitled to do so. Its analysis was that the jurisdictional rules in Section 5 of Chapter II were exhaustive, and as they then were, did not make provision for a claim to be brought against a second joint employer in the court where, in accordance with Article 21, the claimant had the privilege[1324] of suing the first joint employer. It held that what is now Article 8(1) was not available in a case which was based on the jurisdictional privilege given to the employee by Section 5 of Chapter II, for even though he was suing the employer where it was domiciled, he was not doing so on the basis of its general domicile to which a claim against a co-defendant could be joined. The Court saw that its decision was harmful to the sound administration of justice and the economy of procedure,[1325] and it realised perfectly that it made life very difficult for the employee. It denied[1326] that this damaged the interests of the employee, but as Article 8 was to be given a narrow construction, there was no more to be said.[1327] In proceedings to which Regulation 1215/2012 applies, Article 20(1) now reverses the effect of this lamentable judgment in cases in which an employee sues an employer and seeks to join a co-defendant. But the decision illustrates the way in which, until very recently at least, the Court has treated jurisdiction under Article 8(1) in a notably chilly fashion.

2.228 The nature of the claim against the 'anchor' defendant

Several questions arise which have their focus on the quality of the claim against the anchor defendant.

First, it is not a requirement of Article 8(1) that the anchor defendant be the principal target of the claimant, or be the defendant against whom the claim principally lies. The

---

1323 C-462/06, [2008] ECR I-3965.

1324 It appears to have been a privilege that he could not renounce: he was not permitted to rely on what is now Art. 4 rather than on Section 5 of Chapter II.

1325 At [27].

1326 How it persuaded itself of this was a mystery.

1327 At [28]. Were there to be a prize for the most bone-headed judgment of the last two decades, this one would be found to have few serious rivals.

Regulation does not say so, and evaluation of such a condition would be difficult and unpredictable, and therefore damaging to legal certainty. No doubt there are cases in which there is suspicion that, once special jurisdiction has been established over the co-defendant, the claim against the local defendant will not be pursued with any vigour, or may even be discontinued. The question whether to admit such a point to be made, and how to respond to it if it is made, is not easy in a jurisdictional system which does not give the court a general discretion, or perhaps any discretion, in deciding whether to allow jurisdiction to be asserted.[1328] A possible response, evidently favoured by the European Court, is to investigate the purpose for bringing the claim against the local defendant;[1329] but as will be shown, that will not address all the causes of possible concern, and is not, in any event, evidently vouched for by the text of the Article.

Second, what is the relevance of the fact – assuming it to be a fact – that the claim against the anchor defendant is doomed to fail? To judge from the decision in *Reisch Montage AG v. Kiesel Baumaschinen Handels GmbH*,[1330] the fact that the court will not – because it cannot – give judgment against the anchor defendant does not mean that Article 8(1) is not available to establish jurisdiction over a proposed co-defendant.[1331] In that case, proceedings were brought before the Austrian courts in respect of a debt of €8,000. The principal debtor was domiciled in Austria, the guarantor in Germany. The guarantor disputed the application of what is now Article 8(1) on the ground that the claim against the principal debtor had been dismissed *ab initio* as inadmissible, by reason of the latter's insolvency at the date the proceedings were instituted. There was therefore no possibility of a judgment against the principal debtor, and therefore no possibility of irreconcilable judgments – because it was not legally possible for there to be two judgments – if the guarantor was not joined to the Austrian proceedings.[1332] The Court, however, held that the Article was applicable, giving as its reason the principle that a rule of national law could not prejudice the application of the Regulation.[1333] That may be so; but matters of arithmetic are not rules of national law. The decision of the European Court cannot be defended; Article 8(1) should not be applicable if there can in law be no judgment against the anchor defendant with which judgment against the proposed co-defendant could be irreconcilable.[1334]

1328 Contrast this with the position in *AK Investment CJSC v. Kyrgyz Mobile Tel Ltd* [2011] UKPC 7, [2012] 1 WLR 1804, dealing with service out of the jurisdiction on a necessary or proper party with leave of the court, in which the Privy Council accepted that discretion had a considerable part to play in determining whether service should be authorised. Article 8(1) gives no such freedom to the court, and the result is that legal analysis has become rather strained.

1329 See the paragraphs which follow.

1330 C-103/05, [2006] ECR I-6827.

1331 The fact that the court has given judgment in default of his appearance against the anchor defendant does not prevent the application of the Article to the claim against a co-defendant: *Linuzs v. Latmar Holdings Corp* [2013] EWCA Civ 4.

1332 In some sense, of course, non-proceedings.

1333 *Cf ET Plus SA v. Welter* [2005] EWHC 2115 (Comm), [2006] 1 Lloyd's Rep 251, [57], where proceedings against a local defendant were stayed for arbitration and the judge concluded that, as a result, that defendant was not available as the anchor defendant. This, it is submitted, is a much preferable construction and application of the Article: as there was not going to be a trial against the defendant who had obtained the stay for arbitration, the application of what is now Art. 8(1) was unnecessary according to its terms.

1334 An English judge may be obliged to be more circumspect, but it is pretty clear that the view is that *Reisch Montage* does not make rational sense: see the summary of English judicial evaluation in *Bord na Mona Horticulture Ltd v. British Polythene Industries plc* [2012] EWHC 3346 (Comm), [78]–[83].

A different situation arises where the court considers that the claim against the anchor defendant is one which the claimant was at liberty to bring, but which will fail on the merits.[1335] It has been said in such a case that the proposed co-defendant may object to the availability of special jurisdiction under Article 8(1), rather as a defendant served out with the leave of the court may apply to have service made by reference to CPR Part 6, PD 6B, para. 3.1(3) on the basis that there is not a claim against the anchor defendant which it is reasonable to ask the court to try.[1336] At first sight, this may seem sensible, and may appear to be aligned with a principle of interpretation which would give Article 8(1) a narrow interpretation. But it is not easy to support it. There will in such a case be a judgment – quite possibly a summary one – for the anchor defendant against the claimant; and there is, in those circumstances, a theoretical possibility, at least, that proceedings brought in another country against the co-defendant could result in irreconcilable decisions: there will, at least, be two judgments from two courts.

As to whether there is a risk of irreconcilable judgments, it is not realistic to expect a court to determine the outcome of foreign proceedings which have not yet been brought against the proposed co-defendant. The weakness of the claim against the anchor defendant does not therefore affect the existence of the risk of irreconcilable judgments: it just makes it possible to say, summarily, which party will prevail in the English proceedings. Could it then be said that it is not expedient to try the claims together in order to alleviate that risk? That would not be an easy point to sustain. It may fairly be said that the claim against the anchor defendant should not be allowed to proceed to trial because it can be determined here and now, but Article 8(1) does not appear to take any account of that: it simply asks whether there is a risk of two judgments being irreconcilable, and whether that is a risk which should be avoided by allowing the claimant to assert special jurisdiction.[1337] It can, of course, be argued that if it is not expedient to allow the claim to proceed against the anchor defendant, it can hardly be expedient to expose the co-defendant to the special jurisdiction of the court; but that is not what Article 8(1) says. The conclusion may simply have to be that, at this point, as well as elsewhere, the correct operation of Article 8(1) is problematic and requires remedial attention.

2.229 The nature and degree of connection between the claims against the defendants

Article 8(1) applies only where the claims against the co-defendants are so closely connected that it is expedient to hear and determine them together to avoid the risk of irreconcilable judgments which might result[1338] from separate proceedings. The analysis of this point is not

---

1335 At this point, the concern is with a claim brought against an anchor defendant in good faith but which appears to be hopeless on its merits; the case in which the claim against the anchor defendant appears to have been brought for the (illicit) purpose of subjecting a co-defendant to special jurisdiction which will remove him from the court in which he would otherwise have to be sued is examined in the paragraphs which follow.

1336 See below, para. 4.65.

1337 There is some discussion of the point in *Sabbagh v. Khoury* [2014] EWHC 3233 (Comm), esp. around [97], but it cannot be said to resolve any of the questions raised here.

1338 Or might have resulted, if the anchor defendant had not defaulted in appearance and allowed judgment to be entered in default: *Linuzs v. Latmar Holdings Corp* [2013] EWCA Civ 4. If it is disputed, the court must be satisfied that there is a good arguable case (in the sense that the claimant has the better of the argument) that the link between the claims is established. It is not necessary to show that there is a good arguable case on the merits of the claim against the co-defendant: any contention that the claim is so weak does not arise as an objection to

as clear as one would wish, no doubt because the concepts used at this point are particularly malleable.[1339]

One may start by taking a step back. The proviso is the statutory clarification or confirmation of something which was originally established by the Court in *Kalfelis v. Bankhaus Schröder Münchmeyer Hengst & Co.*[1340] Proceedings had been brought in Germany against a German bank and a Luxembourg bank. In addition to the allegation that what is now Article 7(2) conferred special jurisdiction over the Luxembourg bank in matters relating to tort or delict, the claimant also invoked Article 8(1) to justify joining the Luxembourg bank to the proceedings against the German bank. The Court, alert to the possibility that Article 8(1) might be open to abuse by a claimant instituting sham or collusive proceedings against a local defendant, in order to invoke special jurisdiction over a defendant with a domicile in another Member State, ruled that jurisdiction under what is now Article 8(1) was not available unless it was expedient to hear the claims against the two defendants together in order to prevent the possibility of irreconcilable verdicts from their being tried separately.[1341] It seems clear that 'expedient' was chosen to serve as a less demanding requirement than 'necessary' would have been.

The requirement of connection between the two claims, now set out in Article 8(1), was taken from the judgment in *Kalfelis*, but although it sounds sensible, it is easier to state in principle than it appears to be to apply in practice.[1342] For example, if proceedings are brought against D1 and D2 in respect of a tort claim, would a finding that D1 is liable to the claimant be irreconcilable with a finding that D2 is not? In some circumstances it may be, in others not so. If proceedings are brought against the vendor and his agent or representative, is a finding that the vendor is not liable inconsistent with a finding that the agent or representative is not either? It is impossible to give a broad or simple answer to such a question, which requires a careful analysis of the pleading advanced by each party;[1343] it would make sense for a court to consider that it has a reasonable freedom to reach its own conclusion about the expedience, and the risk of irreconcilable judgments.[1344] The literal application of the *Kalfelis* ruling may therefore be difficult.

Though they have not quite sung in perfect harmony, English courts have tended to take a commonsense or pragmatic approach to the question whether the connection was

---

jurisdiction but as a basis for an application to strike out: *JSC Aeroflot-Russian Airlines v. Berezovsky* [2013] EWCA Civ 784, [2013] 2 Lloyd's Rep 242.

1339 As it raises distinct and particular issues, the operation of Art. 8(1) in cases concerned with intellectual property rights is dealt with separately, below, para. 2.230.

1340 189/87, [1988] ECR 5565.

1341 It follows that, if there is no real basis for a claim against D1, but he is merely used as the anchor for the joinder of D2, or if there is no claim against D2 save that he may have documents of which P seeks discovery, the special jurisdiction of Art. 8(1) should not be available. See *The Rewia* [1991] 2 Lloyd's Rep 325; *Mölnlycke v. Procter & Gamble Ltd* [1992] 1 WLR 1112. See also *The Xing Su Hai* [1995] 2 Lloyd's Rep 15.

1342 In *Kalfelis* itself, the Court did not apply its ruling to the facts: it made its ruling and left the implementation of it to the national court that referred the question in the first place.

1343 Which at the jurisdictional stage, before the defendant has entered its defence (so as to avoid being found to have entered an appearance), is extremely difficult, and often impossible. See also *Mölnlycke v. Procter & Gamble* [1992] 1 WLR 1112.

1344 It would be wrong to call it a discretion, for it is a matter of judgment, not discretion. It would be unhelpful to call it a 'margin of appreciation' because no one really knows what that means. It is a matter of judicial judgment, neither more nor less.

sufficiently made out.[1345] In *FKI Engineering Ltd v. De Wind Holdings Ltd*,[1346] for example, the claims were considered to be sufficiently connected because damages in the claim against one defendant could be assessed only in the light of the value of the connected claim: the court described the two claims as 'inextricably linked':[1347] it seems that in the light of *Land Berlin v Sapir*,[1348] it was entirely justified to reach the conclusion which it did. In the end, the fundamental choice may lie between a literal interpretation and a sensible application of the rule, and the Court of Appeal has shown its preference for the latter. In *Gard Marine & Energy Ltd v. Lloyd Tunnicliffe*[1349] the practical arguments in favour of having a single insurance and reinsurance dispute determined by a single court pointed to the conclusion that the requirements of the Article were satisfied; the court showed little enthusiasm for the more awkward jurisprudence which is examined below.

But literal interpretation is made more difficult by the fact that 'irreconcilable' is one of the more slippery terms used in, and in explaining, the Regulation. It appears to exist in a broad and a narrow form. Some guidance may be obtained from *The Tatry*,[1350] which held, in effect, that the meaning of the term 'irreconcilable', when used in what is now Article 30 of Regulation 1215/2012, denotes a less strict condition than is created by the same form of words in what is now Article 45(1)(c), and in the former context indicates simply that the contents of the judgments may be conflicting and contradictory. On the footing[1351] that it is this broader sense of 'irreconcilable', as used in *The Tatry*[1352] which is used in Article 8(1), it would follow that a court should simply ask itself whether there is a possibility of conflicting or contradictory judgments, even though there is no risk of mutually exclusive legal consequences, if the claims against the two defendants are tried separately.

The approach of the European Court to this issue has not been easy to follow, but a fair summary would be that though the Court originally took a remarkably strict approach to the interpretation of 'irreconcilable' as used in Article 8(1), in its most recent judgments it has adopted a more sensible position. In *Réunion Européenne SA v. Spliethoff's Bevrachtingskantoor BV*,[1353] there was an unanswerable reason why what is now Article 8(1) was inapplicable in proceedings brought before the French courts: none of the defendants was domiciled

---

1345 *Gascoine v. Pyrah* [1994] ILPr 82; *Casio Computer Co Ltd v. Sayo* [2001] EWCA Civ 661, [2001] ILPr 694, [31]–[38]; *ET Plus SA v. Welter* [2005] EWHC 2115 (Comm), [2006] 1 Lloyd's Rep 251, [59]; *Masri v. Consolidated Contractors International (UK) Ltd* [2005] EWCA Civ 1436, [2006] 1 Lloyd's Rep 391. For the application of the rule in cartel cases, where the application of the test to the facts will be particularly intricate, see *Cooper Tire & Rubber Co v. Dow Deutschland Inc* [2010] EWCA Civ 864, [2010] Bus LR 1697.

1346 [2008] EWCA Civ 316, [2009] 1 All ER (Comm) 118.

1347 At [16].

1348 C-645/11, EU:C:2013:228, [2013] ILPr 481.

1349 [2010] EWCA Civ 1052, [2011] Bus LR 839 (a case on the Lugano Convention, but the point is general). See also *Sibir Energy Ltd v. Tchigirinski* [2012] EWHC 1844 (QB), [2012] ILPr 894 (a case on the Lugano Convention); *Linusz v. Latmar Holdings Corp* [2013] EWCA Civ 4.

1350 C-406/92, [1994] ECR I-5439. As to this aspect of *The Tatry*, see below, para. 2.267.

1351 There is admittedly no clear authority for this; but it seems essentially reasonable. Article 30 deals, in a limited way, with allocation of jurisdiction prior to the hearing, whereas Art. 45(1)(c) is concerned with the consequences of two courts having pronounced inconsistent verdicts. Of the two, Art. 8(1) is clearly closer in function to Art. 30; and it is accordingly submitted that the more flexible meaning given to 'irreconcilable' by *The Tatry* is the appropriate model for Art. 8(1).

1352 At [53] *et seq.*

1353 C-51/97, [1998] ECR I-6511.

in France.[1354] But on the question whether claims raised in the proceedings – against a sea carrier for damage done to the cargo, and against the issuer of the bill of lading in respect of the same damage to the same cargo – fell within the Article, the Court, in unhelpful *obiter dicta*, held that they did not. It explained that 'two claims in one action for compensation, directed against different defendants and based in one instance on contractual liability and in the other on liability in tort or delict, cannot be regarded as connected'. As will be seen below, this approach was taken to extreme lengths in cases concerned with parallel-but-territorial intellectual property rights.

The view that such claims could not be regarded as connected[1355] was not convincing,[1356] though it certainly illuminated the Court's hostility to jurisdiction under Article 8(1). It may however be that it may now be put to one side. In *Freeport plc v. Arnoldsson*[1357] the Court ruled, in effect, that special jurisdiction under Article 8(1) was available where the legal bases for the claims against the two defendants were as distinct as they had been in *Réunion Européenne*. Although the Court stated that the Article was to be construed restrictively, it appeared to distance itself from the very proposition which it had stated in *Réunion Européenne*.[1358] It held instead that the Article applied if there was such a connection between the claims as made it expedient to try them together to avoid the risk of irreconcilable judgments, 'irreconcilable' in this sense meaning a 'divergence in the outcome of the dispute [which arises] in the context of the same situation of law and fact'.[1359] There was no requirement that the claims have identical legal bases. That appears to confirm that the sense in which 'irreconcilable' is used in Article 8(1) is the one derived from the judgment of the Court in *The Tatry*.

The result is that the test the court has to apply is somewhat imprecise, and in the end it may be better to stick to the language of the Article and pay little attention to the guidance the Court has given (and even less to the efforts of commentators to make sense of it). But an indication of what is involved can be gathered from a passage taken from the judgment in *Painer v. Standard Verlags GmbH*[1360] and only lightly edited. It would read as follows:

'It is not apparent from the wording of Article 8(1) of Regulation 1215/2012 that the conditions laid down for application of that provision include a requirement that the actions brought against different defendants should have identical legal bases. As regards its purpose, the rule of jurisdiction in Article 8(1), meets the wish to facilitate the sound administration of justice, to minimise the possibility of concurrent proceedings and thus to avoid irreconcilable outcomes if cases are decided separately... In that regard, the Court has stated that, in order for judgments to be regarded as irreconcilable within the meaning of Article 8(1), it is not sufficient that there be a divergence in the outcome of the dispute, but that divergence must also arise in the same situation of fact and law. However, in assessing whether there is a connection between different claims, that is to say a risk of irreconcilable judgments if those claims were determined separately,

---

1354 See also on this point C-645/11 *Land Berlin v. Sapir* EU:C:2013:228, [2013] ILPr 481.

1355 It is obvious that they were not the same, but connected is surely a looser idea.

1356 The view that the judgment was wrong, expressed in the text of an earlier edition, was accepted as correct in *Andrew Weir Shipping Ltd v. Wartsila UK Ltd* [2004] EWHC 1284 (Comm), [2004] 2 Lloyd's Rep 377. Professor Gaudemet-Tallon had been scarcely any more enthusiastic: she described the decision as *trop catégorique*: [1999] Rev crit DIP 339.

1357 C-98/06, [2007] ECR I-8319.

1358 It refused to concede that this is what it was doing, but *res ipsa loquitur*. For those less inclined to latin, the abrupt change in direction is known in journalistic circles as a 'reverse ferret'.

1359 At [39]–[40]. See also *Linuzs v. Latmar Holdings Corp* [2013] EWCA Civ 4.

1360 C-145/10, [2011] ECR I-12553, [81].

the identical legal bases of the actions brought is only one relevant factor among others. It is not an indispensable requirement for the application of Article 8(1). Thus, a difference in legal basis between the actions brought against the various defendants, does not, in itself, preclude the application of Article 8(1), provided however that it was foreseeable by the defendants that they might be sued in the Member State where at least one of them is domiciled. That reasoning is stronger if, as in the main proceedings, the national laws on which the actions against the various defendants are based are, in the referring court's view, substantially identical. It is, in addition, for the referring court to assess, in the light of all the elements of the case, whether there is a connection between the different claims brought before it, that is to say a risk of irreconcilable judgments if those claims were determined separately. For that purpose, the fact that defendants against whom a copyright holder alleges substantially identical infringements of his copyright did or did not act independently may be relevant.'

The most significant element of the new approach to Article 8(1) may well prove to be the question whether it was foreseeable by a proposed co-defendant that he might be sued where another defendant was domiciled. In the light of that advice an English judge should be able to ask the question in the terms in which it is set out in the Article, and to answer it without much elaboration being called for. Bearing in mind that the claimant seeking to establish special jurisdiction will need to have the better of the argument on the issue, there should be no great danger that special jurisdiction under Article 8(1) will over-reach itself.

2.230 The connection between the claims against the defendants in cases concerned with intellectual property rights

The requirement that the risk of divergence in outcome should arise 'in the same situation of law and fact' may indicate that it is not sufficient for the risk of divergence to arise in related situations of law and fact. It provided the basis for the decision in *Roche Nederland BV v. Primus*,[1361] ruling that the Article may not be relied on where the holder of several separate national patents, all derived from a European patent, and therefore practically identical but legally distinct, brings proceedings against defendants who have, as he alleged, each infringed a separate national patent.[1362] As each case, and judgment, will deal with a separate patent, there will be nothing to reconcile or find to be irreconcilable, even if the factual and technical evaluations involved are very similar, for the situations of fact and law are, almost as a matter of definition, not the same.[1363]

Right or wrong as this may be as a matter of abstract logic, it only contributed to a pervasive sense that the Regulation was poorly attuned to the needs of intellectual property litigation. However, the restrictions, insofar as they might have applied to copyright, were relaxed in *Painer v. Standard Verlags GmbH*,[1364] in which a photographer complained of breaches of copyright in photographs taken by her. The defendants were a number of newspaper publishers who had published the photographs, in Austria and Germany and on their websites. The claimant sought to bring the whole claim alleging breach of copyright

---

1361 C-539/03, [2006] ECR I-6535.

1362 C-593/03 *Roche Nederland BV v. Primus* [2006] ECR I-6535; *Sandisk Corp v. Koninlijke Philips Electronics NV* [2007] EWHC 332 (Ch), [2007] Bus LR 705, [39].

1363 For proposals to provide a better mechanism for dealing with disputes concerning national patents devived from the common stock of a European patent, see para. 2.75, above.

1364 C-145/10, [2011] ECR I-12553, [81].

before the Austrian courts, where one defendant was domiciled. It was admitted that the technical formulation of the complaints varied from one Member State of publication to another, but if the copyright laws which had been infringed were substantially the same, the national court was entitled to find that the conditions of the Article were satisfied. If there were substantially identical infringements, Article 8(1) might be relied on. In this respect the decision is good and sensible.

Patents are another matter, however. In *Solvay SA v. Honeywell Fluorine Products Europe BV*,[1365] after a European patent had been granted, it was alleged that several defendants had acted together to infringe the national patents derived from it, in several Member States. One defendant was Dutch, and the claimant sought to join several non-Dutch associates of the Dutch defendant under what is now Article 8(1); it was held that the claimant was entitled to do so. Insofar as there was, say, a Finnsh patent infringed by the three defendants acting in concert, the Dutch court was entitled to exercise jurisdiction over the non-Dutch defendants; insofar as there was a Swedish patent infringed by the three defendants, the Dutch court was entitled to exercise jurisdiction, and so on. But the decision did not cast doubt on the decision in *Roche Nederland* that if the allegation had been that D1 had infringed a Dutch patent, D2 had infringed a Belgian patent, and so forth, jurisdiction on the basis of Article 8(1) would not be available. In that respect, *Solvay* may be a rather unusual case, and the apparent relaxation of the law in *Painer* may not apply so easily to infringement of patents, even where the acts complained of are essentially the same.

2.231 Proceedings brought against a defendant designed to remove a co-defendant from the court otherwise competent over him

The final, and difficult, point on the operation of Article 8(1) may have arisen precisely because the operation of the Article, particularly when the claim against the anchor defendant is weak or worse, is unsatisfactory. If it is not open to a court to deny special jurisdiction on the approximate ground that the claim against the anchor defendant looks weak on the merits, or may have been instituted as a tactical measure which will, once it has served its primary purpose, be ignored, the possibility of abusive behaviour is evident. But so far as the text of the Article is concerned, there is no other limitation on the existence of special jurisdiction under Article 8(1). The Article does not require the claimant to meet a further condition which is, however, applied in relation to Article 8(2), that the proceedings have not been instituted solely with the object of removing the person over whom special jurisdiction is to be asserted from the jurisdiction of his domiciliary court. This limitation makes rational sense in relation to Article 8(2), as will be seen. On the face of it, it is not a prior condition to the exercise of special jurisdiction under Article 8(1); though it may be that it has developed in response – in some sense, at least – to the apparent shortcomings in Article 8(1).

As a matter of history, the concern was that a claimant might seek to use what is now Article 8(1) to bring a claim he did not really intend to prosecute to judgment as the hook or basis for proceedings against another person, domiciled in another Member State, but who by this means could be dislodged from the courts in which the claimant would otherwise have to sue him. The issue first arose in *Kalfelis v. Bankhaus Schröder Münchmeyer Hengst &*

1365 C-616/10, EU:C:2012:445, [22].

Co.[1366] The Court's response to the problem which it had identified was to rule that what was then Article 6(1) was limited to cases in which the claims against the defendants were connected in such a way that it was expedient to try them together to avoid the risk of irreconcilable judgments. This, in the opinion of the Court, was the proper response to the possibility of misuse of Article 6(1), as it then was; and in due course this judicial solution was taken up into and enacted in the Regulation. To repeat: the Court in *Kalfelis* saw the requirement of connection between the claims as a sufficient antidote to the prospect of misuse of what was then Article 6(1). It is wrong to infer from the judgment in *Kalfelis* a further limitation to the effect that the Article is unavailable if proceedings are brought for the purpose of removing a defendant from the court which would otherwise be competent in relation to him, for the judgment says the opposite. And anyway, if it really is expedient to try the claims together to avoid the possibility of irreconcilable judgments, it would be surprising for a court to be prevented from acting on that conclusion, and extraordinary that it be prevented by a principle which the legislator did not enact.

Despite this, in *Reisch Montage AG v. Kiesel Baumaschinen Handels GmbH*,[1367] the Court said[1368] that what is now Article 8(1) could not be used for the sole purpose of removing a defendant from the courts of the Member State in which he was domiciled. As has been suggested above, the judgment was not at all convincing.[1369] The Court first held that what is now Article 8(1) could be relied on even though the local defendant had gone into insolvent administration with the legal consequence that there could never be a judgment against it. The conclusion that one judgment might be irreconcilable with another which could never be given is not one which will leap to every mind, but having taken itself off down the wrong path, the Court sought to make amends by saying that what is now Article 8(1) could not be interpreted in such a way as to allow a claimant to make a claim against several defendants for the sole purpose of removing one of them from the court which would otherwise have been competent.[1370]

The correctness of that limitation was raised and answered in *Freeport plc v. Arnoldsson*.[1371] It was contended that proceedings against the Swedish defendant had been brought before the Swedish courts for the sole purpose of providing a basis for proceedings to be brought in Sweden against an English co-defendant. The Court, however, ruled,[1372] clearly and precisely, that even if the action against the Swedish defendant had been brought solely to remove the English co-defendant from the court which would otherwise be competent in a claim against him, this did not make what is now Article 8(1) inapplicable. The justification, correctly given, was that the requirement of connexity, first expressed in *Kalfelis*, then taken up into the legislated terms of the Article itself, was considered sufficient to prevent any misuse of this rule of special jurisdiction.[1373]

1366 189/87, [1988] ECR 5565.

1367 C-103/05, [2006] ECR I-6827.

1368 At [32].

1369 It also appears to have been translated into English by a Scottish translator, as it refers (e.g. at [26]) to proceedings against a defender. This is not the terminology in which the Regulation is written.

1370 Two wrongs do not make a right, as some might be moved to say.

1371 C-98/06, [2007] ECR I-8319.

1372 As the second point of the ruling.

1373 See, consistent with this conclusion, *Sibir Energy Ltd v. Tchigrinski* [2012] EWHC 1844 (QB), [2012] ILPr 894.

It is regrettable that the Court in *Freeport* did not refer to *Reisch Montage* by name and say that it had been wrongly decided. It would have been easy enough to do so, for on this point the Court was departing from the advice of its Advocate General who had used *Reisch Montage* as the basis for the proposed answer which the Court declined to adopt. But it did not do so. It may be that the apparent lack of a formal denunciation allowed the point made in *Reisch Montage* to rise from its undead state and be repeated (without any elaboration[1374]) by the Court in *Painer v. Standard Verlags GmbH*,[1375] and in *Solvay SA v. Honeywell Fluorine Products Europe BV*.[1376] It seems that this non-textual requirement must now be taken to be part of the law.

The whole sorry mess proceeds from a mis-reading of the judgment in *Kalfelis* and a failure of judicial analysis; but it is fair to say that the many shortcomings in Article 8(1), particularly in relation to those issues on which an English court could fall back on the exercise of discretion, left the European Court with a range of problems and a shortage of tools. It may be that the test of whether the proceedings have been brought with the *sole* purpose of removing a co-defendant from the court in which he would otherwise have to be sued will turn out to set a standard which is hard to attain, but it is really the right solution to the wrong problem. The problems with Article 8(1), and the cases in which a court should be able to refuse to make it available to a claimant, are many. Not only does the solution adopted by the European Court not dovetail with them, it does not even make for a workable bodge. Article 8(1) shows no one in a flattering light.

2.232 International jurisdiction in the courts of the United Kingdom

If the 'anchor' defendant is domiciled in the United Kingdom, and is sued there, the other defendants may be sued in the *place* where the first defendant is domiciled; that is, to the courts of that place. In other words, Article 8(1) gives international jurisdiction to the courts for a place, not just to the courts of a Member State. Paragraph 9 of Schedule 1 to the 2001 Order[1377] accordingly provides a definition of when a defendant is domiciled in a part of or place in the United Kingdom; the courts for that part or place will therefore be given international jurisdiction over the other defendants.

2.233 Special jurisdiction over claims against third parties: Article 8(2)

Article 8(2) of Regulation 1215/2012 provides that:

> *A person domiciled in a Member State may also be sued: (2) as a third party in an action on a warranty or guarantee or in any other third-party proceedings, in the court seised of the original proceedings, unless these were instituted solely with the object of removing him from the jurisdiction of the court which would be competent in his case.*

Article 8(2) of the Regulation is identical with Article 6(2) of Regulation 44/2001.

1374 Save for the false attribution to *Kalfelis*.

1375 C-145/10, [2011] ECR I-12553, [78]. 'Secondly, that rule cannot however be applied so as to allow an applicant to make a claim against a number of defendants with the sole object of ousting the jurisdiction of the courts of the State where one of those defendants is domiciled (see, to that effect, 189/87 *Kalfelis* [1988] ECR 5565, [8] and [9], and C-51/97 *Réunion européenne and Others* [1998] ECR I-6511, [47]).'

1376 C-616/10, EU:C:2012:445, [22].

1377 SI 2001/3929, as amended by SI 2014/2947, Sch. 2, para. 3(11).

2.234 Jurisdiction in the main proceedings

The first point to notice about Article 8(2)[1378] of the Regulation is that there is no requirement that the main proceedings be brought in the courts of the defendant's domicile. It does not, at first sight at least, require the defendant to the (main) proceedings to be domiciled in a Member State: even if jurisdiction over him is taken pursuant to Article 6 of the Regulation and the residual rules of national law which it incorporates by reference, it appears that the third party may be joined to the proceedings.[1379]

It may be questioned, however, whether that should be the position. If jurisdiction over the primary defendant is based upon one of the grounds which may not be asserted over a defendant domiciled in a Member State,[1380] it could be considered an indirect or constructive assertion of such jurisdiction over a third party for him to be joined to such proceedings. If there is anything in that point, it would be possible to argue that jurisdiction over the defendant ought to be asserted in accordance with the remainder of the Regulation, and should not be derived from Article 6. And in the Heidelberg Report which paved the way for Regulation 1215/2012, the view was expressed that the Article should be 'clarified' to confirm that jurisdiction over a third party should not be possible where jurisdiction in the the main proceedings is based on what is now Article 6.[1381]

But no change was made to the wording, and therefore the lack of clarity to which the Heidelberg Report drew attention remains as before. On the other hand, the broader public interest in consistent adjudication and the free movement of judgment would suggest that the basis on which jurisdiction is taken over the defendant is irrelevant to the assertion of jurisdiction over the third party. Each view has something to be said for it, and someone else will have to deliver the definitive answer.

The guidance offered by the Court in *Kongress Agentur Hagen GmbH v. Zeehaghe BV*[1382] was not conclusive. The Court declined to read any limitation by reference to the ground of jurisdiction asserted against the defendant in the main proceedings, saying that there was no warrant for it, and because the beneficial effect of what is now Article 8(2) is that it allows the entire dispute to be heard in a single court. But jurisdiction in the main proceedings was based on what is now Article 7(1), and nothing in the judgment suggests that the Court also had in mind jurisdiction under what is now Article 6. When it said that, so far as the main proceedings were concerned, there was an equivalence between jurisdiction based on what are now Articles 4 and 7, it may have suggested, but certainly did not say, what the answer would have been if jurisdiction in the main proceedings is based on Article 6. The question therefore remains an open one.

It is unclear whether the main proceedings must still be actively being pursued when the application to join the third party is made. But the principle which justifies the jurisdiction is that it is preferable to have one court deal with all such claims together. It may be

---

1378 But see also Art. 65 (it is believed that the list referred to in Art. 65(1) contains Austria, Germany, and Hungary).

1379 For support for the view that Art. 8(2) does apply in such a case, see Dicey, Morris and Collins, *The Conflict of Laws*, 15th edn, 499 n. 866.

1380 Articles 3 and 4.

1381 Hess, Pfieffer & Schlosser, *The Brussels I Regulation 44/2001* (Beck, Munich, 2008), para. 238.

1382 C-365/88, [1990] ECR I-1845.

argued that as a stay may always be lifted, the conditions for the application of the Article are not affected by what may only be a temporary order.[1383]

2.235 Jurisdiction over the third party

Given its position in the hierarchy of jurisdictional rules, it is unnecessary to say that Article 8(2) may not be invoked in circumstances in which this would contradict a jurisdiction agreement between the defendant and the third party: this is obvious. But the point has arisen and has been decided in a predictable and correct fashion.[1384] If this appears to put the defendant in an awkward position, or to be contrary to the public interest in obtaining a single, consistent and efficient resolution of connected matters which are in dispute, the only response is that a better-drafted jurisdiction agreement could have provided for this situation, and it is for the parties, and not for the court, to draft the agreements that they actually want.

2.236 Proceedings brought to remove the third party from the courts of his domicile

By contrast with the muddled position under Article 8(1), it is expressly provided in Article 8(2) that 'these' proceedings must not have been instituted 'solely with the object of removing [the third party] from the jurisdiction of the court which would be competent in his case'. The trouble is that when the Article provides that 'these' proceedings must not have been instituted with this improper object, it is not clear whether the reference is to the main proceedings brought by the claimant, or the third-party proceedings brought by the defendant.

An initial response might be that it is not easy to see how this condition can be taken completely seriously, whichever way it is interpreted. At the jurisdictional stage, especially in England in which jurisdiction is finally determined before any step is taken towards determination of the merits of the dispute, there is limited scope for a detailed examination of the merits of the claim, and not much more scope for an examination of the motivation of the claimant and defendant in doing what they have done. But it was made clear in the Jenard Report[1385] that the material question was whether the original proceedings, not the third-party proceedings, appeared to have been brought solely with the object of removing the third party from the courts of his domicile. This would suggest that the impropriety or abuse which the qualification had in its sights was collusion between claimant and defendant with the aim of disadvantaging the third party.[1386] This still seems to be the rational interpretation of any such limitation.

1383 *Cf Waterford Wedgwood plc v. Nagli* [1999] 3 All ER 185. It may be otherwise where the anchor claim appears to be utterly dormant: *Alfa Laval Tumba AB v. Separator Spares International Ltd* [2012] EWCA Civ 1569, [2013] 1 WLR 1110.

1384 *Hough v. P & O Containers* [1999] QB 834; *Craft Enterprises (International) Ltd v. AXA Insurance Co* [2004] EWCA Civ 171, [2004] 2 All ER (Comm) 123.

1385 [1979] OJ C59/1, 28.

1386 This is the plain interpretation taken in *Hough v. P & O Containers Ltd* [1999] QB 834 ('where the plaintiff and defendant are effectively in collusion to bring a claim against a third party in the plaintiff's or defendant's domicile ...'), which derived its answer from the Jenard Report.

But in *Réunion Européenne v. Zurich España*[1387] the Court stated that it was the third-party proceedings, rather than the main proceedings, which were required to satisfy the condition of not having been brought for this improper purpose. Quite apart from the fact that the Court has departed from the advice of Jenard, it is difficult to see what this might mean in practice, for if the defendant does have a claim against the third party, which arises from or is connected to the claim made against it in the main proceedings, it should be dealt with in third-party proceedings. If that is not so, the defendant, if he loses against the claimant, will have to assert his claim, and his liability as providing the basis for that claim, in separate proceedings. The 'third party', who was not party to the original proceedings, will not be bound to accept that the person claiming against him really was liable to the original claimant, and the problem rapidly spins out of control.

The solution may be to note the discrepancy between the Jenard Report and the judgment, but to conclude that unless the effect of the application of Article 8(2), and the joinder of the third party by the defendant, is a plain and obvious abuse of process, it will satisfy the requirements of Article 8(2). Only where one of the two[1388] claims seems to be spurious, or not advanced in good faith, should the court be expected to make further enquiry. And the use of 'solely' should ensure that this remains a very infrequent objection to the special jurisdiction of the court seised of the main proceedings.

2.237 The types of proceedings falling within Article 8(2)

It is probable that 'third-party proceedings' has a uniform definition. The fact that such proceedings would not be seen in national procedural law as being third-party proceedings is therefore not decisive. According to the Jenard Report,[1389] the wording refers to proceedings 'in which a third party is joined as a party to the action. They are intended to safeguard the interests of the third party, or of one of the parties to the action…'. They are not confined to those where the defendant joins the third party, but include proceedings where the third party voluntarily appears if this is provided for by national law.

It was held in *Kinnear v. Falconfilms NV*[1390] that even though not all the proceedings which are capable as a matter of English procedural law of being brought against third parties would automatically fall within what is now Article 8(2), if the nexus which was prescribed by the then Rules of Court[1391] were satisfied on the facts, such connexity would bring the proceedings within the scope of the Article. Moreover, if there is a strong practical reason for bringing defendant and third party before the same court – such as where a defendant tortfeasor is seeking contribution from a third party[1392] – the case will fall within both the letter and the spirit of Article 8(2).

1387 C-77/04, [2005] ECR I-4509, [29]. See also *Barton v. Golden Sun Holidays Ltd* [2007] EWHC B6 (*sic*: a decision from the Birmingham District Registry) (QB), where the judge followed *Réunion Européenne v. Zurich España* to the letter, noting at [23] that this was at variance with the view which had been proposed in this book.
1388 Original, and third party.
1389 [1979] OJ C59/1, 28.
1390 [1996] 1 WLR 920.
1391 Then RSC Order 16, r. 1(1); now replaced by CPR Part 20, which describes these, and others, as 'Part 20 claims'. The test of nexus has been watered down, and now appears in CPR r. 20.9.
1392 For the other aspects of such claims, see *Arab Monetary Fund v. Hashim* (29 July 1994; noted [1995] LMCLQ 437). For the analogous situation of one insurer seeking a contribution from a co-insurer, see C-77/04 *Réunion Européene v. Zurich España* [2005] ECR I-4509.

It was suggested[1393] in *The Ikarian Reefer (No 2)*[1394] that Article 8(2) may be resorted to when a defendant who has defeated a claim brought against him by the claimant, and has obtained an order for costs, applies under Senior Courts Act 1981, section 51, for an order that a non-party pay all or some of the costs of the action and which the defendant was held to be entitled to recover. It is conceded that, where the application is made by a defendant and the application is made against a non-party, this will bear some resemblance to a third-party claim by that defendant; but as the same form of order could also be applied for by a claimant, it would not be correct in those circumstances to describe it as a third-party claim, for the respondent is not brought into the action by the defendant, but is proceeded against, after the event, by the claimant. Either Article 8(1) is then applicable; or (as the court preferred to say) the non-party is not being 'sued';[1395] or the proceedings should be seen as in the enforcement of a judgment, and within the exclusive jurisdiction of the court in which the enforcement is taking place.[1396]

2.238 The discretion to decline to exercise jurisdiction under Article 8(2)

It is now clear that it is, to some extent at least, open to a national court to decline to exercise special jurisdiction under Article 8(2). This follows from the decision in *Kongress Agentur Hagen GmbH v. Zeehaghe BV*.[1397] In that case, a claim was brought in the Dutch courts against a German defendant. The Dutch courts had special jurisdiction over the defendant by reason of what is now Article 7(1) of the Regulation. The German defendant sought to join the third party, also domiciled in Germany, from whom it claimed to be entitled to an indemnity. The defendant argued that the Dutch courts had special jurisdiction over the third party under Article 8(2), and that they were therefore obliged to exercise it when it was invoked by a defendant. It appears that the Dutch court was unwilling to exercise jurisdiction over the third party, on the apparent basis that the late admission of the indemnity claim would have complicated the proceedings which were pending and close to trial. The European Court agreed that the Dutch courts had special jurisdiction over the third party, but accepted that they were not obliged to exercise it. The question raised by the case before the national court was whether the third-party claim was an admissible one, not whether they had jurisdiction over the third party in respect of it. The Court ruled that the Dutch courts were entitled to apply their own procedural law to determine whether the claim was admissible, in other words, to determine whether to exercise their admitted jurisdiction.[1398]

The immediate decision is understandable. It is one thing to enact a rule that gives jurisdiction over third-party claims, but quite another to say when that jurisdiction may be, and may not be, exercised. The law must have criteria which specify whether the permission of the court is needed, at what point in the procedure the third party may be joined, and so on. The silence of the Regulation upon these matters, which is entirely rational, means that they

---

1393 This not being the basis on which the court preferred to rest its conclusion that it had jurisdiction.
1394 [2000] 1 WLR 603.
1395 *Cf* para. 2.161, above.
1396 *Cf* para. 2.78, above.
1397 C–365/88, [1990] ECR I-1845.
1398 *Cf* the irrelevance of admissibility under national law in C–103/05 *Reisch Montage AG v. Kiesel Baumaschinen Handels GmbH* [2006] ECR I-6827.

must be resolved by the procedural law of the court seised.[1399] It is inevitable that there will be circumstances in which the court has special jurisdiction but, under its own procedural rules, will have reason to not exercise it. That is the result sanctioned by *Hagen*. All that is required of the national court is that it refrain from operating its procedural rules in such a way as to undermine the practical effect of the Regulation.[1400]

In an English court, the procedural rules in CPR Part 20 in particular will modify the operation of Article 8(2). It appears desirable, however, that national courts be as willing as possible to take jurisdiction over third-party proceedings.[1401] In *Hagen*, a decision by the Dutch courts that the defendant was liable to the claimant would not obviously be conclusive of the liability[1402] of the defendant when he makes a later claim against the third party for an indemnity: the third party may not be[1403] prevented from contesting, as against himself, the findings made by a court in proceedings to which he was not party.[1404] There is, therefore, a risk of irreconcilable verdicts if the claim against the third party is not heard as part of the main proceedings; and the court seised of the main proceedings should only be permitted on narrow and compelling grounds to decline to exercise jurisdiction over the third-party claim. If it is otherwise, the practical effect of the Regulation, as a means of preventing irreconcilable judgments, will indeed be jeopardised.

2.239 Proceedings in the English court

As Article 8(2) of the Regulation gives international jurisdiction to the courts already seised of a dispute, there is obviously no need for a rule of national law to deal with national jurisdiction.

2.240 Special jurisdiction over counterclaims: Article 8(3)

Article 8(3) of Regulation 1215/2012 provides that:

> *A person domiciled in a Member State may also be sued: (3) on a counter-claim arising from the same contract or facts on which the original claim was based, in the court in which the original claim is pending.*

Article 8(3) of the Regulation is identical to Article 6(3) of Regulation 44/2001.

1399 Schlosser [1979] OJ C59/71, [135].

1400 By, for example, refusing to accept jurisdiction on the simple basis that the third party is domiciled in another Member State: that would directly contradict a jurisdictional rule of the Regulation. In fact, in *Hagen*, there would be a possible risk of irreconcilable verdicts created by the non-exercise of jurisdiction by the Dutch court, unless the Dutch proceedings were held to be decisive of the liability of the defendant to those proceedings when he later sues in Germany for the indemnity, which seems unlikely, as the party against whom that order is intended to be used was not party to the original proceedings at all.

1401 *Cf Kinnear v. Falconfilms NV* [1996] 1 WLR 920.

1402 To the claimant.

1403 In English law he will not normally (but see *House of Spring Gardens Ltd v. Waite* [1991] 1 QB 241) be bound by a decision to which he was not party. The provisions of CPR r. 19.8A concerning 'notice parties' are restricted to cases relating to the estate of a deceased person or property subject to a trust.

1404 For one reason, if the original action is collusively lost by the defendant in order that the defendant might bring a claim against the guarantor, this should not prejudice the guarantor. But if the first action *is* decisive of the liability of the defendant to the claimant, the guarantor would lose the opportunity to challenge the legal basis of his liability.

2.241 General

It obviously makes sense, and contributes to the administration of justice, if a counterclaim is dealt with in a court which is hearing a claim. Article 8(3) provides the mechanism by which the Regulation authorises this.

As was also the case with Article 8(2), it is not expressly said whether the original claim must be based upon jurisdictional rules other than those of Article 6, or includes cases where jurisdiction over the defendant has been founded on Article 6. But this time it is completely clear that there is no reason here to read in any such limitation. If a claimant who is domiciled in a Member State[1405] has commenced proceedings in the courts of a Member State, there is no reason to doubt that he has laid himself open to being counterclaimed against: he has selected the court, and cannot be heard to complain if his choice of court is used against him. As long as the counterclaim is based upon the same contract or facts as the original claim, without which Article 8(3) is inapplicable, it will be irrelevant that the court has taken jurisdiction in the original proceedings on the basis of Article 6 or on any other basis.[1406]

It is necessary that the original claim is still pending in the original court, but the Regulation does require it to be pending at first instance. If national law were to allow a counterclaim to be made for the first time on appeal (which seems improbable), there is no reason to consider Article 8(3) to be inapplicable. But the admissibility of a counterclaim in such circumstances must be determined by the procedural law of the court in which it is proposed to bring it.[1407]

2.242 The nature of a counterclaim

The counterclaim must arise from the same contract or be based upon the same facts as the original claim. It is for the national court to decide for itself whether this condition is satisfied. By contrast, something which is a mere cross-claim by way of set-off, in a sum which does not exceed the amount of the claim, is not within the autonomous definition of a counterclaim, and may be brought without any restriction imposed by the Regulation: in this context, the question is the admissibility of a simple defence, and that is a matter exclusively governed by the procedural law of the court seised.[1408] It is irrelevant that the claim is for a sum which may exceed the sum awarded by way of judgment against the defendant: this amount will remain unknown until judgment; as long as the set-off is less than the amount claimed, no issue arises under Article 8(3).

As a matter of English procedural law, a counterclaim may be brought against someone other than the existing claimant.[1409] It is unclear whether a claim which took this form would fall within Article 8(3) so that it could be brought against someone other than the original claimant even if that other person is domiciled in another Member State. It seems

---

1405 Of course, if he is not domiciled in a Member State, this provision and its limitation do not apply to the counterclaim: *Balkanbank v. Taher* [1995] 2 All ER 904, 926, 928.

1406 In English law, a set-off by way of defence may be used instead of, and more liberally than, a counterclaim. It seems that this procedure allows a set-off to be pleaded in circumstances where a counterclaim would not be permitted by Art. 8(3). But there may be a possible limitation in cases where this may be seen as an abuse of the jurisdictional rules of the Regulation: 220/84 *A-S Autoteile Service v. Malhé* [1985] ECR 2267.

1407 By analogy with C-365/88 *Kongress Agentur Hagen GmbH v. Zeehaghe BV* [1990] ECR I-1845.

1408 C-341/93 *Danvœrn Production A/S v. Schuhfabriken Otterbeck GmbH & Co* [1995] ECR I-2053.

1409 CPR r. 20.5.

unlikely that it can, for if the justification for the existence of Article 8(3) is that a person who has seised the court as claimant cannot be heard to complain if his choice of court bounces back upon him, it is not at all obvious that this sense can provide a proper explanation for a counterclaim against someone who has, so far, never come anywhere near the court. On the other hand, a counterclaim against someone other than the claimant looks very similar to a third-party claim, and if such a claim is considered in the context of Article 8(2), there is no jurisdictional problem if the person against whom it is proposed to be made is domiciled in another Member State.

As a matter of authority, a counterclaim against someone other than the claimant was held to fall outside what is now Article 14(2) of Regulation 1215/2012.[1410] That provision deals with counterclaims in the context of jurisdiction in matters relating to insurance; and the same reasoning would exclude it from Articles 18(3) and 22(2).[1411] It is true that to allow the counterclaim against an insured, a consumer, or an employee, none of whom is party to the original action, would run the risk of depriving a privileged individual of the jurisdictional advantage conferred on him by Sections 3, 4 and 5 of Chapter II of the Regulation. However that may be, it does not follow that outside this area, a counterclaim against a new party must likewise be excluded from the scope of Article 8(3). But if it is excluded, then, as suggested above, Article 8(2) may provide for special jurisdiction instead.

2.243 Proceedings in the English court

As Article 8(3) of Regulation 1215/2012 gives international jurisdiction to the court in which the original claim is pending, there is no need for a rule of national law to deal with internal jurisdiction.

2.244 Special jurisdiction in personal claims connected to proceedings *in rem* relating to land: Article 8(4)

Article 8(4) of Regulation 1215/2012 provides that:

> *A person domiciled in a Member State may also be sued: (4) in matters relating to a contract, if the action may be combined with an action against the same defendant in matters relating to rights in rem in immovable property, in the court of the Member State in which the property is situated.*

Article 8(4) of the Regulation is identical to Article 6(4) of Regulation 44/2001.

Article 8(4) really speaks for itself. It is unsaid, but seems to be implicit, that the claimant must be the same in each case;[1412] the provision is principally intended to allow actions by the mortgagee in relation to charged or mortgaged land[1413] to be combined with an action upon the personal covenant of the defendant to repay. The limitation to the action being

---

1410 *Jordan Grand Prix Ltd v. Baltic Insurance Group* [1999] 2 AC 127. See also *Dollfuss Mieg & Compagnie v. CDW International Ltd, The Times*, 19 April 2003 (only cross-claim by original defendant will count). On a related point, where the provisions of Section 3 of Chapter II were given an interpretation which gave primary to the protection of the protected party, see C-112/03 *Soc Financière et Industrielle de Peloux v. AXA Belgium* [2005] ECR I-3707.

1411 Certain consumer contracts and employment contracts, respectively.

1412 See the Report on the San Sebastián Convention: [1990] OJ C189/35, 46, though separate claimants between whom there is privity of interest may be enough.

1413 For example, for an order for sale of the land.

against the same defendant means that Article 8(4) cannot be used to bring a claim against a guarantor or surety, but Article 8(1), as now understood, should be available if special jurisdiction is required in such a case.

2.245 Land in the United Kingdom

As Article 8(4) of the Regulation gives special jurisdiction only to the courts of the Member State in which the land is situated, it gives international jurisdiction to the courts of the United Kingdom. Accordingly, a rule of internal United Kingdom law is required to identify the part of the United Kingdom the courts of which have national jurisdiction under Article 6(4). It appears that section 16 of the 1982 Act, and rule 5(d) of Schedule 4 to the 1982 Act,[1414] give jurisdiction to the courts for the part of the United Kingdom in which the property is situated.

2.246 Special jurisdiction to limit liability resulting from use of a ship: Article 9

Article 9 of Regulation 1215/2012 provides that:

> *Where by virtue of this Regulation a court of a Member State has jurisdiction in actions relating to liability from the use or operation of a ship, that court, or any other court substituted for this purpose by the internal law of that Member State, shall also have jurisdiction over claims for limitation of such liability.*

Article 9 of the Regulation is practically identical with Article 7 of Regulation 44/2001.

Article 9, which applies to maritime proceedings for a decree limiting liability, establishes a form of special jurisdiction so that there is no impediment, attributable to the fact that an interested party has a domicile in another Member State, to proceedings to obtain a decree limiting liability for use of a ship. Its effect is that a party who will be, or who fears that he will be, defendant in a maritime claim may commence proceedings for limitation of his liability in any court which would have jurisdiction over him if he were to be sued as defendant. Article 9 does not apply to actions brought by a claimant against the shipowner or fund administrator, but only to the independent proceedings for a decree of limitation instituted by a shipowner against a potential claimant or against claimants as a whole.[1415]

2.247 Conclusion

If any of the provisions of Articles 7 to 9 of the Regulation gives special jurisdiction to the English court, service out will be available as of right.[1416] If the defendant has a domicile in another Member State, but Articles 7 to 9 do not give the English court special jurisdiction over that defendant, Article 5 of the Regulation leads to the conclusion, which is now final and marks the end of the road, that the English court does not have jurisdiction and cannot exercise it.

1414 As inserted by Civil Jurisdiction and Judgments Order 2001, SI 2001/3929, Sch. 2, para. 4.

1415 For the proposition that an action to limit liability does not have the same cause of action as a claim for damages against the defendant, even if the underlying facts are the same, see C-39/02 *Mærsk Olie & Gas A/S v. Firma M de Haan en W de Boer* [2004] ECR I-9657.

1416 CPR r. 6.33.

If the defendant is not domiciled in a Member State, however, Articles 7 to 9 will have been inapplicable to him; and he falls instead to be dealt with on the basis of Article 6, as a defendant who does not have a domicile in any Member State.

(11) RESIDUAL JURISDICTION OVER DEFENDANT NOT HAVING A DOMICILE IN A MEMBER STATE

2.248 General

Article 6 of Regulation 1215/2012 provides that:

> *(1) If the defendant is not domiciled in a Member State, the jurisdiction of the courts of each Member State shall, subject to Article 18(1), Article 21(2) and Articles 24 and 25, be determined by the law of that Member State. (2) As against such a defendant, any person domiciled in a Member State may, whatever his nationality, avail himself in that Member State of the rules of jurisdiction there in force, and in particular those of which the Member States are to notify the Commission pursuant to point (a) of Article 76(1), in the same way as nationals of that Member State.*

Article 6 of Regulation 1215/2012 is substantially similar to Article 4 of Regulation 44/2001.

2.249 Residual jurisdiction

If the defendant is not domiciled in the United Kingdom or in any other Member State,[1417] Article 6 authorises a court to exercise the rules of jurisdiction found in its own national or common law in civil or commercial proceedings against such a defendant. The Brussels I Regulation has not yet adopted the terminology of 'residual jurisdiction' for the rules picked up and made applicable in such cases, but it is increasingly used elsewhere, most noticeably in the Brussels II Regulation,[1418] and it is appropriate to adopt this terminology. It has two principal advantages. One is that it is accurate: the jurisdictional rules deal with the residue of cases for which the Regulation has not made, or has not yet[1419] made, more specific jurisdictional provision. The second is that it serves to distinguish the rules picked up and applied by virtue of Article 6 from the same rules as applied to cases which are not within the scope of the Regulation. Superficially these are the same rules, but in practice they are substantially different in effect.

In such a case the jurisdiction, being authorised for use by the Regulation, must be exercised subject to such further conditions, such as to *lis alibi pendens* in other Member States, and as to the discretionary refusal to exercise jurisdiction,[1420] as the Regulation may impose. These conditions distinguish residual jurisdiction from the unmodified version

---

1417 If he is domiciled in Iceland, Norway or Switzerland, the Lugano Convention will govern jurisdiction; if he is domiciled in one of the remaining territories to which the Brussels Convention still applies to govern jurisdiction.

1418 Regulation 2201/2003, [2003] OJ L338/1: see Art. 7.

1419 The proposal supported by the Commission that legislation should provide uniform jurisdictional rules for some of the cases which fell under Art. 4 of Regulation 44/2001 (and which remain under Art. 6 of Regulation 1215/2012) was not successful. It will, no doubt, be repackaged and put forward again.

1420 See generally paras 1.03 and 2.260 *et seq.*, above.

of the rules of common law applied to cases which fall wholly outside the domain of the Regulation.

Article 6 draws specific attention to certain provisions of the Regulation which may have effect even though the defendant does not have a domicile in a Member State. For the most part these are instances in which a provision of the Regulation operates without regard to the domicile of the defendant: the most obvious examples are exclusive jurisdiction regardless of domicile, and prorogation of jurisdiction by agreement: indeed, if the advice given in this book to address the jurisdictional questions in the order presented here is taken, these qualifications to Article 6 will not arise. There is no reference to Article 26, from which it may be wondered whether prorogation of jurisdiction by voluntary appearance is confined to defendants domiciled in a Member State; the answer to that, as said above, should be no, it should not be understood to be so confined, but if that is correct, it is unfortunate that Regulation 1215/2012 does not make it clear.

The references to Articles 18 and 21 are to those provisions of the privileged jurisdictional scheme for consumer contracts and contracts of individual employment, according to which a professional or an employer, with no domicile in a Member State, may be sued in a court designated by the Article in the same way as a professional or a employer who is domiciled in a Member State may be. The issue was sufficiently discussed above; it needs no further attention here.

2.250 Consequences of taking jurisdiction on the basis of the residual rules

If the court finds that the defendant does not have a domicile in any of the Member States, and if none of the earlier provisions of the Regulation has operated to allocate jurisdiction to the courts of a Member State, the defendant falls outside the primary provisions of the Regulation so far as these relate to the exercise of jurisdiction over him.

The Brussels Convention, when originally conceived, was entered into, among other reasons, 'to strengthen in the Community the legal protection of persons therein established', and though this recital is not reproduced in precise terms in the Regulation, it is likely that its sentiment is not displaced. It is inevitably the case that, when dealing with a defendant who is not domiciled in a Member State, there is a rather different reason for the Regulation to define the rules for the taking of jurisdiction. The Regulation takes the jurisdictional rules of national law and incorporates them into itself by reference, by means of Article 6, for the residual cases for which the Regulation makes no more specific provision. Jurisdiction under Article 6 is within the Regulation; it is not external to the Regulation.[1421]

It follows that Article 6 jurisdiction is subject to the other constraints upon jurisdiction which are derived from the Regulation. For one thing, the Regulation will provide for the recognition and enforcement of judgments given against those without a domicile in a Member State.[1422] For another, and perhaps because of the previous point, the Regulation is still concerned to prevent the possibility of irreconcilable judgments being handed down

---

1421 See Jenard [1979] OJ C59/1, 20–21. And *cf* the technique adopted in what is now Art. 71 of the Regulation, and on which, see Schlosser [1979] OJ C59/71, [240].

1422 As to this, see para. 7.05, below.

by the courts of Member States, so the *lis abili pendens* provisions will apply in their full force: a conclusion was confirmed by the decision of the European Court in *Overseas Union Insurance Ltd v. New Hampshire Insurance Co.*[1423] In that case, the Court observed that what is now Article 29 made no exception for the case of jurisdiction taken under the residual rules now provided for by Article 6. On the contrary, it said, the provisions on *lis alibi pendens* were to be applied without regard to the basis upon which the two courts had or had taken jurisdiction. There is no more to be said.

2.251 Service of process on the defendant in cases to which the residual rules apply

If the English court is permitted to exercise jurisdiction under Article 6, service out of the jurisdiction, if it is needed, will be available only with the permission of the court.[1424] This is because the requirement that permission be obtained, and the limitation of this grant of permission to claims falling within the paragraphs of a Practice Direction, is part and parcel of the residual rules of jurisdiction which Article 6 authorises the court to exercise. If the court refuses to grant permission, or having first granted it later declares that it has no jurisdiction and sets service aside, it will thereupon not be seised, and the claimant will have to find somewhere else to sue the defendant.

If the residual rules of jurisdiction are applicable by reason of Article 6, and the defendant is within the jurisdiction, so that he may be served as of right, the court may be seised without further ado. If this happens, but the defendant wishes to contend, for example, that England is a *forum non conveniens*, and that proceedings should be stayed in favour of the court which is the *forum conveniens*, the question whether it may do so is one which is considered at length below, as part of the broader question whether there is an inherent discretion to decline to exercise a jurisdiction which has been conferred by the Regulation.

(12) JURISDICTION TO ORDER PROVISIONAL OR PROTECTIVE RELIEF

2.252 General

A court which has jurisdiction in a civil or commercial matter has power, in the exercise of that jurisdiction, to grant interim or interlocutory orders so long as its doing so does not conflict with principles of European law of general application. It cannot, for example, order a person not to take proceedings in a civil or commercial matter before the courts of another Member State, whether on an interim or a final basis.

But if it does not have jurisdiction over the defendant in relation to the substance of the proceedings, it may be applied to for provisional, including protective, measures, on the basis of Article 35 of Regulation 1215/2012, which provides as follows:

1423 C-351/89, [1991] ECR I-3317.
1424 See paras 4.57 *et seq.*, below; and CPR r. 6.36.

Application may be made to the courts of a Member State for such provisional, including protective, measures as may be available under the law of that Member State, even if the courts of another Member State have jurisdiction as to the substance of the matter.

Article 35 of the Regulation is practically identical to Article 31 of Regulation 44/2001.

2.253 The operation of Article 35

The manner in which Article 35 operates is peculiar. It operates by removing any objection, made by the person against whom the relief is applied for, to the jurisdiction of the court to which the application is made. It does not state the grounds on which jurisdiction exists; it merely un-states the grounds which would otherwise have been an impediment to the jurisdiction. The jurisdictional grounds are therefore supplied by the national law of the court seised; and these are not always straightforward.

But relief sought in accordance with Article 35 is obviously not sought outside the Regulation; and the manner in which it relates to the Regulation is complex. It therefore makes sense to deal with the relief, the rules which determine jurisdiction to apply for or order it; the scope of the orders which can be made; the effect of the orders which are made; and other related questions, all together as part of a general examination of interim relief. It is therefore postponed to Chapter 6.

(13) EXAMINATION OF JURISDICTION IN CERTAIN CIRCUMSTANCES

2.254 General

Section 8 of Chapter II of the Regulation deals with the circumstances in which a court which has been seised by a claimant is under a duty to ascertain for itself whether a conclusion that it has jurisdiction would be consistent with the Regulation. Although much tends to be made of this provision as a demonstration of the respect paid to due process, natural justice and the right to be heard, there are in fact only two sets of circumstance in which the court is obliged to examine the basis (or lack of basis) for its own jurisdiction.

2.255 Examination of jurisdiction to check for exclusive jurisdiction: Article 27

Article 27 of Regulation 1215/2012 provides that:

Where a court of a Member State is seised of a claim which is principally concerned with a matter over which the courts of another Member State have exclusive jurisdiction by virtue of Article 24, it shall declare of its own motion that it has no jurisdiction.

Article 27 of the Regulation is identical with Article 25 of Regulation 44/2001.

2.256 The nature of the examination required of the court

Article 27 requires the court to act of its own motion to ensure that it is not being called upon to hear a claim which is principally concerned with a matter over which the courts of another Member State have exclusive jurisdiction. This requirement reinforces the primacy of exclusive jurisdiction under Article 24 within the Regulation scheme.

According to Schlosser,[1425] a court, when examining its own jurisdiction, may not exercise such jurisdiction unless it is sure of those facts which give it jurisdiction; in cases where it is not sure it is required to request from the parties evidence as to those facts which might confer jurisdiction. However, the entering of an appearance by a defendant will itself confer jurisdiction by reason of Article 26. It is only in proceedings to which Article 24 applies that the entering of an appearance will not confer jurisdiction on the court. It follows that the duty of a court to examine its jurisdiction under Article 27, where the defendant appears, is confined to those cases in which Article 24 may be applicable. It is understood that 'sure' means 'sure to the standards applied in the context of jurisdictional disputes', and not anything more demanding.

If a court at first instance raises the question of the operation of Article 24 with the parties, and is assured by them that there is no such jurisdictional impediment, a problem may arise if at a later point one of the parties changes his mind and seeks to rely on Article 24 or Article 27. The issue, or one very similar, has arisen before the Supreme Court in relation to what is now Article 29, and it makes sense to examine it in that context. The issues are inevitably slightly messy.

2.257 Examination of jurisdiction where the defendant does not appear: Article 28

Article 28 of Regulation 1215/2012 provides that:

> *(1) Where a defendant domiciled in one Member State is sued in a court of another Member State and does not enter an appearance, the court shall declare of its own motion that it has no jurisdiction unless its jurisdiction is derived from the provisions of this Regulation. (2) The court shall stay the proceedings so long as it is not shown that the defendant has been able to receive the document instituting the proceedings or an equivalent document in sufficient time to enable him to arrange for his defence, or that all necessary steps have been taken to this end. (3) Article 19 of Regulation (EC) No 1393/2007 of the European Parliament and of the Council of 13 November 2007 on the service in the Member States of judicial and extrajudicial documents in civil or commercial matters (service of documents) shall apply instead of paragraph 2 of this Article if the document instituting the proceedings or an equivalent document had to be transmitted from one Member State to another pursuant to that Regulation. (4) Where Regulation (EC) No 1393/2007 is not applicable, Article 15 of the Hague Convention of 15 November 1965 on the Service Abroad of Judicial and Extrajudicial Documents in Civil or Commercial Matters shall apply if the document instituting the proceedings or an equivalent document had to be transmitted abroad pursuant to that Convention.*

Article 28 of the Regulation is identical with Article 26 of Regulation 44/2001.

2.258 The nature of the examination required of the court

It is said to be a fundamental principle of the scheme put in place by the Regulation that if the defendant does not appear, the court is under an obligation to ascertain that it does have jurisdiction under the provisions of the Regulation. Article 28 therefore obliges a court to examine its jurisdiction if a defendant who is (which presumably means that it may be

---

1425 [1979] OJ C59/71, [22]. For an illustration, see *Coin Controls Ltd v. Suzo International (UK) Ltd* [1999] Ch 33.

apprehended by the court that he is) domiciled in a Member State other than that in which he is sued does not appear. In such a case, the court (i) must assure itself that any exercise by it of jurisdiction is consistent with the provisions of the Regulation,[1426] and (ii) must stay proceedings until it is shown that either the defendant has received the document instituting the proceedings in sufficient time to arrange his defence, or that if not, all necessary steps have still been taken to that end.[1427]

It is sometimes said that the Article forms an important part of the protection of the rights of the defence, and this is justifiable. But it has also been acknowledged more openly in recent cases that the rights of the defence are not absolute or unfettered, and the claimant also has a qualified right to obtain judgment, with the result that a balance therefore has to be struck.[1428] And it is a striking fact that if the defendant does not appear to be domiciled in a Member State, the obligation arising under Article 28(1) does not apply; but the duty to enquire into the effectiveness of service, imposed by Article 28(2), is not restricted to proceedings against defendants who are domiciled in a Member State.

In deciding whether its jurisdiction is derived from the Regulation, it is obvious that residual jurisdiction under Article 6 is excluded.[1429] The court will therefore have to ascertain that it has jurisdiction on a basis other than Article 26, as the defendant has not appeared. It is in this context that the claimant will need to adduce evidence sufficient to satisfy the court that it has jurisdiction under the Regulation.[1430]

The duty on the court to stay its proceedings means that judgment in default of appearance may be entered against a defendant domiciled in a Member State, other than that of the court in which the proceedings are taking place, only if the document instituting proceedings, or an equivalent document, is shown to have been served in time for the defendant to arrange for his defence. It has been made clear that this is a reference to the document, or documents, if they are intrinsically linked, which the defendant needs, or would need, to allow him to understand the subject matter of the claim and the grounds on which the claim is made against him. The principle of the matter is clear enough: the defendant must have been served[1431] with such documentation as he requires or would require so as to be able to exercise the right of defence.[1432] But on the other hand, the claimant is entitled to a hearing of his claim, and he cannot be held up forever by an evasive defendant. The obligation on the claimant is to make all proper attempts to locate and make service upon a defendant, but if all that has led only to failure, because the defendant has managed to

---

1426 And if the court is not so assured, it must declare that it has no jurisdiction. But if the court has jurisdiction according to the rules of a particular Convention to which Art. 71 applies, it does have jurisdiction according to the rules of the Regulation: C-148/03 *Nürnberger Allgemeine Versicherungs AG v. Portbridge Transport International BV* [2004] ECR I-10327.

1427 On the case in which the impossibility of locating defendant means that the attempt to serve him has been by public notice as provided for by national law (held sufficient), see C-292/10 *G v. De Visser* EU:C:2012:142, [2013] QB 168.

1428 C-394/07 *Gambazzi v. Daimler Chrysler Canada Inc* [2009] ECR I-2563; C-292/10 *G v. De Visser* EU:C:2012:142, [2013] QB 168; C-327/10 *Hypoteční Banka AS v. Lindner* [2011] ECR I-11543; but *cf* C-112/13 *A v. B* EU:C:2014:2195 (defendant still free to argue that proceedings and judgment were in default of (his) appearance, even if a legal representative has been appointed by the court).

1429 Not available in respect of a defendant domiciled in a Member State.

1430 On the extent to which a court is bound to conduct its own enquiry, or can instead rely on the bare allegations of the claimant (which it may not do), see Schlosser [1979] OJ C59/71, [22].

1431 Or all necessary steps have been taken to serve him.

1432 C-14/07 *Ingenieurbüro Michael Weiss & Partner GbR v. Industrie- und Handelskammer Berlin* [2008] ECR I-3367.

hide himself from public view and private discovery, the court may, and should, allow the claimant to enter judgment in default.[1433] After all, the defendant who was not served may still rely on Chapter III of the Regulation[1434] to resist recognition or enforcement of the default judgment.

If the claimant rushes to enter judgment in default of appearance, he runs the risk that the court will refuse to allow it,[1435] or[1436] that a court in another Member State, called upon to recognise that judgment, will decline to do so.[1437] The question will be examined again in the context of the recognition of judgments under Chapter III of the Regulation, in which context it has been examined by the European Court. But there may be much to be said for re-serving process, or at least writing to a defendant who has not appeared to offer him another chance, to reduce the chance that a court in another Member State, called upon to recognise the judgment, will invoke Article 34(2) of Regulation 44/2001, or Article 45(1)(b) of Regulation 1215/2012 and refuse recognition.

Paragraph (2) of Article 28 of Regulation 1215/2012 is substantially superseded by Article 19 of the Service Regulation,[1438] which makes alterations of detail, though not of major substance, in cases in which the document has had to be served within the territory of a Member State[1439] upon a person whose address for service is known.[1440] Article 19 states that it applies:

> 'where a writ of summons or an equivalent document has had to be transmitted to another Member State for the purpose of service, under this Regulation, and the defendant has not appeared, judgment shall not be given until it is established that (a) the document was served by a method prescribed by the internal law of the Member State addressed for the service of documents in domestic actions upon persons who are within its territory, or (b) the document was actually delivered to the defendant or to his residence by another method provided for by this Regulation; and that in either case the service or the delivery was effected in sufficient time to enable the defendant to defend.'

As the Service Regulation permits other means of transmission and service, such as through diplomatic or consular channels, or by post, or by direct service, it will not always be necessary to show that the official channels described in Section 1 of Chapter II of the Service Regulation were used. Where service was required to be effected outside the territory of a Member State, the Service Regulation is inapplicable.[1441] But as these instruments do not apply if the address of the defendant is not known, there is no requirement to effect service in accordance with them in such a case.[1442]

1433 C-292/10 *G v. De Visser* EU:C:2012:142, [2013] QB 168; C-327/10 *Hypoteční Banka as v. Lindner* [2011] ECR I-11543.

1434 Regulation 44/2001, Art. 34(2): Regulation 1215/2012, Art. 45(1)(b): C-292/10 *G v. De Visser* EU:C:2012:142, [2013] QB 168; C-327/10 *Hypoteční Banka AS v. Lindner* [2011] ECR I-11543.

1435 In England he will need to comply with CPR rr 12.10 and 12.11 and para. 4 of the Practice Direction if the claim is one to which the Regulation applies, so ensuring that the court will have to consider the propriety of its jurisdiction and the quality of service.

1436 Which may well be more inconvenient, because it may now be too late to go back to the original court and cure the perceived defect in the judgment.

1437 As will be seen, the court called upon to recognise the default judgment is bound and entitled to make its own assessment of whether the document was served in time for the defendant to arrange for his defence.

1438 Regulation (EC) 1393/2007, [2007] OJ L324/79, replacing Regulation (EC) 1348/2000.

1439 See also CPR r. 6.41.

1440 But not otherwise: C-292/10 *G v. De Visser* EU:C:2012:142, [2013] QB 168.

1441 In which case, however, Art. 15 of the Hague Convention may apply.

1442 C-292/10 *G v. Visser* EU:C:2012:142, [2013] QB 168.

2.259 Conclusion

If a court, having if necessary examined its jurisdiction, concludes that it has jurisdiction, the rules on *lis alibi pendens* must next be considered by the court, for these may override that conclusion, and deprive it of the jurisdiction which the Regulation would otherwise have given it.

(14) *LIS PENDENS* IN ANOTHER MEMBER STATE

2.260 The general effect of a *lis pendens* in another Member State: Articles 29 to 32

The rules which are set out in Section 9 of Chapter II of the Regulation explain when the jurisdiction which would be or has been provided or justified by the provisions examined so far may be overridden or undercut by the fact that a court in another Member State has also been seised. The question whether or when the jurisdiction which has been or would be conferred on the court by the Regulation may be affected (and if so, in what way) by the fact that a court in a non-Member State has also been seised is examined as the following Question.[1443] If any provisions of the Regulation are to be seen as more important than others in making the Regulation work properly, those in Section 9 of Chapter II will be at the top of the list.

2.261 Possible consequences of *lis alibi pendens*

If the dispute falls within the domain of the Regulation,[1444] the application of the jurisdictional rules so far described may lead to a number of possible outcomes. Viewed from the perspective of the English court, it may arise in the following ways. First, if the English courts have exclusive[1445] jurisdiction, they may exercise it, subject only to Article 31, if another court also has exclusive jurisdiction; this rarely happens. Second, if the courts of another Member State have exclusive jurisdiction, they may exercise it, subject only to Article 31, and the English court has no jurisdiction, which requires no more elaboration. Third, the rules examined so far may not have given the English courts a basis for jurisdiction, which requires no more elaboration. Fourth, the rules examined so far may have given the English courts jurisdiction. If they do, they may and must exercise it, unless the existence of proceedings before the courts of another Member State, which were commenced before the English proceedings, contradict that jurisdiction after all: if Article 29 applies, the English court will be required to stay its proceedings until the jurisdiction of the court seised first is established, and to decline jurisdiction if and when the jurisdiction of the court seised first is established. If Article 30 applies, the English court has power, though it has no duty, to dismiss or to stay the proceedings before it. At this point we are concerned with Articles 29 to 32.

1443 See para. 2.288, below.

1444 Of course, where proceedings do not, the provisions which are to be discussed, which regulate *lis abili pendens*, are entirely inapplicable: C-129/92 *Owens Bank Ltd v. Bracco* [1994] ECR I-117; *Moore v. Moore* [2007] EWCA Civ 361, [2007] ILPr 481.

1445 For the meaning of this, see para. 2.274, below. Jurisdiction under Art. 25 is not within it.

It will be seen that the rules on *lites alibi pendentes*, in relation to proceedings in other Member States,[1446] apply whenever a claim falls within the scope of the Regulation[1447] and the English courts are asked to exercise jurisdiction;[1448] the uncompromising nature of their application underlines the absolute importance of being the first to commence proceedings.[1449]

2.262 Identical proceedings pending before court in another Member State: Article 29

Article 29 of Regulation 1215/2012 provides that:

> *(1) Without prejudice to Article 31(2), where proceedings involving the same cause of action and between the same parties are brought in the courts of different Member States, any court other than the court first seised shall of its own motion stay its proceedings until such time as the jurisdiction of the court first seised is established. (2) In cases referred to in paragraph 1, upon request by a court seised of the dispute, any other court seised shall without delay inform the former court of the date when it was seised in accordance with Article 32. (3) Where the jurisdiction of the court first seised is established, any court other than the court first seised shall decline jurisdiction in favour of that court.*

Article 29 of the Regulation differs from Article 27 of Regulation 44/2001 in two principal ways. First, the reference to Article 31(2), which is designed to reverse the rule of temporal priority in favour a court designated by an agreement on jurisdiction, did not appear in Regulation 44/2001. Second, Article 29(2), which seeks to eliminate uncertainty over another court's date of seisin, was not part of Regulation 44/2001: any such enquiry made of a foreign court was a matter of judicial initiative only.

There is no reason to suppose that Article 29 is a provision which the parties may contract out of. In some cases the parties may have bound themselves to a contract which provides that one of the parties – often one providing finance – may bring proceedings against the other – usually a borrower and now a non-repaying debtor – before more than one court at the same time. Nothing in Article 29 suggests that such an agreement is jurisdictionally effective; there is every reason to suppose that it is not. Given the relative ease with which a judgment from one Member State may be enforced in other Member States under Chapter III of the Regulation, there is no obvious hardship to a creditor if such an agreement is held to be ineffective within the territory of the Member States.

1446 For the impact of proceedings before a non-Member State, see further below. For proceedings before a Lugano State, see the Lugano II Convention, which is discussed to the extent necessary in Chapter 3.

1447 The proceedings before the other court must obviously be within the material scope of the Regulation as well: *Fondazione Enasarco v. Lehman Brothers Finance SA* [2014] EWHC 34 (Ch).

1448 And whether the jurisdiction is based upon the direct rules of the Regulation, or upon those of a Convention incorporated by Art. 71, or upon the basis of Art. 6.

1449 For the question how (if at all) these provisions apply if the court first seised was a non–Member State when proceedings were commenced before it, but had become a Member State when the proceedings in the court seised second were commenced, see C-163/95 *Von Horn v. Cinnamond* [1997] ECR I-5451; *Davy International Ltd v. Vöst Alpine Industrieanlagenbau GmbH* [1999] 1 All ER 103 (where both sets of proceedings predate accession of a new Member State, provisions on *lis alibi pendens* did not apply); *Advent Capital plc v. GN Ellinas Imports-Exports Ltd* [2005] EWHC 1242 (Comm), [2005] 2 Lloyd's Rep 607 (injunction granted before Cyprus became Member State not affected by accession of Cyprus).

2.263 General approach to Article 29: duty of the court seised second

Though the requirements of Article 29 of Regulation 1215/2012 are not free of technicality, Article 29 is meant to be interpreted reasonably broadly, to serve one of the overriding purposes of the Regulation, which is to prevent parallel litigation of civil and commercial[1450] matters which might result in irreconcilable judgments.

The point has been made many times. In *Gubisch Maschinenfabrik KG v. Palumbo*,[1451] a dispute arose between a buyer and a seller of a woodworking machine. The seller commenced proceedings against the buyer in Germany, for the unpaid purchase price. The buyer retaliated by commencing proceedings in Italy against the seller for rescission of the contract of sale. It was contended by the buyer that he was free to pursue the Italian proceedings, as the cause of action (rescission) in Italy was different from that (action for the price) being pursued in Germany. The Court, rejecting the advice of its Advocate General, disagreed. It observed that what is now Article 29 was intended to prevent parallel proceedings being pursued before the courts of different Member States, and to avoid the conflict which could arise if two such proceedings were permitted to run independently of each other. What is now Article 29 was designed to preclude, 'in so far as possible and from the outset', the risk of inconsistent verdicts within the single community of Member States. 'In so far as possible and from the outset' is strong language, not given to much complication. The court seised second is required to observe this overriding principle and to read, understand and apply Article 29 accordingly.

In *Overseas Union Insurance Ltd v. New Hampshire Insurance Co*,[1452] a reinsured party brought proceedings in France on the basis of the residual rules of jurisdiction now in Article 6 of Regulation 1215/2012, against a reinsurer, for payment in respect of claims made. The reinsurer retaliated by commencing proceedings in England, based also on what is now Article 6, for declarations of non-liability under the terms of the policies. In ruling that what is now Article 29 deprived the English court, which had been seised second, of jurisdiction, the Court repeated that the Article must be interpreted and applied 'to preclude, in so far as possible and from the outset' a possible clash of inconsistent verdicts, and that the Article 'must be interpreted broadly so as to cover, in principle, all situations of *lis pendens* before courts in [Member] States, irrespective of the parties' domicile'.[1453] There was no question of discretion; when the rule applies, it applies without flexibility.

Until the coming into force of Regulation 1215/2012, no exception was made for the case in which the court seised second concluded that it had jurisdiction by virtue of an agreement prorogating its jurisdiction and excluding the jurisdiction of other Member States. No exception was made to allow for a different answer where the proceedings in the court seised first were instituted in bad faith and to frustrate the claimant who was seeking to rely on the jurisdiction agreement. In *Erich Gasser GmbH v. MISAT Srl*,[1454] the Court was unmoved by the argument that the whole point of jurisdiction

---

1450 It is improbable that the Article applies if the other proceedings are civil and commercial but excluded from the Brussels I Regulation by (say) Art. 1(2)(b), though the issue was left open in *Rahman v. GMAC Commercial Finance Ltd* [2012] EWCA Civ 1467.

1451 144/86, [1987] ECR 4861.

1452 C-351/89, [1991] ECR I-3317.

1453 At [16]. For a broad interpretation in the context of intellectual property disputes, see *Football Dataco Ltd v. Sportradar GmbH* [2011] EWCA Civ 330, [2011] 1 WLR 2044.

1454 C-116/02 [2003] ECR I-14693.

agreements was to prevent such shenanigans, or by the evidence of chicanery on the part of the Italian party. Few troubled to persuade themselves that this was the Court's finest hour. The antidote to this particular problem is now provided by Article 31(2), which is examined below.

Despite the exhortation, Article 29 of the Regulation, as it now stands, does contain technical component parts. It must be shown that the proceedings involved the same cause of action: that is to say, identity of *objet* and identity of *cause*; and that they were between the same parties. Together these are sometimes known as the 'three identities'. It must then be shown that the court in question was seised first.[1455]

It is oddly unclear whether Article 29 of the Regulation is confined to proceedings seeking final or substantive relief, or is also applicable to proceedings seeking orders for interim relief from the courts of two or more Member States. At first sight the answer would appear to be that it does not apply to these latter measures: as will be seen,[1456] the scheme of the Brussels I Regulation is to allow applications for provisional or protective measures to be brought before any court of a Member State, without interference from the jurisdictional provisions of the Regulation, even where another court has exclusive jurisdiction regardless of domicile.[1457] That appears to allow for parallel applications for relief which may overlap. But in *Italian Leather SpA v. WECO Polstermöbel GmbH*,[1458] the Court applied the rules on irreconcilable judgments[1459] to the question of recognition of orders for provisional and protective relief. It also explained that the application of the rules on the recognition of judgments was indifferent to whether the orders were for provisional or for final relief;[1460] and it allowed the court to refuse recognition to a foreign order for provisional measures which was irreconcilable with a local one. Whether it would have gone further, and allowed what is now Article 29 to be used at the point of seeking the relief was not said. Of course, the issue could arise only if the relief actually applied for in the two sets of proceedings was actually overlapping: if the relief sought from each court is confined to assets or activities wholly within the jurisdiction of the court applied to, this condition will not be met. And it may be that provisional and protective measures represent an area in which the *lis alibi pendens* provisions do not apply but the rules on irreconcilable judgments do, in the hope that it will be a rare case in which this needs to be done. But the position is uncertain.

2.264 General approach to Article 29: duty of the court seised first

The duty on the court seised first is to get on with the proceedings before it. If its jurisdiction is not contested, it should proceed with the determination on the merits (or give judgment if these are not contested); if its jurisdiction is contested, it should determine whether it has jurisdiction in order that a court seised second not be kept waiting longer than necessary. Whether this requires a court which would not otherwise do so to determine jurisdiction

---

1455 In certain admiralty proceedings, these requirements may be a little more difficult than in other cases.
1456 Chapter 6, esp. at para. 6.07, below.
1457 C-616/10 *Solvay SA v. Honeywell Fluorine Products Europe BV* EU:C:2012:445.
1458 C-80/00, [2002] ECR I-4995.
1459 Article 34(3) of Regulation 44/2001; Art. 45(1)(c) of Regulation 1215/2012, and discussed in para. 7.22, below.
1460 Especially at [41].

as a preliminary point is not clear, but this is not an issue in England in which this is the manner in which jurisdiction is determined.

The point that the court seised first, considering itself to have jurisdiction, must get on with its work and adjudicate is neatly illustrated by *JP Morgan Chase Bank NA v. Berliner Verkehrsbetriebe.*[1461] In that case, the court accepted that it had jurisdiction under what is now Article 25, and that the case was not one in which Article 24(2) gave exclusive jurisdiction, regardless of domicile, to the German courts. The German entity then brought proceedings before the German courts, seeking in effect to persuade the German court to give a judgment which would have hampered the enforcement of an English judgment against it. The German court made a reference to the European Court; and once this wrecking effort had been got underway, the German entity applied for a stay of the English proceedings, in effect to allow the German proceedings to catch up and interfere with them. The Court of Appeal refused to stay; it was absolutely right to do so. Having determined that it had jurisdiction, it would be absurd for it to have second thoughts and act as though it did not have jurisdiction after all. It saw its duty as being to adjudicate, and got on with it.

Article 29(1) and Article 31(2) of Regulation 1215/2012 make an exception for the case in which the jurisdiction of the court seised second has been prorogated by agreement: Article 31, in material part, says that:

> (2) Without prejudice to Article 26, where a court of a Member State on which an agreement as referred to in Article 25 confers exclusive jurisdiction is seised, any court of another Member State shall stay the proceedings until such time as the court seised on the basis of the agreement declares that it has no jurisdiction under the agreement. (3) Where the court designated in the agreement has established jurisdiction in accordance with the agreement, any court of another Member State shall decline jurisdiction in favour of that court.

In other words, the court seised first may be called upon to stay its proceedings if it is informed, before the defendant has entered an appearance, that a court prorogated by an exclusive jurisdiction agreement has been seised. When that happens, the first court is required to wait for the second court to rule on whether it does have jurisdiction; and when the second court has ruled on whether the agreement does, does only partially, or does not, give it jurisdiction, the court seised first will fall into line by declining, or by partially declining, or by confirming its jurisdiction.

The objection to the jurisdiction of the court seised first will need to be taken on the first possible occasion, both as a matter of policy, but also because voluntary appearance in the court seised first will confirm its jurisdiction according to Article 26. It will not be possible for a defendant to wait to see which way the wind is blowing and only then play his card in favour of the prorogated court. Whether the court seised first is entitled to look at Article 31(2) and refuse to stay its proceedings because it does not consider the jurisdiction agreement to be exclusive, or sufficiently broad to apply in relation to the proceedings before it, is not clear. It may be argued that if the first court really regards the matter before it as falling outside the scope of the agreement, so that the decision of the second court that it has exclusive jurisdiction would make no difference to it, it is hard to see why it should stay the proceedings before it. But if that were admitted, it would open the door to the antics exemplified in *Erich Gasser GmbH* which this provision was designed to deal with. The better view is, therefore, that the court seised first should just wait for the court prorogated

---

1461 [2010] EWCA Civ 390, [2012] QB 176, [108] *et seq.*

by agreement to give its ruling, and when the ruling has been given, recognise it,[1462] and deduce the effect this has on the matter before it.

If as a result of this analysis the court seised first observes that a part of the proceedings before it do not fall within the terms of the jurisdiction agreement, its duty is still to proceed to adjudicate. It is not required to decline jurisdiction over this fragment in favour of the court with 'exclusive jurisdiction', because Article 27 applies only to courts whose jurisdiction is exclusive in the sense of Article 24. It is not permitted, so it appears, to stay or dismiss its proceedings in favour of the prorogated court, because Article 30 provides for that to be done only by the court seised second, which it was not. It is possible that a procedural stay on grounds of case management would be permissible, and proper, but a court will need to be careful that any order does not have the effect of contradicting the rule that if the court has jurisdiction, it should adjudicate.[1463]

2.265 The same cause of action under Article 29: identity of *objet* and identity of *cause*

From what has been said about *Gubisch Maschinenfabrik KG v. Palumbo*, it will be clear that 'the same cause of action' has an autonomous meaning, and is not to be viewed through the lens of national law.[1464] Other language versions of the Regulation speak more distinctly of the proceedings having the same *objet* and the same *cause*,[1465] and it has been held[1466] that the English text must be interpreted as if both requirements were distinctly mentioned. Accordingly, the sets of proceedings must have the same *cause*: that is, the same facts and rule of law as the basis for the action; and they must have the same *objet*: that is, the same end in view. If those criteria are satisfied, the fact that the substantive arguments are formulated differently in the two actions is irrelevant.

For example, in *Gubisch*, an action to enforce a contract, and an action to have that contract declared void, rescinded or dissolved, had the same *cause*, because they were based on the same facts and rule of law, namely the same contractual relationship. They had the same *objet*, having in view a judicial determination of whether the contract was valid and binding. The same principle can be illustrated by *The Tatry*.[1467] Proceedings were brought in the Netherlands by two shipowners for a declaration that they owed no liability for damage to the cargo which they had carried, and proceedings were brought in England by various cargo interests for damages from the shipowners for damage done to the cargo. The claims in the two sets of proceedings had the same *cause*, because they were based on contracts for the carriage of goods by sea containing the same terms and in respect of the same damage

---

1462 C-456/11 *Gothaer Allgemeine Versicherung AG v. Samskip GmbH* EU:C:2012:719, [2013] QB 548.

1463 In *Skype Technologies SA v. Joltid Ltd* [2009] EWHC 2783 (Ch), [2011] ILPr 103 the court used the imagery of not allowing in through the back door something which had been locked out of the front. There may be half a point to be made along those lines, but the orderly management of its business by a court must on any reasonable view remain within its power.

1464 Though for its meaning in English law, see *The Indian Grace* [1993] AC 410; see also para. 7.74, below. See also *Berkeley Administration Inc v. McClelland* [1996] ILPr 772 (whether enquiry as to damages the same cause of action as claim to establish liability).

1465 It is not clear that it would be accurate to render these expressions, which are not used in the English language text of Art. 29, as 'the same cause of action' and 'the same object'. Accordingly, and by convention, they are rendered in their French language form.

1466 *Gubisch*, [14]; C-406/92 *The Tatry* [1994] ECR I-5439, [37].

1467 C-406/92, [1994] ECR I-5439.

to cargo. They had the same *objet*, because the issue of liability for the damage to the cargo was central in both actions.

Another way to approach the issue might be to examine whether a decision in the one set of proceedings would have been[1468] a conclusive answer to the question raised in the other: in both *Gubisch* and *Tatry* it is evident that it would have.[1469] But if the two decisions could stand alongside each other, albeit a little awkwardly, Article 29 will not apply, as the proceedings will not have the same *objet*.[1470] So, for example, if the claim of the buyer in *Gubisch* had been for damages for late delivery, or for breach of warranty of quality, rather than for rescission, the allegations made would not have had the same end in view, and would not be found to be at risk of being found to be irreconcilable with each other. Article 29 would, therefore, not have applied to them. The same point is also liable to be expressed by asking, as the Supreme Court did in *The Alexandros T*,[1471] whether the proceedings are mirror images of each other. The court may be required, as it was in that case, to conduct a close and careful analysis of the causes of action in the proceedings before the two courts to determine whether they are (or whether judgments given on them would be) legally irreconcilable. If the causes of action are distinct, even though the issues pleaded by way of defence in the one action are essentially the same as the claims in the other, Article 29 will not apply. If a decision in the one court would annul the legal basis for the claim in the other, Article 29 will be likely to apply; but where a decision in the one court will simply lead to financial set-off against the decision in the other, it probably will not.

In order to assess whether the claims have the same *objet* and *cause*, the comparison is made by reference to the claims made in each case. If these do not fulfil the requirements of Article 29, the fact that an issue which is raised by way of defence reflects the claim in the other proceedings has no bearing on the application of Article 29, though as far as the court seised second is concerned, it may be material to the operation of Article 30. The Court in *Gantner Electronic GmbH v. Basch Exploitatie Maatschappij BV*[1472] ruled that the fact that the defendant to one set of proceedings had pleaded a defence of set-off, the substance of which had been raised by him as claimant in other proceedings, did not trigger the application of what is now Article 29. The effect of this interpretation is to prevent a second-seised court properly concluding from an analysis of the claim raised in the matter before it that it has jurisdiction, only for this to be called into question when a defence is filed in the first-seised set of proceedings.[1473] Such a conclusion was necessary to prevent manipulation of Article 29 and to promote a version of legal certainty. It will, however, weaken the policy against allowing parallel proceedings to produce irreconcilable judgments.

1468 Or might be; it is the appreciable risk of irreconcilable judgments, rather than their certainty, which is the key. In *JP Morgan Europe Ltd v. Primacom AG* [2005] EWHC 508 (Comm), [2005] 2 Lloyd's Rep 665 it was held that the more restrictive approach proposed here was *too* restrictive, and that the positions of the parties in relation to the facts in the dispute needed also to be considered. It is open to question whether this is a wider formulation than in *Gubisch*, but even if it is, that is not to say that it must be wrong.

1469 So also in *Secret Hotels 2 Ltd v. EA Traveller Ltd* [2010] EWHC 1023 (Ch), [2010] ILPr 616.

1470 This submission was referred to with seeming approval in *Lloyd's Syndicate 980 v. Sinco SA* [2008] EWHC 1842 (Comm), [2009] Lloyd's Rep IR 365, [26].

1471 [2013] UKSC 70, [2014] 1 Lloyd's Rep 223.

1472 C-111/01, [2003] ECR I-4207. And *cf* para. 2.36, above.

1473 Though the court seised second may be called on to consider whether Art. 30 requires it to grant relief: see below.

2.266 The same cause of action: examples and complexity in identity of *objet* and identity of *cause*

The case law provides several further examples which illustrate the identities of *cause* and *objet* in advance of looking at more challenging cases below. In *Gantner Electronic GmbH v. Basch Exploitatie Maatschappij BV*,[1474] to which reference has already been made, a claim for damages for breach of contract did not involve the same cause of action as a claim for payment for goods supplied prior to the repudiation. In *Mærsk Olie & Gas A/S v. Firma M de Haan en W de Boer*,[1475] proceedings to limit liability for use of a ship did not have the same cause of action as a claim for damages for damaging a pipeline: a conclusion which had already been reached in England in *Glencore International AG v. Shell International Trading and Shipping Co Ltd*.[1476] *Glencore* also held that a claim for substantive relief in relation to property whose ownership was in dispute did not share identity with a claim for interpleader relief: the court suggested that the test is one which requires a judge to identify 'the essential issue' which arises in the two sets of proceedings in the sense of two claims. In *Eli Lilly & Co v. Novo Nordisk A/S*,[1477] it appears to have been held that an action to obtain relief on the basis of a contract did not share identity with a claim to rectify that contract: if this is correct, it will presumably depend on a close analysis of the extent to which, or grounds upon which, rectification is sought. And in *Mecklermedia Corp v. DC Congress GmbH*,[1478] it was held that an action for passing off was not identical with one based on infringement of trademark.

If a party puts forward a number of grounds in support of his claim, some of which are alternative to others, the application of Article 29 will be more complex. Suppose the buyer in *Gubisch* had argued that he was entitled to rescind, but if unsuccessful on that point, advanced an alternative claim for damages for late delivery. The first claim would have the same *objet* and the same *cause* as that brought by the seller for the unpaid price; the second would not. It would follow that the court, if seised second, would have no jurisdiction to determine the claim for rescission, but would have jurisdiction to hear the claim for damages for late delivery. In such circumstances, it should presumably declare that it has no jurisdiction in respect of the first, but has jurisdiction over the second of the two claims.[1479] Authority for the proposition that the court is required to examine its jurisdiction or lack of jurisdiction over the claims individually, and to apply Article 29 separately, is probably to be found in *The Tatry*, in the same way as it applies to proceedings involving different parties.[1480] To the extent that the application of Article 29 does not result in there being only one set of proceedings, there would be a very strong case for the court seised second in respect of any claim over which it does have jurisdiction, to consider ordering relief under Article 30. That relief, as we shall see, might allow it to dismiss the proceedings before it for consolidation with those in the first-seised court, always assuming that the first-seised court

---

1474 C-111/01, [2003] ECR I-4207.
1475 C-39/02, [2004] ECR I-9657.
1476 [1999] 2 Lloyd's Rep 692. To the extent that there was any doubt about it expressed in *The Happy Fellow* [1998] 1 Lloyd's Rep 13, there is no need to pay attention to it, for the analysis in *Glencore* was approved by the Supreme Court in *The Alexandros T* [2013] UKSC 70, [2014] 1 Lloyd's Rep 223.
1477 [2000] ILPr 73: a case decided at common law, and therefore not directly authoritative on the Regulation.
1478 [1998] Ch 40.
1479 But as to which, Art. 30 may apply: see below.
1480 Judgment, at [29] *et seq.* See also *Lloyd's Syndicate 980 v. Sinco SA* [2008] EWHC 1842 (Comm), [2008] 2 CLC 187.

would have jurisdiction over them, or stay its proceedings to wait for the outcome of the proceedings in the court first seised.[1481]

It may be less easy to apply Article 29 in a case where there are issues common to the two claims but the orders sought by way of relief are significantly different.[1482] Take, for example, *Continental Bank NA v. Aeakos Compania Naviera SA*.[1483] In that case, proceedings were commenced first in Greece for damages for wrongful exercise of legal rights under a contract,[1484] and at a later date, in England for an anti-suit injunction to restrain the Greek proceedings.[1485] No doubt it was controversial whether the Greek courts properly had jurisdiction to entertain the claim brought before them; but it was also argued that the English court, as the court seised second, had no jurisdiction at all over the claim brought before it (an issue which was logically anterior to any question whether it was entitled to grant an injunction[1486] if it did have jurisdiction), by reason of what is now Article 29.[1487] The Court of Appeal rejected the argument that what is now Article 29 deprived it of jurisdiction; it was right to do so. The proceedings in England and in Greece clearly overlapped on the question whether the underlying contract between the parties gave exclusive jurisdiction to the English courts. But they could not be said to have the same end in view. In Greece the proceedings claimed damages for the abusive or immoral exercise of legal rights. In England the claim was for an injunction which did not pretend to examine, still less to adjudicate upon, the merits of the substantive claim at all. To put the same point another way, the Greek proceedings sought relief in relation to the substantive contract, while the English proceedings sought to enforce the (distinct, separate, severable) agreement on the resolution of disputes. The two sets of proceedings were not aimed at obtaining judgments in which the one would annul the claim in the other; and as a result there was no identity of *objet* and *cause*.[1488] Analysed in these terms, the explanation given in *The Tatry* lends support to the approach taken by the Court of Appeal.

It follows from this that if proceedings are brought in England for damages for breach of a jurisdiction agreement, and proceedings are brought before the courts of another Member State in respect of a cause of action which fell within the jurisdiction agreement, the proceedings do not have the same *cause* (because the contractual terms relied on as the basis for the two proceedings are distinct) or the same *objet* (as the relief sought is quite different).[1489]

1481 See below, para. 2.281.

1482 See also *Research in Motion (UK) Ltd v. Visto Corp* [2008] EWCA Civ 153, [2008] 2 All ER (Comm) 560.

1483 [1994] 1 WLR 588.

1484 Reminiscent of an old equitable suit to restrain the unconscientious exercise of common law rights, or of the civilian quasi-delict of abuse of rights.

1485 For anti-suit injunctions generally, see Chapter 5 at paras 5.34 *et seq.*, below.

1486 In the light of C-159/02 *Turner v. Grovit* [2004] ECR I-3565 it plainly did not.

1487 Or, in fact, that until the Greek court had ruled on its jurisdiction, it was required to stay its proceedings; if the Greek court ruled that it did have jurisdiction, then to dismiss them.

1488 But see the more relaxed interpretation of these requirements in *J P Morgan Europe Ltd v. Primacom AG* [2005] EWHC 508 (Comm), [2005] 2 Lloyd's Rep 665. See also *Alfred C Toepfer International GmbH v. Molino Boschi Sarl* [1996] 1 Lloyd's Rep 510, where an anti-suit injunction was held not to have the same end in view as the substantive proceedings which it was designed to stop; and similar analysis was applied to the declaratory proceedings designed to establish that P was obliged to arbitrate and was not entitled to litigate the claim: these had different ends in view as well.

1489 *The Alexandros T* [2013] UKSC 70, [2014] 1 Lloyd's Rep 223, [36]–[38], and cases there cited. The decision was applied in the resumed proceedings: *Starlight Shipping Co v. Allianz Marine & Aviation Versicherungs AG* [2014] EWCA Civ 1010, [2014] 2 Lloyd's Rep 554; see also *Starlight Shipping Co v. Allianz Marine & Aviation Versicherungs AG* [2014] EWHC 3068 (Comm), [2014] 2 Lloyd's Rep 579.

As long as the two causes of action have distinct legal bases, Article 29 will not apply to them. By contrast, if in *Continental Bank*, the Greek proceedings had simply been for a declaration or a preliminary ruling that the shipowners were entitled, notwithstanding the terms of the contract, to sue the bank in Greece. Had that been so, then the relationship between the two sets of proceedings would fall much closer to the template for application of Article 29.

This approach is supported by the decision in *The Alexandros T*,[1490] where it was held that proceedings for contractual relief arising from breach by one of the parties to a settlement agreement which contained a jurisdiction agreement, did not have the same cause of action as proceedings for damages for defamation and for loss resulting from late payment of sums due under the settlement agreement. There was no doubt that the allegations and cross-allegations arose from a maritime accident and the resolution of disputes following from it, but the causes of action were not the same. The fact that the causes of action were in the one court contractual and in the other founded on what appeared to be torts was not, perhaps, decisive. But the rights relied on to found the contractual claims were separate and quite distinct from the rights relied on to found the claims in the other court. It is therefore necessary to examine the respective causes of action carefully, paying particular attention to the legal basis on which the claims for relief are based, as distinct from 'standing back' and considering whether overall results sought by the parties in the two proceedings are contradictory only in a more general or economic sense.[1491]

2.267 The same parties under Article 29: identity of parties

As long as the same persons are before each of the two courts as parties, the fact that there may be additional parties on one or both sides of the claim will not prevent the operation of Article 29 of the Regulation: as between the same parties, but only as between the same parties, the particular condition of Article 29 will be satisfied.[1492] It therefore follows, as was made clear in *The Tatry*, that insofar as there is a *lis* between pairs of parties who are not identical, the proceedings do not fall within what is now Article 29. The potential inconvenience of this – for example, in a cargo claim there may be a very large number of parties, not all of whom are joined in all the proceedings – is partially ameliorated by Article 30[1493] and the options it gives to the court seised second.

Some uncertainty had arisen in the English courts in connection with maritime claims, commenced by service of a claim form[1494] upon a ship. The uncertainty arose from the question whether or when the action is to be regarded as one *in rem*, *in personam*, or both, and from the issue how the uniform interpretation of what is now Article 29 applies to a

---

1490 [2013] UKSC 70, [2014] 1 Lloyd's Rep 223.

1491 See *The Alexandros T* [2013] UKSC 70, [2014] 1 Lloyd's Rep 223, [49]-[54]; *Starlight Shipping Co v. Allianz Marine & Aviation Versicherungs AG* [2014] EWCA Civ 1010, [2014] 2 Lloyd's Rep 554. The courts declined to refer a question to the European Court on this issue as the answer was clear.

1492 *AGF v. Chiyoda* [1992] 1 Lloyd's Rep 325, 340–341.

1493 See *The Tatry* at [29] *et seq.*; see also *Grupo Torras SA v. Sheikh Fahad Mohammed al-Sabah* [1996] 1 Lloyd's Rep 7.

1494 In accordance with Art. 71 of the Regulation, the court may assume jurisdiction in accordance with the 1952 Arrest Convention, without regard to the Brussels I Regulation. This applies to jurisdiction taken when the ship has been arrested, but not to jurisdiction taken when it might have been, but has not been, arrested: see *The Deichland* [1990] 1 QB 361.

form of action for which it was not evidently designed. For as a matter of English law, an action *in rem* against a ship was differently constituted from an action *in personam* against the owner of a ship or other interested party. If an action is commenced *in rem*, and an appearance is then entered by the owner or other person interested, that person submits to the jurisdiction of the court. An action *in personam* is then also pending against him, presumably from the original date on which the action *in rem* was instituted, and the action is thenceforth a hybrid one.

If proceedings are commenced in one Member State against a defendant who has an interest in a ship, and thereafter process is served upon a ship in England, the questions are whether Article 29 applies, and whether the answer changes if the interested party enters an appearance. The answer is, for the purposes of the Brussels I Regulation at least, that the action may still be seen as being between the same parties. The Court of Appeal in *The Deichland*[1495] held that, where the English action was only *in rem*, nothing turned upon the technical or procedural manner in which it was constituted. For the purposes of applying what is now Article 4, it was necessary to look behind the technicality and to determine who 'in effect' was being sued. In *The Deichland*, this was Deich Navigation SA, even though that entity had not been served personally, and had entered an appearance only in order to dispute the jurisdiction of the court. The correctness of this approach, in the context of English Admiralty law at least, was confirmed in *The Indian Grace (No 2)*.[1496] In that case, the House of Lords relied on *The Tatry* to reinterpret the approach of English Admiralty law that an Admiralty action *in rem* was a thing apart.[1497]

This approach was supported by *The Tatry*, where the Court had explained[1498] that what is now Article 29 was not excluded from application where the English proceedings were *in rem* and *in personam*, and the Dutch proceedings were *in personam*. The procedural nature of Admiralty claims was just that: a rule of national law concerning the constitution of actions, which did not affect the uniform jurisdictional rules of what is now the Regulation. If the parties may be seen as the same, and if the two cases may lead to irreconcilable judgments, Article 29 should apply. In the light of *The Tatry* and *The Indian Grace (No 2)*, it is unlikely that the particular context of admiralty claims will be problematic in future.[1499]

In *Mecklermedia Corp v. DC Congress GmbH*,[1500] a licensee had been permitted to use the licensor's trade name. But this did not mean that the licensor and licensee were the same parties for the purposes of Article 29. The decision is correct, because there was no reason to suppose that the interests of licensor and licensee could never be opposed to each other: licensee–licensor disputes are not infrequent. The judge did not reject the proposition that a wholly-owned subsidiary could, for these purposes, sometimes be seen as the same party as its parent.[1501] To the extent that this asks whether the interests of the two ostensibly distinct

---

1495 [1990] 1 QB 361.

1496 [1998] AC 878.

1497 And, in this respect, to distance English law from the admiralty law of Australia: *Comandate Marine Corp v. Pan Australia Shipping Pty Ltd* (2006) 157 FCR 45.

1498 At [46]–[48].

1499 On the application of these principles to civil claims advanced in the context of criminal proceedings, see *Haji-Ioannou v. Frangos* [1992] 2 Lloyd's Rep 337.

1500 [1998] Ch 40.

1501 This had been proposed as a case where there would be identity in *Berkeley Administration Inc v. McClelland* [1995] ILPr 201. But for greater caution, see *WMS Gaming Inc v. B Plus Giocolegale Ltd* [2011] EWHC 2620, [2012] ILPr 109.

parties are inseparable or indivisible, the analysis in *Mecklermedia Corp* is aligned with the important decision in *Drouot Assurances SA v. Consolidated Metallurgical Industries*.[1502] The context in which the Court in *Drouot* had to interpret 'the same parties' was a claim by the insurer of a ship's hull against the insurer of the cargo, and a claim by the insurer of the cargo against the owner and charterer of the vessel, the causes of action being essentially the same. As it was not the task of the European Court to apply its ruling to the facts of the individual case, it was sufficient for it to rule that the parties would be the same if their interests were identical and indissociable from each other. Whether the interests of the insurer and its insured fall within that definition was left to the national court to determine.[1503] One can imagine circumstances in which the insurer and the insured have interests which are opposed, particularly where the insurer may be seeking to disavow its liability under the insurance.[1504] Even so, the test is reminiscent of that found in the common law of estoppel by *res judicata*, where privity of interest is sufficient to meet the requirement that the issue be between the same parties.[1505]

The principle in *Drouot* was applied by the Court of Appeal in *Kolden Holdings Ltd v. Rodette Commerce Ltd*.[1506] In that case, A brought proceedings against B in England, and then gave notice of an assignment of its interests to C. In the gap between the giving of notice and the execution of the assignment, B instituted proceedings against C in Cyprus, and then had the nerve to contend before the English court that it had no jurisdiction, or had lost jurisdiction, over the claim when constituted as one between C and B. The court rejected the contention on the facts of the case before it, accepting that the interests of A and C, in relation to B, were one and the same, indissociable from each other,[1507] and that the English court was seised of the proceedings, whether brought in the name of A or C, who were in this sense to be seen as the same single party, before the Cypriot court was seised of the proceedings brought by B. It was absolutely right.

2.268 Date on which a court is seised: background

The rule in what is now Article 29 of the Regulation is clear enough: save in the case provided for by Article 31(2), the court first seised has jurisdiction and unless it finds that its jurisdiction is unfounded, must exercise it; any court seised second or later must stay its proceedings until the jurisdiction of the first court is established, and if it is established,[1508]

1502 C-351/96, [1998] ECR I-3075.

1503 The insurer and insured did not have the same interest, and Art. 29 did not apply, in *Sony Computer Entertainment Ltd v. RH Freight Services Ltd* [2007] EWHC 302 (Comm), [2007] 2 Lloyd's Rep 463 (Art. 30 applied).

1504 From which point of view, the interests of licensor and licensee of intellectual property rights are not identical, and they are not liable to be regarded as the same party: *Mölnlycke Health Care AB v. BSN Medical Ltd* [2009] EWHC 3370 (Pat), [2010] ILPr 171.

1505 *Cf House of Spring Gardens Ltd v. Waite* [1991] 1 QB 241; and see further, para. 7.80.

1506 [2008] EWCA Civ 10, [2008] Bus LR 1051. See also *Re Cover Europe Ltd* [2002] EWHC 861 Ch, [2002] 2 BCLC 61 (English action against liquidator under Insolvency Act 1986 to require him to admit a claim as proof of debt; Italian action by company against claimant for declaration of invalidity of debt claim is between the same parties, even though one case involved the company and the other its liquidator). The decision of the Regional Court of Appeal of Cologne in Case 16 U 110/02 (8 September 2003) [2004] IPRax 521, noted, *ibid.*, 505 is to the same effect as the decision in *Kolden*.

1507 It was of no significance that the validity of the assignment was contested.

1508 Which expression includes being not contested: C-1/13 *Cartier parfums-lunettes SAS v. Ziegler France SA* EU:C:2014:109, [2014] ILPr 359. In that case no challenge to the jurisdiction had been raised by the time of the

must decline jurisdiction. The general idea is that the winner takes it all, that there are no prizes for seising second.[1509] It was equally clear that under the Brussels Conventions it was left to national procedural law in the court seised to specify the conditions, and therefore the date, upon which the court is seised of a claim in proceedings brought before it. The point was decided in *Zelger v. Salinitri (No 2)*.[1510] The sequence of procedural steps was: issue of German writ in August 1976; issue of Italian writ in September 1976; service of Italian writ in September 1976; service of German writ in January 1977. In order to decide which court was seised first, the Court ruled that it was necessary to apply German procedural law to decide when the German action became 'definitively pending' before that court, and Italian procedural law in respect of the Italian action to decide when it became 'definitively pending' before that court.[1511]

It was therefore necessary to decide, according to the national law of the particular court seised, when an action was definitively pending before it. It was believed for some time that, as far as civilian systems were concerned, this was the date of service of the document instituting proceedings, whereas in England the corresponding date was the date of issue of process.[1512] In other words, an English court could be seised in an action without this fact having been brought to the attention of the other party. But this understanding of English procedural law was rejected by the Court of Appeal, in *Dresser (UK) Ltd v. Falcongate Freight Management Ltd*.[1513] In that case, a writ in respect of a cargo damage claim was issued in England in July 1988 and served in July 1989. But in February 1989, proceedings had been commenced in the Dutch courts by the charterers, and these proceeded with despatch. Publication of the orders of the Dutch court was made in May 1989. Although the case did not fall within what is now Article 29 of the Regulation, as the causes of action and the parties thereto were not identical, it fell within what is now Article 30, as the claims were clearly related. In addressing the issue of which court was seised first, the Court of Appeal concluded that the service of the English writ, rather than its earlier issue, had activated the English process of litigation so far as the Brussels Convention was concerned. Though certain time periods were, for the purposes of English procedural law, measured as from the date of issue, it was not until service was actually made that the claimant went public and the defendant brought into the process. For this reason, the court determined that an English

---

first defence, so the jurisdiction was established in the perfectly sufficient sense that it had not been challenged, or was uncontested, and now could be neither challenged nor contested. The establishing of jurisdiction needs no fanfare.

1509 If the court seised second is unclear as to whether it was in fact seised second, it may, and it may be appropriate to, adjourn the jurisdiction application to await the decision of the other court as to when it was seised: *Polly Peck International v. Citibank NA* [1994] ILPr 71; *Chorley v. Chorley* [2005] EWCA Civ 68, [2005] 1 WLR 1469; *Bentinck v. Bentinck* [2007] EWCA Civ 175, [2007] ILPr 391 (a case on the Lugano Convention). It may instead make a direct request of the foreign court in accordance with Art. 29(2). The question will usually be one of foreign law, even in cases to which Art. 31 applies, and this will be good way to reduce the chance of contradictory adjudications.

1510 129/83, [1984] ECR 2397.

1511 In order to avoid difficulties, it is desirable and perhaps essential that the decision of the first court to decide the point be recognised by the other court.

1512 *Kloeckner & Co KG v. Gatoil Overseas Inc* [1990] 1 Lloyd's Rep 177. But for the special problems caused by those systems which require a formal conciliation before the institution of adversary proceedings, see *Chorley v. Chorley* [2005] EWCA Civ 68, [2005] 1 WLR 1469 (a family law case, holding the English judge should have allowed the issue to be determined by the foreign court, and not otherwise ruling on the question); also *Deutsche Bank AG v. Petromena ASA* [2013] EWHC 3065 (Comm); *Lehman Brothers Finance AG v. Klaus Tschira Stiftung GmbH* [2014] EWHC 2782 (Ch) (Swiss conciliation procedure prior to judicial proceedings); see further below.

1513 [1992] 1 QB 502.

court was seised, for the Brussels Convention,[1514] only when process was served. Bingham LJ went so far as to characterise the view that an English court was seised on the issue of process, as 'artificial, far-fetched and wrong', though he reserved his position for exceptional cases in which a court might be seised prior to service.[1515]

In its subsequent decision in *The Sargasso*,[1516] the Court of Appeal confirmed the general rule in *Dresser v. Falcongate*, and denied that there were any exceptions to the rule that a court was seised on, and not before, service. In particular, an English court was not seised in relation to the substantive dispute if it had only been seised with an application for what is now known as a freezing injunction. An invitation to reconsider this point was put to the House of Lords in *Phillips v. Symes (No 3)*[1517] but was not taken up by the majority, mainly because the point was considered to be of historical interest only,[1518] and would have no bearing on the outcome of the actual case. But the argument that a court is seised of substantive proceedings when an application has been made for provisional or protective measures would have been unsound, because the two procedures are plainly distinct, as a matter of fact and for the purposes of the Conventions and the Regulation.[1519]

2.269 A uniform approach to the date of seisin for the purpose of the Regulation

Article 32 of Regulation 1215/2012 provides that:

> *(1) For the purposes of this Section, a court shall be deemed to be seised: (a) at the time when the document instituting the proceedings or an equivalent document is lodged with the court, provided that the claimant has not subsequently failed to take the steps he was required to take to have service effected on the defendant; or (b) if the document has to be served before being lodged with the court, at the time when it is received by the authority responsible for service, provided that the claimant has not subsequently failed to take the steps he was required to take to have the document lodged with the court. The authority responsible for service referred to in point (b) shall be the first authority receiving the documents to be served. (2) The court, or the authority responsible for service, referred to in paragraph 1, shall note, respectively, the date of the lodging of the document instituting the proceedings or the equivalent document, or the date of receipt of the documents to be served.*

Article 32 of the Regulation is practically identical to Article 30 of Regulation 44/2001. Article 30 did not contain the clarificatory final sentence at the end of paragraph 1, and paragraph (2) is new. But neither addition alters the substance of the law.

Significant practical difficulties had arisen from the decision that the date of seisin was to be determined by the individual national laws' answers to the question when proceedings were 'definitively pending'. Litigants could find it surprisingly difficult to obtain

---

1514 But not for the purpose of rules of domestic English law: *Arab Monetary Fund v. Hashim (No 4)*, *The Times*, 24 July 1992.

1515 This did not mean that the Dutch court was seised first. As the judge at first instance had decided that the issue of the English writ, which was the first procedural step taken anywhere, meant the English court was seised first, he had not needed to decide at what date the Dutch court had, as a matter of Dutch law, become seised of the limitation proceedings. The case was therefore remitted to him for that issue to be tried.

1516 [1994] 3 All ER 180.

1517 [2008] UKHL 1, [2008] 1 WLR 180 (a case on the Lugano Convention).

1518 It was irrelevant to the Brussels I Regulation, and would soon be irrelevant to the revised Lugano Convention. It would remain of relevance only to those few scraps of territory to which the Brussels Convention will continue to apply.

1519 The jurisdictional rules which apply to substantive proceedings do not apply to applications for provisional and protective measures: see below, para. 6.09.

reliable advice as to the content of foreign civil procedural law; obtaining clear, reliable, and presentable advice on the point could be problematic.[1520] Another made a naked appeal to chauvinism: the proposition that some courts were seised prior to service, but others only afterwards, was unjustifiable, particularly in a case in which there were many defendants, and the first one to be served could tip off the others. To address these short-comings, and to impose a uniform approach to the date of seisin, the rule now comprising Article 32 was established. It is necessary to decide whether the law of the country whose document[1521] is to be served applies an issue-and-then-serve, or a serve-and-then-file, system to the seisin of the court in question: there is no reason why the answer may not vary, within the one Member State, as between the courts and tribunals which have jurisdiction in civil and commercial matterss.[1522] English law generally conforms to issue-then-serve pattern, and the effect of this new provision is that an English court will be seised when the claim form is issued by the court[1523] at the behest of the claimant, provided that it is thereafter served. French law follows the serve-then-file approach to seisin, with the result that if the defendant is in England, a French court will be seised when the writ is received in the Foreign Process Section of the Royal Courts of Justice for onward transmission.[1524]

Article 32 therefore reflects the principle that the first public step to involve the judicial authorities – having the court issue the claim form, or arranging for the document to be served by the competent authority, as the case may be – marks the formal point at which the proceedings begun by that document are definitively pending before the court in question. Though some points of detail, not all of them minor, may remain to be sorted out,[1525] there will be a much more straightforward basic rule where seisin under the Regulation is concerned, and it would be churlish to complain. The law has been changed, and certainly for the better.

If the Member State in question is one which follows the issue-then-serve approach, it is obvious that service will only take place after issue. It is equally obvious that when service[1526]

1520 For example, it may simply not be clear whether a court is seised on service, on attempted service, on an attempt to serve even though irregular, or only if service is made by particular means. See for an excellent illustration of the problems posed by the position taken by Greek law: *Tavoulareas v. Tsavliris* [2004] EWCA Civ 48, [2004] 1 Lloyd's Rep 445. For the conclusion that an English court was seised on service even though service was irregular, see *Phillips v. Symes (No 3)* [2008] UKHL 1, [2008] 1 WLR 180. In the light of *Abela v. Baadarani* [2013] UKSC 44, [2013] 1 WLR 2043, this conclusion is even more certain to be correct; and see also *Olafsson v. Gissurarson* [2007] EWCA Civ 152, [2008] 1 WLR 2016. Irregularity does not mean there has been no service.

1521 As to which document, in the context of jurisdictions which require conciliation before litigation, see *Chorley v. Chorley* [2005] EWCA Civ 68, [2005] 1 WLR 1469. It does not appear that Art. 32 deals directly with the identification of the document whose issue or service defines the date of seisin. For the question of seisin when the process has begun with the obtaining of an 'order to pay' from a national enforcement agency, which has been objected to, and which objection has not yet been lifted by judicial order, see *MacKew v. Moore* [2012] EWHC 1287 (QB).

1522 If an English court suspects that it was seised second, and that all depends on analysis of what was done in the court which may have been seised first, it may be appropriate to wait for that court to rule on its seisin in its own time: *UBS Ltd v. Regione Calabria* [2012] EWHC 699 (Comm), [2012] ILPR 468.

1523 As on the date stamped on the form: CPR r. 7.2(2). This will meet the point in Art. 32(2).

1524 As the FPS is the authority responsible for service in such a case. Receipt by fax will be sufficient, in the light of the Service Regulation 1393/2007: see *Arbuthnot Latham & Co Ltd v. M3 Marine Ltd* [2013] EWHC 1019 (Comm), [2014] 1 WLR 190.

1525 For example, *Nordea Bank Norge ASA v. Unicredit Corp Banking SpA* [2011] EWHC 30 (Comm).

1526 Particularly because this is a proviso, it does not seem sensible to interpret this as meaning 'faultless service': effective or sufficient service should suffice: *Benatti v. WPP Holdings Italy Srl* [2007] EWCA Civ 263, [2007] 1 WLR 2316.

is made, the proviso at the end of Article 32(1)(a) will have no application, and the court's seisin on the date of issue will not be called into question. But in some cases, the date of service has been delayed, for reasons which the court appeared to consider egregious; and the conclusion which was found to follow was that the original date of seisin had been lost, together with the temporal priority which this had given. While this appeals to an intuitive sense of there being a difference between normal and blameless and therefore insignificant delays,[1527] on the one hand, and culpable delays[1528] on the other, it is more difficult to see where the line is to be drawn and to determine whether the issue has lost its priority.[1529] The law on this point cannot yet be regarded as clear.

Article 32 will allow a solution to the question which may arise[1530] when seeking to pinpoint the date of seisin in those Member States in which conciliation proceedings are (or are required to be) commenced before the formal institution of adversary proceedings.[1531] It would make little sense if it were to be held that the foreign court is not seised while this process of conciliation is underway, for it would simply mean that judicial proceedings, instituted before the end of the conciliation process, before the courts of another Member State would have temporal priority. As long as the conciliation process may be regarded as being sufficiently judicial in character,[1532] sufficiently part of the civil procedure in a system which treats judicial adjudication as a measure of last resort, the institution of such measures should mean that the court is seised from the date on which they are commenced.[1533]

In the paragraphs that follow it is necessary to examine how the seisin rule applies in cases involving multiple defendants, and where there is an amendment of pleadings. In doing so, it will be seen that the issues are, as was pointed out in *The Alexandros T*, dependent on a close analysis of the facts.

1527 *Benatti v. WPP Holdings Italy Srl* [2007] EWCA Civ 263, [2007] 1 WLR 2316; *UBS AG v. Kommunale Wasserwerke Leipzig GmbH* [2010] EWHC 2566 (Comm), [2010] 2 CLC 499 (where the delay in service was to allow time for negotiation: surely a risky justification).

1528 For example, failing to pay the fee for service of process to be made (*SK Slavia Praha Fotbal AS v. Debt Collect London Ltd* [2010] EWCA Civ 1250, [2011] 1 WLR 866); failing to provide the information which the body which will effect service requires (but not where the reason is that the defendant is being evasive, so that the information cannot be obtained and cannot therefore be given: *Benatti v. WPP Holdings Italy Srl* [2007] EWCA Civ 263, [2007] 1 WLR 2316), etc.

1529 For a case in which the delay was such that temporal priority was lost, and an extension of time to serve was refused as this might be seen to reclaim temporal priority from the foreign court (this consequence is legally debatable, but the point stands), see *Katsouris Bros v. Haitoğlu Bros* [2011] EWHC 111 (QB).

1530 See also *Chorley v. Chorley* [2005] EWCA Civ 68, [2005] 1 WLR 1469, a case on the corresponding rule of Regulation 1347/2000, the now-superseded Matrimonial Regulation.

1531 For example, *Deutsche Bank AG v. Petromena ASA* [2013] EWHC 3065 (Comm); *Lehman Brothers Finance AG v. Klaus Tschira Stiftung GmbH* [2014] EWHC 2782 (Ch) (Swiss conciliation procedure prior to judicial proceedings). In the context of the Brussels II Regulation, see also *De La Ville De Barge v. China* [2014] EWHC 3975 (Fam) (Italian separation proceedings distinct from but a necessary condition for subsequent divorce proceedings; held in effect that there was one uninterrupted period of seisin).

1532 *Lehman Brothers Finance AG v. Klaus Tschira Stiftung GmbH* [2014] EWHC 2782 (Ch) (a case on the Lugano II Convention). Swiss conciliation procedure prior to judicial proceedings was, on the balance of the evidence, regarded as a matter of Swiss law as part of the ordinary proecdure for the resolution of civil disputes. It might be otherwise if the 'conciliation' is before a panel which is less obviously associated with a court but more obviously part of a government ministry.

1533 And it would be rational to consider there to be no hiatus if the conciliation is then followed by judicial proceedings instituted within the time period allowed by the foreign system: *Moore v. Moore* [2007] EWCA Civ 361, [2007] ILPr 481.

2.270 The date of seisin: multiple defendants

In straightforward cases an English court will now be seised of proceedings on the issue of a claim form. A difficulty had arisen under the Brussels Convention was how to determine the date of seisin in proceedings in which claims were made against more than one defendant. If there were several defendants, for example, would the rule in *Dresser v. Falcongate* mean that the court was seised of proceedings against each defendant only when that individual defendant had been served? Or was it instead sufficient that process had been served on one, in order to establish that the proceedings were definitively pending in relation to every person named in the writ? The question had no obviously correct answer.

The decision at first instance in *Grupo Torras SA v. Sheikh Fahad Mohammed al-Sabah*[1534] that, as soon as process had been served on one defendant, the action was definitively pending in relation to all defendants named in the writ, had practical attractions. The Court of Appeal[1535] disposed of the case on other grounds, and neither explicitly endorsed nor repudiated the sensible view of the judge. But it noted that *The Tatry*[1536] required a *lis*-by-*lis* approach to decide whether proceedings were between the same parties, and that it was possible to infer[1537] that the same approach could be applied when deciding whether and when proceedings were definitively pending and the court was seised.

But where the Brussels I Regulation applies, the effect of what is now Article 32 is that a court is seised of proceedings, as against all named defendants, when the claim form is issued. No question of having to serve any or all of the defendants will arise, unless it is alleged that there has been a failure by the claimant to confirm or perfect the seisin by service. One assumes that this will be a rare case. In this respect the law has become more straightforward.

2.271 Problems arising from the amendment of pleadings

Amendment is problematic, for several reasons. It may be proposed to make and add allegations which were not originally spelled out in the claim, or to add or substitute parties to the proceedings. The problems only really arise when the doing of any of these is complicated by the existence of proceedings in another Member State, across which the proposed amendment may be said or seen to cut. The issues are almost always tangled, for they may raise all or any of a number of questions: is this a new claim, or not a new claim, or something else? If the substance of the new claim is before the courts of another Member State in proceedings which were instituted after the English proceedings, does this affect the jurisdiction of the court to permit the amendment, or the exercise of any discretionary power which the court may have in relation to the proposed amendment? If the court does allow the amendment, is it then to be regarded as seised second in relation to the issues raised on amendment, or first seised because the proceedings into which the amendment is to be added were still instituted before the proceedings in the other Member State? So far as

---

1534 [1995] 1 Lloyd's Rep 374.

1535 [1996] 1 Lloyd's Rep 7.

1536 Which was decided after the decision at first instance. It was said by the Court of Appeal that this was significant; in the light of the analysis put forward below, it is not clear that this is as well founded as it seems.

1537 Although there is a suggestion (at 21) that the Court thought it was actually incumbent upon them to adopt such an approach to all issues arising within what is now Arts 29 and 30. The defendant-by-defendant approach seems to have found favour in *Fox v. Taher* [1997] ILPr 441, CA; petition for leave to appeal to the House of Lords dismissed: 6 March 1997.

the court in the other Member State is concerned, is it correct that it could regard itself as first seised of a matter which is raised in proceedings before it, only for it to become second seised once the proceedings in the first State are amended?

The answers are not altogether easy to see; and in advance of an authoritative answer from the European Court, the analysis which follows is offered with rather more diffidence than is usual in these pages. It is sensible, however, to start with a practical point. A difficulty is always liable to arise when proceedings which have been commenced are proposed to be amended by the addition of a new *lis* (whether this is by the addition of new defendants to an existing claim, or by introducing entirely new claims against existing defendants)[1538] in cases where the amendment may be made only with permission of the court.[1539] The amended proceedings will be pending only once an order allowing the amendment has been made.[1540] If the claimant has had to make an application for permission to amend, the application notice may have been taken by the respondent as notice of a window of opportunity to commence proceedings in mirror image elsewhere, before the application comes on to be heard.[1541] This may put the claimant at a tactical disadvantage, as a result of which it may be better to apply for leave to amend without notice to the intended defendant, and leave it up to the new defendant, once served with the reissued claim form, to apply to have the permission to amend set aside. If a claimant is not permitted to act in this way, the procedure of his having to seek leave by application heard *inter partes* may be damaging, and for no good or intended reason.

The amendment of proceedings to alter the names of parties on the claim form will not always be seen as adding new parties, and the question whether there is a new date of seisin, for some purposes, will not then arise. As was explained above,[1542] an amendment which is made to take account of an assignment of the interests of the claimant does not affect the date of seisin, as the assignor and assignee are regarded for this purpose as the same person.[1543] Subject to that, a court is seised of a claim which adds a properly new party to proceedings on the date on which the new party is added to the proceedings.[1544]

The proper analysis where the addition is of new claims into existing proceedings is more elusive. Before getting down to the detail, it is well to be reminded of the wise way it was put in *The Alexandros T*:[1545] 'it is never easy to decide what is an entirely new claim, what is

---

1538 In this context, the introduction of new (in the sense of extra) claimants raises the same issue as the addition of new defendants.

1539 See CPR rr 19.2, 19.4.

1540 And the amended claim form reissued. It appears that, although the amendment dates back to the date of the original claim form, which it replaces as a matter of procedural law, the claim is definitively pending only on the date on which the amended claim form was actually reissued: *cf Grupo Torras SA v. Sheikh Fahad Mohammed Al-Sabah* [1996] 1 Lloyd's Rep 7 (a case decided under Art. 21 of the Brussels Convention, and where the equivalent date was that of service). Where there was need to cure an irregularity in service, the court was not seised until that was done: *Molins plc v. GD SpA* [2000] 1 WLR 1741. But the court might make an order declaring that the earlier irregular service had been good service, and as a result the court will have been seised from the date of original service: *Phillips v. Symes (No 3)* [2008] UKHL 1, [2008] 1 WLR 180. But the issue, which arose under the Brussels and Lugano Convention, under which the date of seisin was the date of service, will not arise in this form under the Brussels I Regulation.

1541 For (thwarted) illustration, see *Kolden Holdings Ltd v. Rodette Commerce Ltd* [2008] EWCA Civ 10, [2008] Bus LR 1051.

1542 Paragraph 2.267, above.

1543 *Kolden Holdings Ltd v. Rodette Commerce Ltd* [2008] EWCA Civ 10, [2008] Bus LR 1051.

1544 *The Alexandros T* [2013] UKSC 70, [2014] 1 Lloyd's Rep 223, [60].

1545 [2013] UKSC 70, [2014] 1 Lloyd's Rep 223, [90].

a new claim and what is an expansion of an old claim'. An attempt to draw lines in this area is liable to run into difficulty of various kinds. It may also be necessary to address a question which arises tangentially, which reflects the fact that a court cannot be seied in the abstract, but must be seised of something. Whether that something is causes of action or proceedings is a question which will certainly arise when a court has to consider whether, for the purpose of these rules, it was seised first or second in time.[1546]

In principle, and as *The Alexandros T* shows, the first question for the court will be whether the proposed amendment has the same *cause* and *objet* as anything raised in proceedings before a court in another Member State.[1547] Only once that has been done is it possible to sort out the difficulties resulting from the first seised rule of Articles 29 to 32. Take for example a case in which it is sought, some time after issue and service, to add claims to proceedings already pending and proceeding against an existing defendant. Suppose A has commenced proceedings against B for breach of contract, and only later seeks to amend to add a claim in respect of a distinct loss. It may be that B, having seen the limited nature of the claim advanced by A, had commenced proceedings of his own in the courts of another Member State for a declaration that he owed no liability in respect of the distinct loss. The question for the court considering the proposed amendment would be whether the pendency of the claim raised in proceedings before another Member State would preclude A from making the amendment sought.

One will therefore ask whether the proposed amendment is, as it was put in *The Alexandros T*, an entirely new claim, a new claim, or the expansion of the pending claim. If it is seen as no more than an expansion, or elaboration, of a pending claim, there should be no impediment to the amendment which simply draws out the implications of a claim which is already pending before the court. The majority would in such a case see the original date of seisin as applying to this claim as well, as though (notwithstanding that it was not put quite this way) it was latent in the original claim and before the court from the same date as the original claim.[1548]

If, by contrast, it is correct to see the proposed amendment as an entirely new claim,[1549] the next question to determine will be whether it has the same *objet* and *cause* as the proceedings pending before the courts of another Member State. In answering that question, the fact that the issue arises on amendment is irrelevant: the court will be required to carry out a careful analysis of the legal basis of each claim. If, as was the case with almost all the claims in *The Alexandros T*, they are not mirror images of the claims in the proceedings pending before another court, but are related to them, for example by being claims which are consequential on the anticipated judgment in the foreign court, Article 29 will not pose a problem.

If the claims proposed to be added are the mirror image of claims before the other court, which is already seised, there is a harder question to answer. However, if the matter sought

---

1546 See also and in particular *Research in Motion (UK) Ltd v. Visto Corp* [2008] EWCA Civ 153, [2008] 1 Lloyd's Rep 434; *Stribog Ltd v. FKI Engineering Ltd* [2011] EWCA Civ 622, [2011] 1 WLR 3264.

1547 See *The Alexandros T* [2013] UKSC 70, [2014] 1 Lloyd's Rep 223.

1548 Lord Mance, who dissented on this point, would not have agreed, as he appeared to find it just too difficult to accept that a court could be seised of a claim which had not been made. He would have regarded the notion that this amounted to upsetting the chronological priority which the Regulation established: see esp. at [160].

1549 The case of a new claim which is not wholly new is the most problematic. The only solution which appears to work is to deny the existence of the category, and to require the court to decide whether the claim is a (wholly) new one, or one which was always in the writ even though it had not been clearly drawn out.

to be raised by amendment would, if it had stood alone, have fallen on the wrong side of Article 29, it cannot in principle make any difference that as a matter of English procedure it may be brought before the court by way of amendment of existing proceedings. Rules of procedural law apply to the extent that they do not call into question the practical effect of the Regulation; and for a procedural rule to undermine or overturn the practical effect of Article 29 would be challenging.

If amendment were to take place in such circumstances, the real question would be one concerning the date of seisin. If the true position were to be that the English court was first seised of the proceedings – on the footing that Article 29 is concerned with the date on which proceedings were first pending, not with the date on which the court was seised with individual causes of action within proceedings – the English court would be able to consider itself to be first seised. But so also would the court in the other Member State: it may be unwilling to accept that although it was the first court before which the particular matter had been raised, it was relegated to the status of court seised second when the English proceedings were amended,[1550] even though it was the second of the two courts to be seised. This would suggest that the scheme of the Regulation should not allow a wholly new claim to be added by amendment when the substance of that proposed amendment is already pending in proceedings before a court in another Member State. In *The Alexandros T* it was admitted that at this point the answer is not clear, and that it would need a reference to be made to the European Court to obtain an answer which the court could then simply apply.[1551] In the light of the conclusion of the Supreme Court, the next time the question arises and needs an answer, a reference must be made.

It is believed that this explanation is broadly in line with the analysis in *The Alexandros T*, and is aligned with the broad purposes of the Regulation. If, therefore, there is a claim before the court for damages for breach of contract, and then by reason of proceedings taken before a foreign court it appears that the contract, or the individual term, is being re-breached, it is not difficult to see claims added into the existing proceedings as unaffected by Article 29, as they are really only amplification of what was already there. Proceedings which seek relief in relation to a distinct breach of a contractual settlement of disputes will be liable to be added into the proceedings still pending before the court because they arise naturally from the original proceedings, over which the English court was first and is still seised.[1552]

In such circumstances, the view to be taken by the court seised second, but with proceedings which it considered itself, quite possibly correctly, to have jurisdiction to entertain, will be a matter for it, though in the light or analogy of *The Tatry*, it may be that it is required to decline jurisdiction in accordance with Article 29. If that seems unsatisfactory – that a court with jurisdiction subsequently discovers that it does not have jurisdiction after all – that is perhaps better seen as a problem for the claimant more than it is for the court. If he commences before another court proceedings which are in some sense related to proceedings already and still pending before another court, there is always this risk.

1550 Of course, it is not accurate to say that is is relegated to the status of court seised second. The truth is that it was seised of proceedings between the parties; and as a court seised second, Art. 30 will determine whether it should order jurisdictional relief.

1551 At [58] it was indicated that a question might be referred on the relationship (or the mirror-imageness of the proposed English and pending Greek claims); and at [72] on the application of the first seised rule in such a case.

1552 *Starlight Shipping Co v. Allianz Marine & Aviation Versicherungs AG* [2014] EWHC 3068 (Comm), [2014] 2 Lloyd's Rep 579.

Even if this is broadly correct, there will be cases where such an analysis is simply too strained to be put forward. In those cases it appears that a defendant, who sees his opponent's claim as being limited or potentially incomplete, may be able to pre-empt later amendment by commencing proceedings of his own to steal the gap. Until the law is completely clear, which it currently is not, there may be a high price to be paid if the original claim form is not drafted as fully and completely as the claimant's capacity for foresight permits.[1553] If it is possible to make a general, place-saving, allegation of liability which may emerge and require the pleading to be supplemented, or to plead the absence of any basis for the defendant to make any allegation of non-liability, it may be worth considering how to do so.

2.272 Court ceasing to be seised or staying its proceedings

Article 29 provides no immediate solution to the problems which may arise if one of the courts ceases to be seised, or decides to stay its proceedings. The various permutations therefore need to be explored separately.

If the foreign court was seised first, but is no longer seised when the English proceedings are instituted, there is no objection to the exercise of jurisdiction by the English court.[1554] If the dismissal of the proceedings before the foreign court has come about through a successful[1555] challenge to its jurisdiction, the English court may proceed to hear the matter before it: this, after all, is the way Article 29 is designed to work.

If the foreign court was seised first but has given its judgment, and is as a result *functus officio* by the time the English proceedings are instituted, there is also no *lis pendens* barrier to the exercise of jurisdiction by the English court. But the obligation under Chapter III of the Regulation to recognise the foreign judgment will affect the course of the English proceedings.[1556]

There may be circumstances in which a court remains seised of proceeding after what may be thought of as the effective end of the trial. An easy case is where the court has stayed its proceedings on the basis of the parties' agreement to settle the matter and to carry into effect the terms of the settlement which they have agreed. An order in this form is usually known as a *Tomlin* order, and according to the decision in *The Alexandros T*, the court

---

1553 A predecessor version of this passage was cited with apparent approval in *Lloyd's Syndicate 980 v. Sinco SA* [2008] EWHC 1842 (Comm), [2008] 2 CLC 187, [62].

1554 *International Nederlanden Aviation Lease BV v. Civil Aviation Authority* [1997] 1 Lloyd's Rep 80; *Prudential Assurance Co Ltd v. Prudential Insurance Co of America* [2003] EWCA Civ 327, [2003] 1 WLR 2295. The same has been held to be true even where the foreign court was definitively seised when the English proceedings were commenced but the foreign court has since given judgment and has ceased to be seised: *Tavoulareas v. Tsavliris* [2005] EWHC 2643 (Comm), [2006] 1 All ER (Comm) 130 (though it is harder to explain why it was not incumbent on the English court to dismiss the English proceedings *in limine litis*, on the ground that the foreign court was seised, that its jurisdiction was confirmed, and that what is now Art. 29 therefore gave the English court no choice but to dismiss). It is also arguable that it is not open to a party to commence (fresh) proceedings in respect of a matter in which a foreign court has already given judgment: 42/76 *De Wolf v. Cox* [1976] ECR 1759; *T v. L* [2008] IESC 48, [2009] ILPr 46, though this principle must be confined to cases in which a claimant institutes a second set of proceedings in a case in which the judgment of the court seised first is entitled to recognition under Chapter III of the Regulation.

1555 This must mean a final challenge which is not further subject to appeal; decisions which are subject to appeal cannot be regarded as decisive in this context. On the other hand, the Northern Irish courts have held that a court is no longer seised of proceedings if all that remains is an appeal against having been struck out, *Lough Neagh Exploration Ltd v. Morrice* [1999] NI 258.

1556 *Berkeley Administration Inc v. McClelland* [1995] ILPr 201; *Gamlestaden plc v. Casa de Suecia SA* [1994] 1 Lloyd's Rep 433.

remains seised of the substantive case, as it must if it is to be able to police the parties' compliance or not with the terms of their settlement. Any suggestion that the court has ceased to be seised of a case which it has stayed – no matter the cause for the stay, or expectation of the court – is heretical and wrong.[1557] It follows that complaints which are based on the non-observance, or subversion, of the settlement may be brought in and considered as part of the original proceedings, even though it is true, as a matter of logic and chronology, that they could not have been alleged when the claim was first made. Perhaps the explanation is that they form a 'procedural unit' with the original claim,[1558] but whatever the technical explanation, the common sense is obvious, even if the relationship of this sense with the Regulation may need clarification.[1559]

It may, but less persuasively, be argued that even after it has given what is intended by the court to be final judgment, it remains seised of the proceedings for the purpose of enforcement; the orders made by the Court of Appeal by way of enforcement and reinforcement of its judgment in *Masri v. Consolidated Contractors International Co SAL (No 2)*[1560] were held to be justified on the ground that as the court had been seised of the claim, it had power to make, and to continue to make, orders in its capacity as the court with 'full possession' of the proceedings to determine the substance of the dispute. Even so, once the court has given final judgment on the issues raised in the *lis*, it is hard to see how it is still seised of a dispute on the merits as set out in the claim.[1561] Accordingly, any continued engagement with the case should not prevent a court in another Member State from asserting jurisdiction. Whether that court will be required to recognise the first judgment will be a matter principally determined by Chapter III of the Regulation.

A court does not cease to be seised as soon as it rules that it has no jurisdiction if the losing party may still appeal and the appeal has not yet been determined.[1562] A court does not cease to be seised until the challenge to its jurisdiction is finally determined. It would make no sense at all for it to be held that an English court is no longer seised when the master or judge in chambers upholds a challenge to the jurisdiction brought under CPR Part 11, and declares that the court has no jurisdiction, only for this to be reversed on appeal. It is only rational to accept that the English court remains seised at all times during the period in which an appeal may be lodged, without hiatus and until the final determination of the appeal or appeals on jurisdiction. After all, if the appeal has the effect of reinstating the proceedings as on the date of their issue, the court is seised with retrospective effect. If it were otherwise, and the effect of the order was that the court had ceased to be seised, there would be an incentive for an unseemly attempt to commence foreign proceedings in the meantime, and even to argue that by virtue of this fact the English court has been relegated to the

---

1557 *The Alexandros T* [2013] UKSC 70, [2014] 1 Lloyd's Rep 223, approving in this respect *ROFA Sport Management AG v. DHL International (UK) Ltd* [1989] 1 WLR 902.

1558 *The Alexandros T* [2013] UKSC 70, [2014] 1 Lloyd's Rep 223, [89], considering C-296/10 *Purrucker v. Vallés Pérez* [2010] ECR I-11163.

1559 *The Alexandros T* [2013] UKSC 70, [2014] 1 Lloyd's Rep 223, [89].

1560 [2008] EWCA Civ 303, [2009] QB 450 (receivership), [2008] EWCA Civ 625, [2009] QB 503 (injunction), [2008] EWCA Civ 876, [2009] 2 WLR 699 (examination of debtor's officer: however, a person who is not within the territorial jurisdiction of the English court is not subject to CPR Part 71 in any event: *Masri v. Consolidated Contractors International Co SAL (No 4)* [2009] UKHL 43, [2010] 1 AC 90).

1561 It will have exclusive jursidction over enforcement of the judgment in England according to Art. 24(5), which is a preferable explanation for its jurisdiction to make post-judgment orders.

1562 If the claimant indicates that he will not appeal, this point falls away.

status of having become seised second.[1563] For the good order of litigation, and to protect the power of courts to rule properly and effectively upon their jurisdiction, an English court remains seised until the final determination of any appeals in the procedure which disputes the jurisdiction;[1564] the same must also be taken to be true of courts in other Member States.

If a claimant commences proceedings in England, but now prefers to sue in another Member State, the issues are different again. If the cause of action is the same, pending English proceedings may well make a difficulty for him, as the court in the second Member State will be precluded by Article 29 from assuming jurisdiction. The claimant may in such a case seek to discontinue the English proceedings,[1565] though this is not always available as of right. In the cases in which the permission of the court is needed, it is not obvious that this always will, or should, be easily obtained. An application for permission failed in *Internationale Nederlanden Aviation Lease BV v. Civil Aviation Authority*[1566] as the judge considered that, on the facts of the case, the English proceedings had gone too far to allow discontinuance; but he also stated his opinion that it would generally be contrary to the policy of what is now the Regulation for the court first seised to permit discontinuance simply to enable the claimant to change his mind and sue in another Member State instead.[1567] It is possible, however, to question this conclusion. If the policy of the Regulation is to ensure that only one court hears a case, and that there will not be conflicting judgments in respect of a single cause of action, there is no need to refuse permission to discontinue. But it is undeniable that a claimant who has elected to launch proceedings in one country, perhaps before he was really ready, will have prevented his opponent from exercising any right to choose where to seek to have the dispute heard. The perception that the claimant has made his own bed and must now lie in it would be perfectly understandable, and it may well be a sufficient reason for a court to exercise its procedural discretion by refusing leave to discontinue;[1568] it is not quite so obvious that this result is also required by the general policy of the Regulation. Even so, the court appears to have assumed[1569] that only a formal termination, or dismissal, or discontinuance, of the proceedings would allow the court seised second to exercise jurisdiction; and this appears to be correct.

1563 It is true that this could be forestalled by seeking a stay of the order declaring that the court has no jurisdiction and setting aside service, but not all courts may be persuaded of the legitimate need for such an order.

1564 *Moore v. Moore* [2007] EWCA Civ 361, [2007] ILPr 481. See also *Internationale Nederlanden Aviation Lease BV v. Civil Aviation Authority* [1997] 1 Lloyd's Rep 80 (court may still be seised of a case even though its jurisdiction was not established); *J P Morgan Europe Ltd v. Primacom AG* [2005] EWHC 508 (Comm), [2005] 2 Lloyd's Rep 665 (court seised even though its jurisdiction not established, with the result that a court could grant protective measures without regard to the restraints otherwise imposed by Art. 31 of the Regulation). The principle is broadly consistent with *Kolden Holdings Ltd v. Rodette Commercial Ltd* [2008] EWCA Civ 10, [2008] Bus LR 1051 in its desire to see a rational and stable approach to the issue whether and when a court is (still) seised.

1565 CPR Part 38.

1566 [1997] 1 Lloyd's Rep 80. The application was made under RSC Order 21, which was considerably more restrictive than the current CPR Part 38.

1567 *Cf* (in a related context) *Knauf UK GmbH v. British Gypsum Ltd* [2001] EWCA Civ 1570, [2002] 1 Lloyd's Rep 199.

1568 Though outside the domain of the Brussels I Regulation, the appropriate response would be to put the claimant to his election as between proceedings, not to deprive him of choice in the matter: *Australian Commercial Research and Development Ltd v. ANZ McCaughan Merchant Bank Ltd* [1989] 3 All ER 65. For a far more stringent reaction, see *Glencore International AG v. Exter Shipping Ltd* [2002] EWCA Civ 524, [2002] 2 All ER (Comm) 1 (not a case on the Brussels I Regulation, but taking a very dim view of the attempt to discontinue and so be free of the jurisdiction of the court which had been seised).

1569 The court was at pains neither to guess, nor dictate, how the court seised second (*in casu*, Belgian) would appreciate its situation. But it considered the application for leave to discontinue as this was before it for decision.

If it is not the claimant, but the defendant who wishes the proceedings to be brought in another Member State, he may try to challenge the jurisdiction of the court over him. But if that is unsuccessful, it may be asked whether it would be useful for him to seek a stay of the English proceedings. This will be a possibility only where jurisdiction was taken on the basis of Article 6, of course, and the answer will depend upon how the foreign court understands the status of proceedings which have been stayed. A similar question may arise for an English court if proceedings have been commenced in Ireland, and then stayed. In short, is a court which has stayed its proceedings still seised of those proceedings?

Although there was an occasional suggestion[1570] that a court which has stayed proceedings in the expectation that the claimant will sue in another court is not seised any more, or should be treated as though it was not seised any more,[1571] this was not consistent with what had been decided in *ROFA Sport Management AG v. DHL International (UK) Ltd*;[1572] and the correctness of *ROFA Sport* has now been confirmed by the Supreme Court:[1573] an English court which stays proceedings remains seised of them. No other answer makes any sense, especially in the context of the Regulation where certainty is especially required. The court may always lift the stay on the claimant's application; no fresh claim form needs to be issued to bring the matter back before the court; no question of limitation will have arisen, and so forth: this makes it impossible to see that the court has ceased at any point to be seised of the proceedings. Anyway, the point is now settled.

This presents a significant obstacle for an applicant who applies to the English court in proceedings which have been commenced on the basis of Article 6 for a stay in favour of the courts of another Member State on the ground of *forum non conveniens*. If the English court remains seised, the stay application will fall at the first hurdle: there will not be a court of competent jurisdiction outside the English court in which the action could be brought.[1574] This argument troubled the Court of Appeal in *Haji-Ioannou v. Frangos*,[1575] but it did not need to be resolved once the court found, as it did, that its own jurisdiction could not be derived from what is now Article 6. Even so, it would be surprising if a court was precluded from ordering a stay, with the result that its Article 6 jurisdiction would have been effectively (and, no doubt, unintentionally) widened by the Regulation.[1576] The court in *Haji-Ioannou* suggested that if the foreign court would still have been troubled by its perception that the claim was still definitively pending in the English courts, it would have been prepared, in principle, to dismiss rather than stay the action. This would have been a novel departure from the structure of a stay of proceedings, and all the more so in a case in which the defendant applicant has given undertakings to the court as a condition of the stay, but as the issue is one of English procedural law as much as European law, it may be a matter for the Supreme Court rather than the European Court.

1570 *Haji-Ioannou v. Frangos* [1999] 2 Lloyd's Rep 337.

1571 On the footing that it had neither intention to adjudicate nor expectation that it would adjudicate.

1572 [1989] 1 WLR 902.

1573 *The Alexandros T* [2013] UKSC 70, [2014] 1 Lloyd's Rep 223, [81]–[83].

1574 See below, paras 4.19 *et seq.*

1575 [1999] 2 Lloyd's Rep 337.

1576 The observation that a plea of *forum non conveniens* leads a Scottish court to dismiss the action was not wholly convincing: all it shows is there is no jurisdiction unless the claimant can survive such a challenge. In this respect the jurisdiction of the Scottish courts appears to resemble that based on service out with the permission of the court, in which case there is no jurisdiction, and permission will not be granted, unless England is the natural forum. Sometimes considerations of *forum conveniens* are built into the jurisdiction of the court; sometimes not.

2.273 The court seised second considers that it has general, special, or residual jurisdiction and that the court seised first does not have jurisdiction

If the court seised second believes that it has general, special, or residual jurisdiction and that the court seised first does not have jurisdiction, it is required to act in accordance with Article 29, no matter how plain it appears to be that the court seised first does not have jurisdiction. This was decided in *Overseas Union Insurance Ltd v. New Hampshire Insurance Co,*[1577] and reaffirmed on several occasions.[1578] The Court emphasised the overriding need to apply what is now Article 29 so as to avoid the risk of parallel proceedings leading to irreconcilable judgments, and ruled that where the jurisdiction of the court seised first was established,[1579] the court seised second must decline jurisdiction. No exception was made for cases in which jurisdiction was based on Article 6, or for cases in which the jurisdiction of the first court was wrongly established, for it was not the function of the court seised second to decide for itself whether a court in another Member State had jurisdiction. *Overseas Union Insurance* made it plain that collateral attack on the jurisdiction of the court seised first by the court seised second is not consistent with the broader purposes of the Regulation.[1580]

If one accepts that the jurisdictional provisions of the Regulation are common to all Member States, it is as easy for the court seised first, as for the court seised second, to determine whether the court seised first has jurisdiction. Often a decision about the jurisdiction of the first court will require the application of some element of the domestic law of that State;[1581] it will be rare for a decision about the jurisdiction of the first court to turn upon the domestic law of the second court. It would be anarchic if each court were entitled to reach an individual view and to act on the strength of it. For these reasons, the court seised second must consider itself obliged to defer to and accept the conclusions of the court seised first, and may not second-guess the jurisdiction of the first court.[1582] Indeed, the decision of the first court on jurisdiction enjoys a special status as a judgment required to be recognised in other Member States.[1583]

2.274 The court seised second believes it has exclusive jurisdiction regardless of domicile and that the court seised first does not

If the court seised second believes, on analysis, that the court seised first did not have jurisdiction because the issue is one over which the court seised second has exclusive jurisdiction regardless of domicile, it is not required to stay or dismiss its proceedings, but may (and

---

1577 C-351/89, [1991] ECR I-3317.

1578 C-116/02 *Erich Gasser GmbH v. MISAT Srl* [2003] ECR I-14692 is a notorious example.

1579 Which simply means that the point at which a challenge could have been made has passed: C-1/13 *Cartier parfums-lunettes SAS v. Ziegler France SA* EU:C:2014:109, [2014] ILPr 359. In that case no challenge to the jurisdiction had been raised by the time of the first defence, so the jurisdiction was established in the perfectly sufficient sense that it had not been challenged, or was uncontested, and now could be neither challenged nor contested.

1580 Reiterated in C-163/95 *Von Horn v. Cinnamond* [1997] ECR I-5451.

1581 Most notably when an issue of domicile within that State arises as the basis for jurisdiction.

1582 If each court considers that it was seised first, there will be a clash of jurisdiction which the Regulation cannot resolve. All the European Court can do is interpret the Articles of the Regulation. It does not, and cannot, apply this interpretation to the law of courts before which the question has arisen. If the two courts each conclude that they were seised first, they will both be entitled to determine the case, and the provisions of Art. 34 of Regulation 44/2001 and Art. 45 of Regulation 1215/2012 will resolve any eventual clash of judgments.

1583 C-456/11 *Gothaer Allgemeine Versicherung AG v. Samskip GmbH* EU:C: 2012:719, [2013] QB 548: below, para. 7.07.

therefore must) proceed to adjudicate the matter before it. Although Article 29 does not say so, this welcome clarification of the law was given by the Court in *Weber v. Weber*.[1584]

The question had been raised but left open in *Overseas Union Insurance Ltd*: the answer given by the Court in that case was expressed to be 'Without prejudice to the case where the court seised second has exclusive jurisdiction under the Convention and in particular under Article 16 thereof...'. But as Chapter III of the Regulation would impose an obligation to deny recognition to any judgment conflicting with what is now Article 24, it ought to follow that the court seised second in such circumstances may proceed to hear the case, for otherwise there will be no judicial determination of the issue capable of being recognised: to put it another way, there is nothing for the court seised second to wait for. The Court of Appeal accepted this conclusion in *Speed Investments Ltd v. Formula One Holdings Ltd*.[1585] It is now clear that it was right to do so.

In *Weber v. Weber* the Court simply accepted the argument that a court seised second was entitled to consider whether it had exclusive jurisdiction regardless of domicile. If it did, then unless the court seised first also had such jurisdiction,[1586] it should adjudicate. To do otherwise would undermine Article 24 and the rules of exclusive jurisdiction which it put in place. The judgment is concise and sensible. It does not make a substantial breach in the principle of mutual respect for the decisions of courts in other Member States, and to the extent that it does so, it is justified by the higher authority of Article 24 in the scheme of the Regulation.

2.275 The court seised second believes it has exclusive jurisdiction on the basis of Sections 3, 4, or 5 of Chapter II and that the court seised first does not

The Court in *Weber v. Weber* said nothing specific about the case in which the court seised second considers that its jurisdiction is derived from Sections 3, 4, or 5 of Chapter II of the Regulation and that the assertion of jurisdiction in the court seised first is in conflict with those provisions. Two principles clash, and it must be for the European Court to determine which one prevails. On the one hand, it will be reluctant to allow a court seised second to act in such a way as increases the likelihood of a judgment from a non-Member State being unrecognised because it is irreconcilable with a judgment from another Member State. On the other hand, the reasoning used in *Weber* fits the case perfectly, for a judgment which conflicts with Sections 3, 4, and 5 of Chapter II of Regulation 1215/2012 must be refused recognition. There is no point in waiting for a judgment which will be bound to be refused recognition, and in such circumstances, for a court with jurisdiction according to these provisions to not adjudicate would be to undermine these important provisions. The latter argument appears to be much more persuasive than the former, and it is submitted that it should be accepted as the consequence of *Weber v. Weber*. The fact that the word 'exclusive' is not used in Sections 3, 4, and 5 of Chapter II is of no significance, for the scheme of those Sections is to give jurisdiction to a number of courts on the basis of specific defined

---

1584 C-438/12, EU:C:2014:212, [2015] 2 WLR 213.

1585 [2004] EWCA Civ 1512, [2005] 1 WLR 1936. Note that in *Evialis v. SIAT* [2003] EWHC 863 (Comm), [2003] 2 Lloyd's Rep 377, a case on the Brussels Convention, the court had refused to extend this principle to a case in which the court seised second was violating the insurance contract provisions in Section 3 of Chapter II: the issue may be reconsidered in the light of *Weber*.

1586 Article 27 deals with this case.

connections. It could hardly be said than any of them had exclusive jurisdiction, but that is a point about the use of language, not the content of the law.

2.276 The court seised second believes it has exclusive jurisdiction on the basis of prorogation by agreement and the court seised first does not

The point of departure is the decision in *Erich Gasser GmbH v. MISAT Srl*,[1587] where the Court, in a judgment of some force but rather less strength, held that an agreement on jurisdiction for the courts of a Member State, the courts of which had been seised second, did not permit that court which had been so prorogated to adjudicate while proceedings were pending before the courts of another Member State in such a way that what is now Article 29 would apply. The Court was dismissive of the reasons which might be offered in support of letting a party who has agreed the jurisdiction of a court in a Member State take advantage of that agreement without interference from a party whose disregard of that agreement may be blatant and cynical: it considered that the arguments advanced in favour of allowing the chosen court to exercise jurisdiction 'are not such as to call in question the interpretation of any provision of the Brussels Convention, as deduced from its wording and its purpose'.[1588]

The Court had also been invited to accept that if it allowed the blocking action brought in Italy to torpedo[1589] the opportunity for the claimant to bring proceedings in the agreed court, and given the chronic delays in the Italian judicial system, there was a risk of violating Article 6 of the European Convention on Human Rights.[1590] But the Court did not accept the premise, and did not engage with the argument. It observed that the European Convention was not mentioned in what is now Article 29 of the Regulation, with the consequence that it had no relevance to the interpretation of the Article which it was required to give. It noted that to accept the argument based on Article 6 of the European Convention would undermine the mutual trust and confidence between courts which underpinned the Brussels Convention. It might have said that as the Austrian party had access to the Italian courts, its rights under Article 6 of the ECHR were secured, or that there is no right under Article 6 of the ECHR to have access to the particular court one wishes so long as there is access to a fair and impartial court, which the Italian court certainly was.

The judgment will have encouraged some to turn their attention to the idea of developing jurisprudence of damages to compensate for breach of agreements on jurisdiction. But it is not without rational justification, even if the reasoning is less so. For it may not be correct to assume that, whenever one party to litigation alleges the existence of a jurisdiction agreement which is valid and which on its true construction applies to the matter in question, that party has right on their side. A litigant who says that he is not bound by such an agreement may also be right, and if that may be so, a rule of strict temporal priority is justifiable. On the other hand, in the light of *Erich Gasser*, it may not be justifiable enough. It may also be

---

1587 C-116/02, [2003] ECR I-14693. The reference was made from the Austrian courts; the court seised first and in breach of contract was the Italian.

1588 At [53]. The reasoning in support of the conclusion was paltry.

1589 The wrecking tactic of launching proceedings in Italy is sometimes labelled as the 'Italian torpedo', as the expression appears to have been coined by an Italian lawyer, Mario Franzosi, at [1997] 7 EIPR 382. But in France it would appear that the torpedo is ascribed to the Germans: Cadet [2013] JDI/Clunet 779. Further comment is unnecessary.

1590 See also, in relation to Art. 71 of the Regulation, para. 2.63, above.

said that it would have been difficult to provide collateral support from Chapter III of the Regulation for the argument that the progogated court, seised second, should be allowed to press on, full steam ahead, for a judgment given by a court in conflict with Section 7 of Chapter II may not be refused recognition. For good or ill, and as said above, that makes jurisdiction taken under what is now Article 25 a jurisdiction which is rather less exclusive than some.

2.277 The effect of Article 31 (2)–(4) of Regulation 1215/2012

Article 31 of the Regulation provides as follows:

> *(1) Where actions come within the exclusive jurisdiction of several courts, any court other than the court first seised shall decline jurisdiction in favour of that court. (2) Without prejudice to Article 26, where a court of a Member State on which an agreement as referred to in Article 25 confers exclusive jurisdiction is seised, any court of another Member State shall stay the proceedings until such time as the court seised on the basis of the agreement declares that it has no jurisdiction under the agreement. (3) Where the court designated in the agreement has established jurisdiction in accordance with the agreement, any court of another Member State shall decline jurisdiction in favour of that court. (4) Paragraphs 2 and 3 shall not apply to matters referred to in Sections 3, 4 or 5 where the policyholder, the insured, a beneficiary of the insurance contract, the injured party, the consumer or the employee is the claimant and the agreement is not valid under a provision contained within those Sections.*

Article 31 was examined above in the context of jurisdiction agreements and their effect, but it is now necessary to address the precise effect on the rules of *lis alibi pendens* as explained by the Court in *Erich Gasser GmbH v. MISAT Srl*.[1591]

In matters to which Regulation 1215/2012 applies, and when the point is taken, it is the duty of the court seised first to have regard to Article 31(2), and to be prepared to stay its proceedings if the court on which exclusive jurisdiction has been (arguably) conferred by agreement has not yet declared that it has no jurisdiction under the agreement. The meaning of this was examined above,[1592] but a number of points need to be addressed here. As the rule in Article 31(2) places a duty on the court seised first, it will apply when the proceedings before that court commenced on or after 10 January 2015. It will not apply, because it will place no obligation on the court first seised, if the proceedings pre-date 10 January 2015, or are before the courts of a State to which Regulation 1215/2012 does not apply.

Next, although this new rule places an obligation on the court seised first, the text of the Article does not give the court seised second any power or right to proceed to adjudicate if the court seised first appears to have failed to act in accordance with Article 31(2). If the first seised court were to decide, for example, that the matter before it did not fall within the terms of the jurisdiction agreement, or that it was not an exclusive jurisdiction agreement, with the consequences that (as it sees it) Article 31(2) does not bite on the proceedings before it, there does not appear to be anything that the court seised second may do about it: indeed, it may actually be required to recognise the ruling of the court seised first on the proper effect of the jurisdiction agreement.[1593] Of course, if the court seised first does stay its proceedings, and the court seised second rules that the agreement on jurisdiction does give it

---

1591 C-116/02, [2003] ECR I-14693.
1592 Para. 2.127.
1593 C-456/11 *Gothaer Allgemeine Versicherung AG v. Samskip GmbH* EU:C:2012:719, [2013] QB 548, below, para. 7.07.

jurisdiction to adjudicate, there appears to be no impediment to its continuing to determine the merits of the dispute, not least because the court seised first will be required to recognise its decision on the jurisdictional issue.[1594]

Next, but in partial contradiction of the point previously made, there is a suggestion in the Recitals that the court seised second is *not* obliged to wait for the court seised first to do the right thing, but that it may examine and rule on its own jurisdiction regardless, for Recital (22) appears to go considerably further than the text of the Article would itself suggest.[1595] The fifth sentence, which provides that 'the designated court should be able to proceed irrespective of whether the non-designated court has already decided on the stay of proceedings' suggests that a court which considers itself to be designated by an exclusive jurisdiction agreement may proceed to rule on its own jurisdiction and, it is fair to infer, proceed to adjudicate if it finds that it has jurisdiction. The possibility therefore arises that there will be parallel adjudications to which – it would appear – Article 29 is not meant to apply and Article 30 will not.[1596] This suggests that the measure in Article 31(2), and the failure of the legislator to amend Chapter III to put jurisdiction agreements on a par with exclusive jurisdiction regardless of domicile, may lead to trouble in any case in which the court seised first comes to the conclusion – which may well be entirely reasonable – that Article 31(2) does not apply to the proceedings before it.

It is not possible to give a clear view on what a court seised second should do if it concludes that an exclusive jurisdiction agreement applies to the proceedings before it and gives it jurisdiction, but the court seised first has, one way or the other, arrived at the conclusion that its jurisdiction is not impaired by the agreement to which the second court would ascribe decisive force. There are arguments on each side; it will be for the European Court to remedy the shortcomings in the statutory words and the Recital.

2.278 The court which is seised is informed by the parties that Article 29 is not an impediment to its jurisdiction

The final question arises when a court which has been seised is informed by the parties that there is no issue of *lis alibi pendens* which would prevent its having and exercising jurisdiction. The issue arises because Article 29(1) requires the court to stay proceedings of its own motion if it appears that the conditions of Article 29 are met. The questions which arise are whether the court has discharged whatever duty was laid upon it if it asks the parties

---

1594 C-456/11 *Gothaer Allgemeine Versicherung AG v. Samskip GmbH* EU:C:2012:719, [2013] QB 548.

1595 Recital (22). However, in order to enhance the effectiveness of exclusive choice-of-court agreements and to avoid abusive litigation tactics, it is necessary to provide for an exception to the general *lis pendens* rule in order to deal satisfactorily with a particular situation in which concurrent proceedings may arise. This is the situation where a court not designated in an exclusive choice-of-court agreement has been seised of proceedings and the designated court is seised subsequently of proceedings involving the same cause of action and between the same parties. In such a case, the court first seised should be required to stay its proceedings as soon as the designated court has been seised and until such time as the latter court declares that it has no jurisdiction under the exclusive choice-of-court agreement. This is to ensure that, in such a situation, the designated court has priority to decide on the validity of the agreement and on the extent to which the agreement applies to the dispute pending before it. The designated court should be able to proceed irrespective of whether the non-designated court has already decided on the stay of proceedings. This exception should not cover situations where the parties have entered into conflicting exclusive choice-of-court agreements or where a court designated in an exclusive choice-of-court agreement has been seised first. In such cases, the general *lis pendens* rule of this Regulation should apply.

1596 A court which has jurisdiction by prorogation in these circumstances will be most unlikely to order a stay or dismissal in favour of a court which, as it sees it, should not be exercising jurisdiction at all.

whether Article 29 requires it to stay or decline jurisdiction and is told that Article 29 does not apply; and whether, if this happens, the position may be reconsidered if it is later contended by the defendant that Article 29 should have applied after all.

The issue arose in *The Alexandros T.*[1597] At first instance the court was told by counsel for the defendant that what is now Article 29 did not apply to or prevent the proceedings before the English court; and no challenge to the jurisdiction of the court was made. The court accepted what it had been told and exercised its jurisdiction. There was then a change of heart, and the defendant contended that the Court of Appeal was entitled and bound to take the Article 29 point for itself. The Supreme Court disagreed, citing among many reasons for its conclusion the fact that English procedural law makes provision for challenges to the jurisdiction and for the consequences of not making a challenge. It saw this as supporting, not as jeopardising the proper operation of the Regulation. There was also a threat to the principle of legal certainty in the proposition that a defendant could decide not to rely on Article 29 to challenge the jurisdiction, wait and see how the wind blew in the substantive hearing, and if things appeared to be going badly, then play the Article 29 card.[1598]

The decision plainly accords with common sense.[1599] Though rules of national procedural law may not impair the practical effect of the Regulation, it is very hard to see how the application of English procedural law as set out in CPR Part 11 could seriously be said to do that. There is no reason to suppose that a system which provides a clear mechanism for a defendant to object to the jurisdiction of the court, whether by reference to Article 29 or otherwise, does any damage to the operation of the Regulation. Unless it is said that the words 'of its own motion' mean 'upon its own investigation', which seems unlikely, the court is entitled to rely on what the defendant tells it. In the very rare case in which the court has reason to suppose that the parties are colluding to prevent the proper application of Article 29, the court has powers of its own to meet the point.

2.279 The duty of the court seised first and the power of case management

It is not always appreciated that Articles 29 and 30 impose duties only on the court seised second. Unless Article 31(2) applies, or unless the court has exclusive jurisdiction regardless of domicile, Article 29 obliges the court seised second to accept that it has no jurisdiction; Article 30 permits it to stay or to dismiss proceedings to allow them to be consolidated with the proceedings pending at first instance in the court seised first (or to do neither). But neither Article 29 nor Article 30 places an obligation on the court seised first.

It follows that unless Article 31(2) applies, the court seised first is under a duty to rule on its own jurisdiction if this is challenged, or if the defendant does not appear and Article 28 applies, with reasonable despatch. It may not be asked to find that, where it has jurisdiction,[1600] the *forum conveniens* for the resolution of the issues before it is another

---

1597 [2013] UKSC 70, [2014] 1 Lloyd's Rep 223, esp. at [98]–[123].

1598 As authority for the view that a court has no duty to revisit a jurisdictional question which has been determined in accordance with the law and procedure of the court, see C-234/04 *Kapferer v. Schlank & Schick GmbH* [2006] ECR I-2585 and *Interfact Ltd v. Liverpool City Council* [2010] EWHC 1064 (Admin), [2011] QB 744.

1599 The court would have been prepared to make a reference to the European Court on the point, but this was not, in the end, necessary.

1600 Except in the case of Art. 6, on which see above.

Member State or non-Member State, and to stay its proceedings on the ground that the cause of action raised before it should be determined by that other court.[1601] Its duty is to adjudicate.

This does not exclude the possibility of the court seised first ordering a stay of proceedings on grounds of case management, or granting an interim stay in the exercise of its inherent power to do so.[1602] In truth, of course, at this point we are not now speaking of the court seised first, but of any court which has jurisdiction under the Regulation. As long as it does not cross the line by ordering a stay, or granting other relief, on grounds which conflict with the Regulation,[1603] it may still order and arrange the process of adjudication of the matter before it. It *may* stay its proceedings to await the determination of another court, whether it is the court of a Member State in a matter which falls outside the scope of the Regulation,[1604] or even a court in a non-Member State which is hearing a matter outside the material scope of the Regulation,[1605] or an arbitral tribunal.[1606] But it has no obligation to do so; and a court which reasons that as it has jurisdiction it would not be right for it to stay its proceedings to allow courts elsewhere to deliver judgments of which account would then have to be taken, certainly does nothing wrong.[1607] If it has jurisdiction by reason of an agreement on jurisdiction to which Article 25 applies, the case against a stay on grounds of case management (which really means, if one is being candid about it, to allow a court elsewhere to do something which might put a spoke in a wheel which will otherwise turn in an unwelcome direction) is overwhelming.[1608]

2.280 Court seised first in another part of the United Kingdom

Article 29 of the Regulation applies in cases where the courts of another Member State were seised first. It has no application if proceedings are brought before a court elsewhere within a single Member State: this raises a question of internal or national, but not one of international, jurisdiction. Within the United Kingdom, therefore, any such problem will be determined by application of the principles of *forum non conveniens*,[1609] and not by application of rules based on Article 29.[1610] It follows that the principle of *forum non conveniens* may still be applied even if there are no proceedings yet pending in the courts of another part of the United Kingdom.[1611]

1601 See below, para. 2.303.

1602 A power confirmed but not created by Senior Courts Act 1981, s. 49.

1603 See *Skype Technologies SA v. Joltid Ltd* [2009] EWHC 2783 (Ch), [2011] ILPr 103 (not permissible to be seen to let in the back door something which had been locked out of the front); see also *Plaza BV v Law Debenture Trust Corp* [2015] EWHC 43 (Ch).

1604 See *Mazur Media Ltd v. Mazur Media GmbH* [2004] EWHC 1566 (Ch), [2004] 1 WLR 2966; *Jeffries International Ltd v. Landsbanki Islands HF* [2009] EWHC 894 (Comm).

1605 *Abbassi v. Abbassi* [2006] EWCA Civ 355, [2006] 1 FCR 648 (though the proceedings before the English court were not within the material scope of the Regulation either).

1606 *Reichhold Norway ASA v. Goldman Sachs International* [2000] 1 WLR 173 (stay ordered). There are many illustrative decisions at first instance, but none establishes any new point of principle.

1607 *JP Morgan Chase Bank NA v. Berliner Verkehrsbetriebe* [2010] EWCA Civ 390, [2012] QB 174.

1608 *JP Morgan Chase Bank NA v. Berliner Verkehrsbetriebe* [2010] EWCA Civ 390, [2012] QB 174.

1609 Discussed in detail in paras 4.13 *et seq.*, below.

1610 *Cf* Sch. 4 to the 1982 Act, which does not reproduce Arts 29–34 of the recast Regulation.

1611 It was so held in *Cumming v. Scottish Daily Record and Sunday Mail Ltd* (8 June 1995), not following *Foxen v. Scotsman Publication Ltd* [1995] 3 EMLR 145 (on which, see Collins (1995) 11 LQR 541). In these cases, the Regulation gave international jurisdiction to the courts of the United Kingdom, and not to the courts for a place

On the other hand, in those cases for which the Regulation specifies the part of the United Kingdom whose courts have jurisdiction, the Regulation determines the international and the national jurisdiction of the court. There is, therefore, no question of national jurisdiction for the internal law of the United Kingdom to answer, and as a result, no opportunity for the doctrine of *forum non conveniens* to be applied.[1612]

2.281 Related action in another Member State: Article 30

Article 30 of the Regulation provides that:

> *(1) Where related actions are pending in the courts of different Member States, any court other than the court first seised may stay its proceedings. (2) Where the action in the court first seised is pending at first instance, any other court may also, on the application of one of the parties, decline jurisdiction if the court first seised has jurisdiction over the actions in question and its law permits the consolidation thereof. (3) For the purposes of this Article, actions are deemed to be related where they are so closely connected that it is expedient to hear and determine them together to avoid the risk of irreconcilable judgments resulting from separate proceedings.*

Apart from a small matter of clarification in Article 30(2), Article 30 of the Regulation is practically identical to Article 28 of Regulation 44/2001.

2.282 General approach to Article 30

Article 30 is best thought of as the provision which may apply if the English court is seised second but the conditions for the application of Article 29 are not met. It contributes to the coordination of adjudication, but in a discretionary fashion. It permits a court seised second simply to stay its proceedings to await the outcome of an action which is still pending in the court seised first, whether it is pending at first instance or on appeal. It also allows it to decline jurisdiction over the action before it, if this action may be consolidated into the action which is pending at first instance in the court seised first, though only if the court seised first would have, independently, jurisdiction over the action which is proposed to be dismissed: this is because Article 30 does *not* provide a ground for jurisdiction over the second claim but provides only a mechanism for consolidation of two actions over each of which the first court does or would have jurisdiction.[1613] And, of course, it also allows the court to conclude that neither of these things is appropriate, but to press on and adjudicate.[1614] In particular, if proceedings in the court seised first are going to be slow, and especially if the foreign court will take proper account of an English decision given in the meantime, it may well be correct to refuse to grant relief but require the parties to get on with it in England.[1615]

---

within the United Kingdom. They are not, therefore, affected by C-386/05 *Color Drack GmbH v. Lexx International Vertriebs GmbH* [2007] ECR I-3699.

1612 C-386/05 *Color Drack GmbH v. Lexx International Vertriebs GmbH* [2007] ECR I-3699: an exception may be where the Regulation gives (special) jurisdiction to the courts of two places in the United Kingdom.

1613 150/80 *Elefanten Schuh GmbH v. Jacqmain* [1981] ECR 1671. If the contrary is suggested in *Assurances Générales de France IART v. Chiyoda Fire and Marine Co (UK) Ltd* [1992] 1 Lloyd's Rep 325, 334, it is wrong.

1614 A suggestion that the court did not have this third possibility was correctly regarded as unarguable by the court in *The Alexandros T* [2013] UKSC 70, [2014] 1 Lloyd's Rep 223, [97].

1615 *Trademark Licensing Co v. Leofelis SA* [2009] EWHC 3285 (Ch), [2010] ILPr 290; *Cooper Tire & Rubber Co Europe Ltd v. Dow Deutschland Inc* [2010] EWCA Civ 864, [2010] Bus LR 1697.

The question whether a court is first or second seised in a case in which the actions are related, and relatedness may be shown from the contents of the claim and the defence, raises some complexity which does not really arise in relation to Article 29. The issue is therefore revisited below; for the purpose of the paragraphs which follow it is assumed that there is no issue as to which court is first and second seised in the relevant sense.

2.283 Identification of actions as 'related'

Actions are defined as related when they are so closely connected that it is expedient[1616] to hear[1617] and determine them together to avoid the risk of irreconcilable judgments arising from separate proceedings. The assessment of whether actions are related for the purpose of Article 30 permits and may require a court to examine claim and defence: the question is not whether the *claims* are related, but whether the *actions* are. In this respect, Article 30 asks a broader question than the corresponding question for the purpose of Article 29, which is confined to the claims made.[1618]

Though it is easy enough to understand in principle, and is often a matter of common ground between the parties, the application of this definition to the facts of actual cases may sometimes give rise to difficulty. It was held in *The Tatry*[1619] that actions are related for the purpose of what is now Article 30 if they would involve the risk of conflicting decisions, without necessarily involving the risk of giving rise to mutually exclusive legal consequences. This gives the expression 'irreconcilable' as used in Article 30 a relatively loose meaning. This is perfectly sensible – a flexible rule which is designed to prevent the occurrence of conflicting judgments is perfectly comfortable alongside a narrow and restrictive one applicable when it is sought to withhold recognition from a judgment which has already, after what may be much effort and cost, been given. The result of *Gubisch Maschinenfabrik KG v. Palumbo*[1620] is that Article 30 may apply to cases where the same cause of action is in dispute but between different parties, or where there are different causes of action in proceedings between the same parties. Unlike Article 29, Article 30 allows a court to look at issues raised by claim, defence, and counterclaim or cross-claim.[1621] It is, therefore, preferable to interpret *The Tatry* as meaning Article 30 applies to actions which are so closely related, by reason of the closeness of the factual and legal issues in dispute, that it would[1622] serve the interests of justice for them to be heard and disposed of together.[1623]

1616 Again, note that the Article does not say 'necessary'.

1617 This must be, in part at least, a matter of fact, and common sense. See, for example, *Alfred C Toepfer International GmbH v. Molino Boschi Sarl* [1996] 1 Lloyd's Rep 510; *JP Morgan Europe Ltd v. Primacom AG* [2005] EWHC 508 (Comm), [2005] 2 Lloyd's Rep 665. If the court first seised has been seised in breach of a jurisdiction agreement, no question of granting relief under Art. 30 will normally arise, though whether this is because it is not expedient to try the actions together, or because the court may in its discretion refuse to grant relief, is not clear.

1618 *Stribog Ltd v. FKI Engineering Ltd* [2011] EWCA Civ 622, [2011] 1 WLR 3264.

1619 C-406/92, [1994] ECR I-5439.

1620 144/86, [1987] ECR 4861, which defined 'the same cause of action' for the purposes of what is now Art. 29.

1621 *Research in Motion (UK) Ltd v. Visto Corp* [2008] EWCA Civ 153, [2008] 2 All ER (Comm) 560.

1622 It is not a requirement that they actually are capable of being brought in the foreign court if the application is only for a stay: the issue of connectedness depends only on whether it *would be* expedient that they be tried together: *Nomura International plc v. Banca Monte dei Paschi di Siena SpA* [2013] EWHC 3187 (Comm), [2014] 1 WLR 1584.

1623 The expression 'heard together' is also problematic. If this means they may be consolidated and determined in one set of proceedings, the second paragraph seems to cover the case, and this provision adds nothing.

Nevertheless, the guidance given in *The Tatry* is in some respects elusive. It is unclear whether the risk[1624] of inconsistency in judgment, which identifies the actions as related, is concerned (narrowly) with inconsistency as between the potential rulings of the courts, or (more broadly) with inconsistency as between ancillary observations which may be contained in a judgment, but which may not be strictly necessary for the decision of the court. To put it another way, is it sufficient that there may be *obiter dicta* which diverge, or that different courts may come to different views on the credibility of a witness or the authenticity of a document? The judgment in *The Tatry* did not point clearly in one direction.[1625] A moderately restrictive approach is probably appropriate, not least because a decision that a court will not act on and exercise the jurisdiction which it has been given should be one arrived at with some reluctance.[1626] Breadth of application is not necessary to allow Article 30 to achieve its proper aims. As a result, the apprehension that the court first seised may make observations in the course of its reasoning which are relevant to issues before the court seised second, but without its being evident that it will give a judgment requiring decision upon those points, should not necessarily make the actions related ones. Only if the judgments and orders which may be made may themselves contradict each other should actions be seen as related.[1627]

In *Sarrio SA v. Kuwait Investment Authority*,[1628] the House of Lords took a distinctly broad approach to whether actions were related, appearing to hold that if it was expedient to hear the cases together, that single fact sufficed to make the actions related. That approach may be thought to put the cart before the horse; it certainly rejected the contention that the relatedness of actions had to be demonstrated by reference only to those facts which were or would be essential to the judgments which had to be given. The preference[1629] for a simple and wide test, which was not overly sophisticated, will not necessarily ease the task of the judge. It must still be shown that there is an appreciable risk that, if they are tried separately, the two courts may come to conclusions which could not be fitted together so that separate proceedings risk impairing the proper administration of justice, even if the formal judgments are not irreconcilable. Searching for greater precision than that is probably pointless.[1630]

If so, it means 'tried by the same court, but in separate or sequential proceedings'; and the utility of the stay is uncertain. Perhaps the solution is to give the expression an autonomous interpretation. And see below, in relation to *Sarrio SA v. Kuwait Investment Authority* [1999] 1 AC 32.

1624 The degree of probability inherent in this expression has not been explained. For reasons which are set out below, it is thought that the risk should have to be substantial, and not simply a situation capable of being imagined by the court as a possibility.

1625 Opinion, at [28], which gives as an illustration the case of contradictory decisions or decrees, might be thought to support a narrower interpretation, limited to the disposition of the case and not more broadly concerned with observations made in the course of the judgment.

1626 Cf *Seven Licensing Co Sarl v. FFG Platinum SA* [2011] EWHC 2967 (Comm), [2012] ILPr 134.

1627 For a case in which there was, as a result of developments in the foreign proceedings, no risk of irreconcilable judgments, see *Televisión Autonómica Valenciana SA v. Imagina Contenidos Audiovisuales SL* [2013] EWHC 160 (Ch), [2013] ILPr 445.

1628 [1999] 1 AC 32.

1629 At 41. The general tenor of *J P Morgan Europe Ltd v. Primacom AG* [2005] EWHC 508 (Comm), [2005] 2 Lloyd's Rep 665 may also favour a more expansive view of Art. 30, following the approach in *Sarrio SA*.

1630 For an illustration of the complexity which may be generated when this rule is applied in the context of claims and counterclaims which have been brought with a view to stymieing the jurisdictional preferences of the opposite party, see *Research in Motion (UK) Ltd v. Visto Corp* [2008] EWCA Civ 153, [2008] 2 All ER (Comm) 560; *Stribog Ltd v. FKI Engineering Ltd* [2011] EWCA Civ 622, [2011] 1 WLR 3264.

2.284 The forms of relief which the court seised second may order

It bears repeating that the court is given two powers to grant relief, as well as the power to not grant relief. A stay may be ordered in accordance with Article 30(1) if the related actions are pending at first instance. If those conditions are met the court has a discretion to stay its proceedings or to not do so.

The second power given to the court seised second, by Article 30(2) of the Regulation, is to dismiss the action before it, with a view to its being brought before, and consolidated into an action pending at first instance in, the courts of the Member State which had been seised earlier in time. For this to happen, four conditions need to be satisfied. The two actions must be related; the action in the court which was seised first must still be pending at first instance; the court which was seised first must itself have jurisdiction over the related action which was instituted before the court seised second; and the law of the court seised first must permit the consolidation to take place. If those conditions are met the court seised second may dismiss the action for consolidation or decide to not do so. However if, for example, the law of the court seised first will not permit the consolidation of the two actions, for example, because the first is very close to trial and this will delay the entire process, that court is entitled to take this view.[1631] The dismissal conditions will not have been met, and the court seised second will not be permitted to dismiss for consolidation.

2.285 If relief is to be granted, selecting between the options available to the court seised second

Even though a court may have concluded that the criteria for the application of Article 30 are satisfied, and that relief of one kind or the other would be appropriate, Article 30 gives no guidance as to which power is to be preferred. No doubt the court should lean in favour of whichever order will reduce or eliminate the possibility of irreconcilable judgments.[1632] Though Jenard observed,[1633] without further explanation, that the first duty of the court was to stay its proceedings, and though the Advocate General in *Owens Bank Ltd v. Bracco*[1634] evidently agreed, this does not mean that the power to dismiss proceedings is subordinate to the power to stay. A court faced with the choice of stay or dismissal or neither will have to decide what principles – assuming that the selection between the remedies is amenable to exercise on grounds of principle – govern the choice before it. The Opinion in *Bracco* does expressly accept that a court seised second may legitimately ask itself which court is best placed to decide the issues raised in the action before it; the court in *The Alexandros T* appears to have taken and acted on that advice in exercising its discretion against the ordering of any relief. No doubt a perception that the Greek proceedings appeared to have been brought to undermine a settlement agreement and a jurisdiction agreement inclined the Supreme Court against the view that the Greek

---

1631 C–365/88 *Kongress Agentur Hagen GmbH v. Zeehaghe BV* [1990] ECR I-1845.

1632 *Masri v. Consolidated Contractors International Co SAL* [2011] EWHC 1780 (Comm).

1633 [1979] OJ C59/1, 41. But *cf Centro Internationale Handelsbank AG v. Morgan Grenfell* [1997] CLC 870, denying the existence of such 'first duty'.

1634 C–192/92, [1995] ECR I-117; referred to without dissent in *The Alexandros T* [2013] UKSC 70, [2014] 1 Lloyd's Rep 223, [92].

court was the court best placed to decide the matters raised in the action before the English court.[1635]

In cases where further guidance may be looked for, a suggestion follows. As there is no authority to demonstrate that it is correct, no more is claimed for it than that it is a suggestion. It is possible to see Article 30 as covering two situations in which there are related actions before the courts of two Member States. The first occurs where there are different parties in the two sets of proceedings, but the underlying claim is essentially the same in each case. This was so in *The Tatry*,[1636] for example, where the cargo claims which were brought against a shipowner[1637] in England and the Netherlands were identical but for the fact that they involved different cargo-owners. The proceedings were related, in that there was a real risk of contradictory[1638] conclusions if the two actions proceeded to trial separately. If the court seised second had dismissed its proceedings for them to be consolidated with those pending at first instance in the court first seised, the outcome would have been a single piece of litigation, resulting in a decision in which all parties would have been bound: a result which is in accordance with the overall scheme of the Regulation. By contrast, there would have been little point in staying the English proceedings. True, the Dutch court would have made its findings of fact, but these would have been of legal relevance only to the parties to the Dutch litigation. Those claimants in the English proceedings not involved in the Dutch action would not be affected or bound by what the Dutch court had decided in proceedings in which they had played no part and had had no right to be heard,[1639] and there is therefore no reason to suppose that the English trial would be reduced in length, complexity, or that it would alleviate the risk of inconsistency with the Dutch proceedings, by the court having ordered a stay. In this factual circumstance, therefore, there is good reason to use the power given in the second, rather than that contained in the first, paragraph of Article 30 of the Regulation.

By contrast, where the parties to the litigation are the same in the two courts, but the issues in the two claims, though related, are not identical, there is good reason for the court seised second to stay its proceedings. The court first seised will determine certain issues as between those who are also parties to the proceedings in the court seised second. The further consequence of this potential binding of the parties in relation to the second action may be to make the second trial shorter, or even unnecessary. A stay will then have served the purpose of producing an efficient use of time and resources, and will assist the goal of producing consistent judgments. But the same advantage would not be generated by a dismissal-for-consolidation. The principal reason is that the immediate result of the consolidation would, almost inevitably, be to increase the length and complexity of the first trial. Not only that, but the first court may in fact be called upon to determine more issues

---

1635 See also *Nomura International plc v. Banca Monte dei Paschi di Siena SpA* [2013] EWHC 3187 (Comm), [2014] 1 WLR 1584.

1636 C-406/92, [1994] ECR I-5439. The Court disposed of the case on other grounds and did not need to deal with this issue.

1637 The fact that the Dutch claim was brought *by* the shipowner for a declaration of his non-liability to the cargo-owner is irrelevant for the purposes of this argument: the essence of the claims was the same.

1638 In the sense that, although the judgments might not be technically irreconcilable, as the one would not be a complete defence to the other, they would still contain inconsistent factual and legal analyses.

1639 For though the Dutch judgment would qualify for recognition, it would not be given against, and would not therefore bind, those cargo-owners not party to it.

than would be necessary if the two trials were to take place sequentially. This would not be so consistent with the aims of the Regulation.[1640]

For these reasons, it is submitted that the decision as to which of the powers in Article 30 should be applied should be guided[1641] by asking whether it is a 'same issue, different parties' case, or a 'same parties, different issue' case. It may not produce the right answer in every imaginable case, but it does give a workable structure to the unstructured powers apparently conferred by Article 30 in the event that the court decides that some form of relief is appropriate.

However, the decision of the House of Lords in *Sarrio SA v. Kuwait Investment Authority*,[1642] does not support this analysis. There, though the parties were the same, the English action was dismissed for consolidation with the proceedings pending in Spain. If one asks why the court chose this, rather than a stay of the English proceedings, the explanation appears to lie in the very definition of related actions: they are related if it is expedient to hear and determine together to avoid the risk of irreconcilable judgments. If the two actions satisfy this definition, one may suppose that they ought to be tried together. But this would make nonsense of Article 30(1); and for the reasons which are set out above,[1643] it is submitted that the supposition is misguided. It is perfectly true that this involves reading Article 30(3) as though it stated that it was 'expedient to coordinate the hearing and determination of the two actions to avoid the risk of irreconcilable judgments resulting from uncoordinated parallel proceedings'. A purposive reading of Article 30(3) could comfortably manage that.

2.286 The material date of seisin for the purpose of Article 30

It would be easy to suppose that 'first seised' means the same for the purpose of Article 30 as it did for Article 29. That may not be wrong. But a court cannot be seised; it must be seised of something. If it is correct that the focus of Article 29 is on claims, and Article 30 on actions, it is arguable that the operation of Article 32 reflects that difference.

The issue was examined and explained by the Supreme Court in *The Alexandros T*.[1644] The question whether the court is first or second seised for the purpose of what is now Article 30 directs attention to when the court was seised of the proceedings, not of particular causes of action within those proceedings.[1645] Insofar as the amendment added (or drew out) claims which were inherent in the original claim, the English court was able to find that it had been (and was still) seised long before the Greek court was. Insofar as the amendment to the English proceedings introduced new parties to the proceedings, after they had started their Greek proceedings, the English court was seised second. As the court was clear that,

---

1640 For an illustration – a very instructive illustration – of the circumstances in which a stay of proceedings is the proper order in a matter to which Art. 30 applies, where the proper progress of the English proceedings needed to be informed by the decision of a foreign court, already seised, see *Lehman Brothers Bankhaus AG I Ins v. CMA CGM* [2013] EWHC 171 (Comm), [2013] 2 All ER (Comm) 557.

1641 As distinct from being strictly driven.

1642 [1999] 1 AC 32.

1643 As well as by reference to Art. 34(1)(a), which is framed on the basis that if the proceedings are related in this way, the court may stay (but may not dismiss) the proceedings before it. This development supports, though it cannot demonstrate, that the approach of the court in *Sarrio* was not completely sound.

1644 [2013] UKSC 70, [2014] 1 Lloyd's Rep 223. The judgment draws significantly on the analysis of the Court of Appeal in *Stribog Ltd v. FKI Engineering Ltd* [2011] EWCA Civ 622, [2011] 1 WLR 3264, but which, in the light of the Supreme Court's analysis, does not require separate treatment in any detail.

1645 At [79].

if and to the extent that the English court was seised second, there was no proper basis for granting relief under what is now Article 30, no more needed to be said; but it was accepted that had the decision turned on the proper interpretation of the date of seisin for the purpose of Article 30, a reference to the European Court would have been appropriate.

2.287 Concurrent exclusive jurisdictions: Article 31(1)

Article 31 of Regulation 1215/2012 provides that:

> *(1) Where actions come within the exclusive jurisdiction of several courts, any court other than the court first seised shall decline jurisdiction in favour of that court.*

Article 31(1) of the Regulation is identical to Article 29 of Regulation 44/2001.

For the sake of completeness, if a claim falls within the exclusive jurisdiction of the courts of two Member States, the court seised second with such jurisdiction is required to decline jurisdiction in favour of the court seised first with such jurisdiction. If, as is thought it does, this refers to the exclusive jurisdiction conferred by Article 24, it will be an event which occurs only rarely, though as Article 24(1) now allows for concurrent exclusive jurisdictions, the occurrence will not be quite as rare as it once was.[1646]

(15) *LIS PENDENS* IN, AND OTHER POINTERS TO, A NON-MEMBER STATE

2.288 *Lis pendens* in a Lugano State or a Brussels Convention territory

Where the court first seised is in a State which is party only to the Lugano II Convention, which means Iceland, Norway or Switzerland, or in a territory to which the Brussels Convention still applies, the resolution of an issue of *lis alibi pendens* is governed by those Conventions, and not by the Regulation. This follows from Articles 73(1) and 68 of the Regulation, respectively.

As the Regulation has nothing to say about proceedings pending in a non-Member State, the *lis pendens* provisions of the respective Conventions will apply in these cases. They are briefly dealt with in Chapter 3 of this book.

2.289 *Lis pendens* in a non-Member State: general background

Where there are proceedings which were commenced first before the courts of a State which is party to none of these European instruments, there is no room for the application of Articles 29 to 32 of the Regulation. Until the coming into effect of Regulation 1215/2012, the fact that there may have been a *lis alibi pendens* before the courts of a non-Member State was held by some, though not by all, to be irrelevant to the rules of jurisdiction put in place by Regulation 44/2001 and its predecessor instruments. The incoherence of that legislative vacuum, which had been filled by some sane and other less balanced analyses, has been dealt

---

1646 It may also operate in the instance of proceedings which have as their object a tenancy of land which, as a single parcel, straddles the border separating Member States: *cf* 158/87 *Scherrens v. Maenhout* [1988] ECR 3791 (not a case on concurrent proceedings).

with, and a proper legislative scheme has been created to deal with the effect on the courts of a Member State of a *lis alibi pendens* in another Member State. We examine that next.

But the existence of a *lis alibi pendens* before its courts is not the only possible point of connection to the courts of a non-Member State which may be imagined. There may be connections of the kind which, when they point to a Member State, give rise to exclusive jurisdiction regardless of domicile. There may be an agreement for the jurisdiction, or on the exclusive jurisdiction, of the courts of a non-Member State. But these silent deficiencies in Regulation 44/2001 have been left unaddressed in Regulation 1215/2012. They have to be examined, in conditions of uncertainty, after the examination of *lis pendens* in a non-Member State.

2.290 Proceedings involving the same cause of action pending before the courts of a non-Member State: Article 33

Article 33 of Regulation 1215/2012 provides that:

> *(1) Where jurisdiction is based on Article 4 or on Articles 7, 8 or 9 and proceedings are pending before a court of a third State at the time when a court in a Member State is seised of an action involving the same cause of action and between the same parties as the proceedings in the court of the third State, the court of the Member State may stay the proceedings if: (a) it is expected that the court of the third State will give a judgment capable of recognition and, where applicable, of enforcement in that Member State; and (b) the court of the Member State is satisfied that a stay is necessary for the proper administration of justice. (2) The court of the Member State may continue the proceedings at any time if: (a) the proceedings in the court of the third State are themselves stayed or discontinued; (b) it appears to the court of the Member State that the proceedings in the court of the third State are unlikely to be concluded within a reasonable time; or (c) the continuation of the proceedings is required for the proper administration of justice. (3) The court of the Member State shall dismiss the proceedings if the proceedings in the court of the third State are concluded and have resulted in a judgment capable of recognition and, where applicable, of enforcement in that Member State. (4) The court of the Member State shall apply this Article on the application of one of the parties or, where possible under national law, of its own motion.*

This is a new provision. The explanation for it and for the way it is intended to operate is in the Recitals to Regulation 1215/2012, where the following is written:

> *(Recital 23) This Regulation should provide for a flexible mechanism allowing the courts of the Member States to take into account proceedings pending before the courts of third States, considering in particular whether a judgment of a third State will be capable of recognition and enforcement in the Member State concerned under the law of that Member State and the proper administration of justice. (Recital 24) When taking into account the proper administration of justice, the court of the Member State concerned should assess all the circumstances of the case before it. Such circumstances may include connections between the facts of the case and the parties and the third State concerned, the stage to which the proceedings in the third State have progressed by the time proceedings are initiated in the court of the Member State and whether or not the court of the third State can be expected to give a judgment within a reasonable time. That assessment may also include consideration of the question whether the court of the third State has exclusive jurisdiction in the particular case in circumstances where a court of a Member State would have exclusive jurisdiction.*

2.291 Background to Article 33

The question whether a court with jurisdiction under Regulation 44/2001 and its predecessor instruments could take account – and if so, what account – of the fact that proceedings related to or identical with those with which it had been seised were pending before the courts of a non-Member State was never put to the European Court: the one reference which would have required it to answer the question directly appears never to have made it as far as Luxembourg.[1647] The result was a scattering of views at first instance from judges who, at a time when only courts exercising appellate jurisdiction had power to refer questions to the European Court, were faced with an impossible task.

The conclusion that the court had no power to do anything but adjudicate[1648] was derived from the fact that the Court in *Owusu v. Jackson*[1649] had said, on one reading of the judgment, that unless the Regulation gave specific authority to a court to decline to exercise jurisdiction, there was no discretion to not do so. But as the Court in *Owusu* had refused to answer a question framed with specific reference to this issue, the strength of support for this conclusion was debatable. In cases in which the opposite conclusion was reached,[1650] it was on the broad basis that *Owusu* should not be read as standing in its way, and that it simply made no adult sense for a court in a Member State to pretend that proceedings in courts outside the Member States were not happening. This view was the only credible one. Judgments from non-Member States can be enforced in Member States; and persons established in Member States, who may find themselves in litigation before the courts of non-Member States, have a reasonable expectation that the law of the European Union will take sensible account, and will not ignore, the existence and potential effect of such proceedings.

It was not the fault of the English courts that there was divergence in the views at first instance; it was no surprise that appellate courts appeared to be happy to find that the question did not need to be answered. The Regulation was defective in the sense that it did not provide an answer which it should have provided, and the judgment in *Owusu* was seriously defective in the sense that it did not answer a commercially important question which it had been asked:[1651] heaven knows how much money has been wasted in national proceedings as a result of the Court's disinclination to answer a direct question. We will have cause to return to this after dealing with Articles 33 and 34 of Regulation 1215/2012, but for the present it is sufficient to say that Article 33 provides a solution to some of the problem; and if the question should arise in relation to cases to which Regulation 44/2001 applies, but not Regulation 1215/2012, applies, the clear message from *Mittal v. Mittal*[1652] is that an English court will interpret Regulation 44/2001 as though it allowed what Articles 33 and 34 of Regulation 1215/2012 now expressly provide for. The court took the view that the legislature had provided an answer to the question which the Court in *Owusu* had refused to answer, and that is effectively that.

1647 *Goshawk Dedicated Ltd v. Life Receivables Ireland Ltd* [2009] IESC 7, [2009] ILPr 435.

1648 *Catalyst Investment Group Ltd v. Lewinsohn* [2009] EWHC 1964 (Ch), [2010] Ch 218.

1649 C-281/02, [2005] ECR I-1383.

1650 The conclusion in *Catalyst Investment Group Ltd v. Lewinsohn* was not followed in *Ferrexpo AG v. Gilson Investments Ltd* [2012] EWHC 721 (Comm), [2012] 1 Lloyd's Rep 588, [137]; though the case was concerned with a connection to a non-Member State of the exclusive jurisdiction kind, rather than *lis alibi pendens*, the latter judgment is thorough and excellent. The decision in *Catalyst* was also not adopted in *JKN v. JCN* [2010] EWHC 843 (Fam), [2011] 1 FLR 826, in an extremely detailed and persuasive judgment which concluded that in any event it should not be applied in the context of family matters to which the Brussels II Regulation applied. In *Mittal v. Mittal* [2013] EWCA Civ 1255, [2014] Fam 102, on the Brussels II Regulation, the Court of Appeal came to the same conclusion as in *JKN v. JCN*, drawing indirect support for its conclusion from Art. 33 of Regulation 1215/2012 (not then in force). It is correct to observe, however, that the context of disputes in matrimonial cases may be materially different from that within which the Brussels I Regulation operates.

1651 The Court pretended to consider the second question referred by the English court as hypothetical. The contrast with its approach to the supremely ridiculous and completely irrelevant (see the judgment at [38]–[41]) question in C-283/09 *Weryński v. Mediatel 4B Spółka zoo* [2011] ECR I-601 is painful.

1652 [2013] EWCA Civ 1255, [2014] Fam 102.

2.292 Application of Article 33

Article 33 allows the court to stay its proceedings if it has general jurisdiction or special jurisdiction, in the matter before it, but not otherwise. Insofar as the question is whether to cede priority to proceedings in a court in a non-Member State which has aleady been seised, this limitation makes sense, for where the Member State court has jurisdiction on the basis of exclusive, privileged, or prorogated jurisdiction, there is generally a good reason for it to exercise it which is, arguably (but now legislatively) more important than the fact that there are proceedings before the courts of a non-Member State. The only examples of a case which might call into question the sense of this limitation will be, for example, when a contract of employment contains a jurisdiction agreement for a non-Member State, and the courts of that non-Member State have been seised by the employer.[1653] It would appear that the court will have no power under Article 33 to stay proceedings if its jurisdiction is derived from Section 5 of Chapter II. This may or may not be a desirable answer, but it is an answer, and we should be grateful that we do at least know where we stand.

In respect of the other limitations on the court's power to order a stay of its proceedings by reference to Article 33, it is easiest to state them in terms of 'not unless' rather than 'if' propositions.

The court may not order a stay under Article 33 unless the proceedings before the non-Member State court are pending on the date on which the court in the Member State is seised. The latter date will of course be determined by the scheme in Article 32, but the question in relation to the non-Member State will not be. There is no formal definition of 'pending' in relation to the courts of a non-Member State. If a formal test is required, it may be derived either from Article 32, applied by some form of analogy, or from the law which applied prior to the adoption of the uniform definition of the date of seisin, namely that one asks whether the proceedings are 'definitively pending' according to the law of the court in question.[1654] If that leads to the conclusion that the proceedings in the non-Member State are considered by its law to be 'definitively pending' even though the defendant has not been served, for example, the court will be able to take account of that fact by exercising its discretion against the grant of a stay. If, however, the jurisdiction of the non-Member State court is being challenged, it should be held that the proceedings are pending, albeit at an early stage.

The court may not order a stay unless the proceedings before the non-Member State court are between the same parties, and in respect of the same cause of action, as the action before the Member State. This will require the Member State court to apply the 'triple identies' analysis which applies in relation to Article 29, and about which no more need be said at this point. It is not clear whether Article 33 is to be applied by looking at the claims, as distinct from the claims-and-defences, but the similarity with Article 29 probably means that it should be.

2.293 Assessment of the interests of justice

The court may not order a stay unless it is in the interests of justice to do so. Insofar as this will be based on matters of general assessment, such as the degree of progress the

---

1653 *Cf Samengo-Turner v. J & H Marsh & McLennan (Services) Ltd* [2007] EWCA Civ 723, [2008] ICR 18. But Section 5 itself makes *limited* provision for a jurisdiction agreement for a non-Member State: C-154/11 *Mahamdia v People's Democratic Republic of Algeria* EU:C:2012:491, [2013] ICR 1.

1654 C-129/83 *Zelger v. Salinitri (No 2)* [1984] ECR 2397.

proceedings have made so far, the condition does not need general elaboration, in England at least. It seems likely that a court may be permitted to make some sort of assessment of whether the foreign court is one whose procedure seems likely to measure up to standards of procedural fairness and general suitability to serve as the substitute for an adjudication by the courts of a Member State. No doubt there are sensitivies here, and a list of countries whose courts are not to be trusted will need to be found elsewhere; but the issue is whether a court with jurisdiction under Chapter II should decline to exercise it. It should not do if it has doubts about the quality of the adjudication liable to result from the exercise of this declinatory order.

When considering whether to order a stay of the proceedings before it, the court is entitled to consider all the circumstances of the case, but Recital (24) makes particular mention of factors which, were they to point to a Member State, would give that Member State exclusive jurisdiction. Insofar as this means that the proceedings in a non-Member State are in a court which, *mutatis mutandis* would have had jurisdiction under Articles 24 or 25, it is welcome: as will be seen below, little good will come from failing to treat jurisdiction agreements for the courts of a non-Member State as institutionally inferior to those for Member States; and if that is true for jurisdiction agreements, it must be *a fortiori* for connections of the kind indicated by Article 24. Insofar as it may be inferred that these points of contact are irrelevant unless there is a prior and still pending *lis pendens* in the non-Member State concerned, it raises a significant question, examined after the treatment of Articles 33 and 34.

2.294 Problems associated with the status of the foreign judgment

The court may not order a stay unless it is expected that the court in the non-Member State will give a judgment capable of recognition or enforcement in the Member State whose courts are proposed to be seised. In the light of Article 33(2)(b), this means that a judgment from the non-Member State can be expected within a reasonable time. But as to the condition that the judgment which is foreseen be one 'capable' of recognition, it may be said that it will not be known for sure whether it is capable of recognition until it has been given. For example, if it is a permissible objection that a foreign judgment is not capable of being recognised where there was a failure to observe the rules of natural justice, or where the court made an error of a kind which prevents its recognition,[1655] it may not be known whether the judgment will meet the criteria for its recognition in the Member State. It is to be supposed that the court should not take too literal a view of this condition, and if on the date of application for the stay there is no established fact or other clear reason why a judgment from the foreign court would not be recognised, this condition should be taken to be satisfied.

But one particular point does arise. It is not said, neither is it to be inferred, that the judgment from the non-Member State, which is liable to be recognised in the Member State, will by virtue of its status in relation to Article 33, become a Member State judgment for the purpose of enforcement in other Member States. The position therefore is that if the proceedings in the Member State are stayed, the outcome may be a judgment from a non-Member State, which takes the place, in the Member State in question, of the judgment

---

1655 In England, a mistake as a result of fraud; in some other Member States, because it did not adopt the approach to the issue of applicable law which a court in the Member State would have followed, etc.

which will not now be given when, in accordance with Article 33(3), the proceedings which were stayed are dismissed. Sensible as this undoubtedly is, it gives rise to some complications for which the Article offers no immediate solution.

Where the stay is ordered, it means that the judgment creditor will not be able to obtain the recognition or enforcement of the eventual judgment in other Member States, because the decision to recognise a judgment from a non-Member State does not result in a 'judgment' for the purposes of Chapter III of the Regulation.[1656] As Article 33(3) means that there is no prospect of any form of judgment being given in the stayed cause of action before the Member State, the party who succeeds before the court of the non-Member State secures only a local victory. A judgment in his favour does not obtain a European passport. Whether it is effective in Member States other than the one in which a stay was ordered will be a matter for the laws of each Member State. That is a significant potential disadvantage. It must therefore be open to the claimant in the Member State proceedings to object that he wishes to obtain a judgment which can be recognised and enforced under Chapter III, and that if the Member State does not adjudicate in the action before it, he will be deprived of one of the significant aspects of adjudication in accordance with the jurisdictional principles of Chapter II.

From time to time this argument has surfaced in common law analysis of the justice of ordering a stay of proceedings on *forum non conveniens* grounds, but it has not been confronted as directly as perhaps it should have been.[1657] One solution would be for the Court to make a qualification to the absoluteness of the interpretation which it gave in *Owens Bank Ltd v. Bracco*,[1658] long before Article 33 was thought of, to hold that where the judgment from the courts of non-Member State has been obtained in circumstances defined by Article 33, it should not count as a judgment from a non-Member State, properly so called, but be treated as though it were a judgment from the courts of the Member State which had ordered a stay to accommodate it. That may be sensible, but it does involve reading quite a lot of text between lines which may be seen to be too dense or narrow to allow it. And it may be that if someone asks what difference it makes to the status of the foreign judgment, as a judgment, that a court in a Member State had also been seised, the answer may be that it does not appear to make as much difference as the divergence in treatment would suggest. All that said, there is a problem if a court which could give a judgment which would operate under Chapter III of the Regulation makes an order which means that the judgment which will be given in the dispute will not be a Chapter III judgment.

If the proceedings before the non-Member State are likely to result in an order which will be recognised but not enforced in the Member State in question, what is the court to do? The common law only enforces final judgments for sums quantified in money, though it recognises as *res judicata* a much wider range of foreign judgments.[1659] If that appears to be the likely outcome of the proceedings before the foreign court, it seems that an English court could order a stay, but once the foreign court has given judgment, lift the stay, recognise the foreign judgment, and make its own enforceable order. But if this is right, it means that where the foreign court may be expected to give a final judgment in money terms, the judgment creditor will obtain a judgment to which Chapter III does not extend; where the

---

1656 C-129/92 *Owens Bank Ltd v. Bracco* [1994] ECR I-117.
1657 *International Credit & Investment Co (Overseas) Ltd v. Adham* [1999] ILPr 302.
1658 C-129/92, [1994] ECR I-117.
1659 See below, Chapter 7, para. 7.76.

foreign court may be expected to give a final judgment in non-money terms, the judgment creditor will be able to have the stay lifted, obtain a judgment on the basis of the *res judicata* effect of the foreign judgment, and enforce that under Chapter III. If this is correct, it does not feel quite right.

2.295 Lifting the stay

The court which ordered a stay may lift it again if the assumptions on which its imposition had been based turn out to have been unfounded, or were justified at the time but have now been confounded or defeated. The formal position is set out in Article 33(2), but the conditions there identified call for no additional comment.

2.296 Related proceedings pending before the courts of a non–Member State: Article 34

Article 34 of Regulation 1215/2012 provides that:

> *(1) Where jurisdiction is based on Article 4 or on Articles 7, 8 or 9 and an action is pending before a court of a third State at the time when a court in a Member State is seised of an action which is related to the action in the court of the third State, the court of the Member State may stay the proceedings if: (a) it is expedient to hear and determine the related actions together to avoid the risk of irreconcilable judgments resulting from separate proceedings; (b) it is expected that the court of the third State will give a judgment capable of recognition and, where applicable, of enforcement in that Member State; and (c) the court of the Member State is satisfied that a stay is necessary for the proper administration of justice. (2) The court of the Member State may continue the proceedings at any time if: (a) it appears to the court of the Member State that there is no longer a risk of irreconcilable judgments; (b) the proceedings in the court of the third State are themselves stayed or discontinued; (c) it appears to the court of the Member State that the proceedings in the court of the third State are unlikely to be concluded within a reasonable time; or (d) the continuation of the proceedings is required for the proper administration of justice. (3) The court of the Member State may dismiss the proceedings if the proceedings in the court of the third State are concluded and have resulted in a judgment capable of recognition and, where applicable, of enforcement in that Member State. (4) The court of the Member State shall apply this Article on the application of one of the parties or, where possible under national law, of its own motion.*

As with Article 33, Article 34 is new. The explanation given in the Recitals to Regulation 1215/2012, set out above, applies here as well.

2.297 Operation of Article 34

The explanation of Article 34 is substantially the same as that applying to Article 33; there is no need to repeat what has already been said.

The common sense of Article 34 is that if the proceedings in the foreign court do not meet the conditions of triple identity of causes of action – same parties, *objet* and *cause* – relief under Article 33 cannot be given, but relief should still be possible if the pending foreign proceedings are related to those now commenced before the Member State court. Relatedness is defined by Article 34(1(a) in terms which are identical to Article 30(3), to which reference should be made. The relief which can be ordered by the court is, of course, only a stay of proceedings: by contrast with the powers given by Article 30, the court is not given the option of dismissing the proceedings before it to allow the foreign court to take jurisdiction, consolidate the proceedings and deliver a single, comprehensive judgment. The whole question of ordering, and of lifting the stay, is one for the discretion of the court of the Member State, seised after the foreign proceedings became pending.

The only other point of difference between Articles 33 and 34 is that whereas the court to which Article 33 applies is to dismiss the proceedings if the foreign judgment in respect of the same cause of action is to be recognised or enforced; but as the conditions of triple identity do not apply in cases to which Article 34 applies, the court is empowered, but is not directed, to dismiss the proceedings before it. In cases in which dismissal is not appropriate, it may lift the stay, take account of the foreign judgment, and deal with what remains to be decided in the exercise of the jurisdiction which it had from the start.

2.298 Pointers to the courts of a non-Member State in which proceedings have not been instituted and are not pending: the question which needs to be answered

We now come to a more difficult question, or perhaps to a question which has a difficult answer. It may be shortly stated, but will be addressed at far greater length. It may be put this way: should Regulation 1215/2012 be taken to mean that the circumstances in which a connection to a non-Member State may be taken into account by a court which has jurisdiction in accordance with Chapter II of the Regulation are exhaustively stated by Articles 33 and 34? Or, to put the matter another way, if there is a pointer to a non-Member State which would, *mutatis mutandis*, suggest exclusive jurisdiction regardless of domicile, or exclusive jurisdiction by prorogation, may a court take account of it (and if so, when and to what effect) if there are no proceedings pending in the non-Member State in question?

Or to put the matter yet another way, does the principle of interpretation of legislation *ejusdem generis* mean that there is no other basis for taking account of points of contact with a non-Member State? Or to put the matter slightly differently, should Articles 33 and 34 be interpreted as applying to the situations which they define, but as saying nothing about, and not influencing the analysis of, situations of fact and law which fall outside their scope?

In order that the reader know in advance the conclusion which will be proposed as the better one, it is that Articles 33 and 34 do not mean that a court in a Member State is required to ignore points of contact with a non-Member State when there are no prior pending proceedings in the Member State in question. The answers to the four questions posed above are, on this basis, it should not; it may; it does not; and they should.

It is not possible to assess the strength of the arguments on each side without understanding the problems generated by the jurisprudence, and by certain academic writing, prior to the adoption of Regulation 1215/2012.

2.299 Judicial discretion to decline to exercise jurisdiction conferred by the Regulation

The question whether a court with jurisdiction in accordance with Chapter II of the Regulation had power to decline to exercise that jurisdiction was much debated in days gone by. It had led English courts to express the view that the question, or aspects of it, was fit for reference to the European Court;[1660] and it had the effect of drawing writers to sharply opposed positions. But in *Owusu v. Jackson*,[1661] the Court finally and very clearly ruled that, where a court in the United Kingdom had jurisdiction under what is now Article 4 of Regulation 1215/2012, it was not open to that court to decline to exercise that jurisdiction on the ground that the courts of what would now be called a non-Member State would be a more appropriate forum for the trial of the action.

2.300 Some arguments for and against the existence of jurisdictional discretion

The Brussels I Regulation is organised on the basis of a high degree of uniformity, and a low degree of judicial discretion, in its application. The principle of legal certainty, in particular, does not easily accommodate jurisdictional discretion.

The overwhelming opinion of civilian lawyers was and is that an English court with jurisdiction under Chapter II of what is now the Regulation has no general discretion to not exercise it, on the footing that the exercise of jurisdiction, when this was derived from the Regulation and invoked by the claimant, is statutory and mandatory so far as the court is concerned. It would follow that when a claimant seises a court, in accordance with the jurisdictional rules of that court, the judge has a duty to hear the case, and has no discretion to elect not to do so. It is not only a civilian view: there is a perfectly sensible common law view that the inherent power to stay proceedings on the ground of *forum non conveniens* is indissociable from the inherent jurisdiction of the High Court: the two inherent powers, to adjudicate and to not adjudicate, belong together. But where jurisdiction is imposed by legislation which gives effect to an international agreement, the jurisdiction is of a wholly different kind, in relation to which the question is whether the international agreement, or the implementing legislation, allows or accommodates the exercise of a jurisdictional discretion; and it is entirely plausible that the answer is that it does not. Perhaps more attention should be given to the distinction between inherent jurisdiction and statutory jurisdiction than has been given in the past; but rightly or wrongly, the Court in *Owusu v. Jackson* held that an English court with general jurisdiction had no power to stay its proceedings in favour of the courts of a non-Member State on the bare ground that the English court was, in the circumstances of the case, a *forum non conveniens*.

If one asks why the Regulation, or its predecessor instruments, made no allowance for the doctrine of *forum non conveniens*, Professor Schlosser gave a partial answer: that when negotiating its accession to the Brussels Convention, the United Kingdom delegation did not press for a formal amendment to the Convention so as to make provision for it.[1662] But at the time, the doctrine of *forum non conveniens* was known to be part of the law of Scotland only, not of England; and so by accident is legal history made.[1663]

1660 In *Re Harrods (Buenos Aires) Ltd* [1992] Ch 72, the House of Lords referred certain questions to the European Court. But before the case was heard the national litigation settled, and the reference was withdrawn from the Register; see also *Haji-Ioannou v. Frangos* [1999] 2 Lloyd's Rep 337; *Lubbe v. Cape plc* [2000] 1 WLR 1545. In the former case, the court referred, with humbling generosity of spirit, to the discussion in the second edition of this book, but on the view it took of the defendant's domicile, found no need to reach a conclusion or make a reference to the European Court.

1661 C-281/02, [2005] ECR I-1383.

1662 At [78].

1663 There is therefore room for reasonable persons to suspect that the degree of pressure in favour of making allowance for a doctrine of *forum non conveniens* was less than it might have been in different British circumstances.

Even so, even when it is accepted that a general discretion to not exercise it is inconsistent with the jurisdiction created and conferred by the Regulation, there are still cases in which the Regulation, and legal certainty, must allow for the granting of jurisdictional relief, whether the text of the Regulation actually says so or not. If the defendant is sued in England, where he is domiciled, but the parties had contractually agreed that the courts of New York were to have exclusive jurisdiction, it would make no sense at all for the English court to be obliged, notwithstanding the breach of contract by the claimant, to exercise jurisdiction just because the defendant is domiciled in England.[1664] If a dispute arises as to title to land situated in New York, it cannot be correct that a defendant in that dispute may be sued, and if proceedings are instituted, must resign himself to being sued, in England if he is domiciled here. The point was never put more tellingly than by Droz, when he wrote in 1990, that:[1665] '*Si un juge français est radicalement incompétent pour juger d'un immeuble ou d'un brevet allemand, en raison de la specificité, et de la particularité, du droit réel ou droit des brevets allemands, on ne voit pas pourquoi il serait mieux armé pour juger d'un bail rural argentin ou de la validité d'un brevet japonais!*' This appreciation of the matter stands in no need of improvement.[1666]

2.301 The nature of jurisdictional rules made by the Regulation

No doubt it is true that, on a literal or dull-eyed reading of the Regulation, if there are proceedings which have as their object title to land in New York, the defendant remains liable to be sued in a Member State as long as one of the other jurisdictional rules of the Regulation applies to him. This, so the argument runs, follows from the fact that no specific or express provision is made by the Regulation for the case in which the proceedings have as their object rights *in rem* in land in a non-Member State, and from the assertion that no allowance may be made by the court seised for a matter which is not expressed in the Regulation. It is tosh. The fact that the Regulation makes no mention of a particular point is a fact, but it is one which calls for intelligent interpretation.

The 'failure' of the Regulation to refer to certain connections with, or pointers to, non-Member States derives from the way in which the Regulation deals with these jurisdictional connections or pointers to the courts of Member States. Where they point to a Member State, the Regulation can direct one court to exercise jurisdiction, and direct others to not exercise jurisdiction. But it cannot direct a court in a non-Member State to exercise jurisdiction. And because it cannot do this, it cannot know whether the courts of the non-Member State in question will adjudicate. And because it does not know that, it does not have the necessary basis for directing a Member State court to not exercise jurisdiction. It

---

1664 On the footing that the choice of court clause for a non-Member State has no effect under Art. 23, and the defendant is domiciled in the United Kingdom. The Schlosser Report [1979] OJ C59/71, [176], says a court may give effect to such a clause, but gives no further justification for this sensible view. The same may be said of the decision of the Court in C-387/98 *Coreck Maritime GmbH v. Handelsveem BV* [2000] ECR I-9337. On the other hand, the Regulation could hardly state that the courts of a non-Member State were entitled or obliged to exercise jurisdiction, which may have led to the perception that there was nothing for the Regulation to say on the point, leaving it to national law to deal with instead.

1665 [1990] Rev crit DIP 1, 14.

1666 Though translation is another matter: if a French judge is fundamentally without jurisdiction to adjudicate on German immovable property or a German patent, on account of the specific nature of German land law and patent law, one cannot see why he would be better placed to adjudicate an Argentinian agricultural tenancy or a Japanese patent!

is therefore quite wrong to read or to purport to read the Regulation as regarding these pointers to non-Member States as irrelevant, for the truth is quite different. The Regulation regards them as beyond its legislative power, with the consequence, as it is proposed here, that it says nothing, as a result of which the national court is left to answer the jurisdictional question for itself.

The point is made all the more obvious when one observes that the basis of Articles 33 and 34 is that where it is known that the court of a non-Member State has and will exercise jurisdiction, *because it is already exercising it*, the uncertainty is sufficiently resolved. Where that is so, it makes sense, and is proper and right, for the Regulation to deal with the jurisdictional consequences. What does not make sense is reasoning which says, in effect, that because it is not known whether the court in a non-Member State would or will exercise jurisdiction, the fact or matter which points to that court as the proper place to resolve the issue before the Member State court is to be treated as though it did not exist.

2.302 A broad brush answer or a series of separate questions?

It is most improbable that there should be a single, one-size-fits-all, answer to the question whether a court has any discretion to stay proceedings. If there were to be a single and clear answer, *Owusu* would mean that it had to be negative, and there would no sense in that: the authority of M. Droz is sufficient to make that point good. That being so, in order to decide whether the Regulation does permit a court to stay proceedings over which it has jurisdiction it will still be helpful, after we have properly examined the decision in *Owusu v. Jackson*,[1667] to deal individually with a number of cases in which the power to stay proceedings might be in issue.

Six sets of circumstance may be examined, which are (1) where the English court has general jurisdiction under Article 4[1668] but there is a more appropriate forum in another Member State; (2) where the English court has general jurisdiction under Article 4 but there is a more appropriate forum in a non-Member State; (3) where the English court has general jurisdiction under Article 4 but there is an agreement on jurisdiction for the courts of a non-Member State; (4) where the English court has general jurisdiction under Article 4 but the dispute concerns title to land in a non-Member State; (5) where the jurisdiction of the English court is based on Article 6 of the Regulation but there is a material connection with a non-Member State; and (6) where the jurisdiction of the English court is based on Article 6 and the natural forum is in another Member State. What might have been the seventh case, where the English court has general jurisdiction under Article 4 but there are proceedings already pending before the courts of a non-Member State, has now been dealt with under Articles 33 and 34; but it still plays a part in this enquiry, and will be briefly revisited.

1667 C-281/02, [2005] ECR I-1383.

1668 But in this respect, Art. 4 stands for any of those provisions of Chapter II of the Regulation with the exception of Art. 6. No distinction is to be drawn between jurisdiction based on Art. 4, and jurisdiction based on Art. 7, or 25, for example. See *Ace Insurance SA-NV v. Zurich Insurance Co* [2001] EWCA Civ 173, [2001] 1 Lloyd's Rep 618.

2.303 Court has general jurisdiction but a more appropriate forum is in another Member State

If jurisdiction over the defendant is taken on the basis of Article 4 of Regulation 1215/2012, even if the natural forum for the trial would be the courts of another Member State,[1669] the court has no power to stay its proceedings. This is the archetype of a case in which jurisdiction is entirely and solely the concern of the direct jurisdictional rules of the Regulation, which do not yield to arguments, no matter how well-founded, about *forum non conveniens*.[1670] There is no more to be said.

2.304 Court has general jurisdiction but a more appropriate forum is in a non–Member State

The European Court ruled in *Owusu v. Jackson*[1671] that, where the English court has jurisdiction under what is now Article 4 of the Regulation,[1672] it has no power to stay proceedings, on the ground of *forum non conveniens*, in favour of the courts of a non-Contracting State, *in casu*, Jamaica. The claim arose from personal injuries sustained by the claimant while on holiday in Jamaica. According to the Court, it was irrelevant that the facts and matters arising for analysis and decision were more appropriate to be tried in Jamaica, which was the *locus in quo* and the place where the evidence was, and where the law to be applied to the claim would be local to the court applying it. It was also irrelevant that this could result in[1673] Jamaican defendants, who were five of the six named defendants, being served out of the jurisdiction under the Civil Procedure Rules as necessary or proper parties to the claim against the English-domiciled defendant, and therefore being called upon to defend themselves in England where legal proceedings are relatively costly, with the consequence that they will have been, indirectly but catastrophically, affected by the Regulation.[1674] If the English court set aside service on the Jamaican defendants, it was nevertheless irrelevant that proceedings arising from a single accident might have to be tried in proceedings in two countries. It was irrelevant that this might make the enforcement of judgments problematic. And above all, it was irrelevant that the case had nothing to do with any other Member State. As the Court said, in a rather

---

1669 Say, because the claim is founded on a tort, and the court in question is for the place where the tort was committed.

1670 C-282/92 *Custom Made Commercial Ltd v. Stawa Metallbau GmbH* [1994] ECR I-2923.

1671 C-281/02, [2005] ECR I-3565. The reference was made by the Court of Appeal: [2002] EWCA Civ 877, [2002] ILPr 813. For a French comment, see [2005] *Rev crit DIP* 698 (*note* Chalas).

1672 The principle is the same where the jurisdiction of the English court is special jurisdiction over a defendant domiciled in another Member State: *Ace Insurance SA-NV v. Zurich Insurance Co* [2001] EWCA Civ 173, [2001] 1 Lloyd's Rep 618, or jurisdiction over a defendant by virtue of an agreement on jurisdiction which conformed to Art. 23: *Equitas Ltd v. Allstate Insurance Co* [2008] EWHC 1671 (Comm), [2009] Lloyd's Rep IR 227, [64]. The decision in *OT Africa Line Ltd v. Magic Sportswear Corp* [2005] EWCA Civ 710, [2005] 2 Lloyd's Rep 170, which suggests that a court with jurisdiction under what is now Art. 25 has a discretion to stay its proceedings in favour of the courts of a non-Member State, is probably not to be relied on at this point: *Owusu* does not appear to have been cited to the court.

1673 However, if this were a bad thing, the responsibility for bringing it about would be entirely a matter of English law. It is not a fair point to be made against the decision of the Court in *Owusu*, which cannot be affected by the curiosities of English jurisdictional law.

1674 The Court took the view that nothing short of a bilateral Convention between the United Kingdom and Jamaica would support the argument that it was inappropriate to place this burden on the Jamaican defendants, so betraying an alarming misconception about the methods of the common law.

insouciant tone: 'in that regard, genuine as those difficulties may be, suffice it to observe that such considerations, which are precisely those which may be taken into account when *forum non conveniens* is considered, are not such as to call into question the mandatory nature of the fundamental rule of jurisdiction contained in Article 2 of the Brussels Convention'.[1675] No stay on the exercise of jurisdiction on the ground of *forum non conveniens* is permissible.

It may be recorded, if only as a matter of legal history, that the English courts had up to that point taken a different view. In *Re Harrods (Buenos Aires) Ltd*,[1676] a company incorporated in England was defendant to a petition that a minority shareholder was being unfairly prejudiced by the conduct of the company's affairs. As the business of the company was to all intents and purposes carried on in Argentina, it was argued on behalf of the company that the natural forum for the dispute was Argentina. Despite the fact that the company was being sued as defendant in the courts for the place where it was domiciled,[1677] the Court of Appeal held that it had power to stay, and should stay, proceedings in favour of the courts of Argentina.[1678] It took the view that it was not obliged to exercise the jurisdiction which had been invoked. It reasoned that the Brussels Convention had no proper concern with a case with which no other Contracting State was involved,[1679] or that the Convention regulated jurisdiction as between the Contracting States only.[1680] A reference by the House of Lords to the European Court[1681] for a ruling which would have gone to the heart of these issues was later withdrawn.

The disappointment of the judgment in *Owusu* was not so much with the bare answer: indeed, the very idea that the claimant, quadriplegic as a result of the catastrophe, should be told that he should go and start again before the courts of Jamaica, was simply grotesque: no wonder that the European Court was repulsed by the prospect of a stay of proceedings. The fact that the judges misunderstood the doctrine of *forum non conveniens* was one thing, but the fact that they clearly saw what it would lead to, and did not like it, was quite another. It may also be that the distinction between inherent jurisdiction (and the inherent power to regulate inherent jurisdiction) and statutory jurisdiction implementing an international agreement, which may ignore such national idiosyncracies,[1682] was not seen as clearly at the time as it is now. But there it is: the answer is clear, and the debate has moved on.

1675 At [45].

1676 [1992] Ch 72. This decision is now to be regarded as overruled, along with the cases which were bound by and applied it.

1677 According to the definition of corporate domicile in the Brussels Convention, as it then was. It is unclear whether the company would be regarded as domiciled in England according to Art. 63 of Regulation 1215/2012. Though the company was incorporated under English law, it is not known whether it had its registered office outside England; if it did, this will displace the place of its incorporation for the purpose of the Regulation.

1678 [1992] Ch 72. Followed on this point in *The Po* [1991] 2 Lloyd's Rep 206, where the jurisdiction was derived from what is now Art. 71 of the Regulation and the 1952 Collision Convention.

1679 See Dillon LJ at 98.

1680 See Bingham LJ at 103.

1681 C-314/92 *Ladenimor SA v. Intercomfinanz SA*.

1682 In relation to the Warsaw Convention, the inherent power to stay on grounds of *forum conveniens* is excluded: *Milor v. British Airways plc* [1996] QB 702; likewise under the European Patent Convention: *Sepracor v. Hoechst Marion Roussel Ltd* [1999] FSR 746; likewise under the CMR Convention: *Hatzl v. XL Insurance Co* [2009] EWCA Civ 223, [2010] 1 WLR 470.

2.305 Court has general jurisdiction but a pointer to a non–Member State reflects Articles 24 and 25 of the Regulation

The relationship between the Brussels Regulation and the non–Member States is more complex when the connection to the non–Member State is substantially one which is acknowledged in the Regulation itself as one to require one court to exercise jurisdiction and to require all others not to exercise jurisdiction.

The starting point is to consider jurisdiction agreements for the courts of a non–Member State. As was said above, as the European Union could not compel a court in a non–Member State to accept jurisdiction according to the terms of a jurisdiction agreement or otherwise it could not direct a court in a Member State to not adjudicate; and as a result, no reference to such agreements is made in the Regulation. The consequence is that it is for the court seised to determine for itself whether, and if so on what conditions, to give effect to a jurisdiction agreement for a non–Member State. Professor Schlosser said so, and[1683] by its judgment in *Coreck Maritime GmbH v. Handelsveem BV*[1684] the European Court agreed with him.[1685] The point about *Coreck Maritime* has been made and accepted in England;[1686] and one would have thought that its basic common sense was all one needed to put the point to rest.

It follows that where an English court is seised of a dispute which, according to its interpretation and evaluation of the parties' agreement, should have been brought before the courts of a non–Member State, it should apply its rules of private international law and may, in accordance with these, stay the proceedings in favour of the contractually-chosen court. This answer reflects one of the most basic principles for which the Regulation stands: that a well-informed party should be able to predict where he is liable to be sued as defendant, or entitled to bring proceedings as claimant. The proposition that a jurisdiction agreement should be accorded something less than its full weight and intended effect can only be at the expense of legal certainty, and there is accordingly no reason to doubt the efficacy of such agreements, even where jurisdiction over the defendant would otherwise be governed by the Regulation.

The judgment in *Owusu v. Jackson*[1687] did not deal with this point: the Court had been asked to, and its failure to offer any kind of answer is a matter of shame. It has been argued that the Court really thought,[1688] though did not say, that a national court had power to relinquish jurisdiction which existed by reason of what is now Article 4 only in the cases specifically provided for by the text of the legislation. As this made no mention of declining jurisdiction in favour of the courts of a non–Member State where and because there was an agreement for the courts of that non–Member State, it was even argued that *Owusu* has, in effect, reversed this aspect of the decision in *Coreck Maritime*.[1689] But the suggestion that the

---

1683 [1979] OJ C59/71, [176].

1684 C-387/98, [2000] ECR I-9337.

1685 At [19].

1686 *Ferrexpo AG v. Gilson Investments Ltd* [2012] EWHC 721 (Comm), [2012] 1 Lloyd's Rep 588.

1687 C-281/02, [2005] ECR I-1383. See Peel [2005] LMCLQ 363; Briggs *ibid.*, 378.

1688 At [37]. The reason this cannot be taken as a firm conclusion is because of the Court's refusal to answer the second question. If it meant that the only derogations permitted to be made from what is now Art. 4 were those set out in the Convention itself, the second question referred by the Court of Appeal would have been redundant, already answered, and not hypothetical as the Court said.

1689 It may be said that the decision of the Court of Appeal, in *Samengo-Turner v. J & H Marsh & McLennan (Services) Ltd* [2007] EWCA Civ 723, [2008] ICR 18, to give less than no effect (by ordering a party not to rely on the clause before the nominated court) to an agreement for the courts of a non–Member State, has cast doubt on

Court had overturned a decision on which the ink was barely dry, without publicising its intention of doing so, is not credible.

The Court did not mention the issue of non-Member State jurisdiction agreements. At one point[1690] in his Opinion, the Advocate General mentioned the possibility of according 'reflexive effect' to what is now Article 25, to allow a court to treat a jurisdiction clause for a non-Member State as though it was an agreement within the scope of what is now Article 25 of Regulation 1215/2012.[1691] The progenitor of this notion of 'reflexive effect' was Mr Droz,[1692] who suggested that a court might justify its refusal to hear such a claim brought against a local defendant by applying the logic of what are now Articles 24 and 25 by analogy. He suggested that the law might recognise *l'effet réflexive des compétences exclusifs*. It is not clear how far Mr Droz was prepared to allow this principle to extend; it is unclear whether the Advocate General in *Owusu* was in favour of the possibility that a court should be able to give effect to a jurisdiction agreement for a non-Member State. But it would be absurd for this not to be the law, for the principle of legal certainty is served by encouraging parties to make litigation agreements in advance, and by their strict enforcement; it would be unthinkable for the European Court to direct a national court to ignore an agreement for the courts of a non-Member State.[1693] It should in principle be just as willing to acknowledge the jurisdictional significance of other connections with a non-Member State which reflect the provisions of the Regulation itself.

But it is still necessary to pinpoint the legal power which gives the court the authority to make the order applied for. It may be that Droz conceived of the principle of 'reflexive effect' as being a legitimate interpretation and application of the rule of European law, by which case the relevant Article is being read and given effect 'as if' it applied to a category of case to which it literally did not apply.[1694] If that is not so, and all that European law says on the matter is '*nihil obstat*', the basis for jurisdiction must be found in a rule of national law, which in this context may be the inherent power of the court to regulate and control its own jurisdiction.

2.306 The Lugano Opinion

The illusion of a shadow has been considered by some to have fallen[1695] over this conclusion as a result of the Opinion of the European Court given in answer to questions referred to

---

the submission advanced here. If the decision were held to be reliable, this would indeed follow. It is not reliable; it is wrong. For further comment, see [2007] LMCLQ 433, (2007) 78 BYBIL 615.

1690 At [139].

1691 It should not be overlooked that *Coreck Maritime* is absolutely no authority for the principle of reflexive effect. It provides that a court should decide whether to enforce a jurisdiction agreement for a non-Member State by reference to its own private international law and not, if this be different, by applying the rules now in Art. 25 by analogy.

1692 Originally in Droz, *Compétence judiciaire et effets des jugements dans le marché commun* (1972): at [164]–[169] (in relation to exclusive jurisdiction regardless of domicile), and [204] (in relation to jurisdiction clauses).

1693 For the agreement of the English courts, see *Konkola Copper Mines plc v. Coromin Ltd* [2005] EWHC 898 (Comm), [2005] 2 Lloyd's Rep 555, affirmed [2006] EWCA Civ 5, [2006] 1 Lloyd's Rep 410; *Winnetka Trading Corp v. Julius Baer International Ltd* [2008] EWHC 3146 (Ch). See also [2005] Rev crit DIP 722 (note Muir Watt).

1694 For a view sharply critical of the proposition that a non-European legislative rule, which was worded so as not to apply to a matter before the court, may be given effect 'as if' it did apply, see the judgment of Lord Collins in *Singularis Holdings Ltd v. PriceWaterhouseCoopers* [2014] UKPC 36 (a case on cross-border assistance in insolvency). The Judge in *Plaza v Law Debenture Trust Corp* [2015] EWHC 43 (Ch) declined to see *singularis* as having removed the possibility of applying the Regulation with reflexive effect, but this cannot prevent others asking the same question.

1695 If an illusion can do this kind of thing.

it by the Council on whether the European Union had (exclusive) legislative competence to negotiate and settle the terms of what became the Lugano II Convention.[1696] Originally this had been the responsibility of the individual States; but once the European Union had legislated in the field by Regulation 44/2001, a principle of European law meant that legislative competence had forever passed out of the hands of the Member States and into the hands of the European Union.

At one point in its lengthy analysis, the Court considered the problems which would arise if there were a jurisdiction agreement for a Contracting State to the Lugano II Convention which was not also a Member State of the European Union. There would be a conflict between the Lugano II Convention, which would validate the agreement on jurisdiction, and the Brussels Regulation, which would find the court of the defendant's domicile to be competent.[1697] Some[1698] claimed to see in this an indication that, as far as the Court is concerned, in the absence of a new instrument to which the European Union was party, there would be no power to give effect to a jurisdiction agreement for a non–Member State where the defendant is domiciled in a Member State. This, so the reasoning goes, suggests that the Court was back-pedalling from its answer in *Coreck Maritime*.

Such reasoning is not credible. The point of a jurisdiction agreement is to prorogate and derogate jurisdiction at the same time, and to do so with as much of a guarantee of certainty as is legally possible. If the parties agree upon the courts of a State over which the European Union has no legislative authority, no European legislative instrument can direct the court of that non–Member State to accept that it has jurisdiction. If it is intended that European law direct that a non–Member State court exercise jurisdiction, and direct also that a Member State court must consider itself derogated from in favour of that other court, this result is in peril if the enforcement of a jurisdiction agreement for a non–Member State involves remission to national private international law, as *Coreck Maritime* and Professor Schlosser severally explain that it does. Rather, there needs to be, as the Court carefully explained, a legislative, direct, jurisdictional rule, made in relation to the Lugano States only, and which will be mandatory for prorogated and derogated court. This need provides the justification for the legislative competence of the European Union. Rather than casting doubt on the correctness of the decision in *Coreck Maritime*, this Opinion underscores its legal soundness.

All this being admitted, the final question is whether the court, minded to give effect to such a jurisdiction agreement, or to grant relief because the action concerns title to land in a non–Member State, or because the proceedings concern the validity of a patent issued in a non–Member State, should be guided and constrained by the framework of the corresponding Article of the Regulation, or should instead fall back on and apply its traditional rules of jurisdiction. The principle of 'reflexive effect' might suggest the former, but this is not what *Coreck Maritime* says.[1699] Rather, it is submitted, the court should apply its national law, not hemmed or trimmed by the precise structure of the Article in question.

Take the case of the jurisdiction agreement for a non–Member State, for example. When the agreement is for the courts of a Member State, Article 25 prescribes the rules by which a court must decide that it has and will exercise jurisdiction, as well as those by which it finds that its jurisdiction has been removed by agreement. Satisfaction of those rules results

---

1696 C-1/03 *Lugano Convention* [2006] ECR I-1145.
1697 At [153].
1698 No names, no pack drill.
1699 See above, para. 2.141.

in the mandatory jurisdiction of the court chosen, and the mandatory dismissal of the claim by every other court, always excepting the possibility that the parties may agree to vary the contract by agreement. There is no element of discretion. This makes perfect sense within the closed and finite world of the Member States, in which all courts apply the same jurisdictional rules, and within which the principle of mutual trust and confidence justifies the mandatory application of the rules of the Regulation.

Little of that applies where the chosen court is in a non-Member State. The chosen court is under no obligation imposed by the Regulation to accept jurisdiction; it will not apply the jurisdictional rules set out in the Regulation; and the principle of trust and confidence can, by no stretch of the imagination, be said to be part of the relationship between courts. Comity and mutual respect are all very well, but the duty to accept, unquestioningly, that they are, in every single case, the equal of the English or other European court would be irrational. An English court must have discretion to give effect to a jurisdiction agreement for a non-Member State's court, and will therefore apply its own private international law to the question whether and how to enforce the agreement, just as *Coreck Maritime* said. The same should be true where the connection with a non-Member State corresponds to Article 24 of the Regulation. It is submitted that there should be a remission to national law;[1700] we do not need an inflexible rule which inserts the particle 'non-' before 'Member State'. A court called upon to recognise a jurisdictional connection with a non-Member State which corresponds to Articles 24 or 25 should therefore be free to grant relief as far as the Regulation is concerned, and must do whatever its national rules of private international law tell it to do, neither more nor less. The point is amplified below.

2.307 Court has general jurisdiction but the parties made an agreement on choice of court for a non-Member State

It follows from the general analysis just given that a court may decline to exercise jurisdiction if the dispute before it is covered by a choice of court agreement for the courts of a non-Member State. To recapitulate: Schlosser[1701] observes that what is now the Regulation neither validates nor invalidates such clauses, and that a court may apply its own procedural law to give them such effect as its own law determines they should have.[1702] The Court in *Coreck Maritime GmbH v. Handelsveem BV*[1703] confirmed that a court should assess such a clause by reference to its own rules of the conflict of laws, which presumably means that it is entitled to give effect to it. Nothing in *Owusu v. Jackson* compels a different analysis. The Court limited its analysis to cases where the justification for a stay of proceedings was that the courts of a non-Member State were 'more appropriate for the trial of the action', refusing to deal with the second question referred for a ruling, as one which sought 'advisory opinions on general or hypothetical matters'.[1704] And although it is not quite on this precise point, the Court in *Mahamdia v. Algeria*[1705] accepted that a jurisdiction agreement

---

1700 Subject to a question as to formalities, as to which see the following paragraph.

1701 [1979] OJ C59/71, [176].

1702 See *The Nile Rhapsody* [1992] 2 Lloyd's Rep 399, [1994] 1 Lloyd's Rep 382, giving effect to an Egyptian choice of court clause, when an English defendant was being sued in England.

1703 C-387/98, [2000] ECR I-9337.

1704 At [49].

1705 C-154/11, EU:C:2012:491, [2013] ICR 1. The reason that the decision is not quite on point is that Art. 23 makes express provision for effect to be given to jurisdiction agreements for courts, and does not limit this,

for the courts of a non-Member State could be given effect in accordance with Article 23 of the Regulation if it complied – as in that case it did not – with the requirements of Article 23. That offers some support for a conclusion that a court with jurisdiction under the Regulation may give some effect to a jurisdiction agreement for a non-Member State.

It might also be said to follow from *Coreck Maritime*, as distinct from a strict 'reflexive effect' approach, that an English court may give effect to a jurisdiction agreement for a non-Member State even where the agreement is itself one which would not have complied with the formal or other requirements of Article 25. If *Coreck Maritime* is taken literally, the reference back to the conflicts rules of the court seised is therefore different from the proposition that Article 25 is being applied by precise analogy; and it is submitted that there is much to be said for it. But the argument to the contrary is probably stronger. One of the effects of an agreement on jurisdiction is to derogate from the jurisdiction of the courts of a Member State, say the courts of the defendant's domicile, which would otherwise have it. The justification for the formal conditions set out in Article 25(1) is, some may say,[1706] to ensure that the party who is giving up domiciliary jurisdiction does so deliberately, and may properly be held to his agreement. If effect is to be given to a jurisdiction agreement for the courts of a non-Member State, this also has the consequence that the jurisdiction of the Member State court with, say, general domiciliary jurisdiction is being foregone; and in those circumstances, the requirement that the jurisdiction be relinquished in writing, etc, is just as applicable, just as persuasive. It follows that if a court is to give effect to an agreement for the jurisdiction of the courts of a non-Member State, it should be able to do so only if the agreement on jurisdiction complies with the formal requirements set out in Article 25(1) for agreements for the courts of Member States: a derogation from the general jurisdiction of the court of the domicile is just as much a derogation whether the court prorogated is in Dieppe or Djibouti. It is submitted that the derogation must comply with Article 25.

The result is that, as matters stand in 2015, a court should apply its own national law on the effect to be given to an agreement on jurisdiction for the courts of a non-Member State – exercising a discretion if that is what its law provides for – if the agreement on jurisdiction is one which complies with the formal requirements of Article 25(1); but if the agreement is not so compliant, it should not be sufficient to derogate from the jurisdiction of the courts of the Member State which would otherwise have it according to Chapter II of the Regulation.

When the European Union adopts the Hague Convention on Choice of Court Agreements,[1707] this instrument will offer a more transparent basis for giving effect to jurisdiction agreements for the courts of non-Member States which are party to the Convention.

---

by express words at least, to the courts of non-Member States; and that a jurisdiction agreement to which Art. 23(2) applies must be non-exclusive, not derogating from the jurisdiction of the courts otherwise having jurisdiction. That allows it to be said that *Mahamdia* is governed by the express provision of Art. 23 (and in the language of the Opinion in *Owusu*, is a case for which the Regulation makes provision), and has no necessary application to jurisdiction agreements for which no express textual provision is made. On the other hand, there was no suggestion in *Mahamdia* that a jurisdiction agreement for a non-Member State could not be exclusive and given effect under Art. 23(1).

1706 See above, para. 2.125.

1707 Hague Convention of 30 June 2005 on Choice of Court Agreements. The Explanatory Report is by Hartley and Dogauchi. The Convention will take effect in the European Union after the deposit of the instrument of approval, which is to take place within a month of 5 June 2015: Council Decision 2014/887/EU, [2014] OJ L353/5.

It is not expected that the Convention will affect the recast law on jurisdiction agreements falling within Article 25. It would be unlikely that it would apply to jurisdiction agreements for a Lugano II State, but as none of these has signed the Convention the question is of no current importance. So far, the Convention applies to Mexico, and the immediate result of its coming into force in the European Union will be that jurisdiction agreements for the Mexican courts will be given effect according to a common set of rules, no matter which Member State is seised with proceedings; and that judgments from Mexican courts, when these have been seised in accordance with a choice of court agreement to which the Convention applies, will (subject to conditions) be recognised in the Member States according to a common rule for recognition.[1708]

2.308 Court has general jurisdiction but there is an 'Article 24 connection' pointing to the courts of a non-Member State

For reasons described above, if the dispute concerns title to land[1709] in a non-Member State, an English court seised in such a dispute must in principle be permitted to decline jurisdiction. The broad basis for doing so is that the conflict of laws principles of civilised countries usually contains such a rule, which reflects the paramount power and unique concern of the courts of the *situs* of the land; the particular issue is to formulate the precise rule by which it is to be done. The starting point is that if the matter is one which Article 24 would refer to the exclusive jurisdiction of the courts of a Member State, if the land or other pointed is to a non-Member State, the court should be free to decline to adjudicate. This is the very point on which Mr Droz expressed his opinion in 1990; it is as powerful today as it was then;[1710] it is almost incomprehensible that anyone should dissent from it.

Guidance from the English courts gives less support than one might expect to the proposition that there may be a stay or a dismissal when the case concerns land in a non-Member State, but this is, at least in part, attributable to prevent judicial ambivalence about the jurisdictional rule of English law as it is about the interpretation of the Regulation.[1711] The question has not yet directly arisen for decision in relation to foreign land,[1712] but in those other few areas in which an English court traditionally had no subject-matter jurisdiction,[1713] such as adjudication of the validity of rights under foreign intellectual property laws,[1714] and the enforcement of foreign revenue laws, it has been held, or at any rate suggested, that the existence of personal jurisdiction over the defendant served to override the rule of the common law which denied the existence of jurisdiction.

1708 See generally Hartley, *Choice-of-Court Agreements Under the European and International Instruments* (Oxford, 2013).

1709 In principle, what is said in this paragraph must extend to all connections of the type listed in the five paragraphs of Art. 24. But land is taken as the illustrative example of a broader principle.

1710 See Droz [1990] Rev Crit DIP 1, 14: the material passage is set out in para. 2.300, above.

1711 *Lucasfilm Ltd v. Ainsworth* [2011] UKSC 39, [2012] 1 AC 208; *Hamed v. Stevens* [2013] EWCA Civ 911, [2013] ILPr 623.

1712 *Cf Re Polly Peck International plc (No 2)* [1998] 3 All ER 812. But for company law issues to which Art. 24(2) provides the analogy, see *Ferrexpo AG v. Gilson Investments Ltd* [2012] EWHC 721 (Comm), [2012] 1 Lloyd's Rep 588.

1713 See below, para. 4.05.

1714 *Pearce v. Ove Arup Partnership Ltd* [2000] Ch 403; *Lucasfilm Ltd v. Ainsworth* [2011] UKSC 39, [2012] 1 AC 208.

The appropriate answer appears to be found by analogy with the approach of the Court in *Coreck Maritime GmbH v. Handelsveem BV*.[1715] This would mean that if the proceedings had as their object rights *in rem* in, or a tenancy of, immovable property in a non-Member State, the court would be permitted to apply its rules of private international law to determine whether to adjudicate. This would mean that the rule in *British South Africa Co v. Companhia de Moçambique*[1716] would continue to apply where the land was in a non-Member State, for example. Once again, the only reason the Regulation cannot say this for itself is because of the legal impossibility of enacting a rule that the courts of a non-Member State have jurisdiction.

2.309 Court has jurisdiction based on Article 6, but there is a material connection to the courts of a non-Member State

Though *Owusu v. Jackson* establishes that a court with jurisdiction under Article 4 is not entitled to stay its proceedings in favour of the courts of a non-Member State, on the ground of *forum non conveniens*, the case where the court has jurisdiction under the residual jurisdictional rule in Article 6 remains to be considered. It might be argued that where the jurisdiction asserted over the defendant is by virtue of Article 6 of the Regulation, and the claimant has[1717] seised the court in accordance with it, there is no more power to stay proceedings than there is when jurisdiction is based on other provisions of Chapter II. On the other hand, the case for there being a power to stay is clearly much stronger than in the preceding cases: if the Regulation refers the exercise of jurisdiction to the rules of the common law, and those rules are actually rules of inherent jurisdiction which come with an inherent power to stay proceedings on the ground of *forum non conveniens*, a stay may be ordered consistently with the overall scheme of the Regulation. It is difficult to mount a convincing contrary argument, for if there is no power to stay, the jurisdiction of the English court, taken on the basis of rules that are too wide to be used against those with a domicile in a Member State, would have been made wider still. That would make no sense.[1718] A stay may be ordered.

2.310 Court has jurisdiction based on Article 6, but there is a material connection to the courts of another Member State

As has been said above, where jurisdiction over the defendant is taken on the basis of Article 4 of the Regulation, and it is demonstrated that the natural forum could be in another Member State, there is no practical doubt that a court is precluded from staying its proceedings. There is less certainty[1719] where the natural forum would be in another Member

---

1715 C-387/98, [2000] ECR I-9337.

1716 [1893] AC 602; see below, para. 4.05.

1717 If he has not done so by service as of right he will need permission to do so outside the jurisdiction. The court may, of course, refuse; and if it does so the claimant remains free to seek to sue in another Member State. Accordingly, there may be disparity between cases where service has been made (the court is now seised) and those where the court refuses to grant permission to serve or sets aside permission previously given (the court is not seised).

1718 *Haji-Ioannou v. Frangos* [1999] 2 Lloyd's Rep 337.

1719 As reflected in the fact that the court was in principle prepared to make a reference to the European Court in *Haji-Ioannou v. Frangos* [1999] 2 Lloyd's Rep 337.

State but the court has jurisdiction over the defendant on the basis of Article 6, that is to say, proceedings have been commenced against a defendant with no domicile in a Member State and in respect of whom no other provision of the Regulation is applicable. It was suggested[1720] at first instance in *Sarrio SA v. Kuwait Investment Authority*[1721] that this was a very different case from one where jurisdiction was based on the 'direct' rules of the Brussels Convention, and was one where the Convention imposed no restriction on the power of the court to order a stay. This view was generally approved by the Court of Appeal in the same case.[1722] In *Haji-Ioannou v. Frangos*,[1723] the Court of Appeal was generally sympathetic to the decision in *Sarrio*, but eventually found that, as the defendant had a domicile in Greece, and not just in Cyprus as the judge below had found, it did not need to reach a decision on the point. The present state of the authorities therefore favours the availability of a power to stay of proceedings. At first sight the argument may be attractive, for the discretion to stay on the ground of *forum non conveniens* may easily be seen as an integral part of the jurisdictional rules of the common law whose use for residual purposes is authorised by Article 6. It is not completely clear that it is correct, but the idea that a court cannot stay in such a case has to be rested on the proposition that a court in another Member State cannot be a court in favour of which a stay may be ordered.

2.311 Court has jurisdiction based on Article 6, but there is a *lis pendens* before the courts of another Member State

The question whether a court should be permitted to stay its proceedings if substantially the same dispute had been commenced at an earlier point in time and is still pending, before the courts of a non-Member State had been debated along with all the other cases in which it would be arguable that relief should be granted on grounds not mentioned in the Regulation. Decisions given in the immediate aftermath of *Owusu* tended to say that relief could not be granted;[1724] later decisions tended to, or took, the opposite view,[1725] as well they might.

The answer is now provided by Articles 33 and 34. It bears repetition that these Articles make sense as legislative provisions in the Regulation because it is known that a court in a non-Member State would adjudicate, and the inability of the Regulation to direct a court in a non-Member State (and to provide for the derogation from jurisdiction as a consequence of it) is not a problem. However, for the reasons put forward above, this provides no basis for any deduction as to the intended answer in cases in which there is a material connection or pointer to a non-Member State but in which no proceedings are currently pending. To repeat the point: it does not follow from the limited scope of Articles 33 and 34 of Regulation

---

1720 Though the point did not arise for decision.

1721 [1996] 1 Lloyd's Rep 650.

1722 [1997] 1 Lloyd's Rep 113.

1723 [1999] 2 Lloyd's Rep 337.

1724 The question was to have been referred by the Irish Supreme Court in *Goshawk Dedicated Ltd v. Life Receivables Ltd* [2009] IESC 7, [2009] ILPr 435, but according to *Catalyst Investment Group Ltd v. Lewinsohn* [2009] EWHC 1964 (Ch), [2010] Ch 218, [85], the reference was not in fact made.

1725 *Ferrexpo AG v. Gilson Investments Ltd* [2012] EWHC 721 (Comm), [2012] 1 Lloyd's Rep 588, [137] (though the case was concerned with a connection to a non-Member State of the exclusive jurisdition kind, rather than *lis alibi pendens*); *JKN v. JCN* [2010] EWHC 843 (Fam), [2011] 1 FLR 826 (a case on the Brussels II Regulation); *Mittal v. Mittal* [2013] EWCA Civ 1255, [2014] Fam 102 (a case on the Brussels II Regulation, drawing some inspiration for its answer from the prospective Art. 33 of Regulation 1215/2012).

1215/2012 that no relief may be granted in cases in which there is a material connection or pointer but no pending proceedings. Where that is the case, the 'reflexive approach' or application of national law by analogy with the Regulation, is still the rational answer.

(16) INTERNATIONAL JURISDICTION
IN 'THE UNITED KINGDOM'

2.312 Allocation of national jurisdiction to a part of the United Kingdom

The Regulation may allocate international jurisdiction to the courts of the United Kingdom, but at some points it will also allocate national jurisdiction to the courts for a part of the United Kingdom. If it allocates jurisdiction to the courts for a particular part of the United Kingdom – such as where parties agree in writing upon the jurisdiction of the High Court in London,[1726] or where the defendant enters an appearance before that court;[1727] or where special jurisdiction[1728] is given to the courts for a place where something happened or was supposed to happen – the court identified will have international and national jurisdiction, and there is no further jurisdictional question to answer.[1729] It also follows that if the particular court is identified by the Regulation, it is not[1730] open to that court to exercise a procedural discretion such as *forum non conveniens* in favour of the courts of another part of the United Kingdom which, *ex hypothesi*, do not have international jurisdiction in the first place.

But where the Regulation allocates international jurisdiction only to the courts of a Member State, and hence to nothing more precise than the courts of the United Kingdom, the work of the Regulation is complete once the United Kingdom has been identified as the Member State with international jurisdiction. In such cases, the further allocation of the case to a court which has national or internal jurisdiction is a matter for internal United Kingdom law. The statement of these rules is the concern of this sixteenth Question.

The rules which provide for these cases are set out in Schedule 4 to the 1982 Act, as amended by the Civil Jurisdiction and Judgments Order 2001,[1731] Schedule 2, paragraph 4. The original version of Schedule 4 to the 1982 Act made provision for national jurisdiction as a reflection, though not a photocopy, of the provisions of the Brussels Convention; these were made to apply to cases where international jurisdiction was ascribed by the Lugano Convention as well.[1732] But the rules as inserted by the 2001 Order,[1733] which take the form of a new Schedule 4 to the 1982 Act, apply whether the international jurisdiction of

---

1726 Regulation 1215/2012, Art. 25.

1727 Article 26.

1728 Articles 7 and 8 of Regulation 1215/2012 mostly give jurisdiction to the courts for a place, or to a court in which a claim is being prosecuted.

1729 Of course, rules which specify whether the High Court or County Court, or some other tribunal, may hear the case will still apply, but as both courts have national jurisdiction, there is no further question of territorial jurisdiction to be concerned with.

1730 On the footing that this conclusion is the correct one in relation to jurisdiction taken by virtue of the Regulation itself: see the material at paras 2.288 *et seq.*, above.

1731 SI 2001/3929. The amendments to that Order, made in SI 2014/2947, do not materially affect the issues discussed at this point.

1732 Civil Jurisdiction and Judgments Act 1991, Sch. 2, para. 11.

1733 SI 2001/3929, Sch. 2, para. 4.

the courts of the United Kingdom is derived from the Regulation (original or recast), the Lugano Convention, or the Brussels Convention. They also apply where there is no international question of jurisdiction, but simply a question as between the national jurisdictions of England, Scotland and Northern Ireland.[1734] It would have been needlessly complex for parallel versions of the intra-UK rules to be drafted so as to differ according to the particular instrument which conferred international jurisdiction on the United Kingdom. Accordingly the version of Schedule 4, as inserted by the 2001 Order, has been applicable to all proceedings instituted on or after 1 March 2002.

Where they are required for this purpose, definitions of domicile are contained in Schedule 1 to the 2001 Order. These definitions closely follow their predecessors in sections 41–45 of the 1982 Act, and have been discussed above. It has also been noted that sections 41–45 of the 1982 Act do not apply when it is necessary to determine the international jurisdiction of the courts for the purposes of the Regulation (original and recast): instead, the rules in Schedule 1 to the 2001 Order do this.[1735] They do still apply to determine the international jurisdiction of the courts of the United Kingdom under the Brussels or Lugano Conventions; but where these instruments confer jurisdiction on the courts of the United Kingdom, the national jurisdiction of the courts of a part of the United Kingdom, including any question of domicile in a part of the United Kingdom, is determined by Schedule 4 as inserted by the 2001 Order.

Where the courts of the United Kingdom have international jurisdiction on the basis of the defendant's domicile, or because section 16 of the 1982 Act confers it, the rules of national jurisdiction are, as explained above, those contained in the amended version of Schedule 4 to the 1982 Act. In other cases where international jurisdiction is given to the courts of the United Kingdom by the Regulation, as with special jurisdiction in relation to trusts,[1736] and in relation to certain consumer contracts, Schedule 1, paragraph 7[1737] identifies which court is to have national jurisdiction under the Regulation: jurisdiction is conferred on the part of the United Kingdom in which the trust or the consumer is domiciled.[1738] The right of the courts of the United Kingdom to exercise their traditional *forum non conveniens* discretion as between themselves will continue to be applicable, because the jurisdictional question which arises for answer is now one of internal United Kingdom law. In those cases where the Regulation confers international jurisdiction on the courts of the United Kingdom, it was explained in the context of analysis of each particular rule how such a case will be allocated as between the courts of the parts of the United Kingdom. It is not proposed to repeat that material here; it may generally be found at the end of each section dealing with the particular provision of the Regulation. But where the United Kingdom has international jurisdiction on the ground that the defendant was domiciled in the United Kingdom, pursuant to Article 4 of the recast Regulation, the rules for sub-allocation within the United Kingdom are detailed and complex. They are noted here; but they do not regulate national jurisdiction in this context alone.

1734 SI 2001/3929, Sch. 2, para. 3, amending Civil Jurisdiction and Judgments Act 1982, s. 16.
1735 SI 2001/2939, Sch. 1, paras 9–12, as amended by SI 2014/2947, Sch. 2, para. 3(11)–(13).
1736 Regulation 1215/2001, Art. 7(6).
1737 As amended by SI 2014/2947, Sch. 2, para. 3(9).
1738 In accordance with 2001 Order, Sch. 1, para. 9.

2.313 Internal jurisdiction in non-international cases

As the Brussels I Regulation is not designed to apply to a case which is wholly internal to a single Member State, then if the case is not one which concerns the international juris-diction of the courts of the United Kingdom, the Regulation does not apply to the case. Typically this will be the case where both parties are English, or a Scottish claimant wishes to sue an English defendant, and so on. In such a case, the only jurisdictional issue is as to the part of the United Kingdom whose courts have national or internal or local jurisdiction. In a civil or commercial matter,[1739] the rules to be applied are those of United Kingdom law; they are to be found in section 16 of, and in Schedule 4 to, the 1982 Act as amended by 2001 Order, Schedule 2, paragraph 4, and which are examined below. For example, therefore, when Kleinwort Benson Ltd, an English merchant bank, sought to sue Glasgow City Council for the return of money paid under a void agreement which had been wrongly supposed to be valid, section 16 of the 1982 Act, and therefore Schedule 4 to the Act, was the legislative text which determined whether the claim could be brought in the English courts, or had to be brought in Scotland.[1740] It follows that Schedule 4 may apply (i) when, in a civil or commercial matter, the courts of the United Kingdom have international juris-diction on the ground that the defendant is domiciled in the United Kingdom,[1741] and (ii) when, in a civil or commercial matter, the defendant is domiciled in the United Kingdom, but no question of international jurisdictional arises, and the issue is simply one of internal United Kingdom law. The remainder of this chapter therefore gives a brief summary of the contents of Schedule 4 to the 1982 Act, as amended.

2.314 Schedule 4 to the 1982 Act: general

The rules set out in Schedule 4 to the 1982 Act are rules of internal United Kingdom law. Their interpretation is not a matter upon which the European Court has competence, for they are not rules of European law. Nor may a court in the United Kingdom, believ-ing that an interpretive ruling on a corresponding provision of the Regulation would be of assistance in its interpretation of Schedule 4, make a request for such a ruling.[1742] The reason appears to be that the English courts would not, as a matter of European law, be bound to apply the ruling given: they would, as a matter of European law, be entitled to thank the Court for its ruling, and then proceed to reach an independent conclusion anyway. Nor is it relevant that, as a matter of United Kingdom law, the referring court would be obliged to, and would indeed, apply the ruling of the court in the case before it: to allow the Court to give a ruling in such a case would, in effect, be to permit the expansion of the jurisdiction of the European Court by individual national legislation.[1743] Even so, as a matter of United

---

1739 Section 16 of the 1982 Act as amended by SI 2001/3929, Sch. 2, para. 3; the exclusions from Art. 1 of the Regulation also exclude the operation of Art. 16. If the matter is not a civil or commercial one, the traditional rules of jurisdiction will apply.

1740 *Kleinwort Benson Ltd v. City of Glasgow DC* [1999] 1 AC 153.

1741 And also when Art. 24 of the Regulation gives exclusive jurisdiction to the courts of the United Kingdom. But in such a case, r. 11 of Sch. 4 will almost always solve the question of national jurisdiction.

1742 C-346/93 *Kleinwort Benson Ltd v. City of Glasgow DC* [1995] ECR I-615.

1743 It is true that in *Kleinwort Benson* the Court appeared to justify its decision that it had no jurisdiction on the ground that the English court had *as a matter of English law* no obligation to follow and apply the ruling of the Court in the interpretation of Sch. 4. But this cannot be correct: the Court had no jurisdiction to make such a finding as to the content of English law in any event; and as the Court of Appeal in *Kleinwort Benson Ltd v. City*

Kingdom law, Schedule 4 is to be interpreted in accordance with the Regulation itself; and the slightly different form of wording as between sections 3 and 16(3) of the 1982 Act reflects only the fact that the wording of the two texts is not in every case identical.

2.315 Schedule 4 to the 1982 Act: detailed provisions

If the courts of the United Kingdom have jurisdiction by reason of Article 24 of the recast Regulation, Schedule 4 will determine national jurisdiction. If the English courts have international jurisdiction by reason of the fact that the defendant is domiciled in the United Kingdom, or no question of international jurisdiction arises because all the geographical connections are within the United Kingdom, the rules in Schedule 4 apply. The structure and detail of Schedule 4 is similar to the Regulation, generally providing that, where the Regulation refers to the United Kingdom, Schedule 4 refers in turn to a part of the United Kingdom. It is sufficient to draw attention here to the points of divergence. In relation to the 15 questions by which jurisdiction under the Regulation was discussed, they are as follows:

(Q1)   The subject-matter scope of Schedule 4 to the 1982 Act is the same as that of the Brussels I Regulation, though the rules of Schedule 4 apply whether or not the Regulation itself applies to the proceedings in question. But Schedule 4 does not apply to certain matters, which are excluded from its scope by section 17 of, and Schedule 5 to, the 1982 Act: (1) proceedings for the winding up of companies; (2) proceedings concerned with the registration or validity of patents, trademarks, etc; (3) proceedings under section 6 of the Protection of Trading Interests Act 1980; (4) appeals from or review of tribunals; (5) certain maintenance cases; (6) proceedings covered by a particular Convention on jurisdiction and judgments, and to which Article 71 of the Regulation gives effect.

(Q2)   The Rules in Schedule 4 do not apply where there is a Convention to which Article 71 of the Regulation applies.[1744]

(Q3)   As to exclusive jurisdiction regardless of domicile, rule 11 of Schedule 4 contains provisions which copy Article 24 of the recast Regulation, except that there is no provision which reproduces Article 24(4) of the Regulation.[1745]

(Q4)   As to submission by appearance, rule 13 of Schedule 4 copies Article 26 of the recast Regulation.

(Q5)   As to jurisdiction in relation to contracts of insurance, the provisions of Section 3 of Chapter II of the Regulation are not reproduced in Schedule 4. In such cases, the other general and contractual provisions of Schedule 4 will have to be applied.

(Q6)   As to jurisdiction in relation to certain consumer contracts, rules 7 to 9 of Schedule 4 reproduce almost exactly the provisions of Section 4 of Chapter II of the Regulation. The only differences reflect the fact that the consumer's relevant connection must be with, or the activity of the other party must be directed to, a part of the United Kingdom; and the rules specifically exclude contracts of insurance.

---

of Glasgow DC [1996] QB 678 later ruled that the English courts were obliged to decide issues under Sch. 4 in harmony with the Convention, this would appear to affect the reasoning given by the Court. The better answer is that a national court cannot unilaterally enlarge the jurisdiction of the European Court.

1744 Schedule 5, para. 6(a) to the 1982 Act as amended by SI 2001/3929, Sch. 2, para. 5.

1745 *Cf* Sch. 5, para. 2 to the 1982 Act.

(Q7)   As to jurisdiction in relation to individual contracts of employment, rule 10 of Schedule 4 reproduces almost exactly the provisions of Section 5 of Chapter II of the Regulation.

(Q8)   As to agreements on the jurisdiction of the courts of a part of the United Kingdom, rule 12 of Schedule 4 enacts a much simplified version of what is now Article 25 of the recast Regulation. As long as the agreement is effective under the law of the part of the United Kingdom whose courts have been nominated, the chosen court has jurisdiction. No formalities as to writing need to be satisfied, and it is to be assumed that the agreement will be given the interpretation which it was intended to have.

(Q9)   As to general jurisdiction based on the domicile of the defendant, rules 1 and 2 of Schedule 4 make provision which is almost exactly the same as that contained in Articles 4 and 5 of the recast Regulation. In cases in which it is necessary to ascertain the part of the United Kingdom in which a corporation, other legal person, or association of persons has its seat, section 43 of the 1982 Act continues to apply.[1746] Accordingly, a corporation or association has its seat in a part of the United Kingdom if, and only if, it has its seat in the United Kingdom, and either it was incorporated or formed under the law of that part, or it was incorporated under the law of a State other than the United Kingdom but its central management and control is exercised in the particular part of the United Kingdom.

(Q10)   As to special jurisdiction over those domiciled in another part of the United Kingdom, rule 3 of Schedule 4 makes provision which resembles, but does not completely copy, the provisions of Article 7 of the recast Regulation.

The significant differences are as follows. For jurisdiction in matters relating to a contract, rule 3(a) provides that the court with special jurisdiction is that for the place of performance of the obligation in question. In other words, the provisions which were introduced into Regulation 44/2001 as Article 5(1)(b) and (c), and which are reproduced as Article 7(1)(b) and (c) of the recast Regulation are not made part of the internal jurisdictional law of the United Kingdom.

Rule 3(h) gives special jurisdiction, in proceedings concerning a debt secured on immovable property or which are brought to determine certain rights in immovable property, to the courts for the part of the United Kingdom in which the property is situated.

Rule 4 gives special jurisdiction to proceedings which have as their object a decision of an organ of a company or other legal person or association of persons, to the part of the United Kingdom in which the company, legal person, or association, has its seat. This is stated to be without prejudice to the other provisions of Schedule 4; and for this purpose and as indicated above, 'seat' is defined by section 43 of the 1982 Act, as amended, rather than by Schedule 1, paragraph 10 to the 2001 Order, which has no provision for identifying a seat within a part of the United Kingdom.

Rules 5 and 6 of Schedule 4 are effectively copies of Articles 8 and 9 of the recast Regulation.

1746 As a result of the amendments made to s. 43 by the 2001 Order, Sch. 2, para. 16. Section 43 will, therefore, apply to cases where international jurisdiction is a matter for the Conventions (but not the Regulation, for which purpose it is replaced by Sch. 1, para. 10 to the 2001 Order), and to all cases within Sch. 4.

(Q11)   As to jurisdiction over those not domiciled in the United Kingdom, there is no reproduction of Article 6 of the recast Regulation, for the traditional jurisdictional rules of the parts of the United Kingdom apply to such a case by force of the Regulation, speaking through Article 6, itself.

(Q12)   As to jurisdiction to obtain provisional or protective relief, Schedule 4, rule 16 corresponds to Article 35 of the recast Regulation.

(Q13)   As to the examination of its own jurisdiction, rules 14 and 15 of Schedule 4 are in effect a copy of Articles 27 and 28(1) and (2) of the recast Regulation, and the obligation on a court to examine its own jurisdiction over a defendant who makes no appearance is the same as under the Regulation.

(Q14)   As to *lis alibi pendens*, though rule 14 means that a court must decline jurisdiction if the courts of another part of the United Kingdom have exclusive jurisdiction regardless of domicile under rule 11, there is no further reproduction of the provisions of the Regulation which deal with *lis alibi pendens*. Articles 29 to 32 of the recast Regulation have no counterpart in Schedule 4.

(Q15)   As to the power of a court to exercise a discretion not to exercise jurisdiction, it is accepted that, when a court is applying the jurisdictional rules of Schedule 4 to the 1982 Act, the doctrine of *forum non conveniens* may still apply when it is contended that the claim should proceed instead in the courts of Scotland or Northern Ireland. The precise legal basis for this conclusion is not wholly clear, but is presumably that the doctrine of *forum non conveniens* is a part of English law which is not specifically excluded by Schedule 4.

CHAPTER 3

Jurisdiction under the Lugano II Convention

3.01 The Lugano II Convention

Three States are party, with the European Union, to the revised Lugano Convention of 30 October 2007, here and elsewhere referred to as 'Lugano II'. Article 73 of Regulation 1215/2012 provides that the Brussels I Regulation is not to affect the application of the Lugano II Convention, and it is therefore necessary to deal with it, if in abbreviated fashion, at this point.

The original Lugano Convention, concluded in 1988, closely reflected the terms of the Brussels Convention. It was revised and remade in 2007 to bring it closely into line with the Brussels I Regulation 44/2001. The parties to the Lugano II Convention are, on the one hand, the European Union (which has taken over the role of the Member States in this respect) and on the other, Iceland, Norway, and Switzerland. Liechtenstein became a member of the European Free Trade Association in 1991, but for reasons peculiar to the manner in which it processes money for those who find it convenient to use its services, did not accede to the Lugano Convention, and therefore remains a non-Contracting State. It is therefore convenient to refer to the three States party to the Lugano II Convention as 'Lugano States'; the other party to the Convention being the European Union, it is convenient to use the designation of 'Member States' to refer to the States which, as members of the European Union, are bound by the Lugano II Convention.

When the Lugano II Convention[1] came into effect, the result was that the rules for the determination of jurisdiction and the effect of foreign judgments were functionally identical to those of the Brussels I Regulation 44/2001, with the result that separate treatment of the Lugano II Convention and the Lugano II States would have been redundant. However, the recast version of the Brussels I Regulation 1215/2012 was not accompanied by any apparent attempt to renegotiate the terms of the Lugano II Convention. As the Swiss electorate has directed its Government to breach the terms of one of its treaties with the European Union,[2] it seems that sitting down to renegotiation of the terms of the Lugano II Convention will not be high on the to do list in Brussels or in Bern. For these reasons, the Lugano II Convention remains, in effect, as a copy of Regulation 44/2001; and a substantial part of the analysis will therefore depend on the way in which the recast Regulation

---

1 The Lugano II Convention is published at [2007] OJ L339/1. For the determination of the European Court that the negotiation of the new Lugano Convention was a matter within the competence of the European Union, rather than the Member States, see Opinion 1/03 *Lugano Convention* [2006] ECR I-1145. An expert Report on the Lugano II Convention by Professor Pocar is published at [2009] OJ C319/1.

2 Referendum of 9 February 2014 on the 'initiative against mass immigration'.

1215/2012 has moved away from Regulation 44/2001 and therefore from the Lugano II Convention.

The Lugano II Convention took effect in the United Kingdom under the general framework of the European Communities Act 1972. For the sake of good order, but also to reflect the fact that the Lugano II Convention was intended to supersede the original version, the original enactment of the Lugano Convention in the United Kingdom was repealed.[3] Supplementary and consequential legislation was adopted[4] in terms closely resembling that which had been made to accompany the original Brussels I Regulation 44/2001.

The principal practical effect of this is that, where there is a question of jurisdiction or the recognition of judgments in civil and commercial matters, which is alleged to touch the legal order of, say, Switzerland – suppose the defendant had a domicile in Switzerland, or the land is situated in Switzerland, or the company had its seat in Switzerland, or there was an agreement on the jurisdiction of a Swiss court, or there is a *lis alibi pendens* in the Swiss courts which may have been seised first – the rules of the Lugano II Convention are used to verify the fact or matter relied on and, if the jurisdictional or judgment-related connection is found to exist, the Lugano II Convention, and the national legislation which implements it, will be used to provide the answer to the issue raised.

It follows that the question whether the defendant is domiciled in Switzerland will be determined in accordance with the provisions of the Lugano II Convention on domicile; the question where the company has its seat for the purposes of the Lugano Convention will be determined by the rules in the Lugano II Convention on the domicile of companies; the question whether the Swiss court or an English court was seised first will be determined by the rules of the Lugano II Convention as these define and determine the date of seisin; and so forth. In other words, where there is alleged to be a relevant Swiss (Icelandic, Norwegian) connection, the Lugano II Convention will be applied to the issue, because it is the instrument which regulates jurisdiction as between the Member States of the European Union, on the one hand, and the Contracting States party to the Lugano II Convention, on the other.[5]

On the other hand, a defendant who is domiciled in Switzerland for the purposes of the Lugano Convention may also have a domicile in, say, England for the purposes of the Brussels I Regulation. In such a case, the defendant will have a domicile in a Member State for the purposes of the Brussels I Regulation, and the Brussels I Regulation will therefore apply to him.[6] If, however, the parties have agreed on the jurisdiction of a Swiss court, Article 23 of the Lugano II Convention will govern the question of its impact on the jurisdiction the English courts. This follows from the hierarchy of jurisdictional rules in the Brussels I Regulation and the Conventions, which applies to the Lugano Conventions the specific provision which is contained in Article 64 of the Lugano II Convention.

---

3 SI 2009/3121, regs 4 and 25.

4 SI 2009/3131.

5 According to the French Supreme Court, that is the case even when the jurisdictional question concerns an agreement for the French courts: *Natixis Banques Populaires SA v. X* (Cass I Civ, 30 Jan 2013). It is not clear that this is correct, though it will rarely make a significant difference, as even after the coming into force of Regulation 1215/2012, the rules of the Brussels I Regulation will frequently be the same as those of the Lugano II Convention.

6 Lugano II Convention, Art. 64, as explained by Pocar [2009] OJ C319/1, [20], where the point is made that the Lugano Convention will apply only if 'the Regulation does not'. That must mean that if the defendant has a domicile in a Member State, the Regulation applies by reason of Art. 64(1), and the point which would have been made by Art. 64(2) does not arise.

In the light of Article 63 of the Lugano II Convention, the Convention will have applied to all proceedings instituted after its coming into effect in relation to the State in question, though the effect of Article 63(2) is to treat it almost as though it had been in force since the date of the original 1988 Lugano Convention.

3.02 The Brussels Convention

The Brussels Convention continues to apply only to the French Overseas Collectivities,[7] namely New Caledonia, French Polynesia, Mayotte, Wallis & Futuna Islands, St Pierre & Miquelon, and to Aruba, which is a non-metropolitan part of the Kingdom of the Netherlands. The governing text of the Brussels Convention is the one which was given the force of law in England by statutory instrument in 1991.[8] Even if a practitioner hopes that the next jurisdictional question, which is just around the corner, will raise the question of the jurisdiction of the courts of Tahiti, which would almost certainly require an expedition to investigate the *locus in quo*, the practical significance of the Brussels Convention is now so close to nil that it is not justifiable to deal with it in this Chapter. Previous editions of this book will have to suffice.

3.03 Interpretation of the Lugano II Convention

The general canons of interpretation applicable to the Brussels I Regulation will apply also to the Lugano II Convention. The general jurisdiction of the courts of the defendant's domicile will continue to be favoured, and exceptions to it will tend to receive an interpretation which will be no broader than is necessary to achieve the purposes of the particular rule. The autonomous definitions of terms will continue to be applicable; and the provisions for *lis alibi pendens* will continue to do the most they can to prevent a situation of parallel litigation of disputes.

The procedural mechanisms for securing consistency or uniformity as between the Brussels I Regulation and the Lugano II Conventions are made more complicated by the fact that the Lugano States are not Member States of the European Union, and therefore have neither the general obligation to pay attention to decisions of the European Court nor the power to refer questions to that Court for a preliminary ruling. The original Lugano Convention dealt with this slightly unsatisfactory state of affairs by means of a Protocol which contained declarations by which the Member States of the European Union, and the EFTA States, stating that their respective courts were to 'pay due account' to decisions handed down in other countries. This ramshackle mechanism was never really put to the test;[9] and anyway, it was not really appropriate when the Lugano II Convention was made as a treaty by the European Union rather than by the Member States.

---

7 Until 28 March 2003, known as Territories (territoires d'outre-mer, or 'TOM's).

8 SI 2000/1824.

9 In C-394/07 *Gambazzi v. Daimler Chrysler Canada Inc* [2009] ECR I-2563 the European Court (for the first time, so far as can be seen) made reference to the obligation to pay attention to the decisions of courts of Contracting States (*in casu*, the Swiss Federal Tribunal so far as it had made a ruling at an earlier stage of the complex litigation between the parties). But it is not clear that this was anything other than a cosmetic or diplomatic reference, as nothing appeared to flow from it.

Protocol 2 to the Lugano II Convention requires any court applying it to have regard to any relevant decision in relation to the original Lugano Convention and on the Brussels I Regulation 44/2001,[10] but it goes further. If a Member State refers a question on the interpretation of the Lugano Convention to the European Court, a Lugano State is entitled to make written submissions to the European Court; and this opportunity is widened to allow the Lugano States to make submissions when references are made in respect of the Brussels I Regulation. All this is designed to produce harmonious decisions as between the respective instruments; this is bound to suffer if amendment of the Lugano II Convention, in the light of the recast Brussels I Regulation 1215/2012, is derailed by the Swiss referendum result referred to above.

3.04 The jurisdictional rules of the Lugano II Convention

The jurisdictional rules of the Lugano II Convention are more or less identical with those of the original Brussels I Regulation 44/2001, from which they were copied. But as these diverge from the recast Regulation 1215/2012, it is sensible to summarise the differences here, by considering the 16 questions which framed the analysis for the purposes of the recast Brussels I Regulation 1215/2012, to show how the provisions of the Lugano II Convention differ from the corresponding provisions of that Regulation. As explained above, these questions will apply, and those which were posed in relation to the Regulation will not, when the defendant is domiciled in a Lugano II Contracting State, in the sense of a State Party to a Convention but not bound by the Regulation; or the proceedings concern rights *in rem* in land, etc.,[11] in such a State; or there is an agreement on choice of court for the courts of such a State; or there is submission by appearance before the courts of such a State; or there is a *lis alibi pendens* before the courts of such a State.

3.05 (Q1) Scope of the Convention: Lugano II Articles 1 and 63

Article 1 of the Lugano II Convention, which defines its material scope, is the same as Article 1 of Regulation 44/2001, and therefore substantially the same as Article 1 of Regulation 1215/2012.

The one point on which the scope of the Lugano II Convention might be thought to diverge from the recast Regulation 1215/2012 is over the exclusion of 'arbitration' from the material scope of Regulation 1215/2012; but it is very unlikely that any divergence is measurable, depending, in effect, on whether there is any difference between the original and recast Brussels I Regulations on this matter. The view taken here is that although Regulation 1215/2012 contains statements in the Recitals which were designed to indicate that the recast Regulation took more account of arbitration proceedings than had been the case under the original Regulation 44/2001, these statements are almost entirely cosmetic. Recital (12) to Regulation 1215/2012 does little more than state what was already

---

10 There would be nothing but arid technicality in a contention that Art. 64(1) does not mention Regulation 1215/2012 (which it obviously could not have done) and that Protocol 2 to the Lugano II Convention does not therefore direct attention to rulings on this Regulation. And anyway, it will be some time yet before the interpretation of Regulation 1215/2012 comes before the European Court.

11 That is to say, a factor which produces exclusive jurisdiction regardless of domicile.

known; and the specific reference, in Article 73(2) of the recast Regulation, to the New York Convention, adds nothing of substance to the more general statement about the integrity of Conventions on particular matters which was in the Article 71 of Regulation 44/2001 and Regulation 1215/2012. The sum and substance of this is that the material scope of the Lugano II Regulation will be essentially the same as that of the Brussels I Regulation 1215/2012, because this has changed very little, if at all, from the material scope of Regulation 44/2001.[12]

So far as the temporal scope of the Lugano II Convention is concerned, there is nothing to say. Its jurisdictional provisions will apply in all proceedings instituted after its commencement date in the Member State bound by the Convention. The personal scope of the Lugano II Convention was never complicated: it applies without regard to the nationality of claimant[13] or defendant.

As to the question of the international scope of the Lugano II Convention, the preamble to the Convention makes, as the Regulation now does not, explicit reference to its purpose being to determine the international jurisdiction of the courts of the parties to the Convention. It follows that an element of internationality in the facts will be required if the Lugano II Convention is to apply. In the context of English proceedings, though, such an element will inevitably be present if there is a factual connection which makes the Lugano Convention applicable in the first place. This is therefore no longer an issue in relation to the application of the Lugano II Convention in England.

The result of all of this is that the material examined in Chapter 2 in relation to the corresponding issue of scope which was discussed in relation to the Brussels I Regulation will be transferable to and applicable in the context of the Lugano II Convention.

3.06 (Q2) Jurisdiction derived from other Conventions: Lugano II Article 67

So far as concerns jurisdiction derived from other international Conventions on particular matters, Article 67 of the Lugano II Convention is functionally identical to Article 71 of the Brussels I Regulation, save that Article 67 of the Lugano II Convention makes provision for the States which are not Member States to enter into further such Conventions. There is no obvious reason to suppose that the restrictive way in which Article 71 of the Brussels I Regulation has been interpreted by the European Court, appearing to limit the scope within which the rules of the particular Convention will be permitted to apply, will not be considered (by it, at least) to apply with equal force to the interpretation of Article 67 of the Lugano II Convention. On the other hand, if the effect of the jurisprudence of the Court really is that the particular Convention may only have effect in such a way as not to contradict the provisions of the Brussels I Regulation, it may not be regarded as persuasive by the courts of the non-Member States party to the Lugano Convention.

---

12 The material scope of the Brussels Convention will be the same. It will be very interesting to see whether a Swiss court would be willing to accept C-49/12 *HMRC v. Sunico ApS* EU:C:2013:545, [2014] QB 391, which decides that English proceedings for damages against a defendant engaged in tax fraud are brought in a civil or commercial matter, and which means that such a judgment may be enforced under Chapter III of the Regulation, as an accurate statement of the material scope of the Lugano II Convention.

13 C-412/98 *Group Josi Reinsurance SA v. Universal General Insurance Co* [2000] ECR I-5925.

3.07 (Q3) Exclusive jurisdiction regardless of domicile: Lugano II Article 22

Article 22 of the Lugano II Convention corresponds very closely to Article 24 of the recast Brussels I Regulation 1215/2012. The general principle is, of course, common to all the instruments alike: if there is a connection of the kind listed in Article 24 of the Brussels I Regulation to a Lugano State, it is very likely that Article 22 of the Lugano II Convention will give exclusive jurisdiction regardless of domicile to the courts of that Lugano State. There are no substantial divergences between the text of the corresponding Articles; the discussion in Chapter 2 will be equally applicable to Article 22 of the Lugano II Convention.

3.08 (Q4) Jurisdiction by entering an appearance: Lugano II Article 24

Article 24 of the Lugano Convention is identical to Article 26 of Regulation 1215/2012, save for one point. The Lugano II Convention does not reproduce (or pre-produce) the provision which forms the second paragraph of Article 26 of the Brussels I Regulation 1215/2012, and there is therefore no obligation on the court before which an insured, consumer, or employee appears to explain that he could, if he wished to, object to the jurisdiction of the court which the claimant has seised. It is improbable that such a requirement would be read into Article 24 of the Lugano II Convention.

3.09 (Q5) Privileged jurisdiction in relation to insurance: Lugano II Articles 8 to 14

The substance of Section 3 of Chapter II of the Lugano II Convention is for all practical purposes the same as that of the Brussels I Regulation 1215/2012, with the consequence that the analysis proposed in Chapter 2 is applicable to the Lugano II Convention. Only the numbering is altered.

3.10 (Q6) Privileged jurisdiction in relation to consumer contracts: Lugano II Articles 15 to 17

The jurisdictional rules of the recast Brussels I Regulation 1215/2012, which in Section 4 of Chapter II deal with certain consumer contracts, differ in one significant respect from the corresponding provisions of the Lugano II Convention. Where proceedings are brought by the consumer against a professional who does not have a domicile in a Member State, the Lugano II Convention does not provide that the consumer may sue in the courts of his domicile unless the professional has a branch in a Member State out of the operations of which the dispute arises, in which circumstance the professional is deemed to be domiciled in that Member State.[14] The widening of privileged jurisdiction in Article 18(1) of Regulation 1215/2012 is not reflected in the Lugano II Convention.

---

14 Article 15(2) of the Lugano II Convention.

3.11 (Q7) Privileged jurisdiction over individual contracts of employment: Lugano II Articles 18 to 21

The jurisdictional rules of the recast Brussels I Regulation 1215/2012, which in Section 5 of Chapter II deal with individual contracts of employment, differ in two significant respect from the corresponding provisions in the Lugano II Convention. Where proceedings are brought by the employee against an employer who does not have a domicile in a Member State (and in cases in which the dispute does not arise out of the operations of a branch situated in a Member State), the Lugano II Convention does not give the employee the option of suing in the courts for the place in the Member State in which he carries out the duties of the employment, or, if there is no such place, in the courts for the place where the business which engaged him was or is situated. The widening of privileged jurisdiction in Article 21(2) of Regulation 1215/2012 is not reflected in the Lugano II Convention.

The second difference is that the unfortunate decision of the European Court in *GlaxoSmithKline v. Rouard*,[15] which held that jurisdiction by joinder of a co-defendant was unavailable to an employee in matters which fell within Section 5 of Chapter II, presumably remains applicable to the Lugano II Convention. It was necessary for this decision to be reversed by legislation in Regulation 1215/2012,[16] but it would take a bold reading of the Lugano II Regulation to treat it as though it did not produce the result which *GlaxoSmithKline v. Rouard* had approved.

It is also worth noting (though it is not directly a matter of jurisdiction) that if a court exercises jurisdiction in a way which conflicts with Section 5 of Chapter II of the Lugano II Regulation, this fact does not justify a court in another State bound by the Convention in refusing to recognise the judgment. Article 35(1) of the Lugano II Convention does not reflect the full extent of the rule which appears in the recast Brussels I Regulation 1215/2012 as Article 45(1)(e)(i), any more than Article 35(1) of the original Regulation 44/2001 had done.

3.12 (Q8) Agreements on jurisdiction for the courts of a Lugano State: Lugano II Article 23

The law on jurisdiction agreements underwent considerable development, which some see as improvement, in the recast Brussels I Regulation 1215/2012. When set alongside Articles 25 and 31(2) of the recast Brussels I Regulation, it can be seen that Article 23 of the Lugano II Convention is considerably different. The principal differences are as follows.

First, according to its Article 23(1), the application of Article 23 of the Lugano II Convention depends on one of the parties to the agreement on jurisdiction being domiciled in a State to which the Lugano II Convention applies: Brussels I Regulation 1215/2012 no longer makes such a requirement. But where this condition is not met, the Lugano II Convention provides that the States to which the Convention applies have no jurisdiction unless and until the designated court has declined jurisdiction.[17]

---

15 C-462/06, [2008] ECR I-3965.

16 Article 20(1) of Regulation 1215/2012.

17 The material date for the domicile is that of the conclusion of the contract, rather than the date of proceedings but though this was agreed, it was decided not to make the point in the text of the Convention (which seems rather strange): see Pocar [2009] OJ C319/1, [103].

Second, the Lugano II Convention does not provide, in express terms at least, that the jurisdiction agreement shall be effective unless it is null and void as to its substantive validity under the law of the State whose courts have been chosen. This qualification was introduced into the recast Brussels I Regulation to respond to a concern that the Regulation made no sufficient provision for an argument, which will sometimes be well-founded, that there was an objection to the alleged agreement on jurisdiction which is not really a matter of formal validity, or for which compliance with the requirement of writing would be a sufficient protection. While it is obviously right that complaints of, for example, duress, forgery, mistake, misrepresentation, lack of certainty or precision, etc., be dealt with, it is, for reasons which have been set out in Chapter 2, not clear that the form of words inserted into Article 25 of Regulation 1215/2012 was the way to go about it. But in the absence of such wording in Article 23 of the Lugano II Convention, a court will simply ask itself whether there is an agreement, in the form provided for in Article 23(1), for the jurisdiction of a court. An autonomous interpretation of 'agreement' will have to bear the burden of dealing with objections which go to the legal validity of the agreement; the question will simply be whether the person to be held to the alleged agreement on jurisdiction agreed in writing to the jurisdiction of the court.

Third, a very significant change was made by the recast Brussels I Regulation 1215/2012 to the rule of temporal priority as it applies to proceedings within the scope of that Regulation. Regulation 1215/2015 has the effect that where a court has been seised prior to the institution of proceedings in a court evidently designated by an agreement that it should have exclusive jurisdiction, the non-designated court is required, in most circumstances, to stay its proceedings and allow the court identified in the alleged agreement to determine whether it has exclusive jurisdiction by virtue of that alleged agreement. But this innovation does not apply to proceedings within the scope of the Lugano II Convention, which remain regulated by the original rule of strict temporal priority. If, for example, the Swiss courts are seised of proceedings in respect of a claim before proceedings between the same parties are instituted in England in accordance with an agreement for the exclusive jurisdiction of the English courts, the English court will be required to consider itself to be second seised, and to wait for (and abide by) the decision of the Swiss court on whether it has jurisdiction. To put the point another way, proceedings which have and bring about the effect which was exemplified by *Erich Gasser GmbH v. MISAT Srl*[18] will have the effect which they had in that case when deployed within the framework of the Lugano II Convention. It is possible, one supposes, that the European Court might overrule *Erich Gasser*, or the courts of a Contracting State refuse to apply it, but there is no rational basis to suppose that either of these things may happen.

3.13 (Q9) Defendant domiciled in the United Kingdom: Lugano II Article 2

General jurisdiction on the basis of the domicile of the defendant is the linchpin of the Lugano II Convention as it is – though the definition of domicile is slightly different – of the Brussels I Regulation, and Article 2 of the Convention is identical to Article 4 of the recast Brussels I Regulation.

---

18 C-116/02, [2003] ECR I-14693.

For the purpose of the Lugano II Convention, the definition of the domicile of an individual is given by section 41A of Civil Jurisdiction and Judgments Act 1982.[19] The definition of the seat of a company for the purpose of Article 22(2) of the Lugano II Convention is given in section 43A of the 1982 Act; and the deemed domicile of insurers, professionals and employers in the United Kingdom is given by section 44A of the Act. The content of the definition of domicile is, however, the same for the Convention and the Regulation alike.

3.14 (Q10) Special jurisdiction over defendant domiciled only in another Contracting State: Lugano II Articles 5 to 7

The provisions of the Lugano II Convention which make provision for special jurisdiction over defendants domiciled in another State to which the Convention applies are very similar to those set out in Articles 7 to 9 of the recast Regulation 1215/2012. There are only two real points of difference to be noted.

First, special jurisdiction in matters relating to maintenance is provided for by Article 5(2) of the Lugano II Convention. The corresponding provision was removed from the Brussels I Regulation, and does not appear in the recast Regulation, because a dedicated European Regulation[20] now makes comprehensive provision for matters of maintenance.

Second, the Lugano II Convention contains no provision for special jurisdiction over a defendant in a claim for the recovery, on the basis of ownership, of a cultural object.

It may be possible to argue that the strictness or restrictiveness in interpretation which has been developed in relation to Article 8(1) of Regulation 1215/2012 does not necessarily apply to the Lugano Convention.[21] But the authority is not sufficiently robust to make the contention a solid one.

3.15 (Q11) Residual jurisdiction over defendant without a domicile in a Contracting State: Lugano II Article 4

Subject to what was said above about employers (sued by employees) and professionals (dealing with consumers), for which Article 6 of the recast Brussels I Regulation 1215/2012 makes reference for the sake of good order, Article 4 of the Lugano II Convention is in substance identical with Article 6 of the recast Regulation 1215/2012.

3.16 (Q12) Jurisdiction to order provisional including protective measures: Lugano II Article 31

Article 31 of the Lugano II Regulation is identical to Article 35 of the recast Regulation 1215/2012.

---

19 Inserted by SI 2009/3131.
20 Regulation 4/2009.
21 *Cf* the approach in *Gard Marine & Energy Ltd v. Lloyd Tunnicliffe* [2009] EWHC 2388 (Comm), [2010] Lloyd's Rep IR 62.

3.17 (Q13) Examination of jurisdiction on limited grounds: Lugano II Articles 25 and 26

The obligation which is placed on a court by Article 25 of the Lugano II Convention, to relinquish jurisdiction if it is seised of a claim which is principally concerned with a matter over which the courts of another State bound by the Convention have exclusive jurisdiction, regardless of domicile, under Article 22 is identical to that set out in Article 27 of the recast Brussels I Regulation. The obligations placed on the court by Article 26 of the Lugano II Regulation, to make a limited examination of the basis for its jurisdiction, and to check that proper efforts have been made to serve a defendant who has not appeared, are identical to those in Article 28 of the recast Regulation.

3.18 (Q14) *Lis pendens* in another State to which the Convention applies: Lugano II Articles 27 to 30

The provisions for preventing or managing a situation of *lis pendens* before the courts of two States, which are set out in Articles 27 to 30 of the Lugano II Convention, are substantially the same as those in Articles 29 to 32 of the recast Brussels I Regulation, but with the following points of difference.

First, and as has been explained above, the Lugano II Convention makes no specific provision for the case in which the court seised second has or appears to have exclusive jurisdiction under the terms of an agreement which complies with the requirements of Article 23 of the Lugano II Convention. This means that proceedings brought first in a different court may torpedo the jurisdiction agreement. It is very hard to see how the Lugano II Convention might be interpreted as though it contained the words inserted into the recast Brussels I Regulation as Article 31(2)–(4) (and, for the sake of good order, as the opening words of Article 29(1) of that Regulation). The argument has been advanced that as *Erich Gasser GmbH v. MISAT Srl* was not a decision on the interpretation of the Lugano II Convention, a court dealing with the interpretation of the Lugano II Convention would be entitled to ignore it. How this is supposed to be consistent with Article 1(1) of Protocol 2 to the Lugano II Convention is not apparent. If – which is not admitted – *Erich Gasser* is to be regarded as a completely bad decision, on the basis (one supposes) that the majority of proceedings brought outside a court which has been designated for some kinds of action are brought illicitly, it will require an amendment to be made to the Convention to do anything about it.

Second, there is no formal mechanism, corresponding to Article 29(2) of the recast Regulation 1215/2012, for a court to be asked to confirm the date on which it was seised for the purpose of the Convention. It is hard to see that this has any practical significance.

Third, the Lugano II Convention does not say in express terms, as it is said in Article 32 of the recast Regulation, that the 'authority responsible for service' is the first authority to which the documents for service are delivered. This probably elucidates what was already the settled understanding of Article 30 of the Lugano II Convention.

Fourth, the Lugano II Convention deals more helpfully than does the Brussels I Regulation with the question whether proceedings before a body are to be seen as before a court for the purpose of ascertaining the date of seisin. This, no doubt, reflects the fact that in two of the three Contracting States a process of conciliation is required to precede the opening of more obviously adversary proceedings. Article 62 of the Convention gives a definition of 'court' which is more illuminating than anything found in the Brussels I Regulation.[22] This is likely to mean that a dispute, which has been subjected to a conciliation process which is recognised in the Contracting State concerned as being sufficiently (or even necessarily) part of the process of civil dispute resolution, will be pending in the State in question from the date of institution of the conciliation, rather than only from the date of judicial proceedings instituted after the failure of conciliation;[23] and the 'courts' of that country will remain seised, without hiatus, if the dispute moves from conciliatory body to regular court in the manner and within the time frame prescribed by the law of that State.

3.19 (Q15) *Lis pendens* in a State in which the Lugano II Convention does not apply; and other points of contact with such a State

There is nothing in the Lugano II Convention which corresponds to Articles 33 and 34 of the recast Brussels I Regulation 1215/2012. If the question has to be addressed whether a court which has jurisdiction on the basis of the Lugano II Convention should take account – and if so, what account – of points of connection with a State in which the Lugano II Convention does not apply, it will require a court to consider the extent to which it may, for example, apply the provisions of the Convention by analogy, or with reflexive effect.

However, this is far more likely to be an issue for the courts of Iceland, Norway and Switzerland than it is for the courts of the United Kingdom, and there is no need to say any more than was said in Chapter 2.

3.20 (Q16) International jurisdiction given by the Conventions to the courts of the United Kingdom

Where the Lugano Convention gives international jurisdiction to the courts of the United Kingdom, it is for the law of the United Kingdom to specify the part of the United Kingdom whose courts have jurisdiction in the particular case. As with the case where international jurisdiction is conferred by the Brussels I Regulation, this is governed by Schedule 4 to the 1982 Act as amended by Schedule 2 to the 2001 Order.

---

22 The Lugano II Convention states as follows: 'Article 62: *Definition of the term "court"*. For the purposes of this Convention, the expression "court" shall include any authorities designated by a State bound by this Convention as having jurisdiction in the matters falling within the scope of this Convention.'

23 *Deutsche Bank AG v. Petromena ASA* [2013] EWHC 3065 (Comm); *Lehman Brothers Finance AG v. Klaus Tschira Stiftung GmbH* [2014] EWHC 2782 (Ch): Norwegian and Swiss conciliation procedures, respectively. It may be different if the conciliatory body appears to be less independent but more like a process before a civil servant in a government ministry.

CHAPTER 4

The Common Law Rules of Jurisdiction

INTRODUCTORY MATTERS

4.01 Introduction

In this chapter we examine what are sometimes called the traditional,[1] or common law,[2] rules of jurisdiction.[3] Whatever they are called, they apply in two discrete areas which must be thought about separately: in cases which fall wholly outside the domain of the Brussels I Regulation,[4] where they may be called 'common law rules', and in cases where their application is required by Article 6 of the Brussels I Regulation 1215/2012, in which context they may be called 'residual rules'.

Suppose that, in the light of the material looked at in Chapters 2 and 3, the direct rules set out in Chapter II of the Regulation do not determine the jurisdiction of the court. This may be because the subject matter of the claim lies outside the scope of the Regulation, or because even though the subject matter of the claim falls within the scope of the Regulation, Article 6 directs the court to use its own traditional rules on the taking of jurisdiction.[5] In the former case, the Regulation makes no claim at all to regulate the jurisdiction of courts, and the jurisdictional rules set out in this chapter apply without modification, though if the reason for the matter falling outside the scope of the Brussels I Regulation also means that the matter falls within the domain of (say) the Insolvency Regulation[6] or the Matrimonial Regulation,[7] the rules in those instruments will apply in place of the rules which will be examined in this chapter.[8]

But in the latter case, the result of taking up and incorporating jurisdictional rules from national law into the Regulation is that the rules undergo certain modifications, and their

---

1 Except for the fact that much of the law is modern.

2 Except for the fact that much of the law is statutory, or at least contained in Civil Procedure Rules.

3 For the proposition that 'jurisdiction' is a word with many meanings, and that care needs to be taken to identify the particular sense in which it is being used – a warning which has been issued on many occasions – see for example *Fourie v. Le Roux* [2007] UKHL 1, [2007] 1 WLR 320, [25].

4 Regulation 1215/2012. In fact, the common law rules apply to cases which fall outside the domain of the Regulation, and to cases which fall within it in accordance with what is now Art. 6 of Regulation 1215/2012 (the same is true for Regulation 44/2001 and the Lugano II Convention, where Art. 4 does the job which Art. 6 now does in Regulation 1215/2012).

5 There is no need to consider the third possibility, that the matter falls outside the temporal scope of the Regulation, because, if it does, it will fall within the temporal scope of the original Regulation 44/2001.

6 Regulation (EC) 1346/2000.

7 Regulation (EC) 2201/2003 ('Brussels II'), replacing Regulation (EC) 1347/2000.

8 They also may provide, in residual cases, for the application of the jurisdictional rules of the common law.

character is slightly changed, most obviously in that they become subject to the provisions of the Regulation on *lis alibi pendens*.[9]

This chapter examines these jurisdictional rules. It does not examine the provisions of the Insolvency or Matrimonial Regulations, as these particular instruments are more appropriately examined in specialist works. It therefore limits itself to the traditional rules of the common law.

THE COMMON LAW PRINCIPLES OF JURISDICTION

4.02 General

The rules themselves can be summarised very simply: the jurisdiction of the court depends upon service of process. Whereas the scheme of the rules examined in Chapter 2 is that where the Regulation provides that there is jurisdiction the claimant is entitled to serve the claim form, the common law views the issue in mirror image: where the claimant has served the claim form, with permission where this is needed, the court will have jurisdiction.

The question then becomes one of how and when the claimant may serve process upon a defendant. If the defendant is present within the territorial jurisdiction of the court, the claimant has a right to serve him. If the defendant is not within the territorial jurisdiction of the court, and has not appointed an agent within the jurisdiction to accept service of process on his behalf, the claimant has no right to serve him. Instead, permission must be obtained from the court for service to be made out of the jurisdiction, unless legislation[10] provides that the claim is one in which service out of the jurisdiction may be made without prior permission.

A defendant who submits to the jurisdiction of the English court confirms the court's personal[11] jurisdiction over him:[12] any points which might have been raised to dispute that jurisdiction, aside from the points of subject matter jurisdiction examined below, are made redundant by the defendant's personal submission to the jurisdiction of the court. Submission may take several forms. The most obvious is by acknowledging service of process and not invoking the procedure to dispute the jurisdiction of the court, which is examined in the following chapter. A person who has been served may fail to tick the box which indicates that he intends to dispute the jurisdiction, though the box-ticking is not decisive (many people fail to tick boxes, by oversight) and its absence is not conclusive. A defendant may still dispute the jurisdiction within the timeframe given by the rules so long as he has done nothing unequivocal to waive his privilege to dispute the jurisdiction; and a failure to tick a box on a form is not an unequivocal act.[13] On the other hand, a defendant

---

9 See above, para. 2.310.

10 There is rather little such legislation; see below, para. 4.56.

11 An absence of subject matter jurisdiction, however, cannot be cured (is not affected) by the purported submission of the parties: see below, para. 4.05.

12 *Derby & Co Ltd v. Larsson* [1976] 1 WLR 202 (HL); *Republic of Liberia v. Gulf Oceanic Inc* [1985] 1 Lloyd's Rep 539; *Balkanbank v. Taher (No 2)* [1995] 1 WLR 1067; *SMAY Investments Ltd v. Sachdev* [2003] EWHC 474 (Ch), [2003] 1 WLR 1973.

13 *IBS Technologies (Pvt) Ltd v. APM Technologies SA (No 1)* (unrep.), 7 April 2003.

who ticks the box to indicate his intention to dispute the jurisdiction but who fails to follow with an application to that effect may be held to have submitted after all.[14]

A party who appoints a solicitor with authority[15] to accept service of process within the jurisdiction submits to the jurisdiction.[16] A litigant who had previously invoked the jurisdiction of the court will usually be taken to have submitted generally to the jurisdiction of the court: he will not be heard to say that he submitted for some purposes convenient to him, but not for others which he finds to be somewhat less congenial,[17] though common sense places limits on the argument.

Matters stand differently for the defendant who has been served out of the jurisdiction but who objects to the jurisdiction of the English court, and who seeks to have service on him set aside. To begin with, such a defendant may dispute the jurisdiction of the court, and may do so on a claim-by-claim basis, for the court's grant of permission to serve out is assessed separately for each distinct claim made.[18] However, once a defendant has submitted to the jurisdiction, only in rare cases will he be permitted to have second thoughts and withdraw the submission. In *Somportex Ltd v. Philadelphia Chewing Gum Corp*[19] an American company was served out of the jurisdiction, and did the equivalent[20] of acknowledging service without indicating an intention[21] to dispute the jurisdiction. In due course it applied to be allowed to withdraw the appearance, to be treated as though it had made no response whatever to the writ served on it.[22] The Court of Appeal considered that as the original decision had been taken on the basis of professional advice, a change of heart or professional advice was not sufficient to allow the appearance to be withdrawn. The courts have since followed the same general line, refusing to allow a party who has submitted to the jurisdiction, but who now sees some perceived advantage in subsequently changing its mind, to be treated as not having submitted after all. Indeed, in a number of cases it has expressed its refusal in notably strong terms.[23]

---

14 *Maple Leaf Macro Volatility Master Fund v. Rouvroy* [2009] EWHC 257 (Comm), [2009] 1 Lloyd's Rep 475, [186]–[187]. If it is contended that the defendant ticked the box to indicate an intention to dispute the jurisdiction but then acted in such a way as to show that he had abandoned that position, the conduct to which the claimant points will need to be 'wholly unequivocal': *SMAY Investments Ltd v. Sachdev* [2003] EWHC 474 (Ch), [2003] 1 WLR 1973, [41]; *Pacific International Sports Clubs Ltd v. Soccer Marketing International Ltd* [2009] EWHC 1839 (Ch), [29]; *Zumax Nigeria Ltd v. First City Monument Bank Ltd* [2014] EWHC 2075 (Ch).

15 But the extent of the submission must be limited by the scope of the authority given.

16 *Sphere Drake Insurance plc v. Gunes Sigorta AS* [1987] 1 Lloyd's Rep 139. Questions of construction of the authorisation will be dealt with objectively, as though the document were a commercial contract: *Actavis Group HF v. Eli Lilly & Co* [2013] EWCA Civ 517, [2013] RPC 37.

17 *Republic of Liberia v. Gulf Oceanic Inc* [1985] 1 Lloyd's Rep 539; *Balkanbank v. Taher (No 2)* [1995] 1 WLR 1067; *Glencore International AG v. Exter Shipping Ltd* [2002] EWCA Civ 528, [2002] 2 All ER (Comm) 1; *Marketmaker Technology Ltd v. CMC Group plc* [2008] EWHC 1556 (QB).

18 *Glencore International AG v. Exter Shipping Ltd* [2002] EWCA Civ 528, [2002] 2 All ER (Comm) 1: it is impermissible to obtain service out in respect of a claim which, standing alone, would not have justified a grant of permission by the device of including it in a claim form which does contain a claim or claims for which permission is available.

19 [1968] 3 All ER 26. In due course the US courts held that the English default judgment, which was entered when the defendant walked away from the English proceedings, was entitled to be enforced in the US: *Somportex Ltd v. Philadelphia Chewing Gum Corp* 453 F 2d 435 (1971).

20 That is to say, it entered a conditional appearance, but which it later sought to withdraw altogether.

21 In fact, it did give that impression to begin with, but then changed its mind.

22 Evidently the reason had to do with the enforceability of any English judgment in the United States.

23 *Glencore International AG v. Exter Shipping Ltd* [2002] EWCA Civ 528, [2002] 2 All ER (Comm) 1; *CNA Insurance Co Ltd v. Office Depot International (UK) Ltd* [2005] EWHC 456 (Comm), [2005] Lloyd's Rep 658, [2007] Lloyd's Rep IR 89 (the judgment appears to have been reported twice).

4.03 Consequences of service effected within the jurisdiction

Where jurisdiction is asserted under the rules of the common law, a significant question is whether service of process was made in accordance with the how-and-when-and-where rules which govern such service: these are examined in brief in Chapter 5. If service has taken place in apparent accordance with these procedural rules, the jurisdiction of the court may still be disputed on the ground that there was no lawful basis for service to have been made, but unless the defendant is able to say that the Brussels I Regulation, or Lugano II Convention, or some other statute, provided that he was not subject to the jurisdiction of the English court in respect of the claim, and that the claimant therefore had no right to serve him, there is little scope for such arguments to be advanced.

If an application to dispute the jurisdiction succeeds, the court will declare that it has no jurisdiction, and service will necessarily be set aside. However, even though a defendant may not be able to dispute the propriety of service and the existence of jurisdiction, if the defendant wishes the court to not exercise the jurisdiction it has, and to decline to hear the case on the basis that the proper forum lies elsewhere, he may apply for a stay of the proceedings.[24] If this application succeeds, the court will remain seised of the case,[25] but will suspend the hearing of it, leaving[26] the claimant to bring proceedings elsewhere. In cases where it is appropriate to do so, the court may lift the stay at a later date and allow the case to proceed; alternatively, it may resume the proceedings after judgment has been given in the foreign court. But in most cases the stay of proceedings is never lifted and the case does not proceed in England.

The power to grant a stay of proceedings is part of the court's inherent power to control its own procedure.[27] As the jurisdiction of the High Court based on service within the jurisdiction is an inherent jurisdiction, not created by or dependent on any statute,[28] the inherent power to control the exercise of that jurisdiction is a natural adjunct to it.[29]

4.04 Service out of the jurisdiction

If service has to be made out of the jurisdiction, and the case is not one of the relatively rare[30] ones in which a statute provides that service may be made out of the jurisdiction of England and Wales[31] without the need to obtain permission in advance, the claimant must obtain an order granting him permission to make that service,[32] and he must then serve

---

24 See paras 4.16 *et seq.*, below.

25 *The Alexandros T* [2013] UKSC 70, [2014] 1 Lloyd's Rep 225.

26 Not *require* as the court generally has no power to order proceedings to be brought, whether in a foreign jurisdiction or elsewhere.

27 Senior Courts Act 1981, s. 49(3).

28 Senior Courts Act 1981, s. 19.

29 The significance of this is plain when considering the inherent power to stay proceedings founded on a jurisdiction conferred and defined by statute or by international instrument.

30 Though always remembering that where the Brussels I Regulation gives the court jurisdiction, service out may be made without the need to obtain permission. It is outside the context of the Regulation that this is rare.

31 In cases in which service may be made out of England without the need to obtain permission, the Civil Procedure Rules draw a further distinction between service in Scotland and Northern Ireland (CPR r. 6.32), and service out of the United Kingdom (CPR r. 6.33). For present purposes, the two cases may be treated alike.

32 In cases where the Brussels I Regulation or the Brussels or Lugano Convention give the court direct jurisdiction, service out is permitted as of right: CPR r. 6.33(1), (2). Other statutes may allow service to be made out of the jurisdiction without permission, under CPR r. 6.33(3), on which see further below, para. 4.56, but it

in the manner prescribed for such a case.[33] If permission is granted, it is the service made pursuant to that order which gives the court jurisdiction over the defendant in respect of the claim set out in the claim form.

The defendant may, however, challenge the grant of permission to serve, and therefore the service made pursuant to it, on either or both of two broad grounds. First, he may contend that the court had, on the facts of the case, no basis in law for granting the claimant permission to serve process out of the jurisdiction. If this argument is sustained, the court will declare that it has no jurisdiction, will set aside the order for permission to serve out, and will set aside service of the claim form. Second, he may argue that, even though the court had a basis in law to grant permission to serve out, the case was not a proper one for the exercise of that power, and that the order should, in all the circumstances, not have been made. If this argument is sustained, the outcome will be the same: the court will declare that it has no jurisdiction, and will set aside the order granting permission, together with service of the claim form. And the defendant-applicant will frequently advance both arguments in support of his application, as there is no inconsistency between them.

4.05 Cases where jurisdiction at common law does not and cannot exist

There are some persons who are entitled to immunity from the jurisdiction of the English courts.[34] There are also matters in which the common law considers that the court has no jurisdiction over the substance of the claim, on the approximate basis that such cases are not justiciable in an English court;[35] and where that is so, there is no question of submission conferring jurisdiction.

4.06 Claims which depend on showing title to foreign land: the *Moçambique* rule

At common law, an English court has no jurisdiction to adjudicate a claim whose substance depends on establishing title to foreign land. The rule is sometimes put in terms of the court having no jurisdiction to resolve a dispute over title to foreign land, but that is inaccurate: the House of Lords confirmed that if the claim depends on title to foreign land, the court has no jurisdiction to try it as a matter of common law, whether or not title is in dispute.[36]

---

was held that the predecessor provision would not apply unless the enactment in question makes it plain that it specifically contemplates proceedings being brought against persons out of the jurisdiction, as distinct from persons generally: *Re Harrods (Buenos Aires) Ltd (No 2)* [1992] Ch 72, 116; *Re Banco Nacional de Cuba* [2001] 1 WLR 2039. It is assumed that this is still the position.

33 If he does not manage to serve, however, because the defendant manages to evade (or perhaps even only avoid) service, it will be usual to make an order deeming such steps as have been made to be sufficient: *Abela v. Baaradani* [2013] UKSC 44, [2013] 1 WLR 2043.

34 Paragraph 4.11, below.

35 If according to these rules the court has no jurisdiction, it is not open to the claimant to contend that the defendant is estopped from taking the point: *J & F Stone v. Levitt* [1947] AC 209; *R Griggs Group Ltd v. Evans* [2004] EWHC 1088 (Ch), [2005] Ch 153, [20].

36 *Hesperides Hotels Ltd v. Aegean Turkish Holidays Ltd* [1979] AC 508. In that case, despite appearances, title to land was not in dispute, because if the court ignored the pretended laws of the occupation forces in the north of Cyprus as illegal, as it was bound to do, there was no dispute as to whose the land was.

The fundamental statement and theoretical justification of the rule is made in *British South Africa Co v. Companhia de Moçambique*.[37] Theory aside, it also reflects the practical[38] fact that only at the *situs* of the land can there be an effective determination of title. Even if an English court were to hear the case, and were to apply the law which a court at the *situs* would itself have applied, it is likely that its judgment will be ignored at the *situs*, on the ground that it was still a judgment given by a court with, as it appears to the judge at the *situs* of the land, no jurisdiction to adjudicate on the issue at all. It is this fact which provides the pragmatic reason why the court has no jurisdiction to try questions which dispute title to foreign land. It might have been argued that where there is no real dispute as to title, but damages are claimed, for example for trespass, this rationale does not apply. But the House of Lords refused to draw such a distinction, and that was that so far as the common law was concerned.[39] And because the issue is one where the court has no jurisdiction over the subject matter of the claim, the purported personal submission of the defendant to the jurisdiction of the court is irrelevant: what the court lacks is subject matter jurisdiction, not personal jurisdiction. The point is underscored by the fact that in *Hesperides Hotels Ltd v. Aegean Turkish Holidays Ltd*,[40] claims for damages for trespass, and for conspiracy to trespass, on foreign land were struck out; by contrast, the claim for damages for trespass to chattels on the land was unaffected and remained in the writ.

In addition to the two exceptions, examined below, to the absolute character of the *Moçambique* rule, it is evident that some consider the rule to have outlived its usefulness. The Supreme Court exhibited little obvious enthusiasm for it when it expressed the view that it had been 'undermined', that it had no application to cases founded on the infringement of foreign copyright in any event, and that its application to patents was not before them for decision.[41] More recently, the Court of Appeal went out of its way – out of its way, because the rule plainly had no application to the claim before it – to suggest that the rule had become narrower than it had been, and that it was in some sense analogous to the rule now in Article 24(1) of the Brussels I Regulation 1215/2015, which applies only when proceedings have as their object rights *in rem* in immovable property in another Member State.[42] Neither case gives any reason to question the rule. As will be seen,[43] in making a statutory exception to the rule, Parliament legislated against the background of a unanimous decision of the House of Lords on which the ink was barely dry. It is to be assumed that it knew precisely how and how far it wished the common law exclusionary rule to be pruned.

---

37 [1893] AC 602; approved and applied in *Hesperides Hotels Ltd v. Aegean Turkish Holidays Ltd* [1979] AC 508.

38 In truth, it reflects a historical decision that actions concerning title to foreign land were local and not transitory, and therefore had to be brought where the land was. This may be historically interesting, but is of no practical significance today.

39 *Hesperides Hotels Ltd v. Aegean Turkish Holidays Ltd* [1979] AC 508.

40 [1979] AC 508.

41 *Lucasfilm Ltd v. Ainsworth* [2011] UKSC 39, [2012] 1 AC 208: on the point concerning patents, see [102], [107].

42 *Hamed v. Stevens* [2013] EWCA Civ 911, [2013] ILPr 623. The judgment, at [11], is plainly wrong, as in *Hesperides Hotels Ltd v. Aegean Turkish Holidays Ltd* [1979] AC 508 Lord Wilberforce is clear that the decision of the court in that case does not involve any extension of the exclusionary rule. The fact that this was simply lifted from *Lucasfilm Ltd v. Ainsworth*, at [72], does not make it any more right. The statement of the common law in Dicey & Morris, 9th edn (Stevens, London,1973) does not confine the exclusionary rule to cases in which title to land was in dispute.

43 Paragraph 4.08, below.

4.07 Exceptions to the *Moçambique* rule (1): enforcing personal obligations ancillary to the land

The non-statutory exception to the *Moçambique* rule is so ancient that it pre-dates by over a century the case which has given its name to the common law rule. It is equitable in origin, and very useful in application.[44]

According to the principle laid down in *Penn v. Lord Baltimore*,[45] though a court may have no jurisdiction to try a question based on title to land situated outside the territorial jurisdiction of the court, this does not affect its jurisdiction to adjudicate on and enforce a contract, or fiduciary or other equitable obligation, made between and binding on the parties to it, even though the obligation relates to that foreign land. In the case itself the court ordered specific performance of a contract to settle a boundary dispute by proceeding to arbitration, even though the question where the boundary between Maryland (owned by Lord Baltimore) and Pennsylvania (owned by Mr Penn) was to be drawn was not one which the court had jurisdiction to determine for itself. It certainly could enforce a contract, and could deal with the consequences of any disregard of its order in the usual fierce way, and that was enough.

For the principle in *Penn v. Baltimore* to apply, there must be, or be alleged to be, a pre-existing personal relationship between the parties which the court may be asked to enforce,[46] such as a contractual duty to sell,[47] or the fiduciary duty of a trustee to convey land to a beneficiary. By contrast, a claim for equitable relief[48] in the form of a 'remedial constructive trust' to reverse an enrichment resulting from trespass to foreign land neither relies on nor seeks the enforcement of the rights and obligations of a voluntary and pre-existing relationship, and does not fall within the *Penn v. Baltimore* exception.[49]

The bare fact that there is a claim made for equitable relief is therefore insufficient to take the claim outside the *Moçambique* rule. But a contractual claim which has foreign land as its subject matter, and a suit to enforce rights created under a trust of foreign land, fall within this exception to the *Moçambique* rule, and are within the subject matter jurisdiction of the court. The 'contract or other equity' rule, which allows jurisdiction to be taken despite the fact that the broader subject matter of the claim is foreign land, fastens or relies on a pre-existing relationship between the parties. In cases in which the land comes into the hands of a third party, and it is asserted that he too falls within the *Penn v. Baltimore* principle, difficulty is bound to arise. For the obligations of the third party, if they exist at all, are not based on a voluntary relationship with the other, but on notice of that relationship (say, the estate contract) in relation to the property acquired. It has been suggested that this is enough to bring the third party within the principle, but the point is open to further question.[50]

It is worth pointing out that the principle in *Penn v. Baltimore* is of more general application than its peculiar historical context might suggest. It may apply in the context of the

---

44 See, for example, *Pattni v. Ali* [2006] UKPC 51, [2007] 2 AC 85.

45 (1750) 1 Ves Sen 444.

46 *Minera Aquiline Argentina SA v. IMA Exploration Inc* [2008] 10 WWR 648; *cf Catania v. Giannattasio* [1999] ILPr 630, in which the Ontario Court of Appeal declined to apply the exception to a case concerning the validity of a deed of grant.

47 Including a claim is for the rescission of a contract for the sale of land and the repayment of sums paid under it: *Hamed v. Stevens* [2013] EWCA Civ 911, [2013] ILPr 623.

48 Assuming for the sake of argument that there is such a principle of equity in English law.

49 *Re Polly Peck International plc*. In fact, the Court considered that there was no basis in English law for the imposition of such a trust in any event.

50 *R Griggs Group Ltd v. Evans* [2004] EWHC 1088 (Ch), [2005] Ch 153.

enforcement of foreign judgments when it is alleged that the judgment may not be enforceable on the ground that it was a judgment *in rem*, and that the *res* in question was not within the territorial jurisdiction of the foreign court.[51] If the judgment may (also) be seen as one which imposes obligations on the defendant *in personam*, it may be recognised and enforced on that basis instead. And as will be seen more generally in relation to foreign judgments,[52] it is aligned with, or may even be, the theoretical basis on which an English court enforces a judgment from a court within whose territory the defendant was not present when proceedings were begun.

4.08 Exceptions to the *Moçambique* rule (2): claims based on tort or trespass to foreign land

There is usually no contractual or equitable relationship between tortfeasor and victim, with the consequence that *Penn v. Baltimore* will not give the court jurisdiction to enforce the obligation allegedly owed by a tortfeasor or trespasser to a landowner.[53] Judging that this particular impediment to the jurisdiction of an English court was unsatisfactory, Parliament enacted Civil Jurisdiction and Judgments Act 1982, section 30(1), which provides that the court may entertain proceedings for trespass or other torts to foreign land 'unless the proceedings are principally concerned with a question of title to, or the right to possession of' that land. The practical[54] justification for the exception is that, if there is no real dispute over title to the foreign land, and the claim is only for personal relief in respect of a tort, there is no compelling need for a court with personal jurisdiction to be prevented from adjudicating: the possibility, or even the fact, that the courts at the *situs* of the land would take no notice of a damages judgment is of limited practical importance.

One way of looking at section 30 of the 1982 Act is that it creates for relationships governed by the law of tort a jurisdictional rule roughly analogous to that established by *Penn v. Baltimore* for those personal claims arising from voluntary obligations. But where the court would have to make a genuine investigation of title to foreign land, whether to determine the validity of the claim or (it is to be supposed) to assess such damages as depend on the nature or extent of title to land, section 30(1) is inapplicable and the *Moçambique* rule will apply.

In *Re Polly Peck International plc (in administration) (No 2)*,[55] it was held that section 30(1) of the 1982 Act gave the court jurisdiction unless the 'real issue' raised by the claim[56] was that of title to the land, and all other issues could be said to be merely incidental thereto.[57] The claimant asked the court to impose a 'remedial constructive trust', to reverse enrichment unjustly derived from the illegal use of land in the occupied territory in the northern part of Cyprus, licence to use which having purportedly been granted by the regime which was carrying on business as the 'Turkish Republic of Northern Cyprus'. The court held

---

51 *Pattni v. Ali* [2006] UKPC 51, [2007] 2 AC 85.

52 Paragraph 7.62, below.

53 *Hesperides Hotels Ltd v. Aegean Turkish Holidays Ltd* [1979] AC 508; *Re Polly Peck International plc (in administration) (No 2)* [1998] 3 All ER 812.

54 There is nothing in the way of *travaux préparatoires*, and little in the Parliamentary debates.

55 [1998] 3 All ER 812.

56 This is probably more accurate than saying 'the claimant': if an issue of title is raised by the defendant so that its resolution can be seen to be the real issue in the case, the court should conclude that it lacks jurisdiction.

57 At 829.

that the case was not principally concerned with title to the disputed land, and that if the claim had been arguable on its facts, section 30(1) would have given the court jurisdiction to adjudicate it. That seems perfectly correct. For as a matter of English law, the pretended laws of the regime were not recognised, and once that was appreciated there was no issue, still less a principal issue, of title. By contrast, the issues of trusts law and remedies which the court would have been[58] required to address would be formidable. It is not helpful to gloss the words of the Act, or to propose tests which (it seems) do not reflect what the case actually decided:[59] the court is required to ask itself, in effect, whether the matter before it for decision is 'more about this or more about that'.[60]

4.09 Jurisdiction over claims which turn on the validity of foreign intellectual property rights

Until recently it was not controversial that an English court had no jurisdiction to adjudicate claims involving the validity of foreign intellectual property rights. The English authorities may not have been strong, but they agreed that the *Moçambique* rule, or something resembling it, excluded jurisdiction to adjudicate on the validity of foreign patents,[61] copyrights[62] and trademarks. Quite apart from that, even if the claim were framed in tort, as a claim for damages for infringement of the particular foreign right, the common law rules of choice of law rules for claims in tort[63] would have meant that an action before the English courts, founded on infringement of a foreign intellectual property right, would fail. This was because acts infringing such foreign rights would not have given rise to liability as a tort even if committed in England, for a foreign right was territorial and had no effect in England. There was, therefore, no incentive for a claimant to challenge the application of the *Moçambique* rule in this area.

That settled understanding, or misunderstanding, of the law was questioned by the Court of Appeal in *Pearce v. Ove Arup Partnership Ltd*,[64] which held that in proceedings founded on an alleged infringement of a Dutch copyright by a defendant over whom the Brussels Convention (as it then was) gave the court personal jurisdiction, it was incompatible with the Convention for a common law jurisdictional rule to prevent the jurisdiction of the court. But rather than confine its attention to the impact of the Brussels Convention, the court considered the broader question whether the *Moçambique* rule had any proper application to intellectual property disputes at all, and concluded that no English authority required it to hold that it did apply. It took the view that the early authority of the High Court of

---

58 In fact, the claim was substantively hopeless, and the claim was struck out.

59 The suggestion in Dicey Morris & Collins, *The Conflict of Laws*, 15th edn (Sweet & Maxwell, London, 2012), para. 23–040, is, it is submitted, not reliable. It was originally formulated as a suggestion well before the decision in *Polly Peck* (see Dicey & Morris, 11th edn (1987), 927) and does not appear to have been reconsidered in the light of that decision which, on the face of it, did not adopt it but said something rather different.

60 It may be a difficult question to answer: see *The Bodo Community v. Shell Petroleum and Development Co of Nigeria Ltd* [2014] EWHC 1973 (TCC).

61 *Potter v. Broken Hill Pty Ltd* (1906) 3 CLR 479; *Norbert Steinhardt & Son v. Meth* (1961) 105 CLR 440; *Mölnlycke v. Procter & Gamble Ltd* [1992] 1 WLR 1112. But on the correct reading of *Potter v. Broken Hill*, see *Habib v. Commonwealth of Australia* (2010) 183 FCR 62; *Lucasfilm Ltd v. Ainsworth* [2011] UKSC 39, [2012] 1 AC 208.

62 *Tyburn Productions Ltd v. Conan Doyle* [1991] Ch 75.

63 The rule of 'double actionability' in *Boys v. Chaplin* [1971] AC 356.

64 [2000] Ch 403.

Australia on the point was not, or was no longer, persuasive,[65] and that the rule, at least in a broad formulation, was and ought to be inapplicable in the context of intellectual property disputes in the twenty-first century. It might have been different if an issue of validity were squarely raised, for in such cases the court of the country under which the property right had been granted or arose would alone have jurisdiction to determine it. But where there was no such issue of validity, there was no need to conclude that the *Moçambique* rule was applicable in the context of infringement claims.

The approach of the Court of Appeal was generally approved by the Supreme Court in *Lucasfilm Ltd v. Ainsworth*,[66] which held that if there was a common law exclusionary rule applicable to issues of foreign intellectual property, it had no application to cases founded on the infringement of foreign copyright, or perhaps to copyright at all; and the question whether or how it applied to patents was not one which the court needed to determine. A fair reading of the judgment, though, would suggest that where a genuine dispute as to the validity of a patent is raised, whether as a claim or as a defence to an allegation of infringement, the exclusionary rule may still apply. The grant of a patent right is closer to an act of sovereign power than many; if a court considers that a patent should be held to be invalid and cancelled as a result, it is hard to see how this can be done and made effective by a court other than at the place where the patent was granted and must now be cancelled. Moreover, as the Brussels I Regulation reserves proceedings which have as their object the validity of a patent to the courts of the Member State under which it was granted, it would be difficult to attack a rule of the common law which was built on the same foundation.

To the extent that the *Moçambique* rule still applies to disputes concerning the validity of a foreign patent, it is also modified by the rule in *Penn v. Baltimore*, with the consequence that the court will have jurisdiction to enforce a contract, or other equity, between the parties which relates to the foreign patent.[67] It is, however, more difficult to see that the wording of section 30 of the 1982 Act is apt to allow it to apply to foreign intellectual property rights in the way that it applies to foreign land.

4.10 Jurisdiction over claims which require a court to enforce a foreign penal, revenue or public law of an analogous kind

According to Rule 3 of Dicey, Morris and Collins, *The Conflict of Laws*, and by long tradition, the English courts have no jurisdiction to enforce, directly or indirectly, a foreign penal law, or a foreign revenue law, or other[68] foreign public laws.

It is clear that there is a principle which prevents enforcement of such laws in an English court. But it is less clear that it is illuminating to describe this as a rule which goes to the jurisdiction of the court if this means that, even if the defendant does not take the point, the court has no legal power to adjudicate the claim. In *Re State of Norway's Application (Nos 1*

---

65 To the same effect: *R Griggs Group Ltd v. Evans* [2004] EWHC 1088 (Ch), [2005] Ch 153, doubting that there was an exclusionary rule for copyright, but in any event applying the rule in *Penn v. Baltimore* to conclude that the court had jurisdiction to adjudicate the claim.

66 [2011] UKSC 39, [2012] 1 AC 208.

67 *R Griggs Group Ltd v. Evans* [2004] EWHC 1088 (Ch), [2005] Ch 153.

68 It is customary to qualify the reference to 'other public laws' with the explanation that the authority for and scope of such a third category is less well established. The correct position today is that there is no doubt that such a rule exists, but that the identification of 'other public laws', and the application of a rule that these may not be enforced, as distinct from having an effect other than enforcement, is more problematic.

and 2),[69] Lord Goff of Chieveley acknowledged that the editors of Dicey and Morris, as it then was, had questioned the proposition that the rule was to be understood as one which went to the jurisdiction of the court. He suggested that the better analysis may be that the jurisdiction of the court is not exercised, as distinct from its being legally non-existent. It is implicit in this that the defendant may apply for the claim to be struck out as non-justiciable, but that, if he chooses not to, the court will not be prevented from adjudicating.

Some observations made by the Privy Council in *Equatorial Guinea v. Royal Bank of Scotland*[70] may suggest that the issue is one which does go to jurisdiction, and that where submissions are not addressed to the court on the issue of whether the court has jurisdiction to entertain a claim which will require it to enforce a foreign public law, there is a risk that the court will be led into making an error of law, but the decision of the Privy Council was that, as the point had not been taken by the defendant below, it could not be taken before the Judicial Committee, and the order made at first instance was upheld. If that is correct, then the objection is not one which goes to jurisdiction properly so called, but is one by reference to which a defendant may invite a court not to exercise the jurisdiction it has.

4.11 Jurisdiction denied by general principles of public international law

Apart from these cases where an English court lacks, or may lack, subject matter jurisdiction as a matter of private international law, properly so called, the principles of public international law may operate to deny or remove the jurisdiction of the court over the defendant in relation to the claim made.

In some instances the defendant will have personal immunity from the jurisdiction of the English courts: if the defendant has such personal immunity, the courts will have no jurisdiction to adjudicate the matter set out in the claim.[71] The most important of these exceptions to the jurisdiction of the court lies in the field of State and sovereign immunity. The detail of the law on sovereign immunity is beyond the scope of this book. It is sufficient to say that it is governed in large part by the common law as now restricted by the State Immunity Act 1978, and by international Convention.[72] This grants immunity to a foreign State,[73] to the sovereign of the State in his public capacity, to the Government of the State, and to any department of its Government.[74] Such immunity is extended to a 'separate entity' which acts in, and is sued in relation to, the exercise of sovereign authority where, if it had so acted, a State would have been immune.[75] Questions of state immunity must be decided as a preliminary issue, even if the State does not appear. But a State may put aside

---

69 [1990] 1 AC 723, 807–808 for examination of the true basis for the exclusionary rule as defined in *Government of India v. Taylor* [1955] AC 491.

70 [2006] UKPC 7 (PC, Guernsey), esp. at [23].

71 See for a recent example, *Grovit v. De Nederlandsche Bank* [2007] EWCA Civ 953, [2008] 1 WLR 51 (applying the rule in a case in which the defendant was subject to the personal jurisdiction of the English court according to the Brussels I Regulation.

72 For immunity (or not) in relation to a claim for damages for torture committed within and on behalf of a foreign State, see *Jones v. Saudi Arabia* [2006] UKHL 26, [2007] 1 AC 270; *cf Belhaj v. Straw* [2014] EWCA Civ 1394; *Rahmatullah v. Ministry of Defence* [2014] EWHC 3846 (QB).

73 Section 1(1). For the interrelationship between the Act and the common law, see *Holland v. Lampen-Wolfe* [2000] 1 WLR 1573 (action for defamation against employee of US Government at military base in England stuck out on ground of immunity at common law).

74 Section 14.

75 Section 14.

its immunity shield by submission to the courts. This may be done after the dispute has arisen, or by prior written agreement,[76] or by taking a step in the proceedings for purposes which go beyond seeking to establish or defend its immunity.[77] And in any event, there is no immunity in relation to a commercial transaction entered into by the State, or in relation to an obligation under any contract which fell to be performed wholly or in part within the United Kingdom.[78] Further cases in which there is no immunity include acts or omissions in the United Kingdom causing death or personal injury, or damage to or loss of tangible property,[79] and claims in relation to use or possession of immovable property in the United Kingdom.[80]

An English court does not have jurisdiction over a person entitled to immunity under the Diplomatic Privileges Act 1964 or the Consular Relations Act 1968. Finally, if an international organisation benefits from an Order made under the International Organisations Act 1968,[81] it will enjoy such immunity (if any) as may be conferred on it by that Order. In the absence of such an Order, an international organisation would enjoy no such immunity.[82]

There is a separate and reasonably distinct principle of non-justiciability, by reference to which a court may conclude that the matter raised is not one for a municipal court to try. One traditional explanation for the absence of jurisdiction, in some of these cases at least, is the 'act of State' doctrine, but the danger with using this particular label is that it distracts attention from the real basis on which the law is organised. Equality of respect for sovereign States, and the principles of international comity limit the judicial power of an English court to investigate and adjudicate upon the sovereign acts of States. The proper basis of the leading case of *Buttes Gas & Oil Co v. Hammer (No 3)*[83] was recently examined and clarified by the Supreme Court in *Shergill v. Khaira*,[84] to which reference may be made.

But in the same way that private law has long held that there is no confidence in iniquity,[85] it increasingly appears that English international law holds that there is no non-justiciability in barbarity. The boundaries of the exception to the rule of non-justiciability are somewhat fluid, as is inevitable. On the one hand there is a strong public interest in

---

76 *NML Capital Ltd v. Argentina* [2011] UKSC 31, [2011] 2 AC 495 (submission by contractual term to jurisdiction of court)

77 Section 2. See *Kuwait Airways Corp v. Iraqi Airways Co* [1995] 1 WLR 1147.

78 Section 3. Note that there is separate treatment for claims in relation to contracts of employment in s. 4.

79 Section 5.

80 Section 6. Other cases include succession and the winding-up of companies (s. 6), certain intellectual property rights governed by United Kingdom law (s. 7), certain cases of membership of a body corporate, or an unincorporated body (s. 8), proceedings in relation to an arbitration which has been agreed to (s. 9), certain admiralty proceedings (s. 10), certain taxes and levies (s. 11).

81 Or under analogous statutes making particular provision for an individual organisation, such as the Commonwealth Secretariat Act 1966.

82 Such Orders may be made under the Act only in respect of international organisations of which the United Kingdom is a member; and there is no immunity otherwise than under the Order: *Standard Chartered Bank v. International Tin Council* [1987] 1 WLR 641. The Act also allows legal capacity to be conferred on such organisations of which the United Kingdom is not a member but which maintain establishments in the United Kingdom: s. 4. See *JH Rayner (Mincing Lane) Ltd v. Department of Trade and Industry* [1990] 2 AC 418. An international organisation of which the United Kingdom is not a member, and which has no establishment in the United Kingdom, may still be recognised as having legal personality if it has legal personality under the domestic law of the State in which it had been incorporated: *Arab Monetary Fund v. Hashim (No 3)* [1991] 2 AC 114; but (of course) in such a case no question of immunity can arise.

83 [1982] AC 888.

84 [2014] UKSC 33, [2014] 3 WLR 1.

85 *Gartside v. Outram* (1856) 26 LJ (NS) 113.

respecting the sovereignty of States. It is proper for a court to avoid taking steps which will impair the public interest in the conduct of diplomatic and security relations between the United Kingdom and other States. On the other, there is an increasingly strong acceptance that the judicial protection of human rights is also a matter of public policy, and that for a claimant to be shut out of court by a plea that it will damage the interests of the United Kingdom if his claim is heard is unattractive, and the more barbarous the alleged behaviour of the foreign State, the less attractive it will be for the claimant to be denied a fair hearing of his claim. It appears that the court will conduct a balancing exercise, and that this is perfectly capable of taking account of the variable nature of the facts and matters complained of. It seems plausible that the more outrageous is the actual allegation of abuse of human rights, the less likely it is that the court will be receptive to contentions that it is inappropriate to shine a light on the conduct of a foreign State, or of those acting in its name.[86]

It is difficult to envisage a case in which the Brussels I Regulation would, apart from these rules, confer jurisdiction on the English courts; these jurisdictional immunities may be applied by an English court without regard to it.[87]

4.12 Jurisdiction in relation to multi-State defamation

The subject matter jurisdiction of an English court has recently been cut back in the context of defamation in which publication of a statement, to which the claimant takes exception, in England, is part of a more substantial publication which has its centre of gravity overseas. Until very recently, certain opportunistic individuals with nothing better to do, who fancied themselves to have been traduced in the media, hit upon the wheeze of suing the defendant in England. The trick was to complain only of publication in England and of damage to their reputation resulting from English publication. So localised, the claim would be one over which it was practically impossible for the English court to refuse to exercise jurisdiction. English law would be applied to such a claim; and as this requires the defendant to justify what he had said, pressure and pain could be brought to bear in England in a way which – because its law has a rather different approach to free speech – might not be possible in the place where the lion's share of the publication had taken place.[88] This was thought in many quarters to be something of a scandal.

Rather than legislate to give or to confirm the power of an English court to stay such proceedings on the defendant's application, on the ground that whether or not the complaint was limited to publication in England, the appropriate forum was overseas where

---

86 See for example *Oppenheimer v. Cattermole* [1976] AC 249; *Kuwait Airways Corp v. Iraq Airways Co (No 2)* [2002] UKHL 19, [2002] 2 AC 883; *Yukos Capital Sarl v. OJSC Rosneft Oil Co* [2012] EWCA Civ 855, [2014] QB 458; *Belhaj v. Straw* [2014] EWCA Civ 1394; see also European Convention on Human Rights, Art. 6.

87 The reasons include the fact that there is no general immunity for commercial matters in any event; and in other cases, the immunity from the jurisdiction of the English courts derives from a Convention to which Art. 71 of the Brussels I Regulation will accord precedence.

88 For example (though there were plenty of others), see *Berezovsky v. Michaels* [2000] 1 WLR 1004, a case on service out of the jurisdiction, discussed further below, para. 4.90; see also *King v. Lewis* [2004] EWCA Civ 1329, [2005] ILPr 185; *Richardson v. Schwarzenegger* [2004] EWHC 2422 (QB) (affirmed [2005] EWCA Civ 25) (both applying the same principle to libel by material downloaded from the world wide web and complained about only insofar as there was an alleged English readership (and on all of this madness, see (2004) 75 BYBIL 565). But when the principle was pushed to the point that its use could be seen as an abuse of the process of the court, the action could be dismissed on the application of the defendant: *Dow Jones & Co Inc v. Jameel* [2005] EWCA Civ 75, [2005] QB 946.

the totality of publication had its centre of gravity, the Defamation Act 2013 removed the subject matter jurisdiction of the English court. The effect of section 9 of the Act is that the English court does not have jurisdiction to hear and determine the action unless it is satisfied that, of all the places in which the statement complained of has been published, England and Wales is clearly the most appropriate place in which to bring an action in respect of the statement. The rule certainly appears to be one which removes the jurisdiction of the court, leaving no room for discretionary considerations or exceptions of any kind. The Act may be an effective remedy for some forms of abusive behaviour, but the possibility that an English victim will have been deprived of the only remedy which was within his reasonable means is not a happy one.

According to section 9, the new jurisdiction-denying rule does not apply to cases where the defendant is domiciled in a Member State. No doubt this was intended to mean that if the court has jurisdiction according to the Brussels I Regulation, the jurisdiction-denying provisions of the Act are inapplicable. This appears to suppose that where the defendant is not domiciled in a Member State, any jurisdiction over him would be based, and based only, on what is now Article 6 of the Regulation. That may not be correct: if a defendant submits to the jurisdiction by prorogation or voluntary appearance, Articles 25 and 26 appear to mean that the court has jurisdiction by virtue of the Regulation, no matter where the defendant may actually be domiciled. If that is correct,[89] Section 9 purports in part to remove a jurisdiction which the Regulation has conferred, which suggests that something has gone wrong with the drafting.

PROCEEDINGS COMMENCED BY SERVICE WITHIN THE JURISDICTION: APPLYING FOR A STAY OF PROCEEDINGS

4.13 General

As stated above, where proceedings may be instituted by making service upon the defendant within the jurisdiction, as a consequence of which service the court has jurisdiction, any disputing of the jurisdiction of the court will be based on whether the service was made in accordance with the law governing the manner and form of service of the document in question. These rules about how service may be made are examined in more detail in Chapter 5.

If it is established or conceded that service was effected lawfully, the defendant may still apply for a stay of the proceedings. If he succeeds, the court will remain seised of the proceedings,[90] but will suspend further consideration of them, usually *sine die*, leaving the claimant to prosecute his claim, if so advised, before the courts of another State. The power to order a stay is inherent: according to the Senior Courts Act 1981, section 49(3): 'Nothing in this Act shall affect the power of the Court of Appeal or the High Court to stay any proceedings before it, where it thinks fit to do so, either of its own motion or on the application of any person, whether or not a party to proceedings.' Civil Jurisdiction and Judgments Act

---

89 On whether Art. 26 of the Brussels I Regulation applies when a defendant does not have a domicile in a Member State, see above, para. 2.85.

90 *The Alexandros T* [2013] UKSC 70, [2014] 1 Lloyd's Rep 223, approving *ROFA Sport Management AG v. DHL International (UK) Ltd* [1989] 1 WLR 902.

1982, section 49, echoes this, providing that: 'Nothing in this Act shall prevent any court in the United Kingdom from staying, sisting, striking out or dismissing any proceedings before it, on the ground of *forum non conveniens* or otherwise, where to do so is not inconsistent with' the Brussels Convention (as it then was).[91] The remainder of this section examines the law which governs the granting of such stays of proceedings.

4.14 Legislative limitations on the general power to stay proceedings

Before examining the law on the staying of proceedings, it is necessary to ask whether Parliament has legislated, in a particular case or context, to remove the court's inherent power to stay from the claim with which the court is concerned.

This may be found to have happened, in particular, where a statute provides that a court shall have jurisdiction, and the court reaches the conclusion, from a construction of the Act as a whole, that it would be contrary to the intention of Parliament for that jurisdiction to be not exercised. For example, in *The Hollandia*,[92] the essential question for the court was whether exclusion clauses contained in a bill of lading should be subjected to the control provisions of the Hague-Visby Rules, as would have happened if the action were to proceed in England, or governed by the rather more lax provisions of the original Hague Rules, as they would have been if the dispute were to be brought before a Dutch court. The defendant applied for a stay of English proceedings, on the basis that the parties had expressly agreed on the jurisdiction of the Dutch courts. But the Hague-Visby Rules had been given the force of law in England by the Carriage of Goods by Sea Act 1971, and the Rules provided, in effect, that any contract term which lessened the liability of a defendant more than was permitted by the Rules was to be null and void. The House of Lords concluded that Parliament had prohibited a court from giving effect to a contractual agreement on jurisdiction, by way of a stay of proceedings, where the result of its doing so would be to prevent the Hague-Visby Rules from being applied to the case.[93] A stay of proceedings, in order to give effect to an agreement on jurisdiction, was therefore precluded by the 1971 Act.

Similar conclusions have been reached when the courts have had to consider other domestic legislation enacted to give effect to other international Conventions. It has been held that the implementing legislation forbade a stay of proceedings where the claim was

---

91 The Act was not amended to make reference to the Brussels I Regulation, for as the Regulation is directly effective, it is not open to the United Kingdom to legislate within the sphere of its operation, and the decision was evidently taken to refrain from even amending s. 49 in what would, surely, have been a helpful and wholly uncontroversial way. For a case on *forum non conveniens* as between Scotland and England in a matter falling outside the material scope of the Regulation in any event, see *Tehrani v. Secretary of State for the Home Department* [2006] UKHL 47, [2007] 1 AC 521.

92 [1983] 1 AC 565.

93 It does not follow that a stay would have been refused if the basis for its grant had been that the foreign court was the natural forum. The material question is whether Parliament has legislated to prevent a stay being ordered *on the ground advanced by the applicant.* In *The Hollandia*, the true construction of the 1971 Act and of the Hague-Visby Rules was that a term of the contract, which would have the effect of lessening the protection extended by the Rules, was null and void. The application for a stay, rested on a term of the contract, was therefore unsuccessful. Contrast *The Herceg Novi and the Ming Galaxy* [1998] 2 Lloyd's Rep 454, where the court refused to see the intention of Parliament as having been to remove the power to stay proceedings on the ground that the foreign forum was the natural forum. And *cf* also the approach of the Canadian Federal Court of Appeal in *OT Africa Line Ltd v. Magic Sportswear Corp* [2007] 1 Lloyd's Rep 85 (Can Fed CA), refusing to interpret mandatory legislation as precluding the power of the court to order a stay.

one which the court was given jurisdiction to adjudicate by the Warsaw Convention,[94] the CMR Convention,[95] and by the European Patents Convention.[96] A still similar construction has been taken to the legislation governing jurisdiction to order matrimonial relief, in a case concerned with assets held in a trust which contained an exclusive jurisdiction clause.[97] A similar conclusion was reached in a case in which an English court would be required to apply the Commercial Agents' Regulations 1993 but where the agreed court, which was in a non-Member State, would not apply them.[98] In all cases it was possible to justify the conclusion by observing that the particular jurisdiction was a statutory one, not an inherent one; and for this reason there was perhaps no expectation that an inherent power to regulate procedure was to be associated with jurisdiction of that kind.

The provisions of the Brussels I Regulation may, or must, also be seen as a set of jurisdictional rules which, just as with these other international agreements, specify where proceedings may be brought. It is, once again, no surprise that there is no room, where statutory jurisdiction is conferred on a court in the United Kingdom by that Regulation, for an English court to exercise an inherent, or inherent-and-then-confirmed-by-statute discretion to decline to exercise that jurisdiction: the two forms of jurisdiction are very different.

But there is no reason to suppose that this exclusion of the inherent power to stay is confined to cases in which the legislation is made to enact an international agreement. It is, in principle at least, always possible to construe a statute as being sufficiently emphatic on the issue of its application that it excludes the possibility of its being defeated by a stay ordered under the inherent jurisdiction of the court. The difficulty is that statutory language is only very rarely that clear.

A particular aspect of this issue arises when a claimant, seeking to sue in England and to rely on a particular cause of action, is able to show that a court[99] overseas would not give effect, in proceedings before it, to the cause of action which would be available to him in an English court. In many cases, the English court will simply consider this along with all the other indications of what justice may require in deciding whether to order a stay of proceedings, and the fact that proceedings will follow a different path in a foreign court will be seen as insignificant and unremarkable. But on other occasions it may be contended that the English legislation is of mandatory application, in the sense that it must be applied by the English judge to the matter before him and that this leads to certain consequences which

---

94 Carriage by Air Act 1961; *Milor v. British Airways plc* [1996] QB 702.

95 *Royal & Sun Alliance Insurance plc v. MK Digital (Cyprus) Ltd* [2005] EWHC 1408 (Comm) (appeal allowed on other grounds: [2006] EWCA Civ 629, [2006] 2 Lloyd's Rep 110) (CMR Convention: power to stay excluded); *Hatzl v. XL Insurance Co* [2009] EWCA Civ 223, [2010] 1 WLR 470 (CMR Convention: agreed that power to stay was excluded).

96 *Sepracor v. Hoechst Marion Roussel Ltd* [1999] FSR 746; *Innovia Films Ltd v. Frito-Lay North America Inc* [2012] EWHC 790 (Pat), [2012] RPC 557.

97 *C v. C (Ancillary Relief: Nuptial Settlement)* [2004] EWCA Civ 1030, [2005] Fam 250.

98 *Accentuate Ltd v. Asigra Inc* [2009] EWHC 2655 (QB), [2009] 2 Lloyd's Rep 599 (which led to the refusal of a stay for arbitration, and to the disregarding of a choice of Ontario law: the decision goes as far as it is possible to go along this path, and then further. It was not followed in *Fern Computer Consultancy Ltd v. Intergraph Cadworx & Analysis Solutions Ltd* [2014] EWHC 2908 (Ch), [2015] 1 Lloyd's Rep 1, but as the jurisdiction of the court in the latter case required permission to serve out of the jurisdiction, for which no basis was found to be satisfied, the point was not precisely the same.

99 In principle the same argument could be made when the parties have agreed to arbitrate before a tribunal which will likewise not give effect to this cause of action. But the duty to stay proceedings for arbitration is statutory and derived from international Convention; and it will be much more difficult to see that duty overcome by other forms of legislation.

disrupt the usual structure of argument concerning stays of proceedings. It may lead to the conclusion that an agreement on choice of law made by the parties should be overridden; but it may also lead to the conclusion that an agreement on jurisdiction should be overridden as well.[100] If this argument does not find favour, it may be contended that the foreign court is not available for the trial of the action[101] (the first limb of the *Spiliada* test),[102] or that it cannot be seen as the natural forum for the trial of the action[103] (the first limb of the *Spiliada* test), or that it would be unjust to deprive the claimant of his reliance on the English cause of action (the second limb of the *Spiliada* test), or all of the above. As can be seen, the limbs of the test tend to slide into one another, and the drawing of rigid lines to demarcate them is sometimes difficult.

As a matter of simple observation, English judges in reported cases have been generally unimpressed by claimants who complain that the court has no power to deprive them of a cause of action which would be available in England: the prevailing attitude is that different legal systems establish their own rules for dealing with litigation, and it is wrong to harbour an institutional preference for causes of action or remedies[104] or measures of damages[105] offered by English law. By contrast, the approach of the Australian courts would appear to suggest a wider acceptance of the proposition that a cause of action created by an[106] Australian legislature should be available to a claimant, and that if it is shown that a foreign court would not or could not give effect to it, the action will be allowed to remain before the Australian courts.[107] This may be defended as giving effect to the intention of the legislature; and whenever it does arise in recognisable form, this expression of parliamentary intention certainly overrides the ordinary rules for the staying of proceedings. But in the absence of a legislative abrogation of the power to order a stay of proceedings, it is necessary to consider the general rules which govern this form of relief.

It is finally necessary to mention certain points which were made in Chapter 2 in connection with the analysis of the Brussels I Regulation for, as said above, the Regulation is a statute which prevents a court which has jurisdiction from ordering a stay of proceedings. If the proceedings are brought in a civil or commercial matter, and the jurisdiction of the English court is confirmed by Chapter II of the Regulation, apart from Article 6, there is no general power to order a stay of proceedings even though the courts of a non-Member State would be clearly more appropriate than England for the trial of the action;[108] it makes no difference whether the claimant is domiciled in a Member State or a non-Member State.[109] But if jurisdiction is founded on Article 6 of the Regulation, then the power of the court to

---

100 *The Hollandia* may also be seen as a case of this kind.

101 Below, paras 4.19 *et seq*.

102 The reference is to *Spiliada Maritime Corp v. Cansulex Ltd* [1987] AC 460, which is discussed in detail below.

103 Below, paras 4.20 *et seq*.

104 *Re Harrods (Buenos Aires) Ltd* [1992] Ch 72.

105 *The Herceg Novi and The Ming Galaxy* [1998] 2 Lloyd's Rep 454.

106 Commonwealth or State, as the case may be.

107 *Akai v. People's Insurance Co* (1997) 188 CLR 418 (effect of Insurance Contracts Act 1982 that jurisdiction agreement for London was a nullity); *Reinsurance Australia Corp Ltd v. HIH Casualty and General Insurance Ltd (in liq)* (2003) 254 ALR 29 (esp. at [293]: Australian court cannot be inappropriate, and therefore no stay will be granted, if it is the only one of the possible fora in which a claim under the Trade Practices Act 1974 (as it then was) could be fully and properly entertained).

108 C-281/02 *Owusu v. Jackson* [2005] ECR I-1383.

109 C-412/98 *Universal General Insurance Co v. Group Josi Reinsurance Co SA* [2000] ECR I-5925.

stay proceedings is still liable to be exercised, as part and parcel of the inherent jurisdictional rules which are picked up and incorporated into the Regulation, even where it is the court of another Member State which is clearly more appropriate than England.[110]

4.15 Staying proceedings: private interests and public interest

In some jurisdictions the doctrine of *forum non conveniens* takes account of certain matters of public interest or public policy, and weighs these alongside the private interests of the parties. In the United States,[111] in particular, the fact that there may be a long queue of cases waiting to get on before a judge has been held to entail a right and duty of a judge to bear this in mind in deciding whether to stay proceedings, and to respect the wishes of an American claimant to sue in his own courts more highly than the desire of a non–American claimant to invoke American jurisdiction;[112] though whether this is a matter or private or public interest is harder to say.

In *Lubbe v. Cape plc*,[113] the House of Lords held that considerations of this type were irrelevant to the analysis undertaken in an English court. It is possible, though, that there is marginally more to be said for the American approach, and for allowing it to be debated openly, than was publicly acknowledged in *Lubbe*. If justice delayed may be justice denied, the public interest in allowing international cases with small connection to England to proceed, and delaying cases involving those local litigants whose taxes fund the courts, is not so easily identified. And in terms of the overriding objective of the Civil Procedure Rules, it may well be that a case which has only a small connection to England is one to which rather fewer of the resources of the court should be allocated.[114] It may not be wholly desirable to limit the analysis to the claimed private interests of the parties, and to disregard any public interest. But, on the face of it at least,[115] this does not form part of the current approach of the English courts.

4.16 Staying proceedings commenced by service within the jurisdiction: general

Suppose that proceedings have been commenced in a case to which the Brussels I Regulation provides that a court shall exercise its own rules of jurisdiction, or in a case which falls outside the material scope of the Regulation. If the defendant has been served with process within the jurisdiction, the court has jurisdiction over the claim against him. Unless and until the service of the process is set aside on application, any argument that the court should not act upon its jurisdiction proceeds by way of an application for a stay of proceedings,

---

110 *Haji-Ioannou v. Frangos* [1999] 2 Lloyd's Rep 337.

111 *Piper Aircraft Co v. Reyno* (1981) 454 US 235; *Union Carbide Corporation Gas Plant Disaster at Bhopal* (1986) 634 F Supp 842.

112 *Gulf Oil Corp v. Gilbert* 330 US 501 (1947); *Piper Aircraft Co v. Reyno* 454 US 235 (1981); *Sinochem International Co v. Malaysia International Shipping Corp* 549 US 422 (2007); *Gullone v. Bayer Corp* 484 F 3d 951 (7th Cir, 2007); *SME Racks Inc v. Sistemas Mecanicos Para Electronica SA* 382 F 3d 1097 (11th Cir, 2004); *King v. Cessna Aircraft Co* 562 F 3d 1374 (11th Cir, 2009).

113 [2000] 1 WLR 1545, in the speech of Lord Hope.

114 CPR r. 1.1(2)(e).

115 The alternative may be that it is smuggled into an analysis of what the parties' private interests may be said to be.

which is made pursuant to CPR Part 11. For though CPR Part 11 may give the impression that it provides for jurisdiction to be disputed, rule 11.1 makes it clear that it also provides the framework for an application to be made for a stay of English proceedings.[116]

A stay of proceedings is a characteristic feature of many common law jurisdictions,[117] but is known in few[118] civil law systems. The English common law now acknowledges that, if the parties agree to English jurisdiction and adjudication, they may have it if they want it. Leaving aside cases in which there is no subject matter jurisdiction, the parties will not be driven away from the English court in the face of their common wish to resolve their dispute there. However, if the defendant is not content to have his case heard by the English courts, he is entitled to show the English court that it is a *forum non conveniens* because the natural forum lies elsewhere. If he does show this to the court, the court is likely[119] to stay its proceedings to leave the claimant to proceed against the defendant elsewhere.

The doctrine of *forum non conveniens*, though a relatively late arrival so far as the common law of England is concerned, naturalised very quickly and struck deep roots. A number of factors may have contributed to this. One is that the initial choice of court is effectively that of the claimant,[120] who issues the claim form, but that there is no convincing reason why the important, maybe critical, decision about where the trial should take place should be entirely under the control of only one of the parties. To put it another way: it may be the claimant's claim, but is also the parties' dispute. Clearly the selection of forum is important; it may load the dice substantially against the defendant if the selection of court to adjudicate is that of the claimant alone. In this regard, to fail to ensure that the parties are on an equal footing may contradict an important aspect of the overriding objective of the Civil Procedure Rules.[121] Another factor is the realisation that, no matter how effective and professional the English trial process may be, other courts are also effective and professional, and they are often significantly cheaper. Moreover, if the choice lies between an English court seeking to resolve a dispute by applying foreign law, or a foreign court applying that law as its own, it is far from obvious that the English court will do the job with greater ease, efficiency or accuracy, not least because appeals to correct mistakes made in the application of foreign law are not really possible in England. And if the fact that the dispute arose overseas means that factual matters relating to it can be more efficiently resolved there, the policy basis of the doctrine is clear. In short, the principle is civilised and sound and rational and right.

The rule, fashioned for English purposes almost entirely by the House of Lords, made its debut in *The Atlantic Star*.[122] That decision was followed and further refined by *MacShannon v. Rockware Glass Ltd*,[123] and *The Abidin Daver*.[124] The principle was restated in classic form

---

116 *Texan Management Ltd v. Pacific Electric Wire & Cable Co Ltd* [2009] UKPC 46. And also where the issue arises in the context of the Brussels I Regulation: *The Alexandros T* [2013] UKSC 70, [2014] 1 Lloyd's Rep 223.

117 Even if it has arrived fairly recently; its antecedents lie in Scottish law.

118 Though Scotland and Québec are notable and instructive exceptions.

119 But, of course, not certain: it has a discretion.

120 Though the 'defendant' may himself choose to bring his own proceedings in a court of his choice, either for substantive relief, or for a declaration of his non-liability to his opponent. See Chapter 5.

121 CPR r. 1(2)(a).

122 [1974] AC 436. Historically they grew out of a very restrictive power to stay domestic proceedings on the ground that they were oppressive or vexatious (*St Pierre v. South American Stores (Gath & Chaves) Ltd* [1936] 1 KB 382).

123 [1978] AC 795.

124 [1984] AC 398.

in *Spiliada Maritime Corporation v. Cansulex Ltd*.[125] It was elaborated and further refined in *Connelly v. RTZ Corporation plc*[126] and *Lubbe v. Cape plc*.[127] It was most recently reviewed and refreshed in *VTB Capital plc v. Nutritek International Corp*,[128] but for most practical purposes, *Spiliada* is still the case to which attention needs to be directed, for it has worn extremely well and shows no sign of wearing out. Reference to the earlier decisions – aptly described as stepping-stones to the modern law – is appropriate only to throw light upon parts of the developed *Spiliada* doctrine;[129] and reference to the later decisions is necessary only to deal with points which have emerged as significant issues since the decision in *Spiliada*. In the most recent judgment of the Supreme Court, *Spiliada* was described as the '*locus classicus* in relation to issues of appropriate forum at common law'.[130] It is that, and more. It may have been a case which was directly concerned with the law on service out of the jurisdiction, but it is well understood, as *Spiliada* itself made clear and no one has doubted since, that it applies to the law on stays of proceedings just as directly.[131]

STAYING PROCEEDINGS ON THE GROUND OF *FORUM NON CONVENIENS*

4.17 General structure of the *Spiliada* test: two limbs to answer a single question

Two preliminary points need to be made and got out of the way. First, it is usual, even if it may not be strictly necessary,[132] to deal separately with the cases where the parties have, and have not, agreed in advance upon the court which is to have, as far as the parties are concerned,[133] jurisdiction to settle the dispute which has arisen.

Second, even if the parties have made a choice of court agreement for the English courts, or have made a contractual promise that neither will argue that the English court is a *forum non conveniens*, the court may still entertain an application for a stay of proceedings, albeit that it will be very hard for the applicant to persuade the court to allow him to obtain a stay by doing the very thing he has promised and bound himself not to do.[134] In effect, a promise not to challenge the jurisdiction of the English court is treated as though it were

---

125 [1987] AC 460. This will be referred to as the *Spiliada* test, and individual points identified as having been made by Lord Goff of Chieveley, or Lord Templeman: see further, paras. 4.19 *et seq*.

126 [1998] AC 854.

127 [2000] 1 WLR 1545. There have been more recent decisions, but none has established new law or improved on the formulation of the law as set out in *Spiliada*.

128 [2013] UKSC 5, [2013] 2 AC 337.

129 See, for example, *E.I. Du Pont de Nemours v. Agnew (No 1)* [1987] 2 Lloyd's Rep 585, 588.

130 *VTB Capital plc v. Nutritek International Corp* [2013] UKSC 5, [2013] 2 AC 337, [12].

131 Such differences as there may be, which suggest that the law on stays and service out are not exact mirror images, will be dealt with at the conclusion of examination of the law in relation to service out, at para. 4.92, below.

132 It is indeed true that if there is a choice of court agreement, the defendant's argument that the court should stay proceedings is not, at first sight, based upon the question of appropriateness, but upon the fact that the claimant is breaking his contractual promise to sue in the chosen court. The approach to such cases is set out separately at paras. 4.41 *et seq*., below.

133 Whether the agreement of the parties will establish the judicial jurisdiction of the court will be a matter for the public law of the court in question.

134 *UBS AG v. Omni Holdings AG* [2000] 1 WLR 916; *Marubeni Hong Kong & South China Ltd v. Mongolian Government* [2002] 2 All ER (Comm) 873.

an exclusive jurisdiction agreement for the English courts.[135] As the relief will be granted only in extreme cases, there is probably no difficulty in allowing an application which will rarely be successful; but if events have occurred which allow it to be argued that what has happened really falls outside what the parties must have had in mind, then in a proper case a stay may be ordered.

In the absence of any agreement on choice of court, the defendant[136] who wishes the court to stay proceedings commenced against him is required to show that the interests of justice favour a stay of proceedings. In order to make the plea good, the applicant is required to show that there is another available[137] forum, which is clearly or distinctly more appropriate than England for the resolution of the dispute: this is the *first limb* of the *Spiliada* test. If the applicant (defendant) succeeds in that task, the burden then passes to the respondent (claimant), to show why it would nevertheless be so unjust to prevent his suing in England and, in effect, to expect him to proceed in the natural forum overseas, that the English proceedings should not be stayed after all: this is the *second limb* of the *Spiliada* test. But if the applicant (defendant) does discharge the burden placed upon him at the first stage, the presumption in favour of a stay is a heavy one. The respondent (claimant) should expect to have a hard task to show, at the second stage, that there is still sufficient reason why the case should not be heard in the forum clearly more appropriate for it.

The test is, at least to begin with, constructed to operate sequentially: it has two limbs, operated one after the other, not two lists operating side by side. However, when the second stage is reached, and it is necessary to decide whether to allow the case to continue to be heard in England, notwithstanding that a more appropriate forum is overseas, the fact that the overseas forum is clearly or distinctly more appropriate than England will be a factor which bears on whether, overall, it would be just or unjust to stay the proceedings. With this in mind, it is correct to analyse the two limbs of the test separately, but it is important not to lose sight of the fact that the ultimate issue, or the overarching question, is whether the interests of justice require a stay of proceedings. This is an important point, because certain factors, such as the existence of an actual *lis alibi pendens*, or the possibility that other parties may join or be joined to the litigation at a later date, or the fact that an English judgment would not be recognised by a foreign court before which the defendant would need to claim over against a

---

135 *General Motors Corp v. Royal & Sun Alliance Insurance plc* [2007] EWHC 2206 (Comm), [2008] Lloyd's Rep IR 311. In *National Westminster Bank v. Utrecht-America Finance Corp* [2001] EWCA Civ 658, [2001] 3 All ER 733, it was thought that such an express promise was fatal to a stay application for a stay; the view of the Court of Appeal in *UBS AG v. HSH Nordbank AG* [2009] EWCA Civ 585, [2009] 2 Lloyd's Rep 272, [100], was probably not quite so pronounced.

136 The claimant may exceptionally apply to stay his own proceedings pending parallel proceedings in a foreign court if this is what good management of the litigation requires: *A-G v. Arthur Andersen & Co* [1989] ECC 224. If, for example, the claimant issues the claim form merely to save limitation, it may be proper to grant him a stay of the proceedings he has commenced if the natural forum is an overseas court and the application is made immediately after service of the claim form. See also *Deaville v. Aeroflot Russian International Airlines* [1997] 2 Lloyd's Rep 67; but *cf Centro International Handelsbank AG v. Morgan Grenfell* [1997] CLC 870, where the court was notably more sympathetic to the view that if the claimant had commenced proceedings, he was obliged to move them along and allow the defendant actively to defend them; see also *Insurance Co of the State of Pennsylvania v. Equitas Insurance Ltd* [2013] EWHC 3713 (Comm). The broad question will be one of what justice demands in the individual circumstances of the case.

137 Normally it will be available, because the defendant undertakes to submit to its jurisdiction. But if the court would not have jurisdiction, because there was a jurisdictional impediment which the defendant could not waive, or because the claimant's action is not admissible in that court, the case is one where there is not an available forum elsewhere; and an application for a stay will be rendered much more difficult. See below, para. 4.19.

third party, do not fit neatly and tidily within only one but not the other of the limbs of the *Spiliada* test. It may also be that points of legitimate concern about the quality of adjudication available from the foreign court, which have assumed prominence in recent cases, do not neatly fit, either. It does not appear worthwhile to seek to force them to do so; it is more realistic to recognise that, although the *Spiliada* limbs are an excellent starting point, the goal in every case is to identify whether the interests of justice favour a stay. The two limbs of the test in *Spiliada* help to answer this question, but they do not constrain it. To use another idiom, they are 'pointers rather than boundary marks'.[138]

4.18 Nature and length of applications for a stay

It was said in plain terms in *Spiliada v. Cansulex*,[139] and has been reiterated on several occasions since, that the decision whether to stay proceedings is largely one for the evaluation[140] of the first instance judge, and that appeals against the decision, especially when given by a Commercial Court judge, should be rare. It was also said that the judge should be able to proceed by refreshing his memory of what was said in *Spiliada*, and that submissions of the parties' legal representatives should be measured in hours rather than days. Sage though this advice may have been, it represented the triumph of hope over experience. In some cases the hearings have been lengthy, and the evidence placed before the court very substantial. It is not surprising that this has provoked some courts to suggest that matters are getting out of control.[141]

But the issue of where a dispute will be tried will very often be the most significant factor in the parties' appraisal of the likely outcome of the case.[142] Not only does the determination of forum tend to determine which system of law or laws will be applied to the merits of the case, but it will also determine which system of procedural law will govern the pre-trial procedure. These factors, whose impact on the dispute may become clear as soon as any issue as to forum is settled, may be sufficient by themselves to encourage the parties to come to terms. A preliminary skirmish on the question of jurisdiction, even if expensive, may

---

138 *The Atlantic Star* [1974] AC 436, 468 (Lord Wilberforce, referring to the requirements of a predecessor test).

139 [1987] AC 460, 464–465.

140 As distinct from a discretion: *VTB Capital plc v. Nutritek International Corp* [2013] UKSC 5, [2013] 2 AC 337, [156].

141 There are many; a couple will do as samples (though for a highly colourful version, see *Friis v Colbourn* [2009] EWHC 903 (Ch)). In *Cherney v. Deripaska* [2009] EWCA Civ 849, [2010] 1 All ER 456, [7], in which the court said that the parties' money would have been better spent on a trial of the merits: a conclusion which was, in the circumstances of the particular case, more than a little challenging. In *AK Investment CJSC v. Kyrgyz Mobil Tel Ltd* [2011] UKPC 7, [2012] 1 WLR 1804, [7] (a service out case), the complaint was directed at the volume of material placed before the court ('wholly disproportionate to the issues of law and fact raised by the parties') rather than at the cost of the application, though there is probably a linear relationship between the two. A more measured comment, but to the same overall effect, is to be found in *VTB Capital plc v. Nutritek International Corp* [2013] UKSC 5, [2013] 2 AC 337, [81]–[94] (a service out case). If the parties see the question of where the trial will take place as the most vital factor in their assessment of how to bring the dispute to an end, it is hard to see why they should not litigate it as though it were a trial; but if it is believed that the defendant is taking every conceivable preliminary point and trying to break a claimant whose financial resources are under strain (for which the defendant may be responsible in the first place) the issue certainly looks very different. It may not be easy to persuade a court to make findings at so early a stage, but this is part of the calculation which the parties make in deciding whether to spend money on such a challenge.

142 But they may be quite wrong in their appraisal of likely outcome: see *UBS AG (London Branch) v. Kommunale Wasserwerke Leipzig GmbH* [2014] EWHC 3615, [922].

assist the early settlement of cases, and the occasional burdensome application, and judicial scolding, may be a price worth paying.[143] For similar reasons, the procedure to obtain a stay of proceedings may conduce to the overriding objective of the Civil Procedure Rules, namely that of dealing with a case justly by saving expense, ensuring that the case is dealt with expeditiously and fairly, and allotting to it an appropriate share of the court's resources while taking into account the need to allot resources to other cases.[144] Not everyone will agree, but this aspect of *Spiliada* should not be undersold: a significant number of the cases in which the issue of jurisdiction is fought at the preliminary stage appear to go no further. This almost inevitably means that they consume a smaller share of the resources of the court than they otherwise would.

The material date for the purposes of the evidence and other material to which the court may be taken on the application for a stay is the date of the hearing of the application for a stay, rather than the date on which the proceedings were instituted or the application notice was issued.[145] It was correctly explained in *Mohammed v. Bank of Kuwait and the Middle East KSC*[146] that this was the most practical solution, for by contrast with the case of an application to set aside an order granting permission to serve out, there is no prior act of the court which is being challenged.[147] The question whether another court is more appropriate than England may well be affected, for example, by the nature of the defence which the defendant may intend to run. This may be unknown at the date proceedings are issued, and may not be clear when the application notice is issued. No doubt it will be necessary to put in evidence as to facts and matters which may be expected to arise at trial; this evidence may not be served until very shortly before the hearing. The decision in *Mohammed v. Bank of Kuwait*, to look at all this material as at the date of the hearing, is rational. However, if the circumstances change materially after the hearing, this fact may furnish grounds for an application by the defendant to lift the stay, or justify a fresh application by the claimant for a stay, but does not give ground for an appeal, for it does not establish that there was anything wrong with the original order when it was made.[148]

4.19 First limb of the *Spiliada* test: the 'availability' of the foreign forum

The first requirement is that the forum which the defendant proposes as being clearly more appropriate than England for the trial be available for the trial of the action.[149] There are

---

143 For example, the Commercial Court Working Party, in commenting on the proposed Woolf reforms of civil procedure stated in its memorandum of 16 February 1996 that, so far as the Commercial Court was concerned, 'unlike other parts of the High Court, there are very many cases that involve *"forum conveniens"* issues. Many cases are principally concerned with this point, and are resolved by the parties once jurisdiction issues have been decided, even in favour of the English courts'. There is no reason to doubt the continuing truth of that observation.

144 CPR Part 1.

145 Implicitly approved in *Lubbe v. Cape plc* [2000] 1 WLR 1545, 1556, 1558. Contrast the relevant date for an application to set aside the order granting permission to serve out of the jurisdiction (the date is that of the order granting permission), or to set aside service where this was made where permission was not required (the date is the date of service).

146 [1996] 1 WLR 1483.

147 For confirmation, in a case of service out, see *Sharab v. Al-Saud* [2009] EWCA Civ 353, [2009] 2 Lloyd's Rep 160.

148 In such a case it is unlikely that the application could be made under CPR Part 11; but CPR r. 3.1(2) may be used instead, the application now being made in the context of the court's case management powers.

149 *Spiliada* at 477 (Lord Goff). Lord Templeman did not, in express terms, deal with this as a separate requirement.

potentially three[150] aspects of availability; and depending on how many of them are properly seen as part of the definition of 'availability' (the view taken here is that only the first of the three is part of 'availability'), the defendant will have the burden of proof in relation to all of them.

The first requirement is that the foreign court must be shown[151] to have personal jurisdiction over the defendant.[152] In a case in which the defendant is otherwise present or resident within the territorial jurisdiction of the foreign court, or has contractually submitted in advance to its jurisdiction, it will be likely that the foreign court is one whose jurisdiction is available to the claimant[153] In such a case, the claimant will have been able as of right to bring proceedings in the foreign court, which will therefore be available; but it may be otherwise if the defendant has judicial immunity from suit under the law applicable in the foreign court.[154] An apparent difficulty had arisen in cases where the claimant would not have been able to proceed against the defendant as a matter of right, but would have needed the permission of the foreign court, or a voluntary submission by the defendant, in order to commence proceedings there. In *Lubbe v. Cape plc*[155] it was held that, as long as the defendant has undertaken to submit to the jurisdiction of the foreign court by the time of the hearing of the application for a stay,[156] the condition that the foreign court be available will have been satisfied. Any concern[157] that a defendant might be able to contrive a natural forum, or engineer a form of reverse forum shopping, by undertaking to submit to an inappropriate court, is unreal, for the naturalness of the forum has nothing to do with the will of the parties, but everything to do with the objective facts. If a court is one of competent jurisdiction only by reason of a voluntary submission, this may be a further indication, at a later stage, of its unnaturalness; and a late-delayed submission to the jurisdiction may, and probably should, be reflected in the costs order made by the court, but it is irrelevant to availability. Very much more doubtfully,[158] it has been held that even if the defendant has not undertaken to submit, and does not do so at the hearing, the court may infer that this is his position.[159]

---

150 Treatment of the third, which is more controversial, is found at the end of this paragraph.

151 If it is uncertain whether the foreign court will accept that it has jurisdiction, it may be appropriate to stay, and to lift the stay if it is held that the foreign court does not have jurisdiction after all: *BMG Trading Ltd v. A S Mackay Ltd* [1998] ILPr 691; *cf Baghlaf Al Zafer v. Pakistan National Shipping Co (No 2)* [2001] 1 Lloyd's Rep 1. For something similar under the law of California, see *Gambra v. International Lease Finance Corp* 377 F Supp (2d) 810 (CD Cal 2005).

152 The question whether it must also have (subject matter) jurisdiction over the claim is examined below, as part of the broader question whether the claimant must have a right to prosecute a cause of action to success in the foreign court: see para. 4.20, below.

153 Though if this is not common ground, evidence will need to be given.

154 *Harty v. Sabre International Security* [2011] EWHC 852 (QB) (a service out case, but the point is general).

155 [2000] 1 WLR 1545.

156 But if he only proffers an undertaking to submit at the hearing of the appeal to the Court of Appeal it will be too late and will be disregarded, at least in the context of an application to set aside service out; it seems probable that the same will be true in a stay case, for the appeal is still an appeal against the order of the judge made on the evidence before him: *Sharab v. Al-Saud* [2009] EWCA Civ 353, [2009] 2 Lloyd's Rep 160.

157 This had been a concern for the Court of Appeal in the first *Lubbe* decision: [1998] CLC 1559.

158 Because he bears the burden of proving the point.

159 Though this seems quite unprincipled. In *Gheewala v. Hindocha* [2003] UKPC 77 (Jersey), [2004] WTLR 1119, some among the applicants for a stay were not obviously subject to the jurisdiction of their preferred court (Kenya) and had not undertaken to submit to the jurisdiction of those courts. This apparently did not prevent the ordering of a stay, though this may well have been because the point had not been taken below and was therefore not available before the Privy Council. The decision goes to (and perhaps beyond) the very edge of what is acceptable, for if a defendant is not prepared to undertake to submit, a court may be right to be very wary of his alleged

4.20 Availability and the claimant's prospects of success on the merits

The second possible aspect of 'availability' is more controversial. It is not completely settled how the court is to evaluate a contention by the claimant that the foreign forum is not 'available' to him, because the cause of action which he has raised before the English court is not one which would be open to him in the foreign court.

There has been occasional suggestion in the cases that, in such a case, either the foreign court is not 'available', or the case falls right outside the sphere of operation of the *Spiliada* principle, on the basis that *Spiliada* applies to cases, but only to cases, in which there is a choice between two courts which are available for the trial.[160] But neither of these is persuasive; this factor, if it is a factor, belongs to the second limb of the *Spiliada* test, for its effect is to support an argument that it would in the circumstances be so unjust to stay the proceedings that no stay should be ordered.

This is consistent with authority and common sense. As to authority, in *Re Harrods (Buenos Aires) Ltd*[161] proceedings were commenced in England, against the company as defendant, under what was then section 459 of the Companies Act 1985,[162] alleging unfair prejudice in the conduct of the company's affairs. One of the remedies available to the English court would have been to order the majority shareholder to buy the minority shareholder's shares. The court held that though such a remedy was unavailable from a court in the country which was the natural forum (*in casu* Argentina), that did not prevent the court ordering a stay of proceedings. And in *Spiliada* itself, the House of Lords accepted that a stay of proceedings was possible in favour of a court before which the claim would be barred by lapse of time:[163] in such a case not all will agree that the foreign court can be described as available.

And as to common sense, in every case, somebody wins and someone loses. This is the nature of justice rather than a symptom of injustice, and the fact that it happens in a particular way in a particular case cannot really mean that a foreign court is not available. It therefore makes sense to address the issue in relation to the second limb of the test.

4.21 Availability and the prospects of a fair trial

The third aspect of availability is that there must actually be a functioning court or court system in the place to which the defendant can point. In the rare case in which civil administration has broken down and there is no sensible judicial process in the foreign place, it will not be possible to show that there is a court available for the trial of the action.[164] Such

---

preparedness to be sued elsewhere before a court which he says is available to the claimant. For a more principled decision, see *Sharab v. Al-Saud* [2009] EWCA Civ 353, [2009] 2 Lloyd's Rep 160, where such trickery was less successful.

160 The issue has arisen most frequently in relation to claims for an anti-suit injunction, where the claim as formulated before the foreign court (an arguable example is a claim under the Clayton-Sherman Act) could not be proceeded with in England.

161 [1992] Ch 72.

162 Now s. 994 of the Companies Act 2006.

163 Not, perhaps, if the claimant was not at fault in not instituting proceedings in the foreign court, but if he had been negligent in not doing so, a stay would not be refused on this account.

164 *889457 Alberta Inc v. Katanga Mining Ltd* [2008] EWHC 2679 (Comm), [2009] ILPr 175 (Kolwezi area of Democratic Republic of Congo). For cases in which it is contended that the claimant cannot expect a fair trial before the courts of the otherwise-available foreign forum, see below, para. 4.35. It seems undeniable that the

extreme circumstances are not frequently raised in commercial litigation, but when they are, it must be possible to say that there is no court in the foreign territory, and therefore no court which is available.

A more controversial sense of this aspect of availability may require the defendant to show that the foreign forum is available in the sense that the claimant can expect to receive a fair trial there. As with the previous point, the better view is that this argument, even if it can be made, has no bearing upon whether the foreign forum is available, and that its proper place is at the second stage of the *Spiliada* enquiry, when it is incumbent on the claimant to establish that it would be so unjust, to send him, in effect, to the foreign court that the order sought by the defendant should not be made.[165] It is true that in *Mohammed v. Bank of Kuwait and the Middle East KSC*,[166] the Court of Appeal decided that, where this objection could on the facts be raised, the fact that the claimant had a well-founded fear that he would not be able to get a fair trial in Kuwait meant that Kuwait had not been shown by the defendant to be an available forum for the trial of the action. Or, to put it another way, the foreign court had to be available for the *fair* trial, rather than for the pretence of trial, of the action.

Although this will be significant only as to the question who has the burden of proof, there may well be cases which turn on this point, and in which the burden of proof is crucial. Although it is understandable that, if the defendant wishes to remove the claim and claimant to another jurisdiction, the defendant should have the task of showing that the alternative which he proposes is satisfactory in the eyes of the English court, at least some of the matters relevant to proof will more obviously lie within the knowledge of the claimant. More to the point, the general approach in *Mohammed* is inconsistent with *Spiliada*, and was fatally undermined by both *Connelly v. RTZ Corp*[167] and *Lubbe v. Cape plc*.[168] In both cases the claimants were faced with a submission that Namibia and South Africa were, respectively, clearly or distinctly more appropriate than England. The claimants showed that they were, on financial grounds, wholly unable to fund and therefore to bring a claim in the natural forum. It was accepted that this contention was relevant only at the second stage of the *Spiliada* enquiry, where one asks whether it is unjust to send the claimant away from the English court, and had no bearing on the first stage. *Connelly* and *Lubbe* were not cases where the foreign court was said to offer only an unfair trial to the claimant. But if *Mohammed* were applied, then if the claimant can obtain no access to court at all, the court could be regarded as unavailable. The analysis in *Connelly* and *Lubbe*, treating the capacity of the foreign court to offer a system of adjudication which was objectively fair to the claimant as a matter falling under the second limb of the *Spiliada* test, should suffice to consign this aspect of *Mohammed* to history.

As a result of *Connelly* and *Lubbe*, and in conclusion, all that need be shown, so far as the availability of the foreign court is concerned, is that the court proposed by the defendant as being more appropriate than England is one to whose personal jurisdiction the defendant is amenable. Arguments which tend to show that the claimant may, in effect, be bound to

---

list of failing States in which a half-decent trial would be unimaginable, is considerably longer than it was in the recent past.

165 Unless it has already been decided that Parliament has legislated, by giving effect to Art. 6 of the ECHR, to remove completely the power to stay in such cases.

166 [1996] 1 WLR 1483. The claimant was an Iraqi; the defendant argued that the natural forum was Kuwait.

167 [1998] AC 854.

168 [2000] 1 WLR 1545, reversing [2000] 1 Lloyd's Rep 139, and affirming, but on different grounds, [1998] CLC 1559. It is to be noted that Lord Bingham was well aware of the potential impact of the ECHR in such a case.

lose if the action is stayed may be relevant at the second stage of the *Spiliada*, when the issue is whether it is unjust to send him to the natural forum. They do not challenge, still less disprove, the availability of the natural forum; and the cases which have suggested otherwise are not to be relied on.

4.22 The first limb of the *Spiliada* test: the 'natural forum' or the 'appropriate forum'

It has become common to refer to the court identified by the defendant under the first limb of the *Spiliada* test, as 'the natural forum'. It is more correct, though still not quite right, to refer to it as 'the forum with which the action has a closer and more real connection than it has with England'.[169] In *VTB Capital plc v. Nutritek International Corp*,[170] the court referred to 'the appropriate forum', which is probably the best choice. But whichever is used, three preliminary points may be made about it.

First, it is clear that there may be cases in which there is *no* forum which can be said to be the most appropriate forum: this is not fatal to the application for a stay. In an international commercial dispute, there may be points of contact with a number of possible courts, but distributed in such a way that no single court can be said to be *the* most appropriate forum. That, however, is not what the first limb of the *Spiliada* test requires to be identified. The defendant, applying for the stay, is required to show that the court to which he points is 'clearly or distinctly more appropriate than England' for the trial of the action. If he cannot do so, there will be no stay of proceedings.[171] But it also follows that, if the other forum *is* clearly or distinctly more appropriate than England, a stay should be granted, or should not be ruled out, even though that forum could not be described as *the* most appropriate forum. At least, it would appear to follow; one can, however, understand that a court might conclude that the defendant had not sufficiently discharged the burden of proof upon him by showing the foreign court to be something less than *the* appropriate forum. To put it another way, although the *Spiliada* test is expressed in comparative terms, it may be understood in more absolute terms.

Second, it is not obvious that if the defendant can show a court to be clearly more appropriate than England for the trial of the action, he will have identified 'the natural forum'. That expression would suggest that the search is for, and only for, a court which can be shown to be most appropriate for the trial of the action; but in almost every case in which the issue arises for decision, the question is whether the defendant has shown the court outside England, in favour of which he seeks the stay, to be the natural forum.

Third, there may be cases in which the foreign court is the natural forum, at least when this expression is assessed in terms of the strength of connection between the facts of the particular case and the court or country in question, but where it cannot be said that the foreign court is clearly more appropriate than England for the trial. This may be because the particular dispute is part of a larger picture,[172] which alters the impression. It may also

---

169 *Deutsche Bank AG v. Highland Crusader Offshore Partners LP* [2009] EWCA Civ 725, [2010] 1 WLR 1023, [55].

170 [2013] UKSC 5, [2013] 2 AC 337.

171 *Spiliada*, at 477. For illustration, *European Asian Bank v. Punjab & Sind Bank* [1982] 2 Lloyd's Rep 356; *The Coral Isis* [1986] 2 Lloyd's Rep 166; *MacSteel Holdings Ltd v. Thermasteel (Canada) Inc* [1996] CLC 1403.

172 See below, para. 4.28.

be argued[173] that the foreign court cannot be more appropriate than England if the foreign country is one in which a fair trial is not possible, for how could it be more appropriate that the trial take place in a corrupt court?[174]

The terminology of the 'natural forum' has become so embedded in the language of the law that it is useless to object to it. But that does not alter the law: the test is a comparative one, not an absolute one.

4.23 The first limb of the *Spiliada* test: the pointers to appropriateness

Whether the forum to which the defendant points is referred to as 'natural' or 'appropriate', the factors which help to identify it depend on the circumstances of the individual case: many may be listed, but the weight of any of them depends on the context in which it arises. Their evaluation in a particular case is a matter of evaluation (rather than discretion), for the judge hearing the application for a stay.[175]

The factors which have been found to be relevant can probably be organised under five points, though this is for convenience of exposition only. For just as the *Spiliada* test comprises one question which is initially analysed in two limbs, the first limb of *Spiliada* comprises one question which may be initially examined under five points. Insofar as these are separate, they are: first, the personal connections which the parties to the litigation have with particular countries; second, the factual connections which the events which make up the story have with particular places; third, the question of which law should or will be applied to resolve the substantive issues in the dispute; fourth, the possibility of there being a *lis alibi pendens* in another court; and fifth, the possibility that other persons may become party to, and affect the overall shape of, the litigation.

Of course, it is for the applicant (defendant) to identify the specific issues which arise for decision and which show it, as he says, to be more appropriate that the trial take place in another forum: it will not usually be enough for him to allege generally that the foreign court is more appropriate than England and to hope that this will suffice. The test is more specific than that: it requires the defendant to show that the foreign court is more appropriate than England for the investigation and the adjudication of those particular issues which need to be resolved in the case.[176]

4.24 Appropriateness (1): personal connections of the parties

As to the first point, if the residences[177] of the claimant and defendant are in the same State, it may well be that the litigation will appear to belong in the courts of the State of their

---

173 Wrongly, as it is suggested: see the following footnote.

174 However, in the case of stay applications, it is clear that complaints of this kind do not arise at the first stage of the enquiry; they do not affect the debate whether the foreign court is clearly more appropriate than England. Instead, they arise at the second, corrective, stage of the *Spiliada* test: see below, para. 4.30. This conclusion is not affected by *Cherney v. Deripaska* [2009] EWCA Civ 849, [2010] 1 All ER (Comm) 456, or *AK Investment CJSC v. Kyrgyz Mobil Tel* [2011] UKPC 7, [2012] 1 WLR 1804, which are service out cases.

175 Lord Templeman, in *Spiliada*, at 465; *VTB Capital plc v. Nutritek International Corp* [2013] UKSC 5, [2013] 2 AC 337, esp. at [156].

176 *VTB Capital plc v. Nutritek International Corp* [2013] UKSC 5, [2013] 2 AC 337, [36], [192].

177 Residence, rather than domicile in its common law sense, connotes a real and present connection. Domicile in the sense in which it is defined in the 1982 Act would be very close to residence, and could be used interchangeably with it.

common residence. The practical convenience of litigation being in one's home court is considerable,[178] and in this case doubly so. On the other hand, where a residence in a particular country has been acquired, or is self-inflicted, for tax avoidance or for other unnatural reasons, and is not in any other sense the home of the party, or if the litigation is actually being driven by an insurance company with a residence different from that of the notional party in whose name the claim is made, the residence of the parties will be less weighty a factor in the identification of the natural forum.[179]

In the specific context of disputes concerning the internal management of companies created under foreign laws, the place of incorporation has a strong claim to be seen as the natural forum,[180] though there is no particular reason to suppose that this principle has any application to external disputes to which a company is party, even if one of the other parties is an officer or employee.

4.25 Appropriateness (2): evidence in relation to the events

If the dispute has arisen or has come to light in a particular country, it will sometimes appear that that will be the most appropriate place for it to be resolved. For example, if a motor accident has occurred in Canada, it is likely that those who can bear witness to the facts, and the witnesses to what happened after the accident, are in Canada. It makes some sense for the trial to take place where the ordinary witnesses of fact can most conveniently give their evidence.[181] The point is all the more pressing if the ordinary witnesses will give their evidence in a language which then has to be translated: this is bound to affect, adversely, the ability of a court to gauge their credibility.

In the context of tort claims, it has been said that the place where a tort was committed will have a very strong claim to be seen as the natural forum for the resolution of disputes arising from it. This point is all the more persuasive if it is borne in mind that the law which will be applied to the merits will frequently be the law of that place. But it is less persuasive if the tort is one of those in which the elements which make it up are more delocalised, and if the witnesses whose evidence will be decisive are not local to the place considered to have been the place of the tort.[182] If a cargo has been unloaded at a port in Mexico,[183] and it is alleged (and denied) that the cargo was decomposed on arrival, or was damaged in

---

178 It is implicit in the Brussels I Regulation, and in the law of most of Western Europe, that for a defendant it is a matter of basic right, rather than mere convenience.

179 *Spiliada*, at 481–482.

180 *Konamaneni v. Rolls Royce Industrial Power (India) Ltd* [2002] 1 WLR 1269 (fraud on minority shareholder); *Československa Obchodni Banka AS v. Nomura International plc* [2003] ILPr 321 (internal management); *SMAY Investments v. Sachdev* [2003] EWHC 474 (Ch), [2003] 1 WLR 1973; *Reeves v. Sprecher* [2007] EWHC 17 (Ch), [2008] BCC 49; *Incorporated Broadcasters v. CanWest Global Communications Corp* (2003) 223 DLR (4th) 627. But it is otherwise if the companies are not being wound up compulsorily, and no issue of corporate governance arises: *Islamic Republic of Pakistan v. Zaidari* [2006] EWHC 2411 (Comm), [2006] 2 CLC 667. See also *Pacific International Sports Clubs Ltd v. Soccer Marketing International Ltd* [2010] EWCA Civ 753 (shareholder dispute as to ownership or control of Dinamo Kiev Football Club; common ground that natural forum Ukraine); *Zumax Nigeria Ltd v. First City Monument Bank Ltd* [2014] EWHC 2075 (Ch).

181 This factor looms more largely in those systems which rely on oral rather than documentary evidence.

182 *The Albaforth* [1984] 2 Lloyd's Rep 91; *Berezovsky v. Michaels* [2000] 1 WLR 1004; for a more delocalised tort, in which this factor may be of reduced significance, see *VTB Capital plc v. Nutritek International Corp* [2013] UKSC 5, [2013] 2 AC 337, making the point that the strength of the factor will vary from case to case and that there is no invariable rule.

183 See, for example, *The El Amria* [1981] 2 Lloyd's Rep 119.

the course of unloading and storage, it may be that the relevant evidence is to be found in Mexico, and will be given in Spanish, and that this may contribute to Mexico emerging as the natural forum. But the witnesses will not always be where the tort was committed or where the damage occurred. It is therefore appropriate to look at the witnesses who will be called on to testify separately from any issue of applicable law, at least at this stage. Of course, if the evidence is in documentary form, or will take the form of expert testimony,[184] its geographical situation or the language in which it will be given may be less compelling as a factor.

If the claimant identifies witnesses who will be willing or could be compelled to give evidence in England, but who cannot be compelled to give evidence, and whose evidence will not otherwise be available to the court, in the foreign country, this may make it harder for the defendant to show that the foreign forum is more appropriate than England. Alternatively, this fact may be relevant under the second limb of the *Spiliada* test, as tending to show why it would be unjust to prevent the trial from taking place in a court where evidence can be given. However, the development of methods and procedures for the taking of evidence for use in proceedings in other countries may have reduced the significance which this point might otherwise have had.

4.26 Appropriateness (3): the law which will be applied to decide the issues raised

The significance to be attached to the identification of the law which is to be applied to the merits of the dispute is a little more complex. The obvious point of departure is that a court will be presumed to apply its own law better than a foreign court will apply that same law. One may start close to home. If claims arise from insurance contracts made on the London market, there is a clear tendency to see England as the natural forum, for English law will be very likely to be the applicable law; and England will therefore tend to be the most appropriate forum.[185]

By contrast, if it is clear that a dispute is going to be resolved by the application of Russian law, and that Russian law is likely to differ from English law, and not only on account of the language, there will be a strong *prima facie* reason for considering the Russian court to be a more appropriate court than an English court would be.[186] This is not just because a first instance court in Russia should apply Russian law better than an English court may be expected to, but also because there will be an opportunity to take the case to a Russian appellate court if it is contended that the law was applied incorrectly: no such correction is available from the English Court of Appeal. This conclusion is underscored by the fact that

---

184 It is assumed that experts are willing and able, and even keen, to travel, and are used to giving their evidence wherever in the world it is called for. Documents can be put in a box and sent by courier.

185 *Arkwright Mutual Insurance Co v. Bryanston Insurance Co Ltd* [1990] 2 QB 649; *CGU International Insurance plc v. Szabo* [2002] 1 All ER (Comm) 83; *Lincoln National Life Insurance Co v. Employers' Reinsurance Corp* [2002] EWHC 28 (Comm), [2002] Lloyd's Rep IR 853; *Markel International Insurance Co Ltd v. La Republica Compania Argentina de Seguros Generales SA* [2004] EWHC 1826 (Comm), [2005] 1 Lloyd's Rep IR 90; *Carvill America Inc v. Camperdown UK Ltd* [2005] EWCA Civ 645, [2005] 2 Lloyd's Rep 457 (a case concerning reinsurance brokerage in the London market).

186 *Trendtex Trading Corp v. Credit Suisse* [1982] AC 679; *The Nile Rhapsody* [1994] 1 Lloyd's Rep 382; *ED & F Man Ltd v. Kvaerner Gibraltar Ltd* [1996] 2 Lloyd's Rep 206; *Tryg Baltica International (UK) Ltd v. Boston Compania de Seguros SA* [2004] EWHC 1186 (Comm), [2005] Lloyd's Rep IR 40, [42].

a Russian court will apply Russian law and procedure; but if the case is heard in England, Russian law will be applied to the substantive, but English law to the procedural, issues: the amalgam has the potential to produce less than satisfactory results, and (in cases in which the applicable law is a law which the parties have expressly chosen) may also distort the bargain the parties believed themselves to have made. All in all, this makes a clear case for this as a pointer to the natural forum; and if one substitutes for Russian a law which is even more foreign to the common law, the argument is *a fortiori*. The point is stronger still if the issues of foreign law which need to be decided are intrinsically difficult.[187]

As against this, four factors may weaken the argument that the identification of the governing law is a clear pointer to the appropriate forum. The first is that not all foreign laws are equally difficult for an English court to apply. Whereas the difficulty of understanding and applying some laws, from legal and cultural traditions wholly alien to the common law, may be just too great for an English court to have confidence and give assurance that it would be able to offer a reliable adjudication, other laws are just not so very different from English law, and a court should not be so easily persuaded that the other court is clearly more appropriate than England for the adjudication simply because its law is to be applied. Second, the reasoning assumes that the foreign court will itself share the view of the English court as to choice of law. An example may make the point. Suppose that a contractual dispute has arisen, and that according to English private international law, the contract in question is governed by the law of Mexico. But suppose also that a Mexican court would consider it to be governed instead by English law, on the footing that such a dispute is governed by the law of the place where the contract was made. This, assuming it is shown to be so, should weaken the proposition that Mexico may be a more appropriate forum, for the choice is now shown to lie between two courts, each of which will be struggling, equally but differently, with the application of what they will see as foreign law. Third, there may be more than one legal issue to be decided. If two legal issues arise, to which different laws apply, the persuasive strength of this factor may be reduced.[188] And fourth, of course, a vague and general assertion that 'foreign law applies' will not get anyone anywhere: the contention that foreign law has to be applied must be demonstrated by identifying the particular issues on which that law will be applicable.[189] If the evidence is that the foreign court can and will determine the case in accordance with English law (which is the *lex causae*), the case for holding that the foreign court is not the appropriate forum is rather weaker than it would otherwise be.

For these reasons, the identification of the law governing the dispute may not be as persuasive a factor pointing to the appropriateness of a court as may at first sight appear. In *Spiliada* itself, though for no stated reason, Lord Goff said[190] that the identification of the governing law may, but need not, be of significance in the search for a more appropriate forum: it is possible that some of this is what he had in mind.[191] Much more significantly,

---

187 *Pacific International Sports Clubs Ltd v. Surkis* [2010] EWCA Civ 753. For a gruesome illustration of the difficulties which may arise if the court does have to decide very difficult issues of foreign law (*in casu*, Thai), see *Dornoch Ltd v. Westminster International BV* [2009] EWHC 1782 (Admlty), [2009] 2 Lloyd's Rep 420.

188 But if one of these is a matter of English public policy, such a matter can generally be decided only by an English court: *E.I. Du Pont de Nemours v. Agnew (No 1)* [1987] 2 Lloyd's Rep 585; see also *CGU International Insurance plc v. Szabo* [2002] 1 All ER (Comm) 83.

189 *Cf VTB Capital plc v. Nutritek International Corp* [2013] UKSC 5, [2013] 2 AC 337, [36], [192].

190 *Spiliada*, at 481.

191 For a case where there was no real law in the claim, and the identification of the *lex causae* was not material to the identification of the natural forum, see *Navigators Insurance Co v. Atlantic Methanol Production Co LLC* [2003]

perhaps, in *VTB Capital plc v. Nutritek International Corp*[192] the Supreme Court diluted the significance of the governing law to a factor of the 'if everything else is equal' kind.[193] The case was one in which the governing law of the claims in tort was (according to English rules of private international law) English law, but there was nothing before the court to suggest that a Russian court would be unable or unwilling to apply English law. That prevented the identification of the *lex causae* being the killer point which it might have been expected to be.

Separate consideration may be given to the case in which the *lex causae* is what it is because of a contractual term which expresses the parties' agreement on the point. Though the courts have been careful to avoid treating a choice of English law to govern a contract as though it were exactly the same as a choice of the English courts,[194] there is no doubt that an express choice of English law will make it more difficult to show a foreign forum, even where the foreign court will try to apply English law, to be clearly more appropriate. Indeed, as will be shown below,[195] it may make it relatively easy to show that England is the most appropriate forum; and it may even support a contention that it is positively wrongful for the claimant to think of bringing the claim anywhere other than before a court which will decide the issues in accordance with the parties' express agreement on choice of law.[196]

4.27 Appropriateness (4): the effect of a *lis alibi pendens*

The existence of a *lis alibi pendens* has no particular impact on the identification of a more appropriate forum: English law does not have rigid rules or formal doctrine of *litispendence*.[197] At first sight it seems wrong that factors beyond the actual dispute between the parties may affect the decision of where it is most appropriate for it to be tried. But it is probable[198] that the fact of actual or foreseeable related litigation may influence the identification of a forum as more appropriate.[199]

EWHC 1706 (Comm); *Royal & Sun Alliance Insurance plc v. Retail Brand Alliance Inc* [2004] EWHC 2139 (Comm), [2005] 1 Lloyd's Rep IR 110.

192 [2013] UKSC 5, [2013] 2 AC 337. And in the context of an application for an injunction to restrain foreign proceedings, it has been made clear that the fact that English law will (or, according to the rules of English private international law, should) be applied to the claim falls a long way short of furnishing a cause of action for the injunction: *FR Lürssen Werft GmbH & Co KG v. Halle* [2009] EWHC 2607 (Comm), [2010] 2 Lloyd's Rep 20; *Golden Endurance Shipping SA v. RMA Watanya SA* [2014] EWHC 3917 (Comm).

193 At [46].

194 *MacSteel Commercial Holdings (Pty) Ltd v. Thermasteel Canada Inc* [1996] CLC 1403; *BP Exploration Co (Libya) Ltd v. Hunt (No 2)* [1976] 3 All ER 879; *The Elli 2* [1985] 1 Lloyd's Rep 107; *Sawyer v. Atari Interactive Inc* [2005] EWHC 2351 (Ch), [2006] ILPr 8; *Novus Aviation Ltd v. Onur Air Tasimacilik A/S* [2009] EWCA Civ 122, [2009] 1 Lloyd's Rep 576.

195 Paragraph 4.89, below,

196 See below, para. 5.37.

197 This is the term usually found in civilian systems. The non-technical nature of the English approach is in contrast to the technical character of certain civilian notions of when a situation of *litispendence* has arisen.

198 But it is not certain. Although some judges have referred to the potential catastrophe of different courts reaching irreconcilable verdicts (*The El Amria* [1981] 2 Lloyd's Rep 119), others have observed that it may properly lie beyond the powers of any common law to prevent this occurring (*E.I. Du Pont de Nemours v. Agnew (No 2)* [1988] 2 Lloyd's Rep 240), or have not regarded it as particularly crucial (*Meadows Indemnity Co v. Insurance Corp of Ireland* [1989] 2 Lloyd's Rep 298).

199 *Cleveland Museum of Art v. Capricorn Art International SA* [1990] 2 Lloyd's Rep 166. If the claimant brings the same claim in two courts he may be required to elect to pursue only one.

If the claimant brings the same claim in two courts he may be required to elect to pursue only one,[200] though this point is very much weaker if the parties have specifically agreed in advance that no objection will be taken to parallel litigation.[201] Subject to that substantial point, the interests of justice are not generally served by two courts each hearing the same dispute, or each hearing only part of a larger, complex, dispute. Indeed, the possibility that there may be parallel litigation of a complex claim may be a reason which is sufficiently powerful to prevent effect being given to a choice of law agreement for the English court:[202] if it can do that, it can certainly influence the search for the appropriate forum.

It has also been held that if there is or has been litigation of a particularly high degree of factual or legal complexity, which has already been commenced; and it is alleged that this 'team expertise' makes the court in which it exists more appropriate than otherwise it might be, this factor will have some persuasive weight.[203]

4.28 Appropriateness (5): standing back to take a broader view

There are cases in which the appropriateness of a court seems clear (though one man's clarity may be another's illusion), but the reasons for this do not quite emerge from the usual list of factors and the careful judicial weighing exercise. After this examination of individual points of contact has been done, it may be right to stand back and view the issue with the wisdom of the common law. An excellent illustration of this is to be found in *VTB Capital plc v. Nutritek International Corp.*[204] The claims made were framed in tort, principally for deceit and conspiracy. Part of the complaint was that the alleged tortfeasor had induced the claimant to enter into contracts with another entity, connected with the tortfeasor, which provided for the exclusive jurisdiction of the English courts. On the issue whether the existence of this agreement on jurisdiction was directly binding on the alleged tortfeasor, the answer was no: such an outcome could only be arrived at by getting behind the corporate veil, and on a jurisdiction application, the intense analysis of facts relationships which might justify this result is simply not sensible.[205] But on the issue whether the jurisdiction agreement had a separate impact, contributing to the general argument that England was the appropriate forum for proceedings against the tortfeasor arising in connection with the contract which the other entity had concluded, the Supreme Court divided. In holding that the jurisdiction agreement was admissible as part of the *res gestae* helping to identify the appropriate forum for the claim against the tortfeasor, the minority may have drawn strength from a decision

---

200 *Australian Commercial Research & Development Ltd v. ANZ McCaughan Merchant Bank Ltd* [1989] 3 All ER 65. Alternatively he may seek to stay one set: *A-G v. Arthur Andersen & Co* [1989] ECC 244; though the defendant may oppose this manoeuvre on the ground that he has a right actively to defend allegations made against him: *Centro Internationale Handelsbank AG v. Morgan Grenfell* [1997] CLC 870.

201 A provision not uncommon in banking contracts: see *Royal Bank of Canada v. Cooperative Centrale Raiffeisen Boerenleenbank* [2003] EWCA Civ 7, [2004] 1 Lloyd's Rep 471; *Deutsche Bank AG v. Highland Crusader Offshore Partners LP* [2009] EWCA Civ 725, [2010] 1 WLR 1023.

202 *Donohue v. Armco Inc* [2001] UKHL 64, [2002] 1 All ER 749.

203 It did in *Spiliada* itself, where it was described as the 'Cambridgeshire' factor (named after the vessel in which an earlier shipment of corrosive sulphur had taken place). There the court with the expertise was England, but the principle must be reciprocal. Attempts to rely upon this point since *Spiliada* have been pretty unsuccessful, though it may have played a minor (but unacknowledged) part in the reasoning of the court in *Teekay Tankers Ltd v. STX Offshore & Shipping Co* [2014] EWHC 3612 (Comm), [73].

204 [2013] UKSC 5, [2013] 2 AC 337.

205 For the law on corporate veils, see also *Prest v. Petrodel Resources Ltd* [2013] UKSC 34, [2013] 2 AC 415.

to this effect from the New South Wales Court of Appeal;[206] in being unwilling to follow this line, the majority may have sensed that there was a range of possibility on the general issue whether a defendant could be fairly said to have 'engineered' the jurisdiction agreement in such a way that allowed it to have an indirect effect on him, and that in taking a view on this, the court would be forming a view on the facts which cannot be assumed, at the jurisdictional stage, to be reliable.

Whatever the right answer – the view preferred here is that the minority was onto something, but that the reservations of the majority were entirely understandable – the judgments illustrate the fact that appropriateness cannot be measured entirely by the listing and weighing of factors. A sense of the overall shape of the litigation needs to be taken, so far as it can be seen by the judge before whom the application comes. The process is, as the court said, an evaluative one, and unless the first instance judge has careered right off the rails, his decision should be respected. The problem, then, is not so much the effort put into the original application, but the rules which allow for appeals against decisions on this kind of application.

It is apparent from some cases that the 'overall shape' issue can be affected by the selective pleading of facts by the claimant. We have seen above how this reached abusive levels in the case of multi-state defamation, but the phenomenon is also evident in certain personal injury cases. For example, in *Lubbe v. Cape plc*,[207] the claimants who sought compensation for injuries said to have been sustained while working in the asbestos mining and processing industry, framed their claims against the English parent company which had, as they said, culpably failed to direct its subsidiaries which ran the mines to take proper care for the health and safety of their employees. Though a personal injury claim against the companies which operated the mines may well have had its natural forum where the mines were operated, such a claim was not advanced; and the tactic of claiming only against the English parent company was presumably designed to give the action more of an English flavour and to inoculate it against a stay application. The Court of Appeal[208] took the view that, though the claimants were entitled to tailor their claim so as to make only such allegations as they chose to make, such selective highlighting of some aspects of the story and suppression of others did not prevent the court looking more widely for the issues which identified the natural forum.[209] It is not clear whether the House of Lords endorsed this approach, for there was no suggestion of any impropriety in selecting only the parent company as defendant, neither in seeking to show that the defendant owed a duty of care without regard to whether other parties not sued might have done also.

Even-handedness[210] would require that the natural forum be assessed in the light of the anticipated defence as well as the claim. It would follows that though the defendant is not entitled to ask the court to read the particulars of claim as if they advanced a case which is not made, he is entitled to say, credibly and in evidence, that the defence will[211] raise issues which certainly bear on the location of the natural forum. So a defendant should not be

---

206 *Global Partners Fund Ltd v. Babcock & Brown Ltd* (2010) 79 ASCR 383.

207 [2000] 1 WLR 1545.

208 [2000] 1 Lloyd's Rep 139, in this respect taking a rather broader view than had a differently constituted court at the earlier hearing: [1998] CLC 1559.

209 At 160–161.

210 Inherent in the judicial function, and reinforced by CPR r. 1.2(a).

211 The defence will not have been served, for the time-frame imposed by CPR Part 11, and the need to avoid being seen to have waived objection to the jurisdiction of the court, prevents it.

heard to say that the claimant might also have sued D2, D3 and D4, and that if he had done so, the natural forum would have looked different from the way it does. But he may say that his defence to the claim as formulated against him will raise issues which give the overall litigation a different cast, and that the identification of the natural forum must be undertaken against that broader background.

4.29 The first limb of the *Spiliada* test: the consequences

If the defendant is unable to point to and show a court elsewhere to be clearly or distinctly more appropriate than England, a stay on this ground will not be granted.[212] But if he can, the burden passes to the claimant to justify his desire to proceed in an English forum which is clearly or distinctly less appropriate.

4.30 The second limb of the *Spiliada* test: whether it is unjust to stay the proceedings

In cases which were the stepping stones to the principle fully developed in *Spiliada*, most notably in *MacShannon v. Rockware Glass Ltd*,[213] it was said that if a stay would deprive the claimant of a legitimate personal or juridical advantage, a stay would not be ordered. The use of the indefinite singular article was noticeable but, as is now clear, this was liable to tilt the law too heavily in favour of the claimant.

It is now understood that if there is a clearly more appropriate forum overseas, the demands of justice lean in favour of a stay of the English proceedings and of the trial taking place overseas. This presumption may be overcome, or resisted, but it is not sufficient for the claimant to single out some advantage which he will have to forgo if not permitted to proceed in his preferred court. What is required of the claimant is that he establish, by clear and cogent evidence, the grounds on which he says it would be unjust to leave him to go to a foreign court.[214] An English court will not proceed on the basis of whisper or suggestion, and it will not be at all receptive to a general disparaging of the foreign court's procedure. Despite the occasional surprising decision, it is only rarely that the strong presumption of a stay will be rebutted on these grounds. If he is to succeed, the claimant must establish the reality, and the significance, of the alleged injustice that will befall him: for example, if he asserts that the injustice results from the fact that he would not be entitled to attend the court in person, he must explain why it is true, and why that fact makes it unjust for the trial to take place there.[215] The claimant must assert, but must also persuade the court of, the real injustice on which he says the decision should turn.

It is comparatively easy to state the principle in general terms. It is also possible to identify particular factors which have been relied on by claimants seeking to rebut the *prima facie* case for a stay; but it is not always possible to predict the impact which they will have on a court.

---

212 *Spiliada*, at 478.
213 [1978] AC 795.
214 *The Abidin Daver* [1984] AC 398.
215 *Zambia v. Meer Care & Desai* [2006] EWCA Civ 390 (not sufficiently unjust, as evidence may be given by video link and trial may be followed in the same way); *cf Cherney v. Deripaska* [2008] EWHC 1530 (Comm), [2009] 1 All ER (Comm) 333 (appeal dismissed without specific reference to this point: *Cherney v. Deripaska* [2009] EWCA Civ 849, [2010] 1 All ER (Comm) 456).

Nevertheless, cases decided before *Spiliada*, particularly where they were based on the earlier approach in *MacShannon v. Rockware Glass*,[216] are likely to be less reliable today.

The following paragraphs examine factors and arguments which might be said to demonstrate the injustice of ordering a stay of proceedings.

4.31 Pointers to injustice (1): differences in matters of law and procedure

On the basis of the decision in *Spiliada*, the broad question appears to be whether the foreign court would be able to try the dispute between the parties in a manner which is procedurally and substantively fair: if it appears that it will be able to, the fact that the procedural rules of the foreign court are said to be disadvantageous to the claimant is irrelevant.

It is convenient to consider ordinary procedural differences first. In general,[217] the fact that the foreign court would apply rules on documentary disclosure which were more[218] or less thorough than those of English law does not make it unjust for the case to be heard in that court.[219] It would appear to follow that the fact that the foreign court would allow the taking of depositions from potential witnesses, or provides for oral discovery, which would not be available against the claimant in England, is not a source of manifest injustice either.[220] The fact that the foreign court would proceed by inquisitorial rather than adversarial methods cannot properly be objected to,[221] and neither can the fact that the foreign court would appoint and rely on an independent expert to examine the facts.[222] This general approach is wholly correct. All civilised systems of civil procedure strike their own balance to protect the rights of the parties and to get at and expose the truth. It is, therefore, inappropriate to point to an isolated difference by comparing a rule of English law, and one of foreign law, each wrenched out of its context, and to contend that the comparison shows that the claimant is exposed to the risk of an injustice if not permitted to proceed in England.[223]

There are nevertheless some particular instances of differences in civil procedural rules where, contrary to the general approach outlined above, the court has been open to persuasion that the difference connotes an injustice which may be sufficient for it to refrain from ordering a stay.[224] For example, if there is evidence that the length of time before a case will come on hearing is very great, it may be inappropriate to order a stay: justice delayed may, in this context, be justice denied.[225] This may not be a major concern in a commercial

---

216 [1978] AC 705.

217 The matters set out below are dealt with at the level of generality. It is clear that the trial judge has a substantial margin of appreciation, and there will be cases where the general rule should and will be departed from.

218 As may be the case in the United States.

219 *Spiliada*, at 482.

220 But for a contrary view in relation to American anti-trust procedures, see *Midland Bank plc v. Laker Airways Ltd* [1986] QB 689.

221 *The El Amria* [1981] 2 Lloyd's Rep 119.

222 This was the basis for the attempt to sue in England in *The Atlantic Star* [1974] AC 436, and in the light of CPR r. 35.7, this would be a most unexpected objection to a stay of proceedings.

223 *Spiliada*, at 482.

224 See too *Midland Bank plc v. Laker Airways Ltd*, where the characteristic features of American anti-trust pre-trial investigation were thought, in the circumstances of a case with no real connection with America, to be sufficiently objectionable to justify an anti-suit injunction.

225 *The Vishva Ajay* [1989] 2 Lloyd's Rep 558; *Marconi Communications International Ltd v. PT Pan Indonesia Bank Ltd TBK* [2004] EWHC 129 (QB), [2004] 1 Lloyd's Rep 594; aff'd [2005] EWCA Civ 422, [2007] 2 Lloyd's Rep 72, [77]; but *cf Radhakrishna Hospitality Service Private Ltd v. EIH Ltd* [1992] 2 Lloyd's Rep 249. In a personal

dispute between two substantial businesses, but in cases of personal injury, where the injured claimant is in urgent need of a decision on a claim for compensation, the prospect of having to cope with delay before the foreign court may be intolerably unjust. Indeed, there is good reason to suppose that the *Spiliada* principles should, and do, operate distinctively and to the advantage of the claimant, in cases of personal injury. Certainly, the leading cases in which the House of Lords declined to order a stay in favour of the natural forum were cases of personal injury.[226] The leading authorities in the High Court of Australia, which has taken a rather critical view of the principle established by *Spiliada*, are predominantly cases of personal injury rather than commercial disputes;[227] and the one case in which the European Court was asked to consider the compatibility of the *Spiliada* principle with what is now the Brussels I Regulation was a personal injury claim in which it was evidently to be supposed that, eight years after he had been rendered quadriplegic in a diving accident for which he blamed the defendants, the claimant could, and should, have been told to start all over again, before the courts of Jamaica.[228] Seen from an English vantage point, the doctrine developed in *Spiliada* is perfectly well able to accommodate these atypical cases[229] (except in the last case, in which the idea that there might have been a stay was insane), but it cannot be denied that what some may see as plain right strikes others quite differently.

If there is evidence that the costs order made by the foreign court will be seriously disadvantageous to the claimant when compared with what an English court would do, this may persuade the court to decline to stay proceedings.[230]

More complexity arises if the claimant, who has financial support for the prosecution of his claim in England, would have none for (and so would have to abandon) a claim in the natural forum and contends that this is by itself a sufficient reason to show that it would be unjust to impose a stay. The *Spiliada* test is flexible enough to conclude that justice may exceptionally demand that a claim be allowed to proceed in England without a stay, even though the natural forum is overseas. In *Connelly v. RTZ Corporation plc*,[231] the House of Lords accepted that the impossibility of obtaining financial support for a claim before the courts of Namibia meant that the claimant's English action (for which civil Legal Aid or a

---

injury case this may very well be a significant matter. On the other hand, if the English court can offer an expedited trial, this may be a relevant factor: *XN Corp Ltd v. Point of Sale Ltd* [2001] ILPr 525.

226 *Connelly v. RTZ Corp plc* [1998] AC 854; *Lubbe v. Cape plc* [2000] 1 WLR 1545.

227 *Oceanic Sun Line Special Shipping Co Ltd v. Fay* (1988) 165 CLR 197; *Régie Nationale des Usines Renault SA v. Zhang* (2003) 210 CLR 491: and not only that: the natural forum in those cases was, as it usually will be, a very long way away from the claimant's Australian home. A similar sentiment underpinned a defamation claim brought by a local claimant against a large foreign corporation, though the thrust of the case was more directed at choice of law: *Gutnick v. Dow Jones & Co Inc* (2003) 210 CLR 575. The one case which was not so openly hostile to *Spiliada* was a commercial dispute: *Voth v. Manildra Flour Mills Pty Ltd* (1991) 171 CLR 538, but its influence has clearly waned.

228 C-281/02 *Owusu v. Jackson* [2005] ECR I-1383.

229 Even if a court occasionally appears to go wrong in applying them.

230 *Roneleigh v. MII Exports* [1989] 1 WLR 619; see also *The Vishva Ajay*; *The Oinoussin Pride* [1991] 1 Lloyd's Rep 126; *The Nile Rhapsody* [1994] 1 Lloyd's Rep 382; *The Al Battani* [1993] 2 Lloyd's Rep 219; *Agrafax Public Relations Ltd v. United Scottish Society Inc* [1995] ILPr 753. But the limited recovery of a successful claimant's costs is a feature of many systems, including certain of the United States, and Japan. It may therefore not be appropriate to take so critical a view of it for it does involve extracting one procedural rule from its context and examining it in dangerous isolation.

231 [1998] AC 854. Lord Hoffmann dissented, on the ground that the reasoning of the majority meant that a claimant of limited means may resist a stay which would have been ordered against a wealthy claimant. It was undeniable that this is so, and difficult to see why it was a matter of remark, still less ground for dissent. In *Lubbe v. Cape plc* [2000] 1 WLR 1545, Lord Hoffmann did not press the point.

conditional fee arrangement was available) would not be stayed; and in *Lubbe v. Cape plc*[232] a stay was also refused for, as Lord Bingham put it: 'I cannot conceive that the court would grant a stay in any case where adequate funding and legal representation of the plaintiff were judged to be necessary for the doing of justice and these were clearly shown to be unavailable in the foreign forum although available here.'[233]

Lubbe was a case in which the complex scientific evidence would have been costly to prepare, present, and put to the test; and this highlighted the perception that the claimants would have to bring their claims in England or nowhere at all.[234] It may not have been intended to extend to a case in which the claimant might have relatively rudimentary, as opposed to no, support for the costs of litigation in the natural forum; but it is almost inevitable that claimants with conditional fee arrangements in England will test the limits of the principle. But in the final analysis, the *Spiliada* test is one in which the overall ends of justice are the dominant concern. It all goes to show that the occasional exceptional decision can serve those ends just as loyally as can a long string of routine ones.

If the foreign court could not accept jurisdiction over all parties in a complex or multipartite dispute, with a consequent risk that irreconcilable verdicts may follow from separate trials, it may be appropriate to refuse to stay proceedings. If the foreign court would submit a complex commercial dispute to a civil jury with little or no provision for review of its monetary award, there is more than a suspicion that this ought to help tilt the scales against granting a stay.[235] In such a case, where he may feel that certain aspects of foreign procedure may be open to such objection, and will defeat an application for a stay which would otherwise be liable to succeed, a defendant may be prepared, and may be wise, to undertake to the court to renounce certain procedural advantages which may be thought by an English court to tend towards the unacceptable.[236]

4.32 Pointers to injustice (2): differences in time bar rules

The operation of time bars within the context of applications for a stay of proceedings is now less complex than it was where a claimant would be out of time if the English proceedings were to be stayed and he were left to start his action in the court which is the natural forum for the claim,[237] or where the stay is sought on the basis of an exclusive jurisdiction

---

232 [2000] 1 WLR 1545.

233 At 1561. Having reached this conclusion it was unnecessary to consider, and will generally be unnecessary to consider, whether a decision to stay the proceedings might have involved infringing Art. 6 of the European Convention on Human Rights, for Art. 6 made no demand on the English court which *Spiliada* had not already met. See further, para. 1.21, above.

234 It is not known why Texas lawyers had not made the claimants an offer they could not refuse.

235 No case has actually held that the prospect of being tried by an American civil jury is *prima facie* a reason not to stay proceedings, but one has only to look at the nature of jury awards to realise that this would be a perfectly reasonable view to adopt. On the other hand, this submission gains no support from *Airbus Industrie GIE v. Patel* [1999] 1 AC 119.

236 *Cf* the undertakings given in *SNI Aérospatiale v. Lee Kui Jak* [1987] AC 871. It may also be sensible for him to offer to put up security against the later enforcement of a foreign judgment in England, to rebut the claimant's argument that it would be unjust to deprive him of a right to sue in England where he has security for his claim; *cf Spiliada*, at 483.

237 A good question is how the court should proceed if the claimant was not out of time when the English proceedings were instituted or when the application for a stay was first made, but will be out of time in the foreign court by the time the stay application is before the court for final decision. In *Spiliada*, for example, it will have taken a couple of years for the English courts to decide finally whether the English proceedings should be allowed

clause which nominates a court in which the claimant would now be out of time. The predominant question is whether the claimant has only himself to blame.

The starting point is that the fact that a claimant would be out of time if the English proceedings were stayed has been accepted by the courts as a reason why it *may* be unjust to stay English proceedings in favour of a (non-)trial in the natural forum. Lord Goff said so in *Spiliada*,[238] thereby making this a practical exception to the general proposition that the differences in procedure and choice of law were part of the swings and roundabouts of international commercial litigation. He said that a court could properly examine whether the claimant had been at fault in allowing time to run out in the natural forum. If he had been culpable in allowing time to run in the natural forum, he would not generally be allowed to use this to support a contention that he would not be able to sue in the foreign court and that this would be unjust; but if he had not been at fault, a limitation defence which the defendant proposed to take[239] before the foreign court may be an injustice to the claimant, sufficient to overcome the case for a stay.

This makes perfect sense, for, at the stage when a claimant has to decide whether, where and when to institute proceedings, it may not be apparent whether there is a natural forum or where it is; and it would be wrong to allow this to deprive the claimant of a hearing of his claim when he has brought proceedings in good time in England. And in many cases in which the court relies on this factor as the basis for exceptionally refusing to stay proceedings, no injustice will be done to the defendant because the Foreign Limitation Periods Act 1984, section 1, requires[240] an English court to apply the time bar rules of the law which governs the substance of the case, and not to apply the limitation period prescribed by English domestic law unless English law is the law which governs the substance of the claim. Only if the foreign court would have applied a different choice of law rule to the merits of the claim, or to the issue of time barring,[241] will there be a difference between the outcomes in the courts of England and the natural forum.

Where the application for a stay is founded on an exclusive jurisdiction agreement for the foreign court the analysis of this point should be different.[242] The proposition that the claimant was not at fault in failing to save limitation in the contractually agreed exclusive forum is harder to accept, at least where the claim advanced falls plainly within the scope

---

to continue; and if the foreign time bar has come down during that decision period, it is hard to see how the court should balance the principle of the matter. Even if it is correct that the evidence be assessed as at the date of the decision, rather than the date of the institution of proceedings (*Mohammed v. Bank of Kuwait and the Middle East KSC* [1996] 1 WLR 1483), it is uncertain whether this will mean the date of the original decision of the High Court, or any subsequent decision on the appeal. The latter is preferable, albeit that this means that the decision of the court may change in the course of the procedure.

238 At 483. See also *The Blue Wave* [1982] 1 Lloyd's Rep 151.

239 Faced with this, a defendant may undertake not to take the defence before the foreign court, so shooting the claimant's fox: *Baghlaf al Zafer v. Pakistan National Shipping Co* [1998] 2 Lloyd's Rep 229. But if the foreign court will apply the limitation defence in any event, the court will reconsider the case as one in which the defendant will defeat the claim by reference to limitation: *Baghlaf al Zafer v. Pakistan National Shipping Co (No 2)* [2001] 1 Lloyd's Rep 1.

240 Subject to exceptions on grounds of public policy: s. 2 of the 1984 Act. Where choice of law is governed by the Rome I and Rome II Regulations, these instruments produce the same outcome.

241 Presumably on the basis that it sees them as procedural, a view which was thought in England to be so wrong that the 1984 Act was passed to eradicate it.

242 In principle this should be dealt with below (paras 4.41 *et seq.*), but the coherence of the analysis requires that it be examined at this point.

of the agreement.[243] But some courts have been more indulgent than one would have expected, and have accepted that a stay of proceedings for the contractually agreed forum may be unjust if the claim would be time barred in the foreign court but not in England. If one takes seriously the proposition that contracts are made to be kept, at least where there is no third-party interest in the subject matter of which the court should take notice, condoning a claimant's failure to commence proceedings in good time and in the right place seems simply wrong.[244]

4.33 Pointers to injustice (3): differences in applicable law and effect of judgments

Other arguments advanced in opposition to a stay may focus on the substantive law which will be applied by the foreign court. As has been noted already, the fact that the claimant will only be able to obtain a lower level of damages will not generally be a reason to refuse a stay:[245] all systems draw lines to limit the amount or extent of recovery. The same is, or should be true, even where the damages which would be awarded by an English court are fixed by an international Convention to which the United Kingdom is party, but which will not be applied in the natural forum. The argument that, in such a case, English law was in some sense superior to that applied in the natural forum, so that a stay should not be ordered, was condemned in *The Herceg Novi and The Ming Galaxy*,[246] which is clearly correct. It will be different, of course, if the Convention as enacted into English law is interpreted as forbidding the court to order a stay of proceedings in the first place.[247]

If the court will apply a choice of law rule which is different from that applicable in an English court, this may, but will only in rare cases, lay the ground for an argument that it would be unjust to leave the claimant to go to the foreign court.[248] In *Banco Atlantico SA v. British Bank of the Middle East*,[249] it was decided not to stay proceedings in favour of the courts of Sharjah on the principal ground that the court would decide the dispute by the application of the domestic law of Sharjah, so giving effect to choice of law rules so different from the English ones that they were manifestly wrong. In *Cadre SA v. Asigurari SA*[250] the

---

243 It is different if the claim may not fall within the material scope of a jurisdiction agreement which is not worded widely or clearly, or if it is not clear which court is nominated by the agreement (such as where the court is defined as that for the carrier's 'principal place of business').

244 See also *The Pioneer Container* [1994] 2 AC 324; *Citi-March Ltd v. Neptune Orient Lines* [1996] 2 All ER 545; *Baghlaf al Zafer v. Pakistan National Shipping Co* [1998] 2 Lloyd's Rep 229; *Pirelli Cables Ltd v. United Thai Shipping Corp* [2000] 1 Lloyd's Rep 663.

245 *Spiliada*, at 482.

246 [1998] 2 Lloyd's Rep 454: the United Kingdom applied the 1976 Convention on Limitation of Liability for Maritime Claims; Singapore applied the 1957 Convention, which applied a lower financial limit. Different issues arise in connection with the Hague-Visby Rules, as given effect by Carriage of Goods by Sea Act 1971. That Convention annuls a choice of court agreement for a country where the limit on damages would be set lower than that under the Hague-Visby Rules. In such a case the 1971 Act strikes out the choice of court agreement, and the decision not to stay proceedings is a consequence of that, and not of the inadmissible preference for English law: *The Hollandia* [1983] 1 AC 565; *Baghlaf al Zafer v. Pakistan National Shipping Co* [1998] 2 Lloyd's Rep 229; *Pirelli Cables Ltd v. United Thai Shipping Corp Ltd* [2000] 1 Lloyd's Rep 663.

247 *Cf* para. 4.14, above.

248 But see, in the context of the enforcement of foreign judgments, para. 7.68, below.

249 [1990] 2 Lloyd's Rep 504. For an analogous decision which pre-dates *Spiliada*, see *Britannia Steamship Insurance Association v. Ausonia Assicurazioni SpA* [1984] 2 Lloyd's Rep 95.

250 [2005] EWHC 2504 (QB). For the subsequent decision to grant an anti-suit injunction to restrain the proceedings before the Romanian courts, see *Cadre SA v. Asigurari SA* [2005] EWHC 2626 (Comm), [2006] 1

court refused to stay proceedings in favour of the courts of Romania, in part at least because the Romanian court would not apply the English law upon which the contracting parties had agreed. But other decisions regard the differences in national choice of law rules as essentially irrelevant to this question.[251] And there may be a narrower basis upon which the exceptional cases may be supported: that if the parties have expressly chosen a law to govern their contract, then for the defendant to seek to have the case heard in a court which will not give effect to that express choice of law will be for him to undermine the contractual bargain.[252] If that analysis were considered to be sustainable, it seems correct to refuse to stay proceedings. But any wider principle would be difficult indeed to defend, or to control. If a foreign judgment will not be denied recognition just because the court applied the wrong law, it is not really coherent to refuse to stay proceedings because the foreign court, which is the natural forum, will apply a law different from that which would be applied by an English court.[253] But express agreement on choice of law is a distinct point, to which a distinct approach may conceivably apply.[254]

A more problematic argument is raised if the claimant contends that a stay of English proceedings would deprive him of the possibility of obtaining a judgment which would be enforceable under Chapter III of the Brussels I Regulation. The complaint is not now that the claimant will lose, or will be awarded only diminished damages, if sent abroad, but that his victory will be much less useful if he needs to enforce the judgment against assets of the defendant in other Member States. His non-Member State judgment will be in the equivalent of non-convertible currency. The argument appears to have been accepted as legitimate in *International Credit and Investment Co (Overseas) Ltd v. Adham*,[255] and if it is justified on the facts, it is difficult to see any obvious limit which may be used to circumscribe it. As a judgment from a non-Member State which is subsequently recognised in England remains outside the scope of Chapter III of the Regulation,[256] the loss of the prospect of pan-European enforceability does appear to be a very significant factor in suggesting that it is unjust to leave the claimant to obtaining judgment from the courts of a non-Member State.

Lloyd's Rep 560. More generally, the issue was discussed, but without conclusive resolution, in *Golden Ocean Group Ltd v. Salgaocar Mining Industries Pvt Ltd* [2011] EWHC 56 (Comm), [2011] 2 All ER (Comm) 95, esp. at [143] (a service out case, but the point is general; the point was not dealt with on appeal); *Baturina v. Chistyakov* [2014] EWCA Civ 1134.

251 For an excellent example, see *Navig8 Pte Ltd v. Al-Riyadh Co for Vegetable Oil Industry* [2013] EWHC 328 (Comm), [2013] 2 Lloyd's Rep 104, [27].

252 *Cf The Magnum* [1989] 1 Lloyd's Rep 47.

253 Though it can be argued that it is one thing to act to prevent an imperfect judgment coming into existence, but quite another to deny recognition to a regular judgment which is disagreed with.

254 The point is discussed in Chapter 5 below, in relation to anti-suit injunctions. It is sufficient to say, at this point, that English authority does not support the contention that an express choice of law for English law may be used as a cause of action for an anti-suit injunction to restrain proceedings before a foreign court: see for example *Navig8 Pte Ltd v. Al-Riyadh Co for Vegetable Oil Industry* [2013] EWHC 328 (Comm), [2013] 2 Lloyd's Rep 104, [27]; *Golden Endurance Shipping SA v. RMA Watanya SA* [2014] EWHC 3917 (Comm).

255 [1999] ILPr 302 (a case on service out of the jurisdiction). It had been taken by the judge as a relevant factor, and the Court of Appeal did not take issue with his analysis; it was also applied in *Sharab v. Al-Saud* [2009] EWCA Civ 353, [2009] 2 Lloyd's Rep 160 (another case on service out of the jurisdiction) as part of the justification for permitting an order for service out of the jurisdiction to stand. *Adham* was also applied in *Inter-Tel Inc v. OCIS plc* [2004] EWHC 2269 (QB), where the court refused to stay proceedings for the courts of Arizona, admittedly the natural forum, as the practical unenforceability of an Arizona judgment made it unjust to expect the claimant to sue there; it was accepted in *Karafarin Bank v. Mansoury-Dara* [2009] EWHC 1217 (Comm), [2009] 2 Lloyd's Rep 289 as part of the reason why English proceedings would not be stayed even though there were proceedings in Iran which seemed likely to result in a judgment enforceable in Iran but not in England.

256 Case C-129/92 *Owens Bank Ltd v. Bracco* [1994] ECR I-117.

It is surprising that this argument does not appear to have been given greater attention, but it cannot properly be restricted to cases involving claimants from Member States; and given that, it may yet have wide-ranging implications.

4.34 Pointers to injustice (4): claimant may win in England but will lose overseas

If the claimant establishes that, by reason of the choice of law or other rules of the natural forum, he will win in England but will lose if forced to claim overseas, it is sometimes suggested that it is unjust to stay proceedings.[257] This is a very unattractive argument.[258] It flies in the face of *Spiliada*, and it appears to suggest that the claimant has a vested right to be victorious. There is no earthly reason why this should be so; every reason why it should be not so. It would follow that the fact that a cause of action would be available to the claimant in England but not overseas should be given little weight; the reverse proposition is, after all, that the defendant would have a defence in the foreign court but not in England, and this will presumably be given no great weight either. In cases where the parties cannot agree where to litigate, strict impartiality has much to commend it and nothing to be said against it.

But some cases have suggested that the law makes distinct provision for 'single forum' cases, according to which a claimant is treated more favourably if England is the only country in which he may advance a cause of action with any prospect of success. By contrast, it has never been contended that, if there is only one court in which the defendant has a chance of raising a successful defence, this is the court in which he must be allowed to defend himself and answer the claim: there is no precedent for a court accepting a 'defendant's single forum' submission: a fact which surely shows the fundamental unsoundness of the argument. The correct solution, it is submitted, is that no special rule, or special application of a general rule, should provide for cases in which the claimant could formulate a cause of action before an English court but not before the courts of the natural forum: as long as the defendant is personally amenable to the jurisdiction of the foreign court there should be no further enquiry designed to establish the unavailability of the foreign forum.[259] To go beyond this and to institutionalise a preference for the claimant is to depart from the basic principle of even-handedness,[260] and also to ignore part of the overriding objective of the Civil Procedure Rules.[261]

---

257 Cf *Banco Atlantico SA v. British Bank of the Middle East* [1990] 2 Lloyd's Rep 504. For refusal to stay Australian proceedings on this ground, where a claim under the Trade Practices Act could not be brought outside Australia, see *Francis Travel Marketing Pty Ltd v. Virgin Atlantic Airways Ltd* (1996) 39 NSWLR 160; *Reinsurance Australia Corp Ltd v. HIH Casualty and General Insurance Ltd (in liq)* (2003) 254 ALR 29 (esp. at [293]: Australian court cannot be inappropriate, and therefore no stay will be granted, if it is the only one of the possible fora in which a claim under the Trade Practices Act 1974 could be fully and properly entertained).

258 Cf *The Hamburg Star* [1994] 1 Lloyd's Rep 399, 410.

259 See, for an illustration in the context of claims against a sovereign, which will fail in the foreign forum, *Garsec Pty Ltd v. Sultan of Brunei* (2008) 250 ALR 682 (though the case was probably one in which the claim would have failed in Australia as well, for the Australian court would have applied the substantive law of Brunei, under which there was no claim).

260 And see, for support for the dominant principle of even-handedness, the judgment of Callinan J in *BHP Billiton Ltd v. Schultz* (2004) 221 CLR 400, [258]; *Golden Endurance Shipping SA v. RMA Watanya SA* [2014] EWHC 3917 (Comm).

261 CPR r. 1(2)(a).

Because the idea of the 'single forum' case has arisen most obviously in relation to anti-suit injunctions, we will examine the authorities there. But on the view taken here, unless the case is an exceptional one, perhaps where the justification for the plea is that the foreign court will disregard an agreement on choice of law, the plea should surely be inadmissible. As in life, so in law: some you win, some you lose.

4.35 Pointers to injustice (5): direct attacks on the integrity of foreign court

Within the last decade a point has arisen and obtained considerable significance. To appreciate the sea change in the approach of the English courts, a little time may be given to the previous practice. For although in 1984 the House of Lords had admitted the principle that if the claimant might resist a stay by adducing clear and cogent evidence to show that he would not receive a fair hearing of his claim before the foreign court,[262] the cases in which the defendant rose to the challenge and the court accepted that he had met the standard required to prevent a stay, were few in number. Where the point was taken, the English court would tread carefully to avoid giving the impression that it was impugning the conduct or quality of the foreign court,[263] and direct attacks on the integrity of the foreign court were rare. As recently as the 1980s, the English courts were strikingly unsympathetic to fears or apprehensions that the courts of Turkey were so cowed by the military that they would not do justice;[264] they were no more willing to accept that a Turkish court would not do justice in a dispute between a Turkish claimant and a Cuban[265] State corporation.[266] From time to time it would be complained that the judges in a foreign court were unreliable, or impoverished and so unable to resist bribes, or in thrall to the political leadership of the State and simply incapable of deciding a case contrary to its interests.[267] The unspeakable truth probably was that there were some countries and courts in relation to which criticism along those lines fitted like a glove, but that it would have been invidious for an English judge to be required to go on the record and make such a finding, quite apart from the point that it would have been quite wrong to tar all judges in every court with the same brush. No doubt the idea that a fair trial can be guaranteed in courts in certain troubled, or even untroubled, parts of Africa or Asia involves a developed sense of the absurd. But where the States in question are friendly States, the idea that an English court might conduct some kind of quality audit of their judicial systems is not an appetising prospect. Even if there

---

262 *The Abidin Daver* [1984] AC 398.

263 It does not disparage a foreign court to say that it is overworked and under-resourced. Where the shortcoming is that the court may not be assisted by the expert analysis it will need to try the case properly, this is less likely to be seen as an impermissible attack on the court itself: see *Lubbe v. Cape plc* [2000] 1 WLR 1545. But for other (unrepresentative) cases, which do not directly find fault with the court as a court, see *Askin v. Absa Bank* [1999] ILPr 471; *Merrill Lynch v. Raffa* [2001] ILPr 437; *Purcell v. Khyatt, The Times*, 23 November 1987.

264 *Muduroğlu v. TC Ziraat Bankası* [1986] QB 1225. The case was unfortunate for the defendant, who had gone on the record to make rather lurid allegations about the awfulness of what passed for justice in Turkey, and who, when the stay was ordered, was faced with the need to go before a Turkish court to make his claim. The further proceedings are not reported.

265 And therefore communist: the Turkish state and army, if indeed there was distinction between the two, were busy running a thuggish military regime of notable and anti-communist brutality.

266 *The Abidin Daver* [1984] AC 398.

267 *Jeyaretnam v. Mahmood, The Times*, 21 May 1992. Not followed on this point (and allowing evidence tending to show that judges were not independent of the Sudanese State): *Al-Koronky v. Time-Life Entertainment Group Ltd* [2006] EWCA Civ 1123; and now to be considered as overruled: *AK Investment CJSC v. Kyrgyz Mobil Tel Ltd* [2011] UKPC 7, [2012] 1 WLR 1804.

were judicially-manageable standards by which this could be done, which is surely to be questioned,[268] it was not subject matter on which an English court might be asked to rule.[269]

However, the Human Rights Act 1998 may require an English court to address and rule on submissions that a person's human rights will not be respected by the judicial system of a foreign country if (for example) he is required to return to it. And in 2008 a flurry of first instance decisions removed the stopper from the bottle, accepting in a number of service out cases, in a manner which sometimes appeared to be decisive, that a foreign court could not be trusted to do justice to the particular claimant or against the individual defendant, or at all, and that the jurisdictional issue should be decided in the light of that fact. Adverse judgment was made of the courts of Russia in a claim made between powerful businessmen;[270] the margin by which the submission failed in relation to the courts of the Ukraine, after lengthy judicial recitation of all the depressing reasons for scepticism, was very slender;[271] and in each case the Court of Appeal found no vitiating flaw in what had gone on below. It was made in relation to the courts of the Democratic Republic of Congo.[272] In similar vein, it was held that the recognition of a judgment from what was said to be a court in North Korea might be opposed on grounds which included an allegation that the judicial arm of the State had participated in or connived at a criminal conspiracy with the political leadership of the State, to defraud a foreign insurance company by giving judgment on a false and inflated claim.[273] Almost overnight, the courts had discovered that they were prepared to make adverse judgments about the judicial qualities of a foreign court.

This development was ratified by the Privy Council,[274] and it may be taken to be the law. In proceedings which turned on whether the courts of Kyrgyzstan offered the prospect of justice served up in accordance with the law, in circumstances in which it had been argued that service out should be permitted to allow proceedings to be brought in the Isle of Man which were otherwise wholly rooted in Kyrgyzstan, the conclusion of the court was that 'the better view is that, depending on the circumstances as a whole, the burden can be

---

268 The court in *Yukos Capital Sarl v. OJSC Rosneft Oil Co* [2012] EWCA Civ 855, [2014] QB 458, had rather fewer doubts, taking the view that the standards of the rule of law were universal.

269 *Cf Attorney General (UK) v. Heinemann Publishers Australia Pty Ltd* (1988) 165 CLR 30.

270 *Cherney v. Deripaska* [2008] EWHC 1530 (Comm), [2009] 1 All ER (Comm) 333, appeal dismissed: [2009] EWCA Civ 849, [2010] 1 All ER (Comm) 456 (a case on service out of the jurisdiction). But for contrast, *OJSC Oil Co Yugraneft v. Abramovich* [2008] EWHC 2613 (Comm); *JSC VTB Bank v. Skurikhin* [2014] EWHC 271 (Comm); *OJSC Alfa Bank v. Trefilov* [2014] EWHC 1806 (Comm) (cases on recognition of Russian judgment).

271 *Pacific International Sports Clubs Ltd v. Soccer Marketing International Ltd* [2009] EWHC 1839 (Ch) (appeal dismissed: [2010] EWCA Civ 753). But a different conclusion was reached in *Ferrexpo AG v. Gilson Investments Ltd* [2012] EWHC 721 (Comm), [2012] 1 Lloyd's Rep 588, where the evidence purporting to find fault with the foreign system was characterised as sweeping and imprecise. For a remarkable judgment, which may say that mere fears and personal suspicions concerning the foreign court are not enough (which, if it does, is correct), see *Mengiste v. Endowment Fund for the rehabilitation of Tigray* [2013] EWHC 599 (Ch) (proceedings stayed, so that case might resume if a fair trial was denied by the Ethiopian courts and for further proceedings, see *Mengiste v. Endowment Fund for the Rehabilitation of Tigray* [2014] EWHC 4196 (Ch)).

272 *889457 Alberta Inc v. Katanga Mining Ltd* [2008] EWHC 2679 (Comm), [2009] ILPr 175. In fact, the case was determined by the application of the provisions of the Brussels I Regulation; and insofar as it was not, it was probably safer to hold that the courts of Congo were not an available forum (except for those seeking an early death).

273 *Korea National Insurance Co v. Allianz Global Corporate and Specialty AG* [2008] EWCA Civ 1355, [2009] Lloyd's Rep IR 480. It is fair to say that no one seems ever to have had sight of a North Korean court judgment in a civil or commercial matter; if [2014] NKLR has been published, it has not yet made it to Oxford. But for contrast, *BCEN Eurobank v. Vostokrybprom Co Ltd* [2014] 1 Lloyd's Rep 449 (E Caribbean CA).

274 *AK Investment CJSC v. Kyrgyz Mobil Tel Ltd* [2011] UKSC 7, [2012] 1 WLR 1804, [95].

satisfied by showing that there is a real risk that justice will not be obtained in the foreign court by reason of incompetence or lack of independence or corruption. Of course, if it can be shown that justice "will not" be obtained that will weigh more heavily in the exercise of the discretion in the light of all other circumstances.' If that is the law when the court is considering whether to allow service out of the jurisdiction, it must be *a fortiori* when the court is being asked to stay proceedings commenced by service as of right. The result is that if the court may be satisfied that there is a risk that the foreign court will, in the circumstances of the individual case, not do justice according to the law, a court will be free to conclude that a stay of proceedings will not be in the interests of justice.

There can be no objection to this development if there is proper and focused[275] evidence that the foreign court will not (or would be acting quite out of character if it were to) do justice according to the law.[276] But 'a real risk' may set the bar rather low. It immediately raises the question what manner of evidence would be needed to sustain such a contention, and the answer is that there is no answer. Evidence of judicial propensity in general, or of judicial propensity when one of the litigants is well connected, may suffice; rather less focused observations from organisations which have given themselves grand names and which compile 'indexes of corruption', for example, may be accorded rather less weight. But as the circumstances of each case will be individual, the question how to discharge the burden of proof will vary from case to case.

Is the law well served by this development? For even if the courts insist on cogent evidence, there are few bright lines to be drawn. The objections to such an enquiry, which can be derived from *Attorney General (UK) v. Heinemann Publishers Australia Pty Ltd*,[277] in particular, are substantial. Even so, for the claimant, facing the prospect of having to sue in dreadful places in the middle east or west Africa, or in a perfectly safe place but in which the Government or ruling family has never lost a case, what else can he do but protest that, whatever is on offer from the alleged courts in those places, it is not justice according to the law as the English or other European courts know it? It is certainly difficult, especially if there is no system of certification by which the Government might inform the court of its view of the judicial system of a foreign State. The task of the judge is not, or should not be, an enviable one; but in some cases it cannot be shirked. It is this which the Privy Council faced up to in *AK Investment CJSC v. Kyrgyz Mobil Tel Ltd*, and it is very hard to say that it did otherwise than it should.

4.36 The *Spiliada* test: relevance of the merits of the claim or the defence

If the claimant contends that the defendant has no defence to the claim, and is seeking a stay only to harass the claimant in the hope that he will abandon the claim, the court may conclude that the defendant does not seriously seek a trial in the foreign court, and that it would on that account be wrong to stay proceedings.[278] On occasion a claimant has sought

---

275 *Cf* what was put before the court in *Ferrexpo AG v. Gilson Investments Ltd* [2012] EWHC 721 (Comm) [2012] 1 Lloyd's Rep 588.

276 A suggestion that justice in Iran would be denied because of delay said to be attributable to excessive judicial holidays was not regarded as substantial in *Surrey (UK) Ltd v. Mazandaran Wood & Paper Industries* [2014] EWHC 3165 (Comm).

277 (1998) 165 CLR 30.

278 *Cf Agrafax Public Relations Ltd v. United Scottish Society Ltd* [1995] ILPr 753.

to bolster his contention by applying for summary judgment on the same date as the hearing of the stay application, or by arguing that there is no defence to the claim and that the defendant is simply seeking to 'avoid' a trial.[279]

There is good reason for a court to be distinctly cautious before acting on any perception that the defendant has no defence. If the motives of the defendant are apparently disreputable, this may be a contributory factor in the argument why a stay should be withheld, but if the stay is sought on the basis of a jurisdiction clause, it is hard to see that a defendant who seeks to rely on the advantages accruing to him from a contract freely entered into can fairly be criticised for what he has done. And, indeed, it does not follow that, just because the claimant would have a clear and summary victory in England, there is no defence to the claim. Another court may apply a different choice of law rule, or may admit different evidence, or may place the burden of proof differently; or may for a variety of reasons conclude that the defendant has an arguable or a good defence. In any such case it is undesirable for an English court to conclude that its assessment of who will win at trial is the only tenable one; the question of who will win may well be affected by the decision where the case is to be fought. To conclude that, because the claimant is going to win, there is no issue as to where the natural forum might be is to put the cart before the horse, which is not generally profitable.

It has also been suggested[280] that if a claim is obviously bad, there is no purpose in staying the proceedings, for the sense in 'exporting' a bad claim is not evident. To put the matter another way, there is no natural forum for a claim which is plainly bad. The court should dismiss the application for a stay, leaving the claimant with the possibility of applying to amend the claim or the defendant to apply to have the claim struck out. The practical sense of this is clear, and any sense that the defendant has sought the wrong relief is answered by the observation that if he had simply applied to have the claim struck out, it would have been strongly arguable that he had foregone the possibility of jurisdictional relief by submitting to the merits jurisdiction of the court.

4.37 The *Spiliada* test: various responses to *lis alibi pendens*

The problems created by the fact that there is litigation pending in another court may manifest themselves in a number of different procedural contexts. First, X may have brought proceedings against Y in another court, at some time after which, Y brings proceedings against X in England.[281] In such a case, an English court may be asked by X to stay the English proceedings,[282] or may be asked by Y to restrain X from proceeding in the foreign court. An application for a stay will be resolved by *Spiliada* and the doctrine of *forum non conveniens*: a question will be whether the foreign court is, in the light of the

---

279 And courts have shown some sympathy for the approach *cf Adria Services YU v. Grey Shipping Co Ltd* (30 July 1993); *Bank of Credit and Commerce Hong Kong Ltd v. Sonali Bank* [1995] 1 Lloyd's Rep 227; *Standard Chartered Bank v. Pakistan National Shipping Corp* [1995] 2 Lloyd's Rep 365; *Sonali Bank v. Bank Austria AG* (16 May 1996); *Merrill Lynch v. Raffa* [2001] ILPr 437 (*cf Speed Investments Ltd v. Formula One Holdings Ltd* [2004] EWHC 1777 (Ch), taking a more measured view where the defendant was challenging the jurisdiction rather than seeking a stay; the point was not directly dealt with on appeal: [2005] EWCA Civ 1512, [2005] 1 WLR 1936).

280 *Baturina v. Chistyakov* [2014] EWCA Civ 1134.

281 For the case where the same party brings proceedings in two courts, see below.

282 There may, it appears, be a temporary stay to allow the foreign court to determine certain factual issues: see *Henry v. Henry* (1996) 185 CLR 571; *Sterling Pharmaceuticals Pty Ltd v. The Boots Co (Australia) Pty Ltd* (1992) 34 FCR 287. This would appear to be wholly consistent with the overriding objective of the Civil Procedure Rules.

proceedings there, the *forum conveniens*. In the latter case, an application for an anti-suit injunction will be made; the applicable principles are different as it is the *lis alibi pendens* itself which is to be prevented from continuing.[283] Second, X may have commenced proceedings in a foreign court, after which Y seeks permission to serve out of the jurisdiction to commence proceedings in England. A challenge to Y's right to ask for permission will be governed, in large part, by the version of the *Spiliada* test which applies in the context of applications for permission to serve out: a question will arise whether England is, despite the foreign proceedings, the proper place to bring the claim. Third, Y may simply seek to restrain X from suing in a foreign court: he will seek an anti-suit injunction to restrain the *lis* which is *alibi pendens*. In most, but not necessarily all, applications for an anti-suit injunction it is necessary to show that England is the proper place for the proceedings, the *forum conveniens*.

English law, as this may suggest, treats the existence of a *lis alibi pendens* as a factor which is relevant as a part of, and which is to be accommodated within, the general law on discretionary stays, or the law on service out, or the law on anti-suit injunctions. As the law on these three procedural topics is different, so will be the effect and treatment of a *lis alibi pendens* within it. English law has not therefore developed a uniform, separate, or technical doctrine of '*litispendence*'; and the definition, or the effect, of a *lis alibi pendens* has not been made subject to uniform rules. Rather, it is necessary to deal with the impact of a *lis alibi pendens* in the particular context of the procedural application made. It is fair to say that the cases do not paint a wholly consistent picture. In some instances the court adopts an approach which appears to strain every sinew to prevent parallel litigation, even to the extent of allowing a party to an agreement on jurisdiction to breach his contract.[284] In others, however, the courts seem more resigned to accepting that parallel litigation is, in complex cases at least, just a part of life.[285]

When an application is made to stay English proceedings, the *lis alibi pendens* will usually be in the form of proceedings brought in the foreign court by the party who is defendant in the English proceedings.[286] In this context, it will usually be the defendant who relies on the *lis alibi pendens*: his argument will be, in effect, that the existence of the foreign proceedings tends to make that foreign court the appropriate forum. At first sight this might not appear to follow. Just as the fact that litigation is already pending in England does not make England the natural forum for the litigation, the fact that litigation has been commenced in a foreign court might not be thought to make a foreign court the natural forum either. But the precise form of the *Spiliada* test asks whether there is another forum which is (as distinct from another forum which would have been) clearly or distinctly more appropriate than England; and it is obviously arguable that the fact that litigation has progressed a long way in another court may have had the effect of helping that court appear to be a clearly more appropriate forum than the English court for the resolution of the dispute.[287] As a result, the existence of a *lis alibi pendens* may be a significant, though

---

283 They are examined in Chapter 5.

284 *Donohue v. Armco Inc* [2001] UKHL 64, [2002] 1 All ER 749.

285 *Deutsche Bank AG v. Highland Crusader Offshore Partners LP* [2009] EWCA Civ 725, [2010] 1 WLR 1023; *Lloyd's Underwriters v. Cominco Ltd* (2007) 279 DLR (4th) 257 (BC CA).

286 For the case where they are brought by the same party, see below.

287 This may be because costs incurred in the foreign proceedings would be wasted (or, more accurately, costs in the English proceedings would result in needless duplication), or because the foreign court is believed to have acquired an expertise in the factual issues before it.

certainly not a decisive, factor in determining whether there is, at the time of the application for a stay, another forum which is clearly or distinctly more appropriate than England for the trial of the dispute.[288]

Certain guidelines have, however, emerged. If the foreign proceedings have made some headway, it may well have become appropriate for these to be left alone to determine the parties' rights;[289] but if they were not commenced long before the English proceedings, less importance will be given to this fact.[290] If the English proceedings are in the form of an application for a negative declaration,[291] or appear to have been contrived simply to allow them to be commenced before proceedings in the foreign court got going, the temporal priority of the English proceedings may be irrelevant to the operation of the *Spiliada* test. If the foreign proceedings will continue despite the existence of the English proceedings, it may be more appropriate to allow the parties' rights to be determined by the foreign court than to create the conditions for a conflict of judgments by permitting the English proceedings to continue.[292] But if the foreign proceedings are themselves open to objection, for example, if they were contrived for forum shopping purposes, or if they will resolve only a fraction of the matter in actual dispute, it may be that rather less weight should be given to them.[293] In the end it has to be asked whether the interests of justice favour allowing the foreign court a clear run, and the fact that proceedings have been commenced before that court is a factor in coming to the answer.

Finally, if the claimant in the English proceedings is also claimant in the foreign proceedings, the defendant may ask the court to put the claimant to his election as to which set of proceedings to discontinue, as opposed to seeking a stay of the English proceedings.[294] It will be unusual for the claimant to be permitted to maintain both sets of proceedings in the absence of special reasons. However, if the parties have made an express agreement that there may be parallel proceedings, or if it appears that the defendant, by not submitting to the jurisdiction of the foreign court may be preventing the claimant from obtaining a judgment which may be enforced in England,[295] or if there are proceedings relating to patent infringement in several countries at once, there is no reason to impose a stay, as in the former case the parties have made an agreement to which it is not unreasonable that they be held,[296] and in the latter, the territorial nature of patents and

---

288 Though see *Henry v. Henry* (1996) 185 CLR 571 and *CSR Ltd v. Cigna Insurance Australia Ltd* (1997) 189 CLR 345, in which the High Court of Australia held that the institution of local proceedings after the institution of foreign ones was *prima facie* vexatious and oppressive, and therefore gave rise to a strong presumption in favour of a stay. This runs counter to the English approach and denies the court the right to assess which set of proceedings would more appropriately be left to continue, and which stopped.

289 *De Dampierre v. De Dampierre* [1988] AC 92, 108; *Meadows Indemnity Co Ltd v. Insurance Corp of Ireland plc* [1989] 1 Lloyd's Rep 181, 189; *Cleveland Museum of Art v. Capricorn Art International SA* [1990] 2 Lloyd's Rep 166; *The Varna (No 2)* [1994] 2 Lloyd's Rep 41, 48–49.

290 *Banque Paribas v. Cargill International SA* [1992] 1 Lloyd's Rep 19.

291 But this objection may be less significant today: *cf Messier Dowty Ltd v. Sabena SA* [2000] 1 WLR 2040; *CGU International Insurance plc v. Szabo* [2002] 1 All ER (Comm) 83.

292 *First National Bank of Boston v. Union Bank of Switzerland* [1990] 1 Lloyd's Rep 32.

293 *Meridien BIAO Bank GmbH v. Bank of New York* [1997] 1 Lloyd's Rep 437.

294 *Australian Commercial Research & Development Ltd v. ANZ McCaughan Merchant Bank* [1989] 3 All ER 65; *A-G v. Arthur Andersen & Co* [1989] ECC 224.

295 *Karafarin Bank v. Mansoury-Dara* [2009] EWHC 1217 (Comm), [2009] 2 Lloyd's Rep 289: to recover the whole of the sums due on the cheques in question, the bank needed to sue in Iran and in England.

296 A term not uncommon in banking contracts: see *Royal Bank of Canada v. Cooperative Centrale Raiffeisen Boerenleenbank* [2003] EWCA Civ 7, [2004] 1 Lloyd's Rep 471; see also *Deutsche Bank AG v. Highland Crusader Offshore Partners LP* [2009] EWCA Civ 725, [2010] 1 WLR 1023.

patent actions makes this the only way in which cross-border infringement can be dealt with.[297]

4.38 Time (limit) for making the application for a stay

Prior to the coming into effect of the Civil Procedure Rules, an application for a stay of proceedings was regarded as conceptually, and treated as procedurally, distinct from one challenging the very jurisdiction of the court. After all, the results of the two arguments were different: one resulted in the court concluding that it had no jurisdiction, the other in it concluding that it did have a jurisdiction which it would retain but would, for the time being at least, not exercise. For this reason a stay of proceedings on the ground of *forum non conveniens* was not applied for under the procedure which challenged the jurisdiction, and there was even some suggestion, driven by impeccable logic, that to seek a stay of proceedings was, therefore, to concede and submit to the jurisdiction of the court.[298] This has now changed, and 'a defendant who wishes to… argue that the court should not exercise its jurisdiction' may apply for an order to that effect pursuant to CPR Part 11,[299] the details of which are examined in Chapter 5.

In *Texan Management Ltd v. Pacific Electric Wire & Cable Co Ltd*,[300] the Privy Council, after a thorough review of the law prior to and as established in CPR Part 11, came to the conclusion that CPR Part 11 and its timetable furnished the framework within which an application for a stay of proceedings was to be made. Despite the fact that much of CPR Part 11 seems to apply naturally to challenges to the jurisdiction, properly or strictly so called, the language of the Rule was clear enough[301] to mean that a stay is to be applied for within the timetable set by the Rule. However, the court has a general discretion to extend time in an appropriate case; and the power to order a stay on discretionary grounds has not been abolished.[302] It follows that a defendant will be expected to comply with the timetable established by CPR Part 11 if he wishes to apply for a stay of proceedings, but that if the case is a sufficient one – say the shape of the litigation changes in the course of pleading[303] – a later application will be permitted.[304] The approach adopted by the Privy

---

297 *Affymetrix Inc v. Multilyte Ltd* [2004] EWHC 291 (Pat), [2005] FSR 1.

298 *Cf* (in the context of recognition of foreign judgments): *Henry v. Geoprosco International* [1976] QB 726.

299 Replacing, but also extending the scope of what was, RSC Order 12, r. 8.

300 [2009] UKPC 46. It will also apply to stays sought on the basis of Art. 30 of Regulation 1215/2012: *Cooper Tire & Rubber Co v. Shell Chemicals UK Ltd* [2009] EWHC 2609 (Comm), [2009] 2 CLC 619.

301 There was a possible argument that CPR Part 11 did not apply to a stay, but that r. 11(1)(a) applied to contentions that the basis for service was not satisfied and r. 11(1)(b) to contentions that the case was not one in which the court should have exercised its discretion in favour of permission to serve out. However, r. 11(6)(d) was not consistent with the argument that CPR Part 11 did not apply to stays on the ground of *forum non conveniens*; and the 'possible argument' was not favoured by the Privy Council.

302 *Sawyer v. Atari Interactive Inc* [2005] EWHC 2351 (Ch), [2006] ILPr 8; *Zumax Nigeria Ltd v. First City Monument Bank Ltd* [2014] EWHC 2075 (Ch).

303 It is to be observed that in *Owusu v. Jackson* [2002] EWCA Civ 877 (subsequently referred to the European Court) the first defendant had served a defence prior to making the application for a stay under CPR Part 11, and the Court did not seem at all concerned. This suggests that applications for a stay on *forum non conveniens* grounds are not invariably hemmed in by the CPR Part 11 procedure and timetable, though the point does not appear to have been directly addressed: see the judgment at [10] and [15].

304 There is no reason why an application, if unsuccessful the first time, should not be repeated if, in the course of the process of preparation for litigation, facts emerge which suggest there are good grounds for it. An unsoundly-based repeat application will be foolish and costly; but the principle of reapplication is supported by principle and by the Court of Appeal in *Owens Bank Ltd v. Bracco* [1992] 2 AC 433 at 474. The point was not addressed by the

Council is sensible and practical, and it will put an end to any uncertainty which may have existed previously.

4.39 The *Spiliada* test: critical views

For the sake of completeness it should be said that the *Spiliada* doctrine has not escaped criticism from common lawyers.[305] It is usual, perhaps nowadays essential, for applications for a stay to be made early in the process of litigation, not least because the longer it is left undone, the greater will be the unwillingness of the court to abort the English proceedings and see the expense wasted. That being so, the application for a stay may be dealt with long before the final shape of the claim and of the defence has emerged. Certainly it may be done long before it is known who the witnesses will be and what their evidence will be. Parties, it is sometimes said (but never, so far as one can discover, by parties to the litigation), want to spend their money fighting on the merits, not on the merits of where to fight.[306]

None of this is untrue; none of it is conclusive. If a court is to decide whether it or another court is best placed to adjudicate in a dispute, it is better done early than late. Applications for permission, or to set aside permission, to serve out of the jurisdiction, and jurisdictional issues arising under the Brussels I Regulation, are decided at the earliest stage possible; an application for a stay is not so very different. If the claimant were to object that he has to oppose a stay application before he is ready, the proper response should be that he should not have instituted the claim, in England at least, in such a state of unpreparedness. And the proposition that defendants want to spend their money otherwise than on a stay application is just rhetoric.[307] No one forces them to apply for a stay of proceedings or to make any other form of jurisdictional application. The law as finally put in place by *Spiliada*, striking the balance as it now stands, is the brilliant product of true judicial creativity. As Lord Goff of Chieveley put it, the principle of *forum non conveniens* is 'one of the most civilised of legal principles'.[308] Further comment would be impertinent. Even so, no account of the law would be complete without an acknowledgment of the rejection of this civilised legal principle, as it applies in England, by the High Court of Australia.[309] This fact supplies a ground of rejection which is limited, but quite distinct from those examined above.

House of Lords at 480. And though CPR Part 11 appears to suggest or require that an application for a stay needs to be made within 14 days of filing an acknowledgment of service, and this will usually be what is required of the defendant, the possibility of a stay granted under the court's inherent discretion has not been eliminated, and this may provide the procedural mechanism for a subsequent or delayed application: a stay could be applied for as part of the court's powers of case management under CPR r. 3.1(2)(f). Alternatively, time may be extended under CPR r. 3.1(2)(a): see generally *Texan Management Ltd v. Pacific Electric Wire & Cable Co Ltd* [2009] UKPC 46.

305 See, for an early practitioner's complaint, Slater (1988) 104 LQR 554. For a much more balanced and far more detailed analysis, see Bell, *Forum Shopping and Venue in Transnational Litigation* (OUP, 2003).

306 But it is clear that a decision upon where the case will be heard will sometimes settle whether the claimant will decide to sue in the foreign court, or simply throw in the towel.

307 Perhaps because, in some cases at least, they see it as a way of preventing the claimant suing on the merits at all.

308 *Airbus Industrie GIE v. Patel* [1999] 1 AC 119, 141.

309 For an extraordinary assertion, that the Australian formulation may be seen as being 'more globally responsible', see Prince (1998) 47 ICLQ 573. The remarkable claim that the Australian doctrine has this amazing power is made at 593.

In *Oceanic Sun Line Special Shipping Co Inc v. Fay*,[310] a bare majority of the High Court held that *Spiliada* did not represent the law in Australia. Though the reasoning may be questioned, not least as the case was one where jurisdiction was founded on service out of the jurisdiction, to which considerations of *forum conveniens* are surely admissible, even in Australia, it may have been right to look on *Fay's* case as one involving a consumer who was not to be defeated by a take-it-or-leave-it jurisdiction agreement for a court half the world away. Indeed, most of the leading Australian decisions have involved a local claimant, equivalent to a consumer, bringing proceedings against a foreign entity of considerably greater economic power and for whom a trial in Australia would hardly be a bother. The English authorities prior to *Spiliada* were not of this character; and when later decisions[311] did involve economically weak claimants suing economically powerful entities who preferred to defend themselves overseas, the second limb of *Spiliada* was available to prevent a stay being ordered in favour of a faraway foreign court. It is interesting to wonder whether the House of Lords would have developed the doctrine as it did if it had been faced with a series of local consumers seeking to sue foreign suppliers in respect of injuries sustained at home and overseas. So far as the Australian cases are concerned, if this was a part of the thinking of the majority, it would have been preferable to have had it said openly, for such a point would have real substance.

Be that as it may, *Fay's* case was concerned with the setting aside of service out of the jurisdiction, and it was not obvious, at least to those outside Australia, that what *Spiliada* had to say about stays of proceedings should have been seen as relevant at all. However, in the opinion of Deane J, the gap between *Spiliada* and the approach of the majority was likely to be small. The decision of the majority was then approved in *Voth v. Manildra Flour Mills Pty Ltd*,[312] though with a further modification to acknowledge the distinct nature of the jurisdictional issues in service out cases.

But so far as stay cases were concerned, what resulted from this was a test which held that such relief would be granted only if Australia was a clearly inappropriate forum for the trial of the claim. This condition would be satisfied if the continuation of proceedings in Australia would be oppressive ('seriously and unfairly burdensome, prejudicial or damaging') or vexatious ('productive of serious and unjustified trouble and harassment'). It appeared that, in sharp contrast to the assumptions underpinning *Spiliada*, this test was formulated to protect an Australian judge from being asked or required to make any form of comparative judgment as to where a case should be allowed to proceed to trial.[313] This became clearer in *Henry v. Henry*,[314] when local proceedings were stayed on the ground, apparently conclusive, that they had been commenced a year after foreign proceedings brought in respect of the same matrimonial subject matter. And in *CSR Ltd v. Cigna Insurance Australia Pty Ltd*,[315] proceedings in New South Wales were stayed on the ground that their being

---

310 (1988) 165 CLR 197.

311 *Connelly, Lubbe*: see para. 4.20, above.

312 (1991) 171 CLR 538.

313 *Optima est lex quae minimum relinquit arbitrio judicis, optimus judex qui minimum sibi* as Brennan J put it in *Oceanic Sun Line Special Shipping Co Inc v. Fay* (1988) 165 CLR 197 (that system of law is the best which leaves least to the discretion of the judge; that judge is the best who relies least on his own opinion).

314 (1996) 185 CLR 571.

315 (1997) 189 CLR 345. The case was predominantly concerned with Australian law on anti-suit injunctions, but having refused to make such an order, the court dealt briefly with, and granted, an application to stay proceedings in the courts of New South Wales.

brought within days of an action commenced in the courts of New Jersey meant that they were inherently oppressive or vexatious. As this conclusion was reached in contradiction of the trial judge, it appears that it followed as a matter of law that the Australian action was necessarily oppressive or vexatious.

In *Fay's* case, as said above, Deane J had predicted that the difference between the English and Australian formulations might be small in practice. But it appears that this was a mis-prediction. In *Régie Nationale des Usines Renault SA v. Zhang*,[316] a majority of the High Court took the law back to an earlier and undeniably more parochial position: indeed, in *BHP Billiton Ltd v. Schultz*[317] the view was expressed by three of their Honours that the developed state of Australian law bore overtones of the original, pre-*Atlantic Star*, common law approach as established by *St Pierre v. South American Stores*.[318] It results in the conclusion that an action commenced by service out of the jurisdiction will be allowed to continue in Australia unless Australia is a clearly inappropriate forum, in the sense that it is vexatious or oppressive for the defendant to be subjected to a trial in Australia: if this is the law for service out, it will be even more loaded against the granting of a stay when proceedings have been commenced by service within the jurisdiction.

One takes from this the conclusion that it will be very difficult, especially for a corporate defendant, to persuade an Australian court to decline to exercise jurisdiction, whether the action was commenced by service within or service out of the jurisdiction.[319] In the light of the decision in *CSR Ltd v. Cigna Insurance Australia Pty Ltd*, there will instead be a premium on the local proceedings being commenced before those in any competing foreign court, with the arresting consequence that the Australian common law has eschewed *Spiliada* but adopted an outlook very similar to that legislated in Article 29 of the Brussels I Regulation.

The merits of the formulation aside, the result[320] is that the modern Australian law on the principles which govern applications for a stay of proceedings places its focus on the local proceedings, and the sufficiency of their connection with Australia. The partial attraction in this is not hard to see: in *Lubbe v. Cape plc*, Lord Bingham of Cornhill trod a careful line between saying that the claim of the asbestos victims could not be properly tried without the group action procedure and financial resources available to the claimants in England, and saying that the civil procedures in South Africa were simply not up to the task of delivering justice to the claimants. But, one might have thought, being a judge involves making judgments, even when the issues are difficult; and it is hard to believe that justice can be fully done while being reluctant to assess and evaluate the strength of competing connections with different courts. Once this is permitted, the line which the High Court of Australia sought to hold in *CSR v. Cigna* becomes untenable.

By further contrast, the Supreme Court of Canada has taken the doctrine of *forum non conveniens*, in its *Spiliada* form, as the basis for a modern re-evaluation of the law on jurisdiction, anti-suit injunctions, and the recognition of foreign judgments, with few or none of the High Court of Australia's inhibitions about making judgments about the manner in which a

---

316 (2003) 201 CLR 491; see Briggs (2002) 2 OxUCLJ 133.
317 (2004) 221 CLR 400.
318 See above, para. 4.16.
319 Service out in most of Australia does not require prior permission.
320 The significance of this is much more acute in the law relating to anti-suit injunctions, examined in Chapter 5.

foreign court exercised, or was proposing to exercise, jurisdiction.[321] The 'most civilised of legal principles' has certainly got lawyers thinking.

4.40 Stay of proceedings on the ground of case management

If the case is not made out for a stay on the basis of the principle of *forum non conveniens*, it may still be open to a party who wishes the English proceedings to be dealt with before or after some procedure in a foreign court or before an arbitral tribunal to apply for a stay of proceedings[322] on the basis of the court's powers of case management. Such procedural law, which has no particular connection to the law on civil jurisdiction and judgments, really lies beyond the scope of this book, but it is clear that the stay ordered on the ground of case management is a useful, distinct, component of the court's procedural powers of control.[323]

STAYING PROCEEDINGS BY REFERENCE TO AGREEMENT ON CHOICE OF COURT

4.41 General approach

Pacta sunt servanda: agreements are made to be kept. The case law deals separately with stay applications which are founded on an agreement made for the jurisdiction of a foreign court and for the non-exercise of jurisdiction by the English court.[324] Two reasons in particular justify doing so. First, in *Spiliada* itself, Lord Goff of Chieveley expressed doubt as to whether there should be any cross-fertilisation between this area and the law on stays where there was no prior agreement on choice of court.[325] Second, in applying for a stay, the defendant is making an allegation of specific wrongdoing: the claimant is breaking his contract, and should be prevented from doing so, just as any other party in breach should.

An agreement on jurisdiction for the English courts does not, as a matter of common law,[326] establish the jurisdiction of the court: only service does that. But it does mean that jurisdiction established by service will be most unlikely to be stayed; and where the

---

321 On provincial judgments, *Morguard Investments Ltd v. De Savoye* [1990] 3 SCR 1077; on anti-suit injunctions, *Amchem Products Inc v. British Columbia (Workers' Compensation Board)* [1993] 1 SCR 897; on jurisdiction, *Spar Aerospace Ltd v. American Mobile Satellite Corp* [2002] 4 SCR 205 (on an appeal from Québec, where jurisdiction is codified but probably of general application); and on foreign judgments, *Beals v. Saldanha* [2003] 3 SCR 410.

322 Or even a stay of the application to challenge the jurisdiction.

323 Representative decisions of the Court of Appeal are *Reichhold Norway ASA v. Goldman Sachs International* [2000] 1 WLR 173; *Racy v. Hawila* [2004] EWCA Civ 209; *Konkola Copper Mines plc v. Coromin Ltd* [2006] EWCA Civ 5, [2006] 1 Lloyd's Rep 410; *Amlin Corporate Member Ltd v. Oriental Assurance Corp* [2012] EWCA Civ 1341. Of the High Court decisions, see in particular *Equitas Ltd v. Allstate Insurance Co* [2008] EWHC 1671 (Comm), [2009] 1 All ER (Comm) 1137; *Isis Investments Ltd v. Oscatello Investments Ltd* [2013] EWHC 7 (Ch); *Citicorp International Ltd v. Shiv-Vani Oil & Gas Exploration Services Ltd* [2014] EWHC 245 (Comm).

324 If there is a choice of court for the English court, it will be rare, but will not be inadmissible, for a stay of proceedings to be applied for. For the possibility, see *UBS AG v. Omni Holding AG* [2000] 1 WLR 916; *Marubeni Hong Kong & China Ltd v. Mongolia Government* [2002] 2 All ER (Comm) 873; *Sinochem International Oil (London) Co Ltd v. Mobil Sales and Supply Corp* [2001] 1 Lloyd's Rep 670, 678–680. And for a case where a stay was actually ordered, see *Bouygues Offshore SA v. Caspian Shipping Co (Nos 1, 3, 4 and 5)* [1998] 2 Lloyd's Rep 461, discussed further below.

325 At 480.

326 It is quite different under the Brussels I Regulation, where the legislation provides that certain types of jurisdiction agreement establish in law the jurisdiction of the court.

defendant is out of the jurisdiction, it does provide a firm basis for permission to serve out of the jurisdiction, as will be shown later in this chapter. An agreement for the jurisdiction of a foreign court does not, as a matter of common law, oust or deny the jurisdiction of the English court where this has been established by service,[327] but it does provide a firm basis for an application for a stay of those proceedings, as will be shown in the paragraphs which follow. And an agreement on jurisdiction for the English courts may provide a cause of action for an injunction to restrain the party in breach of it from suing in a court overseas,[328] or a cause of action for damages for breach of contract if any loss is proved.[329]

An agreement on choice of court does not confer a *right* to obtain a stay of English proceedings which conflict with or breach it. A stay of proceedings may not be equitable relief, but procedural relief of this kind is also a matter of judicial discretion. However, the defendant has a greatly enhanced expectation of obtaining a stay of proceedings; and whether or not he obtains that relief, he may argue that the common law gives him a right to claim damages for breach of contract. Where proceedings are brought in a foreign court in breach of an agreement for the English courts, the general expectation is that the breach of contract will justify an application for an injunction to restrain the party in breach. The private international law issues which arise in that context go beyond the law on choice of court agreements, but the two situations overlap, particularly where the issue upon which the case turns is the construction of the agreement on choice of court. In the account which follows in this chapter, some of the authorities referred to will be cases in which the application to the English court was for an anti-suit injunction; on questions of construction, validity, nature and scope of a contract term, the case law is interchangeable.

Rights come before remedies; grounds come before relief. Before coming to the question of enforcement, a court will need to determine any questions of construction, validity, nature, and scope (material and personal) of the parties' agreement on choice of court on which the application will turn.[330] These questions or issues do rather run into one another, but in the account which follows they will be disentangled to the extent that it seems possible.

The courts have been careful to avoid equating a choice of English law to govern a contract as though it were a choice of English courts.[331] If the parties have chosen a law to govern their contract, but have not identified a court as the one which is to have jurisdiction, the maxim of *expressio unius, exclusio alterius* may suggest that there is no agreement on choice of court (by contrast, it may make it relatively easy to show that England is the most appropriate forum). However, it can be argued that a choice of law connotes, by necessary implication, a jurisdictional choice of any court which will apply that agreed-upon law to the resolution of the issue in dispute, and that the approach to jurisdictional applications

---

327 Only statute can define the conditions in which service does not establish the jurisdiction of the court (the Brussels I Regulation is the most important such statute).

328 Paragraph 5.36, below.

329 Paragraph 5.53, below.

330 In connection with the material examined in the following paragraphs, further detail and analysis may be found in Joseph, *Jurisdiction and Arbitration Agreements and Their Enforcement*, 3rd edn (Sweet & Maxwell, London, 2014); Briggs, *Agreements on Jurisdiction and Choice of Law* (OUP, Oxford, 2008); and Briggs [2012] LMCLQ 364.

331 *MacSteel Commercial Holdings (Pty) Ltd v. Thermasteel Canada Inc* [1996] CLC 1403; *BP Exploration Co (Libya) Ltd v. Hunt (No 2)* [1976] 3 All ER 879; *The Elli 2* [1985] 1 Lloyd's Rep 107; *Sawyer v. Atari Interactive Inc* [2005] EWHC 2351 (Ch), [2006] ILPr 8; *Novus Aviation Ltd v. Onur Air Tasimacilik A/S* [2009] EWCA Civ 122, [2009] 1 Lloyd's Rep 576. For a related point, that a choice of law is not *ipso facto* a submission to the jurisdiction (though it does furnish a ground for application for permission to serve out of the jurisdiction: see para. 4.58, below), see *Ace Insurance Ltd v. Moose Enterprise Pty Ltd* [2009] NSWSC 724, [47].

which characterises cases in which there is an agreement on choice of court ought to be applicable, if with modification, to cases involving an express choice of law. The matter is considered below.[332]

Of course, if there is a statutory obligation to give effect to a jurisdiction agreement (just as where there is with an arbitration agreement to which Arbitration Act 1996 applies[333]), the common law analysis, which is used to shape the exercise of discretion by the court, is sidelined. The primary example is where the Hague Convention on Choice of Court Agreements, which takes effect in the United Kingdom via Article 67 of the recast Brussels I Regulation, requires an English court to give effect to an exclusive jurisdiction agreement for the courts of a non-Member, Contracting, State. But outside the Brussels I Regulation and the Lugano Convention, there are very few such statutory provisions, and the issue need not be considered further.

In the paragraphs which follow, therefore, the context of the enquiry will be on the common law principles which apply to the staying of English proceedings which have been commenced by service of process within the jurisdiction. The role of an agreement on choice of court usually is, in such a context, to provide a basis for an application to the English court for a stay of proceedings, this made on the broad ground that the parties chose and agreed to the courts of another country and that they should now abide by that choice.

4.42 Construction of the choice of court agreement: its scope, validity, and nature

If the basis upon which a stay of proceedings is sought is that the claimant is breaking his contractual agreement in instituting proceedings in England, the factual basis for this argument must be established. Accordingly, the defendant will need to show (i) that on its proper construction, the proceedings brought by the claimant in England fall within the material and personal scope of the agreement,[334] (ii) that the agreement remains valid and enforceable as between the parties, and (iii) that the agreement obliged, as distinct from merely permitting, the claimant to sue in the foreign court. Failure to satisfy these three conditions will mean that any application for a stay will be determined by the ordinary *Spiliada* principles. It is convenient to examine these three elements separately, though the first is the most complex.

In *Fiona Trust & Holding Corp v. Privalov*,[335] the House of Lords significantly re-stated English private international law as it applies to disputed agreements on jurisdiction and arbitration.[336] As a result of this heroic judgment, many troublesome earlier authorities are relegated to history, and are mentioned below only for their appalling curiosity value. The decision in *Fiona Trust* needs to be separately understood in relation to the three issues with which we are concerned. On the *scope* of the agreement, it provides clear authority for the

---

332 See para. 5.58, below.

333 See further below, para. 4.55.

334 For a more detailed analysis of drafting such clauses, see Appendix IV to this book.

335 [2007] UKHL 40, [2007] Bus LR 1719. The case is reported in the House of Lords as *Premium Nafta Products Ltd v. Fili Shipping Co Ltd*, but is more generally referred to by the name under which it was reported below. Why it was not reported in the regular (Weekly) Law Reports is a mystery which does no credit to the system of law reporting in England.

336 In principle, they also apply to settlement agreements: *Starlight Shipping Co v. Allianz Marine & Aviation Versicherungs AG* [2014] EWCA Civ 1010, [2014] 2 Lloyd's Rep 544, [8]–[9].

view that words of ambiguous scope will be given as broad a meaning as they may properly bear. This is because it is not rational to suppose that parties who were of sound mind will have wished some aspects of a possible dispute, for which they have made provision, but not others, to fall within the scope of a choice of court. On the issue of the *validity* of the agreement, the decision means that the agreement will be regarded as effective, even though one party has persuasive-looking grounds to challenge the validity of the contract in which the choice of court agreement is contained and uses this to contest the validity of the agreement on jurisdiction as well.[337] This is because it is rational to suppose that the parties intended the court which they identified, in the contract which they made, to have jurisdiction to determine whether the contract between them was legally valid: a moment's reflection is enough to see that a jurisdiction agreement which would allow the nominated court only to hold the contract valid and binding would be a strange and useless thing. But on the issue of *nature* of the agreement *Fiona Trust* has nothing to say: the question whether the agreement is exclusive or non-exclusive, or of a nature which is not clearly one or the other, is not one to which only one rational answer is possible.

The principles established by *Fiona Trust* will apply whether the agreement is for the English courts or for the courts of a country outside England: the relief will differ, but the approach to construction will, in principle, be the same. In principle the approach to construction supported by *Fiona Trust* should apply only if the agreement on jurisdiction is itself governed by English law, but the persuasive force of the judgment is so great that it is bound to apply unless the evidence that foreign law is different is extremely clear. If it is, however, the conclusion will be that the contractual term, for jurisdiction or arbitration, covers only so much as it is drafted to cover.

4.43 Scope of the choice of court agreement: the law to which the issue is referred

The question whether the claim falls within the four corners of the parties' agreement as to choice of court raises a question of construction; and construction of the agreement, where this is in dispute and the words are not unambiguous, is referred to the law which is applicable to that agreement, which will usually be the law of the larger agreement or contract of which it is a term.

The common law took it as settled law that a choice of court clause, like any other term in a contract, was interpreted by the proper law of the contract, as it was one contractual promise among many.[338] The law which governs contracts made in civil and commercial matters after 17 December 2009 will usually be identified by the Rome I Regulation,[339] which makes no claim to apply to agreements on choice of court.[340] But if it is asked how this affects the determination of the law which governed an agreement on choice of court,

---

337 *El Nasharty v. J Sainsbury plc* [2007] EWHC 2618 (Comm), [2008] 1 Lloyd's Rep 360.

338 *Hoerter v. Hanover Telegraph Works* (1893) 10 TLR 103; *The Sindh* [1975] 1 Lloyd's Rep 372; *The Sennar (No 2)* [1985] 1 WLR 490. This did give rise to problems when the proper law was not chosen by the parties but might then be affected by whether there was a choice of court agreement from which to infer it. The problem of circularity was never far away from the common law method.

339 Superseding in this respect the Rome Convention (Contracts (Applicable Law) Act 1990), which was in materially identical terms and which applied to contracts made after 1 May 1991.

340 Article 1(2)(e). The same provision also excludes the Regulation from arbitration agreements.

the most plausible answer is that it will usually[341] be governed by the law – identified by the Rome I Regulation if this applies to the contract – which governs the contract of which it is a term. For though the Regulation makes no demand to govern the validity and scope of an agreement on choice of court, it does not prevent the private international law rules of the common law taking their own decision to refer the issue to the law which governs the contract in which the agreement on jurisdiction is contained.[342]

The foregoing assumes, but surely correctly,[343] that the definition and scope of an agreement is a matter for the law which governs it. In the common law scheme of jurisdiction, the role of an agreement is to provide data for the court's decision whether to set aside service which has been made, or to authorise service to be made. In that context, it makes sense to treat the agreement as though it is a contractual term, part of the package agreed to.

But by way of contrast, it is clear that other systems may look on agreements as to jurisdiction rather differently.[344] If one has a rule – as the Brussels I Regulation does – that an agreement on jurisdiction establishes the jurisdiction of a court, as a matter of public law, the agreement is more obviously a matter of civil procedure or statutory jurisdictional law which may be conceptualised as a submission in advance to the jurisdiction of one court and a waiver of the jurisdiction of another. For this, some degree of formality might be required,[345] but there is no particular reason to see the process as one which is framed by the apparatus of contract. And if *that* is the way agreements on jurisdiction are understood, the case for referring questions to the law of the forum,[346] or even the law of the nominated court said to have jurisdiction by virtue of the agreement, may be more persuasive than any reference to a *lex contractus*. This may help explain why there was no consensus to extend the Rome Convention to regulate this issue: the point was explored at greater length in relation to the Brussels I Regulation, in which agreements are, as was submitted, understood in the submission–and–waiver sense just described.

4.44 Material scope of an agreement on choice of court governed by English law

Where a contractual[347] agreement on jurisdiction is governed by, or is construed according to, English domestic law, it is a general rule of English law that it be construed amply,

---

341 The parties may, obviously, specify a separate law to govern the dispute resolution agreement, or may make such an agreement quite distinctly and separately from (and for the purpose of resolving disputes arising under) the substantive contract by which they are bound. This rarely happens.

342 This approach may derive loose support from *Egon Oldendorff v. Libera Corp* [1995] 2 Lloyd's Rep 64 (incorporation of arbitration clause examined in light of law applicable to the contract according to the Rome Convention).

343 The application of the law which governs the agreement, and the irrelevance of the law of the court whose derogated from, was assumed to be correct in *Youell v. Kara Mara Shipping Co* [2000] 2 Lloyd's Rep 102, 117.

344 See, for example, Gaudemet-Tallon, *Compétence et exécution des jugements en Europe*, 4th edn (LDGJ, Paris, 2010), [152]. For the view that as matter of Spanish law, these agreements are to be seen as contractual, and as supporting actions for breach of contract, see the decision of the Spanish Supreme Court in *Sentencia (TS) 6/2009* (12 Jan 2009) [2009] Rep Jur 542.

345 See para. 2.128, above.

346 On the footing that the ouster of, or agreement to forgo, the forum's jurisdiction must be a matter for the *lex fori*.

347 A slightly less broad interpretation may be appropriate for a jurisdiction provision in a trust instrument, in which context a court designated as a 'forum of administration' may not be seen as the place agreed upon for the resolution of disputes: *Crociani v. Crociani* [2014] UKPC 40.

broadly.[348] The court should not accede to a contention that (for example) because the claim is framed in tort or in equity it is not within the scope of a clause which deals with 'all disputes arising under this contract', and so forth. It would make no sense for parties to a commercial agreement to foresee that disputes may arise and that jurisdiction needs to be provided for, but then to include some but not other kinds of dispute within the material scope of their jurisdiction agreement. What would be the point?

Though there had been earlier decisions in support of a rational construction,[349] disapproving of the nit-picking which had evidently been preferred in other cases, this had not prevented practitioners routinely citing the much larger pile of older cases to the courts.[350] The need to rectify law which had got out of hand struck the appellate courts in England[351] and Australia[352] at roughly the same time. As will be seen, the analysis may be different if more complex contractual provisions are concerned, but as a general principle *Fiona Trust* makes a fresh start.

The authorities therefore give less support than they once did to the argument that the words defining the scope of an agreement as to jurisdiction (or arbitration: no material distinction is drawn at this point) should be read restrictively. It is probably harmful to trawl through cases which debated whether 'arising under' or 'in connection with' were synonymous, or if not, how not. For as Lord Hoffmann observed in *Fiona Trust*, these decisions

---

348 But that is not to say that there will not be some applications and proceedings which will fall outside the material scope of the agreement on jurisdiction: it is all a matter of construction. For illustration, see *AWB Geneva SA v. North America Steamships Ltd* [2007] EWCA Civ 739, [2007] 2 Lloyd's Rep 315 (no breach of jurisdiction clause for trustee in bankruptcy to bring proceedings in the insolvency to obtain a determination of rights under a contract); *Brave Bulk Transport Ltd v. Spot On Shipping Ltd* [2009] EWHC 612 (QB), [2009] 1 Lloyd's Rep 115 (no breach of English jurisdiction clause to enforce judgment obtained in England against a non-party on the basis that it was the 'alter ego' of the defendant and liable as a matter of New York law to have the judgment enforced against it); *Vitol SA v. Capri Marine Ltd (No 2)* [2010] EWHC 458 (Comm), [2011] 1 All ER (Comm) 366 (no breach of jurisdiction agreement to obtain order to help with the enforcement of the judgment which had been obtained in the agreed court; *Oceanconnect UK Ltd v. Angara Maritime Ltd* [2010] EWCA 1050, [2011] 1 Lloyd's Rep 399 (proceedings in the US in respect of maritime lien did not breach jurisdiction clause contained in escrow agreement); *Louis Dreyfus Commodities Kenya Ltd v. Bolster Shipping Co Ltd* [2010] EWHC 1732 (Comm), [2011] 1 All ER (Comm) 540 (joinder as party to proceedings in Mexico for purpose of obtaining evidence no breach of arbitration clause); *U&M Mining Zambia Ltd v. Konkola Copper Mines plc* [2013] EWHC 260 (Comm), [2013] 2 Lloyd's Rep 218 (no breach of arbitration agreement to seek interim relief from foreign court); *Ryanair Ltd v. Esso Italiana Srl* [2013] EWCA Civ 1450 [2015] 1 AUER (Comm) 152 (jurisdiction clause did not apply to claims founded on liability for participation in an unlawful cartel); *Bank St Petersburg v. Arkhangelsky* [2014] EWCA Civ 593, [2014] 1 WLR 4360 (no breach of English jurisdiction clause by attempting to rely on Russian judgments in those proceedings, but there would be a breach if those Russian judgments were enforced if the bank were to lose in the English proceedings).

349 Prime examples of this are *The Pioneer Container* [1994] 2 AC 324 (PC, HK); *Harbour Assurance Co (UK) Ltd v. Kansa General International Insurance Co Ltd* [1993] QB 701, which seems to have originated the idea that parties draft agreements to provide for 'one-stop shopping'. See also *ET Plus SA v. Welter* [2005] EWHC 2115 (Comm), [2006] 1 Lloyd's Rep 215.

350 For example, *Heyman v. Darwins Ltd* [1942] AC 356 ('arising under' narrower than 'arising out of'); *Union of India v. E B Aaby's Rederi A/S* [1975] AC 797 (no difference between the two formulations discussed in *Heyman's* case); *Fillite (Runcorn) Ltd v. Aqua-Lift* (1989) 26 Con LR 66 ('under a contract' did not apply to obligations not created by the contract itself); *Mackender v. Feldia AG* [1967] 2 QB 590 ('arising thereunder' applied to claim to avoid for non-disclosure); *El Nasharty v. J Sainsbury Plc* [2003] EWHC 2195 (Comm), [2004] 1 Lloyd's Rep 308 ('in relation to' is wider than 'under'); *Beazley v. Horizon Offshore Contractors Inc* [2004] EWHC 2555 (Comm), [2005] ILPr 123 ('this insurance' is wider that 'this policy of insurance'); *Incitec Ltd v Alkimos Shipping Corp* (2004) 206 ALR 558 ('arising out of or in connection with' is wider than 'arising from').

351 *Fiona Trust & Holding Corp v. Privalov* [2007] EWCA Civ 20, [2007] Bus LR 686; aff'd with specific approval of this aspect of the judgment in particular: [2007] UKHL 40, [2007] Bus LR 1719.

352 *Comandate Marine Corp v. Pan Australia Shipping Pty Ltd* (2006) 157 FCR 45, [2008] 1 Lloyd's Rep 119, [165].

'reflect no credit upon English law'.[353] It may still be prudent to draft contractual agreements for the resolution of disputes in broad terms, but those which are framed less comprehensively may themselves take advantage of this benevolent approach to interpretation.[354] When one remembers that a number of these agreements will have been drafted by persons for whom English is a second, and legal English a third, language, it would be perverse to ascribe a meaning to the words which the individuals concerned did not intend. It may also be observed that the view that if an agreement on jurisdiction may be seen as an exclusion clause – excluding remedies by excluding the jurisdiction of courts from which that relief might have been claimed – ambiguity should, in the final resort, be resolved by construction *contra proferentem*. But reference to it in English authorities has so far been limited to a small number of cases concerned with conflicting agreements on jurisdiction.[355]

4.45 Material scope of a choice of court agreement: more complex contractual structures

Some agreements which provide for the resolution of disputes are less straightforward than the one in *Fiona Trust*, which was dealt with as though it made a single reference to arbitration.[356] In fact, it provided for English jurisdiction, subject to the right of either party to opt for arbitration. The decision for the court was therefore whether the reference to arbitration was valid and binding on the party objecting to it (it was), and which body – English court or London tribunal – should decide the issue in the first instance (London tribunal). But arbitration and jurisdiction were in England, and the internal hierarchy of choices was clear enough.

However, many clauses are more complex, though whether by accident or design is not always easy to tell. It is to be supposed, at least to begin with, that every part of the agreement was intended to be effective alongside the others. An insurance policy might provide for London arbitration, but also contain a 'service of suit' clause, by which the insurer agrees to accept the jurisdiction of another court, usually American, if it refuses to pay sums claimed on the policy. A 'service of suit' clause is an agreement to accept the jurisdiction of a court, and is close in nature to an agreement on jurisdiction which is initially optional or non-exclusive,[357] but which becomes mandatory or exclusive when invoked by one of the parties.[358] It seems probable that in such a case, the agreement to arbitrate is binding,

---

353 *Fiona Trust & Holding Corp v. Privalov* [2007] UKHL 40, [2007] Bus LR 1719, [12].

354 But see the speech of Lord Scott of Foscote in *Donohue v. Armco Inc* [2001] UKHL 64, [2002] 1 Lloyd's Rep 425 for the proposition that an 'all disputes' clause is ineffective to encompass claims arising under a foreign law which could, however, not be successfully brought in an English court. This was a minority view, and is, it is submitted, not convincing. For an extended essay on the complexity of meaning in written contracts, see *Chartbrook Ltd v. Persimmon Homes Ltd* [2009] UKHL 38, [2009] 1 AC 1101; for a rather more accessible explanation, see *Rainy Sky SA v. Kookmin Bank* [2011] UKSC 50, [2011] 1 WLR 2900.

355 *Credit Suisse First Boston (Europe) Ltd v. MLC (Bermuda) Ltd* [1999] 1 Lloyd's Rep 767, 777; *UBS AG v. HSH Nordbank AG* [2009] EWCA Civ 585, [2009] 2 Lloyd's Rep 272; *Sebastian Holdings Inc v. Deutsche Bank AG* [2010] EWCA Civ 998, [2011] 1 Lloyd's Rep 106. In *Ace Insurance Ltd v. Moose Enterprise Pty Ltd* [2009] NSWSC 724, [33], it was suggested that construction *contra proferentem* may apply to insurance contracts. See also *Sumukan Ltd v. Commonwealth Secretariat* [2007] EWCA Civ 243, [2007] Bus LR 1075.

356 *Fiona Trust & Holding Corp v. Privalov* [2007] UKHL 40, [2007] Bus LR 1719, [4].

357 *Cinnamon European Structured Credit Master Fund v. Banco Comercial Portugues SA* [2009] EWHC 3381 (Ch), [2010] ILPr 232.

358 *Cf* the clause in *Sabah Shipyard (Pakistan) Ltd v. Islamic Republic of Pakistan* [2002] EWCA Civ 1643, [2003] 2 Lloyd's Rep 571; *BNP Paribas SA v. Anchorage Capital Europe LLP* [2013] EWHC 3073 (Comm).

and if invoked, overrides the agreement to accept American jurisdiction, even where the insured has brought American proceedings. Whether the American jurisdiction provision could properly be confined to judicial proceedings to supervise a London arbitration and the subsequent enforcement of any award is more difficult to say;[359] but the result would be that a more complex set of provisions for the resolution of disputes may be given effect without regarding any part as otiose or redundant.[360] As it is to be supposed that the parties mean what they write down and agree to, some moderately intricate case law can result.[361]

There are also cases in which the parties, who have entered into complex financial transactions, bind themselves to a number of interlinked contractual relationships, each containing its own jurisdiction clause, and these pointing to different courts. It is obvious in such a case that any presumption that a jurisdiction clause was intended to be comprehensive and to cover all the ground needs to be applied with care, especially where this would have the effect of conflicting with other agreements which were, presumably, also intended to be effective.[362] The material question will be as to the construction of the particular jurisdiction provision in the light of the transaction as a whole; although it may not be an easy question to answer, the complexity results from the commercial transaction itself not from anything in private international law.[363] The result may be that proceedings based on various complaints arising from the broad relationship or transaction may properly be brought before more courts than one;[364] such an outcome would be consistent with the upholding of jurisdiction agreements in which the parties agree that proceedings may be brought in more than one court at the same time.[365] It does, however, mean that the parties can bring about, by accident or design,

---

359 Such division of function derives some support from *Paul Smith v. H & S International Holding Inc* [1991] 2 Lloyd's Rep 127. See *Braes of Doune Wind Farm (Scotland) Ltd v. Alfred McAlpine Business Services Ltd* [2008] EWHC 426 (TCC), [2008] 1 Lloyd's Rep 608 (Scottish arbitration and English exclusive jurisdiction: English courts entitled to deal with appeal on point of law under Arbitration Act 1996, s. 69, otherwise jurisdiction clause meaningless).

360 *Ace Capital Ltd v. CMS Energy Corp* [2008] EWHC 1843 (Comm), [2008] 2 CLC 318.

361 *Indian Oil Corp v. Van Oil Inc* [1991] 2 Lloyd's Rep 634; *Shell International Petroleum Co Ltd v. Coral Oil Co Ltd* [1991] 1 Lloyd's Rep 76; *NB Three Shipping Ltd v. Harebell Shipping Ltd* [2004] EWHC 2001 (Comm), [2005] 1 Lloyd's Rep 509; *Axa Re v. Ace Global Markets Ltd* [2006] EWHC 216 (Comm), [2006] Lloyd's Rep IR 683; *King v. Brandywine Reinsurance Co (UK) Ltd* [2005] EWCA Civ 235, [2005] 1 Lloyd's Rep 665; *C v. D* [2007] EWCA Civ 1282, [2008] Bus LR 843. And see further, Briggs, *Agreements on Jurisdiction and Choice of Law* (2008) [4.53]–[4.58]; further developed at [2012] LMCLQ 364.

362 See *Credit Suisse First Boston (Europe) Ltd v. MLC (Bermuda) Ltd* [1999] 1 Lloyd's Rep 767. In *ACP Capital Ltd v. IFR Capital plc* [2008] EWHC 1627 (Comm), [2008] 2 Lloyd's Rep 655, the judge observed that jurisdiction agreements 'carefully drafted with the assistance of lawyers' had to be interpreted according to their terms, even where the carving out of a sphere of operation for each part of the agreement on dispute resolution led to the partial fragmentation of the totality of disputes between the parties (it may have been significant that there were no third parties involved, with the consequential possibility of overriding a jurisdiction agreement binding only some of them). To similar effect, *Satyam Computer Services Ltd v. Upaid Systems Ltd* [2008] EWCA Civ 487, [2008] 2 All ER (Comm) 465; *UBS AG v. HSH Nordbank AG* [2009] EWCA Civ 585, [2009] 2 Lloyd's Rep 272; *Sebastian Holdings Inc v. Deutsche Bank AG* [2010] EWCA Civ 998, [2011] 1 Lloyd's Rep 106; *Lornamead Acquisitions Ltd v. Kaupthing Bank HF* [2011] EWHC 2611 (Comm) (a case on the Lugano Convention, but on this issue that makes no difference); *Mauritius Commercial Bank Ltd v. Hestia Holding Holdings Ltd* [2013] EWHC 1328 (Comm), [2013] 2 Lloyd's Rep 121. The entire question is one of ascertaining the rational commercial construction of the various contracts, and the fact-specific nature of that exercise means that the law cannot be laid down in narrow and precise terms. To different effect, distinguishing the approach taken in *Satyam* and applying *Fiona Trust* in plain form, *Cavell USA Inc v. Seaton Insurance Co* [2008] EWHC 3043 (Comm), [2009] Lloyd's Rep IR 616.

363 *UBS AG v. HSH Nordbank AG* [2008] EWCA Civ 585, [2009] 2 Lloyd's Rep 272, [83]; *Amtrust Europe Ltd v. Trust Risk Group SpA* [2014] EWHC 4109 (Comm).

364 Though it did not in *UBS AG v. HSH Nordbank AG*, where the court found that the English court did not have jurisdiction over the action brought before it in purported reliance on the English jurisdiction agreement.

365 See para. 4.50, below.

the fragmentation and, to some extent, duplication of judicial effort; and it will sometimes be right to ask whether their drafting should always be permitted to have this effect: after all, the common law sees the parties' agreement as to jurisdiction as data to be taken into account by a court, rather than as something which ties its hands tightly. And if the parties cooperate in the timetabling of jurisdiction applications in the various courts, with the assistance of the court if need be, a practical resolution of the issues may be available.[366]

4.46 Scope of choice of court in one contract having effect on parties to a related contract

In cases in which the substantive contract is not otherwise in dispute, the most frequent question will be whether a particular individual[367] may be bound by, or is entitled to take advantage of, an agreement on choice of court. This question, which is also an aspect of the scope of the agreement, raises a question of contractual construction, which will be governed by the law which governs the alleged agreement on jurisdiction. It should, however, be remembered that agreement to or acceptance of the jurisdiction clause may be held to have arisen in law by less direct means, especially when the jurisdiction clause appears in a dispute concerning carriage of goods. For example, it may be alleged that the agreement may be found in the consent of a bailor of goods to their sub-bailment on terms which may include a choice of court. In such cases the principles of bailment, or other exceptions to the privity rule, may produce the result that there is enough of an agreement for the parties to be bound.

Whether an agreement on jurisdiction is included in a contract also raises a question of the construction of that contract[368] and, therefore, the question whether a jurisdiction agreement appearing as a term of contract 1 may be and has been incorporated into and is part of contract 2 must therefore be a matter for the law governing contract 2. It appears from the authorities that this proposition may be easier to state than to apply, not least because the identification of the law which governs contract 2 may be affected by whether the agreement on jurisdiction is included as a term of contract 2: there are chickens and eggs wherever one looks. There is much to be said for the court taking a practical view, that if there is a good arguable case for the incorporation, then the finer points of legal analysis, which as often as not will lead nowhere, may be overlooked.[369]

In those cases in which contract 2 is governed by English law, or the question is approached as though the contract were governed by English law,[370] the traditional approach of the

---

366 *UBS AG v. HSH Nordbank AG* [2009] EWCA Civ 585, [2010] 1 All ER (Comm) 727, [105]; *Deutsche Bank AG v. Highland Crusader Offshore Partners LP* [2009] EWCA Civ 725, [2010] 1 WLR 1023, [104]; *Sebastian Holdings Inc v. Deutsche Bank AG* [2010] EWCA Civ 998, [2011] 1 Lloyd's Rep 106.

367 Whether originally or by assignment or succession: *Schiffahrtsgesellschaft Detlev von Appen GmbH v. Vöst Alpine Intertrading (The Jay Bola)* [1997] 2 Lloyd's Rep 279; *West Tankers Inc v. RAS Riunione Adriatica di Sicurta* [2005] EWHC 454 (Comm). On the question whether the assignment from an 'original defendant' to another also serves to alter the court which has jurisdiction where an international Convention determines jurisdiction by reference to the 'defendant', see *Hatzl v. XL Insurance Co Ltd* [2009] EWCA Civ 223, [2010] 1 WLR 470.

368 Including, therefore, the rules by which a court may construe the written words of a contract in such a way as corrects an obvious mistake: *Caresse Navigation Ltd v. Zurich Assurance Maroc* [2014] EWCA Civ 1366, [2015] 2 WLR 43 (reference to incorporation of 'law and arbitration' clause from charterparty (which contained only a law and jurisdiction clause) interpreted as incorporation of law and jurisdiction clause).

369 For an excellent illustration, see *Dornoch Ltd v. Mauritius Union Assurance Co Ltd* [2006] EWCA Civ 389, [2006] 2 Lloyd's Rep 475; see also Briggs, *Agreements on Jurisdiction and Choice of Law* (2008), para. 3.72.

370 For example, by assessing the issue by reference to the *lex fori*, on the ground that one has to start with the *lex fori* and assemble the data according to it before any conclusions about choice of law can be drawn.

court was that the use of general words in contract 2 such as 'terms as original', where 'original' refers to contract 1, would not, reliably at least, suffice to pick up and incorporate a jurisdiction agreement, certainly in the context of insurance and reinsurance,[371] but by parity of reasoning, in some other contexts as well. This was said to be because the jurisdiction agreement may be regarded as ancillary to the main subject matter of the contract,[372] and therefore as something which will not be taken, without more, to be picked up and incorporated by general and non-specific words of incorporation.[373]

However, more recent cases have doubted this more cautious approach, preferring the view that the issue is simply one of construing the language of contract 2, approached without presumptions.[374] Although this may be said to impair certainty, in the sense that presumptions against incorporation allow an answer to be given without needing to deal with the actually-intended meaning of the words used, it is hard to see that there is any rational objection to it. It appears that some courts, at least, will favour an approach which means that the parties had incorporated a dispute resolution agreement, on the footing that each would then know where they stood. For all that, the use of a shorthand expression to do a complex job is always risky, and it is hardly the court's fault if the results are occasionally surprising.

Where the jurisdiction agreement is one to which what is now Article 25 of the Brussels I Regulation applies, a similar approach has been taken to support the conclusion that a consensus is, in the absence of special considerations such a trade custom or practice, not clearly and precisely demonstrated by the use of such general words.[375]

4.47 Personal scope of choice of court agreement: privity and related issues

A distinct problem arises in cases in which a jurisdiction agreement governed by English law is said to affect a third party as a matter of common law reasoning. Several situations should be distinguished. A third party may be said to be bound by a jurisdiction agreement in a contract to which he was not party. In *The Pioneer Container*[376] the question arose whether an agreement on jurisdiction entered into between bailee and sub-bailee of goods bound the bailor

---

371 *Dornoch Ltd v. Mauritius Union Assurance Co Ltd* [2006] EWCA Civ 389, [2006] 2 Lloyd's Rep 475.

372 A conclusion aided by the treatment of such terms as 'severable' from the substantive agreement.

373 The origin of the incorporation principle seems to be *TW Thomas & Co Ltd v. Portsea Steamship Co Ltd* [1912] AC 1: see *AIG Europe (UK) Ltd v. The Ethniki* [2000] 2 All ER 566, CA; *AIG Europe SA v. QBE International Insurance Ltd* [2001] 2 Lloyd's Rep 268; *Assicurazioni Generali SpA v. Ege Sigorta A/S* [2002] Lloyd's Rep IR 480; *Siboti K/S v. BP France SA* [2003] EWHC 1278 (Comm), [2003] 2 Lloyd's Rep 364. However, for a less demanding standard for incorporation from one agreement to another when both agreements are between the same persons, and holding the question to be simply one of construction, see *Sea Trade Maritime Corp v. Hellenic Mutual War Risks Association (Bermuda) Ltd (The Athena)* [2006] EWHC 2530 (Comm), [2007] 1 Lloyd's Rep 280; and for the view that there is a general distinction in approach between the case in which the incorporation is from a contract to which both were party, and (on the other hand, less easily shown) incorporation from a contract which one side made with a third party, see *Habaş Sınai ve Tıbbi Gazlar İstihsal Endüstrisi AS v. Sometal SAL* [2010] EWHC 29 (Comm), [2010] Bus LR 880. And for the inevitable conclusion that the issue is in the final analysis one of construing the language used in contract 2, in all cases, see *Caresse Navigation Ltd v. Zurich Assurances Maroc* [2014] EWCA Civ 1366, [2015] 2 WLR 43.

374 *Sea Trade Maritime Corp v. Hellenic Mutual War Risks Association (Bermuda) Ltd (The Athena)* [2006] EWHC 2530 (Comm), [2007] 1 Lloyd's Rep 280; *Axa Re v. Ace Global Markets Ltd* [2006] EWHC 216 (Comm), [2006] Lloyd's Rep IR 683; *Caresse Navigation Ltd v. Zurich Assurances Maroc* [2014] EWCA Civ 1366, [2015] 2 WLR 43.

375 And see also above, para. 2.134, where the issue is discussed in the context of Art. 25 of the recast Brussels I Regulation.

376 [1994] 2 AC 324.

owner of the goods when he sued the sub-bailee. It was held that such an arrangement could, and on the facts did, constitute an agreement between the owner and sub-bailee for the purposes of the rule, and therefore bound the owner, because he had consented to the sub-bailment 'on any terms'. This form of words was wide enough to cover an agreement on choice of court.[377] By contrast, an attempt by a third party to take advantage of a clause in a contract to which he was not party failed in *The Mahkutai*,[378] where a choice of court agreement was contained in a time charterer's bill of lading. The cargo-owners sued the time charterer's sub-contractor[379] who sought to invoke the jurisdiction clause against the cargo-owner via a Himalaya clause in a bill of lading. It was held that the jurisdiction clause was not within the scope of the Himalaya clause, as it was not inserted for the carrier's protection, thereby for the protection of his sub-contractor. Complex as these authorities are, they represent no more than the English doctrine of privity of contract as applied in a particular factual context.[380]

More difficult was the approach in *Through Transport Mutual Insurance Association (Eurasia) Ltd v. New India Assurance Association Co Ltd.*[381] In the context of carriage of goods by road, A had insured B who had sustained loss at the hands of C who had been insured by D. The contract of insurance between C and D contained a dispute resolution agreement for arbitration in London.[382] A settled with B and became subrogated to his rights against C but who had, by then, gone into insolvency. A brought a direct claim against D before the Finnish courts; D objected, and contended that A was bound by the agreement to arbitrate which D had made with C.[383] It was held that A was bound by the dispute resolution agreement, but that it would not be enforced against him by anti-suit injunction. This was a rather difficult conclusion. One would have supposed that either A was bound to arbitrate because the claim which he advanced was subject to the term which provided for arbitration, in which case the injunction should have followed as a matter of course, or A was not bound by the agreement to arbitrate made between C and D, because he had never agreed to it and may never have been aware of it. Predictably enough, in further proceedings, the Commercial Court granted an application by D that an arbitrator be appointed, in order that D be able to seek a determination from the tribunal that D owed no liability to A. At the same time A

---

377 In *Dresser UK Ltd v. Falcongate Freight Management Ltd* [1992] QB 502 it was held that the principle subsequently applied in *The Pioneer Container* was not sufficient to constitute an agreement on jurisdiction for the purposes of Art. 17 of the Brussels Convention (now Art. 25 of the recast Brussels I Regulation). This conclusion may now be due for reconsideration.

378 [1996] AC 650.

379 In fact, the shipowner.

380 Issues of privity will now require reference to the Contracts (Rights of Third Parties) Act 1999; but see s. 6 of the Act for exclusions.

381 [2004] EWCA Civ 1598, [2005] 1 Lloyd's Rep 67. Insofar as the court proceeded on the basis that it was within its power to grant an injunction in support of an agreement to arbitrate, to restrain the respondent from bringing proceedings before the courts of a Member State, it was overtaken by C-185/07 *Allianz Srl v. West Tankers Inc* [2009] ECR I-663.

382 In fact, a London arbitration clause. But the reasoning is unaffected by the particular type of clause as arbitration or choice of court. For application in the context of arbitration, see *London Steamship Owners Mutual Insurance Association Ltd v. Spain* [2013] EWHC 3188 (Comm), [2014] 1 Lloyd's Rep 309.

383 Under Finnish legislation corresponding to the Third Parties (Rights Against Insurers) Act 1930. The reasoning was applied in *London Steamship Owners Mutual Insurance Association Ltd v. Spain* [2013] EWHC 3188 (Comm), [2014] 1 Lloyd's Rep 309, though the question of an injunction did not arise. For a case in which the bringing of a similar direct action was held not to be in breach of the agreement to arbitrate, see *Markel International Co Ltd v. Craft* [2006] EWHC 3150 (Comm), [2007] Lloyd's Rep IR 403: everything turns on the true construction of the agreement. And see also *Shipowner's Mutual P&I Association (Luxembourg) v. Containerships Denizcilik Nakliyat ve Ticaret as* [2015] EWHC 258 (Comm).

was reported to be pressing on with its claim before the Finnish courts. It is probably correct to say that this combination of subrogation and direct claims against a liability insurer is a difficult context in which to ask whether the parties are bound by an agreement on jurisdiction, and certainly one which is more complex than cases of simple assignment of rights.

For contracts governed by English law[384] and made after 11 May 2000, the Contracts (Rights of Third Parties) Act 1999 will also, and much more straightforwardly, allow agreements on jurisdiction to affect those who were not party to the contract in which the agreement was contained.[385] Under the scheme of the Act, a non-party[386] may take advantage of a contract, and therefore of an agreement on jurisdiction, if it is expressly provided in the contract that he may, or if the contract purports to confer that benefit on him.[387] No particular difficulty arises with the simple proposition that a non-party may claim a contractual benefit. If a non-party claims the benefit of a contract made between others, as he was intended to, and that contract provided that an action by the non-party to enforce the contract must be brought in a nominated court,[388] this also will be binding on the non-party as a matter of English law,[389] even though the jurisdiction agreement may be, when viewed in isolation, a burden rather than a benefit. No doubt layers of complexity will develop in time, but the basic understanding of the Act seems clear enough; and, as usual, the issue is almost entirely one of construction.[390] After all, if A has promised B that he will not bring proceedings against C, it would be a remarkably poor state of affairs if the promise could be ignored with impunity.

Finally, a distinct issue of personal scope arises when considering the operation of jurisdiction agreements which are contained in contracts made by a company, but in litigation

---

384 The Act was not intended to apply to contracts governed by a foreign law: Law Commission Report No 242 (1996), para. 14.12.

385 The rights conferred by the Act are in addition to any rights which may exist at common law.

386 Section 1 of the Act defines these as 'third parties'. The usage preferred here may be pedantic, but appears to be more accurate. Section 6 lists the contracts to which the Act does not apply.

387 Section 1. For application, see *Starlight Shipping Co v. Allianz Marine & Aviation Versicherung AG* [2014] EWHC 3068 (Comm) [2014] 2 Lloyd's Rep 579. For illustration of a contract where this effect was excluded by express words (the 1999 Act may be excluded by the parties), see *Global Partners Fund Ltd v. Babcock & Brown Ltd* (2010) 79 ASCR 383.

388 Whether the jurisdiction agreement, on its true construction, makes promises in relation to proceedings against non-parties to the agreement is a matter of contractual construction. For a case in which it was held that no such promise had been made, see *Morgan Stanley & Co International plc v. China Haisheng Juice Holdings Co Ltd* [2009] EWHC 2409 (Comm), [2010] 1 Lloyd's Rep 265; to the opposite effect, construing the clause as broad in personal scope, see *Royal Bank of Scotland plc v. Highland Financial Partners LP* [2012] EWCA Civ 328, [2013] 1 CLC 596.

389 *Nisshin Shipping Co Ltd v. Cleaves & Co Ltd* [2004] 1 Lloyd's Rep 38. Whether this is also correct in relation to jurisdiction agreements falling within the scope of Art. 25 of the Brussels I Regulation is discussed above, para. 2.107. For the express extension of the 1999 Act to arbitration agreements, see s. 8 of the Act.

390 *Morgan Stanley & Co International plc v. China Haisheng Juice Holdings Ltd* [2009] EWHC 2409 (Comm), [2010] 1 Lloyd's Rep 265; *Whitesea Shipping & Trading Corp v. El Paso Rio Clara Ltda (The 'Marielle Bolten')* [2009] EWHC 2552 (Comm), [2010] 1 Lloyd's Rep 648; *Global Partners Fund Ltd v. Babcock & Brown Ltd (in liq)* (2010) 79 ASCR 383. These cases also show, on entirely orthodox grounds, that if the promisee (that is, *not* the third party) applies for relief in the form of a stay, which will prevent the promisor suing the non-party in breach of the undertaking given to the promisee, as may happen where the 1999 Act does not apply, the promisee will need to show that he has a sufficient pecuniary (*cf Snelling v. John G Snelling Ltd* [1973] 1 QB 87) or other (*Royal Bank of Scotland plc v. Highland Financial Partners LP* [2013] EWCA Civ 328, [2013] 1 CLC 596) interest in applying for the relief, such as where there is an obligation or expectation that the promise will indemnify the non-party. This is an elementary part of the common law on privity of contract.

But where the promise is only worded to apply to proceedings against A, associates of A have no rights in relation to it, and any attempt to hang onto the coat-tails of the promise and promisee, and to be joined as claimants 'in order to give effect to the jurisdiction clause' by obtaining an injunction for themselves will be rejected: *Donohue v Armco Inc* [2001] UKHL 64, [2002] 1 Lloyd's Rep 425.

which seeks to impose liability on[391] persons hidden behind the corporate veil. Until very recently the law on this issue was rather uncertain, reflecting a lack of clarity whether a substantive claim, otherwise within the material scope of a jurisdiction agreement, may be brought against the 'veiled person' as though he were a party to the contract which contained the jurisdiction agreement. Some judges had allowed themselves to be persuaded that if the veil is liable to put aside, the hidden-but-now-exposed person somehow becomes, or may be proceeded against as though he were, party to the substantive contract, with the result that he became bound by the jurisdiction agreement. Others found that to be altogether too adventurous an application of a general equitable maxim to the effect that the Companies Acts may not be used to perpetrate a fraud, and which puts that into specific, but limited, effect by allowing liabilities which have been established in proceedings against contracting parties to be enforced against the assets of persons who were behind the veil of incorporation. So far as the common law is concerned the law probably comes down to this. *If* the legal effect of lifting the veil were to be that the revealed person becomes in law a party to the contract, even though the counterparty clearly did *not* intend to contract with him, he is party to the jurisdiction agreement as well; but otherwise it is not. If the correct analysis is that if there is one contract, and the veiled person is considered to be a party to it – this is, after all, how we think of principals in respect of contracts made by their agents – it is not conceptually difficult to see him as party to the jurisdiction agreement which is a separable part of it. But if the effect of lifting the veil is only that the judgment may be enforced against assets of the veiled person, the jurisdiction clause, which *ex hypothesi* applies only to proceedings brought to establish liability, will have nothing to do with such enforcement proceedings. The most recent guidance from the Supreme Court suggests that the law of lifting the corporate veil is to be read in a conservative fashion,[392] and that in any event, the prospect of being satisfied that this may be done at the jurisdictional stage is low.[393] Though it appears to raise issues of some substance, this may be on the way to becoming a non-point.

4.48 Legal validity of the agreement on choice of court: enforceable despite the voidability or rescission of the contract in which it is contained

If the basis of the application for a stay of proceedings is that the claimant is acting in breach of his contract by suing in England, it must be open to the claimant to show that he is not in breach of the agreement[394] after all. Questions of construction aside, one would suppose that the alleged agreement on jurisdiction may be impeached on the ground that it was never agreed to by the party against whom it is being asserted;[395] if that is so, he will not be, indeed, cannot be, bound by it. Though this may appear to have logic on its side, the

---

391 The logic of the situation would be that if the answer to 'brought against' is yes, the same should be true if the claim is 'brought by' the veiled party. But in this area, logic does not have the law in a vice-like grip.

392 *Prest v. Petrodel Resources Ltd* [2013] UKSC 34, [2013] 2 AC 415.

393 *VTB Capital plc v. Nutritek International Corp* [2013] UKSC 5, [2013] 2 AC 337.

394 The agreement does not have to be contractual: the principles of bailment, or closely related principles, may bind the parties in law to jurisdiction clauses in contracts to which they were not party and to which they did not, in that narrow sense, agree. In some senses it may be more accurate to speak of consenting to the (exclusive) jurisdiction of a court, but the terminology of 'agreement' is hallowed by usage, and does require that the agreement be one which is enforceable by legal action. It is therefore used, and in this sense used, here.

395 Because, for example, there was a battle of forms whose result was in dispute. For an illustration of the battle of forms (and of crossings out) see *Brotherton v. Asseguradora Colseguros SA (No 1)* [2002] EWHC 498 (Comm), [2002] Lloyd's Rep IR 848.

proposition that a party may invalidate an alleged agreement on jurisdiction by impugning the contract in which it is said to be contained, is not currently in fashion. Or, to put the matter more precisely, an agreement on jurisdiction may be contested, but this will generally not be achieved by asserting, even on credible grounds, that the contract in which it was contained, or with which it is associated, was itself invalid as a source of legal obligation.

This follows, as a point of general principle, from the decision in *Fiona Trust & Holding Corp v. Privalov.*[396] If one party claims to be entitled to rescind the agreement with the other, this will not release him from the agreement for the resolution of disputes, which has already had its effect. Of course, if he alleges that any contract which may have been made was not made by him – that the case is one of mistaken identity, or of *non est factum*, or of forgery of documents or signatures – there is no contract, and nothing to rescind, and that will be quite different.[397] But if his contention is that the contract which he made, or which was made on his behalf, is one which he is entitled to rescind, this plea will not invalidate the dispute resolution agreement, at least to begin with. The principle is clear: a party who admits that he made a contract which contained a jurisdiction clause remains bound by the provision on jurisdiction, even if he purports to rescind, or has indeed rescinded, the contract. The jurisdiction agreement is severable from the contract to which it relates; on rescission of the substantive contract it breaks free and binds the parties independently. It may also be found that the parties made an agreement as to jurisdiction prior to any substantive agreement which may or may not be later made. In such a case, the jurisdiction agreement should also be seen to be effective.[398]

The principle of severability was first established, as an antidote to the unacceptable argument described above, in the closely related context of arbitration.[399] A related principle has been deduced in the context of what is now Article 25 of the recast Brussels I Regulation:[400] 'related', because the nature of agreements on jurisdiction within the Regulation is that they are not contract terms at all, but written (or otherwise formal) acceptances of the jurisdiction of a court. There is therefore no need to sever the one contract from the other; they were not integral to the contract in the first place. But the language of severance is useful and graphic.

There are limits to this principle; and despite the terms of the judgment in *Fiona Trust*, it cannot be read as being free of all limitation. For example, if the evidence shows that the parties negotiated, but did not finally settle and bind themselves to, a contract which would have contained an agreement on jurisdiction, it would be odd to reason that the failure to conclude an agreement meant that there were no substantive obligations by which the parties were bound, but that this could not be used to support the proposition that there was no agreement on jurisdiction. It must also be accepted that where the contention is that the contract was not made by or on behalf of the party to be held to it, or that there was some

---

396 [2007] UKHL 40, [2007] Bus LR 1719.

397 [2007] UKHL 40, [2007] Bus LR 1719, [17].

398 *Cf UR Power GmbH v. Kuok Oils & Grains Pte Ltd* [2009] EWHC 1940 (Comm), [2009] 2 Lloyd's Rep 495 (a case on arbitration, but the principle is general).

399 See *FAI General Insurance Co Ltd v. Ocean Marine Mutual Protection and Indemnity Association* [1998] Lloyd's Rep IR 24 (NSW SC); *Ash v. Corporation of Lloyd's* (1991) 87 DLR (4th) 65, rev'd on other grounds (1992) 94 DLR (4th) 378 (Ont CA). For statutory intervention, see Arbitration Act 1996, s. 7.

400 C-269/95 *Benincasa v. Dentalkit Srl* [1997] ECR I-3767; see further above, para. 2.146. Article 17 of the Brussels Convention, which became Art. 23 of Regulation 44/2001, is now substantially reproduced as Art. 25 of the recast Brussels I Regulation.

other fundamental flaw which meant that the parties did not come to agreement at all, with the result that no question of severance from, or of rescission of, a voidable contract can consequentially arise, then the so-called agreement on jurisdiction is mis-named, and will not be binding. Presumably a court will proceed by asking which side has the better of the argument at the point at which a decision has to be taken.

It is not helpful to enquire whether this aspect of the decision in *Fiona Trust* is justified by previous authority, for the conclusions will be mixed. It draws strength from a more fundamental principle: that the law cannot allow a party to what was enough of an agreement on jurisdiction to undermine it again by contending that the substantive contract was voidable because procured by duress, fraud, or misrepresentation, or because made by an agent without authority. It may also be justified by collateral argument from the common law of causation. The business of the shipowner in *Fiona Trust* was to charter its vessels. That was what it did; that was all it did. Had it not been bound, as it contended that it was not, to the charterparties which had been procured and made by the alleged bribery of their agent, it would have entered into other charters. These charters would have contained provisions for the arbitration of disputes, as this is the common form of such agreements in the trade. Seen in this light, the shipowners would still have been bound to arbitrate. It therefore follows that the shipowners' agreement and obligation to arbitrate was not caused by the alleged bribery: it, or something very like it, would still have bound the shipowners, no matter who the vessels had been chartered to, and whether or not there would have been bribery. It is the way of the world of business for those who use the Shelltime 4 form.[401]

4.49 Legal validity of the choice of court agreement: challenges to validity based on arguments specific to the agreement itself

It follows from *Fiona Trust* that the only allegations of facts and matters which would lead to justify rescission which may be deployed to undermine the agreement on jurisdiction are those which are specific to the agreement on jurisdiction itself.

If the position is that the alleged agreement on jurisdiction between the parties[402] was made, but was procured by specific misrepresentation or duress, targeted at the jurisdiction agreement alone, this should relieve the claimant of the allegation that he is acting in breach of the agreement. To take a simple example: suppose a customer asks the supplier whether the contract he is asked to sign contains a jurisdiction agreement, and the answer which is given is negative, when the document really did contain such a provision. In principle, the law which governs the jurisdiction agreement, or which would have governed it if it were valid, should determine the consequences. Likewise, if it is argued that the jurisdiction agreement has been discharged by consent, frustration[403] or breach, this should also be referred to the law governing the jurisdiction agreement.

---

401 *Cf*, for this pattern of reasoning in a judgment of Lord Hoffmann in another context, but which appears to be strikingly relevant to the issues, *South Australia Asset Management Corp v. York Montague Ltd* [1996] UKHL 10, [1997] AC 191 (investor would still have invested in (other, similar) property if not lied to by surveyor, and would therefore still have sustained the losses resulting from the fall in the market. That component of the loss was not, therefore, caused by the surveyor's wrongdoing).

402 That is, excluding any case in which the party alleged to be bound contends that he was not party to the agreement, whether it was valid or otherwise.

403 In *Carvalho v. Hull Blyth (Angola) Ltd* [1979] 1 WLR 1228, it was held that the agreement to sue in the courts of (pre-independence) Angola was frustrated by the revolution in that country, with the result that to force

If the nominated court would not accept jurisdiction, this should be seen as a case of mistake or frustration of the jurisdiction agreement, depending upon the time at which the ground of refusal came about. If it is alleged that the jurisdiction agreement, though valid and binding according to its governing law, is nevertheless denied legal effect in England by an overriding or mandatory provision of English law, the jurisdiction agreement will obviously have no legal effect in an English court.[404] If it is alleged that the written jurisdiction agreement should be rectified, this might be thought to be a matter also for the law governing the agreement; but there is some authority for seeing this as a matter for English law as *lex fori*.[405]

4.50 Nature of the choice of court agreement: bringing the objected-to proceedings as a breach of contract

An agreement may oblige the claimant to sue in the foreign court; but if, on its proper construction, it merely obliged the defendant to submit to the jurisdiction of the foreign court if the claimant took steps to invoke its jurisdiction, there is, on the face of it, no breach or other wrong if the claimant institutes proceedings in England: he will have done nothing which he promised not to do.[406] This, after all, is the only material question: is a person bound by the agreement on choice of court doing something he promised not to do ?

The issue is sometimes reformulated as one which asks whether the agreement was one which conferred exclusive or non-exclusive jurisdiction on the designated court. If one accepts that this is the right question to ask, it is to be answered by reference to the law which governs the agreement,[407] and is not for English law as *lex fori*, even if English courts were formerly occasionally encouraged to construe the agreement as if it involved no more than a simple question of English domestic law.[408]

Notwithstanding the analysis which will be set out below, there is a view, which some consider to be persuasive, that a simple dichotomy of exclusive and non-exclusive

---

the claimant to sue in the post-revolutionary courts of Angola would be to enforce an obligation radically different from that which had been undertaken.

404 *The Hollandia* [1983] 1 AC 565 (agreement for the Netherlands ineffective by reason of the Carriage of Goods by Sea Act 1971; but note that Art. 25 of the Brussels I Regulation would today probably validate such a clause); perhaps also Consumer Credit Act 1974, s. 141(1); Law Reform (Personal Injuries) Act 1948; Employment Rights Act 1996, s. 203. For invalidity under the Unfair Terms in Consumer Contracts Regulations, SI 1999/2083, enacting Council Directive 93/13/EC, see C-240/98 *Océano Grupo Editorial SA v. Quintero* [2000] ECR I-4941. See also *Baghlaf Al Zafer v. Pakistan National Shipping Co* [1998] 2 Lloyd's Rep 229; *Pirelli Cables Ltd v. United Thai Shipping Corp Ltd* [2000] 1 Lloyd's Rep 663. See also *Akai Pty Ltd v. The People's Insurance Co Ltd* (1997) 188 CLR 418. But *cf* the view of the Canadian Federal Court of Appeal in *OT Africa Line Ltd v. Magic Sportswear Corp* [2007] 1 Lloyd's Rep 85.

405 *The Nile Rhapsody* [1994] 1 Lloyd's Rep 382. As a matter of common law, *Mackender v. Feldia AG* [1967] 2 QB 590 would suggest the application of English law *qua lex fori*; *Oceanic Sun Line Special Shipping Co Inc v. Fay* (1988) 165 CLR 197 might suggest a combination of both. For the suggestion that a dispute resolution agreement, if perceived as onerous, may need to be written in red capital letters with a red hand pointing to it, see *Kaye v. Nu Skin UK Ltd* [2009] EWHC 3509 (Ch), [2010] 2 All ER (Comm) 832: the decision may be better regarded as an application of rules of English public policy.

406 A contractual promise not to challenge the jurisdiction of the English courts was construed as an agreement for the exclusive jurisdiction of the English courts in *General Motors Corp v. Royal & Sun Alliance Insurance plc* [2007] EWHC 2206 (Comm), [2008] Lloyd's Rep IR 311.

407 *Hoerter v. Hanover Telegraph Works* (1893) 10 TLR 103; *Nova (Jersey) Knit Ltd v. Kammgarn Spinnerei GmbH* [1977] 1 WLR 713; *Evans Marshall & Co v. Bertola SA* [1973] 1 WLR 349, 361; *Ocarina Marine v. Macard Stein & Co* [1994] 2 Lloyd's Rep 524; *FAI General Insurance Co Ltd v. Marine Mutual Protection and Indemnity Assn* (1996) 41 NSWLR 117. See also Fawcett [2001] LMCLQ 234.

408 *Cf. The Cap Blanco* [1913] P 130.

jurisdiction agreements is simple and clear and well-known, and that in many cases the question whether the agreement on jurisdiction was exclusive or non-exclusive may be all that needs to be asked in order to answer the questions which arise.[409] According to this view, if one construes the jurisdiction agreement as exclusive or non-exclusive, the question whether it has been breached is easily answered. But it does, however, assume that the template of jurisdiction agreements is limited to two. That is not self-evidently correct; and there is no reason why it should be accepted. The question is one of construction; the material question is whether the bringing of the proceedings, of which complaint is made, is a breach of contract.[410]

Where the agreement is to be construed according to English law, there is some authority that ambiguity in the construction of this aspect of the agreement should be resolved in favour of giving exclusive jurisdiction to the nominated court. Whether or not this is correct – it is submitted that it is not – the presence or absence of the word 'exclusive' is not decisive.[411] It has been reasoned that if the nominated court would have had jurisdiction, without reference to the jurisdiction agreement, in any event, a court may wish to attribute some further effect to the agreement, which will tend to lead in turn to its being seen as exclusive.[412] But this is not at all persuasive: the parties may not have known whether the court would have had jurisdiction, or may have made the agreement for the avoidance of doubt. None of that suggests that the agreement must be taken to have been exclusive, on the ground that it would otherwise have been without effect. This is a non-point.[413]

---

409 See, for example, *Ace Insurance Ltd v. Moose Enterprise Pty Ltd* [2009] NSWSC 724, [11]–[33].

410 But there will still be some proceedings which will fall outside the material scope of the agreement on jurisdiction; it is all a matter of construction. For illustration, see *AWB Geneva SA v. North America Steamships Ltd* [2007] EWCA Civ 739, [2007] 2 Lloyd's Rep 315 (no breach of jurisdiction clause for trustee in bankruptcy to bring proceedings in the insolvency to obtain a determination of rights under a contract); *Brave Bulk Transport Ltd v. Spot On Shipping Ltd* [2009] EWHC 612 (QB), [2009] 1 Lloyd's Rep 115 (no breach of English jurisdiction clause to enforce judgment obtained in England against a non-party on the basis that it was the 'alter ego' of the defendant and liable as a matter of New York law to have the judgment enforced against it); *Vitol SA v. Capri Marine Ltd (No 2)* [2010] EWHC 458 (Comm), [2011] 1 All ER (Comm) 366 (no breach of jurisdiction agreement to obtain order to help with the enforcement of the judgment which had been obtained in the agreed court; *Oceanconnect UK Ltd v. Angara Maritime Ltd* [2010] EWCA 1050, [2011] 1 Lloyd's Rep 399 (proceedings in the US in respect of maritime lien did not breach jurisdiction clause contained in escrow agreement); *Louis Dreyfus Commodities Kenya Ltd v. Bolster Shipping Co Ltd* [2010] EWHC 1732 (Comm), [2011] 1 All ER (Comm) 540 (joinder as party to proceedings in Mexico for purpose of obtaining evidence no breach of arbitration clause); *U&M Mining Zambia Ltd v. Konkola Copper Mines plc* [2013] EWHC 260 (Comm), [2013] 2 Lloyd's Rep 218 (no breach of arbitration agreement to seek interim relief from foreign court); *Ryanair Ltd v. Esso Italiana Srl* [2013] EWCA Civ 1450, [2015] 1 ALL ER (Comm) 152 (jurisdiction clause did not apply to claims founded on liability for participation in an unlawful cartel); *Bank St Petersburg v. Arkhangelsky* [2014] EWCA Civ 593, [2014] 1 WLR 4360 (no breach of English jurisdiction clause by attempting to rely on Russian judgments in those proceedings, but there would be a breach if those Russian judgments were enforced if the bank were to lose in the English proceedings).

411 *Continental Bank NA v. Aeakos SA* [1994] 1 WLR 588.

412 *Sohio Supply Co v. Gatoil (USA) Inc* [1989] 1 Lloyd's Rep 588 (held exclusive); *Cannon Screen Entertainment Ltd v. Handmade Films (Distributors) Ltd* (11 July 1989: held non-exclusive); *S & W Berisford plc v. New Hampshire Insurance Co* [1990] 1 Lloyd's Rep 454 (held non-exclusive); *Continental Bank NA v. Aeakos* [1994] 1 WLR 588 (held exclusive); *British Aerospace plc v. Dee Howard Co* [1993] 1 Lloyd's Rep 368 (held exclusive); *A/S D/S Svendborg v. Wansa* [1997] 2 Lloyd's Rep 183 (held exclusive); *Sinochem International Oil (London) Co Ltd v. Mobil Sales and Supply Corp* [2000] 1 Lloyd's Rep 670 (held exclusive); *Ace Insurance Ltd v. Moose Enterprise Pty Ltd* [2009] NSWSC 724 (held exclusive).

413 *British Aerospace*, where the defendant would not have been subject to the jurisdiction of the English court. This was approved in *Ace Insurance Ltd v. Moose Enterprise Pty Ltd* [2009] NSWSC 724, though the case also suggests at [33] that in the event of ambiguity, the clause will be construed as non-exclusive, on the basis that it is so easy to draft it exclusively, a failure to do so is significant: *sed quaere*.

What is alleged to be a strictly grammatical approach has been occasionally resorted to, but as a tool for illuminating what the parties, who may well not have been English and will not have been grammarians, actually intended, it has nothing to commend it.[414] According to this, it is evidently necessary to ask whether the parties agreed to submit *themselves* to the jurisdiction of a court, or agreed to submit *disputes* to the jurisdiction of a court. But the difference between 'the parties agree to submit' and 'the parties agree to submit their disputes' is one which will elude most minds.[415] In the former case, the verb is used reflexively: the parties submit themselves. In the latter case, the verb is used transitively: the parties submit something, disputes, to the court; and if anyone sees anything of legal significance in this, they must have very peculiar eyesight, for the idea that parties submit themselves to the jurisdiction of a court for something *other* than the resolution of a dispute is surreal. If one were to ask what the parties meant when they agreed to submit, the answer will be that they agreed to submit to trial. It is improbable, and the more so where the drafting is done by those not expert users of the English language, that the parties appreciated that there could be a difference between the two forms, and even more improbable that they predicted the consequences which followed from the difference. Most graduates of English universities would be hard put to see and explain the distinction; it is beyond all reason to proceed on the basis that non-native speakers of English must have done so.[416] Despite the authority which has vouched for this principle of construction, it ought to be a non-point.

And anyway, there is no general reason why exclusive, rather than non-exclusive, jurisdiction should be taken to reflect the rational intention of commercial parties. Parties who enter into a contractual relationship which might result in litigation several years later may wish to determine and be sure about the law which will be applied by the court which has ultimately to resolve any dispute between them, so express a choice of law, but may wish not to tie their hands to a particular court, to the exclusion of all others, for that litigation. The wisdom of being free to sue where the defendant has assets when proceedings are begun would point away from the 'exclusive' construction of an agreement which is ambiguous on the point.[417] It may therefore be that a jurisdiction clause which allows, but does not require, litigation to take place in a particular court is a perfectly sensible provision, and one which purports to tie the hands of the parties, several years in the future, is not. There should, on this view of the matter, be no presumption of exclusivity. There is just a question of construction, with no presumption that anything other than commercial common sense has anything to do with answering it.

---

414 See the cases cited above; and also *McGowan v. Summit at Lloyd's* 2002 SLT 1258. This is not to deny the principle that where parties reduce their agreement to written form, there is great value in regarding the written form as the sum and substance of the agreement. The issue is not where the agreement is to be found, but what that written form tells us about the parties intended: *Rainy Sky SA v. Kookmin Bank* [2011] UKSC 50, [2011] 1 WLR 2900.

415 *Sea Trade Maritime Corp v. Hellenic Mutual War Risks Association (Bermuda) Ltd* [2006] EWHC 2530 (Comm), [2007] 1 Lloyd's Rep 280, [98].

416 And see, for striking judicial confirmation, *BNP Paribas SA v. Anchorage Capital Europe LLP* [2013] EWHC 3073 (Comm), [85]–[87].

417 The point could be met by an agreement that the parties will not object to concurrent proceedings in more courts than one, but the Brussels I Regulation places severe limitations on the legal effect of such agreements, so this may not be a reliable alternative solution.

If it is held that the agreement is in substance non-exclusive, an application for a stay of proceedings[418] will be determined by *Spiliada* principles, though with appreciable differences: the foreign court will be assumed[419] to be available as a forum, and the agreement may, almost by itself, identify the nominated court as being more appropriate than England. If the jurisdiction agreement is coupled with a choice of the law of that forum, the case for a stay under *Spiliada* may be almost as strong as if the agreement had conferred exclusive jurisdiction on the nominated court.[420] If the claimant has the nerve to allege that deficiencies in the process of that court will mean that it will be unjust for him to be held to his contract and sent to that chosen court, then unless these were unforeseeable (which does not mean unforeseen), he should expect to receive distinctly unsympathetic treatment.[421]

4.51 Non-exclusive agreement as optional agreement for exclusive jurisdiction

Though it takes a moment to appreciate the point, and though some people regard it as conceptually impossible, a non-exclusive jurisdiction agreement may be broken, bringing proceedings in a court other than that designated. It all depends on the careful and full construction of the clause in question, and on the nature of the conduct said to amount to a breach.

In *Sabah Shipyard (Pakistan) Ltd v. Islamic Republic of Pakistan*[422] proceedings were brought in Pakistan in order to seek to frustrate proceedings which had been brought in England. The parties had agreed to the non-exclusive jurisdiction of the English courts. As the claimant had instituted proceedings in England, it was held to be a breach of the particular contract for the defendant to institute proceedings in Pakistan which were designed to frustrate the English proceedings;[423] and to this extent the decision is entirely orthodox. But the court indicated that pre-emptive proceedings in Pakistan would have been open to the same objection. It may have been right to see the agreement on jurisdiction as initially

---

418 The same will be true, *mutatis mutandis*, if an anti-suit injunction is sought, on which see further below, para. 5.41.

419 Though the contrary may be shown.

420 *Standard Steamship Owners' P & I Association (Bermuda) Ltd v. Gann* [1992] 2 Lloyd's Rep 528. In *BP plc v. Aon Ltd* [2005] EWHC 2554 (Comm), [2006] 1 Lloyd's Rep 549 it was held that there was no breach involved in applying to serve out where there was a non-exclusive jurisdiction agreement for Illinois, for there were at the date of the application no proceedings pending in the Illinois court; but that in all the circumstances it was not possible to show that England was clearly the more appropriate forum for the trial of the issues. See also *Winnetka Trading Corp v. Julius Baer International Ltd* [2008] EWHC 3146 (Ch), [2009] Bus LR 1006, where the narrowing of the distinction between exclusive and non-exclusive jurisdiction clauses is noted (non-exclusive jurisdiction for Guernsey; stay of English proceedings), but for a rather different perspective, taking the view that the differences are rather more sharply drawn, see *Winnetka v. Bank Julius Baer & Co Ltd* [2009–10] Guernsey LR 260.

421 *Cf British Aerospace plc v. Dee Howard Corp* [1993] 1 Lloyd's Rep 368 (but which involved a choice of court for England). To the same broad effect, *Mercury Communications Ltd v. Communication Telesystems International* [1997] 2 All ER (Comm) 33; *JP Morgan Securities Asia Pte Ltd v. Malaysian Newsprint Industries Sdn Bhd* [2001] 2 Lloyd's Rep 41; *Import Export Metro Ltd v. Compania Sud Americana de Vapores SA* [2003] EWHC 11 (Comm), [2003] 1 Lloyd's Rep 405; *Antec Ltd v. Biosafety USA Inc* [2006] EWHC 47 (Comm); *Middle Eastern Oil LLC v. National Bank of Abu Dhabi* [2008] EWHC 2895 (Comm), [2009] 1 Lloyd's Rep 251; *Bankhaus Wolbern & Co AG & Co KG v. China Construction Bank Corp* [2012] EWHC 3285 (Comm); *Cuccolini Srl v. Elcan Industries plc* [2013] EWHC 2994 (QB).

422 [2002] EWCA Civ 1643, [2003] 2 Lloyd's Rep 571. See also *BP plc v. Aon Ltd* [2005] EWHC 2554 (Comm), [2006] 1 Lloyd's Rep 549 (no breach as no proceedings pending in foreign chosen court).

423 Which it would if the *lis pendens* made it more difficult, or impossible, for the claimant to seise the nominated court with jurisdiction, or if the court wrongly seised had issued an anti-suit injunction at the behest of the contract-breaker.

being non-exclusive, but one which became exclusive, and binding in that sense, once it had been invoked by the claimant summoning the defendant before the English courts:[424] hardly a novel idea, for options to purchase operate in exactly the same way. If that were its true construction, the granting of an injunction to enforce it is right in principle.

Where, by contrast, the jurisdiction clause in question is construed as allowing for[425] parallel proceedings, as a non-exclusive jurisdiction clause may be taken to do,[426] or if it makes it express that the parties contemplated the possibility that parallel proceedings might be brought,[427] it can hardly be said to involve a legal wrong when one party to the dispute resolution agreement does exactly what the agreement provides that he may do and takes his stand on his contract. For if the contract, on its true construction, envisaged that a party would be entitled to sue in more courts than one, there can hardly be a breach in doing what the parties envisaged and the contract provided for.[428] The proposition that there could be any form of contractual wrong in simply implementing and acting in accordance with the express terms of a dispute resolution agreement is very challenging.[429]

And if that is correct, it suggests that a binary classification of jurisdiction clauses as exclusive or non-exclusive is not always helpful, and is not always enough by itself to fully explain the bargain which the parties struck. The question whether the bringing of a particular set of proceedings is or is not a breach of contract raises a question of construction: to determine precisely what the parties promised to do and when, and where, they promised that it would be done; to determine what the parties agreed that they would not object to if it were done; and to determine what the parties promised would not be done, or would be brought to an end if it had already been begun. A task of such potential complexity cannot be discharged simply by applying the labels of exclusive or non-exclusive to a jurisdiction agreement and making mechanical deductions from the label applied to the clause: the conclusions which follow from finding a choice of court agreement to be non-exclusive are not of the kind where two sizes fit all. The question is one of substance, not of appearance; of construction, not of characterisation.

---

424 In other words, if the true construction of the agreement was that, whenever the claimant issued proceedings in London, the defendant would abandon any proceedings overseas and thenceforward defend or counterclaim only in London, such a clause would be breached by the bringing of and refusal to discontinue foreign proceedings. Everything will turn on a precise analysis of the structure of the jurisdiction agreement. See also *BNP Paribas SA v. Anchorage Capital Europe LLP* [2013] EWHC 3073 (Comm), which appears to accept this very argument in relation to what is now Art. 25 of the Brussels I Regulation.

425 Or, maybe more properly, not raising any objection to: the issue of whether the proceedings will be allowed to run in parallel is not one over which the parties have sole control.

426 *Deutsche Bank AG v. Highland Crusader Offshore Partners LP* [2009] EWCA Civ 725, [2010] 1 WLR 1023.

427 As it did in *Royal Bank of Canada v. Cooperative Centrale Raiffeisen Boerenleenbank* [2003] EWCA Civ 7, [2004] 1 Lloyd's Rep 471 and *Deutsche Bank AG v. Highland Crusader Offshore Partners LP* [2009] EWCA Civ 725, [2010] 1 WLR 1023.

428 A term not uncommon in banking contracts: see *Royal Bank of Canada v. Cooperative Centrale Raiffeisen Boerenleenbank* [2003] EWCA Civ 7, [2004] 1 Lloyd's Rep 471. It does not close off the possibility of obtaining one on the ground that the proceedings are oppressive or vexatious, but it makes it much harder than it would be if the agreement had not been entered into in the first place. For a case in which the parties provided for one court to deal with any patent infringement action, though another would deal with validity of a patent, see *Celltech R & D Ltd v. MedImmune Inc* [2004] EWCA Civ 1331, [2005] FSR 491; see also *Affymetrix Inc v. Multilyte Ltd* [2004] EWHC 291 (Pat), [2005] FSR 1. Of course, in the context of the Brussels I Regulation, this will not work, as it is very unlikely indeed that Art. 29 of the Regulation can be contracted out of.

429 *Royal Bank of Canada v. Cooperative Centrale Raiffeisen Boerenleenbank* [2003] EWCA Civ 7, [2004] 1 Lloyd's Rep 471 and *Deutsche Bank AG v. Highland Crusader Offshore Partners LP* [2009] EWCA Civ 725, [2010] 1 WLR 1023.

4.52 Staying proceedings brought in England in a breach of contract

If there is a statutory duty to grant relief by reference to the jurisdiction agreement, there is little more to be said on the issue of relief. If the jurisdiction agreement is one to which the Hague Convention on Choice of Court Agreements applies, the duty of the court to give effect to it is established by the Convention, which takes effect in the European Union by virtue of Article 67 of the Brussels I Regulation. So far the only non-Member State to which it extends is Mexico, and there is therefore no need to say any more about it at this stage.

If there is an agreement which means that the claimant is breaching his contract by bringing the proceedings which he has brought in England, the courts will, on application, stay the proceedings, and thereby restrain the breach of contract and give specific effect to the agreement on jurisdiction, unless the claimant makes a very convincing case for his being allowed to break his contract.

The leading case is the decision of the House of Lords in *Donohue v. Armco Inc*,[430] which overtakes the trio of decisions which paved the way for it.[431] The House of Lords confirmed that contractual agreements on jurisdiction, just like any other contractual term, should be enforced according to their plain meaning: the judgment is so compelling that one wonders how it could ever have been in doubt.[432] A stay of proceedings brought in breach of a jurisdiction agreement for a foreign court will be ordered unless the circumstances are exceptional. An exception is not established by showing the natural forum for the litigation to be in England: it will be necessary to point to some additional reason, 'strong cause', to condone the breach of contract by the claimant, which there will rarely be.[433]

Older English cases, now only of curiosity value, show a degree of fidelity to choice of court agreements for foreign courts which may have reflected the court's feelings towards the court chosen.[434] In cases decided before the First World War, choices for Budapest,[435] Leipzig[436] and Hamburg[437] were enforced with short, sharp judgments. Between the wars, a choice for Calcutta[438] was treated similarly. But by contrast, a choice of court for Germany was denied enforcement in 1939;[439] and in the days when they indicated courts behind

---

430 [2001] UKHL 64, [2002] 1 Lloyd's Rep 425 (a decision in relation to an English, not foreign, jurisdiction clause). For the same approach taken to a 'no-action' contractual term, see *Elektrim SA v. Vivendi Holdings 1 Corp* [2008] EWCA Civ 1178, [2009] 1 Lloyd's Rep 59. The law of Québec gives effect to agreements on choice of court and arbitration because autonomy in commercial law is a virtue of the first order: *GreCon Dimter Inc v. JR Normand Inc* [2005] 2 SCR 401.

431 *The Eleftheria* [1970] P 94; *The El Amria* [1981] 2 Lloyd's Rep 119; *The Sennar (No 2)* [1985] 1 WLR 490.

432 *Donohue v. Armco Inc* [2001] UKHL 64, [2002] 1 Lloyd's Rep 425 (a decision in relation to an English, not foreign, jurisdiction clause). For the same approach taken to a 'no-action' contractual term, see *Elektrim SA v. Vivendi Holdings 1 Corp* [2008] EWCA Civ 1178, [2009] 1 Lloyd's Rep 59.

433 The more the courts show their willingness to uphold such clauses, the less incentive there will be for a claimant to try to break his contact and provoke litigation whose cost he will ultimately have to bear. And see the US Supreme Court in *Carnival Cruise Lines Inc v. Shute* 111 S. Ct. 1522 (1991). For the possibility that a court may be justified in giving slightly less weight to a jurisdiction agreement in a trust instrument, see *Crociani v. Crociani* [2014] UKPC 40.

434 It is certainly not intended to suggest that these reactions are in all cases ill-founded.

435 *Austrian Lloyd Steamship Co v. Gresham Life Assurance Society Ltd* [1903] 1 KB 249.

436 *Kirchner v. Gruban* [1909] 1 Ch 413.

437 *The Cap Blanco* [1913] P 130.

438 *The Media* (1931) 41 Ll LR 80.

439 *Ellinger v. Guinness Mahon & Co* [1939] 4 All ER 16.

the iron curtain, choices for the USSR[440] and Poland[441] were said to raise no more than a presumption for a stay; in more recent times, choices for the Egyptian[442] courts were said to raise a presumption, but not more, in favour of a stay.[443]

But *Donohue v. Armco Inc* represents a new dawn, settling any lingering doubts. The principal means of dealing with a party who has breached his agreement to sue in a particular court is by specific relief directly enforcing the primary obligations of the agreement. It may now be that, aside from the case of multipartite proceedings, which raise distinct considerations and which are considered below, the courts will be equally unprepared to countenance arguments that a claimant should be allowed to break his contract to sue in any court – English or foreign – in which he has promised not to.[444]

Donohue v. Armco Inc confirmed that only in exceptional cases will English proceedings brought in breach of a foreign jurisdiction agreement not be stayed. Earlier cases had paid lip service to such a rule while suggesting that exceptions were not so hard to find. For example, in *The El Amria*,[445] an exclusive jurisdiction agreement for the court for Alexandria was not enforced by a stay of the English proceedings because the witnesses (factual and expert) were English and in England, and because related litigation[446] was already pending in the English courts: the latter point is plausible, at least if the litigation is genuine and not contrived; the former, in the context, inconsequential. For all that, the orthodox view is that the court leans in favour of a stay unless exceptional reasons dictate otherwise; and the management of multipartite litigation may be the only real exception.

In *The Pioneer Container*,[447] it was suggested that if proceedings would be time-barred in the chosen court, and if there had been no fault in failing to save limitation there, this might furnish an exceptional reason not to stay proceedings. But this rather unwelcome possibility – unwelcome, because the short limitation period for actions before the foreign court may have been one of the factors which led the defendant to contract for it in the first place – may be more apparent than real, for it will be hard to see why it is not negligent, or worse, to fail to save limitation in the court which has been agreed to by contract. Even so, if political changes in the country whose court was chosen mean that the claimant would not now get a fair trial, the jurisdiction clause – even if not technically frustrated by this event – would not be enforced.[448]

---

440 *The Fehmarn* [1959] 1 WLR 159. But cf *The Kislovodsk* [1980] 1 Lloyd's Rep 183.

441 *The Adolf Warski* [1976] 1 Lloyd's Rep 107.

442 *The El Amria* [1981] 2 Lloyd's Rep 119; *The Nile Rhapsody* [1994] 1 Lloyd's Rep 382; *The Al Battani* [1993] 2 Lloyd's Rep 219.

443 It was occasionally said, in a quite unsatisfactory way, that the contract-breaker may be able to get away with it because equity's remedies are discretionary: cf *Citi-March Ltd v. Neptune Orient Lines Ltd* [1996] 2 All ER 545. For damages for breach of jurisdiction agreements, see below, paras 4.55 and 5.55.

444 Certainly, if he now seeks to complain about the law and procedure of the court he agreed to, he should not be given any sympathy.

445 [1981] 2 Lloyd's Rep 119. See also *Evans Marshall v. Bertola* [1973] 1 WLR 349, where a similar result had been reached.

446 Against the port authority; the actual case was against the carrier. The same reasoning led to the same result in *Citi-March Ltd v. Neptune Orient Lines Ltd* [1996] 2 All ER 545.

447 [1994] 2 AC 324. But cf *Citi-March Ltd v. Neptune Orient Lines Ltd* [1996] 2 All ER 545. In the light of *Baghlaf Al Zafer v. Pakistan National Shipping Co* [1998] 2 Lloyd's Rep 229 and *Pirelli Cables Ltd v. United Thai Shipping Corp Ltd* [2000] 1 Lloyd's Rep 663 it may be reasonable not to save limitation in the foreign court if it has jurisdiction only by reason of an agreement which is void as a matter of English law (*in casu*, under the Hague-Visby Rules).

448 *Ellinger v. Guinness Mahon & Co* [1939] 4 All ER 16 (Germany, but which went Nazi); *Carvalho v. Hull Blyth (Angola) Ltd* [1979] 1 WLR 1228 (Portuguese Angola, but which went revolutionary).

4.53 The effect of agreements on choice of court in the context of multipartite litigation

In the context of genuine multipartite litigation, where some but not all of those genuinely involved in the dispute are party to the jurisdiction agreement, the approach foreshadowed in *The El Amria* has been developed further. The principle is an even-handed one, and English proceedings may be stayed where England is the contractual forum. Thus in *Bouygues Offshore SA v. Caspian Shipping Co (Nos 1, 3, 4 and 5)*[449] an English action arising out of a towage contract was stayed, even though the towage contract provided for the exclusive jurisdiction of the English courts. It was held that the court should look at the broad picture presented by the litigation, and not blinker itself and concentrate on the rigid enforcement of the contract as between those party to it.[450] As the web of liabilities arising out of the maritime accident could be litigated in a manner which bound all interested parties if it proceeded in South Africa, but not if part of the trial took place in England, it was inappropriate to allow the jurisdiction agreement to stand in the way of the overall best result.

The rightness of this general approach was confirmed by the House of Lords in *Donohue v. Armco Inc*:[451] although there may be a contractual agreement on jurisdiction, this will not be specifically enforced where to do so would fracture the coherent adjudication of a multipartite dispute. The potential for abuse of this principle is understood, and if a court believes that non-parties to the jurisdiction agreement – affiliates and subsidiaries, or 'friends and relations' as they were memorably described in *Donohue v. Armco Inc*[452] – have been put up by one party, in order to contend that they were not bound by the jurisdiction agreement, with a view to fabricating an exception, a court should detect it. On the other hand, the court will not be deflected from giving effect to a choice of court agreement for the English courts by the fact that there may be, or are, proceedings before a foreign court which is disregarding the agreement: it will allow the proceedings to continue in England, and may restrain the claimant in the foreign proceedings by injunction.[453]

It is apparent that strong legal policies collide at this point. There is a strong public interest in encouraging and enforcing agreements on where proceedings will be brought: the avoiding of litigation about where to litigate has an intuitive appeal. But there is a strong public interest in preventing conflicting judgments from coming into existence, and therefore in having all the interested parties before the court and bound to and by a single

---

449 [1998] 2 Lloyd's Rep 461. Approved and applied (in the sense that an anti-suit injunction against strangers to the agreement was set aside) in *Donohue v. Armco Inc* [2001] UKHL 64, [2002] 1 Lloyd's Rep 425. For further authority, see *Marubeni Hong Kong & South China Ltd v. Mongolian Government* [2002] 2 All ER (Comm) 873.

450 A similar approach was approved in principle, though did not need to be applied (as the English proceedings were held to fall outside the English jurisdiction clause) in *UBS AG v. HSH Nordbank AG* [2009] EWCA Civ 585, [2009] 2 Lloyd's Rep 272, [100]. At this point, there is a sharp divergence from the approach which has, almost certainly, to be taken under Art. 25 of the recast Brussels I Regulation, though *UBS AG v. HSH Nordbank AG* at [102]–[103] left the issue open for later decision.

451 [2001] UKHL 64, [2002] 1 Lloyd's Rep 425.

452 [2000] 1 Lloyd's Rep 579, 590–591. But the House of Lords did not share this analysis of the proceedings and therefore saw no reason to disregard the effect of the doctrine of privity: [2001] UKHL 64, [2002] 1 Lloyd's Rep 425.

453 *OT Africa Line Ltd v. Magic Sportswear Corp* [2005] EWCA Civ 710, [2005] 2 Lloyd's Rep 170; see also *Akai v. People's Insurance Co Ltd* [1998] 1 Lloyd's Rep 90. In *OT Africa Line Ltd* the Court considered the possibility of staying the English proceedings. But it is arguable that it was wrong to do so, as the agreement on jurisdiction fell within what is now Art. 25 of the Brussels I Regulation.

adjudication,[454] and the question is whether the latter is sufficient to overcome the private interest of one party in holding the other to his bargain. After all, the choice of court in the commercial agreement will have been part of the contractual bargain,[455] and there is certainly no general jurisdiction in English courts to rewrite the terms of a contract which is not impeachable on grounds of misrepresentation, duress, and so on. The defendant who argues that *pacta sunt servanda* makes a case which some will consider overwhelming.[456]

But the courts have duties which go beyond the issue presented by the *lis* between claimant and defendant. And as a matter of principle, the legal position of non-parties should not be affected by a contract made between others, and an increasing exercise of judicial case-management may encourage judges to overcome the conclusive effect of a bilateral agreement on jurisdiction, at least where multilateral litigation is in issue.[457] And as to the principle that *pacta sunt servanda*, it is worth remembering that the refusal of one form of specific relief is not the same thing as absolving the breaching party of all the consequences of his breach, or the wrongdoer of all the consequences of his wrong. It is all a matter of balance.

4.54 Enforcing a choice of court agreement by an action for damages for breach

If the court accepts that the bringing of proceedings in England amounts to a breach of contract, but declines to stay its proceedings, is it open to the defendant to claim or counterclaim for damages for breach of contract or tort? If[458] the defendant can show that he will (or did) suffer demonstrable and quantifiable financial loss as a result of having to defend the case in England, which would not have been sustained had the choice of court clause been honoured, the proposition that loss caused by another's breach of contract gives rise to a right to damages seems uncontroversial. There has been a breach of contract, or a deliberate interference with contractual rights, and loss has resulted. The secondary obligation to pay damages arises as a matter of law as the consequence of breach. No more is needed to make out a claim for compensation.

---

454 The point being that not all those who may be involved in the factual dispute will be party to, and liable to be affected by, the agreement. For a case of multipartite litigation involving jurisdiction clauses for England and for Hong Kong (where the court elected to uphold the English and accordingly not to enforce the Hong Kong one) see *Sinochem International Oil (London) Co Ltd v. Mobil Sales and Supply Corp* [2000] 1 Lloyd's Rep 670, 680.

455 It is surely irrelevant that there may have been little actual bargaining, for the theory is that the parties reached agreement by such means as seemed sufficient to them.

456 As it was put by Sir Owen Dixon in *Huddart Parker Ltd v. The Ship 'Mill Hill'* (1950) 81 CLR 502, 509, the court should exercise a 'strong bias in favour of maintaining the special bargain'.

457 It led the House of Lords to overcome the provisions of the jurisdiction agreement in *Donohue v. Armco Inc* [2001] UKHL 64, [2002] 1 Lloyd's Rep 425. But for the very different approach where the Brussels I Regulation is concerned, where no judicial flexibility whatever is allowed for, see *Hough v. P&O Containers Ltd* [1999] QB 834. Likewise for arbitration, where there is no real discretion to refuse effect to an agreement on arbitration on grounds of wider dispute management: Arbitration Act 1996, s. 9.

458 It may be a big if, but it is in principle no more than another issue of foreign law, required to be proved as a fact, on a balance of probability. See *Mantovani v. Carapelli* [1980] 1 Lloyd's Rep 375 (arbitration clause); *cf The Lisboa* [1980] 2 Lloyd's Rep 546 (jurisdiction clause). The possibility was viewed without enthusiasm in *Tracomin v. Sudan Oil Seeds (No 2)* [1983] 1 WLR 1026 and in *The Eastern Trader* [1996] 2 Lloyd's Rep 585, 602; and it was said in *Continental Bank NA v. Aeakos SA* [1994] 1 WLR 588 that a claim for damages for breach of contract arising out of breach of an English jurisdiction clause 'would be a relatively ineffective remedy'. No further explanation was given. But the law has moved on since then; it is discussed in the more obvious context of actions for damages for breach of a jurisdiction agreement for the English courts, in Chapter 5, para. 5.53, below.

It may seem surprising that such a claim or counterclaim[459] could be raised; two strong points against it may be made. The first is that, if the English court has allowed the action to proceed, it is contradictory for the court to order damages against a party who is doing only what it has sanctioned: it would be a tacit admission that the refusal to stay proceedings was itself wrong. If a party is doing what the court has refused to prevent, how can he be liable in damages for so doing? The second argument is that a contract to oust the jurisdiction of the English courts is, as a matter of English law, not legally effective. It would follow that an action for damages could not be founded upon a void contractual term.

Each argument can be sensibly responded to. As to the first, when in a domestic case a court is applied to for, but declines to make, an equitable or similar order,[460] such as an injunction to restrain a breach of contract, it does not follow that there is no breach.[461] Rather, the claimant is left to his common law remedy of damages: as there, so here. A court may decline to stay proceedings, but without prejudice to other remedies which may be available to the victim of a breach of contract.[462] As to the second, even though the ouster doctrine may apply to a contract governed by a foreign law, the claimant's breach of contract may be found in his asking the court *at this stage* to exercise the jurisdiction which it is admitted to have. The contractual term requires the parties to litigate their dispute elsewhere, but allows them, after that, to enforce the judgment by action in the English court. In other words, the clause neither ousts nor purports to oust the jurisdiction of the court, but rather as a *Scott v. Avery*[463] clause, pinpoints when in the proceedings recourse to the English court may be had. The defendant or counterclaimant does not plead that the court had no jurisdiction, but that even though it did, the claimant was in breach of contract by invoking it when he did. An action for damages, even though without unambiguous precedent where the breaching proceedings are brought before the English courts, would be available.

In 2001 the Court of Appeal accepted that an action for damages may be brought against a defendant who broke a contractually binding jurisdiction agreement by bringing proceedings before a foreign court.[464] The first case in which it did so was when a claim was brought for damages in respect of costs and expenses incurred, in proceedings before the foreign court, in applying to have the foreign action struck out. The claim before the English courts

---

459 A counterclaim raises a difficulty as the loss will not be quantifiable at the point where the counterclaim is made: everything depends on what happens to the claim. If the claim is framed as one for breach of contract, it may be pleaded by way of counterclaim, for the cause of action is complete on the occurrence of the breach, and everything else is then the quantification of damage. The rational form of the claim may therefore be for an indemnity against losses incurred, as was (in a related context) ordered in *A/S D/S Svendborg v. Akar* [2003] EWHC 797 (Comm).

460 Such as a stay: a stay is not equitable in origin.

461 It follows that, if he seeks a stay, he has not waived the breach and thereby deprived himself of a right to claim damages, but has merely sought one remedy as opposed to another. It may, however, be that the claim should be brought as a counterclaim, rather than as a separate, later action, to avoid problems with the principle in *Henderson v. Henderson* (1843) 3 Hare 100, though it may also be that the cause of action for damages is not established until the proceedings brought in breach of contract have run their course and damage has been sustained.

462 Indeed, in *A/S D/S Svendborg v. Wansa* [1997] 2 Lloyd's Rep 183 it appears to have been assumed without particular difficulty that such a claim for damages for breach of contract could be advanced, in principle at least. In *Svendborg*, the breach lay in suing in a *foreign* court, but the reasoning is presumably the same if there is a choice of court clause for a foreign court and the action is in England.

463 (1855) 5 HLC 811.

464 *Union Discount Co Ltd v. Zoller* [2001] EWCA Civ 1755, [2002] 1 WLR 1517; see further below, para. 5.55.

was founded on an exclusive jurisdiction agreement for the English courts, and the contention that it had been breached. The court accepted that the territory was not well mapped, but it had no need to go further than to rule that the claimant was, in principle, entitled to plead his claim for damages for breach of contract. It will be seen below[465] that this was the starting point for a string of subsequent cases, including several at the highest level, in which it was said that damages were recoverable for loss resulting from breach of an English jurisdiction clause.

It has yet to be authoritatively decided whether this same principle would extend to allow a counterclaim for damages, brought in respect of loss which may not yet have been incurred, when an English court permits a claimant to proceed to bring his claim in English in spite of his contractual promise not to do so. But contractual rights, when breached, give rise to a *right* to damages unless some other legal rule abrogates that common law right. The general issues raised by pleading a cause of action for damages for breach of a jurisdiction clause is examined in greater detail in relation to breaches of contract committed by suing in a foreign court;[466] but in one respect the present context is more, not less, suitable for a damages claim. Some consider that an action in England, which claims damages for breach of contract in suing overseas, has the potential to create dissonance between the English and foreign judgments. But where the English court allows an action to proceed in England, there is much less chance of a breach of comity if it also allows a counterclaim for damages for breach of contract. Judicial analysis of the issue is awaited.

4.55 Stays sought and obtained on the basis of agreements on arbitration

The third broad justification for a stay of proceedings which have been commenced as of right by service within the jurisdiction is that proceedings have been brought in breach of a binding agreement to arbitrate.

The law on stays ordered to enforce an agreement to arbitrate can be found in outline in Chapter 8, but the summary answer is that such a stay must be granted on application. The Arbitration Act 1996 provides that a party to an arbitration agreement to which the Act applies[467] may apply for a stay after the acknowledgment of service, and before taking a step in the proceedings to answer the substantive claim.[468] The court is obliged to stay proceedings unless the arbitration agreement is null and void, inoperative or incapable of being performed;[469] it is irrelevant that the seat of the arbitration is not England,[470] or that the law governing the arbitration agreement is not English law,[471] or that the enforcing of the agreement will fracture the broader picture of dispute resolution. In other words, there

---

465 Paragraph 5.53.

466 See at para. 5.53, below.

467 Defined by s. 6(1) as 'an agreement to submit to arbitration present or future disputes (whether they are contractual or not)'. The arbitration agreement must be in writing: s. 5(1). Section 5 proceeds to amplify the definition of 'agreement in writing', as to which see Chapter 8, below. For agreements to settle disputes by alternative means, but this not being regarded as an agreement to arbitrate, see *Halifax Financial Services v. Intuitive Systems Ltd* [1999] 1 All ER (Comm) 303, where the court even refused a stay of proceedings in the exercise of its discretion.

468 If a defendant takes a step in proceedings brought in a foreign court in breach of an arbitration agreement for England, he will have lost the right to specific enforcement of the agreement, but may not have waived his right to sue for damages for its breach: *The Eastern Trader* [1996] 2 Lloyd's Rep 585.

469 Section 9.

470 Section 2(2)(a).

471 Section 4 and Sch. 1.

is a mandatory stay in relation to valid arbitration agreements, and (by extension) in relation to disputed arbitration agreements which the court considers should be treated, at this stage, as though they were valid.

It is counter-intuitive that there is a general, mandatory, duty to stay proceedings brought in breach of an arbitration agreement, but less of a duty to do so where the agreement is for adjudication in the courts of another country. Some may consider it rather odd that the common law would not regard choice of court agreements as being as effective as Parliament has seen fit to make arbitration agreements. But the enforcement of arbitration agreements derives its force from international Convention, and the distinct legal and commercial policies which underpinned it. Agreements on choice of court agreements have quite different roots. Outside the context of the Brussels I Regulation, and until there is legislative change, the effect of an agreement on choice of court is a matter for the common law principles of private international law, and these will always be more receptive to special circumstances than will a statutory rule.

PROCEEDINGS COMMENCED BY SERVICE OUT OF THE JURISDICTION WITHOUT THE PRIOR PERMISSION OF THE COURT

4.56 Statutory claims which allow service to be made without permission

If one takes a step back, it will be recalled that where jurisdiction is established under the Brussels I Regulation, the claimant may effect service of process on a defendant out of the jurisdiction as of right, subject to making the requisite declaration of his right to invoke the jurisdiction on which he relies. The right to effect service in such cases is confirmed by CPR rules 6.33(1) and 6.33(2), respectively, which has been dealt with above.

However, in a small number of other cases, a statute will, on its face and on a true construction, allow a claim to be made and service to be made out of the jurisdiction without prior permission, and even though the facts giving rise to the claim did not occur within the jurisdiction. In such cases CPR rule 6.33(3) allows the claimant to serve out of the jurisdiction without the need to obtain the permission of the court.[472] Where this happens, although the permission of the court is not needed, the defendant may seek to dispute the jurisdiction on the basis that the statute was not one which allowed for this exceptional form of service: in effect, his contention will be that the statute was not one of the special ones, and that prior permission had been required and should not now be given with retrospective effect. All this comes to pass because the identification of a statute as one of the special kind is not as precise a science as it should be.

The number of statutes to which his principle applies is not large.[473] Rather than make service without prior permission, only to be faced with argument by a defendant, disputing the jurisdiction, that the statute did not, on a true construction, allow for such service to be

---

472 The claimant must file a notice stating the grounds on which he was entitled to serve out of the jurisdiction without permission, and this notice must be served together with the claim form: CPR r. 6.34(1).

473 It applies to certain legislation implementing international conventions in circumstances in which the convention gives jurisdiction to the courts of the United Kingdom. It also applies to Protection of Trading Interests Act 1980, s. 6 (clawback actions). It has not been held to apply to very much else. It does not apply to a claim for payment under the Commercial Agents (Council Directive) Regulations 1992, SI 1993/3053, as nothing on the

made, a claimant may find it expedient to apply for permission under CPR rule 6.36 and Ground 20(a) of Paragraph 3.1 of Practice Direction 6B. The rules governing service out the jurisdiction with the permission of the court are discussed in the next section, and in the case of liability arising under a statute, there may be little to be gained by serving out of the jurisdiction without the permission of the court, when permission is so simple to obtain.

PROCEEDINGS COMMENCED BY SERVICE OUT OF THE JURISDICTION WITH THE PRIOR PERMISSION OF THE COURT

4.57 General structure of the rules

If it is not possible to serve the defendant within the jurisdiction,[474] and the claim does not arise under a statute which permits service out of the jurisdiction without the need for permission, it is necessary to obtain permission to serve process on the defendant out of the jurisdiction. This involves showing that the court has legal power to grant permission and (if it does) that the discretion of the court should be exercised in favour of granting permission.

Although doubt has recently been cast on the explanation or upon its modern utility,[475] it was always understood that the summoning of a defendant to court is or involves an assertion of sovereign power, and that if the defendant is not within the jurisdiction, it is not something which the claimant has a right to do, not even if the defendant had agreed in advance to submit to the jurisdiction of the English courts.[476] For this reason, until relatively recently, what was actually served on a defendant out of the jurisdiction was not the writ but notice of the writ. This is no longer done, but the fact that it was demonstrates the possible delicacy of the situation. After all, there are some countries in Europe in which it is a serious criminal offence to serve process issued by a foreign court unless this is done through official channels.[477]

It was also the reason for describing the assertion of jurisdiction in cases as 'exorbitant'. As recently as 2012 the Supreme Court[478] was able to observe that 'it has frequently been said that the jurisdiction exercised under what used to be RSC Ord 11, 1 (and is now CPR Practice Direction 6B, para. 3.1) is an exorbitant one, in that it was a wider jurisdiction than was recognised in English law as being possessed by courts of foreign countries in the

---

face of the Regulations makes such provision for jurisdiction: *Fern Computer Consultancy Ltd v. Intergraph Cadworx & Analysis Solutions Ltd* [2014] EWHC 2908 (Ch), [2015] 1 Lloyd's Rep 1.

474 For service out of the jurisdiction with permission in relation to arbitration, see Chapter 8, and CPR Part 62, esp. r. 62.5.

475 *Abela v. Baadarani* [2013] UKSC 44, [2013] 1 WLR 2043.

476 But, of course, if he had appointed an agent within the jurisdiction who had authority to accept service of process, there would be no problem, and in particular, no need to (obtain permission to) serve out of the jurisdiction.

477 Swiss Penal Code, Art. 271: 'Whoever, without being authorised, performs acts for a foreign state on Swiss territory that are reserved to an authority or official, or performs such acts for a foreign party or another foreign organisation, or aids and abets such acts, shall be punished with imprisonment for up to three years, or a monetary penalty, in serious cases with imprisonment for not less than a year'. This is the Swiss view of the service of foreign process outside the framework of international treaties to which Switzerland is party. Anyone who thinks that the service of English process overseas has nothing to do with conceptions of sovereignty should try serving English process on a Swiss private bank in Zürich and see what happens next.

478 *Rubin v. Eurofinance SA* [2012] UKSC 46, [2013] 1 AC 236, [126] (Lord Collins).

absence of a treaty providing for recognition: see *The Siskina (Owners of cargo lately laden on board) v. Distos Cia Naviera SA*,[479] *per* Lord Diplock; *Amin Rasheed Shipping Corpn v. Kuwait Insurance Co*,[480] *per* Lord Diplock; *Spiliada Maritime Corp v. Cansulex Ltd*,[481] *per* Lord Goff of Chieveley', though in truth, the characterisation of this jurisdiction as 'exorbitant' went much further back than its repeated reaffirmation in those more recent decisions.

Yet when the Court of Appeal followed what it took to be the approach settled at the highest level, and held that the English court should declare that it had no jurisdiction in circumstances in which a claimant had failed to effect the service out of the jurisdiction which he had been given permission to make, on the ground that if it did otherwise it would make an exorbitant jurisdiction even more exorbitant, it was criticised in surprisingly sharp terms by the Supreme Court. The result of the judgment in *Abela v. Baadarani*[482] is that use of the term 'exorbitant' will generate only heat but no light at all. Rightly or wrongly, the discussion of the law in the paragraphs which follow will seek to avoid use of this incendiary adjective: the law is what the law is, and labels are a distraction. It is sufficient to say that the court will not grant permission to serve out unless England is the proper place to bring the claim – notice, *the* proper place – and that if it is, arguing about use of the 'e' word is an odd thing to be doing when there is work to be done.[483]

4.58 Jurisdiction founded on service out of the jurisdiction: position of the defendant

A brief, scene-setting, summary of the position in which the defendant may find himself if service has been made on him is as follows. If the claimant serves process outside the jurisdiction without having obtained permission, the service will, no doubt, be irregular, but it will not be a nullity: it is always alarming to be informed by a defendant that he realised that process had been served without permission so he ignored it, or that he did not acknowledge service because this would have given a validity to the service which it did not have.[484] The defendant may, but also should, apply to have service set aside, because service was effected; whether service should have been effected does not affect the proposition that it was effected. Where service has been made, the defendant needs to respond to it. By contrast, ignoring it will risk being seen as having decided not to dispute the jurisdiction; and not disputing the jurisdiction risks being seen as having submitted to the jurisdiction of the court and as having waived any irregularity which went before.

In the more usual case, in which the defendant has been served with the permission of the court, he may, if so advised, dispute the jurisdiction of the court. This is done by application made under CPR Part 11. The application will be made for an order declaring that the court has no jurisdiction, for an order setting aside the grant of permission to serve process, for an order setting aside service, and for such other relief as may be appropriate.[485]

---

479 [1979] AC 210, 254.

480 [1984] AC 50, 65.

481 [1987] AC 460, 481.

482 [2013] UKSC 44, [2013] 1 WLR 2043. The judgment of the Court of Appeal is at [2011] EWCA Civ 1571.

483 See, in this spirit, [2013] LMCLQ 415.

484 One might just as well ignore the symptoms of malaria because 'it does not exist in England'. Ignoring facts is usually a very bad idea; pretending that they are not facts is a bad idea coupled with a pretence.

485 See, for the procedure, paras 5.25 *et seq.*, below.

If the defendant indicates that he is going to dispute the jurisdiction, but then does nothing to make the necessary application, he will be taken to have abandoned or withdrawn his challenge and to have accepted the jurisdiction of the court.[486] If the defendant simply enters an appearance as a defendant in the ordinary course of events, he will be taken to have submitted to the court and to have waived any objection to service which he might have been entitled to make. If the defendant simply ignores the service, the claimant may apply for judgment in default,[487] but if permission to serve out had not been obtained, doing so may not be straightforward, given that the fact of service must be proved by evidence, and the question of the regularity of service will emerge as a result of the claimant's own act.

4.59 Jurisdiction founded on service out of the jurisdiction: position of the claimant

So much for the position of the defendant; let us now focus on the position of the claimant. The claimant, having no right to act without it, will have needed the permission of the court before serving the claim form out of the jurisdiction. This is applied for in accordance with Part 6, Section IV, of the Civil Procedure Rules.

The application is made without the opponent's being notified that it is being made; the court will almost always grant permission unless there is a very obvious flaw in the application. If permission is granted, as in practice it almost always is,[488] and service is effected in accordance with it, the defendant may dispute the jurisdiction by challenging the order which granted permission, and the service which was made pursuant to it, by applying under CPR Part 11. The *inter partes* procedure which then follows marks the point in the process at which the court will investigate whether permission to serve should have been granted.[489] The fact that permission was granted to the claimant in the first place is largely irrelevant at this point: it leaves no footprint; no onus is placed upon the defendant who applies to have the permission set aside; the application is in effect a rehearing of an application for permission, with the onus lying on the party who needed the permission in the first place.[490] The court is not inhibited from discharging or varying the order, and for which the claimant now in substance (if not in form) reapplies, by reason of the fact that it has already been made.[491]

When the claimant makes the application for permission to serve out, a high degree of frankness and openness is required of him. This includes an obligation to return to court

---

486 *Maple Leaf Macro Volatility Master Fund v. Rouvray* [2009] EWHC 257 (Comm), [2009] 1 Lloyd's Rep 475.
487 CPR Part 12.
488 At this stage the court will have seen only the claim form and the written evidence in support of the application for permission. Unless the application is plainly bad, or plainly fails to comply with the rules governing it (see in particular CPR r. 6.37), or the written evidence can be regarded as incredible, permission will be granted, for there is little basis for doing otherwise. See *Attock Cement Co Ltd v. Romanian Bank for Foreign Trade* [1989] 1 WLR 1147.
489 The question is whether it was proper to grant permission on the date upon which it was granted, not (in the light of changed circumstances, or fresh evidence) whether it would be right to grant it as of today: *ISC Technologies v. Guerin* [1992] 2 Lloyd's Rep 430; *Mohammed v. Bank of Kuwait and the Middle East KSC* [1996] 1 WLR 1483; *Sharab v. Al-Saud* [2009] EWCA Civ 353, [2009] 2 Lloyd's Rep 160; *Vitol Bahrein EC v. Nasdec General Trading LLC* [2014] EWHC 984 (Comm).
490 *Artlev AG v. Almazy Rossii-Sakha* (8 March 1995), *Navig8 Pte Ltd v. Al-Riyadh Co for Vegetable Oil Industry* [2013] EWHC 328 (Comm), [2013] 2 Lloyd's Rep 104, [10].
491 *WEA Records v. Visions Channel 4 Ltd* [1983] 1 WLR 721.

for further directions if circumstances materially change between the granting of permission and the actual service.[492] If he is found to have fallen short of what may properly have been expected of him, permission may, in principle at least, be set aside on this ground alone.[493] It is fair to say, however, that the precise standards actually set by the general formula of frankness are hard to pin down, the case law is very fact-specific, and setting aside on this ground is rarely made[494] (or said to be called for in cases in which the setting aside has already been justified on the basis that the conditions for the grant of permission were not met in any event.)[495]

In deciding whether permission will be granted, the questions which need to be addressed fall into two parts. The first is to show that the claim made satisfies CPR rule 6.36. That will mean that the claim, or if more than one claim is made, that each one of them, falls within one or more of the 20 paragraphs of paragraph 3.1 of 'Practice Direction B supplementing CPR Part 6':[496] for convenience of reference we will in this chapter refer to this as 'Paragraph 3.1', and its several provisions as the 'heads' of jurisdiction. To the extent that the claim does or the claims do, the court is empowered to grant permission to serve out. To the extent that the claim does not or the claims do not, the court has no power to grant permission. If service out may be authorised for some but not for other claims made by the claimant, the claim form will need to be amended to remove those for which service may not be authorised.[497] It also follows that where permission is given to serve out, the claimant should not be permitted to amend the claim,[498] after the defendant has entered an appearance, to add a claim for which permission would not have been given in the first place: the claim form for which permission is given will not be allowed to serve as a 'Trojan horse'.[499]

If the court is satisfied in terms of Paragraph 3.1 that there is a legal basis to grant permission, the next stage, framed by CPR rule 6.37, is to determine whether the case was a proper one for the court to exercise its discretion to authorise service, which means to allow jurisdiction to be established.[500] This in turn breaks down into three sub-issues, which ask: (i) whether England is the proper place in which to bring the claim, (ii) whether it

---

492 *Network Telecom (Europe) Ltd v. Telephone Systems International Inc* [2003] EWHC 2890 (Comm), [2004] 1 All ER (Comm) 418, but which does seem to take the law into new territory.

493 In general, see *The Hagen* [1908] P 189; *R. v. Kensington Income Tax Commissioners, ex parte de Polignac* [1917] 1 KB 486, 509; *Electric Furnace Co v. Selas* [1987] RPC 23; *Newtherapeutics Ltd v. Katz* [1991] Ch 226 at 256; *Arab Business Consortium International Finance & Investment Co v. Banque Franco-Tunisienne* [1996] 1 Lloyd's Rep 485 aff'd [1997] 1 Lloyd's Rep 531; *Knauf GmbH v. British Gypsum Ltd* [2001] EWCA Civ 1570, [2002] 1 Lloyd's Rep 199; *Ophthalmic Innovations International (UK) Ltd v. Ophthalmic Innovations International Inc* [2004] EWHC 2948 (Ch), [2005] ILPr 109.

494 Some authorities appear to demand a very high degree of frankness, see for example *R. v. Kensington Income Tax Commissioners, ex parte de Polignac* [1917] 1 KB 486; *Brink's Mat v. Elcombe* [1988] 1 WLR 1350; *Lloyd's Bowmaker v. Britannia Arrow* [1988] 1 WLR 1337. Other decisions appear to stand for a less rigid view, see *The Hida Maru* [1981] 2 Lloyd's Rep 510; *Beecham Group plc v. Norton Healthcare Ltd* [1997] FSR 81. But it is only on the material relevant to the grant of permission that the duty really bites: *MRG (Japan) Ltd v. Engelhard Metals Japan Ltd* [2003] EWHC 3418 (Comm). As to the consequences, the general issue is examined at length in *Millhouse Capital UK Ltd v. Sibir Energy plc* [2008] EWHC 2614 (Ch), [2009] 1 BCLC 298, [67]–[109] (not a case on service out of the jurisdiction).

495 *Surrey (UK) Ltd v. Mazandaran Wood & Paper Industries* [2014] EWHC 3165 (Comm).

496 In relation to arbitration, CPR r. 62.5.

497 *Holland v. Leslie* [1894] 2 QB 450; *Waterhouse v. Reid* [1938] 1 KB 743; *Metall & Rohstoff AG v. Donaldson Lufkin & Jenrette Inc* [1990] 1 QB 391; *Donohue v. Armco Inc* [2001] UKHL 64, [2002] 1 All ER 749, [21].

498 If the defendant takes this particular point.

499 *Donohue v. Armco Inc* [2001] UKHL 64, [2002] 1 All ER 749, [21], and cases there cited.

500 On whether the correct formulation is 'the proper place' or 'the natural forum', see further below, paras 4.88 *et seq.*

would nevertheless be unjust to require the defendant to defend himself in England, and (iii) whether the claimant has shown there to be a serious issue to be tried upon the merits of his claim. Given answers in the claimant's favour, the grant of permission will be made or confirmed; if any issue is decided against him, the permission and the service may[501] be set aside. Even so, if the claimant would be free to make a fresh application on which he would succeed, there may be little practical point in setting aside the first order, even if an objection on these grounds would have been well founded, and the court may simply deem irregular service to stand as good service and deal with the irregularity by an appropriate costs order.[502]

The provisions governing permission for service out of the jurisdiction have been amended from time to time. Those now contained in Part 6 of the Civil Procedure Rules are the successors in title to the provisions of RSC Order 11 which had, in various respects, stated the law for over a century. Although numerous changes have been made to the text of the rules under which service may be permitted to be made out of the jurisdiction, it is, unfortunately, not always clear whether alterations to the previous wording were intended to be substantial, or were instead meant to express the same ideas in more modern but less dextrous language.

It is generally supposed[503] that the authorities on RSC Order 11, rule 1(1), and on the earlier textual versions of CPR Part 6, will remain relevant, but to be used with care for it may not be assumed that where the wording was altered it did not change the law. The same is true of RSC Order 11, rule 4(2), which provided that the court should not authorise service out of the jurisdiction 'unless it shall be made sufficiently to appear to the court that the case is a proper one for service out of the jurisdiction under this Order'. It was this provision which provided the foundation for the three sub-issues[504] set out above. But though the former rule 4(2) was not remade in express terms in CPR Part 6, and though the precise requirements which it was held to impose may not have been carried forward, entirely intact, into the structure of CPR Part 6, the former Order 11, rule 4(2) had not given rise to any dissatisfaction, and decisions on this aspect of the law retain their authority almost intact.

4.60 Legal basis for permission: CPR rule 6.36, and the heads of jurisdiction

Paragraph 3.1 of the Practice Direction sets out, in 20 sub-paragraphs, the cases in which court has power to authorise service out of the jurisdiction under CPR rule 6.36. Although they are amended from time to time, for convenience of reference they are set out here:

> *General grounds: (1) A claim is made for a remedy against a person domiciled within the jurisdiction. (2) A claim is made for an injunction ordering the defendant to do or refrain from doing an act within the jurisdiction. (3) A claim is made against a person ('the defendant') on whom the claim form has been or will be served (otherwise than in reliance on this paragraph) and (a) there is between the claimant and the defendant a real issue which it is reasonable for the court to try; and (b) the claimant wishes to serve the claim*

---

501 It is probable, as is shown below, that the claimant must succeed on all points.

502 CPR r. 6.15, on which see *Abela v. Baadarani* [2013] UKSC 44, [2013] 1 WLR 2043.

503 For the view of the courts, see also *Cool Carriers AB v. HSBC Bank USA* [2001] 2 Lloyd's Rep 22 on the continuing authority of the old rules in the interpretation of the new.

504 England and Wales the natural (or the proper) forum; not unjust to authorise service; serious issue on the merits of the claim.

*form on another person who is a necessary or proper party to that claim. **(4)** A claim is an additional claim under Part 20 and the person to be served is a necessary or proper party to the claim or additional claim. **Claims for interim remedies: (5)** A claim is made for an interim remedy under section 25(1) of the Civil Jurisdiction and Judgments Act 1982. **Claims in relation to contracts: (6)** A claim is made in respect of a contract where the contract (a) was made within the jurisdiction; (b) was made by or through an agent trading or residing within the jurisdiction; (c) is governed by English law; or (d) contains a term to the effect that the court shall have jurisdiction to determine any claim in respect of the contract. **(7)** A claim is made in respect of a breach of contract committed within the jurisdiction. **(8)** A claim is made for a declaration that no contract exists where, if the contract was found to exist, it would comply with the conditions set out in paragraph (6). **Claims in tort: (9)** A claim is made in tort where (a) damage was sustained within the jurisdiction; or (b) the damage sustained resulted from an act committed within the jurisdiction. **Enforcement: (10)** A claim is made to enforce any judgment or arbitral award. **Claims about property within the jurisdiction: (11)** The whole subject matter of a claim relates to property located within the jurisdiction. **Claims about trusts, etc: (12)** A claim is made for any remedy which might be obtained in proceedings to execute the trusts of a written instrument where (a) the trusts ought to be executed according to English law; and (b) the person on whom the claim form is to be served is a trustee of the trusts. **(13)** A claim is made for any remedy which might be obtained in proceedings for the administration of the estate of a person who died domiciled within the jurisdiction. **(14)** A probate claim or a claim for the rectification of a will. **(15)** A claim is made for a remedy against the defendant as constructive trustee where the defendant's alleged liability arises out of acts committed within the jurisdiction. **(16)** A claim is made for restitution where the defendant's alleged liability arises out of acts committed within the jurisdiction. **Claims by HM Revenue and Customs: (17)** A claim is made by the Commissioners for H.M. Revenue and Customs relating to duties or taxes against a defendant not domiciled in Scotland or Northern Ireland. **Claim for costs order in favour of or against third parties: (18)** A claim is made by a party to proceedings for an order that the court exercise its power under section 51 of the Senior Courts Act 1981 to make a costs order in favour of or against a person who is not a party to those proceedings. **Admiralty claims: (19)** A claim is (a) in the nature of salvage and any part of the services took place within the jurisdiction; or (b) to enforce a claim under section 153, 154, 175 or 176A of the Merchant Shipping Act 1995. **Claims under various enactments: (20)** A claim is made (a) under an enactment which allows proceedings to be brought and those proceedings are not covered by any of the other grounds referred to in this paragraph; or (b) under the Directive of the Council of the European Communities dated 15 March 1976 No 76/308/EEC, where service is to be effected in a Member State of the European Union.*

The first question, which is not quite as trivial as it seems, is how to refer to these provisions. 'Sub-paragraphs' is correct,[505] though it is cumbersome. The terminology of 'gateways' is sometimes used, but this does not feel quite right, not least because once through the 'gateway' the claimant has to negotiate the further requirements of CPR rule 6.37. The nearest the rules themselves come to nomenclature is when they refer to the 'ground' in Paragraph 3.1,[506] but it is most convenient to refer to the 'heads' of jurisdiction under which the court has power to authorise service out of the jurisdiction. It was the usage for many decades before the Practice Direction, and there is no need to abandon it.

4.61 Strictness in the interpretation of the heads of jurisdiction

It is noticeable that the provisions which are now set out in Paragraph 3.1 have suffered something of a reduction in apparent status. They were first made in primary legislation;[507] they were then remade in Rules of the Supreme Court,[508] and then in the Civil Procedure

---

505 They are referred to in this list as 'paragraphs': see sub-Paragraphs (3) and (8). This is unfortunate, for though the sense of the law is clear enough, this may cause occasional confusion. Anyway, it is wrong.

506 CPR r. 6.37(1)(a).

507 Common Law Procedure Act 1852.

508 Order 11 of the Rules of the Supreme Court.

Rules.[509] They now appear in a Practice Direction, which is the end of the line. There is nowhere left to go, except to abolish them altogether, and to rest the whole jurisdictional decision on whether England is the proper place to bring the proceedings.

Indeed, this might not be a wholly bad idea; and in the opinion of the Supreme Court it may be time to take the step. Originally it made sense for the law, which first made provision for service out by the Common Law Procedure Act 1852, to be developed by reference to the legal category of claim. But as it is understood that service out will not be permitted unless England is shown, clearly and distinctly, to be the proper place for the trial of the claim, one may fairly ask why there is a need also to fit the claim within one of the heads. The distinct acceptance of the principle of *forum non conveniens* may have made this appear to be a rather purposeless additional requirement.[510]

In *Abela v. Baadarani*, the Supreme Court appears[511] to have agreed that the adoption of the principle of *forum conveniens*, and the fact that 'litigation between residents of different states is a routine incident of modern commercial life', meant that the decision to allow service out 'is generally a pragmatic one in the interests of the efficient conduct of litigation in an appropriate forum'. The logic of this point of view is that the heads under which service may be authorised are not points of cardinal importance. The court, obviously, could not act as though the heads were not there, but it certainly gave the impression that it saw them as performing no function which needed to be performed.

If the law were to be reoriented in line with this approach, it would ask whether England was the proper place to bring the claim, and would regard service out of the jurisdiction as being to notify the defendant of the imminent commencement of proceedings, or of inviting him to participate in the proceedings. It would reduce the formal significance of service; and it would, by relaxing the procedural rules governing service, widen the effective jurisdiction of the courts. There are reasons – far from conclusive, but still significant – to express reservations about any such development.

It was explained above that the basic assumption of the common law is that where there is service there is jurisdiction. In that context, to make it easier to effect service is, directly and inescapably, to widen the jurisdiction of the court. If one takes the view that the latter function is, today, one for the legislature, judicial slackening of the rules for service could not be correct. It was then also explained that in a system such as that put in place by the Brussels I Regulation, in which the statutory grounds for jurisdiction are specified in some detail, the basic supposition is that where there is jurisdiction there may be service. In that context, by contrast, there can be no rational objection to relaxing rules on service which perform no useful function, for it has no effect on the jurisdiction of the court.

The significance of *Abela v. Baadarani* is that it deals with a case which sits between the two kinds of jurisdictional system. Service out has elements of a common law jurisdictional system, in that the entire concern is with when service may be made; and it has elements of

---

509 CPR r. 6.20 (until 1 October 2008).

510 However, for a note of caution, that a jurisdictional rule written simply in terms of there being 'a real and substantial connection' with the court would not be an adequate basis for the jurisdiction of the Canadian courts, or that it would not serve as a sufficient guarantee of order and fairness, but more concrete and ascertainable points of connection are required, see *Club Resorts Ltd v. Van Breda* [2012] 1 SCR 572; see also (in the context of defamation) *Banro Corp v. Éditions Écosociété Inc* [2012] 1 SCR 636; *Beeden v. Black* [2012] 1 SCR 666.

511 The point is made by Lord Sumption at [53]; the rest of the court, speaking through Lord Clarke, agreed: at [45].

a statutory system of jurisdiction, in that the jurisdictional heads which allow the claim to be brought before the English court are set out in considerable detail. Small wonder, then, the question whether legislative requirements relating to service out should be relaxed has pulled academic writers in opposite directions:[512] it is a reflection of the hybrid nature of service out of the jurisdiction in English law. The view taken here was that if it was right to signal some relaxation in the rules on service of process, it would have been wrong to suggest, at the same time, that the bases of jurisdiction, set out in CPR Part 6, should be materially loosened.[513] If by suggesting that 'it should no longer be necessary to resort to the kind of muscular presumptions against service out which are implicit in adjectives like "exorbitant"'[514] the court was also suggesting that the heads of jurisdiction in Paragraph 3.1 should be interpreted in a new and looser way, this would be unfortunate. But if the court was suggesting that the jurisdiction of the court was, in effect, defined in terms of England being the proper place to bring the claim, then it is perfectly understandable that fussy or unnecessary requirements of service should not stand in the way of the exercise of that jurisdiction. The broad issue will need to be examined further when there is more material to do it with.

Back to the heads of jurisdiction. There is considerable case law upon the meaning of the heads of jurisdiction, or upon the meaning of their predecessors in CPR rule 6.20, as it then was, or in RSC Order 11, rule 1(1), as it more remotely was. It has already been explained that each claim in the claim form must fall within one (or more) of the heads: although the text of the rules is not explicit on this point, the cases are completely clear.[515] Accordingly, it is not possible to obtain permission to serve out of the jurisdiction in respect of a claim which does fall within Paragraph 3.1, and to annex to it other claims which do not themselves fall under any of the heads;[516] it is not proper to obtain permission to serve out of the jurisdiction and, once the defendant has entered an appearance, to seek to add by amendment a claim for which, if permission had been sought at the outset, permission would not have been granted.[517]

The claim form, rather than the witness statement in support of the application for permission, identifies the claims for which service out is sought and permitted.[518] It will not be proper to seek to supplement the contents of the claim form if it appears, under a harsher light, that it was poorly or incompletely drafted.[519] Moreover, if the defendant was prevailed upon to accept service within the jurisdiction, to save the cost and inconvenience of an application for permission to serve out of the jurisdiction, the court should also be

---

512 Briggs [2013] LMCLQ 415; Dickinson (2014) 130 LQR 197.

513 To this effect, see *Cruz City 1 Mauritius Holdings v. Unitech Ltd* [2014] EWHC 3704 (Comm).

514 At [53].

515 See, for further illustration, *The Volvox Hollandia* [1988] 2 Lloyd's Rep 361, 371–372, using the idiom of the curate's egg (rather unhelpfully, for the separation of a breakfast egg into good and bad parts is not always easy).

516 *Metall & Rohstoff v. Donaldson Lufkin & Jenrette Inc* [1990] 1 QB 391.

517 *Waterhouse v. Reid* [1938] 1 KB 743; *Trafalgar Tours Ltd v. Henry* [1990] 2 Lloyd's Rep 298. See also *Parker v. Schuller* (1901) 17 TLR 299; *SCOR v. Eras* [1992] 1 Lloyd's Rep 570, 612; *ED & F Man (Sugar) Ltd v. Lendoudis* [2007] EWHC 2268 (Comm), [2007] 2 Lloyd's Rep 579.

518 And a defective claim form is not cured by a fuller statement: *Express Insurance Co Ltd v. Astra SA Insurance and Reinsurance Co Ltd* [1997] ILPr 252. For defective witness statements, see *The Kurnia Dewi* [1997] 1 Lloyd's Rep 552.

519 *Arab Business Corporation International Finance & Investment Co v. Banque Franco-Tunisienne* [2003] EWCA Civ 205, [2003] 2 Lloyd's Rep 146; *BAS Capital Funding Corp v. Medfinco Ltd* [2003] EWHC 1798 (Ch), [2004] 1 Lloyd's Rep 652.

slow to permit the addition of a claim in respect of which service out of the jurisdiction would not have been authorised, at least if the defendant takes the point by way of objection.[520]

It is now an express requirement that the written evidence in support of the application for permission specify the head or heads of jurisdiction upon which the claimant applies for permission to serve.[521] This will identify for the defendant the argument he will have to meet at the hearing of the application to set aside the permission, pursuant to which service was made. That being so, it was until recently understood that the claimant would not be permitted, at the hearing of the application to set aside, to seek to rely upon a different head when permission had not originally been sought on that particular basis.[522] However, in *NML Capital Ltd v. Argentina*,[523] the Supreme Court repudiated this approach to service out cases, explaining that if the claimant could have relied on different heads to justify the service of the actual claim form,[524] he would be allowed to change horses in mid stream and do so. There would, after all, be little sense in setting aside the permission wrongly obtained, only for the claimant to make a fresh application on a basis which could not be spoken against. Any prejudice could be dealt with by a costs order; and no injustice would be done as a result. So long as the claim form does not require amendment for an application for permission to serve it to be soundly based, there is no real problem. Any suggestion that this relaxation of the rules would 'make an exorbitant jurisdiction more exorbitant' will now be inadmissible and irrelevant. Even so, the danger that a court will take the view that an imprecisely drafted claim form or inadequate witness statement was simply not good enough to impose on a defendant the obligation to come to England, means that real care should be taken to get this first step right.[525]

4.62 Definition and interpretation of the statutory heads of jurisdiction

It will be seen below that if the question is whether the claimant has done enough to meet the requirements of the jurisdictional head relied on, the court will require him to show a good arguable case that he has done so.

But the current enquiry is a different one. The heads set out in Paragraph 3.1 contain various definitional elements. A question which appears important, but which is oddly free of convincing authority, is whether these are to be interpreted by reference to English domestic law, or English rules of private international law, or something else.[526] Suppose

---

520 *Beecham Group plc v. Norton Healthcare Ltd* [1997] FSR 81; *Beck v. Value Capital Ltd* [1975] 1 WLR 6; *Youell v. Kara Mara Shipping Co Ltd* [2000] 2 Lloyd's Rep 102, 120–121; *Donohue v. Armco Inc* [2001] UKHL 65, [2002] 1 Lloyd's Rep 425, [21]. If service was accepted voluntarily, it is a question of construction of the acceptance whether the defendant reserved the right to challenge it on the basis that it did not fit within the Grounds of Paragraph 3.1: *Baghlaf Al Zafer v. Pakistan National Shipping Corp* [1998] 2 Lloyd's Rep 229.

521 CPR r. 6.37(1)(a). But though the rule is expressed as mandatory, a failure to comply with it is an irregularity which can be cured under CPR r. 3.10 if no prejudice has resulted from the failure.

522 *Metall & Rohstoff*, at 436. To similar effect: *Schiffahrtsgesellschaft Detlev von Appen GmbH v. Vöst Alpine Intertrading GmbH* [1997] 2 Lloyd's Rep 279.

523 [2011] UKSC 31, [2011] 2 AC 495. It follows that if *Parker v. Schuller* (1901) 17 TLR 299 and *Youell v. Kara Mara Shipping Co Ltd* [2000] 2 Lloyd's Rep 102 say something different, they are not now reliable.

524 That is, without any need to amend it.

525 *ED & F Man (Sugar) Ltd v. Lendoudis* [2007] EWHC 2268 (Comm), [2007] 2 Lloyd's Rep 579.

526 Such as by asking whether the claim advanced is to be characterised as, or is in the nature of, a tort, a contract, and so on.

the claimant wishes to serve out on the basis 'the claim is in respect of a contract where the contract was made within the jurisdiction'.[527] Is the question whether there actually was a contract for the claim to be made in respect of answered by reference to English domestic law, or by reference to the rules of English private international law?[528] And is the place where it was made answered by applying the offer and acceptance rules of English domestic law, or the corresponding rules of whichever law is picked out by the rules of private international law, or in some other way altogether?

Take by way of example a case in which English domestic law would consider that there was a contract, but where the rules which English private international law would point to – say Ruritanian law – would say that there was no contract. If the question is whether the claim relates to a contract, and the rules of English law, in its broad and complete sense, would conclude that there was no contract, it seems to follow that there is no contract for the purpose of this jurisdictional head. If the position is reversed – English domestic law would say that there was no contract, say for lack of consideration, but the law to which English private international law would point, say Italian law, would consider that there was a contract, it would seem surprising if the jurisdictional head were held to be unavailable simply because English domestic law would consider that the arrangement was not contractual.[529] That suggests that the term 'a contract' may be satisfied if there is a contract as a matter of English domestic law, and will not be satisfied if there is not; but if either party raises the issue, the reference should instead be to whichever law, as a matter of English private international law, would be used to determine the existence and validity of the alleged contract. This conclusion is supported by *Amin Rasheed Shipping Corp v. Kuwait Insurance Co*,[530] which will be discussed below.

The question where the contract was made is not so much legal as geographical. The view that it is answered, via rules of private international law, by a law which might not be English domestic law, has been rejected.[531] It probably follows that one therefore asks, by reference to English domestic law, where the acceptance was effective;[532] though it has also been held that a contract may be considered to be made in two places if a contractual document is signed in two places.[533] It may therefore be that on these issues, which are really matter of geography rather than law, reference to a law is not always made, and that a purely factual determination is all that is called for.

Of course, it may fairly be said that this is all too complicated, and that the jurisdictional head should be satisfied if there is a good arguable case that there is a contract without making further enquiry into whether there really is a contract (or into which law defines the term). But as matters currently stand, the definitional terms used in Paragraph 3.1 are subjected to an interpretation which may turn on identification of the law which supplies that definition. The law is complicated as a result.

---

527 Paragraph 3.1(6)(a) of the Practice Direction.

528 If this, it is to be supposed that it means the rules of private international law which would apply to the alleged contract: the Rome I Regulation if it falls within the scope of that Regulation; the Rome Convention, or the common law, as the case may be, if it does not, for otherwise the law would be impossibly difficult to operate.

529 *Cf Re Bonacina* [1912] 2 Ch 394.

530 [1984] AC 50.

531 *The TS Havprins* [1983] 2 Lloyd's Rep 356.

532 *Brinkibon Ltd v. Stahag Stahl und Stahlwarenhandels GmbH* [1983] 2 AC 34.

533 *Conductive Inkjet Technology Ltd v. Uni-Pixel Displays Inc* [2013] EWHC 2968 (Ch), [2014] 1 All ER (Comm) 654, following *Apple Corps Ltd v. Apple Computer Inc* [2004] EWHC 768 (Ch).

Finally, the construction of the heads will not be allowed to be any wider than is properly suggested by the natural construction of the words used.[534] Until recently, this approach would have been seen as rock-solid orthodoxy, affirmed and reaffirmed at the highest level. It is fair to say, however, that it occasionally appears to be less orthodox than it was, as more seductive contentions are put to a court which is invited to find the language of the jurisdictional head to be more malleable. But the wording of the paragraph represents the legislator's intention. There is no obvious justification for the court to widen it further, by stretching the limits of the jurisdictional heads out beyond their proper meaning.[535] Given the nature of the imposition upon a defendant who is served with process out of the jurisdiction,[536] the construction of the heads should not be strained.[537] To put the same point in other language, which until recently was frequently heard, the claim actually made must fall within the letter and the spirit of the particular jurisdictional head.[538] To put the same point in language which is not so frequently heard,[539] CPR rule 6.36 and Paragraph 3.1 make exceptions to the general provision that a defendant who is not within the jurisdiction should not be sued here, and the heads of jurisdiction should therefore be given a restrictive interpretation.

The 'letter and spirit' principle of construction was, until recently at least, reasonably well vouched for by authority,[540] but there has been some questioning of the principle in the most recent cases.[541] It is debatable whether the law would be improved by such a change. In any event, it must remain the law that genuine problems of construction of the heads of jurisdiction will be resolved in the defendant's favour. On the other hand, if the claimant will satisfy the requirement of showing, clearly or distinctly, that England is the proper place to bring the claim, and bearing in mind the question raised earlier, as to whether the heads of jurisdiction set out in Paragraph 3.1 now serve the useful purpose which they once did, as well as the decision in *Abela v. Baadarani*, a loosening of the restrictions on the interpretation of these jurisdictional rules could be defended. It may be that the current state of the law is slightly unstable.

---

534 *The Hagen* [1908] P 189, 201; *George Monro Ltd v. American Cyanamid Corp* [1944] KB 432, 437; *The Brabo* [1949] AC 326, 357; *Mackender v. Feldia AG* [1967] 2 QB 590, 599; *The Siskina* [1979] AC 210, 254; *Newtherapeutics Ltd v. Katz* [1991] Ch 226, 256.

535 But there are a few older cases where an opposite tendency had been seen: see *Bowling v. Cox* [1926] AC 751 (contract sub-rule in what was RSC Order 11 encompasses a quasi-contractual claim); *Official Solicitor v. Stype Investments Ltd* [1983] 1 WLR 214 (contract sub-rule in what was RSC Order 11 encompassed claim based on covenant contained in declaration of trust). Now that the Grounds have been extended beyond the earlier list of heads of the then Order 11, there would be no need for such a construction today.

536 It is plainly arguable that in *Abela v. Baadarani* [2013] UKHL 44, [2013] 1 WLR 2043, [53], Lord Sumption rather understated the nature of this imposition. It may be 'a routine incident of modern commercial life', but the rules apply to non-commercial cases as well; and the very basis of the jurisdictional rules set out in the Brussels I Regulation is that defendants may expect to defend at home, not to be summoned to make their defence overseas.

537 *Seaconsar Far East Ltd v. Bank Markazi Jomhouri Islami Iran* [1994] 1 AC 438: see at 455 for the observation about the imposition of an English trial on a defendant out of the jurisdiction.

538 *Johnson v. Taylor Bros* [1920] AC 144, 153; *Metall & Rohstoff*, at 434–435; *Mercedes Benz AG v. Leiduck* [1996] 1 AC 284, 299.

539 But which is borrowed from the interpretation of the Brussels I Regulation.

540 In addition to the cases in the previous note, see also *Johnson v. Taylor Bros* [1920] AC 144, 153; *Rosler v. Hilbery* [1925] Ch 250, 259; *George Monro Ltd v. American Cyanamid Corp* [1944] KB 432, 437, 442; *Beck v. Value Capital Ltd (No 2)* [1978] 1 WLR 6.

541 *Sharab v. Al-Saud* [2009] EWCA Civ 353, [2009] 2 Lloyd's Rep 160, [35] reads rather less into the 'letter and spirit' point, regarding the 'spirit' aspect as being concerned solely with the exercise of discretion once the claim has been shown to fall within the letter of the head relied on; see also *Citigroup Global Markets Ltd v. Amatra Leveraged Feeder Holdings Ltd* [2012] EWHC 1331 (Comm), [2012] 2 CLC 279, [36].

4.63 Claims against a defendant domiciled in England: Paragraph 3.1(1)

The domicile head of jurisdiction applies if relief is sought against a person (whether individual, corporate or a partnership)[542] domiciled within the jurisdiction. Domicile, in this context, means domicile as this is defined by Schedule 1 to the Civil Jurisdiction and Judgments Order 2001,[543] and not domicile according to its common law definition. Usually, if the defendant is domiciled in England the court will have jurisdiction under the Brussels I Regulation,[544] so this head of jurisdiction is largely confined to those cases where the claim falls outside the domain of the Regulation (for example, because it is not in a civil or commercial matter), and to those cases in which the jurisdiction of the English court is governed by Article 6 of the recast Regulation in circumstances where the residual jurisdictional rules of national law – including rules on service out of the jurisdiction with permission – continue to apply.

4.64 Claims for an injunction: Paragraph 3.1(2)

The injunction head of jurisdiction[545] applies if an injunction is sought to order the defendant to do, or to refrain from doing, an act within the jurisdiction.

The injunction must be a substantial part of the relief sought; it is not permissible to make a spurious claim for an injunction as a peg upon which to hang a claim for damages or other relief,[546] or to make a claim in which only some of the acts to be restrained were within the jurisdiction.[547] While it is easy to see that an order that the defendant not do something which he is threatening to do within the jurisdiction is within this jurisdictional head, it is more difficult to argue that it applies if the claim is that he should not perform an act anywhere except England. If such a claim could be presented as one in which it is sought to order the defendant to do an act, if anywhere at all, within the jurisdiction,[548] an application for an injunction to restrain the plaintiff in foreign proceedings might conceivably be brought within this head; but no case establishes this to be the law, and it would seem to extend the provision beyond its natural meaning.

---

542 Interpretation Act 1978, Sch. 1.

543 See above, para. 2.153; and CPR r. 6.31(1)(i). This is to all intents and purposes identical to the definition in ss 41–46 of the Civil Jurisdiction and Judgments Act 1982. The 2001 Order (SI 2001/3929) is made to apply in this context by SI 2001/4015. For the meaning of domicile, and the connection which it requires, see the authority examined in para. 2.153.

544 Where, therefore, permission to serve is not needed: CPR r. 6.32 (service in Scotland or Northern Ireland), CPR r. 6.33 (service outside the United Kingdom).

545 Formerly RSC Order 11, r. 1(1)(b), which added the words 'whether or not damages are also claimed in respect of a failure to do or the doing of that thing'. Their omission is not significant if it is assumed that a claim for damages in the alternative to an injunction will not be struck out as falling outside this head of jurisdiction, and bearing further in mind the fact that a claim for damages in lieu of an injunction must be within this head.

546 *Rosler v. Hilbery* [1925] 1 Ch 250; *GAF v. Amchem* [1975] 1 Lloyd's Rep 601.

547 *Conductive Inkjet Technology Ltd v. Uni-Pixel Displays Inc* [2013] EWHC 2968 (Ch), [2014] All ER (Comm) 654 (worldwide injunction not within the sub-Paragraph): in this respect the sub-Paragraph does not reflect the way in which sub-Paragraph (9) is read, which is satisfied if some acts or damage are located within the jurisdiction, even though other acts and damage are not: see below, para. 4.73.

548 Or to refrain from issuing instructions from within the jurisdiction. In a very different context, but where the obligation lacked any particular place for performance and was therefore to be performed everywhere and nowhere in particular, see C-256/00 *Besix SA v. WABAG* [2002] ECR I-1699.

An application for an order against the defendant requiring him to account within the jurisdiction was held[549] not to fall within a predecessor version of the injunction head. An order for payment of money was not in this context to be regarded as falling within the natural meaning of the reference to an injunction.[550] That seems correct.

It was also held in relation to an earlier version of this head of jurisdiction[551] that it applied only to an injunction sought in relation to substantive rights. It was for that reason inapplicable to proceedings brought to obtain only a freezing order[552] against a defendant who was out of the jurisdiction but who had assets within the jurisdiction, and over whom the only basis of jurisdiction was service out under the predecessor to what is now Paragraph 3.1(2).[553] This conclusion was supported by the fact that RSC Order 11 allowed service to be authorised 'if in the action begun by the writ … an injunction was sought…'. As an application for a freezing order did not seek to determine substantive rights, and did not constitute an action, it did not fall within the rule as it then was. The current version of the rule might have removed this limitation, so that a court could grant permission to serve a claim form out of the jurisdiction if a claim were made for an injunction even if not in relation to substantive rights, thereby reversing the effect of *Mercedes Benz AG v. Leiduck*;[554] but this view did not commend itself to the court in *Cool Carriers AB v. HSBC Bank USA*.[555] As there is a separate head of jurisdiction[556] for service out of a claim form in which an interim remedy is claimed, this question may now be of limited practical importance. Nevertheless, the result is that, if the claim for an injunction, of whatever kind, is well founded as a matter of arguable fact and law, the injunction head presents no obvious additional obstacle to an application for permission to serve out.

4.65 Claims made against someone who is a necessary or proper party to a claim against another: Paragraph 3.1(3)

The necessary or proper party head of jurisdiction[557] applies if the claim is made against a defendant, D1, who has been or will be served, and D2 is a necessary or proper party to that claim.

An earlier version of this head[558] had required that D1 have been served, whether within or out of the jurisdiction, before the application for permission to serve a necessary or proper party was made. But this limitation has been removed, and all that is required is that D1 have been served, or be someone who will be served otherwise than in reliance on this same head. It is not entirely clear whether this condition is satisfied if an application for permission

---

549 *ISC Technologies v. Radcliffe*, 7 December 1990. The court was unwilling to stretch the meaning of the sub-rule. The decision was followed in *ISC Technologies v. Guerin* [1992] 2 Lloyd's Rep 430.

550 In the light of Paragraph 3.1(15) and (16), which had no direct predecessor in Order 11 as it applied to that case, this conclusion may be of reduced importance.

551 RSC Order 11, r. 1(1)(b).

552 Then known as a *Mareva* injunction.

553 *Mercedes Benz AG v. Leiduck* [1996] 1 AC 284.

554 [1996] 1 AC 284.

555 [2001] 2 Lloyd's Rep 22.

556 Paragraph 3.1(5).

557 Formerly RSC Order 11, r. 1(1)(c). There is no basis for the submission that Paragraph 3.1(3) is any narrower than sub-rule (c) had been: *United Film Distribution Ltd v. Chhabria* [2001] EWCA Civ 416, [2001] 2 All ER (Comm) 865, applied in *Trumann Investment Group Ltd v. Société Générale SA* [2004] EWHC 1769 (Ch).

558 RSC Order 11, r. 1(1)(c).

to serve D1 out of the jurisdiction is made at the same time as the application to serve D2, for until permission is obtained it cannot be said, and therefore cannot really be said in the witness statement, that D1 *will* be served. But nothing prevents the applications being made sequentially, so that if the court grants permission in respect of D1 it can immediately hear and determine an application to grant permission in respect of D2; and, if this is accepted, it will suffice that D1 is someone in respect of whom an application for permission to serve[559] will also be made.[560] This head of jurisdiction is available only when the claimant who is proceeding against D1 wishes to serve D2 as well; it does not apply to Part 20 claims, which are covered by Paragraph 3.1(4).[561]

This head of jurisdiction imposes distinct conditions in respect of the claims against D1 and D2.[562] So far as concerns D1, it is required that he be someone on whom the claim form has been or will be served, but the basis on which the court has jurisdiction over him is immaterial. It is no longer required[563] that D1 have been *duly* served, but if D1 has been served in a manner which is irregular and could be contested by D1, it may be argued that the jurisdiction is not available. On the other hand, irregular service is still service, and irregularity is almost always curable;[564] and an application for service by alternative means may be made in an appropriate case. And anyway, if the claimant is in any event able to re-serve D1, and thereby allow him to be described as someone who will be served, there appears to be no reason to read back into the rule a limitation that D1 must have been *duly* served.[565] It seems that this requirement is, one way or another, very easy to satisfy.[566]

Second, there must be between the claimant and D1 a real issue which it is reasonable for the court to try.[567] The justification for this is the obvious one that D1 may not be put up as a spurious defendant to give jurisdictional cover for a claim which is, in reality, only intended to be advanced against D2 who could not otherwise be brought within the jurisdiction;[568]

---

559 But not under Paragraph 3.1(3), obviously. It would have been better if the legislative text had made it clear that service on D1 had to be based on something other than this *sub*-paragraph, rather than *paragraph*, but the sense of the law is clear enough without it: see *Alliance Bank JSC v. Aquanta Corp* [2012] EWCA Civ 1588, [2013] 1 Lloyd's Rep 175, [77]–[79].

560 *Joint Stock Asset Management Co Ingosstrakh-Investments v. BNP Paribas SA* [2012] EWCA Civ 644, [2012] 1 Lloyd's Rep 649 holds that it is sufficient that D1, who has not been served, will be served by alternative means. Indeed, it now seems improbable that this part of the rule furnishes any obstacle to service on D2 unless the court is of opinion that the claimant has no intention to sue the other person whose name appears on the writ.

561 See para. 4.66, below.

562 For a general analysis which serves as a convenient starting point, see *AK Investment CJSC v. Kyrgyz Mobil Tel Ltd* [2011] UKPC 7, [2012] 1 WLR 1804.

563 As it was under RSC Order 11, r. 1(1)(c).

564 Both points are supported by CPR r. 3.10, which deals with errors of procedure and the powers of the court to remedy them; see also *Joint Stock Asset Management Co Ingosstrakh-Investments v. BNP Paribas SA* [2012] EWCA Civ 644, [2012] 1 Lloyd's Rep 649.

565 It may be different if the claim form is no longer valid for service on D1, at least until an application to extend the validity of the claim form for service has been successfully made, or a new claim form issued. Otherwise the proposition that D1 *will* be served is tenuous.

566 *Joint Stock Asset Management Co Ingosstrakh-Investments v. BNP Paribas SA* [2012] EWCA Civ 644, [2012] 1 Lloyd's Rep 649.

567 Paragraph 3.1(3), condition (a).

568 This may be so where the claim against D1 is mostly spurious, or where D1 has few assets and the claim against it is not really serious and may be discontinued soon after permission to join D2 has been granted and acted upon: *OJSC Oil Co Yugraneft v. Abramovich* [2008] EWHC 2613 (Comm) *Cf Witted v. Galbraith* [1893] 1 QB 577; *Derby & Co Ltd v. Larsson* [1976] 1 All ER 401.

the claim against D1 must be substantive in nature.[569] On the other hand it is certainly no part of the rule that D1 be the principal defendant: the question is simply whether there was, when permission was applied for, a claim against the local defendant which the court may be asked to try.

CPR rule 6.37(2) requires the claimant's written evidence to state the grounds on which the person making the statement believes this condition to be met. The Privy Council has concluded that if a court considers that if D1 is sued only for the purpose of bringing D2 before the court, the head of jurisdiction is available in relation to D2, but the court may exercise its discretion against permitting service;[570] it seems that the same approach will apply when there is good reason to suppose that the claim against D1 will not be prosecuted once D2 has been served. However, the condition in rule 6.37(2) cannot be satisfied if the claim against D1 is manifestly doomed to fail;[571] it is also unlikely that it can be satisfied if the claim against D1 is liable to be stayed on grounds of *forum non conveniens*.[572]

In a case in which D1 is domiciled in England, this is liable to produce a remarkable effect. In *Owusu v. Jackson*[573] the second to sixth defendants were Jamaican, but D1 was domiciled in England. Once the European Court had ruled that the English court had no power to stay proceedings against D1, it appeared to follow that the second to sixth defendants were liable to have service on them out of the jurisdiction upheld, on the wholly orthodox ground that the claim against the six defendants should be disposed of in a single proceeding. It is not known whether this actually happened, but the consequence of widening the effective jurisdiction of the English court over D1 seemed likely to have an impact on defendants who, but for the decision in *Owusu v. Jackson*, would have been allowed as a matter of English private international law to make their defence in their home courts. No clear conclusion can be drawn. It is startling to think that the non-European defendants ought to be prejudiced by a Regulation which has no application to them; but it is for English law, not for the Regulation, to ensure that national rules of jurisdiction do not misfire or overreach themselves. The issue is whether the traditional concern for disposing of the issues in a single trial still operates in a case in which the Regulation prevents the English court from exercising a jurisdictional discretion, in the way in which the common law allowed, over one of the defendants.[574]

In partial response to this, it has been suggested that where the claim against a local defendant is really too peripheral to the main dispute to allow it to be used as a hook with which to catch the overseas defendant, even if it appears to be sustainable on the facts and liable to be pursued to judgment, the judge might 'loose the chain' and set aside service

---

569 *Cruz City 1 Mauritius Holdings v Unitech Ltd* [2014] EWHC 3704 (Comm).

570 *AK Investment CJSC v. Kyrgyz Mobil Tel Ltd* [2011] UKPC 7, [2012] 1 WLR 1804, [79], relying on *The Brabo* [1949] AC 326; *Derby & Co Ltd v. Larsson* [1976] 1 All ER 401.

571 *AK Investment CJSC v. Kyrgyz Mobil Tel Ltd* [2011] UKPC 7, [2012] 1 WLR 1804, [80]; *The Brabo* [1949] AC 326. The question whether the claim against D1 is doomed to fail is, in principle, the same as asking whether it would be struck out: *AK Investment CJSC v. Kyrgyz Mobil Tel Ltd* [2011] UKPC 7, [2012] 1 WLR 1804, [81]–[86].

572 *Pacific International Sports Clubs Ltd v. Surkis* [2010] EWCA Civ 753, [55]; see also *JSC BTA Bank v. Granton Trade Ltd* [2010] EWHC 2577 (Comm), [2011] 2 All ER (Comm) 542.

573 Case C-281/02, [2005] ECR I-1383.

574 For the view that the English court should not allow *Owusu* to overshadow the analysis and cause an English court to assert a jurisdiction which would otherwise be inappropriate, see *Pacific International Sports Clubs Ltd v. Soccer Marketing International Ltd* [2010] EWCA Civ 753, [42]–[44].

made under this head.[575] But the precise basis for this was not explained. The correct analysis may be that if the court would have set aside service if it had not been for the decision in *Owusu*, it should still generally set it aside notwithstanding the effect of *Owusu*. Perhaps there is a sense, still underdeveloped in the jurisprudence, that a court has power to prevent abusive use of the Regulation, and that this is an area in which the extension of the effect of the Regulation goes beyond its proper purpose. But the answer is, as yet, not clear to see.

So far as concerns D2, he must be a necessary or proper party to the claim against D1. The terms are disjunctive. The point of departure is to ask whether, if D2 were subject to the jurisdiction of the court, it would be appropriate for the claimant to join him to the claim against D1 as co-defendant.[576] If the answer is affirmative, he will in all probability be a proper party to the claim, but if the two claims, though each is sustainable, are not, on analysis, bound up with each other, the court should not exercise its discretion in favour of service out.[577] It is at this point that a court will need to be astute to distinguish between cases in which the connection between the claims against D1 and D2 are genuinely or naturally connected, and those in which the apparent connection really only arises from artful or self-servingly broad pleading.

Of course, if there is no pleaded or sustainable claim against D2, or the claim against D2 is not well founded in fact and law, the present state of the law is that he will not be a proper party no matter how closely bound up with the claim against D1 he may be.[578] For example, it has been held that a defendant is not properly joined if the only purpose of applying to do so is to obtain an order for disclosure[579] against him,[580] but there is inevitable pressure to relax this view where there is reason to believe that D2 is sufficiently mixed up in the activity of D1 for there to be a risk of injustice, even if no substantive relief is sought against D2, if D2 is not made party to the proceedings, even if only for procedural purposes.[581] But if the addition of D2 will secure no real advantage to the claimant, it is harder to see that he will be a proper party.[582] It is unnecessary, however, for the claimant to plead that D1 and D2 are jointly or

---

575 *OJSC Oil Co Yugraneft v. Abramovich* [2008] EWHC 2613 (Comm), [490].

576 *AK Investment CJSC v. Kyrgyz Mobil Tel Ltd* [2011] UKPC 7, [2012] 1 WLR 1804, [87]; *Carvill America Inc v. Camperdown UK Ltd* [2005] EWCA Civ 645, [2005] 2 Lloyd's Rep 457. If he is scheming to undermine a contract by which D1 is bound to the claimant he will be liable to be served under this provision: *Joint Stock Asset Management Co Ingosstrakh-Investments v. BNP Paribas SA* [2012] EWCA Civ 644, [2012] 1 Lloyd's Rep 649.

577 *AK Investment CJSC v. Kyrgyz Mobil Tel Ltd* [2011] UKPC 7, [2012] 1 WLR 1804. The point is made in various ways, including occasional use of the imagery of tails not being permitted to wag dogs, but in the end the analysis will be intensely fact-specific, and each case is really only authority for its own facts. For an illustration (only), see *Standard Bank plc v. Just Group LLC* [2014] EWHC 2687 (Comm).

578 For the proper interpretation of this description of the claim, see *Citigroup Global Markets Ltd v. Amatra Leveraged Feeder Holdings Ltd* [2012] EWHC 1331 (Comm), [2012] 2 CLC 279, [64]–[66].

579 Previously 'discovery'.

580 *Mölnlycke v. Procter & Gamble Ltd* [1992] 1 WLR 1112; *Unilever plc v. Chefaro Proprietaries Ltd* [1994] FSR 135 (cases under what is now Art. 8(1) of the recast Brussels I Regulation). Given the specific power under the Senior Courts Act 1981, s. 34 and CPR r. 25.1(1)(j) to order disclosure against non-parties, this careful scheme is not intended to be circumvented by the routine joinder of non-parties.

581 For example, *C Inc plc v. L* [2001] 2 Lloyd's Rep 459 (joinder of party against whom no substantive relief sought on ground of being trustee of assets for D1, and a proper party for the purposes of freezing those assets in aid of enforcement; though held that procedure was by application notice rather than claim form, in light of *Mercedes-Benz AG v. Leiduck* [1996] 1 AC 284). But for the view that so far as the claim against D1 is concerned, it must be in respect of a substantive claim, rather than something such as enforcement proceedings, see *Cruz City 1 Mauritius Holdings v. Unitech Ltd* [2014] EWHC 3704 (Comm).

582 *Electric Furnace Co v. Selas Corp of America* [1987] RPC 23, 32–33 (distinguished *Apex Global Management Ltd v. Fi Call Ltd* [2013] EWHC 1652 (Ch)).

severally liable.[583] If to allow service out would violate an agreement on choice of court, the court will need to balance the competing interests – in enforcing agreements on jurisdiction; on ensuring that those who ought to be dealt with in a single set of proceedings appropriately – with care. It seems reasonable to suppose that the answer will be very fact-specific.

By contrast with the corresponding rule of the Brussels I Regulation,[584] it is not specifically required that the claims against D1 and D2 be so closely connected that it is necessary to hear them together to avoid the risk of irreconcilable judgments: the necessary *or proper* party head is more flexible and wider in its scope. So if there are common questions of fact arising out of the same series of transactions, a decision to permit service out cannot be criticised. It is obviously irrelevant that there is no other basis on which jurisdiction over D2 could be asserted, for if this were so Ground (3) would be redundant.[585] However, this also means that D2 may be made subject to the jurisdiction of the English court even though he has, by himself, done nothing whatever which would have allowed the court to take jurisdiction over him apart from this rule: a state of affairs which some may consider to be unprincipled, and which may appear to offer too much of an opportunity for creative pleading. This fact should, no doubt, cause a court to be cautious before concluding that D2 is sufficiently involved with D1 to render him jurisdictionally liable by association: personal jurisdiction by association is, in some minds, only marginally more attractive than guilt by association. Of course, the fact that D2 would have had a complete defence if sued where he resided will not necessarily mean that he is not a proper party to the claim before the English court.[586]

4.66 Claims made under Part 20 of the Civil Procedure Rules: Paragraph 3.1(4)

The Part 20 claim head of jurisdiction[587] extends the principles underpinning the necessary or proper party head of jurisdiction to what are now called Part 20 claims and what were previously, and perhaps more transparently, known as counterclaims and third party claims.

Service in respect of a claim falling within CPR Part 20 may be authorised if the person to be served is a necessary or proper party to the claim made against the Part 20 claimant. It was found to be necessary to make separate provision for Part 20 claims as the wording of what now appears as Paragraph 3.1(3) did not allow[588] a defendant to a claim to take advantage of it when seeking to join a third party from whom he sought a contribution or an indemnity, or when seeking to extend the scope of a counterclaim to parties other than the existing claimant.[589] Such procedural possibilities are grouped together as 'Part 20 claims'; and Paragraph

---

583 *Österreichische Export Co v. British Indemnity Co Ltd* [1914] 2 KB 747. If the claim is that either D1 or D2 is liable, but the claimant does not currently know which, jurisdiction may be established under this rule: the idea that this conclusion is prevented by a requirement that the claimant have much the better of the argument that D2 is liable is misconceived: *Virgin Atlantic Airways v. KT Holdings Co Ltd* [2014] EWHC 1671 (Comm).

584 Article 8(1) of the recast Brussels I Regulation; see further above, paras 2.225 *et seq.*

585 Joinder of *claimants* is not covered by the paragraph, but for a case of joinder where it was hard to see that the claimants had any substantive basis for a claim against the defendants at all, see *Donohue v. Armco Inc.* [2000] 1 Lloyd's Rep 579. The reversal of this decision by the House of Lords: [2001] UKHL 64, [2002] 1 Lloyd's Rep 425 appears to confirm that the Ground (or previous sub-rule) does not apply to the joinder of claimants.

586 *Petroleo Brasiliero SA v. Mellitus Shipping Inc* [2001] EWCA Civ 418, [2001] 2 Lloyd's Rep 203, discussed below in relation to Paragraph 3.1(4).

587 Formerly RSC Order 11, r. 1(1)(c); RSC Order 16, r. 3(4).

588 By contrast with its predecessor, RSC Order 11, r. 1(1)(c) as extended by RSC Order 16, r. 3(4).

589 There is no need to obtain permission to serve a claimant, even if foreign, who has invoked and submitted to the jurisdiction of the court.

3.1(4) deals with service of the document by which they are claimed. The principles are essentially those which underpin the necessary or proper party head of jurisdiction, except that as the defendant or Part 20 claimant will already have been served and will participate in the proceedings as a defendant, there is no need to show that anyone else will be served. All that is required to satisfy this jurisdictional rule[590] is that the non-party, against whom the Part 20 claimant wishes to advance a claim of his own, is a necessary or proper party to the claim. Where the defendant to the Part 20 claim can show that he would not be liable if sued in the State of his residence, this fact does not necessarily mean that he is not a proper party to the claim, although, in the exercise of its discretion, the court may consider whether it is unjust to expose the Part 20 defendant to such liability as an English court will impose on him.[591]

4.67 Claims for interim remedies: Paragraph 3.1(5)

The interim remedy head of jurisdiction[592] provides that a claim form by means of which the claimant seeks interim remedies under Civil Jurisdiction and Judgments Act 1982, section 25(1) may be served out of the jurisdiction. Section 25, as extended, gives the court a wide power to grant interim relief in aid of proceedings to be brought in England or elsewhere; it would be irrational if there were no means of serving the claim form seeking such relief on a defendant or respondent who happened to be out of the jurisdiction.

As a matter of English law, permission to serve out will not be granted unless England is the proper place to bring the claim for such relief,[593] and if the English court has no jurisdiction over the substantive claim, the court may conclude that it is inexpedient to grant the relief sought and, if that is so, permission to serve out will be refused. But where the defendant is domiciled in a Member State, and is subject to the international jurisdiction of the English court only by reason of Article 35 of the recast Regulation, as the case may be, the Regulation places further limitations on the power of the court to grant relief. The interlocking of these various provisions is not free of complexity, and is examined in detail in Chapter 6. But in cases where the defendant is not within the territorial jurisdiction of the English court, and can be served only with the permission of the court, this head of jurisdiction provides the basis for making the application.

4.68 Claims made in respect of a contract: Paragraph 3.1(6), (7), and (8)

The contract heads of jurisdiction, which allow service out of the jurisdiction to be authorised when the claim is made in respect of a contract, are simpler and more straightforward than were their predecessors.[594] The current version contains three provisions which deal with contract claims. Paragraph 3.1(6) deals with claims made in respect of a contract in cases in which the contract meets one of four requirements: that it was made in England, or that it was made through an agent trading or residing in England, or that it was governed by English law, or that it provides for the English court to have jurisdiction. If the contract

---

590 There are, however, additional requirements and limitations which are imposed by Part 20 itself for the making of a Part 20 claim. See also *Knauf (UK) GmbH v. British Gypsum Ltd* [2002] EWHC 739 (Comm), [2002] 2 Lloyd's Rep 416.

591 *Petroleo Brasiliero SA v. Mellitus Shipping Inc*; see below, para. 4.92.

592 Formerly RSC Order 11, r. 8A.

593 CPR r. 6.37(3).

594 RSC Order 11, r. 1(1)(d) and (e).

falls within any one of these, the only further requirement is that a claim is made in respect of the contract. Where the claim is made for a declaration that no such contract exists, the claim falls within Paragraph 3.1(8).

Paragraph 3.1(7), by contrast, deals with claims made in respect of a breach of any contract. The breach must have taken place within the jurisdiction, but the contract is not required to fall within the conditions applicable to the other paragraphs. For the purposes of exposition, it makes sense to consider sub-Paragraphs (6) and (8) together, and sub-Paragraph (7) separately.

For the contract heads of jurisdiction to apply at all, there must first be 'a contract'. Previous versions of the rule interpreted this as meaning that there was required to be a contract[595] to which both the claimant and defendant were parties.[596] Some doubt has been raised by the observation that to interpret 'a contract' as though it said 'a contract between the claimant and defendant' was to read in words which were not there,[597] though later decisions have been more sceptical, and have preferred and followed the more traditional construction.[598] But the rule is surely satisfied by a showing that the claimant is a person to whom the contract gave enforceable rights, albeit as a third party; and if a claim in such a case is to fall within the rule, it cannot be denied that there is a degree of flexibility in the requirement that the parties be privy to the contract in question. That being so, the proper question is whether the claim is sufficiently connected to the contract to be able to say that it arises 'in respect of' that contract. Cases in which the relief claimed is not founded on the existence of a contractual right, but will determine the liability of contracting parties to each other, are bound to test the meaning and extent of the words 'in respect of' a contract.[599] It

---

595 *Bowling v. Cox* [1926] AC 751 and *Re Jogia* [1988] 1 WLR 484 established that a quasi-contractual claim was also within the previous sub-rule. It is not clear that this interpretation should be followed today as more obvious provision is made for such cases by Paragraph 3.1(15), (16); and in *Sharab v. Al-Waleed* [2012] EWHC 1798 (Ch), [2012] 2 CLC 612 it was held that a claim founded on there being no contract and seeking payment of a *quantum meruit* was not within sub-paragraph (6). On the other hand, if the claimant seeks to enforce a contract, but in the alternative claims *quantum meruit* if the court finds that there is no contract, it would surely be unacceptable for the court to have jurisdiction over only part of the claim.

Whether 'a contract' will include an agreement to share ownership of property, which agreement equity will protect and give effect to by finding that the registered proprietor holds the legal estate on constructive trust, is unclear. In *Lloyd's Bank plc v. Rossett* [1991] 1 AC 107 and *Stack v. Dowden* [2007] UKHL 17, [2007] 2 AC 432, the House of Lords established that an agreement, which had been detrimentally relied on, to share ownership of land, was enforceable in equity, and that what was enforced was the parties' agreement. In such cases of casual co-ownership, there will frequently not be a *contract*; it is uncertain whether such a claim, founded on a looser form of agreement, would come within this rule.

596 *Finnish Marine Insurance Co v. Protective National Insurance Co* [1990] 1 QB 1078; originally, or by assignment or by statutory means: *Schiffahrtsgesellschaft Detlev von Appen GmbH v. Vöst Alpine Intertrading GmbH (The Jay Bola)* [1997] 2 Lloyd's Rep 279; *Maritrop Trading Corp v. Guangzhou* [1998] CLC 224; *Youell v. Kara Mara Shipping Co* [2000] 2 Lloyd's Rep 102 (direct statutory action against insurer).

597 *Greene Wood & McClean LLP v. Templeton Insurance Ltd* [2009] EWCA Civ 65, [2009] 1 WLR 2013.

598 *Alliance Bank JSC v. Aquanta Corp* [2012] EWCA Civ 1588, [2013] 1 Lloyd's Rep 175; *Erste Group Bank AG v. JSC 'VMZ Red October'* [2013] EWHC 2926 (Comm); *Navig8 Pte Ltd v. Al-Riyadh Co for Vegetable Oil Industry* [2013] EWHC 328 (Comm), [2013] 2 Lloyd's Rep 104; *Brownlie v. Four Seasons Holdings Inc* [2014] EWHC 273 (QB) (where there was no doubt that there was a contract, but service on the hotel was only permissible if it was sufficiently shown to be a party to the contract); *Surrey (UK) Ltd v. Mazandaran Wood & Paper Industries* [2014] EWHC 3165 (Comm) (where it was taken to be obvious that if the claimant could not show that it was party to the contract, this head of jurisdiction could not be satisfied).

599 See for example *Albon v. Naza Motor Trading Sdn Bhd* [2007] EWHC 9 (Ch), [2007] 1 WLR 2489 (restitutionary claim relating to contract, and making point that 'in respect of' a contract is wider in material scope than 'under' a contract); *Global 5000 Ltd v. Wadhawan* [2012] EWCA Civ 13, [2012] 1 Lloyd's Rep 239; *Greene Wood & McLean LLP v. Templeton Insurance Ltd* [2009] EWCA Civ 65, [2009] 1 CLC 123 (contribution claim

may be that excessive attention to the precise ambit of the phrase 'in respect of' may give rise to fussy points of interpretation, in an unconscious echo of the case law which grew up around the interpretation of similar language in jurisdiction agreements, and which was condemned as bringing no credit on the law by *Fiona Trust & Holding Corp v. Privalov*.[600] For example, may a claim against a defendant who negligently induced the claimant to enter into a contract with another be brought under this head of jurisdiction? There is a clear and obvious sense in which a claim may be said to relate to the contract, for the entry into the contract is the event which completes the cause of action for negligent misrepresentation; and it may be thought to follow that the claim is in respect of the contract. But this path does not appear to have been trodden yet. For another, can a claim against a defendant which alleges that he induced another to breach a contract be brought within this head of jurisdiction? The indications from the case law are ambivalent, but if one interprets 'in respect of' in a looser sense, to mean that the contract is an essential part of the cause of action even if not the legal foundation of the claim against the defendant, it may yet be possible.[601]

Service out may still be authorised if the claimant asserts that there was a contract which he was entitled to rescind; and in the light of sub-Paragraph (8), service out may be authorised even though the claimant asserts that the contract alleged against him was, as far as he is concerned, a nullity: the reference to 'a contract' therefore means 'a contract or a contract which is alleged by one party but denied by the other'. The question whether the provisions will apply to a case in which both parties are agreed that there was no contract between them, but relief is still sought, is considered below.[602]

As indicated above, the requirement that there be a contract as a matter of English private international law follows from *Amin Rasheed Shipping Corp v. Kuwait Insurance Co*,[603] which established that whether there is a contract must be determined in an appropriate case by the rules of the English conflict of laws. The method of enquiry would appear to be as follows. It must first be asked whether the defendant admits that there is a contract. If he does, no difficulty arises. If instead he denies that there is a contract, English law must be used to decide whether there is a contract. This may, if either party takes the point, involve the application of the rules of English private international law: in *Amin Rasheed* the answer was provided by the common law principle that the validity and existence of a contract is

---

against person not party to the contract still 'in respect of' the contract: this may not be wholly reliable); *Cherney v. Deripaska* [2009] EWCA 849, [2010] 1 All ER (Comm) 456 (claim to enforce trust said to arise from contract 'in respect of' the contract alleged to provide the basis for it. A claim for relief which is ancillary to a contractual claim will fall within the paragraph if the contract itself does, but it was also held that a claim for financial relief in relation to unconscionable or inequitable conduct is not within the paragraph, as it is not sought in relation to a contract: *Golden Endurance Shipping SA v. RMA Watanya SA* [2014] EWHC 3927 (Comm); to similar effect, *Navig8 Pte Ltd v. Al-Riyadh Co for Vegetable Oil Industry* [2013] EWHC 328 (Comm), [2013] 2 Lloyd's Rep 104. In *Fern Computer Consultancy Ltd v. Intergraph Cadworx & Analysis Solutions Ltd* [2014] EWHC 2908 (Ch), [2015] 1 Lloyd's Rep 1 it was considered that a claim for a statutory payment under the Commercial Agents (Council Directive) Regulations 1992 could be said to be made in relation to a contract, but as the substantive contract was, by express choice, governed by Texas law, there was no provision of sub-paragraph (6) which applied to it. See also *Shipowner's Mutual P&I Association (Luxembourg) v. Containerships Denizcilik Nakliyat ve Ticaret as* [2015] EWHC 258 (Comm).

600 [2007] UKHL 40, [2007] Bus LR 1719; see above, para. 4.42.

601 However, *Alliance Bank JSC v. Aquanta Corp* [2012] EWCA Civ 1588, [2013] 1 Lloyd's Rep 175, is sceptical about the proposition that a non-party may be served by reference to sub-Paragraph (6) where the allegation is that he induced another to breach a contract. In such a set of facts, it is not the contract, but his alleged tort, which links the defendant to the jurisdiction. See also *Shipowner's Mutual P&I Association (Luxembourg) v. Containerships Denizcilik Nakliyat ve Ticaret as* [2015] EWHC 258 (Comm).

602 See para. 4.69 below.

603 [1984] AC 50.

determined by its proper law. If there is a contract according to the law which would determine this issue as a matter of English private international law,[604] this part of the rule may be satisfied. But if English private international law yields the answer that there is no contract, this jurisdictional rule is not satisfied.

4.69 Claims relying on sub–Paragraphs (6) and (8): the contract and its connection to England

In order for the claim to fall within sub–Paragraphs (6) or (8), whatever the relief sought, the contract must satisfy one of four possible connections to England. These four connections are set out in sub–Paragraph (6).

The first point of connection is that the contract was made in England.[605] On the face of it, a contract is made in England if, according to the rules on English domestic law governing when, where and how contracts are made, the contract in question was made in England: this question, which is essentially one of geography, is not answered by making reference to rules of private international law, and is not therefore answered by reference to the law which governs the contract according to those rules. It was once generally assumed that it is instead answered by English domestic law. So if acceptance is made by post, the contract was made where the letter of acceptance is posted; if acceptance is made by electronic means, such as a telephone, telex or fax, then at the place where the acceptance is (or should be) received by the offeror.[606] However, there are some cases which appear to treat this requirement as though it raised little more than a question of fact:[607] it has been held that a contract may be made within the jurisdiction even though there had been a prior, rather less formal, agreement made elsewhere;[608] it has been held that a contract may be made in two places at once, with the consequence that if one of those places is England, the rule still applies.[609] This conclusion may be open to question, but if the rule asks where the contract was *made*, as distinct from where it was *concluded*, the answer may be that it is right: a contract may be concluded in one place but made in two.

It will appear in some cases that the place where the contract was made was a matter of chance,[610] or (which is much the same thing) the result of the forum's domestic law of offer and acceptance. It may follow that claims which are brought under this head will not routinely appear as those for which England is clearly the appropriate forum. However, where the facts disclose that the contract was deliberately, or at least consciously, made in England, the fact that the claim falls within this sub–Paragraph will make it a little easier to show England as the most appropriate forum for disputes relating to it.[611]

---

604 Which today is likely to mean the Rome I Regulation.

605 Paragraph 3.1(6)(a).

606 *Entores v. Miles Far East Corp* [1955] 2 QB 327; *Brinkibon Ltd v. Stahag Stahl und Stahlwarenhandels GmbH* [1983] 2 AC 34. There appears to be no reported decision on contracts made by electronic mail, though ordinary contractual principle would suggest that it is where the acceptance comes, or should have come, to the attention of the offeror: this will be where he reads his email in the ordinary course of events.

607 *Arab Business Corporation International Finance & Investment Co v. Banque Franco-Tunisienne* [2003] EWCA Civ 205, [2003] 2 Lloyd's Rep 146; *cf Surrey (UK) Ltd v. Mazandaran Wood & Paper Industries* [2014] EWHC 3165 (Comm) (various acts done in England falling short of being an acceptance).

608 *Gibbon v. Commerz und Creditbank AG* [1958] 2 Lloyd's Rep 113.

609 *Apple Corps Ltd v. Apple Computer Inc* [2004] EWHC 768 (Ch), [2004] ILPr 597; *Conductive Inkjet Technology Ltd v. Uni-Pixel Displays Inc* [2013] EWHC 2968 (Ch), [2014] 1 All ER (Comm) 654.

610 *Brownlie v. Four Seasons Holdings Inc* [2014] EWHC 273 (QB).

611 So deduced from *Sharab v. Al-Saud* [2009] EWCA Civ 353, [2009] 2 Lloyd's Rep 160.

The second point of connection is that the contract was made by or through an agent trading or residing in England.[612] Because the sub-Paragraph says 'by or through', it is not necessary that the agent concluded the contract himself; it is sufficient that he acted as the conduit through which the principal and claimant made the contract.

The third point of connection is that the contract is governed by English law.[613] In relation to contracts not made in a civil or commercial matter this will mean that English law is the proper law of the contract. In relation to contracts made after 1 April 1991, this means that the contract is governed by English law according to the rules of the Rome Convention on the Law Applicable to Contractual Obligations;[614] and in relation to contracts concluded after 17 December 2009, it will mean that the contract is governed by English law according to the rules of the Rome I Regulation. But the discrepancies between the three, mutually-exclusive, systems for discerning the law which applies to the contract are relatively small.[615]

It has been said that where sub-Paragraph (6)(c) is relied on, and the contract is governed by English law, the court is required to be particularly cautious about applications for permission to serve out.[616] It is hard to see why this should be so. The fact that English law governs the contract will assist in arriving at the conclusion that England is the proper place in which to bring the claim, with the consequences, surely, that there is no need for any particular caution about the application of this sub-Paragraph. If, despite the fact that English law governs the contract, the claimant is unable to show that England is the proper place to bring the claim, there is no need to dwell on the application of sub-Paragraph (6)(c). If English law has been expressly chosen but it is apprehended that the relevant foreign court may not apply English law, the case for allowing service out will be strong; where English law may be said to be applicable by reason of an implied choice of law, the argument will be a little less strong;[617] and where it applies in the absence of choice, the case for service out will be the least strong. All this can be taken into account as part of the enquiry whether England is the proper place to bring the claim, which provides the context in which the

---

612 Paragraph 3.1(6)(b). It is the defendant, not the claimant, who must be the principal to the contract which was made through an agent within the jurisdiction: *Union International Insurance Co Ltd v. Jubilee Insurance Co Ltd* [1991] 1 WLR 415. Note also that if the conditions of sub-Paragraph (6)(b) are satisfied, and also at the time of application for permission to serve the agent's authority has not been terminated, or he is still in business relations with the principal, the court may authorise service of the process to be made on the agent instead of the principal: CPR r. 6.12. A copy of the claim form and the order giving permission must also be sent to the principal who is out of the jurisdiction.

613 Paragraph 3.1(6)(c). Though the issue arises later in this chapter, it should be noted that the fact that a contract is governed by English law does not necessarily compel the conclusion that permission to serve out must be granted; the earlier view that it was sufficient in almost every case was doubted in *Amin Rasheed Shipping Corp v. Kuwait Insurance Co* [1984] AC 50, 68; *Novus Aviation Ltd v. Onur Air Tasimacilik A/S* [2009] EWCA Civ 122, [2009] 1 Lloyd's Rep 576. The fact that the contract is governed by English law is a factor whose weight will vary from case to case. But it is submitted that if the parties have expressly chosen English law, and if the court which would otherwise have jurisdiction would not give effect to such a clause, there is a strong case to grant leave to serve out in order to avoid what would, indirectly, amount to a breach of contract. And see para. 4.50, above.

614 Contracts (Applicable Law) Act 1990; see also *Bank of Baroda v. Vysya Bank Ltd* [1994] 2 Lloyd's Rep 87; *Egon Oldendorff v. Libera Corp* [1995] 2 Lloyd's Rep 64.

615 *Egon Oldendorff v. Libera Corp.*

616 *Ilyssia Compania Naviera SA v. Bamaodah, 'The Elli 2'* [1985] 1 Lloyd's Rep 107, 113; *Spiliada Maritime Corp v. Cansulex Ltd* [1987] AC 460, 480; *Amin Rasheed Shipping Corp v. Kuwait Insurance Co* [1984] AC 50, 65, 66 (all referred to without further comment in *Novus Aviation Ltd v. Onur Air Tasimacilik AS* [2009] EWCA Civ 122, [2009] 1 Lloyd's Rep 576, [53]).

617 *Stonebridge Underwriting Ltd v. Ontario Municipal Insurance Exchange* [2010] EWHC 2279 (Comm), [2011] Lloyd's Rep IR 171.

evaluation of the significance of English as the governing law will take place, and that is enough.[618]

The fourth point of connection is that the contract contains a term giving the English courts jurisdiction: here there must be a good arguable case that there is a contract, as well as a good arguable case that it contains a term giving jurisdiction to the English court.[619] Unless the matter before the court is not a civil or commercial one, such a case will almost always confer jurisdiction under the Brussels I Regulation, in which case this rule will have no application, and permission to effect service out of the jurisdiction will not be required.[620]

If the contract falls within sub-Paragraph (6), there is no explicit limitation or restriction upon the cause of action to be relied on, nor on the relief which may be claimed in respect of it. An earlier version of this provision had required that the claim be brought 'to enforce, rescind, dissolve, annul or otherwise to affect a contract, or to recover damages or obtain other relief in respect of the breach of a contract'. That form of words had been said to draw the bounds of the provision widely, and to include within them all varieties of relief which were consequent on the existence of a contract and the events that had occurred.[621] It extended to cover cases in which a claimant contended that a contract had been frustrated,[622] or had been lawfully rescinded,[623] and it had generally been held that it covered actions for declarations on non-liability by a party alleged by his opponent to be contractually bound.[624] But it was not considered to cover an action for inducing a breach of contract;[625] and as was said above, this still seems largely right, for such a claim is not naturally said to be in respect of a contract to which the claimant and defendant are party, or which confers rights and correlative duties on claimant and defendant.

A claim to enforce fiduciary duties which are created by, or which arise by reason of, a contract is to be seen as brought in respect of a contract, and as within the rule. A claim for the restitution of money paid, or in respect of other benefits conferred, pursuant to a void supposed contract, on the other hand, might be said on one analysis of the matter not to arise in respect of a contract, but from some non-contractual obligation. But it is hard to see that such a reading of the jurisdictional rule would make practical sense, and it is submitted that such a claim may be brought within sub-Paragraph (6).[626] It has been held that a claim

---

618 See further, *Novus Aviation Ltd v. Onur Air Tasimacilik AS* [2009] EWCA Civ 122, [2009] 1 Lloyd's Rep 576, [71]–[81].

619 *Rimpacific Navigation Inc v. Daehan Shipbuilding Co Ltd* [2009] EWHC 2941 (Comm), [2010] 2 Lloyd's Rep 236.

620 Paragraph 3.1(6)(d). It is liable to arise only when the claim is wholly outside the Regulation, or no party to the agreement has a domicile in a Member State.

621 *EF Hutton & Co (London) Ltd v. Moffarij* [1989] 1 WLR 488. It includes an action for a final anti-suit injunction: *Youell v. Kara Mara Shipping Co* [2000] 2 Lloyd's Rep 102.

622 *BP Exploration Co (Libya) Ltd v. Hunt* [1976] 1 WLR 788.

623 *The Olib* [1991] 2 Lloyd's Rep 108.

624 *Gulf Bank KSC v. Mitsubishi Heavy Industries Ltd* [1994] 1 Lloyd's Rep 323; *DR Insurance Co v. Central National Insurance Co of Omaha* [1996] 1 Lloyd's Rep 74, 79. But to opposite effect, *Finnish Marine Insurance Co Ltd v. Protective National Insurance Co* [1990] 1 QB 1078. The previous uncertainty is now resolved by the provision which is now Paragraph 3.1(8), discussed below.

625 *EF Hutton & Co (London) Ltd v. Moffarij* [1989] 1 WLR 488, 494. But to opposite effect in Australia, *South Adelaide Football Club v. Fitzroy Football Club* (1988) 92 FLR 117.

626 It may be that such a claim falls within sub-Paragraph (8), but this deals only with a claim for a declaration that no contract exists, and does not expressly extend to a claim for consequential relief. It may also be that sub-Paragraph (16) applies when the acts relied on as founding liability were committed within the jurisdiction.

for a statutory payment under the Commercial Agents (Council Directive) Regulations 1992 is a claim for a statutory entitlement, but not a claim which is founded on a breach of contract.[627]

If the claimant seeks a declaration that no contract exists, the claim will fall within sub-Paragraph (8) if the disputed contract would have fallen within sub-Paragraph (6). This provision means that it was no longer necessary to perform the gymnastics which accompanied attempts to locate such claims within the predecessor versions of the contract provisions. The result is that if the claimant alleges that a contract is voidable, or was voidable and has been avoided, sub-Paragraph (6) will, and sub-Paragraph (8) may well, cover the case. If it is claimed that the alleged contract was void, or non-existent, *ab initio*, or may have bound someone other than the claimant but did not bind the claimant, or was void for illegality, sub-Paragraph (6) will cover the case; and it would be sensible for sub-Paragraph (8) also to cover claims for the relief which is consequential upon the court declaring that the contract does not exist. Sub-Paragraph (8) does not cover the case where the claimant admits a contract but denies that he owes any unperformed obligations under it: in such a case sub-Paragraph (6) will apply.

4.70 Claims relying on sub-Paragraph (7): contracts breached in England

This head of jurisdiction[628] applies if the claim is in respect of a contract which was breached within the jurisdiction.

For the purpose of sub-Paragraph (7), the contract is not required to fall within the framework of sub-Paragraph (6). So long as the breach is committed within the jurisdiction the court may authorise service out in respect of claim. An earlier version of this rule confirmed that the head of jurisdiction was available in cases in which a breach outside the jurisdiction made it impossible to perform within the jurisdiction; it is unclear whether the absence of this clause from sub-Paragraph (7) is intended to be significant.[629] It is to be noted that, by contrast with the rule of special jurisdiction under the Brussels I Regulation, it is the place of the breach, as opposed to the place where the obligation in question was required to be performed, which provides the basis for jurisdiction under this sub-Paragraph. And although the place of performance may be a manageable concept, the place of the breach is less so.

It may be useful to divide cases of breach into two categories: breach by failure to perform, and breach by repudiatory act. In the case of failure to perform the contractual obligation, the place of the breach will be England if the obligation was required to be (according to the law governing the contract) performed within the jurisdiction:[630] it will be insufficient to show that England was only one of the places at which the broken obligation might lawfully have been performed. So if the contract price is payable in England or Scotland,

---

627 *Fern Computer Consultancy Ltd v. Intergraph Cadworx & Analysis Solutions Ltd* [2014] EWHC 2908 (Ch), [2015] 1 Lloyd's Rep 1. This is not wholly convincing, for the agency arises by way of contract, and the failure to pay is therefore a breach of an entitlement which arises by virtue of the contract. The court suggested that the claim was instead in the nature of a tort of breach of statutory duty, which in the circumstances seems rather strained. *Cf Accentuate Ltd v. Asigra Inc* [2009] EWHC 2655 (QB), [2009] 2 Lloyd's Rep 599.

628 Formerly RSC Order 11, r. 1(1)(e).

629 One reason for thinking that it is not is that the amendment of the sub-Paragraphs only ever seems to widen their scope. It is not clear whether this is a legitimate aid to construction, but it appears to be true.

630 *Cuban Atlantic Sugar Sales Corp v. Compania de Vapores San Elefterio Lda* [1960] 1 QB 187.

breach by non-payment cannot be said to have occurred in England: it has occurred, but did not occur in England.[631]

The most common case of breach within the jurisdiction will be the failure to pay money due under the contract: identification of the place where payment of money was legally due is not always easy. If the contract makes express provision for place of payment, the rule is easy to apply. If it does not, the answer depends upon ascertaining the implied intention of the parties, or the default rule which applies when no contrary intention can be found. This place must be identified by the law which governs the contract. If the contract is governed by English law, the general rule is that the debtor must seek out his creditor, and pay where the creditor resides or has his place of business.[632] The rule may be an arbitrary one, but it is only a general one, and is no worse than the equally arbitrary alternative to be found in other systems and which gives the jurisdictional advantage to the party in debt or default, which always seems rather surprising.

Where the breach takes the form of acting inconsistently with the contractual obligation, it is likely that the place of breach is where the inconsistent act is done.[633] The rule, in contrast to that which gives special jurisdiction under Article 7(1) of the Brussels I Regulation, is concerned not with the place where the obligation in question should have been performed, but with where the breach took place. So, if goods which should have been delivered in England are wrongfully disposed of in New York, the breach probably takes place in New York, rather than in England,[634] even though it has consequences in England. If a settlement agreement binds parties not to reopen a dispute, the breach takes place where subsequent proceedings are instituted, not in the place where, as a matter of common law, the defendant should otherwise have been sued.[635] It may be necessary for the court to take a reasonably flexible view as to where in substance the breach occurred. In the case of breach of the settlement agreement, the fact that process may have been served in England should not prevent the conclusion that the breach occurs where the substantial conduct occurs.[636]

Even so, the distinction between breach by omission and breach by commission is sometimes more apparent than real. If a seller of goods fails to deliver as obliged, and sells them elsewhere,[637] the idea that one, but not the other, is the place of the breach is difficult. Either view – that the breach was where they were required to have been delivered, and that the breach was where they were wrongly sold – seems justifiable; the answer may have to depend on the way the claim is put in the claim form. Of course, if this sub-Paragraph were interpreted in accordance with the somewhat different rule in the Brussels I Regulation,[638]

---

631 *Sharab v. Al-Saud* [2009] EWCA Civ 353, [2009] 2 Lloyd's Rep 160 applying *The Eider* [1893] P 119; *Cuban Atlantic Sugar Sales Corp v. Compania de Vapores San Elefterio Lda* [1960] 1 QB 187.

632 *The Eider* [1893] P 119. But *cf Royal Bank of Scotland v. Cassa di Risparmio* [1991] ILPr 411, aff'd *Financial Times*, 21 January 1992, emphasising that the general rule is not an inflexible one; a conclusion reaffirmed in *Deutsche Ruckversicherung v. La Fonderia Assicurazioni SpA* [2001] 2 Lloyd's Rep 621. See also *Commercial Marine Piling Ltd v. Pierse Contracting Ltd* [2009] EWHC 2241 (TCC), [2009] 2 Lloyd's Rep 659.

633 *Mutzenbecher v. La Asseguradora Española* [1906] 1 KB 254.

634 Unless it can be argued that the failure to deliver in London amounts to a breach in London.

635 For a case which would point (indirectly, but unconvincingly) to the opposite conclusion, see *AMT Futures Ltd v. Marzillier et al GmbH* [2014] EWHC 1085 (Comm), [2015] 2 WLR 187.

636 Although in *Hambros Bank Ltd v. Thune & Roll* (18 January 1991), it was held that the service in England of the document instituting proceedings in a foreign court did bring the case within this provision.

637 It would be unsatisfactory if the answer turned on whether the wrongful sale was before or after the contractual date for delivery, but a technical approach to the rule may indeed produce this result.

638 Though without the elaboration contained in the corresponding provision of the Brussels I Regulation.

one would ask simply where the broken obligation should have been performed. Such an approach, at least, appears to identify only one place as that of the 'breach', but it may not be consistent with the wording of the particular head of jurisdiction.

In practice, if England is shown to be the proper place to bring the claim, there may be a perceptible, if illicit, temptation to see England as the place of the breach, and to resolve the anterior issue accordingly. A similar approach may also be useful where the breach is a continuing breach, arguably committed in more than one country, or where it is alleged that the breach committed in England, while still a breach, is still only a rather minor breach in the context of the claim as a whole.[639]

4.71 Claims made in tort: Paragraph 3.1(9)

The tort head of jurisdiction[640] applies to claims 'made in tort'. If this condition is satisfied, service out of the jurisdiction may be authorised if either of two further conditions is satisfied: that damage was sustained within the jurisdiction,[641] or the damage resulted from an act committed within the jurisdiction. The immediate predecessor to this provision applied where 'the claim is founded on a tort'.[642] The question whether this alteration in wording is substantial or merely cosmetic is problematic.[643]

The definition of tort – the question whether it connotes a completed cause of action is a separate point, discussed in the following paragraph – is probably wider than those wrongs which English law regards as a tort. But it has been held that though the infringement of a patent is a tort, and misuse of private information is a tort, claims founded on a breach of confidence are not made in tort.[644] Insofar as claims founded on equitable obligations, including that of confidence, may now fall within sub-Paragraph (15) or (16), this may not be crucial; but it is perhaps surprising that the jurisdictional accident, which saw certain kinds of claim develop in equity rather than the common law, has such consequences for the modern law on service out of the jurisdiction. As the rules for determination of the applicable law now divide into contractual and non-contractual obligations, it would be convenient if sub-Paragraphs (6) to (8), on the one hand, and (9), on the other, could be held to reflect it, even though it is hard to say that this is what the rule-maker had intended.

4.72 Claims made under sub-Paragraph (9): claim 'made in tort' as meaning that there must be a completed cause of action?

Sub-Paragraph (9) refers to claims made in tort, but in order to understand what is meant by this form of words, it is first necessary to examine the manner in which the courts interpreted

---

639 *Cf Hambros Bank Ltd v. Thune & Roll* (18 January 1991).

640 Previously RSC Order 11, r. 1(1)(f).

641 Which includes on a ship in English waters: *Saldanha v. Fulton Navigation Inc* [2011] EWHC 1118 (Admlty), [2011] 2 Lloyd's Rep 206.

642 RSC Order 11, r. 1(1)(f). An even earlier version of this rule required that there be a tort committed within the jurisdiction.

643 See generally *Cool Carriers AB v. HSBC Bank USA* [2001] 2 Lloyd's Rep 22 for the view that differences in wording do not necessarily lead to a different interpretation.

644 *Kitechnology BV v. Unicor GmbH Plastmaschinen* [1995] FSR 765, 777, which the judge in *Vidal-Hall v. Google Inc* [2004] EWHC 13 (QB), [2014] 1 WLR 4155, held that he was bound to follow: at [71].

the provision in the predecessor rule, that 'the claim is founded on a tort'. As will be seen, the important element was the use of the indefinite article; and the consequent question of the effect of not reproducing it in the current version of the rule, is just as important.

The previous rule had been held to import two conditions. First, the claimant had been required to demonstrate, to the requisite level of certainty,[645] that he had a completed cause of action in tort. It was not sufficient that he could show that a duty of care was owed to him, or that a duty of care had been broken but gave rise to no damage:[646] in neither case would there have been *a* tort for the claim to be founded on. Second, the completed cause of action had to constitute a tort, as opposed to giving rise to some other form of liability;[647] and in determining whether this condition was satisfied, if it was not admitted, the court was liable to apply the English rules of private international law applicable to torts if it was alleged that the question was not a wholly domestic one. In other words, there had to be a tort, by reference to English rules of private international law, unless the point was conceded by the defendant for the purposes of jurisdiction.

These propositions were conclusively established in *Metall & Rohstoff AG v. Donaldson Lufkin & Jenrette Inc.*[648] Until that decision, there was a credible alternative view to the effect that all a claimant was required to do was to plead a claim which was framed in the language of tort, or to advance a claim whose general nature was tortious, but that it was unnecessary for him to go further, on a jurisdictional application, and show that his claim was founded on a good cause of action.[649] However, confronted by wording which required the claim to be founded on '*a* tort', it was not easy to see how the court could have taken this to require no more than that the claim was formulated as something with a 'tort-like appearance'. The rule required a tort, and a tort is an actual cause of action. In this respect there was a sharp contrast with the contract heads of jurisdiction which did not require then, and do not require now, that there was a completed cause of action for breach of contract.[650] The fact that this may have flowed from the asymmetrical terminology used by English law – contracts are not causes of action, but torts are causes of action – may have been an accident, but it was justifiably held to be the law.

And as the earlier rule required there to be *a* tort, satisfaction of this element, if not conceded, had to be demonstrated by reference to the rules of English private international law. At the time of *Metall & Rohstoff* these were the common law rules of private international law, according to which it was necessary to decide first where the alleged tort was committed, by asking where in substance the cause of action arose.[651] For causes of action which

---

645 That is, to the standard of a good arguable case: see further below, para. 4.86.

646 Except in the case of a tort, such as defamation, in which no proof of damage is required to substantiate the claim.

647 Such as equitable liability, liability as a fiduciary, liability as a constructive trustee, or liability under some form of action unknown to English domestic law: *Metall & Rohstoff AG v. Donaldson Lufkin & Jenrette Inc* [1990] 1 QB 391.

648 [1990] 1 QB 391.

649 Collier [1989] All ER Annual Review 49 at 53 summarised, quite brilliantly, why recourse to choice of law rules at a jurisdictional stage may be inappropriate: 'The method by which the Court of Appeal proceeded entails, in effect, that the defendant's liability is being tried in order to decide whether the court has jurisdiction to determine the defendant's liability'.

650 But just that the contract was, for example, made in England. Different considerations apply, of course, to sub-Paragraph (7), where the jurisdictional rule requires there to be a breach of contract and, therefore, a completed cause of action.

651 *Distillers Co Ltd v. Thompson* [1971] AC 458 (product liability: at the place of sale and consumption); *Castree v. Squibb & Sons Ltd* [1980] 1 WLR 1248 (product liability: at the place of sale and use); *Bata v. Bata* [1948]

arose in England, the English domestic law of tort had to be satisfied; for causes of action which arose overseas the claimant was required to show double actionability: liability in tort under English domestic law, and civil liability under the law of the place where the cause of action arose, but with a degree of flexibility in suitable cases.[652] No doubt this rather complicated common law rule would be superseded by the provisions of the Rome II Regulation if the same analytical framework were still in place today.[653]

It was undeniable that this analysis, which required an exercise in choice of law to determine whether there was a tort on which the claim could be shown to be founded, was the product of unassailable logic. It also had the potential to make jurisdictional disputes quite strikingly complex.[654] The important question is therefore whether Paragraph 3.1(9) is to be approached in the same way.

Sub-Paragraph (9) requires that 'a claim is made in tort'. On one possible reading it does not re-enact the requirement that there be 'a tort', but, instead, alters and simplifies the law to require no more than that the claim be one pleaded in the form and manner of a tort, or that the claim be one which is tortious in nature. It may, therefore, open the gate wider than its predecessor did, in two respects. First, it may no longer be necessary to show that there is a good and completed cause of action: some claims fail, and a claim is no less a claim if it fails at trial. Second, it may no longer be necessary to show that the cause of action is founded on something which would be a tort, as distinct from (say) an equitable wrong, such as breach of confidence, or even a non-contractual obligation arising from tort or delict.[655] It would follow that a claimant need only plead a claim which would be characterised as one in tort for the purposes of private international law; but the proposition that this would result in a simplification of the law is not completely sound. Though a claimant would not need to show a completed cause of action for the purpose of satisfying[656] sub-Paragraph (9), there will still need to be a serious issue to be tried on the substance of the claim.[657] As this will require investigation of whether he has a good cause of action, albeit to a lower level of certainty, the complexities of the facts and the law will arise within the framework of the same jurisdictional application, albeit at a different point. For this reason, an analysis of the rules of private international law as they apply to claims in tort cannot in practice be avoided. As to the second of these points, it would make the law tidier if the jurisdictional rule of sub-Paragraph (9) covered the same ground as the Rome II Regulation, but it is quite unclear whether the rule can properly be read this way.[658]

WN 366, *Berezovsky v. Michaels* [2000] 1 WLR 1004 (defamation: where material made available to readers with consequent damage to reputation of victim, not where broadcast from); *Diamond v. Bank of London & Montreal Ltd* [1979] QB 333 (negligent misrepresentation: where material received and relied on, not where prepared and transmitted from; but for a conflicting analysis in the context of negligent accountancy advice, see *Voth v. Manildra Flour Mills Pty Ltd* (1991) 171 CLR 538); *Metall & Rohstoff AG v. Donaldson Lufkin & Jenrette Inc* [1990] 1 QB 391, *Arab Business Consortium International Finance and Investment Co v. Banque Franco-Tunisienne* [1997] 1 Lloyd's Rep 531 (economic torts: where acts were aimed and damage intended to be caused).

652 *Boys v. Chaplin* [1971] AC 356; *Red Sea Insurance Co Ltd v. Bouygues SA* [1995] 1 AC 190.

653 For detail, see Dickinson, *The Rome II Regulation* (2008).

654 That the two adjudications operated to different burdens of proof was probably insufficient to deflect the implicit criticism.

655 In other words, the jurisdictional rule would be aligned with the choice of law rule set out in the Rome II Regulation, Chapter 2.

656 To the standard of a good arguable case.

657 CPR r. 6.37(1)(b); see below, para. 4.93.

658 See *Erste Group Bank AG v. JSC 'VMZ Red October'* [2013] EWHC 2926 (Comm) for the refusal to align sub-sub-Paragraph (a), which requires that damage be sustained within the jurisdiction, with the corresponding

Until these points are clarified by the courts, the conclusion must be put this way. If sub-Paragraph (9) has not altered the earlier law in this respect, the law as described above will still be applicable; but if it has departed from the previous position, all the claimant will have to do is plead a cause of action which, for the purposes of private international law, would be characterised as tortious in nature. The view preferred[659] here, on the ground that it would simplify law which had been allowed to become far too complicated, is that the law has indeed changed, and that it is not necessary to demonstrate (a good arguable case that there was) a tort, but only a claim formulated in the nature of tort; but this uncertainty is not to the credit of the law.

It is not clear whether a claim is made in tort when it is brought, not by the victim, but by one tortfeasor for a contribution from another tortfeasor. But the claim does appear to be made in (the context of a) tort.[660]

4.73 Claims relying on sub-Paragraph (9)(a): damage sustained within the jurisdiction

If the claim is made in tort, service out will not be authorised unless damage was sustained within the jurisdiction or resulted from an act committed within the jurisdiction.[661] Only one of these conditions needs to be met.

So far as the quantum of damage is concerned, it is not necessary that the whole of the damage have been sustained within the jurisdiction. In relation to the earlier rule, all that was required was that 'some significant damage has been[662] sustained in England'.[663] As this aspect of the rule has not changed, it follows that even if the greater part of the damage was sustained outside the jurisdiction, sub-Paragraph (9)(a) could still be satisfied. Presumably a court could still exercise its discretion against service if the greater part of the damage was sustained in a foreign country, but if the claimant elects to limit the scope of his claim and plead a cause of action which is limited to the damage sustained in England, there will be no difficulty in satisfying this requirement, though the material scope of the claim, and the claim for relief, will be correspondingly restricted.[664]

---

provisions of what is now Art. 7(2) of the Brussels I Regulation, which requires the immediate damage to occur within the jurisdiction.

659 Until the courts confirm that this is so.

660 *Cf FSSB Ltd v. Seward & Kissel LLP* [2007] UKPC 16 (PC Bah) (a case on the Bahamian rule); *cf Hewden Tower Cranes Ltd v. Wolffkran GmbH* [2007] EWHC 857 (TCC), [2007] 2 Lloyd's Rep 138 (a case on the Brussels I Regulation).

661 Considered in the following paragraph.

662 It appears that the rule may be relied on in a case where no damage has yet been sustained but if the anticipated tort is committed it will cause damage within the jurisdiction. The suggestion appears most clearly (and appropriately) in cases of patent infringement: see *Beecham Group plc v. Norton Healthcare Ltd* [1997] FSR 81. But it has been thought to apply to other cases of anticipated economic loss (*cf SCOR v. Eras* [1992] 1 Lloyd's Rep 570), and the suggestion is sound in principle, so long as the evidence for the feared occurrence of such damage is sufficient to meet the standard of a good arguable case. And see *Kitechnology BV v. Unicor Plastmaschinen GmbH* [1995] FSR 765; and now see the new wording of Art. 7(2) of the recast Regulation, discussed at para. 2.209.

663 *Metall & Rohstoff*, at 437; applied *Booth v. Phillips* [2004] EWHC 1437 (Comm), [2004] 1 WLR 3292.

664 *Cf Berezovsky v. Michaels* [2000] 1 WLR 1004 (defamation claim in international magazine limited to complaint about dissemination in England); for limitations, see *Dow Jones & Co Inc v. Jameel* [2005] EWCA Civ 75, [2005] QB 946. But now see Defamation Act 2013, s. 9, which removes the jurisdiction of the court in such cases.

So far as the location of damage is concerned, it is in some cases uncertain where it was sustained. By way of general introduction, two particular points have been established by the case law. The first is that damage which is the consequence of other damage which has already been inflicted may be used to satisfy this rule. So for example, medical expenses incurred in England, or the loss of earnings which would otherwise have been gained in England, will satisfy the requirement of damage sustained within the jurisdiction, even though this may be the consequence of damage which was more immediately done else-where.[665] The second point is that pure financial loss may be more difficult to pin down to a specific location, but that it is probably unnecessary to take too technical a view of the point, for the reason which follows.

It is certainly true that the immediate predecessors of sub-Paragraph (9) were said[666] to have been drafted to bring the tort head of jurisdiction into line with the special jurisdictional rule which now appears as Article 7(2) of the Brussels I Regulation,[667] as this had been elucidated in *Handelskwekerij GJ Bier BV v. Mines de Potasse d'Alsace SA*.[668] Were that view to be understood strictly, damage would be sustained where it occurred, rather than where it may later ramify;[669] and this approach was initially supported.[670] But there was no credible reason to apply this line of Brussels authority outside the Regulation itself. The function of Article 7(2) as an exception to the general jurisdiction of Article 4, and as a rule of special jurisdiction not further controlled in its application by a principle of *forum conveniens*, is quite separate and distinct, and has a function quite different, from sub-Paragraph (9)(a). For where jurisdiction is to be asserted under that rule, the claim-ant must also, separately, clearly and distinctly, satisfy the requirement of *forum conven-iens*[671] before the court will authorise service to be made out of the jurisdiction. There is therefore no need for 'alignment' with a jurisdictional rule which serves a quite different function.[672]

Where the damage is physical, it should not be problematic to show where it was sus-tained.[673] Where it is economic, however, there is more scope for differences of opinion and analysis, but as the court has a discretion to allow service out in any event, there is no compelling need to be restrictive about what is needed to satisfy this element of sub-Para-graph 9(a). However, if the gist of the complaint is that money should have been received

---

665 *Booth v. Phillips* [2004] EWHC 1437 (Comm), [2004] 1 WLR 3292; *Cooley v. Ramsay* [2008] EWHC 129 (QB), [2008] ILPr 345; *Harty v. Sabre International Security* [2011] EWHC 852 (QB); *Wink v. Croatia Osiguranje DD* [2013] EWHC 1118 (QB); *Stylianou v. Toyoshima* [2013] EWHC 2188 (QB); *Erste Group Bank AG v. JSC 'VMZ Red October'* [2013] EWHC 2926 (Comm), where the contrary argument was described, at [147] as 'hopeless'; *Pike v. Indian Hotels Co Ltd* [2013] EWHC 4096 (QB).

666 See Dicey, Morris and Collins, *The Conflict of Laws*, 15th edn (Sweet & Maxwell, London, 2012), para. 11–214.

667 See above, para. 2.243.

668 21/76, [1976] ECR 1735.

669 *Cf C-220/88 Dumez France SA v. Hessische Landesbank* [1990] ECR I-49; C-364/93 *Marinari v. Lloyds Bank plc* [1995] ECR I-2719.

670 *Arab Business Corporation International Finance & Investment Co v. Banque Franco-Tunisienne* [2003] EWCA Civ 205, [2003] 2 Lloyd's Rep 146.

671 See below, paras 4.88 *et seq.*

672 *Booth v. Phillips* [2004] EWHC 1437 (Comm), [2004] 1 WLR 3292; *Cooley v. Ramsay* [2008] EWHC 129 (QB), [2008] ILPr 345; *Wink v. Croatia Osiguranje DD* [2013] EWHC 1118 (QB); *Erste Group Bank AG v. JSC 'VMZ Red October'* [2013] EWHC 2926 (Comm).

673 But what if the claimant ingests poison in one country but the symptoms do not manifest themselves until he has arrived within the jurisdiction? Or vice versa? The answer may be to say that there was significant damage in each place, and to conclude on that account that the case falls within the rule.

in England, but was not received, financial loss is sustained within the jurisdiction,[674] even if it may be said to have been sustained elsewhere as well. Likewise, if money is paid away, as a result of a fraud, from London, damage will have been sustained in London.[675] If the claimant becomes legally liable to pay out money within the jurisdiction, it seems that he does sustain damage, in the sense of economic loss, within the jurisdiction, maybe whether or not he actually pays it.[676]

Where the victim of a tort such as misrepresentation sends instructions from England to an overseas bank, directing and authorising it to pay money out from an account there, it is certainly true that loss is sustained out of the jurisdiction, for that is where the money passes out of his ownership, possession or account; but that does not rule out the possibility that damage was also sustained within the jurisdiction. If one were to regard the sending of the instruction to pay as a part of the damage which was brought about, it would be easy to contend that it was sustained within the jurisdiction. Where the claimant is deprived of sales, say as a result of an anti-competitive conspiracy, the damage may be sustained where the sales would have been expected to take place, or where the money paid pursuant to those putative (lost) sales would have been received,[677] though perhaps not where the shares in the company are traded and the company is valued.[678] In the result, the correct approach is, in practice, not to be too clever or analytical when it comes to the location of intangible, or financial, losses, but to rely on the principle of *forum conveniens*[679] to screen out those cases in which the damage connection with England is too weak or tenuous to justify service out.

4.74 Claims relying on sub-Paragraph (9)(b): damage resulting from act committed within the jurisdiction

The alternative requirement of sub-Paragraph (9) is that the damage resulted from an act (which must surely be interpreted to include an omission in the face of a duty to act) committed within the jurisdiction. The predecessor to this provision was interpreted to mean that there was no requirement that the act be one committed wholly within the jurisdiction, but that the damage 'resulted from substantial and efficacious[680] acts committed within the jurisdiction, whether or not other substantial and efficacious acts have been committed elsewhere'.[681] There is no reason to think that this has changed. Where the defendants

---

674 *Erste Group Bank AG v. JSC 'VMZ Red October'* [2013] EWHC 2926 (Comm).

675 *VTB Capital plc v. Nutritek International Corp* [2013] UKSC 5, [2013] 2 AC 337.

676 *SCOR v. Eras* [1992] 1 Lloyd's Rep 570, 591. See also *Newsat Holdings Ltd v. Zani* [2006] EWHC 342 (Comm), [2006] 2 Lloyd's Rep 707, in the context of costs incurred by way of legal expenses, but which may need to be reconsidered.

677 This is supported in the context of inducing breach of contact by *Metall & Rohstoff*, at 449. Indeed, where the acts are aimed at a claimant in England, it will be easier to accept that the damage was sustained in England. For passing off, the damage is sustained where the deception occurs and goodwill is lost: *Mecklermedia Corp v. DC Congress GmbH* [1998] Ch 40.

678 *Shahar v. Tsitsekkos* [2004] EWHC 2659 (Ch) (diminution of value of shareholding in an English company).

679 CPR r. 6.37(3). For support, see *Cooley v. Ramsay* [2008] EWHC 129 (QB), [2008] ILPr 345.

680 It may be argued than an act is not efficacious as an act giving rise to damage if it is reversible: *Shahar v. Tsitsekkos* [2004] EWHC 2659 (Ch) (amendment of register at Companies House which could be reversed if it were shown to have been procured improperly): this is not clearly right, because there is no requirement that the act be an irreversible one, not least because if damages are paid by the defendant, all torts involve reversible inflictions of loss or damage. Only those *not* tortious are irreversible.

681 *Metall & Rohstoff*, at 437.

are joint tortfeasors, the act of one is the act of all, and therefore, in such a case, an act by one defendant will be sufficient to bring all of them within range of this jurisdictional provision.[682]

4.75 Claim made to enforce a judgment or arbitral award: Paragraph 3.1(10)

The enforcement head of jurisdiction[683] applies if the claim is brought to enforce any judgment or arbitral award. If it is necessary to enforce a foreign judgment which cannot be registered for enforcement under the various statutory schemes,[684] it will be necessary to bring an action at common law, by suing on the obligation imposed on the defendant by reason of his submission to, or voluntary presence within the jurisdiction of, the foreign court which gave the judgment; and process may be served out of the jurisdiction under this provision.

It is not said explicitly that the judgment or award has to be one which is entitled to be enforced as a matter of English private international law, but the court could not properly exercise its discretion in favour of service unless this were so. It is not necessary for the claimant to show that the defendant has assets in England: this is not a condition for a claimant to bring an action in the first place, and even though it may bear on the utility of the proceedings, it does not lie in the mouth of the judgment debtor to say so, or to resist service out so that he may thereafter bring assets into the jurisdiction with no fear of execution against them.[685] But it has been held that the jurisdiction does not extend to cases in which the judgment or award relied on has not yet been given, presumably because such a claim would not fall within the natural meaning of the rule.[686]

4.76 Claim whose whole subject matter relates to property located within the jurisdiction: Paragraph 3.1(11)

The property head of jurisdiction[687] applies if the whole subject matter of the claim relates to property located within the jurisdiction. Unlike its predecessors, it is not confined to real property situated within the jurisdiction, and the extent to which the removal of this limitation has widened the jurisdiction of the court may take the unwary by surprise. It has been held that it applies 'to any claim for relief, whether damages or otherwise, so long as

---

682 *Puchsner v. Palmer* [1989] RPC 430; *Unilever plc v. Gillette UK* [1989] RPC 583; *Mölnlycke AB v. Procter & Gamble* [1992] 1 WLR 1112. On joint tortfeasors, or joint enterprises, see also *Douglas v. Hello! Ltd (No 2)* [2003] EWCA Civ 139, [2003] EMLR 28 (photographer and magazine editor); *Morin v. Bonhams & Brooks Ltd* [2003] EWCA Civ 1802, [2004] 1 Lloyd's Rep 702 (branches of auctioneers' business). Once again, the approach taken under Art. 7(2) of the Brussels I Regulation is very different indeed, which does nothing to call into question the proper interpretation of sub-Paragraph 9(b).

683 Formerly RSC Order 11, r. 1(1)(m).

684 These have their own provisions for service out of the jurisdiction, permission to serve not being required: CPR r. 74.6.

685 On both points: *Tasarruf Mevduati Sigorta Fonu v. Demirel* [2007] EWCA Civ 799, [2007] 1 WLR 2508. This case was not drawn to the attention of the court in *Linsen International Ltd v. Humpuss Transportasi Kimia* [2011] EWCA Civ 1042, which is to be regarded as wrong (though for the difficulty this causes for a first instance judge, see *Parbulk II AS v. PT Humpuss Intermoda Transportasi TBK* [2011] EWHC 3143 (Comm)). See also (generally agreeing with *Tasarruf v. Demirel*) *Yaiguaje v. Chevron Corp* [2013] ONCA 758 (permission granted to appeal to the Supreme Court of Canada).

686 *Mercedes Benz AG v. Leiduck* [1996] 1 AC 284.

687 Formerly RSC Order 11, r. 1(1)(g), (h), (i).

it is related to property[688] located within the jurisdiction',[689] and is not limited to a claim to ownership or possession of such property.[690] There is no reason to suppose that intellectual property rights are excluded from this expression,[691] and every reason why they, as well as other forms of intangible property, should be included.

4.77 Claims made about trusts: Paragraph 3.1(12)

The trusts head of jurisdiction[692] applies if the claim is brought to execute the trusts of a written instrument, being trusts that ought to be executed according to English law, and of which the person to be served is a trustee, or for any other relief or remedy which might be obtained in such an action. The trust or its administration must be governed by English law,[693] but it is not required that the trust property be situated in England.

4.78 Claims made in proceedings for the administration of estates: Paragraph 3.1(13)

The administration head of jurisdiction[694] applies if the claim is made for the administration of the estate of a person who died domiciled within the jurisdiction, or for any relief or remedy which might be obtained in such an action. The term 'domicile' here refers to domicile in the sense of Schedule 1 to the Civil Jurisdiction and Judgments Order 2001 and not to the common law meaning of the expression.[695] It may therefore give jurisdiction where the deceased died domiciled in another country so far as concerns the substantive issue of succession, but domiciled in England for jurisdictional purposes: in such a case England may not be the proper place for the proceedings, and permission may be refused.[696]

---

688 Including an investment account, or the chose in action by which it is represented: *Walanpatrias Stiftung v. Lehman Brothers International (Europe)* [2006] EWHC 3034 (Comm).

689 In *Re Banco Nacional de Cuba* [2001] 1 WLR 2039 (distinguished on the facts in *Shahar v. Tsitsekkos* [2004] EWHC 2659 (Ch)), where the claim related to shares situated within the jurisdiction. Of course, the court still has a discretion as to whether to grant permission.

690 *Islamic Republic of Pakistan v. Zardari* [2006] EWHC 2411 (Ch), [2006] 2 CLC 667 (constructive trust claim to land in England: claim falls within this rule even though land is the target of the trust as distinct from the case being one about title to land within the jurisdiction: cf C-242/92 *Webb v. Webb* [1994] ECR I-1717).

691 A view now confirmed by *Ashton Investments Ltd v. OJSC Russian Aluminium* [2006] EWHC 2545 (Comm), [2007] 1 Lloyd's Rep 311. For the view that a domain name is property, and that it may be within the jurisdiction, see *Tucows.com Co v. Lojas Renner SA* (2011) 106 OR (3d) 561 (Ontario CA).

692 Formerly RSC Order 11, r. 1(1)(j).

693 *Chellaram v. Chellaram* [2002] EWHC 632 (Ch), [2002] 3 All ER 17. The material date is the date of the application for permission, not any earlier date. For how to determine the governing law, see *Re Carapiet's Trusts, Manoogian (Armenian Patriarch of Jerusalem) v. Sonsino* [2002] EWHC 1304 (Ch); and cf *Gómez v. Gómez-Monche Vives* [2008] EWCA Civ 1065, [2009] Ch 245 (a case on the Brussels I Regulation).

694 Formerly RSC Order 11, r. 1(1)(k). Cf *Weinstock v. Sarnat* [2005] NSWSC 744.

695 CPR r. 6.31(1)(i).

696 It is not clear that this curious wrinkle was seen in *Deller v. Zivy* [2007] EWHC 2266 (Ch), [2007] ILPr 868. The court found that the deceased died domiciled (as a matter of the common law of domicile and the substantive law of succession) in England, and that therefore the case fell within what is now sub-Paragraph (13). This overlooks the fact that the meaning of 'domiciled' in sub-Paragraph (13) was that set out in CPR r. 6.31(1)(i) and SI 2001/3929, Sch. 1, para. 9. This may not have affected the outcome, but it makes the reasoning unreliable.

4.79 Claims made in probate proceedings: Paragraph 3.1(14)

The probate and wills head of jurisdiction[697] applies if the claim is brought in probate proceedings, including a claim for the rectification of a will.[698] No further comment is required.

4.80 Claims made against a defendant as constructive trustee: Paragraph 3.1(15)

There is no head of jurisdiction in Paragraph 3.1 which allows permission to be granted simply because there was a breach of fiduciary duty[699] committed within the jurisdiction. However, if the claim is brought for relief against the defendant as constructive trustee, and the defendant's alleged liability arises out of acts committed within the jurisdiction, sub-Paragraph (15) may allow service out of the jurisdiction.

The provision is ostensibly designed to give jurisdiction over those whose equitable liability derives from acts done within the jurisdiction. Typically these will be cases where it is alleged that a breach of fiduciary duty has occurred by reason of acts done within the jurisdiction. It draws an inexact parallel with breaches of contract committed within the jurisdiction, and torts where acts were committed within the jurisdiction, and allows service out upon those who are liable to be held to be a constructive trustee, presumably to account. The predecessor to sub-Paragraph (15)[700] contained an express provision that the acts which had to be committed within the jurisdiction were not required to be those of the defendant himself: if there were acts committed within the jurisdiction by someone else, the defendant confining his activity to things, such as receipt of property or funds, done outside the jurisdiction, the provision was satisfied. The omission of the words 'whether by himself or otherwise' left it unclear whether it was intended to restrict the scope of the rule to cases in which the defendant had himself done something within the jurisdiction.[701] In many cases this would not be critical, for where another defendant has done acts within the jurisdiction, Paragraph 3.1(3) would furnish a basis for seeking permission to serve the defendant as a necessary or proper party to a claim against that defendant. If the defendant has not done anything at all within the territorial jurisdiction of the English court, it may be argued that he should not be subject to its jurisdiction; the discretion of the court may be exercised with that in mind.

On the other hand, there was no real reason to suppose that the rule was intended to restrict the existing power of the court to deal with fraudsters, and if the words used in the predecessor rule were understood to be, and read as, words of confirmation rather than limitation, it would be unnecessary that the acts done within the jurisdiction be those of the defendant himself. It should be enough for the defendant to have had something to do with the acts done within the jurisdiction. If that is so, the only question is how substantial must be the acts which were done within the jurisdiction, or which were the acts which must be done within the jurisdiction;[702] and on that, a need for substantial and efficacious acts, even

---

697 Formerly RSC Order 11, r. 1(1)(l).

698 For confirmation of the pretty obvious proposition that the natural forum for a case on the interpretation of a will is the courts for the (common law) domicile of the testator, see also *Jaiswal v. Jaiswal* [2007] Jersey LR 305.

699 By analogy with breaches of contract, and torts, within the jurisdiction.

700 Formerly RSC Order 11, r. 1(1)(t).

701 The issue is discussed but not decided in *Islamic Republic of Pakistan v. Zardari* [2006] EWHC 2411 (Ch), [2006] 2 CLC 667.

702 *Nabb Brothers Ltd v. Lloyds Bank International Guernsey Ltd* [2005] EWHC 226 (Ch), [2005] ILPr 506 accepted that there had to be some link between the defendant and the territorial jurisdiction, but what that link might be was not specified. The proposition in the text therefore remains unimpaired.

if accompanied by substantial acts done elsewhere, would set a sensible standard.[703] The exercise of discretion by the court should be able to allow for the variable degrees of connection between the acts within the jurisdiction and the proposed defendant to the claim based in part upon them.

A defendant may become liable as a constructive trustee on the basis of his wrongful receipt of trust funds. According to *ISC Technologies Ltd v. Radcliffe*,[704] such liability must be imposed by reason of the receipt having occurred within the jurisdiction. It was held to be insufficient that a fraud or breach of fiduciary duty occurred within the jurisdiction, in consequence of which the defendant's liability arises. Rather, the act which gave rise to the defendant's own liability had itself to be committed within the jurisdiction, and so it was the receipt, or the knowing assistance, rather than the original fraud, which was required to have been committed within the jurisdiction. By contrast, in *ISC Technologies Ltd v. Guerin*, it was said that such a construction may be unduly narrow, and that as long as some of the acts underpinning the defendant's liability were to have occurred in England, it would not be necessary for the actual receipt to have occurred in England. In principle the latter construction is to be preferred. On the footing that the defendant's liability exists by reason of the original fraud and his subsequent participation[705] in it (for without one or the other there would be no liability), it should be sufficient that there was substantial conduct within the jurisdiction, even if there was other essential conduct outside the jurisdiction.[706] If the paragraph is designed to apply to international fraud, it would be as surprising as it would be disappointing if it could be defeated by the stratagem of arranging the receipt of the money outside England.

4.81 Claims made for restitution: Paragraph 3.1(16)

The restitution head of jurisdiction[707] allows service out to be authorised where a claim is made for restitution and the defendant's alleged liability arises out of acts committed within the jurisdiction. The law of restitution in England still appears to be going through an identity crisis, and its boundary disputes with the laws of contract, tort, equity and trusts, and that fact that it now appears to go under the name of unjust enrichment, do not make it easy to see its role in private international law.

On the footing that 'restitution' for the purposes of the conflict of laws describes claims which are founded on the principle that gains made from an unjust enrichment should be reversed,[708] the scope of sub-Paragraph (16) is reasonably clear; and in many cases, claims which may be brought under it will also fit under others. As with sub-Paragraph (15), alongside which it is to be read, it is not made clear whether the acts relied on must be the acts of the defendant himself, or must be some of the totality of the acts which found the liability, or be defined in some third way. But for the reasons which were given in relation

---

703 *Cf Metall & Rohstoff AG v. Donaldson Lufkin & Jenrette Inc* [1990] 1 QB 391; see further above, para. 4.74.

704 7 December 1990, referred to in *ISC Technologies v. Guerin* [1992] 2 Lloyd's Rep 430. This latter decision was followed in *Polly Peck International plc v. Nadir*, 17 March 1993.

705 By wrongful receipt, or by dishonestly rendering assistance.

706 By direct analogy with *Metall & Rohstoff AG v. Donaldson Lufkin & Jenrette Inc* [1990] 1 QB 391.

707 Formerly RSC Order 11, r. 1(1)(t).

708 On whether the provision applies to claims based on alleged equitable property in a trust fund, see *Nabb Brothers Ltd v. Lloyds Bank International Guernsey Ltd* [2005] EWHC 226 (Ch), [2005] ILPr 630, where the question was not answered.

to sub-Paragraph (15), it is submitted that such limitation would be wrong in principle, and that as long as the defendant has something to do with the acts which were committed within the jurisdiction, the requirements of the paragraph should be seen as satisfied. As to whether an omission to perform an act within the jurisdiction – such as the failure to pay contractual consideration – would suffice to bring the claim within the paragraph, principle suggests that it should, if the act complained of as not done was one which was required to be done within the jurisdiction.[709]

It is to be expected that sub-Paragraph (16) will now provide the natural home for restitutionary claims or those based on the law against unjust enrichment, and that earlier authorities which had allowed a quasi-contractual claim to be brought, for want of anything better, within the contract head, will not now need to be followed.[710]

4.82 Claims made by HM Revenue and Customs: Paragraph 3.1(17)

The tax head of jurisdiction[711] applies if a claim is made by the Commissioners for HM Revenue and Customs relating to duties or taxes against a defendant not domiciled in Scotland or Northern Ireland. No further comment is required.

4.83 Claims made for costs orders in favour of or against third parties: Paragraph 3.1 (18)

The third-party costs order head of jurisdiction allows for service out of the jurisdiction if a party to proceedings applies for an order pursuant to Senior Courts Act 1981, section 51, that costs be paid by or to someone not a party to the proceedings. As the court has power to make such orders in relation to proceedings, it would unduly restrict its powers if they could not be made against someone who fell within the statutory definition of the liability but who was outside its territorial jurisdiction.[712] This head, therefore, makes it clear that the court may assert jurisdiction over such a person even where he is out of the jurisdiction.

Whether this Ground needs to be relied on when the non-party is domiciled in a Member State is unclear. If the non-party is to be seen as being 'sued' in the sense in which the Brussels I Regulation uses the term, service on him may be made without permission if Chapter II of the Regulation gives the English court jurisdiction and CPR rule 6.33 is satisfied, but not otherwise. On the other hand, if the non-party is not being 'sued', so that the Regulation does not bear on the jurisdiction of the English court, permission is needed and this head will be the vehicle for making the application.[713] It is too early to see the correct answer. The view preferred above was that the non-party was being

---

709 This submission was accepted by the court in *AstraZeneca UK Ltd v. Albemarle International Corp* [2010] EWHC 1028 (Comm), [2010] 2 Lloyd's 61.

710 *Cf Bowling v. Cox* [1926] AC 751; *Rousou's Trustee v. Rousou* [1955] 3 All ER 486; *Re Jogia* [1988] 1 WLR 484.

711 Formerly RSC Order 11, r. 1(1)(n).

712 *Cf The Ikarian Reefer (No 2)* [2000] 1 WLR 603, decided before the adoption of CPR r. 6.36 and Ground (18), and discussed above, para. 2.77.

713 Though this conclusion would contradict, in part at least, the view established in *Mercedes-Benz AG v. Leiduck* [1996] 1 AC 284 in the context of RSC Order 11 that the service out provisions apply only to claims against defendants who are being sued for substantive relief.

sued in relation to the enforcement of a judgment from a court in a Member State.[714] As proceedings which have as their object the enforcement of judgments from the courts of a Member State are within the exclusive jurisdiction of the Member State in which enforcement is taking place,[715] service of the claim form out of the jurisdiction without permission would be justified, regardless of the domicile of the non-party.[716] If that were correct, sub-Paragraph (18) would be redundant, which seems unexpected. Until the doubt is cleared up, a claimant would be well advised to apply for permission to serve out, in all cases where the non-party is outside the jurisdiction, on the footing that, if it was unnecessary after all, the fact of obtaining an unnecessary permission cannot jeopardise his right to serve the claim form.

4.84 Claims made in certain admiralty proceedings: Paragraph 3.1(19)

The admiralty head of jurisdiction allows a claim form to be served out of the jurisdiction if the claim is in the nature of salvage and any part of the services took place within the jurisdiction, or the proceedings are to enforce a claim under sections 153, 154 or 175 of the Merchant Shipping Act 1995.

4.85 Claims made under other enactments: Paragraph 3.1(20)

The other enactment head of jurisdiction is a rather awkward thing. In earlier versions of the rule there was a list of certain statutes, claims made under which might ground an application for permission to serve out of the jurisdiction. The list is no longer given, and Ground (20)(a) simply provides that service out may be authorised if a claim is made under an enactment which allows proceedings to be brought, and the proceedings are not covered by any of the other sub-Paragraphs.

At first sight, this is odd, for it allows permission to be given in respect of every claim which is founded on a statute, without any further formal limitation: whether by reference to the particular statute, or by reference to who may be sued, or by reference to where the acts complained of were committed, and so forth. Quite why it would be right to treat claims based on statutes so sharply differently from claims based on the common law is not clear. The only effective limitation appears to be that the court will not authorise service out of the jurisdiction unless England is the proper place in which to bring the claim.[717] But if England is, in this sense, the natural forum, and if on a true construction the statute imposes liability on the defendant in respect of the facts and matters complained of, it is hard to see why service out should not be liable to be authorised.[718]

---

714 There being nothing overt in Art. 24(5) to limit its application to judgments from *other* Member States. If the matter is seen as something over which the court has jurisdiction by virtue of its having had jurisdiction to adjudicate the substantive action, the question whether the party out of the jurisdiction is being sued will not arise.

715 Article 24(5) of the recast Brussels I Regulation.

716 CPR rr 6.32, 6.33.

717 CPR r. 6.37(3). For illustration (based on Companies Act 2006, s. 994), see *Apex Global Management Ltd v. Fi Call Ltd* [2013] EWHC 1652 (Ch); (based on Insolvency Act 1986, s. 423) *Erste Group Bank AG v. JSC 'VMZ Red October'* [2013] EWHC 2926 (Comm).

718 *Erste Group Bank AG v JSC 'VMZ Red October'* [2013] EWHC 2926 (Comm), [150]. For the few cases in which a claim based on statutory liability may be served out of the jurisdiction without the permission of the court, see above, para. 4.56.

Sub-paragraph (20)(b) makes separate provision for claims made under EC Council Directive 76/308/EEC where service is to be effected in a Member State of the European Union.

4.86 The standard of proof needed to satisfy the elements of Paragraph 3.1

In order to establish whether the claimant has brought himself within the head of jurisdiction on which he relies, it is necessary to distinguish two possible areas of uncertainty.

It may first be argued that, even though the facts are not in dispute, the head of jurisdiction relied on, on its true construction, does not cover the claim set out in the claim form. In this case, the court must conclude that the meaning or interpretation of the sub-Paragraph for which the claimant is contending is the right one: a 'good arguable case' that it is right is not enough. According to *EF Hutton & Co (London) Ltd v. Moffarij*,[719] and as was explained above, the construction of Paragraph 3.1 of the Practice Direction, when the facts are not in dispute, is a matter of law for the court to decide; it is a matter of legal interpretation, on which the court must rule.

Distinct from this is the question whether the claimant has shown with sufficient certainty that the facts are such that his claim satisfies the components necessary, or that the claim ticks the boxes needed, for it to fall within the head of jurisdiction relied on.[720] Upon this point, although it had once been said[721] that the claimant was called upon to show that his version of the facts was, on balance, right, the prevailing view was that this set too high a standard. It was for all practical purposes decided in *Seaconsar Far East Ltd v. Bank Markazi Jomhouri Islami Iran*[722] that the claimant was required to show a 'good arguable case' that any disputed elements of the sub-Paragraph relied on were satisfied on the facts: a form of words which was sufficiently well understood for the judge to know it when he saw it, even though it was hard to express in words, and misleading to express it in percentage numbers.

At any rate, and as a matter of common law, a 'good arguable case' did not require the claimant to demonstrate that he was probably right, or that he had 'much the better of the argument' on the jurisdictional question which is disputed by the defendant.[723] The practical reason for this may have been that, at this stage the court simply does not know whether the conditions for its exercise of jurisdiction, so far as these are stated in Paragraph 3.1, are satisfied. It cannot be expected to resolve differences revealed by the various witness statements.[724] So

---

719 [1989] 1 WLR 488 (the case was decided under RSC Order 11, but the principle is not in dispute).

720 That is, that there is a contract, and one which was made within the jurisdiction; that there was a contract which was broken within the jurisdiction, etc.

721 *Attock Cement Co Ltd v. Romanian Bank for Foreign Trade* [1989] 1 WLR 1147.

722 [1994] 1 AC 438. See also *Agrafax Public Relations Ltd v. United Scottish Society Inc* [1995] ILPr 753. It may appear from this that the same test applies as in relation to jurisdiction under the Brussels I Regulation and Brussels Convention, but it is also clear that the test of a 'good arguable case' is a flexible one, and that flexibility may lead to some differences in application as between the Civil Procedure Rules and the Brussels I Regulation.

723 For example, *Seaconsar Far East Ltd v. Bank Markazi Jomhouri Islami Iran* [1994] 1 AC 438 (drawing the distinction between the test of a 'good arguable case' and the 'serious issue to be tried' standard which is applied to the merits of the claim).

724 Though there appears to be nothing to prevent the parties agreeing that the court's decision on the jurisdiction application (say on whether there was a contract, or whether it was governed by English law) should be taken as conclusive on the issues which arise as a matter of substance. In such a case it seems inevitable that the court will be asked to decide the issue on the balance of the material before it. Such cases, though, which depend on the agreement of the parties and of the court, and which may be a form of estoppel by convention, do not establish a wider principle applicable in cases in which the jurisdiction is disputed on the traditional basis that there was no proper basis for granting permission to serve out.

in *Sharab v. Al-Saud*,[725] for example, the court simply confirmed that it was necessary for the claimant to show a good arguable case that a contract which she wished to enforce was a contract made within the jurisdiction. The suggestion that this required her to show that she had 'the better of the argument', or 'much the better of the argument', on the point was not supported.

By contrast, where the jurisdiction of the court is based on the rules of the Brussels I Regulation, the formulation of 'a good arguable case' was, correctly, interpreted to mean that the claimant had to have '(much) the better of the argument'.[726] It was therefore very surprising that the need to show a 'good arguable case', when the question was whether the claimant had satisfied Paragraph 3.1, was equated with having 'much the better of the argument' in *AK Investment CJSC v. Kyrgyz Mobil Tel Ltd*.[727] The decision is, in this respect, wrong, and it should not be followed. The justification for this submission follows.

Where the decision for a court is whether one Member State or another has jurisdiction, as it is when a court is deciding whether it has special jurisdiction, or whether there is an agreement on choice of court for a Member State, it is deciding a jurisdictional question which will be effective in all Member States; it is, in effect, deciding which Member State will adjudicate. Moreover, the jurisdictional rules which it is applying are rigid and unmoderated by any jurisdictional discretion: the court either has jurisdiction, which it must exercise, or it does not. In those circumstances, a test which asks which side has the better of the argument, or much the better of the argument, on the jurisdictional question, is right in principle.

But where the question is whether to exercise jurisdiction under CPR rule 6.36, the only court to consider is the English court. It is not deciding between the jurisdiction of two courts of equal authority. And it will exercise jurisdiction only if England is the proper place to bring the claim. That means that much of the heavy jurisdictional lifting is done by CPR rule 6.37(3); and if England is the proper place to bring the claim, it is very far from obvious why jurisdiction should not be exercised. In such circumstances the need to satisfy the requirements of Paragraph 3.1 is questionable; but the idea that this requirement should be made *more* demanding than hitherto understood is not rational.[728] To repeat: the exercise of jurisdiction on the basis of service out, with the permission of the court which has a discretion to exercise, is a very different thing from the decision whether the Brussels I Regulation requires the court to exercise jurisdiction. The functions of the question which asks whether the jurisdictional rule is satisfied are quite different; there is no reason for the tests to be the same. In the circumstances, it was an error to say that 'a good arguable case' was an expression whose meaning and content was variable. It is time to stop it. For the satisfaction of Paragraph 3.1, the law should be restated in its traditional terms.

As English courts are not bound by decisions of the Privy Council, this aspect of *AK Investment* is one which need not be followed. It is, admittedly, more difficult to advance

---

725 [2009] EWCA Civ 353, [2009] 2 Lloyd's Rep 160.

726 *Canada Trust Co v. Stolzenberg (No 2)* [2002] 1 AC 1 (though the expression was first used by Waller LJ in the court below); *Bols Distilleries BV v. Superior Yacht Services Ltd* [2006] UKPC 45, [2007] 1 WLR 12.

727 [2011] UKPC 7, [2012] 1 WLR 1804, [71]. The use of the 'much the better' test in *Erste Group Bank AG v. JSC 'VMZ Red October'* [2013] EWHC 2926 (Comm) may be regarded as the loyal application of an unfortunate authority.

728 Unless, of course, Paragraph 3.1 is approached as though it defined an exorbitant jurisdiction, which *Abela v. Baadarani* [2013] UKSC 44, [2013] 1 WLR 2043 explains that it is not.

this point of view in the light of *VTB Capital plc v. Nutritek International Corp*,[729] but in that decision it was only Lord Clarke who qualified the 'good arguable case' test in the way proposed in *AK Investment*. As his was a dissenting judgment, and as the other judgments did not elaborate on the meaning of 'good arguable case' as it applied to service out of the jurisdiction, and as it is not apparent that the arguments on this point were squarely raised and squarely addressed,[730] there is no need to accept that the law has been changed.[731] It is not necessary for the claimant to show that he has '(much) the better of the argument' that the elements of Paragraph 3.1 were satisfied.

4.87 Discretion to authorise service out of the jurisdiction: CPR rule 6.37

Once the claimant has shown (if any of the jurisdictional facts is disputed, to the standard of a good arguable case) that his claim falls within one or more of the heads of jurisdiction in Paragraph 3.1 of the Practice Direction, the court is empowered to make an order granting permission to serve out of the jurisdiction. Whether it will do so depends upon the court's being satisfied by the claimant on two further points which regulate its discretion to make the order: the appropriateness of England as the forum for the trial, and the apparent strength of the merits of the claim against the defendant. It is well established that these are separate and distinct requirements, the case law establishing that the ample satisfaction of the one could not condone a marginal failure to satisfy the other.[732] This continues to be the law today.

If on the hearing to dispute the jurisdiction, under CPR Part 11, the defendant succeeds in showing that the claimant could not have satisfied, or should not have been held to have satisfied, the requirements of CPR rule 6.36, the court will (or should) declare that it has no jurisdiction, and the order granting permission to serve process, and service of the process itself, will all be set aside.

4.88 Pointers to the exercise of discretion (1): England is the proper place to bring the claim: CPR rule 6.37(3)

The requirement that England and Wales be shown to be the proper place in which to bring the claim is the successor to the requirement, set out in RSC Order 11, rule 4(2), which required the claimant to shown that the case was a proper one for service out of the jurisdiction. This requirement was interpreted as requiring, among other things, that the claimant show, clearly and distinctly, that England is the most appropriate forum for the bringing of the claim. There is no reason to suppose that the wording of CPR rule 6.37(3) intended to make substantial alteration to the law which had been established under the predecessor rule, though there will be cases in which the two tests produce different answers, and when they do, the version set out in rule 6.37(3) is obviously the one to be applied.

---

729 [2013] UKSC 5, [2013] 2 AC 337. It is not clear that the argument advanced here was put to the court, or to the Court of Appeal, which also (perhaps also regrettably) took its law from *AK Investment*.

730 It may eventually have been common ground that Paragraph 3.1 was satisfied on the facts.

731 See further, *BNP Paribas SA v. Anchorage Capital Europe LLP* [2013] EWHC 3073 (Comm); *Virgin Atlantic Airways Ltd v. KI Holdings Co Ltd* [2014] EWHC 1671 (Comm), which show that the law is still perturbed by the apparent change in the traditional understanding of the common law.

732 *Seaconsar Far East Ltd v. Bank Markazi Jomhouri Islami Iran* [1994] 1 AC 438.

As a result, the claimant will be required to show that England is the proper place to bring the claim by satisfying the requirements which the previous case law identified as establishing a proper case for service out. The old cases will continue to be useful on what is required to demonstrate that England is the proper place in which to being the claim.[733]

The landmark decision which established this requirement was the decision of the House of Lords in *Spiliada Maritime Corp v. Cansulex Ltd*.[734] In that case it was alleged that the defendants were party to a contract governed by English law,[735] and that service out of the jurisdiction should be authorised on that basis. In the opinion of the House of Lords, to obtain permission to serve the defendants outside the jurisdiction, it was necessary for the claimants to show that England was 'the forum in which the case can suitably be tried for the interests of all the parties and the interests of justice',[736] or, putting it another way, 'the burden of proof rests on the plaintiff to persuade the court that England is the appropriate forum for the trial of the action ... he has to show that this is clearly so. In other words, the burden is, quite simply, the obverse of that applicable where a stay is sought of proceedings started in this country as of right'.[737]

It follows that those facts and matters described above[738] which were used to help determine whether a foreign forum was clearly or distinctly more appropriate than England, apply equally, but in mirror image, when the claimant is seeking to show, clearly or distinctly, that England is the appropriate forum, or the proper place in which to bring the claim. It would be repetitious to set them out again here, but certain particular observations may be justified.

4.89 England as the proper place: English law as the governing law

A significant question arises as to the degree to which the identification of English law as the law which will or should be applied to determine the merits of the claim bears on the requirement that England be the most appropriate forum for the trial of the action. It obviously has *some* bearing, but how much?

In cases based on a contract, the courts accept that the bare fact that English law governs the contract will not automatically lead to the grant of permission to serve out;[739] but where it appears that a party is resisting English jurisdiction in order to avoid the results which the application of English law would produce, the court should be astute to detect and frustrate undermining behaviour.[740]

---

733 In the case of an application for permission to serve in Scotland or Northern Ireland, CPR r. 6.37(4) requires that the court, in deciding whether to grant permission, compare the comparative cost and convenience of suing in the two jurisdictions.

734 [1987] AC 460. See also *Berezovsky v. Michaels* [2000] 1 WLR 1004, which shows that a claimant may select which facts and matters to rely on in order to enhance his argument that England is the proper place to bring the claim.

735 Paragraph 3.1(6)(c) of the Practice Direction; previously RSC Order 11, r. 1(1)(d)(iii).

736 At 480.

737 At 481. The fact that an English judgment would be enforceable under Chapter III of the Brussels I Regulation may conceivably contribute to the seeing of England as a proper place to bring the claim: *International Credit and Investment Co (Overseas) Ltd v. Adham* [1999] ILPr 302; *Sharab v. Al-Saud* [2009] EWCA Civ 353, [2009] 2 Lloyd's Rep 160.

738 Paragraphs 4.22 *et seq.*, above.

739 *MacSteel (Holdings) Ltd v. Thermasteel (Canada) Inc* [1996] CLC 1403.

740 *The Magnum* [1989] 1 Lloyd's Rep 47, 51; *HIB Ltd v. Guardian Insurance Co Inc* [1997] 1 Lloyd's Rep 412.

Where the parties have made an express choice of English law to govern the contract, it may be thought that they expected the English courts to be ready to exercise jurisdiction over it. To tell the truth, it is more often than not artificial to try to interpret the intentions which led the parties to express a choice of law but not to express a choice of court. A possible explanation may be that the parties sought to create certainty as to which law would govern the substance of their relationship, and which law would be applied if they reached the point of litigation, but saw no need, or did not wish, to tie their hands to a particular choice of court. It would follow that a choice of English law should not be too quickly seen as an actual but unexpressed choice of an English court, but should be taken at face value: the courts have been correct in not equating a choice of English law to govern a contract as though it were in every respect the same as a choice of English courts.[741]

On the other hand, an express choice of law deserves to be given its proper weight. If the evidence suggests that the foreign court would be unable or unwilling to apply the law chosen by the parties,[742] or if the evidence suggests that the fact that the foreign court will be applying what is for it a foreign law, in circumstances in which the absence of an avenue of appeal to correct errors of law may pose a real risk that the law chosen by the parties would not be properly applied,[743] the court should be rather more willing to see England as the proper place to bring the claim, because it will be the only place in which the parties may obtain the adjudication they bound themselves to seek and settle for.[744] The fact that a foreign legal system will not be able, reliably at least, to correct errors of English law, does not involve disparaging that foreign system, for the same, *mutatis mutandis*, is true of an English court when it seeks to apply foreign law. It reflects the fact that court systems apply and correct errors in their own laws far better than they do in respect of foreign laws.

In the absence of an express choice of English law,[745] where all that may be said is that the rules for choice of law suggest that English law should be applied, greater caution will precede the grant of permission, perhaps because there is no reason to suppose that the English approach to the issue of applicable law is universal. However, in some categories of case there is an institutional view, which tends to displace individual assessment that England will be the most appropriate place to bring the claim, for reasons which include the fact that English will be the applicable law. For example, insurance written on the London market will almost always be governed by English law, and the proposition that England will be the most appropriate forum will be easily sustained.[746] Defamation arising from publication

---

741 *MacSteel Commercial Holdings (Pty) Ltd v. Thermasteel Canada Inc* [1996] CLC 1403; *BP Exploration Co (Libya) Ltd v. Hunt (No 2)* [1976] 3 All ER 879; *The Elli 2* [1985] 1 Lloyd's Rep 107; *Sawyer v. Atari Interactive Inc* [2005] EWHC 2351 (Ch), [2006] ILPr 8; *Novus Aviation Ltd v. Onur Air Tasimacilik A/S* [2009] EWCA Civ 122, [2009] 1 Lloyd's Rep 576.

742 If there is an issue of English public policy, such a matter can generally only be decided by an English court, and this will make England more obviously the natural forum: *E.I. Du Pont de Nemours v. Agnew (No 1)* [1987] 2 Lloyd's Rep 585; see also *CGU International Insurance plc v. Szabo* [2002] 1 All ER (Comm) 83; *Novus Aviation Ltd v. Onur Air Tasimacilik A/S* [2009] EWCA Civ 122, [2009] 1 Lloyd's Rep 576.

743 *Wright v. Deccan Chargers Sporting Ventures Ltd* [2011] EWHC 1307 (QB), [2011] ILPr 781.

744 *Golden Ocean Group Ltd v. Salgaocar Mining Industries Pvt Ltd* [2011] EWHC 56 (Comm), [2011] 2 All ER (Comm) 95, esp. [143]; *Baturina v. Chistyakov* [2014] EWCA Civ 1134 (a stay case, but the point is general). But if the foreign court will be well able to apply English law, this point is much diminished: *Baturina v. Chistyakov* [2014] EWCA Civ 1134; also *Mujur Bakat Sdn Bhd v. UNI Asia General Insurance Bhd* [2011] EWHC 643 (Comm), [2011] Lloyd's Rep IR 465.

745 English law nevertheless being the law which governs the contract.

746 *Arkwright Mutual Insurance Co v. Bryanston Insurance Co Ltd* [1990] 2 QB 649; *CGU International Insurance plc v. Szabo* [2002] 1 All ER (Comm) 83; *Lincoln National Life Insurance Co v. Employers' Reinsurance Corp* [2002]

to an English readership will be governed by English law, and this fact alongside others will make England the most appropriate forum for the litigation which is confined to such a complaint.[747] Where the claim in question falls within the scope of a statute which imposes a liability which would not be applied by a foreign court, it is arguable that England is the most appropriate forum because it is the only forum in which the legislation can be applied. This may be of particular importance when dealing with applications falling within Paragraph 3.1(20) of the Practice Direction.[748]

In tort cases which are committed outside a contractual relationship,[749] in particular, it had at one time been understood and accepted that the fact that the tort took place in England would be very likely to make England the proper place to bring the claim, for in many such cases there will a coincidence of applicable law and witness convenience.[750] It has been made clear, however, that if this is a presumption, it is certainly not a rule. In *VTB Capital plc v. Nutritek International Corp*[751] the tort was held to have taken place in England, but the facts of the dispute were, in the evaluation of the court, overwhelmingly Russian, and this meant that England was not the proper place to bring the claim, or was not the most appropriate place for the trial of the action. Two reasons in particular support this: first, it is no longer the rule of English private international law that a tort is governed by the law of the place of its commission;[752] and second, for some torts, particularly those of inflicting pure economic injury, there will often be no place where the tort can sensibly be said to have been committed. In those cases, to look for the place of the tort may be to look for something which is not really there, and to find it is to pick up something of no great value. As *VTB Capital plc v. Nutritek International Corp* demonstrates, the identification of the applicable law is a variable part of the overall evaluation, but in the end it is no more than that.

4.90 England as the proper place for the trial of the claim: other factors

A number of other factors may help sustain the argument that England is the proper place for the trial of the action. One such is the 'Cambridgeshire' factor, as it has come to be known, which played an important part in *Spiliada* in helping to determine whether the natural forum

---

EWHC 28 (Comm), [2002] Lloyd's Rep IR 853; *Swiss Reinsurance Co Ltd v. United India Insurance Co* [2003] EWHC 741, [2004] ILPr 4; *Prifti v. Musini* [2003] EWHC 2796 (Comm); *Markel International Insurance Co Ltd v. La Republica Compania Argentina de Seguros Generales SA* [2004] EWHC 1826 Comm, [2005] 1 Lloyd's Rep IR 90; *Carvill America Inc v. Camperdown UK Ltd* [2005] EWCA Civ 645, [2005] 2 Lloyd's Rep 457 (a case concerning reinsurance brokerage in the London market). But in many such cases, English law will be expressly chosen.

747 *Berezovsky v. Michaels* [2000] 1 WLR 1004, a case on service out of the jurisdiction, discussed further below, para. 4.91. But in the case of mass publication, the court may not now have the jurisdiction it had in those cases: Defamation Act 2013, s. 9, on which see above, para. 4.12.

748 And see, in the Australian context, *Akai v. People's Insurance Co* (1997) 188 CLR 418; *Reinsurance Australia Corp Ltd v. HIH Casualty and General Insurance Ltd (in liq)* (2003) 254 ALR 29, [293]: Australian court cannot be inappropriate, and therefore no stay will be granted, if it is the only court in which a claim under the Trade Practices Act 1974 could be fully and properly entertained.

749 It may be different if the torts are associated with contracts which contain choice of law or choice of court agreements: the contracts may exercise an influence on the law governing the tort, or on the proper place to sue in respect of it: see *VTB Capital plc v. Nutritek International Corp* [2013] UKSC 5, [2013] 2 AC 337.

750 *The Albaforth* [1984] 2 Lloyd's Rep 91; *Berezovsky v. Michaels* [2000] 1 WLR 1004.

751 [2013] UKSC 5, [2013] 2 AC 337; see also *Navig8 Pte Ltd v. Al-Riyadh Co for Vegetable Oil Industry* [2013] EWHC 328 (Comm), [2013] 2 Lloyd's Rep 104, [27].

752 Both the Rome II Regulation, and the Private International Law (Miscellaneous Provisions) Act 1995 before it apply, as a starting point, a 'place of the damage' rule.

was in England. There had recently been litigation concerning a claim factually and scientifically similar to the one in *Spiliada*, between closely related parties, and which had involved many of the witnesses who were expected to give evidence in *Spiliada* itself. The scientific learning curve, which had been climbed once, was a steep one in cases such as those,[753] and the interests of justice were found to favour that experience being recycled. Although in later cases this factor has been relied on without much apparent success,[754] it remains a factor which may possibly help identify a court, if there is one, as clearly or distinctly more appropriate for the trial in the interests of all the parties and for the ends of justice.[755]

Second, if the court is asked to grant permission to serve D1, but will be unable to exercise jurisdiction over D2 and D3, it will be much harder to show that the interests of justice favour service on D1. The interests of justice are more likely to favour having all issues between all parties resolved coherently, in a single trial.[756] Likewise, if there are proceedings before the foreign court, instituted before the English proceedings and liable to continue in any event, it will be difficult to justify an application to serve out and, by doing so, to create a real risk of conflicting judgments.[757] By contrast, if England is the only place where comprehensive justice can be done in a complex dispute involving many parties, this may well incline the court to authorise service out.[758]

Third, there may be relationships or transactions, for which the relevant parties had agreed to English jurisdiction, which allow it to be said that the defendant knew or should have known that this would make England the proper place to sue him, or sue him as well. For example, where the controller of a company who has caused it to make a jurisdiction agreement for the English courts, and a claim which is associated with that relationship is made against that individual, it may be argued that England is the proper place to being the claim in question: not because he is bound by the jurisdiction agreement as though a party to it, but because it is still the proper and predictable place for him to be sued. The argument is legally sound, but its application to the facts of an individual case will naturally be variable.[759]

---

753 Apparently the factual issues as to the corrosive properties of allegedly damp sulphur are difficult to understand and determine. By contrast, for a refusal to see this factor as being of particular importance, see (in the context of the Australian test, and refusing to see the Dust Diseases Tribunal of NSW as having comparable claims to pre-eminent suitability) *BHP Billiton Ltd v. Schultz* (2004) 221 CLR 400.

754 See, for example, *SNI Aérospatiale v. Lee Kui Jak* [1987] AC 871; *Royal & Sun Alliance Insurance plc v. Rolls-Royce plc* [2010] EWHC 1869 (Comm), [2010] Lloyd's Rep IR 637. It may have played a minor (but unacknowledged) part in the reasoning of the court in *Teekay Tankers Ltd v. STX Offshore & Shipping Co* [2014] EWHC 3612 (Comm), [73].

755 It is possible to construe the judgment in *Spiliada* as having treated the 'Cambridgeshire' factor as something which could be relied on as an advantage taken into account only once the natural forum has been identified by the party charged with identifying it. This would be a misreading: not only does it fit more easily within the process of identifying a natural forum, but if the claimant has shown the natural forum to be England, it is for the *defendant* to assert the advantages of which it would be an overriding injustice to deprive him. The 'Cambridgeshire' factor here operated to the advantage of the claimant, not the defendant, so operates, if at all, at the first stage, not the second stage, of the enquiry.

756 *New Hampshire Insurance Co v. Strabag Bau AG* [1992] 1 Lloyd's Rep 361. On the other hand, to allow the absence of one possible defendant to destroy the case for service out may be to allow the tail to wag the dog, and it will not be guaranteed to succeed: *Münchener Rückversicherungs GmbH v. Commonwealth Insurance Co* [2004] EWHC 914 (Comm).

757 *Galaxy Special Maritime Enterprise v. Prima Ceylon Ltd, The 'Olympic Galaxy'* [2006] EWCA Civ 528, [2006] 2 Lloyd's Rep 27.

758 *Groupama Insurance Co Ltd v. Channel Islands Securities Ltd* [2002] Lloyd's Rep IR 843; *BAT Industries plc v. Windward Prospects Ltd* [2013] EWHC 4087 (Comm), [2014] 2 All ER (Comm) 757.

759 *VTB Capital plc v. Nutritek International Corp* [2013] UKSC 5, [2013] 2 AC 337: see esp. [102]–[110], [221]–[222], [234]–[235].

Fourth, a claim may have been tailored by the claimant so that it appears that England is the proper place for it to be brought.[760] The clearest examples were found in the law of defamation as it stood before the coming into force of Defamation Act 2013, section 9. Under the previous law, if a claimant has been defamed in a journal or other publication with international circulation, or on the Internet, it is improbable that England is the natural forum for a claim in respect of the damage done by the totality of publication to all those who read it. But if the complaint and claim is confined to the damage done by publication in England, it appeared to be hard to counter the submission that England is the natural forum for its resolution. But the abuse of this freedom resulted in changes to the law of jurisdiction over defamation claims.[761]

Fifth, it was considered at one time that, where proceedings were brought by a claimant for a declaration of non-liability, that fact gave a clear indication that England is not the proper place to sue, but had instead been contrived as an artificial and inappropriate place, in which to bring the claim.[762] If this was ever true, it is submitted that it is now of next to no significance, or has altogether disappeared today. As Paragraph 3.1(8) now makes express provision for service out in proceedings for a declaration that there is no contract, and hence no liability owed by the claimant, it is very difficult to argue that the fact that the claim seeks negative declaratory relief is of any particular jurisdictional significance. It is now recognised that the claim for declaratory relief can be an entirely proper and useful procedural measure.[763] The court will not grant permission to serve out if there is no live dispute between the parties, and will in any event not grant permission if England is not shown to be the most appropriate place for the trial of the issues; and the appreciation of these matters is peculiarly within the discretion of the judge. Beyond that it is unlikely that the form in which the claim is framed or the relief sought is of any additional significance. The point is re-examined in Chapter 5.[764]

4.91 England as the proper place for the trial of the claim: even though England is not the natural forum for the claim

The previous paragraph tried to avoid using the terminology of the natural forum. This was deliberate, for in almost all cases in which England is the proper place to bring the claim (as CPR rule 6.37(3) expressed it), or clearly or distinctly the most appropriate forum (as *Spiliada* put it), it will also be the natural forum for the trial of the claim. It may, however, be that even if England is not shown to be the natural forum it may still be the proper place in which to bring the claim. For example, if England has been chosen by the parties in a valid

---

760 This may be done by bringing proceedings against a parent or holding company, rather than against the individual entity which did the injury directly, and relying on what the parent alone did or was responsible for: see, for example, *Lubbe v. Cape plc* [2000] 1 WLR 1545. See also *Friis v. Colborn* [2009] EWHC 903 (Ch), where the court took the view that it was not open to the claimant to make England the natural forum for a claim to restrain the use of confidential information when the natural place for that issue to be resolved was California.

761 See above, para. 4.12.

762 Or under the pre-CPR rules, that the case was not a proper one for service out of the jurisdiction.

763 *Messier Dowty Ltd v. Sabena SA* [2000] 1 WLR 2040; *Youell v. Kara Mara Shipping Co* [2000] 2 Lloyd's Rep 102. See also *New Hampshire Insurance Co v. Phillips Electronics North America Corp* [1998] ILPr 256; *Gan Insurance Co Ltd v. Tai Ping Insurance Co Ltd* [1998] CLC 1072; *CGU International Insurance plc v. Szabo* [2002] 1 All ER (Comm) 83; *Smyth v. Behbehani* [1999] ILPr 584 (a stay case).

764 See paras 5.55 *et seq.*, below.

choice of court agreement,[765] England is the proper place to bring the claim; the question whether England is the natural forum will not arise.[766]

If England is not the natural forum, but there is no other forum available, England may still be the proper place in which to bring the claim. If, for example, the defendant is in a territory where the administration of civil justice has utterly broken down or has utterly degenerated,[767] it is not really credible that the common law would require a claimant, whose claim falls within Paragraph 3.1 of the Practice Direction, to go without a judicial resolution of his dispute. It will be a rare case, but its solution should be obvious. So if the other court were to be in a State in civil war or overrun with lethal viral diseases, it should be open to an English court to find that England is the proper place to being the claim. If the claimant cannot travel to the foreign country, because no sane person would go there and for that reason cannot obtain a trial there, this may suggest, without undue difficulty, that England is the proper place to bring the claim.[768]

The third category of case is far more controversial, and its recent development is rather unsettling. The starting point is that there are some places in which civilisation has broken down in so fundamental a way that it is unrealistic to suppose that anyone could expect a fair trial from the courts. Places, such as Nazi Germany,[769] and of Lebanon[770] in its years of kidnapping and civil war, and of the eastern Congo in its state of anarchy,[771] were so uncivilised that nobody could expect a fair trial, either because the infrastructure of the State had broken down, or because the State was institutionally evil. But there are many countries in which one could reasonably apprehend that the quality of justice would be far lower than anything to be found in London. It was for a long time the law that this was a thought which a litigant must keep to himself: general disparaging of a foreign system is not permissible. But more recently, some claimants faced with this have succeeded in persuading the English courts that there is a risk that *they* would not receive justice from the foreign court in question, perhaps because there is a State interest in the matter which would pervert the course of justice, and have secured a decision that, as a result, England is the proper place to bring the claim.[772] In other words, it may not need to be said that the courts of that foreign country are incapable of doing justice, only that when certain litigants are involved the scales of justice do not work as they otherwise would.

---

765 This is subject to the large proviso that if the case falls within the scope of the Brussels I Regulation, or Brussels or Lugano Conventions, the particular instrument contains provisions on agreements on choice of court which will give the court exclusive jurisdiction if the clause complies with the formalities therein set out, and one of the parties to the agreement is domiciled in a Member or Contracting State. In such a case permission will not be needed: CPR r. 6.33.

766 If the parties have chosen English law but not English jurisdiction, it may well indicate that they did not want English jurisdiction: *MacSteel (Holdings) Ltd v. Thermasteel (Canada) Inc* [1996] CLC 1403.

767 *Oppenheimer v. Rosenthal* [1937] 1 All ER 23; *889457 Alberta Inc v. Katanga Mining Ltd* [2008] EWHC 2679 (Comm), [2009] ILPr 175.

768 Unless, of course, the defendant has brought this misfortune upon himself by, for example, being a fugitive from justice in the foreign country: see *Askin v. Absa Bank* [1999] ILPr 471; *Merrill Lynch v. Raffa* [2001] ILPr 437; *Purcell v. Khyatt, The Times*, 23 November 1987.

769 *Oppenheimer v. Rosenthal* [1937] 1 All ER 23.

770 *Purcell v. Khyatt, The Times*, 23 November 1987.

771 *889457 Alberta Inc v. Katanga Mining Ltd* [2008] EWHC 2679 (Comm), [2009] ILPr 175.

772 *Cherney v. Deripaska* [2009] EWCA Civ 849, [2010] 1 All ER (Comm) 456; *AK Investment CJSC v. Kyrgyz Mobil Tel Ltd* [2011] UKPC 7, [2012] 1 WLR 1804. There are others, but these two authorities define the principle.

But however broadly or narrowly the point it put, the methodology by which an English court may make such an assessment in advance of any hearing,[773] of what the foreign court may do in the instant case is elusive. It is not altogether satisfactory for an English court to be asked to find that England is the proper place for the trial of a claim because the courts of a foreign country, which may otherwise be the place with which the dispute has its closest factual and legal connection, cannot be trusted to dispense justice according to their law. In some cases in which this contention is advanced there is room for the suspicion that the claimant, fearing that he will lose before the foreign court, seeks to cloak that irrelevant fact in allegations of unjudicial behaviour by foreign judges. English private international law may not have much to gain by lending encouragement to it; English law has not yet accepted that its courts may be asked to provide a 'forum of necessity',[774] as it is sometimes called.[775] Yet what is a court to do if the evidence before it appears to show that there really is a risk that a claimant will not get a fair trial unless allowed to sue in England? The truth may be that bad countries make hard law; and if the common law does not require the English court to exercise jurisdiction, it is possible that Article 6 ECHR would fill the gap, so the common law might as well do it for itself.

In the end, in an atypical case a court may depart from the structure by which it usually regulates its discretion to authorise service out. In *Agrafax Public Relations Ltd v. United Scottish Society Inc*,[776] permission to serve out was upheld in a 'finely balanced' case on the basis of the fact that the costs rule to be applied by an American court would make it wholly uneconomic for the claimant to pursue his claim in the United States; a similar approach may be seen in *Roneleigh v. MII Exports*,[777] where the American law and practice on litigation costs was a good reason for the claimant to abandon a claim if it could not be brought in England. But this does appear to take the principle to its limit: that if the claimant would enjoy only a Pyrrhic victory in the foreign court, service out may be authorised, even though England is not otherwise the proper place to bring the claim, or is clearly not the natural forum for the claim. This would not appear to be aligned with *Spiliada*, unless – as it considered the case to be – the *Spiliada* test is a reliable pointer to the interests of justice, but not a straitjacket which will sometimes require the court to produce an unjust result. That would be to pervert *Spiliada*, not to apply it.

4.92 The overall shape of the 'proper place' or 'most appropriate forum' test

If the claimant has shown that England is the proper place to bring the claim, a test which was formulated as the mirror image of the rule which applies to stays of proceedings, which is certainly what *Spiliada* suggested, the burden would then pass to the defendant to show that it would (still) be unjust to allow service to be made out of the jurisdiction. But it has been held that this two-stage approach is not quite right, and that by contrast with the manner in which the law applies to applications for a stay of proceedings, where the analysis

---

773 The matter is rather different when dealing with the question whether to deny recognition to a judgment which was given in proceedings which fell far short of what looks like the administration of justice.

774 The point that the claim has also to satisfy Paragraph 3.1 does not materially affect the argument.

775 The doctrine appears to be found in some civilian systems: see Retornaz and Bolders [2008] Rev crit DIP 225.

776 [1995] ILPr 753. It is, however, arguable that this can be reconciled with *Spiliada* in the speech of Lord Templeman, at 465.

777 [1989] 1 WLR 619.

is certainly conducted in two stages, at least to begin with, in service out cases there is a single test, not a test in which the burden is first on the claimant, then on the defendant. Such, at least, was the view of the Court of Appeal in *VTB Capital plc v. Nutritek International Corp*,[778] though it is not so clear that the Supreme Court considered the issue of whether the test was to be conducted in two stages or one to be a significant one.[779] So long as the judge before whom the application to dispute the jurisdiction comes asks whether England has been shown to be the proper place to bring the claim, or the most appropriate place, in the interests of justice for the trial of the action, his decision will not be impeachable. If he finds it more convenient or transparent to organise the material before him into two provisional parts, it is hard to see the error or the harm.

Whether there should be seen to be a one stage or two-stage test, therefore, is not really the issue. The question whether England is the proper place to bring the claim, or whether England is the most appropriate place, in the interests of justice, for the trial of the action, may appear straightforward, but the facts and matters which bear on it will, from one case to another, vary widely. In those circumstances, the judge should be allowed to organise the material, and his analysis of it, in the way which seems most suitable. In the end there is a single question, but it is in the nature of single questions to be built on more complex foundations. There is really no point to be made here, as the Supreme Court seems rather to have accepted.

4.93 Pointers to the exercise of discretion (2): there is a serious issue on the merits

If the claim falls within one or more of the sub-Paragraphs of the Practice Direction, and if the court is satisfied that England is the proper place to bring the claim, the court still has one final issue to address before granting permission to serve out of the jurisdiction. It will not grant permission unless the claimant shows (unless the issue is conceded for the purpose of the jurisdiction application) that there is a serious issue to be tried on the merits of his claim; and it will set the permission aside again if, when the defendant disputes the jurisdiction, the claimant is, when challenged on the point, unable to show that he has a serious case on the merits of the claim.[780] This is now taken to mean that the prospects of success are real, as distinct from being imaginary or fanciful.[781]

The origin of this rule lay in the requirement in RSC Order 11, rule 4(2), that leave to serve out should not be made 'unless it shall be made sufficiently to appear to the court that the case is a proper one... ' for the making of the order. In *Seaconsar Far East Ltd v. Bank Markazi Jomhouri Islami Iran*,[782] the House of Lords interpreted this as meaning that an order

---

778 [2012] EWCA Civ 808, [2012] 2 Lloyd's Rep 313, [128] *et seq.*

779 *VTB Capital plc v. Nutritek International Corp* [2013] UKSC 5, [2013] 2 AC 337, [44], [99], [156], [230].

780 Of course, where service was not dependent on the permission of the court, this requirement is not applicable. But a defendant who has been served as of right may apply to have the claim struck out on the ground that it does not have a reasonable prospect of success, and though this is not a challenge to the jurisdiction, and should not be made until after any challenge to the jurisdiction has been disposed of, it achieves a superficially similar result: superficially, because the decision is taken by reference to the merits of the claim, and may therefore be recognised as *res judicata* in foreign proceedings.

781 *AstraZeneca UK Ltd v. Albemarle International Corp* [2010] EWHC 1028, [2010] 2 Lloyd's Rep 61.

782 [1994] 1 AC 438. The High Court of Australia has adopted a very similar standard: *Hyde v. Agar* (2001) 201 CLR 552.

authorising service would not be made unless the claimant showed that there was a serious issue to be tried on the merits of the claim. The rule, as interpreted in *Seaconsar*, imposed on the claimant a relatively modest burden in relation to the merits of the claim, it being for the court to adjudicate on whether he had discharged it. There was no justification for making more demands on the claimant, given that he will have shown England to be the natural forum as well as satisfying one or more of the heads of jurisdiction provided in the Civil Procedure Rules.

The formal position under CPR rule 6.37 is at first sight slightly different. CPR rule 6.37(1)(b) requires the claimant's written evidence to state that he believes that his claim has a reasonable prospect of success. This does not mean that a genuine belief in the prospects of success on the merits at trial is sufficient. It means that the claimant has to make a formal statement of his belief that he has a reasonable prospect of success. That statement made, it is up to the court to decide, if it is not conceded, whether there really is a serious issue as to the merits of the claim. This is sensible: it would make no sense for a defendant to have to make a separate application for summary judgment under CPR rule 24.2 when one of his contentions is that the claimant has not raised a serious issue which is fit to go to trial; and for this reason the law established in *Seaconsar* prior to the adoption of CPR rule 6.37 remains reliable.

That the burden on the claimant should be a low one is also justifiable by reference to *Seaconsar*. If the claimant has shown that England is clearly or distinctly the most appropriate forum, and if it is not unjust to require the defendant to come to England to defend himself or suffer judgment in default, there is no good reason to place a further significant hurdle in the claimant's way. As long as the claim on the merits is, and is not merely believed to be, sufficiently strong to survive a notional application for its being struck out, that will suffice.[783] The practicality of this is also pretty clear: all the court will have seen will be the claim form and certain written evidence. It is not really sensible to ask the court at this stage to do other than to ascertain whether the case looks as though it deserves a hearing.

There will be cases, therefore, in which the factual and legal issues are so complex that it will be practically impossible for a court to conclude, on a jurisdiction application, that the claim is so obviously doomed to fail that the proceedings should be terminated there and then. It seems likely that the cases in which the courts have taken the strongest exception to the length and complexity of the application to dispute the jurisdiction are those in which the defendant seeks to show that there is no serious issue on the merits, and that the claim should (notionally, at least) be struck out. Some courts have responded to this by requiring the defendant to identify a 'killer point'.[784] This may sound good, but the jurisdiction of the court depends on a test which is, in effect, that which applies on applications to strike out. That may make for complicated hearings, not least because an application to strike out a claim does not require a 'killer point' if a more complex analysis will make the submission equally well. If it were to be suggested at this point that the rules of jurisdiction are excessively elaborate, it would be hard to disagree.

---

783 At 455–456; *Barings plc v. Coopers & Lybrand* [1997] ILPr 576.
784 *Erste Group Bank AG v. JSC 'VMZ Red October'* [2013] EWHC 2926 (Comm), [11]; *Standard Bank plc v. Efad Real Estate Co WLL* [2014] EWHC 1834 (Comm), [2014] 2 All ER (Comm) 208, [5].

4.94 Disputing jurisdiction and the exercise of jurisdiction: CPR Part 11

The defendant who has been served out of the jurisdiction will be entitled to dispute the jurisdiction of the court over him, or over the cause of action asserted against him, by applying under CPR Part 11 for a declaration that the court does not have jurisdiction over him in respect of the claim. The application must be made within 14 days (but in the Commercial Court, 28 days) of filing the acknowledgment of service. The procedure is not limited to those who were served out of the jurisdiction with permission, but applies generally to any defendant whose contention is that the English court does not have jurisdiction over him; and is not limited to those who challenge the jurisdiction *stricto sensu*, but extends to include all those who seek an order that the jurisdiction be not exercised. The details of the procedure, and of related issues, are examined in Chapter 5.

CHAPTER 5

Procedural Issues Relating to Jurisdiction

INTRODUCTORY MATTERS

5.01 Scope of this chapter

The material in this chapter is something of a miscellany. But it seeks to address the remaining questions of procedure and ancillary matters which may arise, whether the jurisdiction of the court is based on the rules of the Brussels I Regulation or the traditional rules of English law which apply in relation to the jurisdictional rules examined in Chapters 2, 3, and 4, but not identically in each jurisdictional context.

First, whatever the legal basis for the jurisdiction of the court, it will be necessary for the claimant to serve process in accordance with the rules applicable to mode and manner, and time and place, of service on the particular defendant. If it may be shown that service has not been properly made, it will be open to the defendant to dispute the jurisdiction and to ask the court to declare that it has no jurisdiction; it may be open to the claimant to ask the court to cure or overlook any shortcoming which may be regarded as an irregularity. The rules on how service is effected, as distinct from the question whether permission is required to effect it, are not significantly affected by the question whether jurisdiction is based on the Brussels I Regulation, but they are moderately complex. Those governing service of the claim form within the jurisdiction are summarised in Section (A) of this chapter; and some issues relating to service out of the jurisdiction in Section (B).

Next, the defendant may contend that he is simply not subject to the jurisdiction of the English court in respect of the particular claim. There may be several bases for this contention. One would be that he has not been properly served by reference to the material in Sections (A) and (B). But others would focus on his legal liability to be sued in England, as opposed to being sued before a foreign court. In a case in which jurisdiction is determined by the rules of the Brussels I Regulation, he may argue that he is not liable to be sued in the United Kingdom, and that service of process was therefore impermissible and should on that account be set aside. In a case where jurisdiction is determined by the traditional rules of English law, he may argue that the court should not have given the claimant permission to serve him out of the jurisdiction, and that the order granting permission, and the actual service made pursuant to it, should all be set aside. In all cases the procedural application is made pursuant to CPR Part 11; and the way it works is summarised in Section (C) of this chapter.

Separately from this, the defendant may have no basis for contending that the English court has no jurisdiction over him, but may wish to argue that the case against him would be more appropriately pursued in another court, or is already being pursued in another court. If so, he may apply, this also pursuant to CPR Part 11,[1] for a stay of proceedings. The grounds on which a stay may be obtained have been discussed above, in relation to jurisdiction conferred by the Brussels I Regulation and in relation to jurisdiction not based on the Regulation; but as the procedure for making this kind of argument is that which applies to challenges to the very existence of jurisdiction, more properly so called, this is dealt with in Section (C) as well.

Next, the claimant may discover that, although he is suing, or is proposing to sue, or is entitled to sue but has not yet decided whether to sue, in England, his opponent has commenced or is threatening to commence proceedings in another court. In such a case the claimant may bring proceedings, or apply,[2] for an anti-suit injunction. In principle he may do this whenever the respondent to the application is or can be made subject to the personal jurisdiction of the English court; the grounds on which the relief may be obtained are examined here; the material is examined in Section (D) of this chapter. It is followed, because this is where it seems most naturally to fit, by an examination of pecuniary remedies which may be applied for and awarded as a response to what one might describe in general terms as 'wrongful litigation', this including the bringing of actions contrary to a prior agreement as to where to sue and not sue. This jurisprudence is important, but may be particularly so as an alternative to an anti-suit injunction: the material is in Section (E), though that is certainly not its only role in commercial litigation.

Finally, the claimant may find that he is sued in another jurisdiction, or that he is threatened with being sued in another jurisdiction; and may be anxious to do what he can to pre-empt the judgment, or neutralise the possible consequences of the judgment which may be given against him. He may bring proceedings in England which may even take the form of seeking purely declaratory relief. Any question of jurisdiction to bring such proceedings will be answered by the rules examined in Chapters 2 and 4, as the case may be. Insofar as questions arise from the fact that the court has discretion to grant or not grant such relief, they are examined here, in Section (F) of this chapter.

(A) SERVING THE CLAIM FORM IN ENGLAND AND WALES

5.02 Service of the claim form in the jurisdiction: general

The rules for the service of process were recast by the Civil Procedure Rules, with the intention of making them more straightforward and less liable to trap the unwary. As a general rule, however, most of the rules about service of process are procedural rather than strictly statutory. Errors of procedure do not of themselves invalidate the step which has been taken, and it generally lies within the power of the court to remedy an error of procedure.[3] The Supreme Court has recently indicated that it regards service as a process of

---

1 This represents a significant procedural change from the law prior to the enactment of the Civil Procedure Rules in 1998. But for further consideration of whether the application is required to be under CPR Part 11, see above, para. 4.38.

2 If the application is made in the context of proceedings already on foot before the English court.

3 CPR r. 3.10. There had traditionally been a less forgiving attitude to failures to comply with the rules governing applications for permission to serve out of the jurisdiction (*Leal v. Dunlop Bio-Processes International Ltd* [1984] 1 WLR 874; *Camera Care Ltd v. Victor Hasselblad AB* [1986] 1 FTLR 348) though this was watered down in *Kuwait*

giving notice of the proposed commencement of proceedings, and, at least by implication, that honest and reasonable failures in the process of service will be unlikely to have serious consequences if the defendant knew perfectly well of the attempts being made to serve in accordance with the rules.[4]

Insofar as the law imposes particular requirements, the law on the service of documents requires it to be decided *how* service may be effected, *when* service must be made, and *where* service by the chosen means must be or may be effected. This section is not concerned with the service in England of foreign process. But the Service Regulation, which is examined below,[5] will apply in many cases where service is made in England of process, in a civil or commercial matter, originating in another Member State.

Part 6 of the Civil Procedure Rules makes provision for service of the claim form within the jurisdiction in its Section II, and service of other documents within the jurisdiction in its Section III.[6] The contents of the two Parts are very substantially the same, but for convenience it is the service of the claim form which is examined below.

5.03 Service of the claim form within the jurisdiction: methods

In general, and unless provision is made to the contrary, a claim form may be served by any of the methods listed in CPR rule 6.3(1). These methods may also be used to effect service on a company, in addition to the forms of service provided for by statute.[7] In practice, service on a company in accordance with CPR rule 6.3 will usually be simpler and easier than service under statutory schemes: the schemes are, and are designed to be, distinct.[8] The Rules deal with the methods of transmission of the claim form, but do not specify whether it must be accompanied by words or deeds which make clear that it is delivered by way of service, as distinct from delivery by way of information that a claim has been formulated and may be served later. The probable answer is that delivery in accordance with the methods set out below is delivery by way of service unless the contrary is made clear.[9]

According to CPR rule 6.3(1), a claim form may be served in England and Wales (a) by personal service in accordance with CPR rule 6.5, or (b) by first class post or by document exchange, or by other service which provides for delivery on the next business day, in accordance with the Practice Direction, or (c) by leaving the document at a place specified

---

Oil Tanker Co SAK v. Al Bader [1997] 1 WLR 1410 and *Youell v. Kara Mara Shipping Co Ltd* [2000] 2 Lloyd's Rep 201, 121–122. For errors of procedure in relation to service of process in a case where jurisdiction was conferred by the Lugano Convention, and where the effect of curing irregularity in service was to (re-)instate the English court as first seised, see *Phillips v. Symes (No 3)* [2008] UKHL 1, [2008] 1 WLR 180; *Ólafsson v. Gissurarson (No 2)* [2008] EWCA Civ 316, [2008] 1 WLR 2016. This, rather than the earlier approach, plainly represents the current attitude of the courts: see *Abela v. Baadarani* [2013] UKSC 44, [2013] 1 WLR 2043; *Integral Petroleum SA v. SCU-Finanz AG* [2014] EWHC 702 (Comm). For a claim for damages against the Foreign and Commonwealth Office for negligence in failing to serve English process properly, *Ólafsson v. Foreign and Commonwealth Office* [2009] EWHC 2608 (QB).

4 *Abela v. Baadarani* [2013] UKSC 44, [2013] 1 WLR 2043.

5 Paragraph 5.22, below. For the supporting rules, see CPR 6, Section V.

6 For service of documents in insolvency proceedings, see *Re T&N Ltd* [2006] EWHC 842 (Ch), [2006] 1 WLR 2831; Insolvency Rules, SI 1986/1925, Parts 12 and 13.

7 CPR r. 6.3(2). For a case illustrating the advantage of service in accordance with the CPR on an unregistered company, over that provided by the Companies Act 1985, see *Sea Assets Ltd v. PT Garuda Indonesia* [2000] 4 All ER 371. The position under the Companies Act 2006 is no different, and the advantage remains the same though now see *Ashley v Tesco Stores Ltd* [2015] EWCA Civ (Jan 15th), on the time allowed for service on a company.

8 *Cranfield v. Bridgegrove Ltd* [2003] EWCA Civ 656, [2003] 1 WLR 2241.

9 *Asia Pacific (HK) Ltd v. Hanjin Shipping Co Ltd* [2005] EWHC 2443 (Comm).

in CPR rules 6.7 to 6.10, or (d) by fax or other means of electronic communication in accordance with Practice Direction 6A, or (e) by any method authorised by the court under CPR rule 6.15. The significance of this is that personal service of the claim form is not the only method of making service of it, and that service by post to an address within the jurisdiction, leaving it at a place within the jurisdiction, and fax transmission within the jurisdiction are permissible alternatives to personal service of the claim form.

Personal service can be made only on a defendant who is physically present in the jurisdiction.[10] It was widely understood that the same limitation applied in the case of service by posting and by leaving: that it was also conditional on the defendant being within the jurisdiction at the date of actual or deemed service:[11] it is hard to see how there can be service on a defendant within the jurisdiction if the defendant is not within the jurisdiction at the material time. But, perhaps in accordance with a recent, more relaxed, approach to service, it has been held that service may be made by post to an address within the jurisdiction when the individual on whom service is to be made is not.[12] As a matter of first impression, this appears to treat the rule as being designed to state how service of process may be made, and to regard where the defendant is, in or out of the jurisdiction, as of secondary concern. On the other hand, if the defendant is only temporarily out of the jurisdiction, it does not seem sensible to require service, if made during that short period, to be in accordance with the more elaborate processes for service out of the jurisdiction.[13] The sensible, practical result is that, as far as English law is concerned, service may be made within the jurisdiction even though, and when, the defendant is temporarily overseas. If a foreign court, called on in due course to recognise the judgment, sees in this a reason to refuse recognition, that is the risk the claimant takes.

The claimant may arrange for process to be served, personally or by his agent. Alternatively, the court may serve the claim form, in the manner which it chooses,[14] unless a rule provides that a party must serve the document in question, or a practice direction or the court orders otherwise. If the court has failed to effect service, and has sent a notice of non-service[15] to the party on whose behalf the document was to be served, it will not make a further attempt to serve.

5.04 Service of claim form: period of validity for service

A claim form must be served during the period for which it is valid for service. If service is to be made within the jurisdiction, the period is four months from the date of issue; if it is to be served outside the jurisdiction it is six months.[16] More precisely, for service to be made within the jurisdiction, the claimant must complete the step required for the particular

---

10 Personal service is not made by leaving the claim form with a security guard or manservant, as this does not count as leaving it with the defendant: *Cherney v. Deripaska* [2007] EWHC 956 (Comm).

11 *Chellaram v. Chellaram* [2002] EWHC 632 (Ch), [2002] 3 All ER 17; *Cadogan Properties Ltd v. Mount Eden Land Ltd* [2000] ILPr 722; *Fairmays v. Palmer* [2006] EWHC 96 (Ch).

12 *City & Country Properties Ltd v. Kamali* [2006] EWCA Civ 1879, [2007] 1 WLR 1219.

13 *Murrills v. Berlanda* [2014] EWCA Civ 6, [2014] ILPr 605 (not permissible to serve in England at a former work address; if the principle in *City & Country Properties Ltd v. Kamali* is relied on, service must be at a residential address during what is only a temporary absence).

14 CPR r. 6.4.

15 CPR r. 6.18 (postal service by court), r. 6.19 (service by court bailiff).

16 CPR r. 7.5(2). See *The Byzantio* [2004] EWHC 3339 (Comm), [2005] 1 Lloyd's Rep 531. But see also *Ashley v Tesco Stores Ltd* [2015] EWCA Civ (Jan 15th).

mode of service, which is set out in the rules,[17] before midnight on the calendar day four months after the issue of the claim form.[18] When a claim form is served in accordance with Part 6, it is deemed to have been served on the second business day after completion of the relevant step set out in the Table under rule 7.5(1).[19]

No doubt service of the claim form after the date limiting its validity for service, but without the claimant having obtained an order to extend its period for service,[20] is irregular, but it may be contended that the irregularity is a remediable error of procedure,[21] at least in cases where this would not subvert the rules on service out of the jurisdiction, or where it would still be open to the claimant to issue and serve a new claim form. In general, applications may be made for extension of the period of validity for service within the period of validity for service of the claim form.[22] If the application is made after the expiry of the claim form's validity for service, the court may make an order of renewal only if the court was unable to serve the claim form at all, or the claimant has taken all reasonable steps to serve the claim form, but was unable to do so, and in any case only if the claimant has acted promptly in making the application.[23]

5.05 Service of the claim form by personal service in England: the necessary steps and the effective date

Personal service of the claim form is permitted in every case[24] except where a solicitor is authorised to accept service on behalf of a party and the party serving the claim form has been so notified by the solicitor:[25] in that case service must be made on the solicitor unless provided otherwise by legislation, rules or Practice Direction. The step which has to be taken to complete personal service is as set out below; and the date of service will be taken to be the second business day after that step is taken.[26]

The step which needs to be taken to effect personal service of the claim form on an *individual* is to leave the claim form with that individual.[27] The step which needs to be

---

17 CPR r. 7(5)(1).

18 This is so even if the claimant has been given six months to serve the defendant out of the jurisdiction: it is not permitted to use this permission to serve the defendant within the jurisdiction after the end of the fourth month but before the end of the sixth month: *American Leisure Group v. Garrard* [2014] EWHC 2101 (Ch), [2014] 1 WLR 4102.

19 CPR r. 6.14.

20 CPR r. 7.6.

21 CPR r. 3.10. Even so, there are limits, and if a failure to serve is comprehensive enough, it will be regarded as incurable: *Credit Agricole Indosuez v. Unicof Ltd* [2003] EWHC 77 (Comm).

22 CPR r. 7.6(1), (2). See *Cummins v. Shell International Manning Services* [2002] EWCA Civ 933; *Sodastream Ltd v. Coates* [2009] EWHC 1936 (Ch).

23 CPR r. 7.6(3). But the gist of the authorities suggests that the court will not easily be persuaded that a claimant has taken all reasonable steps when service has not been made, especially if all that was needed was to put the claim form on a fax machine and press the send button. See also *Cecil v. Bayat* [2011] EWCA Civ 135, [2011] 1 WLR 3086.

24 CPR r. 6.5(1).

25 See *Nanglegan v. Royal Free Hampstead NHS Trust* [2001] EWCA Civ 127, [2002] 1 WLR 1043; *Arab National Bank v. El Abdali* [2004] EWHC 289 (Comm), [2005] 1 Lloyd's Rep 541. A solicitor on the record, therefore, may not refuse to accept service. If he finds himself without instructions and unable to act, he must apply under CPR r. 42.3 for an order that he has ceased to act, and until he does he will be considered still to be acting for the party, and service may be effected on him.

26 CPR r. 6.14 (date), r. 7.5(1) (step).

27 CPR r. 6.5(3).

taken to effect personal service of the claim from on a *company* or *other corporation* is leaving it with a person holding a senior position within the company or corporation.[28] In the case of a registered company or corporation, this means a director, the treasurer, secretary, chief executive, manager or other officer; in the case of a corporation which is not a registered company, the list is extended to add the mayor, chairman, president, town clerk or similar officer. The step which needs to be taken to effect personal service on the claim form on a *partnership*, when the partners are being sued in the name of their firm, is leaving it with a partner, or leaving it with a person who, at the time of service, has the control or management of the partnership business at its principal place of business.[29]

5.06 The place of service in England: general

The claimant must give an address within the jurisdiction at which the defendant can be served with the claim form, unless the court has made an order permitting service by an alternative method or at an alternative place.[30] Where the defendant has given in writing the business address, within the jurisdiction, of a solicitor at which the defendant may be served with the claim form, or a solicitor acting for the defendant has notified the claimant that he is authorised to accept service at an address within the jurisdiction, the claim form must be served there.[31] In the absence of this notification, service may be made at an address within the jurisdiction which the defendant has given for the purpose of service of proceedings.[32]

In the absence of that notification, and if personal service is not to be made, service is made at a place which is specified by a Table, and which sets out different rules according to the character of the defendant.[33] The date of effective service will be the second business day after the required step is taken.[34]

5.07 Service of claim form in England by first class post

There is nothing more to be said about service by first class post, except to make the obvious point that, though postal services other than first class post are not within the rule, their inadvertent use may be seen as a remediable error of procedure.[35] The required step to effect service of the claim form by first class post is posting it, which means placing the claim form in a post box,[36] and service is deemed to be made on the second business day after the posting.

5.08 Service of claim form in England through a document exchange or other next-day delivery service

Service of the claim form through services which are equivalent to the post may also be made: the commonest will be by Document Exchange (DX). Service may be made through

---

28 CPR r. 6.5(4), as amplified by CPR Part 7, Practice Direction, Paras 5A and 5B.
29 CPR r. 6.5(5).
30 CPR r. 6.6(1).
31 CPR r. 6(7).
32 CPR r. 6.8(a).
33 CPR r. 6.9.
34 CPR r. 6.14.
35 CPR r. 3.10.
36 CPR 6 PD, Para. 3.1(1).

a document exchange where the party's address for service includes a numbered DX box, or the writing paper of the party to be served or that of his legal representative[37] sets out the DX box number, and the party or legal representative has not indicated in writing his unwillingness to accept service by DX.[38] The required step to effect service of the claim form by DX is leaving the document with or delivering the document to the DX service provider; and service is deemed to be made on the second business day after that leaving or delivering.

Where another service provider is used, there is no need for a prior expression of willingness to accept service of the claim form by such means. The required step to effect service of the claim form by next-day delivery service is delivering the claim form to, or having the claim form collected by, the service provider; and service is deemed to be made on the second business day after that delivering or collecting.

5.09 Service of claim form in England by fax

Where a claim form is to be served by fax, the party to be served or his legal representative must previously have indicated in writing to the party serving that he is willing to be served by fax,[39] and the fax number to which it should be sent. If the party on whom the document is to be served is acting by a legal representative, the fax must be sent to the business address of the legal representative (that is, the physical location of his office, within the jurisdiction; and an electronic address given in conjunction with that business address is deemed to be at the business address). The requirement of a written indication may be satisfied by a party acting in person providing in writing a fax number expressly for the purpose of accepting service, or by a fax number being printed on the writing paper of the legal representative.[40] It is not strictly necessary also to send an additional hard copy, but this will be useful if it is found that the document served by fax was not received.[41] The required step to effect service of the claim form by fax is completing the transmission of the fax, and service is deemed to be made on the second business day after that completion.[42]

5.10 Service of claim form in England by other means of electronic communication

Service of the claim form by other electronic means may take place subject to certain conditions. It is necessary that the party to be served had previously expressly indicated in writing to the party serving that he is willing to accept service by this means and that he or his legal representative has provided his email address or other electronic identification, for the purpose of service. This indication may also be provided by an email address in a statement of claim or a response filed with the court. It is not strictly necessary also to send an additional hard copy, but this will be useful if it is found that the document served by

---

37 CPR r. 2.3(1) defines this as 'a barrister, or a solicitor, solicitor's employee or other authorised litigator (as defined in the Courts and Legal Services Act 1990) who has been instructed to act for a party in relation to a claim'.

38 That is, there is a presumption that service by Document Exchange is agreed to.

39 Service by fax without that prior consent was considered to be a seriously irregularity in *Kuenyehia v. International Hospitals Group Ltd* [2006] EWCA Civ 21 (not a case on private international law).

40 PD 6A, Para. 3.1(2).

41 PD 6A, Para. 3.4.

42 CPR rr 6.14, 7.5(1).

electronic means was not received. The required step to effect service of the claim form by these other electronic methods is sending the email or other electronic transaction; and service is deemed to be made on the second business day after such sending.[43]

5.11 Service of claim form by leaving it at a specified place in England

If a person has not given an address within the jurisdiction for service of the claim form, and no solicitor is acting for him, service of the claim form may be effected by leaving the claim form at the place specified in the Table in CPR rule 6.9.

Accordingly, an *individual* may be served at his usual or last known residence.[44] The *proprietor of a business* may be served at his usual or last known residence, or at the place of business or last known place of business.[45] An *individual sued in the business name of a partnership* may be served at his usual or last known residence, or at the principal or last known place of business of the firm. A *limited liability partnership* may be served at the principal office of the partnership, or at any place of business of the partnership within the jurisdiction which has a real connection to the claim. A *corporation incorporated in England, other than a company*, may be served at the principal office of the corporation, or at any place within the jurisdiction where the corporation carried on its activities and which has a real connection to the claim. A *company registered in England* may be served at the principal office of the company or at any place of business[46] within the jurisdiction which has a real connection with the claim. Any *other company or corporation* may be served at any place within the jurisdiction at which it carries on its activities,[47] or at any place of business which it maintains within the jurisdiction. A place of business, for the purposes of this rule, presumably bears the same meaning as it had in relation to the previous rules for the service of companies and for the purpose of statutory service. It is examined in detail in the context of statutory service on companies.[48] Where the required step to make service is the delivery of the claim form to, or leaving it at, the relevant place, service is deemed to be made on the second business day after that delivery or leaving.[49]

In any case where service is proposed to be made at the usual or last known residence of the individual, but the claimant has reason to believe that the address is no longer one at which the defendant resides or carries on business, the rules require the claimant to take reasonable steps to ascertain the defendant's current address.[50] If these reasonable steps lead the claimant to ascertain the defendant's current address, the claim form must be served

---

43 CPR rr 6.14, 7.5(1).

44 Obviously not an address at which he used to work: *Murrills v. Berlanda* [2014] EWCA Civ 6, [2014] ILPr 605.

45 See for illustration *Mersey Docks Property Holdings Ltd v. Kilgour* [2004] EWHC 1638, [2004] BLR 412.

46 *Harrods Ltd v. Dow Jones & Co Inc* [2003] EWHC 1162 (QB) (local office not a place of business); *Reuben v. Time Inc* [2003] EWHC 1430 (QB) (likewise). Both suggest that a place of business is what is needed.

47 See *Actavis Group hf v. Eli Lilly & Co* [2013] EWCA Civ 517, [2013] RPC 985: what amounts to a place of business, or activities, will depend on what the company actually does. In *Lakah Group v. al-Jazeera Satellite Channel* [2003] EWHC 1231 (QB), *The Times*, 18 April 2003, it was held that the expression 'carries on its activities' was a wider concept than that of having a 'place of business' under the Companies Act 1985. It is to be questioned whether this view is reliable.

48 But if the company is not carrying on business in England, it is not present in England, and service on this basis is not possible, even if a director of the company passes through: *SSL International plc v. TTK LIG Ltd* [2011] EWCA Civ 1170, [2012] 1 WLR 1842.

49 CPR rr 6.14, 7.5(1).

50 CPR r. 6.9(3).

there. But if the claimant cannot ascertain the defendant's current address, the claimant must consider whether there is an alternative place where, or an alternative method by which, service of the claim form may be made. If there is not, the claimant must[51] apply for an order permitting service to be made by an alternative method or at an alternative place.[52]

5.12 Obtaining permission to serve the claim form by an alternative method or at an alternative place in England; deeming the sufficiency of attempts made to serve

Where it appears to the court that there is a good reason to authorise service within the jurisdiction by a method not permitted by the Rules, or at a place other than provided for by the Rules, the court may make an order for service of the claim form to be made by an alternative method or at an alternative place.[53] The application for permission is made without notice and must be supported by evidence; and the court will specify the manner and deemed date of such alternative service.[54] Permission under the Rule may be given to effect service in England, or overseas, by means which would not otherwise be regular.

The requirement of a good reason[55] is not met by the claimant merely wishing to commence English proceedings in advance of a foreign court being seised.[56] More importantly, it would be wrong to make orders for service by alternative means simply because it would be more convenient for the claimant to be dispensed from the effort of effecting service (for example) in accordance with the requirements of the Hague Convention.[57]

In relation to an earlier provision for what was then known as substituted service,[58] it had been held that an order would not be made if it would not have been possible to effect good personal service on a defendant who was not within the jurisdiction, but that the position was otherwise if the defendant had left the jurisdiction before the issue of the writ in order to evade service. But the authority for this proposition was dubious, and the principle underpinning it equally so.[59] Even so, as the rules for service by an alternative method are not restricted to cases in which service is to be made within the jurisdiction, it follows as

---

51 CPR r. 6.9(5).

52 CPR r. 6.15.

53 CPR r. 6.15: '(1) Where it appears to the court that there is a good reason to authorise service by a method or at a place not otherwise permitted by this Part, the court may make an order permitting service by an alternative method or at an alternative place. (2) On an application under this rule, the court may order that steps already taken to bring the claim form to the attention of the defendant by an alternative method or at an alternative place is good service.'

54 For an illustration, *Albon v. Naza Motor Trading Sdn Bhd* [2007] EWHC 327 (Ch), [2007] 2 Lloyd's Rep 1.

55 The requirement is of good reason, not of the need to show exceptional circumstances: *Abela v. Baadarani* [2013] UKSC 44, [2013] 1 WLR 2043, [33]; see also *Ólafsson v. Gissurarson (No 2)* [2008] EWCA Civ 316, [2008] 1 WLR 2016.

56 *Knauf UK GmbH v. British Gypsum Ltd* [2001] EWCA Civ 1570, [2002] 1 Lloyd's Rep 199; applied (in a non-Brussels case) in *Cecil v. Bayat* [2011] EWCA Civ 135, [2011] 1 WLR 3086 (though as an English court is now seised on issue rather than service of process, this will be less of a concern).

57 *Cecil v. Bayat* [2011] EWCA Civ 135, [2011] 1 WLR 3086; *Deutsche Bank AG v. Sebastian Holdings Inc* [2014] EWHC 112 (Comm), [2014] 1 All ER (Comm) 733.

58 RSC Order 65, r. 4.

59 *Porter v. Freudenberg* [1915] 1 KB 857, 887; disapproved by the High Court of Australia: *Laurie v. Carroll* (1958) 98 CLR 301, itself applied *Mondial Trading Pty Ltd v. Interocean Marine Transport Inc* (1985) 65 ALR 155.

a matter of principle that an order permitting service by alternative means should not be made in respect of a defendant who could only be served out of the jurisdiction with the permission of the court unless the court is satisfied that it would have been prepared to grant permission to serve the defendant out of the jurisdiction. Otherwise the court would have widened the provisions which define the power to allow service out of the jurisdiction beyond the limits, already broad, set by the rules.[60] This conclusion is not called into question by the proposition that service within the jurisdiction may be made even though the defendant is out of the jurisdiction, for that is really only permissible in the case of temporary absence from the jurisdiction.[61]

This rule also allows a court to make an order declaring that steps which had been taken to make service on the defendant should be deemed to be good service.[62] The rule applies to service which was attempted to be made within the jurisdiction as well as out of the jurisdiction,[63] and it is this retrospective deeming of the sufficiency of steps taken to serve which is probably the more important effect of this rule. There needs to be good reason to make the order, but it is not necessary that there be 'exceptional reasons' for making it.[64] It will not be sufficient to say that the contents of the claim form came to the knowledge or notice of the defendant, not least because this would make service an optional, but pointless, formality. But where efforts have been made, unavailingly, and where the claimant cannot really be blamed for failing to effect service on the defendant, a court is certainly entitled to find that there is good reason to make the declaratory order.

5.13 Service of claim form in England by contractually agreed method

Where the parties have agreed by contract that a claim form may be served by a particular specified method, and a claim form is issued containing only a claim in respect of that contract, service in accordance with that method is good service; but if service by the agreed method is to be made out of the jurisdiction, it will not be good service unless any permission which may be required has been obtained.[65]

There is no reason to doubt that the parties are free to agree to service taking place by a means which is acceptable to them, without the need for an order of the court.[66]

---

60 This is not called into question by *Abela v. Baadarani* [2013] UKSC 44, [2013] 1 WLR 2043, for in that case the grounds for granting permission to serve out of the jurisdiction were agreed to be satisfied, and the only problem was the consequent one of accomplishing service in accordance with that permission; see also *Cruz City 1 Mauritius Holdings v. Unitech Ltd* [2014] EWHC 3704 (Comm).

61 *City & Country Properties Ltd v. Kamali* [2006] EWCA Civ 1879, [2007] 1 WLR 1219 (on which, see *SSL International plc v. TTK LIG Ltd* [2011] EWCA Civ 1170, [2012] 1 WLR 1842); *Murrills v. Berlanda* [2014] EWCA Civ 6, [2014] ILPr 605. If the defendant has informed a court in another jurisdiction that his home is in England, service may be made at that English address: *Varsani v. Relfo Ltd (in liq)* [2010] EWCA Civ 560, [2011] 1 WLR 1402.

62 For example, *Phillips v. Symes (No 3)* [2008] UKHL 1, [2008] 1 WLR 180.

63 Even though it appears in CPR Part 6 within the section which deals with service within the jurisdiction: *Abela v. Baadarani* [2013] UKSC 44, [2013] 1 WLR 2043, [20]. The only limitation is that the rule does not allow the deeming of service as valid if it would have been unlawful to effect it in the place in which it was made: at [24].

64 *Abela v. Baadarani* [2013] UKSC 44, [2013] 1 WLR 2043, [33]; see also *Ólafsson v. Gissurarson (No 2)* [2008] EWCA Civ 316, [2008] 1 WLR 2016.

65 CPR r. 6.11.

66 This had been held under the previous rules in *Kenneth Allison Ltd v. Limehouse & Co (a firm)* [1992] 1 AC 105, but it will not constitute the exclusive means by which service may be made unless it has been specifically so agreed: *Cranfield v. Bridgegrove Ltd* [2003] EWCA Civ 656. See also *McCulloch v. Bank of Nova Scotia (CI) Ltd* [2006] EWHC 790 (Comm), [2006] 2 All ER (Comm) 714.

5.14 Service of claim form in England on agent of principal who is out of the jurisdiction

Where the defendant is out of the jurisdiction the court may, in certain circumstances, permit a claim form to be served on his agent within the jurisdiction.[67] The conditions for the obtaining of permission are that the contract to which the claim relates was entered into within the jurisdiction with or through the defendant's agent, and at the time of the application the agent's authority has not been terminated, or he is still in business relations with his principal. This power is in addition to the power to authorise service by alternative means.

5.15 Service of claim form in England on companies: under the Companies Acts

In the light of CPR rule 6.3, it will usually be simpler and more straightforward for service of the claim form on a company to be made in accordance with the Civil Procedure Rules, and for the greater complexities of statutory service on companies to be left well alone. But if for some reason it is intended to effect service on a company pursuant to the statutory scheme, it is necessary to distinguish between a company registered under the Companies Act 2006, served within the jurisdiction under section 1139(1) of that Act; an overseas company, which means a company incorporated outside the United Kingdom which has registered particulars for the purpose of service of process, which may be served within the jurisdiction under section 1139(2);[68] and a company registered in Scotland or Northern Ireland which carries on business in England, which may be served within the jurisdiction under section 1139(4). Having said all that, it is rather difficult to see any general practical advantage in preferring to effect service by statutory means if service may be made according to CPR rule 6.3(2).

5.16 Statutory service of claim form in England on a United Kingdom company

The Companies Act 2006 provides that a claim form may be served on a company registered under the Act: section 1139 allows service to be made by serving or leaving it at, or sending it by post to, its registered office. It appears that this may be done even though the company carries on no business in the United Kingdom. If the company is in liquidation, the leave of the court must first be obtained,[69] and service is made on the liquidator.

If a company is registered in Scotland or Northern Ireland and carries on business in England, service may be made by sending the claim form to the company's principal

---

67 CPR r. 6.12.

68 There is no restriction which would limit service in such cases to claims in which the claim arises out of the activities of the English establishment: *Teekay Tankers Ltd v. STX Offshore & Shipping Co* [2014] EWHC 3612 (Comm) (confirming that Overseas Companies Regulations 2009, reg. 7, did not impose any such limitation on the broad terms of ss 1139(2), 1046 and 1056).

69 Insolvency Act 1986, s. 130. If the company is subject to an administration order, *either* the consent of the administrator *or* the leave of the court is required: Insolvency Act 1986, s. 11(3)(d).

place of business in England, with a copy to the registered office in Scotland or Northern Ireland.[70]

5.17 Statutory service of claim form in England upon an overseas company

If a company is incorporated outside the United Kingdom, it is classed by the Companies Acts as an 'overseas company'.[71] The Secretary of State may require the company to deliver certain particulars with the Registrar of Companies.[72] There are two schemes for registration of overseas companies which open a branch in the United Kingdom. These systems are mutually exclusive, as appears from the texts of the legislation. The company must be required to register these particulars if it is not a Gibraltar company; it may be required to register them if it is a Gibraltar company.[73] In this context, a 'branch' means a branch within the meaning of the Eleventh Company Law Directive.[74] But the Directive does not give a meaning to the expression 'branch', which is not entirely helpful. A branch, as an indication of the right of establishment,[75] may connote an office managed by the undertaking's own staff, which is authorised to act on a permanent basis for the undertaking.[76] It may also be relevant to refer to the definition of 'branch, agency or other establishment' as used in Article 7(5) of the recast Brussels I Regulation[77] in order to determine whether the presence in Great Britain is sufficient to constitute a branch of the overseas company.

If the overseas company has registered the particulars required, service of the claim form may be made by leaving it at or sending it by post to the registered address of any person in the United Kingdom authorised to accept service on the company's behalf. If there is no such person, or if such person refuses to accept service, the claim form may be served by leaving it at or sending it by post to any place of business of the company in the United Kingdom.[78] But in cases where the company has not complied with the requirement to register the particulars, the Act does not provide for the making of service, and service will instead have to be made under CPR Part 6. If the company does not carry on business within the jurisdiction, it cannot be served within the jurisdiction, for it will not have a place at which it carries on its activities within the jurisdiction.[79]

A company other than one registered in England and Wales may be served within the jurisdiction at any place at which it has a place of business. The rule requires that the place

---

70 Companies Act 2006, s. 1139(4). And see *Ashley v Tesco Stores Ltd* [2015] EWCA Civ (15 Jan).

71 Companies Act 2006, s. 1044.

72 Companies Act 2006, s. 1046.

73 Companies Act 2006, s. 1046(2).

74 Companies Act 2006, s. 1046(3).

75 Article 49 TFEU.

76 *Cf* 205/84 *Commission v. Germany* [1986] ECR 3755. Note also that the Second Banking Directive (89/646/EEC), which is almost directly contemporaneous with the Eleventh Company Law Directive, defines branch as 'a place of business which forms a legally dependent part of a credit institution... and which carries out directly all or some of the transactions inherent in the business of a credit institution... '.

77 See para. 2.213, above.

78 Companies Act 2006, s. 1139(2). For the nature of the address at which service may be made, see Companies Act 2006, s. 1141(2), and Companies Act 2006 (Annual Return and Service Addresses) Regulations 2008, SI 2008/3000, reg. 10.

79 See *The Theodohos* [1977] 2 Lloyd's Rep 428. It is in principle not open to a claimant to contend that the company should be estopped from denying that it has a place of business, for estoppel may not be used to enlarge the statutory jurisdiction of the court: *J & F Stone v. Levitt* [1947] AC 209; *Bethlem Steel Corp v. Universal Gas & Oil Co Inc* (HL; *The Times*, 3 August 1978).

of business be fixed and definite,[80] and that what is transacted there constitutes 'business'.[81] This in turn suggests that the personnel in the place of business have authority to enter into transactions on behalf of the company, or that they have been given autonomy to act in the name of the company without reference back to the head office for authorisation.[82] If the alleged place of business is merely a letter-box for the overseas company, the company will not be seen as carrying on business within the jurisdiction;[83] but if some decision-taking is done, or negotiation conducted, on behalf of the company, this could amount to the carrying on of business[84] within the jurisdiction. It is not required that the particular claim arise out of the activities carried on at that place of business within the jurisdiction.[85] It was perhaps for this reason that the courts were not zealous to find that a company was carrying on its activities within the jurisdiction unless it did so to such a degree that it had fairly exposed itself to the risk of being sued there in respect of any and all of its activities, wherever arising or occurring. The alternative is to serve the claim form at any place within the jurisdiction where the corporation carries on its activities. For the purpose of this rule, one must ask where the corporation carries on its activities, and whether that place has a real connection with the claim.

Even though the rules for the service of process on companies have been simplified, when contrasted with the very complex provisions of the Companies Act 1985, there is still something of a puzzle about the relationship, or maybe the deliberate lack of relationship, between CPR Part 6 and the statutory provisions in the Act. It is hard to understand why there should be two, quite separate, codes for the service of process, and this has led some to wonder whether there should be some reconsideration. But as matters stand, service under CPR Part 6, and under the Companies Act 2006, represents a choice of manner of service for the claimant.

5.18 Service of claim form in England in claims brought against partnerships

The law as it applies to claims brought against persons who were in partnership has been considerably simplified. If they were partners and carried on business within the jurisdiction when the cause of action arose, the persons concerned may be sued, unless it is inappropriate to do so, in the name of the partnership which carried on the business.[86] Service of the claim form may be by any of the methods set out in the rules. Personal service is made by leaving the claim form with a partner, or with a person who, at the time of service, has control or

---

80 *Okura & Co Ltd v. Forsbacka Jernverks A/B* [1914] 1 KB 715, dealing with whether an English court has jurisdiction over a foreign corporation; *Rakusens Ltd v. Baser Ambalaj Plastik Sanayi Ticaret AS* [2001] EWCA Civ 1820, [2002] 1 BCLC 104. See also *Adams v. Cape Industries plc* [1990] Ch 433 applying this line of authority to the question whether a corporation is present within the jurisdiction of a foreign court for the purposes of recognition of a foreign judgment against it: this was expressly adopted in *Harrods Ltd v. Dow Jones & Co Inc* [2003] EWHC 1162 (QB) (local office not a place of business); *Reuben v. Time Inc* [2003] EWHC 1430 (QB) (to same effect).

81 See *Harrods Ltd v. Dow Jones Inc* [2003] EWHC 1162 (QB), *Reuben v. Time Inc* [2003] EWHC 1430 (QB). But the analysis is fact-specific.

82 *Actavis Group hf v. Eli Lilly & Co* [2013 EWCA Civ 517, [2003] RPC 985.

83 And not, therefore, as having a place of business within the jurisdiction.

84 *South India Shipping Corporation v. Export-Import Bank of Korea* [1985] 1 WLR 585; and if it does so from a fixed place, this will be a place of business. See also *Re Oriel Ltd* [1986] 1 WLR 180.

85 This contrasts with the corresponding rule of special jurisdiction under the Brussels I Regulation relating to jurisdiction over the activities of a branch, agency or other establishment of a defendant domiciled in another Member State, where the claim must arise out of the operations of the branch.

86 CPR Part 7, PD, Paras 5A and 5B.

management of the partnership business at its principal place of business.[87] A limited liability partnership formed under the Limited Liability Partnerships Act 2000 may be served at the principal office of the partnership or at any place of business of the partnership within the jurisdiction which has a real connection with the claim,[88] but as the service provisions of the Companies Act 2006 have been extended to limited liability partnerships, service may also[89] be made in accordance with that regime if that is more convenient.[90]

(B) SERVING THE CLAIM FORM OUTSIDE ENGLAND AND WALES

5.19 Service of claim form outside England and Wales, without permission

When dealing with the question how to make service of the claim form outside England and Wales, it will have been seen that there is a distinction between cases in which the permission of the court is not required, and service may be made without it, and cases in which the permission of the court is required. When the claimant considers that his claim is one the court has jurisdiction to hear, and that that permission is accordingly not required to serve the claim form outside England, it is necessary further to distinguish between service elsewhere in the United Kingdom, and service outside the United Kingdom. The most obvious case will be the one in which the claimant considers that the Regulation justifies his invocation of the jurisdiction of the court, and that service may be made without permission as a result.

Part 6, Section IV of the Civil Procedure Rules deals with the service of the claim form, as well as other service of other documents, out of the jurisdiction. In principle, where permission would be required to serve the claim form out of the jurisdiction, permission is likewise needed to serve other documents out of the jurisdiction.[91]

Rule 6.33 of the Civil Procedure Rules establishes the basis for service of the claim form out of the jurisdiction[92] in those circumstances in which permission to do so is not required. Its wording gives rise to some difficulties, and it is therefore convenient to set it out verbatim. It provides as follows:

> *(1) The claimant may serve the claim form on a defendant out of the United Kingdom where each claim made against the defendant to be served and included in the claim form is a claim which the court has power to determine under the 1982 Act and*
>> *(a) no proceedings between the parties concerning the same claim are pending in the courts of any part of the United Kingdom or any other Convention territory; and*
>> *(b) (i) the defendant is domiciled in the United Kingdom or in any Convention territory; (ii) the proceedings are within Article 16 of Schedule 1 or Article 16 of Schedule 3C to the 1982 Act; or (iii) the defendant is party to an agreement conferring jurisdiction, within Article 17 of Schedule 1 or Article 17 of Schedule 3C to the 1982 Act.*

---

87 CPR r. 6.5(3)(c).

88 CPR r. 6.9(2).

89 CPR r. 6.3(3).

90 Limited Liability Partnerships (Application of Companies Act 2006) Regulations 2009, SI 2009/1804, reg. 75.

91 CPR r. 6.38.

92 In fact, service in Scotland or Northern Ireland is dealt with by CPR r. 6.32, which is in substantially identical terms, but which is not of major practical significance.

(2)   *The claimant may serve the claim form on a defendant out of the United Kingdom where each claim made against the defendant to be served and included in the claim form is a claim which the court has power to determine under the Judgments Regulation*[93] *and*

    (a)   *subject to paragraph 2A, no proceedings between the parties concerning the same claim are pending in the courts of any part of the United Kingdom or any other Member State; and*

    (b)   *(i) the defendant is domiciled in the United Kingdom or in any Member State; (ii) the defendant is not a consumer, but is party to a consumer contract within article 17 of the Judgments Regulation; (iii) the defendant is an employer and party to a contract of employment within article 20 of the Judgments Regulation; (iv) the proceedings are within Article 24 of the Judgments Regulation; or (v) the defendant is party to an agreement conferring jurisdiction within Article 25 of the Judgments Regulation.*

(2A)   *Paragraph 2(a) does not apply if the jurisdiction conferred by the agreement referred to in paragraph (2)(b)(v) is exclusive.*[94]

(3)   *The claimant may serve the claim form on a defendant out of the United Kingdom where each claim made against the defendant to be served and included in the claim form is a claim which the court has power to determine other than under the 1982 Act or the Judgments Regulation, notwithstanding that*

    (a)   *the person against whom the claim is made is not within the jurisdiction*

    (b)   *the facts giving rise to the claim did not occur within the jurisdiction.*[95]

5.20 Service of claim form out of the jurisdiction: uncertainty as to the need for permission

It follows that two régimes apply: in one, the permission of the court to serve out of the jurisdiction is not needed, and in the other, permission is required. Unfortunately, the two régimes are expressed to be mutually exclusive, and this gives rise to a problem.

If the claim form is to be served out of the jurisdiction without permission, the claimant is required to file a notice[96] which identifies the grounds on which he is entitled so to serve the claim form, and a copy of that notice must accompany the claim form.[97] But CPR rule 6.36, which allows an application to be made for permission to serve out of the jurisdiction, opens with the words 'in any proceedings to which rule 6.32[98] or 6.33 does not apply…', from which it follows that if the claim falls clearly and unambiguously outside CPR rule 6.32 or 6.33, permission to serve must be applied for.

But not all cases are so clear-cut, and two, in particular, cause difficulty. First, a claim form may contain a number of claims, only some but not others of which would fall within CPR rule 6.32 or 6.33. In such a case, a claimant would appear to have a choice. He may issue separate claim forms, seeking permission to serve the one containing the claims falling outside (say) CPR rule 6.33, and making the statement of entitlement and serving the other as of right;[99] or he can apply under CPR rule 6.36 for permission to serve the single claim

---

93   This terminology is used in the Civil Procedure Rules as it was used in SI 2001/3929 and continues to be used: see SI 2014/2947. In every other context the usual reference is to the Brussels I Regulation, not least because this Regulation is not primarily about judgments, but jurisdiction.

94   This provision, inserted into CPR r. 6.33 by SI 2014/2948, reflects Art. 31(2) of the recast Regulation.

95   CPR r. 6.33(3) is nowhere near as wide as it may appear. It applies to those cases in which an enactment makes it plain (as distinct from arguable) that it is envisaged that proceedings may be brought against persons even though they are out of the jurisdiction: *Re Harrods (Buenos Aires) Ltd (No 2)* [1992] Ch 72, 116; *Re Banco Nacional de Cuba* [2001] 1 WLR 2039. Enactments which do this are relatively few in number; see further above, para. 4.56.

96   Form N510.

97   CPR r. 6.34.

98   That is, service in Scotland or Northern Ireland.

99   Applying later to consolidate the two claims.

form, on the ground that he does not satisfy the opening words of CPR rule 6.33(1). This may be an inconvenience, but it is no more than an irritant.

The second case is rather more difficult. The claimant may believe that his claim falls within CPR rule 6.33; may also know that, if it does not, it will fall within one or more of the paragraphs of the Practice Direction 6B, to which CPR rule 6.36 refers; but above all he may be aware that there is some doubt about it. There may be uncertainty as to whether the claim arises in a civil or commercial matter,[100] or (assuming that it does) whether the defendant is domiciled in a Member State,[101] or whether the agreement on jurisdiction which is relied on was formally valid or will be construed as being broad enough to cover the claim, and so forth. All such points may leave it uncertain whether the claim will in due course be seen to have fallen within CPR rule 6.33. Again, there may be proceedings already commenced in another Member State in relation to which the claimant intends to challenge jurisdiction and expects to succeed, but the pendency of which prevents his filing the notice which identifies the grounds on which he is entitled to serve the claim form out of the jurisdiction.

The problem arises from the specific wording which the claimant or his agent must subscribe to: the form requires, with a statement of truth, the person signing it to state that the court has jurisdiction to hear the claim according to the relevant legislative provision, and that no proceedings are pending between the parties in another court.[102] The claimant or his agent may not be able to say that the court does have power to hear the claim: the truth may be that they believe it does, but that is a rather different point. It is unattractive to conclude that, where there is doubt in the mind of a conscientious solicitor, his client may not rely on CPR rule 6.33, and as CPR rule 6.36 applies only to cases in which CPR rule 6.33 does not, an application for permission may be technically irregular.[103] Moreover, in a case in which speed of issue and effectiveness of service may be critical, the delay in seeking permission which may turn out to have been unnecessary is something it may be well to avoid.

There is no completely satisfactory answer to the question. One analysis might be that a claimant may rely on CPR rule 6.33, and file the notice stating the grounds of the entitlement to serve, if he has, or believes that he has, a good arguable case that this procedural rule is complied with. But a rule which was developed to deal with uncertainty as to jurisdictional facts does not necessarily extend to the statutory scheme for service of process, and may even contradict the prescribed wording, which does not appear to allow for a claimant to state that there is only a good arguable case that he is entitled to serve out of the jurisdiction without permission.[104] If this is nevertheless to be the solution, it would be welcome if this were to be confirmed by the rules, and the form of the prescribed statement which

---

100 See above, para. 2.29.

101 The facts and matters which will be relevant to this are peculiarly within the knowledge of the defendant: the claimant can do no more than guess at what will be later said. For an illustration of the problems facing a party who does not have the right of access to the primary facts, see *Canada Trust Co v. Stolzenberg (No 2)* [2002] 1 AC 1.

102 Problems with the prescribed form of words were identified by the Court of Appeal in *Royal & Sun Alliance Insurance Co plc v. MK Digital FZE (Cyprus) Ltd* [2006] EWCA Civ 629, [2006] 2 Lloyd's Rep 110, [109]. It is not apparent that they have been addressed by the wording of Practice Form N510.

103 So treated in *Agrafax Public Relations Ltd v. United Scottish Society Incorporated* [1995] ILPr 753. No doubt it is a remediable error of procedure (CPR r. 3.10), but that is hardly the point.

104 Unless the proposition that there is a good arguable case that the court has jurisdiction under the Brussels I Regulation or the 1982 Act is identical in substance with the proposition that the court has jurisdiction under the Regulation or the 1982 Act.

is required to be made amended to reflect it. Even so, all this would achieve would be to lower the hurdle which the claimant is required to clear. If, when the defendant contests the jurisdiction, facts emerge which show that the claimant had not reached the standard of certainty, whatever it is held to be, the claimant will have served out of the jurisdiction when not entitled to do so and without obtaining permission. And it is of no help at all in the case mentioned above, in which the prescribed statement cannot be made because proceedings which should never have been brought are nevertheless pending in the courts of another Member State.

Another, more cumbersome but probably safer, analysis is that the claimant should issue two copies of the one claim form:[105] make the prescribed statement on one of them to enable it to be served under CPR rule 6.33, and apply in accordance with CPR rule 6.36 for permission to serve the other, explaining the background to, and reason for, the procedure which he has adopted, including his reservations about the statement of entitlement he will have made, but also the ways in which (as he sees it) facts may emerge which would mean that he was entitled to serve under CPR rule 6.33 all along.[106] There is an obvious drawback to this: a defendant will be served with two copies of what is substantially the one claim form. But until there is an authoritative clarification on the dilemma faced by the claimant, who believes on balance that he satisfies CPR rule 6.33 but sees the possibility that he may not, and who needs to be very sure that the service he is effecting will be impregnable to challenge, this may be the least bad way to minimise the risk.

5.21 Service of claim form out of the jurisdiction: outside the territory of the Member States

When process is to be served out of the jurisdiction, either with the permission of the court granted under CPR rule 6.36, or in cases where there is no requirement for permission to be obtained, CPR rule 6.40 explains how such service must be made.[107] For it may, in principle at least,[108] be as good an answer to a claim that the claim form has not been properly served on these technical grounds, as is the contention that the service should be set aside because the court should not have granted permission in the first place. English process is to be served in accordance with the rules of English law as these apply to service of English

---

105 It appears that the power to issue a concurrent claim form is no longer provided for by the Civil Procedure Rules (see *Pirelli Cables Ltd v. United Thai Shipping Corp* [2000] 1 Lloyd's Rep 663), though this may well have been an accident, for the procedural need for a concurrency procedure is manifest. In *The Byzantio* [2004] EWHC 3339 (Comm), [2005] 1 Lloyd's Rep 531, the judge simply assumed that the deletion was no impediment to the issue of a concurrent writ. But there appears to be no reason why the variant proposed in the text cannot be adopted, for the point is no more than that the claimant wishes to make doubly sure that service is made once and effectively.

106 It is not certain that there is anything which can be done to assist the claimant who would have had an incontestable claim to serve out under CPR r. 6.33 until the moment when manifestly unfounded proceedings were commenced in the courts of another Member State, but the dismissal of which the claimant has not yet been able to procure: after all, Art. 29 of Regulation 1215/2012 does not preclude the institution of proceedings, just their being proceeded with while the jurisdiction of the first court is being established. A practical solution would be for the court to authorise a variant on the statement in the prescribed Notice and for service then to be made (so securing that the English court will count as first seised once the foreign proceedings are disposed of; but it remains to be discovered whether the wording of CPR r. 6.33(2) can so easily be circumvented. The alternative of applying for permission under CPR r. 6.36 seems singularly inappropriate.

107 For service of foreign process in England, see CPR Part 6, Section V.

108 But maybe less so in practice today than hitherto: *Abela v. Baadarani* [2013] UKSC 44, [2013] 1 WLR 2043; see also *Weston v. Bates* [2012] EWHC 590 (QB), [2013] 1 WLR 189 (service of copy of claim form).

process in the particular country for service to be regular. The claimant must also act in accordance with (which means not in a way which is prohibited by)[109] the law of the place in which service is to be made.[110]

The basic principle is that service will be good if it is made by any method permitted[111] for the service of English process by the law of the country in which it is to be served,[112] and if it is contrary to the law of the country in which it is made, the service will not be service authorised by the civil procedure rules. In general, for service of an English claim form in the United States, therefore, the question is what are the rules which govern or restrict service of an English claim form in the United States? As this is a matter of local knowledge, the reliable[113] advice of a local practitioner will be required. Accordingly, no general answer can be given to the question whether the claim form may be served by the claimant personally, or by his agent, or by a process-server, or by the court, or by the local police, or by posting it, or by faxing it or by emailing it, in order to be effective. In all cases the answer is that it depends on the law of the country in which service is to be made.[114]

As an alternative,[115] service may be made through official channels, or by the manner prescribed for service on a State, or as permitted by a Civil Procedure Convention.[116] Where service is to be effected in a country[117] which is party to the Hague Convention on the Service Abroad of Judicial and Extrajudicial Documents of 15 November 1965, the claim form may be served through the authority designated by the State in question or, if the law of the country permits, through the judicial authorities of that country or through a British consular authority in that country.[118] Similar provision is made for service in a country which is party with the United Kingdom to a bilateral civil procedure Convention. If the country in which service is to be effected is not party with the United Kingdom to a relevant Convention, process may be served through the government of that country if

---

109 As distinct from merely not being provided for under the law of the state in question: see *Embassy of Brazil v. de Castro Cerqueira* UKEAT/456/13, [2014] 1 WLR 3718.

110 CPR r. 6.40(4).

111 That is to say, not forbidden by the law of the country in which service is to be made: *Habib Bank Ltd v. Central Bank of Sudan* [2006] EWHC 1767 (Comm), [2007] 1 WLR 470; *Abela v. Baadarani* [2013] UKSC 44, [2013] 1 WLR 2043.

112 CPR r. 6.40(3). In *Knauf UK GmbH v. British Gypsum Ltd* [2001] EWCA Civ 1570, [2002] 1 Lloyd's Rep 199, the court expressed uncertainty why a claim form to be served in Germany could not be served by first class post. The answer appears to be that English first class post (CPR r. 6.3(1)(b)) does not operate outside the United Kingdom and service by post is not permitted by German law. For confirmation, see *Burns-Anderson Independent Network v. Wheeler* [2005] EWHC 575 (QB), [2005] 1 Lloyd's Rep 580.

113 As the law of the particular country in question may change, reliable means up to date.

114 CPR Part 6 PD B, para. 4.2, invites enquiries to the Foreign Process Section (Room E02), Royal Courts of Justice, Strand, London WC2A 2LL. For an illustration of the potential problems, see *Shiblaq v. Sadikoglu* [2004] EWHC 1890 (Comm), [2004] ILPr 826, dealing with service of documents in Turkey in circumstances where Turkish law did not make it easy to understand whether service by notary public (which is valid for service of Turkish documents in Turkey) was valid service for English documents: held no); *Arros Invest Ltd v. Nishanov* [2004] EWHC 576 (Ch), [2004] ILPr 366 (service by post inside Russia); *BAS Capital Funding Corp v. Medfinco Ltd* [2003] EWHC 1798 (Ch), [2004] 1 Lloyd's Rep 652 (service in Malta before Malta became a Member State).

115 Unless a bilateral Convention specifies that service in accordance with the Convention is the only permitted basis for service to be made.

116 CPR r. 6.42(1). For the documents and procedure generally, see CPR r. 6.43.

117 See *Knauf (UK) GmbH v. British Gypsum Ltd* [2001] EWCA Civ 1570, [2002] 1 WLR 907.

118 CPR r. 6.42(1). The Hague Convention allows the States to impose restrictions on methods of service, such as on service by post. Guidance in relation to this is also available from the Foreign Process Section (Room E02) at the Royal Courts of Justice.

the government is willing, or through a British consular authority in that country if the State permits it. But unless service is to be made under the Hague Convention, service through official channels is not permitted for service in Scotland, Northern Ireland, the Isle of Man, the Channel Islands, any Commonwealth State, or any British Overseas Territory.[119]

No general answer can therefore be given to the question whether service must, or may (but need not) be done in accordance with the Hague Convention, nor to the question whether all the options provided for in the Hague Convention apply in relation to all States Party to that Convention: reservations are permitted in relation to various forms of service on the territory of individual Contracting States. Anyone reasoning, for example, that the Hague Convention allows for personal service, and that as Switzerland is a Contracting State, it is lawful as a matter of Swiss law to appoint an agent to serve an English claim form in Switzerland, would have a very rude shock indeed.[120]

5.22 Service of claim form out of the jurisdiction: within the territory of a Member State

Where service is to be made on the territory of Member State in respect of a civil or commercial matter, service is regulated by the Service Regulation, Council Regulation (EC) 1393/2007.[121] This instrument makes improved provision for the service within the territory[122] of the Member States[123] of judicial and extrajudicial documents issued in civil or commercial proceedings and which have to be transmitted from one Member State to another for service in the latter. Its stated purpose is to speed up and to simplify provisions for service in Member States through official channels,[124] and to give the necessary degree of protection to those upon whom service of foreign process is to be made. This is achieved, in part at least, by the Service Regulation being treated as an exhaustive code for the service of documents to which it applies.[125] It is not open to a claimant to 'serve' a defendant who is in another Member State by means not provided for in the Regulation. As a result, rules of national procedural laws which would have permitted, for example, service by leaving documents on the court file, or other pretended methods, are inapplicable in cases which fall within the scope of the Service Regulation.[126]

In addition to service made through and by the authority referred to by the Regulation and designated by the individual Member States, the Regulation confirms that service made

---

119 CPR rr 6.40.2, 6.42(3)

120 See Art. 271 of the Swiss Penal Code, which was set out in para. 4.57 above.

121 [2007] OJ L324/79. The Regulation repealed and replaced the original Service Regulation 1348/2000.

122 That is, it is a Regulation about service of judicial and extrajudicial documents on the territory of a Member State. It is not concerned with the domicile or residence of the party on whom service is to be made; it is inapplicable if service is to be made in a non-Member State, even if the party on whom service is to be made is domiciled in a Member State. On the nature and meaning of extrajudicial documents, see C-14/08 *Roda Golf & Beach Resort SL* [2009] ECR I-5439 (a case on Regulation 1348/2000): extrajudicial documents are not limited to those related to actual or proposed legal proceedings, so a notarial act to terminate a contract for the sale of land fell within the material scope of the Regulation).

123 Denmark is now a Member State, despite what is said in Art. 1(3) of the Regulation.

124 Though the speediest solution would be for all the states to allow the claimant to serve directly, without the restriction of these formalities.

125 C-325/11 *Alder v. Orłowska* EU:C:2012:824: see esp. [24], [25].

126 *Tavoulareas v. Tsavliris* [2004] EWCA Civ 48, [2004] 1 Lloyd's Rep 445 had already arrived at this conclusion, and has therefore been vindicated.

through consular channels is permitted save where a State has given notice that it opposes such service otherwise than on nationals of the State whose document is to be served.[127] It confirms that service by post, which means by registered letter with acknowledgment of receipt, is permitted:[128] the predecessor Regulation had added the qualification that postal service was to be permitted unless the Member State in which service is to be made has made it known that it is opposed to service of judicial documents by post, but this limitation has now been removed.[129] And it confirms the validity of direct service though 'judicial officers, officials, or other competent persons of the Member State addressed', unless the Member State in which service is to be made has made it known that it is opposed to service of judicial documents by these direct means:[130] some States do, others do not. This information about whether Member States permit or do not permit service within their territory by diplomatic or consular agents, or by direct service, and the information about what else is required or permitted in the individual Member States, is collected, updated, and most usefully made available in the electronic 'European Judicial Atlas'.

The Regulation imposes some uniformity as to the language in which documents which are to be served must, or may be, drafted;[131] it specifies the grounds on which a person served must be informed that he may refuse to accept service.[132] The Annexes to the Regulation set out standard forms which accompany the document to be served. If there were to be a concern that the need to arrange for service under the Service Regulation may be to the disadvantage of a claimant seeking to seise the English courts before his opponent has the opportunity to seise a court in another Member State, it should be remembered that an English court is now seised on the issue, rather than upon service, of the claim form,[133] so this is now much less of a concern than it once was.

The receiving agency is required to take all necessary steps to effect service as soon as possible, and within one month of receipt.[134] If it is necessary to determine it, the date of service is the date on which the document is served in accordance with the law of the Member State in which it is served.[135]

Of course, service in those Member States which have not opted out of service by diplomatic and direct means may be made in accordance with those procedures, within the parameters of the Regulation and the notifications made by the Member State on whose territory service is to be made. But it is now settled that, where service of English process is to be made in another Member State, service of the document on the defendant in that Member State must be made in conformity with the requirements of the Service Regulation. It will be unwise to act without the reliable advice of a local practitioner, but notwithstanding that, to be confident that service of English process in a particular Member

---

127 Article 13 of the Service Regulation.
128 Article 14 of the Service Regulation.
129 This has not prevented some Member States making some specification of the circumstances in which they permit service to be made by post in the European Judicial Atlas. Unless this national information simply reproduces other provisions of the Regulation as to translations, etc., it is hard to see how it can be proper.
130 Article 15 of the Service Regulation.
131 Articles 5, 8.
132 Article 8.
133 See above, para. 2.269.
134 Article 7.
135 Article 9.

State will be effective, it is essential that it be made by a method provided for in the receiving Member State by the Service Regulation.

(C) DISPUTING THE JURISDICTION OF THE COURT

5.23 General

In the terminology now used in English law, the jurisdiction of a court may be disputed in two very distinct senses. The defendant may contend that the basis for jurisdiction over him is absent, and that the court should therefore declare that it has no jurisdiction, and should set aside any service which has been made as the necessary consequence of the decision on jurisdiction. This may be thought of as a challenge to the very existence of jurisdiction; and it is provided for in CPR rule 11(1)(a).

But a defendant who has no basis for making a challenge which alleges that the court did not have jurisdiction over him in relation to the claim, and who therefore has no basis for asking the court to set aside service which had been made on him, may nevertheless argue that the court should not exercise the jurisdiction which it has, by applying for a stay of proceedings. This is, to a purist mind, not a challenge to the jurisdiction in a strict sense, but if the relief is ordered it results in the court not adjudicating the merits of the claim; and it is therefore provided for by CPR rule 11(1)(b). In this Section the primary focus is on disputing the jurisdiction in the stricter sense of CPR rule 11(1)(a); the argument that a court with jurisdiction should not proceed to exercise that jurisdiction is discussed later.

If therefore a claim form has been served, but the defendant wishes to challenge the propriety of service or the existence of jurisdiction over him, the procedure by and according to which this is to be done is set out CPR Part 11.[136] Even though service within the jurisdiction may have blatantly contravened the rules governing service, the service of the process of an English court in circumstances which do not comply with the rules governing service will be merely irregular;[137] and irregularity may, because it is ultimately only an error of procedure, be remedied by the court.[138] Irregularity of service is a basis upon which the defendant may succeed in having service upon him set aside, but it is no more than that.

Service outside the jurisdiction in circumstances where the necessary permission[139] was not obtained is also irregular. Even if – as sometimes happens – a claim form is received by a defendant out of the jurisdiction, without any indication that permission was sought or obtained to serve it, this is only an irregularity: maybe a serious one, but always a potentially curable one. It is sometimes said that in such a case the irregularity is less susceptible to cure, but that only goes to show that where service has been made, the court has jurisdiction. Every now and then a defendant will decide to ignore the delivery of a claim form on the pretended ground that he should not have been served with it: this, when it happens, is a terrible error of thought and analysis. When the claim form has been served upon him, whether this was done in conformity with the rules or otherwise, the defendant has been

---

136 Previously RSC Order 12, r. 8.
137 But is not a nullity: CPR r. 3.10.
138 *Leal v. Dunlop Bio-Processes International Ltd* [1984] 1 WLR 874; *Camera Care Ltd v. Victor Hasselblad AB* [1986] 1 FTLR 348; *The Goldean Mariner* [1990] 2 Lloyd's Rep 215; *The Oinoussin Pride* [1991] 1 Lloyd's Rep 126; *Shiblaq v. Sadikoglu (No 2)* [2004] EWHC 1890 (Comm), [2004] ILPr 826.
139 Paragraphs 4.57 *et seq.*, above.

made subject to the jurisdiction of the English court. It is therefore quite wrong to ignore it, or to assume that the flaw (if flaw there actually was) means that nothing with any legal significance has happened. The proper response is to acknowledge service, and apply for the setting aside of the service and for an appropriate costs order.

A defendant who has been served may challenge the jurisdiction of the court over him. It could hardly be otherwise. The claim form will have been issued at the behest of, and frequently served by, the claimant or his legal adviser. It will have been stamped in and issued by the appropriate judicial office, but no judicial officer will have scrutinised it; still less will a judge have decided that it is a proper case to bring before the court. Even where the claim form is served out of the jurisdiction with the permission of the court there will have been no judicial or other detailed investigation of whether the case is one in respect of which the court has, or should exercise, its power to grant permission to serve: all the court will have seen will be the claim form (or a draft), and the witness statement in support of the application for permission for service out of the jurisdiction. In no sense does the court determine whether it is jurisdictionally proper to bring the case: it is the claimant, rather than the court, who invokes jurisdiction; it is the claimant who says why he considers himself entitled to invoke the jurisdiction; and it is his act of service which gives the court the basis for its exercise of jurisdiction.

What happens next is up to the defendant. He may elect to fight the claim on its merits. Once he takes a step towards doing so, he may be seen to have submitted to the jurisdiction of the court.[140] But he may instead ignore the service; or may make an application to dispute the jurisdiction.

5.24 Making no response to service of the claim form

The defendant may decide to ignore, or otherwise not respond to, service of the claim form upon him. If he does so, he does not object to the jurisdiction of the court, and without such a challenge being made, the court may proceed to give judgment in default of acknowledgment of service. As a matter of common law procedure, the court does not ask itself whether, if he had chosen to contest the jurisdiction, the defendant might have succeeded. If the claim form has been served within the jurisdiction, or outside with permission (where this is required), and it appears that service has been effected, the court may proceed to give judgment against a defendant who chooses not to appear.[141]

The common law, set out above, is partially modified in cases where the claim falls within the scope of the Brussels I Regulation. According to Article 28, as explained above,[142] the court has a limited obligation to examine the basis of its jurisdiction if the defendant is domiciled in another Member State but does not appear.

With that single qualification, the court may proceed to give a default judgment. It will do so by giving such judgment as it appears to the court that the claimant is entitled to

---

140 In cases in which his response to the service of the writ is ambiguous, it may be more difficult to say whether he has submitted to the jurisdiction. In principle the test must be one of objective appearance.

141 Nor does the court make a detailed examination of the merits of the claim: it gives judgment in default, under CPR Part 12.

142 See para. 2.257, above; for the form of evidence of service, see CPR r. 12.10 and Practice Direction, Paras 4.3, 4.5.

on his statement of case.[143] Once this is done, the defendant is at a strategic disadvantage. For the judgment of an English court in a civil or commercial matter is, subject to limited objections,[144] entitled to be recognised and enforced under Chapter III of the Brussels I Regulation.[145] When enforcement is sought, but a challenge to it is raised, it is generally irrelevant and inadmissible that the jurisdiction of the original court could have been successfully challenged. The court has given judgment, and both the jurisdiction of the court and the merits of the matter are regarded as having been determined.

5.25 Uncertainty as to the satisfaction of the basis on which the jurisdiction, pursuant to which service was made, is asserted

In a case falling within the scope of the Regulation otherwise than under Article 6, the claimant will have exercised his power to serve the claim form on the defendant without permission, regardless of whether the defendant was within or outside[146] the jurisdiction when service was made. The first occasion, therefore, upon which a court may be asked to decide for itself the question whether the Regulation actually justified the claimant's assertion of jurisdiction will be if the defendant makes an application to dispute the jurisdiction of the court: to have the court declare that it has no jurisdiction, by application made under CPR Part 11. The defendant may deny, for example, that he was domiciled in the United Kingdom;[147] he may deny that there was an agreement for the jurisdiction of the English court to have jurisdiction over him in relation to the dispute;[148] he may deny that there was a contract entered into between the parties of which the obligation in question was to be performed in England;[149] he may deny that the place of the harmful event was England,[150] and so on. He may assert that there was an agreement that the courts of another Member State should have exclusive jurisdiction; he may contend that the proceedings have as their object a tenancy of land in another Member State: it all depends, but it all invites the court to come to the same conclusion: that the justification for service to be made out of the jurisdiction without permission was not present, and that service should now be set aside. The question is, by what standard or test is the court to assess whether the claimant made out so sufficient a case on jurisdiction that he should be allowed to proceed to have the merits of his claim determined in the English courts in circumstances where the defendant contests the matter.

According to authority, the answer falls into two parts.[151] The precise nature of the test to be applied is a matter of national procedural law.[152] In England the content of the test was generally understood to mean, at least at a level of general principle, that the claimant

---

143 CPR r. 12.11.

144 See paras 7.10 *et seq.*, below.

145 It may also be entitled to recognition in other States if so permitted by the law of such State.

146 Subject to the claimant's filing and serving a notice which states the grounds on which this service was entitled to be made: CPR r. 6.34.

147 Article 4. He may also deny that he was domiciled in England (as distinct from Scotland); but this raises a question of internal United Kingdom jurisdiction, not a question of international jurisdiction.

148 Article 25.

149 Article 7(1).

150 Article 7(2).

151 See also above, para. 2.126, where this issue was also discussed in the particular context of disputed jurisdiction agreements.

152 *Shevill v. Presse Alliance SA* [1995] ECR I-415; proceedings resumed at [1996] AC 980. See also, for confirmation, C–375/13 *Kolassa v. Barclays Bank plc* EU:C:2015:37, at [58]–[65].

was required to demonstrate a good arguable case that the jurisdiction on which he relies is established. This in turn meant that the claimant, who seeks to invoke the jurisdiction which the court would not otherwise have, must demonstrate a good arguable case that the jurisdictional facts, or jurisdictional prerequisites, on which he relies to establish the jurisdiction of the court, are present. This did not require him to show that he was probably right on the jurisdictional point on which he relied.

In relation to the Regulation, the formal adoption of this test can be traced back to *Tesam Distribution Ltd v. Schuh Mode Team GmbH*.[153] Its application, again in principle, was confirmed by the House of Lords in *Canada Trust Co v. Stolzenberg (No 2)*,[154] but in a rather particular sense. An interpretation was adopted which required the claimant to have the better of the argument that the jurisdictional rule on which he sought to place reliance was satisfied. In the context of the Regulation, this made sense. Take for example a claim to be brought against a defendant domiciled in England, but who disputes the jurisdiction by contending that there is an agreement on choice of court for the courts of Germany, to which the claimant responds by arguing that there was no choice of court to which Article 25 would give effect. If the English court were to reach the view, on the material before it, that the agreement on choice of court was effective, but were still to accept that there is a good arguable case that it could be impeached, it might be said that the claimant has shown a good arguable case that the English court has jurisdiction, even though that same court also considers that the German courts have, on balance, a stronger jurisdictional claim. It would not be right in those circumstances for the English court to conclude that it has jurisdiction; and for this reason the appropriate test to apply is whether the claimant has the better of the argument on the jurisdictional issue which the court has to decide.

As a matter of principle, the point of departure must be that the national court establishes, as a matter of its own procedural law, the standard of jurisdictional certainty which must be met for it to proceed to hear the case on its merits. But rules of national procedural law may not impair the practical effect of the Regulation.[155] English procedural law could not properly mean that a court may decide that its jurisdictional base under the Regulation is, on balance, not present, yet nevertheless proceed to adjudicate. As the decision on personal jurisdiction, interlocutory though it is, is not capable of being postponed till later, or revisited and reversed at trial, a court should not accept jurisdiction when it believes, on balance, that the jurisdictional ground relied on is absent, or (to make the same point even more tellingly) that the Regulation gives jurisdiction to the courts of another Member State at the same time as it withholds it from the English court. In other words, the court should not ask whether there is a good arguable case that the English court has jurisdiction, but should ask whether the claimant has 'the better of the argument' on the issue. To this extent the approach of the English courts to the question whether the Regulation justified the claimant in the assertion of jurisdiction is principled and correct.

But is there any reason to interpret a test of 'who has the better of the argument on the point of jurisdiction?' as though it required either party to establish its case to the more robust standard of a balance of probability. In many cases the court will be all too aware

---

153 [1990] ILPr 149.
154 [2002] 1 AC 1.
155 C-365/88 *Kongress Agentur Hagen GmbH v. Zeehaghe BV* [1990] ECR I-1845.

that it can do no more than decide whose contentions on jurisdiction are currently the least unpersuasive, and in that sense the more persuasive, while being perfectly well aware that 'the limitations which an interlocutory process imposes'[156] mean that neither side even comes close to the standard of making his case to the standard of a balance of probabilities. The question who has the better of the argument is a rational, and easily understood, standard, which should not be complicated by excessive analysis.[157]

A further strand in the recent jurisprudence concerned with the Regulation, that the law may require the court to ask whether one party has 'much the better of the argument',[158] is definitely not an improvement. A test which requires one party to have *much* the better of the argument inevitably prompts the questions, which party has to shoulder the greater burden which this adjective suggests, and how much more burdensome 'much' makes the test. It would surely be wrong for a court to say that it finds that, on balance, the claimant has satisfied the requirements for jurisdiction under the Chapter II of the Regulation, but that he has not satisfied them by such a clear margin that he is entitled to bring his claim before the court. Yet this is what a requirement that the claimant have 'much the better' of the jurisdictional argument would mean. It is an unprincipled distortion of the law.

And anyway, the difference between 'the better of' and 'much the better of' is not measurable. Its continued use would damage the principle of legal certainty, and would therefore jeopardise the operation of the Regulation. In all the circumstances the bothersome qualifier 'much' should not form part of the test applied by the court. The Court of Appeal has recently said so,[159] and there is good reason to support its sensible approach. The question, in the context of jurisdiction given or refused by the Regulation, is whether the claimant has the better of the argument that the jurisdiction on which he seeks to rely was available to him.

One final point needs to be made: what has just been said applies to jurisdiction taken on the basis of (or denied by) the Regulation. As the jurisdiction of the court is assessed once and for all at the outset of proceedings, and as there is no separate role for a principle of *forum (non) conveniens*, the entire weight of the jurisdictional question is borne by the question whether the provision of the Regulation relied on is available. Where, by contrast, the question is whether the court has jurisdiction on the basis of service out with the permission of the court under CPR rule 6.36 and the Practice Direction, in the context of which it is additionally necessary to show that England is the proper place for the proceedings to be brought, it is sufficient to show that there is a good arguable case, in the traditional, non-Regulation sense, that the paragraph of the Practice Direction relied on was satisfied. The two forms of jurisdiction are, in this respect, very different, and what is right and proper in the one context would be unwarranted in the other.

---

156 *Bols Distilleries BV v. Superior Yacht Services Ltd* [2006] UKPC 45 (Gib.), [2007] 1 WLR 12, [28].

157 It was proposed by Lawrence Collins J in *Bank of Tokyo-Mitsubishi Ltd v. Baskan Gida Sanayi ve Pazarlama AS* [2004] EWHC 945 (Ch), [2004] 2 Lloyd's Rep 395.

158 The leading case on the 'much the better' test, in the context of Art. 25 agreements on jurisdiction at least, is *Bols Distilleries BV v. Superior Yacht Services Ltd* [2006] UKPC 45 (Gib.), [2007] 1 WLR 12 (a case on the law of Gibraltar)

159 See in particular *JSC Aeroflot-Russian Airlines v. Berezovsky* [2013] EWCA Civ 784, [2013] 2 Lloyd's Rep 242, [49]–[50]. It did not put forward all the points made here, but the decision is clear enough.

5.26 Disputing the jurisdiction of the English court: the framework

The defendant may choose to challenge the legal foundation for the jurisdiction which the claimant has invoked or purported to invoke.[160] In doing so he will make a formal[161] acknowledgment of the jurisdiction of the court which results from the fact of service, but will contend that the court should declare there to be no proper basis for that jurisdiction and grant such consequential relief as flows from the declaration that it has no jurisdiction. If the defendant succeeds, the court will declare that it does not have jurisdiction.[162] But if the court dismisses the defendant's application disputing its jurisdiction, the defendant's original acknowledgment of service lapses. What the defendant then does is examined below.[163]

CPR Part 11 provides that a defendant wishing to dispute the court's jurisdiction to try the claim, *or to argue that the court should not exercise its jurisdiction*,[164] must first acknowledge service of process in accordance with CPR Part 10.[165] This is done without prejudice to any objection which may be taken to the jurisdiction.[166] The defendant must then apply, within 14 (or, in the Commercial Court, 28) days of acknowledging service,[167] for relief pursuant to CPR Part 11.

There may be several possible bases for the application. In a case of service out, the argument may be that permission to serve the defendant out of the jurisdiction should not have been granted, and should now be set aside, together with its consequences. In a case of service within or out of the jurisdiction, the argument may be that service was not made in accordance with the rules governing the time, manner and place of service. In a case of service within or out of the jurisdiction, the argument may be that the defendant was not subject to the jurisdiction of the court: perhaps because of a personal immunity, but perhaps because statute – for example, the Brussels I Regulation – provides that the court does not have jurisdiction over the defendant in relation to the claim. Even though the contention that the court had no jurisdiction may be based on the rules of the Brussels I Regulation, the framework within which the application for relief must be made is CPR Part 11.[168]

If, instead, the defendant applies within the framework of CPR Part 11 for a stay of proceedings, he may do so on the basis of a plea of *forum non conveniens*, that there is a court in another country which is clearly more appropriate than England for the trial of the claim, as a result of which the interests of justice favour the suspension of the exercise of jurisdiction by the English court. He may also apply for a stay of proceedings by reference to Article 30 of the Brussels I Regulation, on the ground that a court in another Member State was seised of related proceedings prior to the seisin of the English court and that the court should, in

---

160 He may also allege that service was irregular.

161 But one which may not be held against him if he proceeds to make his challenge to the jurisdiction: CPR r. 11(3).

162 If he is successful in relation to part, but not all, of the claim, the claim form will be amended by deletion.

163 See para. 5.30, below.

164 Or, naturally, to argue both in the one application.

165 CPR r. 11(2). According to *IBS Technologies (Pvt) Ltd v. APM Technologies SA (No 1)*, 7 April 2003, it is not strictly necessary that the defendant tick the box on the acknowledgment of service form, so long as the application is made within the time fixed by CPR Part 11, though this cannot possibly be recommended as a sensible way to proceed. On the other hand, if the box is ticked, so indicating that the defendant will challenge the jurisdiction, he must then get on and actually do it, or else he will be taken to have waived his challenge: *Maple Leaf Macro Volatility Master Fund v. Rouvroy* [2009] EWHC 257 (Comm), [2009] 1 Lloyd's Rep 475, [186]–[187].

166 CPR r. 11(3).

167 CPR r. 11(4). For the position in the Commercial Court, CPR r. 58.7(2).

168 *The Alexandros T* [2013] UKSC 70, [2014] 1 Lloyd's Rep 223.

the circumstances, order a stay. But as said before, jurisdictional relief by reference to the Brussels I Regulation is applied for under CPR Part 11, in exactly the same way (and within the same time limits)[169] as jurisdictional relief sought by reference to the common law rules.

5.27 Application to dispute the jurisdiction of the court: CPR rule 11(1)(a)

The application for relief must be made within 14 or 28 days, as the case may be, of filing an acknowledgment of service.[170] The actual period for filing the acknowledgment, however, varies according to how and where the claim form and particulars of claim were served. If the defendant leaves it until the last moment to file the acknowledgment of service, he will maximise the time period for making the application to dispute the jurisdiction. But the period allowed for filing an acknowledgement of service varies according to where service was made. The point of departure is the date of service of the particulars of claim. If service was made in England, the period for filing the acknowledgment of service is 14 days from the service of the particulars of claim.[171]

If service out of the jurisdiction was made in a case in which the permission of the court was not required, the period allowed for acknowledging service depends on where service was made. If service was made in Scotland or Northern Ireland, the period is 21 days. If service was made in a (Brussels or Lugano) Convention territory within Europe, or in the European territory of a Member State, the period is 21 days.[172] If service was made in a Brussels Convention territory outside Europe, the period is 31 days.[173] If the defendant was served elsewhere, the period for acknowledgment of service is specified by a Table printed in Practice Direction 6B.[174]

If service was made in a case in which permission was sought and obtained under CPR rule 6.36, permitting the service of the claim form out of the jurisdiction, the order granting permission must itself specify the period for filing an acknowledgment of service.[175] This is set in accordance with the Table in Practice Direction 6B,[176] which states the number of

---

169 *The Alexandros T* [2013] UKSC 70, [2014] 1 All ER 590.

170 For the power of parties to agree to an extension of time, see CPR r. 3.8(3), (4). For the suggestion that a case may be commenced in the Chancery Division of the High Court, rather than in the Commercial Court where it naturally belongs, for the purpose of forcing the defendant into a shorter time period to make the application than would have been the case in the Commercial Court, see *SET Select Energy GmbH v. F&M Bunkering Ltd* [2014] EWHC 192 (Comm), [2014] 1 Lloyd's Rep 652: in such circumstances, the propriety of overlooking a small delay in meeting the deadline is obvious.

171 CPR r. 10.3.

172 CPR r. 6.35(2).

173 CPR r. 6.35(3).

174 CPR r. 6.35(4).

175 CPR r. 6.37(5).

176 The actual periods for acknowledging service as set out in this Table are completely fascinating: the insight which gave rise to them is a complete mystery. For example, a defendant served in the dreadful chaos that is Somalia has 22 days, but one served in the comfort of Bermuda 31 days, to acknowledge service. A defendant has 25 days if served in Australia, but only 23 if served in Burkina Faso, as Upper Volta is now known. He has 50 days if served in the Cook Islands, but 31 days on Tristan da Cunha; 24 days if served in China (a day less if served in Taiwan), but 31 days in Hong Kong or Macau, and 34 if served in Tibet. The 24 days allowed if served in South Korea are extended by four days if service is made in North Korea. Though a defendant is allowed 31 days if served in Gibraltar, only 22 days are allowed if served in Paraguay or darkest Peru, and a truly punishing 21 days if process is served in the icy wasteland of the South Shetland Islands, a part of the British Antarctic Territory, and which contrasts oddly with the 31 days allowed to a defendant served in South Georgia. That this magnificent curiosity should have survived, untouched by modern political geography, is oddly comforting.

days by reference to the country in which service was made: the tabular number of days is counted from the date of service of the particulars of claim, whether served with or after the claim form.

As said above, a defendant who wishes to dispute the jurisdiction must do so within 14 (or in the Commercial Court, 28) days of acknowledging service, or must apply[177] within that period for an extension of time to make an application disputing the jurisdiction. If no such application is made in advance of the time running out, the court still has discretion to allow the application to be made, out of time;[178] but if the defendant has allowed time to run out and has done nothing to suggest[179] that he intends to dispute the jurisdiction, he is at risk of being told that he appears to have submitted and it is now too late.[180] A defendant who applies for an extension of time for filing a defence is also at risk of being held to have submitted to the jurisdiction of the court, for the intelligent bystander may well interpret this as a step towards filing a defence on the merits of the claim, not as a challenge to the jurisdiction.[181]

If he disputes the jurisdiction of the court by application under CPR Part 11, the primary relief for which a defendant will apply is a declaration that the court has no jurisdiction;[182] but further and consequential relief[183] may be granted, including an order setting aside service of the claim form,[184] and an order discharging any order made before the claim was commenced or the claim form was served.[185]

Having issued an application to challenge the jurisdiction of the court, the defendant must take care not to jeopardise it by appearing to submit to the jurisdiction of the court after all. He will need to make progress with the application, for if he does not he may appear to (and so be taken to) have abandoned it.[186] It is advisable to take only steps which are consistent with the contention that the court does not have jurisdiction and should so declare, and that the technical jurisdiction invoked by service should be annulled by the setting aside of service. If he does anything which goes beyond this, he risks being held to have taken a step in the proceedings to decide the merits, and he will have thrown away his right to dispute

---

177 Under CPR r. 3.1(2)(a), unless this can be agreed to by the claimant within the limited scope of CPR r. 3.8(3), (4).

178 *Sawyer v. Atari Interactive Inc* [2005] EWHC 2351 (Ch), [2006] ILPr 129; *CNA Insurance Co Ltd v. Office Depot International* [2005] EWHC 456 (Comm), [2005] Lloyd's Rep IR 658. For consideration of the strictness or otherwise of these limits, see *Deutsche Bank AG v. Highland Crusader Offshore Partners Ltd* [2009] EWCA Civ 725, [2010] 1 WLR 1023, [18]–[20]; *Zumax Nigeria Ltd v. First City Monument Bank Ltd* [2014] EWHC 2075 (Ch); *cf SET Select Energy GmbH v. F&M Bunkering Ltd* [2014] EWHC 192 (Comm), [2014] 1 Lloyd's Rep 652.

179 It is a matter of the objective appearance which would have been given to an interested bystander, and so the answer will be fact-specific: *Sage v. Double A Hydraulics Ltd* [1992] Times LR 165; *Spargos Mining v. Atlantic Capital Corp* (unrep), *The Times*, 11 December 1995; *SMAY Investments Ltd v. Sachdev* [2003] EWHC 474 (Ch), [2003] 1 WLR 1973; *Burns-Anderson Independent Network plc v. Wheeler* [2005] EWHC 575 (QB), [2005] 1 Lloyd's Rep 580; *Marketmaker Technology Ltd v. CMC Group plc* [2008] EWHC 1556 (QB).

180 *Global Multimedia International Ltd v. ARA Media Services* [2006] EWHC 3612 (Ch), [2007] 1 All ER (Comm) 1160.

181 *Midland Resources Ltd v. Gonvarri Industrial SA* [2002] ILPr 74; *Burns-Anderson Independent Network v. Wheeler* [2005] EWHC 575 (QB), [2005] 1 Lloyd's Rep 580; and see generally for the modern approach *Zumax Nigeria Ltd v. First City Monument Bank Ltd* [2014] EWHC 2075 (Ch).

182 CPR r. 11(1).

183 CPR r. 11(6).

184 In any case in which the court determines that it does not have jurisdiction.

185 Including any order under CPR r. 6.36 granting permission to serve out of the jurisdiction, but also any other interim relief.

186 *Maple Leaf Macro Volatility Master Fund v. Rouvray* [2009] EWHC 257 (Comm), [2009] 1 Lloyd's Rep 475.

the jurisdiction. If a general principle illuminates the way the law works at this point, it is probably that of estoppel by representation: if the defendant does something which would convey to an intelligent observer the message or impression that he has abandoned his argument that the court does not have (or, in the case of the application for a stay, should not exercise) jurisdiction, he risks being held to the outward appearance which he gives. It may not be correct to say that the tiniest foot fault will be taken as a submission; but equally, a requirement that the act said to be by way of submission be unequivocal may put the point rather high. The question should be to ask what a reasonable man would think on the question whether the defendant has (now) accepted the jurisdiction of the court; the answer will be distinctly fact-specific.

But the defendant would do well to refrain from participation, even incidentally, in the procedure for resolution of the merits of the case. On the face of it, if he does take part in any such process, it will risk looking like a submission. The position may appear to be complicated by the fact that where jurisdiction was asserted by service out with permission under CPR rules 6.36 and 6.37, a court will set aside service if shown that there is no serious issue on the merits of the claim, and the defendant may fairly seek to show that the position in relation to the merits are such that service should be set aside.[187] Even so, if he decides to make this part of his jurisdictional challenge, it may be prudent to say that this, and only this, is the purpose for which the court is being asked to examine the merits of the claim. Otherwise there is a risk of facts being misconstrued.

The defendant must certainly not file a defence, for if he does that he will be taken to have thrown away his shield and submitted to the jurisdiction;[188] but if he indicates in the evidence in support of his application what his defence will be, so as to bolster a contention that there was not a serious issue to be tried and that permission to serve out should be set aside for that reason, this obviously will not amount to a submission.[189] Unless and until a court clearly holds that the serving of a defence does not prejudice the right to dispute the jurisdiction or to seek a stay, it would appear to be a perilous adventure for the defendant to file a defence until after the determination of his application under CPR Part 11, this including any appeals. After all, even if the application for a declaration that the court has no jurisdiction is unsuccessful, the defendant has a fresh opportunity to acknowledge service of process,[190] and this would make no sense if a defence had already been filed. The safest path is straight and narrow.[191]

---

187 *Ryanair Ltd v. Esso Italiana Srl* [2013] EWCA Civ 1450, [2015] 1 AU ER (Comm) 152, [20].

188 Because in England the court will determine jurisdiction before it embarks on the merits phase of the matter. It would be different if England had followed the path of those other States – Member States and non-Member States – which expect a defendant to file all his defences, to jurisdiction and to merits, in a single pleading.

189 By contrast, and as will be seen, for a defendant seeking only a stay of proceedings under CPR r. 11(1)(b), service of a defence may not be fatal to the application, for a stay may in some circumstances be properly applied for at a later stage in the proceedings.

190 CPR r. 11(8).

191 The view expressed in the text is the cautious one. It is not impossible that a court may take a more flexible view and overlook an act which was done, but which was not strictly required as part of the jurisdictional challenge, while the defendant was still maintaining that the court should declare that it has no jurisdiction. The cautious view is supported by *Ngcobo v. Thor Chemicals Holdings Ltd, The Times,* 10 November 1995, where the taking of a step in the action was held to prevent further appeal to obtain a stay; and the same principle was said to apply to Order 11 (as it then was) cases. However, a similar submission had been made in a service out case in *Lubrizol Corp v. Esso Petroleum Co Ltd* [1992] RPC 467, and had been rejected by Dillon LJ as 'impertinent'. The service of a defence and counterclaim pending the appeal in the application to dispute the jurisdiction did not constitute a submission, as the claimants 'knew perfectly well at all times... that the third defendant was... struggling to get out

To put the same point in positive rather than negative terms, CPR Part 11 allows the defendant to obtain an order declaring that the court has no jurisdiction, setting aside service, and similar relief.[192] If service of the claim form is set aside, there is no longer jurisdiction over the defendant. The defendant may, therefore, do whatever is consistent with his taking this stance: applying for an extension of time to make this challenge,[193] or seeking disclosure and inspection of documents that are material to this application.[194] If the application is successful, the court will declare that it has no jurisdiction, and service will be set aside. If the application is unsuccessful, the jurisdiction of the court is confirmed, but the original acknowledgment of service will lapse and the defendant has a further period in which to decide whether to enter a fresh one.[195] If he elects to do so, he takes the first step in what will now be the trial of the merits,[196] and through this act of submission the defendant will confirm the jurisdiction of the court;[197] but if he decides not to, his position is as though he had ignored service of the claim form in the first place.

Where the application seeks an order that the original order granting permission to serve out be set aside, the material date for the purpose of deciding whether the original order should be set aside is that on which the order granting permission to serve out was made. This is because the application is designed to show, and obtain relief on the basis, that the order should not have been made, and this cannot logically be affected by events which have taken place since the original order was made. So the evidence[198] must

---

of the action and taking steps to do so. They knew that everything done by the third defendant was done subject and without prejudice to the right of appeal, and they did not suppose for one moment that the right to appeal, or the appeal, had been abandoned.' To similar effect, in the context of arbitration, is *Capital Trust Investments Ltd v. Radio Design TJ AB* [2002] EWCA Civ 135, [2002] 2 All ER 159, following in this respect *Patel v. Patel* [2000] QB 551. The authorities are therefore in a little disarray: *Lubrizol* was not referred to in *Ngcobo*. While it can be contended that both cases establish that the sole question is one of external or objective appearances, the attitudes represented by the judgments are not aligned. Either a single, unforced, step in the action is fatal to the jurisdictional challenge (*Ngcobo*), or a factual assertion (on reasonable grounds) that the challenge is being maintained, and not abandoned, will shield the defendant from the allegation of submission (*Lubrizol*). It is possible that the cases may all be reconciled by asking whether a disinterested bystander would have assumed, or whether the defendant actually knew, that any challenge to the jurisdiction had been abandoned: if the answer to either question is affirmative, the defendant has submitted and it is too late to dispute the jurisdiction.

192 And a stay of the proceedings in a case where he cannot claim that the court lacks jurisdiction. The earlier decision in *The Messiniaki Tolmi* [1984] 2 Lloyd's Rep 284, that an application for a stay was not a challenge to the jurisdiction, has been overtaken by CPR Part 11.

193 It will be otherwise if the defendant simply applies for an extension of time to serve a defence and by doing so conveys the opposite message: *Montrose Investments Ltd v. Orion Nominees* [2002] ILPr 267; *Midland Resources Ltd v. Gonvarri Industrial SA* [2002] ILPr 74; *Burns-Anderson Independent Network v. Wheeler* [2005] EWHC 575 (QB), [2005] 1 Lloyd's Rep 580. But the defendant ought to be allowed (time) to find out more about the claim in order to determine whether he has grounds to dispute the jurisdiction: *Bilta UK Ltd v. Nazir* [2010] EWHC 1086 (Ch), [2010] Bus LR 1086 (a case concerning a stay for arbitration, but the point is a general one). It will all, therefore, depend on the objective appearance of the things the defendant has done, in a manner which resembles the principles of estoppel by representation.

194 *Kurz v. Stella Musical Veranstaltungs GmbH* [1992] Ch 196; *Canada Trust Co v. Stolzenberg* [1997] 4 All ER 983; *Bilta UK Ltd v. Nazir* [2010] EWHC 1086 (Ch), [2010] Bus LR 1086. Or responding to the administration of interrogatories: *BCCI v. Al Kaylani* [1999] ILPr 278.

195 CPR r. 11(7).

196 *ED & F Man (Sugar) Ltd v. Haryanto (No 2)* [1991] 1 Lloyd's Rep 429, 438.

197 It follows that, if the application is dismissed but the defendant wishes to appeal, he should seek an extension of the time for entering a fresh acknowledgment of service pending the determination of the appeal. If not, the claimant will be entitled to apply for default judgment: *Sithole v. Thor Chemicals Holdings Ltd, The Times*, 15 February 1999.

198 That is, all the evidence placed before the court: *Electric Furnace Co v. Selas Corp of America* [1987] RPC 23, *Lubrizol Corp v. Esso Petroleum Co Ltd* [1992] RPC 467, 470.

establish that as on the date of making the order granting permission to serve out (or the date of service if permission was not required), the order should not have been made. By contrast, in the case of an application for a stay, the significant date is the date of the hearing of the application; and though any change of circumstance after that date may justify a fresh application, it should not provide the basis for an appeal against the original order.[199]

5.28 Disputing the jurisdiction of the English court under CPR rule 11(1)(a): other points

The defendant may argue that the manner in which the service took place was irregular, and that service should be set aside on that ground alone. Aside from such points,[200] he may argue that the court does not have, or should declare that it does not have, jurisdiction over him in respect of the claim. This may be for two broad reasons. First, the rules of the Brussels I Regulation, examined in Chapter 2, may provide that the courts of another Member State do, and that those of England do not, have jurisdiction. Second, he may say that, although permission was required prior to service out, and although it was obtained without notice, it should not have been granted, and should now be rescinded. If it is, service pursuant to such permission will also be set aside. The rules regulating this were set out in Chapter 4.

These are the most common grounds upon which a jurisdictional challenge is made. But there are others. For example, if the defendant is immune from the jurisdiction of the English courts on the ground of State or diplomatic immunity,[201] an application may be made under this procedure. If the claim is one over which the court has no subject-matter jurisdiction, such as where the claim will require the court to determine the validity of a foreign patent, or to try questions principally concerned with title to foreign land, an application to dispute the jurisdiction may be made under this procedure. The precise form of the relief granted will be adapted to fit the facts of the case.

There is some uncertainty over the precise meaning of certain aspects of CPR rule 11(1). Three may be mentioned. First, it is sometimes said, particularly in relation to banking cases, that whilst a court may have personal jurisdiction over a branch of a bank, it may lack subject-matter jurisdiction over the claim brought (such as, for example, where an order is sought that another branch produce records for use in the English proceedings). It has been said that subject-matter jurisdiction marks the extent to which the court can claim to regulate the conduct of those persons who are in law amenable to its personal jurisdiction.[202] But there is no authority for requiring such an argument to be advanced

---

199 *Mohammed v. Bank of Kuwait and the Middle East KSC* [1996] 1 WLR 1483. See also *ISC Technologies Ltd v. Guerin* [1992] 2 Lloyd's Rep 430. It may be argued that in *Lubbe v. Cape plc* [2000] 1 WLR 1545, the House of Lords took a slightly more relaxed view and considered all the evidence available by the date of the appeal. It is hard to deny that this has certain practical attractions.

200 Which may be curable by the court on the basis that they indicate irregularity, but not nullity: CPR r. 3.10. *The Goldean Mariner* [1990] 2 Lloyd's Rep 215; *Kuwait Oil Tanker Co SAK v. Al Bader* [1997] 1 WLR 1410; *Abela v. Baadarani* [2013] UKSC 44, [2013] 1 WLR 2043.

201 Paragraph 4.05, above.

202 *MacKinnon v. Donaldson Lufkin & Jenrette Inc* [1986] Ch 482, 493. See also *R. v. Grossman* (1981) 73 CAR 302, 307; *Power Curber International Ltd v. National Bank of Kuwait* [1981] 1 WLR 1233, 1241; *Libyan Arab Foreign Bank v. Bankers' Trust Co* [1989] QB 728. In *Masri v. Consolidated Contractors International (UK) Ltd (No 2)* [2008] EWCA Civ 303, [2009] QB 450, [30]–[47], the Court of Appeal appears to regard matters of 'subject-matter

by application pursuant to CPR Part 11: instead, these arguments appear, notwithstanding the language used, to be matters which go more to the discretion of the court, rather than being determinants of its technical jurisdiction. They do not dispute the jurisdiction of the court in the material sense.

Second, in relation to claims for a declaration of non-liability,[203] it will sometimes be objected by a defendant that the court has, in the circumstances, no jurisdiction to grant such a declaration.[204] If this were to be taken literally, it would suggest that the defendant was both entitled and required to make his objections in the form of an application under CPR Part 11; and that if he does not do so, he may no longer advance an argument based on the alleged lack of jurisdiction to grant such relief. But this too would be wrong. Where the claim form has been properly served, the court undoubtedly has jurisdiction to make the declaration; the question whether it will do so is one for its discretion. Accordingly, the objection that the court should not make such a declaration should not be seen as one which is entitled or required to be brought under this procedure. It does not dispute the jurisdiction of the court.

Third, a defendant who disputes the jurisdiction will sometimes seek an order that the action against him be dismissed. If the court declares that it has no jurisdiction and sets aside the service of the claim form, it does follow that the action sought to be commenced by that claim form has failed, and should be dismissed. But dismissal of the action on jurisdictional grounds is not the same thing as judgment for the defendant; and the decision of the court will not give rise to any form of estoppel in relation to the merits of the claim if the claimant should seek to institute fresh proceedings in respect of the same claim: there will have been no decision on the merits, after all. But for the avoidance of confusion in the mind of a foreign court, it may be preferable if the court did not make an order dismissing the action.

According to English procedural law, it is entirely correct that at this preliminary stage a court should be called upon to give a ruling on whether it has jurisdiction, so that if it does not, the defendant can be immediately released from the proceedings. But it is worth observing that in many other jurisdictions[205] a court does not necessarily segregate and make a preliminary ruling on the issue of jurisdiction, but may decide instead to hear all the evidence and rule on jurisdiction at the conclusion of the hearing, going on to rule on the merits only if it has rejected the jurisdictional defence. Though this may appear rather unsatisfactory, for a defendant who says that the claimant has no right to expose him to this peril may still find that he has been forced to participate in the trial all the way through to the end,[206] it has a practical sense in those cases in which the facts and matters which will determine the issue of jurisdiction also bear on the issues raised by the substance of the claim. If the claim arises out of a disputed contract, it may be inefficient for a court to make a provisional ruling about the effect of the contract for the purpose of jurisdiction and then, after another hearing, a conclusive ruling on much the same matters later on. But CPR Part 11 does not

---

jurisdiction' as affecting the question whether it would be internationally proper, or consistent with comity, for the court to exercise its jurisdiction.

203 See Section (F) below; paras 5.60 *et seq.*

204 Perhaps because it would be premature, or because the defendant has never threatened to bring proceedings, etc.

205 Both European and other common law.

206 A conclusion which is especially objectionable if there is no indemnification in respect of costs if the jurisdictional defence is upheld.

appear to give this power to an English court, and it is improbable that the power of case management[207] can be stretched to do so either.

5.29 Disputing the jurisdiction by arguing that the court should not exercise its jurisdiction: CPR rule 11(1)(b)

CPR Part 11 provides, in effect, that a defendant who has no ground upon which to dispute the jurisdiction of the court, but who seeks a stay of the proceedings over which the court does have jurisdiction, is permitted, *and is generally required*, to make his application within the framework of CPR Part 11.[208] A stay of proceedings on *forum non conveniens* grounds is now applied for as though it were a challenge to the jurisdiction of the court in the more traditional sense; the fact that it is required to be made within CPR Part 11 offers a cast-iron guarantee that the applicant, applying for a stay of proceedings, will not be taken to have submitted to the jurisdiction of the court. This clarifies a point on which the common law had been less clear, or was actually, simply, different.[209] But the departure from previous law is deliberate, and results from the express wording of CPR rule 11(1)(b), which provides that a defendant who wishes to argue that a court should not exercise its jurisdiction may apply under CPR Part 11; and if there was any doubt about it, it was removed by the decision in *Texan Management Ltd v. Pacific Electric Wire & Cable Co Ltd*.[210] The order the court will make, if the application is successful, will be a stay of proceedings.[211]

It is entirely convenient that the application for a stay of proceedings be brought within the framework of CPR Part 11. Prior to this, it was understood that a stay of proceedings was not a challenge to the jurisdiction of the court, and therefore was not properly brought within the predecessor of CPR Part 11 which provided only for applications disputing the jurisdiction of the court in strict sense.[212] This was awkward for a defendant whose two-legged contention was that the court should find that it had no jurisdiction, or that if it did have jurisdiction, should stay the proceedings in any event. The suggestion that an application for a stay was an admission that there was jurisdiction – for unless a court has jurisdiction, there is nothing for it to stay – led to some awkwardness, and meant that there was some level of risk in running the two arguments in parallel.[213] The enormous advantage of CPR Part 11 is that all such difficulty is swept away. That said, if the actual basis for disputing the jurisdiction is that the court should not have given permission to serve out, making an application for a stay, whether concurrent, or subordinate or whatever else, is not based on coherent reflections. For if the court upholds the decision to allow service out of

---

207 CPR r. 3.1(2) makes it clear that these powers do not extend to setting aside the Rules themselves.

208 For the power to apply for a stay outside that framework, see *Texan Management Ltd v. Pacific Electric Wire & Cable Co Ltd* [2009] UKPC 46.

209 The argument having been that a defendant who applies for a stay necessarily acknowledges that a court has jurisdiction, and therefore submits to it; *cf The Messiniaki Tolmi* [1984] 2 Lloyd's Rep 266.

210 [2009] UKPC 46. The court rejected a construction of CPR r. 11(1)(b) which would have restricted it to disputes based on the exercise of discretion to permit service out (and CPR r. 11(1)(a) to disputes based on the satisfaction of Para. 3.1 of the Practice Direction).

211 CPR r. 11(6)(d).

212 *The Messiniaki Tolmi* [1984] 2 Lloyd's Rep 266.

213 For an illustration of the problem, see the illuminating judgment of the Singapore Court of Appeal in *Zone Communications Ltd v. Broadcast Solutions Pte Ltd* [2014] SGCA 44.

the jurisdiction, it will have decided that England is the proper place to bring the claim; and if that is so, an application for a stay on the ground of *forum non conveniens* is quite useless.[214]

It is therefore no longer necessary to reason – even though there may be nothing intellectually wrong with the reasoning – that a defendant who applies for a stay submits to the jurisdiction of the court to rule on its jurisdiction, not to its jurisdiction to decide the merits, as was said in *Williams & Glyn's Bank v. Astro Dinamico*.[215] The clear effect of CPR rule 11(7) is that a defendant who applies under CPR Part 11 does not thereby submit to the jurisdiction. As long as the defendant restricts the application, and the steps taken within that application, to what is appropriate to dispute the jurisdiction of the court, in either of the ways provided for by CPR rule 11(1), there is no problem. It is, of course, different if he invites the court to take (and act on) a view on matters which are not material to the question of jurisdiction. The risk of being seen thereby to have waived the objection to the jurisdiction of the court, and so submitted, is still there.

If an application for a stay of proceedings is not made within the timetable set out in CPR Part 11, the court may allow it to be made later. It is true that a challenge to the jurisdiction which falls within CPR rule 11(1)(a), and which is founded on the argument that the conditions for service to be made were not satisfied at the point at which the proceedings were instituted, will need to be made within that tight procedural timetable; and any failure to meet the deadlines, in any way which is more than marginal, may not be easily forgiven,[216] an application for a stay of the kind provided for by CPR rule 11(1)(b) may be made outside that period if in all the circumstances it was not unreasonable for it not to have been made earlier: *Texan Management Ltd v. Pacific Electric Wire & Cable Co Ltd*[217] accepted that one consequence of the otherwise wholly beneficial incorporation of applications for a stay within the framework of CPR Part 11 was that a court would need to be prepared to extend time[218] to allow a stay to be made at a later stage in proceedings if, for example, the question whether a foreign court was clearly more appropriate than England for the trial of the action became clear only after the pleadings had developed.

5.30 Application by the defendant served without permission to have the claim struck out on substantive grounds

If the question is whether the defendant should make an application to strike out the claim on substantive grounds at the same time as he contests the jurisdiction, the cautious view would be that he should not. The question only arises in the case of service within the jurisdiction or service out without prior permission: where service was made out of the jurisdiction with permission, a contention that the merits of the claim are hopeless will form

---

214 *Zone Communications Ltd v. Broadcast Solutions Pte Ltd* [2014] SGCA 44.

215 [1984] 1 WLR 438. See also *Rein v. Stein* (1892) 66 LT 469.

216 It will presumably be a matter of degree: the court in *Polymer Vision R&D Ltd v. Van Dooren* [2011] EWHC 2951 (Comm) was forgiving; *Zumax Nigeria Ltd v. First City Monument Bank Ltd* [2014] EWHC 2075 (Ch) very much less so.

217 [2009] UKPC 46. The court rejected a construction of CPR r. 11(1)(b) which would have restricted it to disputes based on the exercise of discretion to permit service out (and confined CPR r. 11(1)(a) to disputes based on the satisfaction or not of Para. 3.1 of the Practice Direction). The court was plainly right to do as it did, for otherwise the old problems of applying for a stay and submitting to the jurisdiction of the court, and running the risk of accident by not fully appreciating the nuances of the law on submission, would have remained in place.

218 Or even to entertain an application under the inherent jurisdiction (i.e. outside CPR Part 11) of the court.

part of the general jurisdictional argument that there was not a serious issue on the merits of the claim and that for this reason permission should not have been given and service should be set aside. But if service was made without permission, the strength of the merits of the claim will not form part of the jurisdictional analysis; and the question is whether a defendant objecting to the jurisdiction may additionally ask for the claim to be struck out on the ground that the merits are wholly in favour of the defendant.

To ask the court to strike out the claim on the basis that it has no real prospect of success,[219] or on the basis that the claim form discloses no reasonable ground for bringing the claim,[220] is to ask the court to make a judgment, albeit a summary one, upon the merits, and there is a risk that it may appear to be a submission to the adjudicatory merits jurisdiction of the court. A cautious view would be that such an application should not be made until any proceedings under CPR Part 11 have come to an end.[221] In *Eagle Star v. Yuval*,[222] the court held that such an application might, in exceptional cases, not constitute a submission, but in general the making of such a combined application would appear to be needlessly risky. The defendant might contend that he is not asking the court to determine the merits, but to decide that the claim has no merits and that there is, therefore, nothing to adjudicate; but the sense that this is just playing with words is palpable. If the court is asked to examine the merits, it is hard to see why that does not amount to a submission to its jurisdiction to adjudicate those merits.

This view, admittedly cautious, is challenged by a passage in *Ryanair Ltd v. Esso Italiana Srl*,[223] in which it appears to have been said that a defendant may challenge the jurisdiction of the court under the Brussels I Regulation by contending that the substance of the claim is hopeless, if he does so making it clear that the contention is advanced for the purpose of disputing the jurisdiction, almost as if there were a legal principle that there is no jurisdiction to adjudicate a groundless claim.[224] It is difficult to see how this can be recommended. A challenge to the jurisdiction of the court, established by service without permission, on the ground that the claim is bound to fail is, it is submitted, a risky novelty. It is not a basis for asking the court to find that it has no jurisdiction to adjudicate the merits, or for asking the court not to exercise its jurisdiction to adjudicate the merits. It is an application for a quick and conclusive decision *on* the merits; it is not, strictly or in any other way, a challenge to the jurisdiction of the court.

---

219 CPR r. 24.2.

220 CPR r. 3.4.

221 In the light of *Seaconsar Far East Ltd v. Bank Markazi Jomhouri Islami Iran* [1994] 1 AC 438, such an argument can in essence be advanced as part of the jurisdictional challenge that permission to serve out should not have been given. A separately-founded application appears to offer nothing of value.

222 [1978] 1 Lloyd's Rep 357. See also *The Messiniaki Tolmi* [1984] 2 Lloyd's Rep 266. Note, though, that in *Capital Trust Investments Ltd v. Radio Design TJ AB* [2002] EWCA Civ 135, [2002] 2 All ER 159, and in this respect, following *Patel v. Patel* [2000] QB 551, an application for a summary judgment for the defendant, if the court refused to stay proceedings under Arbitration Act 1996, s. 9 did not amount to the taking of a step in the proceedings, because the application was expressly subordinate to the stay application, and was justifiable in terms of case management as well.

223 [2013] EWCA Civ 1450, [2015] 1 ALL ER (Comm) 152, [20].

224 It might just be different if he were to dispute the existence of special jurisdiction under Art. 7(1), say, by arguing that the claim that there was a contract, whose obligation required performance within the jurisdiction of the court, was hopeless because the contention that there was a contract was hopeless. But even that does not appear to work, for a matter may relate to a contract even though the opposite party denies that there is a contract at all.

5.31 Application by the claimant for summary judgment

Where the defendant has acknowledged service and has made an application under CPR Part 11, it should not generally be open to the claimant to seek summary judgment under CPR rule 24.2 on the ground that there is no real prospect of the defendant successfully defending the claim.[225] Although it is obvious that, if the defendant puts in evidence in answer to the application for summary judgment, this cannot be seen as submission[226] on his part, it seems contrary to principle that a defendant whose contention is that the court has no jurisdiction over him should be drawn into any form of investigation of, or a contest in relation to, the merits of the claim itself.[227] There is nothing obvious in the rules to prevent an application from being made on these grounds, although as the acknowledgment of service, the filing of which generally precedes an application for summary judgment under CPR Part 24,[228] will lapse at the end of the application to dispute the jurisdiction,[229] it would be a welcome step for a court to rule that an acknowledgment of service which has been followed by an application under CPR Part 11 is not to be seen as an acknowledgment of service for the purposes of an application for summary judgment. At the very least, the court should consider itself obliged to hear the jurisdictional challenge before the application for summary judgment, even if the claimant has contrived to have his application listed for hearing earlier or at the same time.[230] For even though there may be no defence to the claim when the matter is viewed as an English court would see it, it may be that there is a perfectly good defence when this is looked at by the court which ought to be allowed to exercise jurisdiction.

(D) ANTI-SUIT INJUNCTIONS

5.32 General

So far the concern has been for a party who, when sued in an English court, would prefer the proceedings to be brought overseas. It is now necessary to examine steps which may be taken by a party who is being, or who fears being, sued before a foreign court, but who considers that any proceedings which are to be brought against him should be brought in England. In some ways this question is connected to the rules which define the jurisdiction of the English courts, but what may be done to impede or derail proceedings before foreign courts has no necessary or mirror-image relationship to the exercise of jurisdiction by a

---

225 Similarly, the claimant may apply for judgment in default if the defendant is debarred from defending, even though there may still be a challenge to the jurisdiction which has not been heard: *JSC BTA Bank v. Ablyazov* [2010] EWHC 2219 (QB), though the overall fairness of the procedure will have to be considered carefully.

226 *Artlev AG v. Almazy Rossii-Sakha* (8 March 1995).

227 Of course, if he challenges jurisdiction on the ground that the claimant does not have a serious issue on the merits of the claim, and that permission to serve out should not therefore have been granted, he invites the court to make some form of examination of the merits, but only because this is an inherent part of the jurisdictional challenge to an order granting permission to serve out.

228 Though CPR r. 24.4 does allow the court power to hear an application for summary judgment against a defendant who has not made an acknowledgment of service, the present case is a rather particular one.

229 CPR r. 11(7).

230 This general approach was approved by the judge in *Speed Investments Ltd v. Formula One Holdings Ltd* [2004] EWHC 1777 (Ch), [2005] 1 WLR 1233, subject to the proviso that under CPR r. 24.4 the court does have power to hear an application for summary judgment against a defendant who has not acknowledged service.

court in England. But the steps open to a party wishing to impede foreign proceedings by obtaining a remedy from the English court are an integral part of the broader, overall, and common law picture of jurisdiction – asserting, establishing or challenging that jurisdiction, as the case may be – in international cases.[231]

There are two approaches which a party in such a position may wish to consider. The first is to bring proceedings before the English court. This may be for an injunction, addressed to the party who is, or who threatens to become, claimant in the foreign proceedings, directing him to discontinue, or not commence, those proceedings. Another possibility is to bring a counter-action in England to obtain judgment, which may be declaratory as to the merits of the dispute, with the aim of making the substantive issue *res judicata* as a matter of English law. Both are considered in this chapter.

The second is to seek a remedy from the foreign court itself. This is, of course, the most direct approach, but it may be unavailable in law or in practice. Moreover, it is even possible that for the applicant to seek it is to expose himself to the accusation of having submitted, in some material sense, to the foreign court.[232]

In the paragraphs which follow,[233] the remedy of an injunction against a party proceeding or threatening to proceed in a foreign court is examined: this is the 'anti-suit injunction'.[234] The party against whom the injunction is sought is the claimant in the foreign proceedings, and may be described for convenience as the respondent. The actual or prospective defendant to the foreign proceedings, who seeks the injunction, is referred to here as the applicant, even though he may also be claimant in substantive proceedings pending before the English court.

It is obvious that an English court may not direct a foreign judge to stop hearing a case. But the court may make orders against individuals subject to its personal jurisdiction to require them to behave in a certain way. The court may order them to stop proceedings which they have instituted before a foreign court. It is therefore necessary to consider (i) whether the court has jurisdiction over the respondent to grant an injunction and, if so, (ii) the rules and principles upon which it acts to grant or not grant the relief.

---

231 See, to this effect, Lord Goff of Chieveley in *Airbus GIE v. Patel* [1999] 1 AC 119, for the human rights implications of the law on anti-suit injunctions: see above, paras 1.19–1.21; and see also *OT Africa Line Ltd v. Hijazy* [2001] 1 Lloyd's Rep 76.

232 See paras 7.56 *et seq.*, below. If by doing so the applicant is regarded by the foreign court as submitting to its jurisdiction, he may have made things worse for himself in the foreign proceedings. He may not be taken by an *English* court to have submitted if it is later sought to have the judgment recognised and enforced in England (s. 33 of the 1982 Act), but this arises by virtue of a specific English statute, and not from general principles of the common law: see *Henry v. Geoprosco International* [1976] QB 726; *cf Re Dulles (No 2)* [1951] Ch 842.

Moreover, if issue estoppel may arise out of the decision of the foreign court, the position of the applicant will have become very difficult: *cf Desert Sun Loan Corp v. Hill* [1996] 2 All ER 847. This is not an unimportant possibility, for a decision on the issue of *forum conveniens* may be final, in that it represents the last and un-reviewable decision of a foreign court on the point. Moreover, in *Barclays Bank plc v. Homan* [1993] BCLC 680, and in *SNI Aerospatiale v. Lee Kui Jak* [1987] AC 871, it was accepted in general terms that the decision of the foreign court should be 'respected': it may well not give rise to an estoppel, but its influence on the mind of a subsequent English judge may be difficult to distinguish in practice. To the same general effect, see *Deutsche Bank AG v. Highland Crusader Offshore Partners LP* [2009] EWCA Civ 725, [2010] 1 WLR 1023, [22]–[29], [117], [119].

233 For a detailed account, but which does not come to all the conclusions proposed here, see Raphael, *The Anti-Suit Injunction* (OUP, 2008).

234 Objection has been taken to this expression in *Turner v. Grovit* [2001] UKHL 65, [2002] 1 WLR 107, [23]. But there is no reason to abandon the common terminology, which describes with perfect accuracy what the respondent is ordered to do: not to sue.

Although it is technically correct that the injunction is made against an individual and not against a foreign court,[235] it obviously has a dramatic practical impact upon the foreign court's control of its own procedure. The abstract principles of comity, if nothing else, require that the application be approached, and any order made, with regard to the proper interest and concern which a foreign court may have in the matter before it.[236] The foreign court may not appreciate[237] the distinction (which seems obvious enough to English lawyers) between an order enjoining it, and enjoining a party before it, and it may, among other things, refuse to cooperate with the party who seeks to comply with the English injunction.[238] The modern rules have been developed against a partial[239] background of a perceived need for judicial self-restraint, and with an increasing awareness that the proper place to obtain an order which will stop a court hearing a case will sometimes be before the foreign court itself.[240]

5.33 Jurisdiction *in personam* over the respondent: the general principle

An English court has jurisdiction to grant an injunction against a respondent if it has personal jurisdiction over him. Originally inherent, the basis for the power of the court to act is now (also) statutory, as is confirmed by section 37 of the Senior Courts Act 1981.[241]

In order to establish personal jurisdiction over the respondent in a particular case, it will be necessary to serve the respondent with process in the application for an injunction, and any jurisdictional defence which the respondent has to the assertion of jurisdiction over him will be a complete answer to the application. Prior to the coming into force of the Brussels Convention, this would have meant that the respondent had to be physically present to be served within the jurisdiction of the English court, or had otherwise to be subject to it,[242] failing which, permission to serve out of the jurisdiction would need to be obtained pursuant to what is now CPR rule 6.36.[243] But the impact of the rules which are now in the Brussels I Regulation has been to restrict the personal jurisdiction of the English courts over defendants or respondents who are domiciled in Member States other than the United Kingdom. The difficulties which this has thrown up are far from being all resolved; but the outlines of the problems are clear. It is necessary to consider a number of points which, when taken together, will establish whether the English court has personal jurisdiction over the respondent.

---

235 See *Bushby v. Munday* (1821) 5 Madd 297. See also *Airbus Industrie GIE v. Patel* [1999] 1 AC 119.

236 *Cohen v. Rothfield* [1919] 1 KB 410; *Laker Airways Ltd v. Pan American World Airways* 559 F Supp 1124 (1983), 1128.

237 In the sense of not understanding, or in the sense of understanding but not being persuaded by.

238 See *Re the Enforcement of an English anti-suit injunction* [1997] ILPr 320, where the Regional Court of Appeal in Düsseldorf, in a judgment cast in particularly emphatic language, held such injunction to be an infringement of German sovereignty, and had refused to authorise service of the injunction in Germany; see further, paras 7.13 *et seq.*, below.

239 But where the basis for the application is that the respondent is in breach of contract in bringing the foreign proceedings, there is much less self-restraint on the part of the court.

240 *Barclays Bank plc v. Homan* [1993] BCLC 680; *Pan American World Airways v. Andrews* 1992 SLT 268.

241 *OT Africa Line v. Hijazy* [2001] 1 Lloyd's Rep 76, which also makes the point that Art. 6 of the European Convention on Human Rights is not material, as the Convention does not guarantee access to *any and every* court of the respondent's choice, but only to *a* court.

242 For example, by being party to related proceedings pending before the English court.

243 Even if the only relief sought was the injunction: *Youell v. Kara Mara Shipping Co Ltd* [2000] 2 Lloyd's Rep 102.

5.34 Jurisdiction *in personam* over the respondent: effect of the Brussels I Regulation

If the subject matter of the dispute between the parties falls within the domain of the Brussels I Regulation, an assertion of jurisdiction *in personam* over the respondent must comply with the provisions of the Regulation or it will have no legal basis. If, according to the Regulation, the respondent is not subject to the jurisdiction of the English courts, there will be no legal basis for instituting the proceedings or claiming the relief, and there will be no more to be said about it. Accordingly, the rules of the Regulation will need to be considered and, if applicable, satisfied.

For example, if the respondent is bound by a jurisdiction agreement for the English courts which confirms to Article 25 of the Regulation, an English court will have jurisdiction *in personam* if the claim for an injunction falls within the scope of the agreement.[244] If the respondent is domiciled in the United Kingdom, Article 4 will give the courts of the United Kingdom general jurisdiction over the respondent. And if the English court is seised of substantive proceedings, it has jurisdiction to make orders against the defendant as part of those proceedings.[245] However if, for example, the respondent is domiciled in another Member State, and there is no other basis within the Regulation for asserting jurisdiction over him in relation to the claim, there is no basis for an English court to take jurisdiction to grant a final injunction or any other final relief.

There is no convincing argument available to undermine this conclusion. It cannot be argued that proceedings for an anti-suit injunction fall outside the scope of the Brussels I Regulation, unless the broader subject matter of the claim is not a civil or commercial matter, or is otherwise excluded from the scope of the Regulation.[246] Neither can it be argued that the respondent is not being 'sued' within the meaning of Article 4 and the rest of the Regulation. Though the merits of the underlying dispute may not be in issue before the court, the relief sought against the respondent makes it hard to argue that he is not being sued. A submission that the respondent was not being sued might derive limited support from *The Ikarian Reefer (No 2)*,[247] in which it was proposed that 'suing' involved pursuing a substantive cause of action, and excluded 'the making of orders ancillary to substantive proceedings pending before a particular court'. In that case, a claim against a non-party for a costs order was considered not to involve suing the non-party. But even accepting this, an anti-suit injunction is not usually – and certainly has no need to be – relief which is ancillary to that sought in substantive proceedings.[248] It is, therefore, submitted that the respondent to the application for an anti-suit injunction is being sued.

It cannot be argued that an anti-suit injunction is a provisional or protective measure within the meaning of Article 35.[249] If this argument could be made good, then there would

---

244 If there is such an agreement for the courts of another Member State, the English court will not have jurisdiction.

245 C-391/95 *Van Uden Maritime BV v. Deco-Line* [1998] ECR I-7091; *Masri v. Consolidated Contractors International (UK) Ltd (No 3)* [2008] EWCA Civ 625, [2009] QB 503.

246 Such as where the subject matter in which the claim for an injunction arises is arbitration: C-185/07 *Allianz SpA v. West Tankers Inc* [2009] ECR I-663.

247 [2000] 1 WLR 603, 615–616.

248 *Turner v. Grovit* [2001] UKHL 65, [2002] 1 WLR 107 suggested that if there are no proceedings pending in the English court, the claimant may lack a sufficient interest to justify the granting of an injunction, at least if there is no contractual right to support the claim: this is to be doubted.

249 *Cf* C-261/90 *Reichert v. Dresdner Bank (No 2)* [1992] ECR I-2149.

be no need for the court to have jurisdiction under the provisions of Articles 4 to 34 of the Brussels I Regulation.[250] But the argument is not tenable. Even though the intended effect of the anti-suit injunction is to prevent another court making the question of substance *res judicata* by giving a judgment upon it, so preserving the *status quo ante*, a final anti-suit injunction is not provisional because it is not a temporary and reversible order for payment restricted to assets within the territory of the English court.[251] The truth is that it is a final determination in relation to certain rights, including procedural rights; and it is therefore thought extremely unlikely that an application for a final[252] anti-suit injunction can fall within Article 35.[253]

5.35 Jurisdiction *in personam* over the respondent: where the Brussels I Regulation does not specify it

In cases where the subject matter of the dispute falls outside the domain of the Brussels I Regulation, or where the Regulation provides[254] that jurisdiction is to be determined by the traditional rules of English law, it must be possible to serve the claim form within the jurisdiction as of right, or out of the jurisdiction with permission granted pursuant to CPR rule 6.36.[255]

If the claimant intends to commence proceedings in England, and applies to restrain the defendant, as respondent, by injunction, the availability of service out will be governed by the question whether there may be service of process out of the jurisdiction in the main proceedings.[256] The court will have jurisdiction over these proceedings (and hence jurisdiction to grant injunctive relief in relation to them), or it will not. If, however, an injunction is the only relief sought from the English court, the claim form seeking the injunction must be entitled to be served in its own right.

CPR rule 6.36 contains no provision which is tailor-made for such cases. One untried possibility is that Paragraph 3.1(2) of the Practice Direction may be used.[257] If it were possible to argue that the injunction is in form an order which requires the respondent to sue, if anywhere, within the jurisdiction, or which directs him to refrain from issuing instructions from England to his legal advisers outside England, the provision may just be stretched to cover the case, though it is not obvious that it would fall within the natural meaning of the words of the rule. If the injunction is sought against an associate of a party who is bound by an agreement on jurisdiction, and who is trying to undermine that agreement by bringing proceedings before a foreign court and claiming not to be affected by the agreement on jurisdiction, he should be served as a necessary or proper party under Paragraph 3.1(3), or

---

250 See below, Chapter 6; and in particular C-391/95 *Van Uden Maritime BV v. Firma Deco-Line* [1998] ECR I-7091 and C-99/96 *Mietz v. Intership Yachting Sneek BV* [1999] ECR I-2277.

251 C-391/95 *Van Uden Maritime BV v. Firma Deco-Line* [1998] ECR I-7091.

252 A claim for an interlocutory anti-suit injunction may be differently regarded.

253 It is not clear that the approach of the Court of Appeal in *Masri v. Consolidated Contractors International (UK) Ltd (No 3)* [2008] EWCA Civ 625, [2009] QB 503, is consistent with this submission.

254 Article 6 of the recast Regulation 1215/2012.

255 If, by contrast, the claim for an injunction is made if the course of proceedings which are already underway, the application will be made by way of notice, but service will not be an issue.

256 For illustration, see *Sohio Supply Co v. Gatoil (USA) Inc* [1989] 1 Lloyd's Rep 588.

257 But *ISC Technologies v. Radcliffe*, 7 December 1990 and *ISC Technologies v. Guerin* [1992] 2 Lloyd's Rep 430 (see above, para. 4.64) favour a narrow construction of the Ground.

proceeded against as a tortfeasor, to whom sub-Paragraph (9) applies, for wrongful interference with a contract.[258]

If the respondent has already commenced proceedings of his own, or has otherwise submitted to the jurisdiction of the English court, he is subject to its jurisdiction and liable to be restrained. The possibilities may be illustrated by reference to three cases. In *Castanho v. Brown & Root (UK) Ltd*,[259] the respondent had commenced proceedings in England but then, having left the country, decided[260] that self-interest required him to commence proceedings in Texas instead. It was held that he was amenable to the court's jurisdiction to grant an injunction as, having invoked the jurisdiction of the court, he remained subject to it.[261] In *Glencore International AG v. Exter Shipping Ltd*,[262] the respondent was party to proceedings before the court, as claimant and defendant, and yet sought to argue that his participation was insufficient to give the court jurisdiction over him for the purpose of ordering an injunction. The court was memorably scornful of such a contention: there had been a submission to the jurisdiction of the English courts, and that was that. In *CNA Insurance Co Ltd v. Office Depot International*[263] the respondent underwent an apparent change of mind, after having submitted to the English court's jurisdiction and participated in the trial; its attempt to then pursue those claims in Florida was restrained by injunction on the ground that the change of heart had come too late, and that the injunction was needed to restrain unconscionable behaviour which threatened to undermine the jurisdiction of the English court.

And it has been held that a respondent is liable to be found to have submitted to the jurisdiction of a court which is exercising, or which is liable to exercise, a supervisory jurisdiction. For example, if the respondent has lodged a claim in the winding up of an insolvent company, he is liable to be held to have submitted generally to the jurisdiction of the court supervising the insolvency, even though the lodging of a proof of debt is not closely analogous to the issue and service of a claim form.[264] The same principle will justify the conclusion that a party to an English arbitration agreement submits thereby to the supervisory – including enforcement – jurisdiction of the English courts, with the consequence that he is exposed to the jurisdiction of the English court as court supervising the arbitration.[265]

---

258 *Horn Linie GmbH v. Panamericana Formas e Impresos SA (The Hornbay)* [2006] EWHC 373 (Comm), [2006] 2 Lloyd's Rep 44. See also *Starlight Shipping Co v. Tai Ping Insurance Co* [2007] EWHC 1893 (Comm), [2008] 1 Lloyd's Rep 230 (party to arbitration agreement restrained to enforce the legal right; ship's manager not party to the arbitration agreement, so restrained to prevent vexatious behaviour); *The Kallang* [2008] EWHC 2761 (Comm), [2009] 1 Lloyd's Rep 124 and *The Duden* [2008] EWHC 2762 (Comm), [2009] 1 Lloyd's Rep 145 treat the acts of the non-party in undermining the arbitration agreement as torts, but on any view they are wrongs and are liable to restraint as wrongs. And see, more tangentially, *AMT Futures Ltd v. Marzillier et al GmbH* [2014] EWHC 1085 (Comm),[2015] 2 WLR 187. And see also *Shipowners' Mutual P&I Association (Luxembourg) v Containerships Denizcilik Nakliyat ve Tocaret a.s. [2015] EWHC 258 (Comm), in connection with sub-paragraph (6).*

259 [1981] AC 557: the decision not now reliable on the exercise of discretion, but is still authoritative upon this point.

260 American lawyers whispered damages beyond the wildest dreams of a Portuguese manual worker.

261 But for the conditions upon which a party may discontinue proceedings, see CPR Part 38.

262 [2002] EWCA Civ 528, [2002] 2 All ER (Comm) 1, (2002) 73 BYBIL 463.

263 [2005] EWHC 456 (Comm), [2005] Lloyd's Rep IR 658.

264 *Rubin v. Eurofinance SA* [2012] UKSC 46, [2013] 1 AC 236; *Stichting Shell Pensioenfonds v. Krys* [2014] UKPC 41, [2015] 2 WLR 289.

265 *AES Ust-Kamenogorsk Hydropower Plant JSC v. AES Ust-Kamenogorsk Hydropower Plant LLP* [2013] UKSC 35, [2013] 1 WLR 1889.

5.36 Granting the injunction: principles upon which the order is made and not made

Once the court has jurisdiction over the respondent, it is necessary to show that there is a proper basis for the court to exercise its jurisdiction to grant the injunction. There must be a cause of action, or the equivalent of a cause of action, which justifies the remedy of an injunction. Despite some recent authority which rather muddies the waters, an injunction may be obtained in two categories of case. The first is that the applicant has a legal right not to be sued in the foreign country. This may be based on a contract, which is valid and binding between the parties and which, on its true construction,[266] means that the particular proceedings before the foreign court are brought in breach of contract; it may also be based on a contract which settles an earlier dispute and which provides that no proceedings, of any kind, shall be brought, anywhere. In that case, the cause of action for relief is established, and equity, acting in its auxiliary jurisdiction, may order an injunction to restrain the breach.

An injunction may also be granted if the applicant has an equitable right[267] not to be sued in the foreign country or, which may be to say the same thing, if the bringing of proceedings there is an equitable wrong. The applicant may obtain an injunction if it is oppressive or vexatious for him to be sued in the foreign court, but as this may also mean that he is the victim of an equitable wrong, it may be that this is yet another way of saying much the same thing.[268] Whichever the correct formulation is, in this case equity defines the right, the wrong, and the remedy, acting this time in its exclusive jurisdiction. The proposition that there is an equitable right to an injunction may, in this sense, add nothing of definitional value. This account will deal separately, therefore, with injunctions to enforce legal rights and injunctions to restrain equitable wrongs.

It is not sufficient merely to show that the natural forum is England,[269] though in the majority of cases this will be a necessary element of the claim for relief.[270] It is not necessary in every case for there to be proceedings already pending in the English court, though often there will be. It is not necessary for the applicant to argue that proceedings should be brought in England at all, if his case is that the proceedings should not be brought before a court at all, as is most obviously the case when the injunction seeks to restrain proceedings

---

266 But see in particular *Donohue v. Armco Inc* [2001] UKHL 64, [2002] 1 Lloyd's Rep 425 (application to foreign statutory causes of action); *Bankgesellschaft Berlin AG v. First International Shipping Corp Ltd* [2001] 1 CL 61 (application to claim for ancillary relief).

267 This is not quite the same thing as having a cause of action, but having the basis for a suit.

268 It is unclear whether these are two distinct categories, or the one category with two forms of description; but for the view that there is a *single* category, see *Youell v. Kara Mara Shipping Co Ltd* [2000] 2 Lloyd's Rep 102; *Masri v. Consolidated Contractors International (UK) Ltd (No 3)* [2008] EWCA Civ 625, [2009] 2 QB 503.

269 The case in which the House of Lords held, contrary to the proposition in the text, that this *was* enough (*Castanho v. Brown & Root (UK) Ltd* [1981] AC 557) is now unreliable: see below. If an injunction cannot be obtained, a claimant who has chosen to sue in two courts may in a proper case be required to elect between them: *Australian Commercial Research & Development Ltd v. ANZ McCaughan Merchant Bank Ltd* [1989] 3 All ER 65. But *Channel Tunnel Group Ltd v. Balfour Beatty Construction Ltd* [1993] AC 334 suggests that this degree of categorisation may be too rigid, and if the parties have agreed in advance that there may be parallel proceedings, no question of election between them should arise.

270 The doubt comes, as explained below, in relation to cases founded on a legal right not to be sued in a foreign court.

by reference to a contractual agreement to settle differences by arbitration,[271] or to settle them, full stop.[272]

No reported case holds, clearly and precisely, that an applicant will forfeit the right[273] to ask for an injunction if he has already submitted to the jurisdiction of the foreign court.[274] But if the applicant has taken a step in the foreign proceedings which goes beyond a challenge to that court's jurisdiction, it will be more difficult to persuade an English court that the respondent should now be restrained from continuing with those proceedings.[275] Whether this is put on the basis of the applicant's having waived his legal (or equitable) right not to be sued before the foreign court, or by contending that by appearing to answer the merits of the claim against him the respondent is estopped from complaining to the English court about the proceedings in which he has appeared, or on some other basis, it still reflects broad common sense. It also reflects the fundamental rule of English law that, once a defendant has submitted to the jurisdiction of the English courts, he cannot then dispute its jurisdiction over him.[276] Of course, there will be room for debate where the applicant has appeared before the foreign court in such a way as makes it unclear whether he should be taken to have submitted to its jurisdiction,[277] and there may still be exceptional cases in which a submission by appearance should not forfeit the right to apply for an anti-suit injunction. But the principle of the matter seems reasonably clear: an applicant who has already submitted to the jurisdiction of a foreign court should find that this is a substantial obstacle to his obtaining an anti-suit injunction from an English court.

And if the party seeking the injunction has himself behaved unconscionably, with the result that he comes to equity without clean hands, he will have disentitled himself to the relief for which he would otherwise have been entitled to ask. The clean hands principle is fundamental to equitable jurisprudence; there is no reason to question its application to those applying for equitable relief in the form of an anti-suit injunction.[278]

As said above, an applicant is neither entitled to an injunction, nor entitled to expect that he may obtain one, simply by showing that England is the natural forum for the proceedings: that may be necessary in some contexts, but it is not sufficient in any.[279] The result may be that, when the injunction is not ordered, proceedings run in parallel in two jurisdictions.

---

271 *AES Ust-Kamenogorsk Hydropower Plant JSC v. AES Ust-Kamenogorsk Hydropower Plant LLP* [2013] UKSC 35, [2013] 1 WLR 1889.

272 *The Alexandros T* [2013] UKSC 70, [2014] 1 Lloyd's Rep 223.

273 In the sense of a right to ask the court to exercise its discretion in his favour.

274 The point is not quite established by *Akai v. People's Insurance Co Ltd* [1998] 1 Lloyd's Rep 90, though it is entirely consistent with it. In that case it was held that the appearance of the applicant before the Australian courts was not sufficient to establish that the Australian judgment was *res judicata* as against the applicant, and the application for an injunction proceeded on the basis of the applicant's having a legal right not to be sued in Australia. Had the applicant been held to have submitted, the status of the Australian judgment as *res judicata* would have rendered the application for an injunction baseless.

275 *Enercon GmbH v. Enercon (India) Ltd* [2012] EWHC 689 (Comm), [2012] 1 Lloyd's Rep 519.

276 As is implicit in CPR Part 11. And see *Akai v. People's Insurance Co Ltd* [1998] 1 Lloyd's Rep 90; *Glencore International AG v. Metro Trading International Inc* [2002] EWCA Civ 524, [2002] CLC 1090; *Masri v. Consolidated Contractors International (UK) Ltd (No 3)* [2008] EWCA Civ 625, [2009] 2 QB 503.

277 *Akai v. People's Insurance Co Ltd* [1998] 1 Lloyd's Rep 90; *Advent Capital plc v. GN Ellinos Importers-Exporters Ltd* [2003] EWHC 3330 (Comm).

278 *Royal Bank of Scotland plc v. Highland Financial Partners LP* [2013] EWCA Civ 328, [2013] 1 CLC 596. It has no obvious application to a common law claim for damages for breach of a dispute resolution agreement, though.

279 The suggestion that it was sufficient (*Castanho v. Brown & Root (UK) Ltd* [1981] AC 557) was disavowed in *SNI Aerospatiale v. Lee Kui Jak* [1987] AC 871 (PC, Brunei). See, accepting the conclusion even though the result would be that proceedings ran in two courts at the same time, *E.I. Du Pont de Nemours & Co v. Agnew (No 2)* [1988]

But this is the kind of outcome which will, outside a closed system such as that put in place by the Brussels I Regulation, always be a risk. It may also be regrettable, but that does not make it a wrong which has to be avoided.[280]

5.37 Injunction to enforce legal right not to be sued in foreign court: general

If the applicant can show that he has a legal right not to be sued in the foreign court, he has a cause of action which allows him to apply for an injunction to enforce that right. Authority that the existence of a legal right not to be sued is a sufficient justification for an anti–suit injunction,[281] and that this is a distinct and discrete basis for an injunction, can be traced to the decision of the House of Lords in *British Airways Board v. Laker Airways Ltd*,[282] though in truth the general principle goes much further back than that. In *British Airways Board v. Laker Airways Ltd*, an English company, acting by its liquidator, took proceedings in the United States, under American competition legislation which permitted the victim of an unlawful conspiracy to recover treble damages against the alleged conspirators.[283] The English company, respondent to the application for an anti–suit injunction, was within and therefore subject to[284] the personal jurisdiction of the English court. The House of Lords held that an injunction could be ordered if the applicant had a legal right not to be sued[285] in the foreign proceedings. Such a right, it said, might arise under an exclusive jurisdiction clause or an arbitration clause, or under a legally–binding settlement between parties with a clause forbidding the bringing of proceedings to subvert it.[286] There was, however, no such right shown on the facts of the case.[287]

As there was no basis for the claimant in *British Airways Board v. Laker Airways Ltd* to assert that it had a legal right not to be sued, the question of what law was to be resorted to in order to test the basis for that assertion was not addressed. But on the footing that the legal right must lie in a contract or in an analogous legal relationship, the law which governs that contract or analogous legal relationship will determine the existence, validity and scope of the promise, and will, if the matter is in dispute, answer the question whether there is a legal right not to be sued.

A legal right in the requisite sense cannot be formulated as 'the right to have the provisions of the Brussels I Regulation applied properly', and it follows that an application for

---

2 Lloyd's Rep 240; *Deutsche Bank AG v. Highland Crusader Offshore Partners LP* [2009] EWCA Civ 725, [2010] 1 WLR 1023, [63] (in which the case before the US courts was not on all fours with that in England).

280 *Cf Airbus Industrie GIE v. Patel* [1999] 1 AC 119; *Deutsche Bank AG v. Highland Crusader Offshore Partners LP* [2009] EWCA Civ 725, [2010] 1 WLR 1023, [63].

281 For the alternative of enforcement of a legal right by a common law action for damages, see further below, paras 5.53 *et seq*.

282 [1985] AC 58.

283 If the costs of defending the proceedings do not ruin the defendants in the meantime.

284 At least, when served, which the applicant was entitled to do as of right.

285 Lord Diplock, at 81. See also *Pena Copper Mines v. Rio Tinto* (1912) 105 LT 846; *Ellerman Lines Ltd v. Read* [1928] 2 KB 144; *Tracomin v. Sudan Oil Seeds Co Ltd (No 2)* [1983] 1 WLR 1026.

286 See *ED & F Man Ltd v. Haryanto (No 2)* [1991] 1 Lloyd's Rep 429 and *National Westminster Bank Ltd v. Utrecht-America Finance Co* [2001] EWCA Civ 658, [2001] 3 All ER 733. For a legal right arising from a 'no action' clause, see *Elektrim SA v. Vivendi Holdings 1 Corp* [2008] EWCA Civ 1178, [2009] 1 Lloyd's Rep 59.

287 Nor was there an equitable right not to be sued. For a case refusing to restrain a respondent from seeking to enforce a foreign judgment in a third state, see *ED & F Man Ltd v. Haryanto (No 2)* [1991] 1 Lloyd's Rep 429; *Mamidoil-Jetoil Greek Petroleum Co SA v. Okta Crude Oil Refinery AD* [2002] EWHC 2210 (Comm), [2003] 1 Lloyd's Rep 1.

an injunction formulated on such a basis is misconceived.[288] The ordinary rules of the Regulation establish whether courts have jurisdiction, but this[289] gives rise to no private law right, still less one enforceable by injunction. Unfortunately, the authority and principle which justifies and supports this conclusion was not referred to in the judgment of the Court of Appeal in *Samengo-Turner v. J & H Marsh & McLennan (Services) Ltd*,[290] with the result that the court ordered an injunction to prevent proceedings being taken before the courts of New York, on the ground that the applicant, who had signed an exclusive jurisdiction agreement for the courts of New York, had, according to the court's rather bold reading of Chapter II, Section 5 of the Brussels I Regulation, a 'legal right' to be sued in England. On any reasonable view of the matter, this interpretation of the Regulation, or of the expression 'a legal right not to be sued', or both, is insupportable, quite apart from the dizzying implausibility of the argument that a person who has agreed in writing to the jurisdiction of the courts of a non-Member State has a legal right, enforceable by injunction, to restrain the other party from suing him in that court.

The principal condition is, therefore, that the applicant has a legal right not to be sued by the respondent[291] in the foreign court;[292] as will be seen, a subsidiary condition is that the grant of an injunction to enforce the right is a proper exercise of the court's discretionary remedial power.[293] Indeed, it is now settled that, where there is a jurisdiction agreement for the English courts which is broken by the taking of proceedings elsewhere,[294] the court will grant an injunction to restrain the breach unless there is a strong reason not to do so. *Donohue v. Armco Inc*[295] settles the law along lines which run parallel to those governing the enforcement of foreign jurisdiction agreements: they will be given specific effect by the staying of English proceedings which breach the agreement unless there is a strong reason not to do so; the approach to the granting of injunctions where the clause is plainly exclusive is the mirror image.[296] The fragmenting impact which an injunction may have on complex proceedings involving many parties may be one powerful reason;[297] but

---

288 *The Eras EIL Actions* [1995] 1 Lloyd's Rep 64. In *Airbus Industrie GIE v. Patel* the Court of Appeal lent some support to the argument that there was a legal right to the correct application of the Brussels Convention: [1997] 2 Lloyd's Rep 8, but this was disapproved (implicitly if not explicitly) by the House of Lords: [1999] 1 AC 119, 138.

289 But if it can be argued that the respondent bound himself to the applicant not to invoke the jurisdiction of the court in question, the obligations arising from that undertaking may be separately enforced.

290 [2007] EWCA Civ 723, [2008] ICR 18: see also [2007] LMCLQ 433, (2007) 78 BYBIL 615.

291 As distinct from his friends and relations: *Mamidoil-Jetoil Greek Petroleum Co SA v. Okta Crude Oil Refinery AD* [2003] 1 Lloyd's Rep 1.

292 For the issue of contractual construction which arises at this point, see above, paras 4.50 *et seq.*

293 As a matter of general law, injunctions are not ordered unless common law remedies are inadequate. But English judges are not inclined to see a damages remedy as adequate, as made plain, for example, in *Continental Bank NA v. Aeakos SA* [1994] 1 WLR 588; *Donohue v. Armco Inc* [2001] UKHL 64, [2002] 1 All ER 749.

294 The agreement need not be exclusive for it to be a breach of it for proceedings to be taken elsewhere, though this will certainly be the commonest example: *Sabah Shipyard (Pakistan) Ltd v. Islamic Republic of Pakistan* [2002] EWCA Civ 1643, [2003] 2 Lloyd's Rep 571. If it is not exclusive, it will be much harder to show a legal right not to be sued outside the nominated court; and if the contract expressly provides for parallel proceedings, it will be impossible: *Deutsche Bank AG v. Highland Crusader Offshore Partners LP* [2009] EWCA Civ 725, [2010] 1 WLR 1023.

295 [2001] UKHL 64, [2002] 1 Lloyd's Rep 425. Applied in *OT Africa Line Ltd v. Magic Sportswear Corp* [2005] EWCA Civ 710, [2005] 2 Lloyd's Rep 170.

296 *Horn Linie GmbH v. Panamericana Formas e Impresos SA (The Hornbay)* [2006] EWHC 373 (Comm), [2006] 2 Lloyd's Rep 44.

297 It certainly was in *Donohue v. Armco Inc* and in *Verity Shipping SA v. Chartworld Shipping Corp* [2008] EWHC 213 (Comm), [2008] 1 CLC 45. It was not in *Welex AG v. Rosa Maritime Ltd* [2003] EWCA Civ 938,

case law has produced very few other examples of arguments which will defeat a claim for an injunction which is applied for and shown to be justifiable on this ground. The fact that a foreign court would exercise jurisdiction because its law would require it to ignore the agreement on choice of court does not furnish such a good reason.[298]

It is surely obvious that if the parties have agreed to the arbitration of differences, the bringing of proceedings in a foreign court is a breach of a legal right not to be sued in the foreign court. It is not necessary for the applicant to say that he should be sued in the English courts, or that he intends to sue in the English courts, instead. The negative promise necessarily inferred from the promise to go to arbitration is perfectly sufficient as a basis for the claim for relief.[299]

It has not, or has not yet, been held that a party to a contract which provides for an English choice of law has, by virtue of that contractual term, a legal right not be sued before the courts of a country which will not apply English law to a dispute falling within the terms of the agreement, still less one which may be enforced by injunction.[300] On the other hand, where there is an agreement on choice of court *and* law, the proposition that an injunction to restrain a breach of contract is ordered to enforce the choice of court, but is not ordered to enforce the choice of law as well, does not feel correct.[301] In principle it appears to be possible to construct an argument to the effect that an agreement on choice of law may[302] generate legal rights and obligations in relation to the manner and place of resolution of disputes. It has been said that every exclusive right imports a negative, and the person who confers such a right impliedly[303] enters into a negative undertaking to do

---

[2003] 2 Lloyd's Rep 509, or in *Bank of New York Mellon v. GV Films Ltd* [2009] EWHC 2328 (Comm), [2010] 1 Lloyd's Rep 365.

298 *OT Africa Line Ltd v. Magic Sportswear Corp* [2005] EWCA Civ 710, [2005] 2 Lloyd's Rep 170.

299 *AES Ust-Kamenogorsk Hydropower Plant JSC v. AES Ust-Kamenogorsk Hydropower Plant LLP* [2013] UKSC 35, [2013] 1 WLR 1889.

300 The contention that for a party to an agreement on choice of law to behave in this fashion was for him to commit a breach of contract was not accepted in *Ace Insurance Ltd v. Moose Enterprise Pty Ltd* [2009] NSWSC 724, at least in those cases in which the drafting does clearly show an intention to pre-define such behaviour as a breach: a plain vanilla agreement on choice of law was not considered to achieve this result: at [41]–[53]. Still, the judge was able to grant an injunction on the basis of the breach of (as he found it to be) an exclusive jurisdiction clause, and it was therefore only sensible of him to refrain from offering a second, controversial and appealable, justification for the order he had decided to make.

301 *Horn Linie GmbH v. Panamericana Formas e Impresos SA (The Hornbay)* [2006] EWHC 373 (Comm), [2006] 2 Lloyd's Rep 44. In that case, however, the injunction was founded on the vexatious behaviour of an associated party seeking to bring an undermining action while claiming to be free of the contractual agreement on dispute resolution. If necessary, the associated party should be joined to the action as a necessary or proper party, and served out, if necessary, under CPR r. 6.36: *Joint Stock Asset Management Co Ingosstrakh-Investments v. BNP Paribas SA* [2012] EWCA Civ 644, [2012] 1 Lloyd's Rep 649. Also, on restraint of associated non-parties, *Standard Bank plc v. Agrinvest International Inc* [2007] EWHC 2595 (Comm), [2008] 1 Lloyd's Rep 532.

302 But when coupled with a choice of court agreement which expressly allows a party to seise the courts of another jurisdiction (*in casu*, Nebraska), the risk that the Nebraska court might not apply English law is one which the parties must be taken to have foreseen and agreed to, with the result that there is no basis to contend that there was a breach of contract, or other objection which might be taken to the Nebraska proceedings: *Caitlin Syndicate Ltd v. Adams Land & Cattle Co* [2006] EWHC 2065 (Comm), [2006] 2 CLC 425. This cannot be the last word of the Commercial Court on the subject.

303 Although in *The Kallang* [2008] EWHC 2761 (Comm), [2009] 1 Lloyd's Rep 124 and *The Duden* [2008] EWHC 2762 (Comm), [2009] 1 Lloyd's Rep 145 the promise not to undermine a choice of law was regarded as expressed by the arbitration agreement.

nothing to contravene it,[304] or to abstain from any act which would deprive the contract of its efficacy[305] or the efficiency of the bargain which the parties have made.[306] The parties' promise that their relationship shall be governed by, or their disputes determined by the application of, a particular law could be seen as intended to be contractually enforceable, and as something which gives rise to a legal right not to be sued otherwise.[307] It may be that where the parties have not made an express agreement about choice of court to accompany their choice of law,[308] the basis for restraint to give effect to an express choice of law may be more appropriately[309] rested on the proposition that to bring proceedings before a foreign court in such circumstances may[310] be seen as vexatious or oppressive, and susceptible of restraint on that ground in any event.[311] In *Ace Insurance Ltd v. Moose Enterprise Pty Ltd*[312] the judge preferred to see agreements on choice of law as generally declaratory of the parties' wishes, or even as supplicative, rather than promissory; and rejected the 'implied negative stipulation' analysis set out above. But his conclusions were probably *obiter dicta*,[313] and he did accept that a differently drafted choice of law might support the breach analysis.[314]

5.38 Injunction to enforce legal right not to be sued in foreign court: where England is not the chosen court

Some uncertainty hangs over a possible further condition: that England be the natural forum for the resolution of the dispute between the parties, or that England be the contractually chosen forum for the resolution of the dispute.

Where the injunction is sought on the equitable ground, discussed below, it is generally[315] required that England be shown to be the natural forum for the resolution of the

---

304 *O'Keefe & McKenna v. Williams* (1910) 11 CLR 171, 211 (Isaacs J). For the proposition that a court will normally enforce a negative covenant by injunction, see *Elektrim SA v. Vivendi Holdings 1 Corp* [2008] EWCA Civ 1178, [2009] 1 Lloyd's Rep 59, [81].

305 *O'Keefe & McKenna v. Williams* (1910) 11 CLR 171, 197 (Barton J).

306 *Ibid.*, 191 (Griffiths CJ).

307 This does not mean that if the foreign court would apply the 'wrong' law, in the sense that it is not the law an English court would apply, there will be a remedy. It may yet be held that to act inconsistently with an express choice of law is a restrainable wrong, but this conclusion was, however, rejected in *Navig8 Pte Ltd v. Al-Riyadh Co for Vegetable Oil Industry* [2013] EWHC 328 (Comm), [2013] 2 Lloyd's Rep 104, and in *Golden Endurance Shipping SA v. RMA Watanya SA* [2014] EWHC 3917 (Comm).

308 For example, because when the commercial agreement was originally made, they agreed as to the law which would define the rights and applied in any litigation, but did not tie themselves to a court in which, by the time proceedings came to be issued, the defendant might have no local assets.

309 And in a manner which leaves the decision less vulnerable to an appeal.

310 It is not said that it must be.

311 *Cadre SA v. Astra Asigurari SA* [2005] EWHC 2626 (Comm), [2006] 1 Lloyd's Rep 560; *Trafigura Beheer BV v. Kookmin Bank Co* [2006] EWHC 1921 (Comm), [2007] 1 Lloyd's Rep 669 (on which see (2007) 123 LQR 18); *Standard Bank plc v. Agrinvest International Inc* [2007] EWHC 2595 (Comm), [2008] 1 Lloyd's Rep 532. And a judgment based on this ground is much less vulnerable to appeal than one which stakes out a radical position, even if that position is rational and defensible. See also Briggs, *Agreements on Jurisdiction and Choice of Law* (2008), ch. 11, for support for the argument that an agreement on choice of law is a promissory term of a contract which gives rise to legal rights in relation to the resolution of disputes; and see *Ace Insurance Ltd v. Moose Enterprise Pty Ltd* [2009] NSWSC 724 for the contrary view.

312 [2009] NSWSC 724.

313 As he found that an exclusive choice of court agreement grounded the claim for relief in any event.

314 At [47]. He suggested that the drafting would need to be unambiguous, though it is not clear why.

315 *Airbus Industrie GIE v. Patel* [1999] 1 AC 119, 138, 140.

dispute between the parties. One reason for this is that the requirements of comity require an English court to respect the corresponding expectations of other courts, even when dealing with those over whom personal jurisdiction is found to exist; and that this is the particular mechanism by which this respect is shown.[316] If the parties have agreed to settle their disputes by litigation or arbitration in England, the satisfaction of any such condition presents no difficulty.

But if the contractual choice is for dispute resolution in another country, England is not the chosen forum: indeed, it may even be said to be a breach of the contractual agreement on jurisdiction for an application for an injunction to be brought in England in the first place.[317] It can be said, by way of denying that the English court should intervene, that two wrongs do not make a right; and given the respect accorded by English law to jurisdiction agreements, England is unlikely to be the natural forum for any legal proceedings. Even so, whether this generally prevents the court granting injunctive relief to enforce the agreement is still unsettled by English authority. In *Airbus Industrie GIE v. Patel*,[318] the general statement of principle was expressed to be without prejudice to this case.[319] There is much to be said for the argument that if it is a breach of contract to sue in the United States, it is just as much a breach of contract if the agreement had been to sue in England as it would be if it had been to sue in India. Reasoning along these lines led the Court of Appeal for Bermuda to grant an injunction to restrain a party who had agreed to settle disputes by arbitration even though Bermuda was not the seat of the arbitration, and the issues in dispute appeared to have little or nothing to do with the Bermuda courts.[320]

It may be that the decision of the Supreme Court in *AES Ust-Kamenogorsk Hydropower Plant JSC v. AES Ust-Kamenogorsk Hydropower Plant LLP*[321] provides the answer. According to that decision, a court may issue an injunction to restrain the respondent from bringing legal proceedings in circumstances in which it would *also* amount to a breach of contract for the proceedings to be brought in England, as it was in that case, where it had been agreed that no court should have jurisdiction and that disputes should be referred to arbitration. If that is so, the proposition that an English court may only enforce a negative covenant when it is coupled with a positive covenant to bring any proceedings before an English court is not soundly based. It can make no material difference that the seat of any arbitration had been agreed to be in England. All that would mean is that it would have been a breach of contract to institute proceedings before the English courts, just as it would have been in the case before the Bermuda courts. The conclusion to be taken from the *Kamenogorsk* case is that where the injunction is ordered to enforce a negative covenant, a promise not to bring the proceedings which have been brought, there is no requirement that the English courts be the proper place to bring the proceedings. The approach of the Bermuda Court of Appeal has been shored up, and quite right, too. A breach is a breach is a breach.

---

316 There are other ways in which it might be done: see further below, para. 5.49.

317 If the point is raised it will have to be approached as a matter of the construction of the contract.

318 [1999] 1 AC 119.

319 At 138.

320 *IPOC International Growth Fund Ltd v. OAO CT Mobile* [2007] Bermuda LR 43. To contrary effect, suggesting that the application be made to the courts at the seat of the arbitration, *Econet Wireless Ltd v. Vee Networks Ltd* [2006] EWHC 1658 (Comm), [2006] 2 Lloyd's Rep 428. It may be that neither case should be taken to establish an absolute rule.

321 [2013] UKSC 35, [2013] 1 WLR 1889.

5.39 Injunction to enforce legal right not to be sued in foreign court: appropriateness of injunctive relief

In *Sohio Supply Co v. Gatoil (USA) Inc*[322] the applicant had a contractual, legal, right not to be sued before the foreign court. The Court of Appeal said that an injunction could be obtained if it was oppressive or vexatious to proceed in the foreign court, and that to do so in breach of a choice of court clause 'may well in itself be vexatious and oppressive'.[323] The language, though not the result, seems rather odd.[324] It is a legal wrong to breach a contract; it is hard to see what is added or taken away by enquiring whether it is oppressive as well. However, the court was feeling its way, and the application of a more familiar equitable principle may have been seen as safe. But it is now clear that where there is a jurisdiction agreement for the English courts, its breach by the respondent will normally lead to an injunction, and that no reference need be made to concepts of vexation or oppression.

In *Continental Bank NA v. Aeakos Compania Naviera SA*,[325] where proceedings were brought in Greece in breach (as the court found) of an exclusive choice of court agreement for the English courts, the Court of Appeal appeared to come close to saying that an injunction was the only effective remedy for such a breach, and that an injunction would be the natural remedy. In *The Angelic Grace*,[326] where proceedings were brought in Italy in breach (as the court found) of a binding contractual agreement for English arbitration, the court was, if anything, even more clear about it: it was said that, as long as the application was made promptly, good reason would need to be shown why the discretion to order an injunction should *not* be exercised. Considerations of comity were considered to be largely irrelevant, in the interests of upholding and giving full effect to the parties' contract.[327] And finally, in *Donohue v. Armco Inc*,[328] where various proceedings were brought in the United States in breach of an English jurisdiction agreement, the court went even further than it read the decision in *The Angelic Grace* as having done. The House of Lords accepted that the claimants were entitled to an injunction unless strong grounds or strong reasons were shown why it should not be ordered.[329] The court saw no difference of broad principle

---

322 [1989] 1 Lloyd's Rep 588.

323 As will be seen, these are the indicators of an equitable right not to be sued. A similar blending of legal rights and equitable wrongs is seen in *Royal Bank of Scotland plc v. Hicks* [2011] EWHC 287 (Ch), but where the conclusion of the court is (as it appears to have been) that the foreign proceedings breach a jurisdiction agreement if, as a matter of construction, it applies, but are oppressive or vexatious if as a matter of construction it does not, the blending of lines of doctrine is understandable.

324 Though it was adopted in *National Westminster Bank v. Utrecht-America Finance Co* [2001] EWCA Civ 658, [2001] 2 All ER (Comm) 7.

325 [1994] 1 WLR 588. At this point we are not concerned with the fact that the proceedings to be restrained were before the courts of another Member State, though this is a reason why today the result in *Continental Bank* would be different; see further below, para. 5.45.

326 [1995] 1 Lloyd's Rep 87; *Schiffahrtsgesellschaft Detlev von Appen v. Vöst Alpine Intertrading GmbH, The 'Jay Bola'* [1997] 2 Lloyd's Rep 279.

327 To similar effect, see *Petromin SA v. Secnav Marine Ltd* [1995] 1 Lloyd's Rep 603. But if the foreign measures have been taken only in order to obtain security for a (counter-)claim there may, on a true construction of it, not be a breach of the agreement, and so no injunction and *cf Bankgesellschaft Berlin AG v. First International Shipping Corp* [2001] 1 CL 61.

328 [2000] 1 Lloyd's Rep 579. The decision of the Court of Appeal was reversed: [2001] UKHL 64, [2002] 1 All ER 749, but not on this point: the House accepted the strong approach in favour of granting an injunction but found exceptional reasons (in the consequential fragmentation of the litigation) not to make such an order.

329 At 589, 594–595.

between the enforcing of a jurisdiction agreement by staying proceedings brought in England in breach of a foreign jurisdiction clause, and restraining proceedings brought in a foreign court in breach of an English one, with comity having nothing much to do with the matter. Indeed, in *Sabah Shipyard (Pakistan) Ltd v. Islamic Republic of Pakistan*[330] an injunction was granted on the basis of what was from one point of view a non-exclusive jurisdiction agreement for the English courts, albeit on the footing that the bringing of proceedings brought in Pakistan were, on a true construction of the contract and in the very particular circumstances of the case, a breach of the jurisdiction agreement.[331] It is clear that cases decided before *Donohue v. Armco Inc*, which had followed a more cautious line, are not now reliable.[332]

The justification for the settled modern approach is a commercial pragmatism which sees dispute resolution agreements as inherently desirable, and their summary enforcement as valuable. No substantive distinction is to be drawn between English and non-English choices of court: as long as the agreement which founds the legal right not be sued is one which the court may be asked to enforce, it will enforce it by injunction or stay, as the case may be. There is conspicuous even-handedness in the enforcing of English jurisdiction agreements (by injunction to restrain the party in breach) and foreign jurisdiction agreements (by the staying of English proceedings brought in breach), and any suggestion of chauvinism would be without foundation.

Even so, some of the language used by the courts may be thought to have tested the limit which comity, in this respect at least, may be taken to impose. And it is a simple, further, fact that, though it may appear plain to an English court that the foreign proceedings are being brought in breach of contract, a foreign court may not construe the contract in the same way or may, just as an English court may, see exceptional reasons of its own why the proceedings should be allowed to continue despite the agreement the parties may have made. Given all this, the lines of future development should perhaps be these: a court should not intervene unless England is the chosen court,[333] and then should not do so unless its conclusion that the bringing of the foreign proceedings involves a breach of promise, of contract, is one from which the foreign court could be expected not to dissent.[334] And in this respect, if the foreign court has rejected a jurisdictional challenge brought on the basis of the jurisdiction agreement, it is necessary to examine its reasons with care before granting an anti-suit injunction.

5.40 Injunction to restrain commission of equitable wrong: general

In *British Airways Board v. Laker Airways Ltd*, Lord Diplock also said that an injunction could be ordered if the applicant had an equitable right not to be sued in the foreign court. This

---

330 [2002] EWCA Civ 1643, [2003] 2 Lloyd's Rep 571.

331 In that they were designed to prevent the claimant from taking advantage of the non-exclusive jurisdiction agreement to which the defendant had bound itself as soon as the claimant invoked it (and, as was explained in para. 4.50 above, converted it into an exclusive jurisdiction agreement). For a more sceptical view, see *Deutsche Bank AG v. Highland Crusader Offshore Partners LP* [2009] EWCA Civ 725, [2010] 1 WLR 1023, [85] (citing Raphael, *The Anti-Suit Injunction* (OUP, 2008), para. 9.10).

332 In particular *Toepfer International GmbH v. Soc Cargill France* [1998] 1 Lloyd's Rep 379.

333 There may be room for an exception where the basis of the claim for an injunction is that the respondent should not be bringing proceedings anywhere.

334 But the fact that it would or would not order a particular remedy would be irrelevant.

may be found in estoppel, or in laches, and more generally in all conduct capable of being labelled as 'unconscionable'.[335] It is therefore necessary to ascertain the meaning of such 'unconscionable' conduct. By far the most important version of this particular wrong occurs when England is the natural forum for the resolution of the dispute between the parties, and the respondent vexes or harasses the applicant by suing him in a foreign court. There are other examples of unconscionable conduct, which will also be mentioned, but this is by far the most important example of it.

The nomenclature must not, however, be allowed to become a distraction or a straitjacket.[336] One possible explanation for the approach of Lord Diplock was a logical deduction from his view[337] that, as injunctions are available only for the vindication of rights, legal or equitable, all anti-suit injunctions had to be, but also could properly be, accommodated within this framework. A rather different analysis was proposed in *South Carolina Insurance Co v. Assurantie Maatschappij 'de Zeven Provincien' NV*,[338] namely that injunctions ordered as a remedy against vexatious or oppressive litigation are doctrinally separate from those ordered to protect legal or equitable rights which have been threatened with invasion. But it is evident that these are merely differences of form, not of substance, and the leading cases have been insistent throughout that classification may lead to a rigidity which is the very antithesis of what the law, and this particular remedy, requires. If that is so, the only category of injunction clearly calling for separate treatment is that which is founded on a *legal* right not to be sued in the foreign court, and which is obtained in equity's auxiliary jurisdiction.

The one point upon which there may be a distinction between injunctions to vindicate equitable rights and those ordered to restrain vexatious or oppressive behaviour, is the role played by questions of applicable law.[339] Where injunctions are ordered in aid of *legal* rights not to be sued, an anterior choice of law question arises, and has to be answered in order to decide whether there really was a legal right which will found the claim to relief. Where equitable rights are concerned, it might reasonably have been supposed that there was a corresponding question of applicable law to be dealt with before any question of remedy could arise, whereas where the complaint is founded on vexatious or oppressive behaviour, no such question necessarily arose. But even if this is a theoretical ground for distinction, there is no indication in the case law that a question of applicable law ever arose for answer outside the context of an alleged legal right not to be sued. As in all such cases, the court will generally require England to be the natural forum for the dispute; it may well be that this forum requirement is a rational alternative to an applicable law rule, or even a surrogate applicable law rule, and means that English law will only ever be applied in cases where the closest and most real connection of the litigation to anywhere is to England in any event, in which case the application of English law to determine whether there is wrongful behaviour in suing elsewhere is rational.

---

335 Lord Diplock, at 81.

336 See [1997] LMCLQ 90. See, for further judicial caution about reading too much into an 'equitable right not to be sued', *Masri v. Consolidated Contractors International (UK) Ltd (No 3)* [2008] EWCA Civ 625, [2009] 2 QB 503. The court was wary about forms of words which might be thought to tie its hands in the face of conduct which ought to be restrained simply because it is wrongful.

337 *The Siskina* [1979] AC 210.

338 [1987] AC 24.

339 See [1997] LMCLQ 90, where the issue is examined. The suggestion that the court incorporate a concern for choice of law was not adopted by the House of Lords in *Airbus Industrie GIE v. Patel* [1999] 1 AC 119; and did not feature at all in *Turner v. Grovit* [2000] QB 345, [2002] 1 WLR 107.

In the absence of any serious reason to suppose that these differences have practical significance,[340] it is proposed to follow Lord Diplock, to treat injunctions to protect an applicant from vexatious or oppressive behaviour as being granted in aid of an equitable right not to be victimised by vexatious or oppressive behaviour, and to treat all such cases as belonging to the same broad and flexible category.[341] But for the reasons given, it is doubtful that anything of substance turns upon this exercise in classification, and even more doubtful that anything should do.

5.41 Injunction to restrain commission of equitable wrong: vexatious or oppressive conduct in bringing proceedings before a foreign court

The modern restatement of the law is found in the decision of the Privy Council in *SNI Aerospatiale v. Lee Kui Jak*.[342] An alleged tort had occurred in Brunei in which a local man had been killed. His widow commenced proceedings in Brunei, but American lawyers finally caught up with the ambulance and persuaded her to abandon the Brunei proceedings and sue in Texas instead. The Privy Council, on appeal from the courts of Brunei, reviewed the authorities upon the granting of an injunction in support of an equitable right not to be sued, and decided that whilst rigid categorisation[343] was impossible, one type of unconscionable conduct was of particular relevance: that an injunction would be granted if (a) England were the natural forum for the trial of the action,[344] (b) it would not be unjust to deprive the respondent of the advantages sought in the foreign proceedings and (c) it was vexatious or oppressive for the respondent to sue in the foreign court.[345]

The requirement that England be shown to be the natural forum, as a general rule at least, was reiterated in *Airbus Industrie GIE v. Patel*.[346] In that case an air accident in India had led to desultory litigation in India, but then, as a result of more transnational ambulance chasing, to litigation in Texas. Though the Indian courts had ordered an anti-suit injunction to order restraint by the parties bringing the Texas proceedings,[347] and though the Court of Appeal encountered little difficulty in finding the Texas proceedings to be vexatious or oppressive in nature, Lord Goff explained that it was a general precondition to the grant of relief that England be the natural forum for the litigation. That condition was not satisfied, and the requirements of comity therefore meant that an English court had no business to interfere: the issue was, he might have said, *res inter alios acta*. Lord Goff explained that

---

340 *Masri v. Consolidated Contractors International (UK) Ltd (No 3)* [2008] EWCA Civ 625, [2009] QB 503.

341 For support, see *Youell v. Kara Mara Shipping Co Ltd* [2000] 2 Lloyd's Rep 102.

342 [1987] AC 871.

343 And see *Channel Tunnel Group Ltd v. Balfour Beatty Construction Ltd* [1993] AC 334.

344 The fact that the claim brought in the foreign proceedings could not be brought in an English court (*British Airways plc v. Laker Airways Ltd*) should be irrelevant. There is still an available forum in England in which proceedings could be brought; that the respondent would lose on the merits or the law if he brought them there is in principle irrelevant. It is therefore wrong to see *Laker Airways* as a special case in which there was only one available forum. See below, para. 5.47.

345 At 896.

346 [1999] 1 AC 119.

347 But the respondents had elected to ignore it, on the presumed ground that they had no fear of being found to be in contempt in India, and knew perfectly well that the order of the Indian court could not be enforced outside India. In this regard it is perhaps a little unexpected that, as the courts at the undoubted natural forum had ordered an injunction, and had done so in circumstances in which an English court would have done likewise, the demands of comity were taken to favour not interfering with the Texas litigation as opposed to seeking to make the Indian order effective.

this was a general rule, not an invariable one;[348] but aside from special cases, such as those 'single forum'[349] cases in which the respondent argues that he can bring his claim only in the foreign court or nowhere at all, England will have to be shown to be the natural forum before it is proper for the court to act.[350] As a result, the matters which make England the natural forum are relevant here too; the applicant who alleges the unconscionable behaviour of the respondent will bear the burden of proof on this point. Again, it is true that advantages of which it would be unjust[351] to deprive the respondent may be used to resist the application: these may be few in number, and mere advantages accounted for by the incidental differences between two systems should be disregarded. The real meat of the law is found in the definition of vexatious or oppressive conduct.

'Vexation' may exist if the foreign proceedings 'are so utterly absurd that they cannot possibly succeed',[352] or if the respondent sues in two courts at the same time when there is no real or tangible advantage to him in doing so.[353] 'Oppression', as a term of art, has a wider meaning, and covers other varieties of conduct unfairly[354] prejudicial to the applicant.[355] In *Aérospatiale*, the consequence of the respondent's suing in Texas would have been to deprive the applicant of a right to claim contribution from other parties, with some of whom there had already been a settlement. In subsequent proceedings which would have to be brought if a contribution were to be sought, it would be far from clear that a Texan judgment on the liability of the applicant would be recognised as conclusive on the question of the original liability of the contributors; that, taken together with the fact that Brunei was the natural forum (and the connection with Texas very weak) made it oppressive, and unconscionable, to proceed in Texas. But if a litigant starts proceedings in a foreign court with a view to stealing a march on his opponent, it is not natural to see this as oppressive. It is no more than – indeed, it is a telling example of – sensible litigation strategy.[356]

---

348 At 138.

349 See below, para. 5.47.

350 Or, at any rate, clearly more appropriate than the forum in which the foreign litigation is pending.

351 But advantages accruing only in an inappropriate forum may well be disregarded: this aspect of *Amchem Products Inc v. British Columbia (Workers' Compensation Board)* [1993] 1 SCR 897, 933, is likely to be applicable in the context of a slightly different English test. For the distinctive Canadian approach, see below, para. 5.49.

352 *Peruvian Guano Co v. Bockwoldt* (1883) 23 Ch D 225. It is lack of success in the foreign forum, rather than the impossibility of subsequent enforcement in England, which is presumably relevant. See also *Shell International Petroleum Co Ltd v. Coral Oil Co Ltd* [1999] 2 Lloyd's Rep 606. But for the view that the case must be really extreme, truly hopeless, before the English court is entitled to restrain it on this ground, see *Vitol Bahrein EC v. Nasdec General Trading LLC* [2013] EWHC 3359 (Comm) (*obiter*, as England was in any event not the natural forum for resolution of the question).

353 But if there are assets in two countries, neither of which freely allows the enforcement of judgments from the other, the claimant may be forced to sue in both jurisdictions.

354 If there was an unspoken assumption that proceedings would be brought in England, but they were then instituted in another court, this may be regarded as unsatisfactory, but in the absence of detrimental reliance it may not be oppressive: *Insurance Co of the State of Pennsylvania v. Equitas Insurance Ltd* [2013] EWHC 3713 (Comm), [2014] Lloyd's Rep IR 195.

355 It is possible that the Privy Council would, notwithstanding the general reluctance to make comparisons between systems, have been willing to see some aspects of Texan procedure – jury trial, strict liability, punitive damages and the distortions of the contingency fee system – as pointers towards oppression: at 899. There is tension between this part of the decision and *The Abidin Daver* [1984] AC 398. And in the light of *Lubbe v. Cape* [2000] 1 WLR 1545, if the respondent sues in a court in which the applicant cannot possibly afford to defend himself, this may point to oppression.

356 *Star Reefers Pool Inc v. JFC Group Co Ltd* [2012] EWCA Civ 14, [2012] 1 Lloyd's Rep 376; *Golden Endurance Shipping SA v. RMA Watanya SA* [2014] EWHC 3917 (Comm). This approach was not taken in *Joint*

There is some authority for the view that if a claimant has commenced proceedings in the forum, it may be oppressive and/or vexatious for the defendant to institute proceedings in a foreign court which will duplicate[357] or otherwise frustrate[358] the first set of proceedings. If this were to be applied as a general rule it would put a premium on winning the race to commence proceedings first; and as this is too crude a basis for the decision whether to order an injunction, the relative timing of proceedings should not be decisive. In the end, the questions are whether the behaviour of the party to be restrained can be shown to be objectively wrongful even though it is in accordance with the law of the (foreign) court in which it is taking place, and whether, if it is, the case is one in which the English court ought to take upon itself the decision whether it should be allowed to continue.

It follows that, when an injunction is sought on this basis, the analysis must be a holistic one. If England is the natural forum, the applicant has satisfied one, but only one, of the criteria on which the grant of an injunction depends; but by doing only this he has not shown oppression.[359] Indeed, ten years before the decision in *Airbus Industrie GIE v. Patel*, the Court of Appeal, in *E.I. Du Pont v. Agnew (No 2)*,[360] concluded that as an injunction could no longer be ordered on the bare ground that England was the natural forum, the way was open to the parties to rush to judgment in their preferred forum, and that this was the inevitable consequence of self-restraint in the granting of injunctions.[361] Cases which have identified oppression tend to be fact-specific. But to take one example, in *Midland Bank plc v. Laker Airways Ltd*,[362] an injunction was ordered on the ground of oppression when an English bank, which had a mere presence, but had done none of the acts complained of, in the United States, was to be subjected to the unbearable burden and harassment of American anti-trust proceedings. The result is that a finding of oppression is quite distinct from any question whether England is the most appropriate forum. It requires proof of wrongful behaviour; and more than that it is difficult to usefully say. And, of course, it bears repetition that if the parties have agreed that the foreign proceedings may be brought, even

---

Stock Asset Management Co Ingosstrakh-Investments v. BNP Paribas SA [2012] EWCA Civ 644, [2012] 1 Lloyd's Rep 649, in which pre-emptive proceedings were found to have been brought with a view to undermining an English arbitration. For the proposition that proceedings which were properly brought before a foreign court became liable to restraint once proceedings had been commenced in the forum court, see *Stichting Shell Pensioenfonds v. Krys* [2014] UKPC 41, [2015] 2 WLR 289 (where the foreign proceedings, though not originally objectionable, became liable to restraint once the company was being wound up in its home jurisdiction). It is possible that the decision is confined to the particular context of insolvency proceedings, and is motivated by the public interest which requires the court to ensure that the interests of the general body of creditors are protected.

357 *Henry v. Henry* (1996) 185 CLR 571, *CSR Ltd v. Cigna Insurance Australia Ltd* (1997) 189 CLR 345. But *cf Administracion Nacional de Combustibles Alcohol y Portland v. Ridgley Shipping Inc* [1996] 1 Lloyd's Rep 570. For the possible impact of *Turner v. Grovit* [2002] 1 WLR 107, [2001] UKHL 65, see para. 5.45, below.

358 *Sabah Shipyard (Pakistan) Ltd v. Islamic Republic of Pakistan* [2002] EWCA Civ 1643, [2003] 2 Lloyd's Rep 571. Likewise if the respondent has (or should have) submitted to the jurisdiction but then goes to a foreign court to institute proceedings there; and it will be even more oppressive or vexatious if he seeks relief overseas which will impede the English court in ruling on its jurisdiction: *General Star International Indemnity Ltd v. Stirling Cooke Brown Reinsurance Brokers Ltd* [2003] EWHC 3 (Comm), [2003] ILPr 314; *Tonicstar Ltd v. American Home Insurance Co* [2004] EWHC 1234 (Comm), [2005] Lloyd's Rep IR 32; *Goshawk Dedicated Ltd v. ROP Inc* [2006] EWHC 1730 (Comm), [2006] Lloyd's Rep IR 711; *CNA Insurance Co Ltd v. Office Depot International* [2005] EWHC 456 (Comm), [2005] Lloyd's Rep IR 658.

359 *Aerospatiale* at 895 in particular.

360 [1988] 2 Lloyd's Rep 240.

361 What follows from or may be done about it is examined below.

362 [1986] QB 689. The case was one in which the claim advanced in the United States under federal legislation could not be successfully brought in England. How such cases fit into the law now established by *Airbus* is examined below, para. 5.47.

if there are proceedings in England, the idea that it may be wrongful to bring them is almost unarguable: the maxim that *volenti non fit injuria* will be a good guide when looking for a wrong.[363]

5.42 Injunction to restrain commission of equitable wrong: undermining the jurisdiction of the English court

There are several kinds of case which illustrate the point that foreign proceedings may be wrongful, and the pursuit of them restrained, when they undermine the jurisdiction of an English court.[364] For example, if the court is exercising jurisdiction in a winding-up or bankruptcy, or the administration of a deceased estate,[365] but an action is commenced or continued[366] overseas, by creditors or would-be successors, with a view to obtaining the sole benefit of overseas assets at the expense of the general body of creditors for whose benefit the company is being wound up, the court may treat this as a wrongful attempt to subvert or frustrate its jurisdiction, and may order an injunction to restrain the respondent.[367] In a development which surprised some, the French Supreme Court confirmed that such relief may be granted as a matter of French law.[368] But the particular context of cross-border insolvency may well mean that the law on anti-suit injunctions is applied in a

---

363 *Royal Bank of Canada v. Cooperatieve Centrale Raiffeisen-Boerenleenbank* [2004] EWCA Civ 7, [2004] 1 Lloyd's Rep 471; *Deutsche Bank AG v. Highland Crusader Offshore Partners LP* [2009] EWCA Civ 725, [2010] 1 WLR 1023.

364 Likewise, the same principles allow an English court, when England is the seat of an arbitration, to grant an anti-suit injunction to prevent a party from taking steps overseas which are calculated to undermine an English arbitration.

365 *Weinstock v. Sarnat* [2005] NSWLR 744 (administration of deceased estates: injunction granted); *cf Al-Bassam v. Al-Bassam* [2004] EWCA Civ 857 (where the court was markedly more reluctant to grant the injunction and preferred to give directions for trial of a preliminary issue). For injunctions to restrain proceedings designed to hamper the administration and sale of a company as a going concern, see *Harms Offshore AHT Taurus GmbH & Co KG v. Bloom* [2009] EWCA Civ 632, [2010] Ch 187.

366 *Stichting Shell Pensioenfonds v. Krys* [2014] UKPC 41, [2015] 2 WLR 289 (where the foreign proceedings, though not originally objectionable, became liable to restraint once the company was being wound up in its home jurisdiction).

367 *Aérospatiale* at 892–893; see also *South Carolina Insurance Co v. Assurantie Maatschappij 'de Zeven Provincien'* [1987] AC 24, and *Bank of Tokyo v. Karoon* (noted) [1987] AC 45. See also *Elektrim SA v. Vivendi Holdings 1 Corp* [2008] EWCA Civ 1178, [2009] 1 Lloyd's Rep 59. But in *Barclays Bank plc v. Homan* [1993] BCLC 680, an application in the context of the insolvency of an English company, the application to restrain proceedings in the United States proceeded under the rubric of oppression or vexation, not the protection of the jurisdiction. The principle was extended to the case of a company in administration, granting relief on the ground of unconscionable behaviour by the respondent, who had set a trap for the company by quietly obtaining *ex parte* attachment orders in New York and then attaching funds transferred by the company to pay post-administration suppliers, in such a way as to hinder the administration and sale of the company by the administrators as a going concern: *Harms Offshore AHT Taurus GmbH & Co KG v. Bloom* [2009] EWCA Civ 632, [2010] Ch 187 (but *cf*, to opposite effect, *Kemsley v. Barclays Bank plc* [2013] EWHC 1274 (Ch), where there was no undermining of the English bankruptcy). See also *Carlyle Capital Corp Ltd v. Conway* [2013] 2 Lloyd's Rep 179 (Guernsey CA).

368 *Banque Worms v. Brachot* [2003] Rev Crit DIP 816 (*note* Muir-Watt); also noted by the same commentator at [2003] CLJ 573. However, it is not clear whether this is properly to be seen as an anti-suit injunction, as distinct from some form of asset preservation order, though the difference in nomenclature may not be significant. In *Stolzenberg v. Daimler Chrysler Canada Inc* (Cass, 30 June 2004), [2005] JDI/Clunet 112 (*note* Cuniberti), [2005] ILPr 266, the French Cour de Cassation, in granting enforcement of an English freezing order, was at pains to distinguish such orders from anti-suit injunctions, of which it expressed seeming disapproval. See also, for what may be French recognition of a US anti-suit injunction (but which may be, less dramatically, the recognition of an American court's ruling on its jurisdiction, from which the injunction was merely a procedural consequence which did not call for recognition as such), *Beverage International SA v. In Zone Brands Inc* (Cass Civ 1, 14 Oct 2009), [2010] Rev Crit 158 (*note* Muir-Watt), [2010] ILPr 598; [2010] JDI/Clunet 146 (*note* Clavel).

distinctive way, not easily translated to other areas. For another example, injunctions have been ordered to restrain parties who, having submitted to the jurisdiction of the English courts and participated in the judicial process, then undergo an apparent change of heart and seek to bring proceedings before a foreign court which are designed to undermine the English action.[369] For a third, where parties have made a contractual agreement for the non-exclusive jurisdiction of the English courts which one party wishes to activate, but the other party to the agreement brings proceedings before a foreign court, an injunction may go to restrain those proceedings, even if they are not being continued in breach of contract, if it may be said that their undermining effect on the agreed jurisdiction is positively wrongful, particularly where the foreign proceedings include an application for an anti-suit injunction.[370] And an associate of a person who is party to an agreement on choice of court or law, who brings foreign proceedings which are designed to frustrate that agreement, may be held to be acting vexatiously in undermining the agreement for the resolution of disputes in England.[371] The same principle applies to a person who seeks to undermine an arbitration agreement by which an associate is bound, though whether the behaviour is regarded as a tort or as vexatious, it is still a wrong and is liable to restraint on that basis.[372] All of these are examples of substantive proceedings overseas, restrained on the ground that their undermining of English jurisdiction is vexatious or oppressive.

On the other hand, if there are no proceedings in England, and no contract by which the parties have bound themselves to each other only to litigate in England, there is nothing to undermine when proceedings are brought in the foreign court, and in such circumstances it will be rare that an injunction will be justified.[373] Indeed, some had gone even further than that: it had been suggested that it was an absolute requirement for the grant of an injunction on the vexatious and oppressive ground that there be proceedings in England. But this is probably going too far. In *Turner v. Grovit*,[374] Lord Hobhouse, in delivering a speech on the decision to refer a preliminary question to the European Court, stated that in the absence of a legal right not to be sued, an applicant requires a 'sufficient interest' to justify his obtaining an injunction, and that such an interest will not exist unless he is a party to proceedings actually pending before the English court.[375] It is not to be taken literally, not least because it is not supported by *Airbus Industrie GIE v. Patel*.[376] That said, it is certainly much harder

---

369 *Glencore International AG v. Exter Shipping Ltd* [2002] EWCA Civ 528, [2002] 2 All ER (Comm) 1; *CNA Insurance Co Ltd v. Office Depot International* [2005] EWHC 456 (Comm), [2005] Lloyd's Rep IR 658; *Credit Suisse AG v. UP Energy Group Ltd* [2014] EWHC 2852 (Comm). *Cf Star Reefers Pool Inc v. JFC Group Co Ltd* [2012] EWCA Civ 14, [2012] 1 Lloyd's Rep 376.

370 *Sabah Shipyard (Pakistan) Ltd v. Islamic Republic of Pakistan* [2002] EWCA Civ 1643, [2003] 2 Lloyd's Rep 571 (wrongful; injunction granted); *Deutsche Bank AG v. Highland Crusader Offshore Partners LP* [2009] EWCA Civ 725, [2010] 1 WLR 1023 (not wrongful; injunction not granted).

371 *Horn Linie GmbH v. Panamericana Formas e Impresos SA (The Hornbay)* [2006] EWHC 373 (Comm), [2006] 2 Lloyd's Rep 44; *Credit Suisse AG v. UP Energy Group Ltd* [2014] EWHC 2852 (Comm).

372 *The Kallang* [2008] EWHC 2761 (Comm), [2009] 1 Lloyd's Rep 124 and *The Duden* [2008] EWHC 2762 (Comm), [2009] 1 Lloyd's Rep 145 treat the acts of the non-party in undermining the arbitration agreement as torts, but on any view they are wrongs and are liable to restraint as wrongs.

373 *Star Reefers Pool Inc v. JFC Group Co Ltd* [2012] EWCA Civ 14, [2012] 1 Lloyd's Rep 376; distinguished in *Joint Stock Asset Management Co Ingosstrakh-Investments v. BNP Paribas SA* [2012] EWCA Civ 644, [2012] 1 Lloyd's Rep 649, in which pre-emptive proceedings were found to have been brought with a view to undermining an English arbitration.

374 [2001] UKHL 65, [2002] 1 WLR 107.

375 At [27].

376 [1999] 1 AC 119.

to show that there is anything wrong and restrainable about foreign proceedings when there are no proceedings before the English court, and no contractual obligation to sue only in England. If all that can really be said is that one's opponent saw which way the wind was blowing and wasted no time in commencing proceedings before his preferred court, there is no criticism to be made, and no wrong to be restrained. One should really praise, rather than blame, those who get about their proper business with alacrity.

5.43 Injunction to restrain commission of equitable wrong: vexatious or oppressive conduct by invoking foreign procedural laws?

The obtaining of evidence by recourse to the civil procedures of a foreign court for later use in English proceedings, which were already underway, was held in *South Carolina Insurance Co v. Assurantie Maatshappij 'de Zeven Provincien' NV*[377] not to be an unconscionable interference with the jurisdiction of the English court. Obtaining evidence in a country by means lawful in that country could not be said to interfere with the jurisdiction of the English court; the procedures were not unconscionable simply because they increased the costs burden upon the applicant. He was entitled to make his own decision whether to resist and incur costs, but was not entitled to blame his opponent for the consequences of his own decision.

It may be asked whether this is really correct. There will be cases where the foreign procedures invoked – for example, the subjecting of potential witnesses to the taking of depositions close to the beginning of the English trial – has too disruptive or distorting an effect on the English jurisdiction to be allowed to proceed. Indeed, it is far from clear why it is not oppressive, or an interference with the jurisdiction, to allow depositions to be obtained in a foreign jurisdiction for use in local proceedings. English law does not allow oral discovery; to permit it to be obtained may be too greatly to affect the balance between the parties at trial. In *South Carolina*, it may be significant that the respondent, who had formerly sought both oral and documentary discovery, had abandoned any claim to the former by the time the case came to the House of Lords. It may therefore be possible to read too much into the refusal of the House of Lords in that case to order an injunction.

More recently, two English decisions show a greater preparedness to see steps taken in a foreign court as a wrongful encroaching on the jurisdiction of the English court and its inherent right to control its proceedings. In *Omega Group Holdings Ltd v. Kozeny*,[378] an injunction was ordered to restrain the taking of depositions in the United States under USC §1782, on the basis that the witnesses to be deposed were liable to be cross-examined in the English proceedings, and it was, therefore, unconscionable to expose them to what was, in effect, double cross-examination. And in *Glencore International AG v. Metro Trading International Inc*,[379] where a huge piece of commercial litigation was under close and active case management by the Commercial Court, an injunction was ordered to restrain an action brought in the United States which had or would have the effect of interfering with the proceedings before the Commercial Court, and which would have created a great burden in additional costs. It may be expected that, as the courts become increasingly concerned to

---

377 [1987] AC 24; *Arab Monetary Fund v. Hashim (No 6)*, *Financial Times*, 23 July 1992. But for an odd contrast, see *Singularis v PricewaterhouseCoopers* [2014] UKPIC 36, [29].

378 [2002] CLC 132.

379 [2002] EWCA Civ 524, [2002] 2 All ER (Comm) 1. Followed and applied in *Benfield Holdings Ltd v. Richardson* [2007] EWHC 171 (QB).

manage cases actively, anti-suit injunctions granted on the basis of protecting this scheme of early case management will become a more frequent phenomenon.[380]

5.44 Injunction to restrain commission of equitable wrong: vexatious or oppressive conduct by wrongfully undermining an English judgment

It is possible to demonstrate vexatious or oppressive behaviour by taking steps to undermine the conclusiveness of an English judgment. In *Masri v. Consolidated Contractors International (UK) Ltd (No 3)*[381] it was held that a defendant who had submitted to the jurisdiction of the English courts, and had been ordered to pay damages, was liable to be restrained by injunction from bringing proceedings before a foreign court, where it feared that enforcement against its assets might be sought, for a declaration that it owed no liability to the judgment creditor. The precise ground on which this was to be done was a little unclear, but the best reading of the judgment would appear to be that by submitting to the jurisdiction of an English court, and seeking substantive relief, the respondent had assumed an obligation to abide by and obey the judgment, and to seek to underline or annul this judgment by mounting what was, in effect, an extra-curial appeal, was wrongful.

But the court appeared to prefer the justification that the injunction protected the jurisdiction of the English court, which was not spent once it had given judgment. At first sight, this is not as persuasive as the explanation that it is oppressive to re-litigate the merits of a claim which has already been fought to judgment. This explanation is founded on the behaviour of the judgment debtor and respondent as being (equitably) wrongful, which it plainly was. It will be legitimate to ask the courts at the place where enforcement is anticipated to find that the judgment is not enforceable, but to ask them to re-try the merits is as objectionable after the first trial as would be parallel litigation during it. The case is a good illustration of the proposition that the grounds on which an injunction can be obtained overlap.

The case is to be contrasted with *ED & F Man (Sugar) Ltd v. Haryanto (No 2)*,[382] in which a dispute between an Indonesian citizen, Haryanto, and an English corporation was settled after proceedings had been commenced in the English courts. Thereafter Haryanto sued in Indonesia and obtained a judgment annulling the underlying contracts in respect of which the English proceedings had been brought, and the settlement. The corporation then sought an injunction to restrain Haryanto from relying, anywhere in the world including Indonesia, upon his Indonesian judgment. The Court of Appeal held that the later Indonesian judgment was not entitled to recognition in England, where the substantive matter was *res judicata*; but beyond that it would not be so unconscionable for Haryanto to rely upon his Indonesian judgment in Indonesia, or anywhere else where he was entitled to do so, that the court should order an injunction to restrain him. The settlement agreement contained no express term[383] that proceedings would not be taken elsewhere to challenge it, so the company had no legal right not to be sued in Indonesia.

---

380 On injunctions granted to protect the jurisdiction of an English court to rule on its own jurisdiction, see *Tonicstar Ltd v. American Home Insurance Co* [2004] EWHC 1234 (Comm), [2005] 1 Lloyd's Rep IR 32. This sits uncomfortably alongside cases in which an English court states that its injunction does not interfere with the foreign court or its procedure.

381 [2008] EWCA Civ 625, [2009] QB 503.

382 [1991] 1 Lloyd's Rep 429.

383 And none was to be implied.

Neither was it unconscionable for Haryanto to use the civil procedure of other countries in aid of his cause. In the light of *Aérospatiale*, the Court of Appeal may have paid too little regard to the possibility of proceedings having to be fought and defended by the English company in third countries, but the case was, as Neill LJ admitted, 'very difficult'. That may be so; but the question is a simple one: one asks whether the steps now being taken by the respondent are wrongful.

The fact that the foreign proceedings may result in a judgment in which account needs to be taken of a prior English judgment does not itself make it vexatious to bring the proceedings before the foreign court: as the previously-mentioned cases show, it must be wrongful for the foreign proceedings to have been brought. In *Seismic Shipping Inc v. Total E & P UK plc*[384] a decree limiting a shipowner's liability[385] had been obtained from an English court, but an attempt to obtain an injunction to restrain substantive proceedings before the Texas courts failed, on the approximate ground that the party claiming in Texas was doing nothing wrong. He had not claimed in the English proceedings, had not contractually agreed to the exclusive jurisdiction of the English courts, and had a good claim under the law of Texas. Leaving aside the effect this might have on the limitation decree, he had done nothing which could remotely be described as unconscionable. The fact that an English court had limited liability by decree did not make the Texas action wrongful; the Texas action did not undermine the jurisdiction of the English court or demonstrate wrongful behaviour by the claimant; it could not be correct that an injunction could be obtained every time there was a risk that a foreign judge would say something inconsistent with what an English court had already decided. It would, of course, be for the Texas court to decide for itself what to make of the English limitation decree, which is precisely how private international law is supposed to work.

5.45 Restraining a party to civil or commercial proceedings before the courts of another Member State

It is incompatible with the scheme of mutual trust and confidence which was put in place by the European Union, in legislation which includes the European Treaty[386] as well as Brussels I Regulation, for the courts of one Member State to grant an injunction to restrain another person from taking proceedings in a civil or commercial matter[387] before the courts of another Member State.[388]

In *Turner v. Grovit*,[389] proceedings were commenced in England by an employee against his employer; and a spoiling action was then brought against the employee by, or on behalf

---

384 [2005] EWCA Civ 985, [2005] 2 Lloyd's Rep 359.

385 Under Merchant Shipping Act 1995.

386 The current version of this is the Treaty on the Functioning of the European Union (TFEU): [2012] OJ C326/1.

387 But if the matter is outside the material scope of the Regulation, this principle is inapplicable: *Morris v. Davies* [2011] EWHC 1272 (Ch) (probate proceedings: the judgment shows that the application of the principles in cross-border probate cases is intensely fact-specific). For further consideration of the grant of anti-suit injunctions in cases of cross-border litigation of multiple wills, see *Re Tadros* [2014] EWHC 2860 (Ch).

388 But the restraint of arbitral proceedings in a Member State, in circumstances in which the court has already decided that the parties had not bound themselves to arbitrate but were instead bound by an exclusive jurisdiction clause for England, is another case entirely, and the injunction may be ordered: *Claxton Engineering Services Ltd v. TXM Olaj-és Gázkutató KFT* [2011] EWHC 345 (Comm), [2011] 1 Lloyd's Rep 510.

389 C-159/02, [2004] ECR I-3565, noted (2004) 120 LQR 529.

of, the employer before the Spanish courts. In the circumstances, the behaviour of the employer, in seeking to grind down the impecunious employee, was about as egregiously oppressive as it gets.[390] In addition, the English court was undoubtedly seised before the Spanish court. It was the view of the Court of Appeal, expressed in a judgment of remarkable rhetorical force, that the integrity of the English proceedings needed to be protected by the injunction, as well as the injunction being needed to protect the impecunious former employee from what was, on any view, unfair litigation; and England was, on any view, the proper forum for the action.

Despite all this, the Court of Justice held that the English court had no power to grant the injunction. The justifications proposed by the United Kingdom in defence of the power of its courts to grant anti-suit injunctions, such as the technical lack of direct interference with the foreign court, and the fact that the injunction strikes at unmeritorious or wrongful behaviour on the part of the respondent and not at all at the foreign court, and the fact that this may be necessary to defend the integrity of proceedings before the courts, and the like, were dismissed as being beside the point. The correct approach was to recognise that mutual trust and confidence was to be reposed in the judicial institutions of other Member States, and that it was for the Spanish court, and for it alone, to determine whether there was any jurisdictional flaw in the Spanish proceedings. For an English court to tell a foreign court, whether directly or indirectly, that it should not be exercising the jurisdiction which a party before it has invoked[391] and that it may not even examine for itself whether it has jurisdiction, was incompatible with that scheme. So if the matter is one which falls within the domain of the Brussels I Regulation,[392] no anti-suit injunction may be ordered against a party who has brought (or who may bring) proceedings in respect of it before a court in another Member State, to order him not to do so.[393]

It is irrelevant that proceedings have not been commenced before the court in the other Member State: the dominating question is not the jurisdictional one of which court was seised first,[394] but a substantive one of whether English courts have the power to grant anti-suit injunctions. It is irrelevant that the foreign proceedings appear to have been brought from the basest of base motives: this is a matter to be raised, if anywhere, before the court before which the objectionable proceedings have been brought. In the context of foreign proceedings brought in breach of an arbitration agreement, the answer is the same. For even though arbitration, as a process for dispute resolution, is outside the material scope of Article 1, the civil or commercial matter which the parties have agreed to arbitrate remains

---

390 The decision of the Court of Appeal at [2000] QB 345 left little room for doubt about it.

391 Ever since C-351/89 *Overseas Union Insurance Ltd v. New Hampshire Insurance Co* [1991] ECR I-3317 it was pretty clear that an English court had no power to assess for itself the jurisdiction of a foreign court; and it was a surprise that this disability had not been referred to in the judgment in *Continental Bank*. The die was finally cast in C-116/02 *Erich Gasser GmbH v. MISAT Srl* [2003] ECR I-14693, where the Court refused to allow a court which had jurisdiction on the basis of a jurisdiction agreement to proceed to hear the case while a spoiling action was still pending in the court of another Member State.

392 That is to say, in a civil or commercial matter.

393 It is clear that this decision is irrelevant to proceedings where the injunction is sought in relation to an action in a non-Member State: *Beazley v. Horizon Offshore Contractors Inc* [2004] EWHC 2555 (Comm), [2005] Lloyd's Rep IR 231. It is to be questioned whether it is applicable where the foreign court is acting in violation of Sections 3, 4, 5 or 6 of Chapter II of the Regulation, as in such cases the obligation to trust the adjudicating court is expressly contradicted by Art. 35(1) of Regulation 44/2001, and by Art. 45(1)(e) of Regulation 1215/2012.

394 Which would be answered by what is now Art. 29 of the recast Brussels I Regulation.

a civil or commercial one despite the agreement to arbitrate differences arising out of it. That being so, judicial proceedings relating to that subject matter still fall within the domain of the Brussels I Regulation, even if it is said that the parties have agreed that no court has jurisdiction to adjudicate and the foreign court is in error in believing that it is entitled to adjudicate.[395] This follows from *Allianz SpA v. West Tankers Inc*,[396] where the proceedings before the Italian court were in a civil or commercial matter, with the result that restraint of a party to those proceedings by anti-suit injunction was contrary to the scheme of the Regulation. It is not that the point shall not be decided, but that it shall be decided by the court in which the objected-to proceedings are brought.

The result of *Turner* and *West Tankers* is clear. The reasoning may not be to every taste, but perhaps the point actually is a short one, on which less is more: the jurisdictional rules of the Regulation are made so that each judge is able to read them and determine whether his court has jurisdiction to adjudicate. He does not need any help with that; and he certainly does not need any interference from another who thinks that he can make the decision better. The Spanish court in *Turner*, and the Italian court in *West Tankers*, was able to take its own decision whether it had jurisdiction, and that was more or less that.

Is it a matter of regret that an English court should be deprived of the power to impose a remedy which could be deployed to prevent breaches of contract? It is. Is it obvious that an English court is better placed to decide whether a case proceeding before the Italian courts should continue before the Italian courts? Perhaps it is not. At best, perhaps, the English court would have equal authority; but if the real question is whether the New York Convention, as adopted into Italian law, requires an Italian court to refer the parties to arbitration, the answer to that question is one for Italian law, and for an Italian court, to give. Is it helpful to observe that the English court is not actually assessing whether the foreign court has jurisdiction – it assumes that it does – but is examining whether there was a bilateral agreement to not invoke it, and is enforcing the obligations of that bilateral agreement? It is not helpful. For although it is entirely true, it is, at the same time, intervening in proceedings in a civil or commercial matter before the courts of another Member State. It is the latter which makes the former an irrelevance.

One possible response to the decision in *West Tankers* might be to apply for a decree of specific performance, ordering the respondent to perform and observe the obligations of a contract which it made. If those obligations connote a promise not to bring further judicial proceedings in respect of a matter which has been compromised, that promise may be enforced by a decree of specific performance, the fatal word 'injunction' being left unspoken and unordered.[397] The argument that the making of such an order does not interfere with the power of a foreign court to rule on its own jurisdiction is superficially correct, for the foreign court will form its own decision, though in the light of its obligations under Chapter III of the Regulation. Even so, this does look very much like a case of swapping around the labels on the bottle, and it would be surprising if this decision were to be accepted without question or demur.

---

395 For this analysis, see C–391/95 *Van Uden Maritime BV v. Deco-Line* [1998] ECR I-7091.

396 C–185/07, [2009] ECR I-663. It is possible that this conclusion will be reassessed by the European Court when it gives judgment in C–536/13 *Re Gazprom OAO*. Certainly the Opinion of the Advocate General (EU:C:2014:2414) invites it, in effect, to accept that its decision in *Allianz* was wrong. As a decision will be to hand soon after the manuscript of this book is handed in, further comment would serve no useful purpose.

397 *Starlight Shipping Co v. Allianz Marine & Aviation Versicherungs AG* [2014] EWHC 3068 (Comm) [2014] 2 Lloyd's Rep 579.

5.46 The exercise of discretion: public interest factors

Leaving aside the particular issues presented by the Brussels I Regulation, it will have become clear that in the decision whether to grant an injunction to restrain a respondent from instituting or continuing with proceedings in a foreign court, a balancing of private interests must be undertaken in order to decide whether to make the order. An injunction will not automatically be granted simply on the applicant's being able to show a legal right not to be sued, or to demonstrate that the respondent is behaving vexatiously or oppressively, or in some other way wrongfully, in circumstances in which England is the natural forum for the litigation. There are factors of the public interest to be taken into account as well; and the *prima facie*, or private interest, case for an injunction may be overridden by these issues of public interest.

The main concern is that the court should remember that its order may be seen by the foreign court as interference with its own decision on whether the proceedings before it should be allowed to proceed.[398] The technical point that the restraint is ordered against the party and not the judge should be understood in the light of a notable opinion of the Düsseldorf Regional Court of Appeal, namely that under German procedure, the courts are dependent on the cooperation of the parties, and that an anti-suit injunction directed against a party has a direct impact on the activities of the court; that free access to the courts is a constitutional right of every German citizen; that it is the right and the duty of the German courts, not foreign courts, to decide their competence in particular cases.[399] In the light of that, an English court should perhaps be cautious about making an order which may be viewed with such unease. As against this, the proposition that the court in *The Angelic Grace*[400] was unable to 'accept the proposition that any court would be offended by the grant of an injunction to restrain a party from invoking a jurisdiction which he had promised not to invoke and which it was its own duty to decline' needs reconsideration. In practice, matters may yet turn on which side adduces the more convincing evidence of what the foreign court would make of an English order. So even when the foreign proceedings are before the courts of a non-Member State, there is a need for caution.

Next, the court should be slow to indulge an applicant who invites it to make disparaging judgments about the civil procedures of foreign States. Although there have been occasional

---

398 See para. 5.32, above. But it is not only foreign judges who take umbrage when finding themselves on the blunt end of an injunction. The cat was well and truly let out of the bag in *General Star International Indemnity Ltd v. Stirling Cooke Brown Reinsurance Brokers Ltd* [2003] EWHC 3 (Comm), [2003] ILPr 314, and a very cross and contrary cat it turned out to be. A court in New York had ordered an anti-suit injunction against a party who had commenced proceedings before the English courts. So badly did the English judge take this that he ordered an anti-anti-suit injunction to prevent it. It does not appear that the observation that the American court's injunction was not aimed at the judge, but just at the supposed wrongdoer, would have lowered the temperature. The judge was perfectly clear that it prevented him from doing his job, and he was having none of it. See also *Tonicstar Ltd v. American Home Insurance Co* [2004] EWHC 1234 (Comm), [2005] Lloyd's Rep IR 32. See further, Briggs (2003) 74 BYBIL 532.

399 *Re an English Anti-suit Injunction* [1997] ILPr 320; see also *West Tankers Inc v. RAS Riunione Adriatica di Sicurta SpA* [2005] EWHC 454 (Comm), [2005] 2 Lloyd's Rep 257.

400 [1995] 1 Lloyd's Rep 87. See also *Bankers Trust plc v. RCS Editori SpA* [1996] CLC 899; and *Donohue v. Armco Inc* [2000] 1 Lloyd's Rep 579 (reversed without specific reference to this point: [2001] UKHL 64, [2002] 1 Lloyd's Rep 425). In *West Tankers Inc v. RAS Riunione Adriatica di Sicurta SpA* [2005] EWHC 454 (Comm), [2005] 2 Lloyd's Rep 257 the judge interpreted the evidence as suggesting that a foreign court (*in casu*, in Italy) would simply ignore the anti-suit injunction, rather than being offended by it. This may provide a fig-leaf to cover the court's embarrassment, but it is difficult to take it completely seriously, not least because evidence on whether the foreign court would disregard or be offended by the injunction must be practically impossible to furnish.

derogatory, if colourful,[401] appreciations of certain aspects of American civil procedure, a court should be circumspect before deciding that it is justifiable to hold up to the light of English law and examine a single aspect of civil procedure, or even a single cause of action, and reach the conclusion that its pursuit is objectionable when measured against English standards. Detached from their context, there are many aspects of English law and procedure which could be thought to be pretty odd. There is a suggestion that such adverse criticism may be entertained when the foreign court is not the natural forum;[402] but it is unclear that such a conclusion is defensible in principle. In the end, these factors may be taken by an applicant to assist an argument that there is oppression in the foreign proceedings; but if they are part of a serviceable system of civil justice, it is not right that they should be lightly or easily disparaged.

A distinct element of public interest recognises that a court has a public duty to secure the proper administration of justice, and that this may sometimes override the private interest of parties in holding each other to an agreement on jurisdiction. In *Donohue v. Armco Inc*,[403] the House of Lords refused to enforce by way of anti-suit injunction[404] an exclusive jurisdiction agreement for the English courts to which some, but not all, of the applicants and respondents were party. There being no question of allowing non-parties to derive any benefit from an agreement to which they were strangers,[405] and even less question of using it to impose restrictions on respondents who were not party to it and who had genuine claims which they wished to, and would, prosecute in the American courts in any event, it was accepted that there was strong reason for not enforcing the agreement by way of injunction against those parties who had bound themselves to the agreement on jurisdiction. The same point would arise if the material scope of the agreement were to be significantly narrow, so that the bringing of some claims did not fall within its range and would, even as between parties to the agreement, not involve a breach of its terms.[406] As it cannot be correct that parties may, by private agreement (otherwise than for arbitration), prevent the court from securing an orderly resolution of complex or multipartite disputes, the decision is wholly

---

401 *Smith Kline & French Laboratories Ltd v. Bloch* [1983] 1 WLR 730 ('As a moth is drawn to the light, so is a litigant drawn to the United States. If only he can get his case into their courts he stands to win a fortune. At no cost to himself, and at no risk of having to pay anything to the other side…There is also in the United States a right to trial by jury. These are prone to award fabulous damages. They are notoriously sympathetic and know the lawyers will take their 40% before the plaintiff gets anything …'); *Midland Bank plc v. Laker Airways Ltd* [1986] QB 689 ('That the United States pre-trial procedure in an anti-trust suit is, by English thinking, oppressive has been said many times…'").

402 This was also said to be the reason why the criticisms were evidently entertained in *Smith Kline & French Laboratories v. Bloch* and in *Midland Bank plc v. Laker Airways Ltd*. If the foreign forum is an inappropriate one on the facts, such arguments will probably receive a more sympathetic hearing. But if these are objectionable factors, they should be so wherever the natural forum may lie; and if they are not, it is hard to see why the location of the natural forum should alter this characterisation of them.

403 [2001] UKHL 64, [2002] 1 All ER 749.

404 But it was proposed that, if the agreement were broken by proceedings in the American courts, it could be enforced by an action for damages: at [36] and [48]. For a further analysis of the issues of difficulty which may arise in this context, especially where the action for damages involves contradiction of conclusions reached by the foreign court in the proceedings before it, see the comment on this case and on *Union Discount Co v. Zoller* [2001] EWCA Civ 1755, [2002] 1 WLR 1517: see also (2001) 72 BYBIL 437, 446; Tan and Yeo [2003] LMCLQ 435; Tham [2004] LMCLQ 46; Tan (2005) 40 Tex Int LJ 623 (on the relatively undeveloped state of American authority).

405 The case was unaffected by the Contracts (Rights of Third Parties) Act 1999, but in any event the jurisdiction agreement did not purport to confer a benefit on any non-party.

406 On this, see also differences in appreciation as between Lord Bingham of Cornhill and Lord Scott of Foscote.

rational,[407] and marks a limit on the power of the parties to write the rules of civil litigation for themselves. Of course, even if an anti-suit injunction is not available, a separate question will arise as to whether a damages remedy may be available instead.[408]

5.47 The exercise of discretion: if the respondent can win only by suing overseas

If the respondent will fail in his claim on the merits if he is prevented from suing in the foreign court, it is sometimes suggested that the principles which determine whether an injunction may be granted are distinct. It is proper to observe that the balance of authority does vouch for this distinction: the terminology of 'single forum' has its origins in *British Airways Board v. Laker Airways Ltd*[409] and *Airbus Industrie GIE v. Patel*,[410] and in advancing the submission that it is unprincipled to draw a distinction in these terms it has to be first acknowledged that little attempt is being made to derive the analysis from these leading cases. But sometimes these things cannot be avoided.

In *British Airways Board v. Laker Airways Ltd*, the cause of action relied on in the American courts by the respondent, the liquidator of Laker Airways, was created by the Clayton and Sherman Acts.[411] An action in the English courts could not be founded on this legislation, for English choice of law rules, or public policy,[412] or both, would have precluded it. It was therefore contended that the respondent could sue in the United States or nowhere at all; and Lord Diplock appeared to regard this as justifying some form of departure from the principles which would have been applied when an injunction was applied for in an 'alternative forum' case. In *Airbus Industrie GIE v. Patel*, Lord Goff travelled some distance down this road, and noted that the general requirement, that England be the natural forum, could not be relied on to secure the interests of comity in this context.[413] But he did not need to develop the particular rules which would be applied to such cases. By contrast, the Court of Appeal in *Midland Bank plc v. Laker Airways Ltd*[414] had felt able to restrain the party bringing proceedings of a similar nature without being deflected by the fact that the liquidator would have been unable to prosecute a successful claim in the English courts; and in *Through Transport Mutual Insurance Association (Eurasia) Ltd v. New India Assurance Co Ltd*,[415] the Court of Appeal, though in the end it set aside the injunction, seemed to regard as irrelevant the fact that the respondent would win in Finland but lose if required to advance the same claim in England.

It is submitted that all that is required to bring a sense of balance and reason to this corner of the law is to express the *Airbus v. Patel* criterion in terms of whether England is the natural forum for the resolution of the dispute between the parties. If it is, it is appropriate for the court to restrain the respondent if the proceedings in the foreign court infringe the

---

407 Following and approving *Bouygues Offshore SA v. Caspian Shipping Co (Nos 1, 3, 4, 5)* [1998] 2 Lloyd's Rep 461; also *Society of Lloyd's v. White* [2002] ILPr 11.

408 See below, para. 5.53.

409 [1985] AC 58.

410 [1999] 1 AC 119.

411 Regulating anti-competitive practices, allowing for treble damages, and so forth.

412 The claim was for treble damages, which may offend whatever policy underlies the Protection of Trading Interests Act 1980, s. 5.

413 At 138. For the validity of the distinction, see 134.

414 [1986] QB 689.

415 [2004] EWCA Civ 1598, [2005] 1 Lloyd's Rep 67. For further proceedings, see [2005] EWHC 455 (Comm), [2005] 2 Lloyd's Rep 378.

applicant's legal or equitable right not to be sued. Nothing more is needed. It is, after all, contrary to the guiding philosophy of *Spiliada Maritime Corporation v. Cansulex Ltd* [416] to refuse to order a stay of English proceedings just because the claimant will fare less well in the natural forum than he would in England: the law should not, and the test in its proper form does not, contain a bias in favour of a claimant.[417] Neither should the law on anti-suit injunctions contain an inherent preference for the respondent: the fact that he can win only in the foreign court should be as irrelevant as the fact, if it be the case, that the defendant to English proceedings can successfully defend only in England: one may perhaps call this a 'defendant's single forum' case. Impartiality really does not allow for any significant departure from this approach.

It further follows that it was not helpful to characterise *British Airways Board v. Laker Airways Ltd* and *Airbus Industrie GIE v. Patel* as 'single forum cases'. Nothing except discouraging legal advice prevented the liquidator of Laker Airways Ltd from suing British Airways, or Midland Bank, in England. It might be different if the English court would have no personal or subject-matter jurisdiction at all, such as where the claim concerned title to foreign land. But such cases are rare, and are not what the nomenclature of 'single forum cases' currently seeks to describe.

5.48 Active case management as an alternative solution

In a number of recent cases a claimant has brought proceedings in the courts of two countries at more or less the same time. In some, the relief sought from each court appears to be much the same; in others, some or all the relief available from the one court would not be available from the other. Although these may be seen as cases which lend themselves to the ordinary form of anti-suit injunction,[418] and which may be analysed in terms of legal or equitable rights not to be subjected to such litigation, a discernible trend has developed of seeing this as a problem which sometimes lends itself to resolution by taking effective case management decisions, presumably because case-management orders are less likely to cause offence to other courts in which their effects may be felt than the anti-suit injunction is.

If the two actions are brought by the claimant for practically identical relief, and if judgment in either would appear to be likely to be enforceable for the full sum said to be owing, the likelihood is that the claimant will be put to his election and required to choose one and submit to the staying or dismissal of the other;[419] though, if it has been expressly agreed by the parties that this may happen, the chances of intervention from the court to override the parties' explicit agreement are substantially reduced.[420] But if the relief is not substantially

---

416 [1987] AC 460. See the discussion at paras 4.30 *et seq.*, above.

417 It is different if, as in *Lubbe v. Cape plc* [2000] 1 WLR 1545, the difficulty facing one party is one of finance and funding. This has nothing to do with a preference for one party being more likely to succeed in one or the other court.

418 But which will, according to principle, sometimes not be available even if there are parallel proceedings: see above, para. 5.36.

419 *Australian Commercial Research and Development Ltd v. ANZ McCaughan Merchant Bank Ltd* [1989] 3 All ER 65. On the other hand, the court may consider that the respondent has behaved sufficiently badly that it is oppressive for the foreign proceedings to have been brought, and these will therefore be restrained without a question of election: *CNA Insurance Co Ltd v. Office Depot International* [2005] EWHC 456 (Comm), [2005] Lloyd's Rep IR 658.

420 *Royal Bank of Canada v. Cooperatieve Centrale Raiffeisen-Boerenleenbank* [2004] EWCA Civ 7, [2004] 1 Lloyd's Rep 471.

overlapping, a court may order some form of temporary restraint, or may adjourn its own proceedings,[421] or may give directions for a speedy trial of an issue in English action,[422] so as to make the substantive issues *res judicata* and liable to be recognised as such by the other court. The advantage of such an approach, which may require some muscular encouragement from the court, is obvious: it is preferable that an orderly resolution of disputes be brought about without the need for injunctions;[423] and in the context of the Brussels I Regulation, where anti-suit injunctions have now been generally proscribed, it will offer the possibility of a solution[424] which is not inconsistent with that instrument, even if it has the appearance of encouraging a race to judgment.

It has been held that a court may issue an interim anti-suit injunction in the exercise of its powers of case management where the proper order is for a speedy trial of the issue before the English court and it is thought desirable to preserve the situation in order to allow the decision of the English court to be effective.[425] But it would be quite wrong to see the anti-suit injunction as liable to be granted whenever the abstract interest of case management would have made it attractive for a foreign action to be interrupted or prevented. The anti-suit injunction protects jurisdiction and prevents wrongdoing. It is not part of the ordinary toolkit of case management.

5.49 Canadian and Australian authority and its irrelevance

It is necessary to say something about the distinctive directions in which the law has developed in Canada and Australia, partly in order to illuminate the jurisprudence of the English courts, and partly to mark the limited extent to which authorities from these jurisdictions are useful in England. For although the principle has a common root, and as *SNI Aerospatiale v. Lee Kui Jak*[426] has been approved by the highest courts in the two countries, there are surprisingly large divergences within the present state of the common law.

In Canada, the Supreme Court has embarked on something which looks like an ambitious project to bring an intellectual unity to the law on Canadian jurisdiction, the recognition of foreign judgments,[427] and anti-suit injunctions. In *Amchem Products Inc v. British Columbia (Workers' Compensation Board)*,[428] an attempt was made to obtain an anti-suit injunction to prevent proceedings before the Texas courts. The Supreme Court approached the issue by enquiring whether the foreign court had taken jurisdiction on principles which were in general accordance with the Canadian principles of *forum conveniens*. If it had, its

---

421 *Abbassi v. Abbassi* [2006] EWCA Civ 355, [2006] 2 FLR 415.

422 *Reichhold Norway ASA v. Goldman Sachs International* [2000] 1 WLR 173; *Ledra Fisheries Ltd v. Turner* [2003] EWHC 1049 (Ch); *Duke Group Ltd v. Alamein Investments Ltd*, 14 April 2003; *Racy v. Hawila* [2004] EWCA Civ 209; *Al Bassam v. Al Bassam* [2004] EWCA Civ 857, [2004] WTLR 757.

423 See on this, *Deutsche Bank AG v. Highland Crusader Offshore Partners LP* [2009] EWCA Civ 725, [2010] 1 WLR 1023, [104].

424 Always assuming that the English court is not precluded by the rules of the Regulation on *lis alibi pendens* from exercising jurisdiction over the merits of the claim.

425 *Midgulf International Ltd v. Groupe Chimiche Tunisien* [2009] EWHC 963 (Comm).

426 [1987] AC 871.

427 *Morguard Investments Ltd v. De Savoye* [1990] 3 SCR 1077. In that case, a judgment was held to be entitled to recognition by reason of its coming from a court having a real and substantial connection with the dispute. It was followed and extended in *Beals v. Saldanha* [2003] 3 SCR 416. It may be that, in time, this will come to be read as a reference to a judgment from the courts of the natural forum.

428 [1993] 1 SCR 897.

decision to adjudicate would be respected and an injunction would not be ordered.[429]. But by contrast, if the foreign court was exercising a jurisdiction inconsistent with the principles of *forum conveniens*, as understood in Canada, there would be a presumption in favour of an anti-suit injunction. The question for the Canadian court would then be whether it would be unjust to deprive the respondent of the right to proceed in the foreign court, but if it would not be unjust,[430] an injunction will be liable to be granted, because the foreign court 'not having, itself, observed the rules of comity, cannot expect its decision to be respected on the basis of comity'.[431] In other words, the Canadian interpretation of comity concerns itself with, and makes its evaluation of the foreign proceedings by measuring against Canadian standards the jurisdiction exercised by the foreign court. One effect of placing this primary focus on the jurisdictional rules of the foreign court and the manner in which it applies them is that the applicant will normally be expected to have applied to the foreign court for jurisdictional relief before he seeks an injunction from the Canadian court.[432]

In Canada, therefore, the Canadian court makes its own assessment of the jurisdiction being asserted by the foreign court. In Australia, the analysis is almost diametrically opposite. In *CSR Ltd v. Cigna Insurance Australia Ltd*,[433] the High Court of Australia did not consider that it was appropriate for an Australian court to make an assessment of the jurisdiction of the foreign court, *in casu* the courts of New Jersey. The High Court held instead that the equitable basis for an injunction may be made out in either one of two ways. The first basis would be by pointing to a transaction between the parties which in equity obliged the respondent not to sue;[434] the second would be by proof of vexation or oppression.[435] But according to the High Court, there was no vexation or oppression by a respondent if any part of the relief claimed by him in the foreign court would be unavailable from an Australian court; and once that conclusion was reached the enquiry was complete. Any appraisal of the jurisdiction of the foreign court was ruled out, and the fact that enforcement of the judgment of the American court would be forbidden enforcement in Australia by statute[436] was, in effect, the very factor which immunised it from the allegation of vexation: if the judgment could not be imported into Australia, it would not be doing any harm which an Australian court could properly prevent.[437] By way of qualification to this, it appears that if an action

---

429 At 932, 934.

430 It will not be unjust to deprive him of an advantage available in a forum with which the claim has little or no connection.

431 At 934.

432 At 931.

433 (1997) 189 CLR 345. See also (1998) 114 LQR 27, Bell (1997) 71 ALJ 955. In effect this was a 'single forum' case, in which the relief available from the court in New Jersey was available only from it. In that the High Court saw this as a powerful argument against the grant of an injunction, it lends a little support to the existence of a separate category of case in which it will be more than usually difficult to obtain the injunction.

434 In this respect it represents the equitable counterpart of the legal right not to be sued generated by contracts. It will be exemplified by estoppel or representation.

435 The Court also acknowledged that an injunction may be granted to protect the jurisdiction of the local court; and it reiterated its distinctive approach, noting its difference from the English approach (at least prior to *Turner v. Grovit* [2001] UKHL 65, [2002] 1 WLR 107) in *Australian Broadcasting Corporation v. Lenah Game Meats Pty Ltd* (2001) 208 CLR 199, esp. at [94]. Equally, Australian law does not require the applicant to first seek relief from the foreign court itself: *Ace Insurance Ltd v. Moose Enterprise Pty Ltd* [2009] NSWSC 724.

436 The respondent was claiming treble damages, with the result that enforcement would be precluded by Foreign Proceedings (Excess of Jurisdiction) Act 1984 (C'th), legislation resembling the Protection of Trading Interests Act 1980.

437 Such relief being unavailable from an Australian court.

is commenced after, and with a view to frustrating, an earlier action, it will be oppressive or vexatious: this was the reason given for staying the Australian action brought in *CSR* a few days after the institution of proceedings in New Jersey. But whether this would be applied in mirror image to foreign proceedings brought after an action commenced in Australia is hard to tell from the judgment.

The Australian approach is irreconcilable with the position taken by English law. The decision in *Midland Bank plc v. Laker Airways Ltd*[438] could not have been derived from the reasoning in *CSR*, and the broad proposition that, as long as the claimed relief is different, the proceedings cannot be vexatious is unhelpful if one wishes the anti-suit injunction to remain a flexible and case-sensitive remedy. If the Australian approach means that the odder the relief claimed from the foreign court the harder the order will be to obtain, any lawyer worth his salt will see how to inoculate his client against the threat of an Australian anti-suit injunction. Neither does the case appear to allow the court to consider, as was done in *Aérospatiale*, the consequences and the injustices of allowing the foreign action to proceed; nor the closeness of the connection between the dispute and the local court. It is, therefore, submitted that, notwithstanding the courteous reference to *CSR* which was made in *Airbus v. Patel*, the decision is so distant from the English approach as to be irrelevant to it.

5.50 The timing of the application for an injunction

Apart from the question of jurisdiction to order the injunction, it is also noteworthy that the timing of the application may be crucial. If foreign proceedings have progressed too far, it may be too late for the court to make an order that these be aborted;[439] and it may even be that if the applicant has submitted to the jurisdiction of the foreign court, an injunction should in principle not be granted.[440] But if made too early, the application may also fail. The point is illustrated by the first instance Scottish decision in *Pan American World Airways v. Andrews*.[441] After the explosion of a passenger aircraft in Scottish airspace and subsequent crash, it was feared by the airline that proceedings were about to be commenced against it in the American courts. An attempt was made to obtain an injunction from the Scottish courts on the ground that Scotland was the natural forum, that the estimated cost of the American proceedings would hugely exceed the corresponding Scottish equivalent, and that to sue the airline in the United States was oppressive. The application failed *in limine*: the court observed that, if American proceedings were commenced, they could be challenged in America on *forum conveniens* grounds; and that it was premature to order an injunction to prevent the institution of the proceedings. It appeared that the court might have been willing to order an injunction had it been much clearer than it was that the Scottish forum was the only proper one; and also that if a *forum conveniens* challenge were made unsuccessfully in the American courts, the application for an injunction could be revived. At first sight

---

438 [1986] QB 689. In *Airbus Industrie plc v. Patel*, Lord Goff of Chieveley declined to express a view on *Midland Bank v. Laker*. Yet the facts were so extreme it is hard to believe it could be held to have been wrongly decided.

439 *Toepfer International GmbH v. Molino Boschi Srl* [1996] 1 Lloyd's Rep 510; *Schiffahrtsgesellschaft Detlev von Appen v. Vöst Alpine Intertrading GmbH, The 'Jay Bola'* [1997] 2 Lloyd's Rep 279; *The Skier Star* [2008] 1 Lloyd's Rep 652.

440 See above, para. 5.36.

441 1992 SLT 268.

it may be thought that the balance of convenience lay just where the court thought it did.[442] That the first port of call should be the foreign court was also accepted as being generally correct in *Barclays Bank plc v. Homan*.[443]

By contrast, the approach in *The Angelic Grace*[444] would suggest that the more quickly the English application is made, the greater is the prospect of its success; and as to the proposition that the applicant should first be required to make an application to the foreign court for jurisdictional relief, Leggatt LJ pointed out that for the English court then to sit, as it were, as a court of appeal or review from that decision was the very opposite of what comity may be expected to require. Indeed, in cases where the English court grants relief after the foreign court has refused to,[445] it has been necessary to treat the foreign court as having been, in one way or another, misled to the conclusion it reached. The delicacy of the position is obvious.

It is submitted that the correct analysis is that application to the foreign court should not be a precondition to an English application, though an applicant who wishes to have two bites at the cherry is well advised to consider it. In the light of *Amchem Products Inc v. British Columbia (Workers' Compensation Board)*,[446] it can be seen that the Canadian version of comity is constructed in such a way as to make application to the foreign court an integral element of the test. But in *Airbus v. Patel*, Lord Goff honoured the requirement of comity in quite a different way:[447] by refusing to consider an application for an injunction unless England is the natural forum for the litigation. If England *is* the natural forum for the litigation, comity will be satisfied, and it does not need to be satisfied further by prior application to the foreign court; if England is the natural forum, it is hard to see that objection could be taken to its courts' entertaining the application on the ground that an application had not been first made to the courts of an inappropriate forum. For this reason it is submitted that the suggestion in *Barclays Bank plc v. Homan* should not now[448] be taken as correct. It follows that prior application to the foreign court is not and should not be a prerequisite to an application for an anti-suit injunction to restrain proceedings which are pending or are imminent; but if England may not be shown to be the natural forum, such an application may be the only one the applicant may make.

5.51 Measures ancillary to a final anti-suit injunction

An anti-suit injunction is a powerful remedy, even if its use is no longer generally permissible to grant it in relation to proceedings in civil and commercial matters brought elsewhere

---

442 If the airline were to seek, but fail to obtain, such relief from the American court, it is implicit that it would not be faced with a plea of estoppel if it revived its application in the Scottish court. It is not wholly clear why this is so, unless it can be argued that the American judgment was not final and conclusive. Indeed, for the proposition that it might be so embarrassed, see *Desert Sun Loan Corp v. Hill* [1996] 2 All ER 847. The question of issue estoppel to which this gives rise is far from straightforward, and this may tilt the balance in favour of making the first application to the English court.

443 [1993] BCLC 680.

444 [1995] 1 Lloyd's Rep 87. This aspect of the reasoning of the court is unaffected by the decision in C-159/02 *Turner v. Grovit* [2004] ECR I-3565.

445 *Donohue v. Armco Inc* [2000] 1 Lloyd's Rep 579 (this aspect was not dealt with on the further appeal to the House of Lords); *Society of Lloyd's v. White* [2000] CLC 961.

446 [1993] 1 SCR 897.

447 It is proper to observe that while he paid a generous tribute to Sopinka J, author of the judgment in *Amchem*, he did not specifically endorse it for use in England.

448 In this respect it has been overtaken by the elucidation of principle in *Airbus*.

within Europe. It may be used to achieve many aims. One of these may be to prevent a case being heard in a foreign court. Another may be to delay or impede progress in proceedings pending in a foreign court, so that local proceedings may catch up and come on for trial sooner in time than these competing proceedings. The recognition of these facts of commercial life has led to the development of two further[449] ancillary measures, both important in protecting the effectiveness of an anti-suit injunction.

The first is that an applicant for such an injunction may also seek an interlocutory anti-suit injunction, to hold the ring until the claim for a final anti-suit injunction can be heard.[450] If the interim injunction is treated like any other interlocutory injunction, its being granted should be determined on the basis of a simple balance of convenience,[451] rather than according to the more demanding standard which the applicant or claimant is required to meet to obtain a final injunction. But if the injunction, even though interim, will have the practical effect of being final, it should be ordered only on meeting the standard of proof required for a final injunction.[452]

Second, the applicant may have a well-founded fear that the respondent, if he gets wind of the fact that an anti-suit injunction may be sought against him, may seek relief of his own from the court in which he wishes to sue. This relief may take the form of an anti-anti-suit injunction.[453] The applicant in his turn, who fears that his opponent may act in this way, may seek to protect his position by seeking an anti-anti-anti-suit injunction.[454] Such orders have been made, inevitably without notice in the first instance;[455] and whatever their legitimacy or other abstract virtues, they bear striking testimony to the importance of winning jurisdictional battles in modern trans-national commercial litigation. It is, after all, inevitable that such judicial paralysing of each party by the other will give rise to some form of negotiation.

---

449 That is, in addition to case management techniques.

450 In relation to these, the Brussels I Regulation might at first sight appear to provide no jurisdictional obstacle, as the non-final interlocutory injunction should be seen to fall, as a provisional or protective measure which will be accompanied by an undertaking in damages, within Art. 35 (as to which see Chapter 6, below). On the other hand, if a final anti-suit injunction is precluded by *Turner v. Grovit*, it is difficult to see that an order ancillary to it could properly be granted; and the conclusion probably is that *Turner v. Grovit* prevents these as well.

451 *Apple Corps Ltd v. Apple Computer Inc* [1992] RPC 70, 76–77. There will still be a need, in the interlocutory application, for caution in granting anti-suit injunctions: see also *National Westminster Bank Ltd v. Utrecht-America Finance Co* [2001] EWCA Civ 658, [2001] 2 All ER (Comm) 7, [28]–[29]. But in principle, *American Cyanamid Co v. Ethicon Ltd* [1975] AC 396 will be the applicable doctrine.

452 *Malhotra v. Malhotra* [2012] EWHC 3020 (Comm), [2013] 1 Lloyd's Rep 285; *cf Rimpacific Navigation Inc v. Daehan Shipbuilding Co Ltd* [2009] EWHC 2941 (Comm), [2010] 2 Lloyd's Rep 236 (which appears to suggest that if there is a very good arguable case that there is a jurisdiction agreement, an injunction may be ordered).

453 To order the applicant, as respondent to the pre-emptive application in the foreign courts, not to seek relief by way of anti-suit injunction. It appears to be a common form of order to obtain from certain American courts, sometimes apparently issued spontaneously by the court. See for illustration *Shell (UK) Exploration and Production Ltd v. Innes* 1995 SLT 807. In England, anti-suit injunctions have tended to be retaliatory rather than pre-emptive: *General Star International Indemnity Ltd v. Stirling Cooke Brown Reinsurance Brokers Ltd* [2003] EWHC 3 (Comm), [2003] ILPr 314; *Sabah Shipyard (Pakistan) Ltd v. Islamic Republic of Pakistan* [2002] EWCA Civ 1643, [2003] 2 Lloyd's Rep 571, but this must be an accident of case reporting rather than a matter of principle.

454 To restrain the respondent from seeking an anti-anti-suit injunction from the court in which he wishes the proceedings to go ahead.

455 *Shell (UK) Exploration and Production Ltd v. Innes* 1995 SLT 807 (evidently there was a similar order obtained from the English courts).

5.52 Consequences of disobedience to an anti-suit injunction

If the respondent fails to comply with the anti-suit injunction, two consequences are liable to follow.

The first is that he is liable to be proceeded against in England for his contempt of the English court's order. This may be inconvenient; he is at risk if he is present in, or returns to, England, or has assets within reach of the English court. The remedy may not be completely effective, but the threat of such coercion will often be sufficient to secure compliance. Second, it should follow that the foreign judgment obtained will not be entitled to recognition or enforcement in England at the behest of a party who has disobeyed an injunction in obtaining it: public policy must, at the very least, require this sanction to be available to discourage contempt.[456] There is a faint counter-argument, capable of being derived from the provisions of the European Convention on Human Rights, which would contend that for a court to refuse to enforce a judgment as a punishment for contempt of court may be disproportionate to the wrong committed by the respondent, and so may constitute a breach of Article 6 ECHR. Whether this is correct depends first on whether the refusal to enforce a judgment, which is presumably enforceable where it was given, amounts to a refusal of access to a court for a determination of rights; and in any event, if a court considers the matter carefully and considers that a refusal to enforce the judgment is proportionate to the wrong, there should be little scope for a successful challenge. But the consequences of breach of an anti-suit injunction are internal to England. They do not, and cannot, assert any extraterritorial effect.

(E) DAMAGES FOR WRONGFUL LITIGATION

5.53 A cause of action for compensation for wrongful litigation

If the court declines[457] to issue an anti-suit injunction, or if it accepts that where an injunction may not be ordered, the gap may not be filled by an artful application for a decree of specific performance,[458] the applicant may not be completely without remedy for the legal or equitable wrong which has been done to him. A party to a contract who breaches that contract is in principle liable to pay damages for its breach; a person who tortiously seeks to undermine or interfere with a contract may be liable to pay damages in tort; and a court which declines to issue an injunction has a statutory power[459] to order damages in lieu.

---

456 *Cf Ellerman Lines Ltd v. Read* [1928] 2 KB 144; *Phillip Alexander Securities & Futures Ltd v. Bamberger* [1997] ILPr 73, 115. However, a rather different view was taken in *Golubovich v. Golubovich* [2010] EWCA Civ 810, [2011] Fam 88, where the foreign judgment was a decree of divorce obtained contrary to the terms of a Hemain order. Either the distinct nature of the proceedings, or the fact that a Hemain order is slightly different from an anti-suit injunction in commercial cases, may explain the outcome which is otherwise surprising.

457 Or is prohibited, as in *Turner v. Grovit*.

458 In *Starlight Shipping Co v. Allianz Marine & Aviation Versicherungs AG* [2014] EWHC 3068 (Comm) [2014] 2 Lloyd's Rep 579, the court was willing to grant a decree, even though one effect of the order – only one effect, but never mind – was to require the respondent not to bring proceedings before the courts of another Member State. The view taken here is that this may be seen as an exercise in sophistry which cannot be allowed to subvert a broader principle of European law.

459 Chancery Amendment Act (Lord Cairns' Act) 1858, s. 2; now Senior Courts Act 1981, s. 50. The power is given whenever there is jurisdiction (as distinct from a jurisdiction which would in fact be exercised) to grant the injunction.

These principles apply to contracts, torts and equitable wrongs relating to dispute resolution as they apply to all other legal relationships.[460]

If the court has jurisdiction over the defendant, proof of the claimant's or applicant's having sustained loss which resulted from the breach should lay the basis for a claim for compensation. It is necessary to consider, first, a claim for damages for breach of a jurisdiction agreement or arbitration agreement, and second, the extent to which a claim for equitable compensation or damages may be brought in an English court against one whose behaviour in suing in a foreign court is unconscionable or otherwise inequitable.

It is important to notice that the basis for the claim is that it rests on a bilateral relationship between claimant and defendant according to the terms of which (and for consideration) promises were exchanged on the time, manner and place of dispute resolution. Such an agreement may have consequences for the jurisdiction of courts, for example, by prorogating or derogating from jurisdiction; but it also has a discrete function as a mutually binding agreement as to when, how and where the parties will and will not issue proceedings against each other. It is this separate, bilateral, agreement whose breach sounds in damages; and the damages are, in principle, the losses caused by the institution and continuation of legal proceedings which the defendant had contracted not to bring.

The principle that damages may be awarded against a party who sued in a foreign court and obtained judgment when he was under a legal obligation not to can certainly be traced back to *Ellerman Lines Ltd v. Read*.[461] In that case the defendant, who had agreed to pursue any claim by arbitration in London, arrested the claimant's vessel and sued in the courts at Constantinople. The Court of Appeal ordered the defendant to refrain from seeking to enforce the Turkish judgment he should never have sought, and awarded damages to reverse the judgment debt.[462] The principle that damages could be obtained for breach of an agreement on where to sue then appears to have gone to sleep until it was awakened by the decision of the Court of Appeal in *Union Discount Co Ltd v. Zoller*.[463] Though that decision rested on a rather narrow basis, it breathed new life into the rule of the common law that breach of an agreement on choice of court sounded in damages. It was quickly followed by the acceptance of the House of Lords, if by way of *obiter dicta*, of a concession by counsel in *Donohue v. Armco Inc*,[464] that there may be a rather wider principle at work in such cases; and thereafter by *dicta* at the highest level[465] which mean that the soundness of the principle

---

460 See generally, Briggs, *Agreements on Jurisdiction and Choice of Law* (2008), ch. 8. See also Briggs (2001) 72 BYBIL 437, 446; Tan and Yeo [2003] LMCLQ 435; Tham [2004] LMCLQ 46; Tan (2005) 40 Tex Int LJ 623; Merrett (2006) 55 ICLQ 315.

461 [1928] 2 KB 144.

462 It did so by characterising the defendant's behaviour as having been fraudulent (a term with a long history in the common law of foreign judgments) as distinct from a breach of contract (which was at that stage less frequently referred to in the law of foreign judgments), but nothing turns on this, as the wrong which gave rise to the epithet of fraudulent was the plain breach of contract.

463 [2001] EWCA Civ 1755, [2002] 1 WLR 1517: the claim was for losses caused by successfully challenging the jurisdiction of a foreign court but not getting a complete indemnity in costs.

464 [2001] UKHL 64, [2002] 1 All ER 749: the concession was that if proceedings were brought in the United States in respect of claims within the scope of an English jurisdiction clause, damages for breach of contract would in principle be recoverable.

465 *AES Ust-Kamenogorsk Hydropower Plant JSC v. AES Ust-Kamenogorsk Hydropower Plant LLP* [2013] UKSC 35, [2013] 1 WLR 1889, [25]; *The Alexandros T* [2013] UKSC 70, [2014] 1 All ER 590, [36]–[39], [131]–[132], [135]; *Starlight Shipping Co v. Allianz Marine & Aviation Versicherungs AG* [2014] EWCA Civ 1010, [2014] 2 Lloyd's Rep 554, (which applied the law as laid down in *The Alexandros T* and concluded that there was no infringement of European law in permitting the claim for damages to be made; for the view that the same approach is taken to

cannot be considered to be in any doubt. It may be unusual for the soundness of a principle to be established almost entirely by *dicta*, but the view of the Supreme Court is so settled that it does not seem that a challenge to this judicial understanding would be fruitful.

A contractual agreement on jurisdiction may, if broken,[466] support a claim for damages for breach: the issue is not whether such claims are well founded, but whether there are any limits which are specific to the particular kind of contract and particular kind of breach. In principle, the right to recover damages will, if not admitted, be held to depend on the law which governs the particular agreement relied on,[467] or if the claim is formulated as a tort or other non-contractual obligation, upon the law which governs that obligation doing likewise. But in the absence of proof that it is different, foreign law will be taken to be the same as English law which, as the cases now show as a response to wrongful litigation, does allow a damages claim.

5.54 Damages for breach of a jurisdiction agreement: principle

The modern law starts with *Union Discount Co v. Zoller*. There, a claim had been brought by an investor before an American court. The defendant to those proceedings challenged the jurisdiction of the American court by reference to an exclusive jurisdiction agreement for the English courts. The American court held that the agreement on jurisdiction was valid and binding, and dismissed the proceedings, but its procedural law meant that it could not award costs to the successful party. The victim of this breach of contract, substantially out of pocket as a result, brought a claim against the investor for damages before the English courts. When the investor applied to have the claim struck out, on the ground that English domestic law[468] precluded a civil claim for damages in respect of unrecovered costs, the application was dismissed in terms which made it pretty clear that, as far as the Court of Appeal was concerned, the claim was so well founded that it could have given summary judgment in the claimant's favour.[469]

Though the result was that the court accepted that damages could be awarded for breach of an agreement on jurisdiction, it could not be said that the decision to award damages to the claimant, who had won in the United States, subverted or undermined, still less contradicted, the American judgment: it built on it, and drew further consequences from it. In *Donohue v. Armco Inc*, the concession made by counsel and accepted by the court did not need to test the limits of the principle that breach of a jurisdiction clause gave a cause of action for damages. The case was one in which there was an unquestioned contractual right not to be sued in

---

an application for a decree of specific performance of contractual obligations, see *Starlight Shipping Co v. Allianz Marine & Aviation Versicherungs AG* [2014] EWHC 3068 (Comm) [2014] 2 Lloyd's Rep 579. The question whether all or any of this is right, and whether it may be held to violate the European principle of effectiveness, remains to be addressed on another day.

466 Potentially complicated issues of mistake or frustration will arise if the nominated court could not have exercised, or has declined to exercise, jurisdiction. Their resolution would appear to rely on orthodox principles of the law of contract.

467 *Cf A v. B* [2007] EWHC 54 (Comm), [2007] 1 Lloyd's Rep 358 (where the issue was dealt with as costs).

468 *Quartz Hill Consolidated Gold Mining Co v. Eyre* (1883) 11 QBD 674; *Berry v. British Transport Commission* [1962] 1 QB 306; applied to foreign judgments in *The Ocean Dynamic* [1982] 2 Lloyd's Rep 88 (which was distinguishable).

469 No doubt with damages to be assessed. But the rule in *Berry v. British Transport Commission* [1962] 1 QB 306 still applies where the proceedings wrongfully brought are brought in England, which was why costs were awarded on the indemnity basis in *A v. B* [2007] EWHC 54 (Comm), [2007] 1 Lloyd's Rep 358.

the United States, which derived from a valid and binding promise not to bring proceedings elsewhere than in an English court. Subject to its being shown what loss had flowed from its breach, it was accepted by counsel and the court that if proceedings brought in the United States were not restrained, and invoked or relied on claims and causes of action which could not have been maintained before an English court, damages for breach would be recoverable.

In *AES Ust-Kamenogorsk Hydropower Plant JSC v. AES Ust-Kamenogorsk Hydropower Plant LLP*[470] the court issued an injunction to restrain a party to an arbitration from bringing proceedings in Kazakhstan on the basis that an arbitration agreement for London connoted a promise not to bring proceedings in any other forum; but the court observed, as though it were a matter of course, that the *prima facie* right to damages for bringing or continuing proceedings in breach of a jurisdiction agreement had been established in *Donohue v. Armco Inc.* And in *The Alexandros T*[471] the Supreme Court considered that the only real issue which arose when proceedings in England sought damages for breach of an exclusive jurisdiction agreement was whether the court had jurisdiction in the light of proceedings which had been brought before the Greek courts which had been (as it turned out, wrongly) argued to raise the same cause of action and to have been started before the date on which the English court was seised of the claim. It does not appear to have struck any member of the court that there was any inherent problem with such a claim for damages. And anyway, in the light of what was originally decided in *Ellerman Lines Ltd v. Read*,[472] it could not possibly be said that these recent decisions took the law into territory which it had not previously occupied.

It is implicit in these decisions that the cause of action is a straightforward one for breach of contract. That seems right, even though the view has been expressed that a claim in tort for the unlawful interference with contractual rights would also be possible.[473] There is no need for such an analysis in the context of a claim between contracting parties, but it is certainly right that a non-contractual claim could be made against a non-party who may be accused of wrongfully interfering with the agreement on jurisdiction, say by funding or otherwise maintaining litigation by one of the parties to that agreement in a different court.[474] Once it is accepted that a contractual jurisdiction agreement contains a perfectly ordinary commercial bargain, whatever else it may do, there are no conceptual difficulties with proceedings brought to give effect to it and to defend it from attack. It is possible that if this line of authority is developed, *post hoc* satellite litigation – litigating about where the claimant should (not) have litigated – may attract the disapproval of those who rebuke the parties for *ante hoc* litigation about where to litigate. But it has not happened yet; and a breach is a breach is a breach.

And if a promise to behave or act in a certain way has been bargained and paid for by contracting parties, a claim for damages to compensate for losses caused by its unlawful breach or unlawful subversion seems justified in terms of ordinary common law theory, never mind anything more sophisticated. A contractual promise as to where proceedings will or will not

---

470 [2013] UKSC 35, [2013] 1 WLR 1889, esp. at [25].

471 [2013] UKSC 70, [2014] 1 Lloyd's Rep 223. See esp. at [36]–[39], [131]–[132], [135]; for whether it is affected by the Brussels I Regulation (correctly held not), see the resumed proceedings, reported as *Starlight Shipping Co v. Allianz Marine & Aviation Versicherungs AG* [2014] EWCA Civ 1010 [2014] 2 Lloyd's Rep 554. It appears that the Spanish Supreme Court also agrees that damages for breach are recoverable and raise no issue of special principle: *Soga USA Inc v. D Angel Jesús (Decision 6/2009*, 12 Jan. 2009) [2009] Rep Jur 542.

472 [1928] 2 KB 144.

473 This view is preferred by Tham [2004] LMCLQ 46.

474 *AMT Futures Ltd v. Marzillier et al GmbH* [2014] EWHC 1085 (Comm), [2015] 2 WLR 289 (a case on jurisdiction, but the cause of action is illustrative of the point made here).

be instituted is a promise by a party as to steps which he will or will not take. There is no novelty in the conclusion that, if a party makes a promise as to his behaviour, then departs from it, and in so doing causes loss to the other, he is liable for breach of contract, and is therefore liable to pay damages. It is difficult to see that matters are, or need to be, any more complex than that.

5.55 Damages for breach of a jurisdiction agreement: assessment of loss

The principle is clear; the manner of its application will require more work. The issue may be examined by reference to the various things a foreign court may have done.

A preliminary objection may be disposed of at the outset: there is nothing strange, or invidious or objectionable in asking a court to determine what another court would have done had the case been before it: cases on solicitor negligence, or insurance cases,[475] involve and depend upon that very assessment. The material question is what the outcome would have been if the case had been tried as it should have been tried. It is neither conceptually difficult nor practically challenging to answer that question.

One may therefore suppose that the foreign court had refused jurisdictional relief while acknowledging that the agreement was contractually valid and binding;[476] or that it construed the jurisdiction agreement more narrowly than an English court would have done and therefore decided that it did not cover the claim brought; or that it rejected the jurisdictional challenge but found on the merits for the party who had sought to rely on the clause; or that it rejected the jurisdictional challenges and then found for the party who had broken the agreement. The question will be in how many cases a right to claim damages will be supportable. These examples given mark a progression from the point where an award of damages would not conflict very markedly with the decision of the foreign court, to the point where an award of damages might seek to reverse, unwind, or annul the decision of the foreign court after trial of the merits of the claim, just as it did in *Ellerman Lines Ltd v. Read*, and will have done in *Starlight Shipping Co v. Allianz Marine & Aviation Versicherungs AG*.[477] It is hard to see that anyone can sensibly criticise the decision in *Union Discount Co v. Zoller*, that damages be awarded, and it is equally hard to see that the routine awarding of damages at common law to reverse the finding of a foreign court which has tried the merits could be correct. The question is not so much where to draw the line, but how.

The answer will presumably have to take into account whether the claimant, sued in the foreign court contrary to the parties' agreement, submitted to the jurisdiction of the foreign court or counterclaimed in the proceedings.[478] If he did so submit, principle would suggest that he should be estopped from asking the English court to revisit a question or issue which has already been decided against him. On the other hand, if one regards his decision to fight the case in the foreign court as an attempt to mitigate the losses liable to flow from the breach, it is harder to see that this should prejudice the right to argue after the event

---

475 *Enterprise Oil Ltd v. Strand Insurance Co Ltd* [2006] EWHC 58 (Comm), [2006] 1 Lloyd's Rep 500.
476 Which an English court may also do if strong cause is shown: see para. 4.52, above.
477 [2014] EWCA Civ 1010 [2014] 2 Lloyd's Rep 554.
478 See for comparison, Civil Jurisdiction and Judgments Act 1982, s. 32. On the other hand, the victim of a breach of contract is required to take reasonable steps to mitigate his loss, and it would be ironic if his appearance before the foreign court, to try and keep damages to a minimum, should be taken to worsen his position. There is a cultural issue here which focuses on whether the principles of ordinary contract law are modified when applied to this situation.

that he was the victim of a breach: a party who mitigates his losses does not condone the breach.[479] If he did not, but challenged the jurisdiction, he should not be estopped from reopening what the foreign court decided;[480] and the case is *a fortiori* if he seeks to build on what the foreign court decided in his favour. But what if he challenged the jurisdiction, then withdrew from the proceedings, and suffered judgment in default of defence? No estoppel will flow from such a judgment.[481] Again, if the foreign court ruled that there was a breach of contract but that it was inappropriate to give specific relief, what are the limits of any estoppel which would be derived from that decision?

As to the measure of damages, the authority is not yet strong, so principle must do the work which authority has yet to do. So far it has been decided that the party who was the victim of breach, who wins in the foreign court but does not get a proper costs order, may recover in damages on the footing that if he had obtained the same relief in England he would have been entitled to costs on the indemnity basis.[482] That is plainly right. Next, if the contention of the claimant is that he would not have lost if he had been sued in England, he should be entitled to claim in damages a sum equivalent to all his losses, on the judgment and in legal fees, as sums which would not have been lost if the contract had not been broken: why ever not? If the party who breached his contract by bringing proceedings before a foreign court is able to show that, had he abided by his contract and sued in England instead, the other party would still have lost, it will be up to him to show it on the evidence. In the end, the principle is clear enough: to put the injured party, so far as money can do it, in the position he would have been in if the contract had been performed according to its terms. Working out what that means is a matter of detail, not of principle.[483]

Much or all of this could be answered by recourse to the plain and robust common sense of the Court of Appeal in *Ellerman Lines Ltd v. Read*: Atkin and Scrutton LJJ saw the matter clearly and plainly as one where the breach of contract was pretty scandalous, and the duty of the court as being to deprive the wrongdoer of the fruits of his fraud.[484] If that decision is applied according to its tenor, there will be little more to be said.[485] In *Starlight Shipping Co v. Allianz Marine & Aviation Versicherungs AG*,[486] the parties had agreed to an indemnity against future acts, of which bringing certain proceedings before a foreign court was one; there was therefore no problem with assessment.

---

479 See, perhaps, *Midgulf International Ltd v. Groupe Chimiche Tunisien* [2009] EWHC 963 (Comm), [47].

480 Civil Jurisdiction and Judgments Act 1982, s. 33.

481 Civil Jurisdiction and Judgments Act 1982.

482 *National Westminster Bank plc v. Rabobank Nederland* [2007] EWHC 1056 (Comm), [2008] 1 All ER (Comm) 243 (principle of liability); *National Westminster Bank plc v. Rabobank Nederland* [2007] EWHC 3163 (Comm), [2008] 1 All ER (Comm) 266 (assessment of damages).

483 *CMA CGM SA v. Hyundai Mipo Dockyard Co Ltd* [2008] EWHC 2791 (Comm), [2009] 1 Lloyd's Rep 213 (arbitrators awarding damages to reverse effect of compliance with wrongfully-obtained French judgment).

484 The fact that it was described as fraud is of no significance: the non-recognition of foreign judgments has long used fraud (but did not, until 1982, use breach of jurisdiction agreement) as a basis for non-recognition. The 'fraud' in this case was the breach of contract, and no broader point remains to be considered.

485 See also, for more stirring good sense, *CMA CGM SA v. Hyundai Mipo Dockyard Co Ltd* [2008] EWHC 2791 (Comm), [2009] 1 Lloyd's Rep 213 (arbitrators awarding damages to reverse effect of compliance with wrongfully-obtained French judgment). Some cold water was poured on the judgment by the Court of Appeal in *National Navigation SA v. Endesa Generacion SA* [2009] EWCA Civ 1397, [2010] 1 Lloyd's Rep 193, but this really relates to whether the arbitrators, or the court on an issue arising from the arbitration, were bound to accept as conclusive the decision of a Spanish court on the effect of an arbitration agreement. It does not call into question the basis of the claim for damages.

486 [2014] EWCA Civ 1010 [2014] 2 Lloyd's Rep 554.

It is true that two public interests – in bolstering the sanctity of bargains and in putting an end to litigation – come into conflict at this point. It now seems pretty clear that, whatever else might be said, *Ellerman Lines Ltd v. Read* and *Starlight Shipping Co v. Allianz Marine & Aviation Versicherungs AG* decide that, as far as English law is concerned, the enforcement of contractual promises made in relation to where proceedings will and will not be brought is dominant. The best prediction is that a claim for damages for breach of contract, or for damages in tort, may be advanced by a claimant who appears to have a basis for it; and that any defence or answer derived from the law on foreign judgments and the principles of estoppel by *res judicata* will need to be tested by reference to the rules on the recognition of foreign judgments, and then by recourse to public policy.[487]

5.56 Wrongful litigation before the courts of another Member State

The account so far has taken no particular account of the identity of the foreign court in which the wrongful litigation is taking place. Where the wrongful litigation takes the specific form of bringing proceedings in a civil or commercial matter before the courts of a Member State, account needs to be taken of the further difficulty which may result from the bringing of proceedings which are designed, if for plausible reasons, to allow proceedings in England to counter or balance the economic effect of proceedings brought before the courts of another Member State. There is no question of any interference with the proceedings before the other Member State if these have run their course, or with the decision, to be taken by that court alone. Instead, the English proceedings take the foreign judgment as the basis for the claim for financial relief and proceed from there.[488] The prevailing English view of the matter – and, it is submitted, the correct view of the matter – is that there is no impediment from the Brussels I Regulation or from the general principles of European law which assist in its application.

It is important to observe that the judgments will not be irreconcilable: indeed, the opposite is true. At any rate, the Supreme Court in *The Alexandros T* saw no conceptual problem with an English claim for damages for breach of contract in which the loss which is to be compensated is that which results from litigation before the Greek courts which, *ex hypothesi*, the defendant to the English proceedings had undertaken not to bring. In *Starlight Shipping Co v. Allianz Marine & Aviation Versicherungs AG*[489] the Court of Appeal confirmed that the terms of the parties' contract were sufficiently well drafted as to oblige the party in breach of the contractual promise to indemnify the other against the loss resulting from the bringing of proceedings which that party had promised not to breach. Neither is there an objection along the lines of the impermissibility of reviewing the judgment of the courts of a Member

---

487 See also *J P Morgan Europe Ltd v. Primacom AG* [2005] EWHC 508 (Comm), [2005] 2 Lloyd's Rep 665.

488 The issue would not fall within the principle relied on in *Turner v. Grovit*; and *Starlight Shipping Co v. Allianz Marine & Aviation Versicherungs AG* confirms that the principle does not apply by analogy, for there is no analogy to be drawn. On the other hand, the English court will have to find that, on a balance of probability, the jurisdiction agreement was broken. The fact that a foreign court, derogated from by the agreement, may have entertained the case (in *Starlight Shipping Co v. Allianz Marine & Aviation Versicherungs AG* it had not yet ruled on its jurisdiction, so there was no complication) is not necessarily irreconcilable with that conclusion, especially where the decision of the foreign court (as would be the case where the corresponding decision were that of an English court) is founded on the finding only that there is a good arguable case that there is no jurisdiction agreement to prevent the hearing of the case.

489 [2014] EWCA Civ 1010, [2014] 2 Lloyd's Rep 544.

State on its merits. The merits of the underlying claim are not in dispute; the promise which is enforced is the promise not to bring the proceedings whatever the merits might have otherwise proved to be; and for this reason, a decree of specific performance to require performance of the contractual agreement is similarly permissible.[490] It is the behaviour of the party who has asked the foreign court to examine those merits which is in issue, not the merits of the claim promised not to be brought. In the end, a contract is a contract is a contract, and however much work there is still to be done, the principles that English courts uphold bargains, and that the common law gives a right to damages for breach of contract and for losses tortiously inflicted,[491] is a powerful one, even (or perhaps especially) in this particular context.

All that said, there must be a reasonable likelihood that a court somewhere will ask the European Court to rule on the compatibility of this with the general scheme of the Brussels I Regulation, and when that happens, the contractual, commercial, and coherent approach of the common law will need to address the distinct concerns of the Regulation which aims to secure and to strengthen the recognition and enforcement of judgments from and across the Member States.

5.57 Damages for breach of a jurisdiction agreement: disentangling the twin functions of a jurisdiction agreement

It is only superficially more difficult to justify an action for damages for breach of a choice of court agreement where the proceedings were brought before a court in another Member State, for the obligation to recognise the judgment is statutory, and the Brussels I Regulation does not allow recognition of judgments to be refused on the ground that the court which adjudicated did so in breach of an agreement on choice of court, any more than it allows recognition to be refused on the ground of any other jurisdictional error by the adjudicating court. But there are two reasons to suppose, or to support the argument, that there is nothing in this point, and that to see a problem in the Regulation is to be frightened by a paper tiger.

First, and most importantly, the Supreme Court in *The Alexandros T* saw nothing in the point. At no stage was it suggested that the English proceedings for damages for breach of the jurisdiction agreement were in any sense unsustainable because they identified proceedings before the Greek courts as the source of the loss. One may fairly suppose that if there had been any basis for doubt about the very legitimacy of the claim, either the court would have mentioned it, or it would have referred a question to the European Court. It did neither. In the resumed hearing, in *Starlight Shipping Co v. Allianz Marine & Aviation Versicherungs AG*, the Court of Appeal simply confirmed that the Greek proceedings were brought in breach of a binding contractual settlement and indemnity agreement, and ordered an indemnity against the loss inflicted and continuing to be inflicted by bringing proceedings which a party to that agreement had bound itself, for consideration, not to bring.

Second, it is necessary to re-state the important distinction between two issues, which are related but which are conceptually distinct. One is whether an agreement on jurisdiction can confer jurisdiction on a court, or can remove the jurisdiction a court would otherwise have, or may cause a court to not exercise a jurisdiction which it would otherwise have

---

490 *Starlight Shipping Co v. Allianz Marine & Aviation Versicherungs AG* [2014] EWHC 3068 (Comm), [2014] 2 Lloyd's Rep 579.

491 And that equity will compensate a victim of wrongdoing, or that damages may be awarded in lieu of an injunction or other specific relief.

exercised: these may be thought of as the external, or public law, incidents of the agreement on jurisdiction. Whether one or the other consequence follows in an individual case will depend, in its entirety, on the jurisdictional law of the court before which the issue arises. It has been seen that, as far as an English court is concerned, it will usually give specific effect to an agreement on jurisdiction, but it will not do so invariably. In other words, as a matter of English jurisdictional law, the parties' agreement on jurisdiction will influence, but does not determine, the jurisdiction of an English court.

But the agreement as to jurisdiction is also a promise made by the parties, one to another, by which they undertake to each other where they will, or will not, resolve their disputes. It is a promise about the institution of legal proceedings; and there is no reason to think that this promise, as to personal behaviour in relation to the resolution of disputes, is not enforceable according to its terms.[492] The content of this obligation is not affected by whether a court, in the exercise of its public or statutory law of civil jurisdiction, was prepared to give effect to the agreement on jurisdiction,[493] because the personal obligation assumed by the parties to the agreement on choice of court is something whose performance lies entirely within their own control and autonomy. The justification for enforcing it, by damages claim if necessary, is that it represents a promise of performance to the other in a particular way.

In this sense the mutual obligations assumed to each other are separate and quite distinct from the external impact of the contract.[494] The fact that a court is called upon to recognise a judgment, whether under the Brussels I Regulation or otherwise, is irrelevant to the separate question whether the party who obtained that judgment, whether or not it is entitled to recognition, did so in breach of contract.[495]

All that having been said, the claimant will need to establish that there was a breach of contract. Whether this is possible in circumstances – assuming it to be so – in which a court in another Member State has determined that its jurisdiction is not removed by an agreement on jurisdiction to which Article 25 would give effect, depends at least in part on the effect of that foreign judgment in England. The ruling of the foreign court, insofar as it determines its jurisdiction, must obviously be recognised,[496] and this recognition will extend to the reasoning of the court in support of its decision. It will therefore be necessary to establish exactly what the foreign court has decided (and whether it did so on the balance of probabilities), to determine whether the claimant is free to say that, even despite what the foreign court has conclusively held, the defendant breached his promise to the claimant in instituting proceedings before the Member State court in question. The analysis of that question will be determined by reference to the particular judgment, and no more needs to be said about it at this point.

---

492 Such was the analysis of the Spanish Supreme Court in *Soga USA Inc v. D Angel Jesús* (*Sentencia 6/2009*, 12 Jan. 2009) [2009] Rep Jur 542.

493 Though it is in principle open to argue that the contractual agreement on where to sue may have been frustrated by unforeseen and unprovided-for supervening events, or vitiated by common mistake.

494 At this point, see *Penn v. Baltimore* (1750) 1 Ves Sen 444; and Briggs, *Agreements on Jurisdiction and Choice of Law* (2008), where the analysis is pursued at greater length, and the suggestion is made that the reasoning may be extended to agreements on choice of law.

495 Which was the very point in *Ellerman Lines Ltd v. Read* [1928] 2 KB 144. And see also *CMA CGM SA v. Hyundai MIPO Dockyard Co Ltd* [2008] EWHC 2791 (Comm), [2009] 1 Lloyd's Rep 213.

496 In general, as it is a judgment on a civil or commercial matter; and in particular by reason of C-456/11 *Gothaer Allgemeine Versicherung AG v. Samskip GmbH* EU:C:2012:719, [2013] QB 458.

5.58 Damages for breach of a jurisdiction agreement: extension to breach of agreement on choice of law?

The reasoning used to justify a claim for damages for breach of an agreement on choice of court or arbitration may also apply to a party who has breached an agreement on choice of law. English authority is not supportive, but the issue of principle may not be entirely closed.[497]

The argument would proceed along these lines. An agreement on choice of law, at least when it is express, may be taken as many things. It may provide information from which a court decides which law to apply when called upon to adjudicate a claim between the parties; but it may also be seen as a mutual agreement between the parties as to the law which should be applied. Though an agreement on choice of law obviously cannot tie the hands of a court, which will apply such law or laws as is required by its rules of private international law, it has a supplicative function, which may be admitted as part of the data from which the court determines, in accordance with its rules on private international law, the law which is applicable to the contract.

But it may also bind the parties not to institute proceedings before a court which will do something other than apply the law which the parties agreed for application in the resolution of their disputes. It may make perfect sense for parties to a long-term contractual relationship to make no binding choice of court, for they may not be able to predict where the assets will be when litigation eventually is called for, but to specify the law by which their dispute will be resolved whenever that litigation takes place. If that is so, the bringing of proceedings before a court which will not apply that law is conduct which prevents the agreement from being carried into effect, in other words, which breaches the agreement.[498] There is no reason in principle why this should not be seen as a civil wrong, as a breach of the mutual-performance obligations of the contract, and if departed from, be seen as a breach of a contractual agreement which may give rise to a claim for damages.

Of course, if an agreement on choice of law is not held to have a promissory element, separate and distinct from the role it performs in the identification of the governing law as a matter of private international law, this analysis cannot be applied. But it is hard to see why this is not possible; and in the end the question must be one of construction. If the contract were to provide that, for example 'all disputes arising out of this agreement shall be determined by the application of English law', and proceedings were to be brought in a court which applied a different law, it is not easy to see why the institution of proceedings in that court is not a breach of the promise which the parties made to each other as to how (as distinct from where, or by whom) the dispute would be dealt with.[499]

---

497 However, the submission based on the analysis set out in this paragraph did not persuade the judge in *Ace Insurance Ltd v. Moose Enterprise Pty Ltd* [2009] NSWSC 724, who appeared to require a much clearer form of words to sustain the contention that for a party to bring proceedings in a court which would not apply the law chosen was a breach of contract (as distinct from conduct which was oppressive or vexatious). It fared no better in *Navig8 Pte Ltd v. Al-Riyadh Co for Vegetable Oil Industry* [2013] EWHC 328 (Comm), [2013] 2 Lloyd's Rep 104.

498 In *E.I. Du Pont de Nemours & Co v. Agnew* [1987] 2 Lloyd's Rep 585, the fact that an insurance policy was governed by English law was held, in circumstances in which the material question was as to a rule of English public policy, to require the case to be heard in England, where English law would be applied. It would have been wrong to allow the case to proceed overseas, and so 'introduce an unacceptably random element into a very important commercial undertaking': at 594. No doubt the case would have been stronger still if English law had been expressly chosen to govern the insurance.

499 But, at present, the argument is not supported by judicial authority.

The quantification of loss may be challenging, but in commercial cases this is not rare. A comparison between what would have happened if the chosen law had been applied, and what did happen, is not difficult to formulate as the template for analysis. There ought to be no complication from the proposition that the foreign judgment has to be recognised, and that therefore the principles of *res judicata* destroy the basis for the claim for damages. For one thing, the foreign court will have decided what law its rules of private international law required it to apply; it has not necessarily decided what the parties promised each other as to choice of law. For another, if the recognition of judgments proceeds on the basis that the losing party assumed an obligation to abide by the judgment, it does not seem difficult to argue that if the parties made an agreement as to choice of law, they assumed an obligation to abide by the judgment of a court which applied that law in the resolution of their disputes, but did not assume an obligation to accept and to abide by the judgment of a court which disregarded that aspect of their agreement.[500]

5.59 Wrongful litigation which is not a breach of contract

The complaint that the institution of proceedings before a foreign court is wrongful, and has caused loss, and that there is a cause of action for compensation, is not confined to cases in which the complaint is that the institution of proceedings is a breach of contract. It may take the form of a non-contractual wrong, such as where someone who is not party to a jurisdiction agreement encourages a person who is party to it to institute proceedings elsewhere, and all the more so where the costs of this litigation are met by the encourager. It is difficult to see why this could not be seen as the commission of a tort, or breach of a non-contractual obligation, and complained of accordingly.[501] A question of applicable law may arise, if it is contended that the non-contractual obligation is governed by a law other than English law, but the broad principle seems clear enough.

Where the complaint is that the institution of litigation overseas does not violate a legal right, but is unconscionable or otherwise an equitable wrong, it would seem that the basis for compensation would take the form of damages or equitable compensation in lieu of an injunction. Once again, the authority to show that such a claim for relief would be well founded is not yet to hand, but reason to doubt its availability is hard to formulate, probably because there is no reason to doubt it.

(F) DECLARATORY JUDGMENT ON THE MERITS OF THE DISPUTE

5.60 General

The final issue to consider is the seeking of a pre-emptive ruling and declaration (which may be negative) on the merits of the substantive dispute. The purpose would be to disarm

---

500 See below, para. 7.68. And see also, Briggs, *Agreements on Jurisdiction and Choice of Law* (2008), ch. 11.

501 *AMT Futures Ltd v. Marzillier et al GmbH* [2014] EWHC 1085 (Comm), [2015] 2 WLR 187. See also *Horn Linie GmbH v. Panamericana Formas e Impresos SA (The Hornbay)* [2006] EWHC 373 (Comm), [2006] 2 Lloyd's Rep 44; *Joint Stock Asset Management Co Ingosstrakh-Investments v. BNP Paribas SA* [2012] EWCA Civ 644, [2012] 1 Lloyd's Rep 649.

any judgment which might be obtained by the opposite party in another court. This, by contrast with the anti-suit injunction, will involve the English court ruling on the merits of the claim; the decision may make the merits *res judicata* in the eyes of a foreign court as well as in England.

Declaratory proceedings will sometimes be for positive relief; on other occasions they will involve an action for a declaration that the claimant (who may well be the 'natural' defendant)[502] is under no liability to the defendant (the 'natural claimant'). As this is an action in relation to the merits of the dispute, it may be brought, in principle at least, just like any other action. It may be very effective in saving a party from a worse fate in another court.

Proceedings brought to obtain a negative declaration, however, are also different from more usual forms of action. Where jurisdiction is dependent on the exercise of discretion, jurisdiction may be affected by the perception that the claimant is forum shopping, and where the court has a duty or discretion to discourage this, it may do so. There is also an enhanced risk of there being a situation of *lis alibi pendens*, which the court may also have a duty or discretion to prevent. As a matter of English law, the court has no obligation to grant declaratory relief if the reasons for not granting relief outweigh the reasons for granting it.[503] These factors together make proceedings for negative declaratory relief a special form of action, which merits separate mention.

5.61 Declaratory proceedings: jurisdiction *in personam* over the defendant

In a civil or commercial matter, the main issue is whether jurisdiction over the defendant is governed by the direct rules of the Brussels I Regulation or by the traditional rules of English law as taken up for residual cases by Article 6 of the recast Regulation. In a matter which is not within the scope of the Regulation, these traditional rules apply on their own authority.

5.62 Declaratory proceedings: jurisdiction *in personam* and the direct rules of the Brussels I Regulation

Where the Brussels I Regulation applies, the jurisdictional rules as set out in Chapter 2 determine the issue. In some cases the jurisdictional rule which may be relied upon may make reference to an element – a contract, a tort, an agreement, and so on – the existence of which is denied by the claimant, but which is evidently alleged against him by the defendant.

In *The Tatry*,[504] the Court of Justice examined the application of various jurisdictional rules of what is now the Brussels I Regulation in the context of a case where the proceedings first commenced were for negative declaratory relief. It gave no indication[505] that this fact

---

502 These labels are for illustrative purposes only; it is not intended to convey the idea that one of the parties to the dispute is more properly than the other to be seen as claimant or defendant. That will be determined by the eventual form of the action.

503 CPR r. 40.20.

504 C-406/92, [1994] ECR I-5439.

505 Despite the fact that the reference from the national court, where it is reported as *The Maciej Rataj* [1992] 2 Lloyd's Rep 552, had invited it to do just that.

had any impact at all on the application of the jurisdictional rules, which were indifferent as to the form of the proceedings. The European Court has now confirmed that this approach applies even where an alleged tortfeasor brings proceedings against an alleged victim, and relies on the special jurisdictional rule in what is now Article 7(2) of the Regulation to seise the court.[506]

But the English courts had already taken the point. In *Messier-Dowty Ltd v. Sabena SA*,[507] it was reaffirmed that, where jurisdiction was established in accordance with the Regulation, there was no more to be said. The only proper role for discretion was a substantive or remedial one: that a court may refuse to make a declaration by reference to its law on declaratory proceedings. So, for example, a rule of English law that a declaration will not be made where to do so would be without useful purpose, or where there is no live controversy between the parties which the court may properly be asked to adjudicate, may still be applied. But any attempt to argue that a court lacked jurisdiction, or should decline to exercise jurisdiction because the proper place to sue was somewhere else, was inadmissible.

5.63 Declaratory proceedings: jurisdiction *in personam* otherwise than under the direct rules of the Brussels I Regulation

In cases where the subject matter of the dispute falls outside the scope of the Regulation, or where Article 6 of the Regulation provides that jurisdiction is to be determined by the traditional rules of English law, it must be possible to serve the claim form on the defendant within the jurisdiction, or out of the jurisdiction with permission granted pursuant to CPR rule 6.36. In these cases, the court appears to have more freedom to give effect to considerations of judicial jurisdictional discretion.

If service was made within the jurisdiction, it will be open to the defendant to seek a stay of proceedings on the ground that the *forum conveniens* is elsewhere. In dealing with that application the court has a broad discretion; and it may decide to exercise it with particular reference to the fact that the English proceedings are (negative) declaratory in form. Where jurisdiction has been founded on service out of the jurisdiction under CPR rule 6.36, the form of the proceedings may be significant at two distinct points. First, it may be relevant when the claimant seeks to bring his claim within Paragraph 3.1 of the Practice Direction. For some kinds of claim, such as those which fall within sub-Paragraph (8), there will be no difficulty, for the particular head of jurisdiction has been drafted with negative declaratory proceedings in mind. For other kinds of claim, it is not so certain that the wording of the sub-Paragraph will extend to proceedings which allege, for example, that there was no tort as alleged or at all. But it may be that CPR rule 6.37(3) makes ample provision for judicial discretion; there is no need to strain to keep such claims outside Paragraph 3.1.

Indeed, if the technique of seeking such declarations is open to abuse, as some may consider that it is, the control of that abuse is a proper task for the judicial discretion component of jurisdiction under the rules of the common law. Moreover, if the approach in *Messier Dowty*

---

506 C-133/11 *Folien Fischer AG v. Ritrama SpA* EU:C:2012:664, [2013] QB 523. This rather overtakes the entirely correct decision of the Court of Appeal in *Boss Group Ltd v. Boss France SA* [1997] 1 WLR 351, which was applied by the Court of Appeal in *Youell v. La Réunion Aérienne* [2009] EWCA Civ 175, [2009] 1 Lloyd's Rep 586, and also the entirely correct decision in *Equitas Ltd v. Wave City Shipping Co Ltd* [2005] EWHC 923 (Comm), [2005] 2 All ER (Comm) 301.
507 [2000] 1 WLR 2040.

Ltd v. Sabena SA[508] is taken – as it is submitted it was intended to be – to apply to cases where jurisdiction over the defendant is asserted under the provisions of CPR rule 6.36, there should be no judicial encouragement to exclude the claim from the paragraphs; cases where the proceedings are premature, inappropriate, or otherwise objectionable, can be dealt with by the court exercising its discretion against permitting service to be made out of the jurisdiction by finding that England is not (at the moment) the proper place to bring the claim.

So far as the legitimate exercise of jurisdictional discretion is concerned, there is no need to dwell on older cases in which the courts had exercised jurisdictional powers with clear hostility to proceedings brought in declaratory form.[509] The history of judicial scepticism was treated with clear reservation by the Court of Appeal in *Messier Dowty Ltd v. Sabena SA*.[510] Lord Woolf MR considered that the observations in the earlier cases should be treated with reservation, on the ground that 'the use of negative declarations domestically has expanded over recent years. In the appropriate cases their use can be valuable and constructive'. His approach was that, wherever a useful purpose would be served by the making of a declaration, a court should not be reluctant to entertain the proceedings. In the particular context of applications for permission to serve out under what is now CPR rule 6.36, this presumably means that if it can be seriously argued that it would be useful to make the declaration sought,[511] and always assuming that the claimant has demonstrated that England is the proper place in which to bring the claim, and that the claim falls within one of the heads of jurisdiction given in Paragraph 3.1 of the Practice Direction, permission to serve out should be granted without further ado.

5.64 Declaratory proceedings: making the declaration as a matter of substantive law

CPR rule 40.20 provides that 'the court may make binding declarations whether or not any other remedy is claimed'. The power given to the court is broad and general, and a claimant may therefore institute proceedings to obtain declaratory relief. There is nothing inherently wrong or artificial about doing so: in insurance cases, for example, it is common, proper and desirable for an insurer to ascertain, by seeking such a declaration, whether he is liable to pay a claim which has been or may be made upon the policy. Such declarations are part of the common currency of insurance law and practice.[512] And claims that a contract was rescinded, or that the claimant was entitled to rescind it, are really only claims for a negative declaration by another name.

As a matter of historical fact there has been, in some other areas, a reluctance to grant such declarations, presumably because (i) they deprive the would-be claimant of what had traditionally been seen as his right to select the forum in which the dispute will be heard, and (ii) they may require the victim of a wrong to advance his claim, by way of defence, before he is ready to do so. Further, where the declaration was sought in order to counteract

---

508 [2000] 1 WLR 2040.

509 See, for example only, *The Volvox Hollandia* [1988] 2 Lloyd's Rep 361. The case preceded the coming into force of the Brussels Convention in the United Kingdom.

510 [2000] 1 WLR 2040.

511 That is, the claimant has satisfied the merits condition imposed by *Seaconsar Far East Ltd v. Bank Markazi Jomhouri Islami Iran* [1994] 1 AC 438, discussed above, para. 4.93.

512 See, for example, *CGU International Insurance plc v. Szabo* [2002] 1 All ER (Comm) 83.

the possible or anticipated effect of foreign proceedings, there has been greater reluctance still. A trilogy illustrates the point. In *Guaranty Trust Co v. Hannay*,[513] the court said that the declaration was one which would hardly ever be made, and that the applicant would be left to set up his defence in the substantive proceedings when they were brought (in that case, in America). In *Camilla Cotton Oil Co v. Granadex SA*,[514] the court observed that its power to make the declaration was constrained by an assessment of whether it was useful to do so: if it would have no effect upon the foreign proceedings (*in casu*, in Switzerland), it would not be made. And, in *First National Bank of Boston ('FNBB') v. Union Bank of Switzerland*,[515] the Court of Appeal stated that the court would not act unless it saw some good purpose in making the declaration. Two factors led the court to the conclusion that no useful purpose would be served in that case. First, the substantive claims, in relation to which declarations were sought, were 'properly' brought against FNBB in Switzerland, in that FNBB carried on business in Switzerland. Second, the declaration, if made, would be ignored by the Swiss courts, and its proceedings would continue to judgment in any event. There was, the court considered, no purpose in making the declaration, and, though it had jurisdiction, the court would exercise its discretion not to do so.

But the judgment which repudiated the earlier attitude of jurisdictional hostility also departed from the non-jurisdictional suspicion that such proceedings were inherently unwelcome. In *Messier Dowty Ltd v. Sabena SA*,[516] Lord Woolf MR acknowledged that the declaratory judgment was capable of helping to ensure that the aims of justice were met, and in such cases the court 'should not be reluctant to grant such declarations'.[517] So if the declaration will serve a useful purpose, it would not be wrong to make it.[518] It is proper that a court keep a watchful eye on the proceedings, and exercise its discretion so as not to allow actions to be brought if they are manifestly premature (such as where the opposite party has himself made no real threat to institute proceedings) or if the claimant has in some other sense brought the proceedings for improper or oppressive reasons. But in the adult world of commercial litigation it is at least arguable that, although a claim may be seen as the property of a claimant, a dispute is not to be seen as the property of one party. As a result of this latter point, the choice of whether, where and when to sue should not be the sole prerogative of one party alone. A commercial concern may legitimately need to know whether it is or continues to be bound to another; an insurer may need to know whether he has a contingent liability to his insured.

---

513 [1915] 2 KB 536. See also *Re Clay* [1919] 1 Ch 66; *Insurance Corporation of Ireland v. Strombus International Insurance* [1985] 2 Lloyd's Rep 138; *Booker v. Bell* [1989] 1 Lloyd's Rep 516; *New Hampshire Insurance Co v. Strabag Bau AG* [1992] 1 Lloyd's Rep 361; *New Hampshire Insurance Co v. Aerospace Finance Ltd* [1998] 2 Lloyd's Rep 539.

514 [1976] 2 Lloyd's Rep 10.

515 [1990] 1 Lloyd's Rep 32.

516 [2000] 1 WLR 2040, applied *Youell v. Kara Mara Shipping Services Co Ltd* [2000] 2 Lloyd's Rep 102; *Chase v. Ram Technical Services Ltd* [2000] 2 Lloyd's Rep 418.

517 At 434.

518 It will not be useful to make a declaration of issues as an English court would see them 'for the benefit of' a foreign court when there is little or no evidence that the foreign court would be grateful for it; still less if the purpose of the application is really to establish a 'blocking' judgment of the English court: *Howden North America Inc v. Ace European Group Ltd* [2012] EWCA Civ 1624, [2013] Lloyd's Rep IR 512; see also *Citigroup Global Markets Ltd v. Amatra Leveraged Feeder Holdings Ltd* [2012] EWHC 1331 (Comm), [2012] 2 CLC 279. *Cf Navig8 Pte Ltd v. Al-Riyadh Co for Vegetable Oil Industry* [2013] EWHC 328 (Comm), [2013] 2 Lloyd's Rep 104 (useful to make declaration because English law had been chosen to govern the bills of lading, and it was useful to give a judgment which would prevent enforcement of a contradictory Jordanian judgment).

There will be cases in which a 'natural defendant'[519] should be expected to wait for the 'natural claimant' to institute proceedings when he chooses, if at all. If, for example, it is alleged that a simple debt is owed, there is no obvious reason why it should be considered appropriate, still less essential, for the debtor to bring matters to a head, before the potential creditor has decided whether to sue. To put the point another way, perhaps a right of non-going to a court is a part of, or the counterpart of, the right of access to a court. But if the claimant is facing a defendant who insists that he is entitled to act, or to continue to act, as distributor of the claimant's goods, the claimant wishing to put in place different distributor-ship arrangements, it may be commercially impossible for the claimant to remain commer-cially inhibited or paralysed unless and until the defendant chooses to launch proceedings of his own. A sensible judicial service to commercial parties must allow such difficulties to be resolved in the light of commercial necessities; and the action for declaratory relief is often the best and fairest way for this to be done.

---

519 The terminology is that of Lord Woolf MR in *Messier Dowty Ltd v. Sabena SA*.

CHAPTER 6

Interim Remedies, Provisional Measures and Ancillary Orders

6.01 General

The subject matter of this chapter is the law on interim remedies and 'provisional, including protective' measures which may be sought or obtained in the course of litigation. The full range and detail of the remedies available under English law is described here only in outline. This chapter is mainly concerned with the jurisdiction of the English courts to grant those interim remedies which are available as a matter of English domestic law. It deals with claims for such relief in cases in which the English courts do, and do not, have jurisdiction over the parties in relation to the substantive dispute, paying particular attention to whether the connection (or lack of connection) to England bears on the making or not making of the order applied for. It also examines the effect in England of foreign orders granting interim relief where the foreign court has, and also where the English courts have, jurisdiction over the dispute.

One particularly important measure has already been dealt with. When an English court orders an injunction to restrain a party involved or threatening to become involved in foreign proceedings from continuing to prosecute them, it is not necessarily to be seen as making an order for interim relief or a protective measure, for the order may be a final one. But the grant of an interlocutory anti-suit injunction, to hold the ring until trial, may certainly be seen as an interim remedy.[1]

The point of departure is, of course, that, as the granting of interim remedies is clearly a matter of local procedural law, an English court may grant only such relief as is provided for by English domestic procedural law, even if it does so in aid of proceedings in a foreign court, from which foreign court different forms of relief would be, or are also, available.

The problem of terminology needs to be mentioned at the outset, but should not be a major concern. The expression 'interim remedies' is taken from CPR Part 25, where the orders which are available from an English court are listed. They may also be referred to as interlocutory orders, though that expression is less frequently used today. The expression 'provisional, including protective' measures is taken from the Brussels I Regulation, and refers to the orders which, according to Article 35 of the recast Regulation, may be made by a court which does not have jurisdiction over the merits of a claim. The expression 'ancillary orders' refers to the orders which may be made by a court which has jurisdiction over the merits of a dispute, whether the order is one made before, during or after the conclusion

---

1 Paragraphs 5.32 *et seq.*, above.

of the trial of the merits and which is certainly wider in scope than the list of orders which may be made under the authority of Article 35. Unless there is a particular need to draw a distinction between them, the terms may be used interchangeably.[2]

6.02 Interim remedies: the measures available from an English court

The list of interim remedies that an English court has power to grant is collected together and set out in the Civil Procedure Rules.[3] Though this is a convenient place in which to find the remedies set out in the form of a list, it is necessary to realise that, for some of them, it is statute rather than CPR Part 25 that provides the legal foundation for their availability. Moreover, CPR rule 25.1 is not necessarily an exhaustive list of the remedies that can be obtained,[4] and it is at least still arguable that a court may be prepared to devise a remedy, or to adapt an existing remedy, not specifically provided for in order to facilitate its overall task of doing what procedural justice may require.[5]

Subject to those points, the principal categories of interim remedy which the court may grant are these: an interim injunction;[6] an interim declaration;[7] an order for the detention, preservation, inspection, sampling, and sale of property which is the subject of a claim;[8] an order authorising a person to enter premises in the possession of a party for the carrying out of an order for the detention, etc. of property which is the subject of a claim;[9] an order for the delivery up of goods for the purposes of the Torts (Interference with Goods) Act 1977;[10] a freezing injunction[11] (and an order requiring the provision of information about assets and their location for the purposes of such an injunction[12]); a search order;[13] an order for the inspection and sampling, etc., of property before a claim is made[14] or from a non-party after a claim has been made;[15] an order for disclosure of documents by a non-party;[16] an interim payment;[17] and an order requiring the preparation and filing of accounts.[18] It is not a condition for the grant of these remedies that there be a claim for a corresponding final remedy.

---

2 No account is given here of Regulation 655/2014, [2014] OJ L189/59 on the European Account Preservation Order, which will be in effect from 18 January 2017, as the United Kingdom has elected not to be bound by it.

3 CPR r. 25.1

4 CPR r. 25.1(3).

5 *Astro Exito Navegacion SA v. Southland Enterprise Co Ltd* [1982] QB 1248. Indeed, this may provide the basis for a challenge to the proposition that an English court can award only those interim (and other) remedies which are known to English law. This development was, after all, the way in which the freezing injunction with worldwide effect (formerly the worldwide *Mareva* injunction) was developed.

6 CPR r. 25.1(1)(a).

7 CPR r. 25.1(1)(b).

8 CPR r. 25.1(1)(c); r. 25.1(2).

9 CPR r. 25.1(1)(d).

10 CPR r. 25.1(1)(e).

11 CPR r. 25.1(1)(f), formerly known as a *Mareva* injunction.

12 CPR r. 25.1(1)(g).

13 CPR r. 25.1(1)(h), formerly known as an *Anton Piller* order.

14 CPR r. 25.1(1)(i): Senior Courts Act 1981, s. 33.

15 CPR r. 25.1(1)(j): Senior Courts Act 1981, s. 34.

16 CPR r. 25.1(1)(j): Senior Courts Act 1981, s. 34.

17 CPR r. 25.1(1)(k).

18 CPR r. 25.1(1)(n).

6.03 Interim measures: the freezing or *Mareva* injunction

The freezing injunction describes a form of order known until 1999, and still frequently today, as a *Mareva* injunction. It is dealt with at a little length because of its peculiar effectiveness and evident attractiveness to claimants. It took its name from one of the first cases in which such an order was made.[19] It is an order made against a defendant to an action,[20] against whom there appears to be a good arguable case on the merits of the substantive claim[21] and who, it is reasonably feared, may remove, conceal or dissipate his assets prior to any attempt to enforce a judgment against him. It orders him to preserve, and not to dissipate or conceal, his assets up to the predicted value of the claim. However, if no cause of action has yet arisen, the injunction cannot be granted;[22] and the injunction may not be obtained against someone who neither is nor has yet been made a party to the action.[23] Such an injunction may also be obtained after judgment, in aid of enforcement of the judgment in England or overseas: it is not clear that it is right in that context to regard it in those circumstances as interim, but it is certainly protective.[24]

From time to time the appellate courts issue reminders about the need to apply the law cautiously and carefully, for the order is sought and applied for against persons against whom there is only an allegation, and remind judges to whom applications are in what are often presented as conditions of extreme urgency, of the need to be scrupulous in checking that the application for a measure, whose effect can be severe, is properly prepared and properly made.[25] These reminders are necessary because they are not always

---

19 *Mareva Compania Naviera SA v. International Bulk Carriers SA* [1975] 2 Lloyd's Rep 509. There is now a broad and general statutory basis for its being made, in Senior Courts Act 1981, s. 37(3). It used to attract hostility from certain conservative writers in Australia in particular, but such objections never made any headway in England: *Mercedes Benz AG v. Leiduck* [1996] 1 AC 284, 299. Nevertheless, the perception that the *Mareva* injunction is a parentless novelty may have served to hamper its development in cases where problems of jurisdiction presented themselves: see the difference between the majority and minority judgments in *Mercedes Benz*.

20 Although, in a proper case, a person may be joined as co-defendant, even though there is no substantive claim against him, on the ground that the interests of justice require it: see CPR r. 19.2; *Bullus v. Bullus* (1910) 102 LT 399; *Aiglon Ltd v. Gau Shan Co Ltd* [1993] 1 Lloyd's Rep 164; *Mercantile Group (Europe) Ltd v. Aiyela* [1994] QB 366; *C Inc plc v. L* [2001] 2 Lloyd's Rep 459; *cf Cardile v. LED Builders Pty Ltd* (1999) 198 CLR 380. If this happens, he may be directly restrained: *HMRC v. Egleton* [2006] EWHC 2313 (Ch), [2007] Bus LR 44. And see generally Devonshire [1996] LMCLQ 268; (2002) 118 LQR 124.

21 *Derby & Co Ltd v. Weldon* [1990] Ch 48, 57; *Aiglon Ltd v. Gau Shan Co Ltd* [1993] 1 Lloyd's Rep 164.

22 *Veracruz Transportation Inc v. VC Shipping Co Inc* [1992] 1 Lloyd's Rep 353; *Zucker v. Tyndall Holdings plc* [1992] 1 WLR 1127. This is a controversial restriction, nevertheless: see *Mercedes Benz*, at 308. But it is a rational one, for unless there is a cause of action, it is very hard to see how the court can assess whether there is a good arguable case in respect of it: *Fourie v. Le Roux* [2007] UKHL 1, [2007] 1 WLR 320.

23 Unless joined to the action.

24 Indeed, as a matter of domestic English law, this has always been an easier context for the claimant seeking the injunction, for he has by then conclusively established that he had a good cause of action against the defendant. See *Orwell Steel (Erection and Fabrication) Ltd v. Asphalt and Tarmac (UK) Ltd* [1984] 1 WLR 1097; *Babanaft International Co SA v. Bassatne* [1990] Ch 13; *C Inc v. L* [2001] 2 Lloyd's Rep 459. According to *Masri v. Consolidated Contractors International (UK) Ltd (No 2)* [2008] EWCA Civ 303, [2009] QB 450, a post-judgment order is one the court has jurisdiction to make on the ground that a court with jurisdiction to try the merits has jurisdiction to make all orders which are necessary or convenient for that purpose, including those which will assist with the enforcement of the judgment. See also C-391/95 *Van Uden BV v. Firma Deco-Line* [1998] ECR I-7091. Moreover, the French Cour de Cassation has been prepared, without objection, to recognise and enforce an English post-judgment freezing injunction: *Stolzenberg v. Daimler Chrysler Canada Inc* [2005] JDI/Clunet 112 (*note* Cuniberti), [2005] ILPr 266.

25 *Fourie v. Le Roux* [2007] UKHL 1, [2007] 1 WLR 320.

heeded; it can sometimes seem that as long as there is an allegation of fraud, the court acts as though the merits were all on the one side, and makes orders which are capable of wounding or crippling a defendant.[26] Not all defendants are liable as alleged or at all; and the idea that everything can then be put back as it was with a costs order is plainly unconvincing.

As the injunction is likely to be effective only if applied for without notice to the respondent, the applicant/claimant must make full and frank disclosure of all matters material to the exercise of discretion by the judge.[27] He must also give proper grounds for believing that the defendant has assets, and for his having a well-founded[28] fear of their being dissipated, or otherwise dealt with so as to defeat the ends of justice, unless the order is made. He must give an undertaking,[29] which will usually be required to be fortified by a bank guarantee or other security, to pay damages in respect of any loss suffered in the event that the claim on the merits fails at trial with the consequence that the order will prove to have been one which should not have been made.[30] The injunction may be made to last for such time as the court directs.

Importantly, the respondent/defendant[31] may be ordered to give information as to the existence and whereabouts[32] of his property or assets. This is because the court may make orders ancillary to the freezing injunction on the ground that these are necessary to make the injunction effective.[33] He may be ordered not to remove assets within the jurisdiction, or to deal with assets which are outside the jurisdiction, up to the value of the claim made against him; allowances for living, certain business and legal expenses are usually permitted.[34] He may even be ordered to move assets from one jurisdiction to another.[35] But none of this gives the applicant/claimant any proprietary right or interest in the assets to which the injunction relates: the injunction has no proprietary effect.[36] As a result, in the event of the

---

26 If an anecdote may be permitted, it is only to observe that the writer's pupil master used to say that there was only one law, and that it was the law of merits. In this context, the law is the law of alleged merits, and once these are perceived, everything else follows, in a rather one-sided way.

27 *Brink's Mat Ltd v. Elcombe* [1988] 1 WLR 1350; *Behbehani v. Salem* [1989] 2 All ER 143; *Arab Monetary Fund v. Hashim* [1989] 1 WLR 565.

28 *O'Regan v. Iambic Productions Ltd* (1989) 139 NLJ 1378. See for an example of the respondent's own boasting giving rise to the necessary apprehension *A/S D/S Svendborg v. Wansa* [1997] 2 Lloyd's Rep 183, 188–189.

29 For other kinds of undertaking, given to the court but enforceable by the respondent against the applicant as though they were contractually given to him as well, see *Independiente Ltd v. Music Trading Online (HK) Ltd* [2007] EWCA Civ 111, [2008] 1 WLR 608.

30 The proposition that the order was one which should not have been made does not mean that it was wrong, or was an actionable wrong, to apply for it, for at the time the order is applied for and made, it is not possible to know whether it will turn out to be one which should or should not have been made: *SmithKline Beecham plc v. Apotex Europe Ltd* [2006] EWCA Civ 658, [2007] Ch 71, [25]. The decision also established that the undertaking may be enforced only by the party to whom it was, in effect, given: a non-party acquires no rights under it, even if he appears to have sustained loss as a consequence of the injunction.

31 For such orders against third parties, see *Bankers Trust Co v. Shapira* [1980] 1 WLR 1274.

32 Even if out of the jurisdiction: *Gidrxslme Shipping Co Ltd v. Tantomar-Transportes Maritimos Lda* [1995] 1 WLR 299.

33 CPR r. 25.1(1)(g); *Z Ltd v. A-Z; AJ Bekhor & Co Ltd v. Bilton* [1981] QB 923; *Arab Monetary Fund v. Hashim (No 5)* [1992] 2 All ER 911. For the proposition that a defendant may be required to give disclosure in relation to all his assets, including those in countries in relation to which the court would have no power to grant injunctive relief, see *JSC VTB Bank v. Skurikhin* [2014] EWHC 2254 (QB).

34 *PCW (Undertaking Agencies) Ltd v. Dixon* [1983] 2 All ER 697; *Iraqi Ministry of Defence v. Arcepey* [1981] QB 65.

35 *Derby & Co Ltd v. Weldon (No 2)* [1990] 1 WLR 1139.

36 Such a heretical suggestion had been made in *Z Ltd v. A-Z;* but it was disapproved in *A-G v. Times Newspapers Ltd* [1992] 1 AC 191, 215, and has not been heard of since.

insolvency of the respondent the applicant has no prior claim on the assets subject to the injunction.

The respondent/defendant who disobeys the order of the court may be dealt with for his contempt: his defence to the action may be struck out with the result that default judgment may be entered;[37] he may be fined or imprisoned.

The injunction is in the form of an order made against defendants to the action; it claims to have, and has, no direct effect on a non-party who is, *ex hypothesi*, not addressed by the order made. But a non-party who is notified of the injunction, or who otherwise becomes aware of its having been made, is at risk of being found to be in contempt of court, on the ground that he has interfered with the course of justice, if he assists the defendant/respondent in the disposal of the assets or in other acts which conflict with the injunction.[38] It is for this reason that banks, in which funds attributable to the defendant may be held, may be notified of the injunction before the ink is dry on the order. But because of the difficult position in which this may put them, the injunction and the manner in which it is to affect such a non-party will be spelled out in the order in as much detail as possible. Indeed, the exemplary forms of injunction annexed to the Practice Direction[39] make clear the effect which the injunction may have on non-parties, and the circumstances in which it will do so. The undertaking in damages may be required to be extended to any losses sustained by third parties in complying with the injunction of which they have received notification.[40] Even so, there is some doubt, at the margins, as to the contempt jurisdiction of the court where, for example, a company is directed to act in a particular way, and it is alleged against an officer of the company that he has caused or contributed to the non-compliance of the company.[41] The issue is considered further below.

Although a freezing injunction, and orders requiring the giving of information as to assets, may be made in relation to assets of a defendant out of the jurisdiction, it is neither accurate nor particularly helpful to refer to such an order as being extraterritorial in character. If this terminology is important, then as the order is made against a defendant who is subject to the *in personam* jurisdiction of the court,[42] it may more properly be seen as intra-territorial.[43] But the form of the order when made against the respondent in relation to assets within and outside the jurisdiction is sometimes known as a 'worldwide' freezing injunction;[44] and the perception that the court is making an order of unusual width and

---

37 For an illustration of this, and of the practical difficulties which this may cause for the enforcement of the judgment, see C-394/07 *Gambazzi v. Daimler Chrysler Canada Inc* [2009] ECR I-2563.

38 *Cf A-G v. Times Newspapers Ltd* [1992] 1 AC 191; *Bank Mellat v. Kazmi* [1989] 1 QB 541.

39 CPR Part 25 PD 25A: Practice Direction – Interim Injunctions, para. 6 and Annex. For the specific treatment of banks which are subject to the jurisdiction of the English court but hold customer accounts overseas, see *Baltic Shipping Co v. Translink Ltd* [1995] 1 Lloyd's Rep 673; *Bank of China v. NBM LLC* [2001] EWCA Civ 1916, [2002] 1 WLR 844.

40 *Clipper Maritime Co Ltd of Monrovia v. Mineral Import-Export of Bucharest* [1981] 1 WLR 1262; *Ghoth v. Ghoth* [1992] 2 All ER 920.

41 *Dar ar-Alkan Real Estate Development Co v. Al-Refai* [2014] EWCA Civ 715 [2015] 1 WLR 135.

42 On the manner in which he may be made subject to the jurisdiction of the English court, see below.

43 For unexpected acceptance of this by the French Cour de Cassation, see *Banque Worms v. Brachot* [2003] Rev crit DIP 816 (*note* Muir-Watt), [2003] CLJ 573 (agreeing in principle that such an order may even be made by a French court) and *Stolzenberg v. Daimler Chrysler Canada Inc* [2005] JDI/Clunet 112 (*note* Cuniberti), [2005] ILPr 266, recognising and authorising enforcement of an English post-judgment freezing injunction.

44 For the development of these, see *Ashtiani v. Kashi* [1987] QB 888; *Babanaft International Co SA v. Bassatne* [1990] Ch 13; *Derby & Co Ltd v. Weldon (No 1)* [1990] Ch 48; *Derby & Co Ltd v. Weldon (Nos 3 & 4)* [1990]

scope may be reflected in the exercise of its discretion when determining whether the order should be made.[45] The order will usually specify that it is not to be enforced outside England without the leave of the court, though this does not limit its effectiveness as much as might have been supposed.[46]

In contrast with the above proposition, the rule which allows the court to proceed for contempt against a non-party who was, *ex hypothesi*, not a defendant to the action does raise the theoretical possibility of the court's being asked to hold in contempt a non-party, outside and not subject to the jurisdiction of the English court, for having been notified of the injunction but failing to act to prevent the defendant from breaching the order. Imposing liability upon such individuals would be accurately described as extraterritorial, and at the very least it raises questions about the proper reach of orders made by an English court. In the early cases on worldwide freezing injunctions, attempts were made to formulate a statement which would be incorporated into the injunction, and which would make it clear that the English courts were not seeking to impose liability in this way, or to make orders which went beyond what comity could properly justify.[47] The present version[48] of the notice in respect of third parties (which is to say, non-parties) outside the jurisdiction of the court states that the terms of the order 'do not affect or concern anyone outside the jurisdiction of this court until it is declared enforceable by or is enforced by a court in the relevant country and then they are to affect him only to the extent that they have been declared enforceable or have been enforced unless the person is (i) a person to whom this order is addressed or an officer or an agent appointed by power of attorney of that person, or (ii) a person who is subject to the jurisdiction of this court and (a) has been given written notice of this order at his residence or place of business within the jurisdiction of this court and (b) is able to prevent acts or omissions made outside the jurisdiction of this court which constitute or assist in a breach of the terms of this order'. Usually this will be clear enough to convey its meaning to a person who might be concerned by it, but care must be taken to avoid any ambiguity in the wording.[49]

It follows that the non-parties who are deemed to be affected by the order, and therefore by the possibility of being found to be in contempt of court for not complying with it, include officers and agents of the defendant. That means that an officer of a company against whom the order is made may be, so far as English law is concerned, proceeded against as a person who has acted in defiance of an order framed in these terms. But other orders may be made, to which this exemplary proviso is not attached, but in relation to which it may

---

Ch 65; *Derby & Co Ltd v. Weldon (No 2)* [1990] 1 WLR 1139; *Republic of Haiti v. Duvalier* [1990] 1 QB 202; *Masri v. Consolidated Contractors International (UK) Ltd (No 2)* [2008] EWCA Civ 303, [2009] QB 450.

45 *Rosseel NV v. Oriental and Commercial Shipping (UK) Ltd* [1990] 1 WLR 1387; for reconsideration, *Credit Suisse Fides Trust SA v. Cuoghi* [1998] QB 818.

46 *Babanaft International Co SA v. Bassatne* [1990] Ch 13; *Derby & Co Ltd v. Weldon (No 1)* [1990] Ch 48; *Derby & Co Ltd v. Weldon (Nos 3 & 4)* [1990] Ch 65; *Derby & Co Ltd v. Weldon (No 2)* [1990] 1 WLR 1139; *Republic of Haiti v. Duvalier* [1990] 1 QB 202; *Dadourian Group International Inc v. Simms* [2006] EWCA Civ 389, [2006] 2 All ER (Comm) 385 (which is helpful on the manner in which the court should assess whether to grant such leave to enforce).

47 For the role of comity, see the account in *Masri v. Consolidated Contractors International (UK) Ltd (No 2)* [2008] EWCA Civ 303, [2009] QB 450, at [35]–[39], where the role of comity is made in relation to the appointment of receivers by way of equitable execution.

48 Practice Direction 25A supplementing CPR Part 25 sets out standard forms of the Orders.

49 *Cf Masri v. Consolidated Contractors International Co SAL* [2009] EWCA Civ 36, [2009] 1 CLC 82 (in relation to a receivership order).

be alleged that (for example) a corporate officer has become liable to act, and liable to be proceeded with as a civil contemnor where he does not comply.[50] These are bound to cause difficulty by reason of the ambiguity over who is addressed, who is considered to be bound by the order without having been addressed in specific terms, and who is considered to be liable if they fail to cooperate with the order. It does not seem satisfactory that such questions can still give rise to such difficulty.

6.04 Interim measures: the search, or *Anton Piller*, order

The search order describes what was until 1999 known as the *Anton Piller* order, so named after the first case to clarify that courts had power to grant it.[51] The defendant[52] is ordered[53] to permit his premises to be searched by the claimant or his agents, and to permit property to be removed for the purpose of preserving evidence and so on. From time to time the potential for abusive recourse to this process leads the courts to insist upon its more stringent control,[54] but even after such control has been applied, the defendant may still be left with the impression that a smash-and-grab raid has been sanctioned by the court and carried out on his property. The order may be made in relation to premises inside or outside England,[55] for the jurisdiction in question is personal to the defendant, rather than proprietary in character. Even so, the fact that the premises are outside England will reduce the likelihood that the order will be made, not least by reason of the great practical difficulty of supervising its enforcement.

6.05 Interim measures: interlocutory injunctions in general

The category of interim injunctions covers orders made against a defendant, against whom a final injunction or other relief is ultimately sought, that in the meantime he refrain from doing what is complained of. The leading case is *American Cyanamid Co v. Ethicon Ltd*;[56] the court is required to determine whether granting a temporary injunction, or leaving the parties to their eventual remedies, will more justly preserve the position until trial. Frequently, the granting (or not) of the injunction will effectively dispose of the case, which will not thereafter proceed to trial. In consequence much case law has accumulated around this particular species of application.[57]

---

50 Contrast *Masri v. Consolidated Contractors International Co SAL (No 4)* [2009] UKHL 43, [2010] 1 AC 90 (order for examination of officer of company which had submitted to jurisdiction of court: reach of order not sufficient to apply to officer out of the jurisdiction) with *Dar ar-Alkan Real Estate Development Co v. Al-Refai* [2014] EWCA Civ 715 [2015] 1 WLR 135 (order for preservation of property by company which had submitted to jurisdiction of court: reach of order sufficient to apply to officer out of the jurisdiction).

51 *Anton Piller KG v. Manufacturing Processes Ltd* [1976] Ch 55. It is most commonly used in breach of copyright and trade secret cases. It now has a statutory basis in Civil Procedure Act 1997, s. 7.

52 The remedy cannot be sought against someone not party to the proceedings.

53 On pain of imprisonment for contempt, which does have a rather medieval flavour to it.

54 *Bhimji v. Chatwani* [1991] 1 WLR 989; *Universal Thermosensors v. Hibben* [1992] 1 WLR 840. See now the model form of *Anton Piller* Order in CPR Part 25 PD 25A.

55 *Altertext Inc v. Advanced Data Communications Ltd* [1985] 1 WLR 457.

56 [1975] AC 396.

57 Note that there may be an interlocutory anti-suit injunction, the availability of which is a matter to be decided by the test in *American Cyanamid*: *Apple Corps Ltd v. Apple Computers Inc* [1992] RPC 70, 76–77; *National Westminster Bank Ltd v. Utrecht-America Finance Co* [2001] EWCA Civ 658, [2001] 3 All ER 733, [28]–[29]; *Midgulf International Ltd v. Groupe Chimiche Tunisien* [2009] EWHC 963 (Comm).

6.06 Obtaining an order granting an interim remedy: general

It is next necessary to address the question of the jurisdictional criteria that need to be satisfied before the court may make the order applied for. This jurisdictional issue is quite distinct from, and is without prejudice to, the fact that, even if there is jurisdiction to make the order, all of the above measures are granted only at the discretion of the court. So, for example, even if there is jurisdiction to grant a freezing injunction against the particular defendant in relation to his assets on a worldwide basis, the court may make the order on a narrower basis, or decide not to make the order at all. This will not be because the court lacks the jurisdiction to do so, but because, in the exercise of its discretion, it finds it to be inappropriate to do so.[58]

6.07 Jurisdiction to grant interim remedies: English law

The principal statement of the existence and width of the court's power to grant relief is in section 25 of the Civil Jurisdiction and Judgments Act 1982, as amended,[59] which provides that a court has power to order interim relief where proceedings have been or are to be commenced in another State, or elsewhere in the United Kingdom. As a result of the amendment of the original version of the section, the court's powers are not confined, as they once were, to cases where the foreign proceedings are or will be before the courts of a Member State or a Lugano II State, and they are not confined to cases in which the foreign proceedings are in a civil or commercial matter. But an application under section 25 may not be made for measures in support of an arbitration.[60]

On the other hand, the relief sought from the English court must be related to substantive proceedings in the foreign court, in the sense that the English order could properly be seen as interim relief in relation to the orders sought in the foreign proceedings. If the matter before the foreign court is not properly to be seen substantive in nature, in the sense of section 25, or if the relationship between the relief being sought in the foreign court and the relief applied for from the English court is not such that an English order could be seen as an interim measure in relation to it, the jurisdiction under section 25 will not be available.[61] For example, an order may be made in support of substantive proceedings before the courts of another country which are themselves brought to enforce judgments by attaching debts owed to the judgment debtor;[62] but an order under section 25 may not be made in support of proceedings which take the form of a judicial attachment of assets 'in aid of an

---

58 For the observation that this shows the term 'jurisdiction' to be ambiguous, and maybe unhelpfully so, see *Fourie v. Le Roux* [2007] UKHL 1, [2007] 1 WLR 320, [25].

59 By Civil Jurisdiction and Judgments Act 1982 (Interim Relief) Order 1997, SI 1997/302, removing the limitations originally established by s. 25(1).

60 Instead, Arbitration Act 1996, s. 44, is used, as s. 25(3)(c) of the 1982 Act was repealed without having been brought into force.

61 *Fourie v. Le Roux* [2007] UKHL 1, [2007] 1 WLR 320.

62 *Kensington International Ltd v. Republic of Congo* [2007] EWCA Civ 1128, [2008] 1 Lloyd's Rep 161 (proceedings in Switzerland: the court considered that the orders should be as broad as they would have been if the English court had been seised of the merits of the claim). There is room for respectful doubt whether proceedings in Switzerland to enforce a non-Swiss judgment are substantive for this purpose, but the decision of the Court of Appeal does not question this. The Court of Appeal in *ETI Euro Telecom International NV v. Republic of Bolivia* [2008] EWCA Civ 880, [2009] 1 WLR 665 confirmed that the Swiss proceedings in *Kensington* were substantive for the purpose of s. 25.

international arbitration', for the proceedings before the court are not substantive proceedings brought to resolve the merits of a dispute between the parties.[63]

6.08 Jurisdiction to grant interim remedies: the relevance of European law

Section 25 of the Act states the jurisdictional basis of the court's power to grant interim remedies. The question therefore arises whether any limit or control is placed on that jurisdiction by the provisions of the Brussels I Regulation. The short answer is that, so far as jurisdiction, strictly so called, is concerned, it is not; but the Regulation does limit the circumstances in which certain kinds of order, which the national court would otherwise have power to grant, may be granted.

The Regulation does not state or define the jurisdictional basis for the awarding of interim remedies in civil or commercial proceedings. The result is that the question of jurisdiction is left to national law, with the Regulation confining itself to imposing limits on the grant of relief which are quasi-jurisdictional, but not strictly jurisdictional. It is this combination of national and European law which complicates the explanation, for though English law devises its law in terms of interim remedies, the Regulation makes special provision for 'provisional, including protective, measures' ordered in civil and commercial matters, and the two categories are completely congruent.

The most commercially important of the forms of interim remedy available from the English court is the freezing injunction.[64] It is proposed to examine the complex and interlocking jurisdictional framework for obtaining orders for interim remedies by taking this as the example which illustrates the law. There are three variables which, in combination, serve to define and delineate the jurisdiction of an English court to grant or not grant interim remedies. These are, first, whether the relief sought is in relation to a civil or commercial matter; second, whether the English court has jurisdiction over the substantive claim; and third, whether the courts of another Member State have jurisdiction over the substantive claim. In terms of legal source material, it is necessary to consider the interlocking application of the Brussels I Regulation;[65] the Civil Jurisdiction and Judgments Act 1982; and CPR rule 6.36.[66]

It is therefore convenient to distinguish seven situations in which relief may be applied for from the English courts. These are:

(A) where the relief is sought in a civil or commercial matter in proceedings in which the Regulation provides that the English court has jurisdiction over the defendant in relation to the substance of the claim;[67]

(B) where the relief is sought in a civil or commercial matter in proceedings in which the Regulation provides that the English court does not have jurisdiction over the

---

63 *ETI Euro Telecom International NV v. Republic of Bolivia* [2008] EWCA Civ 880, [2009] 1 WLR 665.

64 It is sometimes said that it is not so much the injunction, but the accompanying order that the respondent give information as to the existence and location of his assets, which is the most valuable measure for, once this order is complied with, the claimant can apply to the courts for the place where the assets are for an attachment. The order used to be considered as ancillary to the *Mareva* injunction; it is now a separately recognised form of interim remedy: CPR r. 25.1(1)(g).

65 The recast Regulation 1215/2012 is taken as the basis for the discussion; its substantive proceedings are not significantly different from the provisions of the original Regulation 44/2001.

66 And Para. 3.1(5) of the Practice Direction.

67 That is to say, under a provision of the Regulation other than Art. 6: Art. 6 cases may raise separate issues, and are discussed in relation to situation (D), para. 6.14, below.

defendant in relation to the substance of the claim but that the courts of another Member State do have jurisdiction;

(C) where the relief is sought in a civil or commercial matter in respect of potential proceedings, not yet instituted, but over which the Regulation provides that the English court may have, and the courts of another Member State may also have, jurisdiction over the defendant;

(D) where the relief is sought in a civil or commercial matter in proceedings in which a court in a Member State has jurisdiction on the basis of Article 6 of the Regulation;

(E) where the relief is sought in a civil or commercial matter, in circumstances in which neither the English court nor the court of any other Member State has jurisdiction;

(F) where the relief is sought in relation to a matter which is not civil or commercial, but in proceedings in which the English court has jurisdiction over the defendant in respect of the substantive claim; and

(G) where the relief is sought in relation to proceedings in a matter which is being litigated before the courts of a non-Member State.

6.09 (A) Relief sought in proceedings in civil or commercial matter pending before English court

This is the straightforward case from which all the others are departures. If the dispute arises in a civil or commercial matter, the Brussels I Regulation will determine whether the English court has jurisdiction over the defendant in respect of the substantive claim. If the English court does have jurisdiction over the defendant in respect of the substantive claim, and this jurisdiction has been invoked, the Regulation allows the English court to make – in the sense that it does not stand in the way of the making of – any ancillary order which it sees fit to impose.

Confirmation that the national court with substantive jurisdiction over a civil or commercial matter does enjoy freedom, so far as the Regulation is concerned, to impose orders for ancillary relief, comes from the explicit statement to this effect in the judgment of the European Court in *Van Uden Maritime BV v. Firma Deco-Line*.[68] In that case, an application for an interim payment had been made to a Dutch court, even though the parties had agreed that the merits of the substantive claim were to be resolved by arbitration. The European Court observed that there was a fundamental distinction between the orders which could be made by a court which had jurisdiction over the merits of the dispute, and those which could be obtained from a court which did not have such jurisdiction. In the former case, there was no further jurisdictional condition required to be satisfied before the court could make orders of a provisional and protective kind, because it had substantive jurisdiction in any event. In the latter case, the jurisdictional basis for the power of the court to act was what is now Article 35 of the recast Regulation, and this is examined in due course.

---

68 C-391/95, [1998] ECR I-7091: see esp. at [22]. The decision builds on and develops, and effectively supersedes, the earlier decision in 125/79 *Denilauler v. SNC Couchet Frères* [1980] ECR 1553. For this purpose, the English court has jurisdiction even where it was seised but, by reference to Art. 29 of the Regulation, the proceedings are stayed while the court seised first determines whether it has jurisdiction: *J P Morgan Europe Ltd v. Primacom AG* [2005] EWHC 508 (Comm), [2005] 2 Lloyd's Rep 665.

This aspect of the decision in *Van Uden* was applied, and just possibly extended a little, by the Court of Appeal in *Masri v. Consolidated Contractors International (UK) Ltd (No 2)*,[69] and *Masri v. Consolidated Contractors International (UK) Ltd (No 4)*,[70] where the court interpreted the first part of the rule in *Van Uden* to mean that the court which was exercising jurisdiction on the merits of the case was free to make any ancillary order permitted and provided for by English[71] law: in other words, there was no restriction or limitation imposed by the Brussels I Regulation upon the orders that may be made by a court with jurisdiction over the merits.[72] It follows that the orders made by the court with jurisdiction over the substantive claim are not confined to being 'provisional, including protective, measures' in the sense in which this expression is used in Article 35, as Article 35 is irrelevant to the case.[73] To put it another way, the court which has jurisdiction over the substantive claim, or full jurisdiction or plenary jurisdiction over the defendant on the merits may grant such ancillary relief as it sees fit. It therefore follows that any or all of the remedies listed in CPR rule 25.1 are available to the applicant.

This principle is clear and straightforward to apply if the English court has actually been seised with proceedings in respect of the claim against the defendant. It appears that matters are, in this respect, not affected by the fact that the court has actually given judgment but remains concerned to supervise and assist the enforcement of that judgment,[74] for the range of ancillary measures available to the court is not obviously limited to orders made before final judgment. After all, the proposition that a court has no power to grant relief which will assist in the enforcement of the judgment which it has just given would be a very strange one.

In two circumstances the application of this clear rule is more problematic. First, if no proceedings have yet been instituted and there is more than one court which may have jurisdiction under the Regulation, the correct interpretation of *Van Uden* may appear to be unclear; the case is considered below.[75] Second, the Court did not deal specifically with the case in which an English court might have had jurisdiction but for the fact that the provisions on *lis alibi pendens* precluded this possibility when substantive proceedings were instituted in the courts of another Member State. But the better conclusion is that, in such a case, it is irrelevant that the English court might have had jurisdiction, because it does not

---

69 [2008] EWCA Civ 303, [2009] QB 450 (appointment of receiver), applied in *Masri v. Consolidated Contractors International (UK) Ltd (No 3)* [2008] EWCA Civ 625, [2009] QB 503 (anti-suit injunction in relation to proceedings in non-Member State); to same effect, see also *The Ikarian Reefer (No 2)* [2000] 1 WLR 603 (third party costs order).

70 [2008] EWCA Civ 876, [2009] 2 WLR 699 (order for examination of director of judgment debtor): reversed on interpretation of CPR Part 71 (on the ground that the power only exists in relation to persons present within the jurisdiction) with no reference to the position under European law which was irrelevant on the facts of the case: *Masri v. Consolidated Contractors International Co SAL (No 4)* [2009] UKHL 43, [2010] 1 AC 90. For the distinct issues of service, which may need to be made on a non-party and out of the jurisdiction, see at [55] *et seq.* and now see also CPR rr 6.38, 6.39.

71 Where, by contrast, the order applied for is unavailable as a matter of English law, there will be no question of making it: *Masri v. Consolidated Contractors International Co SAL (No 4)* [2009] UKHL 43, [2010] 1 AC 90.

72 Excluding, of course, an anti-suit injunction in respect of proceedings before the courts of another Member State, even if this would be justifiable on the ground that it is necessary to protect the jurisdiction of the court, for this is absolutely prohibited in any guise: C-159/02 *Turner v. Grovit* [2004] ECR I-3565; C-185/07 *Allianz SpA v. West Tankers Inc* [2009] ECR I-663; *Masri v. Consolidated Contractors International (UK) Ltd (No 3)* [2008] EWCA Civ 625, [2009] QB 503.

73 As to the definition of these, see the following paragraph.

74 *Masri v. Consolidated Contractors International (UK) Ltd (No 2)* [2008] EWCA Civ 303, [2009] QB 450.

75 Paragraph 6.13, below.

now, with the consequence that the facts should be seen to fall within example (B), which is considered below. However, if the jurisdiction of the court first seised has not yet been determined, with the result that the English court does not yet lack jurisdiction, its power to act may be the same as where it has jurisdiction under the Regulation in the full sense of the term.[76]

As in this case the Brussels I Regulation provides the basis for jurisdiction, and does not place any restriction on the substance of the measures which can be ordered, and as jurisdiction will already have been asserted in the substantive claim in accordance with the rules of the Regulation, and process will already have been served on the defendant, there is no difficulty in relation to the service of any application notice which may be required.[77] The case will be one in which the Regulation provides jurisdiction, and service is a matter of course.

Where the court has exercised jurisdiction and has given judgment on the merits, and its concern is now for the enforcement of its judgment, it will still consider itself to have jurisdiction over the merits of the claim, and its power to make ancillary orders will certainly extend to anything which might have been regarded as interim relief.[78] The only limitation on its power will be Article 24(5) of the Brussels I Regulation, which gives exclusive jurisdiction regardless of domicile to the courts of the Member State on whose territory a judgment from a Member State is to be enforced, but it is generally understood that this refers, and is limited, to measures of execution.

6.10 (B) Relief sought in relation to proceedings in civil or commercial matter over which courts of another Member State have jurisdiction

In this second example, the English court may grant relief in support of the substantive proceedings in a civil or commercial matter which will be brought elsewhere in the Member States. But the Brussels I Regulation limits the specific kinds of remedy which may in these circumstances be ordered by the English court.

Article 35 of Regulation 1215/2012 provides that:

> *Application may be made to the courts of a Member State for such provisional, including protective, measures as may be available under the law of that Member State, even if the courts of another Member State have jurisdiction as to the substance of the matter.*

And it means what it says: Article 35 opens the way to a court making the order applied for, even in circumstances in which the court with jurisdiction over the substance of the claim has it as exclusive jurisdiction, regardless of domicile, in accordance with Article 24. This just goes to show the fundamental separation between proceedings in relation to the substance of the claim, and applications for provisional and protective measures. In *Solvay SA v. Honeywell Fluorine Products Europe BV*,[79] it was pointed out that there is nothing in the text of what is now Article 35 to make an exception for the case in which another court has jurisdiction under Article 24, and that there is no risk of conflicting or irreconcilable decisions, as the provisional order made by reference to Article 35 does not purport to rule on the substantive issues which are before the court with jurisdiction over the merits of the

---

76 *JP Morgan Europe Ltd v. Primacom AG* [2005] EWHC 508 (Comm), [2005] 2 Lloyd's Rep 665.
77 For when an application notice is required, see CPR Part 23 and CPR rr 25.2–25.4.
78 *Masri v. Consolidated Contractors International (UK) Ltd (No 2)* [2008] EWCA Civ 303, [2009] QB 450.
79 C-616/10, EU:C:2012:445.

claim. It followed that a court might grant relief – so far as the Regulation was concerned, at any rate – even though another court has exclusive jurisdiction over the substance of the claim, regardless of domicile.

However, *Van Uden* establishes that the court may order those, but only those, 'provisional, including protective' measures which form the material scope of Article 35 of the Regulation.[80] If the court is asked to go, or may have gone, beyond the kinds of order permitted by Article 35, the person against whom the order is sought will be entitled to object on the basis of the jurisdictional grounds set out in Chapter II of the Regulation.[81] If, however, the measure applied for does fall within the material scope of Article 35, then the Regulation imposes no jurisdictional bar to relief, but opens the way to the application for and grant of relief. It will therefore fall to English law to determine the conditions, including jurisdictional conditions, for the making of the application and the granting of relief. Though the Regulation opens the gate to the making of those orders which count as 'provisional, including protective', the grounds on which the order may be obtained are defined by English law.

Where Article 35 of the Regulation is relied on as the basis for the court to act, the measures which it is open to the court to grant are those which 'are intended to preserve a factual or legal situation so as to safeguard rights the recognition of which is otherwise sought from the court having jurisdiction as to the substance of the case'. Moreover, the ordering of such measures requires particular care on the part of the court, for example, in the imposition of time limits, the scope of the order, the need for security or cross-undertakings to be given by the applicant, and so forth and, in particular, in order to ensure that the measure is properly provisional and does not trespass on the jurisdiction of the court seised with the substantive dispute. As a result, two further restrictions, which are not precisely jurisdictional in nature, have been read into or deduced from Article 35 and its relationship to the structure of the Regulation as a whole.

First, there must be a 'real connecting link' between the United Kingdom and the subject matter of the measures sought.[82] Second, for the measure to be regarded as provisional, it must include a guarantee of repayment in the event of the substantive claim being unsuccessful, and the measure itself must be restricted to specific assets located within the jurisdiction of the English court.[83]

The justification for placing these material limitations upon what the court may order under the authority of Article 35 is to prevent the court acting on the basis of Article 35 trespassing on the territory of the adjudicating court, and to limit the harm that may be done to a defendant by the obtaining of relief, which may bear onerously on him, from a court to whose substantive jurisdiction he is not otherwise subject. The rule in *Van Uden*

---

80 The case was decided in relation to the Brussels Convention, the corresponding provision of which was in identical terms.

81 This means that he will be able to object to the jurisdiction of the English court by reference to the provisions of Chapter II of the recast Regulation, excluding Art. 6. It is less clear that a defendant/respondent sued on the basis of Art. 6 is in the same position, for that defendant has no jurisdictional defence extended to him by the Regulation except for Arts 29 and 30: C-351/89 *Overseas Union Insurance Ltd v. New Hampshire Insurance Co* [1991] ECR I-3317; on this, see further below, para. 6.14.

82 *Van Uden*, at [40]. See further *ICICI Bank UK plc v. Diminco NV* [2014] EWHC 3124 (Comm); *Cruz City 1 Mauritius Holdings v. Unitech Ltd* [2014] EWHC 3704 (Comm).

83 *Mutatis mutandis* if the interim relief is sought from a foreign court in relation to English substantive proceedings (*cf Wermuth v. Wermuth* [2003] EWCA Civ 50, [2003] 1 WLR 942, a case on the Brussels II Regulation (originally Regulation 1347/2000, now replaced by Regulation 2201/2003)).

may be considered to be jurisdictional in the sense that it defines the characteristics of the orders for which Article 35 removes the jurisdictional defence which would otherwise be in place.

The transposition of these restrictions in the context of an English order for interim relief is more difficult. In *Van Uden* itself, the application made to the Dutch court was for an interim payment in respect of four unpaid invoices, pending the adjudication of a substantive claim; and it was in this context that the court established the limitation of Article 35 measures to assets within the territorial jurisdiction of the court ordering the relief. This limitation does not easily translate to, and explain itself in, the context of English law on interim remedies. It is true that the second restriction, which is designed to ensure the provisional and reversible quality of the measure, is not problematic, for in England the grant of interim relief will generally require cross-undertakings in damages to be given, and probably fortified, in cases where the order may turn out not to have been justified after all. But the important question is what is meant by a 'real connecting link' when the remedy being applied for is a freezing injunction.

The problem arises from the fact that, save for atypical cases, freezing injunctions do not take effect against assets at all, but are instead formulated as orders made against an individual in relation to his conduct and behaviour in relation to assets. On one rather cautious view, the effect of *Van Uden* is that the order may now be made only in relation to assets situated either in the United Kingdom[84] or outside the territory of the Member States,[85] but may not be made in respect of dealings with assets which are located within the territory of a Member State. A different view would be that, as the order made is not directed at assets at all, no account need be taken of their actual location: as long as the respondent is within or subject to the territorial jurisdiction of the English court, the existence of a real connecting link, for an order of this kind, which operates *in personam* only, is established. By contrast, when the respondent and his property are both outside the United Kingdom, a real connecting link will not be demonstrable, and the court will not have jurisdiction to make orders by reference to Article 35.[86]

This latter interpretation would derive some support from *dicta* in *Credit Suisse Fides Trust SA v. Cuoghi*.[87] As it is undoubtedly correct, as a matter of English law and theory, which considers that the freezing injunction operates *in personam* against an individual and not *in rem* against assets themselves, this distinction may be justifiable. It is also supported by the approach taken to the appointment of a receiver of assets by way of equitable execution, in *Masri v. Consolidated Contractors International (UK) Ltd (No 2)*,[88] where the contention that the receiver should not be authorised to collect sums due on debts which were not located in England was met by twin answers: that the order appointing the receiver takes effect only *in personam* against the judgment debtor and makes no proprietary claim to, or assertion of

---

84 It would not be the concern of the Regulation to stipulate whether the courts of one part of the United Kingdom could grant relief in relation to assets in another part of the United Kingdom.

85 As to which the Regulation has nothing to say (though see *Masri v. Consolidated Contractors International (UK) Ltd (No 2)* [2008] EWCA Civ 303, [2009] QB 450, [125]–[127] for the possible role of a principle of reflexive effect). See further *ICICI Bank UK plc v. Diminco NV* [2014] EWHC 3124 (Comm).

86 *Belletti v. Morici* [2009] EWHC 2316 (Comm), [2010] 1 All ER (Comm) 142.

87 [1998] QB 818, 827. The decision pre-dates that in *Van Uden* and deals instead with jurisdiction under English law in relation to the granting of interim remedies. See also *Sandisk Corp v. Koninlijke Philips Electronics NV* [2007] EWHC 332 (Ch), [2007] Bus LR 705, [49] *et seq*.

88 [2008] EWCA Civ 303, [2009] QB 450, esp. at [51]–[59].

title over, debts in any foreign jurisdiction,[89] and that any need for a territorial link to the United Kingdom, of the sort mentioned in *Van Uden*, was met by fact that the order operated *in personam* only and the judgment debtor was subject to the jurisdiction of the English court by voluntary submission.[90]

All that being said, it is still debatable whether such an analysis, conducted in purely English terms and based on an English analysis of the relief, will be decisive. The reason for hesitation is that, even though an English anti-suit injunction takes effect only against an individual who is, or who has been made, subject to the jurisdiction of the English court, and has no direct effect against a foreign judge or a foreign court, the European Court, in *Turner v. Grovit*,[91] declined to address the question of jurisdiction under the Regulation by accepting or adopting the English analysis of its own order. Instead, the Court interpreted the injunction as an order which did directly bite on the foreign court, as a result of which it was held to be inconsistent with the scheme of what is now the Brussels I Regulation. The injunction against *Grovit* may not have been an order restraining the Spanish court, but it was perceived to be a measure having equivalent effect. One may see how the English perception of a freezing injunction might be subjected to similarly structured reinterpretation. If this were to happen, Article 35 would not allow a freezing injunction to be made in relation to a defendant's dealing with assets within the territorial jurisdiction of another Member State, but would confine itself to assets in England.[92]

Such is the argument against the analysis put forward in *Cuoghi*. It is unclear whether it would find favour with the European Court. It is worth noting that the final courts of appeal in Switzerland[93] and France[94] have shown no unwillingness to recognise and enforce English freezing injunctions made against a defendant in respect of his assets worldwide, and that fact goes some long way to showing that courts in civil jurisdictions, which generally do not make orders of the freezing injunction kind, see no particular problem with the English court making worldwide freezing injunctions. On the other hand, the two cases in question were both ones in which the English court had, or could be considered to have had, jurisdiction over the defendant in relation to the merits of the case,[95] and in such a context the restrictions imposed by Article 35 of the Brussels I Regulation would be irrelevant in any event. The right answer remains to be confirmed.

---

89 It would be for the receiver to go and recover these, which he would only be able to do if local law permitted.

90 [2008] EWCA Civ 303, [2009] QB 450, esp. at [106]. But if this meant that the court was entitled to make the orders as part of its jurisdiction over the merits of the claim, this part of the reasoning is not relevant to the application of Art. 35.

91 C-159/02, [2004] ECR I-3565.

92 See, consistently with this, *Cruz City 1 Mauritius Holdings v. Unitech Ltd* [2014] EWHC 3704 (Comm).

93 Decision of the Swiss Federal Tribunal (on appeal from the Cantonal Court of Appeal, Zürich), *Uzan v. Motorola Credit Corp* ATF/BGE 129 III 626. See further, (2003) 74 BYBIL 541.

94 Decision of the Cour de Cassation (on appeal from the Paris Court of Appeal), *Stolzenberg v. Daimler Chrysler Canada Inc* [2005] JDI/Clunet 112 (*note* Cuniberti), [2005] ILPr 266, rejecting the appeal from *Stolzenberg v. CIBC Mellon Trust Co* [2002] Rev crit DIP 704 (*note* Muir-Watt).

95 In *Motorola,* this was because the Swiss court was prepared to consider the English court as one with 'virtual' jurisdiction. The substantive case was pending in the United States, but it would have been consistent with the Lugano Convention for the English court to have exercised jurisdiction over the merits. In *Stolzenberg*, it was because the English court was seised on the merits and had entered judgment against Stolzenberg in default of his appearance notwithstanding his having been duly served.

6.11 Making the order once Article 35 has opened the way: jurisdiction

Subject to elucidation of the true construction of the restrictions imposed by Article 35, as interpreted in the light of *Van Uden*, an English court will have power to grant the relief applied for if English procedural law makes provision for it in the circumstances of the case. But the court's jurisdiction over the defendant/respondent must be established, by service of the claim form by means of which the relief is sought, on the respondent. In other words, there must be personal jurisdiction over the respondent to grant the remedy claimed as a matter of English law. For although section 25 of the 1982 Act, as it now is, gives the court the power[96] to grant any interim remedy other than a warrant for the arrest of property or a provision for the obtaining of evidence, jurisdiction over the respondent to the claim for relief must still be established.[97] The English court will apply its own civil procedural law to determine whether there is to be jurisdiction over the respondent.[98]

If the respondent is within the territorial jurisdiction of the English court, he may be served as of right with the claim form by which the relief is sought, and the Brussels I Regulation will furnish no basis for his objecting to the jurisdiction. If he is not within the jurisdiction, an application for permission to serve out must be made pursuant to CPR rule 6.36 and Paragraph 3.1 of Practice Direction 6B. Paragraph 3.1(5) provides for service of a claim form in respect of the claim for an interim remedy, whether or not the English court would have had jurisdiction over the substantive claim. On the other hand, as the most potent characteristic of a freezing order is the power to obtain it without notice[99] to the respondent, section 24 of the 1982 Act[100] makes it clear that the court has power to make an order for interim relief in cases where the jurisdiction of the court is itself doubtful.[101] Often the application for permission to serve out of the jurisdiction will be made at the same time as the application for the freezing injunction is made without notice to the defendant.

Where the defendant is not within the jurisdiction, it is not open to a claimant to circumvent the requirement of applying for permission to serve out by contending that service out may be made as of right under CPR rule 6.33, for the case is not one in which the court has jurisdiction by virtue of the Brussels I Regulation or the 1982 Act. The Regulation, and Schedule 1 to the 1982 Act provide, in effect and as understood in the light of *Van Uden*, that the court may grant these remedies if it has jurisdiction under its national law. It does not provide that it has jurisdiction under the Brussels I Regulation simply because it may order them subject to some further jurisdictional limitations.[102]

In cases in which it is necessary to seek permission to serve the respondent out of the jurisdiction, the court will not grant permission unless England is the proper place to seek the relief. Whether it is will depend in large measure upon whether the court considers that the application for relief would be successful if there were no question about the existence

---

96 Whether it will exercise its discretion to do so in the individual case is examined below.

97 In other words, these two forms of relief may not be applied for, or ordered, whatever CPR r. 25.1 may say.

98 Including, if it should wish, grounds of jurisdiction which are exorbitant and which may not be used to assert jurisdiction to hear a substantive claim against a defendant domiciled in a Member State.

99 For the procedure for application without notice to the respondent, see CPR r. 25.2.

100 As amended by SI 2001/3929, Sch. 2, para. 9.

101 For illustration, see *Thunder Air Ltd v. Hilmarsson* [2008] EWHC 355 (Ch).

102 This clarification of the jurisdictional basis upon which an English court may act means that the earlier and problematic decisions in *Republic of Haiti v. Duvalier* [1990] 1 QB 202, *X v. Y* [1990] 1 QB 220 and *Mercedes Benz AG v. Leiduck* [1996] 1 AC 284 (in all of which the court struggled to find a plausible basis for service process on a respondent who was out of the jurisdiction) are superseded and present no further difficulty.

of jurisdiction: in effect, the question of substance – whether the order should be made even though the court does not have jurisdiction over the merits of the claim – plays a part in the jurisdictional decision whether to authorise service out. It is, therefore, appropriate to say something about it at this point, but to return to it as well when addressing directly the law on granting or not granting relief.[103]

6.12 Making the order when Article 35 has opened the way: substance or discretion

According to section 25(2) of the 1982 Act, the court may refuse to grant the relief sought if the fact that it has no jurisdiction over the substance of the claim makes it 'inexpedient' for the court to grant the relief claimed. The nature of 'inexpediency' is examined here, and it will be considered again when it arises in relation to proceedings before the courts of non-Member States. The reason for this is that what is expedient when there are civil or commercial proceedings before the courts of a Member State, that is to say, proceedings which will almost inevitably result in a judgment which will be recognised in England, may not be the same as the analysis of expediency when the proceedings are before the courts of a non-Member State.[104]

Certain early cases,[105] which had sought to structure the exercise of discretion by making a departure from the literal wording of section 25(2), were disapproved in *Credit Suisse Fides Trust SA v. Cuoghi*,[106] which represents the practical starting point for the analysis of 'inexpediency'. In *Cuoghi*, the court emphasised that the question was one of the expediency or otherwise of granting the relief. It proposed that the answer to the question whether it was expedient to make the order would frequently be found by using a simple rule of thumb. An English freezing injunction takes effect against an individual as a person, rather than against assets as property. It could be presumed to be expedient to grant relief if the defendant resided in England, but inexpedient to grant it if he were resident elsewhere.[107]

By way of derogation from the application of this simple dichotomy, if the foreign court had been applied to for relief and, though having the power to grant it, had elected not to grant the relief, it would not generally[108] be expedient to grant the relief,[109] for this would run the risk of directly contradicting the foreign court's appreciation of the desirability of the measures. However, if the foreign court could be said to 'lack jurisdiction to make

---

103 See also Johnson (2008) 27 CJQ 433.

104 Or before the courts of a Member State in proceedings which are not in a civil or commercial matter.

105 *Rosseel NV v. Oriental Commercial Shipping (UK) Ltd* [1990] 1 WLR 1387; *S & T Bautrading v. Nordling* [1997] 3 All ER 718.

106 [1998] QB 818.

107 At 826–867. In relation to orders which were formulated to take effect against assets as such, the critical issue would be the location of the assets rather than the residence of the respondent.

108 But not invariably: *Ryan v. Friction Dynamics Ltd*, The Times, 14 June 2000. The case also held that if the foreign court had already granted a worldwide freezing order, the court was not prevented from granting overlapping relief (though this would generally be cast in the same terms as the relief granted by the foreign court). For it to be expedient to expose a respondent to such apparent oppression the case must presumably be an unusual one. The order may be made to lapse when the court in which the substantive action is to be brought has made orders of its own, so as not to tread on the toes of the foreign court: *Franses v. Al Assad* [2007] EWHC 2442 (Ch), [2007] BPIR 1233. And see also *Indosuez International Finance BV v. National Reserve Bank* [2002] EWHC 774 (Comm); and on the duty of the applicant to the court, *Lewis v. Eliades*, 1 February 2002 (on the need to justify the application properly).

109 At 29.

an effective order' and as there was said to be, in *Cuoghi*, no reason to suppose that the Swiss court would not 'welcome' the granting of relief by an English court,[110] there would be no reason to consider it inexpedient to make the order against the English resident defendant.[111]

The proposition advanced in *Cuoghi*, that a Swiss court could properly welcome the assistance of an English court in making an order, the power to make which the Swiss lawmakers have withheld from their courts, is a rather curious one. It is not apparent that a Swiss court may be said to welcome a form of judicial intervention which it has no power under the law to order for itself: one may fairly ask how a Swiss court could or would welcome the making of an order by an English court, requiring a person to make disclosure of financial information which, as a matter of Swiss law, he is entitled to preserve without publicity. How, in short, is it to be concluded that the intervention of the English court will be welcome, at least in the absence of a letter or request from the foreign court? In any event, it will presumably be open to a respondent to adduce evidence that the court seised with the substantive dispute cannot purport to, or will not, welcome the intervention made by an English court.[112]

The approach in *Cuoghi* was further developed by the Court of Appeal in *Motorola Credit Corp v. Uzan (No 2)*.[113] However, as that was a case in which the substantive proceedings were before the courts of a non-Member State, it is more appropriate to deal with it at that point.[114] Taken all together, the authorities show that expediency is a concept which has several aspects. The court may be able to highlight certain aspects of it to reach the decision with which it feels comfortable. But the point of departure is the residence of the defendant, and the identification of the court trying the case as one which would or would not welcome assistance (and if so, what form of assistance) from the English court.

It remains to be authoritatively decided whether it can ever be expedient to grant the relief if the parties can be shown to have contracted out of the interim-remedial jurisdiction of the English court.[115] Jurisdiction agreements are often drafted as being concerned to determine only where the substantive proceedings may be brought. But some better drafted ones will also nominate or exclude the court to which recourse may be made for interim remedies. If the parties have contracted to exclude the interim-remedial, as well as the substantive, jurisdiction of the English court, the question is whether this makes it inexpedient to grant the relief. It is submitted that, unless there is a credibly strong challenge to

---

110 At 829, 832.

111 It is implicit that, if the foreign court has made an order, there should be no bar to the English court's acting, but that it is essential that it not go beyond the point which the court hearing the merits would consider appropriate.

112 It has been held that the court should not, in any event, order disclosure of assets on any wider a basis that it could properly order a freezing injunction, so that if the court may not order a freezing injunction, it will not be appropriate to make a disclosure order ancillary to an order which may not, *ex hypothesi*, be made in the first place: *ICICI Bank UK plc v. Diminco NV* [2014] EWHC 3124 (Comm). The contrary may have been suggested in *JSC VTB Bank v. Skurikhin* [2014] EWHC 2254 (QB), where perhaps the merits of the matter were perceived rather differently by the court. The resolution is, no doubt, to say that it will not normally be appropriate for the disclosure order to be deliberately framed so as to apply to assets which could not be referred to in any freezing order made by the court, but that in exceptional cases the court may respond to the needs of the individual case. See also *Singularis v PricewaterhouseCoopers* [2014] UKPC 36, in which the Privy Council held that cross-border assistance in insolvency did not allow the court requested to grant relief which the court-to-be-assisted could not have granted under its own law. This does seem to cast doubt on the general approach of the court in *CuoghiI*.

113 [2003] EWCA Civ 752, [2004] 1 WLR 113; see also *Belletti v. Morici* [2009] EWHC 2136 (Comm), [2010] 1 All ER (Comm) 412; *JSC VTB Bank v. Skurikhin* [2014] EWHC 2254 (QB).

114 Paragraph 6.17, below.

115 For an earlier example, see *Mantovani v. Carapelli SpA* [1980] 1 Lloyd's Rep 375; for general principles of construction in this context, see *Bankgesellschaft Berlin AG v. First International Shipping Corp Ltd* [2001] 1 CL 61.

the validity or scope of the agreement, it should do just that. It is difficult to envisage a case in which it would be expedient to allow a party to break a contractual promise in order to seek an interim remedy from the very court to which he has bound himself not to apply.[116] The factors that may be relied on to allow departure from a jurisdiction agreement in the context of a substantive trial are not easily extended to a claim for interim remedies, for the role of the English court when the trial is taking place elsewhere is necessarily secondary and subordinate.[117] It is, therefore, submitted that a contractual promise not to seek such relief should generally be treated as barring the way to the court's granting of such relief.

Finally, if the English court might have had jurisdiction over the defendant, but is precluded from finding it to be present by the prior seising of a foreign court and the operation of Article 29 of the Brussels I Regulation, it is from the principles set out in this paragraph that the decision whether to grant interim remedies must be derived.[118] The concerns which led to the decision in *Van Uden* are triggered when a defendant is defending himself on the merits before the courts of another Member State. They are not affected by the proposition that he could have been sued in England instead.

6.13 (C) Relief sought in relation to civil or commercial matter in which no Member State court has yet been seised

The decision in *Van Uden* leaves it unclear which approach is to be followed in a case in which both the English and a court in another Member State could in principle be seised with jurisdiction but neither has yet been so seised. In such a case it might be said that the English court has jurisdiction, albeit that it has not yet been asked to exercise it; it might be said that until that jurisdiction is invoked, the court is confined to the relief authorised by Article 35 for a court which does not have jurisdiction over the merits of the claim.

However, the view preferred here is that, until a court has been seised with the claim on the merits of the dispute, which will then have the power to grant unrestricted forms of ancillary relief, as explained in *Van Uden*, all a court can do is consider itself as a court which does not have jurisdiction. The case is not pending before the court, and may never become so pending, and it appears to follow that the court should, in such circumstances, confine itself to provisional, including protective, measures in accordance with Article 35.[119] It would be oppressive for the defendant to be faced with the need to defend himself against applications for measures which were potentially more far-reaching than provisional measures within the scope of Article 35, in the courts of more than one Member State. The scheme of the Regulation is that he should face this only in no more than the one court.

By way of limited exception to this, if the case is one to which Article 24 of the Brussels I Regulation applies, so that the English court has and no other court could have

---

116 *B v. S* [2011] EWHC 691 (Comm).

117 *Refco Inc v. Eastern Trading Co* [1999] 1 Lloyd's Rep 159, 174–175; *Ryan v. Friction Dynamics Ltd, The Times*, 14 June 2000; *Sultan of Brunei Darussalam v. Bolkiah, The Times*, 5 September 2000.

118 It is different if the court *was* seised but has stayed its proceedings while the jurisdiction of the court seised first is established: it is then a court *with jurisdiction: JP Morgan Europe Ltd v. Primacom AG* [2005] EWHC 508 (Comm), [2005] 2 Lloyd's Rep 665.

119 In practice, this may be less of an issue than it seems, for the applicant for relief will presumably, if proceedings are not on foot anywhere, intend to seise the English court and will show the applications judge the claim form which has been, or which is about to be, served. In those circumstances, it is sensible for the English court to act as though it had substantive jurisdiction, and not to consider itself confined by and restricted to Art. 35.

jurisdiction,[120] even by consent, it may be that that court could grant interim remedies as though it already had jurisdiction, and not just as a court exercising limited authority by reason of Article 35. The same cannot so obviously be said of a court which considers that it has been prorogated with jurisdiction, but not yet seised, in accordance with Article 25 of the Regulation. Even though the recast Regulation has adjusted the rules of jurisdictional priority in circumstances in which one court has or may have jurisdiction by agreement, a jurisdiction agreement is capable of being varied or departed from by consent, and there is therefore no guarantee that the prorogated court will have jurisdiction. But the issue remains unresolved.[121]

6.14 (D) Relief sought in civil or commercial matter in relation to proceedings based on Article 6 and the residual rules of jurisdiction

In a case in which the defendant does not have a domicile in any of the Member States, and there is no other material connection to a Member State, jurisdiction over the defendant, in whichever Member State it is taken, will be taken on the basis of Article 6 of the recast Regulation. If proceedings have been commenced in the courts of a Member State, on the jurisdictional basis of Article 6, the principle in *Van Uden* will still apply, and the court which is not exercising jurisdiction will be restricted to granting relief on the basis of Article 35.

A case in which substantive jurisdiction is based on Article 6 is still brought in respect of a civil or commercial matter which falls within the domain of the Regulation. According to *Overseas Union Insurance Ltd v. New Hampshire Insurance Co*,[122] where a defendant is being sued in a Member State on the basis of what is now Article 6, the provisions of the Regulation dealing with *lis alibi pendens* are fully applicable, not least to assist in the subsequent free movement of judgments. One should expect a similar approach to be taken to Article 35, with the consequence that the court exercising jurisdiction on the merits has an unrestricted power to make ancillary orders,[123] and the courts of all other Member States to be restricted to the forms of relief provided for by Article 35. After all, the position of the defendant is just as difficult – maybe more so – if he has to face claims for substantial remedies on more than one front; and it would be altogether wrong for a defendant not domiciled in a Member State to be treated less favourably in this regard than one who was domiciled in a Member State. No reported case appears to have decided this point yet.

By contrast, if the defendant has no domiciliary connection with a Member State, the case has no connection with a Member State, and there are no proceedings yet pending in a Member State, it is difficult to see that the Brussels I Regulation can be concerned to impose any limitation upon the powers of any court to grant interim relief. In this case the English court will be able to exercise its powers to grant relief without restriction. This conclusion is consistent with the approach taken by the Swiss Federal Tribunal in *Uzan v. Motorola*

---

120 See, for the possibility that this makes a material change to the manner in which the Regulation would otherwise generally work, C-438/12 *Weber v. Weber* EU:C:2014:212, [2015] 2 WLR 213.

121 As does the question whether, if the application is successfully made despite the agreement on jurisdiction, a claim for damages for breach of contract could follow proof of loss or damage.

122 C-351/89, [1991] ECR I-3317.

123 After all, in such a case there is even less of a basis for the contention that the court seised with the claim on the merits has no impediment derived from Chapter II of the Regulation, for Chapter II does not grant any protection to the non-Member State defendant other than that derived from Art. 29.

Credit Corp (No 2),[124] where it described the English court in such a case as having 'virtual jurisdiction' in the case, and therefore having power to make orders which the Swiss courts would recognise under the provisions of the Lugano Convention.

6.15 (E) Relief sought in relation to a civil or commercial matter over which no court has jurisdiction

In *Van Uden*, the Court of Justice accepted that the parties' agreement to refer their differences to arbitration meant that, although the matter was a civil or commercial one, no Contracting State had jurisdiction over the substantive claim, at least once one party had invoked the arbitration agreement. There was therefore no court which, having jurisdiction over the merits of the case, could grant relief which went beyond the constraints of what is now Article 35 of the Regulation. What is now Article 35 therefore applied to an application for provisional or protective measures: the court which granted relief was restricted to what that Article allowed it to do. No court could be seen as one with actual or potential jurisdiction so as to allow it to be argued that its powers were wider than those authorised by Article 35.

6.16 (F) Relief sought in relation to proceedings in a matter which is not civil or commercial

If the claim is not in respect of a civil or commercial matter, the Brussels I Regulation is wholly inapplicable to the claim for interim remedies, and the law is unaffected by any jurisdictional or other concerns. The ordinary principles of English law which define the power of the court to grant a freezing injunction, or other interim remedies, will apply; and the more cautious principles which apply when the relief is sought in the form of a worldwide freezing injunction will also apply.

6.17 (G) Relief sought in relation to proceedings before the courts of non–Member State

If proceedings have been brought before the courts of a non-Member State, section 25 of the 1982 Act, as amended,[125] permits the English court to grant interim remedies in respect of them.[126] Jurisdiction to make the order will need to be established by service within the jurisdiction, or out of the jurisdiction under CPR rule 6.36 with the permission of the court.

However, the court will be required to consider again whether its lack of substantive jurisdiction means that it is inexpedient for it to make the order applied for, and the issues raised and partially discussed above[127] in relation to *Cuoghi* will be relevant but with this large difference: as the proceedings in a non-Member State may result in a judgment which will not be enforced in England, or which may not be enforceable in England, the term 'inexpedient' is made to bear considerably more weight. It may need to address this

---

124 ATF/BGE 129 III 626.
125 SI 1997/302, SI 2001/3929, Sch. 2, para. 10.
126 Excluding warrants for the arrest of property, or orders for the obtaining of evidence: s. 25(7).
127 See para. 6.10, above.

issue as part of a jurisdictional enquiry, when considering permission to authorise service of the claim form out of the jurisdiction, or in a case where jurisdiction was established as of right, and the real question is whether the court should exercise its discretion to make the order.

Guidance as to the approach to be adopted was given in *Refco Inc v. Eastern Trading Co*,[128] where proceedings were pending in the United States Federal Court in Illinois, and to which court an application for corresponding relief could not properly be made.[129] The Court of Appeal proceeded on the basis that, if it would have been appropriate to grant the freezing injunction were the substantive proceedings to have been brought in England, it is necessary to ask whether the lack of substantive jurisdiction made it inexpedient to do so after all. As the remedy would not have been granted had the substantive proceedings been brought in England,[130] the further question did not arise for decision. The majority[131] indicated that the inexpediency, the general approach to which had been explained in *Cuoghi*, would arise only if the foreign court, having the same powers (and exercised on similar principles) as in English law, had itself declined to grant corresponding relief. If by contrast the foreign court had declined to grant relief on the basis that it was for the English court, rather than for the foreign court, to make the order,[132] and if there were no reason to suppose that the making of the order would interfere with the case management powers of the foreign court,[133] it would not be inexpedient to grant the relief. The approach of the majority appears to be to favour the making of the order unless it is demonstrated that the foreign judge will be affronted by it.

This, if taken literally, may take *Cuoghi* further than it was intended to go, and would have the potential to make England the presumptive[134] enforcement forum for the world.[135] The court did not deal with, and did not comment on, the distinct argument that it was inexpedient to grant the relief by reason of the allegedly sufficient fact that there was a contractual agreement not to do so.[136]

In *Motorola Credit Corp v. Uzan (No 2)*,[137] the court further assessed the nature of 'expediency', and dealt directly with an argument which had been made in earlier cases, namely

---

128 [1999] 1 Lloyd's Rep 159.

129 It was said that a lawyer could not properly make it, and might be exposed to a personal costs order if he did. Since that decision, the US Supreme Court has held that Federal courts in the United States do not have power to grant an interlocutory injunction to restrain a defendant from disposing of its assets pending the determination of the action: *Grupo Mexicano de Desarrollo SA v. Alliance Bond Fund Inc* 527 US 308 (1999), noted Collins (1999) 115 LQR 601.

130 There was no demonstrated risk of dissipation of assets.

131 Millett LJ, by contrast, focused on what the *foreign* court would have done, and took the view that if it would not have granted the relief even if the defendant and the assets had been within its territorial jurisdiction, that was a powerful indication of inexpediency, whether or not the foreign judge would be offended by the making of the English order. It is submitted that this is more faithful to the decision in *Cuoghi* than is the approach of the majority.

132 In *Refco*, because the assets to be affected by the injunction were located in England.

133 And see *Ryan v. Friction Dynamics Ltd*, *The Times*, 14 June 2000; *Sultan of Brunei Darussalam v. Bolkiah*, *The Times*, 5 September 2000.

134 A presumption rebuttable by evidence that the foreign court will be offended by the English court's making of an order.

135 It may be questioned whether this would be a perception which would bring comfort to the United Kingdom banking industry, whose clients might well fear that maintaining too close a connection with England was a risky business.

136 This is discussed in para. 6.10, above.

137 [2003] EWCA Civ 752, [2004] 1 WLR 113. See further, (2003) 74 BYBIL 541.

that it was inexpedient to order an injunction in support of proceedings before a court which had no legal power to make such an order. What seemed to weigh with the court was the view that, where a court in one country is dealing with an international fraud, courts elsewhere should do whatever their law allows them to do[138] to assist.[139] In that case, the substantive proceedings in question were brought against four alleged Turkish fraudsters before the courts of the United States. It had recently been held by the Supreme Court of the United States[140] that the Constitution prohibited the making of pre-judgment freezing orders. Yet it was held that this fundamental rule of American constitutional law had no impact on the question whether it was inexpedient to make the order which had been applied for from the English courts. The case was not to be seen as one in which the foreign court, seised on the merits, had made an evaluation and had decided that the order should not be made,[141] but was instead a case in which it would welcome the assistance of the English courts. As suggested above, this seems to be a rather controversial interpretation of a constitutional prohibition on such orders being made by an American court.

The court examined other aspects of the issue of expediency. It accepted that if a defendant were resident in England it would generally be expedient to make the order, but it also accepted that other connections, such as the substantial presence of land and other assets in England, would also be sufficient to show expediency in a case where the defendant's residence was clearly shown to be in England. It accepted that it should not ignore the fact that a Turkish court had twice purported to grant an anti-suit injunction against the proceedings taking place in the United States,[142] though having said that it is hard to see what impact that fact really had; and it added that a court should be careful to avoid making orders which would needlessly increase the level of tension in litigation which had evidently been stormy.

The court came close to accepting[143] that it would not be expedient to make an order in circumstances in which a judgment from the foreign court would not be capable of recognition or enforcement in England. This last point, which was clearly accepted as being sound in principle in *Blue Holdings (1) Pte Ltd v. United States*,[144] seems sound: it is hard to see how it could be expedient to make an order in support of what would in due course, as a matter of English private international law, be an unenforceable judgment.[145] Taken

---

138 See the judgment, esp. at [119]. No doubt the court meant to say 'allegations of international fraud'. But if there are only allegations, it is not clear why it is so necessary to assist one litigant at the expense of the other. It may be appropriate to be partisan after judgment on the merits, but one would suppose that it was necessary to be much more cautious beforehand.

139 Which appears to mean to make life difficult for the defendant.

140 *Grupo Mexicano de Desarrollo SA v. Alliance Bond Fund Inc* 527 US 308 (1999).

141 By contrast, this was the analysis of the effect of proceedings in Russia in *JSC VTB Bank v. Skurikhin* [2014] EWHC 2254 (QB), with the consequence that the injunction did not extend to assets in Russia, and in Belarus, China and Cuba (in relation to which the Russian court was taken to have jurisdiction but which it had declined to exercise). However, the judge was prepared to make the asset disclosure order applicable to assets in those countries, on the ground that there was no absolute requirement that the two orders marched in lockstep. The decision contrasts with that in *ICICI Bank UK plc v. Diminco NV* [2014] EWHC 3124 (Comm).

142 This appears to be the first time a Turkish court has made such an order.

143 But the point was not really taken, and there appeared to be no real basis for it to be taken on the facts of the case.

144 [2014] EWCA Civ 1291, [2015] 1 ALL ER (Comm) 1. There may be exceptional cases, but the general position is now clear.

145 But where the foreign judgment will be enforceable, there is no problem. For a case in which the court accepts that a judgment may be enforceable, despite the suggestion that it is based on penal law (see *Robb Evans v. European Bank Ltd* (2004) 61 NSWLR 75, and on which see [2004] LMCLQ 313), see *US Securities and Exchange Commission v. Manterfield* [2009] EWCA Civ 27, [2010] 1 WLR 172, where the freezing order was made.

all together, the decision demonstrates that expediency is a complex and subtle concept which allows a court to highlight certain aspects of it to reach a decision with which it feels comfortable.[146]

If proceedings have not yet been instituted in the courts of a non-Member State, it is submitted that, though an English court will still have the power to grant interim remedies,[147] it will be necessary, in all but egregious cases, to be rather more cautious, as the inexpediency of making an order cannot be tested by reference to what has emerged as the principal criterion: that is, by reference to what the primary court would think of the order being made by an English court.

6.18 Interim remedies when the action is stayed

Where an English action is ordered to be stayed, whether under the Brussels I Regulation, or on the basis of *forum non conveniens*, or under the Arbitration Act 1996, any interim remedies which have been ordered may continue in force.[148] Where the stay is discretionary, this is provided by the power to make the stay conditional.[149] Where the stay is mandatory, imposed under Arbitration Act 1996, section 9, the Act allows interim relief to be obtained from the court in the case of urgency; [150] if not, it may be obtained only with the permission of the arbitral tribunal or consent of the parties.[151] According to *Van Uden*, the English court may be applied to on the footing that the case is one in which no Member State court has jurisdiction,[152] and measures which fall within the scope of Article 35 may be ordered. But as the Arbitration Act 1996 serves to restrict the availability of such measures as a matter of English law, this adds nothing to the powers at the disposal of the court.

It is also clear that the tactic of bringing local proceedings in order to obtain a freezing injunction, which is really sought in aid of proceedings in another jurisdiction, with the intention of then having the local proceedings stayed, is unobjectionable in those common law jurisdictions which have not legislated to confer the power to grant relief in aid of foreign proceedings. The general principle of encouraging international cooperation made the grant of such relief a proper exercise of discretion, and it was sensible to obtain such relief in the place where the respondent was resident and was amenable to measures of enforcement.[153]

---

146 For illustration, *Royal Bank of Scotland plc v. FAL Oil Co Ltd* [2012] EWHC 3628, [2013] 1 Lloyd's Rep 327.

147 Civil Jurisdiction and Judgments Act 1982 (Interim Relief) Order 1997, SI 1997/302 extended the power to grant interim relief under s. 25(1) of the 1982 Act to cases where there are 'proceedings commenced or to be commenced otherwise than in a Brussels or Lugano Contracting State', SI 2001/3929 adding a reference to 'Regulation State'.

148 Or stayed by reason of the first paragraph of what is now Art. 29 of the Brussels I Regulation: *JP Morgan Europe Ltd v. Primacom AG* [2005] EWHC 508 (Comm), [2005] 2 Lloyd's Rep 665.

149 *Spiliada Maritime Corp v. Cansulex Ltd* [1987] AC 460. Where the stay is in admiralty proceedings, s. 26 of the 1982 Act provides a further, statutory, basis for a stay.

150 Arbitration Act 1996, s. 44. See also on this, and on the inapplicability, in this context, of the 1982 Act, *Mobil Cerro Negro Ltd v. Petroleos de Venezuela* [2008] EWHC 532 (Comm), [2008] 1 Lloyd's Rep 684; *ETI Euro Telecom International NV v. Republic of Bolivia* [2008] EWCA Civ 880, [2009] 1 WLR 665.

151 *Ibid.*

152 See para. 6.14, above.

153 *Walsh v. Deloitte & Touche Inc* [2001] UKPC 58, (2001) 59 WIR 30 (Bah).

6.19 Further points

The jurisdictional arrangements examined above do not otherwise affect the substantive law specifying the conditions which limit the availability of the relief applied for, though, as has been seen, the discretionary factors associated with the granting of relief may have a significant impact on the exercise of any discretion to take jurisdiction.

So if a freezing injunction is applied for, it will still be necessary, for example, to show that there is a well-founded fear that a respondent will dissipate his assets unless restrained, for this is a substantive limitation which is built into the remedy itself. And the same reasoning means such an injunction may not be obtained until a cause of action has arisen against the defendant. The limitation on the court's discretion, derived from *Veracruz Transportation Ltd v. VC Shipping*,[154] which defines the bounds of the remedy, is unaffected by the legislative changes made to the jurisdictional competence of the English court. It may be argued that the limitation is itself unsound,[155] and that, to the extent that it is derived from *The Siskina*,[156] it is weakened by legislation which has undermined the basis for that decision. But such an argument would be fallacious, for it has nothing to do with the matters to which the legislation is directed.

Relief may also be obtained against a co-defendant against whom no cause of action is any longer alleged, and against whom the proceedings had been abandoned. There will be no jurisdictional hurdle in such a case, for the party against whom the orders were sought would be a defendant to the action.[157] Even if he had not been a defendant, and had been a mere third party, the orders could have been made by having him joined as a defendant.[158] It appears to be sufficient that the party against whom the orders are sought has become mixed up in the efforts of the judgment debtor to frustrate or evade enforcement of the judgment, and that it would be just and convenient to make the order.[159] If it is necessary that the orders or injunction be incidental to and dependent upon the enforcement of a substantive right, that requirement was satisfied when the right was that of the judgment creditor to enforce his judgment against the judgment debtor, and the party against whom the order was sought had become mixed up in that enforcement process.[160] This will be especially valuable when the beneficial ownership of assets appears to have been disguised by the devious or fraudulent behaviour of the judgment debtor.

Where the measures are taken to obtain security for a maritime claim, the availability of interim remedies and the powers of the court are overshadowed by the maritime context in which the relief is sought. Where the dispute between the parties is to be settled by arbitration, whether in England or overseas, the availability of interim remedies from the English

---

154 [1992] 1 Lloyd's Rep 353.

155 *Cf* Collins (1992) 108 LQR 175.

156 [1979] AC 210.

157 *Mercantile Group (Europe) AG v. Aiyela* [1994] QB 366.

158 *TSB Private Bank International SA v. Chabra* [1992] 1 WLR 231; see also *Bullus v. Bullus* (1910) 102 LT 399; *Aiglon Ltd v. Gau Shan Co Ltd* [1993] 1 Lloyd's Rep 164; *C Inc v. L* [2001] 2 Lloyd's Rep 459; *Cardile v. LED Builders Pty Ltd* (1999) 198 CLR 380. If necessary, service out will be permitted by CPR r. 6.36; CPR Part 25 PD 25A, para. 1.2(3). And s. 25 of the 1982 Act is not expressed to be confined to cases which were brought in a foreign court *and are still pending* there. See generally, on the extent to which it is possible to obtain such orders against persons not party to the substantive claim, Devonshire [1996] LMCLQ 268, (2002) 118 LQR 124.

159 *Cf Norwich Pharmacal Co v. Customs & Excise Commissioners* [1974] AC 133; *Bankers Trust Co v. Shapira* [1980] 1 WLR 1274, and the cases mentioned in the previous note.

160 *Mercantile Group (Europe) AG v. Aiyela* [1994] QB 366; *C Inc v. L* [2001] 2 Lloyd's Rep 459.

courts is overshadowed by the arbitration context in which it is sought. This aspect of the obtaining of interim remedies will be found in greater detail in Chapter 8.

6.20 Measures for the taking of evidence

The relationship between the Brussels I Regulation and orders for the taking or production of evidence was a little uncertain, but is now less so. According to *Masri v. Consolidated Contractors International (UK) Ltd (No 4)*,[161] a court with jurisdiction over the merits of a claim is not impeded by European law from making an order for the examination of individuals who held office in the defendant company, even where they are domiciled in other Member States, on the basis that the court with jurisdiction over the merits may make any order ancillary to that exercise of substantive jurisdiction. However, as a matter of English law, the procedural power to make such an order does not extend to persons who are physically outside the territorial jurisdiction of the English courts when the application is made,[162] and in such cases the effect of European law does not arise.[163]

However, it has also been held that an application for an order that a potential witness to a claim be required to give evidence, to allow the claimant to determine whether he has the basis for the making of a claim, is not a 'provisional, including protective' measure for the purposes of Article 35 of the Regulation, and that Article 35 does not allow such an order to be applied for from a court which does not have jurisdiction over the substance of the potential case, simply on the ground that the national law of the State in question allows for it;[164] and this interpretation has been adopted in the Recitals to the recast Brussels I Regulation.[165] As the Taking of Evidence Regulation[166] makes provision for the direct transmission of requests for the taking of evidence from the courts of one Member State to another, it was once supposed that this alone was the proper means of acquiring the evidence in question. On the other hand, the unavailability of Article 35 as a jurisdictional justification does not contradict the wide and rational decision of the Court of Appeal that a court with jurisdiction, which is exercising that jurisdiction, is not to be hamstrung in

---

161 [2008] EWCA Civ 876, [2009] 2 WLR 699, reversed on the construction of CPR Part 71 without reference to European law: *Masri v. Consolidated Contractors International Co SAL (No 4)* [2009] UKHL 43, [2010] 1 AC 90, with the result that such an order may not be applied for in relation to a person outside the territorial jurisdiction. There is, therefore, no role for European law *unless* the person to be served is present within the jurisdiction but not domiciled in the United Kingdom.

162 Not least because of the absence of any mechanism for serving them with the application notice, though now see CPR r. 6.39.

163 *Masri v. Consolidated Contractors International Co SAL (No 4)* [2009] UKHL 43, [2010] 1 AC 90, reversing *Masri v. Consolidated Contractors International (UK) Ltd (No 4)* [2008] EWCA Civ 876, [2009] 2 WLR 699, [57]. The question how one would serve process on the person to be summoned was also, therefore, not material, but the House of Lords specifically endorsed the view of Tomlinson J in *Vitol SA v. Capri Marine Ltd* [2008] EWHC 378 (Comm), [2009] Bus LR 271 that there was no proper mechanism for serving such a summons on an office-holder out of the jurisdiction. But now see CPR r. 6.39.

164 C-104/03 *St Paul Dairy Industries BV v. Unibel Exser BVBA* [2005] ECR I-3481.

165 Recast Brussels I Regulation, Recital (25). The notion of provisional, including protective, measures should include, for example, protective orders aimed at obtaining information or preserving evidence as referred to in Arts 6 and 7 of Directive 2004/48/EC of the European Parliament and of the Council of 29 April 2004 on the enforcement of intellectual property rights. It should not include measures which are not of a protective nature, such as measures ordering the hearing of a witness. This should be without prejudice to the application of Council Regulation (EC) 1206/2001 of 28 May 2001 on cooperation between the courts of the Member States in the taking of evidence in civil or commercial matters.

166 Regulation (EC) 1206/2001, [2001] OJ L174/1.

the way it would be if it were not to have that jurisdiction, or, to put it another way, that the judgment creditor was entitled to rely on any available measure, and was not confined to proceeding on the basis of the Taking of Evidence Regulation. Indeed, the European Court has since decided that the use of the Taking of Evidence Regulation is optional, not obligatory.[167]

6.21 Post-judgment orders for interim remedies and ancillary relief

A freezing injunction, and an order to provide information about property or assets which may be applied for and ordered in aid of such an injunction, may be made after trial[168] in aid of the enforcement and execution of judgments.[169] From time to time it had been suggested that, as what is now Article 24(5) of the Regulation provides that proceedings which have as their object the enforcement of judgments from Member States are within the exclusive jurisdiction of the courts of the Member State in which the enforcement was sought, the furthest an English court could go, once it had given judgment, was to make orders as though it were a court relegated to the status of one allowed to order provisional, including protective, relief under the authority of Article 35.

But the clear view of the Court of Appeal in *Masri v. Consolidated Contractors International (UK) Ltd (No 2)*[170] was that a court which had exercised jurisdiction over the merits retained the power to make the orders which were recognised as inherent in its having that status by the decision in *Van Uden*, or which were ancillary to its adjudication of the merits. These powers allowed it to make orders for ancillary relief, and did not confine it to the restricted forms of provisional relief which would have been permitted by reference to Article 35. No limitation of jurisdiction or power by reference to Articles 24(5) and 35 therefore arose.

And not only that: English orders which are made in England, such as the asset-freezing-ordering restraint of a party subject to the jurisdiction of the court, or the appointment of a receiver by way of equitable execution, would not infringe Article 24(5) in any event, for they are orders made and taking effect in England, on a person who is subject to the personal jurisdiction of the court in relation to the merits of the claim. That being so, there is no basis for contending that the making of such an order would be inexpedient.

When relief in the form of a freezing injunction is sought in aid of the enforcement in England of a judgment from another Member State, the principles set out in *Cuoghi* and *Van Uden*, as these illuminate the question whether it is expedient or inexpedient to grant relief, will apply. So where there are no assets in England, and where the defendant or judgment debtor is not resident in England, there is no proper basis for the court to exercise its power under section 25 of the 1982 Act to grant relief; and any submission that it has an obligation to grant relief will be unfounded.[171]

---

167 C-332/11 *ProRail BV v. Xpedys NV* EU:C:2013:87, [2013] ILPr 279.

168 Senior Courts Act 1981, s. 37(1); CPR Part 25, PD 25A, para. 1.2(3).

169 Whether English or foreign.

170 [2008] EWCA Civ 303, [2009] QB 450.

171 *Banco Nacional de Comercio Exterior SNC v. Empresa de Telecomunicaciones de Cuba SA* [2007] EWCA Civ 662, [2007] 2 Lloyd's Rep 484.

6.22 Recognition and enforcement of English orders in other Member States

If an order for an interim remedy, such as a freezing injunction, is made by an English court, it may be necessary to seek to enforce it in the courts of another Member State. The starting point is to observe that Article 2 of the Regulation 1215/2012 now provides as follows:

> For the purposes of this Regulation: (a) 'judgment' means any judgment given by a court or tribunal of a Member State, whatever the judgment may be called, including a decree, order, decision or writ of execution, as well as a decision on the determination of costs or expenses by an officer of the court. For the purposes of Chapter III, 'judgment' includes provisional, including protective, measures ordered by a court or tribunal which by virtue of this Regulation has jurisdiction as to the substance of the matter. It does not include a provisional, including protective, measure which is ordered by such a court or tribunal without the defendant being summoned to appear, unless the judgment containing the measure is served on the defendant prior to enforcement;

Although the recognition and enforcement of judgments in civil or commercial matters under Chapter III of Regulation 1215/2012 applies only to judgments obtained in proceedings instituted on or after 10 January 2015, the enforcement of freezing injunctions is likely to trigger the application of Regulation 1215/2012 much sooner than with other forms of judgment.

For recognition to take place, two problems have to be disposed of. First, the order has to be one which the foreign court will accept that the English court was entitled to make; and secondly, the manner by which it is given effect in another Member State will require careful thought.

It was established by the Court of Justice in *Denilauler v. SNC Couchet Frères*[172] that an order for provisional or protective measures, obtained in respect of a civil or commercial matter, was in principle entitled to recognition and enforcement under what was then Title III of the Brussels Convention, but that this was subject to certain limitations. The order in question had first to be regarded as a judgment, and even if characterised as a judgment, it would not be recognised if it had been given in default of appearance without the respondent having been duly served in time to arrange for his defence. Neither the Brussels I Regulation, nor the Convention before it, limited its recognition and enforcement procedures to judgments which were final and conclusive, but each instrument did require that the order have the quality of 'judgment'. This excluded judicial decisions 'which are delivered without the party against which they are directed having been summoned to appear, and which are intended to be enforced without prior service'.[173] In *Denilauler* itself, an order seizing assets, of *saisie conservatoire*, was made by a French court in respect of the German bank account of the defendant. Because the defendant had not been summoned to appear before the French court, and because the order obtained was not capable of being the subject of adversarial proceedings, it did not fall within the recognition scheme of Title III of the Convention.

The policy which appeared to underpin the decision was that such measures should be obtained from the court for the place where the asset is located, so that no question of recognition would need to arise. This policy was weakened by the formulation of Article 34(2)

---

172 125/79, [1980] ECR 1553. See also *Normaco v. Lundman* [1999] ILPr 381.

173 But by contrast with the position under the Conventions, in the context of the Regulation, if the defendant has had the opportunity to challenge the judgment, it may cease to be judgment in default of appearance in the sense of Art. 34(2) of Regulation 44/2001; it must, therefore be seen as a judgment. See more generally below, paras 7.17 *et seq.*

of Regulation 44/2001. It has further been established that recognition may be refused if the order for which recognition is sought (for example, ordering a particular form of interim relief) is irreconcilable with a decision of the local court to opposite effect (for example, refusing to grant the same relief).[174] But the definition of judgment given in Article 2(a) of Regulation 1215/2012 clarifies the definition of what counts as an enforceable judgment and puts it on a more secure footing.

If, therefore, the measure was obtained by proceedings which were, or which were designed to be,[175] adversarial, it qualifies in principle for recognition as a judgment. But being aware of the special nature of applications for provisional measures, the Court of Justice held, in *Mietz v. Intership Yachting Sneek BV*,[176] that a court called upon to recognise and enforce such a measure was required to undertake a preliminary assessment of the measure before proceeding to rule on the general criteria for refusing recognition and enforcement.

According to this, if the order was made by the court which had jurisdiction to adjudicate on the merits of the claim, recognition and enforcement would, in principle,[177] be automatic, for the ancillary order would be one which the court with merits jurisdiction was, as far as the Regulation was concerned, fully entitled to make. But if the court which made the order had jurisdictional authority to act only on the basis of Article 35 of the Regulation, its judgment would be refused recognition unless it was properly characterised as 'provisional, including protective'.[178] If, however, the judgment imposed the kind of measure which was outside the scope of what is now Article 35, and was, therefore, one which only the court with adjudicatory merits jurisdiction could properly have granted, its recognition will be refused.

The Court conceded that this might lead some to suppose that it was inviting the recognising court to make its own assessment of the jurisdiction of the adjudicating court, in a manner which would be contrary to the general operation of Chapter III of the Brussels I Regulation. But any such worry is really an illusion. The recognising court is called upon to evaluate the nature of the order made, rather than the jurisdiction of the court making it; and if it is not an 'Article 35' order, to deny it recognition unless made by the court with jurisdiction over the defendant in relation to the claim on the merits.[179] It appears to follow

---

174 C-80/00 *Italian Leather SpA v. WECO Polstermöbel GmbH & Co* [2002] ECR I-6367. But it is not difficult to envisage cases in which it is hard to determine whether different conclusions amount to irreconcilable judgments, given that 'irreconcilable' has a narrow interpretation, particularly where the property to which they relate is different property, or one court makes orders of attachment while the other makes orders of the freezing injunction kind.

175 The defendant's election to default in appearance is irrelevant if he was served in time to arrange for his defence to the application: see below, paras 7.17 *et seq*.

176 C-99/96, [1999] ECR I-2277.

177 Subject to all the defences to recognition applicable to all Member State judgments under Chapter III: see further, para. 7.12, below.

178 See para. 6.10, above.

179 The judgment appears to envisage that an order could be recognised as being made by the court with jurisdiction over the merits even though no action has yet been commenced: at [50] it is suggested that if the order is made by the court of the place of domicile, and what is now Art. 24 of the recast Brussels I Regulation is inapplicable, an order from this court would be able to be recognised under Title III. In this respect it departs from the analysis put forward at para. 6.13, above. It is submitted that this aspect of *Mietz* is incorrect. The Regulation does not ascribe jurisdiction invariably to the courts of the domicile, except where Art. 24 applies; and it is not, therefore, easy to identify the court which will have jurisdiction over the merits. It is, therefore, submitted that a measure is to be regarded as coming from a court with jurisdiction on the merits only where the court which makes

from *Mietz* that, if the court purporting to exercise Article 31 jurisdiction, has made an order which nevertheless failed to respect the requirement of a 'real connecting link' with the jurisdiction of the court making the order, this will not be capable of being seen as an order whose making was authorised by Article 31, and will be treated as one capable of being made only by the court with jurisdiction on the merits.

The effect of these decisions is that an English freezing injunction will be an order which Article 35 authorises it to make and that, subject to the elucidation of the 'real connecting link' in relation to a freezing injunction which operates only *in personam*,[180] it will qualify for recognition under Chapter III of the Regulation. If a pre-judgment freezing injunction is obtained without notice to the defendant, it will not count as a judgment until it is served on the defendant; but if it is continued or re-made after an application on notice,[181] it will be cured of this initial defect;[182] and no such difficulty arises with a post-judgment order.

Of course, a decisive question should be whether, at the point at which he had the opportunity to be heard, the respondent faced or would have faced a disadvantage which arose from the fact that the original order was obtained without notice to him. In principle, if he was placed under some form of disadvantage, the fact that he appeared at a subsequent hearing, and lost, should not be seen to cure the original order of its birth defect, for in such circumstances the right to appear after the order was made cannot be seen as equal or equivalent to the right to be heard before the order is made. It is, of course, seriously arguable[183] that the respondent to a freezing injunction is placed at a considerable handicap by the very making of the order without notice to him, not least because his freedom to spend money on legal and other expenses is curtailed by the initial order, with the result that he faces a clear procedural handicap as well as all sorts of disruption to his private or commercial life. But it does not appear that this has made it difficult for freezing injunctions to be recognised in other Member States;[184] and, if the views of the Swiss Federal Tribunal[185] or the French Supreme Court[186] are taken into account, the point may prove to have nothing in it: both courts have approved the recognition and enforcement of sweepingly wide freezing injunctions.[187] Other objections which may have been feared, such as that recognition of the freezing injunction may be refused as being contrary to public policy, appear to be insubstantial if the limits of the *Van Uden* principle are observed carefully.

If the order satisfies the test for recognition and enforcement in another Member State, the manner and means of this enforcement must in practice be determined by the

---

the order has been seised with jurisdiction or, in accordance with Art. 24 of the Regulation, is the only Member State court which may be so seised.

180 See para. 6.13, above.

181 CPR r. 23.9 gives the respondent 7 days to have the order set aside or varied; CPR 25 PD 25A, Para. 5.1(3) requires that the initial order obtained without notice specify a return date for a further hearing at which the respondent can be present.

182 By the application of the reasoning in C-420/07 *Apostolides v. Orams* [2009] ECR I-3571.

183 See Zuckerman (1993) 109 LQR 432.

184 Moreover, recognition and a declaration of enforceability will be required from the courts of any foreign State in which it is sought to use the order against third parties: see the proviso (referred to as the '*Babanaft* proviso') in the example order Annexed to CPR 25 PD 25A.

185 *Uzan v. Motorola Credit Corp* ATF/BGE 129 III 626.

186 *Stolzenberg v. Daimler Chrysler Canada Inc* [2005] JDI/Clunet 112 (*note* Cuniberti), [2005] ILPr 266.

187 See above, para. 6.10.

procedural law of the recognising court.[188] For orders to be recognised or enforced under legal instruments made prior to Regulation 1215/2012, where there was no direct equivalent in the foreign law, a degree of judicial creativity might be required. In *European Consulting Unternehmensberatung AG v. Refco Overseas Ltd*,[189] a worldwide freezing injunction was ordered by the High Court,[190] and was presented for enforcement in Germany. The Regional Court of Appeal in Karlsruhe ordered its enforcement,[191] and selected between the measures in the German Code of Civil Procedure to find the nearest equivalent German remedy.[192] Within the limits of what is possible, this is undoubtedly the correct way for a court to proceed. But for orders whose recognition is dealt with by Regulation 1215/2012, this approach has been confirmed. Article 54 of Regulation 1215/2012 provides that:

> *(1) If a judgment contains a measure or an order which is not known in the law of the Member State addressed, that measure or order shall, to the extent possible, be adapted to a measure or an order known in the law of that Member State which has equivalent effects attached to it and which pursues similar aims and interests. Such adaptation shall not result in effects going beyond those provided for in the law of the Member State of origin. (2) Any party may challenge the adaptation of the measure or order before a court. (3) If necessary, the party invoking the judgment or seeking its enforcement may be required to provide a translation or a transliteration of the judgment.*

6.23 Orders for relief granted by the courts of other Member States

The principal difficulty in dealing with the effect in England of orders made by courts in other Member States is a practical one, caused by the variety of measures available as interim relief from the courts of other Member States, and the subtle differences which distinguish one from another. Nevertheless, and as indicated above, the broad proposition is this: a judgment ordering interim relief from the court of a Member State given in a civil or commercial matter is in principle entitled[193] to recognition and enforcement under Chapter III of the Regulation, and the provisions which limit the recognition in England of foreign orders will be identical with those which restrict the recognition of English orders overseas, in particular the requirement, established by the decision in *Mietz*,[194] to examine the nature of the measure to ascertain whether, if it was an order granting ancillary relief made by the court with jurisdiction over the merits, it was within the parameters of Article 35. It is obvious that there may be room for the application of principles of public policy, or for the application of the Human Rights Act 1998, to prevent recognition of orders made, whether by a court with jurisdiction over the merits of the claim, or from a court able to act within the framework of Article 35.

---

188 To this effect, the Schlosser Report: [1979] OJ C59/71, [212].

189 See Zuckerman and Grunert, *Zeitschrift für Zivilprozess International* (ZZPInt) 1 (1996) 89.

190 The report does not disclose whether it was made originally without notice and then continued or re-made after a further hearing on notice.

191 It is noteworthy that in this decision, which pre-dated *Van Uden*, the German court saw no objection in the English court ordering a worldwide injunction. The court – surely correctly – doubted that the order could ever be regarded in Germany as having an effect on non-parties, who had not been present and entitled to be heard at any stage in the procedure; and as against them the order was not to be recognised.

192 It turned out to be under the rules of an injunctive title, para. 890 of the German Civil Code (ZPO).

193 Subject to all defences against recognition: see Chapter 7, below. Accordingly, if the order is not a judgment, but merely a procedural order relating to the gathering of evidence, it does not fall within Chapter III of the Regulation and will not be recognised: *CFEM Façades SA v. Bovis Construction Ltd* [1992] ILPr 561; *cf* C-104/03 *St Paul Dairy Industries NV v. Unibel Exser BVBA* [2005] ECR I-3481.

194 C-99/96, [1999] ECR I-2277.

If the order of the foreign court is not entitled to recognition under the Brussels I Regulation, it may be possible for a party to seek an injunction from the English court, ordering the party who has obtained the foreign order to apply to the foreign court for its complete or partial discharge.[195] If the English court has personal jurisdiction over the party who has sought the foreign order, and if the obtaining of the foreign order can be said to be oppressive or vexatious,[196] an injunction may be ordered requiring the party who sought the order to seek its discharge. Because many of these interim orders are obtained without notice, they will not immediately be entitled to recognition, and if this line of authority is developed, it may often follow that an injunction requiring an application to be made for its discharge will reinforce the decision to deny recognition to the order.

6.24 Orders for relief from the courts of a non–Member State

Unless it is specifically provided for by a statute dealing with the particular matter, the order of a court in a non–Member State providing the interim relief will not be enforceable in England. This follows from the general proposition that only foreign judgments (a) from a court recognised as being jurisdictionally competent according to English law, and (b) which are final, conclusive and for a fixed sum in money, are enforceable at common law.[197] Plainly a foreign interim judgment purporting to freeze assets in London, or ordering the defendant to deliver up property, or to submit to interrogation or oral discovery by way of deposition, cannot be enforced by an application to the English courts for the enforcement of the foreign judgment.

The fact that it cannot ultimately be enforced in England may not be a reason for a party not to seek interim relief from a foreign court. For example, in *South Carolina Insurance Co v. Assurantie Maatschappij 'de Zeven Provincien' NV*,[198] proceedings had been commenced in England, but before a defence had been entered, the claimant sought an order for the pre-trial discovery of documents from an American court.[199] The defendants sought an injunction from the English courts to order the claimant to desist from its American application, but the court refused to grant one. It observed[200] that the English courts do not generally exercise control over the manner in which an English litigant obtains his evidence, but allow a party to gather it by any means lawful in the place where the gathering takes place.[201]

---

195 *Comet Group plc v. Unika Computer SA* [2004] ILPr 10.

196 For example, because (i) the assets to which the foreign order related were in England, (ii) relief could be sought from the English court, (iii) no undertaking in damages was required in the foreign court, and (iv) the main litigation was proceeding in England, it was held in *Steelcase Strafor v. Simpson* (unreported, Sheen J, April 1991); followed in *Dubai Bank Ltd v. Galadari* (29 July 1991)) that the injunction would be ordered requiring the party who had obtained it to seek the discharge of the foreign order.

197 But for the possibility that this limitation may yet be reconsidered, see *Pro Swing Inc v. ELTA Golf Inc* [2006] 2 SCR 612, and see further below, para. 7.76.

198 [1987] AC 24.

199 In fact, before the lower courts the American application appeared to be for oral as well as documentary discovery. This was abandoned by the date of the appeal to the House of Lords.

200 At 41.

201 In the rare case of proceedings to which the Protection of Trading Interests Act 1980 applies, the Secretary of State for Trade and Industry may order a party not to comply or cooperate with a foreign order for interim relief. See *British Airways Board v. Laker Airways Ltd* [1985] AC 58. And for an illustration of an exceptional case where the court did restrain the foreign application, see *Bankers Trust International plc v. PT Dharmala Sakti Sejahetra* [1996] CLC 252; *Allstate Life Insurance Co v. ANZ Banking Corp* (1996) 64 FCR 61; *Omega Group Holdings Ltd v. Kozeny* [2002] CLC 132.

Neither did the court believe that hardship would be caused by allowing the American application to proceed. It appears to follow from this that, whilst a foreign order for interim relief will not be given direct effect in England, recourse to the foreign court for it will not generally[202] be impeded either; and if the party against whom the relief is granted chooses to abide by the foreign order, the order will, it may be said, have succeeded in having indirect effect. Similarly, a foreign order that the party who appears as claimant in English proceedings discontinue them will have no direct effect in England, but if the party so enjoined by the foreign court chooses to discontinue, then (subject to the permission of the court where CPR rule 38.2 makes this necessary)[203] the foreign injunction will have had its intended effect indirectly.

---

202 But if the seeking of the foreign order *is* oppressive or vexatious, for example, because the relief could and should have been obtained from the English court before which the action is pending, an injunction may be granted: *Dubai Bank Ltd v. Galadari* (29 July 1991).

203 See *Castanho v. Brown & Root (UK) Ltd* [1981] AC 557 for a statement of the principles as they applied to RSC Order 21, as it then was, but which was fundamentally different from CPR Part 38.

CHAPTER 7

Recognition and Enforcement of Foreign Judgments

INTRODUCTORY MATTERS

7.01 The schemes by which effect is given in England to foreign judgments

In deciding in which court to commence proceedings, a prospective claimant may consider whether a judgment in his favour will be enforceable outside the jurisdiction of the court which gave it. It is all very well to obtain judgment from a particular court, but if the judgment will not work in the country in which the defendant's assets may be found to be, it will lack practical value. Judged from the point of view of the prospective defendant, the question is whether he can safely turn his back on the foreign proceedings, on the basis that if he does so the judgment will not be enforceable against him outside the State in which it was obtained, or at least not in the States in which he has or plans to keep his assets. This chapter, therefore, examines the rules on the recognition and enforcement of foreign judgments.

The question may arise in at least six ways. First, a defendant[1] may wish to know whether a judgment from a court in a Member State bound by the Brussels I Regulation[2] will be enforceable against him in England. The substance of the law will be found in Chapter III of the Regulation,[3] but so far as the procedure is concerned, a distinction will be drawn between judgments to which Regulation 44/2001 applies, and those which will fall under Regulation 1215/2012. In addition, a judgment from a Member State may also qualify for certified enforcement under a European Enforcement Order ('EEO').[4]

Second, a defendant may wish to know whether a judgment from a court in a territory or State in which the Brussels or Lugano II Convention, but not the Brussels I Regulations, is effective will be enforceable against him in England. This will depend upon the rules of the particular Convention.[5]

Third, a defendant may wish to know whether a judgment from a court of a non-Member, non-Contracting State[6] will be enforceable against him in England. This will depend upon

---

1 A claimant will want to ask these questions with different emphasis.

2 Whether this means Regulation 44/2001 or Regulation 1215/2012 will be dealt with below.

3 As long as the judgment falls within the scope of the Brussels I Regulation. If it does not, the answer must be found elsewhere.

4 Regulation 805/2004, the 'EEO Regulation', as long as the judgment is certifiable under that Regulation: see further below, para. 7.31.

5 If not, the answer will be found in the common law.

6 Or one falling outside the scope of the Regulation and Conventions, for the regimes for recognition are, in principle at least, cumulative rather than exclusive.

the rules of English law, which makes separate (but overlapping) provision according to the origin of the judgment: some may be registered for enforcement pursuant to statute in the High Court; others may need to be sued on at common law.

Fourth, he may wish to know whether an English judgment will be enforceable against him in another Member State. This, as under the first question, is governed by the Brussels I Regulation[7] and the EEO Regulation.

Fifth, he may wish to know whether an English judgment will be enforceable against him in a territory or State in which the Brussels or Lugano II Convention,[8] but not the Brussels I Regulations, is effective.[9] This, as under the second question, is governed by the Brussels or Lugano II Convention, as the case may be.

Sixth, he may wish to know whether an English judgment will be enforceable in a non-Member, non-Contracting State. This will be determined by the private international law of the country in which it is sought to enforce it; the answer will therefore lie beyond the scope of this book, and the advice of a reliable local lawyer will be required.

In fact, it is often just as important for a defendant also to consider whether a judgment from one foreign State would be enforceable against his assets in another foreign State. It will be unsafe to suppose that, just because a foreign judgment – suppose, a default judgment – will not be enforceable in England, it will not be enforceable anywhere else. A State may have bilateral or other treaty arrangements to make its judgments enforceable in another State which is friendly with it: one just has to think about judgments from a court in South America, which could not be enforced in England, being enforced in other South American States to see that there may be a point. Quite apart from that, the judgment debtor may have assets within, or accessible from, the territory of the adjudicating court. These may be vulnerable if the law of that State has adventurous powers of garnishment or debt-seizure, and the defendant has debtors[10] who owe him money, who have a presence within that State, and who are vulnerable to such measures of enforcement or execution 'hijacking' the funds they owe to the judgment debtor. In deciding whether to let judgment be entered in default, a defendant will need to be attentive: where international disputes are concerned, enforcement in England is most unlikely to be the only risk. But the principal concern of this chapter is recognition and enforcement of foreign judgments in England.[11]

---

7 As long as the case falls within the material and temporal scope of the Brussels I Regulation. If it does not, the answer may still be found in the Brussels or Lugano II Convention, but if not, the answer will be found in the internal law of the State in which recognition is sought, and, as such, it lies beyond the scope of this book.

8 That is, from a State or territory which was party to the Convention but not a Member State for the purpose of the Brussels I Regulation, the judgment falling within the domain of the particular Convention.

9 That is, in a State or territory which was a Contracting State to one or another of the Conventions, the judgment falling within the scope of the relevant Convention. If this condition is not satisfied, the answer must be found from the rules of the internal law of that State.

10 A bank, for example.

11 This chapter deals with the general rules of private international law for the recognition and enforcement of judgments. It does not deal with subject-specific statutory schemes creating a statutory framework for allowing cross-border enforcement of orders made for the prevention of crime, as for example in the Proceeds of Crime Act 2002 and the Proceeds of Crime Act 2002 (External Requests and Orders) Order 2005, SI 2005/3181, as amended by SI 2013/2604: for illustration, see *Blue Holdings (1) Pte Ltd v. United States* [2014] EWCA Civ 1291, [2015] 1 ALL ER (Comm) 1.

7.02 Deciding which scheme or schemes of recognition and enforcement will apply

The principal factors which determine the set of recognition and enforcement rules which apply are the identity of the court which gave judgment and the nature of the claim.[12] For example, if the judgment was in a civil or commercial matter from a French court,[13] the answer will depend primarily upon one or other of the Brussels I Regulations,[14] though if judgment was on an uncontested claim for a specific sum of money the judgment may qualify for speeded-up enforcement under the EEO procedure as well. If the judgment was in a civil or commercial matter and from a Swiss court,[15] the answer will be found in the Lugano II Convention. If it is a judgment from an American court, the rules of the common law will give the answer. If it is a judgment from a court in New Zealand, the Administration of Justice Act 1920, which is in large measure a codification of common law principle, will probably apply. If it is a judgment from an Australian court, the Foreign Judgments (Reciprocal Enforcement) Act 1933, which is in essence an approximate codification of the common law, will probably govern. Although the English statutory schemes do not usually prevent the alternative of seeking recognition of the judgment by recourse to the rules of the common law, and although it is technically possible to enforce by action at common law a judgment to which the statutory schemes of registration do not extend, the cases in which this will need to be done are few and rare.[16]

From the point of view of a defendant, it is important to notice from the outset that a sharp and sharpening[17] distinction exists between the enforcement of European civil and commercial judgments under the various European instruments, on the one hand, and under the common law, on the other. Under the European schemes, there will be straightforward, sometimes automatic and unquestioned, recognition and enforcement of judgments as between the States which is hard, sometimes impossible, to derail. In particular, it is generally no defence for the judgment debtor to assert that the adjudicating court was quite wrong in considering that it had jurisdiction or that it decided the case wrongly. Once the judgment has gone against him, the defendant is very much on the back foot. It follows from this that the defendant runs a substantial risk by letting the original proceedings in the courts of a Member State go against him by default, or by not contesting them with vigour

---

12 A subsidiary factor is the date of the institution of proceedings, because the Regulation and the Conventions will apply only if they were in force at the relevant time. This is explained below. Those European Instruments which deal with insolvency (Regulation 1346/2000) and family law matters (Regulation 2201/2003) contain their own provisions for the recognition of judgments given in proceedings falling within their scope. They are not examined further here.

13 And the case falls within the scope of the Brussels I Regulation.

14 The rules on recognition are substantially one and the same; the mechanisms for enforcement are to some extent different, as is shown below.

15 If the case falls within the scope of the Convention.

16 Because the registration schemes either codify the common law, or extend recognition beyond its limits. But the particular *court* may not be one which is specified in the treaty, given the force of law by the relevant Order, and in the case of judgments from such excluded courts, enforcement at common law will still be possible. It follows that it is always necessary to look at the particular bilateral treaty to see which judgments from which courts are covered.

17 Regulation 1215/2012 will make (it applies only to judgments given in proceedings which were commenced on or after 10 January 2015) enforcement of judgments from Member States even more obstacle-free than Regulation 44/2001 did and does; Regulation 44/2001 had removed some obstacles which were contained in the Brussels Convention.

whether on jurisdiction, or on the merits, or both. In Europe, there is little to be gained from keeping one's powder dry; indeed, there may be everything to lose.

By contrast, if the foreign judgment will take its effect in England under the common law rules, or under the statutes[18] which are derived from it, the judgment debtor will be allowed to contend that the adjudicating court did not have what English private international law considers to be 'international jurisdiction' over him. As one of the only two acknowledged bases of such 'international jurisdiction' is submission to the foreign court, a defendant who is not present within the jurisdiction of the foreign court[19] on the relevant date may consider it safe to allow the proceedings to go by default.[20] Moreover, the range of non-jurisdictional objections to the recognition and enforcement of a judgment which are made available by the common law rules is wider than is permitted under the Brussels I Regulation.[21] For these reasons, the tactics which a defendant should deploy will depend upon whether the judgment is likely to be presented for recognition and enforcement under the Brussels I Regulation or related instruments, on the one hand, or take its effect as a matter of common law or its derivative statutes, on the other.

JUDGMENTS IN CIVIL AND COMMERCIAL MATTERS FROM THE COURTS OF MEMBER STATES: REGULATION 44/2001

7.03 Regulation 44/2001 or Regulation 1215/2012?

The recognition and enforcement of judgments given by the courts of Member States in civil and commercial matters is, in principle and in almost every case, governed by Chapter III of the Brussels I Regulation. As there are two versions of the Brussels I Regulation, the original Regulation 44/2001 and the recast version 1215/2012, the question which Brussels I Regulation applies to the particular judgment arises at the outset.

The point of departure is to identify the judgments to which Regulation 1215/2012 applies its provisions on recognition and enforcement. The answer is given by Article 66 of Regulation 1215/2012:

> *(1) This Regulation shall apply only to legal proceedings instituted, to authentic instruments formally drawn up or registered and to court settlements approved or concluded on or after 10 January 2015. (2) Notwithstanding Article 80, Regulation (EC) No 44/2001 shall continue to apply to judgments given in legal proceedings instituted, to authentic instruments formally drawn up or registered and to court settlements approved or concluded before 10 January 2015 which fall within the scope of that Regulation.*

For practical purposes, therefore, it appears that although Regulation 1215/2012 will apply from 10 January 2015, its impact will be felt in questions of jurisdiction rather more quickly than in matters concerned with the effect of judgments from other Member States. For this reason the approach taken in this edition is that Regulation 44/2001 is the basic provision. Regulation 1215/2012, which will not apply unless the original proceedings were instituted after 10 January 2015, is dealt with afterwards, so as to be able to show how much will be

---

18 Administration of Justice Act 1920; Foreign Judgments (Reciprocal Enforcement) Act 1933.

19 Presence being the other basis of 'international jurisdiction' so far as the common law is concerned.

20 Though he will need to consider whether there is still a threat of enforcement in another country in which he has, or may later have, assets, before deciding to take this step.

21 Though almost none is provided for under the EEO procedure.

the same, and how much will be different, in the cases in which it will apply. In the next edition of this book the organisation may need to be different, but it will in fact be several years before Regulation 1215/2012 has a significant impact on the law of foreign judgments.

7.04 Regulation 44/2001 and the recognition of judgments: general

Regulation 44/2001 applies to judgments in civil and commercial matters from the courts of Member[22] States from 1 March 2002;[23] in the ten 2004 Accession States[24] from 1 May 2004; in Bulgaria and Romania from 1 January 2007; in Denmark from 1 July 2007;[25] and from Croatia from 1 July 2013. Insofar as it applies to judgments, Regulation 44/2001 explains the relevance of these dates as follows:

> *(Regulation 44/2001, Article 66): (1) This Regulation shall apply only to legal proceedings instituted and to documents formally drawn up or registered as authentic instruments after the entry into force thereof. (2) However, if the proceedings in the Member State of origin were instituted before the entry into force of this Regulation, judgments given after that date shall be recognised and enforced in accordance with Chapter III, (a) if the proceedings in the Member State of origin were instituted after the entry into force of the Brussels or the Lugano Convention both in the Member State of origin and in the Member State addressed; (b) in all other cases, if jurisdiction was founded upon rules which accorded with those provided for either in Chapter II or in a convention concluded between the Member State of origin and the Member State addressed which was in force when the proceedings were instituted.*

Regulation 44/2001 applies to judgments given in proceedings which were instituted after the date on which the Regulation came into force, but the effect of its Article 66(2) is to extend its temporal scope to cover many judgments which will have been given after that date in proceedings which had been commenced in a Member State prior to this coming into force. In practice, the recognition of a judgment which falls within Article 66 requires[26] no formal step to be taken: the rules on recognition simply apply to a judgment which has been given in a civil or commercial matter in another Member State.

When it comes to the enforcement of a judgment to which Regulation 44/2001 applies, Civil Jurisdiction and Judgments Order 2001, Schedule 1, paragraph 2[27] provides for a qualifying judgment to be registered on application to the High Court. When registered, the judgment 'shall, for the purpose of its enforcement, be of the same force and effect…' as if it had been a judgment of the High Court. The provisions which will be examined define whether and determine when an order for registration of the judgment for enforcement may be obtained by the applicant or, as is in practice the way it works, may be set aside on application by the defendant after its having been obtained, *ex parte*, by the judgment creditor.

The scheme put in place by Regulation 44/2001 is characterised by its comparative simplicity and speed: a constant aim of the European Union has been to create a borderless

---

22 The members of the European Union apart from Denmark, which originally opted out: Art. 1(3) and Recitals 21 and 22 to Regulation 44/2001.

23 Regulation 44/2001, Art. 76.

24 Cyprus, the Czech Republic, Estonia, Hungary, Latvia, Lithuania, Malta, Poland, Slovakia, and Slovenia.

25 Which opted into the Regulation: SI 2007/1655.

26 Though if there is, exceptionally, a need for an order to confirm recognition, and this is the principal issue in the proceedings, Regulation 44/2001, Art. 33(2) permits application for such an order.

27 Which reproduces, in effect, Civil Jurisdiction and Judgments Act 1982, s. 4, which continues to apply to the rare judgment which is to be enforced under the Brussels Convention.

market in judgments, so that a claimant who has obtained judgment from a court within the territory of the European Union is able to enforce that judgment in any and all other Member States with a minimum of fuss. Two important factors contribute to the smooth operation of the Regulation scheme. The first is that it is generally impermissible[28] at the stage of recognition to make objection to the original jurisdiction of the adjudicating court. If grounds existed for such objection, they must generally have been raised before the adjudicating court, and at the outset, or not at all.[29] The reasons are obvious. The European Union comprises a manageable number of developed or deemed-to-be-sufficiently developed countries, the courts of all of which are equally competent to apply the jurisdictional rules of the Regulation which applies to them all. Each one is as well placed as any other to interpret and apply the Regulation, and to refer questions to the European Court where necessary. It would therefore impair the administration of justice in the community and throw sand in the works of the free market in judgments if the jurisdiction of the adjudicating court could, as a matter of course, be retrospectively called into question.[30] This contrasts sharply with the position at common law.

Second, the rules on recognition and enforcement take no[31] account of the domicile or nationality of claimant or defendant. A judgment from a French court in a civil or commercial matter is required to be recognised in other Member States if given against a Belgian just as much as if given against a New Yorker or a Ruritanian, because it is a judgment from the courts of a Member State in a civil or commercial matter. It is as liable to be enforced at the suit of a judgment creditor who is English as one who is Australian, because it is a judgment from the courts of a Member State in a civil or commercial matter. Whereas the rules upon jurisdiction are based in large part upon considerations of the defendant's domicile, the rules on recognition and enforcement are not.

7.05 Regulation 44/2001 and judgment debtors not domiciled in a Member State

Regulation 44/2001 does not discriminate against judgment creditors who are not established in the European Union[32] by withholding its benefits and procedures from them: whoever has a judgment falling within the scope of the Regulation may rely on Chapter III of the Regulation to enforce it. But the position of defendants who do not have a domicile in any of the Member States is a rather different thing.

---

28 The exceptions are in Regulation 44/2001, Art. 35, discussed below.

29 'If anyone knows any lawful impediment why these two parties should not be joined in litigation, let him now declare it or else hereafter hold his peace', as the judge in the adjudicating court might say.

30 Or, to put it another way, as though it were an extra-curial appeal against the jurisdictional decision of the first court. If this is the way to look at it, it makes no sense to allow it. By contrast, where recognition is to take place at common law, the question for the recognising court (was there jurisdiction according to the rules of the common law?) is different from the question before the adjudicating court (was there jurisdiction under the rules of the adjudicating court?), and the sense of there being an extra-curial appeal is plainly absent.

31 There are two exceptions. First, the application of a bilateral treaty made pursuant to Art. 59 of the Brussels Convention and preserved in effect by Regulation 44/2001, Art. 72, may make this a relevant factor. Second, where the exceptions to the rule that the jurisdiction of the adjudicating court may not be reviewed, set out in Regulation 44/2001, Art. 35, apply, the issue of domicile may be marginally relevant. But in general the proposition in the text is accurate.

32 Cf, in the context of jurisdiction, the equal treatment of such claimants: C-412/98 *Universal Groupe Insurance Co v. Group Josi Reinsurance Co SA* [2000] ECR I-5925.

Regulation 44/2001 provides for the recognition and enforcement of judgments from the courts of Member States. Where the adjudicating court has taken jurisdiction over a defendant domiciled in a Member State, the defendant will have had the advantage, or protection, of the primary or detailed jurisdictional rules set out in Chapter II of the Regulation: he will have benefited from the expectation of defending the claim in his home courts unless one of the specific exceptions to the general domiciliary rule[33] applies to him in respect of the claim. If he considers that the claimant is inviting the adjudicating court to misinterpret the jurisdictional rules of the Regulation, he may seek to have a question referred to the European Court for a preliminary ruling. There is no real danger of his finding himself sued on the basis of the traditional, exorbitant or long-arm jurisdictions of national law: in Regulation 44/2001, Article 3(2)[34] forbids the use of these provisions against anyone who has a domicile in a Member State. Given this degree of jurisdictional security, it is balanced and proportionate to prevent the judgment debtor asking a court, called upon by his opponent to recognise the judgment, to re-examine and assess the propriety of the exercise of jurisdiction by the adjudicating court.

A defendant who does not have a domicile in a Member State has none of the benefits, but is still exposed to all of the – to him – disadvantages. He does not benefit from the careful structure of jurisdictional rules established by the Regulation. There is no presumption that he should also expect to be able to defend himself in his home courts. Indeed, Regulation 44/2001 is explicit[35] that the traditional, exorbitant and long-arm jurisdictions of national laws may be used against him: he is at the mercy of jurisdictional rules which have been outlawed for use so far as European defendants are concerned, even though it will, by reason of distance if nothing else, be likely to be more difficult and inconvenient for him to defend in a court of a Member State than it would be for a defendant domiciled in a Member State. But when it comes to recognition and enforcement of judgments, recognition and enforcement is still automatic. The defendant is not entitled to complain that the adjudicating court had no jurisdiction, or that the jurisdictional rules upon which it relied were objectionable, or even contrary to public policy in the recognising court.[36] In short, he may not invoke the jurisdictional protection given to Europeans at the adjudicatory stage; he is not entitled to complain about whatever jurisdiction was taken over him at the recognition stage.[37] It is a honking disgrace.

This very unsatisfactory situation would have been significantly improved had a proposal been adopted at the end of the process of recasting the Brussels I Regulation. Jurisdiction over defendants hitherto (and, as it has turned out, still) liable to be sued on the basis of the 'residual' jurisdictional rules of national law would have been partially replaced with directly legislated rules so that, for example, the rules for taking jurisdiction over a defendant sued outside the courts of his domicile would be, very substantially, common to all defendants. Such a change would have reoriented Chapter III away from the existing (and, as it happened, continuing) unfairness of applying free movement of judgments to residual

---

33 In Regulation 44/2001, Art. 2.

34 Recast in Regulation 1215/2012 as Art. 5(2).

35 Regulation 44/2001, Art. 4.

36 See below.

37 Though if he is within the protection of an Art. 72 treaty, he will be safe from enforcement in the particular State.

jurisdictional rules. The proposal did not survive the legislative process; and from this point of view – there may be others – it is a shame that it did not.

7.06 Recognition of the judgment under Regulation 44/2001: Articles 32 to 37

A judgment cannot be enforced under Chapter III of Regulation 44/2001 unless that Regulation is in force in the State of recognition. In practice, however, the Regulation has been in force in England for 12 years; it is very improbable that any issue will now arise on this point. If an English court is called upon to recognise or enforce a judgment from or in Croatia, the most recent of the Member States to become bound by the Regulation, it may be necessary to address the transitional provision set out in Article 66 of Regulation 44/2001; but in practice there is no need to make further reference to the temporal scope provisions of Chapter III of Regulation 44/2001. The time has passed.

If a judgment meets the criteria for recognition under Chapter III of Regulation 44/2001, its enforcement will be pretty straightforward, if not automatic.[38] As will be seen, the rules which determine whether a judgment, given in proceedings which were instituted on or after 10 January 2015, is entitled to recognition under Regulation 1215/2012, are practically identical with those set out in Regulation 44/2001: the focus of attention when Chapter III was recast was not the grounds for recognition but the mechanism for enforcement of judgments from other Member States.

The question of recognition is best approached by dealing with the questions which need to be addressed. As there are only four of them, the order in which they are considered is not as important as was the case with the rules on jurisdiction. But the logic and economy of Regulation 44/2001 suggests that this order makes sense.

(1) Is the order which is sought to enforce a judgment from a court in a Member State? If it is not, Chapter III of Regulation 44/2001 has no application to it. But if it is such a judgment,

(2) Was the judgment given in proceedings in a civil or commercial matter as defined by Chapter I of the Regulation? If it was not, Regulation 44/2001 has no application to it, and its recognition and enforcement will depend on the rules of the common law.[39] But if it is such a judgment,

(3) Does the respondent have grounds for an admissible objection to the jurisdiction of the adjudicating court? If he does, the objection may be made, and if sustained the judgment will not be recognised under Chapter III of the Regulation. But if he does not have such grounds,

(4) Does the respondent have grounds for an admissible non-jurisdictional (some of which are substantive, others procedural) objection to the recognition of the judgment? If he does, the objection may be made, and if sustained the judgment will not be recognised under Chapter III of the Regulation. But if he does not have such grounds, the judgment must be recognised, for under no circumstances may it be reviewed on its merits.

---

38 It is examined below, paras 7.06 *et seq.*
39 Or on a statute reflecting the rules of the common law.

7.07 A judgment from a court in a Member State: Article 32 of Regulation 44/2001

Little needs to be said about the meanings of 'court' and 'Member State'. As to 'court', the Regulation applies to all courts, whatever they may be called. So even orders made by magistrates' courts[40] are potentially within the scope of Chapter III. The same is probably true of certain bodies designated as tribunals, even if not locally thought of as courts, if they are exercising judicial powers in relation to matters within the material scope of the Regulation. So 'tribunals' which are given jurisdiction in matters of employment law may certainly give 'judgments'. What was said about Member States in Chapter 2 does not need to be repeated here, save only for the fact that a judgment from the courts of Gibraltar is regarded as a judgment from the courts of the United Kingdom, as this European territory for whose external relations the United Kingdom is responsible is included within the geographical scope of the Regulation by Article 355(3) TFEU.[41] But it does not apply to judgments from the Channel Islands or the Isle of Man.[42]

Regulation 44/2001 applies to 'judgments'. This term has a wide, but not an unlimited meaning: it applies to many, but not to all, judicial orders.[43] It expressly includes orders for costs.[44] It includes many interlocutory orders, and injunctions and decrees of specific performance.[45] It includes a decree establishing a limitation fund.[46] It also includes an order decreeing a periodic payment by way of penalty for non-compliance with the order of a court, sometimes known as an *astreinte*, even though the order to pay may not be enforced until the sum due has been 'liquidated' by the courts of the State in which it was handed down.[47] It is not currently known whether it would extend to a court order sanctioning a scheme of arrangement under the Companies Acts.[48] But it does not extend to interlocutory directions upon the conduct of proceedings, such as orders providing for the taking of evidence.[49]

---

40 And other inferior tribunals. This marks a change from the position adopted in most earlier bilateral treaties, where courts below a certain level were excluded. It will also include tribunals where the judge is not legally qualified, such as Tribunals de Commerce in France.

41 Council Document 7998/2000 states that decisions taken by an authority in Gibraltar must be directly enforced in other Member States in accordance with the Regulation. According to the declaration of the United Kingdom [2001] OJ C13/1, documents containing such decisions will be certified as authentic by the United Kingdom Government/Gibraltar Liaison Unit for EU Affairs of the Foreign and Commonwealth Office, in London.

42 TFEU Art. 355(5)(c).

43 It should exclude a refusal to make an order, such as a negative declaration, when the court is in effect refusing to adjudicate at all, but it should include a case where the court refuses to make the order because it has found for the defendant. Everything must turn on the content and context of the decision. It includes judgments as to the scope and effect of the Regulation: see Schlosser [1979] OJ C59/71, [191]; C-456/11 *Gothaer Allgemeine Versicherving AG v Samskip GmbH* EU:C:2012:719, [2013] QB 458.

44 Regulation 44/2001, Art. 32.

45 In sharp contrast to the rules of the common law.

46 At least if the parties had an opportunity to be heard before the provisional decree was made final: C-39/02 *Mærsk Olie & Gas A/S v. De Haan & de Boer* [2004] ECR I-9657.

47 Regulation 44/2001, Art. 49. It is unclear from the text whether the order can be enforced if there has been a liquidation of the sum payable, but that judgment is itself under appeal. At that point, can it be said that the amount of the payment has been finally determined by the courts of the State in which the judgment was given? It is unclear whether the use of the plural form is deliberate.

48 It would need to be a solvent scheme of arrangement to avoid being excluded by Art. 1(2)(b) of the Brussels I Regulation. In the quite different context of its status as a judgment under the common law rules for recognition and enforcement, see *Re Cavell Insurance Co Ltd* (2006) 269 DLR (4th) 679.

49 Schlosser [1979] OJ C59/71, [184]–[187]. In further, if indirect, support, C-365/88 *Kongress Agentur Hagen GmbH v. Zeehaghe BV* [1990] ECR I-1845; see *CFEM Façades v. Bovis Construction SA* [1992] ILPr 561.

Chapter III of Regulation 44/2001 does not extend its recognition rules to orders obtained and designed to be obtained *ex parte* or without notice to the defendant.[50] For if the procedure was one in which the defendant was not entitled to be heard at all, the order cannot be said to have the quality of a 'judgment' to which the mechanism for near-automatic recognition and enforcement should be applied. A freezing injunction, obtained without notice to the defendant is, therefore, for these purposes, not a 'judgment'. This follows from *Denilauler v. SNC Couchet Frères*,[51] where the Court held that a French order of attachment, which had been obtained without notice to the respondent, could not be enforced in Germany, on the ground that it was not an order of a kind obtained or intended to be obtained after enquiry in adversarial proceedings. It was not the fact that the defendant did not appear which deprived the order of the character of a judgment, but the fact that, in the very nature of the procedure, he *could* not have appeared. On the other hand, once the order has been continued after a hearing in *inter partes* proceedings,[52] a confirmed or continued order will qualify as a judgment for the purposes of Article 32 of Regulation 44/2001, for the order is no longer one obtained outside adversary proceedings.[53] The point is considered in greater detail below,[54] but the principle is clear.

A default judgment counts as a judgment. In some circumstances English procedural law allows a claimant to obtain judgment in terms of the claim, without any real judicial scrutiny of the grounds on which the claim is made. This may happen if the defendant does not appear; it may also result from the defendant's being debarred from defending, by reason of non-compliance with a mandatory order made by the court.[55] In such circumstances there is a clear sense in which the order made by the court is not an adjudication: it is certainly not a judicial evaluation of the substance of the claim made, albeit that it results from judicial process and the defendant has no-one to blame but himself.[56] However, if this were held to be correct, and the order were not to be a judgment for the purposes of the Regulation, it would lead to the paradoxical result that a defendant could frustrate the claimant with an unanswerable claim by the simple device of ignoring the proceedings or by behaving defiantly in the face of the court. In the light of this, and of the fact that judgments on uncontested claims may now benefit from the accelerated enforcement procedure of the

---

50 In relation to Regulation 1215/2012, the definition of a judgment in Art. 2(a) makes more specific provision for such kinds of order.

51 125/79, [1980] ECR 1553. The Court also rested its decision upon the basis that what is now the first part of Art. 34(2) of Regulation 44/2001 could be relied upon to oppose recognition.

52 This is certainly so if the application to set aside the order is made by the defendant; if the procedure is one in which the application to continue the order after a short initial period is made by the claimant, the result should still count as a judgment, as the procedure will have been one in which the defendant was entitled to be heard. That is not to say that there will not be other reasons to refuse recognition.

53 This assumption was made by a German court in *European Consulting Unternehmensberatung AG v. Refco Overseas Ltd* (OLG Karlsruhe, 19 December 1994; 9W/32/94); noted in *Zeitschrift für Zivilprozess International*, 1996, 89. But it is also supported, indirectly but clearly (because the debate was whether the objection to recognition in Regulation 44/2001, Art. 34(2) applied), by C-420/07 *Apostolides v. Orams* [2009] ECR I-3571.

54 Paragraphs 7.17 *et seq*.

55 C-394/07 *Gambazzi v. Daimler Chrysler Canada Inc* [2009] ECR I-2563.

56 Though see the very same point being made and accepted in the Privy Council as a matter of Indian statute law (Indian Code of Civil Procedure, Art. 13, which was, one supposes, a statutory formulation of the English common law as then understood), resulting in the non-recognition of an English default judgment because it could not be seen as a judgment on the merits: *Keymer v. Visvanatham Reddi* (1916) LR 44 Ind App 6 (the passage quoted is at 10).

EEO Regulation, a default judgment resulting from proceedings which were designed to be *inter partes* is to be regarded as a judgment; any non-recognition will have to be based on other grounds,[57] such as public policy,[58] or (where the judgment was in default and the defendant was not served in time to enter a defence) on the limited ground made available for such cases.

An order by a court declaring that an arbitral award is enforceable does not count as a 'judgment'.[59] The reason appears to be that judicial rubber-stamping of an award, the determination of which was not undertaken by a judge in the courts of a Member State, does not serve to bring that matter within the Regulation, as the judgment is not that of a court in a Member State.

A decision by a court in a Member State that the judgment of a court of a non-Member State is entitled to recognition in the Member State concerned does not count as a 'judgment' from the courts of a Member State which can then be enforced under Chapter III. There are several ways of justifying this. One would be that a decision that (say) an Algerian judgment is entitled to recognition in France[60] is not a decision of the French courts on the merits of the underlying dispute. Another is that a decision that a judgment from Ruritania is entitled to be enforced in France is no more than that: it may be an order which is, in terms and content, limited in effect to the territorial jurisdiction of France. A third is the observation that '*exequatur sur exequatur ne vaut*': that 'enforcement of an enforcement doesn't count'.[61] However one expresses it, it all comes to the same thing: judgments of Member States upon judgments of non-Member States are, for the purpose of Article 32, not judgments of the courts of Member States. As a matter of authority, this also follows from the decision of the Court in *Owens Bank Ltd v. Bracco*.[62] In that case, judicial proceedings to secure recognition of a judgment from the courts of St Vincent and the Grenadines, and all incidental steps taken within those proceedings, were held to fall wholly outside what is now the Brussels I Regulation, whether the applicant was seeking registration of the judgment, or suing on it as a debt, or disputing an issue which had arisen within that procedure. But it may be different if the judgment creditor instead sues on the original cause of action,[63] relying on the foreign judgment only as evidence of its validity. As the court of a Member State is, in such a case, coming to its own conclusion on the merits of the claim, the judgment which it gives ought to fall within Chapter III of the Regulation. After all, the court's approach to what is admissible evidence can hardly

---

57 C-394/07 *Gambazzi v. Daimler Chrysler Canada Inc* [2009] ECR I-2563.

58 See below, para. 7.13.

59 Schlosser [1979] OJ C59/71, [65]. For the curious consequences of this in relation to Art. 34(3) of the Brussels I Regulation, see below, para. 7.22.

60 It might also be thought that a judgment that it is enforceable in France could not, according to its very terms, be of any effect outside France. Another reason would be that several Member States have arrangements in relation to their colonies or former colonial territories, and while these may justify the recognition of colonial judgments in and under the law of England or France, there is no reason why other Member States should have the consequences of this legacy foisted on them and their laws.

61 Gavalda [1935] JDI/Clunet 113; Kegel, in *FestschriftFestschriftF für Wolfram Müller-Freienfels* (1986), 377. The point is explained in detail by Lenz AG in C-129/92 *Owens Bank Ltd v. Bracco* [1994] ECR I-117. The translation given in the text is loose, but conveys the sense of the rule perfectly clearly.

62 C-129/92, [1994] ECR I-117.

63 Although in England (as distinct from those Member States in which foreign judgments are not recognised as such unless pursuant to treaty, and where suing on the original cause of action but with the aid of the judgment is the only option) Civil Jurisdiction and Judgments Act 1982, s. 34, will make this difficult, if not impossible.

banish the entire dispute beyond the reach of Chapter III. No doubt there may be tricky cases at the margins.

A decision that a court does not have jurisdiction because the courts of another Member State do have jurisdiction counts as a 'judgment'. The reasons are sensible and pragmatic. Authority supports the conclusion, but currently only to a limited extent. If a court decides that it does not have jurisdiction because there is a choice of court agreement for the courts of another Member State, *Gothaer Allgemeine Versicherung AG v. Samskip GmbH*[64] holds that the ruling of the first court, dismissing the matter on jurisdictional grounds, is a judgment and is to be recognised as such:[65] not only as a bare decision that the court seised has no jurisdiction, but also as to the judicial reasoning that there is a jurisdiction agreement for another Member State.[66] That certainly means that another court, seised next, must dismiss the proceedings by reference to the reasons given in the first judgment; and it must surely also mean that the court allegedly prorogated by agreement must accept that it has jurisdiction over the matter which was dismissed in its favour on jurisdictional grounds, whatever it might have thought had the decision been its alone.

The actual decision of the Court in *Samskip* was tied closely to the law on jurisdiction agreements, but the general logic of the decision cannot be so confined,[67] for fear that a claimant may be driven from court to court in search of a hearing, wasting time and money as he goes: a grim illustration of what happens when this simple advice is not heeded or applied can be seen in *Standard Bank London Ltd v. Apostolakis*.[68] But some cases will be more difficult. If a court declares that it has no jurisdiction because another court has exclusive jurisdiction regardless of domicile, when the correct answer would have been that Section 6 of Chapter II did not apply at all, the court in whose favour jurisdiction was declined should recognise the judgment and adjudicate: its exercise of jurisdiction cannot conflict with Section 6 if Section 6 does not apply at all. If an English court declares that it has no jurisdiction because the defendant does not have a domicile in the United Kingdom, it makes no finding as to the existence of a domicile in another Member State, this being irrelevant to general jurisdiction.

But if an English court declares that it does not have special jurisdiction because the defendant is not domiciled in any other Member State according to its law, it is less clear that the courts of other Member States are bound to accept that the defendant does not have a domicile within their territory. In this case, the court is not deciding that it has no jurisdiction because a court in another Member State does have jurisdiction: its decision is qualitatively different. It is not clear that *Gothaer Allgemeine Versicherung AG v. Samskip GmbH*, in which this same conclusion was reached, but on the specific ground that a Member State had jurisdiction by prorogation, would require the totality of the court's findings in relation to jurisdiction to be accepted without question; the cases are not on all fours.

---

64 C-456/11, EU:C:2012:719, [2013] QB 458.

65 *Cf* Schlosser [1979] OJ C59/71, [191].

66 In fact, the jurisdiction agreed to was Iceland, and the decision was governed in that respect by the Lugano Convention. But the point is general.

67 It was construed as having a broad and general effect in *Starlight Shipping Co v. Allianz Marine & Aviation Versicherungs AG* [2014] EWHC 3068 (Comm), [2014] 2 Lloyd's Rep 579.

68 [2003] ILPr 342. Others may prefer the imagery of the Flying Dutchman, but the disastrous result is the same.

7.08 A judgment in a civil or commercial matter: Article 1 of Regulation 44/2001

To be recognised under Chapter III of the Brussels I Regulation, a judgment must have been given in respect of a civil or commercial matter, and must not be excluded from the material scope of the Regulation by Article 1(2).[69] The enquiry is exactly the same as that made when deciding whether a case falls within the domain of the Regulation for the purposes of jurisdiction.[70] Indeed, the earliest cases[71] in which the Court considered the interpretation of Article 1 of the Brussels Convention were concerned with the recognition of judgments rather than with the taking of original jurisdiction. The material examined in Chapter 2 therefore applies in this context as well.

It has not been finally decided whether a court called on to recognise a judgment from another Member State is entitled to examine *de novo* and decide for itself whether the judgment is one given in a civil or commercial matter. It is implicit in *LTU Lufttransport-Unternehmen GmbH & Co KG v. Eurocontrol*[72] that the national court should do this for itself: after all, it could hardly have referred a question, and have received an answer, in relation to Article 1 of the Brussels Convention, if it had not been entitled to assess for itself whether the judgment was given in a civil or commercial matter. And it is apparent that in certain cases the adjudicating court may not have needed to determine whether the proceedings before it fell inside or outside the material scope of the Regulation: for example, if the adjudicating court saw that if the matter were civil or commercial it would have general jurisdiction based on domicile, but that if it were not civil or commercial, it would have jurisdiction under its national law in any event, then it would have no need to decide whether the claim came within Article 1 of the Regulation.[73]

The rules for recognition of judgments in Chapter III of the Brussels I Regulation are not available unless the judgment was given in a civil or commercial matter. As a result, and in principle, the proceedings before the court called upon to recognise the judgment may be the first occasion on which this question has required a decision; and in these cases at the very least the recognising court must decide for itself whether the judgment was given in a civil or commercial matter. But if the adjudicating court has expressly held that the claim was within Article 1 of the Regulation and not excluded by Article 1(2), may the recognising court re-examine this question for itself? The arguments are in balance. In favour of its being allowed to do so is the fact that proceedings for recognition under Chapter III are separate from the adjudicatory proceedings under Chapter II; and the recognising court is obliged to ascertain that the judgment was in proceedings which fell within Chapter III. Also, it may not be easy to distinguish between cases where the adjudicating court has positively decided,

---

69 For a recent illustration, where the foreign judgment was within Art. 1(2) and therefore outside the material scope of the Regulation, see C-111/08 *SCT Industri AB (in liq) v. Alpenblume AB* [2009] ECR I-5565 (a case materially pre-dating the Insolvency Regulation).

70 It includes a judgment from a court which took jurisdiction in a civil commercial matter, but according to the terms of a particular Convention: see Art. 71 of the Regulation (Art. 71 is discussed at paras 2.46 *et seq.*, above).

71 29/76 *LTU Lufttransport-Unternehmen GmbH & Co KG v. Eurocontrol* [1976] ECR 1541; 145/86 *Hoffmann v. Krieg* [1988] ECR 645; C-172/91 *Sonntag v. Waidmann* [1993] ECR I-1963; C-302/13 *flyLAL-Lithuanian Airlines AS v. Starptautiskā lidosta Rīga VAS* EU:C:2014:2319, [2015] ILPr 28.

72 29/76 [1976] ECR 1541. Precisely the same comment may be made in relation to C-111/08 *SCT Industri AB (in liq) v. Alpenblume AB* [2009] ECR I-5565.

73 *Cf* C-220/95 *Van den Boogaard v. Laumen* [1997] ECR I-1147, which is consistent with the proposition that the court addressed may and must do this for itself.

as distinct from having stated (but without the need to decide) that the case is a civil or commercial one. This would suggest that the recognising court should decide the issue for itself. On the other hand, if this issue has been fully argued before and decided in the adjudicating court, one would suppose that the general scheme of the Brussels I Regulation would not encourage allowing it to be re-argued all over again, at least without some regard to what was reasoned and decided in the first court.[74]

An analogy may be drawn with applications for the recognition and enforcement of orders granting provisional or protective measures.[75] According to the Court in *Mietz v. Intership Yachting Sneek BV*,[76] a court called upon to recognise and enforce such an order is required to take account of the basis upon which the first court acted in making its order. If it had stated that it had taken jurisdiction on the basis of Section 10 of Chapter II of the Regulation,[77] the second court would be required to ascertain by its own enquiry that the measure ordered was within the material scope of that Section;[78] but if the first court had expressly based itself on its having jurisdiction over the merits of the substantive dispute, or it were obvious that this was what had been done, it appears that this must be accepted as conclusive and not be open to question in the second court.[79] Transposed by analogy to the present context, it would mean that if the first court had made a finding that the dispute fell within Article 1 of the Brussels I Regulation its decision would bind the second court, but if this had not been clearly established, the second court would be bound and entitled to undertake the analysis for itself. Although some may see such reasoning as involving the use of bootstraps, it probably accords reasonably well with the overall structure of the Regulation.

As a matter of Union law, the question may therefore be still open. But even if the decision of the adjudicating court is held not to be decisive as a matter of Union law, it would still be open to an English court, called on to recognise the judgment as one in a civil or commercial matter, to apply its own national law, of estoppel, *res judicata*, or abuse of process, and to treat the conclusion of the adjudicating court as settling the issue. As principles of issue estoppel[80] appear to operate independently of the Regulation, this may still be the most flexible, and hence the most satisfactory, solution.

7.09 Judgments given in the context of arbitration under Regulation 44/2001

Questions arise in relation to the obligation to recognise a judgment from the fact that the parties may have contractually agreed to settle their differences by arbitration. The explanation which is given at this point takes no account of Regulation 1215/2012, but will address at the end of this paragraph the extent to which, if at all, the proper interpretation of Regulation 44/2001 is affected by anything in Recital (12) of Regulation 1215/2012. In doing so we will get a little ahead of ourselves and will notice arguments which are relevant not so much to whether the order counts as judgment within the scope of Chapter III, but

---

74 For it would impede the free circulation of judgments.
75 The analogy is not perfect, for the issue to be examined is one which arises within the context of civil or commercial matters, and not on its borderline. But the methodology may be of more general application.
76 C-99/96, [1999] ECR I-2277.
77 Regulation 44/2001, Art. 31; Regulation 1215/2012, Art. 35.
78 At [54].
79 At [50].
80 For these, in relation to foreign judgments, see below.

whether, if it is, its recognition may still be resisted on grounds set out elsewhere in Chapter III. But at this point we are principally concerned with whether a court order which has something to do with arbitration is within the scope of Chapter I in the first place, and therefore also within Chapter III, of the Regulation.

Judgments which take the form of orders to establish, regulate, assist and in other respects deal with the arbitration have arbitration as their subject matter; they fall outside the material scope of Chapter I, and therefore Chapter III, of the Regulation. The same will be true of an injunction to enforce the agreement to arbitrate, whether positively or negatively;[81] likewise a judgment ordering damages for breach of an arbitration agreement. All are civil or commercial matters which have arbitration as their sole subject matter; they are not within the material scope of Chapter I, and orders in such matter are not judgments within the scope of Chapter III, of the Regulation.

If the parties have proceeded to arbitration, and after the award an application has been made to a court for leave to enforce the award as if it were a judgment, or that a judgment has been obtained in the terms of the award, the resultant court order does not fall within Chapter I of the Brussels I Regulation. As a result, Chapter III does not require any Member State to recognise it.[82] This is entirely in accord with the proposition that the enforcement of arbitral awards falls within the province of specialist international conventions and national legislation, all of which are wholly separate from the Brussels I Regulation.

Much more troublesome is the problem which arises when it is sought to obtain recognition of a judgment given in a civil or commercial matter by a court which has concluded, contrary to the submission of the defendant and the opinion of English law, that the parties had been under no obligation to settle their differences by arbitration.[83] On the footing that the defendant did not otherwise submit to the proceedings before the foreign court,[84] the question arises as to whether he will be entitled to resist recognition of the judgment on the basis that it concerns arbitration, which falls outside the domain of the Regulation.

Authority on the true interpretation of Regulation 44/2001 was not decisive. There is a view, held by some civilian lawyers,[85] that the judgment must be recognised as one given, even if given wrongly, in a civil or commercial matter. This view treats the 'arbitration point' as a jurisdictional defence to proceedings in a civil or commercial matter, which had been rejected by the court. As jurisdictional error is not a ground for non-recognition of a judgment under Chapter III of Regulation 44/2001, the judgment must qualify for recognition.[86] Acceptance of this point of view by the Court of Appeal was initially limited,[87] but

---

81 *Ust-Kamenogorsk Hydropower Plant JSC v. AES Ust-Kamenogorsk Hydropower Plant LLP* [2013] UKSC 35, [2013] 1 WLR 1889.

82 *Arab Business Corporation International Finance & Investment Co v. Banque Franco-Tunisienne* [1996] 1 Lloyd's Rep 485.

83 It will not be open to the party seeking to uphold the arbitration agreement to obtain an anti-suit injunction to prevent the breach: C-185/07 *Allianz SpA v. West Tankers Inc* [2009] ECR I-663.

84 For if he did, he throws away the shield given by Civil Jurisdiction and Judgments Act 1982, s. 32: see s. 32(1)(c).

85 Though this may mean that it is the view of Professor Schlosser. See also Audit (1993) 9 Arb Int 1; Hascher (1996) 12 Arb Int 223; Beraudo (2001) 18 Jour. Int. Arb. 13; Van Haersolte-Van Hof, *ibid.*, 27. See also *Soc Assurances Générales de France v. Göttgens*, Cass Civ I, 14 November 2000, [2001] Rev Crit DIP 172 (*note* Muir-Watt).

86 And accordingly s. 32(4) of the 1982 Act means that there is no defence to recognition in the violation of the clause. Were it not for s. 32(4), an English court could reach its own independent conclusion that there was a binding agreement to arbitrate, whatever the foreign court may have thought: see s. 32(3).

87 *Marc Rich & Co AG v. Soc Italiana Impianti PA (No 2)* [1992] 1 Lloyd's Rep 624. The point was left open: see at 632–633.

the later opinion of that court was that a judgment given in proceedings in which a Spanish court had rejected a contention that the parties were obliged to proceed to arbitration fell within Chapters I and III of the Regulation, and its recognition was therefore required by Chapter III.[88]

Some support for this view is certainly to be found in *Van Uden Maritime BV v. Firma Deco-Line*.[89] The parties had agreed to arbitrate their differences, but an application had been made to court for an interim payment. In dealing with the question whether what is now Chapter II of the Regulation affected the power of the Dutch court to order payment by the German defendant, the Court confirmed that the proceedings were brought in a civil or commercial matter. It followed that provisional or protective measures could be granted by reference to Section 10 of Chapter II of the Regulation, even though there was no court in any Member State which could be considered to have jurisdiction.[90] In other words, the subject matter of the dispute fell within the material scope of the Regulation, notwithstanding the parties' agreement that disputes arising from it were to be settled by arbitration.[91] It is not difficult to deduce from this that a court which gives judgment in disregard of an arbitration agreement does no more than make an error of jurisdiction, and that as errors of jurisdiction are not admissible as objections to the recognition of judgments, the judgment qualifies for recognition.[92]

It is necessary to mention, though not to dwell on, the arguments to the contrary. First, the decision of the European Court in *Marc Rich & Co AG v. Soc Italiana Impianti PA*[93] said or appeared to say that where the (principal) subject matter of a dispute is arbitration, the entire subject matter was outside the scope of the Regulation. The argument would be that, where a party appears in the foreign proceedings to argue that the matter should be referred to arbitration, then no matter the outcome, arbitration is the subject matter of the proceedings in the claim.

Next is the decision in *Hoffmann v. Krieg*.[94] The case concerned the enforcement of a German maintenance decree as between parties considered by German law as married to each other, but by Dutch law as divorced from each other. The Court held that if a German court refused to recognise a Dutch divorce and ordered the payment of spousal maintenance, a Dutch court, called upon to enforce the maintenance decree, could not be required to recognise the maintenance order and, by doing so, contradict its own law on status, a matter falling outside the Brussels I Regulation. Rather, the Dutch court was entitled to come to its own view on the issue of status law, and to approach the remainder of the judgment in the light of this decision. In other words, if a matter is excluded from the material scope of the Regulation, the exclusion is not to be undermined. The same pattern of reasoning would apply, *mutatis mutandis*, where the alleged obligation to recognise a

---

88 *National Navigation Co v. Endesa Generacion SA, The 'Wadi Sudr'* [2009] EWCA Civ 1397, [2010] 1 Lloyd's Rep 193. The court was unimpressed by the contention that s. 32 of the 1982 Act could be seen as a source of public policy requiring the non-recognition of the judgment, pointing to s. 32(4). This appears to be a rare example of a judgment pulling itself down by its own bootstraps.

89 C-391/95, [1998] ECR I-7091.

90 At [24].

91 At [27]–[29].

92 Article 35 of Regulation 44/2001.

93 C-190/89, [1991] ECR I-3855.

94 145/86, [1988] ECR 645. The decision was approved and interpreted by the Irish Supreme Court in *T v. L* [2008] IESC 48, [2009] ILPr 46.

judgment would require a court to contradict its own legal conclusion on a particular and reserved question of arbitration.

A further argument would point to the obligation, and the extent of the obligation, of the United Kingdom to give effect to an arbitration agreement which is derived in part from international Conventions. It can be argued that Article 71 of the Regulation means that the United Kingdom should not have its international obligations in the field of arbitration injuriously affected by the recognition of a judgment given in breach of such an agreement and which will, inevitably, impair the effectiveness of the arbitration agreement in the eyes of the English court.[95]

It is clear that the judgment of the adjudicating court in circumstances like this is not simply just a judgment on the merits of the case. It is a judgment that there is no binding and enforceable obligation to arbitrate, and that the merits of the case are therefore adjudicated as being thus and so. Seen in those terms, it looks very much like a decision on arbitration, which must fall within Article 1(2)(d) and so outside Article 1; if that is not so, it is a severable judgment,[96] and the part which falls outside the material scope of the Regulation, because its subject matter is arbitration, ought to be refused recognition without impediment from the rest of the Regulation. And finally, this conclusion is not contradicted by the Opinion of the Advocate General in *Allianz SpA v. West Tankers Inc.*[97] A consequence, as she evidently saw it, of the prohibition on the granting of an injunction to enforce the agreement to arbitrate was that the arbitration would run its course and would be likely to result in the non-recognition of any Italian judgment which conflicted with it. This she saw as a problem which required legislation for its solution.[98] It may also be argued that *Van Uden* does not have the effect discussed above, for a further, specific, reason. If a judicial declaration of the enforceability of an arbitration award is not a judgment within the scope of the Regulation, it must follow that a judicial declaration of the unenforceability of an arbitration award is not a judgment either, and if that be so, the Regulation would be of no relevance to its recognition. It would follow that Article 34(3) of Regulation 44/2001[99] would allow the English court to prefer its judgment on a matter of arbitration to a contradictory one from another Member State.[100]

---

95 On the other hand, an argument which sought to show that the New York Convention should result in the non-recognition of a judgment from another Member State, and that Art. 71 should mean that the Regulation does not intrude or override, would be vulnerable to the kind of argument accepted by the Court in C-452/12 *Nipponkoa Insurance Co (Europe) Ltd v. Inter-Zuid Transport BV* EU:C:2013:858 (on which see above, para. 2.48), and which would mean that the New York Convention, to which non-Member States are party, would not be allowed to interfere with the Brussels I Regulation.

96 Regulation 44/2001, Art. 48. But whether or not it is severable, the duty of the English court to apply its law on arbitration would appear to be a complete answer to the contention that it must recognise another part of the judgment and by doing so contradict its law on arbitration.

97 C-185/07, [2009] ECR I-663. The judgment did not deal with the particular point in any detail.

98 The conclusion is not obviously supported by the decision of the Cour de Cassation in *Republic of Congo v. Groupe Antoine Tabet*, 4 July 2007, [2007] Rev crit DIP 822 (*note* Usunier), though it is not clear whether it is contradicted by it either. The conclusion was that a judgment could not be denied recognition under Art. 27(3) of the original Lugano Convention, which corresponds to Art. 34(3) of Regulation 44/2001, as irreconcilability with an arbitral award was not within the scope of the Article. It is not apparent from the judgment whether the court addressed the issue of whether the exclusion of arbitration from the scope of the Lugano Convention meant that there could be no duty under that Convention to contradict the conclusions of French law on a point of arbitration.

99 Assuming, contrary to the view preferred here, that the basis for denying recognition has to be found within the Regulation, and not outside it.

100 But contrast *Republic of Congo v. Groupe Antoine Tabet*, 4 July 2007, [2007] Rev crit DIP 822 (*note* Usunier).

But whatever the logic of the argument against a broad reading of *Van Uden*, and despite the fact that a supposed obligation to recognise the judgment might require a court to contradict its own law on arbitration, it is certainly arguable that a judgment given in a civil or commercial matter in breach of a binding agreement to arbitrate is a judgment which is required to be recognised under Chapter III of the Brussels I Regulation. If this is so, the law will be comprehensible, but it will be bound to damage the conduct of arbitration in Europe, and will be made clear at the expense of arguments whose legal validity does not appear to be questionable.[101]

So far as Regulation 44/2001 is concerned, therefore, the matter is not conclusively determined, though it would probably be safe to predict that an argument, no matter how sound in law, that a judgment from a Member State in a civil or commercial matter should not be recognised will face an uphill struggle. It is plausible, though, that Regulation 44/2001 will be 'interpreted' as to be consistent with whatever it gathered on the issue from Regulation 1215/2012. The relevant sentence of the Recital to that Regulation, which was set out above,[102] says that 'where a court of a Member State, exercising jurisdiction under this Regulation or under national law, has determined that an arbitration agreement is null and void, inoperative or incapable of being performed, this should not preclude that court's judgment on the substance of the matter from being recognised or, as the case may be, enforced in accordance with this Regulation. This should be without prejudice to the competence of the courts of the Member States to decide on the recognition and enforcement of arbitral awards in accordance with the Convention on the Recognition and Enforcement of Foreign Arbitral Awards, done at New York on 10 June 1958 ('the 1958 New York Convention'), which takes precedence over this Regulation.'

If that is so, the matter will appear to stand thus: a judgment in a civil or commercial matter from a court in another Member State will be regarded as a judgment for the purposes of Chapters I and III, and will be required to be recognised under Chapter III. But the permitted grounds of objection to recognition will still be available: of these, the concerns of public policy and irreconcilability may be applicable. It is therefore sensible to postpone further consideration of the recognition of judgments from courts which do not take the view which an English court would have taken about the duty to arbitrate to a later point.[103] A judgment will be within Chapters I and III, even though the foreign court dealt with and determined *en passant* the validity or invalidity of an arbitration agreement.

7.10 Recognition refused for jurisdictional reasons: Article 35 of Regulation 44/2001

It is generally inadmissible to object that the court which gave judgment did not have, or should not have considered that it had, jurisdiction to adjudicate: Article 35 of Regulation

---

101 Further clarification may be given when the European Court gives judgment in C-536/13 *Re Gazprom OAO*, in which the Advocate General has proposed to the Court that it reconsider the law and accept that where a national court is dealing with a matter on which its law of arbitration directs it to disregard a foreign judgment, it should be left in peace to apply its law on arbitration, unaffected by the Regulation (in this respect, relying on the logic of *Hoffmann v. Krieg*). As judgment is to be expected in the first half of 2015, further comment at this stage would be without practical purpose.

102 Paragraph 2.44, above.

103 See below, para. 7.38.

44/2001 is emphatic on this point.[104] It is also forbidden to object, by pointing to the jurisdictional rules of the adjudicating court, that recognition should be rejected as being contrary to public policy.[105] If a defendant, who does not have a domicile in a Member State, objects to the recognition in England of a French judgment against him founded on the jurisdictional rule in Article 14 of the Civil Code, or some other peculiar ground, he may not say that the recognition of a judgment founded on such jurisdiction is contrary to public policy: Article 35(3) makes the point explicitly.[106] And, of course, he gains nothing by pleading that he does not have a domicile in a Member State: the fact, if it is a fact, is irrelevant[107] to the recognition and enforcement of a judgment given by a court in a Member State in a civil or commercial matter against him. This may be startling, but it is the law.

There are four[108] exceptions where, notwithstanding the general rule, the jurisdiction of the adjudicating court may or must be examined prior to recognition and if found to be at fault, recognition of the judgment withheld.[109]

The first three exceptions are provided by Article 35(1) of Regulation 44/2001, which states that a judgment shall not be recognised if it conflicts with the insurance contract provisions of Chapter II,[110] or with the consumer contract provisions of Chapter II,[111] or with the exclusive jurisdiction provisions of Chapter II[112] which means Article 22 of Chapter II.[113] The jurisdictional policy which dictated those particular rules is so powerful that the recognising court is required[114] to reconfirm that there was no violation of these provisions by the adjudicating court. The mischief of this rule is not completely easy to state, and the rule in consequence is imprecise. When a court was called on to take jurisdiction at the outset of proceedings, there may have been uncertainty whether the conditions for it to exercise jurisdiction were satisfied. It may have taken jurisdiction, but now, in the light of the judgment, it may be clear that the basis for its jurisdiction was not there after all. As it is drafted, Article 35(1) of Regulation 44/2001 would appear to require the

---

104 C-7/98 *Krombach v. Bamberski* [2000] ECR I-1935.

105 This is directed at judgments based on the traditional and exorbitant (or residual) grounds of national jurisdiction: these cannot be stigmatised as being contrary to public policy. But if the claimant by lies and fraud persuaded the court it had jurisdiction, public policy may still be relied upon on the footing that it is not the *jurisdictional rules* themselves, but the manner in which the claimant sought to rely on them, which would be against public policy.

106 C-7/98 *Krombach v. Bamberski* [2000] ECR I-1935 (but the jurisdiction in that case did comply with Art. 5(4) of Regulation 44/2001 in any event, so public policy was never likely to be infringed by recognition of the judgment).

107 But see the effect of a bilateral convention, considered below.

108 Three to be found in Regulation 44/2001 in Art. 35(1), and one in Art. 72.

109 Even here, the findings of fact upon which the adjudicating court acted are binding on the court before which recognition arises: Regulation 44/2001, Art. 35.

110 Section 3 of Chapter II. See above, paras 2.91 *et seq*.

111 Section 4 of Chapter II. See above, paras 2.98 *et seq*.

112 Section 6 of Chapter II. See above, paras 2.114 *et seq*.

113 But no such protection is offered by Regulation 44/2001 in relation to the employment contract provisions which comprise Section 5 of Chapter II: the exercise of jurisdiction in conflict with these jurisdictional rules does not result in non-recognition of the judgment (but for alteration of this rule where Regulation 1215/2012 applies to the recognition, see below, para. 7.37).

For the view that a French judgment on a French trademark cannot be recognised in English proceedings concerning an English trademark, for fear of infringing Art. 22(4) of the Regulation 44/2001, see *Prudential Assurance Co Ltd v. Prudential Insurance Co of America* [2003] EWCA Civ 327, [2003] 1 WLR 2295. The supposed inconsistency with Art. 35 is not obvious, and though it may be a rare case when such recognition would actually have any impact at all, it is not precluded by the Regulation.

114 Denial of recognition is expressed to be mandatory.

non-recognition of the judgment on the footing that the judgment does, as is now clear, conflict with Sections 3, 4 or 6 of Chapter II. On the other hand, it may be argued that there is no conflict, in the sense in which this should be understood, if the court exercised jurisdiction on the ground – found in its national law, for example – that the claimant had the better of the argument that Section 3, 4 or 6 did not deprive the court of jurisdiction, even if things look different after the event. In such circumstances it may be that the judgment does conflict with the relevant jurisdictional rule, even if the original decision to adjudicate did not, on the evidence then before the court, do so. Even so, it feels unsatisfactory that fault should be found with an adjudication which has taken every step with proper care; and it may yet be that Article 35(1) should be held to focus on whether the decision to adjudicate, rather than the eventual judgment, conflicted with Sections 3, 4 or 6 of Chapter II.

Similarly, if the correct interpretation of Section 6 of Chapter II that exclusive jurisdiction is conferred on a court only if the case is one which 'principally concerns' the matter which falls within the wording of the Article, it ought to follow that the non-recognition by reason of Article 35(1) will be restricted to cases in which the foreign court was seised of a matter which was principally concerned, rather than simply concerned among other things, with a matter which fell under the exclusive jurisdiction of another court.

It should also be noted that the court may not withhold recognition simply because the adjudicating court was in error in concluding that it *had* jurisdiction under one of these Sections of Chapter II of the Regulation alone. Recognition of the judgment can be said to conflict with these Sections of Chapter II only if those same provisions, properly interpreted, gave the courts of another Member State jurisdiction, not otherwise. So, for example, if an Italian court has taken jurisdiction in a dispute which did not fall within the provision for exclusive jurisdiction at all, the Italian court having erroneously concluded that the claim did and that it had jurisdiction accordingly, recognition of the judgment would not conflict with Article 22 of Regulation 44/2001, which is, *ex hypothesi*, inapplicable to the case, and may not, therefore, be withheld.[115] Only if that Article had operated to give, say, the German courts exclusive jurisdiction regardless of domicile would Article 35(1) be engaged.

If the defendant has entered an appearance before the adjudicating court, recognition of the judgment does not conflict with the insurance or consumer contract provisions in Sections 3 and 4 of Chapter II. As was explained in Chapter 2, jurisdiction may be taken over a consumer who has submitted by then entry of an appearance without infringing Section 4 of Chapter II of the Regulation.[116] But as Article 22 of Regulation 44/2001 says in explicit terms that submission does not confer jurisdiction in a matter which falls within the exclusive jurisdiction of a court under Section 6 of Chapter II, the opposite result would follow where the adjudicating court, to whose jurisdiction the defendant had purported to submit, had acted in conflict with Article 22 of the Regulation by exercising jurisdiction when exclusive jurisdiction was vested in a court in another Member State.

The final jurisdictional objection to recognition may be founded on a bilateral treaty as mentioned in Article 72 of Regulation 44/2001. Take the United Kingdom–Canada

---

115 In effect, the actual infringement would have been of some other jurisdictional rule of the Regulation.
116 C-111/09 *Česká podnikatelská pojišťovna as v. Bilas* [2010] ECR I-4545.

treaty[117] as an example. If the defendant was domiciled[118] or habitually resident in Canada, and was not domiciled in any Contracting[119] State, and if the Contracting State court had jurisdiction only on one of the jurisdictional grounds which may not be used in relation to defendants with a domicile in a Member State,[120] the English court would refuse to recognise the judgment. A similar treaty is in force as between the United Kingdom and Australia.[121] So if a person domiciled in Canada were sued in France in a case where the French court exercised the jurisdiction provided for in Article 14 of the French Civil Code, the judgment will not be recognised in England. But it would be recognised in other Member States unless those States have concluded their own bilateral treaty with Canada. It therefore makes a very limited encroachment upon the rules of automatic recognition; and as no more bilateral Conventions will be made, as the European Commission has responsibility for the 'external relations' component of the Regulation, it will, in England at least, not now extend beyond protection for certain Australian and Canadian defendants.

7.11 Effect under Regulation 44/2001 of judgment in breach of dispute-resolution agreement

It follows from what has been said (but it bears repetition, just to make sure) that a judgment which conflicts with a jurisdiction agreement is not one whose recognition may be refused on jurisdictional grounds. Jurisdictional conflict with Section 7 of Chapter II, which is entitled 'prorogation of jurisdiction', is not stated in Article 35 as an admissible objection to recognition.[122] It follows that a defendant who considers that proceedings have been commenced against him contrary to a jurisdiction agreement must make his objection to the adjudicating court or not at all. Chapter III of the Regulation does not allow him to save it up for use at the point where the judgment is to be recognised against him.[123]

If the adjudicating court has given judgment contrary to an arbitration agreement or a jurisdiction agreement for a non-Member State, Article 35 is not engaged: the jurisdiction of the court will have been based on grounds not mentioned in and protected by that Article. If the judgment is nevertheless to be refused recognition it will have to be (in the case of arbitration only) because it falls outside the Regulation and is not a judgment for the purposes of Article 32 which, as indicated above, is probably not sustainable; or in either case, because a substantive ground for non-recognition, such as public policy, is available, which may not be an easy argument to make.[124]

---

117 SI 1987/468. It provides that the United Kingdom will not recognise or enforce, to the extent permitted by Art. 59 of the Brussels Convention, a judgment given in another Contracting State against a person domiciled or habitually resident in Canada.

118 According to the definition in SI 2001/3929, Sch. 1, para. 9(7), which supersedes Civil Jurisdiction and Judgments Act 1982, s. 41(7): he must be resident in that State and the circumstances of his residence must indicate that he has a substantial connection with that State.

119 'Contracting', because these Conventions were permitted under the Brussels and Lugano Conventions, but are not to be added to under the regime of the Regulation.

120 These are supposed to be notified to the Commission: see Arts 6(2) and 76(1) of the recast Regulation.

121 SI 1994/1901.

122 For confirmation that Art. 23 of Regulation 44/2001 does not confer exclusive jurisdiction in the material sense, see also C-116/02 *Erich Gasser GmbH v. MISAT Srl* [2003] ECR I-14693.

123 Whether he may sue later for damages for breach of contract is considered above, para. 5.54.

124 As will be seen, in *National Navigation Co v. Endesa Generacion SA, The 'Wadi Sudr'* [2009] EWCA Civ 1397, [2010] 1 Lloyd's Rep 193 the court was unwilling to see merit in this point, not approving what had been

7.12 Recognition refused for non-jurisdictional reasons: Article 34 of Regulation 44/2001

Any of four grounds which are listed in Article 34 will prevent recognition, and therefore enforcement, of the judgment. These are the only[125] grounds, other than the limited jurisdictional challenges, upon which recognition of a judgment which falls within the scope of the Regulation may be refused.

If none of these objections applies, the judgment must be recognised: this can produce striking results, but which illustrate the point vividly. In *Prism Investments BV v. Van Der Meer*,[126] a foreign judgment had been given, and the initial stage of registration for enforcement had taken place. The judgment debtor sought to have this set aside on the ground that he had paid the sum due on the judgment, but the Court held that the argument was inadmissible: it was not provided for in Article 34 of Regulation 44/2001, and that was that. The judgment is as arresting as it is odd. As the Court put it:[127] 'In that regard, it must be noted that no provision of Regulation 44/2001 permits the refusal or revocation of a declaration of enforceability of a judgment that has already been complied with because such a situation does not deprive that judgment of its enforceable nature, which is a characteristic specific to that judicial act... compliance with a judicial decision does not in any way deprive that decision of its enforceable nature, or lead to its being given, at the time of its enforcement in another Member State, legal effects that it would not have in the Member State of origin. Recognition of the effects of such a judgment in the Member State in which enforcement is sought, which is precisely the subject of the enforcement procedure, concerns the specific characteristics of the judgment in question, without reference to the elements of fact and law in respect of compliance with the obligations arising from it.'

It followed that the judgment debtor was left to raise his objection when execution on the judgment took place, which seems a rather rigid response. But it certainly makes the point about the exclusivity of the non-jurisdictional objections permitted by Article 34.[128]

In some places these four grounds are described as substantive, but this may mislead, for they are not really directed at the substance of the judgment. They are grounds of objection which are not jurisdictional in nature.

It is not open to the recognising court to make any assessment of the merits of the claim or of the judgment: the point is made twice, in Articles 36 and 45(2). It follows that a judgment may not be denied recognition on the basis that the adjudicating court can be shown to have gone off the rails in its determination of the merits,[129] for the very reason that it *may* not be shown. However, a court is obviously entitled to conduct so much of a review as is necessary to determine whether any of the admissible objections to recognition is made out, even where this involves an examination of the procedure before the foreign court, and even

---

indicated to the contrary in *Phillip Alexander Securities & Futures Ltd v. Bamberger* [1997] ILPr 73, 104; see further below, para. 7.13.

125 C-302/13 *flyLAL-Lithuanian Airlines AS v. Starptautiskā lidosta Rīga VAS* EU:C:2014:2319, [2015] ILPr 28, [46].

126 C-139/10, [2011] ECR I-9511.

127 At [37], [39].

128 For a further and weirder illustration of the inflexibility of these grounds for non-recognition, see C-157/12 *Salzgitter Mannesmann Handel GmbH v. SC Laminorul SA* EU:C:2013:597, [2014] ILPr 83, below, paras 7.23, 7.26.

129 Regulation 44/2001, Art. 36.

where the merits of that procedure are evaluated.[130] If it is possible to refuse to recognise on grounds of public policy where the judgment is for multiple damages,[131] or is otherwise for what appears to be a grossly excessive sum, for example, it must be open to the court to look into the merits so far as this may be necessary to assess the objection which is made.

In principle, the non-jurisdictional grounds of objection in Article 34 of Regulation 44/2001 are self-contained and are designed not to overlap. Accordingly, an objection that a foreign judgment is not compatible with a local judgment must be dealt with within the objection for irreconcilable judgments stated in Article 34(3) alone, and cannot be repackaged and dealt with under the head of public policy in Article 34(1): the consequence is that if Article 34(3) does not lead to its non-recognition, recognition must follow.[132] Likewise, the objection that a defendant was not given a right to be heard falls within Article 34(2) if the judgment is considered to have been given in default of appearance, and not as a matter of public policy under Article 34(1).[133] The reason for this approach may be to prevent the public policy defence from reaching too far, but in *Hendrickman v. Magenta Druck & Verlag GmbH*,[134] it meant that the scope of Article 34(2) was strained. The defendant complained that he had not been heard in the original court because a lawyer had claimed to be acting on his behalf when he had not been authorised: this was held to fall within the rule which appears in Regulation 44/2001 as Article 34(2), even though the judgment was, according to its terms and according to the procedural law of the court which gave it, not given as a judgment in default of appearance.

7.13 Recognition refused on grounds of public policy: Article 34(1) of Regulation 44/2001

The proposition that recognition[135] will be denied where recognition would be manifestly[136] contrary to public policy in the receiving State is a rule to be found, one supposes, in all systems which recognise foreign judgments. The application of the public policy of English law will prevent the recognition of a judgment in cases where the duty to confer recognition would require the court to accept an adjudication, or make an order, which would contravene legal values which English law regards as being fundamental. A proposal that this ground of objection to recognition be removed from the recast Brussels I Regulation was rejected by the Member States, who were not prepared to give up this last ditch measure by reference to which really objectionable judgments may be refused recognition.[137]

---

130 C-78/95 *Hendrickman v. Magenta Druck & Verlag GmbH* [1996] ECR I-4943 (despite the fact that the first question was not answered, the answer to it is clear from the terms of the judgment); C-394/07 *Gambazzi v. Daimler Chrysler Canada Inc* [2009] ECR I-2563, [46].

131 In England, Protection of Trading Interests Act 1980, s. 5. A suggestion in C-302/13 *flyLAL-Lithuanian Airlines AS v. Starptautiskā lidosta Rīga VAS* EU:C:2014:2319, [2015] ILPr 28, [56], that public policy cannot extend to the protection of purely economic interests, would appear to contradict this; it does not appear to have been properly thought through.

132 145/86 *Hoffmann v. Krieg* [1988] ECR 645.

133 C-78/95 *Hendrickman v. Magenta Druck & Verlag GmbH* [1996] ECR I-4943.

134 C-78/95, [1996] ECR I-4943.

135 And not the jurisdiction upon which it was based: para. 7.10, above.

136 'Manifestly' appeared first in Regulation 44/2001; it had not been in the Brussels Convention.

137 To put the matter starkly, the prospect that an English court might be required to recognise and enforce a Greek judgment against the National Gallery, requiring the transfer of the Elgin Marbles to a Greek museum, or an Irish judgment ordering the closure of the nuclear electricity generating plant on the Cumbrian coast, will not have made the proposal seem very attractive.

Though it is the recognition of the judgment, rather than the content of the underlying judgment itself, which must trigger the objection of public policy, the distinction is often more apparent than real. If the underlying claim (such as for payment of a sum offered as an incentive but working as a bribe) is offensive to English public policy, recognition of a judgment founded on it is very likely to be contrary to public policy also.[138]

The public policy defence to recognition is intended to have a narrow field of operation.[139] It is not sufficient that recognition of the judgment would lead to some disquiet in the recognising court. It is necessary to identify a legal rule which requires recognition to be withheld from the judgment; and unless one is, there can be no refusal of recognition under this head.[140]

The content of English public policy is a matter of substantive English law. It is obviously capable of definition only by English legislation or by an English court.[141] But in order to impose some restriction on the permissible outer limits of the doctrine, and in an attempt to secure the more uniform application of the Regulation, the Court of Justice has asserted its right to set the benchmark by reference to which public policy is to be measured. This obviously does not mean that there is some form of 'European public policy' by reference to which non-recognition may be applied: public policy is national, not supranational.

The formulation used by the Court in the cases to which reference will be made requires there to be 'a manifest breach of a rule of law regarded as essential in the legal order of the state in which enforcement is sought, or of a right recognised as being fundamental within that legal order'.[142] This is likely[143] to mean that the defence will be construed amply in relation to fundamental human rights, and more restrictively in relation to most other grounds of objection.[144] Another indication of just how fundamental must be the objection to recognition, before this defence may in principle be taken, may appear from the formulation of the German Federal Supreme Court in a recent case.[145] A French court had given judgment in a claim based on a guarantee. It was held that German public policy was not engaged by the mere fact that a German court might have regarded the guarantee as unenforceable on grounds of undue influence. Non-recognition on the ground of public policy would not be engaged unless the case were one of 'particularly blatant instances of structural inferiority, where the debtor/guarantor would undoubtedly become the defenceless object of heteronomy in the minds of all fair and right-thinking people and would, therefore, be relegated to the financial subsistence level of distraint exemption limits for many years to come'. The manner of expression of the German court makes plain the extremity which must be reached before this defence to recognition is properly

---

138 Cf in the context of arbitral awards, *Soleimany v. Soleimany* [1999] QB 785.

139 C-420/07 *Apostolides v. Orams* [2009] ECR I-3571, [55].

140 C-420/07 *Apostolides v. Orams* [2009] ECR I-3571, [61]. For further proceedings, in which it was sought to be argued that the European Court had failed to focus on the relevant public policy (which was a hopeless contention) see [2010] EWCA Civ 9, [2011] QB 519, 562.

141 See also C-394/07 *Gambazzi v. Daimler Chrysler Canada Inc* [2009] ECR I-2563, [38].

142 *Krombach*, at [37].

143 Though it is not certain that *Gambazzi* wholly supports this view.

144 It has been said that it does not apply to the protection of economic interests, where these would be severely imperilled by recognition of a foreign judgment: see C-302/13 *flyLAL-Lithuanian Airlines AS v. Starptautiskā lidosta Rīga VAS* EU:C:2014:2319, [2015] ILPr 28, [56]. This makes sense in a limited sense, for most judgments will usually put economic strain on the defendant. But it cannot be made into a universal rule which pays no attention to the figures.

145 *Re Enforcement of a Guarantee* (Case IX ZB 2/98) [2001] ILPr 425.

available. It is not clear that an English court would consider that there was a need to go to quite such an extreme before the distinctive policy of English law required the non-recognition of the judgment.

But if the recognising court concludes that the recognition of a judgment would involve an infringement of its own sovereignty, or a violation of the constitutional guarantees conferred upon the judgment debtor or respondent, then it may properly conclude that recognition would violate its public policy. Such a conclusion was reached by a German court, called upon to recognise an English anti-suit injunction ordered against a German respondent and purporting to restrain him from bringing proceedings in German courts.[146] The elastic scope of constitutional guarantees may lead to this line of argument growing in practical importance; it may also provide the proper home, within the Brussels I Regulation,[147] for objections that recognition of a judgment would violate the international obligations of the United Kingdom as contained in the European Convention on Human Rights and as enacted into law by the Human Rights Act 1998.

7.14 Public policy and the right to a fair trial

It is increasingly clear that the European Court sees the function of the public policy objection to recognition as the mechanism by which a court satisfies itself that the defendant has had a fair trial. As the European Convention on Human Rights is not mentioned in Regulation 44/2001, any complaint that the defendant has been dealt with in a way which falls short of the guarantee put in place by Article 6 ECHR has to be accommodated under this ground of objection to recognition, which is another reason why its removal from the Regulation would have been unwelcome.

The point can be seen in in *Krombach v. Bamberski*[148] and in *Régie Nationale des Usines Renault SA v. Maxicar SpA*.[149] These decisions confirm that, where the adjudicating court may be shown to have acted in violation of the principles of the ECHR, the recognising court is free to conclude that recognition of the judgment would be contrary to its public policy. This is because the ECHR may be held to represent a fundamental and integral part of national and Union laws. If the recognising court considers – as one would have supposed that it would[150] – that compliance with the standards of the ECHR is a fundamental principle which is essential in its legal order, a breach of those standards by the adjudicating court will mean that recognition of the foreign judgment must be manifestly contrary to public policy. Accordingly in *Krombach*, where the defendant had been

---

146 *Re the Enforcement of an English anti-suit injunction* [1997] ILPr 320. For the proposition that recognition of an English worldwide freezing injunction does not infringe French public policy, see *Stolzenberg v. Daimler Chrysler Canada Inc* [2005] JDI/Clunet 112 (*note* Cuniberti), [2005] ILPr 266.

147 An alternative location would be Art. 71 of the Brussels I Regulation.

148 C-7/98, [2000] ECR I-1935. The consequences of this unhappy story may have put the principle of mutual trust in the judicial systems of other Member States under a little strain. Bamberski arranged for thugs from Kosovo and Georgia to kidnap Dr Krombach from his home in Germany, and to leave him, bound, gagged and chained to a fence outside a French police station. This Gallic form of extraordinary rendition (*restitution extraordinaire?*), evidently did not perturb the French legal system, which tried and convicted Krombach, sentencing him to 15 years' imprisonment and dismissing all appeals.

149 C-38/98, [2000] ECR I-2973.

150 But for the contrary view, that a foreign judgment may still be recognised even though the adjudicating court has acted in this way, see *Barnette v. United States of America* [2004] UKHL 37, [2004] 1 WLR 2241, criticised below, para. 7.73.

debarred from presenting his defence by counsel by reason of his having earlier been found to be in contempt of court, it was held that the recognising court was entitled to rely on the public policy objection to recognition,[151] by particular reference to the ECHR or to its Basic Law, to refuse recognition of the judgment.[152] The principle was correctly applied in England in *Maronier v. Larmer*,[153] in which a complete failure to notify a defendant that a long-dormant action against him before the Dutch courts had been revived meant that recognition would be contrary to public policy, by reason of its being contrary to Article 6 ECHR.

By contrast, in *Régie Nationale de Usines Renault SA v. Maxicar SpA*, where the adjudicating court was alleged to have made a substantive error in its application of rules of community laws on the free movement of goods and on competition, the shortcoming could not properly be seen as something which meant that recognition of the judgment infringed a fundamental principle or amounted to a manifest breach of a rule regarded as essential or fundamental within the legal order of the recognising State. There was no sense in which the original proceedings had been unfair. The analysis might have been different if there had been no right of recourse against the alleged error in the courts of the adjudicating State, but because there was, and because of the possibility of a reference to the European Court under the law of the adjudicating State, there was no basis for such an objection to be advanced on the facts; the judgment resulted from a procedure which was fundamentally fair.

A procedure is not unfair, and no objection may be taken, if the adjudicating court applied rules of law, including private international law, which diverge from those which the recognising court would itself have used.[154] But – and rather more controversially – it has been held that a procedure is liable to be found to be unfair if it results in a judgment which does not give reasons or grounds[155] and which, as a result, makes it difficult for the defendant to work out whether he has any prospect of an appeal. In *Trade Agency Ltd v. Seramico Investments Ltd*,[156] the European Court held, in effect, that a Latvian

---

151 The fact that the Court did not regard this defect of procedure as falling within what is now Art. 34(2) of the Regulation gives reason to reconsider the broad effect of C-78/95 *Hendrickman v. Magenta Druck & Verlag GmbH* [1996] ECR I-4943: see above, para. 7.12, and below, para. 7.17.

152 See Lowenfeld, 'Jurisdiction, Enforcement, Public Policy and *Res judicata*' in Einhorn and Siehr (eds), *Intercontinental Cooperation Through Private International Law* (TMC Asser Press, The Hague, 2004). For a case of refusal by a French court to recognise an English judgment striking out a claim by a party who had failed to put up security for costs, on the ground that this violated the right of access to justice, see *Pordea v. Times Newspapers Ltd* (Cass, 16 March 1999) [1999] JDI/Clunet 773 (*note* Huet), [2000] ILPr 266. For a Greek decision refusing to recognise an English judgment on the ground that the size of the costs awarded was in conflict with Greek public policy, see Case No 1829/2006, (2007) 55 NV 674, [2007] ILPr 608.

153 [2002] EWCA Civ 774, [2003] QB 620.

154 C-619/10 *Trade Agency Ltd v. Seramico Investments Ltd* EU:C:2012:531, [50]. The possibility that a court in a Member State might have refused to give effect to an express agreement on choice of law – not so uncommon when some non-Member States are borne in mind – does not need to be considered as a possible exception to this statement of law. It will not happen.

155 C-283/05 *ASML Netherlands BV v. Semiconductor Industry Services GmbH* [2006] ECR I-12041, [28]. But this was a case in which there were grounds, but which had not been communicated to the defendant, and it may not apply to a default case, notwithstanding *Trade Agency v. Seramico*, [53].

156 C-619/10, EU:C:2012:531. Contrast with C-302/13 *flyLAL-Lithuanian Airlines AS v. Starptautiskā lidosta Rīga VAS* EU:C:2014:2319, [2015] ILPr 28, where the argument that there was an absence of reasons for the sums assessed, which was true on its face, was answered by contending that it was possible to discern from the court file how the foreign court had conducted the assessment. That seems a poor answer; more persuasive was the observation that there had actually been an *inter partes* hearing before the court of origin, and the basis for arguing that the trial had been unfair was not there.

court would be entitled to refuse recognition of an English default judgment, entered without further analysis of the claim, if the absence of judicial reasons meant that it was impossible for the defendant to determine whether to appeal and that this was, all things considered, seen to be a manifestly disproportionate response to the defendant's failure to appear. This is challenging at several levels. It appears to assume that the defendant will wish to appeal the merits, rather than seek to set aside the judgment, which would come as a surprise to an English lawyer. It sits oddly alongside the recent decision of the Court that there is no invariable human or procedural right to an appeal against a decision at first instance.[157] It may not pay enough attention to the fact that if a defendant has calculated that it would be best for him to act in such a way that reasons need not be given for the judgment which the claimant will obtain, it is inappropriate to allow issue to be taken with the judgment on this very ground. And it looks very odd alongside a policy, put in place by Regulation 805/2004,[158] of seeking to speed up the enforcement of uncontested judgments. It is fair to say that although the basic principle is not plainly wrong, and although a defendant must be allowed to have and be shown to have had a fair hearing, if he wishes to say nothing it should not lie in his mouth to say he had been entitled to a response to a defence which, *ex hypothesi*, he had not troubled to advance. However, it also appears that the claimant who obtains a default judgment, entered without reasons going beyond the default, may face more difficulty than he should in obtaining recognition of the judgment.[159]

It is plausible that some courts will hold that a judgment for a sum in damages which is calculated to be greater than the loss sustained, particularly for the purpose of making a public example of, or punishing, infringes the right to a fair trial. There are reasons for objecting to this, not least the possibility that rules which allow for enhanced damages may be there because the claimant will not recover substantial costs, or because the law which governs the assessment of damages does not make separate provision for heads or extents of damage which would be separately accounted for in other systems. But if the judgment is of the kind which says 'you have lost X; the defendant must therefore pay 3X', it may be said to risk a finding of real unfairness, and trigger this aspect of public policy, even if the recognising court is not supposed to investigate the merits of the underlying dispute, or see an infringement of public policy in the extent of damage done by a judgment to economic interests.[160]

---

157 Case C-413/12 *Asociación de Consumadores Independientes de Castilla y León v. Anuntis Segundamano España SL* EU:C:2013:800.

158 Below, paras 7.31 *et seq.*

159 French courts have long seen this as a ground to refuse recognition: *Soc Polypetrol v. Soc Gen Routière* [1993] ILPr 107; *Soc Transports Internationaux Dehbashi v. Gerling* [1996] ILPr 104; *Masson v. Ottow, Union Discount Ltd v. Casamata* [2007] JDI/Clunet 543; *Society of Lloyd's v. X* (Cass 22 Oct 2008) [2009] ILPr 161: on this, see generally, Cuniberti (2008) 57 ICLQ 25. See also *Camenzuli v. Desira* (Cass, 17 Nov 1999), [2000] Rev Crit DIP 786, and the decision of the Swiss Federal Tribunal in *X Ltd v. Y SA*, 9 Feb. 2001, ATF/BGE 127 III 186 (a case on the Lugano Convention). In order to guard against this threat to recognition of its judgment, an English court may conduct a hearing, or quasi-trial, before giving default judgment, so that it can give judgment on the merits, rather than allowing judgment to be entered in default: *Berliner Bank v. Karageorgis* [1996] 1 Lloyd's Rep 426; *Bhatia Shipping and Agencies Pvt Ltd v. Alcobex Metals Ltd* [2004] EWHC 2323, [2005] 2 Lloyd's Rep 336; *Habib Bank Ltd v. Central Bank of Sudan* [2006] EWHC 1767 (Comm), [2007] 1 WLR 470. It may even set aside a default judgment which has already been entered and give summary judgment instead: *Messer Griesheim GmbH v. Goyal MG Gases Pvt Ltd* [2006] EWHC 79 (Comm), [2006] 1 CLC 283.

160 C-302/13 *flyLAL-Lithuanian Airlines AS v. Starptautiskā lidosta Rīga VAS* EU:C:2014:2319, [2015] ILPr 28, [56].

7.15 Public policy and judgments obtained by fraud

It is most doubtful whether the argument available at common law, that the judgment was procured by fraud,[161] can be accommodated under the public policy head. Schlosser,[162] writing in relation to the equivalent rule of the Brussels Convention, observed that all the Member States permit judgments given by their courts to be impeached on the ground that they were obtained by fraud, and that the availability of a sufficient local remedy may make it improper to rely upon a broad fraud rule, labelled as public policy, in order to withhold recognition from the judgment.[163] There is little doubt that this view will prevail. A contrary view could be advanced, but even if it were sustained, it would lead to the consequence that a judgment obtained in a Member State could be enforced in many Member States, but not in England, where the principle of fraud as an objection to the enforcement of a foreign judgment has a rather wider scope. That is not the outcome which Chapter III of the Regulation strives to produce.

7.16 Public policy and breach of agreements for the resolution of disputes

If the adjudicating court has given judgment in violation of an agreement by the parties to settle their differences by arbitration, then even if the judgment falls within the scope of the Brussels I Regulation,[164] its recognition may be held to violate public policy, at least in England. The argument does not directly infringe the prohibition[165] upon using the doctrine of public policy to object to the jurisdiction of the adjudicating court; but proceeds from the distinct premise that if the parties have contractually bound themselves to arbitrate, it is unacceptable for one of them to seise a court which will, for whatever reason and in the exercise of its unquestionable jurisdiction to adjudicate, decline to give effect to the arbitration agreement. This analysis recently failed to attract the support of the Court of Appeal,[166] but it is respectfully considered that it is entirely sound, and that the court gave insufficient weight to the public policy of holding parties to their agreement to arbitrate and, where it is not possible to do this directly,[167] refusing to give effect to a judgment which, from this point of view, should not have been sought. The court did not see Civil Jurisdiction and Judgments Act 1982, section 32, as requiring the non-recognition of a judgment obtained, as English law saw it, of a binding agreement to arbitrate, but even if its construction of the Act was correct, the public policy is not necessarily illustrated, but rather defined, by the Act.

It was considered above whether the answer to this question will be affected by Recital (12) to Regulation 1215/2012.[168] There is always danger in allowing an existing statute

---

161 See below, para. 7.69.

162 [1979] OJ C59/71, [192].

163 This view was adopted, and the English rule of common law held to be inapplicable in relation to a French judgment, by Phillips J in *Interdesco SA v. Nullifire Ltd* [1992] 1 Lloyd's Rep 180, and by the Court of Appeal in *SISRO v. Ampersand Software BV* [1994] ILPr 55.

164 See para. 7.09, above.

165 Regulation 44/2001, Art. 35.

166 *National Navigation Co v. Endesa Generacion SA, The 'Wadi Sudr'* [2009] EWCA Civ 1397, [2010] 1 Lloyd's Rep 193.

167 Where, for example, an injunction to restrain legal proceedings may not be ordered: C-189/07 *Allianz SpA v. West Tankers Inc* [2009] ECR I-663.

168 The material part of which is set out below, para. 7.38.

to be reinterpreted in the light of legislation adopted many years later, even where the later legislation 'recasts' rather than 'reforms' the earlier. The view taken here is that even under Regulation 1215/2012, though the foreign judgment has to be seen as falling within Chapter III of the Regulation, an objection to recognition which is also provided for within Chapter III may be made to it. If the foreign judgment qualifies for recognition as a judgment, it is also susceptible to an objection to recognition for which Chapter III makes provision;[169] and nothing in the Recital says otherwise. It is well understood that there are opposing views on this issue, but in the end the question whether the enforcement of and respect for arbitration agreements is a matter of fundamental English legal policy is something for English law, and for it alone, to say.

This analysis may be answered by saying, by analogy with what was said about fraud, that if there was a proper opportunity to make the argument based on the agreement to arbitrate to the foreign court, and to appeal against an adverse initial decision, there is no justification for allowing English public policy to allow it to be re-run in England. This is certainly not a spurious argument. But Civil Jurisdiction and Judgments Act 1982, section 32, goes a considerable way to raise the violation of an arbitration agreement to the status of an essential rule of public policy in the sphere of commercial relations; and if more is needed, the courts may find it if they wish. The House of Lords and Supreme Court have explained the fundamental importance, as English commercial law sees it, of holding parties to their agreements to arbitrate.[170] With that in mind, it is open to the English courts to hold that, all things being considered, it offends English public policy to allow a judgment, obtained in breach of an agreement to arbitrate, to be enforced in England; it is, of course, also open to them to hold the opposite.

7.17 Recognition refused in certain cases of judgment given in default of appearance: Article 34(2) of Regulation 44/2001

In principle, at least, the Brussels I Regulation contains various safeguards to prevent defendants being taken by surprise, and the provision which withholds recognition from certain judgments given in default of appearance[171] is one of them.

According to Article 34(2) of Regulation 44/2001 recognition of a judgment will be refused if all of three[172] conditions are satisfied: the judgment was given in default of appearance;[173] the defendant was not served with the document instituting the proceedings, or with an equivalent document, in sufficient time and in such a way as to allow him to arrange for his defence;[174] and it cannot be said against the defendant that though he had

---

169 If it comes in through the front door, it must live with whatever it finds when it gets inside.

170 *West Tankers Inc v. RAS Riunione Adriatica di Sicurta SpA* [2007] UKHL 4, [2007] 1 Lloyd's Rep 391. The fact that this did not persuade the European Court to accept the propriety of an anti-suit injunction is nothing to the point. See also *Ust-Kamenogorsk Hydropower Plant JSC v. AES Ust-Kamenogorsk Hydropower Plant LLP* [2013] UKSC 35, [2013] 1 WLR 1889.

171 It has no application to a case like C-394/07 *Gambazzi v. Daimler Chrysler Canada Inc* [2009] ECR I-2563, as the default was one of defence: the appearance or acknowledgment of service was not struck out.

172 The sub-division is for the purpose of explanation; it does not appear in the Regulation itself.

173 So if the defendant appears, he throws away his shield: C-172/91 *Sonntag v. Waidmann* [1993] ECR I-1963.

174 If the position is that he was not served with the document because he managed to avoid detection, after which the court allowed judgment to be entered in default, he is entitled to take the point that he was not served: the Regulation does not mean that he was not served *by reason of the fault of the claimant*: see C-292/10 *G v. De*

the opportunity to commence proceedings to challenge the judgment, he failed to do so.[175] Among other things, this provision further establishes that orders obtained in proceedings of which the defendant had, and was intended to have, no notice will not be recognised,[176] though the effect of the third of these three conditions may be to limit the period of time for which recognition is forbidden.[177] The underlying purpose of Article 34(2) is to provide for the rights of the defence in general, and in particular, to ensure that the defendant has a proper opportunity to respond to proceedings instituted against him in time to prevent the entry of a judgment in default. But it is not to allow him to take and rely on technical points when he knew perfectly well about the proceedings or about the judgment but calculated that it was a better tactic to sit on his hands and do nothing.

As to the first of the three conditions, namely whether the judgment was given in default of appearance, it was held in *Hendrickman v. Magenta Druck & Verlag GmbH*[178] that a judgment could be considered as having been given in default of appearance even though, as a matter of national procedural law, there was no default in appearance. The limits of this peculiar decision are obscure, not least because the facts disclosed to the European Court were very incomplete. A lawyer who purported to appear on behalf of the defendant was said to have had no authority to do so.[179] Though in one sense this might have meant that the defendant did not appear and had not been heard, the national court did not give its judgment on the ground that there had been a default of or in appearance. The Court nevertheless held that what was then Article 27(2) of the Brussels Convention applied, and thereby established that the concept of a judgment being 'in default of appearance' has an autonomous meaning.[180] A contrary view proposed by the Advocate General in *Sonntag v. Waidmann*,[181] might have been preferable and easier to operate: that a judgment should not be seen as given in default of appearance unless the national court does indeed give judgment in those terms; all other cases would, on this view, be left to be determined by the developing rules on public policy under the provision of what is now Article 34(1) of Regulation 44/2001.

Visser EU:C:2012:142, [2013] QB 168, [57]. It is the fact that the defendant may protect his right to be heard at this stage which justifies the entering of judgment in default in certain circumstances in which he was not served with the document instituting the proceedings.

175 If he did take the opportunity but failed, the case is *a fortiori*: C-420/07 *Apostolides v. Orams* [2009] ECR I-3571, [78].

176 125/79 *Denilauler v. SNC Couchet Frères* [1980] ECR 1553 meant that such an order was not a judgment at all. But whatever results from an *inter partes* procedure after that seems to count as a judgment, and not to fall on the wrong side of Art. 34(2) of Regulation 44/2001.

177 See further below.

178 C-78/95, [1996] ECR I-4943.

179 But the analysis would be the same (and the judgment would also count as having been in default of appearance) if the national court had appointed a 'representative' to act for the defendant who either could not be found or who had not been effectively served: C-112/13 *A v. B* EU:C:2014:2195, for the defendant had not actually appeared, and to say otherwise would be a pretence.

180 As to this, to 'appear' before a court to apply for dismissal of the proceedings on jurisdictional grounds is not to 'appear' for the purposes of this rule: C-39/02 *Mærsk Olie & Gas A/S v. De Haan & De Boer* [2004] ECR I-9657. 'Appear' does not include the making of formal opposition of a claim for payment under the European Order Procedure, even if the opposition to that demand set out the substantive grounds on which the liability was contested: C-144/12 *Goldbet Sportwetten GmbH v. Sperindeo* EU:C:2013:393, [2013] Bus LR 1115. See also *Tavoulareas v. Tsavliris (No 2)* [2006] EWCA Civ 1772, [2007] 1 WLR 1573 (on any view of the word the defendant did not appear, so judgment in default of appearance).

181 C-172/91, [1993] ECR I-1963. The conclusion is, to some extent, also supported by C-7/98 *Krombach v. Bamberski* [2000] ECR I-1935, where a judgment given without the defendant being entitled to be heard was dealt with under the public policy ground.

7.18 The documents whose service will start the clock running

The second of the three conditions, namely whether the defendant has been (duly) served in time to arrange for his defence, gave rise to problems which are now reducing in significance. There is an inevitable tension between two irreconcilable principles. On the one hand, rules of service may be formal, but some will consider that they must be observed strictly if the defendant is to be allowed to know, without any doubt, that proceedings have been instituted against him before a foreign court.[182] On the other hand, for a defendant to take a point about a technical irregularity in service may be disreputable in circumstances where he had perfect knowledge of the institution of proceedings yet chose to store up a technical defect to deploy at the point of enforcement. The resulting ambivalence is reflected in the jurisprudence.

The starting point is to identify *what*, precisely, needs to be served to start the clock running against the defendant. The answer is 'the document which instituted the proceedings, or an equivalent document'. This language reflects the fact that different systems have their own paperwork for the institution of proceedings: it may be a writ; it may be a peremptory order for payment; it may be a statement of the claim which may or may not have the evidence attached to it. It will be for the court called upon to recognise the judgment to identify which was the document, or which were the documents, which instituted the proceedings before the foreign court. In one case,[183] it was found that the peremptory order to pay,[184] combined with the claimant's application, were the documents which instituted the proceedings before an Italian court. The Court has explained that the expression has an autonomous meaning, and it refers to the document (or documents, where they are intrinsically linked) which enables the defendant to understand the subject matter of, and the ground for, the claimant's application, and of his right to assert a defence in a pending action or of his right to challenge an order to pay made *ex parte* where this was made by the original court.

The essential question for the recognising court is, therefore, to identify the document or documents which communicated that essential information to the defendant; and to address the question of the sufficiency and timeliness of their service by reference accordingly.[185] Where a defendant complains that the documents in question should have been served in translation, and that service on him was not therefore made in a way which started the clock running, the true question is whether he had been served with the documents which allowed him to gather the nature of the claim and the cause of action against him; the fact that some evidence was served without the benefit of translation is not necessarily fatal to the allegation that he was served with the document instituting the proceedings.[186] If, therefore, the defendant alleges that he was not served in accordance with the Service Regulation, for the purposes of Article 26 of Regulation 44/2001,[187] it is to the documents so identified that attention is to be given.

---

182 *Abela v. Baadarani* [2013] UKSC 44, [2013] 1 WLR 2043 may be thought to challenge this.

183 C-474/93 *Firma Hengst Import BV v. Campese* [1995] ECR I-2113.

184 A '*decreto ingiuntivo*'.

185 C-14/07 *Ingenieurbüro Michael Weiss & Partner GbR v. Industrie- und Handelskammer Berlin* [2008] ECR I-3367. For comment, see Franzina (2008) 10 *Yearbook of Private International Law* 565.

186 C-14/07 *Ingenieurbüro Michael Weiss & Partner GbR v. Industrie- und Handelskammer Berlin* [2008] ECR I-3367.

187 As to which, see above, para. 2.257.

7.19 The period of time which the defendant had to prevent default judgment

Assuming service to have been in accordance with the law of the State whose document it was,[188] the next question was whether the manner in which that service was made was sufficient to start the clock running against the defendant. In order to guard the rights of the defence, it is open to the court called upon to recognise the judgment to conclude, even if this is contrary to the view of the court of origin, that the method of service used was insufficient to start the clock running against the defendant as from the moment of that service, and to draw the conclusion that he was therefore not served in time or in such a way as to arrange for his defence. This follows from *Debaecker & Plouvier v. Bouwman*,[189] in which the Court of Justice stated that though there had been a form of substituted service of a Belgian document as permitted and provided for by Belgian law, a Dutch court was still entitled to find that the manner of service was such that time had not started to run against the defendant from that moment.[190] It was necessary to show that the defendant was served in such a way as to reasonably permit him, in sufficient time, to take steps to prevent judgment being entered against him in default of his appearance;[191] and the assessment of this time period is a matter of fact for the recognising court, unconstrained by the existence of time periods under the law of the adjudicating court.[192] Although the reasoning in the cases is technical, the principle is clear: the defendant must have been properly served according to the law of the adjudicating court but it is thereafter for the court called upon to recognise the judgment to decide for itself whether the defendant was served in such a way, and in sufficient time, as to reasonably allow him to take steps to defend himself.

7.20 The effect of irregularity in service

The application of these rules, however, is more complicated where there is some irregularity in the manner of service. In principle and in general, if it needs to be asked, the question whether service has been properly made is a matter for the law of the State whose document was to be served.

In its original form, Article 27(2) of the Brussels Convention required the defendant to have been *duly* served. It was therefore necessary to show that the defendant had been served with the document which instituted the proceedings in accordance with the law of the State in which the proceedings were instituted.[193] The justification for giving attention to the requirement that there be *due* service was that, as the Court said in *Scania Finance France v.*

---

188 For the case of irregularity in service, see below, para. 7.20.

189 49/84, [1985] ECR 1779.

190 A German court took the same view of service of a French document by '*remise au parquet*', or pretended service on a person out of the jurisdiction by leaving the document with an officer of the French court for onward transmission: *Re the Enforcement of a French Interlocutory Order* [2001] ILPr 208. The decision of the Court of Justice in C-522/03 *SA Scania Finance France v. Rockinger Spezialfabrik für Anhängerkupplungen GmbH & Co* [2005] ECR I-8639 did not need to deal with the point. But for the illegality of such pretended service today, see C-325/11 *Alder v Ortowska*, EU:C:2012:824.

191 166/80 *Klomps v. Michel* [1981] ECR 1593. A period of five weeks between service and the issuing of judgment was held to be sufficient time in *TSN Kunststoffrecycling GmbH v. Jürgens* [2000] EWCA Civ 11, [2002] 1 WLR 2459.

192 228/81 *Pendy Plastic Products BV v. Pluspunkt Handelsgesellschaft mbH* [1982] ECR 2723.

193 A French document was to be served in accordance with French law: C-123/91 *Minalmet GmbH v. Brandeis Ltd* [1992] ECR I-5661; C-305/88 *Isabelle Lancray SA v. Peters & Sickert KG* [1990] ECR I-2725 (the cure of irregularity in service in accordance with law of State of origin is permissible).

Rockinger Spezialfabrik für Anhängerkupplungen GmbH & Co,[194] the aim of achieving an effective enforcement of judgment must not be allowed to undermine in any way the right to a fair hearing, which a requirement of *due* service went to secure.

But Article 34(2) of Regulation 44/2001 departed in two respects from its predecessor in the Conventions. First, 'duly' no longer qualifies the service to which Article 34(2) of the Regulation refers. It was not at first clear whether this was intended to have any real significance. A defendant might say that he had not been served if the document had not been delivered in strict compliance with the law of the State in which the proceedings have been commenced, even when it had come to his attention in some other and effective way.[195] It initially appeared, to the English courts at least, that the omission of the word 'duly' would make only minor difference to the structure of the argument.[196]

However, in *ASML Netherlands BV v. Semiconductor Industry Services GmbH*[197] the Court drew a much clearer distinction, and put much greater distance, between the Convention and Regulation texts. It interpreted Article 34(2) of Regulation 44/2001 as reflecting the general requirement that the defendant have a right to be heard, making it clear that this was no longer to be secured by a strict insistence that service of the originating process have been 'duly' made. The overriding principle was that the rights of the defence in general, and the right to a fair hearing in particular, should have been respected, and would not be jeopardised by the recognition of the judgment; the original formality or informality of service had no necessary connection with that. The Court was more concerned to specify the conditions needed to satisfy the new additional condition, to make it clear that as long as the defendant was made aware of the judgment entered against him, the material question was whether he had taken, or should have taken, steps to challenge it before the court in which it had been entered. It was not directly said, but it was very strongly hinted, that the focus of enquiry is now on the opportunity to challenge the judgment after its delivery. What takes place prior to this point appears to have been reduced in significance; and if that is so, the removal of the requirement of *due* service marks, or, more properly is part of, a more substantial change. It reflects the fact that if the adjudicating court has ascertained for itself that service was made, and that what was served was sufficient to allow the defendant to exercise the rights of the defence, then the clock will start to run. If judgment is then entered in default of appearance, but the defendant has had a reasonable opportunity to challenge that judgment, then for him to claim that an irregularity in service of process meant that everything which followed was a nullity is not very meritorious; and it will not now succeed in the way it might have done under the Brussels Convention.[198]

---

194 C-522/03, [2005] ECR I-8639, esp. at [15].

195 If it is a French document, it must in principle be served in accordance with French law: C-123/91 *Minalmet GmbH v. Brandeis Ltd* [1992] ECR I-5661; C-305/88 *Isabelle Lancray SA v. Peters & Sickert KG* [1990] ECR I-2725 (the cure of irregularity in service in accordance with law of state of origin is permissible). If, of course, French law requires service to be made in accordance with the law of the place where service is to be made, the latter will be material, but only because of its incorporation by the law of the State of origin.

196 In *Tavoulareas v. Tsavliris (No 2)* [2006] EWCA Civ 1772, [2007] 1 WLR 1573, it was held that some form of service is required, and that the absence of the word 'duly' had some, but probably small, significance.

197 C-283/05, [2006] ECR I-12041; applied in C-14/07 *Ingenieurbüro Michael Weiss & Partner GbR v. Industrie- und Handelskammer Berlin* [2008] ECR I-3367. In C-420/07 *Apostolides v. Orams* [2009] ECR I-3571, [74], the Court reiterated the deliberate and important differences between Art. 27(2) of the Convention and Art. 34(2) of Regulation 44/2001.

198 When the case returned to the national court, it was held that as the defendant had not been served with the judgment, but had learned about it only when served with the enforcement order, he had not had an

7.21 Unreasonably failing to challenge the judgment after the event

The third of the three conditions established by Article 34(2) of Regulation 44/2001 makes the substantial alteration to the law referred to above, in favour of the claimant: a surprising development, perhaps, in the context of a provision which is said to be there to protect the rights of the defence. But Article 27(2) of the Convention had been held to take no account of the fact that the defendant knew perfectly well of the proceedings which had been commenced, or of the judgment which had been given, or of the fact that he knew that he had the right to apply to have the judgment set aside but elected to do nothing.[199] It meant, in effect, that if the judgment was born flawed, it remained flawed if the defendant chose to ignore it: the best defence was to file the papers in the bin; to do nothing.[200] Such calculating behaviour by defendants did produce some distinctly unattractive results. It also meant, or appeared to mean, that if a defendant managed to avoid service, he had an absolute defence to recognition of a judgment on a claim to which, quite possibly, he had had no defence. That tilted the balance too far in favour of one side to the litigation.[201] The Regulation now places on the defendant the practical onus of challenging the judgment, of taking the initiative,[202] so that if he did not do so when he reasonably[203] knew that he could,[204] the judgment may be cured of its birth defect and become one liable to recognition.

It is expected that if the judgment is to be recognised by reference to this particular point, it will still have to be shown that the defendant was placed under no significant handicap when he commenced proceedings to challenge the judgment, and that his procedural position had not been materially weakened by the fact that default judgment had been entered against him.[205] For if he had the right to challenge the judgment, but faced or would face a struggle uphill which he would not have faced had he been served so as to have been able to defend himself in the first place, he will have been prejudiced by orders made in proceedings in which he could not have played a part; and to accept this would contradict a fundamental principle of procedural fairness aimed to be secured by the Regulation:[206] the rights of the defence will not have been sufficiently respected.

---

opportunity to have the judgment set aside, and had not forfeited the protection of Art. 34(2): *ASML Netherlands BV v. Semiconductor Industry Services GmbH* (3 Ob 9/07F) [2009] ILPr 487.

199 C-305/88 *Isabelle Lancray SA v. Peters & Sickert KG* [1990] ECR I-2725; C-129/91 *Minalmet GmbH v. Brandeis Ltd* [1992] ECR I-5661.

200 The position was otherwise if he took steps to have it set aside and the judgment was then confirmed or remade.

201 *Cf* C-394/07 *Gambazzi v. Daimler Chrysler Canada Inc* [2009] ECR I-2563; C-292/10 *G v. De Visser* EU:C:2012:142, [2013] QB 168.

202 C-420/07 *Apostolides v. Orams* [2009] ECR I-3571, [77]. See also *Avotiņš v. Latvia* (ECHR, 25 Feb 2014).

203 C-283/05 *ASML Netherlands BV v. Semiconductor Industry Services GmbH* [2006] ECR I-12041.

204 166/80 *Klomps v. Michel* [1981] ECR 1593 held that an application to set aside which is dismissed as being out of time will not alter the character of the judgment as one given in default of appearance: it is not certain that the case would be decided the same way today.

205 There is room here for a sustained argument that a defendant against whom a freezing injunction is obtained without notice, and upon whom (and whose bankers) the order is served, has to conduct the fight with one hand tied behind his back when he applies to have the order set aside. The disruption and restriction visited on him, directly (on his assets) and indirectly (on his business) by the order, even though it makes some provision for him to spend money on legal fees, means that his position has been weakened by the original order, to such an extent that having a right to set it aside is vastly inferior to having had a right to be heard before it was made. See generally Zuckerman (1993) 109 LQR 432.

206 *Cf* C-474/93 *Firma Hengst Import BV v. Campese* [1995] ECR I-2113.

The final words of Article 34(2) should not be taken to mean that a defendant served with a freezing injunction obtained without notice to him is at risk of finding that the original order becomes entitled to recognition if he fails to move smartly in applying to have it set aside: at least, they should not be so understood. Chapter III is designed to deal with orders made in proceedings which were designed to be adversary, which is why an order obtained in proceedings from which the defendant was, and was designed to be, shut out is not a judgment.[207] That being so, neither Chapter III in general nor Article 34(2) in particular will have any impact upon it. Of course, if the defendant does apply to have the order set aside, something which was not a judgment will, after the application has been determined, be replaced by a judgment to which Chapter III does apply and Article 34(2) does not.[208]

In the end, the question is whether the defendant was given a reasonable opportunity to challenge the judgment after he learned about it. If he had the opportunity, the judgment will lose any default character it may have had, for the rights of the defence will have been sufficiently protected. It follows that the relevance of the earlier conditions is substantially confined to cases in which the defendant has not had that opportunity. Where the defendant has had the opportunity to challenge the judgment, the more relaxed, less technical, approach to original service[209] will be applied; and it will follow that the strictness in the cases decided under Article 27(2) of the Brussels Convention will not apply to Article 34(2) of Regulation 44/2001. The broad question will be whether the procedure of the court in which judgment was given respected the right of the defendant to have a fair hearing.[210] Technical arguments designed to divert the attention of the court from this simple question will be unlikely to succeed.

7.22 Recognition refused because judgment irreconcilable with court's own judgment: Article 34(3) of Regulation 44/2001

If the foreign judgment is irreconcilable with a local judgment given[211] in a dispute between the same[212] parties[213] in the State of recognition, something will already have gone wrong: the provisions in Section 8 of Chapter II which deal with *lis alibi pendens*, and seek to prevent parallel litigation, should have prevented this from coming to pass in the first place. But where it happens, the court called upon to recognise a foreign judgment is bound to follow its own decision in preference to one from another Member State. It could not be otherwise.

---

207 125/79 *Denilauler v. SNC Couchet Frères* [1980] ECR 1553.

208 C-420/07 *Apostolides v. Orams* [2009] ECR I-3571. The contrary English decision at first instance, [2006] EWHC 2226 (QB), [2007] 1 WLR 241 (on which, see (2006) 77 BYBIL 561), was wholly insupportable. Also insupportable, or at least open to doubt and question, is the decision of the German Federal Supreme Court in *Re the Enforcement of a Portuguese Judgment* (Case IX ZB 2/03) [2005] ILPr 362, in broadly the same terms as that of the first instance judge in *Orams*).

209 C-283/05 *ASML Netherlands BV v. Semiconductor Industry Services GmbH* [2006] ECR I-12041; *Ingenieurbüro Michael Weiss & Partner GbR v. Industrie- und Handelskammer Berlin* [2008] ECR I-3367.

210 See also C-420/07 *Apostolides v. Orams* [2009] ECR I-3571.

211 It has been held to be insufficient for there to be pending proceedings but which have not yet resulted in judgment: *Landhurst Leasing plc v. Marcq* [1998] ILPr 822.

212 For elucidation of the requirement that the judgment be in a dispute between the same parties, see the discussion of Art. 29 of Regulation 1215/2012 (where the issues are the same), at para. 2.267, above.

213 To the extent that the dispute is not between the same parties, this provision will not apply: *cf* C-406/92 *The Tatry* [1994] ECR I-5439.

The irreconcilability must arise from comparison with a local *judgment*. This requirement will be satisfied, and non-recognition of a foreign judgment will follow, if the local order has taken the form of a judgment by consent, but it will not be satisfied, and non-recognition of the foreign judgment will not result, if the local measure with which it is irreconcilable was a contractual settlement of claims, even one which has been judicially approved.[214]

If one proceeds from the proposition that 'judgment' is understood to be defined so as to exclude judicial orders giving leave to enforce an arbitral award, on the footing that these fall outside Chapter I and therefore Chapter III of the Regulation, Article 34(3) can have no application to the case in which a foreign judgment is irreconcilable with an arbitral award, even if the English court has given the applicant leave to enforce it, for the irreconcilability is not with something which is a judgment for the purposes of Chapter III of the Regulation.[215] If the logic of this were pursued to its end, the foreign judgment may be enforced, and the fact that it contradicts the local law of arbitration, or is contradicted by something which falls outside the material scope of the Regulation, will be *nihil ad rem* so far as the Regulation is concerned.

This outcome cannot really be correct, though: it is a good example of logic leading one to and over the edge of the cliff, but where a rescue will come from is harder to say. No assistance is to be had from Civil Jurisdiction and Judgments Act 1982, for section 32(4) provides that the duty of a court to withhold recognition from a foreign judgment which was obtained in breach of an arbitration agreement does not extend to cases in which the Brussels I Regulation requires the recognition of the judgment. It is not clear that recourse to the principle of public policy may be had instead, for both *Hoffmann v. Krieg*[216] and *Hendrickman v. Magenta Druck & Verlag GmbH*[217] held that public policy may not be used to deal with objections which fall within the natural domain of other defences to recognition; and it is arguable that the objections based on irreconcilability are exhaustively stated in Article 34(3) of Regulation 44/2001.[218] It may be argued that the whole issue before the court is a matter of arbitration, and is therefore wholly outside the domain of the Brussels I Regulation, but the trouble with that is that it would allow the non-recognition of a foreign judgment on the ground that the foreign court had made an error in believing that it had jurisdiction.[219]

If these points are individually right, the law is in a bit of a mess. It is submitted that the least bad solution is to hold that it is contrary to English public policy to recognise a foreign judgment which is irreconcilable with an arbitral award which the court has given leave to enforce, despite the case law and legislative difficulties which stand in the path of the argument. Alternatively, it could be held that the word 'judgment' in Article 34(3) of Regulation 44/2001 is used in two distinct senses, and that the 'judgment given in a dispute between the same parties in the Member State in which recognition is sought' includes

---

214 C-414/92 *Solo Kleinmotoren GmbH v. Boch* [1994] ECR I-2237, dealing with what is now Chapter IV of the Regulation, but which seems odd in the light of the public interest in supporting the consensual settlement of claims.

215 This appears to have been the conclusion of the French Supreme Court in *Republic of Congo v. Groupe Antoine Tabet* (4 July 2007) [2007] Rev crit DIP 822 (*note* Usunier).

216 145/86, [1988] ECR 645.

217 C-78/95, [1996] ECR I-4943.

218 To say nothing of C-139/10 *Prism Investments BV v. Van Der Meer* [2011] ECR I-9511, on which see above, para. 7.12.

219 See para. 7.09, above.

local judgments which give effect to the award of an arbitral tribunal. This would not be inconsistent with the view that *foreign* judicial orders which give leave to enforce awards are not required to be recognised under the Regulation, while accepting that once an English court has given leave to enforce an arbitral award it would be gravely damaging to legal certainty for it to have to recognise and enforce a foreign judgment which undermined or contradicted that arbitral award.[220]

As to the meaning of 'irreconcilable', judgments are irreconcilable in the sense in which this term is used in Article 34(3) of Regulation 44/2001 if they lead to incompatible consequences though, in the interests of the free circulation of judgments, it is appropriate that this requirement be given a restrictive definition. A judgment that damages be paid for breach of contract is irreconcilable with a decision that the contract has been lawfully rescinded for misrepresentation.[221] A judgment that a man pay maintenance to a person to whom he is married is irreconcilable with a decree of divorce which dissolved that marriage.[222] It applies also to orders made on applications for provisional or protective measures: an interim order that a defendant stop using a particular trade name may be irreconcilable with a judicial decision dismissing an application for the same relief.[223] The rule is easy enough to state as a principle, even if difficulties can be foreseen in its application.[224]

As the law is currently understood, it is *not* necessary that the judgment of the court called upon to recognise the decision precede that of the other court. If it is given afterwards, it is clear that, once the judgment of the local court has been given, the foreign judgment ceases to be entitled to recognition, but it is unclear whether the effect of this is to rescind recognition *ab initio*,[225] or merely to prevent recognition for the future. The interests of legal certainty and expediency favour the latter view, but the position is not free from doubt.

7.23 Recognition refused because judgment irreconcilable with earlier foreign judgment which is recognised: Article 34(4) of Regulation 44/2001

Article 34(4) of Regulation 44/2001 provides that recognition will be denied to a judgment from a Member State if that judgment was irreconcilable with an earlier judgment from a non-Member State which had been given in proceedings between the same parties, involving the same cause of action as the later Member State judgment, and which met the conditions required for its recognition in the state addressed.

---

220 This analysis, or prediction, appears to have been regarded as plausible in *West Tankers Inc v. Allianz SpA* [2011] EWHC 829 (Comm), [2011] 2 Lloyd's Rep 117; see also *African Fertilisers & Chemicals NIG Ltd v. BD Shipsnavo GmbH & Co Reederei KG* [2011] EWHC 2452 (Comm), [2011] 2 Lloyd's Rep 531; *London Steamship Owners Mutual Insurance Association v. Spain* [2013] EWHC 3188 (Comm), [2014] 1 Lloyd's Rep 309.

221 144/86 *Gubisch Maschinenfabrik KG v. Palumbo* [1987] ECR 4861.

222 145/86 *Hoffmann v. Krieg* [1988] ECR 645. This would have been sufficient to deny recognition if the Brussels Convention had applied. In fact, as matters of status are outside the Convention and the Regulation, Art. 27(3) of the Brussels Convention should have been irrelevant to a matter falling outside the scope of the Convention and should not have been resorted to.

223 C-80/00 *Italian Leather SpA v. WECO Polstermöbel GmbH & Co* [2002] ECR I-4995 (though the irreconcilability was rather particular, as the German court did not say that there must never be interim relief: the judgments appear to have been contradictory in the sense in which this expression was used in C-406/92 *The Tatry* [1994] ECR I-5439, rather than strictly conflicting).

224 Its application is, it is thought, a question of fact for the court before which the issue has arisen for decision.

225 With, for example, the associated right to recover money paid in performance of that judgment.

The essence of that provision was found in the Brussels Convention. But the Convention did not offer a solution where a court was confronted by conflicting judgments from two different Contracting States. A solution was needed, and Article 34(4) of the Regulation 44/2001 now covers almost all cases of foreign judgments, whether from Member States or non-Member States, which qualify for recognition but are irreconcilable: the earlier other Member State judgment, or recognised non-Member State judgment, will preclude recognition of the later Member State judgment. The definition of irreconcilability will be the same as under Article 34(3), namely that the judgments lead to or involve legal consequences which are mutually exclusive.

A further illustration of the narrowness of the non-jurisdictional objections to recognition, and of this objection in particular, is found in *Salzgitter Mannesmann Handel GmbH v. SC Laminorul SA*.[226] A Romanian claimant sued a German defendant in Romania, but its claim failed and was dismissed. It then brought what appears to have been the very same claim, before the very same court, all over again; and this time it succeeded. It does not appear that the original judgment was judicially annulled, or anything like that; if there is an explanation for such a state of affairs, it does not emerge from the judgment.[227] The German defendant was not notified of the second set of proceedings, but its attempts to have the judgment set aside in Romania,[228] when it did discover what had happened after it had assumed that the issues were *res judicata* by reason of the first judgment, were rejected on grounds which, to put the matter neutrally, do not appear to have been substantial.[229] When the claimant sought to enforce the second Romanian judgment in Germany, it was held that Article 34(4) had no application, even though the first judgment was bound to be recognised[230] and was irreconcilable with it, because Article 34(4) did not apply to irreconcilable judgments from the same foreign court. No doubt no one considered that this was a problem which had required a legislative solution. They were wrong.[231]

7.24 Recognition and the consequences of recognition

According to Jenard, 'recognition must have the result of conferring on judgments the authority and effectiveness accorded to them in the State in which they were given'.[232] Subject to that point, the principal purpose for which recognition is required will usually be to serve as the springboard for enforcement of the judgment.

---

226 C-157/12, EU:C:2013:597, [2014] ILPr 83.

227 Though an intelligent guess may be possible.

228 In the light of the final words of Art. 34(2) of Regulation 44/2001.

229 This makes the observation of the Court, that the defendant was required to raise its objections before the Romanian courts, almost offensive. It had tried and tried, and had been blocked at every turn. Mutual trust in the judicial institutions of other Member States has never looked as misguided.

230 Article 33(1) of Regulation 44/2001. Presumably it would have been different if the defendant had brought proceedings in Germany for a declaration that the first judgment was liable to be recognised.

231 The first judgment, dismissing the claim, remained one required to be recognised. What the German court was actually supposed to do, if Art. 34(4) did not provide the answer, is anybody's guess.

232 [1979] OJ C59/1, 43. This statement was approved by the Court in 145/86 *Hoffmann v. Krieg* [1988] ECR 645, [10], [11], though it was qualified, if to an uncertain extent, in C-420/07 *Apostolides v. Orams* [2009] ECR I-3571, [66], where it was suggested that a foreign judgment, when recognised, should not, when enforced, have an effect that the judgment would not have had locally.

The rules for enforcing a judgment which is shown to qualify for recognition are examined below; and it is on this point that Regulation 1215/2012 makes a significant departure from Regulation 44/2001.

But Article 33 of Regulation 44/2001 provides that if all a party requires is that the judgment be recognised, no special procedure is required to achieve it: the court must recognise the judgment *ex officio*, though if the judgment is subject to appeal in the Member State in which it was given, the determination whether it qualifies for recognition may itself be stayed.[233] The circumstances in which a party will seek recognition, as distinct from seeking the enforcement, of the judgment, are essentially defensive in nature. The most common case will be where a successful defendant merely wishes to prevent his opponent from raising the same dispute a second time. In such a case, the court will be asked to recognise the first judgment, and the dismissal of the second claim may therefore follow from the national law principles of merger, *res judicata*, cause of action estoppel, or the like.

Case law has been mostly concerned with the recognition of judgments *in personam*; its operation when dealing with the recognition of judgments *in rem* may be less straightforward. Take the example of a foreign court adjudicating, ostensibly *in rem*, that moveable property belongs to a particular person, and therefore not to anyone else. The approach of the Privy Council in *Calyon v. Michailidis*[234] was to deny that a Greek judgment was to be recognised as a judgment *in rem* if the property in question had not been within the territorial jurisdiction of the Greek court. It followed that the Greek judgment did not by itself make it conclusive, as against an alleged dishonest assister who had not been party to the proceedings in Greece, that the property belonged to the claimant. Rational as this appears to be, it must be open to question, for it appears to apply common law principles of judgment recognition and non-recognition, or jurisdictional competence, to a judgment from a Member State in a civil or commercial matter.[235] A preferable route to non-recognition may have been to accept that the judgment was in principle entitled to recognition, and was therefore to be given, in principle at least, the effect it had under the law of Greece,[236] but then to allow Article 34(2) to be used to prevent its being used to prejudice a person who had not been party to the proceedings before the Greek court. Even so, the manner in which the Regulation may provide for the recognition of judgments *in rem*, and therefore as liable to be effective as against non-parties, is unsettling, especially if Article 34(2) were to be taken to impose an effective burden on the individual adversely affected by the judgment to take positive steps to have it set aside once he learns of its existence.[237]

---

233 Regulation 44/2001, Art. 37.

234 [2009] UKPC 34 (Gib). It is debatable whether the judgment fell outside the material scope of the Regulation, as it was concerned with property rights arising from succession to the estate of a deceased person; but this point was not mentioned in the judgment, and it is not clear whether this was the reason why the court made quick reference to the common law rules on the recognition of judgments *in rem*.

235 In the light of C-420/07 *Apostolides v. Orams* [2009] ECR I-3571, [66], where it was suggested that a foreign judgment, when recognised, should not have an effect, when enforced, that the foreign judgment would not have had in the foreign system, it may have been correct to enquire whether the dishonest assister would have been regarded, in Greek law, as bound by the Greek judgment. There was no cause to ask what effect a non-existent English judgment would have had.

236 145/86 *Hoffmann v. Krieg* [1988] ECR 645.

237 However, it is hard to see how an individual can apply to have a judgment *in rem* set aside if he was not named as a party in the foreign proceedings, for only parties to the judgment appear to have that right: C-167/08 *Draka NK Cables Ltd v. Omnipol Ltd* [2009] ECR I-3477. It may therefore be that the final part of Art. 34(2) of Regulation 44/2001 is inapplicable, and the result is that the non-party is not bound by a judgment, which cannot there be recognised as against him, by reason of Art. 34(2).

7.25 Recognition under Regulation 44/2001 as the basis for issue estoppel

A court may be asked to give effect, by way of recognition, to something other than the formal order made by the foreign court. Suppose that, in dismissing a claim, the first court made a finding that a particular document had not been sent, or had been received, or something like that. If a separate second action were to be brought, would the defendant be entitled to ask the second court to give effect to and to consider itself as bound by this particular element of the first court's reasoning or adjudication? Or suppose the first court found that a contract was governed by a particular law: in the second action, would the court be entitled to reach its own conclusion as to the governing law, or would it be obliged to follow the conclusion of the first court?

In the absence of clear authority, it is submitted that one needs to distinguish between principles of European and of national law. As far as European law is concerned, Article 33 of Regulation 44/2001 obliges a court to recognise judgments and orders.[238] It does not, in terms at least, oblige a court to give any, or any particular, effect to statements or reasons mentioned *en passant*. No doubt this is deliberate: the purpose of the Regulation is to assist the free circulation and quick enforcement of judicial orders throughout the legal territory of the Member States. It is no part of that purpose to give effect to statements recorded in judgments, not least because the status of these may differ very sharply from one court to another and from one Member State to another. Of course, if a party to proceedings is able to persuade a court to make declarations on particular points which he wishes to have conclusively determined in his favour, the declaratory judgment would, as a matter of European law, be entitled to be recognised.

But if the foreign court has not made a declaration or other judgment on a particular point, but a party still wishes to place reliance on some step or reason contained in its judgment, nothing prevents an English court applying its own principles of issue estoppel to conclusions reached and expressed by a court in the course of a judgment which otherwise qualifies for recognition.[239] Issue estoppel is a principle of English law of evidence or procedure; and as such it is capable of operating independently of the Regulation, so long as it does not jeopardise its practical effect.[240] It therefore follows that an English court should be free to apply its doctrine of issue estoppel to statements and rulings contained in judgments which otherwise qualify for recognition.

If this analysis is correct, the applicable principles will be those of English law rather than European law.[241] Accordingly, although the Regulation will determine that the judgment is one which is entitled to recognition, and that the adjudicating court was jurisdictionally competent, it must still be shown[242] that the point relied on can be accurately characterised as a finding which the court needed to make, and was final in the court which pronounced

---

238 The separate treatment of decisions on the application of the Brussels I Regulation, in C-456/11 *Gothaer Allgemeine Versicherung AG v. Samskip GmbH* EU:C:2012:719, [2013] QB 458, seems unlikely to extend to this kind of issue.

239 *Berkeley Administration Inc v. McClelland* [1995] ILPr 201.

240 C-365/88 *Kongress Agentur Hagen GmbH v. Zeehaghe BV* [1990] ECR I-1845. Though it is not directly on point, Art. 35(2) of Regulation 44/2001 is broadly consistent with the view that the recognising court should consider itself bound by findings of fact made by the adjudicating court.

241 Though see *Prudential Assurance Co Ltd v. Prudential Insurance Co of America* [2003] EWCA Civ 327, [2003] 1 WLR 2295.

242 As these are, in essence, the basic requirements for an estoppel. See further below, para. 7.83. And see generally Barnett, *Res judicata, Estoppel, and Foreign Judgments* (OUP, Oxford, 2001).

it, and was given in proceedings between the parties or their privies,[243] and was founded on the merits of the point at issue, for these are the elements of common law estoppel by *res judicata*. It would be insufficient for the purposes of issue estoppel if all the court had done was to express a view, but which it did not invest with the status of a judicial conclusion.[244] It would be insufficient for the purposes of issue estoppel – though it would not prevent the recognition of the judgment under the Regulation – if the particular issue could be re-argued in the same court at a later date, with the possible consequence that the later court would not itself be bound by what the earlier court had said.[245] And it would be insufficient for the purposes of issue estoppel – though it would not prevent recognition of the judgment under the Regulation – if the first court had disposed of the issue on grounds which did not involve a consideration of the merits of the point, but which could be labelled as 'procedural' only. Moreover, the fact that the doctrine is one of English law means that the question of who is to be regarded as estopped by the decision is to be answered by the English doctrine concerning parties and their privies, rather than by a principle of European law.[246]

A novel context in which these principles may be called upon for application may be to deal with the effect of a Dutch judgment, ordering that a collective settlement of mass claims be binding on, and enforceable against, all those individuals considered by Dutch law to be bound by it.[247] A Dutch court may make such an order,[248] and may declare that its effect is to prevent any individual within the class of settlement from bringing any action against the defendant company to vindicate private or individual rights: in effect, the Dutch order may preclude a notional class member, or non-participating class member, from bringing proceedings in respect of his or her own claim. For such a judgment to be recognised against the individual to be bound by it,[249] it will need to be shown that, as against the individual class member, the judgment is entitled to recognition. Article 34(1) and 34(2) of Regulation 44/2001 may be particularly material to a contention that a person, who was notified of his entitlement to membership of a class, and of his liability to suffer estoppel by *res judicata* unless he take steps to avoid this outcome, is bound and adversely affected by a judgment in proceedings to which he was not party. It may be hard to understand why someone invited to be a claimant, and who ignores the invitation, should suffer any adverse consequences as a result. But much the same may be said of defendants who are served and who ignore

---

243 In C-351/96 *Drouot Assurances SA v. CMI* [1998] ECR I-3075, a case on the rules of *lis alibi pendens* in Section 9 of Chapter II of the Regulation, the Court said that the parties were to be regarded as the same where they actually were or where, though different, their interests were 'identical to and indissociable from' those of the other. For the proposition that this may yet influence the English doctrine of *res judicata*, see Handley (2000) 116 LQR 191. For a fuller account of the English principles of *res judicata* and estoppel, see below, para. 7.82.

244 And at this point, the English court should be wary of attributing to a judicial statement a quality of finality of determination which it was not intended to have.

245 This would mean that the particular point was not final in the court which pronounced it. It is irrelevant that the finding was made in interlocutory proceedings: see *The Sennar (No 2)* [1985] 1 WLR 490, and *Desert Sun Loan Corp v. Hill* [1996] 2 All ER 847, for the conclusion may still be final. But if the same question can be reinvestigated in the same court at the trial of the main action, it does not have the necessary quality of finality.

246 For the English doctrine, see *House of Spring Gardens Ltd v. Waite* [1991] 1 QB 241. For a loosely analogous issue within the scope of the Brussels Convention, see Schlosser [1979] OJ C59/71, [191] (judgment against debtor binding on surety).

247 The first such example was a judgment by the Amsterdam Court of Appeal on 29 May 2009, in relation to mass claims made against the Shell group of companies.

248 Act on the Collective Settlement of Mass Claims (*Wet collectieve afwikkeling massaschade*) (in force 27 July 2005).

249 That is, to be given the legal effect it will have under Dutch law as the law of the court of origin: 145/86 *Hoffmann v. Krieg* [1988] ECR 645.

the invitation to defend. As long as it is remembered that the rules on recognition have to be applied in relation to the acts and position of the party against whom that recognition is sought, no new issue of principle, as distinct from application of principle, will arise.[250]

Above all, it is important to bear in mind the warning in *Carl Zeiss Stiftung v. Rayner & Keeler Ltd (No 2)*,[251] that, although issue estoppel may be applied to a foreign judgment, care should be taken not to ascribe to a foreign judgment or finding an effect which it was not designed to have.[252] This may be particularly important in relation to statements recited or recorded in judgments, which may not have the weighty significance in their own system which it is customary to attribute to the findings of an English judge in English proceedings. In particular, it may be an error to argue that, just because there is an obligation to recognise a particular judgment, the duties of judicial comity in general, or the Regulation in particular, mean that the judgment must be treated as if it were a judgment given in English proceedings for the purpose of founding an estoppel. Even registration of the judgment in England limits the attribution of statutory equivalence to an English judgment to the purpose of enforcement. That does not have the effect of requiring an English court to regard it for all other purposes as though it were the judgment of an English court. The doctrine of estoppel may well apply once it has been shown that the judgment in question is entitled to recognition under the Regulation, but it should apply as an English doctrine, subject to its own limitations, and, above all, to the *Carl Zeiss* requirement of caution.

7.26 Enforcing a judgment to which Regulation 44/2001 applies: Articles 38 to 52

There are two distinct stages[253] involved in the enforcing of a judgment which is entitled to recognition and which is enforceable in the State of its origin.[254] The first, which involves only the applicant,[255] who applies *ex parte*, is to obtain an order for the registration, or for the enforcement,[256] of the judgment. Once the application has been made and the order for registration obtained, the applicant is entitled[257] to take provisional and protective measures against the party against whom enforcement is sought, to preserve assets until execution of

---

250 For the corresponding principles of the common law, according to which there is practically no chance of recognition and preclusion, see para. 7.81, below.

251 [1967] 1 AC 853.

252 A conclusion which has a faint European echo in 145/86 *Hoffmann v. Krieg* [1988] ECR 645.

253 The substantive rules of English law are contained in paras 2–6 of Sch. 1 to the 2001 Order, and the procedural rules for enforcement of judgments in CPR Part 74, rr 1–11.

254 Regulation 44/2001, Art. 38. If it is not enforceable in the state of origin, or if its enforceability has been suspended by those courts, it may not be declared as enforceable in England. Presumably the appropriate response is to stay enforcement proceedings, rather than to dismiss them outright. In C-420/07 *Apostolides v. Orams* [2009] ECR I-3571 the judgment of the Cypriot court was not completely enforceable, as the order that the defendants demolish their house in the occupied northern part of Cyprus was, in all probability, not specifically enforceable in the occupied northern part of Cyprus. The judgments were not completely unenforceable (see at [67]), and that was sufficient for the judgment to qualify as enforceable for the purposes of Art. 38 of Regulation 44/2001.

255 The other party is not entitled to notice of the application, still less to be heard at this stage. It is deliberate that the applicant should have the benefit of the element of surprise: Schlosser [1979] OJ C59/71, [219].

256 Regulation 44/2001, Art. 38. Which it is depends only upon the civil procedure of the State in question.

257 Regulation 44/2001, Art. 47(2). But the court is not bound to grant such relief; and in *Banco Nacional de Comercio Exterior SNC v. Empresa de Telecomunicaciones de Cuba SA* [2007] EWCA Civ 662, [2007] 2 Lloyd's Rep 484, it was held that it was inexpedient to grant a worldwide freezing injunction in aid of the enforcement of an Italian judgment simply because the judgment had been registered for enforcement in England (no assets in England; defendant not resident in England).

the judgment. The second, *inter partes*, stage comes when the party against whom enforcement is sought has been served with notice of the registration, and has from that date a short period within which to lodge an appeal against (which means, in English terminology, to seek to have set aside) the order for registration made *ex parte*, on any of the grounds which were set out above. He may apply to have the order set aside on the basis that the judgment in respect of which it was made fell outside the scope of Chapters I and III of the Regulation; he may apply to have it set aside on the basis that it did fall within Chapter III but one or more of the jurisdictional or non-jurisdictional grounds for having it set aside applies. It is at the *inter partes* stage that the examination of objections to recognition will take place.

The sharpness of the distinction between the first and second stages of the procedure has become clearer as the role of the court at the *ex parte* stage has been minimised. The present position is illustrated by a recent judgment of the Court,[258] which put it this way: 'It is apparent from recital 17 in the preamble to Regulation 44/2001 that the procedure for making enforceable in the Member State addressed a judgment given in another may involve only a purely formal check of the documents required for enforceability in the Member State in which enforcement is sought. Following the lodging of the application referred to in Article 38(1) of Regulation 44/2001, and as is clear from Article 41 thereof, the authorities of the Member State in which enforcement is sought must, at the beginning of the procedure, not do any more than ensure completion of those formalities with a view to issuing a declaration of enforceability for that judgment.[259] In accordance with Article 43 of Regulation 44/2001, the declaration of enforceability of a judgment delivered in a Member State other than the Member State in which enforcement is sought may, in a second stage of the procedure, be the subject of dispute. The grounds for dispute that may be relied upon are expressly set out in Articles 34 and 35 of Regulation 44/2001, to which Article 45 thereof refers... .'

It is also apparent that if the first stage of the procedure really is such a formality, and if (as is said to be the case) the number of cases in which the person against whom the judgment is to be enforced appeals against the order is very low, the case for simplifying the overall procedure is clear. Indeed, if there is – as there is – agreement on the conditions needed for the judgment to be enforceable, it is not obvious why these must be checked and ticked off by the authority in every separate Member State in which enforcement is sought. It is far more efficient that they be checked and certified once, and that strongly suggests that it should be done by the court which handed the judgment down in the first place. This was a key aim of the programme to recast the Regulation and which culminated in Regulation 1215/2012; the effect of this having been done in Regulation 1215/2012 will be examined below.

7.27 *Ex parte* stage of the procedure under Regulation 44/2001: application for registration of the judgment for enforcement: Articles 38 to 42

Any interested party[260] who seeks the recognition of a judgment from the courts of a Member State will need to produce a copy[261] of the judgment which satisfies the conditions

---

258 C-157/12 *Salzgitter Mannesmann Handel GmbH v. SC Laminorul SA* EU:C:2013:597, [2014] ILPr 83.

259 See C-619/10 *Trade Agency Ltd v. Seramico Investments Ltd* EU:C:2012:531, [29].

260 On whether an heir of the judgment creditor is an interested party for these purposes (held not until, under the law governing the succession, the succession had been established) see *Re Haji-Ioannou, Haji-Ioannou v. Frangos* [2009] EWHC 2130 (QB), [2010] 1 All ER (Comm) 303.

261 For the meaning of copy, see further below in this paragraph.

necessary to establish that it is authentic;[262] and if he is applying for an order which will lead to the enforcement of the judgment, he must[263] also produce a certificate in standard form[264] which gives certain details about the judgment. As indicated above, the judgment must be enforceable in the Member State in which it was given.[265]

Certain prescribed documents must be produced on the application.[266] The applicant, who is required to give an address within the jurisdiction for service of process,[267] applies to the national court identified in Annex II to Regulation 44/2001: in England, the application is made to the High Court, for an order that the judgment be registered for enforcement pursuant to Civil Jurisdiction and Judgments Order 2001, Schedule 1, paragraph 2. The application, which is really only a paper check, and which should not require a hearing, is made without notice[268] to the party against whom the order for registration, and then the enforcement, is sought. To underline this point, according to the second sentence of Article 41, the party against whom the order is sought is not entitled at this stage to make submissions against the making of the order.

When the order is made, paragraph 2(2) of the 2001 Order provides that for the purposes of enforcement the registered foreign judgment is to have the same force and effect as if the judgment had been given by the English court.[269]

The power of the court to reject the application for registration, at this stage, is extremely limited. It involves no more than to check that the documentation appears to be in order;[270] Article 41 of Regulation 44/2001 forbids any review or preview of the possible grounds on which an appeal against registration might be founded.[271] The intention was to restrict to an absolute minimum the grounds upon which a court, minded to be unhelpful to a foreign judgment creditor, for example, could refuse to make an order for registration, or an order for enforcement, in respect of a judgment from another Member State.

---

262 Regulation 44/2001, Art. 53(1). But no proceedings need be brought if recognition is all that is required.

263 He may not sue instead on the original cause of action: 42/76 *De Wolf v. Cox BV* [1976] ECR 1759.

264 Regulation 44/2001, Arts 53(2) and 54; and Annex V to that Regulation. Article 55(1) permits a court to accept an alternative document to this certificate, or even to dispense with its production altogether; but for the implications of this, see further below.

265 Regulation 44/2001, Art. 38(1). This means that it must be formally enforceable; it is irrelevant that the decision may no longer be enforceable by reason, for example, of payment by the debtor (C-139/10 *Prism Investments BV v. Van Der Meer* [2011] ECR I-9511, on which see above, para. 7.12), insolvency, etc.: see C-267/97 *Coursier v. Fortis Bank SA* [1999] ECR I-2543. If the judgment is enforceable in the State in which it was given, because the court in that country has declined to stay the enforcement pending an appeal, then the judgment is enforceable for the purposes of its registration for enforcement in England, and it is not open to the English court to assess for itself the prospects of any appeal succeeding, for this would be to review the judgment on its merits: *Banco Nacional de Comercio Exterior SNC v. Empresa de Telecomunicaciones de Cuba* [2007] EWHC 2322 (Comm), [2007] 2 CLC 690; see also C-183/90 *Van Dalfsen v. Van Loon* [1991] ECR I-4743.

266 Regulation 44/2001, Art. 40(3). In England, they will presumably be exhibited to the witness statement made in support of the application: CPR r. 74.4(6) (as it applied to Regulation 44/2001, for which purpose it is not affected by the amendments made to provide for the recast Regulation: see SI 2014/2948, r. 6(1).

267 Regulation 44/2001, Art. 40(2). If this is not done, he is required to appoint a representative *ad litem*.

268 Regulation 44/2001, Art. 41; CPR r. 74.3(2).

269 This provides the basis for measures of execution to be taken. It does not mean that the judgment has the same legal consequences for other purposes (such as its effect on non-parties) as it would have had if given by an English court, for this would be to confuse execution with the nature of the obligation to recognize a foreign judgment under the Regulation: see further above, para. 7.24; *cf Calyon v. Michailidis* [2009] UKPC 34 (Gib).

270 Regulation 44/2001, Art. 42(1).

271 Or, one supposes, of any other matter, such as whether the judgment falls within the material scope of the Regulation.

When the court has checked the documentation and made the order that the judgment be registered for enforcement, Article 42 of Regulation 44/2001 requires the party against whom the order has been made to be notified by service[272] on him of the order and, if it has not been served on him before, of the judgment. In addition, as soon as the order is made,[273] the applicant is entitled to proceed to claim protective measures, but no other measures, against the property of the party against whom enforcement is sought.[274] The judgment may then be executed unless the process of appeal against the order for registration is invoked.

No doubt it is desirable that the paperwork be in order when making the *ex parte* application for registration. But Article 55(1) of Regulation 44/2001 gives the court a power to dispense with the Annex V certificate; and it would be very unlikely indeed that any other formal objection would be allowed to derail the process of obtaining an order for registration, as long as the rights of the defendant are sufficiently respected.

7.28 *Inter partes* stage of the procedure under Regulation 44/2001: appeals and further appeals by the party disappointed at the first stage: Articles 43 to 47

The losing or disappointed party may appeal against the order made or not made after the first stage of the procedure. Though this does also in theory mean that the applicant may appeal against a refusal to make the order applied for, the chances that the applicant will be in this position are so small that, for the purposes of exposition, it can be ignored; it is assumed that the appeal is brought by the party against whom enforcement has been ordered.[275] There is no allowance under the Regulation for non-parties to appeal, even if they have an interest in the judgment, if they had not formally appeared in the proceedings.[276] To English ears, the nomenclature of appealing against[277] an order made in *ex parte* proceedings, to the court which made the order in the first place,[278] is a little odd, but the principle is clear enough.

The time limits for appealing are tight and rigid. If he is domiciled in the Member State in which enforcement has been ordered, the debtor-appellant has one month from the date

---

272 Under the Brussels Convention it was required that there be due service, made in accordance with the law of the State in which enforcement has been authorised: C-3/05 *Verdoliva v. JM Van der Hoven BV* [2006] ECR I-1579. The fact that the defendant knew of the order for registration, or whatever it is, is not enough to trigger the running of the strict time period limited for him to lodge an appeal. It is not clear that Regulation 44/2001 would be interpreted in the same way, though there is no textual change which would require an interpretation different from that in *Verdoliva*.

273 Prior to that, the applicant may presumably seek relief in accordance with Section 10 of Chapter II of the Regulation: *Babanaft International Co SA v. Bassatne* [1990] Ch 13.

274 Regulation 44/2001, Art. 47. In 119/84 *Capelloni v. Pelkmans* [1985] ECR 3147 it was suggested that there was a right to obtain such measures, but the truth probably is that there is a right to apply and the court has a discretion, which it may exercise in the applicant's favour, to grant the relief applied for. But in *Banco Nacional de Comercio Exterior SNC v. Empresa de Telecomunicaciones de Cuba SA* [2007] EWCA Civ 662, [2007] 2 Lloyd's Rep 484, it was held that it was inexpedient to grant a worldwide freezing injunction in aid of the enforcement of an Italian judgment simply because the judgment had been registered for enforcement in England (no assets in England; defendant not resident in England).

275 For the case where the applicant loses at the first stage, but appeals against the refusal to make the order, Art. 43(4) makes provision for the case in which the other party does not appear.

276 148/84 *Deutsche Genossenschaftsbank v. Brasserie du Pêcheur SA* [1985] ECR 1981; C-172/91 *Sonntag v. Waidmann* [1993] ECR I-1963; C-167/08 *Draka NK Cables Ltd v. Omnipol Ltd* [2009] ECR I-3477.

277 As distinct from applying to set aside.

278 It is possible that this gave rise to the odd analysis in C-619/10 *Trade Agency Ltd v. Seramico Investments Ltd* EU:C:2012:531, and that the Court did not appreciate the distinction between appealing and applying to set aside.

of service of the order for enforcement to lodge his appeal. If he is domiciled in another Member State, the period is extended to two months from the date when service was made on him personally or at his place of residence; and in neither case is the court permitted to extend the time on grounds of distance[279] (though, presumably, time may be extended for sufficient cause other than distance). In the case of an appellant who is not domiciled in any Member State the period is two months which may be extended on grounds of distance.[280]

The *inter partes* appeal against the order for registration is made to the court specified for the purpose in Annex III to the Regulation: in England this is to the High Court, this time to a judge. According to Article 45(1) of Regulation 44/2001, the only grounds upon which the appeal may be allowed are the jurisdictional grounds in Article 35, and the non-jurisdictional grounds in Article 34. But this cannot be read literally. After all, if the appellant were not entitled at this stage to submit that the judgment is not within the domain of the Regulation at all,[281] or that he is protected from enforcement by a bilateral treaty to which Article 72 refers,[282] or on any other ground is not within the ambit of this rule, it must come up at this point or not be raised at all. It follows that all grounds and every ground of opposition to the enforcement of the judgment may be raised at this stage though, of course, the substance of the judgment as such may not be reviewed.[283] Article 45(1) must be taken to be referring to grounds which are internal to and expressly provided by the Regulation for judgments which fall within its scope, and not those which go to define its outer edges.

The court hearing the appeal against registration may[284] also, if the appellant makes an application to this effect, stay the proceedings for enforcement if an 'ordinary appeal'[285] against the judgment is pending in the State of origin.[286] Of course, if the courts of the State of origin of the judgment have suspended the enforceability of the judgment pending the appeal, Article 38 of Regulation 44/2001 will already have prevented the proceedings for enforcement. The court 'may also', which presumably means 'may instead' and probably means 'should usually', order that enforcement is to be conditional on the provision of security.[287]

The party who loses at the *inter partes* stage of the procedure may make one, and only one, further appeal, only on a point of law, against that decision.[288] The grounds on which the court hearing the further appeal on a point of law may make its decision are the same as those open to the court below,[289] and its powers pending an appeal in the State of origin,

---

279 All provided by Art. 43 of Regulation 44/2001. But it appears that compliance with and violation of these time limits is a matter for the national court and not for the Court of Justice: C-220/95 *Van den Boogaard v. Laumen* [1997] ECR I-1147. For a case refusing an extension of time on the merits of the application, see *Citibank NA v. Rafidian Bank* [2003] EWHC 1950 (QB), [2003] ILPr 758.

280 If application for extension of time is made within the period of two months: CPR r. 74.8.

281 Article 1.

282 Paragraph 7.10, above.

283 Regulation 44/2001, Art. 45(2).

284 But there is no obligation: *DHL GBS (UK) Ltd v. Fallimento Finmatica SpA* [2009] EWHC 291 (Comm), [2009] 1 Lloyd's Rep 430.

285 43/77 *Industrial Diamond Supplies v. Riva* [1977] ECR 2175.

286 Regulation 44/2001, Art. 46(1).

287 Regulation 44/2001, Art. 46(3). Which it should do is a matter lying within its own discretion: *Petereit v. Babcock International Ltd* [1990] 1 WLR 350.

288 Regulation 44/2001, Art. 44 and Annex IV.

289 That is, as stated in Regulation 44/2001, Art. 45(1), but not interpreted literally.

to stay or make enforcement conditional on security, are the same as those of the court below.[290] In England, this will almost always mean that the final appeal is to the Court of Appeal.[291]

7.29 Miscellaneous further points concerning enforcement under Regulation 44/2001

A judgment which qualifies for recognition and enforcement under Chapter III of Regulation 44/2001 may be registered for enforcement under Civil Jurisdiction and Judgments Order 2001, Schedule 1, paragraph 2.[292] If the original judgment carried an entitlement to interest, that interest will be recoverable as well.[293] As has been said several times above, when registered for enforcement, the judgment has the same effect for the purposes of execution as if it had been given by the High Court.[294]

Several other points should be noted. First, if on its true construction a judgment is severable, an order for partial enforcement is permissible[295] in those cases where enforcement may be authorised in respect of some, but not in respect of all, parts of the judgment. The principle is clear enough, but it will be dependent, where it is not obvious, on the court which adjudicates making it clear which element of the award of damages, for example, is derived from which part of the claim. The point is illustrated by *Van den Boogaard v. Laumen*[296] in which the court called upon to recognise a judgment given after the dissolution of a marriage had to decide whether it was a judgment for maintenance, which is within the material scope of the Regulation, or one concerned with status or rights in property arising out of a matrimonial relationship, which is not. The same severance may be called for if a judgment contains an element which is otherwise not civil or commercial. If part of the judgment is founded on a claim which is to be identified as revenue law,[297] or possibly[298] penal law, that part of the judgment should also be severed and only enforced in part.

Second, if an applicant for enforcement had complete or partial legal aid in the adjudicating court, he is entitled to the most favourable legal aid under the law of the court to which the application is made in making and prosecuting the application for registration.[299]

Third, no order for security for costs may be made against the party applying for enforcement simply upon the basis that he is not domiciled in the Member State in question.[300]

---

290 Thereby reversing the decision in C-432/93 *SISRO v. Ampersand Software BV* [1995] ECR I-2269.

291 As it did, for example, in C-420/07 *Apostolides v. Orams* [2009] ECR I-3571.

292 SI 2001/3929. This provision of the Order is modelled on the 1982 Act, s. 4.

293 2001 Order, Sch. 1, para. 5.

294 2001 Order, Sch. 1, para. 2. It follows that a stay of execution may be ordered just as may be done in respect of an English judgment: *Noirhomme v. Walklate* [1992] 1 Lloyd's Rep 427. For further consequences, see *Duer v. Frazer* [2001] 1 All ER 249; see also *Re Baden-Württembergische Bank AG* [2009] CSIH 47 (Art. 6 of the ECHR not violated by delay in enforcement proceedings).

295 Regulation 44/2001, Art. 48.

296 C-220/95, [1997] ECR I-1147.

297 Excluded from the material scope of Regulation 44/2001 by Art. 1(2)(b).

298 The hesitation reflects the fact that a penal daily order, imposed to encourage or secure compliance with an order made in the proceedings (*astreinte*) is enforceable under Chapter III of Regulation 44/2001 (Art. 49), and also by C-406/09 *Realchemie Nederland BV v. Bayer CropScience AG* [2011] ECR I-9773 (on which, see para. 2.36, above).

299 Regulation 44/2001, Art. 49.

300 Regulation 44/2001, Art. 50.

Fourth, no case has yet had to ask precisely what follows from the registration of a judgment from another Member State which is of a kind which an English court could not have made for itself. In principle, the answer ought to be that the English court should do its best to make ancillary orders which replicate, as near as possible, the order made by the foreign court. Courts in other Member and Contracting States have been prepared to enforce English orders of a kind which they themselves could not have made, seeming to adopt the strategy of interpreting the English order as though it had been the closest local equivalent. In *European Consulting Unternehmensberatung AG v. Refco Overseas Ltd*,[301] a worldwide freezing injunction was granted in the High Court,[302] and was presented for enforcement in Germany, where the court ordered its enforcement,[303] selecting between the measures in the German Code of Civil Procedure to find and order the nearest equivalent German remedy.[304] Within the limits of what is possible, this is undoubtedly the correct way for a court to proceed.

Fifth, it is should be reiterated that, in sharp contrast to the assumed position at common law, enforcement in England is not confined to judgments for fixed sums of money, but will extend to all judgments from the courts of Member States, wherever the judgment may be called, and whatever the order made.[305]

Finally, it may be asked whether a judgment given on the *inter partes* appeal against registration for enforcement is itself to be seen as a judgment for the purposes of Chapter III, with the consequence that is may have effect outside the Member State in which it was given if, according to its terms, it has decided an issue which might be raised at a later date before a court in another Member State. Although a decision that a judgment shall not be recognised in England because it conflicts with English public policy does not appear to rest on any basis which could be of interest in another Member State, a decision that the judgment shall not be recognised by reference to Article 34(2) of the Regulation would appear to have the potential to be recognised in other Member States; so also a decision that a foreign judgment is irreconcilable with an English judgment, for what arises under Article 34(3) in England would fall under Article 34(4) in another Member State.

No existing authority supports the conclusion that such a degree of recognition is possible as a matter of European law. It could be argued that the approach in *Gothaer Allgemeine Versicherung AG v. Samskip GmbH*[306] would allow the reasons which led a court to refuse recognition to be recognised in their turn, but the context of that case – the overriding need to ensure that issues of jurisdictional competence are done and dusted, quickly and conclusively – was rather different. It may be that if this effect is to be derived from such a decision made by a foreign court, it will have to be brought about by the domestic law

---

301 Unreported, but discussed in *Zeitschrift für Zivilprozess International (ZZPInt)* 1 (1996) 89.

302 The report does not disclose whether it was made originally without notice and then continued or remade after a further hearing on notice.

303 It is noteworthy that in this decision the German court saw no objection in the English court ordering a worldwide injunction. The court doubted that the order could ever be regarded in Germany as having an effect on non-parties, who had not been present and entitled to be heard at any stage in the procedure; and as against them the order was not to be recognised.

304 It turned out to be under the rules of an injunctive title, § 890 of the German Civil Code (ZPO).

305 Regulation 44/2001, Art. 32.

306 C-456/11, EU:C:2012:719, [2013] QB 458. Applied in *Starlight Shipping Co v. Allianz Marine & Aviation Versicherungs AG* [2014] EWHC 3068 (Comm), [2014] 2 Lloyd's Rep 579.

principles of issue estoppel. There is no reason to suppose that this is inappropriate or impossible.

7.30 Authentic instruments and court-approved settlements under Regulation 44/2001

Chapter III of Regulation 44/2001 deals with the recognition and enforcement of judgments. Though this expression includes judgments entered by consent,[307] it does not extend to certain other procedural measures by which a dispute may be brought to an end with the consent of the parties. The recognition and enforcement of two such measures is dealt with in Chapter IV of the Regulation, by Articles 57 and 58.[308]

An authentic instrument is a document which has been formally drawn up or registered as such. It must be drawn up by a public official, who will usually be a civil law notary.[309] Under the law of certain Member States, such as Germany, the instrument may take effect as a conclusive and enforceable statement of indebtedness, without the need to institute court proceedings to obtain an order for payment. According to Article 57 of Regulation 44/2001, authentic instruments may be enforced in another Member State in accordance with the procedures in Articles 38 *et seq.* of the Regulation, but so far as the objections to recognition are concerned, the application for enforcement may be refused by the court hearing the *inter partes* appeal against the order for registration, or hearing the further appeal on a point of law, only if enforcement of the instrument is manifestly contrary to the public policy of the Member State in which its enforcement is sought. As these instruments are not judgments, the rules which provide for the non-recognition of a foreign judgment[310] by reason of irreconcilability with a local judgment do not apply to them.[311]

A settlement which has been approved by a court in the course of proceedings does not amount to a judgment within the scope of Chapter III, for it derives its authority from the parties' agreement, and not from the decision of a court; for this reason it does not enjoy the authority of *res judicata*.[312] But if it is enforceable in the State in which it was concluded, Article 58 of Regulation 44/2001 provides that it may be enforced under the same conditions as govern the enforcement of authentic instruments.

---

307 *Cf* the Opinion of the Advocate General in C-414/92 *Solo Kleinmotoren GmbH v. Boch* [1994] ECR I-2237, 2245, underlining the distinction between a judgment by consent and a court-approved settlement.

308 For the procedural rules relating to the application, see SI 2001/3928. For an illustration of enforcement by registration in Scotland, see *Re Baden-Württembergische Bank AG* [2009] CSIH 47.

309 If the law of the State in question does not require the participation of a public official, the document drawn up will not be an authentic instrument for the purposes of the Regulation: C-260/97 *Unibank A/S v. Christensen* [1999] ECR I-3715 (promissory note formally drawn up and enforceable under Danish law not authentic instrument as there was no authentication by a public official even though Danish law did not require this for the instrument to be enforceable).

310 Article 34(3) and 34(4) of Regulation 44/2001.

311 C-414/92 *Solo Kleinmotoren GmbH v. Boch* [1994] ECR I-2237.

312 C-414/92 *Solo Kleinmotoren GmbH v. Boch* [1994] ECR I-2237. By contrast, an English judgment by consent, though in some sense not an adjudication, has the authority of *res judicata*: *Landhurst Leasing plc v. Marcq* [1998] ILPr 822.

JUDGMENTS WITHIN THE SCOPE OF REGULATION 44/2001 CERTIFIED FOR ENFORCEMENT WITH A EUROPEAN ENFORCEMENT ORDER

7.31 General

To speed up the enforcement of judgments in civil and commercial matters, Regulation 805/2004 on the European Enforcement Order was adopted, coming into force from 21 October 2005,[313] and applying to all judgments given after that date.[314] It applies in principle to all judgments in civil or commercial matters given on uncontested claims for a specific sum of money which has fallen due.[315]

A perceived shortcoming of Chapter III of Regulation 44/2001 was the extent to which a stalling debtor may frustrate a claimant who has an unanswerable claim for judgment and payment. It is well known that an effective way to defend can be to do nothing at all: a defendant who joins issue with the claimant is in many ways easier to deal with than one who ignores proceedings, does not acknowledge service, and so forth. When it comes to the enforcement of judgments under Chapter III, a stalling debtor may still take the relatively few points open to him, and by appealing and further appealing, postpone for months or even years the day when the claimant-creditor is able to proceed to final measures of enforcement by way of execution. In the meantime, the creditor may have run into financial difficulty of his own: a debtor is in a strong position if creditors are weak or have been weakened by the debt, and the larger the debt, the greater may be the debtor's hold over the creditor.

Proceeding therefore from the view that even Chapter III of Regulation 44/2001 was too slow to bring about a final order granting permission to proceed to measures of execution, Regulation 805/2004 provides for the court which has given judgment on an uncontested claim to issue a 'European Enforcement Order' certificate in respect of the judgment. The certificate allows the creditor to present the judgment for recognition and enforcement in any Member State without the need for judicial proceedings to establish the right to enforce the judgment.[316] There is no right of appeal against the decision of the adjudicating court to issue the certificate,[317] and there is little opportunity for steps to be taken to oppose enforcement in any other Member State.

If a defendant is served with process in a claim to which he has no real answer, he will have a choice. If he contests the claim, and loses, he has the chance to fend off the date when enforcement becomes legally irresistible. If he allows the claim to go undefended, he then risks the trial court finding that the claim was uncontested, and certifying the judgment under Regulation 805/2004. From a defendant's point of view, therefore, the cost of allowing a claim to be uncontested is rather high. If, as seems to be the case, the defendant can get away with doing rather little if all he wishes to do is to prevent the claim as being seen

---

313 [2004] OJ L143/15, Art. 33.

314 Regulation 805/2004, Art. 26.

315 On the Regulation generally, see Crifò, *Cross-Border Enforcement of Debts in the EU* (2009).

316 The subordinate legislation providing the administrative details is to be found in CPR Part 74 Section V.

317 Regulation 805/2004, Art. 10(4). There is no mention of what may or may not be done by the judgment creditor if the court refuses to issue the certificate. Presumably he is thereupon thrown back on Chapter III of the Brussels I Regulation, as no mention is made in Regulation 805/2004 of any right to appeal against the refusal of the court to issue a certificate.

as uncontested, it is hard to see the rational argument for doing less than that little. From the perspective of the claimant, this may mean that the opportunity offered by Regulation 805/2004 is easily defeated, but where the defendant allows the claim to be undefended, the claim may count as uncontested, and if it does, the creditor's path to enforcement will be shorter and more direct than before.

In practice, it appears that Regulation 805/2004 has been little used, at least so far as the United Kingdom is concerned. It may therefore be thought that it does not merit much more than a passing mention. However, the principal innovation of Regulation 1215/2012, as will be seen, is that it reflects at least part of the approach in Regulation 805/2004, in providing for the enforcement of judgments on the basis of certification by the original court and without the need for a judicial application for an order that the judgment be registered for enforcement.

7.32 Certification for enforcement in accordance with Regulation 805/2004

The procedure for certification by the original court applies to judgments (which expression is defined widely) in uncontested claims (which is defined restrictively) in civil and commercial matters. Taking the last of these first, the definition[318] of civil and commercial matters, and matters excluded from it, is almost identical with that applicable to Chapter I of Regulation 44/2001, and no more needs to be said about it. A judgment[319] is defined in the same terms as in Article 32 of Regulation 44/2001.[320] There is no requirement that the judgment be a final one, any more than a judgment enforced under Chapter III of Regulation 44/2001 is required to be final. But the judgment may not be certified under Regulation 805/2004 unless it is enforceable under the law of the State of its origin.[321]

Certification is restricted to judgments given on a claim which is uncontested.[322] A claim means a claim for payment of a specific sum of money that has fallen due or for which the date is indicated in the judgment, court settlement, or authentic instrument.[323] It will be considered to be uncontested if (a) the debtor has expressly agreed to it by admission or by a settlement approved by or concluded before a court in the course of proceedings, or (b) the debtor never objected to it, in compliance with the relevant procedural requirements under the law of the Member State of origin, in the course of the court proceedings, or (c) the debtor did not appear or was not represented at a court hearing regarding that claim after having initially objected to the claim in the course of court proceedings, provided that such conduct amounts to a tacit admission of the claim or of the facts alleged by the creditor under the law of the Member State of origin, or (d) the debtor has expressly agreed to it in an authentic instrument.[324]

Despite the rather awkward drafting, the basic idea of a claim as uncontested is clear enough. So far as the claim is concerned, it must have been for a liquidated sum which had a fixed date for payment, or have been for one which was payable on demand, the demand

---

318 Regulation 805/2004, Art. 1.
319 Regulation 805/2004, Art. 4(1).
320 See above, para. 7.07.
321 Regulation 805/2004, Art. 6(1)(a).
322 Regulation 805/2004, Art. 3(1).
323 Regulation 805/2004, Art. 4(2).
324 Regulation 805/2004, Art. 3(1), which is paraphrased here. The original drafting is cumbersome.

having been made. It cannot be extended to a claim for general damages, or for damages to be assessed, for the claim is not for payment of a specific sum but a general one, and because it cannot be said that the payment has fallen due. The paradigm for application will be the unpaid invoice for the sale of goods or the supply of services, where the terms of payment specified a date by which payment was due. If the claim is for a sum which was liable to be calculated, but which was not quantified when the claim was made, it is unclear whether it will be seen as being for a specific sum. But one supposes that this expression will tend to receive a slightly more generous interpretation than might otherwise be expected, and a specific sum should include one which can be made specific by simple arithmetic.

As to the application of the legislative definition of an uncontested claim,[325] judgment in default will be the easy case.[326] If the debtor admits the claim by ticking the relevant box on the form for acknowledgment of service, that is that, and the claim is obviously an uncontested one. Likewise, if in his pleading he admits the debt, that fact will make the claim uncontested. An admission which satisfies CPR rule 14.4 should also make the debt uncontested. In the absence of such an admission, a lack of objection to the debt may also allow the debt to be said to have been uncontested.[327] Presumably a pleaded denial of liability, with as much or as little particularity as the procedure of the court allows or requires, will suffice to make the claim contested and take it outside the scope of Regulation 805/2004. A challenge to the jurisdiction of the court will not count as a denial of liability or a contesting of the debt, as the defendant who contests the jurisdiction of the court is given a fresh opportunity to acknowledge service and so indicate his acceptance or not of the claim. The defendant who ticks the box on the form to acknowledge service to indicate that he does not admit the claim, but who then does no more, is at risk of being taken not to have contested the claim if he fails to file a defence, for judgment in default of defence may be entered against him.[328]

It therefore appears to follow that all a defendant has to do, to prevent the claim being seen as uncontested, is to file a defence at the appropriate time. Though it does not appear that he need proceed to advance it with any particular vigour or at any great length, the serving of a defence in which the claim is denied or not admitted must surely count as contesting the claim.[329] On the other hand, for an argument that it is not enough to issue the challenge, but is also necessary that it be prosecuted or else be at risk of being regarded as waived, there may be an analogy to be drawn with *Starlight International Inc v. Bruce*.[330] As the question raised by Article 3(1)(c) is whether the participation or lack thereof amounts to a tacit admission, it

---

325 Regulation 805/2004, Art. 3(1).

326 There is palpable tension between this Regulation, which seeks to achieve the speedy enforcement of uncontested judgments, of which the default judgment is the most obvious, and Regulation 44/2001, Art. 34(2) of which has been interpreted in such a way as to allow a court in the state of enforcement to go behind the certificate for which Annex V of that Regulation provides, and second-guess the court which gave the judgment and completed the certificate on issues of service and, perhaps, other issues: see C-619/10 *Trade Agency Ltd v. Seramico Investments Ltd* EU:C:2012:531.

327 Regulation 805/2004, Art. 3(1)(b), though what precisely this means is harder to say.

328 CPR r. 12.1(b).

329 On the other hand, for an argument that it is not enough to issue the challenge, but is also necessary that it be prosecuted or else be at risk of being regarded as waived, there may be an analogy with *Starlight International Inc v. Bruce* [2002] EWHC 374 (Ch), [2002] ILPr 617.

330 [2002] EWHC 374 (Ch), [2002] ILPr 617. And see also, to the same general effect in relation to the jurisdiction of an English court, *Maple Leaf Macro Volatility Master Fund v. Rouvroy* [2009] EWHC 257 (Comm), [2009] 1 Lloyd's Rep 475.

would be open to an English court to conclude that the simple filing of a defence, followed by a lack of participation, was a tacit admission of the claim. Until this is clarified, it is dangerous to recommend that the mere filing of a defence will suffice to ward off the possibility of certification of the judgment for enforcement under Regulation 805/2004.

How the rule will apply when a defence is struck out, for example, is not currently clear. The answer may be that one has to ask whether there is a tacit admission of the debt when a defence has been struck out. It does not seem to be very likely that there is, but the possibility that the claim is to be regarded as having become an uncontested one cannot be completely ruled out.

7.33 Issue of, and objection to, the certificate issued under Regulation 805/2004

The certificate for enforcement in accordance with Regulation 805/2004 is issued by the court in which the judgment is given.[331] Once it is issued, recognition and enforcement of the judgment is automatic, in that there is no need to obtain a declaration of enforceability, or to apply for the registration of the judgment for enforcement: that is, the procedure in Chapter III of Regulation 44/2001 is unnecessary,[332] and there is next to no legal possibility of preventing recognition of the judgment.[333] This places a remarkable degree of power in the hands of the claimant and the judge in the court of origin. The form of the certificate is prescribed in Annex I to Regulation 805/2004.

The conditions on which the certificate may be issued are set out in Article 6 of Regulation 805/2004, and are to be policed by, and only by, the court which gave the judgment. The conditions[334] are that the judgment is enforceable in the State of origin;[335] that the judgment did not conflict with the insurance contract provisions;[336] and that the judgment did not conflict with the provisions dealing with exclusive jurisdiction regardless of domicile.[337] Where the judgment is given against a consumer domiciled in a Member State, in respect of a consumer contract,[338] the judgment must be from the Member State in which the consumer is domiciled unless the consumer has expressly agreed to the claim.[339] If there is an error in the certificate, or if it was 'clearly wrong' to grant it, an application for rectification or withdrawal is made to the court which issued the certificate; and there is no appeal against the issuing of the certificate.[340]

In order to offer a guarantee that the debtor had a proper chance to be heard, the certificate may be granted only if certain 'minimum standards' were observed. These are set out in some detail in Chapter III of Regulation 805/2004, and proper observance of them should inoculate the issue of the certificate against any criticism derived from the European Convention on Human Rights. Service on the debtor must have taken place with his written

---

331 Regulation 805/2004, Art. 6.

332 Although the judgment creditor may use Chapter III of Regulation 44/2001 if he prefers: Recital (20) and Art. 27 of Regulation 805/2004.

333 Regulation 805/2004, Art. 5.

334 Regulation 805/2004, Art. 6(1)(b).

335 Regulation 805/2004, Art. 6(1)(a).

336 Section 3 of Chapter II of Regulation 44/2001.

337 Section 6 of Chapter II of Regulation 44/2001.

338 C-508/12 *Vapenik v. Thurner* EU:C:2013:790, [2014] 1 WLR 790.

339 Regulation 805/2004, Art. 6(1)(d).

340 Regulation 805/2004, Art. 10. If it is alleged that the certificate was corruptly issued, for example, there appears to be no recourse to the court of intended enforcement. It is hard to believe that this is really sufficient.

acknowledgment of receipt, or with an attestation from the process-server that the debtor either accepted, or unjustifiably refused to accept, service of the document.[341] But as an alternative, and if the debtor's address is known with certainty, other permissible methods of service are: by service on house-mates, at a place of business on employees, or through a mailbox, or at the post office or competent authorities with notice through the mailbox, or by post to an address in the State of origin, or by electronic means if the debtor has agreed to this in advance.[342] Service may also be made on a debtor's representative.[343] The papers served must contain basic information about the claim[344] and the procedure.[345] If service miscarries, or fails to reach the debtor personally, such irregularity may be cured if the debtor had a chance to challenge the judgment but did not, or if he received the document by other means.[346] And if service was not made personally on the debtor with the result that he did not have time to arrange for his defence (and was not himself at fault), he must be entitled to a review of the judgment.[347] It is not hard to see that there is room for dispute here, but the structure of the Regulation is that it must be resolved by going back to the court of origin.

7.34 Enforcement, and challenges to the enforcement, of the certified judgment

A certified judgment is to be enforced in the same way as a local judgment.[348] All that is required is production to the competent enforcement authorities of a copy of the judgment and of the certificate, with a translation if necessary.[349] The judgment debtor may apply to the court in the State of enforcement for enforcement to be refused if the certified judgment is irreconcilable with a judgment given earlier in another Member State or in a third country, as long as the earlier judgment was between the same parties and involved the same cause of action, the judgment was given in the State of enforcement or satisfies the criteria for its enforcement, and the irreconcilability was not, and could not, have been raised as an objection to the proceedings in the Member State of origin.[350] As to this, if the earlier judgment was raised as an objection, the claim was presumably no longer an uncontested one. It therefore means that the debtor will have to show that it could not have been raised as an objection to the proceedings on the uncontested claim.[351]

Although Regulation 805/2004 provides that there is otherwise no right of recourse to the court at the place of enforcement or execution,[352] if the court at the place of enforcement or execution would consider that the original proceedings did violate the guarantees

---

341 Regulation 805/2004, Art. 13.

342 Regulation 805/2004, Art. 14. It follows that if the defendant's whereabouts are unknown, so that service upon him is not possible, certification for enforcement in accordance with the Regulation is not permissible: C-292/10 *G v. De Visser* EU:C:2012:142, [2013] QB 168.

343 Regulation 805/2004, Art. 15: it is unclear whether this is meant to go beyond legal representative, or to be limited to those who have been authorised by the debtor to accept service of process on his behalf.

344 Regulation 805/2004, Art. 16.

345 Regulation 805/2004, Art. 17.

346 Regulation 805/2004, Art. 18.

347 Regulation 805/2004, Art. 19.

348 Regulation 805/2004, Art. 20(1).

349 Regulation 805/2004, Art. 20(2), (3).

350 Regulation 805/2004, Art. 21. For the procedure, see CPR Part 74, Section V.

351 It is not clear whether this should be read as meaning that it could have been raised *successfully*.

352 Even, it appears, if the EEO is set aside in the state of origin after its registration in England: *Lothschutz v. Vogel* [2014] EWHC 473 (QB).

of Article 6 of the European Convention on Human Rights, it is hard to see that it should, or could, be required to ignore this fact.[353] There may also be cases in which enforcement in accordance with Regulation 805/2004 is not obviously desirable: suppose the courts of Cyprus give judgment for a fixed sum of money against a defendant who acquired land from a vendor whose 'title' was granted by the illegal junta in the northern part of Cyprus:[354] can it really be supposed that such a judgment, if the defendant does not – perhaps cannot – appear to contest it, can be enforced in accordance with Regulation 805/2004 against the assets of the defendant in another Member State? It remains to be seen whether the Regulation can survive the stresses which may be placed on it by challenging cases.[355]

Regulation 805/2004 does not affect bilateral treaties which are preserved in force by Article 72 of Regulation 44/2001.[356] If there is a challenge to the judgment, or to the certificate, in the State of origin, the enforcement may be limited to provisional measures, or be dependent on security; in exceptional cases, the court may stay the enforcement proceedings.[357] Regulation 805/2004 does not affect Regulation 44/2001, which remains available as a means of recognition and enforcement.[358]

Though the aim of Regulation 805/2004 is to prevent proceedings to challenge recognition and enforcement, this cannot be met in its entirety. The irreconcilability defence and the bilateral treaties defence prevent that. It is not wholly clear whether the debtor is prevented from opposing enforcement on the ground that the judgment was not in a civil or commercial matter, or that it was not given in an uncontested claim. But the most natural reading of the Regulation is that as these last matters are necessary preconditions for the certification of the judgment for enforcement, and as they must have been necessarily examined by the court in the State of origin, there is no further room for the debtor to raise them later. At this point, the demands of logic give way to the practical necessity to bring an end to the argument.

JUDGMENTS IN CIVIL AND COMMERCIAL MATTERS FROM THE COURTS OF MEMBER STATES: REGULATION 1215/2012

7.35 Recognition of judgments under Regulation 1215/2012: general

If the judgment was given in civil or commercial proceedings which were instituted on or after 10 January 2015, the judgment will fall within the temporal scope of Regulation 1215/2012, and if it is in other respects a judgment within Chapter I of that Regulation, Chapter III of Regulation 1215/2012 will apply to its recognition and enforcement.

In many respects Regulation 1215/2012 reproduces the substance of Regulation 44/2001. The principle of legal certainty will mean that unless there has been a deliberate alteration

---

353 After all, courts in other Member States do sometimes deliver judgments in proceedings which fall short of what Art. 6 ECHR guarantees. On the French practice of denying recognition to judgments which are given without reasons, and its relationship to the EEO procedure, see Cuniberti (2008) 57 ICLQ 25.

354 *Cf* C-420/07 *Apostolides v. Orams* [2009] ECR I-3571.

355 As a matter of general principle, if the judgment debtor had a right to appeal in the State of origin, there will be a presumption that recognition of the judgment about which he complains does not infringe Art. 6 ECHR: *Avotiņš v. Latvia* (ECHR, 25 Feb 2014).

356 Article 22.

357 Article 23.

358 Article 27.

to the text of the law, what was established under the earlier Regulation will continue to be reliable for the later one. It follows that much of the material examined above, particularly as to the grounds for recognition and non-recognition of judgments, will apply without material alteration. But where it comes to the mechanism by which a judgment is enforced, Regulation 1215/2012 makes a significant change to – many will say an improvement upon – the corresponding mechanism of Regulation 44/2001.

It is therefore necessary to look separately (i) at judgments to which Regulation 1215/2012 applies; (ii) at the grounds for recognition and non-recognition; and (iii) at the procedure for enforcement. It goes without saying, of course, that a judgment may 'under no circumstances' be reviewed as to its substance.[359]

7.36 The meaning of 'judgment' for the purpose of Regulation 1215/2012

For the purposes of Regulation 1215/2012, a judgment means a judgment given in proceedings which were instituted on or after 10 January 2015.

In other respects, the meaning of 'judgment' for the purpose of Chapter III of Regulation 1215/2012 will be the same as that developed in relation to Regulation 44/2001, with one key difference. The similarity results from the fact that the first sentence of Article 2(a) of Regulation 1215/2012 is identical to that given in Article 32 of Regulation 44/2001. However, Regulation 1215/2012 adds two further sentences, which deal with the question of recognition and enforcement of orders for provisional, including protective, measures: whether these are clarification or alteration of the previous law is not wholly clear. According to Article 2:

> For the purposes of this Regulation: (a) 'judgment' means any judgment given by a court or tribunal of a Member State, whatever the judgment may be called, including a decree, order, decision or writ of execution, as well as a decision on the determination of costs or expenses by an officer of the court. For the purposes of Chapter III, 'judgment' includes provisional, including protective, measures ordered by a court or tribunal which by virtue of this Regulation has jurisdiction as to the substance of the matter. It does not include a provisional, including protective, measure which is ordered by such a court or tribunal without the defendant being summoned to appear, unless the judgment containing the measure is served on the defendant prior to enforcement;

It follows that if a court has jurisdiction over the substance of the matter,[360] any order which it makes in those proceedings will count as a judgment, even if the judgment is provisional or protective in nature. It is not clear whether the reference to a court as having jurisdiction means that its jurisdiction must have been invoked, but this would be the better reading, for in many cases it will not be clear, prior to the issue of process, which court will actually have jurisdiction in the matter.

Where the court has made its order on the jurisdictional basis of Article 35 of Regulation 1215/2012, the material scope of the 'judgment' which may be recognised appears to have been widened when compared with the position under Regulation 44/2001. In relation to the earlier Regulation it was assumed that an order made in proceedings from which the defendant was excluded and intended to be excluded, did not count as a judgment at all, and therefore only had effect within the territory of the Member State within which

---

359 Regulation 1215/2012, Art. 52.

360 The expression 'plenary jurisdiction' has been used in England to convey this idea: see *Masri v. Consolidated Contractors International (UK) Ltd (No 4)* [2008] EWCA Civ 876, [2009] 2 WLR 699, [23]–[25].

it was made. The early decision of the Court in *Denilauler v. SNC Couchet Frères*,[361] which was concerned with the recognition and enforcement of judgments under the Brussels Convention, established that an order made in proceedings which were designed to exclude the defendant was not to be seen as a judgment, which meant that no question arose of its being recognised or enforced. In the analysis of Regulation 44/2001 proposed above, it was assumed that *Denilauler* remained the law. Of course, where an order made in such proceedings was confirmed or remade after an *inter partes* process, it was at that point a judgment for all purposes of the Regulation, for a judicial order made after proceedings designed to be *inter partes* proceedings is to be taken on its own terms.

In truth, however, an order made on an application for a freezing injunction looks very like a judgment, for it has an effect on the defendant, and (in this case) also on third parties who come by knowledge of it. There are good reasons why such an order should be subject to special forms of restriction if it is to have any effect outside the territory in which it was given: indeed, there are very good reasons why it should be subject to scrutiny and careful control within the Member State in which it is ordered in the first place. But it is easier to accept, as Regulation 1215/2012 now provides, that the order is a judgment for the purposes of Chapter III if the order has been served on the person against whom it has been made, who will at that point have available to him the full range of measures to challenge it in the State of origin, and to oppose its recognition or enforcement in another Member State. The earlier view, that the order is in this sense not a judgment at all, is one which the law did not need to preserve.

7.37 Grounds for the recognition or non-recognition of judgments: Regulation 1215/2012, Chapter III, Section 1

With a couple of exceptions, the grounds on which a judgment is entitled to be recognised, or to have its recognition opposed (the procedure by which this is done is examined below), are substantially the same as those provided for under Chapter III of Regulation 44/2001. Subject to what is said below, the jurisdictional objections to recognition derived from the insurance contract, consumer contract, and exclusive jurisdiction Sections of Chapter II of the Regulation remain in place, as does the effect of bilateral treaties with Australia and Canada.[362]

But Regulation 1215/2012 also adds, as a new jurisdictional objection to recognition, the case in which the judgment conflicted with the employment contract provisions of Section 5 of Chapter II,[363] so rectifying a historic shortcoming in the predecessor instruments. It follows that a judgment may be refused recognition of enforcement if the jurisdiction of the original court conflicted with Sections 3, 4, 5, or 6 of Chapter II of Regulation 1215/2012.

The non-jurisdictional objections to recognition, based on public policy, judgments in default of appearance, and irreconcilability with a local or foreign judgment, are also available.[364] The analysis of these grounds of objection which were examined in relation to Regulation 44/2001 applies to Regulation 1215/2012 as well.

Though it had been proposed that the public policy ground for non-recognition in Article 34(1) of Regulation 44/2001 should not be reproduced in Regulation 1215/2012, this did not command the agreement of the Member States. The substance of Articles 34

---

361 125/79, [1980] ECR 1553.
362 Regulation 1215/2012, Art. 72.
363 Regulation 1215/2012, Art. 45(1)(e)(i).
364 Regulation 1215/2012, Art. 45(1).

and 35 of Regulation 44/2001 is reproduced, without material change, in Regulation 1215/2012 in Article 45(1).[365] It is true that the language used in Articles 45 and 46 suggests that the recognition of the judgment on the stated grounds shall be refused (only) on the application of a party, and that this raises the possibility that a judgment may be recognised even despite a conflict with Sections 3 to 6 of Chapter II if the judgment debtor does not apply for a refusal of recognition or enforcement, but this may read too much into the language of Article 45, which appears to have been adjusted only to the extent necessary to reflect the fact that the method of enforcement, and therefore the method of bringing these issues before the court for decision, has been altered.

Article 36(1) of Regulation 1215/2012 provides that recognition of a judgment does not require any special procedure, but that any person who wishes to have judicial confirmation of the judgment as one to which no objection is liable to be made may apply for such a declaration that there are no grounds for the refusal of recognition, in accordance with Article 36(2). If he wishes to do that, he will also need to obtain a certificate, issued by the court which gave judgment, for which Article 53 makes provision, and which Annex I to the Regulation sets out in template form.[366] If a person simply wishes a judgment to be recognised, say as *res judicata* for the purpose of proceedings before the English court, it is not clear whether this certificate is also required to be produced, though as it does not appear to require much effort to obtain it, the point has little practical importance.

7.38 Recognition under Regulation 1215/2012 of judgments obtained in breach of agreement to arbitrate

At first sight, Regulation 1215/2012 appears to have paid greater attention to the effect of judgments obtained in civil and commercial matters from the courts of Member States in circumstances in which, as the State called upon to give effect to the judgment would have seen it, the parties had agreed that the dispute should have been dealt with by arbitration. Despite the fact that the text of the Regulation is not materially changed, a passage in Recital (12) to the Regulation, reproduced here for convenience of reference, explains that:

> *A ruling given by a court of a Member State as to whether or not an arbitration agreement is null and void, inoperative or incapable of being performed should not be subject to the rules of recognition and enforcement laid down in this Regulation, regardless of whether the court decided on this as a principal issue or as an incidental question. On the other hand, where a court of a Member State, exercising jurisdiction under this Regulation or under national law, has determined that an arbitration agreement is null and void, inoperative or incapable of being performed, this should not preclude that court's judgment on the substance of the matter from being recognised or, as the case may be, enforced in accordance with this Regulation. This should be without prejudice to the competence of the courts of the Member States to decide on the recognition and enforcement of arbitral awards in accordance with the Convention on the Recognition and Enforcement of Foreign Arbitral Awards, done at New York on 10 June 1958 ('the 1958 New York Convention'), which takes precedence over this Regulation.*

Although this is not part of the legislative text of Regulation 1215/2012, it is reasonable to read it as if it were so. Accordingly, judgments which have arbitration as their principal

---

365 Regulation 44/2001, Art. 34(1)-(4), is reproduced in Regulation 1215/2012 as Art. 45(1)(a)–(d); Regulation 44/2001, Art. 35(1) is reproduced in Regulation 1215/2012 as Art. 45(1)(e); Regulation 44/2001, Art. 35(2), (3) is reproduced in Regulation 1215/2012 as Art. 45(2), (3).

366 Regulation 1215/2012, Art. 37(1).

subject matter fall outside the Regulation, and such a judgment from another Member State will be refused recognition.[367] But if a court in a Member State has, in a civil or commercial matter, given judgment on the substance of the case, even though one party claims (and an English court would consider) that the parties had agreed to arbitrate, the foreign judgment falls within the material scope of the Regulation, and it may be recognised and enforced in accordance with Chapter III.

One therefore turns to Chapter III of the Regulation, where there are two grounds on which it may be argued – it would be premature and optimistic to say argued successfully – that recognition might be refused. The first is in Article 45(1)(a), that it is manifestly contrary to English public policy to allow a judgment to be recognised or enforced in England when it has been obtained by a party who was bound to arbitrate and not to go to court, and who had not been released from that contractual obligation by his counterparty. Although the Court of Appeal did not find this submission to be convincing,[368] the nature of the issue which has to be decided concerns the content of English public policy, not the meaning of the Regulation, and the issue should be revisited.

The other ground for non-recognition foreshadowed by the Recital and provided by the Regulation is in Article 73 of Regulation 1215/2012, which provides that:

> *(2) This Regulation shall not affect the application of the 1958 New York Convention.*

It is, no doubt, possible to read too much into this, not least because of the recent tendency of the Court to read such reservations for international treaties as though it had been enacted that they may take effect so long as they do not interfere with or perturb any of the functions of the Regulation.[369] However, if the New York Convention requires an English court to give effect to an arbitration agreement by dismissing proceedings brought before an English court which disregard it, and by giving effect to an award made by a tribunal to which the Convention applies, it would not be difficult to argue that for the court to recognise and treat as *res judicata* a judgment, which would contradict an award by the tribunal which had been agreed to, is not consistent with the New York Convention.

It might be said that the New York Convention does not impose an express obligation to disregard a judicial judgment which trespasses on an issue which the parties have agreed to settle by arbitration, but a possible explanation for that may be that it was so obvious that it did not need saying. In the end, it can only be the Court which explains the effect of Article 73(2), and in the light of the tendency identified above, one should not be sanguine about the prospect that arbitration agreements have been reinforced in any tangible way. But for a court to take a step which would prevent its giving full and proper (and untrammelled) effect to an award in proceedings which the parties have promised to bring by way of arbitration, would not appear to treat the New York Convention in the way which Article 73(2) appears to require.

---

367 As to whether the party seeking such a decision is required to apply in accordance with Art. 45 or 46 of the Regulation, see below.

368 *National Navigation Co v. Endesa Generacion SA, The 'Wadi Sudr'* [2009] EWCA Civ 1397, [2010] 1 Lloyd's Rep 193. The judgment is not persuasive.

369 Paragraph 2.48, above.

7.39 The enforcement of judgments: Regulation 1215/2012, Chapter III, Section 2

The principal innovation of Regulation 1215/2012 is that when a person who has obtained a judgment in proceedings which (for jurisdictional purposes) fell within the scope of the Regulation, that judgment may be enforced in another Member State without the need for an application to a court for permission to enforce it or for its registration for the purpose of enforcement, as the case may be in the particular Member State. No judicial declaration of enforceability in the State or States in which enforcement is to take place is required: the initial work is all done, instead, by the court which handed down the judgment.[370]

Under Regulation 44/2001 and its predecessor instruments, all cross-border enforcement began with an *ex parte* application, to a court, for a judicial order that the judgment be registered for enforcement within the territory of that court; after the obtaining (and expense) and service of which the person against whom the order had been made would be entitled to appeal in *inter parties* proceedings against the making of the order. However, given (i) the cost and potential delay caused by the need to obtain the order from a court, even though in *ex parte* proceedings, (ii) the fact that this procedure needed to be repeated in each Member State in which enforcement was sought, (iii) the fact that the substantial arguments against recognition and enforcement could only arise for examination at the *inter partes* stage, and (iv) the observation that the proportion of *ex parte* orders which were actually appealed against was a very small one, it was impossible to deny that the procedure could be streamlined with no real loss of legal protection.

Accordingly, the enforcement of a judgment under Regulation 1215/2012 starts with the issue of the certificate, for which Article 53 makes provision, by the court in which the judgment was given.[371] The principal function which this serves is to confirm that the judgment is enforceable under the law of the State which handed it down, to confirm the time and fact of service having been made on the defendant, and to set out in appropriate detail the computation of sums ordered to be paid or the nature of any non-pecuniary order. In other words, the certificate provided for in Annex I of the Regulation covers pretty much all the ground which would otherwise have been regulated by national procedural laws; but it does it once and for all Member States in which enforcement may be intended.

Registration of the certified judgment is then made with the 'competent enforcement authority' in the Member State in which its enforcement is to take place: the identification of the particular authority will, presumably, depend on the form of enforcement measure which is sought. The documentation which must be provided to that authority is prescribed by the Regulation.[372] The certificate and (if he does not already have it) the judgment must be served on the person against whom the judgment was given prior to the first enforcement measure, and that person may demand a translation into a language which he understands if he does not have a domicile in the Member State of origin.[373] Though this procedure does require some paperwork, and an application of an administrative nature, it does not involve application to, or orders made by, a court.

---

370 Regulation 1215/2012, Art. 39; see also Recital (26).
371 The form of the certificate is in Annex I.
372 Regulation 1215/2012, Art. 42. CPR r. 74.4A simply provides that the documents required by Art. 42 must be provided.
373 Regulation 1215/2012, Art. 43.

Novel as this may appear, one may observe that the procedure put in place by Regulation 1215/2012 is not so very novel. The information which is required before a judgment may be enforced has not really changed; it is simply a matter of whether it is produced by the claimant from his own endeavour and placed before the receiving court, or issued by the original court. From this point of view, and from others, it represents a perfectly sensible development of the law. Even if there are some courts in parts of the European Union in whose judicial capability one would hesitate to place unwavering trust, there are also some rather ramshackle places from which judgments may be brought to England for registration under the Administration of Justice Act 1920. This has not caused any obvious problems; it is appropriate to look benevolently on the experiment ushered in by Regulation 1215/2012.

7.40 Application for refusal of enforcement: Regulation 1215/2012, Chapter III, Section 3

The party against whom the judgment was given, and against whom measures of enforcement may be taken, may make an application for refusal of enforcement in accordance with Section 3(2) of Chapter III of Regulation 1215/2012.[374] This corresponds to the *inter partes* appeal when enforcement is under Regulation 44/2001. It is also possible to apply for an order for the refusal of recognition by reference to the grounds given in Section 3(1) of Chapter III,[375] though in practice this will be the rarer application, and we may confine our attention to the application for refusal of enforcement.

The procedure for the making of the application is set out in part in the Regulation, and in part by procedural rules of national law.[376] The application is made to a court,[377] and it succeeds if any of the jurisdictional and non-jurisdictional objections to recognition, set out in Section 3(1) of Chapter III, which means Article 45, can be shown to be satisfied.[378] This means that whereas under Regulation 44/2001 the judgment debtor appeals against an order that the judgment be registered for enforcement, under Regulation 1215/2012 the judgment debtor has to apply for an order that enforcement be refused. The nomenclature and appearance of the two procedures aside, the substance of the applications, and the fact that the judgment debtor has to make an application of one sort or another, means that the differences are almost entirely superficial. By contrast with the position under Regulation 44/2001, in which the judgment creditor has to obtain an order, against which the judgment debtor may appeal, and for which a strict time limit applies to the appeal, there is no statutory time limit for the application for a refusal of recognition or enforcement to be brought.

The grounds on which the application for a refusal of enforcement may be granted have been explained above. Regulation 1215/2012 does not say so in terms, but the procedure in Chapter III, Section 3, for obtaining an order that enforcement be refused, must also apply if the complaint is that the judgment is not one within the scope – material, temporal – of the Regulation. Although this is not specifically provided for in Articles 45 or 46, it is most

---

374 Regulation 1215/2012, Arts 46–51. The application for the refusal of recognition, dealt with in Art. 45, will be a rather less frequent application.
375 Regulation 1215/2012, Art. 45(4).
376 CPR r. 74.7A.
377 According to CPR r. 74.7A(1)(b), to the court in which the judgment is being enforced.
378 Regulation 1215/2012, Art. 46(1).

unlikely that an objection to enforcement under Chapter III based on the contention that the judgment falls outside the scope of the Regulation is to be brought before the court by a different form of application not specified in the Regulation. The only difference may be that if it is said that the judgment falls outside the material scope of the Regulation – because its subject matter is arbitration, for example – it may not be necessary for an application to be made for its recognition or enforcement to be refused: it may be possible to invite a court to reach such a conclusion in whichever form the matter arises before it.

Article 48 of the Regulation requires the court in which the application is made to rule on the application without delay; and Article 49 provides that whichever party loses when that application is determined may appeal. Article 50 provides that whoever loses on the Article 49 appeal may appeal, there being no apparent restriction to the appeal being one confined to points of law.[379]

The effect is that the first occasion on which the grounds on which recognition are debated is the *inter partes* application by the judgment debtor for a refusal of enforcement. After the decision on that application there are two levels of appeal – an appeal[380] and a further appeal[381] – permitted by the Regulation; and the result is that Regulation 1215/2012 provides more opportunities for genuine *inter partes* argument about the recognition or enforcement of the judgment than Regulation 44/2001 did, which is perhaps surprising.

In other respects, the powers of the court during the period within which the application for refusal of enforcement is pending are directly comparable to those given by Regulation 44/2001: to stay the proceedings before it if the original judgment is under appeal or other challenge in the State of origin,[382] to order protective measures as soon as there is an enforceable judgment,[383] and to limit to the grant of protective measures or to allowing enforcement conditional on the provision of security.[384]

7.41 Miscellaneous points relating to recognition and enforcement under Regulation 1215/2012

Section 3(1) of Chapter III of Regulation 1215/2012 allows proceedings for a declaration of refusal of recognition to be brought by any interested party.[385] The grounds on which the application may be granted are the same as are used in the application for refusal of enforcement, but as it is much more likely that the application will be brought for a refusal of enforcement, it made sense to discuss them in that context, and not to repeat them here.

The Regulation deals directly with the problem of judgments from Member States which do not precisely correspond with orders which may be made by the courts of the State in which enforcement is to take place, by requiring the incoming order to be 'adapted' to its nearest local equivalent.[386]

---

379 Regulation 1215/2012, Art. 50.
380 Regulation 1215/2012, Art. 49.
381 Regulation 1215/2012, Art. 50.
382 Regulation 1215/2012, Art. 51.
383 Regulation 1215/2012, Art. 40.
384 Regulation 1215/2012, Art. 44.
385 Regulation 1215/2012, Art. 45.
386 Regulation 1215/2012, Art. 54.

Judgments which order a periodic payment by way of penalty are enforceable, as they are under Regulation 44/2001, when the amount which is to be paid has been finally determined by the court of origin.[387]

As to the question whether the decision of the court on an application for a refusal of enforcement is itself liable to recognised as a judgment for the purposes of Chapter III, the point was raised above in relation to Regulation 44/2001, and there is nothing to add to it in this context.

JUDGMENTS IN CIVIL AND COMMERCIAL MATTERS FROM THE COURTS OF LUGANO II STATES AND BRUSSELS CONVENTION TERRITORIES

7.42 General

Recognition and enforcement under the Brussels and Lugano II Conventions applies to judgments in civil and commercial matters from the courts of those States to which the Lugano II Convention applies, which means Iceland, Norway and Switzerland, and of those few territories in which the Brussels Convention was made to apply but the Regulation does not.[388] As the Lugano II Convention is for all practical purposes the same as Regulation 44/2001, and as judgments from the Brussels Territories are very rarely encountered, the briefest of treatment is sufficient at this point.

7.43 Recognition and enforcement under the Lugano II Convention

The Lugano II Convention[389] was made between the European Union and the three States whose membership of the European Free Trade Association had not been superseded by membership of the European Union. Its substance is very closely modelled on Regulation 44/2001: indeed, it was made to bring the original Lugano Convention of 1988 into line with Regulation 44/2001.

The Convention took effect in relation to Norway on 1 January 2010, Switzerland on 1 January 2011, and Iceland on 1 May 2011. So far as concerns its application to the recognition and enforcement of judgments from the Lugano II States in the European Union, the material scope of the Convention is for all practical purposes the same as that of Regulation 44/2001. As to the question whether the instrument which governs recognition and enforcement of judgments is the Lugano II Convention or its predecessor, the practical answer is that it is the Lugano II Convention. According to Article 63:

> *(1) This Convention shall apply only to legal proceedings instituted and to documents formally drawn up or registered as authentic instruments after its entry into force in the State of origin and, where recognition or enforcement of a judgment or authentic instruments is sought, in the State addressed. (2) However, if the proceedings in the State of origin were instituted before the entry into force of this Convention, judgments given after that date shall be recognised and enforced in accordance with Title III: (a) if the proceedings in the*

---

387 Regulation 1215/2012, Art. 55.
388 See above, para. 2.26.
389 For the text, [2007] OJ L339/1. For a comparison with the 1988 Convention, see Pocar (2008) 10 *Yearbook of Private International Law* 1.

State of origin were instituted after the entry into force of the Lugano Convention of 16 September 1988
both in the State of origin and in the State addressed; (b) in all other cases, if jurisdiction was founded upon
rules which accorded with those provided for either in Title II or in a convention concluded between the State
of origin and the State addressed which was in force when the proceedings were instituted.

Given that proceedings in the Lugano II States will have been based on the 1988 Lugano Convention if they were instituted before the dates set out above, it is practically certain that the judgment in a civil or commercial matter from a Lugano II State will be one to which Article 63 will apply. It therefore provides the rules for the recognition and enforcement of judgments from those States in the European Union, and for the recognition and enforcement of judgments from Member States of the European Union in the Lugano II States.[390]

The definition of the material scope of the Lugano II Convention, the definition of 'judgment', the permitted jurisdictional objections to recognition, the permitted non-jurisdictional objections to recognition, the procedure by which judgments are registered for enforcement, and the procedure by which an appeal against that registration for enforcement may be made, are all the same as found in Regulation 44/2001.

7.44 Recognition and enforcement under the Brussels Convention

The prospect of an English court having to give effect to a judgment from one of the territories left over from the conversion of the Brussels Convention into a Regulation is so remote that, though it may be tiresome, the reader is asked to look at an earlier edition of this book. Judgments from Gibraltar are dealt with at the end of this chapter, along with judgments from other parts of the United Kingdom.

THE EFFECT OF FOREIGN JUDGMENTS TO WHICH THE REGULATION AND CONVENTIONS DO NOT APPLY: ENGLISH RULES OF PRIVATE INTERNATIONAL LAW APPLICABLE TO FOREIGN JUDGMENTS

7.45 General

As cumbersome headings go, this one is a serious contender for an unwanted prize. It reflects the fact that where the effect of a foreign judgment in England is left to English private international law to determine, it is hard to decide where to begin.

The reason is that, for the general run of cases (that is, outside the particular contexts of insolvency, matrimonial and family law, succession, etc.) there are two broad schemes. Under one of them, the person in whose favour a judgment has been given may register it in England for enforcement, after which the person against whom it is liable to be enforced may apply to have the registration set aside. The parliamentary schemes for registration apply to certain countries (and in the case of some countries, to certain courts), and will reflect the terms of a bilateral treaty or some other international agreement. In the cases in which this legislation provides for the registration of the judgment, after which the judgment debtor may apply to have the registration set aside, it is probably correct to say it is the

---

390 For those States, a more complex question will arise if a judgment from Croatia (to take the most recent Member State) is presented for recognition. But this is not our problem.

foreign judgment itself that takes effect in England, though the nature of the effect it has in England is defined and limited by the Act under which it is registered.

The grounds on which a judgment debtor may apply to have registration of the judgment set aside are closely derived from the common law rules relating to foreign judgments, and for this reason – really, only for this reason – it makes sense to deal with the common law first. However, the common law is, in one respect, the very opposite of the registration schemes. For as a matter of common law, a foreign judgment has no effect as a judgment in England. As far as the common law is concerned, and subject to what statute may provide, a foreign judgment cannot be enforced or executed upon in England. Only an English judgment can be enforced in England; and the function of a foreign judgment is, therefore, to provide the basis for English proceedings to be brought to obtain an English judgment which may then be enforced in the usual way.

THE EFFECT OF FOREIGN JUDGMENTS AT COMMON LAW

7.46 General

In principle, the recognition and enforcement of judgments at common law is applicable and available to all final judgments from all courts, wherever they are, without limitation of geography or subject matter, except where legislation has removed the possibility of enforcement under the common law.

The traditional principles of the common law can be summarised shortly. For a judgment to be entitled to be recognised as *res judicata* in England, it must be the final and conclusive judgment of the court which pronounced it, and it must have been given by a court[391] regarded by English law as being competent to do so. In order to be enforceable, it must also be for a fixed sum of money. A party who opposes the recognition of the judgment as *res judicata* may rely upon a number of defences for which the common law makes allowance or statute law superimposes.[392] So far as enforcement of foreign money judgments is concerned, the method of enforcement is to bring an action at common law on the judgment for the debt that the judgment creates, and then to seek summary judgment on the claim; but the irony, and the importance, of that is that the judgment creditor actually then enforces an English, and not the foreign, judgment.

In general the common law takes the view that it is irrelevant that the foreign court had, or did not have, jurisdiction according to its own domestic law. What matters is whether it had 'international jurisdiction' as this is defined by English private international law. The common law likewise takes the view that it is irrelevant that the foreign court decided the

---

391 The adjudicating body must be a court, but an English court will be slow to characterise a body which appears to be a regular part of a foreign legal system as being something other than a court, especially if its procedures appear to be judicial. *Cf Midland International Trade Services Ltd v. Al-Sudairy* (unreported, 11 April 1990; Saudi Chamber for Settlement of Commercial Paper Disputes held to be a court). *Cf Panamanian Oriental SS Corp v. Wright, 'The Anita'* [1971] 1 Lloyd's Rep 487. At first sight, the corresponding provision of Regulation 44/2001 – Art. 32 – is wider. But the exclusion of administrative matters and social security from the scope of the Regulation by Art. 1 much reduces the degree of dissimilarity. Nevertheless, if a State chooses to invest a specialist body with functions which include the adjudication of disputes (*cf* the Intellectual Property Office), there is no reason to consider its determinations of issues in disputes to be not the product of a court: *cf Future New Developments Ltd v. B&S Patente und Marken GmbH* [2014] EWHC 1874 (IPEC).

392 Administration of Justice Act 1920; Foreign Judgments (Reciprocal Enforcement) Act 1933.

case differently from the way an English court would have done. Once the foreign court has given a judgment which is entitled to recognition as a matter of common law, it is generally the case that proceedings may no longer be brought on the underlying cause of action, which is taken to be superseded by the foreign judgment: legislation provides that the underlying cause of action is spent.[393]

It is therefore necessary to examine three broad issues: first, the 'international jurisdictional' competence of the foreign court; second, the defences and other points of objection to recognition of the judgment; and third, the various consequences, as these affect the judgment creditor and the judgment debtor, of a judgment being entitled to recognition.

7.47 Recognition of judgments *in personam*: international jurisdictional competence of the foreign court

A judgment *in personam* will be recognised as binding on and against the party against whom it was given only if it was delivered by a court which, according to English private international law, was competent to deliver a judgment which has this effect in England. This requirement pays no attention to the jurisdictional rules of the foreign court, or to whether they were complied with.

In the case of a judgment against an individual defendant, this competence means that it must have been *either* a court within the jurisdiction of which the defendant was present when proceedings were instituted, *or* a court to the jurisdiction of which the defendant voluntarily submitted himself. Nothing more[394] is required; nothing less[395] will do. These alternative conditions will be examined in turn.

The application of this rule to judgments given against a corporation will be specially and separately noted, though the basic task is one of translating the requirements of the law to a different kind of defendant without significantly altering its meaning. Where one is concerned with judgments against a claimant, the same conditions, *mutatis mutandis*, are applied, but as the claimant will have submitted to the jurisdiction of the court by invoking that jurisdiction in the first place, they are easily met and, save for marginal issues,[396] need no further attention. This allows us to confine the analysis which follows to judgments against defendants.

---

393 Civil Jurisdiction and Judgments Act 1982, s. 34. This changed the rule of the common law: *Black v. Yates* [1992] 1 QB 526; *The Indian Grace* [1993] AC 410. The claimant now generally has only one bite at the cherry, unless the court is prepared to make an exception and, despite the judgment, to allow a second action on the underlying or original claim which it will be notably reluctant to do: see *The Indian Grace (No 2)* [1998] AC 878.

394 Not even, it seems, that the court had jurisdiction according to its own rules; see para. 7.65, below.

395 Even if the court did have jurisdiction according to its own rules.

396 There will be rare cases in which it may be argued that a claimant is bound by a judgment or settlement in class action proceedings, on the footing that he is within the scope of the settlement. The correct analysis of such a case is that the claimant will be so bound only if he submitted to the jurisdiction of the foreign court, a condition which, as will be shown, is defined by reference to English law; see further below, para. 7.52. See also *Rubin v. Eurofinance SA* [2012] UKSC 46, [2013] 1 AC 213, in which (in the conjoined appeal) there was held to be submission to the Australian court, though it is not clear whether this was by the judgment debtor as claimant, or as defendant, or in some other capacity.

7.48 Jurisdictional competence derived from presence: defendant present within the jurisdiction of the foreign court

Though the terminology never quite caught on in England, jurisdiction based on the fact of the defendant's physical presence within the territory of a court is widely known as 'tag' jurisdiction. This evidently reflects the sense, unshakeably lodged in the popular mind, that a writ is served when, and not served unless and until, it is used to touch the defendant, as though the process-server and the defendant were involved in an ancient playground game. The label is debatable, but the principle is clear: presence equates to international jurisdiction.

Until fairly recently, there was room for the view that the rule of jurisdictional competence required the defendant to be resident, rather than present, within the jurisdiction of the court.[397] It may be conceded that residence may indicate a stronger and more durable connection with a particular place than presence, which may be fleeting, and it may therefore be deduced that residence may be a more satisfactory basis for recognising a foreign judgment. In *Adams v. Cape Industries plc*,[398] however, the Court of Appeal held that the presence of the defendant was sufficient, leaving open the question whether residence without presence would also suffice.[399] The court suggested, though had no need to decide, that the relevant time was that of the service of process, this on the presumed footing that it represents the effective start of legal proceedings.[400]

The court observed that presence of a defendant was the traditional basis for the assertion and exercise of jurisdiction by an English court; that the power of a sovereign to summon[401] a defendant to court depended upon presence, not more; and that earlier cases[402] seemed to support it. If this point is to be seen as crucial to the judgment, it is fair to say that the analogy drawn in *Adams v. Cape* with the jurisdiction claimed by an English court is inexact. This is because as a matter of common law, jurisdiction will not be exercised if the defendant pleads and satisfies the doctrine of *forum non conveniens*,[403] this being part and parcel of the practical definition of the jurisdiction which an English court has. If it is accepted that presence forms the basis for the jurisdictional competence of a foreign court, parity of reasoning might suggest that this should not extend to the case in which the foreign court was a *forum non conveniens*. For it would surprise some to learn that English law recognises a foreign jurisdictional competence which was wider than that it claims to exercise for itself.

It is also correct to point out that the court was concerned with the presence of a corporation and, as will be seen below, what amounted to corporate presence was articulated in terms which feel rather more durable and grounded than the fleeting nature of presence may suggest.

---

397 See, for example, Dicey and Morris (as it then was), *The Conflict of Laws*, 11th edn, rule 37.

398 [1990] Ch 433.

399 At 518. In *State Bank of India v. Murjani Marketing Group Ltd* (unreported, 27 March 1991), the Court of Appeal stated, *obiter*, that residence without physical presence at the material time would still suffice to make the court jurisdictionally competent. Sir Christopher Slade suggested that such a defendant 'would be deemed to have continued presence' in the place; Taylor LJ noted that there was still scope for argument; and Fox LJ agreed with both. Of course, if the defendant elects to enter an appearance and submit to the jurisdiction, the point is academic.

400 At 518.

401 This, it thought, was the real basis for the recognition of a judgment. It appears to be a rather theoretical solution to a practical problem.

402 *Sirdar Gurdyal Singh v. Rajah of Faridkote* [1894] AC 670; *Carrick v. Hancock* (1895) 12 TLR 59.

403 See Chapter 4, above.

But the arguments in favour of presence are overwhelming, and the law should be taken to be completely settled. The principle of comity, according to which the rules of private international law respect and give effect to exercises of sovereign authority over things within the territorial jurisdiction of the sovereign, easily accepts that if a person is present with in the territory of a foreign sovereign, exercises of that authority over him should be respected and, within limits, given effect afterwards: what is true for things is true also for persons; territoriality is the very foundation of the common law rules of private international law.[404] Although theory may be out of fashion in some quarters, it explains this aspect of the common law perfectly.

And quite apart from theory, most people can tell where they are present, or were present, on any given day. It may be far more difficult to decide where someone is resident on the same day. Take the foreign student who is in Oxford during term, and back home in the vacation, or even on holiday during the vacation: where is he resident on Monday of the sixth week of term? In college? Probably. At home, overseas, where his things and family are? Possibly also. But in neither case is it certain. What of the person who is subject to immigration control but who has indefinite leave to remain: is he still resident in England if he goes overseas for a month? For three months? For a year? On a two-year secondment?

The purpose of the rule, so far as the common law is concerned, is to allow the reasonably well-informed defendant to be able to decide whether he should appear before and defend the proceedings brought against him before a foreign court. From that perspective, a legal test which asks whether he was resident in that country on the day the proceedings were instituted would be unfit for the purpose for which it were needed. No more should be heard of it. It may be well intentioned, but it is a Very Bad Idea.

7.49 Jurisdictional competence derived from presence: corporation present within the jurisdiction of the foreign court

Where the defendant is a corporation, the idea of its being present anywhere can be understood only in an attenuated form: corporations do not have physical presence, and those entities which have physical presence, such as individual corporate officers, may not 'be' the corporation for the purpose of this common law rule.

This was the precise issue before the court in *Adams v. Cape Industries plc*. The case was one in which the Cape organisation, whose business had been in asbestos, had arranged itself as a complex organisation, made up of a large number of associated companies. The parent company was sued in Texas, within the territorial jurisdiction of which one of these associated mining or processing companies was present.[405] The question for the English court was whether the presence of a local associated company was sufficient to allow the parent company to be regarded as present as well: the answer was that it was not.[406] The court

---

404 The occasional judicial denial that adjudication is an act of sovereign power is plainly wrong, but explicable where a court is seeking to rebut a contention that it has no jurisdiction to find fault with the foreign judgment, just as though the adjudication were an act of state: see *Yukos Capital Sarl v. OJSC Rosneft Oil Co* [2012] EWCA Civ 855, [2014] QB 458.

405 The basis on which, as a matter of Texas or US federal law, the US court had jurisdiction under its own law is not relevant to the issues before the English court on the question of recognition.

406 At least in the absence of evidence of fraud which would have justified lifting the veil of separate incorporation (as to which, now see *VTB Capital plc v. Nutritek International Corp* [2013] UKSC 5, [2013] 2 AC 337; *Prest v. Petrodel Resources Ltd* [2013] UKSC 34, [2013] 2 AC 415).

decided[407] that for a trading[408] corporation[409] to be regarded as present there must be either (a) servants of the corporation carrying on its business from a fixed place of business maintained by the corporation, or (b) a representative of the corporation carrying on the business of the corporation from a fixed place of business. In practice it is the second possibility which is the more difficult to apply. In order for the company to be present, the representative must carry on the business of the corporation, as distinct from his own business, even if he does his own business as well. Most indicative, though probably not decisive, will be his power, if any, to enter into contracts on behalf of the corporation without the need to submit them as proposals for decision-taking by another, elsewhere in the corporation. If he has this power, the corporation is almost certain to be held to carry on business in the fixed place where the representative concluded the contract; if not, this is very much less likely.[410]

Is it right that a corporation is not present within the territorial jurisdiction of a foreign court unless it maintains a fixed place of business there? It may be that the law laid down in *Adams v. Cape* reflects the way commercial business used to be done, rather than the way it is done today. It is not difficult to envisage cases where those who persuade their victims to enter into contracts carry out the business from private residences or sleazy hotel rooms. Should it readily be accepted that the organisation for whom they work was in such a case not present within the jurisdiction of the foreign court? Suppose an organisation carries on its business by electronic means, with a website accessible and intended to be accessible from a customer's computer. Is it really correct to say that it does not have a place of business in the places in which customers are roped into contracts because it has so delocalised or dematerialised its operations that it does not have a place of business at all? Some would argue that the corporation carries on business within the jurisdiction in which it makes contracts, and that this 'purposeful availment' of the particular jurisdiction, as it is described in the United States, is sufficient for the courts of that country to have international jurisdiction over the trading corporation defendant. Such a defendant may, just as the defendant who is present within the territorial jurisdiction of the foreign court, be thought to have laid himself open to being sued there, and to the enforcement of a judgment which came from the proceedings in a court to whose jurisdiction he had laid himself open. It is more than a little galling to watch while a defendant which has taken advantage of a market now claims to have been absent from it throughout.

Yet a pragmatic defence of *Adams v. Cape* as it applies to corporations is easy. It will tend to reduce the number of places in which the corporation is regarded as present. As a matter of common law, the consequence of finding the corporation to be present is that a judgment from the courts of that country will be recognised, even though the claim had nothing to do with that country or with the business which the corporation did in that country. If that is the effect of presence, it is only reasonable that there should be a reasonably strong, as opposed to a fleeting, connection to that country: as the consequences are so dramatic, the connection needs to be robust enough to warrant them.

---

407 At 519–531. See also *Littauer Glove Corporation v. FW Millington (1920) Ltd* (1928) 44 TLR 746, and *Okura & Co Ltd v. Forsbacka Jernverks AB* [1914] 1 KB 715.

408 The rule was formulated for a trading corporation, but was said to apply equally to non-trading corporations: see 524. Even so, the translation from the one to the other will not be straightforward. For if one substitutes 'holding' for 'trading', it is not clear how the principle would apply.

409 In this case, the rule was developed to determine whether Cape plc was present within Texas.

410 At 531. And see *Jabbour v. Custodian of Israeli Absentee Property* [1954] 1 WLR 139. It is sometimes said that if the local representative *makes* contracts, the corporation will be carrying on business, but if he *sells* contracts made elsewhere, it will not be.

In the end, the analysis of the relationship between the corporation and the individuals present within the jurisdiction will often be intricate and case-specific: corporate structures may be complex, and some are designed to avoid the legal consequences which a reasonable man might have expected to be able to have drawn. Some are designed to ensure that although an entity is present within the jurisdiction, it has no assets, and the part of the organisation which has the assets is not present within the jurisdiction of a court in which proceedings are likely to be brought. Indeed, the business organisation shown in *Adams v. Cape plc*, which is common in but not unique to that malign industry, may have been an example of this. This has led some legal systems, particularly in the United States, to consider a company to be present where or wherever an entity which forms a part of the same economic group is present, or to be present wherever its '*alter ego*' may be found to be present. English law, more respectful of separate corporate personality and distinct corporate presences, and more wary of altering the law to the ultimate disadvantage of English trading corporations, has rejected such reasoning. It may yet be that reform is required as a matter of social necessity, but will need to come in the form of legislation.

7.50 Jurisdictional competence derived from presence: federal States and complex countries

In cases which depend upon the presence of the defendant within the jurisdiction of the foreign court, and where this question arises within the context of a federation, it appears[411] that he must be present within the State if sued in the State court, and present within the federation if sued in a federal court. To the extent that the rule depends upon the territorial power of the summoning court, this makes some sense, even if it may appear to lead to capricious results. But it is important to note the limits of this principle. If the defendant is sued in the court in city A when, as a matter of local law, he should have been sued in the court in city B, this raises only a question of local, as distinct from international, jurisdiction; and the error does not affect the question of whether the defendant was present within the jurisdiction of the courts of the *country*.[412]

7.51 Jurisdictional competence derived from submission: defendant submitted to the jurisdiction of the foreign court

As an alternative to his being present, the defendant may have submitted to the jurisdiction of the court. If he did, he is bound to accept and abide by its decision on the merits: *volenti non fit injuria*.

For those who are comforted by the support of a theoretical explanation, one comes quickly to hand. The defendant will not have been present within the territorial jurisdiction of the foreign court, with the result that the principles of comity and territoriality do not require him to abide by the judgment. But if has made an agreement with the

---

411 The court in *Adams v. Cape* did not need to decide the point, but inclined to support the propositions set out here, at 557. What is said here about presence within a country will apply, *mutatis mutandis*, to the alternative jurisdictional basis of submission.

412 It is arguable that a different principle may operate if it be alleged that the defendant *submitted* by contract to the court for city A, and not to the court for city B, where he was sued: *SA Consortium General Textiles v. Sun & Sand Agencies Ltd* [1978] QB 279.

claimant – and all the instances examined under the rubric of submission are cases of agreement with the claimant – to settle their differences before, and to abide by the judgment of, the foreign court, he may be held to that bilateral agreement, and it may be enforced against him. The English court may not enforce the judgment, but as it never actually does, one should not worry too much about that. But it can enforce the parties' bilateral agreement to abide by the judgment of the court.[413]

With that short introduction, it is necessary to distinguish three versions of submission by a defendant to the jurisdiction of the foreign court.

7.52 Jurisdictional competence derived from submission: submission by voluntary appearance

If the defendant appears[414] and defends the merits of the claim he will, in general,[415] be held to have submitted to the jurisdiction of the court. Whether he has submitted by virtue of his voluntary appearance, or by his participation in the action, is in the first place determined by recourse to the common law, though, as will be seen, statute[416] has intervened to establish or confirm the non-submissive character of three particular kinds of act. As a matter of theory, the service of the summons may be seen as an offer by the claimant to accept the jurisdiction and adjudication of the foreign court. If by his words or conduct the defendant accepts it, the common law considers that he is liable to be held to the foreign judgment when it is handed down.

To decide whether the acts of the defendant constituted a submission, the point of departure is to ask whether the defendant took a step in the action which showed an intention to contest the merits before the foreign court.[417] If he did, this will be seen as a submission to the jurisdiction of the court.[418] The court may also ask the question the other way round: were the acts of the defendant 'obviously and objectively inconsistent'[419] with his submission to the jurisdiction of the foreign court? If they were, they should not be seen as

---

413 *Penn v. Baltimore* (1750) 1 Ves Sen 444.

414 For the suggestion that if he makes an attempt to appear but fails to take the requisite steps, there is no submission: *De Santis v. Russo* [2002] 2 Qd R 230.

415 Unless s. 33 of the 1982 Act may apply. See *Marc Rich & Co AG v. Soc Italiana Impianti PA (No 2)* [1992] 1 Lloyd's Rep 624; *State Bank of India v. Murjani* (unreported, 27 March 1991).

416 Civil Jurisdiction and Judgments Act 1982, s. 33.

417 This was the test used prior to the coming into force of the Civil Procedure Rules to determine whether a defendant had submitted to the jurisdiction of the English courts. It is probably still viable, though the actual wording of CPR Part 11 (discussed at para. 5.29, above) now raises some difficulty.

418 There is no clear authority for the view that a defendant can submit to part of a claim but not to some other parts of it. As a matter of English law, a defendant must acknowledge service of process (and submit to the jurisdiction, unless he disputes the jurisdiction pursuant to CPR Part 11) or not acknowledge it at all. If he is willing to submit to some but not all, he must dispute jurisdiction under CPR Part 11 and, after the disposal of his application, decide whether to acknowledge service in relation to the whole of the (but possibly now amended) claim form. It is not, therefore, possible to contend for partial submission by analogy with English proceedings; and it is submitted that it would produce all manner of difficulty if a defendant were entitled to plead that his submission to the causes of action pleaded in the foreign document was partial and was not general. See, for some support, *Marc Rich & Co AG v. Soc Italiana Impianti PA (No 2)* [1992] 1 Lloyd's Rep 624, 633. Submission in relation to additions and amendments to the original claim form is examined below.

419 *Akai Pty Ltd v. People's Insurance Co Ltd* [1998] 1 Lloyd's Rep 90, 97–98; *Advent Capital plc v. GN Ellinas Imports-Exports Ltd* [2005] EWHC 1242 (Comm), [2005] 2 Lloyd's Rep 607, [78] (question is whether defendant acted in a way which was only necessary or useful if no objection were taken to the jurisdiction of the foreign court).

submission to the adjudicatory jurisdiction of the foreign court. The principle is an objective one, which asks whether the response of the defendant to the service of process gives the objective appearance of a defendant accepting the invitation to accept the jurisdiction of the court as binding. Obviously the hardest cases are those in which the appearance which the defendant gives is an ambivalent one.

In principle, at least, an act should not be interpreted as a submission if it would not be so regarded under the law of the foreign court. It would be surprising if an act or response were to be regarded as submission to a court which did not consider itself to have been submitted to.[420] But this point should not be pressed too far, not least because a foreign court's concept of submission may be quite different from that of English law.

7.53 Jurisdictional competence derived from submission: development of a more flexible approach

Although the point that an act taken before a foreign court should not be seen as a submission by voluntary appearance if the foreign court would not interpret it that way was accepted by the Supreme Court in *Rubin v. Eurofinance SA*,[421] the court still concluded (in the part of its judgment dealing with the conjoined appeal) that a defendant had submitted to the insolvency jurisdiction of an Australian court by lodging a claim for payment in the administration. The surprising[422] thing about its conclusion was that the Australian court itself did not appear to consider that the defendant had submitted to its jurisdiction,[423] and the submission was found to have been made, not in response to a writ of summons but by lodging with the administrator a claim for payment out of the insolvent estate. The significance of this will need to be tested to see whether it makes a particular point about participation in insolvency proceedings, or represents a more creative approach to the concept of submission for the purpose of recognition of foreign judgments.

It is true that the administrator is appointed by and is answerable to a court; but the administrator represents, or embodies, the company, and to tell a company that it owes you money, even if this is done by affidavit, is far from submitting to the jurisdiction of a court in respect of a claim in legal proceedings which has not yet been formulated, never mind issued. It is therefore possible to have doubts about this aspect of the decision in *Rubin*: it certainly raises important and fundamental issues.

One certainly sees that when a claim is lodged in an insolvency there is plainly submission to something, or a submission for some purpose, such as the power of the insolvency

---

420 *Adams v. Cape Industries plc* [1990] Ch 433, 461 (aff'd on other grounds, *ibid.* 503); *The Eastern Trader* [1996] 2 Lloyd's Rep 585, 599–601; *Akai Pty Ltd v. People's Insurance Co Ltd* [1998] 1 Lloyd's Rep 90, 97.

421 [2012] UKSC 46, [2013] 1 AC 236. The issue did not arise in relation to *Rubin*, but in the conjoined appeal in *New Cap Reinsurance Corp v. Grant*. See also (expressing the view that the submission of a claim is not necessarily a submission to the foreign court, but that it all depends on the circumstances) *Erste Group Bank AG v. JSC 'VMZ Red October'* [2013] EWHC 2926 (Comm); *Akers v. Deputy Commissioner of Taxation* [2014] FCAFC 57 (court was prepared to assume that the Commissioner's participation in foreign insolvency was a submission to the foreign court, but held that this did not preclude an appearance before the Australian court to oppose claim by liquidator that Australian assets be remitted to the foreign insolvency).

422 The Privy Council in *Stichting Shell Pensioenfonds v. Krys* [2014] UKPC 41, [2015] 2 WLR 289 (also an insolvency case, but not one concerned with the recognition of foreign judgments) did not find it surprising at all, but for reasons developed in this paragraph, the description is not unjustified.

423 Service out of the Australian jurisdiction was considered to be justified on several grounds but which did not include submission to the jurisdiction of the court.

court to make orders.[424] It does not, however, necessarily follow that the 'submission' in this sense is one which leads to the recognition of a foreign judgment given in proceedings on a claim that had not even been made at the date of the alleged submission. In general, it is by the issue and service of a writ that a claimant steps into the legal arena; and in this case the person against whom the judgment was eventually given had not done any such thing. It is by making a response to the service of a writ upon him that a defendant submits, by conduct if not also by words, to the jurisdiction of a court over the matter set out in the writ; it was not in dispute that the person against whom the judgment had been given had not responded to the writ in any way which could be regarded as a voluntary submission. The proposition that there had been a submission to the jurisdiction of the Australian court was, therefore, a rather surprising one.

An alternative analysis might be that the submission is of a different kind: not submission by appearance, but submission by agreement, this being with the other creditors, as though by some form of multipartite contract, to submit to and abide by the insolvency procedure (and all of it) which will be supervised by the foreign court. The conclusion to which this directly leads is that the insolvency court becomes entitled to make orders against the creditor; but once again, it does not necessarily follow that those orders are entitled to recognition as foreign judgments from a court to whose jurisdiction the creditor has submitted, or that submission has a uniform meaning and a universal consequence.[425]

The truth probably is that there are different kinds of submission, or submissions made for different purposes, and that to submit in one particular sense is not to submit for all purposes for which 'submission' is an element of the law. No doubt it is true that the judgment in *Rubin* may reflect a deeper and resonant truth, that the party who claimed that money was owed to him was seeking to have his cake and eat it; to take the plums and leave the duff. He notified a claim in the insolvency administration, but claimed to be untouched by a demand for payment made as part – as a later part, but still as a part – of the same overall process. It may follow that *Rubin*[426] can and, despite what the court said to the effect that the law on foreign judgments given in insolvency proceedings should not be any different from the general law on the effect of foreign judgments, should be confined to the particular context of insolvency, where it may be more illuminating to speak of participation in a process, as distinct from submission to the jurisdiction of a court, as the touchstone for giving effect to foreign judgments. If it is not accepted, and if this aspect of the judgment in *Rubin* has a wider and more general effect, it will mark an increased flexibility in the assessment of whether there has been a submission, according to which a person may be held to have submitted if it would be unconscionable for him to plead that he had not submitted to the jurisdiction of the foreign court. That has an attraction, but it will tend to make the law uncertain at a point at which certainty is a real need.

---

424 *Ex parte Robertson, Re Morton* (1875) LR 20 Eq 333; *Stichting Shell Pensioenfonds v. Krys* [2014] UKPC 41, [2015] 2 WLR 289.

425 *Cf Akers v. Deputy Commissioner for Taxation* [2014] FCAFC 57 (holding that even if the lodging of a proof in a foreign insolvency was a submission to the foreign insolvency court, it did not debar or prevent an application to the local court for relief which it had jurisdiction to grant).

426 And, at this point, *Stichting Shell Pensioenfonds v. Krys* [2014] UKPC 41, [2015] 2 WLR 289.

7.54 Jurisdictional competence derived from submission: appearance followed by amendment of claim

One view of the issue of submission in *Rubin* would be to see it as a case in which a party takes a limited step into a foreign arena, only to find when he has done so that a much larger claim is made against him, with the consequence that although he went in for a penny, he finds that he is in for a pound. If the defendant decided to submit to the jurisdiction of the foreign court, but after he has done so the claimant succeeds in having a new cause of action added to the claim, or another party succeeds in being joined as co-claimant, it may be too late for the defendant to reconsider his position and undo the submission already made.[427] The question is whether he is to be taken to have submitted to the enlarged claim.

It appears that a pragmatic view is to be adopted: if the new claim arises out of the same subject matter as the original claim, or is related to it, the original submission will be likely to extend to it as well. If it is not so related, it will not and, to this extent, the defendant will be entitled to argue in England, if his actions are aligned with the contention, that he submitted to the original, but not to the later, claims made against him.[428] This is more generous to the defendant than the alternative view that when a person submits to the jurisdiction of a court, he submits to all the procedural possibilities, including the adding of parties and claims, which the procedural law of the foreign court allows. But so wide a view of what submission extends to has not yet found favour in England (unless *Rubin* is held to stand for it) and there is good reason to think that it should not, for it would tend to encourage defendants to allow proceedings to go by default, which would not be in the public interest.

A defendant who did not initially submit may, if he subsequently seeks to appeal against a judgment, be taken to submit to the adjudicatory jurisdiction of the court with retrospective effect, and in this sense to throw away his common law shield. The material question will be whether the part played by the defendant after the original judgment was entered was a submission, albeit made late in the day, or was rather an assertion that the judgment which was entered should not have been because the foreign court should have realised that it had no jurisdiction. In the latter case, the appearance should not be taken as a submission to the jurisdiction: the subject matter of the application is a challenge to the jurisdiction, of which the setting aside of the judgment is a legal consequence.[429] But in the former case, the defendant submits to the adjudicatory jurisdiction of the foreign court after all,[430] for in engaging with the merits of the judgment, he necessarily asks the court to adjudicate on those merits. It is all a question of objective appearance, as in the common law it so often is.

---

427 A similar problem confronts a defendant to English proceedings who accepted service of a process in respect of which permission would have been needed to serve it out of the jurisdiction, but who, having accepted service, finds that the claimant seeks to amend and add claims which, had they been included in the original claim form, would have led the defendant to dispute the jurisdiction, or to refuse to accept service within the jurisdiction: see above, para. 4.54.

428 The question is one of fact and degree: *Murthy v. Sivajothi* [1999] 1 WLR 467. The fact that the foreign court applied a similar test in deciding to allow amendment or joinder is not decisive. It may be possible to use this case to contend that a defendant submitted to only part of the claim as originally drafted but, for the reasons given above, this would be an inconvenient result, and one not dictated (though not contradicted) by *Murthy*.

429 The case may in any event be covered by Civil Jurisdiction and Judgments Act 1982, s. 33. See also *Desert Sun Loan Corp v. Hill* [1996] 2 All ER 847.

430 *Guiard v. De Clermont* [1914] 3 KB 145; see also *Karafarin Bank v. Mansoury-Dara* [2009] EWHC 1217 (Comm), [2009] 2 Lloyd's Rep 289.

7.55 Jurisdictional competence derived from submission: appearance protected from being counted as submission by Civil Jurisdiction and Judgments Act 1982, section 33

If the defendant has done something which, looked at in isolation, would be taken to be a submission to the jurisdiction of the foreign court, statute may contradict this answer and provide that he is not to be taken to have submitted after all. There are, therefore, two steps to consider: whether the defendant submitted as a matter of common law definition, and if he did, then whether the Act relieves this of the consequences which would otherwise follow as a matter of common law. But it makes sense to concentrate on section 33, for if it does apply, the question whether the common law would have considered the defendant to have submitted to the jurisdiction of the foreign court does not really matter.

Section 33 was enacted when the common law appeared to have taken an extremely doctrinaire view of what counted as submission: it appears that Parliament intervened rather than wait an indeterminate period before the House of Lords could put the law back on the rails. But as the common law on submission has become more balanced, the work for section 33 to do has lessened. It says:

> **33. Certain steps not to amount to submission to jurisdiction of overseas court** (1) For the purposes of determining whether a judgment given by a court of an overseas country should be recognised or enforced in England and Wales or Northern Ireland, the person against whom the judgment was given shall not be regarded as having submitted to the jurisdiction of the court by reason only of the fact that he appeared (conditionally or otherwise) in the proceedings for all or any one or more of the following purposes, namely (a) to contest the jurisdiction of the court; (b) to ask the court to dismiss or stay the proceedings on the ground that the dispute in question should be submitted to arbitration or to the determination of the courts of another country; (c) to protect, or obtain the release of, property seized or threatened with seizure in the proceedings...

Section 33 was the legislative response to *Henry v. Geoprosco International*,[431] in which a defendant who appeared before a Canadian court to apply for a stay in favour of arbitration was taken to have conceded the technical existence of jurisdiction, and hence to have submitted to the jurisdiction of the court. The Court of Appeal, in this arid decision, reasoned that if a court is asked to not exercise a jurisdictional discretion which it has, the person making the application has already conceded that the court has jurisdiction, and has therefore submitted. The logic is the kind of thing that gets lawyers a bad name. But in similar vein, the Court of Appeal held that a defendant who applied to the English courts for a stay of proceedings on the ground of *forum non conveniens* was not making a challenge to the jurisdiction: it did not expressly state that the application connoted a submission, though the inference is there to be drawn.[432]

In coming to this conclusion, the Court of Appeal had turned its back on the realism of Denning LJ in *Re Dulles Settlement (No 2)*,[433] in which he had said that he could not see that 'anyone can fairly say that a man has voluntarily submitted to the jurisdiction of a court when he has all the time been vigorously protesting that it has no jurisdiction. If he does nothing and lets judgment go against him in default of appearance he clearly does not submit to its

---

431 [1976] QB 726. For a decision not following *Henry v. Geoprosco International* in the context of appearing for a stay in favour of arbitration, see *WSG Nimbus Pte Ltd v. Board of Control for Cricket in Sri Lanka* [2002] 3 Sing LR 603.

432 *The Messiniaki Tolmi* [1984] 1 Lloyd's Rep 266: the case was not about foreign judgments, but about the procedural nature of the application to the English court.

433 [1951] Ch 842.

jurisdiction. What difference in principle does it make if he does not merely do nothing but actually goes to the court and protests that it has no jurisdiction? I can see no distinction at all'. The view of Denning LJ seemed unanswerable; moreover there seemed to be no useful distinction between the defendant who appeared before a foreign court to argue that it had no jurisdiction, to argue that it had been wrong to allow the claimant to invoke its jurisdiction and should now set service aside, or to argue that whatever jurisdiction it might have under its law, it should not exercise it, and should not adjudicate the merits.

The House of Lords, perhaps influenced by section 33, soon took a more nuanced view of applications which a defendant in proceedings in the English courts might make: it was to be supposed that, had the opportunity arisen, it would have applied the same corrective sense to the case of a defendant appearing before a foreign court. In *Williams & Glyn's Bank v. Astro Dinamico*,[434] it drew a distinction between submission to an English court for the purpose of determination of the limits of its exercisable jurisdiction, and submission to an English court to decide the merits. In its opinion, to submit in the first sense was not to submit for the purpose of the second. This decision pointed the law in a much better direction. It makes it possible to ask whether, if section 33 had not been enacted to do the job which needed to be done more immediately than the courts might have been able to do it, *Henry v. Geoprosco International* would have been overruled in any event. It certainly deserved to be. But Parliament got there first.

For the purposes of section 33 of the 1982 Act, it is the *purpose* for which the defendant appears which is decisive, not the procedural nature of the steps which were actually taken. If, for example, local law advises or requires[435] a defendant to file a defence dealing with the merits of the claim prior to or together with any challenge to the jurisdiction, the filing of an omnibus defence is not necessarily inconsistent with the contention that the *purpose* of the appearance was only one of those set out in section 33.

Section 33 protects defendants whose only purpose in making whatever appearance they do make is to seek relief on jurisdictional grounds, and who do only no more than is necessary to support and prosecute their jurisdictional challenge or stay application.[436] On the other hand, if the challenge is made but then not prosecuted or proceeded with, it will risk being seen to have been waived,[437] and the submission otherwise made will remain effective as a matter of English law.

No case has yet examined the precise meaning of 'the jurisdiction' which it must be the defendant's purpose to contest. The issue should have arisen, and maybe did arise, in *Desert Sun Loan Corp v. Hill*.[438] In that case, judgment had been entered against a defendant by a court in Arizona. He then appeared to argue that the lawyer who had purported to represent him had authority neither to accept service of process on his behalf, nor to appear in court on his behalf, and that as a result the court had no jurisdiction over him, and that as a further result, the default judgment should be set aside. The application failed. The claimant sought to enforce the default judgment in England, and the material question was whether

---

434 [1984] 1 WLR 438.

435 Or, equally, if it makes it ill advised for the defendant not to enter his defence, because he will need to seek leave to do so at a later date.

436 In *Marc Rich & Co AG v. Soc Italiana Impianti PA (No 2)* [1992] 1 Lloyd's Rep 624, it was stated by the Court of Appeal that s. 33 was not intended to have a narrow or limited construction: see at 633. See also *The Eastern Trader* [1996] 2 Lloyd's Rep 585.

437 *Starlight International Inc v. Bruce* [2002] EWHC 374 (Ch), [2002] ILPr 617.

438 [1996] 2 All ER 847.

the defendant had submitted to the jurisdiction of the Arizona court. Roch LJ accepted that the defendant was protected from an allegation that he had submitted to the jurisdiction of the court by section 33(1)(a), and that no estoppel could therefore arise from the Arizona judgment on the issue of whether he had submitted in the earlier proceedings. The majority, however, did not refer to section 33, from which it seems safe to deduce that they considered it to be inapplicable.

The question therefore arises whether the purpose for which the defendant appeared was to contend that the court had no jurisdiction over him. It may be that a defendant who appears and who makes such an argument about the validity and scope of powers of attorney, rather than anything else, is certainly seeking to have the judgment set aside, and that without regard to the merits of the claim. It is not quite so clear that his (only) purpose in appearing before the court can be said to be to contest the jurisdiction of the court. It is true that a decision on jurisdiction may be the consequence of the appearance, but the purpose might just be said to be to obtain a ruling on the true construction of a power of attorney. On clear balance, though, the view of Roch LJ is to be preferred.

If a defendant appears to argue that the case should be heard in another court within the same country, but does not challenge or object to the international jurisdiction of the courts of the country, it is less easy to argue that section 33(1)(a) is engaged. The answer is not made explicit in the section, but to concede that the courts of a country *do* have jurisdiction, and to confine the argument to which courts of that country do and do not have jurisdiction, is not the pattern of fact for which section 33(1) was drafted. English private international law does not usually concern itself with a foreign court's local or internal jurisdiction; and if a defendant appears to make an argument which does not really bear on the international jurisdiction of courts, section 33(1)(a) may be held not to apply.[439]

7.56 Jurisdictional competence derived from submission: steps taken in the foreign proceedings which convey a mixed message

English procedural law is easy and clear, and if the rest of the world was modelled on it, litigation would in one respect be a good deal easier than it is. In England, a challenge to the jurisdiction of the court will be heard and finally determined before the defendant is called upon to take any step towards defending the merits of the claim. The English approach to submission in general, and section 33 in particular, assumes that this is the model which applies in foreign courts as well.

But other courts may order their procedural law differently, and when they do, the application of the English law of submission, and of section 33, can be problematic. And it should not for a moment be thought that the English approach is preferable to that found in other places. A court may very quickly see that the issues which go to jurisdiction – whether a contract was made, for example – also underpin the claim on the merits. The idea that a court should hold a set of hearings to answer certain questions once, only to hold a second set of hearings which cover much the same ground, but this time for a non-jurisdictional purpose, will not strike everyone as proportionate and rational. A court which says that a defendant may certainly challenge the jurisdiction, but that this does not arrest progress towards the trial of the merits, may not be doing things the English way, but it does things

---

439 *Cf Future New Developments Ltd v. B&S Patente und Marken GmbH* [2014] EWHC 1874 (IPEC).

in a perfectly sensible manner. When the English rules of private international law of submission, including section 33, come face to face with such procedures, it is not the fault of the foreign system that the answers to the questions which English law asks may be hard to fathom. It may be that the questions are not apt.

Three patterns may be taken for illustrative purposes. First, in some jurisdictions a defendant may issue a motion for the case to be dismissed on jurisdictional grounds, but in the meantime, and before the motion is called on for hearing, find that he is subjected to active case management by way of preparation for the trial of the merits. He may be required to give discovery of documents, to allow his employees or witnesses to be subjected to deposition, and so forth. All this may be demanded of him, even though the motion to dismiss has been issued and has not yet been dismissed. The question is what the defendant can safely do without being held to have submitted to the jurisdiction of the foreign court.

Second, in some jurisdictions a court may decide to deal with the defence that it has no jurisdiction only at trial, not in advance, and that it will rule on the jurisdictional defence in its judgment, and not in advance of the hearing. The defendant may then participate fully in the trial, always maintaining his jurisdictional defence. If he does so, the question is whether he submits as a matter of common law, and if he does, whether he is protected by section 33(1) from having been held to submit.

Third, a foreign court may deal with and reject a challenge to its jurisdiction, and then hear the merits of the claimant's claim, the position being that some form of appeal, on jurisdiction as well as merits may be heard by an appellate court at that point. If the defendant participates in the hearing of the merits of the claim, but still aspires to appeal on jurisdiction, the question is whether he submits as a matter of common law, and if he does, whether he is protected by section 33(1) from having been held to submit.

The authorities are not yet as clear as one might hope for. The view taken here is that as there is no clear answer in the statute or the cases, a court may guide itself by principles of common law common sense, in particular principles such as estoppel by representation. According to this, if a defendant who had raised a jurisdictional defence represents that he has abandoned it, he will thereafter be taken to have submitted to the jurisdiction. As has been said, if a defendant loses on jurisdiction and then goes on to defend the merits, it is easy to interpret what he is saying and doing as an abandoning of the jurisdictional objection. But if the true position is that he does not appear to have abandoned it, and that his outward conduct does not suggest that the defence, originally raised, is now no longer being pursued, then he has not submitted, even if it is also true that he has participated in proceedings directed to the substance of the claim. If this means that a defendant may be able to have his cake and eat it too – to win on the merits, but if he loses, to appeal on jurisdiction, and if he loses on jurisdiction, to claim to be not bound at all – that is just too bad. The defendant did not choose the court into which he was haled, and if the procedural law of that court is organised in such a way that the defendant is allowed to object to the jurisdiction while also trying to win on the merits of the dispute, then as long as he is able to say that his original purpose in appearing was to contest the jurisdiction, unless he appears to have abandoned that contest, and brought that purpose to an end, he should still be safe. Otherwise the answer to the question whether the defendant submitted will vary from court to court, even though in every case the defendant is doing everything he reasonably can to keep his jurisdictional challenge alive and viable. It is hard to think that such variation is what Parliament had in mind when it enacted section 33; and it is equally hard to see that the common law should say that, in any of these cases, the unwilling participation in steps in an unlooked-for procedure running alongside the jurisdictional challenge, there had been submission to the jurisdiction of the foreign court.

It is nevertheless clear that even if the law on submission, and section 33 itself, is ultimately given a pragmatic construction, a defendant may find himself manoeuvred into having to take, or choosing to take, or just taking, steps in the foreign proceedings as a result of which he runs a risk of being accused of having cast away his right to argue that he has, as a matter of English law, not submitted to the jurisdiction of the foreign court. There is no guarantee to be given, save to say that in such cases, all contemporary correspondence, and pleadings filed with the court, which make it objectively clear that participation has the aim of keeping the jurisdictional challenge alive for hearing and purposeful for appeal thereafter, may well be helpful,[440] and may even prove to be decisive.[441] Above all, the English court should be aware of the practicalities of the situation in which the defendant found himself, and should be slow to find a submission where the defendant made it clear that he had done nothing to relinquish his jurisdictional objection.[442]

7.57 Jurisdictional competence derived from submission: submission by prior agreement to appear

If a contract provides that a foreign court[443] is to have jurisdiction to determine a dispute, that court is likely to be recognised as jurisdictionally competent as a matter of English law.[444] If on its proper construction the contractual term applies to the action brought, the judgment in that action is liable on this account to be recognised. If the contractual term does not apply to the foreign proceedings, having subscribed to the clause will not itself constitute the submission of the defendant. It follows that the arguments which are material when interpreting the scope of the clause and its relationship to the claim brought in the foreign proceedings, the question of its validity in circumstances in which that it open to challenge, the issue of whether it is a submission to the courts of a country or to a particular court only, are all as applicable here as they are when the same or similar issues arise on a jurisdictional application.

---

440 One remote possibility might be to bring proceedings in an English court for a declaration that he will not be held to have been submitted. But the chances of getting this heard in time will be small, even if the court is inclined to cooperate. Another might be to resist recognition of the judgment, if he is held to have submitted, on the ground that the lack of an opportunity to make a jurisdictional challenge without submission involves a breach of the rules of natural justice. But there is no strong basis for this in decided cases, even if the argument is not wholly far-fetched. *Cf Amchem Products Inc v. British Columbia (Workers' Compensation Board)* [1993] 1 SCR 897.

441 *Lubrizol Corp v. Esso Petroleum Co Ltd* [1992] RPC 467, 470: a splendidly clear and direct judgment, entirely aligned with the approach proposed here.

442 *AES Ust-Kamenogorsk Hydropower Plant LLP v. AES Ust-Kamenogorsk Hydropower Plant JSC* [2013] UKSC 35, [2013] 1 WLR 1889. The judge at first instance had said, very acutely, that the defendants had not submitted to the foreign court because it could not be said of them that they had failed in their jurisdictional challenge but had gone on to fight the claim on its merits. Neither were they trying to have their cake and eat it. They were trying to prevent the exercise of jurisdiction by the foreign court, and it was absurd to suggest that they were somehow submitting to its jurisdiction.

443 Whether the contractual submission is to courts generally, or to a specific court, in a country is a matter of construction. If the latter, and the claim is brought in a different court, the clause will not constitute submission, but the defendant's voluntary appearance still may. See *SA Consortium General Textiles v. Sun & Sand Agencies Ltd* [1978] QB 279.

444 The same is true if the contract stipulates that the defendant will accept service at an address within the jurisdiction.

It will have been seen that, for the purpose of a jurisdictional application, the current practice of the English courts is to regard the agreement on jurisdiction as severable from the remainder of the contractual or other relationship between the parties, and to give effect to the jurisdiction (or arbitration) clause even though there is a genuine issue between the parties as to the validity of the substantive contract by which the parties are said to be bound. There is, in some sense, a strong presumption that the parties intended the nominated court to have jurisdiction to determine the validity of the contract of which the dispute-resolution provision was, in some sense, a term. It would make sense for the same approach to be taken when asking whether the foreign court was one to which the defendant submitted by agreement. It is perfectly possible to agree to submit to a foreign court in circumstances in which the validity of the contract is going to be denied. It follows that the broad approach of the House of Lords in *Fiona Trust & Holding Corp v. Privalov*[445] should be presumed to be applicable when the question is whether there was submission by agreement to the jurisdiction of a foreign court. In principle the question is simple: did the parties agree with each other that the court in question was to have jurisdiction to determine the question which it has now determined? The answer may be liable to complication (and it may well be different from the question whether the agreement of the parties actually gave the foreign court jurisdiction under its own law), but the principle is clear.

Similarly, if a defendant has bailed goods to a bailee, on terms that there may be a sub-bailment on any terms, it has been held that a jurisdiction agreement in the sub-bailment is effective to govern jurisdiction in an action between the bailor and sub-bailee.[446] If such an arrangement suffices to confer jurisdiction on the nominated court, and to justify a stay of English proceedings brought inconsistently with it, it is right in principle that a judgment from that court should be recognised as being from a court to which the bailor had submitted by agreement. Such a case may look more like one of implied agreement than an express one, but the principled response to that should be that there is no sharp line dividing up the varieties of agreement to accept the adjudication of a court into those which count and those which do not: the question is simply whether there was (enough of an) agreement to accept the jurisdiction and decision of the court in respect of the claim made. To make the law any more complicated than that seems unnecessary.

If the foreign court has ruled that the dispute falls within the scope of the agreement, then it may be asked whether that decision is conclusive if the question arises subsequently before an English court. In principle, the foreign decision upon this point will not prejudice the defendant if all that he did was to appear before the court to contend that the foreign court did not have jurisdiction;[447] his position cannot be worse than if he has failed to appear at all.[448] After all, to appear to argue that the contractual clause does not give the court jurisdiction is only one way, among many, of being sheltered by section 33 of the 1982 Act. It

---

445 [2007] UKHL 40, [2007] Bus LR 1719; and see further above, paras 4.42 *et seq.*
446 *The Pioneer Container* [1994] 2 AC 324.
447 Section 33 of the 1982 Act.
448 This, though reasonable, cannot be deduced from s. 33 of the 1982 Act. The answer may be that in submitting certain actions to the jurisdiction of the courts, the defendant does not submit to the court upon the preliminary interpretation of the clause unless he voluntarily appears in order to do so. The decision reached by the court without his appearance is not, on that account, liable to be recognised as against him, and the English court may decide for itself whether he did contractually submit. For the argument that if a party has sued as claimant in the foreign court, he did submit to the foreign court upon the construction of the clause, and is bound by its determination, see *The Sennar (No 2)* [1985] 1 WLR 104.

might be argued that if the defendant has expressly asked the foreign court to construe the jurisdiction clause and grant relief on the basis of it, he should be estopped from denying the conclusion reached by that court in later proceedings to enforce the judgment, on the ground that he elected, voluntarily, to submit this particular question to the foreign court, and that he is, on that account, bound by the decision of the court whose jurisdiction he invoked on the particular point he brought before it. But notwithstanding *Desert Sun Loan Co v. Hill*,[449] this proposition does not stand up to serious scrutiny, for if the defendant were to be estopped in such a case from challenging the decision of the adjudicating court that he had submitted by contract to its jurisdiction, section 33(1)(a) would be deprived of a substantial part of its effect.

In *Desert Sun Loan Co v. Hill*,[450] the defendant had appeared before a foreign court to argue that it had no personal jurisdiction over him because the lawyer who had purported to accept service and to appear on his behalf had had no authority to do so, seeking as relief the setting aside of a default judgment which had been entered against him. The majority were prepared to accept that he might be estopped from challenging the conclusion of the court on the very point on which he had asked, unsuccessfully, for a decision in his favour. This is barely comprehensible. The defendant appeared before the court to contest the jurisdiction and to seek consequential relief. If the majority were to have been correct, he would be prevented from doing the very thing which section 33 expressly permits him to do. If it were to be objected, in opposition to the view preferred here, that the defendant was claiming to have had a free shot in the Arizona proceedings – that if the decision went as he wanted it to, he would be the winner, but if it went against him, then he was entitled to walk away, scot free – the proper response is that this is exactly what Parliament has, for good or ill, but certainly for law, provided.

The decision was not referred to in the judgment of the Court of Appeal in *A/S D/S Svendborg v. Wansa*.[451] But the court gave no support to the view of the majority. In that case, the court regarded a ruling from a foreign court on the scope of a jurisdiction agreement, given on an application to challenge the jurisdiction brought by the defendant, as not binding on the defendant, albeit that it might have bound the other party to the foreign proceedings. It is submitted that *Svendborg v. Wansa* is precisely right in principle, and that the approach of the majority in *Desert Sun Loan Corp v. Hill* should not be followed.

7.58 Jurisdictional competence derived from submission: claimant submitting to a counterclaim

That the claimant submits to the jurisdiction of the court in respect of a counterclaim against him seems obvious: the claimant should be *volens* with respect to a counterclaim. But there are limits to what the claimant will be taken to have submitted to. It is too broad an approach, to say that the simple fact of bringing a claim in a foreign court exposes the claimant to the jurisdiction of the court in respect of all and any claims introduced against him;[452] and it is difficult to see that anything should turn upon whether the claim against

---

449 [1996] 2 All ER 847.
450 [1996] 2 All ER 847.
451 [1997] 2 Lloyd's Rep 183, 188.
452 See, for example, *Commonwealth of Australia v. Peacekeeper International FZE UAE* [2008] EWHC 1220 (QB) (interpleader applicant in proceedings before the English court does not submit to court for purpose of claim against him).

him is brought as a counterclaim, or as a separate action.[453] It would be rational to limit the extent of his automatic or deemed submission to claims which are in some way related to the claim made by him; in other words, to limit his deemed submission to those matters to which a fair-minded man would say that he had laid himself open. In *Murthy v. Sivajothi*[454] the general principle was accepted, and was stated in terms of the defendant being taken to have submitted to related claims and to those arising out of the same subject matter as the claim. This seems to be an extremely sensible solution to the problem, which will usually be pretty fact specific, and which further analysis will do nothing to improve.

7.59 Jurisdictional competence derived from submission: implied and indirect forms of submission

It is sometimes said that the common law does not acknowledge the possibility of an implied agreement to submit to the jurisdiction of a foreign court.[455] As indicated above, in the case of the bailment, it is hard to see why this should be so. No doubt a court should not infer an agreement to submit in the absence of proper evidence, but that should be the limit of the point. To agree that a contract is governed by New York law is not, on the face of it, to agree to submit to the jurisdiction of the New York court,[456] even if a New York court would hold that this was sufficient to give it jurisdiction. Likewise, to hold office in a Ruritanian company, when Ruritanian law provides that actions against company officials may be brought in a Ruritanian court, should not, it is thought, be seen as sufficient to infer an agreement to submit to those courts; it will be otherwise if shares were taken by a person who thereby became a member of a company whose constitution contains a submission clause.[457] As long as submission is not inferred lightly or loosely it is hard to see a convincing doctrinal objection to the implication of its existence. Implied agreements are a perfectly rational, if minor, part of the common law.

Perhaps there are indications that the traditional framework within which submission operates – voluntary appearance, agreement, and counterclaiming – is breaking down, or becoming slightly more flexible. The case was mentioned above of submission to the courts of New South Wales being found in the lodging of a claim in the insolvency which was being administered under their supervision.[458] The case cannot be seen as one of submission by appearance to the writ, but if one asks whether the creditor appeared to be lowering himself into the arena, in such a way that a reasonable observer would conclude

---

453 For this may depend upon the accident of local procedural law.

454 [1999] 1 WLR 467: a question of fact will be involved in the making of the judgment. See also *Whyte v. Whyte* [2005] EWCA Civ 858, [2006] 1 FLR 400 (where the principle was applied in the context of family proceedings and was said to be particularly apt for use); *Ex p Indiana Transportation Co* 244 US 456 (1917); *Derby & Co v. Larsson* [1976] 1 WLR 202.

455 See the criticism of *Blohn v. Desser* [1962] 2 QB 116 in *Vogel v. Kohnstamm* [1973] QB 133, and in *New Hampshire Insurance Co v. Strabag Bau AG* [1992] 1 Lloyd's Rep 361.

456 It would be far too adventurous to interpret it as an agreement to submit to any court, wherever it may be, which would apply New York law to the dispute.

457 This follows from *Copin v. Adamson* (1874) LR 9 Ex 345, and from the fact that the articles of association constitute a contract between the shareholders (and to which third parties are, presumably, not entitled as being not privy to it). And in the context of the Brussels I Regulation, see C-214/89 *Powell Duffryn plc* [1992] ECR I-1745.

458 *Rubin v. Eurofinance SA* [2012] UKSC 46, [2013] 1 AC 213, though the case discussed in the text at this point was the conjoined appeal in *New Cap Reinsurance Corp v. Grant*.

that he was putting his entitlement – and all of it – into the hands of the foreign insolvency court, the answer that it did so appear is certainly possible. In a decision given only a few years earlier, a unanimous Privy Council had recognised the decision of an American court, given in proceedings in which a Manx company had voluntarily appeared, that the shareholders of the Manx company have their shareholding cancelled and the stock reissued in favour of a committee of unsecured creditors.[459] The shareholders objected that they had not been party to the American proceedings, and still less had submitted to the jurisdiction of the American court. But the Privy Council evidently considered their contention to be unmeritorious, albeit without quite identifying a clear legal basis for showing it to be unfounded in law. In *Rubin v. Eurofinance SA*,[460] a majority of the Supreme Court held the Privy Council to have been wrong to have given effect to the American judgment to the disadvantage of the shareholders; this may not be the final word on what may be developing law.

When a company submits to the jurisdiction of a foreign court, the contention that this brings about the constructive (or attributed) submission of its member shareholders, to the extent that they are shareholders,[461] does not seem untenable. Whereas the submission of a company cannot be taken to connote the submission of its office holders,[462] it may be seen as the submission of a single shareholder who is its *alter ego*.[463] Though the company has a legal personality separate from that of its shareholders, and though a judgment against the company cannot simply be enforced against the assets of the shareholders, the proposition that those who hold shares have their shareholding put at risk when their company submits to the jurisdiction of a foreign court may have had more in it than the majority in *Rubin* was prepared to allow. However that may be, the two cases do suggest that there may be more ways to submit to the jurisdiction of a foreign court than has been traditionally understood, and that when confronted by a case in which there has been some interaction with foreign proceedings, the argument that there has been submission to the jurisdiction of the foreign court may not be impossible: at any rate, *Rubin* has opened the door to further development of the law. The point being made is not that the law on submission has broken down and become a question, more impressionistic than anything else, of whether the person proposed to be bound by a foreign judgment should have expected it, or brought it upon himself.[464] But a more creative approach to submission may still be consistent with principle.

---

459 *Cambridge Gas Transport Corp v. Official Committee of Unsecured Creditors of Navigator Holdings plc* [2006] UKPC 26, [2007] 1 AC 508 (PC, IoM).

460 [2012] UKSC 46, [2013] 1 AC 213. See also (on the issue of submission to a foreign insolvency court and its (non-)preclusive effect) *Akers v. Deputy Commissioner of Taxation* [2014] FCAFC 57.

461 That is to say, not so as to make them liable as though they were judgment debtors for the full debts of the company, but up to the point at which their shareholding is in peril.

462 *Masri v. Consolidated Contractors International (UK) Ltd (No 4)* [2009] UKHL 43, [2010] 1 AC 90. The case was one concerning the liability of officers to attend for examination as to the assets of the judgment debtor company (held no liability where they were outside the jurisdiction).

463 The suggestion to this effect is made in *Masri (No 4)*.

464 An analogous debate took place in the common law of contract formation, with a mechanical approach to offer and acceptance prevailing over a contrary analysis which would have asked, in a less rigid sense, whether the parties had a common expectation that agreement had been reached but in circumstances in which offer and acceptance, as traditionally understood, had not taken place: see *Gibson v. Manchester City Council* [1979] 1 WLR 294.

7.60 No other basis of jurisdiction is accepted as sufficient at common law

Despite some *dicta* which may be found in early cases, and notwithstanding abstract arguments to the contrary, no other basis of jurisdictional competence in respect of an action *in personam* is recognised by English common law on the recognition of foreign judgments. The nationality or domicile of the parties is quite irrelevant,[465] as also is the fact that the cause of action may have arisen within the jurisdiction of the foreign court. The fact that an English court would itself have taken jurisdiction upon similar facts is irrelevant.[466] Even if it were true that the foreign court was the natural forum for the litigation, that does not give the court 'international jurisdiction' under the rules of English private international law.[467]

Though all this seems plain enough to an English private international lawyer, those who try to enforce judgments coming from foreign courts which have exercised a jurisdiction which does not appear to be open to rational objection may not see it in the same way. But the immediate response of the English lawyer is that the question whether the foreign court's jurisdiction was reasonable or unreasonable, rational or irrational, conservative or radical, right or wrong, is nothing to the point.

A number of examples may be given to illustrate the proposition. For one, consider an English manufacturer who produces a defective machine part. Suppose the manufacturer receives in England, via email or fax, an order from an American purchaser, and ships it to the United States. In due course, the part breaks down and causes injury to the purchaser, who brings a personal injury action against the English manufacturer before an American court.[468] The American court may well take 'long-arm' jurisdiction over the English defendant. However, unless the defendant is present within the territory of the particular American court, or submits to its jurisdiction, the judgment against the defendant will not be entitled to recognition or enforcement in England. For a second, consider the case of an English investment adviser who recommends to customers that they put money into a fund which purports to invest in US securities. Suppose the fund in question is poorly managed, makes unwise investments and becomes insolvent. The customers may sue the English investment adviser for his negligence arising out of the mis-selling of the investments and from the failure to exercise proper supervision over the fund; and they may bring the claim in an American court on the basis that the claim involves investments in US securities purportedly traded in New York. The American court may take jurisdiction; but unless the English

---

465 Even though the contrary was stated in *Emanuel v. Symon* [1908] 1 KB 302, and even though the 1982 Act makes the domicile (albeit not in the common law sense) of the defendant the fundamental principle of jurisdiction. Nationality would in any event be unhelpful where the defendant is a national of a federal state; and it is moreover a connection which is defined and conferred by the relevant foreign law, not by English law. It is therefore an uncontrollable connecting factor. The fact that an English judgment was recognised in Australia on the basis of British nationality in *Independent Trustee Services Ltd v. Morris* [2010] NSWSC 1218 is to be regarded as an aberration.

466 This is sometimes said to follow from *Schibsby v. Westenholz* (1870) LR 6 QB 155, but it is made very clear by *Turnbull v. Walker* (1892) 67 LT 767, where the judgment was from New Zealand, and where service out of New Zealand had been based on provisions identical to those found in English law. It appeared to receive some support in *Re Dulles (No 2)* [1951] Ch 842, but it was explicitly rejected in *Henry v. Geoprosco International* [1976] QB 745.

467 It appears that a challenge to the existing state of the law was made at first instance in *Adams v. Cape Industries plc*, but the trial judge was bound by the earlier cases, and the point was not pursued before the Court of Appeal. But see *De Savoye v. Morguard Investments Ltd* [1990] 3 SCR 1077 (noted (1992) 108 LQR 549), where the Supreme Court of Canada held that this would be sufficient for recognition in inter-provincial cases, This principle was followed and extended to non-Canadian judgments in *Beals v. Saldanha* [2003] 3 SCR 416.

468 There is no significance, in this context, in the use of 'American' as distinct from the courts of an American State. The question whether a State or Federal court would have jurisdiction is not the concern of this paragraph.

defendant were present within the territorial jurisdiction of the court when the action was commenced, or submitted or submits to its jurisdiction, any judgment against him will not be entitled to recognition or enforcement in England.

For a third case, one may consider the case of an Englishman who goes to the United States for a vacation, rents a car from a hire company at the airport, and drives out of the airport, sleep-deprived and generally befuddled, causing an accident in which the claimant is injured. Suppose that the defendant is so shaken by the experience that he takes the next flight back to London and does not set foot in the United States again. The injured claimant may sue the English defendant in an American court, but the judgment will still not be recognised in England unless the defendant responds to the summons and submits to the jurisdiction of the court.

It is in every case irrelevant that the American court had jurisdiction according to its own law;[469] it is in every case irrelevant that the English court might well have, if the facts were reversed, allowed a claimant to invoke the corresponding long-arm jurisdiction of the English court, by granting permission to serve process out of the jurisdiction.[470] It is in every case irrelevant that the cause of action arose within the territorial jurisdiction of the American court; and it is in every case irrelevant that the defendant could hardly be heard to say that he was taken by surprise when sued in the place where he has chosen, freely and of his own volition, to undertake the very activity out of which the claim arises.

Though the law is clear enough, abstract[471] arguments may be made for and against its further development.[472] It could not be right that simple reciprocity with the heads of jurisdiction under which an English court is permitted to authorise service out of the jurisdiction[473] would establish international jurisdiction in the foreign court.[474] Those rules, in their plain form, do not necessarily connote a strong connection with the English court as adjudicating court;[475] and it has been clear ever since *Schibsby v. Westenholz*[476] that a foreign

---

469 It is, traditionally at least, equally irrelevant that the foreign court in question did not have jurisdiction according to its own law: the presence or absence of local jurisdiction has no relevance to the recognition of the foreign judgment: see below, para. 7.65.

470 *Schibsby v. Westenholz* (1870) LR 6 QB 155.

471 But it must be clearly understood that is not open to an English court to alter the understanding of the common law which has, in relation to the law on the recognition of foreign judgments, been settled for upwards of a hundred years: *cf Owens Bank Ltd v. Bracco* [1992] 2 AC 443, 489.

472 For a rather unexpected development, giving effect to a foreign judgment or request for the confiscation of shares from a shareholder who did not appear before the foreign court, on the pretext that it is rendering assistance in a cross-border insolvency, see *Cambridge Gas Transport Corp v. Official Committee of Unsecured Creditors of Navigator Holdings plc* [2006] UKPC 26, [2007] 1 AC 508 (PC, IoM). The Privy Council denied that the procedure before the Manx court was to secure the recognition and enforcement of an American judgment *in personam*, though it is hard to see why it was not. The better conclusion may be to accept that orders made in relation to insolvency are inherently different; or that as the company had submitted to the jurisdiction of the American courts, all of its shareholders were bound, to the extent of their shareholding, by the judgment from the court to whose jurisdiction their company had elected to submit. The case was held to have been wrongly decided in *Rubin v. Eurofinance SA* [2012] UKSC 46, [2013] 1 AC 213 and in *Singularis Holdings Ltd v PricewaterhouseCoopers* [2014] UKPC 36, but the flexibility of 'submission' has been noted, and it suggests that the novelty in *Cambridge Gas* may not be as great as it seems at first sight.

473 Now found in CPR Part 6, Practice Direction 6B, Paragraph 3(1).

474 This, it is thought, is the correct, and rather narrow, conclusion to be drawn from *Schibsby v. Westenholz* and from *Henry v. Geoprosco*.

475 The bare fact that a contract was made in England, for example, is about as trifling as a connecting factor can be. As to whether they are fairly described as 'exorbitant' (though the debate is a rather sterile one) see above, para. 4.57.

476 (1870) LR 6 QB 155.

judgment is not to be recognised simply because, if the tables were turned, the claimant might have invoked one of the sub-paragraphs of the Practice Direction[477] which allow a court to authorise service out of the jurisdiction.[478]

However, as a matter of English private international law, jurisdiction is not taken under the provisions for service out under CPR Part 6 unless England is also shown to be the proper place for the litigation.[479] In reality, therefore, English courts now assert jurisdiction if the parties submit to the jurisdiction of the English courts, or if England is the proper place, or the natural forum, for the litigation. One may therefore ask whether this refinement of English jurisdictional rules might be reflected in the English rules which define the competence of foreign courts. If the foreign forum is, in English eyes, the natural forum, or the proper place to bring the proceedings, there is a credible argument that the judgment of that court should, in principle at least, and without regard to whether the defendant elected to submit to its jurisdiction, be entitled to recognition in England.

That conclusion, or one very close to it, has been adopted by the Supreme Court of Canada in its development of the common law of Canada.[480] There is something seductive about the argument; and something resistible about it which explains why it is not part of the common law of England.

7.61 Judgments from the natural forum and Canadian development of the common law

There are several substantial arguments why the path marked out by the Canadian Supreme Court will not be, and probably should not be, followed in England. First, an action commenced in the English courts will not be stayed in favour of a foreign natural forum unless the defendant makes an application for this relief; the judgment of the foreign court will, in due course, be entitled to recognition on the basis that the defendant submitted to its jurisdiction, without reference to the naturalness or otherwise of the forum. Second, it is also true that a defendant could face a difficult choice to make in deciding whether he could safely allow the proceedings to go by default in the foreign court: he would have to consider, at perhaps too early a stage to be able to make a reliable judgment, whether an English court, many facts and several years later, would consider the foreign court to have been the natural forum, or the proper place to sue, or something like that. It will not be a comfortable prediction to have to make; and it would tend to be English defendants who

---

477 Paragraph 3.1 of Practice Direction 6B supplementing CPR Part 6, considered above, paras 4.58 *et seq.* The point is made even more clearly by *Turnbull v. Walker* (1892) 67 LT 767, where the judgment was from New Zealand, and where service out of New Zealand had been based on provisions identical to those found in English law.

478 The point is not improved by appealing to the idea of comity as the basis for recognition: *Schibsby v. Westenholz* (1870) LR 6 QB 155, 159; *Re Trepca Mines Ltd* [1960] 1 WLR 1273, 1281; *Indyka v. Indyka* [1969] 1 AC 33, 58 (a case on matrimonial causes), disapproving a contrary expression of view in *Re Dulles' Settlement (No 2)* [1951] Ch 842, 851; *Travers v. Holley* [1954] P 246 (a case on matrimonial causes).

479 See above, paras 4.88 *et seq.* In fact, the requirement is that England be the proper place in which to bring the claim: CPR r. 6.37(3).

480 *De Savoye v. Morguard Investments Ltd* [1990] 3 SCR 1077 (noted (1992) 108 LQR 549); *Beals v. Saldanha* [2003] 3 SCR 416 (where the question was whether the foreign court had a real and substantial connection to the dispute, rather than whether it was the natural forum).

would be put on the spot of having to make it.[481] Any such change in the common law will therefore make the position of English defendants more difficult than before, and this is Parliament's job, not that of the courts.[482] It is true that one may consider the potential difficulty to be susceptible to overstatement, and even in cases which a defendant could consider as marginal, not everyone will agree that difficulty for an individual defendant should be allowed to outweigh the public interest in encouraging judgments from being obtained in their natural forum. A balance has to be struck; it will be for Parliament to strike it.

7.62 The impact of the doctrine of obligation

The next argument against the developments undertaken in Canada is rather different. The common law approach to the recognition of judgments is to ask whether the party who is now said to be bound by the foreign judgment stood, or behaved in such a way, in relation to the foreign court, for it to be appropriate to say he obliged himself to obey or abide by the judgment. The focus of the law has been on the position of the defendant.

For the last century and more, foreign judgments have been recognised on the basis of the 'doctrine of obligation',[483] and the point of the enquiry is whether the party against whom the foreign judgment is asserted placed himself, voluntarily, in a position where it could fairly be said that he was bound to abide by the adjudication of the foreign court. Judgments, therefore, bind those who by their own actions choose to put themselves in the way of the obligation which they create.

Whether a judgment against the defendant will be enforceable overseas is largely a matter which lies within the choice or control of the defendant. When proceedings are instituted against a defendant in a court within the territorial jurisdiction of which he is neither resident nor present,[484] he has a choice. If he stays away and does not submit to the foreign court, the likelihood is that the judgment against him will be enforceable only against assets within the territorial jurisdiction of the foreign court itself. If, however, he appears, submits to the jurisdiction, and defends the merits of the claim there, an eventual judgment against him will be likely to be enforceable overseas.[485] He may not relish the choice with which he is faced, but the defendant still gets to choose whether to assume the obligation which the foreign judgment may create. His voluntary consent to the jurisdiction of the foreign court, and that alone, is what gives the judgment its passport to international enforceability.

The same point may be made another way. The defendant who is present may be bound by the judgment, but the defendant who is not present is not bound unless he agrees to

---

481 One has to say that the majority of the Supreme Court of Canada in *Beals v. Saldanha* was startlingly unmoved by the predictable plight which this judgment inflicted on Canadian defendants to proceedings overseas.

482 It is to be noted that this point was taken before the Supreme Court of Canada in *Beals v. Saldanha*, and was rejected by a majority of the court. The Supreme Court of Ireland declined to adopt the jurisprudence of the Supreme Court of Canada: *Re Flightlease (Ireland) Ltd (in liq)* [2012] IESC 12, [2012] 2 ILRM 461.

483 *Godard v. Gray* (1870) LR 6 QB 139; *Schibsby v. Westenholz* (1870) LR 6 QB 155. The assertion in *Rubin v. Eurofinance SA* [2012] UKSC 46, [2013] 1 AC 236, [9], that this is 'purely theoretical and historical' is, it is submitted, unhelpful, and can only impair a proper understanding of the law. For a different view, see Briggs (2013) 129 LQR 87.

484 It is not fanciful to regard the choice to be present as the exercise of choice to accept the obligation of judgment.

485 At least in those common law systems which regard submission by appearance as a ground of jurisdictional competence; non-common law systems, if they have an analogous rule, probably express it in different terminology.

waive that immunity, as English private international law sees it, from the international jurisdiction of the foreign court. The explanation appeals to the old reasoning in *Penn v. Baltimore*.[486] A foreign judgment cannot have any effect in the English legal order, for the decision of a foreign sovereign is confined to the territorial jurisdiction of that sovereign. However, if the parties may be seen to have assumed an obligation to each other to abide by and obey the judgment, that obligation (or the consequences which flow from it) may be enforced, just as any other agreement may be enforced, without any need to address the principles of State or judicial sovereignty. However it is viewed, the focus of attention is on the acts of the party who is to be bound, here assumed to be the defendant.

The doctrine of obligation was articulated as the basis for the enforcement of foreign judgments in 1870. The 'obligation' to which the court referred appears to have been understood as a voluntary, or private, or consensual or quasi-contractual obligation, assumed by the party to be bound, rather than one simply imposed by force of the general law. From then on, the obligation was held to arise, or not arise, from the conduct of the party to be obliged, and not from anything else. It was irrelevant to ask what should have happened, or where an action should have been brought. The question was whether the party to be obliged had acted in such as way as to oblige himself to obey the judgment. This puts in perspective many things about the common law doctrine on when a foreign court has jurisdictional competence to bind a party to its judgment.[487] It explains why the English common law does not accept the existence (or concern itself over the lack) of a strong connection between the adjudicating court and the cause of action as a distinct basis for the recognition of a judgment; why the fact that an English court might have exercised jurisdiction is of no relevance; why reciprocity has no part to play in the assessment of whether a foreign judgment should be recognised. These facts and matters tell us nothing about whether the party to be bound by the judgment submitted or consented to the jurisdiction of the foreign court.

The developments illustrated by the common law of Canada[488] are, when viewed in this light and whatever else one may say about them, fundamentally alien to the structure of the English common law on the recognition of judgments. 'I did not submit or consent to the jurisdiction of the foreign court and therefore I am not obliged by its judgment against me' is a sufficient plea[489] in English, but not in Canadian, common law. 'You were sued in a court which had a close connection to the claim and so you are bound to obey its judgment' is a good plea in Canadian law, but cannot be in English law as it is currently understood.[490] It explains why the Canadian approach to the recognition of foreign judgments is not just an updating of the traditional common law, but involves a fundamental change in its basic structure, which is personal rather than geographical.

---

486 (1750) 1 Ves Sen 444. And see above, for its application in the context of jurisdiction, paras 4.06 *et seq*.

487 There is a good argument that this should lead to reconsideration of the view that a judgment obtained by a foreign taxing authority against a defendant may not be enforced in England, on the ground that to allow the judgment to be enforced would infringe the rule prohibiting the enforcement of foreign revenue laws: Dicey, Rule 3; *United States v. Harden* (1963) 41 DLR (2d) 721 (Can SC). If the defendant has consented to the jurisdiction of the foreign court by appearance before it, but has not satisfied the judgment, it is hard to see why the judicial enforcement of the obligation, created by the judgment and the defendant's voluntary submission to the jurisdiction of the court, should be taken to be beyond the proper powers of an English court. It is otherwise, perhaps, if he was present but did not voluntarily submit to the jurisdiction. But the English common law has not yet accepted this distinction; and the impediment to enforcement remains absolute.

488 *Morguard Investments Ltd v. De Savoye* [1990] 3 SCR 1077; *Beals v. Saldanha* [2003] 3 SCR 416.

489 Leaving aside jurisdiction by presence, or 'tag jurisdiction', as to which see para. 7.48, above.

490 At least, unless English law is altered.

And this explains why a change to re-orient English private international law along these lines would be fundamental, and must be a matter for Parliament, and not for the courts. And as to legislative reform, the prospects do not promise much. Bilateral negotiations between the United Kingdom and the United States, which might have resulted in an improved scheme for the mutual recognition of judgments, were abandoned in 1980:[491] among other things, jury awards, punitive damages, and judgments based on long-arm jurisdiction were not on the list of things which the United Kingdom was disposed to find acceptable;[492] it has since become clear that American objections to enforcing English defamation judgments are likely to be, if anything, even more profound. Multilateral negotiations organised by the Hague Conference on Private International Law, designed to produce a template for the mutual recognition of judgments, in what might have been called a 'worldwide Lugano Convention', also came to naught.[493] Of course, even if the task of settling the terms of a bilateral agreement is beyond those charged with negotiating it, this does not necessarily mean that Parliament could not decide unilaterally to change the law. But the idea that it might do so without securing at the same time the greater recognition of English judgments overseas is far-fetched; and it sometimes seems that unless everything can be accepted, nothing can be agreed, with the result that nothing will be agreed.

7.63 Recognition of judgments and orders *in rem*: jurisdictional competence of the foreign court

A foreign court has jurisdiction to give a judgment *in rem*,[494] so far as the common law is concerned, if the *res* in respect of which judgment was given was at the material[495] time situated within the territorial jurisdiction of that court. A judgment *in rem* determines title to a thing, or the status of a person, or the legal existence of a company or corporation. Therefore, a judgment which decrees sale of a thing within the territory of the foreign court[496] to satisfy a claim against the thing in question may be recognised in England: English law recognises the effect of dispositions of property which are effective under the law of the State in which the property was when the disposition occurred,[497] and the effect of the judgment is to adjudicate

---

491 The draft bilateral Convention was published: Cmnd 6771 (1976), though as there was no formal notice of abandonment, it is difficult to vouch for this point. According to the American Embassy in London, the negotiations had 'been taking place since 1971', and had produced a draft Convention: the letter to this effect appears in Lowe, *Extraterritorial Jurisdiction* (1983), 180. It seems probable that heated exchanges about the introduction of the Protection of Trading Interests Act 1980 finished it off for good.

492 The objections to American judgments, which provoked the Protection of Trading Interests Act 1980 (as to which, see below, para. 7.78) revealed a further impediment to the conclusion of a bilateral treaty.

493 See, on the aspiration and the failure, Barceló and Clermont, *A Global Law of Jurisdiction and Judgments: Lessons from The Hague* (Kluwer, The Hague, 2002).

494 This Section does not primarily refer to admiralty actions *in rem*. Rather, it refers to judgments which determine the status or ownership of a thing (most often land: see *Re Trepca Mines* [1960] 1 WLR 1273) situated within the jurisdiction of a court.

495 In principle, and in the interests of legal certainty, this should be at the institution of proceedings.

496 Even in the case of a court somewhere as improbable as North Korea: *BCEN Eurobank v Kostobaybymou Co Ltd (The Phoenix)* [2011] 1 Lloyd's Rep 445 (E. Caribbean CA).

497 *Castrique v. Imrie* (1870) LR 4 HL 414; *Calyon v. Michalilidis* [2009] UKPC 34 (Gib). This applies the rules on recognition of judgments *in rem* to determine whether to recognise a judgment which determines title to property, even though this question arises within the context of proceedings which allege a wrong in relation to that property, such as conversion or dishonest assistance.

the property to its new owner.[498] Likewise, a judgment which determines title to shares in a foreign company will not be recognised or enforced as a judgment *in rem* unless it was given by the courts at the *situs* of the shares. It follows that a foreign judgment purporting to determine title to land, or other property,[499] in England will not be recognised.[500]

On the other hand, a judgment which is properly seen as being *in personam*, enforcing contractual or other obligations in relation to foreign land or foreign shares, may be recognised and enforced as a judgment *in personam*;[501] and the truth of the matter is that it is the order, as distinct from the judgment, which has to be examined to see whether it was made to take effect *in personam* or *in rem*. Indeed, a judgment which may be identified as one *in rem*, and which would not be recognised on that basis, may in an appropriate case be understood to impose a personal obligation on the parties to the proceedings, and the judgment may in that sense be enforced as a judgment *in personam*.[502] In any event it is rare for an order *in rem* to require enforcement, as opposed to recognition, in England. However, if a court at the *situs* of land makes an adjudication of title, there will be no rational basis[503] for the judgment to be denied recognition in England.

According to the private international law of corporations, questions of corporate creation, continuation, dissolution and amalgamation are all governed by the *lex incorporationis*, the law under which the company was created. The principle that what is created by the *lex incorporationis* may be uncreated by it as well is plain;[504] and it applies also to corporate amalgamation.[505] It does not usually require a judgment to bring about the legal result in question, though if a company were to be dissolved by judicial order,[506] a judgment in such terms from the courts of the *lex incorporationis* would be recognised as having been given by a jurisdictionally competent court. But a related issue, namely that of judicial appointments of receivers and liquidators, may raise the issue of recognition of judgments.

---

498 English law will therefore recognise a sale of a ship by a court abroad as giving title to the purchaser. But if the foreign court does not consider its decree as having an effect *in rem*, an English court will not treat it as a judgment *in rem*: *Air Foyle Ltd v. Centre Capital Ltd* [2002] EWHC 2535 Comm, [2003] 2 Lloyd's Rep 753 (noted [2004] LMCLQ 303).

499 *Blue Holdings (1) Pte Ltd v. United States* [2014] EWCA Civ 1291 [2015] 1 ALL ER (Comm) 1.

500 *Duke v. Andler* [1932] 4 DLR 529 and *Shami v. Shami* [2012] Ch 664 (appeal dismissed [2013] EWCA Civ 227 without specific reference to this point) accept the point more or less clearly, though the latter explains that even if this is the law applicable to judgments *in rem*, it has no application to foreign judgments *in personam* (as to the obligations of a trust, for example), even if the land is in England.

501 Though enforcement will be limited to money judgments: see at para. 7.76, below. And on the separate nature of claims *in personam*, see *R Griggs Group Ltd v. Evans* [2004] EWHC 1088 (Ch), [2005] Ch 153.

502 *Pattni v. Ali* [2006] UKPC 51, [2007] 2 AC 85 (PC, IoM) (Kenyan judgment in relation to agreement to transfer of shares in Manx company not, on its true construction, a judgment *in rem*, but one which enforced obligations which the parties had assumed and which bound them *in personam*); applied in *Brunei Investment Agency v. Fidelis Nominees Ltd* [2008] JLR 337; distinguished on entirely orthodox grounds in *Blue Holdings (1) Pte Ltd v. United States* (judgment did not purport to operate *in personam*, and in any event the individuals were not present within and had not submitted to the jurisdiction of the foreign court). And see also (2006) 77 BYBIL 575; Tham [2007] LMCLQ 129.

503 Public policy apart, as when the adjudication is based on disgraceful grounds: *Kuwait Airways Corp v. Iraqi Airways Co (Nos 4 and 5)* [2002] UKHL 19, [2002] 2 AC 883.

504 *Lazard Bros v. Midland Bank* [1933] AC 289; *Russian and English Bank v. Baring Bros* [1932] 1 Ch 435; *Deutsche Bank v. Banque des Marchands de Moscou* (1932) 158 LT 364.

505 *National Bank of Greece & Athens SA v. Metliss* [1958] AC 509; *Toprak Enerji Sanayi AS v. Sale Tilney Technology plc* [1994] 1 WLR 840.

506 If the dissolution were to have been done for thoroughly disgraceful reasons, it may be that it would be refused recognition on grounds of public policy: *Kuwait Airways Corp v. Iraqi Airways Co (Nos 4 and 5)* [2002] UKHL 19, [2002] 2 AC 883.

The question whether to recognise a judgment or order which appoints a person to a particular status is most frequently in the context of matrimonial causes, and therefore falls outside the scope of this book. But it also arises in relation to receivers and liquidators, where a person appointed by a foreign court appears in English proceedings and seeks relief. The common law has in some respects been superseded by statute; but the general view at common law was that a liquidator (but not a receiver) appointed under the law of the place of incorporation would be recognised as such in England. This properly, maybe inevitably, follows from the proposition that the question of who has power to act on behalf of a company is determined by the law under which the company was formed, the *lex incorporationis*.[507] This is not to say that appointments made under another law will necessarily be denied recognition, especially where the appointment would be recognised under the *lex incorporationis*. Whether appointments by a foreign court which is not that of the *lex incorporationis*, and not recognised according to it, would be recognised, for example, by appeal to a principle of reciprocity or comity,[508] must be very doubtful at best. Indeed, it is probably now not possible,[509] or if it is possible, the scope of recognition will be confined to the business of the company within the jurisdiction where the appointment was made.

The appointment of a liquidator by a court of a Member State exercising jurisdiction under the Insolvency Regulation is recognised in accordance with that Regulation;[510] and the appointment of a liquidator under a recognised foreign proceeding may or must also be recognised under the Cross-Border Insolvency Regulations.[511] The detail of these instruments lies outside the scope of this book.

The appointment and status of a receiver is rather different, as these are usually appointed to safeguard the position of investors or creditors, and not the company. However, if the receiver is authorised to act according to the *lex incorporationis*, it seems plausible that his appointment will be recognised as allowing him to act in England. In other cases, a receiver appointed by a foreign court to protect the interests of investors in the company will not be recognised in England.[512] However, the recognition of a receiver appointed by a court whose judgment *in personam* against a defendant is one which an English court will recognise, and who has been appointed by the foreign court to enforce the obligations of the judgment, does not raise any particular issue of principle. As the judgment is one which is binding on the defendant as a judgment *in personam*, according to the ordinary rules, there is no reason to raise objection to the appointment of a receiver who then seeks to enforce that judgment in England by bringing proceedings on the judgment debt in the ordinary way.[513]

---

507 *Bank of Ethiopia v. National Bank of Egypt and Ligouri* [1937] Ch 513; *Felixtowe Dock & Railway Co v. US Lines Inc* [1989] QB 360.

508 *Travers v. Holley* [1953] P 246.

509 *Re Trepca Mines Ltd* [1960] 1 WLR 1273; *Felixtowe Dock & Railway Co v. US Lines Inc* [1989] QB 360; *Soc Coopérative Sidmetal v. Titan International Ltd* [1966] 1 QB 828; *Schemmer v. Property Resources Ltd* [1975] Ch 273.

510 Regulation (EC) 1346/2000.

511 SI 2006/1030. For illustration, and for the conclusion that the person appointed as receiver under the law of the United States was not to be recognised under the Rules (the Rules do not apply to receiverships as such, but only to liquidations and persons appointed under a law on liquidation), and that the person appointed as liquidator under the law of Antigua was to be recognised (as Antigua was the centre of the main interests of the bank), with the further conclusion that the common law should not obstruct him in the performance of his duties, see *Re Stanford International Bank Ltd* [2010] EWCA Civ 137, [2011] Ch 33.

512 *Re Stanford International Bank Ltd* [2010] EWCA Civ 137, [2011] Ch 33.

513 *Robb Evans v. European Bank Ltd* (2004) 61 NSWLR 75, noted [2004] LMCLQ 313. The decision was approved, though not really analysed, in *United States Securities and Exchange Commission v. Manterfield* [2009] EWCA Civ 27, [2010] 1 WLR 172. The reasoning does not apply, obviously, where the foreign judgment orders

7.64 Defences to recognition of a judgment as *res judicata* other than lack of jurisdiction

If the foreign court was not jurisdictionally competent to bind the losing party in the eyes of the English common law, its judgment has no effect at all upon him as a matter of English law. But if the court was jurisdictionally competent, the defendant, assuming him to be the losing party, will in principle be obliged by English law to accept his defeat as *res judicata*, or the unsuccessful claimant, when he is the losing party, will be bound by, and must accept as conclusive, the dismissal of his claim. However, if the party to be bound to the foreign judgment can rely upon one of the defences to recognition provided for by English law, the judgment will not be binding on him after all.

The seven defences to the plea of *res judicata* to be considered at this point are notionally separate, though they do in some significant respects overlap. The first is that the judgment was not 'final and conclusive' on the issue in respect of which its recognition is sought. The second applies if the court gave judgment in breach of a valid dispute resolution agreement:[514] this objection can be relied on only by a party who did not agree to the bringing of the proceedings in the foreign court, which naturally excludes the claimant.[515] The third is that the successful party procured judgment in his favour by fraud.[516] The fourth applies if the court gave judgment contrary to the rules of natural, or perhaps of substantial, justice. The fifth is that recognition of the judgment would be contrary to English public policy. The sixth is that recognition of the judgment would violate the Human Rights Act 1998 and is, therefore, forbidden by force of statute: this defence may well come to supersede a number of those developed as a matter of common law. The seventh defence will apply if the judgment was in conflict with a prior English judgment.

In dealing with and defining the defences, no account appears to be taken of the particular basis on which the foreign court was found to be jurisdictionally competent. But there is an argument to be made to the effect that they should reflect the jurisdictional basis found to be present in the particular case. In particular, a defendant who has contracted or consented to be sued in a particular court should perhaps not have the same freedom to raise a defence of fraud or natural justice as a defendant who did not submit to the jurisdiction of the court but happened to be present when process was served on him. Indeed, a defendant who contracted to accept the jurisdiction of the foreign court may find it more difficult to complain about the procedure followed by the foreign court than one who did not but who was constrained by commercial necessity to appear and defend the proceedings. Moreover, if the English common law were ever to move in the direction marked out by the Supreme Court of Canada, and recognise judgments coming from a court which had a real and substantial connection to the dispute,[517] a more generous allowance for defences may be appropriate, and succeed in striking the right balance between the legitimate interests of all

---

confiscation of assets as a response to crime, in circumstances where the confiscating State is entitled to keep the assets and is under neither obligation nor expectation to turn these over to the civilian victims.

514 Civil Jurisdiction and Judgments Act 1982, s. 32.

515 *Ibid.*, s. 32(1)(b).

516 That is, the successful claimant or the successful defendant may be shown to have committed fraud; and upon such proof the judgment in his favour will be disqualified from recognition.

517 See above, para. 7.60.

the parties. It is possible, of course, that at a subliminal level this is already happening. But no case has yet admitted it openly.[518]

7.65 Complaints which do not amount to defences to recognition as *res judicata*

The seven defences set out above, and examined in detail below, are limited. It is worth making specific mention of facts and matters which – perhaps surprisingly – do not furnish a defence to the recognition or enforcement of the judgment.

One may start with a point relating to jurisdiction. It is understood[519] that even if the foreign court lacked jurisdiction under its own internal law, this is irrelevant to the recognition of the judgment in England. If this proposition is correct, it will save an English court from having to grapple with foreign rules of civil procedure. This makes sense, for it is an English obligation, as distinct from a foreign judgment, which the court acknowledges and enforces; and it is improbable that the defendant assumes an obligation which is defined by reference to the internal jurisdiction of the foreign court.

This is sensible as far as it goes, but it may not go quite far enough. If the foreign court's lack of internal jurisdiction meant that the defendant acted prudently in ignoring the proceedings, which were a nullity under the law of the place where they were instituted, it would be unrealistic and unfair for English law to disregard this fact and to recognise the judgment. If the foreign judgment is a nullity, it should not be regarded in English law as binding the defendant; there can hardly be an obligation in relation to non-existent subject matter.[520] If it is not a nullity, it is valid,[521] and should be regarded as creating an obligation.[522] But it will be rare for a foreign judgment to be a nullity. Much more likely is that a judgment handed down by a court in excess of its local jurisdiction is voidable, or liable to be set aside. A voidable judgment is, by definition, a valid judgment unless and until it is avoided; and it will give rise to an obligation.

So far as concerns what happened at trial, it is no defence to a claim for recognition that the foreign court got the facts wrong, or can plainly be seen to have got the facts completely and utterly wrong, or got the law wrong, or was trying to apply English law and manifestly got that wrong as well.[523] For if arguments which simply allege error could be advanced, there would be no recognition of foreign judgments, just reinvestigation of the grounds for[524] foreign judgments; and the contention that a court should refuse to recognise a judgment from a foreign court which did wrong in 'refusing to apply' English law would lie outside the mainstream of contemporary thinking.[525] Errors of fact or of law do not impugn

---

518 See further Briggs (2004) 8 Singapore Yearbook of International Law 1.

519 Dicey, Morris and Collins, *The Conflict of Laws*, 15th edn (2012), Rule 49(2); *Vanquelin v. Bouard* (1863) 15 CBNS 341; *Pemberton v. Hughes* [1899] 1 Ch 781.

520 *Cf Couturier v. Hastie* (1852) 8 Ex 40 (contract to sell and buy non-existent subject matter is void).

521 No less so if it may be set aside at a later date. On the other hand, if it may be set aside by the very court which pronounced it, it may not be regarded as final and conclusive. This may mean that it cannot be recognised in England, see above, para. 7.66.

522 *Cf Isaacs v. Robinson* [1985] AC 97 for the position in domestic English law.

523 *Godard v. Gray* (1870) LR 6 QB 288.

524 *Godard v. Gray* (1870) LR 6 QB 288; *Carl Zeiss Stiftung v. Rayner & Keeler Ltd (No 2)* [1967] 1 AC 853.

525 The 'perverse and deliberate refusal' of a court in Louisiana to apply English law led to non-recognition of the judgment in *Simpson v. Fogo* (1863) 1 H & M 195, 247. When the common law was used as the basis for Indian law as legislated in the Indian Code of Civil Procedure (1908), Art. 13(c) of the Code provided (and still provides) for non-recognition of a judgment 'founded on a refusal to recognise the law of India in cases in which

the obligation created by the foreign judgment. Indeed, it would hardly be credible for the judgment debtor to say that he agreed to the jurisdiction of the foreign court and assumed an obligation to abide by its judgment only if the court were to make no error of fact or law. When he obliged himself, and obliged himself to the other, to accept the jurisdiction of the foreign court, the obligation was to abide by the judgment of the foreign court, whether it was right or wrong.[526]

For similar reasons, it is no defence that the foreign court applied a choice of law rule which was different from that which an English court would have applied if it had adjudicated the same claim or the same issues. It has never been a requirement of English private international law that the foreign court has applied the same rule for choice of law as would have been applied by an English court, and that unless it did so its judgment would not be entitled to recognition. Such a rule may be found in French private international law;[527] but in England its effect would be to restrict, very severely, the effect given to foreign judgments. However, where the foreign court has applied a law different from that for which the parties made an express agreement, the issues may be somewhat different.[528]

So far as concerns matters which arise after the trial, there is no defence to recognition or enforcement in the fact that the foreign judgment is not, or not yet, enforceable under the law of the foreign court which gave it. The enforceability of the foreign judgment under the law of the court which gave it may well be relevant in relation to those schemes for registration of a foreign judgment,[529] where it is the foreign judgment itself which is given direct effect in England, but as the common law does not enforce the judgment as such, as distinct from the obligations which arise from the adjudication, whether it is enforceable under the law which gave it is a matter of foreign procedure, not applicable in England.

It may follow from this, or if not, then it appears to be correct in principle in any event, that the defences to recognition may be applied to the judgment of an appellate court which has overruled or annulled the decision of a lower court, with the consequence that the lower court judgment is left as liable to recognition in England as though nothing had happened to it. This makes sense: if an appellate judgment is procured by fraud, for example, it will have no effect in England; the result then is that the original judgment is untouched by anything to which English private international law will ascribe legal effect. It may appear strange that the result is that a foreign judgment which is – rightly or wrongly – now void of legal effect in the State in which it was given may be recognised in England. But English law recognises obligations arising from the relationship

---

such law is applicable'. This seems to suggest that *Simpson v. Fogo* was considered to be sound and of more general application. Though the case may be out of favour in England today, its evident acceptance as correct 50 years later by the colonial draftsman, and its continued application in a significant part of the common law world, should not be overlooked.

526 For a very different approach, proceeding from a very different analysis of what parties agree to, where the judgment was obtained by fraud, see below, para. 7.69.

527 The requirement was established by the French Supreme Court in its decision in *Munzer* (Cass, 7 Jan 1964), [1964] Rev Crit DIP 344 (*note* Battifol). But it is understood that this requirement has been watered down and it is no longer insisted on as part of French law on the recognition of judgments.

528 See below, para. 7.68.

529 For example: the Brussels I Regulation, Lugano II Convention, Civil Jurisdiction and Judgments Act 1982, Foreign Judgments (Reciprocal Enforcement) Act 1933 or Administration of Justice Act 1920, all of which provide for the registration of the foreign judgment and for the enforcement of it, once registered, as though it had been a judgment of the High Court.

between the parties or from the presence of the defendant when the proceedings were instituted, rather than the judgment as a judgment. That being so, it is not conceptually difficult to explain why a foreign judgment, as to which English private international law saw no sustainable objection, may give rise to an obligation binding the parties, it being treated as unaffected by a subsequent foreign judicial act which has no effect in the English legal order.[530]

And finally, when it comes to the English proceedings to obtain recognition or enforcement of the foreign judgment, there is no clear authority that a party seeking to enforce the judgment be acting in good faith or come with clean hands,[531] though one can see how the case for such a defence, vague and imprecise as it is, could be made. It is true that the principle has recently been identified as a proper basis for the refusal of equitable relief in the form of an anti-suit injunction,[532] but the obligation to abide by a foreign judgment arises at common law, not in equity. Although an argument based on estoppel might, in an appropriate case, be advanced, the clean hands principle would appear to have no discrete role in the common law of foreign judgments.

We proceed to examine in detail the admissible defences to the plea of *res judicata*, which are seven in number.

7.66 Defence to recognition (1): foreign judgment not final and conclusive on the merits: interlocutory judgments and default judgments

In order to be recognised as *res judicata*, a judgment must be final and conclusive, and must be a judgment upon the merits of the action.[533] This means that the foreign court has given a judgment which is not provisional, but which makes the matter *res judicata* in that court: it is the court's last and final word on the issue in question. If, therefore, the only way to contest the issues in the foreign jurisdiction is to appeal to a higher court, the judgment appealed from will count as final and conclusive. If, by contrast, the judgment can be reopened and reconsidered in that same court, it cannot be said to be final and conclusive, and it cannot be recognised as *res judicata* at common law. It also means that a judicial decision that a foreign judgment meets the criteria for recognition does not itself count as a judgment: *exequatur sur exequatur ne vaut*.[534]

---

530 *Merchant International Co Ltd v. NAK Naftogaz* [2012] EWCA Civ 196, [2012] 1 WLR 3036. In fact the Court of Appeal was able, and evidently preferred, to uphold the decision below on the rather narrower ground that when proceedings in England first relied on the foreign judgment, the first instance judgment had not been reversed by the appellate decision said to have resulted from fraud or a breach of the rules of natural justice or the Human Rights Act 1998. But the broader proposition appears to be perfectly sound: see *Yukos Capital Sarl v. OJSC Oil Co Rosneft* [2014] EWHC 2188 (Comm) (refusal to give effect to a Russian judgment purporting to set aside an arbitral award).

531 See *Beals v. Saldanha* [2003] 3 SCR 416; Briggs (2004) 8 Singapore Year Book of International Law 1.

532 *Royal Bank of Scotland plc v. Highland Financial Partners LP* [2013] EWCA Civ 328, [2013] 1 CLC 596,

533 As distinct from a disposal by application of a foreign procedural rule: *Naraji v. Shelbourne* [2011] EWHC 3298 (QB).

534 A decision by the courts of country B that a judgment obtained in country A is enforceable in country B does not make the issue whether the judgment is enforceable in Canada (and, one would suppose, in England) *res judicata*, as the ruling in country B is not on the merits of the same issue as that which arises in country C: *Cortés v. Yorkton Securities Inc* (2007) 278 DLR (4th) 740. For a very surprising suggestion that an order registering a foreign judgment in Singapore is itself capable of registration as a Singapore judgment in Hong Kong, see *Morgan Stanley & Co International Ltd v. Pilot Lead Investments Ltd* [2006] 4 HKC 93 (on which, see Smart (2007) 81 ALJ 348). One supposes that this must be taken as wrong.

In general the rule causes no difficulty, even if it may have odd effects. In *Nouvion v. Freeman*,[535] proceedings had been brought in Spain. By these, a summary form of procedure resulted in an award of damages being made in favour of the claimant. As a matter of Spanish law, if the defendant wished to contest the order made, he was at liberty to institute 'plenary' proceedings in the same court, possibly even before the same judge. It was held that the order made after the summary proceedings was not final, because it was liable to be reopened and amended, in the ordinary course of events, in the same court which had pronounced it; and the judgment did not qualify for recognition or enforcement. It does not seem satisfactory, however, that a judgment which a defendant could contest, but does not contest, before the same court, could be denied recognition as *res judicata* in England by reason of what may be a tactical decision by a defendant.

However, something very similar could be said of a default judgment: the fact that a default judgment may be later set aside in the court which had entered it cannot in practice be allowed to deprive the judgment of its claim to finality. Otherwise, as is sometimes said, the clearer a claimant's case, the more useless his judgment will be, and the conduct of a defendant who cannot be made to appear and defend the case on the merits will deprive the claimant of a judgment which qualifies as final.[536] But a point very similar to this was approved by the Privy Council when it held that an English default judgment was not entitled to be recognised in India, on the ground that whatever else it was, it was not a judgment on the merits of the case: none of the facts and matters set out in the claim had been examined or considered, and although the proceedings in England had arrived at some form of end, they had not done by judgment on the merits. Lord Buckmaster LC explained that an English 'judgment', entered when the defence was struck out for failure to comply with an order to answer interrogatories, could not be seen as a judgment on the merits which were, *ex hypothesi*, never investigated: as he put it, 'the controversy raised in the action has not, for one reason or another, been the subject of direct adjudication by the Court'. It followed that the judgment could not be sued on in India as a foreign judgment 'given on the merits of the case'.[537] The result of all this would be that a default judgment fails to meet the requirements for recognition in two distinct ways: because it may be set aside in the court in which it was given, but also because it is not a judgment on the merits at all. If the Privy Council was prepared to see that as reason to refuse recognition of an English judgment, there is no reason to question its application to foreign judgments.

However, the proposition that such a resolution is not a judgment on the merits does not appear to have been developed, for the Privy Council decision seems to have been forgotten: it is hard to find any other explanation, for no one has ever sought to explain why the Privy Council was wrong or its decision liable to be distinguished. And as to a default

---

535 (1889) 15 App Cas 1. See also *JSC Aeroflot Russian Airlines v. Berezovsky* [2014] EWCA Civ 20 (evidence of finality of foreign judgment too unclear for summary determination).

536 The possibility that this may lead to the non-recognition overseas of an English default judgment has led to a practice of giving summary, rather than default, judgment in cases in which the defendant does not appear and the claimant apprehends problems with the enforcement overseas: *Messer Griesheim GmbH v. Goyal MG Gases Pvt Ltd* [2006] EWHC 79 (Comm), [2006] 1 CLC 283 (setting aside default judgment under CPR Part 13, and holding that the concept of merger in the judgment did not prevent the court from taking this step to de-merge, as it were, the judgment from the cause of action).

537 *Keymer v. Visvanatham Reddi* (1916) LR 44 Ind App 6 (the passage quoted is at 10). The rule relied on was the Indian Code of Civil Procedure, art. 13(b), but the statutory rule which refused recognition if the judgment was not on the merits of the case was taken directly from the common law as it was then understood. The decision was referred to with evident approval in *Oppenheim & Co v. Mahomed Haneef* [1922] 1 AC 422.

judgment not being final on account of its being liable to be reopened by the same court, the principle may be this: that if there is a specified or ordinary period for applying to set aside a default judgment, and this has not yet expired, the judgment may not yet be seen as final, because it is not yet final in that court, for in the ordinary course the defendant may apply to have it set aside. But once this period has expired, setting aside may be regarded as not being something which happens in the ordinary course; and the judgment should be regarded as being final.[538] Again, if the court which has given judgment retains the power to vary the amount of damages it has awarded, the judgment will be seen as final as to liability, and liable to be recognised as such, but not final as to quantum, so not liable to be enforced by proceedings brought to recover this sum as a debt.

The judgment will be conclusive if none of the defences to its recognition may be raised by the party against whom it is asserted. The judgment is on the merits if it is 'a decision which establishes certain facts proved or not in dispute, states what are the relevant principles of law applicable to such facts and expresses a conclusion with regard to the effect of applying those principles to the factual situation concerned'.[539] If there is judgment for a party on procedural grounds, properly so called, the judgment may not be on the merits.[540]

Decisions on jurisdictional applications or challenges,[541] which may well be interlocutory[542] in the foreign court, may sometimes[543] be seen as final and conclusive for the purposes of English private international law. If, as in *The Sennar (No 2)*,[544] a court dismisses proceedings[545] on the ground that a jurisdiction agreement obliges the claimant to bring it elsewhere, the decision and order will be the last word of the court which

---

538 The rule as stated will not cause injustice on the assumption that the time period permitted for setting aside the judgment is short: as indeed it is likely to be (for otherwise there would be small point in seeking a default judgment in the first place). In *Schnabel v. Lui* [2002] NSWSC 15, the court applied a test derived from *Ainslie v. Ainslie* (1927) 39 CLR 381: was the judgment 'entirely floating as a determination, enforceable only as expressly provided and in the course of enforcement subject to revision' or 'has it been given the effect of finality unless subsequently altered'? This test seems to be entirely appropriate (and it was reaffirmed in *Kuligowski v. Metrobus* (2004) 220 CLR 363, [25]). When the default judgment is set aside in the foreign court, the local judgment to give effect to it must be set aside as well: *Benefit Strategies Group Inc v. Prider* [2007] SASC 250. It would appear to follow, but was not said to follow, that the same is true when a foreign judgment is reversed on appeal if there are grounds to oppose recognition of the appellate judgment (but where there are, the result will be different).

539 Lord Brandon in *The Sennar (No 2)* [1985] 1 WLR 490. This definition was given for the purpose of the expression 'on the merits' as it is used to found an estoppel. But there is no reason to think that it is not of general application.

540 Cf *Black-Clawson International Ltd v. Papierwerke Waldhof-Aschaffenburg AG* [1975] AC 591; *The Sennar (No 2)* [1985] 1 WLR 490; see also *Charm Maritime Inc v. Kyriakou* [1987] 1 Lloyd's Rep 433; *Desert Sun Loan Corp v. Hill* [1996] 2 All ER 847; *Naraji v. Shelbourne* [2011] EWHC 3298 (QB). Care must be taken not to make too much of this proposition. As the more recent cases show, a decision on a question of interlocutory civil procedure can still be on the merits of the point; and a judgment could hardly be denied enforcement if the claimant had won (only) because the defendant had failed to discharge the burden of proof procedurally placed upon him.

541 As they are usually made on the application of the defendant against the claimant, and as the claimant chose the court and, therefore, submitted to its jurisdiction, there is no difficulty in satisfying the requirement that the court have international jurisdiction.

542 It follows that 'interlocutory' is not a useful term of art in this context.

543 There is need for considerable caution. In *Deutsche Bank AG v. Highland Crusader Offshore Partners LP* [2009] EWCA Civ 725, [2010] 1 WLR 1023, [22]–[29], the court was asked to give some effect to a transcript of comments made by a Texas judge in the course of a hearing on a motion to dismiss, where the order made by the judge was, in conformity with Texas procedure, unaccompanied by reasons. This cannot have been an appropriate thing to consider doing.

544 [1985] 1 WLR 490. And see also *Marubeni Hong Kong & South China Ltd v. Mongolian Government* [2002] 2 All ER (Comm) 873.

545 By contrast, if it dismisses a jurisdictional challenge, the defendant will not be regarded as having submitted (see 1982 Act, s. 33(1)) unless he participates further in the proceedings.

handed it down, and will be given and made on the merits of the validity and effect of the jurisdiction agreement. Such a decision will be perfectly capable of recognition in England as *res judicata* against the person who is to be bound by it.[546] It is less clear that the same principle could extend to the decision of a foreign court to stay or dismiss an action of the ground of *forum non conveniens*. Though a foreign court may finally dispose of a case by dismissing it on these grounds in favour of trial in an identified natural forum, there is no authority which clearly holds that such a decision of this kind by a foreign court may qualify for recognition as *res judicata*. The point is not straightforward, for the foreign court may, but need not, have applied principles which are to the same broad effect as an English court would have applied.[547] But if the two versions of the doctrine are sufficiently similar, the reasoning in *The Sennar (No 2)* may be applicable. It is true that, whereas the construction of a contract by a foreign and an English court involves one and the same issue, even if the two courts apply different choice of law rules to determine it, the application of principles of *forum non conveniens* may not be sufficiently similar that the principles of issue estoppel are engaged. In other words, the objection to recognition may not be the finality of the foreign judgment, but directed at the requirement that the same issue must be before the two courts before an issue estoppel can arise. Even so, if the technical principles of issue estoppel are not fully met, it may still be an abuse of process[548] for a claimant to pretend to be unaffected by the jurisdictional decision of a foreign court in circumstances where the English court is called upon to apply jurisdictional principles which operate to similar effect.

7.67 Defence to recognition (2): foreign judgment was obtained in breach of an agreement about the resolution of disputes

If proceedings were brought in the foreign court contrary to[549] a binding arbitration agreement, or in breach of a contractual agreement on choice of court, a judgment in favour of the claimant will not be recognised in England unless the defendant waived the breach by counterclaiming in the proceedings or by otherwise submitting to the jurisdiction of the foreign court. The section needs to be set it out in full:

> **32. Overseas judgments given in proceedings brought in breach of agreement for settlement of disputes.** *(1) Subject to the following provisions of this section, a judgment given by a court of an overseas country in any proceedings shall not be recognised or enforced in the United Kingdom if (a) the bringing of those proceedings in that court was contrary to an agreement under which the dispute in question was to be settled otherwise than by proceedings in the courts of that country; and (b) those proceedings were not*

---

546 And it is of no relevance that the foreign court may have applied a choice of law rule which is not that which would have applied in an English court: see above, para. 7.64. See also *Leibinger v. Stryker Trauma GmbH* [2006] EWHC 690 (Comm). The principle was misapplied by the Australian Federal Court in *Armacel Pty Ltd v. Smurfit Stone Container Corp* (2008) 248 ALR 573, where it was held that a finding made against a defendant who appeared before the foreign court only to challenge jurisdiction was nevertheless binding on him.

547 For the proposition that a court may have to consider whether the foreign doctrine of *forum non conveniens* is sufficiently close to its own, see *Amchem Products Inc v. British Columbia (Workers' Compensation Board)* [1993] 1 SCR 897, 931–932.

548 *House of Spring Gardens Ltd v. Waite* [1991] 1 QB 241; *Owens Bank Ltd v. Etoile Commerciale SA* [1995] 1 WLR 44.

549 That is, the contract containing the clause must be construed in accordance with the relevant law, and according to that law, shown to be broken: this law should be the law that governs the remainder of the contract (a view distantly supported by *Egon Oldendorff v. Libera Corporation* [1995] 2 Lloyd's Rep 64).

brought in that court by, or with the agreement of, the person against whom the judgment was given; and (c) that person did not counterclaim in the proceedings or otherwise submit to the jurisdiction of that court. (2) Subsection (1) does not apply where the agreement referred to in paragraph (a) of that subsection was illegal, void or unenforceable or was incapable of being performed for reasons not attributable to the fault of the party bringing the proceedings in which the judgment was given. (3) In determining whether a judgment given by a court of an overseas country should be recognised or enforced in the United Kingdom, a court in the United Kingdom shall not be bound by any decision of the overseas court relating to any of the matters mentioned in subsection (1) or (2). (4) Nothing in subsection (1) shall affect the recognition or enforcement in the United Kingdom of (a) a judgment which is required to be recognised or enforced there under the 1968 Convention or the Lugano Convention or the Regulation; ...

It may immediately be seen that a judgment *for* the defendant will be recognised as conclusive against the claimant.[550] Such a judgment is given against the claimant; but as the proceedings will have been brought *by* the person against whom the judgment was given, section 32(1)(b) of the 1982 Act will deprive the unsuccessful claimant of an argument based upon his own breach of the agreement.

In its statutory form, this is a relatively new defence, created by section 32 of the 1982 Act, though the common law would not have recognised a judgment obtained in similar circumstances.[551] It makes a different point from that raised when deciding whether there was a contractual submission to a foreign court: the question there is whether the defendant had or had not submitted by virtue of the contractual term. Here the question is whether, even though the court did have jurisdiction in the international sense,[552] it was nevertheless asked to exercise it contrary to a valid and binding agreement on choice of court or for arbitration. In deciding whether there was a breach of the agreement, the decision of the foreign court upon this very point does not bind the English court, which decides the issue for itself; and in deciding whether the defendant counterclaimed or otherwise submitted, the view taken by the foreign court does not bind the English court, which also decides this issue for itself;[553] in deciding whether the clause was enforceable the view of the foreign court does not bind the English court, which also decides this issue for itself.[554]

The policy behind section 32 is that the need to prevent breaches of a valid and binding contract to settle disputes in a particular way overrides the conflicting policy preferring the finality of litigation. Commercial agreements for the resolution of disputes are looked on favourably, and section 32 lends what weight it can to their effectiveness by withholding recognition from the judgments of foreign courts which do not give effect to them. In cases in which the defendant, who has maintained his objection to the foreign court's jurisdiction, has been forced – in the sense of having made a practical decision which he really had no choice but to make – to participate in the substantive proceedings in order to preserve a sensible basis for an appeal on the jurisdictional point, it is most unlikely that he will be

---

550 This shows that the decision in *The Sennar (No 2)* [1985] 1 WLR 490 would be the same today.

551 *Ellerman Lines Ltd v. Read* [1928] 2 KB 144 (considering the applicable common law defence, 50 years before s. 32 was formulated, to be fraud). See also *Bank St Petersburg v. Arkhangelsky* [2014] EWCA Civ 593, [2014] 1 WLR 4360 (no breach of English jurisdiction clause by attempting to rely on Russian judgments in those proceedings, but there would be a breach if those Russian judgments were enforced if the bank were to lose in the English proceedings).

552 On the basis of presence or residence.

553 Section 32(3).

554 Section 32(2). Were it not for s. 32(3), can it be argued that the defendant would have been bound? *Cf Desert Sun Loan Co v. Hill* [1996] 2 All ER 847. The wording of s. 32 appears to preclude the possibility of any estoppel.

taken to have submitted to the jurisdiction of the foreign court in such a way as to prevent subsequent reliance on section 32.[555]

If the judgment is required to be recognised under the Brussels I Regulation,[556] section 32(4) excludes this statutory defence. However, if a judgment is given contrary to the terms of an arbitration agreement, it is still possible (in the sense that it has not yet been held by the European Court to be inadmissible) to argue that English public policy requires recognition of the judgment to be withheld, in which case the defence contained in section 32(1) will assert itself to prevent recognition of the offending judgment.

7.68 Departure from an agreement as to applicable law

It remains to be seen whether section 32 allows a judgment to be refused recognition where it can be said that there was an agreement on choice of law, rather than choice of court or arbitration, and the claimant brought proceedings before a court which, for whatever reason, did not settle the dispute by the application of the contractually agreed law. The starting point obviously is, however, that a contention that the foreign court was in error in applying the wrong law cannot found a defence to recognition. It may be that this is also the finishing point.

On the other hand, section 32(1)(a) requires a court to refuse recognition of a judgment if 'the bringing of those proceedings in that court was contrary to an agreement under which the dispute in question was to be settled otherwise than by proceedings in the courts of that country'. If the parties agreed that disputes were to be resolved by the application of English substantive law, and if proceedings were brought before a foreign court which did not apply English law, it may be argued that the bringing of the proceedings before the foreign court falls within the wording of section 32(1)(a). It may be said that if the contract does not specify a court with exclusive jurisdiction, the most obvious foundation for an argument that the bringing of proceedings in a particular court is contrary to the agreement which the parties made is absent. But if the parties make promises to each other that disputes will be resolved by the application of a particular law, it seems almost inevitable that they must also have agreed that proceedings will not be brought before a court or tribunal which will apply some other law: the logic is inescapable. If the parties make an agreement that their disputes will be resolved by the application of a particular law, and they were then asked how they would characterise the act of one of them bringing proceedings before a court or tribunal which would not apply that law, it is not far-fetched to think that this might be said to breach the promise about the manner in which disputes would be resolved. After all, a law can be applied only by a court; if a law is to be applied it must be applied by a court;

---

555 *AES Ust-Kamenogorsk Hydropower Plant LLP v. AES Ust-Kamenogorsk Hydropower Plant JSC* [2011] EWCA Civ 647, [2012] 1 WLR 920. The point was not directly considered by the Supreme Court (*AES Ust-Kamenogorsk Hydropower Plant LLP v. AES Ust-Kamenogorsk Hydropower Plant JSC* [2013] UKSC 35, [2013] 1 WLR 1889) but there is no reason to doubt the correctness of the decision below. It is, as has been said above, wrong to approach steps taken before a foreign court as though they had been taken before an English court, for foreign procedural systems are not always the same as the English. For earlier decisions to the same general (broad) effect, see *Marc Rich & Co AG v. Soc Italiana Impianti PA (No 2)* [1992] 1 Lloyd's Rep 624; *The Eastern Trader* [1996] 2 Lloyd's Rep 585. However, a suggestion in the judgment of the Court of Appeal that if the defendant had submitted to the foreign jurisdiction, s. 32 did not *require* the court to recognise the foreign judgment (if this really is what was intended) cannot be supported. The point was not raised on appeal to the Supreme Court.

556 And if the Regulation does apply, this is no defence to the recognition of the judgment: Regulation 44/2001, Art. 35; Regulation 1215/2012, Art. 45.

and a choice of law to govern the substantive issues raised at the point when disputes are resolved must be taken to connote that proceedings may be, and will be, brought anywhere, but only in places where this agreement as to governing law will be given effect.[557] If on a true construction of their agreement, the choice of law does not bear this meaning, the analysis will, of course, fail.[558]

It would mean that a choice of law to govern the resolution of disputes connotes the agreement of the parties that proceedings will be brought before a court – any court, but only a court – which will give effect to it. If proceedings are brought before a court which does not respect the agreement on choice of law, section 32(1)(a) would apply. In other words, an agreement on choice of law is an agreement on a court which will adjudicate which is defined by formula or characteristic, rather than by simple geographical designation.

And if the argument can be sustained as far as this point, section 32(3) would then mean that the fact that the foreign court ruled against the application of the law which the parties had selected is irrelevant to the issues arising on the recognition of the judgment. The only remaining impediment to an argument based on section 32(1)(a) is that the defence to recognition is lost if the party against whom the judgment is given counterclaimed in the proceedings or otherwise submitted to the jurisdiction of the court. Does a defendant who appears in the foreign proceedings, who argues that the law chosen by the parties should be applied by the court, submit by virtue of his appearance to the summons and defence of the claim? If the answer is yes, this will defeat reliance on section 32. However, if a party appears before a court, makes a jurisdictional objection on the basis of an agreement on choice of court, it is not inevitable that he submits to the jurisdiction of that court if, for example, the court rules that it will hear evidence and submissions which go to the merits before ruling on the jurisdictional challenge. If to keep the jurisdictional challenge alive the defendant has no real alternative but to participate in the foreign proceedings, it may yet be held that this is not such a submission on his part as casts away the shield given by section 32.[559] If that is correct, then in order to obtain a ruling which results in the application of the law chosen by the parties, the defendant may be left with no real choice but to participate in the procedure before the foreign court; and by parity of reasoning, such participation should not be counted as submission either. If it is anything, it is his attempt to mitigate his loss.

It cannot be denied that a court, if it accepted this reasoning, would be widening the scope of section 32 significantly beyond what has previously been assumed, and that it will, to that same extent, restrict the recognition of foreign judgments. This will not make the argument attractive.[560] On the other hand, it does not mean that a judgment will be denied

---

557 In *E.I. Du Pont de Nemours & Co v. Agnew* [1987] 2 Lloyd's Rep 585, the fact that an insurance policy was governed by English law was held, in circumstances in which the material question was as to a rule of English public policy, to require the case to be heard in England, where English law would be applied. It would have been wrong to allow the case to proceed overseas, and so 'introduce an unacceptably random element into a very important commercial undertaking': at 594. No doubt the case would have been stronger still if English law had been expressly chosen to govern the insurance; the decision comes close to ruling (but did not, and did not need to, rule) that where the parties choose English law, it will be a breach of that agreement for the law of another country to be applied instead.

558 In *Ace Insurance Ltd v. Moose Enterprise Pty Ltd* [2009] NSWSC 724, the judge held that it did fail unless the agreement on choice of law were drafted very clearly to support the contention that it was a promissory, not a declaratory, term.

559 *AES Ust-Kamenogorsk Hydropower Plant LLP v. AES Ust-Kamenogorsk Hydropower Plant JSC* [2011] EWCA Civ 647, [2012] 1 WLR 920. The point was not directly dealt with on appeal.

560 *Cf Ace Insurance Ltd v. Moose Enterprise Pty Ltd* [2009] NSWSC 724.

recognition because a foreign court 'applied the wrong law'. It simply means that a clear legislative policy, in favour of upholding commercial dispute resolution agreements where the defendant has not waived his rights, will take priority over the general common law rules for recognition of judgments as they apply in cases where this is not an issue. Given the importance of choice of law in commercial agreements, this is perhaps unsurprising. Moreover, the doctrine of obligation may point in the same general direction.[561] Whereas it cannot be said that a defendant assumes an obligation to be bound by the foreign judgment only if the foreign court makes no mistake of fact or law, it is not irrational to say that, when he made a contractual agreement as to choice of law, he assumed an obligation to be bound by a judgment which applied that specific law, but not otherwise. The argument may be novel,[562] but it is not irrational.[563]

7.69 Defence to recognition (3): foreign judgment was obtained by fraud: principle

If a judgment is otherwise entitled to recognition, the court will not permit a re-examination of the merits of the claim which gave rise to it, even if it is alleged that the judgment was wrong in fact or in law or in both. That is clear, and the correct policy of the law is to defend that proposition from being undermined.

But an exception is made where it is alleged that the judgment was obtained by fraud: that is to say, if there had not been fraud, the judgment would have been different.[564] If an allegation of operative fraud is credible, that is, there appears to the court to be a *prima facie* case of fraud having caused the judgment,[565] the English court will order that issue to be investigated and ruled on in a separate trial. Even if – as will commonly be the case – this English investigation of the issue whether there was fraud will require the re-examination of the merits of the original judgment, this furnishes no objection to the order that the issue be tried. Fraud unravels most things, and certainly unravels a foreign judgment. A person may not take advantage of his own wrongdoing. If it appears that his wrongdoing may be characterised as the commission of fraud, the allegation must be investigated by the English court; the particular policy of defeating fraud prevails over the general policy favouring the finality of litigation or the conclusiveness of foreign judgments.

The seriousness, separateness, of fraud has been observed on many occasions. In *HIH Casualty and General Insurance Ltd v. Chase Manhattan Bank*,[566] Lord Bingham of Cornhill

---

561 Though for the view that reflection on the doctrine of obligation has nothing to contribute to an understanding of the law (not a view which is not supported here), see *Rubin v. Eurofinance SA* [2012] UKSC 46, [2013] 1 AC 213, [9].

562 Though not perhaps completely so: *British Steamship Insurance Association v. Ausonia Assicurazioni SpA* [1984] 2 Lloyd's Rep 98; *Banco Atlantico SA v. British Bank of the Middle East* [1990] 2 Lloyd's Rep 504.

563 For further analysis, see Briggs, *Agreements on Jurisdiction and Choice of Law* (2008), ch. 11.

564 *Gelley v. Shepherd* [2013] EWCA Civ 1172 (after all, misrepresentations are not actionable at common law unless they are operative, which in turn requires them to have been relied on).

565 In *Codd v. Delap* (1905) 92 LT 810 it was said that the issue should be tried, and summary judgment refused 'unless it is obvious that the allegation of fraud (impeaching the foreign judgment sued on) is frivolous and practically moonshine', *per* Lord Lindley. But for cases in which the assertion of a pretended defence of fraud was dismissed as incredible, see *JSC VTB Bank v. Skurikhin* [2014] EWHC 271 (Comm); *OJSC Alfa Bank v. Trefilov* [2014] EWHC 1806 (Comm).

566 [2003] UKHL 6, [2003] 2 Lloyd's Rep 61.

restated the seriousness with which the common law treats a credible allegation of fraud. He said:[567]

> 'For as Rix LJ observed more than once in his judgment, fraud is a thing apart. This is not a mere slogan. It reflects an old legal rule that that fraud unravels all: *fraus omnia corrumpit*. It also reflects the practical basis of commercial intercourse. Once fraud is proved "it vitiates judgments, contracts and all transactions whatsoever": *Lazarus Estates Ltd v. Beasley*, *per* Denning LJ. Parties entering into a commercial contract will no doubt recognise and accept the risk of errors and omissions in the preceding negotiations, even negligent errors and omissions. But each party will assume the honesty and good faith of the other; absent such assumption they would not deal. What is true of the principal is true of the agent, not least in a situation where, as here, the agent, if not the sire of the transaction, plays the role of a very active midwife. As Bramwell LJ observed in *Weir v. Bell*: "I think that every person who authorises another to act for him in the making of any contract, undertakes for the absence of fraud in that person in the execution of the authority given, as much as he undertakes for its absence in himself when he makes the contract".'

Whether or not the theoretical basis of the recognition of a judgment is that the judgment creates an obligation, if fraud vitiates what would otherwise be a binding commercial obligation, as Lord Bingham says it does, then fraud will vitiate this obligation as well. The only remaining question is what is comprehended by 'fraud'; and on this the common law on the recognition of judgments is open to greater objection. For in the context of the obtaining of foreign judgments, the meaning of fraud is neither narrow nor precise: it extends to encompass 'every variety of *mala fides* and *mala praxis* whereby one of the parties misleads and deceives the judicial tribunal'.[568]

Examples drawn from the cases illustrate the alleged ingenuity of alleged fraudsters. If the allegations are to be believed, in *Abouloff v. Oppenheimer*,[569] a claimant suing for the delivery of goods concealed from the court that he already had them; in *Vadala v. Lawes*,[570] a claimant suing on bills of exchange falsely claimed they were mercantile when they had been given for gambling debts; in *Syal v. Hayward*,[571] a claimant sued for a debt, concealing from the court that half the sum was a usurious interest charge upon the other half; in *Jet Holdings Inc v. Patel*,[572] the claimant intimidated the defendant into not appearing at the trial;[573] in *Owens Bank v. Bracco*,[574] the claimant obtained judgment by forging documents and giving perjured testimony. In none of these cases could the allegations of fraud be dismissed outright as implausible,[575] which means that there had to be an English trial of the allegation of fraud.

---

567 At [15].
568 *Jet Holdings Inc v. Patel* [1990] 1 QB 335.
569 (1882) 10 QBD 295.
570 (1890) 25 QBD 310.
571 [1948] 2 KB 443.
572 [1990] 1 QB 335.
573 In effect, made him an offer he could not refuse.
574 [1992] 2 AC 443.
575 The standard required is that imposed by CPR r. 24.2. As the judgment-creditor will usually apply for summary judgment, he will succeed if the defence can be rejected as having no real prospect of success, but if not, it will be ordered to go to trial: *Jet Holdings v. Patel*. It is plausible that the weight of evidence which will be required to establish a *prima facie* case, or a defence that is more than shadowy, will vary in accordance with the perception which the English court has of the adjudicating court. In this way a judgment from a court with which the English court is very familiar may require a substantially greater weight of evidence to be brought before the allegation of fraud is thought to be well founded enough to be tried again than if the judgment is that of a court the strength and impartiality of which is less well established. This may also be the point made by the Privy Council in *AK Investment CJSC v. Kyrgyz Mobil Tel Ltd* [2011] UKPC 7, [2012] 1 WLR 1804, [116].

A contention that these cases set the bar rather too low is assisted by the more contro-versial aspect of the defence of fraud: that it may be raised in the English recognition or enforcement proceedings even if had been raised before, and even though it had been investigated, and rejected, by the foreign court. It is permitted to raise the facts and matters on which it is based in the English enforcement proceedings, even though these could have been (but were not) raised before the foreign court. Clearly, an allegation of fraud based on newly discovered material should be investigated for its first time. It may be less clear that an old one should be investigated for what may be its second time.

Such reflections have led some common law jurisdictions to reject the English approach to the fraud defence:[576] a chilly wind now blows across the defence. In those systems which have rejected the traditional common law, there is requirement of a new discovery of mate-rial which would justify setting the judgment aside.[577] Indeed, some courts[578] have gone so far as to demand that the new discovery be of material which could not with reasonable dili-gence have been discovered for the original hearing; but this would be very hard to defend, for when it comes to taking sides between a party who may be accused of negligence and another accused of fraud, the decent money is on the former. However, it may be said to show little respect for the forensic abilities of a foreign court if an English court acts as though it has a superior power to make a proper evaluation of the fraud said to have been practised, or if it sits as though it were conducting an extra-curial appeal against the foreign judgment. A submission that an English court would be a more competent or effective tribunal is inadmissible on an application to stay proceedings,[579] and the point is not much more palatable when it is concealed within an attempt to deny recognition to a foreign judgment. Moreover, a cautious approach which may have made sense in the common law of the nineteenth century may be well past its sell-by date in the twenty-first, and the fraud defence should not discriminate on grounds of nationality of judgment.[580]

These are serious points, but they are not decisive, and three points may be made in support of the traditional approach of the common law. First, when an English court is asked to withhold recognition for a foreign judgment on the ground of fraud, it is not saying that the foreign court is an institutionally inferior or less reliable tribunal, but that in this particular case there is evidence that it may have been deceived by the claimant,[581] and that this evidence should be investigated. Second, the English court will allow the losing party to raise the issue of fraud only if there is a sufficient basis shown to support the contention that the particular court was taken in by fraud. By means of this variable test, the material needed to establish a *prima facie* case may be quietly adjusted to reflect the English court's perception

---

576 *Keele v. Findley* (1991) 21 NSWLR 444, but regarded as wrong in *Yoon v. Song* (2000) 158 FLR 295; *Hong Pian Tee v. Les Placements Germain Gauthier Inc* [2002] 2 Sing LR 81; *Beals v. Saldanha* [2003] 3 SCR 416. And see *Owens Bank Ltd v. Bracco* [1992] 2 AC 443 ((1992) 108 LQR 549); *Owens Bank Ltd v. Etoile Commerciale SA* [1995] 1 WLR 44 (PC, St Vin). For a broad and quite excellent survey, see Garnett (2002) 1 J Int & Comm Law 1.

577 This represents the standard which operates when seeking to set aside an English judgment on the ground of fraud: *Hunter v. Chief Constable of the West Midlands* [1980] QB 283. For a decision that the need to demonstrate due diligence is misconceived see *Toubia v. Schwenke* (2002) 54 NSWLR 46, which must be correct, for otherwise the law will favour the fraudulent over the negligent.

578 Notably the Supreme Court of Canada in *Beals v. Saldanha* [2003] 3 SCR 416; see also Briggs (2004) 8 Singapore Year Book of International Law 1.

579 See paras 4.22 *et seq.*, above.

580 For this point in a related context, see *Morguard Investments Ltd v. De Savoye* [1990] 3 SCR 1077.

581 In an extreme case, even conspired with the claimant and the political leadership of the state: *Korea National Insurance Corp v. Allianz Global Corporate & Specialty AG* [2008] EWCA 1355, [2009] Lloyd's Rep IR 480.

of the quality of the foreign court. To put it simply, an English court may require powerful evidence that a court of high international reputation was taken in by fraud, but require less persuasion that it is appropriate to investigate the matter if the judgment came from a court with less of an international reputation for transparency and excellence.

And third, when the court is asked to set aside an English judgment, the defendant is asking for an order which will have international effect, and which will wholly deprive the claimant of his judgment, and of the right to enforce it anywhere and everywhere. In that context, it is unsurprising that English law sets a high hurdle for the defendant to clear. But where an English court is asked to find a foreign judgment to be sufficiently tainted by fraud, it is only being asked to withhold recognition and enforcement *in England*.[582] It will not, and could not, purport to affect the claimant's right to enforce in the country of judgment, or in any third country. It is a much more limited step than it is ever invited to take in respect of its own judgments, and it is wholly rational for the hurdle to be lower. This does not necessarily mean that it is right, but it does mean that the role of fraud in relation to a domestic judgment is not perfectly aligned with the effect it has in relation to a foreign judgment.

There is, therefore, a balance to be struck. There were expressions of judicial unenthusiasm for the traditional rule in *Owens Bank Ltd v. Bracco*[583] and *Owens Bank Ltd v. Etoile Commerciale SA*,[584] and it is not impossible that it is still vulnerable to attack. But in *AK Investment CJSC v. Kyrgyz Mobil Tel Ltd*[585] the Privy Council did not align itself with this criticism, seeing perfectly clearly that it was unwise to throw the baby out with the bathwater. It noted that any reform to the doctrine would need to be legislated, but also that it would be wise to adopt a 'nuanced' approach to the allegations of fraud in individual cases, perhaps so that this could be calibrated according to the circumstances of individual cases. Moreover, in the related[586] context of the enforcement of arbitration awards, the Court of Appeal,[587] though acknowledging the distinction between awards and judgments, did frame the right question, which was whether the award should be enforced *in England*. Once it is recalled that this, and no more, is the territorial scope of the fraud doctrine and the fraud defence, the criticisms of the traditional English approach to foreign judgments evidently obtained by fraud appear to be much less persuasive.

Two further arguments may be offered in support of the common law rule. The first is that the issue before the English court is whether the foreign court was deceived, and that this is not the same as the issue which arose before the foreign court. This has been disparaged as being a technical response to a technical point;[588] but all doctrine is technical, and the point has substance. If the claimant has procured judgment by fraud he has obtained a thing, a judgment and therefore a chose in action, by that fraud. That is, or closely resembles, the commission of a tort: the allegation is that when he induced the court to make an order in

---

582 Whether the courts of another country will regard an English judgment as establishing a *res judicata* is not the concern of the English court.

583 [1992] 2 AC 443.

584 [1995] 1 WLR 44.

585 [2011] UKPC 7, [2012] 1 WLR 1804.

586 The court did not simply apply the fraud rule applicable to judgments to arbitral awards, but its careful formulation of the question whether English public policy precluded enforcement in England was significant and, it is submitted, wholly correct.

587 *Soleimany v. Soleimany* [1999] QB 785; *Westacre Investments Inc v. Jugoimport-SPDR Holding Co Ltd* [2000] 1 QB 288.

588 *Vadala v. Lawes* (1890) 25 QBD 310 (though it was not the court which was doing the disparaging).

his favour, he obtained that thing by fraud. Such an allegation is clearly distinct from the existence of the underlying claim, and amounts to an allegation of a tort or similar wrong committed (or completed) at the moment of judgment, not before. It is not improper that it be investigated by the English court.

The second argument in support of the traditional rule is that the *claimant* chose the court in which to bring his claim. The reasons for his doing so may or may not have been innocent or disinterested.[589] It does not appear to be good policy for the defendant to be required to make his allegation of fraud, once and once only, in a court chosen by the claimant. The legal protection of the rights of the defendant may only really be secured by allowing him to select another forum in which he may advance his allegation of the claimant's fraud. If he makes that choice for England, he will be bound by the result in the court which *he* has seised and to the jurisdiction of which he has elected to submit. If he makes it elsewhere, for example, by bringing fresh proceedings in the country of original judgment to have the judgment set aside,[590] he will be bound by the judgment of the court *he* has seised, for the same reasons. In other words, the defendant is allowed one free, post-judgment, bite at the cherry; not two bites, which would be greedy, but not fewer than one either. It is, therefore, submitted that the fraud defence as presently framed by English law makes a substantial, but rational, inroad on the rule that the merits of a foreign judgment will not be reopened.

7.70 Curtailing the fraud defence where raising it is an abuse of process

Despite the submission above that the common law defence of fraud has more to commend it than is sometimes acknowledged, in theory and in practice, and despite the unwillingness of the Privy Council to align itself with the criticism sometimes heard, one cannot deny that there is a palpable sense of judicial coolness towards the fraud rule. Moreover, in *House of Spring Gardens Ltd v. Waite*,[591] a novel response to the fraud argument was found. After the defendant had been sued to judgment in Ireland, he brought proceedings of his own, also before the Irish courts, to have the judgment set aside on the ground of fraud. The action failed. When the claimant later sought to enforce his judgment in England, the defendant was not entitled to plead that the original judgment had been obtained by fraud. He had seised a court of his own independent choosing (Ireland) in which to allege fraud; and he was estopped from disavowing the judgment he had obtained in order to try and make the plea all over again. If that estoppel argument was not conclusive, it would in any event have been an abuse of process for him to make the plea of fraud for a second time; and the fraud defence was disallowed on that ground also.

The principle that a court has an inherent power to prevent its processes being used abusively (a doctrine said to have developed in equity in response to the technical

---

589 In one extreme case, the courts chosen were those of North Korea: of all the things for a commercial undertaking to agree to, this is the weirdest to be found in the books. The claimant was the national insurance company which alleged that it had paid a truly gigantic sum of money to settle an insurance claim by the national airline (*Korea National Insurance Corp v. Allianz Global Corporate & Specialty AG* [2008] EWCA 1355, [2009] Lloyd's Rep IR 480) and which then sought to recover against a German reinsurer. Even after one has got over the surprise of discovering that there are courts in North Korea, it is rather hard to put out of one's mind the possibility that the choice of the court at Pyongyang had the effect of favouring one side over the other.

590 As in *House of Spring Gardens Ltd v. Waite* [1991] 1 QB 241.

591 [1991] 1 QB 241.

limitations and shortcomings of common law estoppel), according to which the court may prevent a defendant making a plea of fraud to resist recognition of a foreign (*in casu*, French) judgment, was approved by the Privy Council in *Owens Bank Ltd v. Etoile Commerciale SA*.[592] It is clear that a way has now been signposted to permit a court to curtail the fraud defence, in some cases at least. Though no case has yet gone so far, it may one day be argued, for example, that it is an abuse of the process of the English court for a judgment debtor to make an allegation of fraud in circumstances where he would have been free to bring separate proceedings to impeach the judgment in the jurisdiction of the adjudicating court and when, therefore, he has elected not to exhaust his local remedies.[593]

Although there may be something superficially attractive about the possibility that a plea of abuse of process might answer one of fraud, a court should tread cautiously. It cannot always be taken for granted that the court chosen by the claimant will have respected the defendant's rights: the claimant may have chosen his court with a cynical eye. And it may sometimes be possible to read too much into the fact that the judgment debtor has brought proceedings of his own, to have the judgment set aside, in the courts for the place where the judgment was obtained. If the judgment debtor has made a free and unconstrained election to raise the matter and have it resolved in that court, no doubt he should be estopped from seeking to walk away from judgment from the court he chose. But it may sometimes be different, for if the defendant has assets in the country in which judgment was obtained by the claimant (as the defendant says, by fraud), and these were threatened with seizure by way of execution,[594] an application to have the judgment set aside on grounds of fraud may have been so constrained that it should not have been treated as his one and only bite at the fraud cherry.

Before a court accepts that the principle of abuse of process may defeat the doctrine of fraud at common law, it should reflect that a defendant may, despite appearances to the contrary, have had a less than proper opportunity for an impartial investigation of his side of the case. If it is argued that it is an abuse of the process of the English court to raise the issue of fraud without first having applied to do so before the adjudicating court, this should not prevail: it will not be an abuse of process to raise an argument in England unless it could and should have been raised before the foreign court;[595] and it has never been the law that such a challenge must be made before the foreign court. The argument might very well be different if the original proceedings had been brought in a court to whose jurisdiction the defendant had previously agreed to submit by contract: there would then be a reasonable basis for the argument that the defence of fraud should be considered as excluded from being

---

592 [1995] 1 WLR 44, on appeal from St Vincent and the Grenadines, which explains why issues relating to a French judgment were dealt with under rules of the common law; *Desert Sun Loan Corp v. Hill* [1996] 2 All ER 847 (Stuart-Smith LJ; Evans LJ referred to a principle of abuse of justice, which appears to be the same thing). See also, on abuse of process, though not on fraud as a defence, *Virgin Atlantic Airways Ltd v. Zodiac Seats UK Ltd* [2013] UKSC 46, [2014] 1 AC 160.

593 In the different context of the Brussels Convention and doubtless under the Regulation, too, the defendant is expected to pursue his fraud remedy in the foreign jurisdiction and not in England under cover of an argument about public policy: *Interdesco SA v. Nullifire Ltd* [1992] 1 Lloyd's Rep 180; see above, para. 7.13.

594 It is unlikely, but not impossible, that this falls within s. 33(1)(c) of the 1982 Act and, therefore, precludes the argument that the defendant submitted to the jurisdiction of the foreign court, even though he brought the proceedings himself.

595 *Virgin Atlantic Airways Ltd v. Zodiac Seats UK Ltd* [2013] UKSC 46, [2014] 1 AC 160, [24].

available to be raised in the English courts.[596] But in the absence of such additional facts, there is a danger that a slightly impatient dismissal of a plea of fraud, advanced by a judgment debtor, as an abuse of process will run the risk that insufficient attention is directed to genuinely meritorious defences.

7.71 Defence to recognition (4): foreign judgment contravened the principles of natural or substantial justice

It is not clear whether the defence that the judgment should not be accepted as *res judicata* because it was obtained in breach of the rules of natural and of substantial justice is to be seen as one defence or two. But if it can be shown that the foreign court breached the rules of natural justice, the common law will refuse to recognise the judgment. In practice, this defence is liable to be taken over or absorbed by the Human Rights Act 1998, which is considered below. But the common law still needs to be examined.

In principle, foreign procedures, which if followed by a tribunal in England would render its decision reviewable for breach of the rules of natural justice, may be relied on as reasons why a foreign judgment should not be recognised in England. In spite of authority in the cases[597] on (opposing) stays of proceedings which refuses to allow a foreign court's procedure to be criticised in general terms as being inferior to that of English law, a specific allegation[598] made after the judgment, pointing out specific shortcomings in the manner in which the foreign court has operated its procedures, may be examined for its compatibility with standards of natural justice.

Examples of this defence in the case law are few.[599] But if a defendant has not been served,[600] or has not been notified that a moribund case has been revived,[601] or has not been notified that there is to be an appeal against a judgment in his favour,[602] it is likely to be contrary to natural or substantial justice to recognise the judgment. If there has been no judicial or jury[603] assessment of the facts and matters which are alleged to found the claim or the particular head of damages, recognition of the judgment may be denied.[604] It was once

---

596 A similar principle has been applied in the context of challenges to arbitral awards: *Westacre Investments Ltd v. Jugoimport-SPDR Holding Co Ltd* [2000] 1 QB 288, 309; and see above, para. 4.50 (on the inadmissibility of complaints about the procedure of a court which has been chosen for the litigation of disputes).

597 Especially *The Abidin Daver* [1984] AC 398.

598 A matter which requires evaluation, not speculation.

599 For a decision roundly rejecting a contention that the nature of the proceedings before the foreign court had so missed the point that the defendant had not had a hearing at all (but which may just suggest that the point may be available in the very rare case in which the facts support it), see *Jenton Overseas Investment Pte Ltd v. Townsing* (2008) 21 VR 241. The defence plays a more prominent part in Canada, as the nature of 'international jurisdiction' in Canadian private international law is looser. See *USA v. Yemec* (2010) 320 DLR (4th) 96 for the suggestion that there should be a defence of 'denial of a meaningful opportunity to be heard', which was accepted at first instance but rejected as unnecessary on appeal.

600 Which means given proper notice of the commencement of proceedings; it will be irrelevant that there was a technical irregularity in the mode or manner of service.

601 Cf *Maronier v. Larmer* [2002] EWCA Civ 774, [2003] QB 620 (a case on the Brussels Convention).

602 *Boele v. Norsemeter Holdings AS* [2002] NSWCA 363.

603 The fact that a jury does not usually give reasons (unless the foreign court has called for a special verdict) cannot be seen as a reason to refuse to recognise the judgment. It may be different if a judge has given a decision, for which reasons would fairly be expected, without reasons: *Adams v. Cape Industries plc* [1990] Ch 433.

604 *Adams v. Cape Industries plc* [1990] Ch 433 (assessment of damages); *Masters v. Leaver* [2000] ILPr 387 (evaluation of fraud). But, of course, this may also be said of a default judgment, so the point cannot be understood as an absolute one.

believed that the defence could not be taken in England if it had been taken in,[605] and had been rejected by, the foreign court. This may not be correct: it may be that an allegation of breach of natural justice may be made for a second time in England. In *Jet Holdings Inc v. Patel*,[606] the Court of Appeal cast doubt, but did not need to rule, upon the older view. But subject to any argument about its being an abuse of process to raise the point, it is hard to see why, in English private international law, there should be an obligation to abide by the decision of a foreign court which can be shown to have acted in breach of the rules of natural justice.

In *Adams v. Cape Industries plc*,[607] the question arose whether, if there was a procedure in the foreign court for correcting breaches of natural justice, it was incumbent upon the defendant to avail himself of it. The court held that it was not, at least in cases where the breach was fundamental and had deprived the defendant of notice of, or of an opportunity to take part in, the proceedings. But in the case of procedural irregularity[608] of a less fundamental kind,[609] it may be that this objection may not be made to the English court. Clearly it will be difficult for a defendant to be sure how to proceed. If he appears before the foreign court to complain about the procedural irregularity he may, by his act of submission, confer undoubted jurisdiction upon the foreign court. Yet, if he does not do so, he may not be entitled to raise his objection before the English court at the recognition stage, if it is otherwise held that the foreign court had international jurisdiction over him.[610]

The proposition that recognition of a judgment could be opposed on the ground of a breach of substantial justice, though lent some support by *Adams v. Cape*, is more controversial. As a court is not entitled to reinvestigate the merits of a dispute, it may well be that there is little opportunity to examine the substance of a case.[611] But suppose the foreign court had refused to give effect to the parties' choice of law contained in a contract.[612] If it may be said that flagrant disregard of the generally accepted standards of private international law may be a reason for not staying proceedings in favour of such a court,[613] it might be thought that an identical complaint, but revealed *ex post*, would justify the conclusion that the judgment should be denied recognition on grounds of breach of substantial justice. No doubt a court would not rush to reach such a conclusion;[614] and there is no real authority to lend it support. But parity of reasoning with the cases on stays of proceedings may still support it.

---

605 This may be rare: the most common allegation of breach of natural justice may be that the defendant did not have an opportunity to take part in the proceedings.

606 [1990] 1 QB 335.

607 [1990] Ch 433.

608 When measured against the tolerant standards of English private international law.

609 Described in *Adams v. Cape* as a breach of the rules of substantial justice which may, but would not necessarily, have given rise to a breach of natural justice.

610 See, taking the view that the defendant was not required to go to the foreign court and submit to its jurisdiction by taking the points about natural justice before it, *Cortés v. Yorkton Securities Inc* (2007) 278 DLR (4th) 740.

611 The view of the Ontario court in *Society of Lloyd's v. Saunders* [2001] ILPr 18 is that the defence is restricted to procedural fairness, and does not extend to the substantive merits of the claim.

612 But for the proposition that such a complaint falls under s. 32 of the Civil Jurisdiction and Judgments Act 1982, see above, para. 7.68. If that contention is not well founded, then this is the place in which the defence may gain a foothold. It may be that the common law should accept this as a defence. It is, in effect, allowed as a defence to a plea of *res judicata* in the Indian Code of Civil Procedure of 1908, Section 13. It is plausible that such as rule was enacted as a reflection of the common law as it was then understood..

613 *British Steamship Insurance Association v. Ausonia Assicurazioni SpA* [1984] 2 Lloyd's Rep 98; *Banco Atlantico SA v. British Bank of the Middle East* [1990] 2 Lloyd's Rep 504.

614 Which may be why the location of this objection within the scope of s. 32 of the Civil Jurisdiction and Judgments Act 1982 is more attractive.

7.72 Defence to recognition (5): recognition of foreign judgment would be contrary to English public policy

If its recognition would conflict with English public policy, a foreign judgment will not be recognised as *res judicata* in England. The usual colourful examples are an order to pay damages for breach of a contract to kidnap or to sell narcotics, or those based on openly racist laws. No doubt there are others, such as where the judgment has been obtained in defiance of an English anti-suit injunction.[615] The rule as set out here is a rule preventing *recognition* of a thoroughly objectionable judgment.[616] There is a separate rule which prevents the *enforcement* of certain judgments upon the ground, which may be regarded as a particularised aspect of public policy, that this would require enforcement of a foreign penal, revenue, or analogous public law.[617] There is no such barrier to the recognition of a foreign judgment which was given upon the basis of such a law. Even so, there is a small category of foreign laws which are so repugnant to English standards that they will be denied even recognition; and a judgment giving effect to such a law will, in principle, be equally disqualified from recognition.[618]

If it had been argued in the foreign proceedings that the claim should be disallowed on the basis that it contravened the public policy of the foreign forum, it will still be open to the defendant to argue that the recognition of the judgment would be contrary to English public policy: English and foreign public policies are not congruent, and only an English court can properly define and apply English public policy.[619] It is possible that the Court of Appeal in *Israel Discount Bank of New York v. Hadjipateras*[620] took a different view, treating the foreign court's application of its public policy (as this applied to the underlying claim) as relevant to, perhaps even decisive upon, the English law on the public policy against

---

615 *Phillip Alexander Securities & Futures Ltd v. Bamberger* [1997] ILPr 73, 104; *WSG Nimbus Pte Ltd v. Board of Control for Cricket in Sri Lanka* [2002] 3 Sing LR 603 (though *cf Advent Capital plc v. GN Ellinas Imports-Exports Ltd* [2005] EWHC 1242 (Comm), [2005] 2 Lloyd's Rep 607; *Golubovich v. Golubovich* [2010] EWCA Civ 810, [2011] Fam 88). It may just be possible to extend this reasoning to a case where the judgment has been obtained in defiance of an anti-suit injunction granted by a foreign court nevertheless considered to be the appropriate court to have made such an order: *cf Airbus Industrie GIE v. Patel* [1999] 1 AC 119; but the argument awaits judicial acceptance.

616 Or which conflicts with local public policy: *Kidron v. Green* (2000) 48 OR 775, where the Ontario court refused to grant summary judgment in respect of a California judgment awarding $15m for emotional distress. But *cf Beals v. Saldanha* (2004) 234 DLR (4th) 1, [2003] 3 SCR 416, which is hostile to the proposition that, just because the sum awarded is far larger than the local court would have adjudged, enforcement would be contrary to public policy. In *JSC VTB Bank v. Skurikhin* [2014] EWHC 271 (Comm) the possibility was raised that a judgment for manifestly excessive interest might be contrary to English public policy, but this point does not easily translate to the non-recognition (as distinct from enforcement) of the judgment.

617 Dicey, Morris and Collins, *The Conflict of Laws*, 15th edn (2012), Rule 3; and see below.

618 In *Williams & Humbert Ltd v. W & H Trade Marks (Jersey) Ltd* [1986] AC 368, Lord Templeman indicated that the courts might not recognise foreign laws which fail to safeguard human rights. This may have been too widely expressed to be wholly reliable, but the coming into force of the Human Rights Act 1998 may have breathed new life into this as a line of argument. Perhaps judgments for disproportionate or exemplary damages may fall within this need of objection to recognition. And see also *Kuwait Airways Corp v. Iraqi Airways Co (Nos 4 and 5)* [2002] UKHL 19, [2002] 2 AC 883, which was not about judgments but about 'legislative' decrees, but to which the same principles must apply.

619 *Yukos Capital Sarl v. OJSC Rosneft Oil Co* [2012] EWCA Civ 855, [2014] QB 458, [151] (refusing to apply the principles of issue estoppel to a decision of a Dutch court to refuse to recognise a Russian judgment on grounds of public policy. But there is no reason to suppose that findings made by the Dutch court in order to arrive at its conclusion could not be separately recognised as *res judicata*). For further proceedings, see *Yukos Capital Sarl v. OJSC Oil Co Rosneft* [2014] EWHC 2188 (Comm).

620 [1984] 1 WLR 137.

recognition. This appears to be wrong, for a foreign rule of public policy as it applies to the underlying claim is clearly different from a rule of English public policy as it applies to recognition of the judgment. However, if the adjudicating court has determined factual questions in the course of deciding what its public policy required – in *Israel Discount Bank*, whether duress was exercised in procuring the contract – the finding on this point may give rise to an estoppel if it is alleged that the same, or similar, fact gives rise to the English public policy against recognition.[621]

7.73 Defence to recognition (6): recognition of judgment is precluded by Human Rights Act 1998

If the recognition of a foreign judgment would have the effect of depriving a party of his right to a fair trial, it may well be that its recognition will be contrary to natural justice, or to substantial justice, or to public policy. But quite apart from that, if on a true construction of the 1998 Act, and the European Convention on Human Rights ('ECHR') to which it gives legal force, Article 6 ECHR would be infringed by the recognition of a foreign judgment, there will be no power to recognise the judgment, and neither natural justice nor public policy will be the reason for it, for if Parliament has legislated the result there is no more to say. A statute may override, or add to, the grounds for non-recognition of a foreign judgment; and the Human Rights Act 1998, in incorporating the ECHR into English law, has done that.

The principle of the matter is clear. If an English court has a statutory duty to ensure that a person has a right to a fair trial, it must equally have a statutory duty not to recognise a foreign judgment if its recognition, and the making of a judicial order which is consequent upon that recognition, would have the effect of producing the same prohibited outcome. The principle is clear enough; the case law somewhat less so. But if an English court would infringe Article 6 if it were to accept a foreign judgment as making an issue *res judicata* in England, it cannot be consistent with Article 6 for it to recognise a foreign judgment which embodies the same defect. Otherwise the protections guaranteed by Article 6 could be set at naught by suing first in a country which pays less regard to such guarantees.

The apparent difficulty arises when it is argued that a court is imposing the standards of the ECHR on States which are, by choice or by geography, not party to the Convention. There is some sort of balance to be struck, but the European Court of Human Rights in Strasbourg has not maintained a consistent position, which is not helpful. It got off to a bad start. In *Drozd & Janousek v. France and Spain*[622] the Strasbourg Court held that a court in a Contracting State was not precluded from recognising a judgment from the courts of a non-Contracting State (*in casu*, Andorra) even though the procedural standards of the trial court had fallen below the level of the guarantees of the ECHR. And in *Prince Hans-Adam II of Liechtenstein v. Germany*,[623] it stated that the national court seised was not required to assess

---

621 *Cf House of Spring Gardens Ltd v. Waite* [1991] 1 QB 241. And in the context of arbitral awards, it is not contrary to public policy, so as to permit an award to be set aside, to enforce an award alleged to be tainted by procedural defects when these have already been brought before, and considered by, the supervising court: *Minmetals Germany GmbH v. Fercosteel Ltd* [1999] CLC 647. See also *Svenska Petroleum Exploration AB v. Government of Republic of Lithuania* [2005] EWHC 9 (Comm), [2005] 1 Lloyd's Rep 515.

622 (1992) 14 EHRR 745.

623 Judgment of 12 July 2001.

whether the earlier decision of a Czechoslovakian court was compatible with the standards of the ECHR.

However, in *Pellegrini v. Italy*,[624] a contrary and more credible view was taken. Mrs Pellegrini had been summoned to an interview in the offices of the Roman Catholic Church in the Vatican City, and was subjected to some questioning which related to her marriage. Some months afterwards, she was notified that her marriage had been annulled. Her husband, who was behind it all, sought the recognition of the Vatican annulment under Italian law, pursuant to the treaty[625] between the Vatican City[626] and the Italian State. An Italian court considered that it was required to recognise the Vatican decree, but the Strasbourg Court said that as far as the ECHR was concerned, the Italian court was wrong to have done so. Though the Vatican City was not a Contracting State, and could not be required or expected[627] to conform to the standards of the ECHR, Italy was a Contracting State and the Italian courts were required to observe and give effect to the standards of the Convention. It was, therefore, incumbent upon the Italian court to ask whether recognition of the decree, which had been handed down without giving the wife a right to any semblance of a trial in respect of her civil rights, still less a fair one, would be consistent with the Italian court's duties under the ECHR. It seemed pretty clear what the answer was expected to be.

Some may consider that, whatever the Strasbourg Court may have said in *Pellegrini*, the result of the judgment brings the law very close to treating the Vatican City as though it were a Contracting State to the ECHR, and that this is not right. Perhaps sensing this, and the apparent strangeness of it, the House of Lords in *Government of USA v. Montgomery*[628] held that an American judgment would not be denied recognition if all that could be said of it was that the proceedings leading up to it fell short of the standards guaranteed by Article 6 ECHR. What was required before there could be non-recognition was a showing that there had been a *flagrant* falling below those standards.

This, it is submitted, is wrong. The House of Lords purported to distinguish *Pellegrini* on the basis that its outcome depended on the treaty between Italy and the Vatican City. But it is quite impossible to see how that 1929 treaty, as amended, could possibly have incorporated the standards of the ECHR, especially when the Vatican City has taken a deliberate decision not to subscribe to it, and therefore had assumed no obligation, of any earthly kind, to observe such standards itself. The House of Lords next observed that in cases in which an asylum seeker or fugitive has been faced with deportation to a country which is generally weak in its protection of human rights, the ECHR will only arise as a material consideration, which may be used to prevent deportation, if the case is a 'flagrant' one. This is quite right: it would wrong to quash a deportation order just because of a remote possibility that a foreign court or system will not measure up to what the ECHR demands of Contracting States. But to make a prediction about how courts in a foreign country may behave on a future occasions is very different indeed from making a retrospective assessment of what a specific court in

---

624 (2002) 35 EHRR 44. See also, for the proposition that the recognising court is taking its own decision, and must therefore act in accordance with the European Convention, *K v. Italy* (ECtHR Case 38805/97), 20 July 2004.

625 The papacy appears to prefer the designation 'Concordat', but it is all the same thing.

626 An entity which carries on its business under the name of the 'Holy See'.

627 The reasons why the *soi-disant* 'Holy See' cannot be expected to pay heed to human rights, such as equality and respect for the person, are not for this book to explain.

628 [2004] UKHL 37, [2004] 1 WLR 2241. See also Briggs (2005) 121 LQR 185; Muir Watt [2005] Rev Crit DIP 315.

that country has done. In the latter class of case, of which *Montgomery* was one, no element of prediction is required. It is therefore submitted that the court in *Montgomery* applied the wrong test, or applied the correct test but came to a wrong conclusion. The American court was found to have behaved and to have made its orders in a way which, if an English court had done it, would have amounted to a violation of Article 6 ECHR. For an English court nevertheless to recognise its judgment and then to make a judicial decision of its own to require compliance with the order made in the American, non-conforming, proceedings, and to order the confiscation of property, was to apply the rubber stamp to another's breach of, or to commit a constructive breach of, Article 6. It was wrong.[629]

The ECHR has also been pressed into service to deal with a question which has arisen when a foreign judgment, which would otherwise have qualified for recognition in England, has been upset by a higher court on grounds which appear to be open to question. This needs to be treated with more care than it may have received.

In a number of cases originating in Eastern Europe, a decision at first instance was over-turned by a higher court in procedures which appeared to be improper. The Strasbourg Court has explained that the right to a fair hearing before a tribunal as guaranteed by Article 6(1) ECHR is an aspect of the rule of law, and that 'one of the fundamental aspects of the rule of law is the principle of legal certainty, which requires, among other things, that where the courts have finally determined an issue, their ruling should not be called into question'.[630] No objection can be taken to the application of the ECHR if it leads to the conclusion that the procedure of a higher court was so defective that it deprived a person of the right to a fair trial, or that it unfairly deprived that person of the fruits of a judgment in his favour. But the development of a principle of 'legal certainty' does not appear to be a desirable import into the common law rules for recognition of foreign judgments, for there is a risk that it will tend to encourage debates about the meaning of the principle, at the expense of concentration on the particular issue which has arisen.

It has been held that a foreign judgment at first instance, which was set aside in further proceedings in circumstances which gave rise to a strong suspicion that the higher court had departed from the standards required by the ECHR, may be recognised: if the original judgment was affected only by an order which the English court was required to refuse to recognise, the original judgment would remain unimpaired, even though nullified according to the law of the country in which it had been given.[631] This presents no real intellectual problem for the common law, which gives effect to the obligation assumed by the parties in relation to the foreign adjudication, but does not enforce the foreign judgment, as a judicial act, as such. Even so, an English court will need to tread carefully. It is not necessarily improper for a higher court to take points which were not taken below; it is

---

629 For an excellent account of the issues, see Kinsch, 'The Impact of Human Rights on the Application of Foreign Law and on the Recognition of Foreign Judgments', in Einhorn and Siehr (eds), *Intercontinental Cooperation Through Private International Law* (TMC Asser Press, The Hague, 2004), who considers that the ECtHR may have gone too far in requiring the Italian court, in effect, to treat the Vatican judgment as though it were one from a Contracting State.

630 *Pravednaya v. Russia* [2004] ECHR 641; see *Merchant International Co Ltd v. NAK Naftogaz* [2012] EWCA Civ 196, [2012] 1 WLR 3036.

631 *Merchant International Co Ltd v. NAK Naftogaz* [2012] EWCA Civ 196, [2012] 1 WLR 3036. In fact the Court of Appeal was able, and evidently preferred, to uphold the decision below on the rather narrower ground that when proceedings in England first relied on the foreign judgment, the first instance judgment had not been reversed by the appellate decision said to have resulted from fraud or a breach of the rules of natural justice or the Human Rights Act 1998. But the broader proposition appears to be perfectly sound.

not necessarily improper for a court to set aside a lower court's judgment and to direct a rehearing: the broad supervisory role of a higher court may be as important as its function as a reviewer of individual judgments. The fact that a foreign system allows a higher court to call up and quash the judgment of a lower court is, or should be, unremarkable; the fact that a foreign court appeared to be flexing muscles which the English Court of Appeal does not have is not a sign that the rule of law has been cast aside. The nature of the evidence may be difficult;[632] but the fact that a foreign court has powers which an English court does not, does not mean that the foreign system fails to observe the rule of law. The application of the Human Rights Act to the recognition of foreign judgments calls for careful reflection.

7.74 Defence to recognition (7): foreign judgment is inconsistent with a prior judgment

If a foreign judgment is inconsistent with an English judgment, it will be denied recognition as *res judicata*. This has arisen in the context of matrimonial judgments *in rem*,[633] but it applies equally to judgments *in personam*. If a foreign judgment has been given before the English court has reached its decision, it is open to the party in whose favour it was given to apply to amend his pleading and rely upon it. He will succeed if such amendment is allowed and the other party is estopped from contesting the conclusiveness of the judgment. If the foreign judgment is between the same parties there is no difficulty; if not, it may still be decisive in an English court as between persons privy to the parties.[634]

Equally, if the foreign judgment is inconsistent with another foreign judgment between the same parties (or their privies, it is reasonable to suppose) which was prior in time, it will be denied recognition.[635] The general principle, that the first judgment in time prevails, is supported by the decision of the Privy Council in *Showlag v. Mansour*,[636] and the critical timing would appear to be that of judgment, not of other procedural steps, such as the institution of proceedings.[637] On the footing that the first judgment gave rise to an obligation on the date on which it was given, the solution in *Showlag* appears to be logically unimpeachable.

7.75 Effect and consequences of foreign judgment entitled to recognition

If, by the application of the preceding rules, it is decided[638] that a foreign judgment meets the requirements for recognition in favour of the party who seeks to rely on it,

---

632 *JSC Aeroflot Russian Airlines v. Berezovsky* [2014] EWCA Civ 20.

633 A foreign decree of nullity was denied recognition in *Vervaeke v. Smith* [1983] 1 AC 145 on the ground that the validity of the marriage in question was already *res judicata* by virtue of the prior decision of an English court.

634 *House of Spring Gardens Ltd v. Waite* [1991] 1 QB 241. For a fuller examination of the principles of estoppel in relation to foreign judgments, see paras 7.83 *et seq.*, below.

635 Applied to an arbitral award which could no longer be challenged under the Arbitration Act 1996, even though no order had yet been made giving permission to enforce it as a judgment: *People's Insurance Co of China, Hebei Branch v. Vysanthi Shipping Co Ltd* [2003] EWHC 1655 (Comm), [2003] 2 Lloyd's Rep 617.

636 [1995] 1 AC 431.

637 The approach in *The Indian Grace (No 2)* [1998] AC 878, which dealt with the interpretation of s. 34 of the 1982 Act (for which, see below), was to place greater emphasis on the date of institution of proceedings. It is not expected that this statutory approach has any application to the common law of estoppel.

638 The court may, in an appropriate case, but which must be comparatively rare, make a declaration that a foreign (*in casu*, Alberta) judgment will qualify for recognition, even though no challenge to its liability to recognition has been made: *Phillips v. Avena* [2005] EWHC 3333 (Ch).

and therefore binds or obliges the party against whom it was given, it is next necessary to ask what consequences flow from it. In principle, three distinct consequences can be identified; they are summarised in this paragraph and examined in detail in the following paragraphs.

First, a successful judgment creditor may seek to enforce the judgment by action in the English courts. In order to do so, he will commence proceedings to enforce the obligation or debt created by the judgment, by issuing and serving process on the defendant in the usual way.

If the defendant is out of the jurisdiction, permission to serve out in accordance with CPR rule 6.36[639] will have to be sought and obtained. In connection with such an application, it should be noted that this applies only to those judgments which need to be enforced by action at common law; separate arrangements exist for those judgments which are enforced by registration under the 1920 and 1933 Acts.[640] Although in principle the court must also consider, pursuant to CPR rule 6.37(3), that England is the proper place in which to bring the claim, it is extremely unlikely that this will be a significant issue unless the defendant can show the absence of assets, and the highly predictable continuing absence of assets, within the jurisdiction; and even then it may make no difference. Certainly the Court of Appeal took this view in its only fully reasoned decision on the point: if the judgment creditor wishes to obtain an order which he may not be able to execute, at any rate for the time being, there is no good reason to stand in his way.[641]

When the defendant has been served, the claimant may consider his case sufficiently strong to apply for summary judgment. On the hearing of such application, the court will consider whether the defendant has shown a plausible defence to recognition,[642] or any further defence to the enforcement of a judgment entitled to recognition.[643] If the judgment debtor has a real prospect of defending the claim or issue, the court will make no order on, or dismiss, the application for summary judgment, or make a conditional order.[644] But if the defendant has no real prospect of successfully defending the claim, final judgment for the claimant will be given without further ado.

Second, a successful judgment creditor will now be precluded from electing instead to bring an action on the underlying cause of action. It may be that he has obtained judgment in his favour, but is dissatisfied with the extent of his victory. Until 1982 he would have been free, in principle at least, to put the judgment aside and bring fresh proceedings on the underlying cause of action. But statutory reform has substantially abrogated that right.[645]

Third, a successful defendant may seek to rely on the judgment in his favour as creating an estoppel which either prevents the disappointed claimant bringing fresh proceedings on the underlying cause of action,[646] or which at least prevents the claimant seeking to reopen

---

639 The material rule will be CPR 6 PD 6B, Para. 3.1(10).

640 See below, para. 7.89 (1920 Act); para. 7.93 (1933 Act).

641 *Tasarruf Mevduati Sigorta Fonu v. Demirel* [2007] EWCA Civ 799, [2007] 1 WLR 2508. This decision does not appear to have been cited to the court in *Linsen International Ltd v. Humpuss Transportasi Kimia* [2011] EWCA Civ 1042, and the latter decision is not to be preferred.

642 Those previously examined.

643 From those further objections to be considered below.

644 CPR r. 24.4, and Practice Direction, Para. 5.

645 Civil Jurisdiction and Judgments Act 1982, s. 34.

646 Cause of action estoppel.

issues[647] which were decided by the foreign court in favour of the defendant. These three consequences are now examined separately.

7.76 Consequence of recognition (1): action by claimant to 'enforce the judgment'

If a foreign judgment is entitled to recognition, it may be 'enforced' by the claimant[648] or judgment creditor if it is final and conclusive upon the merits of the claim, is for a fixed sum of money, and its enforcement will involve neither the enforcement of a foreign penal or revenue or other public law, nor contravention of the Protection of Trading Interests Act 1980. As explained above,[649] there is no requirement that the foreign judgment be enforceable under the law of the State in which it was given, for the foreign judgment itself is not what is enforced in England.

The action will be commenced by the issue of process in the usual way, claiming the judgment sum as a debt; but the claimant will often seek summary judgment on the basis that the defendant has no real prospect of defending the claim. The claimant has six years from the date of judgment to bring the action,[650] and will then have six years to enforce his English judgment.[651] In an extreme case, for example where the judgment debtor has been unusually assiduous in concealing his assets from the claimant and outside the jurisdiction of the court, the judgment creditor may even obtain another judgment, by way of entitling him to enforce the earlier judgment, so as to pave the way to enforcing an English judgment against assets overseas.[652] It has been held that such a 'judgment on a judgment' may be obtained where the first judgment was obtained under section 26 of the Arbitration Act 1950[653] to make enforceable an arbitration award; there is no reason in principle why the same approach may not be taken to a foreign judgment if there were good reasons for requiring a new *English* judgment for the purposes of possible enforcement. The basis for the second judgment would be the implied[654] contractual promise to honour the first judgment.[655]

The common law generally awarded monetary remedies, and as the action for enforcement of a foreign judgment was originally by an action in debt, it is often said that only

---

647 Issue estoppel.

648 What is said here will apply with equal force to a defendant who makes a counterclaim: he is to all intents and purposes a claimant.

649 Paragraph 7.65, above.

650 It seems that this must be true, even though the foreign judgment remains enforceable for longer than the six years.

651 Limitation Act 1980, s. 24(1); *Berliner Industriebank AG v. Jost* [1971] 2 QB 273; and see *Duer v. Frazer* [2001] 1 All ER 249; *Good Challenger Navegante SA v. Metalexportimport SA* [2003] EWCA Civ 1668, [2004] 1 Lloyd's Rep 67; *Society of Lloyd's v. Longtin* [2005] EWHC 2491 (Comm), [2005] 2 CLC 744.

652 For enforcement against goods, see CPR Part 83 (superseding RSC Order 46).

653 Now s. 66(1) of the Arbitration Act 1996.

654 Which really means 'deemed'.

655 *ED & F Man (Sugar) Ltd v. Haryanto (No 2)*, *The Times*, 9 August 1996; *ED & F Man (Sugar) Ltd v. Lendoudis* [2007] EWHC 2268 (Comm), [2007] 2 Lloyd's Rep 579; *Bennett v. Bank of Scotland* [2004] EWCA Civ 988 (a case only on domestic law); *Kuwait Oil Tanker SAK v. Al Bader* [2008] EWHC 2432 (Comm). Whether such a judgment of the English courts may be enforced overseas is a matter for the law of the particular overseas country. On whether a foreign 'judgment on a judgment' could be enforced in England, there is no authority at common law, but see Foreign Judgments (Reciprocal Enforcement) Act 1933, s. 1(2A), which excludes such things from the material scope of that Act.

final foreign judgments for sums of money can be enforced by the judgment creditor. As the effect of a judgment entitled to recognition is to oblige the defendant to pay the debt adjudicated, and as an action for debt does not lie in respect of an unliquidated sum, a judgment can be enforced only if it has been finally quantified. If the total sum awarded has been finally determined, the fact that the foreign court would have power to vary the instalments of payment within that overall figure is irrelevant: the total sum is fixed, and the speed and mechanics of actual payment are, in England, procedural matters for the English, and not for the foreign, court. If the judgment has been rendered in a foreign currency, there is no reason why the claim for enforcement may not be brought in respect of the debt expressed in terms of the foreign currency in which the judgment was given.[656]

If these propositions, which refine the law on the enforcement of money judgments, were to be taken strictly at face value, it might be supposed that there could be no enforcement of a foreign judgment for an injunction, or of a declaratory judgment, or a judgment ordering other non-monetary relief. But this would not be a reliable impression of the common law. Though the accuracy of the proposition that only money judgments can be enforced at common law has not been seriously challenged, in England at least, this did not prevent the Supreme Court of Canada taking what it considered to be a different view, and holding that, in principle at least, a foreign judgment in terms equivalent or analogous to an equitable decree might be enforced in Canada.[657] This development has been endorsed by the courts in Jersey,[658] of all improbable places. The mechanism by which this was proposed to be done was that the Canadian or Jersey court would make a decree of its own, in terms of the original foreign (American and Brunei, respectively) decree, and this would then be enforced.

The Supreme Court of Canada appeared to think that this was a bold and overdue updating of the common law for Canada, but it may have failed[659] to notice how limited the development really was, and how misleading the traditional statement that only money judgments may be enforced at common law actually is. Consider what happens when an English court is asked to enforce a foreign money judgment. It does so by giving judgment on a claim made by the judgment creditor, the claim being founded on the foreign judgment. The English judgment is usually given for the sum adjudged due under the foreign judgment,[660] frequently summarily;[661] and it will be given without looking into the merits of the underlying claim. It is then this English judgment, rather than the foreign judgment, which provides the basis for execution in England.

---

656 *Miliangos v. George Frank (Textiles) Ltd* [1976] AC 443, which gives the appropriate date for conversion as being the date of actual payment. For the distinct question of the currency in which charging orders may be made, and whether a claimant who obtains an order expressed in a foreign currency may change his mind when the currency depreciates against the pound and it becomes clear that his currency gamble has not paid off (held no), see *Carnegie v. Giessen* [2005] EWCA Civ 191.

657 *Pro-Swing Inc v. Elta Golf Inc* (2006) 273 DLR (4th) 663, [2006] 2 SCR 612. See also *Re Cavell Insurance Co* (2006) 269 DLR (4th) 679.

658 In *Brunei Investment Agency v. Fidelis Nominees Ltd* [2008] JLR 337 a judgment from the courts of Brunei, which had been upheld on appeal to the Privy Council, decreeing the performance of the obligations of a settlement, and in particular the transfer of shares, was accepted as enforceable in Jersey. This is not, perhaps, the wide breakthrough that it seems, especially as the law of Jersey prohibits enforcing a foreign judgment varying a Jersey trust, even if the parties submitted to the jurisdiction of the foreign court which made the order: *Re IMK Family Trust* [2008] JLR 250.

659 The same is to be said of the Royal Court in *Brunei Investment Agency v. Fidelis Nominees Ltd* [2008] JLR 337.

660 Though if part of the judgment is for a penal or revenue sum, this will be excluded from the claim.

661 On the footing that the judgment debtor has no defence to the claim.

There is no reason why this technique cannot be adapted for use when the foreign judgment is one for equitable, specific or other non-monetary relief. There are two ways to think about it. The first possibility is for the judgment creditor to sue on the foreign judgment as creating an obligation by which the defendant is bound,[662] applying for an English judgment in the same terms. If the foreign judgment is entitled to recognition against the losing party, the court will make a judgment of its own, in terms which reflect the obligation created by the original foreign judgment.[663] This works almost as well with equitable or other non-money decrees as it does with a final money judgment. Alternatively, the claimant may bring his claim on the basis of the original cause of action, but will plead that the merits are *res judicata*, as they have already been determined by the foreign judgment, which must be recognised as being final as to liability. If the foreign court's finding of liability satisfies the requirements of the doctrine of *res judicata*, the only question left for the English court is to specify and make the order which it considers to be the appropriate remedy for the right.

However it is viewed, the proposition that only a final money judgment may be enforced, and no other judgments may be enforced, is misleading. The common law provides for the enforcement of foreign judgments by making an English judgment in terms of the foreign judgment, or by provision which is as close to that as makes no difference. In the case of a foreign money judgment, the claimant may not need to make any reference at all to the underlying claim from which the foreign judgment issued; in the case of a non-money judgment he may need to do so, though immediately pleading *res judicata* and so placing the merits of that claim just as far beyond the investigation of the English court. If there is a difference between the two procedures, it is of form rather than substance. But the idea that the English common law will not enforce a foreign judgment unless it is a final judgment for money is really not helpful, for it is really not right.

7.77 Enforcement will not extend to a foreign penal or revenue or other public law

There is a general rule of the common law conflict of laws that a foreign penal, or revenue, or other public, law may not be enforced by action in the English courts.[664] The reasons for it lie beyond the scope of this book, but have to do with the more-than-usually-obvious assertion of sovereign power which such laws reveal. Whatever the theoretical basis may be, a foreign taxing authority may not bring original proceedings in the English courts for the collection of unpaid taxes; a foreign prosecutor may not sue in the English courts to recover payment of unpaid fine; a foreign Attorney-General may not sue in the English courts to obtain property to which he has a right by way of criminal forfeiture.[665] The rule is one of substance, not form, and it therefore applies if the claim under the foreign law has been preceded by an action and judgment in the foreign court. If this has occurred, and the claim

---

662 After all, if the submission of the losing party to the jurisdiction of the foreign court is what creates the obligation to abide by the judgment, the basis for the obligation is unaffected by the nature of the order made.

663 It follows that, where the local judgment asked for is equitable in nature, the usual criteria which limit equitable relief (mutuality, precision in definition, the absence of a need for continual supervision by the court) will be applied by the local court: *Brunei Investment Agency v. Fidelis Nominees Ltd* [2008] JLR 337.

664 Dicey, Morris and Collins, *The Conflict of Laws*, Rule 3.

665 See *Attorney-General for New Zealand v. Ortiz* [1984] AC 1. Such cases are liable to be dealt with by specific legislation, on the basis that the general rules of the common law are not capable of identifying the countries (and the orders) which the United Kingdom wishes to allow to be enforced in England.

is brought in England ostensibly to enforce a foreign judgment debt, the court will look behind the judgment debt to see whether it would (indirectly) be enforcing a foreign law of the proscribed kind.[666]

A penal law, in the present context, almost certainly refers to a law which imposes or requires a payment to State authority.[667] Accordingly, a law which requires payment of sums to an individual should not generally be characterised as penal for the purpose of the present rule, even if the explicit purpose of the award is to mark the court's disapproval of the wrongful conduct of the defendant.[668] A revenue law means a tax payment; this probably indicates a charge which must be paid to the State, whether directly[669] or indirectly,[670] and which cannot in law be avoided by purporting to renounce the benefit notionally given in return for it.[671]

Not all cases easily identify themselves as falling within the prohibited category. One area of challenge is when an action is alleged to involve the indirect enforcement of a revenue law. If a claimant has obtained judgment for a contract debt, part of which represents an element of value added tax, or sales tax, it may be asked whether the enforcement of the foreign judgment will involve the indirect enforcement of a foreign revenue law. It may be thought that it does, in which case either the judgment must be severed,[672] or enforcement wholly disallowed. The answer may, however, be that the enforcement of the judgment does not involve the enforcement of a revenue claim if the tax is payable only on receipt of the money to which it relates: if there is no outstanding revenue claim[673] at the date of enforcement action, the rule may not be infringed by permitting the enforcement of the judgment. But it cannot be claimed that the question is free from all doubt.

Another difficulty arises when a judgment is obtained which requires money to be paid to or collected by an individual who, with the authority of the State in question, will collect these funds from a wrongdoer and distribute them to the individuals who have suffered several losses. For example, a defendant carrying on investment business without authority may cause loss to individual investors; a fraudster may steal funds from, or cause electronic

---

666 See, for illustration, *United States of America v. Harden* (1963) 41 DLR (2d) 721; *United States of America v. Inkley* [1989] QB 225; *Camdex International Ltd v. Bank of Zambia (No 2)* [1997] CLC 714.

667 See *Huntington v. Attrill* [1893] AC 150. But for the view that a sum ordered to be paid to an individual claimant may nevertheless be penal, and denied enforcement, see *Schnabel v. Lui* [2002] NSWSC 15; and *cf* the rule of equity that there is no right to enforce a contract term which is a penalty clause. If the foreign court has ordered payment of a sum which lies to the far side of the line which separates penalty clauses from genuine pre-estimates of loss, it is plausible that equity, looking to the substance and not the form, will prevent enforcement of the judgment. For a careful analysis of foreign public laws, and judgments based on them, see *Robb Evans v. European Bank Ltd* (2004) 61 NSWLR 75; noted [2004] LMCLQ 313; for a completely different analysis where the foreign judgment is unambiguously penal in nature and intent, see *Blue Holdings (1) Pte Ltd v. United States* [2014] EWCA Civ 1291 [2015] 1 ALL ER (Comm) 1.

668 *Cf SA Consortium General Textiles v. Sun & Sand Agencies Ltd* [1978] QB 279 (but the actual award in that case was by way of compensation, not rebuke or punishment). But if the award is of multiple damages, see the Protection of Trading Interests Act 1980, below.

669 As with income tax.

670 As with value added tax.

671 Accordingly, payments to a state monopoly supplier will not be seen as revenue payments, for (if) the supply can be renounced and the payment lawfully avoided.

672 *Raulin v. Fischer* [1911] 2 KB 93 provides authority for severance where this is arithmetically possible.

673 See *Williams & Humbert Ltd v. W & H Trade Marks (Jersey) Ltd* [1986] AC 368, discussing *Buchanan v. McVey* [1955] AC 516 (note). See also, as evidence of the tendency to narrow the scope of this exclusionary rule, *Re State of Norway's Application (Nos 1 and 2)* [1990] 1 AC 723; and as regrettable evidence of the opposite tendency, *QRS 1 Aps v. Frandsen* [1999] 1 WLR 2169. But if the law were otherwise a claim for unpaid wages would be liable to be defeated.

debits to be made against the accounts of, individuals in circumstances where the individual sums are too small to justify litigation and the circumstances liable to cause embarrassment.[674] A foreign judgment ordering that the defendant make such payments and that these be collected by a receiver or other officer has been held in Australia to be enforceable, and not to be prevented by the rule that foreign public laws are not be to enforced directly or indirectly.[675] As the action is in substance the collective enforcement of civil liability brought in the interest of, or on behalf of, individual victims of a civil wrong, there is no reason why it should be excluded from enforcement; each judgment will have to be looked at for its individual terms. If it provides for an appreciable sum to be paid over to the State, however, it will be necessary to grant partial enforcement or, if this cannot be done, to consider excluding the entire judgment from enforcement, which would be an unfortunate consequence, best avoided if at all possible.[676]

7.78 Enforcement may be prevented by Protection of Trading Interests Act 1980

The Protection of Trading Interests Act 1980 may be seen as a particularised head of public policy, but it is in law a statutory bar to proceedings to enforce a foreign judgment. As a response[677] to certain American laws which purport to regulate, to an undue degree, trading activity outside the United States, section 5 of the Act forbids the enforcement in the United Kingdom of any judgment for multiple damages.[678] It is noteworthy, and perhaps unexpected, that the exclusion covers not just the sum reached by multiplication, but also the underlying sum assessed by way of compensation.[679] It is not easy to see why the policy protected by the Act needed to extend its reach quite this far, but the statutory language is in this respect absolutely clear.[680] Furthermore, if such a judgment has been given against a

---

674 For example, debits or charges made for visits to pornographic internet sites; even if the victim had done no such thing, he may decide that a quiet life is to be preferred to the vindication of rights in the glare of publicity: *cf Robb Evans v. European Bank Ltd* (2004) 61 NSWLR 75, [2004] LMCLQ 313.

675 *Robb Evans v. European Bank Ltd* (2004) 61 NSWLR 75, approved in *United States Securities and Exchange Commission v. Manterfield* [2009] EWCA Civ 27, [2010] 1 WLR 172; distinguished in *Blue Holdings (1) Pte Ltd v. United States* [2014] EWCA Civ 1291, [2015] 1 ALL ER (Comm) 1, in which the foreign judgment was unambiguously penal and the sums confiscated would be for the profit of the United States and it alone.

676 It is important to observe that the question whether English law will recognise the appointment of a liquidator by a foreign court will be principally determined by the Insolvency Regulation, Regulation (EC) 1346/2000, [2000] OJ L160/1, where the appointment is made under the law of a Member State, and under the Cross-Border Insolvency Regulations, SI 2006/1030, in other cases (the detail of this substantial question of insolvency law is beyond the scope of this book). These legislative provisions do not apply to foreign-appointed receivers, as distinct from liquidators; and whatever the common law might otherwise have said, it would now be wrong to recognise the title of a foreign-appointed receiver which would, if recognised, interfere with the liquidator in the performance of his duties. For illustration, see *Re Stanford International Bank Ltd* [2010] EWCA Civ 137, [2011] Ch 33.

677 Some would consider the breadth of the 1980 Act as excessive. For the background material, see Lowe, *Extraterritorial Jurisdiction* (Grotius, Cambridge, 1983), 176.

678 Or one based on a law identified by the Secretary of State in an Order made under the Act. This may also be covered by the defence of public policy. Note that even the element of the judgment for the basic compensatory amount cannot be enforced.

679 Though for the argument that treble damages under the Racketeer Influenced and Corrupt Organisations Act (an American statute) are part compensatory and part non-compensatory, see *Faircloth v. Friesod* 938 F 2d 513 (1991); *Abell v. Potomac Insurance Co* 858 F 2d 1104 (1989) (vacated on other grounds: 492 US 914 (1989)). This will not override the clear words of the 1980 Act.

680 Notwithstanding this, the judge at first instance in *Lucasfilm Ltd v. Ainsworth* [2008] EWHC 1878 (Ch),

British citizen, a British company, or a person carrying on business here, and the defendant has (wholly or partly) paid in accordance with the judgment, an action lies[681] for the recovery of so much as exceeds the compensatory element of the award.

It is not clear exactly what is covered by a judgment for multiple damages. Section 5(2) defines it as one 'for an amount arrived at by doubling, trebling or otherwise multiplying' the sum assessed as compensation. This would appear to mean that judgment for any sum which is multiplied, but not for one to which a sum is added, is caught by the prohibition on enforcement contained in the Act. It is not easy to see the policy which draws the line in this place; and it may yet be that a judgment for exemplary damages on top of the compensatory sum could be denied recognition if there is evidence of a subliminal multiplication of the compensatory sum. But if a judgment given in respect of several distinct causes of action comprises an element which is multiple, added to other elements which are not, the judgment may be severed and enforcement withheld from only that element which offends the 1980 Act: the whole of the judgment is not tainted.[682]

It may be appropriate to say a little more about the basic policy which underpins this aspect of the Act, though. One reason why a foreign court may multiply an award of damages may be to reflect the fact that the foreign legal system makes no separate provision for the recovery by the successful party of legal costs. In several of the United States, anti-trust legislation and product liability legislation allow a court to award multiple damages. But, historically at least, part of the reason for this was that the court had no general power to make an award of costs to a successful claimant: an award of multiple damages would, in a rough and ready way, prevent the claimant's litigation costs rendering his victory Pyrrhic. For the 1980 Act to treat all instances of multiple damages as serving no legitimate purpose is, therefore, unsatisfactory, at least in those cases where they may serve the same end as an English costs order. But that is exactly what the Act appears to do.

7.79 Consequence of recognition (2): preventing a successful claimant from suing again

At one time, the approach of English law to a foreign judgment which qualified for recognition was to treat the judgment as giving rise to an obligation, but not to an exclusive obligation. In other words, foreign judgment did not extinguish the cause of action or merge it in the foreign judgment. The reasons for this are principally of interest only to historians; but the result was that a claimant who had won only an unsatisfying or an incomplete victory would be entitled, in principle at least, to sue once again on the original cause of action. The potential unfairness to a defendant who had won a partial victory in the foreign court was obvious. Although the defendant may have been able to argue that the claimant was estopped from reopening certain aspects of the claim which were to be recognised against the claimant as being *res judicata*, and although it may have been possible to argue that

---

[2009] FSR 103 took the view that the un-multiplied, or purely compensatory, element in a judgment for multiple damages was recoverable. This was evidently based on the view that s. 5 of the 1980 Act should not have said what it plainly does say, and was plainly understood by the United States and United Kingdom Governments to say (for confirmation of this, see Lowe, *Extraterritorial Jurisdiction* (1983), 176). The decision, which was not dealt with on this point on appeal, is plainly wrong.

681 Under s. 6
682 *Lewis v. Eliades* [2004] 1 WLR 692.

the conduct of the claimant in suing for a second time was itself an abuse of process, the principle which preserved the claimant's right to sue for a second time remained intact.

Section 34 of the Civil Jurisdiction and Judgments Act 1982 took this right away from the claimant. It provides that 'no proceedings may be brought by a person in England and Wales or Northern Ireland on a cause of action in respect of which a judgment has been given in his favour in proceedings between the same parties, or their privies, in a court in another part of the United Kingdom or in a court in an overseas country, unless that judgment is not enforceable or entitled to recognition in England and Wales or, as the case may be, in Northern Ireland'. The result is that the claimant in the foreign proceedings, who has obtained judgment in his favour, may not bring proceedings on the same cause of action if he is entitled to enforce, or obtain the recognition of, the judgment against the defendant in England. It follows that, if the claimant has lost in the foreign proceedings, the section does not apply, though the principles of estoppel[683] should operate to prevent a successful second action. But if he has had a partial victory only, then unless the judgment in his favour cannot be recognised or enforced,[684] or unless the element of the judgment which was given against him can itself be impeached,[685] he may be barred from bringing a second action in England. If, however, the judgment cannot be enforced in England, section 34 has no application.

Section 34 was examined in detail by the House of Lords in *The Indian Grace*[686] and *The Indian Grace (No 2)*.[687] A shipment of munitions to India was damaged in transit. A small fraction of the cargo was jettisoned in France; the balance was found on unloading in India to be corrupted and useless. The consignee brought an action in the Indian courts against the shipowners in respect of short delivery of the fraction which had been jettisoned. Before judgment in India, and by the arrest of a sister ship, they brought a second action, in the form of an admiralty action *in rem* in the English courts in respect of the balance of the cargo. But once the Indian court had found for the claimant, the defendant relied on section 34 as a defence to the English action. The first decision of the House of Lords was that section 34 did not enact a technical rule of merger, but amounted to one which allowed a claimant to invoke (and, in an appropriate case,[688] to be debarred or estopped from invoking) the defence. The second decision was that there was no basis for lifting the barrier which section 34 presented to the claimant.

The result was that a judgment in the Indian courts for a sum equivalent to a measly £9,000 precluded an action in the English courts in respect of a multi-million pound claim. Five points need to be noted. First, though the subject of the two claims differed, they had the same cause of action. This followed from the fact that the claims were based on breach of contract, for which damage is not a necessary component of the claim. Matters might have stood differently had the proceedings concerned a tort claim, where damage is

---

683 Discussed below. And see generally Barnett, *Res judicata, Estoppel and Foreign Judgments* (2001).

684 *Karafarin Bank v. Mansoury-Dara* [2009] EWHC 1217 (Comm), [2009] 2 Lloyd's Rep 289. But if the reason it cannot is that he has obtained the judgment he did obtain by fraud, it is difficult to believe that he may breathe a sigh of relief and sue once again on the underlying cause of action. Presumably the defendant would not plead fraud as a defence to recognition; or if he did, the court could dismiss the second action as an abuse of process.

685 If, for example, the claimant won only a minor victory because the defendant advanced a fraudulent defence, there should be no bar to his proceeding again.

686 [1993] AC 410.

687 [1998] AC 878.

688 By reason of agreement, waiver, representation or estoppel.

generally required,[689] and two different heads of damage indicate two different causes of action. Second, the fact that the action in India had been *in personam* against the shipowner, whereas the English action had been commenced *in rem* against the ship, did not take the two actions outside the ambit of section 34: the actions were held to be, in substance, between the same parties.[690] Third, though it was possible in principle for section 34 to give way before an argument based on estoppel or representation, the court gave no encouragement to its prospects of success. One may ask whether the operation of section 34 should take more obvious account of whether the claimant's behaviour in not bringing a single, omnibus, claim was reasonable by reference to the law of the court hearing the first claim. It is not obvious why the Government of India, in seeking compensation for its losses from the India Steamship Co Ltd, should be required to bear in mind the possible impact of section 34. But the decision is clear.

Fourth, the court seemed concerned by the fact that the English action had been commenced after the Indian one had been begun, which rather turns section 34 into a rule which says that the second action is procedurally improper, whether or not the first action has come to judgment.[691] Fifth, it is unclear whether section 34 has any application in a case where the English action is commenced first, but a foreign one, commenced second, comes to judgment before the English one. Even so, for all that the decisions may bear harshly on a claimant who had no reason to suppose that his litigation strategy would be assessed by the standards of English law, it is plain that the decision does not indulge the fragmentary prosecution of claims.

In a case in which the defendant fails to satisfy the requirements of section 34, it may still be held to be an abuse of the process of the English court for the claimant to bring a second action in respect of matters which fell within the natural scope of the first. The principle in *Henderson v. Henderson*[692] holds that a court may restrain as being unconscionable the bringing of a claim in respect of a matter which could and should have been brought in an earlier action.[693] So even if the statute constitutes no bar to the claim, equity may still impose one.[694]

---

689 *Cf Black v. Yates* [1992] QB 526, where a dependency claim under the Fatal Accidents Act 1976 was held to involve the same cause of action as a claim for compensation as a civil party to Spanish criminal proceedings, but the claim on behalf of the deceased's estate was not. Moreover, the fact that a claim on behalf of the children had been made in Spain did not prevent their suing again in England, for the court had a power to relieve the children of the effect of the Spanish judgment, which had not been in their interest, and which, when so disposed of, meant there was no foundation for a s. 34 argument.

690 This is a controversial analysis, at least from the perspective of maritime law. Though it appears to follow from C-406/92 *The Tatry* [1994] ECR I-5439 that the two species of action do not prevent the application of what is now Art. 29 of Regulation 1215/2012, it was surprising that this should be used as the foundation for a reinterpretation of a rule of English procedural law in a context to which the Convention has no application. It also creates very real difficulties where the admiralty action is founded on a maritime lien, for as such a right may be enforced by an action against a new owner or other innocent third party, and not just against the party originally obliged, it will be unreal to regard the form of the action as a historical irrelevance.

691 [1998] AC 878, 912. The same comment as was made in the previous footnote, namely that it is inappropriate to use Brussels legislation to justify alterations to English law, applies with equal force.

692 (1843) 3 Hare 100. See also *Virgin Atlantic Airways Ltd v. Zodiac Seats UK Ltd* [2013] UKSC 46, [2014] 1 AC 160.

693 In this respect, it is the equitable counterpart to the doctrine of estoppel at common law, which deals with matters which were litigated in the first action: equity looks on as done that which ought to have been done.

694 The Court of Appeal in *The Indian Grace (No 2)* would have been prepared to apply the abuse of process doctrine; given the view which commended itself to the House of Lords, the point was left open in that court: [1998] AC 878, 916. But see, to broadly similar effect, *Desert Sun Loan Corp v. Hill* [1996] 2 All ER 847, 863.

7.80 Consequence of recognition (3): preventing an unsuccessful claimant from suing again

If the foreign court dismissed the claim on the merits, the defendant may be able to rely on it to prevent the claimant from attempting to litigate the claim for a second time. The mechanism by which the defendant will do this is to plead the foreign judgment as rendering the matter *res judicata* in his favour, and as therefore giving him a defence to the claim.[695] Although this really involves no more than recognition of the judgment, it may be convenient to look on it as enforcement by the defendant of a judgment in his favour. As a result, the judgment must be final and conclusive in the court which pronounced it, and it must be on the merits of the claim.[696]

The defendant will need to establish that the judgment in his favour was given by a court which was competent to bind the claimant, and that the judgment is entitled to be recognised against the claimant. The former condition is unlikely to present any difficulty. For as the claimant selected the court he chose to sue in, he must, *ex hypothesi*, have submitted to its jurisdiction to decide against him. The latter condition may be slightly more of a problem. If, for example, it is alleged and then shown that the defendant procured judgment in his favour by fraud, this would obviously prevent the judgment being recognised as against the claimant.[697] But if no such impediment to recognition against the claimant exists, the defendant may plead the foreign judgment as a defence to the claim.

The effect of the foreign judgment will be to bar the claim if and to the extent that: (i) it was given between the same parties (or their privies)[698] as are party to the English proceedings; and (ii) it involved the same cause of action as is now raised in the English proceedings.[699]

As to the first point, the requirement is that the judgment be or have been between the same parties, or between parties who were privy in or by blood, or by title or by interest. In essence this expression signifies that they had the same interest in the litigation. Privity of interest may be a somewhat elusive concept: it was conceded in *House of Spring Gardens Ltd v. Waite*[700] that 'it is not easy to detect from the authorities what amounts to a sufficient interest' to constitute privity of interest. Although having a mere outsider's interest in the litigation will not suffice, if it can be said that it is just to hold that a finding against one

---

695 There are difficulties here which have yet to be resolved. For one, is it open to a party to plead *res judicata* on the basis of a foreign judgment even though English proceedings were commenced before the foreign ones, or even though the English action was being tried when the foreign court made its finding? So far it has been assumed that it is; but it is not clear that this should be necessarily permitted. Second, suppose that the party seeking to plead an estoppel was able to get his judgment from a foreign court because he managed to slow up or impede the English proceedings, whether by a foreign anti-suit injunction or by other delaying procedural device. In such circumstances, is it clear that a court should simply accept that the foreign court's judgment may give rise to an estoppel? If estoppel is a flexible principle of justice, the answer may be no.

696 See above, para. 7.66. Note that a judgment on a procedural or interlocutory question may still involve a final decision on the merits of the particular point: *The Sennar (No 2)* [1985] 1 WLR 490; *Desert Sun Loan Corp v. Hill* [1996] 2 All ER 847.

697 By parity of reasoning with the material in para. 7.69, above.

698 This will therefore exclude non-parties to the proceedings, even if they seek to argue that a party to an earlier proceeding is estopped from re-opening it: *Sun Life Assurance Co of Canada v. Lincoln National Life Insurance Co* [2004] EWCA Civ 1660, [2005] 1 Lloyd's Rep 606.

699 For examination of the various strands of estoppel by *res judicata*, see *Virgin Atlantic Airways Ltd v. Zodiac Seats UK Ltd* [2013] UKSC 46, [2014] 1 AC 160. See also Spencer Bower, Turner and Handley, *The Doctrine of Res Judicata*, 4th edn (2009); Barnett, *Res Judicata, Estoppel and Foreign Judgments* (2001).

700 [1991] 1 QB 241, 252. Applied in *PJSC Vseukrainskyi Aktsionernyi Bank v. Maksimov* [2013] EWHC 3203 (Comm).

individual should be binding in later proceedings to which another is a party, there will be privity of interest.[701] There appears to be a growing acceptance of the proposition that where a corporate vehicle is owned, controlled, and driven by a single controlling mind, there may be privity of interest between the vehicle and the driver, so that issues decided against the company are conclusive against the driver, and as the incidence of oligarchic ownership (and reckless driving) of corporate vehicles increases, this development seems likely to be increasingly referred to.[702] Indeed, the modern phenomenon of complex and opaque legal structures, designed to hide assets and ownership (to say nothing of the need to obey judicial orders), is likely to require sustained attention, for which a modification of the principle of privity of interest may be suggested.[703]

Where the identification of the non-party as privy in interest with the party bound by judgment is not quite possible, an interpretation of the principle in *Henderson v. Henderson* may bridge the gap and it be held to be an abuse for the non-party to contest the findings previously made by the court.

The question whether the foreign judgment involves the same cause of action as is raised in the English proceedings may also be problematic. In principle, one should examine the minimum facts which were required to be pleaded and proved to permit the claimant to obtain the relief he sought.[704] If the claims arise out of a single contract, they are likely to be seen as involving the same cause of action;[705] if they arise out of a single accident, they may still be held to involve the same cause of action even if the heads of damage claimed differ.

However, if the causes of action are not the same, and the claimant contrives to frame his claim in a way which steers a path around the cause of action adjudicated upon by the foreign court, he may still face two possible barriers to success in proceedings in England. First, even if the causes of action are different, if the foreign court has adjudicated an issue which also arises in the new action, 'issue estoppel' may apply to it, in the same manner

---

701 *Gleeson v. Wippell* [1997] 1 WLR 510; *Society of Lloyd's v. Fraser* [1998] CLC 127; *Powell v. Wiltshire* [2004] EWCA Civ 534, [2005] 1 QB 117. For the leading authority on privity of interest in relation to a foreign judgment, see *Carl Zeiss Stiftung v. Rayner and Keeler Ltd (No 2)* [1967] 1 AC 853. For a narrower view, that it will encompass only the actual parties or their successors in title, see *C v. London Borough of Hackney* [1996] 1 All ER 973; for a rather more expansive view, that it extends to those who stand by and allow others to fight 'their' battles, see *Nana Ofori Atta II v. Nana Abu Bonsra II* [1958] AC 95. A complete stranger will not be entitled to take advantage of a finding adverse to his opponent when he brings subsequent proceedings: *Sun Life Assurance Co of Canada v. Lincoln National Life Insurance Co* [2004] EWCA Civ 1660, [2005] 1 Lloyd's Rep 606. See also Handley (2011) 127 LQR 83.

702 *OJSC Oil Co Yugraneft v. Abramovich* [2008] EWHC 2613 (Comm); *Deutsche Bank AC v. Sebastian Holdings Inc* [2014] EWHC 2073 (Comm); *Secretary of State for Business, Innovation and Skills v. Potiwal* [2015] EWHC 3723 (Ch), [2013] Lloyd's Rep FC 124. But there is unlikely to be privity of interest as between companies if all that can be said is that they were in the same group: *Resolution Chemicals Ltd v. Hundbeck A/S* [2013] EWCA Civ 924.

703 The Supreme Court in *Prest v. Petrodel Resources Ltd* [2013] UKSC 34, [2013] 2 AC 415 declined to liberalise the law on lifting the corporate veil, but that does not prevent sensible modification of the principle of privity of interest. Where an individual is, in effect, the owner and sole controller of a company, the requirements of privity of interest should be satisfied by showing unity of interest: for example, *Deutsche Bank AG v. Sebastian Holdings Inc* [2014] EWHC 2073 (Comm), [2014] 1 All ER (Comm) 733, [31]: 'It would be hard to find a case where a person was more closely connected with a company than Mr Vik and SHI, whether consideration is given to their financial interrelationship, their management interrelationship or the conduct of the English litigation. The complete absence of any corporate formalities in the sense of resolutions, minutes of decisions, corporate books and records illustrate clearly the extent to which Mr Vik identified SHI as his "trading company" and Beatrice as his "savings company" where he could and did decide on the transfer of monies between them without regard to the financial obligations of each considered independently as a corporate entity.'

704 *Letang v. Cooper* [1965] 1 QB 232; *The Indian Grace* [1993] AC 410.

705 *The Indian Grace.*

as with cause of action estoppel. All that is required is that the foreign court have ruled in judicial proceedings: even if, for example, the foreign proceedings are concerned with issues which arise on the enforcement of an arbitral award, a judicial judgment on those issues may provide the basis for an issue estoppel, for the judgment is still a judgment.[706] If the foreign court has decided the issue which is now before the English court, it is quite irrelevant that it may have done so by applying law to answer the question which is different from the law which an English court would have applied.[707] This is because issue estoppel does depend upon the foreign court having the same rules for choice of law as would have been applied in an English court.[708] Were it otherwise, a foreign judgment would not be recognised unless the foreign court had applied the same choice of law rule as an English court would have done; and that has never been the law in England. But it will be necessary to look closely at what the foreign court has decided to ascertain that it has actually decided the very same issue as arises for decision in the proceedings before the English court.

Second, estoppel applies to matters which were decided in, or which were essential (as distinct from collateral) to, the proceedings before the foreign court: if they were not essential, in the sense that the foreign court did not depend upon them in making the order it made, no estoppel arises from them.[709] If the objection is a different one, namely that the matters alleged in the English proceedings could, and in the opinion of the English court, should, have been raised in the foreign proceedings, then the claimant may still be estopped, or quasi-estopped. This time it is not the judgment of the foreign court which generates the defence, but the equitable principle that matters which could properly have been brought in foreign litigation between two litigants should have been brought there, and may not be reserved to later litigation in a separate action in England.[710]

7.81 The practical effect of estoppel by *res judicata*

Just as is found in other areas of the English system, the technical requirements of the common law of estoppel by *res judicata* may appear to be in some form of conflict with the

---

706 *Human SE v. Czech Republic* [2014] EWHC 1639 (Comm), [2014] 2 Lloyd's Rep 283. But if the foreign court has decided, for example, that an arbitral award may not be enforced because to do so would conflict with the public policy of the foreign court, its decision is not on the point which arises when an English court has to determine whether enforcement of the award in England would conflict with English public policy: *Yukos Capital Sarl v. OJSC Rosneft Oil Co* [2012] EWCA Civ 855, [2014] QB 458; for further proceedings, see *Yukos Capital Sarl v. OJSC Oil Co Rosneft* [2014] EWHC 2188 (Comm).

707 *First Laser Ltd v. Fujian Enterprises (Holdings) Co Ltd* [2013] 2 HKC 459.

708 *Leibinger v. Stryker Trauma GmbH* [2006] EWHC 690 (Comm).

709 It follows that if the claimant is successful before the foreign court, any findings of the foreign court made against him do not give rise to an estoppel, for they cannot have been essential to the decision to give judgment in his favour: *Joint Stock Asset Management Co Ingosstrakh-Investments v. BNP Paribas SA* [2012] EWCA Civ 644, [2012] 1 Lloyd's Rep 649, [61].

710 *Henderson v. Henderson* (1843) 3 Hare 100; *Virgin Atlantic Airways Ltd v. Zodiac Seats UK Ltd* [2013] UKSC 46, [2014] 1 AC 160; *Olympic Airlines SA v. ACG Acquisition XX LLC* [2014] EWCA Civ 821. This principle will therefore not apply if the issue which was not raised in the first proceedings is not one which should not have been raised in them. It is debatable whether the principle in *Henderson* is strictly a form of estoppel, or a manifestation of the principle that such behaviour is likely to be an abuse of process, or both. But from the perspective of the claimant there will be no practical difference; indeed, if the defendant is unable to establish the technicalities of the doctrine of estoppel, he may still succeed in reliance on the *Henderson* doctrine. See also *Good Challenger Navegante SA v. Metalexportimport SA* [2003] EWCA Civ 168, [2004] 1 Lloyd's Rep 67. The overriding principle is that one must examine with care what the foreign (or, indeed, earlier English) court said, what it needed to decide, what it did decide, and the range of material and principles of law which it took into account is reaching its decision.

principle that, in civil litigation as elsewhere, equity looks on as done that which ought to be done. It is not always clear that courts have recognised or maintained the significance of this distinction, with the result that courts may be tempted to blur the lines which demarcate the legal and the equitable principles. But it is desirable that the doctrines be maintained as distinct. The following may be given as a summary of their relationship.

First, if in litigation between A and B an issue was raised and ruled on by a court in judicial proceedings, the common law principles of *res judicata* will in principle apply to it;[711] if it was not raised and can be seen to have been not adjudicated on, *res judicata* cannot apply to it. But in this case it may be inequitable or abusive to permit the issue to be raised in a separate action between A and B, given that it could and should have been raised, and would therefore have been determined[712] in the first action. The rule in *Henderson v. Henderson* may preclude the issue being raised before the English court. But if it cannot be said that the issue could and should have been raised, and that if it had been raised it would have been determined in the one trial, there is no abuse in raising it separately, in England.

Second, if an issue was raised and adjudicated in litigation between A and B, the question whether it is open to re-argument in litigation before a different court between A and C depends on whether B and C are regarded as being the same parties or as being in a relationship of privity.[713] If either condition is satisfied, the common law of *res judicata* may operate. If neither condition is satisfied, it may still be inequitable or an abuse of process for C to invite the court to re-examine the issue with a view to obtaining a contradictory answer: if it is, *Henderson* will apply. Whether it does will depend upon whether in equity C should be regarded as bound by the decision given in the litigation between A and B. This requirement will be satisfied if it can be said that C 'should have' participated in the action between A and B,[714] or if C has behaved in some other fashion so as to hold him bound: he may have represented that he will accept the finding of a test case, or representative action or group action, as being binding on him. The court may even go further and regard C as bound by the finding on the basis of the need for sensible case management of large claims or group litigation. But if there is no justification for considering that he could and should have applied to join in the litigation between A and B, or no basis for holding that he represented or should otherwise be taken as bound to accept that its outcome would be applicable to him, there is no basis for regarding it as inequitable for C to exercise his right to raise the issue for determination in his own right.[715]

---

711 And special circumstances will be needed to justify reopening it: *Olympic Airlines SA v. ACG Acquisition XX LLC* [2014] EWCA Civ 821.

712 If it would not have been determined by the foreign court, but would have been left over to be tried after the first action, the defendant is no worse off if a second action is brought in England, and he cannot rely on *Henderson*: *Barrow v. Bankside Members' Agency Ltd* [1996] 1 WLR 257 (a case not involving the conflict of laws). The test may be whether the claimant had the power and opportunity to raise the claim in the foreign action and should have been required to do so: *Johnson v. Gore Wood & Co* [2002] 2 AC 1 (a case not involving the conflict of laws).

713 This principle may be stretched to make it apply to cases of complex litigation: *Society of Lloyd's v. Fraser* [1998] CLC 127 (a case not involving the conflict of laws). For an analysis of the general problems of accommodating these principles to group litigation or test actions brought in the United States, see below.

714 *Society of Lloyd's v. Fraser* [1998] CLC 127 (a case not involving the conflict of laws); *Bradford and Bingley Building Society v. Seddon* [1999] 1 WLR 1482 (a case not involving the conflict of laws).

715 See *Baker v. McCall International Ltd* [2000] CLC 189 (a case involving the conflict of laws: not an abuse of process for a defendant to bring a separate contribution claim rather than join third party into foreign action: Limitation Act 1980, s. 10 lays down a limitation period for such claims, so it can hardly be abusive for them to be brought).

In an appropriate case, a combination of these principles will produce the answer to the question whether a participant or a non-participant in (say) American class action litigation should be bound by the outcome or the decision of a class action and precluded from bringing an independent claim.[716] According to Rule 23 of the Federal Rules of Civil Procedure, an American court, for example, may designate an action as a class action, which has the approximate effect of allowing all those persons who may have an interest in the claim to be notified, and to opt out or else be bound by the result.[717] Local law will determine the extent of the obligation or preclusion established by the judgment, which will determine its effect in the country of origin.[718]

No real difficulty arises if an attempt is made to assert the preclusive effect of the overseas judgment as against an absentee 'claimant' who was notified of, but who played no part in, the proceedings. If such a person positively opted out of the jurisdiction of the American court, it is impossible to see that the American court was jurisdictionally competent to bind him by its judgment or order as a matter of English private international law; indeed, American law may agree that, in such a case, the 'opting out claimant' is not bound.

Where the would-be claimant is notified that he or she is deemed to have opted in unless he or she opts out, but who does nothing, the ordinary common sense of the common law, that one cannot impose an obligation or deem acceptance to have taken place by virtue of silence or lack of response,[719] will provide the right answer: unless the individual has, as a matter of English law, submitted to the foreign jurisdiction, say by instructing or accepting the offer of attorneys to act on his behalf, he is not bound or obliged by the foreign judgment or settlement. It may just be different if the person had such a connection to the adjudicating court as would allow an English court to conclude that he or she had otherwise subscribed to, or placed himself at risk of non-compliance with, the foreign procedure. But otherwise it is hard to see why the common law common sense expressed in *Felthouse v. Bindley*[720] will not settle the argument. A claimant who is not present, and who does not submit to the jurisdiction of a court, cannot be bound by a foreign judgment any more than can a defendant in the same position: the judgment cannot, therefore, be seen as *res judicata* so far as such a claimant is concerned. It does not seem possible to say that such a person should have participated in the class action, except perhaps in the most unusual of circumstances. The result is that, whatever the effect of the judgment may be under the law of the court in which it was given, it is most improbable that it has any impact on a claimant who did not opt in.

---

716 See generally Fairclough and Lein, *Extraterritoriality and Collective Redress* (OUP, Oxford, 2012); also Stiggelbout (2011) 52 Harv Int LJ 435. For a different analysis, but which leads to a conclusion considered here to be plainly wrong, see Dixon (1997) 46 ICLQ 134, who wrote that the prevalence of such actions is likely to increase, which is admitted, and argued that the obstacles to recognition of a judgment or settlement are not insuperable, which is far more controversial. His suggestions cannot be derived from the present rules of English law; whether the law would be improved by legislation of the general sort proposed by Dixon is unclear. It is clear, however, that legislation would be required to do any such thing. For the position where the judgment and settlement is by the courts of a Member State, and the effect of the judgment is governed by Chapter III of the Brussels I Regulation, see para. 7.25, above. And see also Mulheron (2012) 75 MLR 180.

717 Or the settlement, if the case does not proceed to trial.

718 See, for example, *Zhang v. Minister for Immigration* (1993) 45 FCR 384, esp. at pp 400–406; *Carnie v. Esenda Finance Corp* (1995) 183 CLR 398, esp. at pp 423–424.

719 *Felthouse v. Bindley* (1862) 11 CBNS 859.

720 (1862) 11 CBNS 859.

That is the answer given by the common law. As against it, it may be said that the class action has been developed in response to a social problem faced by multiple small claimants confronting a powerful single defendant (and, perhaps, to allow a tortfeasor to draw a line under the litigation to which its business may be exposed, to prevent it dragging on for years), and that the common law rules on the recognition and enforcement of judgments should evolve to accommodate and support, and not to frustrate, such litigation. An argument along these general lines was deployed in a related context, to notably beneficial effect, in *Robb Evans v. European Bank Ltd*.[721] But the common law cannot do it by itself. Consider it this way. If the natural defendant were to bring proceedings for a declaration of non-liability and serve a natural claimant out of the jurisdiction, a judgment in favour of the natural defendant would not be recognised in England if the natural claimant did not submit by appearance. The legal position cannot rationally be different when a natural claimant is made a party to the foreign proceedings by other claimants, or by the court: the foreign court is still not one of competent jurisdiction in relation to him. What, one may ask rhetorically, has the person in question done to assume the obligation to abide by the judgment? The answer is: nothing. It follows that a court should be extremely cautious before proposing to alter the rules on the recognition of foreign judgments in this area.[722] A person outside the territorial jurisdiction of a foreign court, who does not submit to the jurisdiction of that foreign court, is not bound or obliged by its judgment, even if this judgment purports to affect him.[723] And that is that.

7.82 Findings made against the claimant: issue estoppel

Even if the foreign court has not dismissed the whole of the claimant's claim, it may have resolved certain factual or legal issues against him.[724] If so, the principles of estoppel are, as with cause of action estoppel, liable to lead to the result that, if litigation is subsequently commenced in England, those issues determined against the claimant are also treated as *res judicata*. This time the principles are those of issue estoppel.

---

721 (2004) 61 NSWLR 75 (noted [2004] LMCLQ 313).

722 The Ontario Court of Appeal, in *Currie v. McDonald's Restaurants of Canada Ltd* (2005) 250 DLR (4th) 224, was, in principle at least, to recognise a judgment or settlement in a class action proceedings as binding an absent plaintiff who had been notified of the proceedings and had done nothing. A number of first-instance decisions have applied the principle in that decision. But Canadian law is no longer concerned with whether the party to be bound has assumed an obligation to abide by a foreign judgment, being more concerned to ask whether the proceedings were brought in an appropriate court. It is therefore possible for Canadian law to take the view that a class action judgment or order, in proceedings to which a putative claimant was invited to join (or invited to opt out) but who did not respond to the invitation, may be bound. English private international law, which recognises judgments on the basis of the doctrine of obligation, and interprets this in terms of the actions of the party to be bound being such that he has assumed that obligation, could not adopt this reasoning without a change in the law which would need to be legislative. See also *Canada Post Corp v. Lépine* [2009] 1 SCR 549.

723 A contradictory view to the effect that if the *defendant* submits to the jurisdiction of the foreign court, a *person invited to be claimant*, who does nothing to show an intention to opt into or otherwise submit (as this term is understood in English law) to the jurisdiction of the foreign court in respect of the proceedings, may be bound and precluded by the judgment as well, is not coherent. It fundamentally misunderstands the principles of *res judicata* to argue that 'a judgment is recognised' in an abstract sense, and that persons who did not submit, and who were not privy to any party who did submit, can be affected by it. In English private international law, the material question is whether a *party* has so conducted himself as to have assumed an obligation to accept the binding force of the foreign judgment. See also Lemontey and Michon [2009] JDI/Clunet 535, who explain why recognition under French private international law would, for reasons which are similar but not identical to those set out here, be equally unthinkable.

724 In such a case, s. 34 of the 1982 Act may present an obstacle to his proceeding in England.

Issue estoppel is not always easy to tell apart from cause of action estoppel; but the principles are much the same.[725] The court will have been competent to make the finding against the claimant because, in choosing to sue there, he has submitted to its jurisdiction. Unless the conduct of the defendant or the court can be complained about, so as to disentitle the judgment to recognition against the claimant as *res judicata*, findings made by the court will, in principle at least, be capable of founding an estoppel. Some care is needed.[726] First, the proposition that the decision of the foreign court need be final and conclusive is difficult to apply when one is dealing with observations or findings made by the court, but which did not actually form part of its order.[727] Second, it may not be easy to be sure what the court has decided. Third, the court may have recited the considerations on which its judgment was formally based, but without intending them to have the status of decisions on the particular points. On the other hand, the specific reasons for caution before applying issue estoppel against a defendant, discussed in the next paragraph, are inapplicable as against the party who selected the foreign court in the first place.

7.83 Findings made against the defendant: issue estoppel

Just as it is true that a finding made against the claimant may give rise to an issue estoppel,[728] the same is, in principle, true where a foreign court has made a finding against a defendant. In principle, issue estoppel may arise against him as well; and, also in principle, matters of defence which he could and should have raised, but did not, may be shut out by the principle in *Henderson v. Henderson*.

But the need for caution in the application of the principles of issue estoppel to a foreign judgment, clearly expressed in *Carl Zeiss Stiftung v. Rayner & Keeler Ltd (No 2)*,[729] is acute. A defendant may have acted prudently in allowing a claim in a faraway court to be lost or to go by default: it may have been a claim too small to be worth the expense of fighting. In such a case, it may be inappropriate to hold that he is now estopped, in relation to a much larger claim in England, by issues apparently or actually decided by the foreign court. It would be wrong to hold that a defendant who allows judgment to go against him by default in respect of a particular claim, or who defends it on the basis of limited expenditure, is nevertheless to be treated as being bound, for all time and in all future contexts, by decisions made by

---

725 See *Thoday v. Thoday* [1964] P 181; *Carl Zeiss Stiftung v. Rayner & Keeler Ltd (No 2)* [1967] 1 AC 853; *The Sennar (No 2)* [1985] 1 WLR 490; *The Indian Grace* [1993] AC 410; *Desert Sun Loan Corp v. Hill* [1996] 2 All ER 847.

726 *Carl Zeiss*; see also *Berkeley Administration Inc v. McClelland* [1996] ILPr 772; *HJ Heinz Co Ltd v. EFL Inc* [2010] EWHC 1203, [2010] 2 Lloyd's Rep 727; *Abdel Hadi Abdullah Al Qahtani & Sons Beverage Industry Co v. Antliff* [2010] EWHC 1735 (Comm) (no issue estoppel from decision of Saudi Primary Commission).

727 For refusal to estop where the issues before the foreign court were collateral, not central, to those before the English court, see *Good Challenger Navegante SA v. Metalexportimport SA* [2003] EWCA Civ 1668, [2004] 1 Lloyd's Rep 67, which adopts a rather conservative stance, but which was approved in *Sun Life Assurance Co of Canada v. Lincoln National Life Insurance Co* [2004] EWCA Civ 1660, [2005] 1 Lloyd's Rep 606.

728 But only in favour of the other party to the proceedings: it is not open to a non-party in subsequent litigation against a party who lost on an issue determined in separate proceedings, to contend that the latter is bound by the decision, not least because estoppels are mutual, and the non-party could not be regarded as being bound by any matter decided adverse to him in proceedings to which he was a stranger: *Sun Life Assurance Co of Canada v. Lincoln National Life Insurance Co* [2004] EWCA Civ 1556, [2005] 1 Lloyd's Rep 606.

729 [1967] 1 AC 853. The principle was most recently reaffirmed in *Diag Human SE v. Czech Republic* [2014] EWHC 1639 (Comm), [2014] 2 Lloyd's Rep 283, applying it in the context of a foreign judgment on the enforceability of an arbitral award.

the judge in the foreign court. For *The Indian Grace (No 2)* to be extended,[730] as it were, to defendants and defences, would be to take the law in the wrong direction.

7.84 Consequence of non-recognition of a foreign judgment

It is finally necessary to notice that if a judgment is not entitled to recognition as *res judicata*, because the party against whom it is asserted was not present and did not submit to the jurisdiction of the foreign court, it has no effect in the English legal order. In particular, it has no weight as evidence of the truth or otherwise of the issues determined, or of the underlying claim. This follows from the decision in *Hollington v. F Hewthorn & Co Ltd*.[731] In fact, the decision is not concerned with the effect of a foreign decision, but the decision of another English court. The position in relation to a foreign judgment is, of course, *a fortiori*.[732]

DIRECT ENFORCEMENT OF FOREIGN JUDGMENTS BY REGISTRATION UNDER THE 1920 AND 1933 ACTS

7.85 General

'Enforcement of foreign judgments', under the rules of the common law, has been shown to be something of a misnomer: there will be a foreign judgment, but it is in fact a consequent English judgment which is enforced: the common law does not actually allow the enforcement of foreign judgments as judgments, but requires the judgment creditor to obtain an English judgment and to enforce that. It may be a matter of form more than substance, but it is an important matter of form.

However, there are some countries, some judgments from the courts of which are not usually enforced by an action upon the judgment at common law, but which are liable to be dealt with instead by registration under the provisions of the Administration of Justice Act 1920, or the Foreign Judgments (Reciprocal Enforcement) Act 1933.[733]

Broadly speaking, the procedure under the two Acts is that the foreign judgment may be registered for enforcement in accordance with the Act. The court will need (just as any enforcement authority would need) to be furnished with certain basic information: as this is not provided by the foreign court, CPR Part 74 places the burden of assembling it on the applicant.[734] Once the judgment is registered, the statute provides that the foreign, now registered, judgment takes effect for the purpose of execution, for the taking of proceedings,

---

730 See above, para. 7.79.

731 [1943] KB 587; *Secretary of State for Trade and Industry v. Bairstow* [2004] Ch 1; *Calyon v. Michalidis* [2009] UKPC 34 (Gib).

732 Whether the foreign judgment is presented for recognition under the common law, or the Regulation, or otherwise: *Calyon v. Michalidis* [2009] UKPC 34 (Gib).

733 Judgments recognised and enforced under the Brussels I Regulation 44/2001, and the Brussels and Lugano II Conventions, are also registered for enforcement, under Civil Jurisdiction and Judgments Order 2001, SI 2001/3929, Sch. 1, and Civil Jurisdiction and Judgments Act 1982, s. 4A (inserted by SI 2009/3131), respectively. Judgments which will be recognised and enforced in accordance with the recast Brussels I Regulation are dealt with by SI 2014/2947.

734 But under the recast Brussels I Regulation 1215/2012, much of this information will be provided by certificate issued by the original court. It is therefore unnecessary for the applicant for enforcement to provide it by means of his own evidence.

and for the accrual of interest, as if it had been a judgment of the court in which it has been registered. The judgment debtor may make an application to have registration set aside, but if he does not, it is the foreign judgment itself, as distinct from an English judgment derived from it, which is enforced in England.

Though the form and mechanism are sharply different from those of the common law, the criteria for registration are very closely derived from the rules of the common law.[735] It is therefore broadly true to say that the statutes identify the countries and affect the procedure and mechanism for recognition and enforcement of judgments to which they extend, but reflect the common law upon the circumstances in or conditions under which judgments from those countries are entitled to enforcement under the Acts. Summaries of the statutes, their scope and the points of difference from the common law, are now given.

7.86 Registration under the 1920 Act: countries and judgments

The 1920 Act applies to the enforcement[736] of certain judgments from the courts of many colonial and Commonwealth countries.[737] The Act applies to the judgments[738] of superior courts of these countries.[739] A judgment for the purposes of the Act means 'any judgment or order given or made by a court in any civil proceedings… whereby any sum of money is made payable, and includes an award in proceedings on an arbitration if the award has, in pursuance of the law in force at the place where is was made, become enforceable in the same manner as a judgment given by a court in that place'. It is not said that it excludes a 'judgment on a foreign judgment', though it seems reasonable to suppose that it does.

The law is substantially contained in section 9 of the 1920 Act, which it is convenient to set out here:

> **9. Enforcement in the United Kingdom of judgments obtained in superior courts in other British dominions.** *(1) Where a judgment has been obtained in a superior court in any part of His Majesty's dominions outside the United Kingdom to which this Part of this Act extends, the judgment creditor may apply to the High Court in England or to the Court of Session in Scotland, at any time within twelve months after the date of the judgment, or such longer period as may be allowed by the court, to have the*

---

735 And the criteria for setting aside registration are closely modelled on the defences to recognition and enforcement contained in the common law.

736 But not to recognition, which is not mentioned and continues to be governed by the common law.

737 Until 2003 the list of countries appeared in the notes to RSC Order 71, r. 1 (then Sch. 1 to CPR). But RSC Order 71 has been superseded by CPR Part 74, and this list has not been reprinted. Nevertheless, it is as follows: Anguilla, Antigua and Barbuda, Bahamas, Barbados, Belize, Bermuda, Botswana, British Indian Ocean Territory (but which the United Kingdom has cleansed of its native population, and which presumably now has neither judgments nor courts), British Virgin Islands, Cayman Islands, Christmas Island, Cocos (Keeling) Islands, Dominica, Falkland Islands, Fiji, Gambia, Ghana, Grenada, Guyana, Jamaica, Kenya, Kiribati, Lesotho, Malawi, Malaysia, Mauritius, Montserrat, New Zealand, Nigeria, Papua New Guinea, St Christopher and Nevis, St Helena, St Lucia, St Vincent and the Grenadines, Seychelles, Sierra Leone, Singapore, Solomon Islands, the Sovereign Base Areas of Akrotiri and Dhekelia, Sri Lanka, Swaziland, Tanzania, Trinidad and Tobago, Turks and Caicos Islands, Tuvalu, Uganda, Zambia, Zimbabwe. Cyprus and Malta were (or still are) on the list, but in practice (and unless the judgment is one founded on an arbitral award, in which case the 1920 Act will still be relevant) judgments from these countries will fall under the Brussels I Regulation. The Act no longer applies to Australia or to the Australian States or territories: SI 1994/1901. It no longer applies to Gibraltar, judgments from which are dealt with under s. 39 of the 1982 Act: SI 1997/2602. It has not applied to judgments from Hong Kong since the cesser of sovereignty in 1997.

738 A judgment in any civil proceedings that a sum of money be paid, including an arbitral award if the award has become enforceable in the same way as a judgment in the place where it was made: s. 12.

739 Section 9(1).

judgment registered in the court, and on any such application the court may, if in all the circumstances of the case they think it just and convenient that the judgment should be enforced in the United Kingdom, and subject to the provisions of this section, order the judgment to be registered accordingly. (2) No judgment shall be ordered to be registered under this section if (a) the original court acted without jurisdiction; or (b) the judgment debtor, being a person who was neither carrying on business nor ordinarily resident within the jurisdiction of the original court, did not voluntarily appear or otherwise submit or agree to submit to the jurisdiction of that court; or (c) the judgment debtor, being the defendant in the proceedings, was not duly served with the process of the original court and did not appear, notwithstanding that he was ordinarily resident or was carrying on business within the jurisdiction of that court or agreed to submit to the jurisdiction of that court; or (d) the judgment was obtained by fraud; or (e) the judgment debtor satisfies the registering court either that an appeal is pending, or that he is entitled and intends to appeal, against the judgment; or (f) the judgment was in respect of a cause of action which for reasons of public policy or for some other similar reason could not have been entertained by the registering court. (3) Where a judgment is registered under this section (a) the judgment shall, as from the date of registration, be of the same force and effect, and proceedings may be taken thereon, as if it had been a judgment originally obtained or entered upon the date of registration in the registering court; (b) the registering court shall have the same control and jurisdiction over the judgment as it has over similar judgments given by itself, but in so far only as relates to execution under this section; (c) the reasonable costs of and incidental to the registration of the judgment (including the costs of obtaining a certified copy thereof from the original court and of the application for registration) shall be recoverable in like manner as if they were sums payable under the judgment. (4) Rules of court shall provide (a) for service on the judgment debtor of notice of the registration of a judgment under this section; and (b) for enabling the registering court on an application by the judgment debtor to set aside the registration of a judgment under this section on such terms as the court thinks fit; and (c) for suspending the execution of a judgment registered under this section until the expiration of the period during which the judgment debtor may apply to have the registration set aside. (5) In any action brought in any court in the United Kingdom on any judgment which might be ordered to be registered under this section, the plaintiff shall not be entitled to recover any costs of the action unless an application to register the judgment under this section has previously been refused or unless the court otherwise orders.

As may be seen, judgments may be registered within 12 months of the judgment[740] 'if it is just and convenient that the judgment should be enforced in the United Kingdom'.[741] The registration of the judgment is, in the last resort, discretionary. One possible consequence of this is that, where the Act does not expressly reproduce a rule of the common law, it may nevertheless be interpreted in accordance with the common law as part of the court's assessment of whether it is 'just and convenient' to register the judgment.

7.87 Registration under the 1920 Act: jurisdiction of the foreign court

The Act provides that judgment shall not be registered if the court acted without jurisdiction;[742] in practice this means that if the judgment should not have been registered, the registration will be set aside on application. As far as a defendant is concerned, it is a jurisdictional defence[743] to registration if he neither ordinarily resided, nor carried on business, within the jurisdiction of the court, nor did otherwise appear or submit to the foreign court. In other words, ordinary residence, and the carrying on of business,[744] and submission

---

740 Section 9(1); this may be extended by the court.

741 It is not just and convenient to register a Nigerian judgment given against the Nigerian State, for reasons of state immunity: *AIC v. Nigeria* [2003] EWHC 1357 (QB) (approved in *Svenska Petroleum Exploration AB v. Lithuania* [2006] EWCA Civ 1529, [2007] QB 866, [137]).

742 Section 9(2)(a): this is undefined. Section 9(2)(b) then sets out, more or less exactly, the common law principles of jurisdiction, and says that a judgment shall not be registered if these are contravened.

743 Section 9(2)(b).

744 Which is applicable to both individual and corporate defendants.

give the foreign court jurisdictional competence. This is close to, but not precisely the same as, the conditions for jurisdictional competence under the common law.[745]

7.88 Registration under the 1920 Act: substantive defences to registration

Most of the common law defences to recognition of foreign judgments apply to registration under the 1920 Act.[746] The defence of fraud is not confined to newly-discovered fraud, but has the full width of the common law rule as traditionally understood.[747] A defence resembling that of lack of natural justice[748] is framed in terms of lack of due service. To the extent that the judgment did not fall within this provision, but was still rendered in breach of the rules of natural justice, it may well not be just and convenient to register it; and in any event, the Human Rights Act 1998 will apply to proceedings taken under this section. The defence, which is framed in terms of public policy,[749] is directed at the underlying cause of action, rather than at registration of a judgment founded on it; but it is unlikely that this will be a distinction with much practical importance.

There is one addition to the common law defences: if an appeal is pending or is intended to be lodged,[750] the judgment shall not be registered. The Act does not specifically require that the foreign judgment must be enforceable under the law under which it was given, but if there is to be an appeal, registration will not be allowed. The effect is analogous to a requirement that the judgment must be enforceable in the state of origin for registration to be permitted.

7.89 Registration under the 1920 Act: miscellaneous further points

Registration of the judgment[751] is obtained after an application made without notice to any other party.[752] Notice of the registration is then served upon the defendant,[753] who may then apply[754] to have registration set aside. If the claimant prefers,[755] he may, rather than register the judgment, bring an action at common law on the judgment itself; but he may not[756] recover the costs of so doing unless he has sought, unsuccessfully, to register the

---

745 The 1920 Act stipulated residence, rather than presence, as the basis for jurisdictional competence. The reasoning employed by the House of Lords in *Owens Bank Ltd v. Bracco* [1992] 2 AC 443 would strongly suggest that this was, and was intended as, a reflection of the common law as it stood in 1920. That being so, the acceptance, in *Adams v. Cape Industries plc* [1990] Ch 433, of presence, as distinct from residence, may mean either that the common law has moved on since 1920, or that *Adams v. Cape Industries plc* was wrongly decided. If the 1920 Act is intended to harmonise with the common law, the latter is strongly arguable.

746 Section 9(2)(d), (e). The Protection of Trading Interests Act 1980 expressly applies also to the 1920 Act (s. 5(1) of the 1980 Act). Section 32 of the 1982 Act (dealing with judgments in breach of arbitration or choice of court agreements) does not expressly do so. However, that section states that a judgment to which it applies shall not be recognised or enforced, and this ought to cover enforcement under the 1920 Act. Even if this is doubted, it is thought that the registration of such a judgment would not be just and convenient.

747 Section 9(2)(d); *Owens Bank Ltd v. Bracco* [1992] 2 AC 443.

748 Section 9(2)(c).

749 Section 9(2)(f).

750 Section 9(2)(e).

751 CPR r. 74.3.

752 Evidence required is specified by CPR r. 74.4.

753 Section 9(4)(a); CPR r. 74.6. No permission is required to serve it out of the jurisdiction: CPR r. 74.6(2).

754 Section 9(4)(b); CPR r. 74.7.

755 Though he may not sue on the original cause of action: s. 34 of the 1982 Act.

756 Unless the court orders otherwise.

judgment beforehand:[757] it is not obvious why he would wish to proceed in this way, but where the foreign judgment is subject to appeal, it is not registrable under the Act but will be final for the purposes of the common law. The Act is silent as to the currency in which the judgment will be registered. Those covered by the 1933 Act are now registered in the currency in which they were originally given; it would seem desirable if the same were true under the 1920 Act.

7.90 Registration under the 1933 Act: countries and judgments

The 1933 Act,[758] the provisions of which also largely reflect the common law, applies to the enforcement, and to the recognition,[759] of judgments from countries with which a bilateral treaty is concluded, and which, in accordance with the Act, has been enacted into domestic law. The effect of registration under the Act is that the judgment in question is itself enforceable as though it had been given by the High Court; it is logical, and it is so provided, that if the judgment could not be executed on under the law of the court which gave it, it cannot be registered under the Act.[760]

The countries to which the Act applies include some European States,[761] some non-European States[762] and some Commonwealth States and territories.[763] Because the arrangements for the country in question are made on the basis of a bilateral treaty, the particular treaty, which will appear in the provisions of a statutory instrument, must be examined to determine precisely which courts are covered. It is now provided that the 1933 Act applies to the judgments of 'recognised' courts, though in the individual treaty the earlier designation of superior[764] courts may be found. The meaning is the same.

For the purpose of the Act, 'judgment' means a judgment or order given or made by a court in any civil proceedings,[765] or a judgment or order given or made by a court in any criminal proceedings for the payment of a sum of money[766] in respect of compensation or

---

757 Section 9(5).

758 Some amendments were made by Sch. 10 to the 1982 Act.

759 Given that this does not require registration, the application of the Act is not easy. See s. 8; *Black-Clawson International Ltd v. Papierwerke Waldhof-Aschaffenburg AG* [1975] AC 591.

760 Section 2(1), Proviso (b).

761 Austria (SI 1962/1339), Belgium (SI 1936/1169), France (SI 1936/609), West Germany (SI 1961/1199), Italy (SI 1973/1894), Netherlands (SI 1969/1063, SI 1977/2149), Norway (SI 1962/636). Where the Brussels I Regulation, Brussels Convention or Lugano II Convention applies to a judgment, its provisions supersede and for almost all purposes replace the scheme of the 1933 Act. But the fact that the 1933 Act applies to arbitral awards which have become enforceable in the same manner as a judgment (1933 Act, s. 10A) means that it may still have relevance in relation to these Member and Lugano States.

762 Israel (SI 1971/1039, amended by SI 2003/2618), Pakistan (SI 1958/141), Surinam (SI 1981/735).

763 Australia, and Australian States and territories (SI 1994/1901), certain Canadian courts but excluding the courts of Québec (SI 1987/468, SI 1987/2211, SI 1988/1304, SI 1988/1853, SI 1989/987, SI 1991/1724, SI 1992/1731, SI 1995/2708), Guernsey (SI 1973/610), Isle of Man (SI 1973/611), Jersey (SI 1973/612), certain Indian courts (SI 1958/425), Tonga (SI 1980/1523). The 1920 Act is superseded to this extent.

764 Schedule 10 to the 1982 Act substitutes 'recognised' for 'superior'. A judgment from a court which is not a recognised court may still be enforced by action at common law.

765 It includes interest up to the date of registration: s. 2(6). It also includes, as they are not to be seen as penalties, orders to pay a sum for '*résistance abusive*' under French law: *SA Consortium General Textiles v. Sun & Sand Agencies Ltd* [1978] QB 279. It will include insolvency proceedings: *Rubin v. Eurofinance SA* [2012] UKSC 46, [2013] 1 AC 236, [170]–[176].

766 It must be final and conclusive, ordering payment of a sum of money (other than taxes or penalties): s. 1(2), but extends to cover judgments for interim payments.

damages to an injured party.[767] The provisions of the Act apply, as they apply to a judgment, in relation to an award in proceedings on an arbitration which has, in pursuance of the law in force in the place where it was made, become enforceable in the same manner as a judgment given by a court in that place.[768] But the Act does not apply to judgments given on appeal from a non-recognised court, or to a judgment given by the foreign court in proceedings founded on a judgment of a court in another country and having as their object the enforcement of that judgment.[769]

Registration is mandatory[770] if the conditions of the Act are met.

7.91 Registration under the 1933 Act: jurisdiction of the foreign court

The rules of jurisdictional competence under the 1933 Act[771] closely mirror those of the common law. Section 4 sets out the main provisions of the statutory scheme, and it is convenient to reproduce it here.

> **4. Cases in which registered judgments must, or may, be set aside.** *(1) On an application in that behalf duly made by any party against whom a registered judgment may be enforced, the registration of the judgment (a) shall be set aside if the registering court is satisfied (i) that the judgment is not a judgment to which this Part of this Act applies or was registered in contravention of the foregoing provisions of this Act; or (ii) that the courts of the country of the original court had no jurisdiction in the circumstances of the case; or (iii) that the judgment debtor, being the defendant in the proceedings in the original court, did not (notwithstanding that process may have been duly served on him in accordance with the law of the country of the original court) receive notice of those proceedings in sufficient time to enable him to defend the proceedings and did not appear; or (iv) that the judgment was obtained by fraud; or (v) that the enforcement of the judgment would be contrary to public policy in the country of the registering court; or (vi) that the rights under the judgment are not vested in the person by whom the application for registration was made; (b) may be set aside if the registering court is satisfied that the matter in dispute in the proceedings in the original court had previously to the date of the judgment in the original court been the subject of a final and conclusive judgment by a court having jurisdiction in the matter. (2) For the purposes of this section the courts of the country of the original court shall, subject to the provisions of subsection (3) of this section, be deemed to have had jurisdiction (a) in the case of a judgment given in an action in personam (i) if the judgment debtor, being a defendant in the original court, submitted to the jurisdiction of that court by voluntarily appearing in the proceedings; or (ii) if the judgment debtor was plaintiff in, or counter-claimed in, the proceedings in the original court; or (iii) if the judgment debtor, being a defendant in the original court, had before the commencement of the proceedings agreed, in respect of the subject matter of the proceedings, to submit to the jurisdiction of that court or of the courts of the country of that court; or (iv) if the judgment debtor, being a defendant in the original court, was at the time when the proceedings were instituted resident in, or being a body corporate had its principal place of business in, the country of that court; or (v) if the judgment debtor, being a defendant in the original court, had an office or place of business in the country of that court and the proceedings in that court were in respect of a transaction effected through or at that office or place; (b) in the case of a judgment given in an action of which the subject matter was immovable property or in an action in rem of which the subject matter was movable property, if the property in question was at the time of the proceedings in the original court situate in the country of that court; (c) in the case of a judgment given in an action other than any such action as is mentioned in paragraph (a) or paragraph (b) of this subsection, if the jurisdiction of the original court is recognised by the law of the registering court. (3) Notwithstanding anything in subsection (2) of this section, the courts of the country of the original court shall not be deemed*

---

767 Section 11(1).

768 Section 10A (inserted by Sch. 10, para. 4 to the 1982 Act).

769 Section 1(2A).

770 Section 2.

771 Those of the treaty with the particular country may extend beyond these minimum requirements; the particular treaty must therefore be consulted.

> *to have had jurisdiction (a) if the subject matter of the proceedings was immovable property outside the country of the original court; or … (c) if the judgment debtor, being a defendant in the original proceedings, was a person who under the rules of public international law was entitled to immunity from the jurisdiction of the courts of the country of the original court and did not submit to the jurisdiction of that court.*

The combination of sections 4(1)(a)(ii), 4(2), and 4(3) explains the rules which define the jurisdictional competence of the foreign court for the purposes of the Act. These closely resemble the rules of the common law, as it was then understood, but with a number of small, but important, differences; and as the wording of the Act is made to give effect to the bilateral treaties made between the United Kingdom and the States in question, it does not appear to be open to an English court to modify the wording of the Act, whether 'to bring it up to date' or for any other reason.

It is the residence (or principal place of business for corporate defendants), rather than presence, when proceedings were instituted which (along with submission) establishes jurisdiction for the purposes of the Act.[772] In addition, if the defendant had an office or place of business within the jurisdiction, through the transactions of which the claim arose, then there is jurisdictional competence. The grammatical structure of the section appears to require that the defendant had such an office or place within the jurisdiction of the foreign court when proceedings were begun, as distinct from the case in which the defendant *had* had such a place within the jurisdiction, but no longer had it when the proceedings were begun.[773]

7.92 Registration under the 1933 Act: substantive defences to registration

The substantive defences, which lead to the non-registration, or the setting aside of registration, are set out in section 4(1), which appears above. The defences closely resemble those of the common law.[774] The fraud defence[775] is, presumably for the same reasons as were given in *Owens Bank Ltd v. Bracco*,[776] identical with that of the common law; and is not now susceptible to judicial alteration. The defence, which is based on a failure of natural justice, is framed simply in terms of failure to receive notice of the proceedings in time for the defendant to defend himself,[777] but other varieties of breach of the rules

---

772 Section 4(2)(a)(iv). If the defendant were merely present, the common law rules may still be resorted to for the enforcement of the judgment.

773 Section 4(2)(a)(v): the drafting of the subsection states that the court 'shall… be deemed to *have had* jurisdiction… if the defendant *had* an office or place of business…'. If the intention had been to extend jurisdiction to the case in which the defendant *had had* such a place, but *had* that place no longer, the drafting would have been different. It appears to apply equally to individual and corporate defendants. The Report of the Foreign Judgments (Reciprocal Enforcement) Committee 1932 (Cmd 4213), at 63, observed that 'this rule, if not precisely covered by the existing Common Law Rule, at any rate is at the most only a rational extension of it, to which no objection can, it is thought, be taken'. As the whole of the common law rule is framed by reference to facts and matter existing at the date the commencement of proceedings, it follows that s. 4(2)(a)(v) should also be so interpreted.

774 Section 32 of the 1982 Act does not expressly extend to registration under the 1933 Act. But it proscribes the enforcement of judgments within its scope, and as registration is a prelude to enforcement under the 1933 Act, it should extend to the 1933 Act. Alternatively, registration may be found to be contrary to public policy: s. 4(1)(a)(v): as declared by the 1982 Act. The Protection of Trading Interests Act 1980 does apply to the 1933 Act: s. 5(1) of the 1980 Act.

775 Section 4(1)(a)(iv).

776 [1992] 2 AC 443.

777 Section 4(1)(a)(iii).

of natural justice may well fall within the public policy defence,[778] which is expressed in terms of enforcement[779] being contrary to public policy; and in any event, the Human Rights Act 1998 will apply to registrations taking place under the 1933 Act. In addition, there is an express power[780] to set aside registration if the judgment of the foreign court was given after the final and conclusive judgment of another court also having jurisdiction in the matter.

It is not a defence that the judgment is subject to appeal in the foreign court,[781] but this may provide a ground for either setting aside registration, or for staying the application to set aside registration;[782] and in any event, if the judgment is not liable to execution under the law of the State in which it was given, it may not be registered.[783] This makes sense, as the basic scheme of the 1933 Act is to enforce the foreign judgment as a judgment, as distinct from the scheme of the common law, which is to allow the foreign adjudication to pave the way for an English judgment, which is then enforced.

7.93 Registration under the 1933 Act: miscellaneous further points

Registration, which is applied for without notice to any other party,[784] is permitted within six years of the judgment or of the final disposal of any appeal against the judgment.[785] Once the judgment is registered, notice of registration is served upon the defendant,[786] and the judgment takes effect as if it were a judgment of the English court.[787] The defendant may thereafter apply to set aside the registration.[788] Partial registration, in order to obtain partial enforcement, is permitted in appropriate cases.[789] The judgment is registered in the currency in which it was given; if converted into sterling it will be converted at the date of payment, not at any other date.[790]

If the judgment is one to which the Act applies, that is, one capable of being registered under the Act, section 6 prevents any action being brought upon the judgment itself at common law.[791]

---

778 Section 4(1)(a)(v). See *Habib Bank Ltd v. Ahmed* [2001] EWCA Civ 1270, [2002] 1 Lloyd's Rep 444.

779 And not the underlying cause of action itself. For a Canadian decision on the bilateral treaty with the United Kingdom, limiting the scope of public policy to the status of a safety valve to prevent anomalies, see *Society of Lloyd's v. Meinzer* (2002) 210 DLR (4th) 519.

780 But not a duty: s. 4(1)(b).

781 Section 1(3).

782 Section 5.

783 Section 2(1), Proviso (b).

784 Section 3(1)(b); CPR r. 74.3.

785 Section 2(1).

786 Section 3(1)(c); CPR r. 74.6. Permission is not required to serve it out of the jurisdiction: CPR r. 74.6(2).

787 Section 2(2).

788 CPR r. 74.7.

789 Section 2(4), (5).

790 Section 2(3) was repealed by s. 4 of the Administration of Justice Act 1977. On a related point, a charging order may be made in respect of a judgment debt expressed in foreign currency or in sterling; and for issues relating to the date of conversion, or change of mind by the claimant who procured an order in terms of foreign currency but now wishes the order had been made in sterling, see *Carnegie v. Giessen* [2005] EWCA Civ 191, [2005] 1 WLR 2510.

791 Section 34 of the 1982 Act prevents proceedings being brought on the underlying cause of action.

JUDGMENTS FROM SCOTLAND, NORTHERN IRELAND AND GIBRALTAR

7.94 General

Section 18[792] of the Civil Jurisdiction and Judgments Act 1982 provides for the more or less automatic enforcement in England, by registration, of judgments from other courts in Scotland and Northern Ireland. Section 18(8) provides that, for judgments to which the section applies, registration is the sole manner of enforcement. As one would expect, there are very few limitations upon the recognition and enforcement of such judgments within the United Kingdom.[793]

With effect from 1 February 1998, judgments from Gibraltar given in civil or commercial matters became registrable for enforcement in England under section 4 of the 1982 Act, as though Gibraltar were, as far as the United Kingdom was concerned, a Contracting State to the Brussels Convention.[794] The grounds on which registration may be opposed are those contained in the Brussels Convention. Power was given by the 1982 Act to make similar arrangements in relation to the Isle of Man, any of the Channel Islands and any colony.[795] But except in relation to Gibraltar it was not exercised.

MISCELLANEOUS POINTS RELATING TO THE RECOGNITION OF FOREIGN JUDGMENTS

7.95 Sovereign immunity

According to general principles of public international law,[796] a foreign court has no jurisdiction to give judgment against a defendant who is entitled to sovereign immunity, and who did not choose to submit to the jurisdiction of that court. Foreign judgments given against States are covered by section 31 of the 1982 Act, where it is stated that a judgment against a foreign State shall be enforced only if (a) it would have been entitled to recognition and enforcement if not given against a State, and (b) that court would have had jurisdiction if the foreign court had applied rules which were in accordance with sections 2–11 of the State Immunity Act 1978.[797]

---

792 And Schs 6 and 7. For illustration of operation, and in particular for the proposition that the merits of the judgment are not to be questioned, see *Clarke v. Fennoscandia Ltd* 1998 SCLR 568; *Parkes v. MacGregor* [2008] CSOH 43, 2008 SCLR 345.

793 See *Clarke v. Fennoscandia (No 3)* 2003 SCLR 894. For the full story of the litigation between these parties, see *Clarke v. Fennoscandia Ltd* 2004 SC 197. The appeal to the House of Lords, in *Clarke v. Fennoscandia Ltd* [2007] UKHL 56, 2008 SLT 33, is not material to the present point.

794 SI 1997/2602. Gibraltar is now treated as part of the United Kingdom for the purposes of the Brussels Regulation, and judgments from its courts will be (or in the case of Spain, should be) recognised and enforced in other Member States as judgments from the courts of the United Kingdom. But in relation to the purely internal issue of their enforcement elsewhere in the United Kingdom, it is as if Gibraltar were a Contracting State to the Brussels Convention.

795 1982 Act, s. 39 (as amended by SI 1990/2591, art. 10).

796 And, within the 1933 Act, s. 4(3)(c).

797 Did the defendant submit? Did the proceedings relate to a commercial transaction? For illustration, see *NML Capital Ltd v. Argentina* [2011] UKSC 31, [2011] 2 AC 495.

A detailed examination of the principles of state immunity and the 1978 Act is beyond the scope of this book. However, in *NML Capital Ltd v. Argentina* the Supreme Court gave guidance on the common law rules – and, one supposes, the rules which govern registration under the 1920 and 1933 Acts – in cases in which the foreign judgment was given against a State. The Argentine State had issued bonds on which it had defaulted. Judgment had been obtained against it in New York, and an attempt was made to enforce the judgment under the common law rules applicable to judgments from the United States. The Supreme Court interpreted the State Immunity Act 1978 as leading to the conclusion that the State could not rely on its immunity in the English proceedings. This conclusion was not based on section 3 of the Act, which removes immunity for proceedings relating to a commercial transaction, but because the express terms of the bond contained a broadly-worded submission to the courts of New York which was sufficient to waive the immunity the State would otherwise have had.

The first part of this conclusion is not completely persuasive: the assertion that the proceedings before the English court were not proceedings relating to a commercial transaction because they were in fact proceedings relating to the enforcement of a foreign judgment (which was given in proceedings relating to a commercial transaction) is not self-evidently correct, though if it is correct to construe the immunity of a State broadly, and the exceptions narrowly, it may be understood. But the second part of it seems plainly correct: the width of the State's waiver of its immunity would have been sufficient for it to have been sued in the English courts, and as a result the jurisdiction of the New York court conformed to English law as set out in the State Immunity Act 1978. The court also considered that the terms of the State's waiver were independently wide enough to apply to the English proceedings in any event.

7.96 Community judgments

It is probably incorrect to call these foreign judgments. A Community judgment is one from the Court of Justice of the European Communities, or a decision of the Council or Commission of the European Communities, which imposes a monetary obligation upon persons other than States. The legislation is to be found in the European Communities (Enforcement of Community Judgments) Order.[798] The Secretary of State is required to append an order for its enforcement.[799] Upon registration,[800] the judgment takes effect as if it were a judgment of the High Court.

7.97 Judgments given on the basis of other Conventions

A number of other Conventions give jurisdiction to, and contain provisions requiring the recognition of foreign judgments in, the United Kingdom. Many of these relate to international transport. A judgment must be recognised under one of these Conventions when

---

798 SI 1972/1590 as amended by Administration of Justice Act 1997, Sch. 5, Part I. It was further amended by SI 1998/1259 (to make provision for Council Regulation (EC) 40/94 on the Community Trade Mark, and by SI 2003/3204 (to make provision for Council Regulation (EC) 6/2002 on Community Designs).

799 The purpose of which is the authentication of the judgment.

800 The procedure for which is contained in CPR 74, Part IV.

the legislation implementing the Convention so requires it;[801] and Article 71(2)(b) of the Brussels I Regulation, both original and recast, makes the procedures of the Regulation available for the purpose of enforcement where the proceedings fall within the scope of the Regulation.

---

801 See further, Dicey, Morris and Collins, *The Conflict of Laws*, 15th edn (2012), Rule 62.

CHAPTER 8

Arbitration

INTRODUCTORY MATTERS

8.01 General

The preceding chapters of this book have been concerned with the process, and the manipulation and management of the process, of dispute resolution by proceedings before the courts, and with the recognition and enforcement of judicial orders. But no account of the law and practice of commercial dispute resolution can be seen to be complete without acknowledging that a substantial number of such disputes are intended to be, and are, resolved, in the first instance at least, by means of arbitration. This chapter therefore aims to give a brief account of some of the more important aspects and incidents of arbitration, and its relationship to the rules of jurisdiction described in the earlier chapters. It is obvious that arbitration is a large and complex topic, and practitioner works on the subject find it necessary to devote several hundreds of pages to the detail of their subject. This is neither possible nor appropriate in the present context.

One of the principal aims of dispute resolution by arbitration is to detach the process from the judicial system of any particular country, or, as it is sometimes said, to de-localise it. In principle all sensible legal systems are willing to make provision for this, and support it, but unless arbitration is to be recognised as occupying a modern Alsatia, where the King's writ does not run, it is also true that there must, at the beginning or in the end, be some form of supervisory control, which has to mean judicial supervisory control. Striking this balance is never straightforward.[1] Especially at the point where arbitration law came into contact with the conflict of laws, the State of English law was one of considerable complexity. However, two fresh starts were made: one legislative and one judicial. The legislative one came in the form of the Arbitration Act 1996 ('the 1996 Act').[2] This furnished English law with an

---

1 For an illuminating study of the issues from all sides of the debate, see Petrochilos, *Procedural Law in International Arbitration* (Oxford, 2004).

2 The Act came into force on 31 January 1997, apart from ss 85–87 which will not take effect. CPR Part 62, and the Practice Direction supplementing CPR Part 62, provide for certain matters of detail left unspecified by the 1996 Act, and also provide the basis for service of claim forms or notices out of the jurisdiction; see CPR r. 62.5 and r. 62.16. It is not finally settled whether r. 62.5 provides a basis for service on a person not alleged to be party to an arbitration agreement where relief is sought in connection with a matter which is to be arbitrated. The conclusion that it does not is supported by *The Cienvik* [1996] 2 Lloyd's Rep 395, *Vale do Rio Doce Navegação SA v. Shanghai Bao Steel Ocean Shipping Co Ltd* [2000] 2 Lloyd's Rep 1, *Starlight Shipping Co v. Tai Ping Insurance Co Ltd (Hubei Branch)* [2007] EWHC 1893 (Comm), [2008] 1 Lloyd's Rep 320, and *Cruz City 1 Mauritius Holdings v. Unitech Ltd* [2014] EWHC 3074. In *Joint Stock Asset Management Co Ingosstrakh-Investments v. BNP Paribas SA* [2012] EWCA Civ 644, [2012] 1 Lloyd's Rep 649, [79], the court upheld service on the basis of CPR Part 6,

almost entirely new point of departure for the resolution of old problems, and it went a very long way to clarify the relationship between English courts and arbitral tribunals. In doing so it significantly reduced the opportunity for the courts to intervene or interfere in the process and supervision of arbitration. It is therefore appropriate to draw a veil over certain intricacies of the old law, which has now been replaced. No doubt there is still an occasional temptation[3] to revert to cases decided under the common law and the repealed legislation in order to interpret the new; and in some areas[4] this will be sensible. Even so, the 1996 Act is meant to improve the law, and this aim is not likely to be furthered by extensive backwards reference to the law which it replaced.

The judicial one came in the form of an important decision of the House of Lords[5] to limit or exclude the opportunity for one party to an apparent agreement to arbitrate to find reasons to impugn, and to find a court willing to entertain submissions that he had been entitled to impugn, the alleged agreement to arbitrate. The dominant strand of thinking is that if the parties appear to have agreed to arbitrate, or to have put themselves in a position in which it is plausible that they did so agree, it should generally be the arbitrators, rather than the courts, who should take the primary role in dealing with most of the arguments which may then be raised. If there is a pendulum, it has swung a long way in favour of allowing the tribunal to take all the decisions, or to take them first, and against those arguments by which a party might try to bring a dispute before a court instead. But as with all pendulums, which swing to and fro, the point of balance between leaving it to the tribunal, and giving the court a role in determining whether the matter is one for the tribunal, is not a fixed one.

It is therefore principally necessary to examine arbitrations which fall within Part I of the 1996 Act, which will encompass the large majority of commercial arbitrations with which an English court may be concerned. Thereafter we will examine matters which are dealt with elsewhere in the 1996 Act, such as the recognition of certain foreign awards, and finally, a small number of areas of common law doctrine, and preserved statutory law, to the extent that this has not been abolished by the 1996 Act. For a statement of the law which applies to arbitration prior to the coming into force of the 1996 Act, the reader will need to look elsewhere.[6]

---

and declined to examine the availability of service under CPR Part 62, which left the matter open at that level. In *PJSC Vseukrainskyi Aktsionernyi Bank v. Maksimov* [2013] EWHC 3203, [80] it was held to be arguable that r. 62.5 did, in some circumstances at least, provide a basis for service on a non-party; so also in *Shipowners' Mutual P&I Association (Luxembourg) v. Containerships Denizcilik Nakliyat ve Ticaret as* [2015] EWHC 258 (Comm). One may see why this should be: the proliferation of corporate structures designed to create artificial separations between entities which have an intimate relationship is a phenomenon to which the law may see a need to respond in a way which was not previously accepted. But it may be that service out under CPR Part 6 is the proper way of dealing with jurisdiction over non-parties to the arbitration agreement in such cases.

3 For example, *Halki Shipping Corp v. Sopex Oils Ltd* [1998] 1 WLR 726 (stay of proceedings under s. 9 of the 1996 Act).

4 For example, the Arbitration Act 1975 is substantially re-enacted in various places throughout the 1996 Act; provisions of the Arbitration Act 1950 are also, in many cases, reproduced in effect in the 1996 Act. Where it is concluded that the legislature intended to restate, as distinct from improving, the law, it will not be inappropriate to have recourse to old authority.

5 *Fiona Trust & Holding Corp v. Privalov* [2007] UKHL 40, [2007] Bus LR 1719.

6 The standard practitioner works are Mustill and Boyd, *Commercial Arbitration*, 2nd edn (Butterworths, London, 1989, together with companion volume (2001) to the 1996 Act), and Redfern and Hunter, *International Arbitration*, 5th edn (OUP, Oxford, 2009). See also Joseph, *Jurisdiction and Arbitration Agreements and their Enforcement*, 2nd edn (Sweet & Maxwell, London, 2010).

8.02 The problems of agreement or consent to arbitrate

Arbitration derives its status, its reason for being, from the agreement of the parties to have their disagreements – whether called disputes or differences probably does not matter – resolved by a body which will do so in private, with a set of rules or guidelines which, to a greater or lesser extent, the parties may fashion for themselves. If they want arbitration according to the rules and understandings of a religious law, or without reference to any particular law, the parties may agree to it and arbitration may well deliver it. If they want arbitration before adjudicators who understand the particular business or trade, they may have it by appointing or arranging for the appointment of a tribunal whose members will have this form of expertise. If they want three heads rather than one to consider the issues, they can have this as well if they agree upon a tribunal so constituted.

All of this is fine when it is common ground that the parties have agreed to arbitrate the particular dispute in question. But it works rather less well when there is disagreement as to the validity, or the scope (material or personal or both) or the interpretation of the agreement to arbitrate; and even if it is accepted that these issues should, in accordance with principle, be referred to a governing law for their answer, which governing law will that be? The governing law of the arbitration agreement, or the contract of which it may be a part, or something else? It may be appropriate to refer some of these questions to the law of the seat of the proposed arbitration, but if one party argues that there is no seat because there is no agreement to arbitrate in the first place, reference to the law of the place of the seat seems less compelling. The private international law of arbitration works extremely well if the foundation that the parties have agreed to arbitrate this dispute is not in question. Otherwise it is not at all clear.

Likewise, the proposition that arbitral tribunals have jurisdiction to rule on their own jurisdiction is sensible and efficient; but if one party challenges the existence of the alleged arbitration agreement as something by which he is bound, it is not so obvious that the tribunal should have the first and the last word.

In *Dallah Real Estate and Tourism Holding Co v. Government of Pakistan*,[7] the Supreme Court made it clear that a party whose position is that it never agreed to the arbitration is entitled to raise that objection at the point where judicial proceedings are brought to obtain enforcement of the award, and is not to be prejudiced (never mind restrained) by the fact that it did not raise or take the objection before the courts of the seat of the arbitration. In other words, it will be the court, and not the tribunal which will, in the last resort, decide this question. This is a welcome reassertion of the fact that the binding force of arbitration is the consent of the parties, and only the consent of the parties, as well as a welcome reassertion of the fact that, in the final analysis, the question whether a person or party consented to arbitration and to abide by the award is one for a court to answer. Whereas the law may allow a tribunal to determine this issue as a precondition to its going further, by providing that the tribunal has power to rule on its own jurisdiction, the two propositions that 'the tribunal finds that there was consent to its exercise of power' and 'there was consent to the exercise of power by the tribunal' are not the same thing at all. It is not the question which causes the difficulty, but the issue of who is to have the final say about it, and as to that, *Dallah* decides that it is the court. The issue of who is to have the first say is examined below.

---

7 [2010] UKSC 46, [2011] 1 AC 763, esp. [24], [148], [160].

The vortex of circularity in reasoning is at its most dangerous where allegations of consent, limited consent, impugned consent, voidable consent and (waiver of the rights which follow from) absence of consent are made. In arbitration, perhaps more than anywhere else, the problem of circularity in argument is at its most acute. In the final analysis, the law faces a choice of fundamental policy: it can regard the decision of the arbitral tribunal as final, or it can regard the issue as one for the court to take if called upon to decide it. The decision in *Dallah* confirms that questions of whether the parties agreed to arbitrate will be determined by the law which governs that alleged agreement; but where the arbitrators purport to answer that question, their answer is not to taken as the last word.

With that general introduction it will be necessary to examine the structure of the 1996 Act, the significance of the seat or the law of the seat, and the role and the identification of the law which governs the agreement to arbitrate in the first place. It may not be entirely logical, but it makes sense to examine them in this order.

ARBITRATION AND THE ARBITRATION ACT 1996

8.03 The 1996 Act: general

The immediate forerunner of the 1996 Act was a Consultation Paper issued by the Department of Trade and Industry in July 1995,[8] following the work of its Departmental Advisory Committee, under the chairmanship of the then Lord Justice Saville. The Consultation Paper explains that the decision had been taken not to incorporate the UNCITRAL Model Law,[9] holus-bolus, into English law, but that the proposed English legislation had been designed to reflect the provisions of the Model Law wherever this was possible. The opportunity was also taken to put straight and iron out many of the difficulties which had emerged in the existing law of arbitration over the years. It was also considered necessary to write the law in more user-friendly language than had been customary hitherto. In this respect many will consider that the Committee achieved a brilliant success. Certainly the Act is one of the few examples of legislation where a very large part of its intended meaning can be gathered from a single reading of the text.[10]

The preamble to the Act states that it is made '... to restate and improve the law relating to arbitration pursuant to an arbitration agreement, to make other provision relating to

---

8 In fact, the 1995 Paper was the second such paper issued by the Department. The first, issued in February 1994, was limited in its ambitions, and did not attract wide support from those who accepted the invitation to respond to it. The Guides to the Provisions of the Act, produced by the Departmental Advisory Committee, are reproduced in (1997) 13 *Arbitration International* 257, 317.

9 The 'Model Law for International Commercial Arbitration', agreed by the United Nations Commission on International Trade Laws, was approved by resolution of the General Assembly of the United Nations in 1976. The Model Law was adopted into the law of Scotland (Law Reform (Miscellaneous Provisions) (Scotland) Act 1990, Sch. 7); it has been asserted (Aird and Jameson, *The Scots Dimension to Cross-Border Litigation*) that this has led to Scotland's being increasingly used as a centre for international arbitration. In fact the Model Law has been accepted in Hong Kong, Singapore, Canada, India, Australia, California, and in over 30 other countries and territories.

10 One possible exception to this applause may be the provisions on choice of law, and the extent to which various provisions of the Act apply to arbitrations in which England is not the seat of the arbitration and English is not the law which governs the arbitration agreement.

arbitration and arbitration awards, and for connected purposes'. This chapter therefore concentrates on the law as laid down by the Act, and refers to the pre-existing law on arbitration only insofar as may be necessary to explain the working of the 1996 Act.

The 1996 Act is divided into four parts. Part I[11] sets out the law of arbitration pursuant to an 'arbitration agreement', and specifies in detail the powers available to, and the duties imposed upon, arbitrators as well as the English courts. Part II[12] contains other provisions relating to particular forms of arbitration, and which principally take the form of modifications to the operation of Part I.[13] Part III[14] provides for the recognition and enforcement of certain foreign awards. Part IV[15] sets out the final general provisions which apply to the Act. The Act repeals in their entirety the Arbitration Acts of 1975 and 1979, and repeals Part I (but not Part II) of the Arbitration Act 1950.[16]

8.04 The 1996 Act: general principles of interpretation

According to section 1 of the Act, its provisions are founded on three principles, and the provisions of the Act are to be construed accordingly. These principles are that (a) the object of arbitration is to obtain the fair resolution of disputes by an impartial tribunal without unnecessary delay or expense, (b) the parties should be free to agree how their disputes are resolved, subject only to such safeguards as are necessary in the public interest and (c) in matters governed by Part I of the Act, the court should not intervene except as provided by Part I of the Act.

This statement of principle should limit the scope for judicial intervention by means of the court's inherent jurisdiction to interfere. For example, it had been held in *Channel Tunnel Group Ltd v. Balfour Beatty Construction Ltd*[17] that although the power of a court to grant interim relief under section 12(6)(h) Arbitration Act 1950 was not available in relation to an arbitration conducted abroad under foreign law, the court still had power under section 37(1) Senior Courts Act 1981 to grant an interlocutory injunction against defendants subject to the personal jurisdiction of the court. It would now appear from section 1(c) of the 1996 Act that if the arbitration in question falls within Part I of the Act, the intervention of an English court in order to exercise powers not conferred on it by the 1996 Act should not be possible. Accordingly, the application of section 37(1) may well have been modified by section 1(c) of the 1996 Act. Time will tell whether section 1(c) has succeeded in its stated aim.

---

11 Sections 1–84.

12 Sections 85–98 (though ss 85–88, dealing with domestic arbitration agreements, will not be brought into effect); ss 89–91 with consumer arbitration agreements; s. 92 excludes Part I from small claims arbitration in the county court; s. 93 deals with the appointment of judges as arbitrators (a topic not further examined here); and ss 94–98 deal with statutory arbitrations.

13 And is therefore dealt with here at paras 8.26, 8.27 and 8.28 of this chapter.

14 Sections 99–104. Section 99 deals with the enforcement of Geneva Convention awards by the continuation of Part II of the Arbitration Act 1950; ss 100–104 with the recognition and enforcement of New York Convention awards. Sections 100–104 are essentially re-enactments of the corresponding provisions of the Arbitration Act 1975.

15 Sections 105–110.

16 For repeals, see s. 107(2) of and Sch. 4 to the Act. In fact s. 42(3) of Part II of the Arbitration Act 1950 is repealed (but no other section of Part II).

17 [1993] AC 334.

8.05 Operation of the 1996 Act: the arbitrations to which the Act applies, and the law which governs the agreement to arbitrate

In dealing with the scope of arbitrations to which the Act applies, it is necessary to consider separately the seat of the arbitration, and the law which governs the arbitration agreement. Both contribute in defining the scope of the various provisions of Part I of the Act. The identification of the seat of the arbitration will determine which of the provisions of English law set out in the 1996 Act are applicable to the particular arbitration. The law which governs the arbitration agreement determines the validity, scope and interpretation of the agreement, as well as determining whether provisions of the Act dealing with severability and death apply to the arbitration in question.

8.06 Issues which are determined by reference to the seat of the arbitration

The principal statement of the grasp of the 1996 Act, and of the various provisions set out in it, is made in section 2(1). It provides that 'the provisions of this Part apply where the seat of the arbitration is in England and Wales or Northern Ireland'.[18] It follows that, save where the remainder of section 2 modifies[19] this simple provision, the provisions of Part I have no effect if the seat of the arbitration is not in England.[20] This reflects the fact that the main concern of Part I of the Act is to regulate the extent to which the courts may supervise and intervene in and after the arbitration process; such powers as English law confers on the court, and such powers and duties as English law confers on the arbitrators, are appropriate if England is the seat of the arbitration; but they have little or no general claim to be applied if the seat of the arbitration is elsewhere than England: the regulation of the arbitration is then the proper concern of another jurisdiction and another law.

Nevertheless, certain provisions of Part I of the Act still apply if the seat of the arbitration is not England. According to section 2(2), sections 9 to 11 (dealing with stays of legal proceedings[21]), and 66 (dealing with the enforcement in principle of arbitral awards) apply whatever the seat of the arbitration may be. This is self-evidently sensible. If legal proceedings have been brought in England in breach of an agreement to arbitrate in another country, the courts of that other country may not have the power in fact or in law to restrain English legal proceedings by injunction, or may feel unwilling to act in a way which may be thought to trespass on English sovereignty.[22] In such a case there is every reason to permit and require an English court to intervene with its own remedies in aid and support of the agreement to arbitrate. Similarly, if arbitration has resulted in an award,

---

18 Hereafter, references to the seat of the arbitration as being in England are to be read, as is customary, as if they were references to England and Wales.

19 As explained in this paragraph.

20 For the seat of the arbitration, see the following paragraph.

21 See para. 8.13, below.

22 For a view on this point from a jurisdiction into which an English injunction was projected, see *Phillip Alexander Securities and Futures Ltd v. Bamberger* [1997] ILPr 73, 104; *Re the Enforcement of an English Anti-suit Injunction* [1997] ILPr 320 (Düsseldorf Court of Appeal): but contrast *OT Africa Line Ltd v. Hijazy* [2001] 1 Lloyd's Rep 76 (no evidence that anti-suit injunction would be seen by Belgian law as conflicting with its sovereignty or public policy). On the compatibility of anti-suit injunctions with the scheme of the Brussels I Regulation, see C-159/02 *Turner v. Grovit* [2004] ECR I-3565, and C-185/07 *Allianz SpA v. West Tankers Inc* [2009] ECR I-663 (referred from the English courts: *West Tankers Inc v. RAS Riunione Adriatica di Sicurta* [2005] EWHC 454 (Comm), [2005] 2 Lloyd's Rep 257; appeal and reference [2007] UKHL 4, [2007] 1 Lloyd's Rep 391).

it would be absurd if steps could not be taken to secure an order for its enforcement against assets in England.

According to section 2(3), certain other provisions of the Act may be applied if the seat of the arbitration is outside England and Wales, or if no seat has been designated or determined; but the court may refuse to exercise such power if in the opinion of the court the fact that the seat of the arbitration is (or when designated or determined is likely to be) outside England and Wales makes it inappropriate to do so. The powers in question are those in sections 43 (securing the attendance of witnesses) and 44 (court powers exercisable in aid of arbitral proceedings).

As to the remaining powers in the Act, section 2(4) provides that if the seat of the arbitration has not been designated or determined, and if by reason of a connection with England and Wales it is appropriate for it to do so, the court may exercise any other power conferred by Part I of the Act for the purpose of supporting the arbitral process.

Section 2(5) finally provides that the doctrines of severability and non-discharge of an arbitration agreement by the death of one of the parties to it[23] are applicable even if the seat of the arbitration is outside England and Wales, but only if English law is the law applicable to the arbitration agreement.[24]

8.07 Determining the seat of the arbitration

The starting point, when considering the application of the Act, is therefore to identify the seat of the arbitration. As has been seen, the practical application of the provisions of the Act depends in most cases upon whether the seat of the arbitration is in England. According to section 3 of the Act, the seat of the arbitration means the juridical seat of the arbitration *designated* (a) by the parties to the arbitration agreement,[25] or (b) by any arbitral or other institution or person vested by the parties with powers in that regard, or (c) by the arbitral tribunal if so authorised by the parties; or *determined*, in the absence of such designation, by the court, having regard to the parties' agreement and all the relevant circumstances.[26]

The concept of the 'seat' of an arbitration was adopted in the light of its antecedents in international arbitrations. It represents the juridical, as distinct from the strictly geographical, place of the arbitration: the place where it is legally grounded, even though evidence may be taken, and meetings or hearings may be held,[27] and the award itself signed in and sent out from other geographical locations. There will nevertheless be one,[28] and only one, seat, the law of which country will be considered to govern or control the arbitral procedure. In most cases this will in fact be the geographical place in which the arbitration takes place. Where the seat of the arbitration is England, the rules in Part I of the Act will therefore

---

23 Sections 7 and 8.

24 See further paras 8.11, 8.12, below.

25 See *ABB Lummus Global Ltd v. Keppel Fils Ltd* [1999] 2 Lloyd's Rep 24.

26 Up to the point at which the arbitration was begun: *Dubai Islamic Bank PJSC v. Paymentech Merchant Services Inc* [2001] 1 Lloyd's Rep 65. For a surprising example of the choice of an English seat, despite express words to the contrary, see *Braes of Doune Wind Farm (Scotland) Ltd v. Alfred McAlpine Business Services Ltd* [2008] EWHC 426 (TCC), [2008] 1 Lloyd's Rep 608.

27 *Cf PT Garuda Indonesia v. Birgen Air* [2002] 1 Sing LR 393.

28 The common law was unsympathetic to the proposition, less alien to some civilian systems, that there could be a 'delocalised' arbitration. The Act confirms, in this respect, the predisposition of the common law.

be applicable in principle.[29] Where the seat of the arbitration is not in England, the extent to which Part I applies is much reduced.[30] But if the seat of the arbitration is England, the manner and extent to which the Act will then apply will further depend upon whether the provision is a mandatory one;[31] and if not, whether English is the law of the arbitration agreement.[32]

Where the parties have expressly selected the seat of the arbitration to be England, the effect of their doing so has been held to be that English courts have, by reason of the parties' choice, exclusive supervisory jurisdiction over the arbitration:[33] this presupposes, of course, that the court accepts that the parties did indeed agree to arbitration in the first place. By parity of reasoning, where the choice is of a foreign seat, the courts of that country will have exclusive supervisory jurisdiction, including jurisdiction to determine (whether in advance or after the issue has been argued before the tribunal, as local procedure specifies) whether the reference to arbitration is itself valid.[34]

This primacy of, or attribution of exclusivity to, the seat of the arbitration excludes the possibility, which might have otherwise been open, that one party might apply to a court in another jurisdiction for a decision that the agreement to arbitrate was invalid, or that the award should be set aside or vacated or otherwise held to be open to challenge.[35]

To the extent that these conclusions may be deduced as or from the true construction of the agreement to arbitrate there can be no objection to them, even in a case in which the agreement to arbitrate is itself the subject of dispute. But when they are used to support an argument that the losing party is precluded from seeking to establish the enforceability or the unenforceability of the award under the law of another country, it is rather harder to see the justification for the prohibition. If it is accepted that an agreement to arbitrate involves a promise not to take points which would otherwise have been available to be taken against the enforcement of the award, it is possible to explain why an injunction may go to restrain such challenges before a foreign court. But in the ordinary course of things, a party who agrees to arbitrate does not expressly agree to relinquish those arguments which a national law would allow him and which go to determine whether the award is enforceable,[36] and it is far from clear that such a term could be implied in fact or in law. In this sense, the decision in *C v. D*,[37] in particular, which allowed an injunction to restrain a party from raising points before a foreign court in which enforcement of the

---

29 See *Arab National Bank v. El Abdali* [2004] EWHC 2381 (Comm), [2005] 1 Lloyd's Rep 541. Whether they are in a given case will also depend upon which law governs the arbitration agreement, and whether the provision of the Act in question is defined by the Act as mandatory: see para. 8.09, below.

30 See the discussion of s. 2 of the Act in para. 8.05, above.

31 If it is mandatory in the sense of s. 4 of and Sch. 1 to the Act, it applies when Part I applies, even though English is not the law governing the arbitration agreement.

32 As to which, see para. 8.09, below.

33 *C v. D* [2007] EWCA Civ 1282, [2007] Bus LR 843; *Shashoua v. Sharma* [2009] EWHC 957 (Comm), [2009] 2 Lloyd's Rep 376.

34 *Weissfisch v. Julius* [2006] EWCA Civ 218, [2006] 1 Lloyd's Rep 716; *A v. B* [2006] EWHC 2006 (Comm), [2007] 1 Lloyd's Rep 237; *A v. B (No 2)* [2007] EWHC 54 (Comm), [2007] 1 Lloyd's Rep 358.

35 *C v. D* [2007] EWCA Civ 1282, [2007] Bus LR 843; *Shashoua v. Sharma* [2009] EWHC 957 (Comm), [2009] 2 Lloyd's Rep 376.

36 In England, for example, see Arbitration Act 1996, s. 103.

37 [2007] EWCA Civ 1282, [2007] Bus LR 843. The decision is presaged by that in *Noble Assurance Co v. Gerling-Konzern General Insurance Co* [2007] EWHC 253 (Comm), [2007] 1 CLC 85; it was followed and applied in *Shashoua v. Sharma* [2009] EWHC 957 (Comm), [2009] 2 Lloyd's Rep 376.

award was apprehended,[38] on the basis that for it to do so was to breach the promise made by the agreement to arbitrate in England, appears to go to the very limit of the conclusions and promises which can be extracted from an express choice of England as the seat of the arbitration.

8.08 The law which governs an arbitration agreement

The identification of the seat of the arbitration answers the question whether the powers of the court set out in the Act will be available or applicable in the particular case. But it is also necessary to identify the law which governs the agreement, or the alleged agreement, to arbitrate, as this law will govern the validity, scope and interpretation of the agreement to settle differences by arbitration: the question whether it governs the creation, or initial validity, of the agreement is also dealt with in a little more detail below. This is therefore the law which will decide whether (and if so, what) the parties agreed to arbitrate. To answer this question, it is necessary to examine the broader picture presented by the private international law of contracts, and to deal with an agreement to arbitrate in that context.

For contracts concluded after 17 December 2009 the Rome I Regulation contains the choice of law rules which an English court must apply to determine the law applicable to a contractual obligation. Certain exclusions from the Rome I Regulation are listed in Article 1(2), but only one of these is likely to be of significance in the present context.

The Rome I Regulation, by Article 1(2)(e), as was also the case with the Rome Convention which preceded it, excludes 'arbitration agreements and agreements on choice of court' from its material scope. It follows that the Rome I Regulation makes no claim or demand to identify the law which will apply to arbitration agreements, as opposed to substantive contracts; and the answering of the question which law governs an (alleged) agreement to arbitrate is therefore left to the rules of private international law of the court seised.

There is some uncertainty as to what this actually means in practice. On one rather unconvincing view, the exclusion made by Article 1(2)(e) means that the law governing the arbitration agreement has to be determined by the traditional choice of law rules of the common law, almost as though the Rome Convention and Rome I Regulation had never been enacted. If this were correct, one would need to enquire as to the law that the parties had chosen, expressly or impliedly, to govern the arbitration agreement; or if no such choice could be discerned, which was the law with which the arbitration agreement had its closest and most real connection.[39] But there is more than a trace of artificiality in asking such questions, and, subject to one point, a better solution would be to hold that, so far as the English private international law is concerned, an arbitration agreement which is contained in a contract is in general[40] governed by the law which governs the rest of the contract of which it forms a part, albeit a severable part. Though this is not a result which would be dictated or demanded by the Rome I Regulation, it is not prohibited by it either. It would

---

38 It is just arguable that the case depended upon the fact that the proceedings in the US were brought by the party against whom the award had been given. If they had been brought by the successful party, to obtain an order by way of enforcement, it would have looked very odd indeed if the defendant-respondent-losing party were precluded from taking points in its defence which were available under the law of the United States.

39 *Arsanovia Ltd v. Cruz City 1 Mauritius Holdings* [2012] EWHC 3702 (Comm), [2013] 1 Lloyd's Rep 235.

40 But not invariably: *Tamil Nadu Electricity Board v. St-Cms Electricity Co Pte Ltd* [2007] EWHC 1713 (Comm), [2008] 2 Lloyd's Rep 484.

follow that the law which governed the contract as a whole would govern the arbitration agreement, as a term of that contract, as well.[41] If it is a term of a contract, why would this not be the right answer to the question?

The one point which needs to be addressed is the proposition that an arbitration clause may, as far as English law is concerned and for some purposes at least, be separable from the remainder of the contract,[42] and the consequence of this for the purpose of identification of the law governing the agreement to arbitrate. It is true that the application of the *lex contractus* would be completely persuasive if the agreement to arbitrate, agreed to as a contract term, were indissociable from the substantive contract. On the other hand, separable does not mean separate; and although the arbitration agreement may be separable for certain purposes, it does not follow that it has to be regarded as already separated for the purpose of identifying the law which applies to it. The best solution is to accept that an arbitration agreement will be governed by the law which is chosen to govern it; and, save in exceptional cases or where the agreement is not made as part of a substantive contract but is independent and free-standing,[43] this will be the same as the law which governs the contract in which it appears as a term. It may be helpful to take three indicative cases.

First, where the parties have made a contract which contains an express choice of governing law, the explanation for this submission would naturally run along the following lines: if two persons make a contract, in which they choose and express the law which will govern 'this agreement', it makes much sense to interpret that as their choice of law to govern 'these agreements' if the point is taken that the agreement to arbitrate is, in principle and for some purposes, separate from the substantive contract to which it is attached.

Second, where there is no expression of their choice of law to govern the agreement, the law governing the contract will be determined by other means; and in these circumstances the identification of the law which governs the agreement to arbitrate is more difficult. In these circumstances it has been said that the law which governs the arbitration agreement will be the law of the place where the arbitration has its seat.[44] This is both convincing and unconvincing. It is unconvincing because although the law of the seat of the arbitration is the law which will, in principle and in most respects, perform the control and supervision of the arbitration, there is no reason to suppose that the same law should be used to determine the initial validity or material scope of the agreement to arbitrate. To put the same point another way, the law of the seat fulfils its function after the validity and existence of the agreement to arbitrate has been established. It is also rather unhelpful in those cases in which the parties have not identified the seat of the arbitration. On the other hand, if the parties have specified the seat of the arbitration, they may have assumed that the law of the seat will be used to answer all questions which arise in connection with the arbitration agreement. Certainly the manner in which the law which governs the contract is determined in the absence of an express choice would make it a less reliable guide to the intention of the parties as to the law which would govern the agreement to arbitrate; but if the search is for a principled answer, this case remains a difficult one.

---

41 See *The Star Texas* [1993] 2 Lloyd's Rep 445.

42 See s. 7 of the Act, and paras 8.11, 8.12, below.

43 As, for example, in *A v. B* [2006] EWHC 2006 (Comm), [2007] 1 Lloyd's Rep 237. See also *Shegang South Asia (Hong Kong) Trading Co Ltd v. Daewoo Logistics* [2015] EWHC 194 (Comm).

44 *Hamlyn & Co v. Talisker Distillery* [1894] AC 202; *Deutsche Schachtbau- und Tiefbohrgesellschaft mbH v. Ras al Khaimah National Oil Co* [1990] 1 AC 295.

Third, if there is no agreed seat for the arbitration, the only conclusion will be to look to the law which applies in the absence of express choice. It would be possible to do this by reference to the rules in Article 4 of the Rome I Regulation, and use this to determine the validity and scope of the contract and all its terms. This seems preferable to the alternative of reverting to the common law rule, which would be to apply the law with which the contract had its closest and most real connection.

8.09 Application of Part I of the 1996 Act: mandatory and non-mandatory provisions

If the seat of the arbitration is in England, the provisions of Part I of the Act apply. The position is more complex if English law is not the law which governs the arbitration agreement, for if English law governs the arbitration agreement, certain provisions of the Act are excluded by virtue of this fact. This comes about as the Act identifies certain of its provisions as being mandatory.[45] The effect of a particular provision of Part I being mandatory is that it applies to the case, even though the law which governs the arbitration agreement is not English law, and even though the agreement itself may contain a provision to the contrary.

All other provisions of Part I of the Act are non-mandatory, and these apply only to the extent that the parties have not made their own arrangements in the agreement: they are the default options. But the Act also provides[46] that if the arbitration agreement is governed[47] by a law other than English law, that simple fact suffices to constitute an agreement to make contrary provision. As a result, the mandatory rules must be applied whatever the law which governs the arbitration agreement; the non-mandatory rules will apply only when the law governing the arbitration agreement is English law and the parties have not agreed on particular provision to the contrary.

The mandatory provisions of Part I of the Act are set out in Schedule 1 to the Act. They are sections 9–11 (stays of legal proceedings); 12 (power of court to extend agreed time limits); 13 (application of Limitation Acts); 24 (power of court to remove arbitrator); 26(1) (effect of death of arbitrator); 28 (liability of parties for fees and expenses of arbitrator); 29 (immunity of arbitrator); 31 (objection to substantive jurisdiction of tribunal); 32 (determination of preliminary point of jurisdiction); 33 (general duty of tribunal); 37(2) (items to be treated as expenses of arbitrators); 40 (general duties of parties); 43 (securing the attendance of witnesses); 56 (power to withhold award in case of non-payment); 60 (effectiveness of agreement for payment of costs in any event); 66 (enforcement of award); 67 and 68 (challenging the award: substantive jurisdiction and serious irregularity); 70 and 71 (supplementary provisions; effect of order of court, but only so far as relating to sections 67 and 68); 72 (saving for rights of person who takes no part in proceedings); 73 (loss of right to object[48]); 74 (immunity of arbitral institutions, etc); and 75 (charge to secure payment of solicitors' costs).

---

45 Section 4 and Sch. 1.

46 Section 4(5).

47 The Act refers to this as the effect of a 'choice of a law other than the law of England', but immediately this includes an applicable law 'determined in accordance with the parties' agreement, or which is objectively determined in the absence of any express or implied choice'. It might have been easier simply to have said 'governed by'.

48 See on this *JSC Zestafoni G Nikoladze Ferroalloy Plant v. Ronly Holdings Ltd* [2004] EWHC 245 (Comm), [2004] 2 Lloyd's Rep 335.

8.10 Application of Part I of the 1996 Act: formal requirements

It is finally necessary to identify those arbitration agreements to which the provisions of Part I of the 1996 Act apply. According to section 5 of the Act, the provisions of Part I of the Act apply only to arbitration agreements in writing; and any other agreement between the parties as to any matter is effective for the purposes of Part I only if it is in writing. This will mean, among other things, that the variation of an arbitration agreement will be effective only if it is in writing in the sense of section 5.

Section 5 goes on to give a reasonably broad scope to the concept of an agreement[49] in writing. According to section 5(2) there is such an agreement if (a) the agreement is made in writing, whether or not it is signed by the parties, or (b) the agreement is made by exchange of communications in writing, or (c) the agreement is evidenced in writing.

These provisions are extended by the inclusion of particular instances into the section. Section 5(3) includes the case where parties agree otherwise than in writing by reference to terms which are in writing.[50] Section 5(4) includes the case where an agreement made otherwise than in writing is recorded by one of the parties, or by a third party, with the authority of the parties to the agreement. Section 5(5) includes the case where parties to arbitral or legal proceedings exchange written submissions, in which the agreement of the parties otherwise than in writing is alleged by one party and is not denied by the other in his response.[51] Finally, section 5(6) defines something 'written or in writing' as including its being recorded by any means.[52] It is not clear whether, in addition to means of communication which provide a written record, this expression would extend to communication by electronic mail or text message; but if the purpose of the section is to establish a level of objective reliability in relation to the evidence of agreement, there would appear to be no satisfactory reason to exclude these other forms of recording.[53] Beyond that the position is uncertain. It is unclear whether section 5(6) requires the matter in question, or the writing in relation to it, to be recorded by any means. If it is the latter, then the section will require there to be writing of one sort or another. But if the former is intended, then audio-recording of an oral agreement would appear to suffice. If, as was suggested above, the purpose of section 5 is to establish a level of objective reliability in relation to the evidence of agreement, then there is no obvious reason why tape- or other electronic recording would not suffice.[54] But if the transcript of a tape-recorded agreement is made by one of the parties without the authority of the other party, the transcript would not satisfy the requirement of writing: section 5(4). Given that, it would appear that the unilateral tape-recording of a conversation would not satisfy section 5(4).

---

49 Not limited to an arbitration agreement. Therefore these provisions will also determine whether a variation to a written arbitration agreement does itself satisfy the requirement of being in writing. A one-sided agreement which allows one party to refer a dispute to arbitration even if the other has instituted legal proceedings is still an arbitration agreement: *NB Three Shipping Ltd v. Harebell Shipping Ltd* [2005] 1 Lloyd's Rep 509.

50 For example, an oral salvage agreement made by the master of a ship in distress incorporating Lloyd's Salvage Rules, or the engagement of a building contractor by reference to a standard form building contract.

51 *Cf* Art. 7(2) of the UNCITRAL Model Law.

52 An earlier draft of the Bill made express reference to 'letter, telemessage, telex, fax, or any other means of communication providing a record of the agreement': DTI Consultation Paper (July 1995).

53 *Cf* the recast Brussels I Regulation 1215/2012, Art. 25(2): 'any communication by electronic means which provides a durable record of the agreement shall be equivalent to "writing"'.

54 However, oral exchanges before the Beth Din, a Jewish religious tribunal, will not suffice: *Maccaba v. Lichtenstein* [2006] EWHC 1901 (QB).

The requirement that an arbitration agreement be in writing was also to be found in the previous legislation.[55] It does not follow that an oral arbitration agreement is without effect: so long as their operation is consistent with Part I of the Act, rules of the common law as to the effect of an oral arbitration agreement may still be applied by the courts.[56] But to attract the provisions of Part I of the Act, the arbitration agreement must be in writing. No doubt this follows from the perception that the impact on the parties, and on the court, of Part I of the Act will be very substantial, and that it should not be open to one of the parties to rely on evidence which is too flimsy to justify preventing his opponent from having primary recourse to the courts. The extended meaning given to the expression will go a long way to answering the objection that there are other cases of agreement which should be regarded as being sufficient to attract the operation of Part I of the Act. Even so, it has been the experience of the courts in relation to what is now Article 25 of the Brussels I Regulation that there will be cases where insistence by one party on the requirement of writing can be seen as an exercise in bad faith. In such a case it is no doubt open to a court to use the principles of estoppel to prevent such abuses.

8.11 Essential validity, and scope, of an arbitration agreement

According to section 6, an 'arbitration agreement' means an agreement to submit present or existing disputes (whether these are contractual or not) to arbitration.[57] The reference in an agreement to a written form of arbitration clause, or to a document containing an arbitration clause, constitutes an arbitration agreement if the reference is such as to make that clause part of the agreement.[58] Section 6 underlines the point that if there is no agreement to submit disputes to arbitration, there is no agreement on the basis of which the Act could operate. So, for example, if the parties agree that they 'will endeavour to first resolve the matter through arbitration…', their agreement to endeavour to have recourse to arbitration will not be read as though it were a mutual promise to proceed to arbitration. An endeavour to achieve a result is not the same thing as an agreement to do that thing; and a promise expressed in such terms will not, as a matter of English law at least, be construed as amounting to a binding promise to proceed to arbitration to which section 9 of the 1996 Act could be applied.[59]

In accordance with general principle, and as said above, the validity of an arbitration agreement, together with its scope and interpretation, is a matter for the law which governs the arbitration agreement.[60] This is in accordance with the general proposition that obligations arising from an agreement are governed by the law which governs that agreement,

---

55 Arbitration Act 1950, s. 32; Arbitration Act 1975, s. 7. See *JSC Zestafoni G Nikoladze Ferroalloy Plant v. Ronly Holdings Ltd* [2004] EWHC 245 (Comm), [2004] 2 Lloyd's Rep 335.

56 As to these, see para. 8.32, below. In this context, note that the court has an inherent discretion to stay proceedings brought in breach of an oral arbitration agreement: *cf Channel Tunnel Group Ltd v. Balfour Beatty Construction Ltd* [1993] AC 334.

57 *The Paola d'Alessio* [1994] 2 Lloyd's Rep 366.

58 Section 6(2); *Trygg Hansa Insurance Co v. Equitas Ltd* [1998] 2 Lloyd's Rep 439; *The Delos* [2001] 1 Lloyd's Rep 703.

59 *Kruppa v. Benedetti* [2014] EWHC 1887 (Comm), [2014] 2 Lloyd's Rep 421.

60 *West Tankers Inc v. RAS Riunione Adriatica de Sicurta SpA* [2005] EWHC 454 (Comm), [2005] 2 Lloyd's Rep 257 applying this principle in the case of subrogation. For decisions of the Shari'a Council (a self-appointed body which assumed some responsibility for matters concerning the Muslim religion) in London, and their status as arbitration awards, see *Al Midani v. Al Midani* [1999] 1 Lloyd's Rep 923 (held they are not: not a judicial body established under the law of a State).

and what this means was considered above.[61] It follows that if it is denied that an admitted agreement is an arbitration agreement, or that it has any application to the present case, this question must be referred to and answered by the application of the law which governs the 'arbitration' agreement.[62]

Though it is nowhere expressly stated in the 1996 Act, it is to be supposed that the law which would have been the law which governed it if the arbitration agreement had been valid must also determine whether there is a valid agreement where this is denied.[63] Although there is room for objection,[64] the application of the 'putative governing law' to determine whether there is an agreement at all, and then (if there is) the application of that governing law to determine whether the agreement is an arbitration agreement, is in practice the best solution to the issue. As has been seen above, the identification of the law which governs the arbitration agreement may not always be straightforward.

The Act does not require, in express terms at least, the agreement to be one to refer the dispute to arbitration in a particular or single place. As a matter of English law, an agreement to refer disputes to arbitration in X or Y has been upheld as valid;[65] and if English is the law governing the arbitration agreement, there is no reason in principle why such an agreement should not be upheld as valid for the purposes of the Act as well. Of course, until it were decided where arbitration was to be held, there would be no seat of the arbitration designated or determined, and this would affect the manner in which the provisions of the Act would at that stage be applied.

The problems which arise when a contract provides for arbitration and for judicial adjudication are notorious, but just as is the case when parties enter into a number of contracts which have divergent provisions for law and jurisdiction,[66] the task of the court is one of contractual construction, nothing more. If it arrives at the conclusion that the correct interpretation is that the parties identified a court with jurisdiction, but agreed that either party could instead require the matter to be arbitrated, then when one party invoked the agreement to arbitrate, the parties became actively bound by an agreement to arbitrate, which could and should be enforced in the usual ways.[67]

8.12 Rescission of the substantive contract and survival of the arbitration agreement

Two of the problems that may arise if an alleged arbitration agreement formed, or was to form, part of another agreement, are solved by sections 7 and 8. If the law applicable to the

---

61 Paragraph 8.08, above.

62 For the procedure, including the possibility that a court may issue a stay under its inherent jurisdiction so as to allow the arbitral tribunal to rule on its own jurisdiction, see *Al Naimi v. Islamic Press Agency* [2000] 1 Lloyd's Rep 522.

63 *The Heidberg* [1994] 2 Lloyd's Rep 287.

64 On the ground that a proof is defective if it starts by assuming what it is sought to demonstrate.

65 *The Star Texas* [1993] 2 Lloyd's Rep 445.

66 See above, para. 4.45.

67 *Sulamérica Cia Nacional de Seguros SA v. Enesa Engenharia SA* [2012] EWCA Civ 638, [2013] 1 WLR 102 (although the point was not discussed in any detail). Cf *Kruppa v. Benedetti* [2014] EWHC 1887 (Comm), [2014] 2 Lloyd's Rep 421, in which a contractual promise that 'the parties will endeavour to first resolve the matter through Swiss arbitration...', failing which the English court will have jurisdiction, did not create a binding promise to proceed to arbitration to which s. 9 of the 1996 Act could be applied: the promise to 'endeavour' to do something was not the same as a promise to do that something.

arbitration agreement is English,[68] then if the other agreement is impugned on the ground that it was invalid, non-existent or ineffective, or if it is alleged that the other agreement did not come into existence or has become ineffective, this does not affect the arbitration agreement. In other words, the arbitration agreement is, as a matter of English law, separable or separate from the broader agreement of which it may have formed a part.[69]

In this respect, section 7 codified the effect of the common law as established in *Harbour Assurance Co (UK) Ltd v. Kansa General International Insurance Co Ltd*[70] as to the separability, as a matter of English law, of the arbitration agreement from the remainder of the larger, substantive, agreement of which it is part.

The decision is further entrenched by the decision of the House of Lords in *Fiona Trust & Holding Corp v. Privalov*.[71] In that case, one of the parties to an agreement to arbitrate, which had been made by his agent but then rescinded on account of the alleged bribing of that agent, sought to bring proceedings instead before the courts, free of the (now rescinded) agreement to arbitrate. The House of Lords held that the bribery objection went to the legal validity or enforceability of the substantive contract, and may have justified its rescission, but did not so impugn the validity of the agreement to arbitrate that it was open to the complaining party to side-step it and to act as though it had ceased to exist. Only if the objection which was used to justify rescission was one which related distinctly and individually to the agreement to arbitrate, or if it was contended that the agreement was initially and wholly void, would the party complaining about it be entitled to ask a court to adjudicate instead.

There are a number of policies which are in conflict; and the strength of the judgments in *Fiona Trust* is not, perhaps, enough to completely dispel all doubts. For if the plea of the shipowner, that the contract had been concluded by the bribing of his agent, went to anything, it went to the whole of the contract, not simply to the hiring aspect of it. The shipowner did not assert that the bribery of the agent impugned the charterparty but not the agreement to arbitrate. His contention was that the whole contractual relationship, and every part of it, was procured by bribery, and was not binding on him. Likewise, a party who complains that a contract was procured by misrepresentation does not usually assert that he is bound by part of the contract, but that the whole of it is liable to rescission. *Fiona Trust* challenges this piece of contractual orthodoxy, as well as the argument of rhetoric, but avoids that conclusion by using a principle of severance.

On the other hand, the reason for upholding the validity of the agreement on arbitration, even in the face of such an objection, is that when parties agree upon a form of dispute resolution, whether judicial or arbitral or for choice of law, or any combination of these, they presumably intend that court, tribunal or law to be applied to determine whether their contract was valid in the first place. An agreement to arbitrate is almost inevitably an agreement to allow the arbitrator to decide whether, rather than only if, the contract was

---

68 The limitation is imposed by s. 2(5). As to when English law is the law which governs the arbitration agreement, see para. 8.06, above. The irrelevance of invalidity according to some other law, see *JSC Zestafoni G Nikoladze Ferroalloy Plant v. Ronly Holdings Ltd* [2004] EWHC 245 (Comm), [2004] 2 Lloyd's Rep 335.

69 *Cf* Art. 16(1) of the UNCITRAL Model Law. And see, for comparative purposes, *FAI General Insurance Co Ltd v. Ocean Marine Mutual P & I Association* [1998] Lloyd's Rep IR 24 (NSW); *Ash v. Corporation of Lloyd's* (1991) 87 DLR (4th) 65 (Ont); reversed on other grounds: (1992) 94 DLR (4th) 378; *Sonatrach Petroleum Corp v. Ferrell International Ltd* [2002] 1 All ER 627; and Samuel [2000] Arb & Disp Res LJ 36.

70 [1993] QB 701.

71 [2007] UKHL 40, [2007] Bus LR 1719. For a similar principle under the law of the United States, see *Buckeye Check Cashing Inc v. Cardegna* 546 US 440 (2006).

valid and binding, just as much as it was an agreement to allow the arbitrator to determine whether it was discharged by performance, frustration or breach. It would be self-defeating for the dispute resolution agreement to be rendered incapable of performance the moment that there was a dispute which required resolution; and in any event, it is not generally[72] plausible to contend that the agreement to arbitrate, as distinct from the substantive contract itself, will have been procured by misconduct.

If that is accepted, then the logical consequence has to be that complaints which go to the validity of the associated substantive agreement do not *ipso facto* impeach the agreement to arbitrate. For that to happen, the vitiating factor has to be specifically targeted at the agreement to arbitrate,[73] unless the agreement to arbitrate is a freestanding contract not entered into as part of a larger agreement; and even then, there will be a temptation to reject submissions which tend to the conclusion that the agreement to arbitrate is not effective and that the complaining party may commence proceedings before a court rather than before the arbitral tribunal.[74]

Another way of defending the conclusion reached is that if the shipowner had not entered into the particular charterparty, it would have entered into another, and that other would have contained a provision for arbitration, as that is the nature of the shipping business. If that may be plausibly said, the agreement to arbitrate will not have been caused by the alleged bribery, and the discovery of the alleged bribery will not allow it to be avoided. The result is that where the complaint seeks to show that the complaining party was entitled to rescind the contract, the arbitrator will be left to take the first step in deciding whether there is a valid arbitration agreement.[75] It will be otherwise where the party alleges that the supposed contract was, as far as he is concerned, wholly void.

The true principle, therefore, appears to be that where it is made sufficiently to appear that there is an arbitration agreement, which appears to be wide enough to capture the dispute[76] and by which the parties[77] may be bound, then the claimant will be expected to go to the tribunal, and questions as to the validity of the agreement will be raised in the first instance before the tribunal; it will not be permissible for one of the parties to require the other to deal with the arguments before a judge instead, or before the judge first.[78] This is, in effect, what *Fiona Trust* decides: that the agreement to arbitrate is separate from any

---

72 But for a case where this was exactly what was alleged, but the court did not appear to see the significance of the distinction, see *A v. B* [2006] EWHC 2006 (Comm), [2007] 1 Lloyd's Rep 237

73 *Fiona Trust & Holding Corp v. Privalov* [2007] UKHL 40, [2007] Bus LR 1719; *Deutsche Bank AG v. Asia Pacific Broadband Wireless Communications Inc* [2008] EWCA Civ 1091, [2008] 2 Lloyd's Rep 619; *El Nasharty v. J Sainsbury plc* [2007] EWHC 2618 (Comm), [2008] 1 Lloyd's Rep 360; *Habaş Sınai ve Tıbbi Gazlar İstihsal Endüstrisi AS v. VSC Steel Co Ltd* [2013] EWHC 4071 (Comm), [2014] 1 Lloyd's Rep 479.

74 *A v. B* [2006] EWHC 2006 (Comm), [2007] 1 Lloyd's Rep 237.

75 See above, where this analysis is proposed in relation to agreements on jurisdiction, para. 4.44.

76 But if it is not so wide, then there is no point in ordering a stay and leaving the parties to go to the tribunal: *Abu Dhabi Investment Co v. H Clarkson & Co Ltd* [2006] EWHC 1252 (Comm), [2006] 2 Lloyd's Rep 381 (agreement governed by Abu Dhabi law).

77 But it must be otherwise if one 'party' denies that he was party to the agreement at all: pleas of mistake or mistaken identity go to establish that there was no agreement at all; they are pleas tending to show the alleged agreement is void and not voidable. But illegality does not: an allegation that the substantive contract is unenforceable by reason of illegality does not impeach the arbitration agreement, at least in general cases: *Beijing Jianlong Heavy Industry Group v. Golden Ocean Shipping Group Ltd* [2013] EWHC 1063 (Comm), [2013] 2 Lloyd's Rep 61.

78 This does not affect the proposition that objections may be taken at the enforcement of the award (Arbitration Act 1996, s. 103), subject to the principle that a party who has estopped himself from taking any particular point (as the Government had not) will not be permitted to take it: *Dallah Estate and Tourism Holding Co v. Ministry of Religious Affairs, Government of Pakistan* [2010] UKSC 46, [2011] 1 AC 763.

substantive contract which the tribunal will be asked to examine and, for the purpose of deciding whether the agreement gives jurisdiction to the arbitrator, the decision must be first taken by the arbitrator unless both parties are content to have it decided by the judge.

From the perspective of the party who contends that he is not bound to arbitrate, it may appear most unsatisfactory that he should have to commence the arbitration in order to obtain a decision that he is not bound to arbitrate, but this may be the marginal price which is to be paid to secure the larger principle; and maybe it is correct that if one strays too close to a potential arbitration agreement, one has only oneself to blame if it is taken at face value, at least to begin with. It is not that arbitration agreements are assumed to be valid, but the decision whether they are valid is, in the first instance, a decision which the tribunal may be expected to take. But as will be seen below, there will be cases in which a court departs from the proposition that the parties should go to the arbitral tribunal to allow it to take the first look at the issue of agreement and jurisdiction, and will take that decision for itself. When it does so, however, it will still apply the basic principle of severability.

It is further provided in section 8[79] that, unless the parties otherwise agree, an arbitration agreement governed by English law is not discharged by the death of a party and it may be enforced by or against his personal representatives.[80]

If the law which governs the arbitration agreement is not English law, the doctrine of separability, or any similar doctrine, will be applicable only if the law which governs the contract as a whole contains such a doctrine: this follows from section 2(5). It should also follow that what was said above about the approach in *Privalov* will not necessarily apply, though one imagines that a court will easily be persuaded that the *Privalov* approach should be consistent with agreements to arbitrate which are governed by a law other than English law.

8.13 Stays of legal proceedings: application for a stay

If legal proceedings are commenced in England in breach of an arbitration agreement, sections 9–11 confer on the court the power and, in most cases, the duty, to stay the proceedings[81] if[82] an application for such relief is made;[83] if the proceedings are commenced overseas in breach of an arbitration agreement for an English tribunal, the court has an inherent power to order an injunction to restrain the breach so long as the party in breach is subject to the personal jurisdiction of the court; and if it is unsure whether the alleged agreement is valid, it may conduct a mini-trial to determine the issue. The powers conferred on the court by sections 9–11 apply wherever the seat of the arbitration may be,[84] and notwithstanding the fact that the arbitration agreement may be governed by a law other than English law.[85] Unlike the corresponding provision in some other laws, an English court does not refer the parties to arbitration, but leaves the party who wishes to obtain relief against the other to proceed by way of arbitration if so advised.

---

79 Which applies also only if English law is the law governing the arbitration agreement: s. 2(5).

80 But this is expressed by s. 8(2) not to affect the operation of any enactment or rule of law by virtue of which a substantive right or obligation is extinguished by death.

81 *Cf* Art. 8 of the UNCITRAL Model Law; s. 4(1) of the 1950 Act and s. 1 of the 1975 Act.

82 But if no such application is made, the court will not lack jurisdiction to adjudicate: *Youell v. La Reunion Aerienne* [2009] EWCA Civ 175, [2009] 1 Lloyd's Rep 586.

83 *Youell v. La Reunion Aerienne* [2009] EWCA Civ 175, [2009] 1 Lloyd's Rep 586.

84 Section 2(2)(a).

85 As ss 9–11 are mandatory: s. 4 of and Sch. 1 to the 1996 Act.

The applicant for a stay, that is, the party against whom legal proceedings have been brought in respect of a matter which under the agreement is to be referred to arbitration, must give notice to the other parties to the proceedings of his application.[86] He may do so even though the reference to arbitration is not to be immediate, but is to take effect only after the exhaustion of other dispute resolution procedures:[87] recourse to the courts in such a case is, after all, just as much a breach of contract.[88] He may not apply before acknowledging the legal proceedings against him;[89] he may not do so after having taken any step in the proceedings to answer the substantive claim.[90] This last rule is analogous to that which applies when a defendant to legal proceedings wishes to challenge the jurisdiction of the court over him,[91] and the observations made in relation to that procedure apply with equal force to parties who object to legal proceedings on the basis of an arbitration agreement.[92]

8.14 Stays of legal proceedings by reference to an arbitration agreement

The court is required, by section 9(4), to grant a stay of legal proceedings unless satisfied[93] that the arbitration agreement is null and void,[94] inoperative[95] or incapable of being performed. In other words, if there is an effective arbitration agreement which applies to the dispute, the ordering of a stay is mandatory. Where it is said that a rule of European law transposed into English law must be applied, but would not be applied by a tribunal with its seat in a non-Member State, it has been held that a stay of proceedings may not be ordered: it is not clear that this is correct.[96]

However, the question whether there is an agreement to arbitrate in the first place prompts the question whether that question is to be answered, in the first instance at least, by the

---

86 Section 9(1). See CPR r. 62.8, and Practice Direction – Arbitration, para. 6.1.

87 *Cf* the procedures created by the parties in *Channel Tunnel Group Ltd v. Balfour Beatty Group Ltd* [1993] AC 334, where there was to be reference to a panel of experts prior to arbitration. There would now be no doubt that the statute gives the court an immediate power and duty to stay proceedings.

88 Section 9(2); *cf* the observations of Lord Mustill in *Channel Tunnel Group Ltd v. Balfour Beatty Construction Ltd* [1993] AC 334.

89 Section 9(3). If it is not necessary to acknowledge the proceedings (for example, where they are brought by counterclaim), there is no impediment to the immediate making of the application. And see *NB Three Shipping Ltd v. Harebell Shipping Ltd* [2005] 1 Lloyd's Rep 509.

90 Section 9(3). For illustration, see *Patel v. Patel* [2000] QB 551 and *Capital Trust Investments Ltd v. Radio Design AB* [2002] EWCA Civ 135, [2002] 2 All ER 159, which suggest that it would be inconsistent with the policy behind s. 9 of the Act for the court to take too strict a line with the applicant who may have strayed close to the line. For applications for extension of time, see *Grimaldi Compagnia de Navigazione SpA v. Sekihyo Lines Ltd* [1999] 1 WLR 708; *Bilta UK Ltd v. Nazir* [2010] EWHC 1086 (Ch), [2010] Bus LR 1086; and for proceedings taken in a foreign court, see *Thyssen Inc v. Calypso Shipping Corp SA* [2000] 2 Lloyd's Rep 243.

91 As to which, see CPR Part 11, and paras 5.25 *et seq.*, above.

92 For the right to appeal against orders made under s. 9 of the Act, or not, see *Inco Europe Ltd v. First Choice Distribution* [2000] 1 WLR 586 (held possible).

93 The wording strongly suggests that the burden of proof lies on the claimant to justify his breach of contract, and this represents a reversal of the burden of proof as contained in the 1950 Act, where the defendant had the task of proving his case in support of a stay. This change is sound in principle, for if the defendant has proved the agreement, the burden should move to the claimant to show why that agreement is not, after all, still operative and binding upon him. On cases where the court is uncertain whether the conditions for the ordering of a stay are satisfied, see *Al Naimi v. Islamic Press Agency* [2000] 1 Lloyd's Rep 522.

94 Which means from the outset.

95 *Shanghai Foreign Trade Corp v. Sigma Metallurgical Co Pty Ltd* (1996) 133 FLR 417 (contractual settlement); *Downing v. Al Tameer Establishment* [2002] EWCA Civ 721, [2002] 2 All ER (Comm) 545 (repudiation of agreement accepted by issue of proceedings).

96 *Accentuate Ltd v. Asigra Inc* [2009] EWHC 2655 (QB), [2009] 2 Lloyd's Rep 599.

court or by the arbitrator. As to this, the options are for the court to decide whether the parties have bound themselves to arbitrate the particular issue between them, or for the court to stay the proceedings so that the same issue may be determined by the arbitrators (with the possibility of an appeal against their award on this point) instead. It is fair to say that the authorities do little more than disclose that the court, so long as it keeps the wording of section 9 clearly in mind, has a pretty free hand in deciding which course to adopt. After all, the duty imposed by section 9 depends on there being an arbitration agreement; it does not arise merely but conclusively on one party's say-so, and it would distort section 9 to read it as imposing a duty to stay as soon as the defendant alleges that there is an arbitration agreement.

As to the principle of the matter, the court may consider that the conduct of the claimant, in instituting proceedings in court, is really an attempt to undermine an agreement to arbitrate by which he really knows, and the court can see, that he is bound; or that the alleged belief of the claimant that he is not bound to arbitrate is either not genuine or not reasonable or both. In such a case the court should order an immediate stay of proceedings to allow the tribunal to take the initial decision as to the agreement to arbitrate. Alternatively, the court may take the view that the issue of whether there is an obligation to proceed by way of arbitration is bound to be hotly contested, on grounds which appear to be genuine and not unreasonable, and that whatever the arbitrators decide will be liable to be subject to an appeal to the court: in such a case the court is free, and may well be inclined, to decide the question whether there is a duty to arbitrate the particular dispute once and for all (so far as it is concerned) and right at the outset, with the result that there will be no stay, rather a trial of a preliminary issue. Alternatively still, the court may take the view that the claimant believes, genuinely and not unreasonably, that he is not bound by an agreement to arbitrate, and that in such a case, the proposition that he should be required to constitute an arbitral tribunal for the sole purpose of asking it to decide that it has no jurisdiction would be incoherent, and the proposition that there should be a stay of proceedings scarcely less so.

Little light, though plenty of heat, has been generated by judicial decision. It is not surprising that this should be so. The proposition that the arbitrators should enjoy primacy in decision-taking is a fine and proper thing if their status as arbitrators in relation to the dispute has been really or sufficiently agreed to.[97] But the entire basis for arbitration is that it is what the parties agreed to, with the consequence that the cases in which they disagree about what was agreed to are bound to be as difficult as they are in the case in which parties disagree with each other on whether they bound themselves to each other by contract. There is, in this respect, nothing special about arbitration; and in the end it is hard to see that a court can be expected to do any more than feel its way by asking who appears to have the better of the argument that the parties did agree to arbitrate, or the better of the argument that the court or the tribunal should decide the issue of jurisdiction, always being on guard to prevent spurious attacks on a genuine agreement.[98] And it is irrelevant to this issue of *who* shall decide that one of the parties will claim to have released himself from the agreement to arbitrate by rescission or avoidance or whatever else: this point, which goes to the question whether an initial agreement remains binding, will fall within the jurisdiction of whichever

---

97 No doubt it has some bearing on the attractiveness of London as a seat of arbitration.

98 *Golden Ocean Group Ltd v. Humpuss Intermoda Transportasi TBK Ltd* [2013] EWHC 1240 (Comm), [2013] 2 Lloyd's Rep 421 suggests that s. 9(1) of the Act is triggered only if the party relying on it is able to show – as distinct from being arguably able to show – that there was an agreement to arbitrate the dispute. This seems correct in principle, as the freedom to arbitrate is no different in quality from the freedom to not agree to arbitrate.

body is decided to have the responsibility of addressing the question whether the parties agreed to arbitrate their differences.

As to the authority, quite a lot of it supports the proposition that the issue may be determined by the court;[99] some supports referring this issue in the first instance to the arbitral tribunal for its decision[100] if the agreement is on its terms wide enough to cover the dispute in question.[101] English law is, in this respect, really only a collection of reconcilable and irreconcilable decisions, in an overall state of mild disarray.[102]

Under the provisions of the Arbitration Act 1975[103] a court also had power to refuse a stay if it was satisfied that there was in fact no dispute between the parties with regard to the matter to be referred.[104] But even if there is no obvious or apparent defence to the claim, there is still evidently a dispute between the parties, with the consequent obligation to stay legal proceedings, if one side has made a claim against the defendant who has refused to do the thing which the claimant demands. Accordingly, the former restriction on the duty to order a stay of proceedings is no longer in effect.[105] And if the matter in dispute falls partly within and partly outside the scope of an arbitration agreement, a stay must be granted in respect of the part of the dispute which falls within the scope of the agreement,[106] or even though there are parties to the overall dispute who are not bound by the agreement.[107] In this respect the policy of enforcing agreements on arbitration overrides the court's public duty to secure the coherent adjudication of disputes; and in this respect the law is different from that applicable to jurisdiction agreements under the common law.[108] According to section 9(5), if the court refuses to stay the legal proceedings, any provision that an award is a condition precedent to the bringing of legal proceedings in respect of any matter is of no effect in relation to those proceedings.

The effect of section 9 is that if there appears to the court to be an arbitration agreement to which Part I of the Act applies, there is, to all practical intents and purposes, no discretion which permits a court to decline to stay judicial proceedings brought in breach of it; and the alterations made to the law by the 1996 Act have gone even further than hitherto in

---

99 *Law Debenture Trust Corp plc v. Elektrim Finance BV* [2005] EWHC 1412 (Comm), [2005] 2 Lloyd's Rep 755; *Al-Naimi v. Islamic Press Agency Inc* [2000] 1 WLR 522; *Birse Construction Ltd v. St David Ltd* [1999] BLR 194; *Albon v. Naza Motor Trading Sdn Bhd (No 3)* [2007] EWHC 665 (Ch), [2007] 2 All ER 1075; *Albon v. Naza Motor Trading Sdn Bhd (No 4)* [2007] EWCA Civ 1124 (injunction to restrain arbitration while court decides allegation of forgery); *Claxton Engineering Services Ltd v. TXM Olaj-és Gázkutató KFT* [2010] EWHC 2567 (Comm), [2011] 1 Lloyd's Rep 252; *Excalibur Ventures LLC v. Texas Keystone Inc* [2011] EWHC 1624 (Comm), [2011] 2 Lloyd's Rep 289.

100 *Weissfisch v. Julius* [2006] EWCA Civ 218, [2006] 1 Lloyd's Rep 716; *A v. B* [2006] EWHC 2006 (Comm), [2007] 1 Lloyd's Rep 327; *Fiona Trust & Holding Corp v. Privalov* [2007] UKHL 40, [2007] Bus LR 1719.

101 *Fiona Trust & Holding Corp v. Privalov* [2007] UKHL 40, [2007] Bus LR 1719 will favour a broad construction if the agreement is governed by or construed by reference to English law. But other laws may be significantly more restrictive: *Abu Dhabi Investment Co v. H Clarkson & Co Ltd* [2006] EWHC 1252 (Comm), [2006] 2 Lloyd's Rep 381.

102 *Golden Ocean Group Ltd v. Humpuss Intermoda Transportasi TBK Ltd* [2013] EWHC 1240 (Comm), [2013] 2 Lloyd's Rep 421, esp. at [59], contains a very useful summary of the authorities.

103 Section 1; the 1975 Act is repealed in its entirety by the 1996 Act.

104 For the uncertainty as to how this was to be interpreted, see *SL Sethia Lines Ltd v. State Trading Corporation of India Ltd* [1985] 1 WLR 1398; *Home and Overseas Insurance Co Ltd v. Mentor Insurance Co (UK) Ltd* [1990] 1 WLR 153; *Hayter v. Nelson* [1990] 2 Lloyd's Rep 265.

105 *Halki Shipping Corp v. Sopex Oils Ltd* [1998] 1 WLR 726; *Glencore Grain Ltd v. Agros Trading Ltd* [1999] 2 Lloyd's Rep 410.

106 *Kaverit Steel & Crane Ltd v. Kone Corp* (1992) 87 DLR (4th) 129 (a Canadian case).

107 *Wealands v. CLC Contractors Ltd* [1999] 2 Lloyd's Rep 739.

108 See above, para. 4.52.

establishing that the court is obliged to enforce the arbitration agreement, and does not have a discretion to rewrite the contract at the instance of the claimant.

8.15 Stays in Admiralty proceedings

Where Admiralty proceedings are stayed on the ground that the dispute in question should be submitted to arbitration, the court granting the stay may, if in those proceedings property has been arrested or bail or other security has been given to prevent or obtain release from arrest, (a) order that the property arrested be retained as security for the satisfaction of any award given in the arbitration in respect of that dispute, or (b) order that the stay of those proceedings be conditional on the provision of equivalent security for the satisfaction of any such award.[109]

8.16 Injunctions to defend an arbitration agreement from judicial proceedings brought elsewhere

The 1996 Act makes provision for the defence of an arbitration agreement from being undermined by judicial proceedings brought in an English court. But it says nothing about what an English court, or tribunal, is to do when proceedings are brought in a foreign court in breach of an arbitration agreement, so from one point of view this question is not naturally part of the law on arbitration as shaped by the Arbitration Act 1996. The question whether and, if so, when an injunction may be ordered by an English court is therefore a matter for the common law and equity,[110] subject to any restrictions imposed by the Brussels I Regulation; but it is so closely bound up with the manner in which an English court gives effect to agreements to arbitrate that it is necessary to examine it here.

In principle, the rules which apply to the availability and grant of an injunction are therefore those which were set out in Chapter 5.[111] The English courts have made it plain that where foreign proceedings are brought in breach of an agreement to arbitrate, the court should be neither hesitant nor apologetic about ordering an injunction against a respondent who has instituted judicial proceedings overseas in breach of contract: numerous cases make the point. Likewise, where proceedings are brought by an associated party with a view to undermining an arbitration in London to which another is party, an injunction can be ordered against the wrongdoer on the basis that his proceedings are oppressive or vexatious, or brought inequitably to undermine the arbitration.[112]

According to the Supreme Court in *AES Ust-Kamenogorsk Hydropower Plant JSC v. AES Ust-Kamenogorsk Hydropower Plant LLP*,[113] an injunction to restrain a party to an arbitration

---

109 Section 11. This is, in effect, a re-enactment of s. 26 of the Civil Jurisdiction and Judgments Act 1982 so far as this related to arbitration; and references to arbitration in that section are deleted from it: see Sch. 4 to the 1996 Act. The result is that s. 26 of the 1982 Act applies when proceedings are stayed in favour of the courts of another country, and that s. 11 of the 1996 Act applies where the stay is in favour of arbitration.

110 See *Bankers Trust Co v. PT Jakarta International Hotels & Development* [1999] 1 Lloyd's Rep 910.

111 It also follows that if it is necessary to serve the claim form out of the jurisdiction, this takes place in accordance with CPR Part 6 and not under CPR Part 62 or the Practice Direction.

112 *Joint Stock Asset Management Co Ingosstrakh-Investments v. BNP Paribas SA* [2012] EWCA Civ 644, [2012] 1 Lloyd's Rep 649.

113 [2013] UKSC 35, [2013] 1 WLR 1889. For the most recent authorities, see *Nomihold Securities Inc v. Mobile Telesystems Finance SA* [2012] EWHC 130 (Comm), [2012] 1 Lloyd's Rep 442; *Ecom Agroindustrial Corp Ltd v. Mosharaf Composite Textile Mill Ltd* [2013] EWHC 1276, [2013] 2 Lloyd's Rep 196 (injunction particularly

agreement from bringing proceedings before a foreign court does not depend on there being a pending arbitration in England. The function of an injunction is not just to defend an ongoing arbitration from collateral attack, though it certainly can do that, but also to prevent the wrongdoing of a respondent who has departed from his dispute resolution agreement by bringing proceedings he contracted not to bring.

This perspective probably answers the question whether there is any requirement that the arbitration agreement be for arbitration with an English seat, or whether an English court may order an injunction to restrain wrongdoing even though the seat is elsewhere. There had already been common law authority, from Bermuda, for the view that where judicial proceedings are brought in breach of an agreement to arbitrate, a court with jurisdiction over him might restrain the wrongdoer by injunction even if the seat of the arbitration was outside the territorial jurisdiction of the court.[114] In that case, the party to be restrained was resident within the territorial jurisdiction of the court, and therefore the court was able to exercise jurisdiction and to justify its exercise on the ground that relief which operated *in personam* was something which could properly be ordered by the court for the place where the respondent was resident. It did not accept that, in making an agreement to arbitrate, the parties had made an implied agreement that the supervision and enforcement of that agreement was within the exclusive jurisdiction of the courts of the seat.[115] The opposite point of view would make more of a distinction according to where the seat, and therefore the supervision of the arbitration, was to be, and, contrary to the view of the Bermuda court, might presume that there was no sufficient interest for it to be justified in restraining a party to an agreement to arbitrate elsewhere; and in *AES Ust-Kamenogorsk Hydropower Plant JSC v. AES Ust-Kamenogorsk Hydropower Plant LLP*,[116] the seat of the arbitration was England. However, if the justification for intervention by injunction is not the defence and supervision of the arbitration, but the restraint of wrongdoing, the location of the seat assumes a marginal role.

A choice between legal policies has therefore to be made. On balance, the view that the right to restrain breaches of the agreement to arbitrate should be confined to the courts at the seat is not sufficiently persuasive, not least because the law at the place of the seat may not confer such powers on the courts. And anyway, there is a difference between supervision and control, which properly belongs exclusively to the courts at the seat, and the policing of acts done elsewhere with a view to undermining the rights of the parties who agreed to arbitration, which does not necessarily do so. In English terms, the exercise of powers given by the Arbitration Act 1996 generally depend on England being the seat of the arbitration; the exercise of powers conferred or recognised by Senior Courts Act 1981, s. 37 does not. It is arguable that if the wrongful activity is the bringing of legal proceedings before a court, then it should in the first instance be a matter for the court before which the proceedings are brought to put matters right. But where, as in the *Kamenogorsk* case, it shows no sign of doing so, the view of the court before which proceedings have been wrongfully brought is of no interest;[117] and an English court may and should order a final injunction to

---

justified where party in breach had the cheek to get an anti-suit injunction from a foreign court); *Bannai v. Erez* [2013] EWHC 3689 (Comm); *Shipowners' Mutual P&I Association (Luxembourg) v. Containerships Denizcilik Nakliyat ve Ticaret as* [2015] EWHC 258 (Comm).

114 *IPOC International Growth Fund Ltd v. OAO 'CT Mobile'* [2007] Bermuda LR 43 (Bermuda CA).

115 *Cf C v. D* [2007] EWCA Civ 1282, [2008] Bus LR 843.

116 [2013] UKSC 35, [2013] 1 WLR 1889.

117 [2013] UKSC 35, [2013] 1 WLR 1889, [61].

restrain a party from breaching an agreement to arbitrate where it has personal jurisdiction over the respondent.[118]

8.17 Restraint of parties who breach an agreement to arbitrate by instituting proceedings before courts of a Member State

By contrast with what is said above, where the judicial proceedings to be restrained are in a civil or commercial matter and before the courts of another Member State of the European Union, it is clear from *Turner v. Grovit*[119] and from *Allianz SpA v. West Tankers Inc*[120] that there is now no power to order an injunction.[121]

Even though arbitration is a matter which falls outside the domain of the Brussels I Regulation,[122] and is therefore a matter in which the duties of mutual trust and confidence imposed by the Regulation would appear to be inapplicable, it is not to be forgotten that, so far as the court in the other Member State is concerned, it will have been seised with jurisdiction in a civil or commercial matter, and that where this is true, the obligation on the courts of all Member States is to trust and have confidence that the court of that Member State will do its job properly. Of course, the decision has neither application nor relevance to cases in which the objectionable foreign proceedings are before the courts of a non-Member State.[123]

In *Allianz SpA v. West Tankers Inc* itself, an agreement for London arbitration was infringed, as the applicant claimed, by the bringing of proceedings before a court in Sicily. As the proceedings before the Sicilian court were in a civil or commercial matter, just as the Spanish proceedings had been in *Turner v. Grovit*, the idea that an English court might restrain them by injunction was held to be as inconsistent with the Brussels I Regulation as it had been with the Brussels Convention in *Turner v. Grovit*. The logic of the argument works in its own specific terms, for the Court had already explained that where parties had agreed to refer a matter to arbitration, this fact did not contradict the proposition that the matter was a civil or commercial one: all the parties' agreement did was to remove the jurisdiction of courts to adjudicate it.[124]

---

118 The earlier, and more cautious approach in *Toepfer International GmbH v. Cargill France SA* [1998] 1 Lloyd's Rep 379 has therefore been superseded.

119 C-159/02, [2004] ECR I-3565.

120 C-185/07, [2009] ECR I-663. In retrospect, it was unhelpful that the orders were known as anti-suit injunctions. An '*in personam* order in support of the arbitration' might have drawn less fire.

121 It is surely improbable that this prohibition can be got round by applying instead for a decree of specific performance, requiring the party in breach to perform his promise to arbitrate. This distinction was drawn and relied on by the court in *Starlight Shipping Co v. Allianz Marine & Aviation Versicherungs AG* [2014] EWHC 3068 (Comm), [2014] 2 Lloyd's Rep 579 (not a case on arbitration); it is very difficult to believe that it is correct, whatever its non-legal merits might be. The consequences of the decree, breach of which places the respondent in contempt, are such that it is a measure having equivalent effect to an injunction, with the consequence that it must be within the scope of the decision in *Allianz SpA v. West Tankers Inc.*

122 Article 1(2)(d); applied in C-189/90 *Marc Rich & Co AG v. Società Italiana Impianti PA* [1991] ECR I-3855, a case concerning an application to appoint an arbitrator, and therefore having no direct concern with the adjudicatory jurisdiction of the English or the Italian courts. The Italian courts had been seised of a claim by the respondent to the arbitration application. These had been objected to on jurisdictional grounds; but the relief sought in the English proceedings made no reference to, and sought to make no interference with, the proceedings before the Italian courts.

123 *Shashoua v. Sharma* [2009] EWHC 957 (Comm), [2009] 2 Lloyd's Rep 376; *Midgulf International Ltd v. Groupe Chimiche Tunisien* [2010] EWCA Civ 66, [2010] 2 Lloyd's Rep 543.

124 C-391/95 *Van Uden Maritime BV v. Firma Deco-Line* [1998] ECR I-7091.

The consequence of *Allianz SpA v. West Tankers Inc* appears to be that if the party bringing the foreign court proceedings is not to be restrained, there will be nothing to prevent the two procedures – one arbitration, one judicial – from proceeding along parallel tracks.[125] In due course, each will result in a decision which the successful party may wish to enforce against the other. It would appear to follow from *Allianz SpA v. West Tankers Inc* that a judgment from the Sicilian court, if one were ever to have been handed down, would be entitled, in principle and subject to defences,[126] to be recognised and enforced in accordance with Chapter III of the Brussels I Regulation, for it will be a judgment given in a civil or commercial matter, and the possibility that the foreign court made a jurisdictional error in adjudicating is no defence to recognition.[127] It equally follows that the award of an arbitral tribunal will be enforceable in England, and in any other State which has legislated in accordance with the New York Convention. The result will be messy.

It ought to be clear from the judgment in *Hoffmann v. Krieg*,[128] as well as from Article 73(2) of the recast Brussels I Regulation, that an English court will not be required to set aside part of its law on a matter excluded by Article 1 from the material scope of the Regulation, such as arbitration,[129] and will not be bound to recognise a judgment from a court in a Member State which contradicts the agreement to arbitrate, or which contradicts an arbitral award which is required to be recognised. There is also rational support for the conclusion that an English court might refuse to recognise a judgment from another Member State on the ground that a rule of English public policy[130] prevents the recognition of judgments which conflict with the parties' agreement to arbitrate;[131] and the prohibition imposed by Article 35(1) of Regulation 44/2001[132] is not triggered, as the objection is not to the rules of jurisdiction of the foreign court, but to the failure of that court to give effect to the agreement to arbitrate.[133] True, a French court has held that recognition of a judgment may not be refused on the ground that it is irreconcilable with the award of a French tribunal, as the irreconcilability defence to recognition in Article 34(3) of the Brussels I

---

125 For an illustration of the manner in which this may take place, see *Through Transport Mutual Insurance Association (Eurasia) Ltd v. New India Assurance Association Co Ltd* [2004] EWCA Civ 1598, [2005] 1 Lloyd's Rep 67; *Through Transport Mutual Insurance Association (Eurasia) Ltd v. New India Assurance Association Co Ltd (No 2)* [2005] EWHC 455 (Comm); *London Steamship Owners Mutual Insurance Association Ltd v. Spain* [2013] EWHC 3188 (Comm), [2014] 1 Lloyd's Rep 309.

126 Though the public policy defence may be a serious objection to recognition.

127 Regulation 44/2001, Art. 35; Regulation 1215/2012, Art. 45(3).

128 C-145/86, [1988] ECR 645. In his Opinion in C-536/13 *Re Gazprom OAO* EU:C:2014:2414, the Advocate General recommended, in effect, that the Court reconsider the decision in *Allianz SpA v. West Tankers Inc*, and the adverse consequences for commercial arbitration which may flow from it, and reaffirm instead the principle that when a national court is dealing with a matter of arbitration, no provision of the Regulation applies to modify or contradict its application of law which is, as a matter of legislative definition, excluded from the material scope of the Regulation. As the decision of the Court is expected in the first half of 2015, there is no need to seek to predict the conclusion which it will reach.

129 In *Hoffmann v. Krieg*, personal status excluded by what is now Art. 1(2)(a).

130 Civil Jurisdiction and Judgments Act 1982, s. 32.

131 *Phillip Alexander Securities & Futures Ltd v. Zoller* [1997] ILPr 73, 104; *National Navigation Co v. Endesa Generacion SA, The 'Wadi Sudr'* [2009] EWHC 196 (Comm), [2009] 1 Lloyd's Rep 666 (for the result of the appeal, see below).

132 In the recast Regulation 1215/2012, see Art. 45(3).

133 It is correct to observe that in *National Navigation Co v. Endesa Generacion SA, The 'Wadi Sudr'* [2009] EWCA Civ 1397, [2010] 1 Lloyd's Rep 193, the Court of Appeal rejected this possibility and these arguments, holding that if a Spanish court had determined that there was no agreement to arbitrate, it was not open to the English court to take a contrary view. It is respectfully submitted that this was, and is, simply wrong.

Regulation deals only with judgments, not awards;[134] but this just goes to underline the validity of the conclusion to be drawn from *Hoffmann v. Krieg*.

An English court has confirmed that where the judicial proceedings have resulted in expense for the innocent party, the arbitrators may award compensation in respect of it provided that the reference to arbitration is worded widely enough to allow for it:[135] the fact that the foreign proceedings were before the courts of another Member State is irrelevant, for the Brussels I Regulation has no application to arbitration, and as a result the obligation to recognise judgments under Chapter III of the Regulation is not imposed on the arbitral tribunal.[136] Even so, the obligations to give effect to an arbitration agreement and to recognise an arbitral award, and to recognise and enforce a judgment in a civil or commercial matter from the courts of a Member State, may contradict each other.

8.18 The recast Brussels I Regulation 1215/2012 and arbitration

No one seemed to be in much doubt that the relationship between the Brussels I Regulation and arbitration was unsatisfactory, but finding agreement as to what might be done about it proved to be very much more difficult. There is a fundamental difference in philosophy between those who saw, and see, the Brussels I Regulation as having an overarching role in dealing with jurisdiction in civil and commercial matters, from which perspective it is natural to expect that Regulation to specify how and when a court should defer to a potential arbitration, what account it should take of arbitral proceedings and arbitral awards, on the one hand, and those who see the very point and purpose of arbitration as being to distance the resolution of disputes from the courts. As a result, the recast Regulation did little more than set out, in a lengthy Recital, what most probably understood the law already to provide.[137]

The effect of all this was dealt with in Chapter 2, but for convenience it is repeated here. Recital (12) to the recast Regulation made a statement of principle which was intended to strengthen the policy of allowing arbitration to proceed, and where necessary, to be supported, without interference from the Regulation. In material part (and with sentence numbers added, for convenience of reference), it reads:

> *(1) This Regulation should not apply to arbitration. (2) Nothing in this Regulation should prevent the courts of a Member State, when seised of an action in a matter in respect of which the parties have entered*

---

134 *Republic of Congo v. Groupe Antoine Tabet* (Cass, 4 July 2007) [2007] Rev Crit DIP 822 (*note* Usunier): the case was one on the Lugano Convention, but the principle is identical.

135 *CMA CGM SA v. Hyundai Mipo Dockyard Co Ltd* [2008] EWHC 2791 (Comm), [2009] 1 Lloyd's Rep 213.

136 *West Tankers Inc v. Allianz SpA* [2012] EWHC 854 (Comm), [2012] 2 Lloyd's Rep 103.

137 This conclusion is challenged by the Opinion of the Advocate General in C-536/13 *Re Gazprom OAO* EU:C:2014:2414, who considers that the intention of the European Parliament had been to underline the complete separation of arbitration from the Regulation, and to reaffirm the principle that when it was dealing with a matter of arbitration (including, one supposes, the right or duty of a national court to disregard a judgment from another Member State which conflicted with a binding agreement to arbitrate), a national court was entitled to disregard any contrary indication from the Brussels I Regulation. It it not clear, however, whether the European Parliament's intention was finally adopted when the recast Regulation was finalised and made. As the European Court is expected to deliver judgment in the matter in the first half of 2015, and as the Opinion of the Advocate General will be superseded when it does, it is not appropriate to say any more about it, save that it suggests that some at least of the judicial personnel of the European Court consider that *Allianz SpA v West Tankers Inc* was wrong to read down the arbitration exception in the way in which it did.

into an arbitration agreement, from referring the parties to arbitration, from staying or dismissing the proceedings, or from examining whether the arbitration agreement is null and void, inoperative or incapable of being performed, in accordance with their national law. (3) A ruling given by a court of a Member State as to whether or not an arbitration agreement is null and void, inoperative or incapable of being performed should not be subject to the rules of recognition and enforcement laid down in this Regulation, regardless of whether the court decided on this as a principal issue or as an incidental question. (4) On the other hand, where a court of a Member State, exercising jurisdiction under this Regulation or under national law, has determined that an arbitration agreement is null and void, inoperative or incapable of being performed, this should not preclude that court's judgment on the substance of the matter from being recognised or, as the case may be, enforced in accordance with this Regulation. (5) This should be without prejudice to the competence of the courts of the Member States to decide on the recognition and enforcement of arbitral awards in accordance with the Convention on the Recognition and Enforcement of Foreign Arbitral Awards, done at New York on 10 June 1958 ('the 1958 New York Convention'), which takes precedence over this Regulation. (6) This Regulation should not apply to any action or ancillary proceedings relating to, in particular, the establishment of an arbitral tribunal, the powers of arbitrators, the conduct of an arbitration procedure or any other aspects of such a procedure, nor to any action or judgment concerning the annulment, review, appeal, recognition or enforcement of an arbitral award.

The first sentence simply repeats what Article 1(2)(d) of the Regulation provides, though it must be taken to re-enforce the conclusion that arbitrators are not required by the Regulation – what the law of the seat may tell them that they are required to do is a separate issue – to take any account of the Regulation. The second sentence provides, in effect, that when dealing with a matter of arbitration, a court shall ignore proceedings before the courts of another Member State, whether or not it was seised first, but should get on with the matter before it without distraction. It is not clear whether this changes the law, but it is a welcome clarification. The third sentence builds on that, to allow the court to be about its business without the Regulation telling it to take account of any decision by the courts of a Member State on the validity, scope or effect of the arbitration agreement. Of course, there is nothing to say that the national law of the court seised – that is to say, its ordinary law on the effect of foreign judgments – may not take account, but in England, section 32 of the 1982 Act is left to operate without contradiction.

The fourth sentence is problematic, but it is just possible that the problems are really insoluble. If a dispute arises in a civil or commercial matter, judicial proceedings in relation to it are within the scope of the Regulation unless they are excluded by other provisions; and if there is a judicial disagreement as to whether the parties bound themselves to arbitrate, there is no particular reason for supposing one court rather than the other to be correct. Once the Member States were persuaded to abandon a proposal that the definitive decision as to the validity and scope of the arbitration agreement should be taken by the courts of the seat (a proposal which might have been seen to reflect Article 31(2) of Regulation 1215/2012, but which is of little use when the seat is not known, or not in a Member State), the possibility of judicial disagreement is inevitable.

But even if there really is an obligation under Chapter III of the Regulation to recognise the judgment, there is still an opportunity to invoke public policy to withhold recognition again. Despite what was said, most unwelcomely, in *National Navigation Co v. Endesa Generacion SA, The 'Wadi Sudr'*,[138] there is no convincing reason to doubt that an English court would be entitled to come to the conclusion that the public policy of English law required it to give full effect to an arbitration agreement, and to refuse to recognise a judg-

---

138 [2009] EWCA Civ 1397, [2010] 1 Lloyd's Rep 193.

ment that contradicted it.[139] The point may be put another way: the obligation to recognise an award, underpinned as it is by the New York Convention and overpinned by Article 73(2) of Regulation 1215/2012, is arguably reduced if the court is required to allow it to be contradicted: not, as would be unobjectionable, by a separate debt which might be set off, but by a judgment which depends on the (wrong) conclusion that there is no arbitration agreement in the first place.

The fifth sentence is uncontroversial; and the sixth reinstates the ample reading of the exception for which the decision in *Marc Rich* stood, though the idea that it might have opened the door to the possibility of an anti-suit injunction (and the reversal of the effect of *Allianz SpA*) ordered in aid of the arbitration is implausible.[140] As to whether the recast Regulation throws any light on the proposition that a claimant may seek damages at common law for breach of an arbitration agreement, the answer is that it does not. English courts may be expected to continue to allow such claims, resting on the principle that damages for breach of contract is a common law right, and that as arbitration is a private matter between the parties who have agreed to it, its enforcement by private law remedy does not affect the scheme of the Brussels I Regulation. And at some point the propriety of its doing so will be assessed by the European Court.

The result appears to be that very little has been changed, and to the extent that it has, this will be because of the recognition that *The 'Wadi Sudr'* was wrong in any event, and will be allowed to sink without trace. Otherwise, the resolution of the problems created by the laconic reference to 'arbitration' in Article 1(2)(d) of the Regulation must await the decision or decisions of the European Court on a suitable reference. The Court will have to complete the work begun, but rather depressingly left unfinished, by the Regulation. Whatever results will not be entirely the fault of the Court.

8.19 Commencing English arbitral proceedings and the arbitral tribunal

Sections 12 to 29 of the 1996 Act deal with the setting up of the tribunal, the appointment of (and failure to appoint) the arbitral tribunal,[141] the revocation of the authority of arbitrators and their removal, resignation or death. As provided by section 2 of the Act, the application of these rules and procedures to the arbitration in question is affected in large part by the question whether the seat of the arbitration is in England or Wales: if no seat has been designated or determined the court may exercise its powers if there is a connection with England and Wales which makes it appropriate to do so; but otherwise the court may not act in pursuance of the powers given in these sections.[142] In cases where the court may

---

139 An argument to the contrary, but trailed in *The 'Wadi Sudr'*, that s. 32(4) of the Civil Jurisdiction and Judgments Act 1982 disables the contention that public policy may be invoked in such circumstances is unsustainable. The sub-section was enacted to make sure that nothing in the section contradicted the requirements of what is now the Brussels I Regulation. It did not say, and did not purport to say, that s. 32 did not apply where the judgment was given by the courts of another Member State, only that it did not apply if the court was under an obligation to recognise the judgment which came from the courts of another Member State.

140 Though it appears to have been the considered view of the Advocate General in C-536/13 *Re Gazprom OAO* EU:C:2014:2414. The Court will deliver judgment, it is supposed, in 2015, at which point a more definitive answer will be given.

141 The exercise of these powers does not yield to considerations of *forum non conveniens*: *Atlanska Plovidba v. Consignaciones Asturianas SA* [2004] EWHC 1275 (Comm), [2004] 2 Lloyd's Rep 109 (irrelevant to appointment of arbitrators that legal proceedings have been instituted in foreign court).

142 Sections 1(c) and 2(1).

act, its power to do so will be removed if the arbitration agreement is governed by a foreign law, except in relation to provisions which are mandatory. Within sections 12 to 29, the following provisions are mandatory: sections 12 (power[143] of court to extend agreed time limits), 13 (application of Limitation Acts), 24 (power of court to remove arbitrator), 26(1) (effect of death of arbitrator), 28 (liability of parties for fees and expenses of arbitrators) and 29 (immunity of arbitrator); and these provisions will apply regardless of the law governing the arbitration agreement.

8.20 Jurisdiction of the arbitral tribunal

Sections 30 to 32 of the 1996 Act deal with certain issues concerning the jurisdiction of the arbitral tribunal. Section 30 provides that, unless agreed by the parties to the contrary, the arbitral tribunal may rule on its own substantive jurisdiction,[144] that is, it is entitled to rule on (a) whether there is a valid arbitration agreement, (b) whether the tribunal is properly constituted, and (c) what matters have been submitted to arbitration in accordance with the arbitration agreement.[145]

Any such ruling may be challenged by any available arbitral process of appeal or review, or in accordance with Part I of the Act. Sections 31 and 32 set out the procedures provided by the Act for objecting to the substantive jurisdiction of the tribunal, and the manner in which a court may be asked to determine a preliminary point as to jurisdiction. These provisions will apply only if the seat of the arbitration is England and Wales, or, in accordance with section 2(4), if there is no seat designated or determined and there is a connection with England. But sections 31 (objection to substantive jurisdiction of tribunal) and 32 (determination of preliminary point of jurisdiction) are mandatory, and are available even if the arbitration agreement is governed by a foreign law.

8.21 The arbitral proceedings

Sections 33 to 41 of the 1996 Act deal with certain questions concerning the conduct of the arbitral proceedings and the powers of the arbitral tribunal. Among other provisions, section 34 allows the tribunal to decide all procedural and evidential matters, but subject to the right of the parties to agree any matter.[146] The tribunal may order a claimant to put up security for costs,[147] give directions as to property in dispute and as to the examination of witnesses,[148] and, if the parties agree, make provisional awards.[149]

In the event of failure by one party to do something necessary for the proper conduct of the arbitration, the parties may agree on what may be done. But in default of agreement, in the case of inordinate and inexcusable delay by the claimant, where that delay (a) gives rise, or is likely to give rise, to a substantial risk that it is not possible to have a fair resolution

---

143 Which is limited: *Cathiships SA v. Allanasons Ltd, The 'Catherine Helen'* [1998] 3 All ER 714; *Harbour and General Works Ltd v. Environment Agency* [2000] 1 WLR 950.

144 *Vee Networks Ltd v. Econet Wireless International Ltd* [2004] EWHC 2909 (Comm), [2005] 1 Lloyd's Rep 192. *Cf* Art. 16 of the UNCITRAL Model.

145 Section 30(1).

146 *Cf* Arts 19, 20, 22–24, 26 of the UNCITRAL Model Law.

147 Section 38(3).

148 Section 38.

149 But only if the parties agree: s. 39.

of the issues in that claim, or (b) has caused or is likely to cause serious prejudice to the respondent, the tribunal may make an award dismissing the claim.[150] These provisions will apply only if the seat of the arbitration is England and Wales, or in accordance with section 2(4) if there is no seat designated or determined and there is a connection with England. But sections 33 (general duty of tribunal), 37(2) (items to be treated as expenses of arbitrators) and 40 (general duty of parties) are mandatory, and are available even if the arbitration agreement is governed by a foreign law.

8.22 Powers of the court in relation to arbitral proceedings prior to the award

Sections 42 to 45 of the 1996 Act deal with certain powers of the court in relation to the arbitral proceedings themselves. According to section 42, unless the parties have agreed otherwise, an application may be made to the court for an order to require a party to comply with a peremptory order of the tribunal; the section specifies the conditions on which the application may be made and the order granted. According to section 43, a party to arbitral proceedings may use the same court procedures as are available in relation to legal proceedings to secure the attendance of witnesses to give oral testimony or to produce documents or other material evidence.[151] The application may be made only with the permission of the tribunal or the agreement of other parties, and the procedures may be used only if the witness is in the United Kingdom and the arbitral proceedings are being conducted in England.

Further powers to grant interim relief are conferred on the court by section 44.[152] Unless otherwise agreed by the parties, the court has, for the purposes of and in relation to arbitral proceedings,[153] the same power of making orders about the matters listed in section 44(2) as it has for the purposes of and in relation to legal proceedings. The matters listed in subsection (2) are: (a) the taking of evidence; (b) the preservation of evidence; (c) making orders in relation to property, which is the subject of proceedings or as to which any question arises in the proceedings, for the inspection, photographing, preservation, custody or detention of the property, or ordering that samples be taken from, or any observation be made of or experiment conducted upon, the property; and for that purpose authorising any person to enter any premises in the possession or control of a party to the arbitration; (d) the sale of any goods the subject of proceedings; and (e) the granting of an interim injunction or the appointment of a receiver. But the existence of these powers does not implicitly or explicitly remove the general powers of the court in respect of such matters.[154]

The court may act without notice to the other party or parties in cases of urgency for the purpose of preserving evidence or assets,[155] but otherwise only on notice to the other

---

150 Section 41(3).

151 See Practice Direction – Arbitration, para. 16. *Cf* Art. 27 of the UNCITRAL Model Law.

152 See Practice Direction supplementing CPR Part 62, para. 18. *Cf* Arts 9 and 31 of the UNCITRAL Model Law, and also *cf* Arbitration Act 1950, s. 12(6). For an illustration, see *Commerce and Industry Insurance Co of Canada v. Certain Underwriters at Lloyd's of London* [2002] 1 WLR 1323.

153 Section 44 does not apply to ICSID arbitrations, as no such order has been made under Arbitration (International Investment Disputes) Act 1966, s. 3 (as amended): see *ETI Euro Telecom International NV v. Republic of Bolivia* [2008] EWCA Civ 880, [2008] 2 Lloyd's Rep 421.

154 *Kamenogorsk Hydropower Plant JSC v. AES Ust-Kamenogorsk Hydropower Plant LLP* [2013] UKSC 35, [2013] 1 WLR 1889.

155 See *Cetelem SA v. Roust Holdings Ltd* [2005] EWCA Civ 618, [2005] 2 Lloyd's Rep 494. On the application by analogy of *Credit Suisse Fides Trust SA v. Cuoghi* [1998] QB 818, and *Motorola Credit Corp v. Uzan (No 2)*

party with the permission of the tribunal or with the agreement in writing of the other parties.

Section 45 confers on the court a power, subject to specified conditions, to make a determination on a question of law arising in the course of the proceedings which the court is satisfied substantially affects the rights of one or more of the parties. This power can be excluded by agreement between the parties; and an agreement to dispense with reasons for the tribunal's award shall be considered an agreement to exclude the jurisdiction of the court under section 45.

These provisions will apply if the seat of the arbitration is England and Wales.[156] In addition, if the seat of the arbitration is outside England and Wales, or if no seat has been designated or determined, the powers in sections 43 and 44 shall apply unless the fact that the seat of the arbitration is or may be outside England and Wales makes it inappropriate for the court to act.[157] Moreover, the power in section 45 may be exercised if no seat has been designated or determined and there is a connection with England.[158] But apart from section 43, which is mandatory and which applies even though the arbitration agreement is governed by a foreign law,[159] these sections apply only if English law is the law which governs the arbitration agreement.

8.23 The award

Sections 46 to 58 deal with the decision of the tribunal and its award.[160] Section 46 provides that the tribunal shall decide the dispute in accordance with the law[161] chosen by the parties as applicable to the substance of the dispute, or, if the parties so agree, in accordance with such other considerations as are agreed by them or determined by the tribunal. If there is no such choice or agreement, the tribunal shall apply the law determined by the conflict of laws rules which it considers applicable. It follows from section 46(1)(b) that the tribunal may decide the dispute in the light of choice of law rules, but if the parties agree that it should do so,[162] the tribunal shall decide in accordance with what is sometimes called decision *ex aequo et bono* or *amiable composition*.[163] This is a sensible resolution of a problem which had appeared to generate needless rigidity and difficulty at common law. It also appears to mean that the parties'

[2003] EWCA Civ 752, [2004] 1 WLR 113, see *Mobil Cerro Negro Ltd v. Petroleos de Venezuela* [2008] EWHC 532 (Comm), [2008] 1 Lloyd's Rep 684.

156 Section 2(1).

157 Section 2(3).

158 Section 2(4).

159 See above, para. 8.09.

160 Sections 59–65 deal with the costs of the arbitration, and are not examined here.

161 The choice of the law of a country is to be understood as a choice of the substantive law of that country excluding its conflicts laws: s. 46(2). But if the parties do not choose to plead or seek to establish that a foreign law is different from English law, the tribunal is entitled to assume that English law is identical and apply it: *Hussmann (Europe) Ltd v. Al Ameen Development and Trade Co* [2000] 2 Lloyd's Rep 83; *Reliance Industries Ltd v. Enron Oil and Gas India Ltd* [2002] 1 Lloyd's Rep 645.

162 But if the parties do not make their choice, the arbitrators are restricted to the application of a system of law: s. 46(3), and this will exclude the possibility of applying, under this head, the *lex mercatoria*. For the corresponding position under the common law, see *Dallal v. Bank Mellat* [1986] QB 441. On the use or 'justiciability' of the *lex mercatoria*, see also Schultz (2008) 10 *Yearbook of Private International Law* 667.

163 *Cf* Art. 28 of the UNCITRAL Model Law. But note that the formulation in s. 46(1)(b) would also allow the parties to agree that the provisions of public international law, or of the *lex mercatoria*, for example, should be used by the tribunal. But if they do *not* so choose, the tribunal has no power to select such criteria for itself: s. 46(3).

choice of law can range more widely than is permitted in relation to judicial proceedings. For example, there is little doubt that section 46(1) allows them to choose the law to govern a claim in tort which falls within the scope of the agreement to arbitrate; and the restrictions[164] on choice of law for contractual obligations which are imposed on a court by the Rome Convention do not, it seems, apply to the tribunal, for section 46(2) makes it clear that the choice of law is effective, and *excludes* recourse to the conflict of laws. But if no choice of law is made by the parties, section 46(3) requires the tribunal to choose the system of private international law whose rules *are* to apply to identify the law which governs the dispute.

The remainder of these sections[165] deal with the time, form, date, place and notification of the award, the power of the tribunal to grant particular remedies and to order interest, the power to withhold the award if the arbitrators have not been fully paid, and powers of correction. Section 58 provides that unless otherwise agreed by the parties, an award made by the tribunal pursuant to an arbitration agreement is final and binding on the parties and on any persons claiming through or under them;[166] but this is without prejudice to the right of a person to challenge the award in accordance with any arbitral process of appeal or review, or in accordance with Part I of the Act.

These provisions will apply only if the seat of the arbitration is England and Wales, or in accordance with section 2(4) if there is no seat designated or determined and there is a connection with England. Section 56 (power to withhold award in case of non-payment) is mandatory, and is available even if the arbitration agreement is governed by a foreign law; the other sections apply only if English law is the law governing the arbitration agreement.

8.24 Enforcement of, and challenges to, awards to which Part I of the Act applies

According to section 66 of the 1996 Act, an award made by the tribunal pursuant to an arbitration agreement may, by leave of the court, be enforced in the same manner as a judgment or order of the court to the same effect.[167] Where leave is given, judgment may be entered in terms of the award; but leave shall not be given where, or to the extent that, the person against whom it is sought to be enforced shows that the tribunal lacked substantive jurisdiction to make the award.[168] It is made clear that nothing in section 66 affects the recognition or enforcement of an award under any other enactment or rule of law, in particular under Part II of the Arbitration Act 1950[169] or the provisions of Part III of the 1996 Act relating to the New York Convention.[170] And it is no objection to the making of an order

---

164 Admittedly these are limited.

165 On s. 48 (power to select currency of award) see *Lesotho Highlands Development Authority v. Impregilo SpA* [2005] UKHL 43, [2006] 1 AC 221.

166 But this will not extend to a non-party who brings a claim against one of the parties to the original arbitration proceedings: he is not bound by, nor can he take advantage of, any issue decided in the first arbitration, which is essentially private to the parties involved: *Sun Life Assurance Co of Canada v. Lincoln National Life Insurance Co Ltd* [2004] EWCA Civ 1660, [2005] 1 Lloyd's Rep 606.

167 For the procedure to obtain permission to enforce the award in the same manner on a judgment, see CPR r. 62.17; Practice Direction – Arbitration, paras 30–33. For appeals, see *Soinco v. Novokuznetsk Aluminium Plant* [1998] 2 Lloyd's Rep 337. *Cf* Art. 35 of the UNCITRAL Model Law.

168 See *Dallah Real Estate and Tourism Holding Co v. Government of Pakistan* [2010] UKSC 46, [2011] 1 AC 763. For loss of the right to raise such an objection, see s. 73, discussed below at para. 8.25.

169 Enforcement of awards under the Geneva Convention: see para. 8.37 below.

170 See below, para. 8.29.

that the apparent purpose of doing so is to forestall any attempt to enforce a contradictory judgment from the courts of another Member State: indeed, this appears to be considered a proper motivation.[171]

If a party to arbitral proceedings wishes to challenge an award as to the substantive jurisdiction of the tribunal, he may apply to the court under section 67.[172] He may also apply to challenge the award under section 68, alleging serious irregularity affecting the tribunal, the proceedings or the award.[173] The grounds of objection which may constitute a serious irregularity are listed in section 68(2),[174] and they do constitute such an irregularity if the court considers that they caused or will cause substantial injustice to the applicant: the authorities establish, and the intention of the Departmental Advisory Committee was, that this is a long-stop available only in extreme cases, and not a routine ground for seeking to unpick an award. According to section 69, unless otherwise agreed by the parties,[175] a party to arbitral proceedings may appeal to the court on a question of law[176] arising out of an award made in the proceedings; an agreement to dispense with reasons for the tribunal's award shall be considered an agreement to exclude the jurisdiction of the court under this section. Particulars of when the agreement of other parties or the leave of the court is required are set out in detail in the section; as the effect of the appeal is to remove the question to the decision of the court, the requirements for the giving of leave are restrictive.

So far as the challenges under sections 67, 68 and 69 are concerned, section 70 provides that an application may be brought only after the applicant has exhausted any available arbitral process of appeal or review, and any recourse under section 57 for correction of the award. The time for making the application or appeal is limited to 28 days from the date of the award. The court may order the tribunal to state its reasons in greater detail, and may order the applicant to put up security for the costs of the application or the appeal. Section 71 specifies the effects of the orders the court may make.

The provisions of section 66 will apply regardless of the seat of the arbitration.[177] Sections 67 and 68 (and sections 70 and 71 so far as these relate to sections 67 and 68) will apply only

---

171 *West Tankers Inc v. Allianz SpA* [2012] EWCA Civ 27, [2012] Bus LR 1701; also *African Fertilisers & Chemicals NIG Ltd v. BD Shipsnavo GmbH & Co Reederei KG* [2011] EWHC 2452 (Comm), [2011] 2 Lloyd's Rep 531; *Sovarex Ltd v. Romero Alvarez SA* [2011] EWHC 1661 (Comm), [2011] 2 Lloyd's Rep 320; *London Steamship Owners Mutual Insurance Association v. Spain* [2013] EWHC 3188 (Comm), [2014] 1 Lloyd's Rep 309.

172 By means of an arbitration application: Practice Direction – Arbitration, supplementing CPR Part 62. *Cf* Art. 34 of the UNCITRAL Model Law. If he does not, the award then becomes unchallengeable and bound to be enforced on application. If a foreign court then gives a conflicting judgment, it will be denied recognition by reason of *Showlag v. Mansour* [1995] 1 AC 431: *People's Insurance Co of China, Hebei Branch v. Vysanthi Shipping Co Ltd* [2003] EWHC 1655 (Comm), [2003] 2 Lloyd's Rep 617.

173 *Cf* Art. 34 of the UNCITRAL Model Law. But for loss of the right to make such an objection, see s. 73, discussed below at para. 8.25.

174 See also *The Marie H* [2001] 1 Lloyd's Rep 707; *Profilati Italia Srl v. Painewebber Inc* [2001] 1 Lloyd's Rep 715.

175 See *Braes of Doune Wind Farm (Scotland) Ltd v. Alfred McAlpine Business Services Ltd* [2008] EWHC 426 (TCC), [2008] 1 Lloyd's Rep 608 (Scottish arbitration and English exclusive jurisdiction: English courts entitled to deal with appeal on point of law under Arbitration Act 1996, s. 69, otherwise jurisdiction clause meaningless); *Shashoua v. Sharma* [2009] EWHC 957 (Comm), [2009] 2 Lloyd's Rep 376.

176 This applies only in respect of questions of *English* law (see s. 82); where the contract between the parties is governed by Swiss law it cannot apply: *Egmatra AG v. Marco Trading Corp* [1999] 1 Lloyd's Rep 862; *Reliance Industries Ltd v. Enron Oil and Gas India Ltd* [2002] 1 Lloyd's Rep 645 (Indian law not proved to be different from English law); and *cf Sanghi Polyesters Ltd v. The International Investor (KCFC) (Kuwait)* [2000] 1 Lloyd's Rep 480 (English law unless conflicting with Shari'a, which shall prevail). For appeals from the decision of the High Court, and the need for *it* to give leave, see *Henry Boot Construction (UK) Ltd v. Malmaison Hotel (Manchester) Ltd* [2000] EWCA Civ 175, [2001] QB 388.

177 Section 2(2).

if the seat of the arbitration is England and Wales, but will be available even if the arbitration agreement is governed by a foreign law. Section 69 will only apply if the seat of the arbitration is England and Wales and if English is the law governing the arbitration agreement.

8.25 Miscellaneous and supplementary matters

Section 72 of the 1996 Act permits a party who is alleged to be a party to an arbitration agreement but who took no part in the proceedings to seek a declaration or injunction or other relief in questioning whether there was a valid arbitration agreement, whether the tribunal was properly constituted, and what matters have been submitted to arbitration in accordance with the arbitration agreement. He may also make a challenge under sections 67 and 68, and is under no obligation first to exhaust the arbitral remedies. Section 73 is an important provision, which determines whether a party has lost his right to object by reason of his having continued with the arbitral process without making his objection at the time he was, or should have been, aware of it.[178] Sections 76 to 80 deal with the manner in which notices are to be served, the reckoning of periods of time, and the power of the court to extend time limits in the arbitral proceedings. These sections apply only if the seat of the arbitration is in England and Wales, and English is the proper law of the arbitration agreement.

8.26 Domestic arbitration agreements

Sections 85 to 87 of the 1996 Act contained certain modifications to Part I of the Act as it was to apply to domestic arbitration agreements. But shortly before the provisions of the Act were brought into force, it was determined[179] that the principle underpinning the proposed separate treatment was itself incompatible with European law; and the decision was taken that sections 85 to 87 would not be brought into effect. There is, therefore, no need to identify a separate category of 'domestic arbitration agreements' because there is not one.

8.27 Consumer arbitration agreements

Part II of the 1996 Act repeals the provisions of the Consumer Arbitration Agreements Act 1988. In place of that legislation, it extends the Unfair Terms in Consumer Contracts Regulations 1999[180] to an arbitration agreement, and provides that sections 90 and 91 apply whatever the law applicable to the arbitration agreement. The principal control is that a term which constitutes an arbitration agreement is unfair for the purposes of the Regulations so far as it relates to a claim which does not exceed the amount which will be specified by order for the purposes of the section.[181]

---

178 *JSC Zestafoni G Nikoladze Ferroalloy Plant v. Ronly Holdings Ltd* [2004] EWHC 245 (Comm), [2004] 2 Lloyd's Rep 335; *Svenska Petroleum Exploration AB v. Government of Republic of Lithuania* [2005] EWHC 9 (Comm), [2005] 1 Lloyd's Rep 515.

179 *Phillip Alexander Securities & Futures Ltd v. Bamberger* [1997] ILPr 73, 104.

180 SI 1999/2083. For an illustration, see *Heifer International Inc v. Christiansen* [2007] EWHC 3015 (TCC), [2008] 2 All ER (Comm) 831.

181 Section 91; SI 1999/2167. An arbitration agreement will be unfair under the 1999 Regulations if it is related to a claim for a pecuniary remedy not exceeding £5,000. But the Consumer Rights Bill 2014 will when elected into law, revoke the 1999 Regulations and replace them with legislation, in substantially similar terms.

8.28 Small claims arbitration in the county court

Nothing in Part I of the 1996 Act applies to small claims arbitration in the county court under section 64 of the County Courts Act 1984.[182]

RECOGNITION AND ENFORCEMENT OF FOREIGN AWARDS UNDER PART III OF THE 1996 ACT

8.29 Recognition and enforcement of certain foreign awards pursuant to Convention

The recognition and enforcement of foreign arbitration awards under the 1927 Geneva Convention or the 1958 New York Convention[183] awards is dealt with in, though not exclusively governed by the provisions of, sections 99 to 104 of the 1996 Act.

Part III[184] of the Arbitration Act 1950 continues to apply to govern the enforcement of foreign awards within the meaning of Part II of the Arbitration Act 1950 which are not New York Convention awards.[185]

A New York Convention award is defined as an award made in pursuance of an arbitration agreement[186] in the territory[187] of a State (other than the United Kingdom) which is party to the 1958 New York Convention. Such an award is binding on the parties as between whom it was made, and may be relied on by way of defence, set-off or otherwise in any legal proceedings in England and Wales. It may be enforced by leave of the court in the same manner as a judgment or order of the court to that effect, and where leave is given, judgment may be entered in terms of the award.[188] The only grounds[189] upon which it is permitted to deny recognition or enforcement of a New York Convention award are that the party against whom it was invoked proves that:

(a) a party to the arbitration agreement was, under the law applicable to him, under some incapacity, or

(b) the arbitration agreement was not valid under the law to which the parties subjected it or, failing any indication thereon, under the law of the country where the award was made, or

(c) he was not given proper notice of the appointment of the arbitrator or the proceedings or was otherwise unable to present his case,[190] or

---

182 Section 92.

183 The enforcement of these awards was previously dealt with by the Arbitration Act 1975. This Act is repealed in its entirety by the 1996 Act.

184 Part I of the Arbitration Act 1950 is repealed by the 1996 Act, but Part II (apart from s. 42(3)) is not.

185 Section 99. See para. 8.37, below.

186 Which must be in writing: s. 100(2)(a). 'Agreement in writing' bears the same meaning as it has in s. 5 of the 1996 Act.

187 The award is deemed to be made at the seat of the arbitration, regardless of where it was signed, despatched or delivered to any of the parties. For the seat of an arbitration, see paras 8.05 and 8.06 above.

188 Section 101.

189 Section 103(2).

190 Such as where the party objecting did not see the information on which the award was based, and therefore could not comment on it: *Irvani v. Irvani* [2000] 1 Lloyd's Rep 412.

    (d)   the award deals with a difference not contemplated by or not falling within the terms of the submission to arbitration or contains decisions on matters beyond the scope of the submission to arbitration,[191] or

    (e)   the composition of the arbitral tribunal or the arbitral procedure was not in accordance with the agreement of the parties or, failing such agreement, with the law of the country in which the arbitration took place, or

    (f)   the award has not yet become binding on the parties or has been set aside or suspended by a competent authority of the country in which, or under the law of which, it was made.[192]

Recognition of the award may also be denied if the award is in respect of a matter which is not capable of settlement by arbitration or if it would be contrary to public policy to recognise or enforce the award. The public policy[193] defence is one which commonly requires a balance to be struck between the public interest in the finality of arbitral awards, so as to bring an end to the process of dispute resolution, on the one hand, and the unwillingness of a court simply to rubber stamp without further enquiry an award which appears to be objectionable, or which appears to have condoned illicit behaviour. In relation to allegations of procedural errors on the part of the tribunal which render it contrary to public policy to enforce the award, it has been held that where these could be and were brought to the attention of the supervising court at the seat of the arbitration, and were rejected by it, there was no reason to suppose that it was contrary to public policy to enforce the award.[194]

Where the award appears to uphold and enforce a transaction which was unlawful or illicit, there is less clarity. In *Soleimany v. Soleimany*,[195] the tribunal made its award of damages by way of enforcing a contract to smuggle which was illegal under the law of one of its places of performance; the Court of Appeal refused to enforce the award on the ground of public policy. But in *Westacre Investments Inc v. Jugoimport-SPDR Holding Co Ltd*,[196] the allegation of illegality in the underlying transaction had been raised and rejected by the tribunal, and it was held that unless there was a fresh discovery of evidence to impugn the finding of the tribunal, it was not contrary to public policy to enforce the award. If there is a distinction, it appears to lie in the difference between, on the one hand, a tribunal finding or accepting that there was illegal or illicit behaviour but not regarding this as preventing the making of an award, where it will be contrary to public policy to enforce the award, and, on the other, a tribunal which investigates the allegation with a view to not making an award if the allegation is sustained, but which does not find the allegation to be correct and therefore makes

---

191 Unless those matters can be separated from the matters submitted to arbitration: s. 103(4).

192 Though where there has been only an application to suspend or set aside, the court before which the award is sought to be relied on may adjourn its decision: s. 103(5). On whether it will order the debtor to give security as a condition of the adjournment, see *Soleh Boneh International Ltd v. Government of Uganda* [1993] 2 Lloyd's Rep 208; *Ipco (Nigeria) Ltd v. Nigerian National Petroleum Corp* [2005] EWHC 726 (Comm), [2005] 2 Lloyd's Rep 326.

193 Which may include a public policy drawn from the principles of European law: C-126/97 *Eco Swiss China Time Ltd v. Benetton International NV* [1999] ECR I-3055; *Accentuate Ltd v. Asigra Inc* [2009] EWHC 2655 (QB), [2009] 2 Lloyd's Rep 599.

194 *Minmetals Germany GmbH v. Fercosteel Ltd* [1999] CLC 647 (China). See also *Svenska Petroleum Exploration AB v. Government of Republic of Lithuania* [2005] EWHC 9 (Comm), [2005] 1 Lloyd's Rep 515.

195 [1999] QB 785 (Beth Din).

196 [2000] QB 288 (Zürich).

the award: in such a case public policy will not be infringed.[197] There does not appear to be any great scope for the application to arbitration of the principles of the common law in relation to the non-recognition of judgments obtained by fraud.[198]

The party who opposes the enforcement of the award is, according to the very wording of the Act, entitled to maintain the arguments listed in section 103 before the court to which the application for enforcement is made: there is no express or implied requirement that these be taken, or taken only, before the supervisory court.[199] On the other hand, the principles of estoppel apply to the decisions of tribunals in much the same way as they apply to the decisions of courts, though care must be taken to avoid the trap of circularity: if parties have agreed to a particular form of dispute resolution, it is rational and right that they are bound by its outcome. It generally follows that if a challenge is made to the enforcement of the award, an earlier award by the tribunal as to its jurisdiction over the parties may serve as the basis for a plea of estoppel against the party who seeks to controvert it. In accordance with general principle, estoppel will operate against a party who agreed to submit the particular issue to the tribunal for its determination;[200] equally it will not operate against a party who simply maintained that he was not bound to submit the dispute in question to arbitration.[201]

The legal fact that the tribunal has jurisdiction to determine its own jurisdiction does not, therefore, make any award on jurisdiction automatically binding on a party who contends that he did not agree to refer that question to arbitration in the first place; and the party who maintains that he never agreed to go to arbitration is obviously entitled to maintain that contention as a defence to the application to enforce the award.[202] On the other hand, if the award as to jurisdiction has been held to be valid and binding by a court, and the decision of the court has not been, and now cannot be, appealed by the losing party, then the combination of the award and the unchallenged decision of the court will certainly have the potential to support a plea of estoppel.[203]

8.30 Awards purportedly set aside by foreign court

On occasion the award of an arbitral tribunal, which otherwise looks proper on its face, will be set aside by the courts of the seat. The question whether this has any effect on the recognition of the award in England will, it seems, depend on the legal effect according

---

197 For further illustration of the difficulty in reconciling these authorities, see *Omnium de Traitements et de Valorisation SA v. Hilmarton Ltd* [1999] 2 Lloyd's Rep 222 (Switzerland) (noted Hill [2000] LMCLQ 311); see also *Rena Holding SA v. PT Putrabali* (Cass, 29 June 2007) [2008] Rev Crit DIP 109 (*note* Bollée) (according to French legal analysis of arbitration, a court may rule on the effectiveness of an award only within its territorial boundaries; its decision, even if it purports to set aside the award, has no affect beyond them).

198 Though *Soleimany v. Soleimany* does lend some support to the suggestion of approximation.

199 *Dallah Real Estate and Tourism Holding Co v. Government of Pakistan* [2009] EWCA Civ 755, [2011] 1 AC 763, [56], [72].

200 *Svenska Petroleum Exploration AB v. Lithuania (No 2)* [2006] EWCA Civ 1529, [2007] QB 886.

201 *Dallah Real Estate and Tourism Holding Co v. Government of Pakistan* [2010] UKSC 46, [2011] 1 AC 763.

202 Arbitration Act 1996, s. 103: see *Dallah Real Estate and Tourism Holding Co v. Government of Pakistan* [2010] UKSC 46, [2011] 1 AC 763.

203 *Svenska Petroleum Exploration AB v. Lithuania (No 2)* [2006] EWCA Civ 1529, [2007] QB 886; *Dallah Real Estate and Tourism Holding Co v. Government of Pakistan* [2010] UKSC 46, [2011] 1 AC 763. Whether it will do so in the individual case will still depend on the court reaching the conclusion that the objecting party did agree to proceed to arbitration or that his participation in the process by which that contention was evaluated was sufficient to hold that his hands are now tied.

to the private international law rules of foreign judgments: there is no rule which says that the decision of the court of the seat is conclusive. If the foreign judgment is liable to be recognised as a judgment *in personam*, and it meets the requirements for its recognition, the obligation of the parties to abide by the judgment will determine whether the arbitral award continues to be recognised in England. For even if the award would have been entitled to recognition at the time it was made, a subsequent agreement by the parties to release each other from it would be effective. If they are instead party to a foreign judgment which creates an obligation by which they are bound to each other, the outcome is the same. But if the foreign judgment is not entitled to recognition, because the foreign court is not regarded as one having international jurisdiction over the party to be bound, or because it was procured by fraud, or because the Human Rights Act 1998 requires the English court to refuse recognition to the judgment, for example then there will be nothing to impair the arbitral award and the right and duty of the parties to abide by it.[204]

English law does not, therefore, take the view (which is understood to be preferred in French legal thinking) that once an award has been made, it passes from the potential control or jurisdiction of the courts of the seat onto a higher legal plane on which the private international law of foreign judgments cannot touch it. English law simply applies the ordinary principles of the private international law of foreign judgments, using the doctrine of obligation on which recognition rests to deduce the conclusions which follow from a foreign judgment given after the award.

It also follows that if there have been proceedings before a foreign court in which issues relating to the enforceability of the award have been raised and adjudicated, a judicial decision in those proceedings may, in principle at least, give rise to issue estoppel in respect of any point essential to and decided in the foreign proceedings.[205] The fact that the foreign court may have determined an issue in judicial proceedings founded on an arbitral award does not prevent the ordinary application of the principles of estoppel by *res judicata* in later proceedings concerned with enforcement of the award before an English court.[206] For although arbitration may be, to some degree, insulated from the ordinary rules of private international law, judicial decisions are all liable to trigger the application of the principles of estoppel by *res judicata*.

8.31 Other bases of recognition or enforcement of awards

Section 104 preserves the right to enforce New York Convention awards at common law[207] or under section 66 of the 1996 Act.

---

204 *Yukos Capital Sarl v. OJSC Oil Co Rosneft (No 3)* [2014] EWHC 2188 (Comm), [2014] 2 Lloyd's Rep 435; see also *Yukos Capital Sarl v. OJSC Oil Co Rosneft (No 2)* [2012] EWCA Civ 855, [2014] QB 458; *Dallah Estate and Tourism Holding Co v. Ministry of Religious Affairs, Government of Pakistan* [2009] EWCA Civ 755, [2011] 1 AC 763, [91] (Rix LJ).

205 The principles of *res judicata* will need to be observed carefully, to ascertain that the party to be estopped was, as a matter of English private international law, liable to be bound by the foreign decision, and that the precise issue decided by the foreign court was both one which it was required to decide and the same as the English court is required to decide: *Diag Human SE v. Czech Republic* [2014] EWHC 1639 (Comm), [2014] 2 Lloyd's Rep 283.

206 *Diag Human SE v. Czech Republic* [2014] EWHC 1639 (Comm), [2014] 2 Lloyd's Rep 283.

207 As to which, see para. 8.36, below.

THE LAW PRIOR TO THE COMING INTO FORCE OF THE 1996 ACT

8.32 General

The Arbitration Act 1996 came into force on 31 January 1997.[208] Nevertheless, certain questions will still continue to be governed by the old law. For example, the power of the court in its inherent discretion to stay proceedings brought in breach of an oral arbitration agreement will remain effective, for this falls outside Part I of the Act, and section 81(1) of the Act preserves the common law as it relates to oral arbitration agreements.[209] It is also the case that the 1996 Act in various places preserves other rules of the common law. It is therefore necessary to deal briefly with certain questions of law outside the 1996 Act.

8.33 The law governing an arbitration

As a matter of the common law choice of law rules, the validity and effect of an arbitration agreement, and the scope and interpretation of that agreement, was governed by the applicable law of that agreement. As has been shown above, the relationship between that proposition and the Rome I Regulation which, like the Rome Convention[210] before it, makes no claim to include arbitration agreements within its scope, was uncertain, but there was a likelihood that it would be the law of the contract of which the arbitration agreement formed a part.

8.34 The law governing the arbitration proceedings

As a matter of the common law, the law which governed the arbitration proceedings was capable of being chosen by the parties. But if they did not so choose, there was a strong presumption in favour of the domestic law of the place where the arbitration was held.[211] Despite some writings in support of the idea, the proposition that there could be a 'delocalised' arbitration was never seriously accepted by the common law in England.

8.35 Stays of English proceedings

The court had[212] a discretion to stay proceedings brought in breach of a domestic arbitration agreement if the arbitration agreement was in writing. But stays of non-domestic arbitration agreements in writing were mandatory;[213] and where the arbitration agreement did not satisfy the requirements[214] of the Arbitration Act 1975, there was an inherent power to stay proceedings.

---

208 All except ss 85–87, which will not.

209 It also preserves by express words the rules of the common law as to the definition of matters which are not capable of settlement by arbitration (though it is unclear which these may be), and the refusal to recognise or enforce an award on grounds of public policy.

210 Contracts (Applicable Law) Act 1990, Sch. 1. See para. 8.08, above.

211 *Cf Whitworth Street Estates (Manchester) Ltd v. James Miller & Partners Ltd* [1970] AC 583. The concept of the 'seat' of an arbitration was not a creation of the common law.

212 Arbitration Act 1950, s. 4(1).

213 Arbitration Act 1975, s. 1.

214 *Cf Channel Tunnel Group Ltd v. Balfour Beatty Construction Ltd* [1993] AC 334.

8.36 Enforcement of foreign awards at common law

Arbitration awards were capable of enforcement at common law, as well as under the statutory schemes enacted pursuant to the international obligations of the United Kingdom. At common law, there was, and probably remains, some uncertainty whether an action was in fact brought to enforce the agreement to arbitrate, or to enforce the award itself.[215] Of course, if the foreign award had been the subject of a judgment on the award,[216] the enforcement in England could be sought in respect of the foreign judgment. But if the application was to enforce the award as an award, it was required that the parties submit to arbitration by an agreement which was valid according to its governing law, and that the award was valid and final according to the law which governed the arbitration proceedings.[217]

If the award was valid and final, it was irrelevant that under the law governing the arbitration, a court judgment was required before the award would be enforceable:[218] there is a distinction between an award being final and its being enforceable. Even in cases where the award was *prima facie* entitled to be enforced, it would almost certainly be denied recognition and enforcement if the arbitrators had no jurisdiction to make it according to the law of the arbitration agreement, or it was obtained by fraud, or by breach of the rules of natural justice, or where its recognition would be contrary to public policy. The manner of enforcement at common law was by action on the award, or by means of an application for leave to enforce the award under section 26 of the 1950 Act.[219]

8.37 Enforcement of foreign awards under the Arbitration Act 1950, Part II

Part II of the 1950 Act allows[220] enforcement of an award if the arbitration agreement is:

(a) governed by a foreign law to which the Protocol in Schedule 1 to the Act applies;

(b) between parties who are subject to the jurisdiction of different States which are parties to the Geneva Convention; and

(c) made in a territory to which the Convention applies, may be enforced by action, or by application under Arbitration Act 1950, section 26.[221]

The award will be treated as binding on all parties to it. To be enforceable, it must have

(a) been made in pursuance of an agreement for arbitration which was valid under the law by which it was governed,

---

215 Contrast *Norske Atlas Insurance Co Ltd v. London General Insurance Co Ltd* (1927) 28 Ll LR 104 (enforcing the award) with *Bremer Oeltransport v. Drewry* [1933] 1 KB 753 (enforcing the agreement to arbitrate) and *Agromet Motimport Ltd v. Maulden Engineering Co (Beds) Ltd* [1985] 1 WLR 762 (either basis). The significance of the difference may be most apparent in the law of limitation.

216 A decision from the Islamic Shari'a Council in London is not a judgment (it is not a judicial body, established under the law of a State) nor an award, unless the matter referred to it was expressly referred by the parties: *Al Midani v. Al Midani* [1999] 1 Lloyd's Rep 923.

217 *Uniforêt Pâte Port-Cartier Inc v. Zerotech Technologies Inc* [1998] 9 WWR 688. *Cf Svenska Petroleum Exploration AB v. Government of Republic of Lithuania* [2005] EWHC 9 (Comm), [2005] 1 Lloyd's Rep 515.

218 *Union Nationale des Cooperatives Agricoles v. Catterall* [1959] 2 QB 44.

219 Available for foreign awards if the arbitration agreement was in writing: *Dalmia Cement Ltd v. National Bank of Pakistan* [1975] QB 9.

220 Because it has not been repealed by the 1996 Act.

221 Leave will only be given under this section in reasonably clear cases. If there is likely to be a dispute, leave will be refused, and the claimant will have to seek enforcement by action.

(b) been made by the tribunal provided for in the agreement or constituted in the manner agreed upon by the parties,

(c) been made in conformity with the law governing the arbitration procedure,

(d) become final in the country in which it was made,

(e) been in respect of a matter which can lawfully be referred to arbitration according to the law of England;[222]

and the enforcement must not be against the public policy, or the law, of England. The award will not be final if there are pending proceedings in the country in which it was made to contest the validity of it. The award will not be enforceable if the court is satisfied that

(a) the award has been annulled in the country in which it was made, or

(b) the party against whom it is sought to enforce the award did not receive notice in sufficient time to enable him to present his case, or was under a legal incapacity and was not properly represented, or

(c) the award does not deal with all questions referred, or goes beyond the scope of the agreement for arbitration.[223]

8.38 Enforcement under the Civil Jurisdiction and Judgments Act 1982

An arbitration award which has become enforceable in one part of the United Kingdom in the same manner as a judgment given by a court in that part is enforceable by registration under Schedules 6 and 7 to the 1982 Act. This follows from the definition of 'judgment' in section 18(2)(e) of the Act.

8.39 Enforcement under the Administration of Justice Act 1920 or the Foreign Judgments (Reciprocal Enforcement) Act 1933

An arbitration award made in a country outside the United Kingdom in a country to which Part II of the 1920 Act or Part I of the 1933 Act applies is enforceable in the same manner as is a judgment from the courts of that country, provided that the award has, in pursuance of the law in force in the country in which it was made, become enforceable in the same manner as a judgment given by a court in that country.[224]

---

222 It is difficult to know what, if anything, this relates to. The fact that it is defined by reference to the common law is preserved by s. 81(1)(a).

223 In relation to some of these objections, the court is given power by s. 37(3) of the 1950 Act to adjourn the hearing to allow steps to be taken to annul the award.

224 Administration of Justice Act 1920, s. 12(1); Foreign Judgments (Reciprocal Enforcement) Act 1933, s. 10A (as added by Civil Jurisdiction and Judgments Act 1982, Sch. 10, para. 4).

APPENDICES

APPENDIX 1

Text of the Brussels I Regulation (recast), 1215/2012

REGULATION (EU) No 1215/2012 OF THE EUROPEAN PARLIAMENT AND OF THE COUNCIL of 12 December 2012 on jurisdiction and the recognition and enforcement of judgments in civil and commercial matters (recast)

THE EUROPEAN PARLIAMENT AND THE COUNCIL OF THE EUROPEAN UNION,

Having regard to the Treaty on the Functioning of the European Union, and in particular Article 67(4) and points (a), (c) and (e) of Article 81(2) thereof,

Having regard to the proposal from the European Commission,

After transmission of the draft legislative act to the national parliaments,

Having regard to the opinion of the European Economic and Social Committee,

Acting in accordance with the ordinary legislative procedure,

Whereas:

(1) On 21 April 2009, the Commission adopted a report on the application of Council Regulation (EC) No 44/2001 of 22 December 2000 on jurisdiction and the recognition and enforcement of judgments in civil and commercial matters. The report concluded that, in general, the operation of that Regulation is satisfactory, but that it is desirable to improve the application of certain of its provisions, to further facilitate the free circulation of judgments and to further enhance access to justice. Since a number of amendments are to be made to that Regulation it should, in the interests of clarity, be recast.

(2) At its meeting in Brussels on 10 and 11 December 2009, the European Council adopted a new multiannual programme entitled 'The Stockholm Programme – an open and secure Europe serving and protecting citizens'. In the Stockholm Programme the European Council considered that the process of abolishing all intermediate measures (the *exequatur*) should be continued during the period covered by that Programme. At the same time the abolition of the *exequatur* should also be accompanied by a series of safeguards.

(3) The Union has set itself the objective of maintaining and developing an area of freedom, security and justice, inter alia, by facilitating access to justice, in particular through the principle of mutual recognition of judicial and extra-judicial decisions in civil matters. For the gradual establishment of such an area, the Union is to adopt measures relating to judicial cooperation in civil matters having cross-border implications, particularly when necessary for the proper functioning of the internal market.

(4) Certain differences between national rules governing jurisdiction and recognition of judgments hamper the sound operation of the internal market. Provisions to unify the rules of conflict of jurisdiction in civil and commercial matters, and to ensure rapid and simple recognition and enforcement of judgments given in a Member State, are essential.

(5) Such provisions fall within the area of judicial cooperation in civil matters within the meaning of Article 81 of the Treaty on the Functioning of the European Union (TFEU).

(6) In order to attain the objective of free circulation of judgments in civil and commercial matters, it is necessary and appropriate that the rules governing jurisdiction and the recognition and enforcement of judgments be governed by a legal instrument of the Union which is binding and directly applicable.

(7) On 27 September 1968, the then Member States of the European Communities, acting under Article 220, fourth indent, of the Treaty establishing the European Economic Community, concluded the Brussels Convention on Jurisdiction and the Enforcement of Judgments in Civil and Commercial Matters, subsequently amended by conventions on the accession to that Convention of new Member States ('the 1968 Brussels Convention'). On 16 September 1988, the then Member States of the European Communities and certain EFTA States concluded the Lugano Convention on Jurisdiction and the Enforcement of Judgments in Civil and Commercial Matters ('the 1988 Lugano Convention'), which is a parallel convention to the 1968 Brussels Convention. The 1988 Lugano Convention became applicable to Poland on 1 February 2000.

(8) On 22 December 2000, the Council adopted Regulation (EC) No 44/2001, which replaces the 1968 Brussels Convention with regard to the territories of the Member States covered by the TFEU, as between the Member States except Denmark. By Council Decision 2006/325/EC, the Community concluded an agreement with Denmark ensuring the application of the provisions of Regulation (EC) No 44/2001 in Denmark. The 1988 Lugano Convention was revised by the Convention on Jurisdiction and the Recognition and Enforcement of Judgments in Civil and Commercial Matters, signed at Lugano on 30 October 2007 by the Community, Denmark, Iceland, Norway and Switzerland ('the 2007 Lugano Convention').

(9) The 1968 Brussels Convention continues to apply to the territories of the Member States which fall within the territorial scope of that Convention and which are excluded from this Regulation pursuant to Article 355 of the TFEU.

(10) The scope of this Regulation should cover all the main civil and commercial matters apart from certain well-defined matters, in particular maintenance obligations, which should be excluded from the scope of this Regulation following the adoption of Council Regulation (EC) No 4/2009 of 18 December 2008 on jurisdiction, applicable law, recognition and enforcement of decisions and cooperation in matters relating to maintenance obligations.

(11) For the purposes of this Regulation, courts or tribunals of the Member States should include courts or tribunals common to several Member States, such as the Benelux Court of Justice when it exercises jurisdiction on matters falling within the scope of this Regulation. Therefore, judgments given by such courts should be recognised and enforced in accordance with this Regulation.

(12) This Regulation should not apply to arbitration. Nothing in this Regulation should prevent the courts of a Member State, when seised of an action in a matter in respect of which the parties have entered into an arbitration agreement, from referring the parties to arbitration, from staying or dismissing the proceedings, or from examining whether the arbitration agreement is null and void, inoperative or incapable of being performed, in accordance with their national law. A ruling given by a court of a Member State as to whether or not an arbitration agreement is null and void, inoperative or incapable of being performed should not be subject to the rules of recognition and enforcement laid down in this Regulation, regardless of whether the court decided on this as a principal issue or as an incidental question. On the other hand, where a court of a Member State, exercising jurisdiction under this Regulation or under national law, has determined that an arbitration agreement is null and void, inoperative or incapable of being performed, this should not preclude that court's judgment on the substance of the matter from being recognised or, as the case may be, enforced in accordance with this Regulation. This should be without prejudice to the competence of the courts of the Member States to decide on the recognition and enforcement of arbitral awards in accordance with the Convention on the Recognition and Enforcement of Foreign Arbitral Awards, done at New York on 10 June 1958 ('the 1958 New York Convention'), which takes precedence over this Regulation. This Regulation should not apply to any action or ancillary proceedings relating to, in particular, the establishment of an arbitral tribunal, the powers of arbitrators, the conduct of an arbitration procedure or any other aspects of such a procedure, nor to any action or judgment concerning the annulment, review, appeal, recognition or enforcement of an arbitral award.

(13) There must be a connection between proceedings to which this Regulation applies and the territory of the Member States. Accordingly, common rules of jurisdiction should, in principle, apply when the defendant is domiciled in a Member State.

(14) A defendant not domiciled in a Member State should in general be subject to the national rules of jurisdiction applicable in the territory of the Member State of the court seised. However, inorder to ensure the protection of consumers and employees, to safeguard the jurisdiction of the courts of the Member States in situations where they have exclusive jurisdiction and to respect the autonomy of the parties, certain rules of jurisdiction in this Regulation should apply regardless of the defendant's domicile.

(15) The rules of jurisdiction should be highly predictable and founded on the principle that jurisdiction is generally based on the defendant's domicile. Jurisdiction should always be available on this ground save in a few well-defined situations in which the subject-matter of the dispute or the autonomy of the parties warrants a different connecting factor. The domicile of a legal person must be defined autonomously so as to make the common rules more transparent and avoid conflicts of jurisdiction.

(16) In addition to the defendant's domicile, there should be alternative grounds of jurisdiction based on a close connection between the court and the action or in order to facilitate the sound administration of justice. The existence of a close connection should ensure legal certainty and avoid the possibility of the defendant being sued in a court of a Member State which he could not reasonably have foreseen. This is important, particularly in disputes concerning non-contractual obligations arising out of violations of privacy and rights relating to personality, including defamation.

(17) The owner of a cultural object as defined in Article 1(1) of Council Directive 93/7/EEC of 15 March 1993 on the return of cultural objects unlawfully removed from the territory of a Member State should be able under this Regulation to initiate proceedings as regards a civil claim for the recovery, based on ownership, of such a cultural object in the courts for the place where the cultural object is situated at the time the court is seised. Such proceedings should be without prejudice to proceedings initiated under Directive 93/7/EEC.

(18) In relation to insurance, consumer and employment contracts, the weaker party should be protected by rules of jurisdiction more favourable to his interests than the general rules.

(19) The autonomy of the parties to a contract, other than an insurance, consumer or employment contract, where only limited autonomy to determine the courts having jurisdiction is allowed, should be respected subject to the exclusive grounds of jurisdiction laid down in this Regulation.

(20) Where a question arises as to whether a choice-of-court agreement in favour of a court or the courts of a Member State is null and void as to its substantive validity, that question should be decided in accordance with the law of the Member State of the court or courts designated in the agreement, including the conflict-of-laws rules of that Member State.

(21) In the interests of the harmonious administration of justice it is necessary to minimise the possibility of concurrent proceedings and to ensure that irreconcilable judgments will not be given in different Member States. There should be a clear and effective mechanism for resolving cases of *lis pendens* and related actions, and for obviating problems flowing from national differences as to the determination of the time when a case is regarded as pending. For the purposes of this Regulation, that time should be defined autonomously.

(22) However, in order to enhance the effectiveness of exclusive choice-of-court agreements and to avoid abusive litigation tactics, it is necessary to provide for an exception to the general *lis pendens* rule in order to deal satisfactorily with a particular situation in which concurrent proceedings may arise. This is the situation where a court not designated in an exclusive choice-of-court agreement has been seised of proceedings and the designated court is seised subsequently of proceedings involving the same cause of action and between the same parties. In such a case, the court first seised should be required to stay its proceedings as soon as the designated court has been seised and until such time as the latter court declares that it has no jurisdiction under the exclusive choice-of-court agreement. This is to ensure that, in such a situation, the designated court has priority to decide on the validity of the agreement and on the extent to which the agreement applies to the dispute pending before it. The designated court should be able to proceed irrespective of whether the non-designated court has already decided on the stay of proceedings. This exception should not cover situations where the parties have entered into conflicting exclusive choice-of-court agreements or where a court designated in an exclusive choice-of-court agreement has been seised first. In such cases, the general *lis pendens* rule of this Regulation should apply.

(23) This Regulation should provide for a flexible mechanism allowing the courts of the Member States to take into account proceedings pending before the courts of third States, considering in particular whether a judgment of a third State will be capable of recognition and enforcement in the Member State concerned under the law of that Member State and the proper administration of justice.

(24) When taking into account the proper administration of justice, the court of the Member State concerned should assess all the circumstances of the case before it. Such circumstances may include connections between the facts of the case and the parties and the third State concerned, the stage to which the proceedings in the third State have progressed by the time proceedings are initiated in the court of the Member State and whether or not the court of the third State can be expected to give a judgment within a reasonable time. That assessment may also include consideration of the question whether the court of the third State has exclusive jurisdiction in the particular case in circumstances where a court of a Member State would have exclusive jurisdiction.

(25) The notion of provisional, including protective, measures should include, for example, protective orders aimed at obtaining information or preserving evidence as referred to in Articles 6 and 7 of Directive 2004/48/EC of the European Parliament and of the Council of 29 April 2004 on the enforcement of intellectual property rights. It should not include measures which are not of a protective nature, such as measures ordering the hearing of a witness. This should be without prejudice to the application of Council Regulation (EC) No 1206/2001 of 28 May 2001 on cooperation between the courts of the Member States in the taking of evidence in civil or commercial matters.

(26) Mutual trust in the administration of justice in the Union justifies the principle that judgments given in a Member State should be recognised in all Member States without the need for any special procedure. In addition, the aim of making cross-border litigation less time-consuming and costly justifies the abolition of the declaration of enforceability prior to enforcement in the Member State addressed. As a result, a judgment given by the courts of a Member State should be treated as if it had been given in the Member State addressed.

(27) For the purposes of the free circulation of judgments, a judgment given in a Member State should be recognised and enforced in another Member State even if it is given against a person not domiciled in a Member State.

(28) Where a judgment contains a measure or order which is not known in the law of the Member State addressed, that measure or order, including any right indicated therein, should, to the extent possible, be adapted to one which, under the law of that Member State, has equivalent effects attached to it and pursues similar aims. How, and by whom, the adaptation is to be carried out should be determined by each Member State.

(29) The direct enforcement in the Member State addressed of a judgment given in another Member State without a declaration of enforceability should not jeopardise respect for the rights of

the defence. Therefore, the person against whom enforcement is sought should be able to apply for refusal of the recognition or enforcement of a judgment if he considers one of the grounds for refusal of recognition to be present. This should include the ground that he had not had the opportunity to arrange for his defence where the judgment was given in default of appearance in a civil action linked to criminal proceedings. It should also include the grounds which could be invoked on the basis of an agreement between the Member State addressed and a third State concluded pursuant to Article 59 of the 1968 Brussels Convention.

(30) A party challenging the enforcement of a judgment given in another Member State should, to the extent possible and in accordance with the legal system of the Member State addressed, be able to invoke, in the same procedure, in addition to the grounds for refusal provided for in this Regulation, the grounds for refusal available under national law and within the time-limits laid down in that law. The recognition of a judgment should, however, be refused only if one or more of the grounds for refusal provided for in this Regulation are present.

(31) Pending a challenge to the enforcement of a judgment, it should be possible for the courts in the Member State addressed, during the entire proceedings relating to such a challenge, including any appeal, to allow the enforcement to proceed subject to a limitation of the enforcement or to the provision of security.

(32) In order to inform the person against whom enforcement is sought of the enforcement of a judgment given in another Member State, the certificate established under this Regulation, if necessary accompanied by the judgment, should be served on that person in reasonable time before the first enforcement measure. In this context, the first enforcement measure should mean the first enforcement measure after such service.

(33) Where provisional, including protective, measures are ordered by a court having jurisdiction as to the substance of the matter, their free circulation should be ensured under this Regulation. However, provisional, including protective, measures which were ordered by such a court without the defendant being summoned to appear should not be recognised and enforced under this Regulation unless the judgment containing the measure is served on the defendant prior to enforcement. This should not preclude the recognition and enforcement of such measures under national law. Where provisional, including protective, measures are ordered by a court of a Member State not having jurisdiction as to the substance of the matter, the effect of such measures should be confined, under this Regulation, to the territory of that Member State.

(34) Continuity between the 1968 Brussels Convention, Regulation (EC) No 44/2001 and this Regulation should be ensured, and transitional provisions should be laid down to that end. The same need for continuity applies as regards the interpretation by the Court of Justice of the European Union of the 1968 Brussels Convention and of the Regulations replacing it.

(35) Respect for international commitments entered into by the Member States means that this Regulation should not affect conventions relating to specific matters to which the Member States are parties.

(36) Without prejudice to the obligations of the Member States under the Treaties, this Regulation should not affect the application of bilateral conventions and agreements between a third State and a Member State concluded before the date of entry into force of Regulation (EC) No 44/2001 which concern matters governed by this Regulation.

(37) In order to ensure that the certificates to be used in connection with the recognition or enforcement of judgments, authentic instruments and court settlements under this Regulation are kept up-to-date, the power to adopt acts in accordance with Article 290 of the TFEU should be delegated to the Commission in respect of amendments to Annexes I and II to this Regulation. It is of particular importance that the Commission carry out appropriate consultations during its preparatory work, including at expert level. The Commission, when preparing and drawing up delegated acts, should ensure a simultaneous, timely and appropriate transmission of relevant documents to the European Parliament and to the Council.

(38) This Regulation respects fundamental rights and observes the principles recognised in the Charter of Fundamental Rights of the European Union, in particular the right to an effective remedy and to a fair trial guaranteed in Article 47 of the Charter.

(39) Since the objective of this Regulation cannot be sufficiently achieved by the Member States and can be better achieved at Union level, the Union may adopt measures in accordance with the principle of subsidiarity as set out in Article 5 of the Treaty on European Union (TEU). In accordance with the principle of proportionality, as set out in that Article, this Regulation does not go beyond what is necessary in order to achieve that objective.

(40) The United Kingdom and Ireland, in accordance with Article 3 of the Protocol on the position of the United Kingdom and Ireland, annexed to the TEU and to the then Treaty establishing the European Community, took part in the adoption and application of Regulation (EC) No 44/2001. In accordance with Article 3 of Protocol No 21 on the position of the United Kingdom and Ireland in respect of the area of freedom, security and justice, annexed to the TEU and to the TFEU, the United Kingdom and Ireland have notified their wish to take part in the adoption and application of this Regulation.

(41) In accordance with Articles 1 and 2 of Protocol No 22 on the position of Denmark annexed to the TEU and to the TFEU, Denmark is not taking part in the adoption of this Regulation and is not bound by it or subject to its application, without prejudice to the possibility for Denmark of applying the amendments to Regulation (EC) No 44/2001 pursuant to Article 3 of the Agreement of 19 October 2005 between the European Community and the Kingdom of Denmark on jurisdiction and the recognition and enforcement of judgments in civil and commercial matters,

HAVE ADOPTED THIS REGULATION:

CHAPTER I: SCOPE AND DEFINITIONS

Article 1

1. This Regulation shall apply in civil and commercial matters whatever the nature of the court or tribunal. It shall not extend, in particular, to revenue, customs or administrative matters or to the liability of the State for acts and omissions in the exercise of State authority (*acta iure imperii*).

2. This Regulation shall not apply to:
   (a) the status or legal capacity of natural persons, rights in property arising out of a matrimonial relationship or out of a relationship deemed by the law applicable to such relationship to have comparable effects to marriage;
   (b) bankruptcy, proceedings relating to the winding-up of insolvent companies or other legal persons, judicial arrangements, compositions and analogous proceedings;
   (c) social security;
   (d) arbitration;
   (e) maintenance obligations arising from a family relationship, parentage, marriage or affinity;
   (f) wills and succession, including maintenance obligations arising by reason of death.

Article 2

For the purposes of this Regulation:

(a) 'judgment' means any judgment given by a court or tribunal of a Member State, whatever the judgment may be called, including a decree, order, decision or writ of execution, as well as a decision on the determination of costs or expenses by an officer of the court. For the purposes of Chapter III, 'judgment' includes provisional, including protective, measures ordered by a court or tribunal which by virtue of this Regulation has jurisdiction as to the substance of the matter. It does not include a provisional, including protective, measure which is ordered by such a court or tribunal without the defendant being summoned to appear, unless the judgment containing the measure is served on the defendant prior to enforcement;

(b) 'court settlement' means a settlement which has been approved by a court of a Member State or concluded before a court of a Member State in the course of proceedings;

(c) 'authentic instrument' means a document which has been formally drawn up or registered as an authentic instrument in the Member State of origin and the authenticity of which: (i) relates to the signature and the content of the instrument; and (ii) has been established by a public authority or other authority empowered for that purpose;

(d) 'Member State of origin' means the Member State in which, as the case may be, the judgment has been given, the court settlement has been approved or concluded, or the authentic instrument has been formally drawn up or registered;

(e) 'Member State addressed' means the Member State in which the recognition of the judgment is invoked or in which the enforcement of the judgment, the court settlement or the authentic instrument is sought;

(f) 'court of origin' means the court which has given the judgment the recognition of which is invoked or the enforcement of which is sought.

Article 3

For the purposes of this Regulation, 'court' includes the following authorities to the extent that they have jurisdiction in matters falling within the scope of this Regulation:

(a) in Hungary, in summary proceedings concerning orders to pay (fizetési meghagyásos eljárás), the notary (közjegyző);

(b) in Sweden, in summary proceedings concerning orders to pay (betalningsföreläggande) and assistance (handräckning), the Enforcement Authority (Kronofogdemyndigheten).

CHAPTER II: JURISDICTION

SECTION 1: General provisions

Article 4

1. Subject to this Regulation, persons domiciled in a Member State shall, whatever their nationality, be sued in the courts of that Member State.

2. Persons who are not nationals of the Member State in which they are domiciled shall be governed by the rules of jurisdiction applicable to nationals of that Member State.

Article 5

1. Persons domiciled in a Member State may be sued in the courts of another Member State only by virtue of the rules set out in Sections 2 to 7 of this Chapter.

2. In particular, the rules of national jurisdiction of which the Member States are to notify the Commission pursuant to point (a) of Article 76(1) shall not be applicable as against the persons referred to in paragraph 1.

Article 6

1. If the defendant is not domiciled in a Member State, the jurisdiction of the courts of each Member State shall, subject to Article 18(1), Article 21(2) and Articles 24 and 25, be determined by the law of that Member State.

2. As against such a defendant, any person domiciled in a Member State may, whatever his nationality, avail himself in that Member State of the rules of jurisdiction there in force, and in particular those of which the Member States are to notify the Commission pursuant to point (a) of Article 76(1), in the same way as nationals of that Member State.

SECTION 2: Special jurisdiction

Article 7

A person domiciled in a Member State may be sued in another Member State:

    (1) (a) in matters relating to a contract, in the courts for the place of performance of the obligation in question;

        (b) for the purpose of this provision and unless otherwise agreed, the place of performance of the obligation in question shall be:

          — in the case of the sale of goods, the place in a Member State where, under the contract, the goods were delivered or should have been delivered,

          — in the case of the provision of services, the place in a Member State where, under the contract, the services were provided or should have been provided;

        (c) if point (b) does not apply then point (a) applies;

    (2) in matters relating to tort, delict or quasi-delict, in the courts for the place where the harmful event occurred or may occur;

    (3) as regards a civil claim for damages or restitution which is based on an act giving rise to criminal proceedings, in the court seised of those proceedings, to the extent that that court has jurisdiction under its own law to entertain civil proceedings;

    (4) as regards a civil claim for the recovery, based on ownership, of a cultural object as defined in point 1 of Article 1 of Directive 93/7/EEC initiated by the person claiming the right to recover such an object, in the courts for the place where the cultural object is situated at the time when the court is seised;

    (5) as regards a dispute arising out of the operations of a branch, agency or other establishment, in the courts for the place where the branch, agency or other establishment is situated;

    (6) as regards a dispute brought against a settlor, trustee or beneficiary of a trust created by the operation of a statute, or by a written instrument, or created orally and evidenced in writing, in the courts of the Member State in which the trust is domiciled;

    (7) as regards a dispute concerning the payment of remuneration claimed in respect of the salvage of a cargo or freight, in the court under the authority of which the cargo or freight in question:

        (a) has been arrested to secure such payment; or

        (b) could have been so arrested, but bail or other security has been given; provided that this provision shall apply only if it is claimed that the defendant has an interest in the cargo or freight or had such an interest at the time of salvage.

Article 8

A person domiciled in a Member State may also be sued:

    (1) where he is one of a number of defendants, in the courts for the place where any one of them is domiciled, provided the claims are so closely connected that it is expedient to hear and determine them together to avoid the risk of irreconcilable judgments resulting from separate proceedings;

    (2) as a third party in an action on a warranty or guarantee or in any other third-party proceedings, in the court seised of the original proceedings, unless these were instituted solely with the object of removing him from the jurisdiction of the court which would be competent in his case;

    (3) on a counter-claim arising from the same contract or facts on which the original claim was based, in the court in which the original claim is pending;

(4) in matters relating to a contract, if the action may be combined with an action against the same defendant in matters relating to rights *in rem* in immovable property, in the court of the Member State in which the property is situated.

Article 9

Where by virtue of this Regulation a court of a Member State has jurisdiction in actions relating to liability from the use or operation of a ship, that court, or any other court substituted for this purpose by the internal law of that Member State, shall also have jurisdiction over claims for limitation of such liability.

SECTION 3: Jurisdiction in matters relating to insurance

Article 10

In matters relating to insurance, jurisdiction shall be determined by this Section, without prejudice to Article 6 and point 5 of Article 7.

Article 11

1. An insurer domiciled in a Member State may be sued:
    (a) in the courts of the Member State in which he is domiciled;
    (b) in another Member State, in the case of actions brought by the policyholder, the insured or a beneficiary, in the courts for the place where the claimant is domiciled; or
    (c) if he is a co-insurer, in the courts of a Member State in which proceedings are brought against the leading insurer.
2. An insurer who is not domiciled in a Member State but has a branch, agency or other establishment in one of the Member States shall, in disputes arising out of the operations of the branch, agency or establishment, be deemed to be domiciled in that Member State.

Article 12

In respect of liability insurance or insurance of immovable property, the insurer may in addition be sued in the courts for the place where the harmful event occurred. The same applies if movable and immovable property are covered by the same insurance policy and both are adversely affected by the same contingency.

Article 13

1. In respect of liability insurance, the insurer may also, if the law of the court permits it, be joined in proceedings which the injured party has brought against the insured.
2. Articles 10, 11 and 12 shall apply to actions brought by the injured party directly against the insurer, where such direct actions are permitted.
3. If the law governing such direct actions provides that the policyholder or the insured may be joined as a party to the action, the same court shall have jurisdiction over them.

Article 14

1. Without prejudice to Article 13(3), an insurer may bring proceedings only in the courts of the Member State in which the defendant is domiciled, irrespective of whether he is the policyholder, the insured or a beneficiary.

2. The provisions of this Section shall not affect the right to bring a counter-claim in the court in which, in accordance with this Section, the original claim is pending.

Article 15

The provisions of this Section may be departed from only by an agreement:

(1) which is entered into after the dispute has arisen;

(2) which allows the policyholder, the insured or a beneficiary to bring proceedings in courts other than those indicated in this Section;

(3) which is concluded between a policyholder and an insurer, both of whom are at the time of conclusion of the contract domiciled or habitually resident in the same Member State, and which has the effect of conferring jurisdiction on the courts of that Member State even if the harmful event were to occur abroad, provided that such an agreement is not contrary to the law of that Member State;

(4) which is concluded with a policyholder who is not domiciled in a Member State, except in so far as the insurance is compulsory or relates to immovable property in a Member State; or

(5) which relates to a contract of insurance in so far as it covers one or more of the risks set out in Article 16.

Article 16

The following are the risks referred to in point 5 of Article 15:

(1) any loss of or damage to:

    (a) seagoing ships, installations situated offshore or on the high seas, or aircraft, arising from perils which relate to their use for commercial purposes;

    (b) goods in transit other than passengers' baggage where the transit consists of or includes carriage by such ships or aircraft;

(2) any liability, other than for bodily injury to passengers or loss of or damage to their baggage:

    (a) arising out of the use or operation of ships, installations or aircraft as referred to in point 1(a) in so far as, in respect of the latter, the law of the Member State in which such aircraft are registered does not prohibit agreements on jurisdiction regarding insurance of such risks;

    (b) for loss or damage caused by goods in transit as described in point 1(b);

(3) any financial loss connected with the use or operation of ships, installations or aircraft as referred to in point 1(a), in particular loss of freight or charter-hire;

(4) any risk or interest connected with any of those referred to in points 1 to 3;

(5) notwithstanding points 1 to 4, all 'large risks' as defined in Directive 2009/138/EC of the European Parliament and of the Council of 25 November 2009 on the taking-up and pursuit of the business of Insurance and Reinsurance (Solvency II).

SECTION 4: Jurisdiction over consumer contracts

Article 17

1. In matters relating to a contract concluded by a person, the consumer, for a purpose which can be regarded as being outside his trade or profession, jurisdiction shall be determined by this Section, without prejudice to Article 6 and point 5 of Article 7, if:

    (a) it is a contract for the sale of goods on instalment credit terms;

    (b) it is a contract for a loan repayable by instalments, or for any other form of credit, made to finance the sale of goods; or

    (c) in all other cases, the contract has been concluded with a person who pursues commercial or professional activities in the Member State of the consumer's domicile or, by any means, directs such activities to that Member State or to several States including that Member State, and the contract falls within the scope of such activities.

2. Where a consumer enters into a contract with a party who is not domiciled in a Member State but has a branch, agency or other establishment in one of the Member States, that party shall, in disputes arising out of the operations of the branch, agency or establishment, be deemed to be domiciled in that Member State.

3. This Section shall not apply to a contract of transport other than a contract which, for an inclusive price, provides for a combination of travel and accommodation.

Article 18

1. A consumer may bring proceedings against the other party to a contract either in the courts of the Member State in which that party is domiciled or, regardless of the domicile of the other party, in the courts for the place where the consumer is domiciled.

2. Proceedings may be brought against a consumer by the other party to the contract only in the courts of the Member State in which the consumer is domiciled.

3. This Article shall not affect the right to bring a counter-claim in the court in which, in accordance with this Section, the original claim is pending.

Article 19

The provisions of this Section may be departed from only by an agreement:

(1) which is entered into after the dispute has arisen;

(2) which allows the consumer to bring proceedings in courts other than those indicated in this Section; or

(3) which is entered into by the consumer and the other party to the contract, both of whom are at the time of conclusion of the contract domiciled or habitually resident in the same Member State, and which confers jurisdiction on the courts of that Member State, provided that such an agreement is not contrary to the law of that Member State.

SECTION 5: Jurisdiction over individual contracts of employment

Article 20

1. In matters relating to individual contracts of employment, jurisdiction shall be determined by this Section, without prejudice to Article 6, point 5 of Article 7 and, in the case of proceedings brought against an employer, point 1 of Article 8.

2. Where an employee enters into an individual contract of employment with an employer who is not domiciled in a Member State but has a branch, agency or other establishment in one of the Member States, the employer shall, in disputes arising out of the operations of the branch, agency or establishment, be deemed to be domiciled in that Member State.

Article 21

1. An employer domiciled in a Member State may be sued:

(a) in the courts of the Member State in which he is domiciled; or

(b) in another Member State: (i) in the courts for the place where or from where the employee habitually carries out his work or in the courts for the last place where he did so; or (ii) if the employee does not or did not habitually carry out his work in any one country, in the courts for the place where the business which engaged the employee is or was situated.

2. An employer not domiciled in a Member State may be sued in a court of a Member State in accordance with point (b) of paragraph 1.

Article 22

1. An employer may bring proceedings only in the courts of the Member State in which the employee is domiciled.

2. The provisions of this Section shall not affect the right to bring a counter-claim in the court in which, in accordance with this Section, the original claim is pending.

Article 23

The provisions of this Section may be departed from only by an agreement:

(1) which is entered into after the dispute has arisen; or

(2) which allows the employee to bring proceedings in courts other than those indicated in this Section.

SECTION 6: Exclusive jurisdiction

Article 24

The following courts of a Member State shall have exclusive jurisdiction, regardless of the domicile of the parties:

(1) in proceedings which have as their object rights *in rem* in immovable property or tenancies of immovable property, the courts of the Member State in which the property is situated. However, in proceedings which have as their object tenancies of immovable property concluded for temporary private use for a maximum period of six consecutive months, the courts of the Member State in which the defendant is domiciled shall also have jurisdiction, provided that the tenant is a natural person and that the landlord and the tenant are domiciled in the same Member State;

(2) in proceedings which have as their object the validity of the constitution, the nullity or the dissolution of companies or other legal persons or associations of natural or legal persons, or the validity of the decisions of their organs, the courts of the Member State in which the company, legal person or association has its seat. In order to determine that seat, the court shall apply its rules of private international law;

(3) in proceedings which have as their object the validity of entries in public registers, the courts of the Member State in which the register is kept;

(4) in proceedings concerned with the registration or validity of patents, trade marks, designs, or other similar rights required to be deposited or registered, irrespective of whether the issue is raised by way of an action or as a defence, the courts of the Member State in which the deposit or registration has been applied for, has taken place or is under the terms of an instrument of the Union or an international convention deemed to have taken place. Without prejudice to the jurisdiction of the European Patent Office under the Convention on the Grant of European Patents, signed at Munich on 5 October 1973, the courts of each Member State shall have exclusive jurisdiction in proceedings concerned with the registration or validity of any European patent granted for that Member State;

(5) in proceedings concerned with the enforcement of judgments, the courts of the Member State in which the judgment has been or is to be enforced.

SECTION 7: Prorogation of jurisdiction

Article 25

1. If the parties, regardless of their domicile, have agreed that a court or the courts of a Member State are to have jurisdiction to settle any disputes which have arisen or which may arise in connection

with a particular legal relationship, that court or those courts shall have jurisdiction, unless the agreement is null and void as to its substantive validity under the law of that Member State. Such jurisdiction shall be exclusive unless the parties have agreed otherwise. The agreement conferring jurisdiction shall be either:

(a) in writing or evidenced in writing;

(b) in a form which accords with practices which the parties have established between themselves; or

(c) in international trade or commerce, in a form which accords with a usage of which the parties are or ought to have been aware and which in such trade or commerce is widely known to, and regularly observed by, parties to contracts of the type involved in the particular trade or commerce concerned.

2. Any communication by electronic means which provides a durable record of the agreement shall be equivalent to 'writing'.

3. The court or courts of a Member State on which a trust instrument has conferred jurisdiction shall have exclusive jurisdiction in any proceedings brought against a settlor, trustee or beneficiary, if relations between those persons or their rights or obligations under the trust are involved.

4. Agreements or provisions of a trust instrument conferring jurisdiction shall have no legal force if they are contrary to Articles 15, 19 or 23, or if the courts whose jurisdiction they purport to exclude have exclusive jurisdiction by virtue of Article 24.

5. An agreement conferring jurisdiction which forms part of a contract shall be treated as an agreement independent of the other terms of the contract. The validity of the agreement conferring jurisdiction cannot be contested solely on the ground that the contract is not valid.

Article 26

1. Apart from jurisdiction derived from other provisions of this Regulation, a court of a Member State before which a defendant enters an appearance shall have jurisdiction. This rule shall not apply where appearance was entered to contest the jurisdiction, or where another court has exclusive jurisdiction by virtue of Article 24.

2. In matters referred to in Sections 3, 4 or 5 where the policyholder, the insured, a beneficiary of the insurance contract, the injured party, the consumer or the employee is the defendant, the court shall, before assuming jurisdiction under paragraph 1, ensure that the defendant is informed of his right to contest the jurisdiction of the court and of the consequences of entering or not entering an appearance.

SECTION 8: Examination as to jurisdiction and admissibility

Article 27

Where a court of a Member State is seised of a claim which is principally concerned with a matter over which the courts of another Member State have exclusive jurisdiction by virtue of Article 24, it shall declare of its own motion that it has no jurisdiction.

Article 28

1. Where a defendant domiciled in one Member State is sued in a court of another Member State and does not enter an appearance, the court shall declare of its own motion that it has no jurisdiction unless its jurisdiction is derived from the provisions of this Regulation.

2. The court shall stay the proceedings so long as it is not shown that the defendant has been able to receive the document instituting the proceedings or an equivalent document in sufficient time to enable him to arrange for his defence, or that all necessary steps have been taken to this end.

3. Article 19 of Regulation (EC) No 1393/2007 of the European Parliament and of the Council of 13 November 2007 on the service in the Member States of judicial and extrajudicial documents in civil or commercial matters (service of documents) shall apply instead of paragraph 2 of this Article if the document instituting the proceedings or an equivalent document had to be transmitted from one Member State to another pursuant to that Regulation.

4. Where Regulation (EC) No 1393/2007 is not applicable, Article 15 of the Hague Convention of 15 November 1965 on the Service Abroad of Judicial and Extrajudicial Documents in Civil or Commercial Matters shall apply if the document instituting the proceedings or an equivalent document had to be transmitted abroad pursuant to that Convention.

SECTION 9: *Lis pendens* — related actions

Article 29

1. Without prejudice to Article 31(2), where proceedings involving the same cause of action and between the same parties are brought in the courts of different Member States, any court other than the court first seised shall of its own motion stay its proceedings until such time as the jurisdiction of the court first seised is established.

2. In cases referred to in paragraph 1, upon request by a court seised of the dispute, any other court seised shall without delay inform the former court of the date when it was seised in accordance with Article 32.

3. Where the jurisdiction of the court first seised is established, any court other than the court first seised shall decline jurisdiction in favour of that court.

Article 30

1. Where related actions are pending in the courts of different Member States, any court other than the court first seised may stay its proceedings.

2. Where the action in the court first seised is pending at first instance, any other court may also, on the application of one of the parties, decline jurisdiction if the court first seised has jurisdiction over the actions in question and its law permits the consolidation thereof.

3. For the purposes of this Article, actions are deemed to be related where they are so closely connected that it is expedient to hear and determine them together to avoid the risk of irreconcilable judgments resulting from separate proceedings.

Article 31

1. Where actions come within the exclusive jurisdiction of several courts, any court other than the court first seised shall decline jurisdiction in favour of that court.

2. Without prejudice to Article 26, where a court of a Member State on which an agreement as referred to in Article 25 confers exclusive jurisdiction is seised, any court of another Member State shall stay the proceedings until such time as the court seised on the basis of the agreement declares that it has no jurisdiction under the agreement.

3. Where the court designated in the agreement has established jurisdiction in accordance with the agreement, any court of another Member State shall decline jurisdiction in favour of that court.

4. Paragraphs 2 and 3 shall not apply to matters referred to in Sections 3, 4 or 5 where the policy-holder, the insured, a beneficiary of the insurance contract, the injured party, the consumer or the employee is the claimant and the agreement is not valid under a provision contained within those Sections.

Article 32

1. For the purposes of this Section, a court shall be deemed to be seised:
   (a) at the time when the document instituting the proceedings or an equivalent document is lodged with the court, provided that the claimant has not subsequently failed to take the steps he was required to take to have service effected on the defendant; or
   (b) if the document has to be served before being lodged with the court, at the time when it is received by the authority responsible for service, provided that the claimant has not subsequently failed to take the steps he was required to take to have the document lodged with the court. The authority responsible for service referred to in point (b) shall be the first authority receiving the documents to be served.

2. The court, or the authority responsible for service, referred to in paragraph 1, shall note, respectively, the date of the lodging of the document instituting the proceedings or the equivalent document, or the date of receipt of the documents to be served.

Article 33

1. Where jurisdiction is based on Article 4 or on Articles 7, 8 or 9 and proceedings are pending before a court of a third State at the time when a court in a Member State is seised of an action involving the same cause of action and between the same parties as the proceedings in the court of the third State, the court of the Member State may stay the proceedings if:
   (a) it is expected that the court of the third State will give a judgment capable of recognition and, where applicable, of enforcement in that Member State; and
   (b) the court of the Member State is satisfied that a stay is necessary for the proper administration of justice.

2. The court of the Member State may continue the proceedings at any time if:
   (a) the proceedings in the court of the third State are themselves stayed or discontinued;
   (b) it appears to the court of the Member State that the proceedings in the court of the third State are unlikely to be concluded within a reasonable time; or
   (c) the continuation of the proceedings is required for the proper administration of justice.

3. The court of the Member State shall dismiss the proceedings if the proceedings in the court of the third State are concluded and have resulted in a judgment capable of recognition and, where applicable, of enforcement in that Member State.

4. The court of the Member State shall apply this Article on the application of one of the parties or, where possible under national law, of its own motion.

Article 34

1. Where jurisdiction is based on Article 4 or on Articles 7, 8 or 9 and an action is pending before a court of a third State at the time when a court in a Member State is seised of an action which is related to the action in the court of the third State, the court of the Member State may stay the proceedings if:
   (a) it is expedient to hear and determine the related actions together to avoid the risk of irreconcilable judgments resulting from separate proceedings;
   (b) it is expected that the court of the third State will give a judgment capable of recognition and, where applicable, of enforcement in that Member State; and
   (c) the court of the Member State is satisfied that a stay is necessary for the proper administration of justice.

2. The court of the Member State may continue the proceedings at any time if:
   (a) it appears to the court of the Member State that there is no longer a risk of irreconcilable judgments;

(b)   the proceedings in the court of the third State are themselves stayed or discontinued;

(c)   it appears to the court of the Member State that the proceedings in the court of the third State are unlikely to be concluded within a reasonable time; or

(d)   the continuation of the proceedings is required for the proper administration of justice.

3. The court of the Member State may dismiss the proceedings if the proceedings in the court of the third State are concluded and have resulted in a judgment capable of recognition and, where applicable, of enforcement in that Member State.

4. The court of the Member State shall apply this Article on the application of one of the parties or, where possible under national law, of its own motion.

SECTION 10: Provisional, including protective, measures

Article 35

Application may be made to the courts of a Member State for such provisional, including protective, measures as may be available under the law of that Member State, even if the courts of another Member State have jurisdiction as to the substance of the matter.

CHAPTER III: RECOGNITION AND ENFORCEMENT

SECTION 1: Recognition

Article 36

1. A judgment given in a Member State shall be recognised in the other Member States without any special procedure being required.

2. Any interested party may, in accordance with the procedure provided for in Subsection 2 of Section 3, apply for a decision that there are no grounds for refusal of recognition as referred to in Article 45.

3. If the outcome of proceedings in a court of a Member State depends on the determination of an incidental question of refusal of recognition, that court shall have jurisdiction over that question.

Article 37

1. A party who wishes to invoke in a Member State a judgment given in another Member State shall produce:

(a)   a copy of the judgment which satisfies the conditions necessary to establish its authenticity; and

(b)   the certificate issued pursuant to Article 53.

2. The court or authority before which a judgment given in another Member State is invoked may, where necessary, require the party invoking it to provide, in accordance with Article 57, a translation or a transliteration of the contents of the certificate referred to in point (b) of paragraph 1. The court or authority may require the party to provide a translation of the judgment instead of a translation of the contents of the certificate if it is unable to proceed without such a translation.

Article 38

The court or authority before which a judgment given in another Member State is invoked may suspend the proceedings, in whole or in part, if:

(a)   the judgment is challenged in the Member State of origin; or

(b)   an application has been submitted for a decision that there are no grounds for refusal of recognition as referred to in Article 45 or for a decision that the recognition is to be refused on the basis of one of those grounds.

SECTION 2: Enforcement

Article 39

A judgment given in a Member State which is enforceable in that Member State shall be enforceable in the other Member States without any declaration of enforceability being required.

Article 40

An enforceable judgment shall carry with it by operation of law the power to proceed to any protective measures which exist under the law of the Member State addressed.

Article 41

1. Subject to the provisions of this Section, the procedure for the enforcement of judgments given in another Member State shall be governed by the law of the Member State addressed. A judgment given in a Member State which is enforceable in the Member State addressed shall be enforced there under the same conditions as a judgment given in the Member State addressed.

2. Notwithstanding paragraph 1, the grounds for refusal or of suspension of enforcement under the law of the Member State addressed shall apply in so far as they are not incompatible with the grounds referred to in Article 45.

3. The party seeking the enforcement of a judgment given in another Member State shall not be required to have a postal address in the Member State addressed. Nor shall that party be required to have an authorised representative in the Member State addressed unless such a representative is mandatory irrespective of the nationality or the domicile of the parties.

Article 42

1. For the purposes of enforcement in a Member State of a judgment given in another Member State, the applicant shall provide the competent enforcement authority with:
   (a) a copy of the judgment which satisfies the conditions necessary to establish its authenticity; and
   (b) the certificate issued pursuant to Article 53, certifying that the judgment is enforceable and containing an extract of the judgment as well as, where appropriate, relevant information on the recoverable costs of the proceedings and the calculation of interest.

2. For the purposes of enforcement in a Member State of a judgment given in another Member State ordering a provisional, including a protective, measure, the applicant shall provide the competent enforcement authority with:
   (a) a copy of the judgment which satisfies the conditions necessary to establish its authenticity;
   (b) the certificate issued pursuant to Article 53, containing a description of the measure and certifying that: (i) the court has jurisdiction as to the substance of the matter; (ii) the judgment is enforceable in the Member State of origin; and
   (c) where the measure was ordered without the defendant being summoned to appear, proof of service of the judgment.

3. The competent enforcement authority may, where necessary, require the applicant to provide, in accordance with Article 57, a translation or a transliteration of the contents of the certificate.

4. The competent enforcement authority may require the applicant to provide a translation of the judgment only if it is unable to proceed without such a translation.

Article 43

1. Where enforcement is sought of a judgment given in another Member State, the certificate issued pursuant to Article 53 shall be served on the person against whom the enforcement is sought prior to the first enforcement measure. The certificate shall be accompanied by the judgment, if not already served on that person.

2. Where the person against whom enforcement is sought is domiciled in a Member State other than the Member State of origin, he may request a translation of the judgment in order to contest the enforcement if the judgment is not written in or accompanied by a translation into either of the following languages:

    (a) a language which he understands; or

    (b) the official language of the Member State in which he is domiciled or, where there are several official languages in that Member State, the official language or one of the official languages of the place where he is domiciled.

Where a translation of the judgment is requested under the first subparagraph, no measures of enforcement may be taken other than protective measures until that translation has been provided to the person against whom enforcement is sought. This paragraph shall not apply if the judgment has already been served on the person against whom enforcement is sought in one of the languages referred to in the first subparagraph or is accompanied by a translation into one of those languages.

3. This Article shall not apply to the enforcement of a protective measure in a judgment or where the person seeking enforcement proceeds to protective measures in accordance with Article 40.

Article 44

1. In the event of an application for refusal of enforcement of a judgment pursuant to Subsection 2 of Section 3, the court in the Member State addressed may, on the application of the person against whom enforcement is sought:

    (a) limit the enforcement proceedings to protective measures;

    (b) make enforcement conditional on the provision of such security as it shall determine; or

    (c) suspend, either wholly or in part, the enforcement proceedings.

2. The competent authority in the Member State addressed shall, on the application of the person against whom enforcement is sought, suspend the enforcement proceedings where the enforceability of the judgment is suspended in the Member State of origin.

SECTION 3: Refusal of recognition and enforcement

Subsection 1: Refusal of recognition

Article 45

1. On the application of any interested party, the recognition of a judgment shall be refused:

    (a) if such recognition is manifestly contrary to public policy (*ordre public*) in the Member State addressed;

    (b) where the judgment was given in default of appearance, if the defendant was not served with the document which instituted the proceedings or with an equivalent document in sufficient time and in such a way as to enable him to arrange for his defence, unless the defendant failed to commence proceedings to challenge the judgment when it was possible for him to do so;

    (c) if the judgment is irreconcilable with a judgment given between the same parties in the Member State addressed;

    (d)   if the judgment is irreconcilable with an earlier judgment given in another Member State or in a third State involving the same cause of action and between the same parties, provided that the earlier judgment fulfils the conditions necessary for its recognition in the Member State addressed; or

    (e)   if the judgment conflicts with: (i) Sections 3, 4 or 5 of Chapter II where the policyholder, the insured, a beneficiary of the insurance contract, the injured party, the consumer or the employee was the defendant; or (ii) Section 6 of Chapter II.

2. In its examination of the grounds of jurisdiction referred to in point (e) of paragraph 1, the court to which the application was submitted shall be bound by the findings of fact on which the court of origin based its jurisdiction.

3. Without prejudice to point (e) of paragraph 1, the jurisdiction of the court of origin may not be reviewed. The test of public policy referred to in point (a) of paragraph 1 may not be applied to the rules relating to jurisdiction.

4. The application for refusal of recognition shall be made in accordance with the procedures provided for in Subsection 2 and, where appropriate, Section 4.

Subsection 2: Refusal of enforcement

Article 46

On the application of the person against whom enforcement is sought, the enforcement of a judgment shall be refused where one of the grounds referred to in Article 45 is found to exist.

Article 47

1. The application for refusal of enforcement shall be submitted to the court which the Member State concerned has communicated to the Commission pursuant to point (a) of Article 75 as the court to which the application is to be submitted.

2. The procedure for refusal of enforcement shall, in so far as it is not covered by this Regulation, be governed by the law of the Member State addressed.

3. The applicant shall provide the court with a copy of the judgment and, where necessary, a translation or transliteration of it. The court may dispense with the production of the documents referred to in the first subparagraph if it already possesses them or if it considers it unreasonable to require the applicant to provide them. In the latter case, the court may require the other party to provide those documents.

4. The party seeking the refusal of enforcement of a judgment given in another Member State shall not be required to have a postal address in the Member State addressed. Nor shall that party be required to have an authorised representative in the Member State addressed unless such a representative is mandatory irrespective of the nationality or the domicile of the parties.

Article 48

The court shall decide on the application for refusal of enforcement without delay.

Article 49

1. The decision on the application for refusal of enforcement may be appealed against by either party.

2. The appeal is to be lodged with the court which the Member State concerned has communicated to the Commission pursuant to point (b) of Article 75 as the court with which such an appeal is to be lodged.

Article 50

The decision given on the appeal may only be contested by an appeal where the courts with which any further appeal is to be lodged have been communicated by the Member State concerned to the Commission pursuant to point (c) of Article 75.

Article 51

1. The court to which an application for refusal of enforcement is submitted or the court which hears an appeal lodged under Article 49 or Article 50 may stay the proceedings if an ordinary appeal has been lodged against the judgment in the Member State of origin or if the time for such an appeal has not yet expired. In the latter case, the court may specify the time within which such an appeal is to be lodged.

2. Where the judgment was given in Ireland, Cyprus or the United Kingdom, any form of appeal available in the Member State of origin shall be treated as an ordinary appeal for the purposes of paragraph 1.

SECTION 4: Common provisions

Article 52

Under no circumstances may a judgment given in a Member State be reviewed as to its substance in the Member State addressed.

Article 53

The court of origin shall, at the request of any interested party, issue the certificate using the form set out in Annex I.

Article 54

1. If a judgment contains a measure or an order which is not known in the law of the Member State addressed, that measure or order shall, to the extent possible, be adapted to a measure or an order known in the law of that Member State which has equivalent effects attached to it and which pursues similar aims and interests. Such adaptation shall not result in effects going beyond those provided for in the law of the Member State of origin.

2. Any party may challenge the adaptation of the measure or order before a court.

3. If necessary, the party invoking the judgment or seeking its enforcement may be required to provide a translation or a transliteration of the judgment.

Article 55

A judgment given in a Member State which orders a payment by way of a penalty shall be enforceable in the Member State addressed only if the amount of the payment has been finally determined by the court of origin.

Article 56

No security, bond or deposit, however described, shall be required of a party who in one Member State applies for the enforcement of a judgment given in another Member State on the ground that he is a foreign national or that he is not domiciled or resident in the Member State addressed.

Article 57

1. When a translation or a transliteration is required under this Regulation, such translation or transliteration shall be into the official language of the Member State concerned or, where there are several official languages in that Member State, into the official language or one of the official languages of court proceedings of the place where a judgment given in another Member State is invoked or an application is made, in accordance with the law of that Member State.

2. For the purposes of the forms referred to in Articles 53 and 60, translations or transliterations may also be into any other official language or languages of the institutions of the Union that the Member State concerned has indicated it can accept.

3. Any translation made under this Regulation shall be done by a person qualified to do translations in one of the Member States.

CHAPTER IV: AUTHENTIC INSTRUMENTS AND COURT SETTLEMENTS

Article 58

1. An authentic instrument which is enforceable in the Member State of origin shall be enforceable in the other Member States without any declaration of enforceability being required. Enforcement of the authentic instrument may be refused only if such enforcement is manifestly contrary to public policy (*ordre public*) in the Member State addressed. The provisions of Section 2, Subsection 2 of Section 3, and Section 4 of Chapter III shall apply as appropriate to authentic instruments.

2. The authentic instrument produced must satisfy the conditions necessary to establish its authenticity in the Member State of origin.

Article 59

A court settlement which is enforceable in the Member State of origin shall be enforced in the other Member States under the same conditions as authentic instruments.

Article 60

The competent authority or court of the Member State of origin shall, at the request of any interested party, issue the certificate using the form set out in Annex II containing a summary of the enforceable obligation recorded in the authentic instrument or of the agreement between the parties recorded in the court settlement.

CHAPTER V: GENERAL PROVISIONS

Article 61

No legalisation or other similar formality shall be required for documents issued in a Member State in the context of this Regulation.

Article 62

1. In order to determine whether a party is domiciled in the Member State whose courts are seised of a matter, the court shall apply its internal law.

2. If a party is not domiciled in the Member State whose courts are seised of the matter, then, in order to determine whether the party is domiciled in another Member State, the court shall apply the law of that Member State.

Article 63

1. For the purposes of this Regulation, a company or other legal person or association of natural or legal persons is domiciled at the place where it has its:
  (a) statutory seat;
  (b) central administration; or
  (c) principal place of business.

2. For the purposes of Ireland, Cyprus and the United Kingdom, 'statutory seat' means the registered office or, where there is no such office anywhere, the place of incorporation or, where there is no such place anywhere, the place under the law of which the formation took place.

3. In order to determine whether a trust is domiciled in the Member State whose courts are seised of the matter, the court shall apply its rules of private international law.

Article 64

Without prejudice to any more favourable provisions of national laws, persons domiciled in a Member State who are being prosecuted in the criminal courts of another Member State of which they are not nationals for an offence which was not intentionally committed may be defended by persons qualified to do so, even if they do not appear in person. However, the court seised of the matter may order appearance in person; in the case of failure to appear, a judgment given in the civil action without the person concerned having had the opportunity to arrange for his defence need not be recognised or enforced in the other Member States.

Article 65

1. The jurisdiction specified in point 2 of Article 8 and Article 13 in actions on a warranty or guarantee or in any other third-party proceedings may be resorted to in the Member States included in the list established by the Commission pursuant to point (b) of Article 76(1) and Article 76(2) only in so far as permitted under national law. A person domiciled in another Member State may be invited to join the proceedings before the courts of those Member States pursuant to the rules on third-party notice referred to in that list.

2. Judgments given in a Member State by virtue of point 2 of Article 8 or Article 13 shall be recognised and enforced in accordance with Chapter III in any other Member State. Any effects which judgments given in the Member States included in the list referred to in paragraph 1 may have, in accordance with the law of those Member States, on third parties by application of paragraph 1 shall be recognised in all Member States.

3. The Member States included in the list referred to in paragraph 1 shall, within the framework of the European Judicial Network in civil and commercial matters established by Council Decision 2001/470/EC ('the European Judicial Network') provide information on how to determine, in accordance with their national law, the effects of the judgments referred to in the second sentence of paragraph 2.

CHAPTER VI: TRANSITIONAL PROVISIONS

Article 66

1. This Regulation shall apply only to legal proceedings instituted, to authentic instruments formally drawn up or registered and to court settlements approved or concluded on or after 10 January 2015.

2. Notwithstanding Article 80, Regulation (EC) No 44/2001 shall continue to apply to judgments given in legal proceedings instituted, to authentic instruments formally drawn up or registered and to court settlements approved or concluded before 10 January 2015 which fall within the scope of that Regulation.

CHAPTER VII: RELATIONSHIP WITH OTHER INSTRUMENTS

Article 67

This Regulation shall not prejudice the application of provisions governing jurisdiction and the recognition and enforcement of judgments in specific matters which are contained in instruments of the Union or in national legislation harmonised pursuant to such instruments.

Article 68

1. This Regulation shall, as between the Member States, supersede the 1968 Brussels Convention, except as regards the territories of the Member States which fall within the territorial scope of that Convention and which are excluded from this Regulation pursuant to Article 355 of the TFEU.

2. In so far as this Regulation replaces the provisions of the 1968 Brussels Convention between the Member States, any reference to that Convention shall be understood as a reference to this Regulation.

Article 69

Subject to Articles 70 and 71, this Regulation shall, as between the Member States, supersede the conventions that cover the same matters as those to which this Regulation applies. In particular, the conventions included in the list established by the Commission pursuant to point (c) of Article 76(1) and Article 76(2) shall be superseded.

Article 70

1. The conventions referred to in Article 69 shall continue to have effect in relation to matters to which this Regulation does not apply.

2. They shall continue to have effect in respect of judgments given, authentic instruments formally drawn up or registered and court settlements approved or concluded before the date of entry into force of Regulation (EC) No 44/2001.

Article 71

1. This Regulation shall not affect any conventions to which the Member States are parties and which, in relation to particular matters, govern jurisdiction or the recognition or enforcement of judgments.

2. With a view to its uniform interpretation, paragraph 1 shall be applied in the following manner:

(a) this Regulation shall not prevent a court of a Member State which is party to a convention on a particular matter from assuming jurisdiction in accordance with that convention, even where the defendant is domiciled in another Member State which is not party to that convention. The court hearing the action shall, in any event, apply Article 28 of this Regulation;

(b) judgments given in a Member State by a court in the exercise of jurisdiction provided for in a convention on a particular matter shall be recognised and enforced in the other Member States in accordance with this Regulation.

Where a convention on a particular matter to which both the Member State of origin and the Member State addressed are parties lays down conditions for the recognition or enforcement of judgments, those conditions shall apply. In any event, the provisions of this Regulation on recognition and enforcement of judgments may be applied.

Article 71a[1]

1. For the purposes of this Regulation, a court common to several Member States as specified in paragraph 2 (a 'common court') shall be deemed to be a court of a Member State when, pursuant to the instrument establishing it, such a common court exercises jurisdiction in matters falling within the scope of this Regulation.

2. For the purposes of this Regulation, each of the following courts shall be a common court:

    (a) the Unified Patent Court established by the Agreement on a Unified Patent Court signed on 19 February 2013 (the 'UPC Agreement'); and

    (b) the Benelux Court of Justice established by the Treaty of 31 March 1965 concerning the establishment and statute of a Benelux Court of Justice (the 'Benelux Court of Justice Treaty').

Article 71b

The jurisdiction of a common court shall be determined as follows:

(1) a common court shall have jurisdiction where, under this Regulation, the courts of a Member State party to the instrument establishing the common court would have jurisdiction in a matter governed by that instrument;

(2) where the defendant is not domiciled in a Member State, and this Regulation does not otherwise confer jurisdiction over him, Chapter II shall apply as appropriate regardless of the defendant's domicile. Application may be made to a common court for provisional, including protective, measures even if the courts of a third State have jurisdiction as to the substance of the matter;

(3) where a common court has jurisdiction over a defendant under point 2 in a dispute relating to an infringement of a European patent giving rise to damage within the Union, that court may also exercise jurisdiction in relation to damage arising outside the Union from such an infringement. Such jurisdiction may only be established if property belonging to the defendant is located in any Member State party to the instrument establishing the common court and the dispute has a sufficient connection with any such Member State.

Article 71c

1. Articles 29 to 32 shall apply where proceedings are brought in a common court and in a court of a Member State not party to the instrument establishing the common court.

2. Articles 29 to 32 shall apply where, during the transitional period referred to in Article 83 of the UPC Agreement, proceedings are brought in the Unified Patent Court and in a court of a Member State party to the UPC Agreement.

Article 71d

This Regulation shall apply to the recognition and enforcement of:

    (a) judgments given by a common court which are to be recognised and enforced in a Member State not party to the instrument establishing the common court; and

---

1 Articles 71a to 71d were inserted by Regulation 542/2014, [2014] OJ L163/1.

(b) judgments given by the courts of a Member State not party to the instrument establishing the common court which are to be recognised and enforced in a Member State party to that instrument.

However, where recognition and enforcement of a judgment given by a common court is sought in a Member State party to the instrument establishing the common court, any rules of that instrument on recognition and enforcement shall apply instead of the rules of this Regulation.

Article 72

This Regulation shall not affect agreements by which Member States, prior to the entry into force of Regulation (EC) No 44/2001, undertook pursuant to Article 59 of the 1968 Brussels Convention not to recognise judgments given, in particular in other Contracting States to that Convention, against defendants domiciled or habitually resident in a third State where, in cases provided for in Article 4 of that Convention, the judgment could only be founded on a ground of jurisdiction specified in the second paragraph of Article 3 of that Convention.

Article 73

1. This Regulation shall not affect the application of the 2007 Lugano Convention.

2. This Regulation shall not affect the application of the 1958 New York Convention.

3. This Regulation shall not affect the application of bilateral conventions and agreements between a third State and a Member State concluded before the date of entry into force of Regulation (EC) No 44/2001 which concern matters governed by this Regulation.

CHAPTER VIII: FINAL PROVISIONS

Article 74

The Member States shall provide, within the framework of the European Judicial Network and with a view to making the information available to the public, a description of national rules and procedures concerning enforcement, including authorities competent for enforcement, and information on any limitations on enforcement, in particular debtor protection rules and limitation or prescription periods. The Member States shall keep this information permanently updated.

Article 75

By 10 January 2014, the Member States shall communicate to the Commission:

(a) the courts to which the application for refusal of enforcement is to be submitted pursuant to Article 47(1);

(b) the courts with which an appeal against the decision on the application for refusal of enforcement is to be lodged pursuant to Article 49(2);

(c) the courts with which any further appeal is to be lodged pursuant to Article 50; and

(d) the languages accepted for translations of the forms as referred to in Article 57(2).

The Commission shall make the information publicly available through any appropriate means, in particular through the European Judicial Network.

Article 76

1. The Member States shall notify the Commission of:

(a) the rules of jurisdiction referred to in Articles 5(2) and 6(2);

(b) the rules on third-party notice referred to in Article 65; and

(c)   the conventions referred to in Article 69.

2. The Commission shall, on the basis of the notifications by the Member States referred to in paragraph 1, establish the corresponding lists.

3. The Member States shall notify the Commission of any subsequent amendments required to be made to those lists. The Commission shall amend those lists accordingly.

4. The Commission shall publish the lists and any subsequent amendments made to them in the Official Journal of the European Union.

5. The Commission shall make all information notified pursuant to paragraphs 1 and 3 publicly available through any other appropriate means, in particular through the European Judicial Network.

Article 77

The Commission shall be empowered to adopt delegated acts in accordance with Article 78 concerning the amendment of Annexes I and II.

Article 78

1. The power to adopt delegated acts is conferred on the Commission subject to the conditions laid down in this Article.

2. The power to adopt delegated acts referred to in Article 77 shall be conferred on the Commission for an indeterminate period of time from 9 January 2013.

3. The delegation of power referred to in Article 77 may be revoked at any time by the European Parliament or by the Council. A decision to revoke shall put an end to the delegation of the power specified in that decision. It shall take effect the day following the publication of the decision in the Official Journal of the European Union or at a later date specified therein. It shall not affect the validity of any delegated acts already in force.

4. As soon as it adopts a delegated act, the Commission shall notify it simultaneously to the European Parliament and to the Council.

5. A delegated act adopted pursuant to Article 77 shall enter into force only if no objection has been expressed either by the European Parliament or the Council within a period of two months of notification of that act to the European Parliament and the Council or if, before the expiry of that period, the European Parliament and the Council have both informed the Commission that they will not object. That period shall be extended by two months at the initiative of the European Parliament or of the Council.

Article 79

By 11 January 2022 the Commission shall present a report to the European Parliament, to the Council and to the European Economic and Social Committee on the application of this Regulation. That report shall include an evaluation of the possible need for a further extension of the rules on jurisdiction to defendants not domiciled in a Member State, taking into account the operation of this Regulation and possible developments at international level. Where appropriate, the report shall be accompanied by a proposal for amendment of this Regulation.

Article 80

This Regulation shall repeal Regulation (EC) No 44/2001. References to the repealed Regulation shall be construed as references to this Regulation and shall be read in accordance with the correlation table set out in Annex III.

Article 81

This Regulation shall enter into force on the twentieth day following that of its publication in the Official Journal of the European Union. It shall apply from 10 January 2015, with the exception of Articles 75 and 76, which shall apply from 10 January 2014.

This Regulation shall be binding in its entirety and directly applicable in the Member States in accordance with the Treaties.

ANNEX I (omitted)

ANNEX II (omitted)

ANNEX III: CORRELATION TABLE

Regulation (EC) No 44/2001	This Regulation (1215/2012)
Article 1(1)	Article 1(1)
Article 1(2), introductory words	Article 1(2), introductory words
Article 1(2) point (a)	Article 1(2), points (a) and (f)
Article 1(2), points (b) to (d)	Article 1(2), points (b) to (d)
—	Article 1(2), point (e)
Article 1(3)	—
—	Article 2
Article 2	Article 4
Article 3	Article 5
Article 4	Article 6
Article 5, introductory words	Article 7, introductory words
Article 5, point (1)	Article 7, point (1)
Article 5, point (2)	—
Article 5, points (3) and (4)	Article 7, points (2) and (3)
—	Article 7, point (4)
Article 5, points (5) to (7)	Article 7, points (5) to (7)
Article 6	Article 8
Article 7	Article 9
Article 8	Article 10
Article 9	Article 11
Article 10	Article 12
Article 11	Article 13
Article 12	Article 14
Article 13	Article 15
Article 14	Article 16
Article 15	Article 17
Article 16	Article 18
Article 17	Article 19
Article 18	Article 20
Article 19, points (1) and (2)	Article 21(1)
—	Article 21(2)
Article 20	Article 22
Article 21	Article 23
Article 22	Article 24
Article 23(1) and (2)	Article 25(1) and (2)
Article 23(3)	—

—	Article 49
—	Article 50
—	Article 51
—	Article 54
Article 49	Article 55
Article 50	—
Article 51	Article 56
Article 52	—
Article 53	—
Article 54	Article 53
Article 55(1)	—
Article 55(2)	Article 37(2), Article 47(3) and Article 57
Article 56	Article 61
Article 57(1)	Article 58(1)
Article 57(2)	—
Article 57(3)	Article 58(2)
Article 57(4)	Article 60
Article 58	Article 59 and Article 60
Article 59	Article 62
Article 60	Article 63
Article 61	Article 64
Article 62	Article 3
Article 63	—
Article 64	—
Article 65	Article 65(1) and (2)
—	Article 65(3)
Article 66	Article 66
Article 67	Article 67
Article 68	Article 68
Article 69	Article 69
Article 70	Article 70
Article 71	Article 71
Article 72	Article 72
—	Article 73
Article 73	Article 79
Article 74(1)	Article 75, first paragraph, points (a), (b) and (c), and Article 76(1), point (a)
Article 74(2)	Article 77
—	Article 78
—	Article 80
Article 75	—
Article 76	Article 81
Annex I	Article 76(1), point (a)
Annex II	Article 75, point (a)
Annex III	Article 75, point (b)
Annex IV	Article 75, point (c)
Annex V	Annex I and Annex II
Annex VI	Annex II
—	Annex III

****

APPENDICES

(This Table is not part of the Regulation)

Unofficial table of correlation as between Regulation 44/2001 **in bold type** and the Brussels Convention [in plain type and parenthesis]:

1 [1]	**2** [2]	**3** [3]		**4** [4]	**5** [5]	**6** [6]	**7** [6a]	**8** [7]
9 [8]	**10** [9]	**11** [10]		**12** [11]	**13** [12]	**14** [12a]	**15** [13]	**16** [14]
17 [15]	**18** [★]	**19** [¹]		**20** [★]	**21** [²]	**22** [16]	**23** [17]	**24** [18]
25 [19]	**26** [20]	**27** [21]		**28** [22]	**29** [23]	**30** [★]	**31** [24]	**32** [25]
33 [26]	**34** [27]	**35** [28]		**36** [29]	**37** [30]	**38** [31]	**39** [32]	**40** [33]
41 [34]	**42** [35]	**43** [36, 37(1), 40(1)]		**44** [37(2), 4]	**45** [³]			
46 [38]	**47** [39]	**48** [42]		**49** [43]	**50** [44]	**51** [45]	**52** [P⁴]	**53** [46]
54 [47]	**55** [48]	**56** [49]		**57** [50]	**58** [51]	**59** [52]	**60** [53]	**61** [P⁵]
62 [★]	**63** [P⁶]	**64** [⁷]		**65** [P⁸]	**66** [54]	**67** [57(3)]	**68** [★]	**69** [55]
70 [56]	**71** [57]	**72** [59]		**73** [66]	**74** [★]	**75** [★]	**76** [62]	

★ *Indicates completely new provision.*

1. New, but cf. proviso to Article 5(1) of Brussels Convention.
2. New, but cf. Article 17(5) of Brussels Convention.
3. New, though cf. Article **36** [29].
4. Article III of Annexed Protocol to Brussels Convention.
5. Article II of Annexed Protocol to Brussels Convention.
6. Article I of Annexed Protocol to Brussels Convention.
7. Article Vb of Annexed Protocol to Brussels Convention.
8. Article V of Annexed Protocol to Brussels Convention.

838

Text of the Brussels I Regulation 44/2001

COUNCIL REGULATION 44/2001 of 22 DECEMBER 2001, ON JURISDICTION AND THE RECOGNITION AND ENFORCEMENT OF JUDGMENTS IN CIVIL AND COMMERCIAL MATTERS
THE COUNCIL OF THE EUROPEAN UNION,
Having regard to the Treaty establishing the European Community, and in particular Article 61(c) and Article 67(1) thereof,
Having regard to the proposal from the Commission,
Having regard to the opinion of the European Parliament,
Having regard to the opinion of the Economic and Social Committee,

Whereas:

(1) The Community has set itself the objective of maintaining and developing an area of freedom, security and justice, in which the free movement of persons is ensured. In order to establish progressively such an area, the Community should adopt, amongst other things, the measures relating to judicial co-operation in civil matters which are necessary for the sound operation of the internal market.

(2) Certain differences between national rules governing jurisdiction and recognition of judgments hamper the sound operation of the internal market. Provisions to unify the rules of conflict of jurisdiction in civil and commercial matters and to simplify the formalities with a view to rapid and simple recognition and enforcement of judgments from Member States bound by this Regulation are essential.

(3) This area is within the field of judicial co-operation in civil matters within the meaning of Article 65 of the Treaty.

(4) In accordance with the principles of subsidiarity and proportionality as set out in Article 5 of the Treaty, the objectives of this Regulation cannot be sufficiently achieved by the Member States and can therefore be better achieved by the Community. This Regulation confines itself to the minimum required in order to achieve those objectives and does not go beyond what is necessary for that purpose.

(5) On 27 September 1968 the Member States, acting under Article 293, fourth indent, of the Treaty, concluded the Brussels Convention on Jurisdiction and the Enforcement of Judgments in Civil and Commercial Matters, as amended by Conventions on the Accession of the New Member States to that Convention (hereinafter referred to as the 'Brussels Convention'). On 16 September 1988 Member States and EFTA States concluded the Lugano Convention on Jurisdiction and the Enforcement of Judgments in Civil and Commercial Matters, which is a parallel Convention to the 1968 Brussels Convention. Work has been undertaken for the revision of those Conventions, and the Council has approved the content of the revised texts. Continuity in the results achieved in that revision should be ensured.

(6) In order to attain the objective of free movement of judgments in civil and commercial matters, it is necessary and appropriate that the rules governing jurisdiction and the recognition and

enforcement of judgments be governed by a Community legal instrument which is binding and directly applicable.

(7) The scope of this Regulation must cover all the main civil and commercial matters apart from certain well-defined matters.

(8) There must be a link between proceedings to which this Regulation applies and the territory of the Member States bound by this Regulation. Accordingly common rules on jurisdiction should, in principle, apply when the defendant is domiciled in one of those Member States.

(9) A defendant not domiciled in a Member State is in general subject to national rules of jurisdiction applicable in the territory of the Member State of the court seised, and a defendant domiciled in a Member State not bound by this Regulation must remain subject to the Brussels Convention.

(10) For the purposes of the free movement of judgments, judgments given in a Member State bound by this Regulation should be recognised and enforced in another Member State bound by this Regulation, even if the judgment debtor is domiciled in a third State.

(11) The rules of jurisdiction must be highly predictable and founded on the principle that jurisdiction is generally based on the defendant's domicile and jurisdiction must always be available on this ground save in a few well-defined situations in which the subject matter of the litigation or the autonomy of the parties warrants a different linking factor. The domicile of a legal person must be defined autonomously so as to make the common rules more transparent and avoid conflicts of jurisdiction.

(12) In addition to the defendant's domicile, there should be alternative grounds of jurisdiction based on a close link between the court and the action or in order to facilitate the sound administration of justice.

(13) In relation to insurance, consumer contracts and employment, the weaker party should be protected by rules of jurisdiction more favourable to his interests than the general rules provide for.

(14) The autonomy of the parties to a contract, other than an insurance, consumer or employment contract, where only limited autonomy to determine the courts having jurisdiction is allowed, must be respected subject to the exclusive grounds of jurisdiction laid down in this Regulation.

(15) In the interests of the harmonious administration of justice it is necessary to minimise the possibility of concurrent proceedings and to ensure that irreconcilable judgments will not be given in two Member States. There must be a clear and effective mechanism for resolving cases of *lis pendens* and related actions and for obviating problems flowing from national differences as to the determination of the times when a case is regarded as pending. For the purposes of this Regulation that time should be defined autonomously.

(16) Mutual trust in the administration of justice in the Community justifies judgments given in a Member State being recognised automatically without the need for any procedure except in cases of dispute.

(17) By virtue of the same principle of mutual trust, the procedure for making enforceable in one Member State a judgment given in another must be efficient and rapid. To that end, the declaration that a judgment is enforceable should be issued virtually automatically after purely formal checks of the documents supplied, without there being any possibility for the court to raise of its own motion any of the grounds for non-enforcement provided for by this Regulation.

(18) However, respect for the rights of the defence means that the defendant should be able to appeal in an adversarial procedure, against the declaration of enforceability, if he considers one of the grounds for non-enforcement to the present. Redress procedures should also be available to the claimant where his application for a declaration of enforceability has been rejected.

(19) Continuity between the Brussels Convention and this Regulation should be ensured, and transitional provisions should be laid down to that end. The same need for continuity applies as regards

the interpretation of the Brussels Convention by the Court of Justice of the European Communities and the 1971 Protocol should remain applicable also to cases already pending when this Regulation enters into force.

(20) The United Kingdom and Ireland, in accordance with Article 3 of the Protocol on the position of the United Kingdom and Ireland annexed to the Treaty on European Union and to the Treaty establishing the European Community, have given notice of their wish to take part in the adoption and applicable of this Regulation.

(21) (*inapplicable*)

(22) (*inapplicable*)

(23) The Brussels Convention also continues to apply to the territories of the Member States which fall within the territorial scope of that Convention and which are excluded from this Regulation pursuant to Article 299 of the Treaty.

(24) Likewise for the sake of consistency, this Regulation should not affect rules governing jurisdiction and the recognition of judgments contained in specific Community instruments.

(25) Respect for international commitments entered into by the Member States means that this regulation should not affect conventions relating to specific matters to which the Member States are parties.

(26) The necessary flexibility should be provided for in the basic rules of this Regulation in order to take account of the specific procedural rules of certain Member States. Certain provisions of the Protocol annexed to the Brussels Convention should accordingly be incorporated in this Regulation.

(27) In order to allow a harmonious transition in certain areas which were the subject of special provisions in the Protocol annexed to the Brussels Convention, this Regulation lays down, for a transitional period, provisions taking into consideration the specific situation in certain Member States.

(28) No later than five years after entry into force of this Regulation the Commission will present a report on its application and, if need be, submit proposals for adaptations.

(29) The Commission will have to adjust Annexes I to IV on the rules of national jurisdiction, the courts or competent authorities and redress procedures available on the basis of the amendments forwarded by the Member State concerned; amendments made to Annexes V and VI should be adopted in accordance with Council Decision 1999/468/EC of 28 June 1999 laying down the procedures for the exercise of implementing powers conferred on the Commission.

HAS ADOPTED THIS REGULATION:

CHAPTER I: SCOPE

Article 1

1. This Regulation shall apply in civil and commercial matters whatever the nature of the court or tribunal. It shall not exceed, in particular, to revenue, customs or administrative matters.

2. The Regulation shall not apply to:
   (a) the status or legal capacity of natural persons, rights in property arising out of a matrimonial relationship, wills and succession;
   (b) bankruptcy, proceedings relating to the winding-up of insolvent companies or other legal persons, judicial arrangements, compositions and analogous proceedings;
   (c) social security,
   (d) arbitration.

3. (*Inapplicable, now that Denmark is to be treated as a Member State*)

CHAPTER II: JURISDICTION

SECTION 1: General provisions

Article 2

1. Subject to this Regulation, persons domiciled in a Member State shall, whatever their nationality, be sued in the courts of that Member State.

2. Persons who are not nationals of the Member State in which they are domiciled shall be governed by the rules of jurisdiction applicable to nationals of that State.

Article 3

1. Persons domiciled in a Member State may be sued in the courts of another Member State only by virtue of the rules set out in Sections 2 to 7 of this Chapter.

2. In particular the rules of national jurisdiction set out in Annex I shall not be applicable as against them.

Article 4

1. If the defendant is not domiciled in a Member State, the jurisdiction of the courts of each Member State shall, subject to Articles 22 and 23, be determined by the law of that Member State.

2. As against such a defendant, any person domiciled in a Member State may whatever his nationality, avail himself in that State of the rules of jurisdiction there in force, and in particular those specified in Annex I, in the same way as the nationals of that State.

SECTION 2: Special Jurisdiction

Article 5

A person domiciled in a Member State may, in another Member State, be sued:

1. (a) in matters relating to a contract, in the courts for the place of performance of the obligation in question;

    (b) for the purpose of this provision and unless otherwise agreed, the place of performance of the obligation in question shall be:
— in the case of the sale of goods, the place in a Member State where, under the contract, the goods were delivered or should have been delivered,
— in the case of the provision of services, the place in a Member State where, under the contract, the services were provided or should have been provided,

    (c) if subparagraph (b) does not apply then subparagraph (a) applies;

2. in matters relating to maintenance, in the courts of the place where the maintenance creditor is domiciled or habitually resident or, if the matter is ancillary to proceedings concerning the status of a person, in the court which, according to its own law, has jurisdiction to entertain those proceedings, unless that jurisdiction is based solely on the nationality of one of the parties;

3. in matters relating to tort, *delict* or *quasi-delict*, in the courts for the place where the harmful event occurred or may occur;

4. as regards a civil claim for damages or restitution which is based on an act giving rise to criminal proceedings, in the court seised of those proceedings, to the extent that that court has jurisdiction under it own law to entertain civil proceedings;

5. as regards a dispute arising out of the operations of a branch, agency or other establishment, in the courts for the place in which the branch, agency or other establishment is situated;

6. as settlor, trustee or beneficiary of a trust created by the operation of a statute, or by a written instrument, or created orally and evidenced in writing, in the courts of the Member State in which the trust is domiciled;

7. as regards a dispute concerning the payment of remuneration claimed in respect of the salvage of a cargo or freight, in the court under the authority of which the cargo or freight in question:

    (a) has been arrested to secure such payment, or

    (b) could have been so arrested, but bail or other security has been given;

provided that this provision shall apply only if it is claimed that the defendant has an interest in the cargo or freight or had such an interest at the time of salvage.

Article 6

A person domiciled in a Member State may also be sued:

1. where he is one of a number of defendants, in the courts for the place where any one of them is domiciled, provided the claims are so closely connected that it is expedient to hear and determine them together to avoid the risk of irreconcilable judgments resulting from separate proceedings;

2. as a third party in an action on a warranty or guarantee or in any other third party proceedings, in the court seised of the original proceedings, unless these were instituted solely with the object of removing him from the jurisdiction of the court which would be competent in his case;

3. on a counter-claim arising from the same contract or facts on which the original claim was based, in the court in which the original claim is pending;

4. in matters relating to a contract, if the action may be combined with an action against the same defendant in matters relating to rights *in rem* in immovable property, in the court of the Member State in which the property is situated.

Article 7

Where by virtue of this Regulation a court of a Member State has jurisdiction in actions relating to liability from the use or operation of a ship, that court, or any other court substituted for this purpose by the internal law of that Member State, shall also have jurisdiction over claims for limitation of such liability.

SECTION 3: Jurisdiction in matters relating to insurance

Article 8

In matters relating to insurance, jurisdiction shall be determined by this Section, without prejudice to Article 4 and point 5 of Article 5.

Article 9

1. An insurer domiciled in a Member State may be sued:

    (a) in the courts of the Member State where he is domiciled, or

    (b) in another Member State, in the case of actions brought by the policyholder, the insured or a beneficiary, in the courts for the place where the plaintiff is domiciled,

    (c) if he is a co-insurer, in the courts of a Member State in which proceedings are brought against the leading insurer.

2. An insurer who is not domiciled in a Member State but has a branch, agency or other establishment in one of the Member States shall, in disputes arising out of the operations of the branch, agency or establishment, be deemed to be domiciled in that Member State.

Article 10

In respect of liability insurance or insurance of immovable property, the insurer may in addition be sued in the courts for the place where the harmful event occurred. The same applies if movable and immovable property are covered by the same insurance policy and both are adversely affected by the same contingency.

Article 11

1. In respect of liability insurance, the insurer may also, if the law of the court permits it, be joined in proceedings which the injured party has brought against the insured.

2. Articles 8, 9 and 10 shall apply to actions brought by the injured party directly against the insurer, where such direct actions are permitted.

3. If the law governing such direct actions provides that the policyholder or the insured may be joined as a party to the action, the same court shall have jurisdiction over them.

Article 12

1. Without prejudice to Article 11(3), an insurer may bring proceedings only in the courts of the Member State in which the defendant is domiciled, irrespective of whether he is the policyholder, the insured or a beneficiary.

2. The provisions of this Section shall not affect the right to bring a counter-claim in the court in which, in accordance with this Section, the original claim is pending.

Article 13

The provisions of this Section may be departed from only by an agreement:

1. which is entered into after the dispute has arisen, or

2. which allows the policyholder, the insured or a benficiary to bring proceedings in courts other than those indicated in this Section, or

3. which is concluded between a policyholder and an insurer, both of whom are at the time of conclusion of the contract domiciled or habitually resident in the same Member State, and which has the effect of conferring jurisdiction on the courts of that State even if the harmful event were to occur abroad, provided that such an agreement is not contrary to the law of that State, or

4. which is concluded with a policyholder who is not domiciled in a Member State, except in so far as the insurance is compulsory or relates to immovable property in a Member State, or

5. which relates to a contract of insurance in so far as it covers one or more of the risks set out in Article 14.

Article 14

The following are the risks referred to in Article 13(5):

1. any loss of or damage to:
    (a) seagoing ships, installations situated offshore or on the high seas, or aircraft, arising from perils which relate to their use for commercial purposes;
    (b) goods in transit other than passengers' baggage where the transit consists of or includes carriage by such ships or aircraft;

2. any liability, other than for bodily injury to passengers or loss of or damage to their baggage:

(a) arising out of the use or operation of ships, installations or aircraft as referred to in point 1(a) in so far as, in respect of the latter, the law of the Member State in which such aircraft are registered does not prohibit agreements on jurisdiction regarding insurance of such risks;

(b) for loss or damage caused by goods in transit as described in point 1(b);

3. any financial loss connected with the use or operation of ships, installations or aircraft as referred to in point 1(a), in particular loss of freight or charter-hire;

4. any risk or interest connected with any of those referred to in points 1 to 3;

5. notwithstanding points 1 to 4, all 'large risks' as defined in Council Directive 73/239/EEC, as amended by Council Directives 88/357/EEC and 90/618/EEC, as they may be amended.

SECTION 4: Jurisdiction over consumer contracts

Article 15

1. In matters relating to a contract concluded by a person, the consumer, for a purpose which can be regarded as being outside his trade or profession, jurisdiction shall be determined by this Section, without prejudice to Article 4 and point 5 of Article 5, if:

(a) it is a contract for the sale of goods on instalment credit terms; or

(b) it is a contract for a loan repayable by instalments, or for any other form of credit, made to finance the sale of goods; or

(c) in all other cases, the contract has been concluded with a person who pursues commercial or professional activities in the Member State of the consumer's domicile or, by any means, directs such activities to that Member State or to several States including that Member State, and the contact falls within the scope of such activities.

2. Where a consumer enters into a contract with a party who is not domiciled in the Member State but has a branch, agency or other establishment in one of the Member States, that party shall, in disputes arising out of the operations of the branch, agency or establishment, be deemed to be domiciled in that State.

3. This Section shall not apply to a contract of transport other than a contract which, for an inclusive price, provides for a combination of travel and accommodation.

Article 16

1. A consumer may bring proceedings against the other party to a contract either in the courts of the Member State in which that party is domiciled or in the courts for the place where the consumer is domiciled.

2. Proceedings may be brought against a consumer by the other party to the contract only in the courts of the Member State in which the consumer is domiciled.

3. This Article shall not affect the right to bring a counter-claim in the court in which, in accordance with this Section, the original claim is pending.

Article 17

The provisions of this Section may be departed from only by an agreement:

1. which is entered into after the dispute has arisen; or

2. which allows the consumer to bring proceedings in courts other than those indicated in this Section; or

3. which is entered into by the consumer and the other party to the contract, both of whom are at the time of conclusion of the contract domiciled or habitually resident in the same Member State, and

which confers jurisdiction on the courts of that Member State, provided that such an agreement is not contrary to the law of that Member State.

SECTION 5: Jurisdiction over individual contracts of employment

Article 18

1. In matters relating to individual contracts of employment, jurisdiction shall be determined by this Section, without prejudice to Article 4 and point 5 of Article 5.

2. Where an employee enters into an individual contract of employment with an employer who is not domiciled in a Member State but has a branch, agency or other establishment in one of the Member States, the employer shall, in disputes arising out of the operations of the branch, agency or establishment, be deemed to be domiciled in that Member State.

Article 19

An employer domiciled in a Member State may be sued:
1. in the courts of the Member State where he is domiciled; or
2. in another Member State:
    (a) in the courts for the place where the employee habitually carries out his work or in the courts for the last place where he did so, or
    (b) if the employee does not or did not habitually carry out his work in any one country, in the courts for the place where the business which engaged the employee is or was situated.

Article 20

1. An employer may bring proceedings only in the courts of the Member State in which the employee is domiciled.

2. The provisions of this Section shall not affect the right to bring a counter-claim in the court in which, in accordance with this Section, the original claim is pending.

Article 21

The provisions of this Section may be departed from only by an agreement on jurisdiction:
1. which is entered into after the dispute has arisen; or
2. which allows the employee to bring proceedings in courts other than those indicated in this Section.

SECTION 6: Exclusive jurisdiction

Article 22

The following courts shall have exclusive jurisdiction, regardless of domicile:
1. in proceedings which have as their object rights *in rem* in immovable property or tenancies of immovable property, the courts of the Member State in which the property is situated.

However, in proceedings which have as their object tenancies of immovable property concluded for temporary private use for a maximum period of six consecutive months, the courts of the Member State in which the defendant is domiciled shall also have jurisdiction, provided that the tenant is a natural person and that the landlord and the tenant are domiciled in the same Member State;

2. in proceedings which have as their object the validity of the constitution, the nullity or the dissolution of companies or other legal persons or associations of natural or legal persons, or of the validity of the decisions of their organs, the courts of the Member State in which the company, legal person or association has its seat. In order to determine that seat, the court shall apply its rules of private international law;

3. in proceedings which have as their object the validity of entries in public registers, the courts of the Member State in which the register is kept;

4. in proceedings concerned with the registration or validity of patents, trade marks, designs, or other similar rights required to be deposited or registered, the courts of the Member State in which the deposit or registration has been applied for, has taken place or is under the terms of a Community instrument or an international convention deemed to have taken place.

Without prejudice to the jurisdiction of the European Patent Office under the Convention on the Grant of European Patents, signed at Munich on 5 October 1973, the courts of each Member State shall have exclusive jurisdiction, regardless of domicile, in proceedings concerned with the registration or validity of any European patent granted for that State;

5. in proceedings concerned with the enforcement of judgments, the courts of the Member State in which the judgment has been or is to be enforced.

SECTION 7: Prorogation of jurisdiction

Article 23

1. If the parties, one or more of who is domiciled in a Member State, have agreed that a court or the courts of a Member State are to have jurisdiction to settle any disputes which have arisen or which may arise in connection with a particular legal relationship, that court or those courts shall have jurisdiction. Such jurisdiction shall be exclusive unless the parties have agreed otherwise. Such an agreement conferring jurisdiction shall be either:
    (a) in writing or evidenced in writing; or
    (b) in a form which accords with practices which the parties have established between themselves; or
    (c) in international trade or commerce, in a form which accords with a usage of which the parties are or ought to have been aware and which in such trade or commerce is widely known to, and regularly observed by, parties to contracts of the type involved in the particular trade or commerce concerned.

2. Any communication by electronic means which provides a durable record of the agreement shall be equivalent to 'writing'.

3. Where such an agreement is concluded by parties, none of whom is domiciled in a Member State, the courts of other Member States shall have no jurisdiction over their disputes unless the court or courts chosen have declined jurisdiction.

4. The court or courts of a Member State on which a trust instrument has conferred jurisdiction shall have exclusive jurisdiction in any proceedings brought against a settlor, trustee or beneficiary, if relations between these persons or their rights or obligations under the trust are involved.

5. Agreements or provisions of a trust instrument conferring jurisdiction shall have no legal force if they are contrary to Articles 13, 17 or 21, of if the courts whose jurisdiction they purport to exclude have exclusive jurisdiction by virtue of Article 22.

Article 24

Apart from jurisdiction derived from other provisions of this Regulation, a court of a Member State before which a defendant enters an appearance shall have jurisdiction. This rule shall not apply where appearance was entered to contest the jurisdiction, or where another court has exclusive jurisdiction by virtue of Article 22.

SECTION 8: Examination as to jurisdiction and admissibility

Article 25

Where a court of a Member State is seised of a claim which is principally concerned with a matter over which the courts of another Member State have exclusive jurisdiction by virtue of Article 22, it shall declared of its own motion that it has no jurisdiction.

Article 26

1. Where a defendant domiciled in one Member State is sued in a court of another Member State and does not enter an appearance, the court shall declare of its own motion that it has no jurisdiction unless its jurisdiction is derived from the provisions of this Regulation.

2. The court shall stay the proceedings so long as it is not shown that the defendant has been able to receive the document instituting the proceedings or an equivalent document in sufficient time to enable him to arrange for his defence, or that all necessary steps have been taken to this end.

3. Article 19 of Council Regulation (EC) No. 1393/2007 of 13 November 2007 on the service in the Member States of judicial and extrajudicial documents in civil or commercial matters shall apply instead of the provisions of paragraph 2 if the document instituting the proceedings or an equivalent document had to be transmitted from one Member State to another pursuant to this Regulation.

4. Where the provisions of Regulation (EC) No. 1393/2007 are not applicable, Article 15 of the Hague Convention of 15 November 1965 on the Service Abroad of Judicial and Extrajudicial Documents in Civil or Commercial Matters shall apply if the document instituting the proceedings or an equivalent document had to be transmitted pursuant to that Convention.

SECTION 9: *Lis pendens*-related actions

Article 27

1. Where proceedings involving the same cause of action and between the same parties are brought in the courts of different Member States, any court other than the court first seised shall of its own motion stay its proceedings until such time as the jurisdiction of the court first seised is established.

2. Where the jurisdiction of the court first seised is established, any court other than the court first seised shall decline jurisdiction in favour of that court.

Article 28

1. Where related actions are pending in the courts of different Member States, any court other than the court first seised may stay its proceedings.

2. Where these actions are pending at first instance, any court other than the court first seised may also, on the application of one of the parties, decline jurisdiction if the court first seised has jurisdiction over the actions in question and its law permits the consolidation thereof.

3. For the purposes of this Article, actions are deemed to be related where they are so closely connected that it is expedient to hear and determine them together to avoid the risk of irreconcilable judgments resulting from separate proceedings.

Article 29

Where actions come within the exclusive jurisdiction of several courts, any court other than the court first seised shall decline jurisdiction in favour of that court.

Article 30

For the purposes of this Section, a court shall be deemed to be seised:

1. at the time when the document instituting the proceedings or an equivalent document is lodged with the court, provided that the plaintiff has not subsequently failed to take the steps he was required to take to have service effected on the defendant, or

2. if the document has to be served before being lodged with the court, at the time when it is received by the authority responsible for service, provided that the plaintiff has not subsequently failed to take the steps he was required to take to have the document lodged with the court.

SECTION 10: Provisional, including protective, measures

Article 31

Application may be made to the courts of a Member State for such provisional, including protective, measures as may be available under the law of that State, even if, under this Regulation, the courts of another Member State have jurisdiction as to the substance of the matter.

CHAPTER III: RECOGNITION AND ENFORCEMENT

Article 32

For the purposes of this Regulation, 'judgment' means any judgment given by a court or tribunal of a Member State, whatever the judgment may be called, including a decree, order, decision or writ of execution, as well as the determination of costs or expenses by an officer of the court.

SECTION 1: Recognition

Article 33

1. A judgment given in a Member State shall be recognised in the other Member States without any special procedure being required.

2. Any interested party who raises the recognition of a judgment as the principal issue in a dispute may, in accordance with the procedures provided for in Sections 2 and 3 of this Chapter, apply for a decision that the judgment be recognised.

3. If the outcome of proceedings in a court of a Member State depends on the determination of an incidental question of recognition that court shall have jurisdiction over that question.

Article 34

A judgment shall not be recognised:

1. if such recognition is manifestly contrary to public policy in the Member State in which recognition is sought;

2. where it was given in default of appearance, if the defendant was not served with the document which instituted the proceedings or with an equivalent document in sufficient time and in such a way as to enable him to arrange for his defence, unless the defendant failed to commence proceedings to challenge the judgment when it was possible for him to do so;

3. if it is irreconcilable with a judgment given in a dispute between the same parties in the Member State in which recognition is sought;

4. if it is irreconcilable with an earlier judgment given in another Member State or in a third State involving the same cause of action and between the same parties provided that the earlier judgment fulfils the conditions necessary for its recognition in the Member State addressed.

Article 35

1. Moreover, a judgment shall not be recognised if it conflicts with Sections 3, 4 or 6 of Chapter II, or in a case provided for in Article 72.

2. In its examination of the grounds of jurisdiction referred to in the foregoing paragraph, the court of authority applied to shall be bound by the findings of fact on which the court of the Member State of origin based its jurisdiction.

3. Subject to the paragraph 1, the jurisdiction of the court of the Member State of origin may not be reviewed. The test of public policy referred to in point 1 of Article 34 may not be applied to the rules relating to jurisdiction.

Article 36

Under no circumstances may a foreign judgment be reviewed as to its substance.

Article 37

1. A court of a Member State in which recognition is sought of a judgment given in another Member State may stay the proceedings if an ordinary appeal against the judgment has been lodged.

2. A court of a Member State in which recognition is sought of a judgment given in Ireland or the United Kingdom may stay the proceedings if enforcement is suspended in the State of origin, by reason of an appeal.

SECTION 2: Enforcement

Article 38

1. A judgment given in a Member State and enforceable in that State shall be enforced in another Member State when, on the application of any interested party, it has been declared enforceable there.

2. However, in the United Kingdom, such a judgment shall be enforced in England and Wales, in Scotland, or in Northern Ireland when, on the application of any interested party, it has been registered for enforcement in that part of the United Kingdom.

Article 39

1. The application shall be submitted to the court or competent authority indicated in the list in Annex II.

2. The local jurisdiction shall be determined by reference to the place of domicile of the party against whom enforcement is sought, or to the place of enforcement.

Article 40

1. The procedure for making the application shall be governed by the law of the Member State in which enforcement is sought.

2. The applicant must give an address for service of process within the area of jurisdiction of the court applied to. However, if the law of the Member State in which enforcement is sought does not provide for the furnishing of such an address, the application shall appoint a representative *ad litem*.

3. The documents referred to in Article 53 shall be attached to the application.

Article 41

The judgment shall be declared enforceable immediately on completion of the formalities in Article 53 without any review under Articles 34 and 35. The party against whom enforcement is sought shall not at this stage of the proceedings be entitled to make any submissions on the application.

Article 42

1. The decision on the application for a declaration of enforceability shall forthwith be brought to the notice of the applicant in accordance with the procedure laid down by the law of the Member State in which enforcement is sought.

2. The declaration of enforceability shall be served on the party against whom enforcement is sought, accompanied by the judgment, if not already served on that party.

Article 43

1. The decision on the application for a declaration of enforceability may be appealed against by either party.

2. The appeal is to be lodged with the court indicated in the list in Annex III.

3. The appeal shall be dealt with in accordance with the rules governing procedure in contradictory matters.

4. If the party against whom enforcement is sought fails to appear before the appellate court in proceedings concerning an appeal brought by the applicant, Article 26(2) to (4) shall apply even where the party against whom enforcement is sought is not domiciled in any of the Member States.

5. An appeal against the declaration of enforceability is to be lodged within one month of service thereof. If the party against whom enforcement is sought is domiciled in a Member State other than that in which the declaration of enforceability was given, the time for appealing shall be two months and shall run from the date of service, either on him in person or at his residence. No extension of time may be granted on account of distance.

Article 44

The judgment given on the appeal may be contested only by the appeal referred to in Annex IV.

Article 45

1. The court with which an appeal is lodged under Article 43 or Article 44 shall refuse or revoke a declaration of enforceability only on one of the grounds specified in Articles 34 and 35. It shall give its decision without delay.

2. Under no circumstances may the foreign judgment be reviewed as to its substance.

Article 46

1. The court with which an appeal is lodged under Article 43 or Article 44 may, on the application of the party against whom enforcement is sought, stay the proceedings if an ordinary appeal has been

lodged against the judgment in the Member State of origin or if the time for such an appeal has not yet expired; in the latter case, the court may specify the time within which such an appeal is to be lodged.

2. Where the judgment was given in Ireland or the United Kingdom, any form of appeal available in the Member State of origin shall be treated as an ordinary appeal for the purposes of paragraph 1.

3. The court may also make enforcement conditional on the provision of such security as it shall determine.

Article 47

1. When a judgment must be recognised in accordance with this Regulation, nothing shall prevent the applicant from availing himself of provisional, including protective, measures in accordance with the law of the Member State requested without a declaration of enforceability under Article 41 being required.

2. The declaration of enforceability shall carry with it the power to proceed to any protective measures.

3. During the time specified for an appeal pursuant to Article 43(5) against the declaration of enforceability and until any such appeal has been determined, no measures of enforcement may be taken other than protective measures against the property of the party against whom enforcement is sought.

Article 48

1. Where a foreign judgment has been given in respect of several matters and the declaration of enforceability cannot be given for all of them, the court or competent authority shall give it for one or more of them.

2. An applicant may request a declaration of enforceability limited to parts of a judgment.

Article 49

A foreign judgment which orders a periodic payment by way of a penalty shall be enforceable in the Member State in which enforcement is sought only if the amount of the payment has been finally determined by the courts of the Member State of origin.

Article 50

An applicant who, in the Member State of origin has benefited from complete or partial legal aid or exemption from costs or expenses, shall be entitled, in the procedure provided for in this Section, to benefit from the most favourable legal aid or the most extensive exemption from costs or expenses provided for by the law of the Member State addressed.

Article 51

No security, bond or deposit, however described, shall be required of a party who in one Member State applies for enforcement of a judgment given in another Member State on the ground that he is a foreign national or that he is not domiciled or resident in the State in which enforcement is sought.

Article 52

In proceedings for the issue of a declaration of enforceability, no charge, duty or fee calculated by reference to the value of the matter at issue may be levied in the Member State in which enforcement is sought.

SECTION 3: Common provisions

Article 53

1. A party seeking recognition or applying for a declaration of enforceability shall produce a copy of the judgment which satisfies the conditions necessary to establish its authenticity.

2. A party applying for a declaration of enforceability shall also produce the certificate referred to in Article 54, without prejudice to Article 55.

Article 54

The court or competent authority of a Member State where a judgment was given shall issue, at the request of any interested party, a certificate using the standard form in Annex V to this Regulation.

Article 55

1. If the certificate referred to in Article 54 is not produced, the court or competent authority may specify a time for its production or accept an equivalent document or, if it considers that it has sufficient information before it, dispense with its production.

2. If the court or competent authority so requires, a translation of the document shall be produced. The translation shall be certified by a person qualified to do so in one of the Member States.

Article 56

No legalisation or other similar formality shall be required in respect of the documents referred to in Article 53 or Article 55(2), or in respect of a document appointing a representative *ad litem*.

CHAPTER IV: AUTHENTIC INSTRUMENTS AND COURT SETTLEMENTS

Article 57

1. A document which has been formally drawn up or registered as an authentic instrument and is enforceable in one Member State shall, in another Member State, be declared enforceable there, on application made in accordance with the procedures provided for in Articles 38, *et seq*. The court with which an appeal is lodged under Article 43 or Article 44 shall refuse or revoke a declaration of enforceability only if enforcement of the instrument is manifestly contrary to public policy in the Member State addressed.

2. Arrangements relating to maintenance obligations concluded with administrative authorities or authenticated by them shall also be regarded as authentic instruments within the meaning of paragraph 1.

3. The instrument produced must satisfy the conditions necessary to establish its authenticity in the Member State of origin.

4. Section 3 of Chapter III shall apply as appropriate. The competent authority of a Member State where an authentic instrument was drawn up or registered shall issue, at the request of any interested party, certificate using the standard form in Annex VI to this Regulation.

Article 58

A settlement which has been approved by a court in the course of proceedings and is enforceable in the Member State in which it was concluded shall be enforceable in the State addressed under the same conditions as authentic instruments. The court or competent authority of a Member State where a court settlement was approved shall issue, at the request of any interested part, a certificate using the standard form in Annex V to this Regulation.

CHAPTER V: GENERAL PROVISIONS

Article 59

1. In order to determine whether a party is domiciled in the Member State whose courts are seised of a matter, the court shall apply its internal law.

2. If a party is not domiciled in the Member State whose courts are seised of the matter, then, in order to determine whether the party is domiciled in another Member State, the court shall apply the law of that Member State.

Article 60

1. For the purposes of this Regulation, a company or other legal person or association of natural or legal persons is domiciled at the place where it has its:
    (a)   statutory seat, or
    (b)   central administration, or
    (c)   principal place of business.

2. For the purposes of the United Kingdom and Ireland 'statutory seat' means the registered office or, where there is no such office anywhere, the place of incorporation or, where there is no such place anywhere, the place under the law of which the formation took place.

3. In order to determine whether a trust is domiciled in the Member State whose courts are seised of the matter, the court shall apply its rules of private international law.

Article 61

Without prejudice to any more favourable provisions of national laws, persons domiciled in a Member State who are being prosecuted in the criminal courts of another Member State of which they are not nationals for an offence which was not intentionally committed may be defended by persons qualified to do so, even if they do not appear in person. However, the court seised of the matter may order appearance in person; in the case of failure to appear, a judgment given in the civil action without the person concerned having had the opportunity to arrange for his defence need not be recognised or enforced in the other Member States.

Article 62

In Sweden, in summary proceedings concerning orders to pay (*betalningsföreläggande*) and assistance (*handräckning*), the expression 'court' includes the 'Swedish enforcement service' (*kronofogdemyndighet*).

Article 63

(*Ceased to have effect on 1 March 2008*)

Article 64

(*Ceased to have effect on 1 March 2008*)

Article 65

1. The jurisdiction specified in Article 6(2), and Article 11 in actions on a warranty of guarantee or in any other third party proceedings may not be resorted to in Germany, Austria, and Hungary. Any person domiciled in another Member State may be sued in the courts:

    (a) of Germany, pursuant to Articles 68 and 72 to 74 of the Code of Civil Procedure (*Zivilprozessordnung*) concerning third-party notices,

    (b) of Austria, pursuant to Article 21 of the Code of Civil Procedure (*Zivilprozessordnung*) concerning third-party notices.

    (c) of Hungary, pursuant to Article 58 to 60 of the Code of Civil Procedure (*Polgári perrendtartás*) concerning third-party notices.

2. Judgments given in other Member States by virtue of Article 6(2), or Article 11 shall be recognised and enforced in Germany and Austria in accordance with Chapter III. Any effects which judgments given in these States may have on third parties by application of the provisions in paragraph 1 shall also be recognised in the other Member States.

CHAPTER VI: TRANSITIONAL PROVISIONS

Article 66

1. This Regulation shall apply only to legal proceedings instituted and to documents formally drawn up or registered as authentic instruments after the entry into force thereof.

2. However, if the proceedings in the Member State of origin were instituted before the entry into force of this Regulation, judgments given after that date shall be recognised and enforced in accordance with Chapter III,

    (a) if the proceedings in the Member State of origin were instituted after the entry into force of the Brussels or the Lugano Convention both in the Member State or origin and in the Member State addressed;

    (b) in all other cases, if jurisdiction was founded upon rules which accorded with those provided for either in Chapter II or in a convention concluded between the Member State of origin and the Member State addressed which was in force when the proceedings were instituted.

CHAPTER VII: RELATIONS WITH OTHER INSTRUMENTS

Article 67

This Regulation shall not prejudice the application of provisions governing jurisdiction and the recognition and enforcement of judgments in specific matters which are contained in Community instruments or in national legislation harmonised pursuant to such instruments.

Article 68

1. This Regulation shall, as between the Member States, supersede the Brussels Convention, except as regards the territories of the Member States which fall within the territorial scope of that Convention and which are excluded from this Regulation pursuant to Article 299 of the Treaty.

2. In so far as this Regulation replaces the provisions of the Brussels Convention between Member States, any reference to the Convention shall be understood as a reference to this Regulation.

Article 69

Subject to Article 66(2) and Article 70, this Regulation shall, as between Member States, supersede the following conventions and treaty concluded between two or more of them (*list not reproduced save to show Conventions to which the United Kingdom is party*):

— The Convention between the United Kingdom and the French Republic providing for the reciprocal enforcement of judgments in civil and commercial matters, with Protocol, signed at Paris on 18 January 1934,
— The Convention between the United Kingdom and the Kingdom of Belgium providing for the reciprocal enforcement of judgments in civil and commercial matters, with Protocol, signed at Brussels on 2 May 1934,
— The Convention between the United Kingdom and the Federal Republic of Germany providing for the reciprocal recognition and enforcement of judgments in civil and commercial matters, signed at Bonn on 14 July 1960,
— The Convention between the United Kingdom and Austria providing for the reciprocal recognition and enforcement of judgments in civil and commercial matters, signed at Vienna on 14 July 1961, with amending Protocol signed at London on 6 March 1970,
— The Convention between the United Kingdom and the Republic of Italy providing for the reciprocal recognition and enforcement of judgments in civil and commercial matters, signed at Rome on 7 February 1964, with amending Protocol signed at Rome on 14 July 1970,
— The Convention between the United Kingdom and the Kingdom of the Netherlands providing for the reciprocal recognition and enforcement of judgments in civil and commercial matters, signed at The Hague on 17 November 1967.

Article 70

1. The Treaty and the Conventions referred to in Article 69 shall continue to have effect in relation to matters to which this Regulation does not apply.
2. They shall continue to have effect in respect of judgments given and documents formally drawn up or registered as authentic instruments before the entry into force of this Regulation.

Article 71

1. This Regulation shall not affect any conventions to which the Member States are parties and which in relation to particular matters, govern jurisdiction or the recognition or enforcement of judgments.
2. With a view to its uniform interpretation, paragraph 1 shall be applied in the following manner:
   (a) this Regulation shall not prevent a court of a Member State, which is a party to a convention on a particular matter, from assuming jurisdiction in accordance with that convention, even where the defendant is domiciled in another Member State which is not a party to that convention. The court hearing the action shall, in any event, apply Article 26 of this Regulation;
   (b) judgments given in a Member State by a court in the exercise of jurisdiction provided for in a convention on a particular matter shall be recognised and enforced in the other Member States in accordance with this Regulation.

Where a convention on a particular matter to which both the Member State of origin and the Member State addressed are parties lays down conditions for the recognition or enforcement of judgments, those conditions shall apply. In any event, the provisions of this Regulation which concern the procedure for recognition and enforcement of judgments may be applied.

Article 72

This Regulation shall not affect agreements by which Member States undertook, prior to the entry into force of this Regulation pursuant to Article 59 of the Brussels Convention, not to recognise judgments given, in particular in other Contracting States to that Convention, against defendants domiciled or habitually resident in a third country where, in cases provided for in Article 4 of that Convention, the judgment could only be founded on a ground of jurisdiction specified in the second paragraph of Article 3 of that Convention.

CHAPTER VIII: FINAL PROVISIONS

Article 73

No later than five years after the entry into force of this Regulation, the Commission shall present to the European Parliament, the Council and the Economic and Social Committee a report on the application of this Regulation. The report shall be accompanied, if need be, by proposals for adaptations to this Regulation.

Article 74

1. The Member States shall notify the Commission of the texts amending the lists set out in Annexes I to IV. The Commission shall adapt the Annexes concerned accordingly.

2. The updating or technical adjustment of the forms, specimens of which appear in Annexes V and VI, shall be adopted in accordance with the advisory procedure referred to in Article 75(2).

Article 75

1. The Commission shall be assisted by a committee.

2. Where reference is made to this paragraph, Articles 3 and 7 of Decision 1999/468/EC shall apply.

3. The Committee shall adopt its rules of procedure.

Article 76

This Regulation shall enter into force on 1 March 2002.

This Regulation is binding in its entirety and directly applicable in the Member States in accordance with the Treaty establishing the European Community.

Done at Brussels, 22 December 2000.

ANNEX I

The rules of jurisdiction referred to in Article 3(2) and Article 4(2) are the following (*list not reproduced save to show rules of law for courts outside the United Kingdom*):

— in the United Kingdom: rules which enable jurisdiction to be founded on:

(a) the document instituting the proceedings having been served on the defendant during his temporary presence in the United Kingdom; or

(b) the presence within the United Kingdom of property belonging to the defendant; or

(c) the seizure by the plaintiff of property situated in the United Kingdom.

ANNEX II

The courts or competent authorities to which the application referred to in Article 39 may be submitted are the following (*list not reproduced save to show rules of law from the United Kingdom*):
— in the United Kingdom:
  (a) in England and Wales, the High Court of Justice, or in the case of a maintenance judgment, the Magistrates' Court on transmission by the Secretary of State;
  (b) in Scotland, the Court of Session, or in the case of a maintenance judgment, the Sheriff Court of transmission by the Secretary of State;
  (c) in Northern Ireland, the High Court of Justice, or in the case of a maintenance judgment, the Magistrates' Court on transmission by the Secretary of State;
  (d) in Gibraltar, the Supreme Court of Gibraltar, or in the case of a maintenance judgment, the Magistrates' Court on transmission by the Attorney General of Gibraltar.

ANNEX III

The courts with which appeals referred to in Article 43(2) may be lodged are the following (*list not reproduced save to show rules of law from the United Kingdom*):
— in the United Kingdom:
  (a) in England and Wales, the High Court of Justice, or in the case of a maintenance judgment, the Magistrates' Court;
  (b) in Scotland, the Court of Session, or in the case of a maintenance judgment, the Sheriff Court;
  (c) in Northern Ireland, the High Court of Justice, or in the case of a maintenance judgment, the Magistrates' Court;
  (d) in Gibraltar, the Supreme Court of Gibraltar, or in the case of a maintenance judgment, the Magistrates' Court.

ANNEX IV

The appeals which may be lodged pursuant to Article 44 are the following (*list not reproduced save to show rules of law from the United Kingdom*):
— in the United Kingdom, a single further appeal on a point of law.

ANNEX V

Certificate referred to in Articles 54 and 58 of the Regulation on judgments and court settlements

(English, inglés, anglais, inglese, ...)

1. Member of State of origin
2. Court or competent authority issuing the certificate
   2.1. Name
   2.2. Address
   2.3. Tel./fax/e-mail
3. Court which delivered the judgment/approved the court settlement (*)
   3.1. Type of court
   3.2. Place of court
4. Judgment/court settlement (*)
   4.1. Date
   4.2. Reference number

4.3. The parties to the judgment/court settlement (*)

    4.3.1. Name(s) of plaintiff(s)

    4.3.2. Name(s) of defendant(s)

    4.3.3. Name(s) of other party(ies), if any

4.4. Date of service of the document instituting the proceedings where judgment was given in default of appearance

4.5. Text of the judgment/court settlement (*) as annexed to this certificate

5. Names of parties to whom legal aid has been granted

The judgment/court settlement (*) is enforceable in the Member State of origin (Articles 38 and 58 of the Regulation) against:

Name:

Done at ,,   date

Signature and/or stamp

(*) Delete as appropriate.

ANNEX VI

Certificate referred to in Article 57(4) of the Regulation on authentic instruments

(English, inglés, anglais, inglese... ... ...)

1. Member state of origin
2. Competent authority issuing the certificate

    2.1. Name

    2.2. Address

    2.3. Tel./fax/e-mail

3. Authority which has given authenticity to the instrument

    3.1. Authority involved in the drawing up of the authentic instrument (if applicable)

        3.1.1. Name and designation of authority

        3.1.2. Place of authority

    3.2. Authority which has registered the authentic instrument (if applicable)

        3.2.1. Type of authority

        3.2.2. Place of authority

4. Authentic instrument

    4.1. Description of the instrument

    4.2. Date

        4.2.1. on which the instrument was drawn up

        4.2.2. if different: on which the instrument was registered

    4.3. Reference number

    4.4 Parties to the instrument

        4.4.1. Name of the creditor

        4.4.2. Name of the debtor

5. Text of the enforceable obligation as annexed to this certificate

The authentic instrument is enforceable against the debtor in the Member State of origin (Article 57(1) of the Regulation)

Done at ,   date

Signature and/or stamp

APPENDIX 3

List of Decisions of the European Court

In the list of cases printed here, the Articles referred to in the right-hand column are those of the recast Brussels I Regulation 1215/2012. In a number of cases the decision of the European Court will have been on a provision which is not precisely reproduced in that Regulation; indeed (and as can be seen from the Table of Correlation printed in Regulation 1215/2012 as Annex III, in a number of cases, particularly those concerned with enforcement and objections to enforcement, the provision interpreted by the Court has no direct counterpart in Regulation 1215/2012. Where this is the case, the reference given is to the nearest counterpart provision of Regulation 1215/2012.

As many of these decisions were given on the basis of the Brussels Convention, an unofficial Table of Correlation of Brussels Convention to Regulation 44/2001 will be found printed after the official Table of Correlation of Regulation 44/2001 to Regulation 1215/2012.

Seq:	Case:	Parties:	Report:	Neutral ref	Reg 1215/2012, Article
1	12/76	*Tessili v. Dunlop*	[1976] ECR 1473	EU:C:1976:133	7(1)(a)
2	14/76	*De Bloos v. Bouyer*	[1976] ECR 1497	EU:C:1976:134	7(1), 7(5)
3	29/76	*LTU v. Eurocontrol*	[1976] ECR 1541	EU:C:1976:137	1
4	21/76	*Bier v. Mines de Potasse*	[1976] ECR 1735	EU:C:1976:166	7(2)
5	42/76	*De Wolf v. Cox*	[1976] ECR 1759	EU:C:1976:168	39
6	24/76	*Salotti v. RÜWA*	[1976] ECR 1831	EU:C:1976:177	25(1)
7	25/76	*Segoura v. Bonakdarian*	[1976] ECR 1851	EU:C:1976:178	25(1)
8	9/77	*Bavaria Flug v. Eurocontrol*	[1977] ECR 1517	EU:C:1977:132	70
9	43/77	*Industrial Diamond v. Riva*	[1977] ECR 2175	EU:C:1977:188	35, 38
10	73/77	*Saunders v. Van der Putte*	[1977] ECR 2382	EU:C:1977:208	24(1)
11	150/77	*Bertrand v. Ott*	[1978] ECR 1431	EU:C:1978:137	17
12	23/78	*Meeth v. Glacetal*	[1978] ECR 2183	EU:C:1978:198	25(1)
13	33/78	*Somafer v. Saar-Ferngas*	[1978] ECR 2133	EU:C:1978:205	7(5)
14	133/78	*Gourdain v. Nadler*	[1979] ECR 733	EU:C:1979:49	1(2)(b)
15	143/78	*De Cavel v. De Cavel* (I)	[1979] ECR 1055	EU:C:1979:83	1, 35
16	25/79	*Sanicentral v. Collin*	[1979] ECR 3423	EU:C:1979:255	25
17	56/79	*Zelger v. Salinitri* (I)	[1980] ECR 89	EU:C:1980:15	7(1)(a)
18	120/79	*De Cavel v. De Cavel* (II)	[1980] ECR 731	EU:C:1980:70	35
19	784/79	*Porta-Leasing v. Prestige*	[1980] ECR 1517	EU:C:1980:123	2
20	125/79	*Denilauler v. Couchet Frères*	[1980] ECR 1553	EU:C:1980:130	2(a), 45(1)(b)
21	814/79	*Netherlands v. Rüffer*	[1980] ECR 3807	EU:C:1980:291	1
22	139/80	*Blanckaert & Willems*	[1981] ECR 819	EU:C:1981:70	7(5)
23	157/80	*Re Rinkau*	[1981] ECR 1391	EU:C:1981:120	64

---

2 Annexed Protocol to the Brussels Convention relating to Luxembourg defendants: now irrelevant.

24	166/80	*Klomps v. Michel*	[1981] ECR 1593	EU:C:1981:137	45(1)(b)
25	150/80	*Elefanten Schuh v. Jacqmain*	[1981] ECR 1671	EU:C:1981:148	25, 26, 30
26	27/81	*Rohr v. Ossberger*	[1981] ECR 2431	EU:C:1981:243	26
27	38/81	*Effer v. Kantner*	[1982] ECR 825	EU:C:1982:79	7(1)(a)
28	25/81	*CHW v. CJH*	[1982] ECR 1189	EU:C:1982:116	1, 26, 35
29	133/81	*Ivenel v. Schwab*	[1982] ECR 1891	EU:C:1982:199	7(1)
30	228/81	*Pendy Plastic v. Pluspunkt*	[1982] ECR 2723	EU:C:1982:276	28, 45(1)(b)
31	34/82	*Martin Peters v. ZNAV*	[1983] ECR 987	EU:C:1983:87	7(1)
32	201/82	*Gerling v. Italian Treasury*	[1983] ECR 2503	EU:C:1983:217	25, 26
33	80/83	*Habourdin v. Italocrema*	[1983] ECR 3639	EU:C:1983:321	[inadmissible]
34	288/82	*Duijnstee v. Goderbauer*	[1983] ECR 3663	EU:C:1983:326	24(4), 27
35	56/84	*Von Gallera v. Maitre*	[1984] ECR 1769	EU:C:1984:136	[inadmissible]
36	129/83	*Zelger v. Salinitri (II)*	[1984] ECR 2397	EU:C:1984:215	29, 32
37	71/83	*The Tilly Russ*	[1984] ECR 2417	EU:C:1984:217	25
38	178/83	*P v. K*	[1984] ECR 3033	EU:C:1984:272	49
39	258/83	*Brennero v. Wendel*	[1984] ECR 3971	EU:C:1984:363	44
40	241/83	*Rösler v. Rottwinkel*	[1985] ECR 99	EU:C:1985:6	24(1)
41	48/84	*Spitzley v. Sommer*	[1985] ECR 787	EU:C:1985:105	25, 26
42	49/84	*Debaecker v. Bouwman*	[1985] ECR 1779	EU:C:1985:252	45(1)
43	148/84	*G'bank v. B du Pêcheur*	[1985] ECR 1981	EU:C:1985:280	45, 46
44	220/84	*AS-Autoteile v. Malhé*	[1985] ECR 2267	EU:C:1985:302	24(5)
45	221/84	*Berghofer v. ASA*	[1985] ECR 2699	EU:C:1985:337	25
46	119/84	*Capelloni v. Pelkmans*	[1985] ECR 3147	EU:C:1985:388	44
47	22/85	*Anterist v. Credit Lyonnais*	[1986] ECR 1951	EU:C:1986:255	25
48	198/85	*Carron v. Germany*	[1986] ECR 2437	EU:C:1986:313	37, 41
49	313/85	*Iveco Fiat v. Van Hool*	[1986] ECR 3337	EU:C:1986:423	25
50	266/85	*Shenavai v. Kreischer*	[1987] ECR 239	EU:C:1987:11	7(1)(a)
51	144/86	*Gubisch v. Palumbo*	[1987] ECR 4861	EU:C:1987:528	29
52	218/86	*Schotte v. Rothschild*	[1987] ECR 4905	EU:C:1987:536	7(5)
53	145/86	*Hoffmann v. Krieg*	[1988] ECR 645	EU:C:1988:61	1, 36, 45(1)
54	9/87	*Arcado v. Haviland*	[1988] ECR 1539	EU:C:1988:127	7(1)
55	158/87	*Scherrens v. Maenhout*	[1988] ECR 3791	EU:C:1988:370	24(1)
56	189/87	*Kalfelis v. Schröder*	[1988] ECR 5565	EU:C:1988:459	7(2), 8(1)
57	32/88	*Six v. Humbert*	[1989] ECR 341	EU:C:1989:68	7(1)

(from this point, case references are properly C-(no/year), and ECR references are [year] ECR I-(page)

58	115/88	*Reichert v. Dresdner (I)*	[1990] ECR 27	EU:C:1990:3	24(1)
59	220/88	*Dumez France v. HELABA*	[1990] ECR 49	EU:C:1990:8	7(2)
60	365/88	*Hagen v. Zeehaghe*	[1990] ECR 1845	EU:C:1990:203	8(2)
61	305/88	*Lancray v. Peters & Sickert*	[1990] ECR 2725	EU:C:1990:275	45(1)(b)
62	351/89	*Overseas Union v. NHI*	[1991] ECR 3317	EU:C:1991:279	6, 29
63	190/89	*Marc Rich v. Impianti*	[1991] ECR 3855	EU:C:1991:319	1(2)(d)
64	183/90	*Van Dalfsen v. Van Loon*	[1991] ECR 4743	EU:C:1991:379	44, 45
65	280/90	*Hacker v. Euro-Relais*	[1992] ECR 1111	EU:C:1992:92	24(1)
66	214/89	*Powell Duffryn v. Petereit*	[1992] ECR 1745	EU:C:1992:115	25
67	261/90	*Reichert v. Dresdner (II)*	[1992] ECR 2149	EU:C:1992:149	7(2), 24(5), 35
68	26/91	*Jakob Handte v. TMCS*	[1992] ECR 3697	EU:C:1992:268	7(1)
69	123/91	*Minalmet v. Brandeis*	[1992] ECR 5661	EU:C:1992:432	45(1)(b)
70	89/91	*Shearson Lehmann v. TVB*	[1993] ECR 139	EU:C:1993:15	17
71	172/91	*Sonntag v. Waidmann*	[1993] ECR 1963	EU:C:1993:144	1, 7(3), 45(1)(b)
72	125/92	*Mulox IBC v. Geels*	[1993] ECR 4075	EU:C:1993:306	7(1)(a)

73	129/92	*Owens Bank Ltd v. Bracco*	[1994] ECR 117	EU:C:1994:13	1
74	294/92	*Webb v. Webb*	[1994] ECR 1717	EU:C:1994:193	24(1)
75	414/92	*Solo Kleinmotoren v. Boch*	[1994] ECR 2237	EU:C:1994:221	45(1)(c), 59, 60
76	292/93	*Lieber v. Gobel*	[1994] ECR 2535	EU:C:1994:241	24(1)
77	288/92	*Custom Made v. Stawa*	[1994] ECR 2913	EU:C:1994:268	7(1)(a), 25
78	318/93	*Brenner & Noller*	[1994] ECR 4275	EU:C:1994:331	17, 18
79	406/92	*The Tatry*	[1994] ECR 5439	EU:C:1994:400	29, 30, 71
80	68/93	*Shevill v. Presse Alliance SA*	[1995] ECR 415	EU:C:1995:61	7(2)
81	346/93	*Kleinwort Benson v. G'gow*	[1995] ECR 615	EU:C:1995:85	[inadmissible]
82	439/93	*Lloyd's Register v. Bernard*	[1995] ECR 961	EU:C:1995:104	7(5)
83	341/93	*Danvaern v. Otterbeck*	[1995] ECR 2053	EU:C:1995:239	8(3)
84	474/93	*Hengst Import v. Campese*	[1995] ECR 2113	EU:C:1995:243	45(1)(b)
85	432/93	*SISRO v. Ampersand*	[1995] ECR 2269	EU:C:1995:262	44, 49
86	364/93	*Marinari v. Lloyd's Bank*	[1995] ECR 2719	EU:C:1995:289	7(2)
87	275/94	*Van der Linden v. BFE*	[1996] ECR 1393	EU:C:1996:101	42
88	78/95	*Hendrickman v. Magenta*	[1996] ECR 4943	EU:C:1996:380	45(1)(b)
89	383/95	*Rutten v. Cross Medical Ltd*	[1997] ECR 57	EU:C:1997:7	7(1)(a)
90	106/95	*MSG v. Les Gravières*	[1997] ECR 911	EU:C:1997:70	7(1), 25
91	220/95	*V d Boogaard v. Laumen*	[1997] ECR 1147	EU:C:1997:91	1
92	295/95	*Farrell v. Long*	[1997] ECR 1683	EU:C:1997:168	[maintenance]
93	269/95	*Benincasa v. Dentalkit*	[1997] ECR 3767	EU:C:1997:337	17, 25
94	163/95	*Van Horn v. Cinnamond*	[1997] ECR 5451	EU:C:1997:472	29, 66
95	351/96	*Drouot v. CMI*	[1998] ECR 3075	EU:C:1998:242	29
96	51/97	*Réunion Européenne*	[1998] ECR 6511	EU:C:1998:509	7(1), 7(2), 8(1)
97	391/95	*Van Uden v. Deco-Line*	[1998] ECR 7091	EU:C:1998:543	1, 35
98	159/97	*Castelletti v. Hugo Trumpy*	[1999] ECR 1597	EU:C:1999:142	25
99	99/96	*Mietz v. Intership Yachting*	[1999] ECR 2277	EU:C:1999:202	17, 35
100	267/97	*Coursier v. Fortis Bank*	[1999] ECR 2843	EU:C:1999:213	39, 42
101	260/97	*Unibank v. Christensen*	[1999] ECR 3715	EU:C:1999:312	58
102	440/97	*Groupe Concorde*	[1999] ECR 6307	EU:C:1999:456	7(1)(a)
103	420/97	*Leathertex v. Bodetex*	[1999] ECR 6747	EU:C:1999:483	7(1)(a)
104	8/98	*Dansommer v. Götz*	[2000] ECR 393	EU:C:2000:45	24(1)
105	7/98	*Krombach v. Bamberski*	[2000] ECR 1935	EU:C:2000:164	45(1)(a)
106	38/98	*Renault v. Maxicar*	[2000] ECR 2973	EU:C:2000:225	45(1)(a)
107	412/98	*UGIC v. Groupe Josi*	[2000] ECR 5925	EU:C:2000:399	1, 10–16
108	387/98	*Coreck Maritime GmbH*	[2000] ECR 9337	EU:C:2000:606	25
109	518/99	*Gaillard v. Chekili*	[2001] ECR 2771	EU:C:2001:209	24(1)
110	256/00	*Besix SA v. WABAG*	[2002] ECR 1699	EU:C:2002:99	7(1)(a)
111	37/00	*Weber v. UOS*	[2002] ECR 2013	EU:C:2002:122	7(1)(a), 21
112	24/02	*Marseille Fret v. Seatrano*	[2002] ECR 3383	EU:C:2002:220	[inadmissible]
113	69/02	*Reichling v. Wampach*	[2002] ECR 3393	EU:C:2002:221	[inadmissible]
114	80/00	*Italian Leather v. WECO*	[2002] ECR 4995	EU:C:2002:342	29, 35
115	96/00	*Gabriel v. Schlank & Schick*	[2002] ECR 6367	EU:C:2002:436	7(1), 7(2)
116	334/00	*Tacconi v. HWS*	[2002] ECR 7357	EU:C:2002:499	7(1), 7(2)
117	167/00	*VfK v. Henkel*	[2002] ECR 8111	EU:C:2002:555	1, 17, 7(1), 7(2)
118	271/00	*Steenbergen v. Baten*	[2002] ECR 10489	EU:C:2002:656	1
119	437/00	*Pugliese v. Finmeccaniche*	[2003] ECR 3573	EU:C:2003:219	7(1), 21
120	111/01	*Gantner v. Basch*	[2003] ECR 4207	EU:C:2003:257	29
121	266/01	*TIARD v. Netherlands*	[2003] ECR 4867	EU:C:2003:282	1
122	116/02	*Erich Gasser v. MISAT*	[2003] ECR 14693	EU:C:2003:657	25, 29

123	433/01	*Bayern v. Blijdenstein*	[2004] ECR 981	EU:C:2004:21	1
124	18/02	*DFDS Torline v. SEKO*	[2004] ECR 1417	EU:C:2004:74	7(2)
125	265/02	*Frahuil v. Assitalia*	[2004] ECR 1543	EU:C:2004:77	1, 7(1)
126	159/02	*Turner v. Grovit*	[2004] ECR 3565	EU:C:2004:228	[general scheme]
127	168/02	*Kronhofer v. Maier*	[2004] ECR 6009	EU:C:2004:364	7(2)
128	555/03	*Warbecq v. Ryanair*	[2004] ECR 6041	EU:C:2004:370	[inadmissible]
129	39/02	*Mærsk Olie v. de Haan*	[2004] ECR 9657	EU:C:2004:615	29, 45(1)(b)
130	148/03	*Nürnberger v. Portbridge*	[2004] ECR 10327	EU:C:2004:677	22, 71
131	464/01	*Gruber v. Bay Wa*	[2005] ECR 439	EU:C:2005:32	17
132	27/02	*Engler v. Janus*	[2005] ECR 481	EU:C:2005:33	7(1), 7(2), 17
133	281/02	*Owusu v. Jackson*	[2005] ECR 1383	EU:C:2005:120	[general scheme]
134	104/03	*St Paul Dairy v. Unibel*	[2005] ECR 3481	EU:C:2005:255	35
135	112/03	*Peloux v. AXA*	[2005] ECR 3707	EU:C:2005:280	15
136	77/04	*Reunion v. Zurich*	[2005] ECR 4509	EU:C:2005:327	8(2)
137	522/03	*Scania Finance v. Rockinger*	[2005] ECR 8639	EU:C:2005:606	45(1)(b)
138	73/04	*Klein v. Rhodos*	[2005] ECR 8667	EU:C:2005:607	22(1)
139	3/05	*Verdoliva v. V d Hoeven*	[2006] ECR 1579	EU:C:2006:113	43
140	234/04	*Kapferer v. Schlank*	[2006] ECR 2585	EU:C:2006:178	17
141	343/04	*Land Oberösterreich v. ČEZ*	[2006] ECR 4557	EU:C:2006:330	24(1)
142	4/03	*GAT v. LuK*	[2006] ECR 6509	EU:C:2006:457	24(4)
143	539/03	*Roche Nederland v. Primus*	[2006] ECR 6535	EU:C:2006:458	8(1)
144	103/05	*Reisch Montage v. Kiesel*	[2006] ECR 6827	EU:C:2006:471	8(1)
145	283/05	*ASML v. SEMIS*	[2006] ECR 12041	EU:C:2006:787	45(1)(b)
146	292/05	*Lechouritou v. Germany*	[2007] ECR 1519	EU:C:2007:102	1
147	386/05	*Color Drack v. Lexx Int'l*	[2007] ECR 3699	EU:C:2007:262	7(1)(b)
148	98/06	*Freeport v. Arnoldsson*	[2007] ECR 8319	EU:C:2007:595	8(1)
149	463/06	*FBTO v. Odenbreit*	[2007] ECR 11321	EU:C:2007:792	13(2)
150	14/07	*Weiss v. Handelskammer*	[2008] ECR 3367	EU:C:2008:264	45(1)(b)
151	462/06	*GlaxoSmithKlein v. Rouard*	[2008] ECR 3965	EU:C:2008:299	8(1), 20–22
152	372/07	*Hassett v. SE Health Board*	[2008] ECR 7403	EU:C:2008:534	24(2)
153	185/07	*Allianz v. West Tankers Inc*	[2009] ECR 663	EU:C:2009:69	1(2)(d)
154	339/07	*Seagon v. Deko Marty*	[2009] ECR 767	EU:C:2009:83	1(2)(b)
155	394/07	*Gambazzi v. Daimler*	[2009] ECR 2563	EU:C:2009:219	45(1)(a)
156	533/07	*Falco v. Weller-Lindhorst*	[2009] ECR 3327	EU:C:2009:257	7(1)
157	167/08	*Draka v. Omnipol*	[2009] ECR 3277	EU:C:2009:263	45(1)
158	420/07	*Apostolides v. Orams*	[2009] ECR 3571	EU:C:2009:271	24(1), 2(a), 45(1)
159	180/06	*Ilsinger v. Schlank & Schick*	[2009] ECR 3961	EU:C:2009:303	17(1)
160	111/08	*SCT Industrie v. Alpenblume*	[2009] ECR 5565	EU:C:2009:419	1(2)(b)
161	204/08	*Rehder v. Air Baltic*	[2009] ECR 6073	EU:C:2009:439	7(1)(b)
162	189/08	*Zuid-Chimie v. Phillipo's*	[2009] ECR 6917	EU:C:2009:475	7(2)
163	292/08	*German Graphics*	[2009] ECR 8421	EU:C:2009:544	1(2)(b)
164	347/08	*Vorarlberger v. WGV*	[2009] ECR 8661	EU:C:2009:561	13(2)
165	381/08	*Car Trim v. KeySafety*	[2010] ECR 1255	EU:C:2010:90	7(1)(b)
166	19/09	*Wood Floor Solutions*	[2010] ECR 2121	EU:C:2010:137	7(1)(b)
167	533/08	*TNT Express v. AXA*	[2010] ECR 4107	EU:C:2010:243	71
168	111/09	*Česká Podnikatelská v. Bilas*	[2010] ECR 4545	EU:C:2010:290	10–16, 28
169	585/08	*Pammer v. Karl Schluter*	[2010] ECR 12527	EU:C:2010:740	17
170	144/09	*Hotel Alpenhof v. Heller*	[2010] ECR 12527	EU:C:2010:740	17(1)(c)
171	144/10	*BVG v. JP Morgan Chase*	[2011] ECR 3961	EU:C:2011:300	24(2)
172	87/10	*Electrosteel v.Edil Centro*	[2011] ECR 4987	EU:C:2011:375	7(1)(b)

173	139/10	*Prism v. Van der Meer*	[2011] ECR 9511	EU:C:2011:653	45
174	406/09	*Realchemie v. Bayer*	[2011] ECR 9773	EU:C:2011:668	1
175	161/10	*eDate Advertising v. X*	[2011] ECR 10269	EU:C:2011:685	7(2)
176	509/09	*Martinez v. MGN*	[2011] ECR 10269	EU:C:2011:685	7(2)
177	327/10	*Hypoteční Banka v. Lindner*	[2011] ECR 11453	EU:C:2011:745	18(2), 62
178	145/10	*Painer v. Standard Verlags*	[2011] ECR 12553	EU:C:2011:798	8(1)

(from the end of 2011 the European Court Reports were discontinued; official publication was digital only)

179	292/10	*G v. de Visser*	Mar 15, 2012	EU:C:2012:142	7(2)
180	213/10	*F-Tex v. Jadecloud-Vilma*	Apr 19, 2012	EU:C:2012:215	1(2)(b)
181	523/10	*Wintersteiger v. Products 4U*	Apr 19, 2012	EU:C:2012:220	7(2)
182	514/10	*Wolf Naturprodukte v. Sewar*	Jun 21, 2012	EU:C:2012:367	66
183	616/10	*Solvay v. Honeywell*	Jul 12, 2012	EU:C:2012:445	24(4), 8(1), 35
184	154/11	*Mahamdia v. Algeria*	Jul 19, 2012	EU:C:2012:491	20(2), 23(2)
185	619/10	*Trade Agency v. Seramico*	Sep 6, 2012	EU:C:2012:531	53
186	190/11	*Mühlleitner v. Yusufi*	Sep 6, 2012	EU:C:2012:542	17(1)(c)
187	133/11	*Folien Fischer v. Ritrama*	Oct 25, 2012	EU:C:2012:664	7(2)
188	456/11	*GAV v. Samskip*	Nov 13, 2012	EU:C:2012:719	2(a), 36
189	215/11	*Szyrocker v. SiGer Tech*	Dec 13, 2012	EU:C:2012:794	EOP Reg, Art 7
190	325/11	*Alder v. Orłowska*	Dec 19, 2012	EU:C:2012:824	Service, Art 1
191	543/10	*Refcomp v. AXA*	Feb 7, 2013	EU:C:2013:62	25
192	419/11	*Česká spořitelna v. Feichter*	Mar 14, 2013	EU:C:2013:165	7, 17(1)
193	324/12	*Novontech-Zala v. Logicdata*	Mar 21, 2013	EU:C:2013:205	EOP, Art 20
194	645/11	*Sapir v. Land Berlin*	Apr 11, 2013	EU:C:2013:228	1, 8(1)
195	228/11	*Melzer v. MF Global*	May 16, 2013	EU:C:2013:305	7(2)
196	144/12	*Goldbet Sport v. Sperindeo*	Jun 13, 2013	EU:C:2013:393	26
197	147/12	*ÖFAB v. Koot*	Jul 18, 2013	EU:C:2013:490	7(1), 7(2)
198	49/12	*HMRC v. Sunico ApS*	Sep 12, 2013	EU:C:2013:545	1
199	157/12	*Salzgitter v. Laminorul*	Sep 26, 2013	EU:C:2013:597	45(1)(d)
200	170/12	*Pinckney v. Mediatech*	Oct 3, 2013	EU:C:2013:635	7(2)
201	386/12	*Re Schneider*	Oct 3, 2013	EU:C:2013:663	1(2)(a), 24(1)
202	218/12	*Emrek v. Sabranovic*	Oct 17, 2013	EU:C:2013:666	17(1)(c)
203	519/12	*OPT Bank v. Hochtief*	Oct 17, 2013	EU:C:2013:674	1(2)(b), 7(2)
204	478/12	*Maletic v. lastminute.com*	Nov 14, 2013	EU:C:2013:735	18(1)
205	469/12	*Krejci Lager v. Olbrich*	Nov 14, 2013	EU:C:2013:788	7(1)(b)
206	508/12	*Vapenik v. Thurner*	Dec 5, 2013	EU:C:2013:790	EEO Reg, Art 6
207	9/12	*Corman-Collins v. La Maison*	Dec 19, 2013	EU:C:2013:860	4, 7(1)
208	452/12	*Nipponkoa v. Inter-Zuid*	Dec 19, 2013	EU:C:2013:858	71
209	45/13	*Kainz v. Pantherwerke*	Jan 16, 2014	EU:C:2014:7	7(2)
210	1/13	*Cartier Parfums v. Ziegler*	Feb 27, 2014	EU:C:2014:109	26, 29
211	548/12	*Brogsitter v. Montres de N*	Mar 13, 2014	EU:C:2014:148	7(1), 7(2)
212	438/12	*Weber v. Weber*	Apr 3, 2014	EU:C:2014:212	24(1)
213	387/12	*Hi Hotel v. Spoering*	Apr 3, 2014	EU:C:2014:215	7(2)
214	360/12	*Coty Germany v. First Note*	Jun 5, 2014	EU:C:2014:1318	7(2)
215	119/13	*eco cosmetics v. Dupuy*	Sep 4, 2014	EU:C:2014:2144	EOP, Arts 16–20
216	120/13	*St Georgen v. Bonchyk*	Sep 4, 2014	EU:C:2014:2144	EOP, Arts 16–20
217	157/13	*Nickel & Goeldner v. Kintra*	Sep 4, 2014	EU:C:2014:2145	1(2)(b), 71
218	112/13	*A v. B*	Sep 11, 2014	EU:C:2014:2195	26

A Note on Drafting Agreements of Choice of Court And Choice of Law

The point of drafting an agreement on choice of court, or jurisdiction agreement, is to save having to litigate about where to litigate. Two principal factors will determine the level of success: the wording chosen for the clause, and the framework of laws against the background of which it is to operate. At various points in Chapters 2, 3 and 4 we examined, in connection with the Brussels I Regulation, the Lugano II Convention and the common law, how the background laws which interpret and give effect to such agreements actually work. But whatever the law may say, need, require or allow, and whichever may be the court before which the clause may be relied on, the starting point must be for the clause to say what it needs to say. This Appendix offers a short summary of one way to draft jurisdiction agreements, followed by an example of how to do it, and how to make a better job of it. There is, after all, no rational or sensible reason for drafting imprecisely or irresolutely; and if an agreement is drafted properly, it will have the maximum effect which the law allows, even though what the law will allow is beyond the control of a drafter. It is also generally true to say that there are more ways than one of achieving a particular result. A fuller account of the approach may be found in Chapter 5 of Briggs, *Agreements on Jurisdiction and Choice of Law* (Oxford, 2008), together with discussion of whether elaborate drafting or pared-down drafting, is to be preferred.

It will also be sensible to make provision for the law which will be applied to resolve disputes which fall within the terms of the agreement.

A jurisdiction agreement needs to be in writing. The position may not be completely hopeless if it is not, but it will be close. If it identifies the courts in a Member State bound by the Brussels I Regulation, or of a Contracting State to the Lugano II Convention, it is certainly helpful for there to be a signature at the end of the document in which the agreement is written. It is not necessary for there to be a separate signature against the jurisdiction clause, but if there were, it would do good, not harm.

For the purpose of illustration, an example, taken from finance documents which were until recently – and which therefore still are – in common use, is given below. The individual points made in relation to it should be generally adaptable, though this is not a precedent to be copied slavishly or at all; and it is worth noting that the rather different context in which arbitration works will mean that the drafting of agreements to arbitrate is a distinct exercise, guided by different lines. Above all, it is to be remembered that the law develops and alters. A form of words which was considered to be effective and reliable in the recent past may now be seen to have flaws and to need upgrading. For this reason also, the draft which is put forward in this Appendix is merely the current statement of work in continual progress.

Aims of a drafting exercise

The task of drafting may be approached with a number of particular aims in mind. Eight are identified here. There may be others, but these will do to establish the ground rules. It is assumed for present purposes that the court to be chosen is the High Court in London.

(1) To provide for litigation in London (with the possibility of an option for elsewhere)

To ensure that all litigation takes place in London unless it is preferred to pursue it somewhere else, some drafting points must be borne in mind. The clause must be drafted so that its wording obliges, rather than permits, the parties to have recourse to the nominated court, so that it may be seen to be a plain and obvious breach of the promise each party makes to the other for proceedings to be brought elsewhere. Or, to put the same point in language which is often used, it must therefore be *exclusive*, rather than permissive or non-exclusive, in its content; and the wording must say so as clearly as it can. Case-law shows that it is not really good enough to 'submit to the jurisdiction of' a particular court; it is necessary, to submit to the *exclusive* jurisdiction of a particular court. True, the use of the word 'exclusive' is not absolutely necessary, and synonyms for it may yet do as good a job when the question of interpretation arises before an English court. It may even be that non-exclusive jurisdiction agreements may be able to support the argument that certain kinds of foreign proceedings which are brought in the face of them are wrongfully brought. But assuming that the clause is supposed to work equally clearly before a foreign court, which may not follow English canons of construction, it is certainly good practice to use the word 'exclusive': why use synonyms instead of the word itself? If one ends up litigating the issue whether the words actually used really do mean 'exclusive', it is hard to avoid the sense that something will have gone wrong with the drafting.

The clause must also be drafted so as to bring within its material scope all disputes which could conceivably arise between the parties, and all types of claim for relief. It will not be difficult for it to be made to apply to actions for damages for breach of contract. But it will have to be worded more carefully if it is to apply to actions in which the original validity or continuing effect of contract is impugned or denied by one party; and more creatively still if it is to apply to pre-contractual obligations or conduct; or if it is to apply to claims which are framed as torts; or if it is to apply to claims arising under foreign statutes which impose liability which is not obviously contractual or tortious in nature. A clause which specifies 'all disputes arising under this contract' is less likely today than it was to be held to fall short of applying to all these other claims which may be alleged, in some sense, to be non-contractual in nature. And although English law has now committed itself to the view that a jurisdiction agreement worded in general terms will be given the broadest material scope its words can reasonably bear, it cannot be assumed that the laws of other countries will do likewise, for the tradition of some legal systems is to be very wary about the proposition that a defendant has given up, and should be held to have given up, his right to be brought before his natural judge.

Drafting the personal scope of a jurisdiction agreement is, at least in some cases, almost as important: on this issue, English (and Australian) law seems to have become more receptive to the idea that the personal scope of a jurisdiction agreement may go further than the contracting parties themselves. There are two aspects to it.

A contractual promise by which A promises B not to sue B or C otherwise than in a specified court may be one which C can rely on directly (as a third party beneficiary of a contractual promise) or indirectly (by arguing that it should play a part in the exercise of any jurisdictional discretion the court may have); and however that may be, B may well be able to enforce it by intervening in the proceedings which A brings against C. Some courts have appeared to be wary of reading jurisdiction agreements as extending to non-parties in this way (or in any way), but the problem is usually one of imprecise drafting, rather than legal impediment, and may be dealt with accordingly.

It may also be sensible to try to limit, or to declare an intention to try to limit, the bringing of claims by entities which are associated with the other contracting party but which are not actually party to the agreement, or 'friends and relations' claimants, as they are sometimes known. This is much more difficult to do directly, for it has the effect of placing a burden on someone not a party to a contract. But it may be possible to achieve by indirect means an effect which could be accomplished directly.

If the parties do not wish to commit themselves to a particular jurisdiction, but wish to ensure that wherever the proceedings are brought, the rights and duties of the parties are governed by a particular law, a choice of law clause in the form of 'all disputes shall be determined in accordance with' ought to have the desired effect. This may also be seen as an implicit choice of court in the sense of being a choice for any court which will resolve the issues between the parties by the application of the chosen law, and against any court which will not do so.

(2) To provide for the option of suing elsewhere should this seem preferable

It may be that there is a practical preference for a clause which preserves the right of one of the parties to sue elsewhere if it chooses to, but which limits and obliges the other to bring any proceedings which it may wish to commence in the single nominated court. This can be done: indeed, it seems quite commonly to be done, though English case law means that the wording has to be clear and explicit about it. The suggestion from the French Supreme Court that jurisdiction agreements in such terms are void of legal effect is discouraging, but it is plainly wrong. The fact that such agreements may be denied effect by a French court, or by any other court which sees this as a basis to deprive an agreement of its intended effect, is an insufficient reason to question their efficacy, but it may be that clearer drafting will keep trouble at bay.

There is no reason to discourage clauses which give exclusive jurisdiction to two states concurrently.

(3) To persuade a foreign court that it has no jurisdiction

It cannot be guaranteed that a foreign court will consider an agreement to be unimpeachable in legal proceedings before it. But the chance of failure can be reduced by drafting clearly, in printing the text in sensible and legible print, and by obtaining a clear signature from the other party, particularly on the page on which the agreement is printed. All this will reduce the scope for an argument that the agreement on jurisdiction was slipped in, unnoticed by the other party.

It should be drafted using wording which is, as said above, as wide as can sensibly be: this will reduce the scope for an argument that the agreement does not extend to preclude the kind of (for instance, non-contractual) action which has been brought. It must also be remembered that it will be necessary, in particular, to draft in a way which will be effective according to the recast Brussels I Regulation as well as the Lugano II Convention. This means that the drafting exercise becomes more complex as time goes by and the law develops.

(4) To pave the way for an anti-suit injunction

If the foreign action is brought in breach of contract (that is, if the drafting guidelines from the previous section have been observed), the likelihood of being able to obtain an anti-suit injunction from the English courts to restrain it is high if the objected-to proceedings are before the courts of a non-Member State or a non-Contracting State.

It is not possible to obtain an anti-suit injunction to restrain an opponent who brings proceedings in a civil or commercial matter before the courts of another Member State or Contracting State in breach of contract, but if the proceedings are plainly brought in breach of contract, an action for damages for breach may be available as an alternative.

If it cannot be said that the foreign action is being brought in breach of contract, an injunction to restrain it may still be granted if England is the natural forum for the litigation and the bringing of the foreign proceedings is wrongful in the sense of their being oppressive or vexatious. This is the basis on which anti-suit injunctions are applied for against someone who is not breaching a contract in bringing proceedings, and the basis for an injunction against someone who seeks to interfere with or undermine a contractual agreement on jurisdiction which is binding on an ally of his. It may also be a basis for an injunction against someone who contracted not to sue a third party (with whom he did not have a contractual relationship) but whom he now sues.

(5) To prevent the recognition of a foreign judgment from a different court

In order to furnish a defence to the recognition and enforcement of a foreign judgment obtained in breach of a jurisdiction agreement or other provision for the resolution of disputes it is necessary to show that the action was brought in breach of contract. If it was, and if the other party did not take part in the foreign proceedings otherwise than for the purpose of contesting the jurisdiction, Civil Jurisdiction and Judgments Act 1982, section 32 provides a defence to the recognition and enforcement of the judgment. But if the bringing of the proceedings did not amount to a breach of contract, this argument will be unavailable. Moreover, this particular defence is not available where the judgment comes from another Member State or Contracting State, so for these countries, it is necessary to ensure that the clause works first time, in the courts in which the action may (wrongfully) be brought.

(6) To prevent an argument about the material scope of the agreement

To avoid the possibility that proceedings may be brought by a borrower, seeking to rely on the argument that as the particular claim is not a contractual one the choice of English law does not apply to it, the drafting of the agreement on choice of law needs to show an intention that English law, and only English law, govern and be applied to the liabilities of the parties to each other. It is not completely certain that this will always prevent a claimant framing a claim in tort or in equity, or under some statutory cause of action, and contending that as the claim is not contractual the choice of law provision expressed in the contract does not apply to it. It is still not clear whether this would work before a foreign court also. But it is a commercially-sensible ambition, and the drafting of a choice of law agreement which mirrors the choice of jurisdiction can be defended on pragmatic grounds.

(7) To ensure that the dispute is resolved by application of a particular law

It would be strange not to specify the law which should be applied in the resolution of disputes, and with careful attention to wording, it is possible to show an intention that the law which is identified be applied in disputes which are not necessarily or strictly contractual. To show that this is the intention of the parties is not to guarantee that it will be effective before a particular court, for the question whether a court will give effect to an expressly chosen law is a matter for the rules of private international law in the jurisdiction in which the court sits. But nothing ventured, nothing gained; and if the choice of law is framed in language which is clearly promissory, it may even be possible to enforce it as though it were a contractual promise.

(8) To pave the way for enforcement by secondary means

It has become clear, in England at least, that agreements on jurisdiction may in some circumstances be seen as contractual, promissory, terms which may be broken and which, when broken, will support a claim for damages for breach. It is nowhere near as well established (yet) that the same can be said of agreements on choice of law, but that is no reason not to try to establish the applicability of the principle. It is also clear that wherever the law declines to enforce such an agreement by injunction, or is prevented from doing so, the possibility of enforcement by secondary measures, of which damages or an indemnity are the most obvious, moves closer to the top of the list of useful remedies. But it is not clear that other jurisdictions will necessarily take the view that such terms are capable of sustaining such claims. For that reason, it may be sensible to make specific contractual provision for the payment of an indemnity in the event that certain events, which should not take place, are brought about by the voluntary act of one of the parties. The law on this is in its infancy, but intelligent contractual provision can certainly be made.

Illustration and example

In many cases the parties may devise home made, or kitchen-table, jurisdiction agreements, in simple terms, providing, for example, that 'the English courts shall have exclusive jurisdiction over all disputes', or 'the parties submit to the jurisdiction of the English courts'. And in many cases in which these are never put to the test, they will be serviceable. But a substantial commercial transaction needs a serious commercial agreement on jurisdiction. The clause which is examined below is drafted as if for a client Bank: it is the Bank which is given the benefit of various procedural options, and the Borrower whose freedom of manoeuvre is restricted. *It is not a text to be copied*, for this is not an area of the law in which one size fits all: at this point this book is a teaching guide, not a precedent book. Neither is there any guarantee that it will actually do all one might wish it to do: the law moves on, questions of construction get muddled up with other facts and matters, and so on; and whatever may be its effect before an English court, it may not be given the same treatment by a foreign court before which the dispute is brought. But by dint of comparing an actual against a proposed example, it is possible to see some of the principles which will point towards a satisfactory conclusion. Version 1, in which the Clause is numbered X, is taken from an actual document, purely for the purpose of illustration. Version 2, in which the Clause is numbered Y, is a remodelling of it for consideration for future use.

VERSION 1

CLAUSE X: JURISDICTION AND GOVERNING LAW

X.1 *Submission*

For the benefit of the Bank, the Borrower agrees that the courts of England have jurisdiction to settle any disputes in connection with this Agreement, and accordingly submits to the jurisdiction of the English courts.

X.2 *Service of process*

Without prejudice to any other mode of service, the Borrower:

(a) irrevocably appoints N as its agent for service of process in relation to any proceedings before the English courts in connection with this Agreement;

(b) agrees to maintain such an agent for service of process in England for so long as any amount is outstanding under this Agreement;

(c) agrees that failure by a process agent to notify such an Obligor of the process will not invalidate the proceedings concerned;

(d) consents to the service of process relating to any such proceedings by prepaid posting of a copy of the process to its address for the time being applying under Clause [ ] (Addresses for Notices);

(e) agrees that if the appointment of any person mentioned in paragraph (a) above ceases to be effective, each Obligor shall immediately appoint a further person in England to accept service of process on its behalf in England and, failing such appointment within 15 days, the Agent is entitled to appoint such person by notice to the Borrower.

X.3 *Forum convenience and enforcement abroad*

The Borrower:

(a) waives objection to the English courts on grounds of inconvenient forum or otherwise as regards proceedings in connection with this Agreement, and

(b) agrees that a judgment or order of an English court in connection with this Agreement is conclusive and binding on it and may be enforced against it in the courts of any other jurisdiction.

X.4 *Non-exclusivity*

Nothing in this Clause limits the right to the Bank to bring proceedings against the Borrower in connection with this Agreement:

(a) in any other court of competent jurisdiction, or

(b) concurrently in more than one jurisdiction.

X.5 *Governing law*

This Agreement is governed by English law.

VERSION 2

CLAUSE Y: JURISDICTION AND GOVERNING LAW

Y.1 *Exclusive jurisdiction*

The Bank and the Borrower submit to the jurisdiction of the English courts and, subject to Clause Y.3 below, the Borrower and the Bank irrevocably agree that the courts of England are to have exclusive jurisdiction, and that no other court is to have jurisdiction:

(a) to settle any disputes arising out of or in connection with this Agreement or with the relationship otherwise established between the parties, and

(b) to settle any disputes arising out of or in connection with the negotiation, legal validity or enforceability of this Agreement, whether the alleged liability shall be said to arise under the law of England or under the law of some other country and regardless of whether a particular cause of action may successfully be brought in the English courts, and

(c) to grant interim remedies, or other provisional or protective relief.

Y.2 *Service of process*

Without prejudice to any other mode of service, the Borrower:

(a) irrevocably appoints N as its agent for service of process in relation to any proceedings before the English courts in connection with this Agreement;

(b) agrees to maintain such an agent for service of process in England for so long as any amount is outstanding under this Agreement;

(c) agrees that failure by a process agent to notify such an Obligor of the process will not invalidate the proceedings concerned;

(d) consents to the service of process relating to any such proceedings by prepaid posting of a copy of the process to its address for the time being applying under Clause [ ] (Addresses for Notices);

(e) agrees that if the appointment of any person mentioned in paragraph (a) above ceases to be effective, each Obligor shall immediately appoint a further person in England to accept service of process on its behalf in England and, failing such appointment within 15 days, the Agent is entitled to appoint such person by notice to the Borrower.

Y.3 *Right of Bank, but not Borrower, to bring proceedings in any other jurisdiction*

Nothing in this Clause limits the right of the Bank to bring proceedings, including third party proceedings, against the Borrower, or to apply for interim remedies, in connection with this Agreement:

    (a) in any other court of competent jurisdiction, and

    (b) concurrently in more than one jurisdiction

and the obtaining by the Bank of judgment in one jurisdiction shall not prevent the Bank from bringing or continuing proceedings in any other jurisdiction, whether or not these shall be founded on the same cause of action.

Y.4 *Further undertakings by the borrower*

Regardless of whether the courts of any country other than England have or would have jurisdiction to entertain a claim falling within Clause Y.1 or Clause Y.3, the Borrower irrevocably:

    (a) undertakes that it will neither issue nor cause to be issued originating or other process in respect of such a claim in any country other than England;

    (b) in relation to proceedings brought by the Bank in accordance with Clause Y.1:

        (i) waives any and every objection to the exercise of jurisdiction by the English court on the ground of *forum non conveniens* or otherwise, and

        (ii) agrees that a judgment or order of an English court in a dispute falling or intended to fall within this clause is conclusive and binding on the Borrower and may be enforced against the Borrower in the courts of any other jurisdiction or jurisdictions, and

    (c) in relation to proceedings brought by the Bank in accordance with Clause Y.3:

        (i) waives any and every objection to the exercise of jurisdiction by the court in which the Bank has brought proceedings on the ground of *forum non conveniens* or otherwise, and

        (ii) agrees that a judgment or order of an English court in a dispute falling or intended to fall within this clause is conclusive and binding on the Borrower and may be enforced against the Borrower in the courts of any other jurisdiction or jurisdictions

Y.5 *Enforceability despite invalidity of Agreement*

It is hereby declared that the Bank and the Borrower agree that in the event of this Agreement, or any part thereof, being held to be invalid, unenforceable, illegal, discharged or otherwise of no effect, the provisions of this Clause shall continue to apply to all and any legal proceedings which would have fallen within its scope had the Agreement been valid and enforceable in every respect.

Y.6 *Effect in relation to claims by and against non-parties*

    (a) The Bank and the Borrower hereby agree and declare that the benefit of this clause shall extend to, and may be enforced in their own right by any officer, employee, agent, or business associate of the Bank against whom the Borrower brings a claim which, if it were brought against the Bank, would fall within the material scope of this clause.

    (b) The Bank and the Borrower undertake to use their best endeavours to prevent persons not party to this Agreement from bringing against a party to this agreement, otherwise than in the English courts, any action or other proceeding which would, if brought by a party to this Agreement against the other party to the Agreement, have been required to be brought in the English courts.

Y.7 *Further undertaking by Borrower*

The Borrower agrees with the Bank that in the event of the Borrower:

(a) issuing proceedings in a court outside England which, according to this clause should have been issued in England, whether or not the same be found by the court in which the proceedings are brought, and whether or not the Bank defends those proceedings, or

(b) bringing proceedings in a court outside England with the consequence that the Agreement or the relationship between the parties is not determined entirely in accordance with English law, whether or not the same results from argument made to the court by the Borrower,

the Borrower undertakes to pay the Bank, and will pay to the Bank on demand, all such sums as shall represent the whole of the loss to the Bank caused by or resulting from the bringing of those proceedings, or resulting from the application of a law other than English law to the proceedings between the parties.

Y.8 *Governing law*

This Clause, and this Agreement, and the whole of the relationship between the parties, is governed by English law. The parties agree that all disputes arising out of or in connection with it, or with the negotiation, legal validity or enforceability of this Agreement, and the relationship between the parties, and whether or not the same shall be regarded as contractual claims, shall be exclusively governed by and determined only in accordance with English law.

A comparison of some similarities and differences

Some of the reasons for preferring the new wording over the old wording are as follows.

- ***For the benefit of the Bank:*** Clause X is apparently intended to be one-sided, and to give jurisdictional advantage to the Bank. This is sensible, but if the required jurisdictional advantage given to the Bank is set out in detail, it is not clear that is useful to make this statement as well. Clause Y therefore omits it on the ground that it is not necessary, but also because it may actually be disadvantageous to use it. The Brussels Convention contained a specific reference to jurisdiction agreements which were for the benefit of one of the parties, but this particular provision was not reproduced in the Brussels I Regulation or the Lugano II Convention. This fact may have led the French courts to the false conclusion that a jurisdiction agreement which was expressed to be for the benefit of one party no longer worked as such, the legislative basis for its effect having been removed. It would be better not to use language which either draws attention to a change in the law, or risks serving as a distraction, or both. It is sufficient to set out the terms of the jurisdictional agreement without this additional statement of purpose.

- ***Material scope of the agreement:*** Clause X.1 is limited in scope to disputes in connection with this agreement, which is liable to be held to mean the contract. It is not clear from this form of words that it would also be held to apply to disputes which arise from things which occurred before the contract was entered into (pre-contractual misrepresentation or non-disclosure; the effect of bribery or undue influence), or which are not purely contractual in nature (such as claims alleging fraud or negligence, or for breach of fiduciary duty, or liability arising under statute law of England or some other country). Until recently, English law contained a depressingly large number of authorities dealing with such points of interpretation; and although English law has now distanced itself from this approach to jurisdiction agreements, it would be unwise to assume that the rest of the world – particularly those jurisdictions which are wary of jurisdiction agreements in which a party appears to have given up its basic right to litigate before its natural judge – takes the same view.

Comprehensive language is to be preferred. It may not always be effective: a foreign court may take the view that, under the law which it applies, it is not possible to choose the forum for non-contractual disputes, or to choose a forum which would not apply certain laws which the alternative court would apply; but no harm is done by drafting in wider terms.

- **Interim remedies:** Clause X.1 is also silent as to its application to claims for interim remedies. It does not follow from the fact that a court has been given even exclusive jurisdiction over disputes that this excludes recourse to other courts for interim remedies or interlocutory relief. It will always be, first, a question of construction whether the agreement was intended to apply to permit or to prevent such applications. But being on the receiving end of an application for such relief can be almost as vexatious as proceedings in the substantive action itself. If this is a worry, it is sensible to exclude this option by express words, and hope that a foreign court, if it is applied to in breach of the parties' agreement, will give effect to the agreement which excludes its power to grant such relief. Clause Y attends to this.

- **Exclusive or non-exclusive:** Clause X.1 states that the English courts are to have jurisdiction, and that the borrower submits to the jurisdiction of the English courts. It is simply – and indefensibly – unclear whether this means that the English courts are intended to have jurisdiction alongside other courts, or are intended to have jurisdiction to the exclusion of all other courts. There can be no excuse for drafting this critical provision in terms which leave doubt, even if there are authorities which, after a lot of money and anxiety, may assist in resolving the doubt. These authorities, which ask whether the submission is transitive (referring to the submission of disputes) or intransitive (referring to the submission of the parties themselves), or whether the court would have had jurisdiction apart from the agreement (in which case the term will be likely to be seen as exclusive) or would not otherwise have had jurisdiction at all (in which case, probably non-exclusive) have absolutely nothing to recommend them except to the extent that they may serve as *tabula in naufragio*. Clause Y.1 makes the intention clear without any of this nonsense; and Clause Y.3 proceeds to relax the exclusivity to the precise extent intended.

- **Submission:** Clause X.1 does nevertheless confirm the submission of the Borrower to the jurisdiction of the English courts. It is sensible for this to be said, for though from the perspective of English law it may not achieve anything which is not otherwise achieved, it may be relevant to what a foreign court may be asked to do when the judgment comes to be enforced.

- **Service of process:** Clause X.2 is copied across to Clause Y.2, as it is otherwise a good and sensible provision. There is great practical advantage in being able to institute proceedings and serve process in England, for at least two reasons. First, even if service of process is no longer the event which, for the purpose of the Brussels I Regulation and Lugano II Convention, marks the date on which an English court is seised of proceedings, speed of service is still critical if there is likely to be a race between the parties to get proceedings into the preferred court. Moreover, if permission under CPR rule 6.36 will otherwise be needed to serve out of the jurisdiction, the delay may be disastrous. Moreover, there are some countries in which it is remarkably (but also opaquely) difficult and slow to effect service of English process: one occasionally reads that it can take up to two years for service to be made through official channels. The law on service of English process outside the territory of the English court, effectively and lawfully, is beset by hazards and pitfalls, and if it is possible to agree to do without it, it is an enormous advantage to do so.

- **Waiver of objection:** Clause X.3 is substantially satisfactory, but Clause Y.4 makes some changes to it. As to Y.4(b)(i), the renunciation of a right to plead *forum non conveniens* (for which term 'forum convenience' was a horribly inept mistranslation) may be of little

874

effect, for if the English court has been contractually chosen, it should not lie in the mouth of one of the parties to complain about it; and if the court nevertheless overrides the jurisdiction agreement for reasons of supervening public interest, it will not be the submission of the parties which motivates it to do so. As to Y.4(b)(ii), it cannot be known whether a foreign law will recognise and enforce an English judgment, but the effect of a provision in these terms cannot be unhelpful.

In those cases in which the Bank exercises its freedom to sue in a court other than England, which is provided for in Clause Y.3, and which is examined below, it is sensible to replicate the agreement for waiver of jurisdictional objection. Clause Y.4(c) does this.

- **One-sided freedom to sue elsewhere:** Clause X.4 preserved the right of the Bank to sue in any other court instead of or as well as in the nominated English court. As a matter of construction, this has the effect of making the clause one of exclusive jurisdiction so far as concerns claims brought by the Borrower, but of non-exclusive jurisdiction so far as concerns claims brought by the Bank, but without the pitfalls inherent in the term 'non-exclusive'. Clause Y.3 makes certain improvements.

  There have been problematic cases where such a clause has not been seen as preventing the Borrower from bringing claims elsewhere, and the old maxim that *expressio unius est exclusio alterius* has failed to save the day. In principle Clause Y.1 should meet the point by itself, but there is no loss, and possibly some gain, in making it doubly explicit in Clause Y.3 that the clause is intended to be one-sided in its relaxation of exclusivity of jurisdiction.

- **Concurrently in more than one jurisdiction:** Clause Y.3(b) seeks to make it clear that so far as the parties are concerned, the Bank may bring proceedings in more courts than one. In the absence of this provision, the bringing of overlapping or concurrent proceedings may well be seen as oppressive and as being liable to be restrained by injunction, even where it may be justified by the fact that the assets of the Borrower are dispersed. But if it is expressly provided for in the contract, this risk is very substantially reduced. It probably cannot, however, overcome the jurisdictional prohibition on concurrent proceedings in respect of the same cause of action in the courts of the Member States of the European Union which is imposed by the Brussels I Regulation.

- **Promise not to bring proceedings:** Clause Y.4(a) makes a distinct promise about the non-institution of proceedings. It is designed to establish a distinct basis for an argument that, whether or not the court outside England in which the Borrower has instituted proceedings has jurisdiction, the Borrower has made a clear and enforceable promise not to do it. If relief is to be sought against the Borrower, it is good to avoid the distraction of an argument about whether the other court did have jurisdiction. The issue is not whether it did; the issue is whether a promise was made not to invoke it.

- **Contractual invalidity:** Clause Y.5 seeks to address a problem which has emerged in recent years. As is discussed in the text, it is now pretty well established in England that even if the contract as a whole is void or unenforceable, a jurisdiction agreement contained within it is not automatically unenforceable as well. Whether this argument is sound or not may vary from country to country and from law to law; but there is no reason not to make it clear that the parties *intend* the agreement on jurisdiction to survive any and every challenge to the validity of the contract. The clause expresses a sensible contractual intention which will already be familiar to those who practice the law of arbitration, and there is good reason to express it.

- **Non-parties:** claims by the Borrower against those allied to the bank or its officers or employees: The Borrower may seek to evade its jurisdiction agreement with the Bank by bringing a claim, not against the Bank, but against an employee, officer or agent; or against another person or entity which was involved or alleged to be involved in the transaction which has gone wrong. As a matter of common law, such non-parties could not take advantage of this jurisdiction agreement, as they were not privy to it. But the Contracts (Rights of Third Parties) Act 1999, section 1, allows a non-party to take the benefit of a contract if it is expressly provided that he may, or if it appears that the contract intended to confer this benefit on him. It is therefore provided that non-parties, who fall into a defined class and who are sued by the Borrower, are intended to have the benefit and to be entitled to enforce this jurisdiction agreement against the Borrower in the same way as if they were parties to the Agreement, and Clause Y.6(b) spells out that intention.

Even if the non-parties do not have the right to enforce the jurisdiction agreement as though they were parties to it (as when, for example, the 1999 Act is excluded from application), they may still be able to point to the agreement and argue that the court should exercise any jurisdictional discretion which it may have to prevent a claim by the Borrower against the non-party. For though it is one thing to be able to enforce a jurisdiction agreement as though one were a party to it, there is no impediment to relying on it as part of the *res gestae* when contending for the application of a discretionary power which the court possesses.

- **Non-parties:** Claims by those allied to the Borrower: Clause Y.6(a) attempts to deal with issues involving those who were not party to the Agreement. It deals with a practice of there being claims made by other persons, associated or believed to be associated with the Borrower, and whose actions may well be co-ordinated by the Borrower, who claim to be free to sue where they like, and to muddy the waters as a result, on the ground that they are not party to, and hence are not bound by, the jurisdiction agreement. There is no doubt that this happens, and that the claimants in such cases are indeed free of the shackles of the jurisdiction agreements to which they were not party. Insofar as they exercise their jurisdictional freedom in a way which the English court regards as improper, they may be held to account; but there is no reason to doubt that if the Borrower (for instance) is placed under a contractual obligation to prevent this, as best he can, this may furnish indirect means of preventing something which cannot be prevented by direct means. It is drafted as a 'best endeavours' clause.

- **Consequences of breach:** It may well be unclear whether the law of the forum, or the law which governs the jurisdiction agreement, or both, will allow an action for damages for breach of contract or in tort where a party bound by a jurisdiction agreement breaches that agreement by bringing proceedings in another court. It may also be that a court will not grant (or will not be able to grant) an injunction to restrain the breach. But if the Borrower has undertaken not to issue proceedings otherwise than in the named state, it may be easier (it cannot be guaranteed) to argue that the injunction responds to a wrong act done by the respondent, rather than making any judgment about the jurisdiction of the court before which the Borrower seeks to bring the Bank. It may not make a difference of principle, but it is hard to see the objection to an injunction to prevent a person giving instructions of power of attorney to a lawyer when he has specifically promised not to do so. Clause Y.3(a) makes the point.

Separately, if the Borrower has expressly undertaken to pay all such sums as represent the loss to the Bank caused by wrongful litigation, the right to claim damages will be provided for by the express terms of the contract, and this must make it much more difficult for a claim for damages to be rebuffed or refused. Clause Y.7(a) paves the way for such an argument.

- **Choice of law:** Three particular points among many arise. First, the construction of a jurisdiction agreement is, in the opinion of English courts, a matter governed by the law chosen by the parties; and some of the points which it is sought to make may depend upon English being the background law against which this is undertaken. A different view may be taken in a foreign court which may, for example, simply apply its own domestic law to the question, regarding the question as procedural rather than contractual. But the inclusion of an express choice of law to govern the jurisdiction agreement seems a sensible thing to do, and Clause Y.8 does it.

Second, it may also be desirable to deal with the law which will govern the dispute, and not just the jurisdiction agreement, between the parties. So far as concerns the further wording, which widens its material scope and seeks to encompass claims (and to specify the law which governs such claims) which may not be seen as contractual, there is sense in trying to prevent an express choice of law being circumvented by a claimant who formulates a claim in tort or equity or on some statutory basis of liability. It is not likely that this will be completely successful, but if it is not even tried it is certain that nothing will be gained. So the wider wording is strongly preferable.

There is no reason why the reasoning set out in the previous paragraph, about the consequences of breach of the choice of jurisdiction, should not be extended to the agreement on choice of law. Whether there may be a freestanding action for damages for breach of a choice of law agreement is not yet subject to conclusive authority, though it is likely that some significant problems may, in principle at least, be encountered. For this reason, an express promise to indemnify or pay money is a useful addition; and Clause Y.7(b) establishes the basis for it.

INDEX